The Coming of Pakeha Religion

The Spiritual Significance for Maori

New Zealand's Lost Legacy

The Final Edition

A Revisionist Analysis of Maori 'Spirituality'

and Pakeha 'Religion'

Charles Ihaia Hita-Brown

THE COMING OF PAKEHA RELIGION

The Spiritual Significance for Maori

New Zealand's Lost Legacy

The Final Edition

A Revisionist Analysis of Maori 'Spirituality' and Pakeha 'Religion'

Charles Ihaia Hita-Brown

The Last in the Line of the Maori Prophets

http://www.crystalbooks.org

This Edition published by:
Crystal Publishing
P.O.Box 60042, Titirangi
West Auckland, 0642
NEW ZEALAND

First Edition 2006.
Second Edition 2008.
Final Edition 2011.
Copyright © 2006–2008–2011, **Charles S. Brown**.

*   *   *   *   *

Cover design and artwork by **Jack Mackinder**, author of:
"Celtic Design and Ornament for Calligraphers".

Clockwise from top left: **Cook**, **Hongi Hika**, **Williams** and **Marsden**. Centre: **Ratana!**

*   *   *   *   *

ISBN 978-0-473-18888-7

"Soon, very soon in the future you will no longer speak,
but instead a very different person(generation)
will reveal to you all the fruits of these prophecies.
Not only will it be revealed exclusively to you
the morehu only, no but to the whole country..."

T. W. Ratana, 1929.

Reprinted with the kind permission of Keith Newman,
"Ratana Revisited: An Unfinished Legacy".
(Parenthetic addition mine.)

*   *   *   *   *

In connection with Ratana's key prophecy, the reader must understand that this Work, by design and contents, is very different to other publications. In the first place the subject matter and its associated structure places it in a category of its own. In 'edit-speak', moreover, it would be considered too dense and too repetitious.

However, in order to *fully explain* the complete legacy of Ratana's great Spiritual Mission for Maori and New Zealand, the reader must further understand that the revisionist and spiritually-radical concepts herein *are so far removed* from virtually all accepted cultural, educational and even religious and current societal paradigms that they *necessarily require* **constant reinforcement throughout**. It thus occupies a singular place outside standard editing/publishing parameters.

The editing mantra, *"Less is more"*, probably holds true for most books. However, an *aspiritual conditioning-process* of *humanly-derived* education set in place for centuries now has resulted in those above-noted paradigms becoming completely ingrained as more or less the basic foundation of present-day society. So, as a strong countermeasure, the necessary crucial requirement herein is: *"**More needs more.**"*

So those key or necessary words, phrases, whole sentences and even short paragraphs that *require reinforcement*, will be in either 'closed commas', *italics*, **bold**, underlined, or a combination of *'all'*. Moreover, the more *significant statements* will stand separate from the general 'paragraphical flow' and, in some cases, be centred.

Notwithstanding the need to place strong emphasis on that which requires it, the radical aspect of the Work exactly permits the revelation of "all the [spiritual] fruits" of Ratana's prophecies to emerge. The reader should therefore strive to 'absorb' the explanations of the many diverse elements that make up the complete, interconnected picture. The *repetitive necessity* for *constant reinforcement* of exactly those radical Spiritual concepts herein, though perhaps seeming at times to be akin to an 'harangue' or like a 'cracked-record', **are precisely those which** crucially-require *repetitive reinforcement*.

I therefore enjoin you, the reader, to be ***fully cognisant*** of that ***important point*** as you *journey* through the ***many pages*** herein!

This Work, therefore, should not be 'rushed through'!

Charles Ihaia Hita-Brown. [A servant.]

Dedication

This Work – In the very **First Instance** – *unashamedly and absolutely; recognises and confesses*: The:

"I AM!"

THE ALMIGHTY!

For it is **"HIS"** Eternal Beneficence, Grace and Power which ever offers *all* humankind: The **True** and **Pure**:

DIVINE LOVE!

In very deep gratitude, *all* is offered 'UPWARD' to **"THE SOURCE"** for the *singular* Guidance which *Graciously permitted* the recognition of **Its** concomitant **Knowledge**; thus *enabling*, through this Work, the dissemination of **'The Spiritual Truths'** inherent in:

"THE DIVINE!"

        *   *   *   *   *

With love, the 'spiritual journey' *herein* carries along with it my Mother, **Rangihiawe**, [through whom I was *primarily attracted* for my earthly life's work and purpose] yet whose *own* life was lived in a world of unnecessary fear; and confusion. A fear, deep and unreasoning, promoted by a culture that offered little in the way of explanation but simply asserted – *and continues to assert to this day* – that its way was, and is still, the *only* correct spiritual way. And a life lived in confusion; in trying to reconcile two very disparate *cultural ideologies* that never really *harmonised for her* during her lifetime.

Under the **Mantle** of that **Love** and **Knowledge**, therefore, this Work, and its *associated* journey, is offered to *spiritually-clarify* the Maori and Pakeha past. And for the very many who are now a *fusion* of Maori/Pakeha in Aotearoa today; to offer the same *spiritual* clarification and understanding of *their place and purpose* now, and into the future.

iii

Dedication

Acknowledgements

I am extremely grateful to the many people who assisted in various ways with this book. Without their ongoing encouragement to help dispel what began to seem to me to be almost too insurmountable a task, the Work might not even have reached the manuscript stage. Along with that encouragement the clear need to review the Work as it proceeded through its numerous reshaping phases was important.

Special thanks must therefore go to Hazel Morrissey who waded through the very first draft attempt of a first-time writer, and who constantly offered encouragement. And also to my long-time friend, John Copas, who laboured with and helped shape the complete first draft and was kind enough to review that altered format in the second, greatly extended, draft.

Grateful thanks, also, to (Dr.) Stephen Lampe, Author of: *"The Christian and Reincarnation"*, and *"Building Future Societies: The Spiritual Principles"*, for his very kind permission to use essential material from his publications without which my own project would have been deficient. Thanks, also, to Dr. Kanayo Nwanze of Nigeria for his insightful comments and encouragement to strive for publication; and to Mrs N. Van den berg of Western Australia for her review of particular portions of the work and for her kind encouragement in the face of some serious opposition.

Ngaire Bishop of the Auckland Central Library provided vital assistance in locating particular reference material, reviewed key Chapters and offered support and encouragement. And, through her own work in genealogy, particularly, was instrumental in helping to chart, as much as could be correctly determined, the connections to my *whanau tatai/whakapapa*; help that was rarely forthcoming from Maori quarters.

Since the work postulates an absolute premise – and one that cannot be proved empirically – I am extremely grateful to my neighbours and good friends, Jack and Chris Mackinder, for their vital input in providing necessary reference material and for reviewing and analysing the main premise of the Work in terms of its validity within its own stated spiritual and empirical parameters. And, not least, for their valuable advice and ongoing encouragement. [Jack also designed the cover for this book.]

Particular thanks to Sally and Dennis Green, former neighbours and good friends: to Sally for her invaluable computer-savvy in constructing reference charts etc., – a level of expertise that I do not at all possess – for her equally invaluable tutoring skills which offered the greatest single aid for the writing of this Work, and for shaping the original individual Chapters of the early manuscript into book form.

Special mention must go to my sister, Susan Robertson, who, from the very inception of the project, unequivocally understood the need for it for Maoridom in the first instance and reviewed those key Chapters vital to the Maori perspective. My many thanks to her for her insight into that perspective and for her ongoing and vital encouragement.

Thanks, also, to the many, many people to whom I submitted my ideas and thoughts, often unsolicited, to both Maori and Pakeha who nevertheless invariably understood the inherent correctness of a premise that postulates a "middle way". And, indeed, encouraged me to continue to promote a path that transcends the narrow strictures of race and culture.

I cannot leave this page without offering special and grateful thanks to the late Neville (Mac.) Macmillan with whom I had many long talks on the very issues outlined in this Work. Mac., an author in his own right and an able historian, was deeply concerned for the future of this blessed land. In large part his great love for it was set in place through wartime experiences and wonderful memories serving alongside Maori Servicemen. There he saw the huge reservoir of potential within Maoridom. He also understood, however, that without clear direction, it was unlikely that that potential would ever be *fully* realised. Mac's invaluable insight and encouragement thus convinced me that the Work was, perhaps, not only more than just an exercise or pipe-dream, but was vitally needed. Until his review of the early, basic manuscript, I had not seriously regarded it as being something that was potentially publishable, even though that was always the hope. Therefore Mac., wherever you are now, I offer a heartfelt "Thank You!" for allowing me to actually believe it *was* all possible.

Because the First Edition was 'rushed' to publication, so to speak, that 'hurried' process resulted in a number of small but obvious 'typo' and grammatical errors. Careful proof-reading of the stronger **Revised Second Edition** resulted in all offending 'errors' being identified, thereby greatly aiding this **Final Edition**. Grateful thanks, therefore, to Miss Annette K. White and Mr Andrew Law for their 'eyes'.

*   *   *   *   *

The final acknowledgement must go to Mr. R.M. Duraisamy, (M.E. Hons.) author of "*From India to the Truth*" and other publications. Under the politicised protocols of "cultural correctness" now systemically entrenched in New Zealand society, certain Publishers who expressed interest in the manuscript sought endorsement and/or approval from specific Maori academics. Predictably, they did not approve of the Work and recommended that it *not* be published. From the tone of their review notes, particularly their strong reference to *tikanga* (correctness), the "un-named academics" clearly missed a very crucial point of *tikanga*:
"That you state who you are!"
However, since it was *spiritually-ordained from the outset* that this Work see the light of day in this land, and since those New Zealand publishers approached have thus far rejected the opportunity to bring this to pass, a person of *non-New Zealand* origin did so, thus effectively circumventing any attempt by "leading Maori academic nay-sayers and cultural sanitisers" to prevent publication. [The *symbolic* reason for this will become clear to those readers who absorb the contents herein]. Therefore, aside from reviewing the manuscript, the computer skills and publishing expertise of Mr. Duraisamy were especially vital for electronically preparing for printing and publishing *all* the books of **Crystal Publishing**.
In New Zealand these works are available through:

www.publishme.co.nz

They are also obtainable at:

www.crystalbooks.org

Contents

Author's Note

The rapidly-changing face of societal conditions in New Zealand – particularly where the strongly-promoted Maori traditional/cultural ethos impacts on virtually every aspect of New Zealand life more than ever before – seriously requires that *someone* open it all up to the "spiritual scrutiny" it therefore demands. For in this land [where even Maori are not taught their past history *as it really was*] all must simply accept a general kind of 'school/sanitised' version, without question.

As stated in the **Original Edition**, the main reason for writing the book in the first place was principally wrought by particular Maori issues, set in place and moulded by the fear-ridden superstitions of the *whanau* group into which I was born. Those intense experiences thus inculcated the same fears in me during my formative years. A second reason, but perhaps no less an important one, resulted from certain strange and inexplicable incidents that occurred on Military Operations in South Vietnam between the years 1967 and 1972. Seemingly incredulous events that, unfortunately for some of our comrades, resulted in death – in a land where the incredulous and death was *common-place*. Certain later-life experiences offered some clarification as to possible reasons why; for both those aspects of one's life. However, not sufficient to fully understand, in terms of complete answers *then*, either the Maori issues or those associated with 'certain things, Vietnam'.

In the more complete **Second Edition**; whilst the main subject matter necessarily remained the same *overall*, certain crucially-stronger *inclusions* at precise points in the Work brought the Maori reader, particularly, face to face *more decisively* with the inviolable Spiritual Paradigm that —

"*...personal and collective decisions inevitably produce commensurate consequences*".

Now, in 2011, the third and **Final Edition** of **The Coming of Pakeha Religion** cloaks the land and people of Aotearoa/New Zealand. So why the necessity for a definitive **Final Edition** in just a few short years since its first release? It is certainly not because of huge sales. **No!** Challenging *official* Maori history/colonisation in the way that this Work does *should* be of especial interest to *all* in this land.

However, few human beings really want **The Truth** about anything. In terms of so-called *human* truth/s, *everyone* wants the world to be *their* way, and the new Maori ethos is certainly no different in that regard. For it *loudly* demands that *its* truth be *the* truth for *all*. So even though we *all* want the answers to be *our* answers and *all* solutions to be *our* solutions, why do we not use simple *common sense* to see that such a notion is really silly in the extreme. There cannot be, **and there is not**, either an *individual* truth for each person, or a different *truth* for every culture.

The key reason for this **Final Edition**, therefore, is primarily one of timing. The incredible and increasing ferment now engulfing virtually all global societies offers a sure pointer to precise but unfortunate outcomes for we of Planet Earth. We, the participants, can be likened to 'ostriches with their heads in the sand'. Like an insidiously advancing cancer, the lemming-like nature of global societies increasingly degrades the gift of the *taonga* that is 'Mother Earth'.

Not just in the use of the material products we need, but perhaps *more increasingly* in the aspiritual filth and poison of 'anything goes freedom of expression' where even small children –

once protected by *most* cultures and societies – are, for increasing numbers of *very evil humans*, just another commodity for exploitation. The rapid rise of religious intolerance adds just one more dimension to a clearly obvious path of a faster and faster downward slide. Why, ultimately? Simply because we humans do not *really accept* that there are very final **Absolute**, **Inviolable**, **Immutable** – and thus Unchangeable LAWS – to which we are *absolutely subject*. We may *say* 'we know and accept', but the *actual* state of our global societies unequivocally reveals that we hypocritically *do not* accept.

As far back as the eighth century B.C., the Great Prophet, Isaiah [24:4-5], *foresaw* the path that we of Planet Earth **would take**. The present-day state of it and its global societies clearly reveal a **calamitous** and **rapidly-deteriorating** situation. Encapsulated in just one single and very sure sentence is found the ultimate reason for all human miseries and woes, then – in the past; and now – today.

> "The earth also is defiled under the inhabitants thereof; because they have,
> *transgressed the laws*
> *changed the decrees*
> *broken the everlasting covenant.*

What might these **Laws** and **Decrees** actually be that Isaiah so surely prophesies about? Clearly they are not any kind of humanly-derived religious, political or cultural laws. For we humans seem not to be capable of formulating laws that *genuinely* hold both **Truth** and *true* **Justice**. **NO!** The **Law** of which Isaiah speaks is **THE LAW. THE ONE-LAW: THE LAWS OF CREATION. — CREATION-LAW!** —

The continually changing dynamics of the primarily bi-cultural, but also multi-cultural, society that *we* now have is *no different* to all other global societies for it, too, lacks the crucial knowledge of **CREATION-LAW**. To that realisation for the people of this land – but Te Iwi Maori especially – is this **Final Edition** primarily addressed. As in the previous two, in *this* Edition also is offered, explained, that very necessary knowledge.

Whilst there is no real change in the main bulk of the text from the greatly revised **Second Edition**, the *main changes* herein feature *very definitively* towards the **end** of the Work. Those definitive changes represent, *and are*, the **very final poropiti** for Maori, *and* this blessed land. Thus for Pakeha too, *and* for *all* others who have *chosen* to make Aotearoa their *earthly* home. This Edition **is** final simply because what is *now* included towards the end of the Work are the very revelatory explanations that define, **and thereby proclaim**, its finality.

Though prepared for during the developing, step-by-step *spiritual recognitions* of primarily the last four Maori Religious Prophets – Te Kooti Arikirangi, Te Whiti, Kenana and Ratana – the historical time-frame for this crucial revelation was actually Ratana's time. Hence his especial Calling!

The developing recognitions of each of the later Maori Prophets, in turn clearly revealed an ordained path and Spiritual Mission for the Maori race which, very unfortunately, was **not fulfilled** by the greatest of them: Ratana! This **guided Work** prophesied by him, in its three step-by-step Editions explains the *true Spiritual history of what should have been*. Ordained for Ratana in his time, what we later reveal as the **primary recognition** for the *fulfilment* of his *complete* mission, was missed.

This Final Edition, however, not only offers that explanation, but most importantly **why** the **key** to the overall knowledge revealed towards the end of this book *should* have served as the *foundation* for *every* societal, scientific, spiritual and cultural endeavour that we in New Zealand have ever undertaken or otherwise set in place!

Only therewith can the *already-failing* societal consequences and ramifications deriving from *not fulfilling* the *true* collective purpose of all in this **chosen land** be *really* understood. Thus what *was* – **and what should yet still be striven for**.

You may ask why I did not include this very final information, to which I allude, in at least the Revised Second Edition? **Why not?** Simply because that very especial knowledge is, literally in a word: **PROFOUND!** So profound in fact, that it borders on the **Sacred**. It is revealed now because it is **the time** for that **Revelation**. It is also in the time-frame that Ratana prophesied; for he it was who *should* have recognised and revealed it when at the height of *his* Calling. He did not, because he missed it. So it was ordained that another would come in the future to find it; and Proclaim it. That is why this Work is **The Final Edition**, and about which Ratana prophesied!

The catalyst to write did not arrive until the early 1980s when, after many years of reading and 'searching', *spiritual clarification and insight* finally began to arrive. Increasing discernment during that phase of life resulted in the certainty that I would one day write; particularly about the Maori issues. The actual inspiration to begin came in October 1995, after 'seeing', or 'being shown', a vision (picture) of a rainbow-like arc in the sky that gave "three defining impressions".

To the left of the picture, (on the horizontal plane) came the *impression* of a first (Maori) canoe touching onto a beach, with the crew's footprints appearing clearly in the sand [as they took their first steps in this new land]. A second *impression*, this time from immediately above in the centre of the rainbow arc (the 12 o'clock position), was that of the arrival of the Pakeha and a presentiment of the *spiritual meaning of that defining moment* – thus the subsequent long-term effect for Maori.

The third *impression*, which emanated from the horizontal end-point of the extreme right of the arc, represented the collective future of both races and of the land itself. It was one of *uncertainty*, but uncertainty in the sense that it could not be definitively stated or even shown with regard to the human decision-making element that ultimately produces all outcomes. (For that outcome will ultimately be determined, and is still yet to be, by our *collective* decisions in the present. – [Original Edition.])

Now in 2011, however, the end-outcome is much easier to discern. Whilst the potential for a good future is always possible, the whole global societal trend indicates that we *will* follow it if we *do not* make the radical changes *necessary* to stay those strongly-indicated outcomes for all peoples.

The picture of the 'rainbow-arc' also revealed the issues to be written about, which subsequently became the original Chapter headings for the final form of the finished Work. The more I wrote, the more the thread seemed to reveal until, when writing about Ratana, a very deep spiritual experience occurred. Along with the very strong emotions associated with that experience, there arrived a picture that **decisively showed** the major **spiritual significance** for Maori **deriving from** the arrival of the Pakeha. The whole occurrence was exceptionally strong and very emotionally draining. The effect stayed with me for some days.

> The **key legacy** from that revelation, therefore, was the powerful and **clear mandate** given to write this Work – **for Maori in the first instance**.

The knowledge contained herein is thus the final fulfilment given to the line of the later group of Maori Prophets – especially Ratana – to lead the race away from its bind to those beliefs and practices, **strongly resurgent once more** which:

> – **they clearly recognised** as being **spiritually detrimental** to the **ordained path** that they, the Prophets, were blessed **to receive and teach**.

This Work, therefore, *in the fullness of the mandate given*, <u>fulfils</u> the key statement which Ratana, the greatest of them, gave to *all* in the Maori race.

Indeed, his message was to all in this land – then and now:

"I have *opened* the door, but *you yourselves* must go in. I am but a finger post *pointing* to the *true way* of life!"

(Ratana, J.M. Henderson.
Emphases mine.)

This **FINAL EDITION** thus *now finally fulfils – spiritually and symbolically –* what should have been Ratana's **complete mission**. And, moreover, reveals where the final knowledge, the *true way* that Ratana *unfortunately missed*, can be found. The 'spiritual path' for Maori that Ratana unveiled and pointed out obviously has its genesis in the primary face-book of Pakeha religion – **The Bible** – which Ratana powerfully embraced. The "true and final way", however, – **Itself** clearly prophesied in **The Bible** for this 'rapidly-closing time' – is 'pointed out', *explained more completely*, towards the end of this Work. Also in the *primary Work* of "**CRYSTAL PUBLISHING**":

BIBLE "MYSTERIES" EXPLAINED
UNDERSTANDING "GLOBAL SOCIETAL COLLAPSE" FROM THE 'SCIENCE'
IN THE BIBLE
What Every Scientist, Bible Scholar and Ordinary Man Needs to Know.

The reader will find therein *extensions* of the knowledge contained herein. For that particular book is directed, *first and foremost*, to earth-scientists and their very narrow *primarily aspiritual* empiricism, and to Christian fundamentalists and Theologians of every religious 'bent'.

The necessary journey outlined in *this* book, however, primarily traces the thread indicated by the 'rainbow-arc'; from the arrival of the Maori, to the arrival of the Pakeha, and to that later, crucial Spiritual Event for Maori – the "Calling" of:

Tahupotiki Wiremu Ratana!

It is around his key Prophecy; a "...finger-post pointing to the true way...", that this Work is centred as a primary imperative, and to which – *the true way* – we must journey. For from Ratana's ordained task *should have come* concomitant and ongoing spiritual benefit and growth for *all* in the Maori race. Thus the final *impression* of future uncertainty from the rainbow-arc simply indicates that, for Maori: *Truly beneficial future outcomes can **only derive** from correct decision-making **in the present**.*

In the same way, however, all others in this land will also need to similarly choose, if the collective outcome is to be different from that currently indicated by unfortunate present-day social statistics – more particularly in Maoridom.

Because the Work scribes a precise journey, certain Chapters are crucial to its complete understanding. So it is vitally important for the reader to *also* travel that journey – *by reading the Chapters **in sequence**.* My sincere belief is that this book is written with Spiritual clarity and honesty in the first instance. Though uncompromisingly direct at times, I further believe that it also embodies the virtues of sincerity and compassion. My unassailable conviction is, therefore, that by following and understanding *the thread* revealed within its pages, will the door that the right hand end of the rainbow-arc represents as our future, open to a truly harmonious and genuinely spiritual place *for some*.

For even though this particular Work traces precise cultural and historical threads from the past, which intermingle and intertwine with constantly evolving threads in the present, and which would once have led to a golden potential in the future, *that will not now be the case for most*. For the mandate given also permits the insight to state **what is actually going to occur**.

So even though this book still offers the way forward into a spiritually-harmonious future as a *potential* for all, **only the few will actually arrive**. This Work is therefore more a story of an *evolving, collective swansong*. It will be that way simply because most people, as human history has constantly recorded, will stubbornly cling to that which they believe is the only **true way** – that of their *cultural traditions*, their *science*, their *religion*, and their *believed spirituality*.

However, those who are sufficiently awake to recognise the essence of Spiritual Truth revealed in *that* statement will logically travel this journey with an *open* spirit, thereby earning themselves a possible future with the few others of like mind who may also *recognise* the way. It will therefore be a future totally unlike that of this present time. It will be one characterised by societal harmony and beauty, and warm, mutual respect toward one another. And it will be that way by virtue of the fact that *those who refuse to embrace the new knowledge* **will simply not be there**. Their refusal to 'let go' incorrect beliefs will prevent them from completing the journey home, exactly in accordance with the perfect outworking of the inviolable aegis of:

THE LAW!

*   *   *   *   *

This Work, long waiting in the wings for its appropriate time of proclamation, has found its voice through certain, recent key events:

1. The release in 2005 of the Documentary, **"Frontier of Dreams"** –

   – and the publication of the book;

2. **"Fatal Frontiers"**, by Dr. Paul Moon.

For perhaps the very first time in New Zealand's social history, subjects such as slavery, cannibalism and the sale of tattooed heads etc., have gained real traction on National Television. Once considered too racially or culturally-sensitive to be discussed openly, they have now been more thoroughly dissected than at any time previously.

Thus a strong associated mandate for this book automatically derives from my genealogical connection to **Hongi Hika**. Known and feared in his own lifetime as **"Hongi the man-eater"**, that particular mandate originates from the fact that the genealogical line *from which I stem*; – **is senior to Hongi!** Thus is **The Law** for *this Work* fulfilled – even to current, strongly-promoted, earthly Maori protocol.

The path to this point, however, is an amalgam of strange paradoxes. The cycle began with the arrival of the missionaries into **Hongi's** care and protection, thence to his feared raids with the capture and enslavement of thousands of prisoners, further to their attendance at **Mission Schools** in **Ngapuhi-land**, to their release back into their former tribal lands, and thereby to the seeding and subsequent emergence of the line of **Maori Religious Prophets** – to finally culminate in **Ratana**. Thus did **"Hongi the man-eater"**, albeit unknowingly, contribute mightily to a crucially-significant **Spiritual Cycle** for this land and its peoples.

That particular cycle, in accordance with Ratana's prophecy to "...go through the door...", now finds **both its closure and the new beginning** 'beyond that door' **in this Work**. In necessary reinforcement, therefore, few there are who will actually travel the complete road. For in order to arrive at the crucially-necessary recognition that this Work is *spiritually-ordained to reveal and offer*, the *journey itself* must be undertaken. That 'journey', through being travelled *symbolically* through the many pages herein, will *educate* and thus *lead* the *wairua* (spirit) of you, the reader, *through the door* that Ratana opened. And, so, it will only be those *who do* travel this vital path who will thus *recognise – and receive*!

The strong, primary Title of this Work:

THE COMING OF PAKEHA RELIGION
The Spiritual Significance for Maori

New Zealand's Lost Legacy

– perhaps disturbing for many Maori, particularly – *must nevertheless be recognised for the simple and unequivocal truth that it actually and inherently possesses*.

Pakeha "Religion" – *which is quite obviously contained in* **The Bible** – was the **exact, precise and only** reason **why** the line of Maori Prophets could, and **did**, emerge to culminate in the last four strongest; but especially **Ratana** as the very last and **truly Called one**!

And why, therefore, *he* was given the ***Spiritual Power*** to ***destroy*** particular practices and beliefs – as previously stated ***strongly resurgent again in the present culturally and politically-driven 'Maori cultural renaissance'*** – that simply and unequivocally had to be ***expunged/purged/eliminated*** from the very **thought-processes** of Maori if there was to be any saving-grace mechanism to lift Maori out of their debilitating distress at the time.

Most unfortunately, the *spiritual* situation is no different today to what it was then. Even on the global stage, the same *spiritual paucity* holds sway for all cultures and peoples. The surfeit of 'blood and war' on the nightly television news coupled with certain kinds of 'entertainment', therewith unequivocally testifies to the stupidity and foolishness of *all* of global humanity. This Work therefore occupies a *key* position in *this* land, and near-future events will surely bear clear testimony to that statement.

Therefore, in concert with the Mandate thus stated:

All who live in this blessed land, *including those of different religions, cultures and ethnic groups who have chosen – through a free-will decision – to make New Zealand [Aotearoa] their home*, need to embrace the knowledge contained in this Work equally as much as everyone **born** here. For the key aspect **connecting** 'The Coming of Pakeha Religion' **to** 'The Spiritual Significance for Maori' is actually and unfortunately 'New Zealand's Lost Legacy'!

So: For *all* in this land, **New Zealand's** specific **'Lost Legacy'** may be found in the path described herein. All human misfortune and suffering ultimately derives from *choosing not to live* according to the **great truths** that are contained in *all* the major religions of global humanity. For they *all* hold *elements* of **The Truth** and thus **THE LAW**!

[The explanations herein give you, the reader, the knowledge to identify those aspects of *genuine Truth* that are inherent in the key religions.]

0.1   Proclamatory Message to Maori: to Ratana followers: to Politicians

Insofar as *this* Work is concerned, the Maori reader, especially, may wonder at the reason for the final line on the book cover, i.e.: **The Last in the Line of the Maori Prophets.**

Just as the Work was predicated on, and *guided by*, the Vision of the 'rainbow arc' notated at the beginning of this **Note**, so was that particular 'book-cover' statement also *so guided* – for the precise purpose of *strongly-elucidating* the subject matter herein. The reader should know, however, that notwithstanding the clear and unequivocal guidance to write what is now here in print; I, as the author/writer responsible for it, nonetheless *struggled* for very many weeks with the concept and obvious ramifications of incorporating such a statement on the cover.

After that struggle abated, however, the *clear recognition* arrived that *without* such a statement, this Work – as has happened with others that have placed Maori beliefs under close scrutiny – would *probably* have been labelled just another 'Maori-bashing exercise'. *With* that statement included, however, it becomes, **in absolute terms according to "The Spiritual Laws of Creation"** – *of which this Work gives <u>clear</u> explanation* – a non-negotiable Document, *precisely **because** of those inviolable Truths contained herein*. Hence the *clear guidance* to so include that final line on the book cover!

The crucial knowledge and explanation of **The Spiritual Laws of Creation [CREATION-LAW]** – we may call them the Universal Laws, the Laws of Life, the Natural laws etc., etc.. – are, in the final analysis, *the key reason for the writing of this Work*. The clear recognition has finally dawned for global humanity that it must now face the innumerable and serious problems *it **has** created* in its cultures, political systems, its business paradigms and environmental practices; or suffer ***irretrievable collapse***.

More especially in humankind's fracturing religions/cultures, however, do we see perhaps the *greatest harm* in increasingly-bloody practices ultimately deriving from the perverse refusal to live according to the only regime that *can* offer peace and harmony for *all* of man's activities – exactly those **Perfect Laws**. On his journeys away *from* New Zealand, Ratana had the opportunity to find them, *and* **The One** who brought them – as did Gandhi. *Both did not find – [recognise].*

Without fear or favour, the knowledge contained herein is thus also strongly-directed to all those who are either members of the Ratana Church ***and/or*** followers of Ratana himself. These kinds of distinctions must be stated. For in the pivotal Chapter 19 about the ***true*** meaning and purpose surrounding the mission of the greatest **Maori Prophet** – **Ratana** – we specifically include therein, precisely for Ratana followers and Church members – *but more especially for the present 'leadership'* – the **warning** of the Apostle Paul.

That warning from one **Called** by **The Light Above** – *as was Ratana* – should give serious cause for deep thought for all those who have chosen to be part of Ratana's Movement! For that warning is written for all time in the face book of Pakeha Religion – **The Bible!** Moreover, it is precisely that *especial book* and the knowledge contained within upon which Ratana *faithfully built* his Movement and thus also his Service to **The Light**!

This message is also directed to those politicians of the various parts of New Zealand's 'political spectrum' who, each year around 25th January, *dutifully proceed to Ratana Pa* to *attend* the annual celebrations of the founder's birthday. Under the outworking of inviolable and unchangeable **Spiritual Law**, if that is the true intention then no adverse reciprocal effects will ensue. However, if the participation is simply a *political front* for the purposes of currying favour or seeking *political association by numbers* without any *genuine spiritual belief* in the aims and goals of Ratana, then, under the same Perfect outworking of the aegis of **THE LAW**, that stance carries the brand of ***hypocrisy***. And, as such, will bring about the *commensurate reciprocity* at the appropriate time.

*   *   *   *   *

The concepts outlined in this book not only represent a major challenge to *traditional* Maori beliefs, but also to present-day philosophical, academic, medical, political, religious and spiritual notions. Yet, under the aegis of **The Laws of Creation**, those very concepts – herein – *are nonetheless __inviolable__*. "Lone voices in the wilderness" who dare to challenge the status quo – particularly those who possess no *academic* qualifications – inevitably clash with the *current academic thought* of their particular generation. However, the historic reality is such that *every generation* of academics must *re-learn* Kierkegaard's great truth, especially with regard to the *spiritual truths* contained within the great religions:

'That it is not *the truth* that lies with the masses, but the __untruth__!'

Historically, it is the lone voice or small group that holds, in lonely constancy, to the kernel. Very often that lone voice or small group will not possess that level of education or erudition which *the 'establishment' deems necessary* for the retention, understanding and dissemination of such 'elevated concepts' as religious or spiritual truth.

Yet the very same 'learned' from Bible-based Christian-religious academia, particularly, generally laud Paul the Apostle as a key intellectual thinker and scholar. That being the case – for we do not disagree insofar as Paul's access to, then, current knowledge and truth allowed – let us use Paul's sharp intellect and hear what he says to his followers about the 'learned'.

> "For, contemplate your vocation brothers: that not many philosophers, not many powerful, not many high-born – on the contrary, God has **chosen** the **foolish of the world**, so that He might **shame the philosophic**...
>
> Therefore none can boast in the presence of God."

> (1 Corinthians 1:26-29, Fenton.)

> "...how many of you were wise in the ordinary sense of the word, how many were influential people, or came from noble families? No, it was to **shame the wise** that God **chose what is foolish by human reckoning**..."

> (Same Scripture – The Jerusalem Bible.
> Emphases mine.)

Like Ratana, I possess no recognised academic qualifications of any kind, thus no 'mandate' from any 'higher education facility'. Since that is the case, I will, for this Work – which greatly derives from **The Bible** and Teachings of **Jesus** – therefore accept without boast, the **greater mandate** from Paul, the appointed Apostle of that time. For with the Works I have been **directed** to write, I surely count myself blessed in being one of **His** "foolish".

Finally: In seeking *personal help* from the very "**Source**" that has been the *Guiding Hand and Voice* for this now completed Work on how to counter various forms of opposition that, since its original publication, *already has – **and will surely yet still** –* come my way; clear words were given for the purpose.

Since the *primary role* of a Prophet is to *warn*, in the closing part of this **Proclamation** – for the crucially-necessary knowledge herein – the *Message* from that **Sure Source** grants me the Mandate to *proclaim* the following:

If I do not tell you this, who is going to?

So notwithstanding the fact that we have already strongly stated this Work to be crucial for *everyone* in this blessed land, it is the Maori race *in the very first instance* that this book and associated journey *is primarily written for and directed to*. For it was the spiritually-ordained path and task of the key Maori Prophets to so reveal it, *step by necessary step*!

And that task could only be fulfilled through:

The Coming of Pakeha Religion!

This Final Edition not only reveals the final step, but also the consequences and ramifications *already deriving* from our *non-fulfilment*.

Key Maori Prophecies

"The name of their God will be Tama-i-rorokutia (Son who was killed), a good God, however the people will still be oppressed." (Ancient prophecy stated by Toiroa Ikariki [*tohunga* who prophesied Te Kooti] concerning the future arrival of the Pakeha.)

(Redemption Songs, Judith Binney. p.12)

"Kei muri ite awe Kapara
"He tangata Ke
"Mana ite ao
"He Ma." (Origin stated to be from Ngapuhi.)
("Shadowed behind the tattooed face
"A Stranger stands
"He who owns the world
"And he is White!")[1]

"Kingi Nui rawa ki te Rangi!"[2]

"O chiefs of the Ngapuhi, listen to me; let not the Treaty of Waitangi be covered by the flag but let it be enshrined in a cloak of this land... Seeing that you Ngapuhi will not listen to me, a spider will inhabit this house. There is a man coming, however, who will be carrying two books: the Bible and the Treaty. You will listen to him."

(Aperahama Taonui – Ngapuhi prophet, 1863. Ratana, J.M. Henderson.)

"From Katikati to Cape Runaway there will be one child. If he arrives within six years there will be great tribulation. If his advent does not take place within that time, in twenty six years he will arise from the west and unite the people."

"The canoe for you to paddle after me is the law. Only the law can be set against the law."

(Te Kooti Arikirangi, 1893. Ratana, J.M. Henderson.)

"The days remain when man will bow down in the presence of the Creator and climb onto the canoe to paddle as one. It will be known on the day for Taitoko.
"Then also Te Whiti will bow down to the one faith.
"After that another day will be called there. I will not call it but he himself will...
"Then we will all know that that is the day of the prophecies concerning the teaching and the Churches, on which we will come together, to be one in our direction and our canoe."

---

[1]The term white in this case *could* be taken to mean the Pakeha race today who financially own and utilise most of the resources of the material 'world'. From the *spiritual* point of view, however, the prophecy is imbued with far greater power if it is recognised that the actual "**Owner** of the **World**" is of "**The Light**", and not "white". Thus, the *Owner of the World* is **The Light Warrior**. Since all the colours of the spectrum (rainbow) make up white light, we can perhaps also designate Him to be **The Rainbow Warrior** (of Native American prophecy!).

[2]According to one particular "kaumatua" within Ngapuhi, this prophecy (though I do not think it is complete) was made by Turikatuku – *matakite* and blind wife of Hongi – after apparently 'seeing' water-bleached bodies floating in an arm of rough sea. It ostensibly predicts the coming of a Truth or the Teacher of that Truth. His teaching will have the effect of eventually sweeping the land of all that is wrong, thus returning it to a once natural and harmonious state. (i.e., Before the arrival of man.)

(Te Kooti Arikirangi. Redemption Songs, Binney. p.458)

"I have opened the door, but you yourselves must go in. I am but a finger post pointing to the true way of life!"

(Ratana, J.M. Henderson.)

"The day when the 'white thread' is revealed is the day when Ngapuhi will fulfil its spiritual destiny. The 'white thread' will be woven into the present 'unfinished tapestry' to complete it."

(Ngapuhi Prophecy, Anecdotal – origin not stated.)[3]

"Kotahi te [porowhao] o te ngira e kuhina [kanohi] ai te miro maa, te miro pango, te miro whero.
I muri, kia mau ki te aroha, ki te ture, me te whakapono."

**"There is but one eye of the needle through which the white, black and red threads must pass.
After I am gone, hold fast to the love, to the law, and to the faith."**

(Taawhiao Matutaera Potatau Te Wherowhero.)

"And a Prophecy was given to the People..."

"We came to Aotea roa to nurture the land and walk in peace. And we followed the gentle ways of Rongo Marae Roa down the ages and sheltered the kete that held the sacred songs of our ancestors. There was joy in the land from generation to generation and then came the greatest sorrow.
"Strange sails took shape before the wind and Tu Ma Tauenga visited the land with his vengeful warriors. We did not take up weapons, for that is not our way, but in the strength of our minds we stood against them offering healing where there was pain and returning kindness for anger.
"And the Fires of War seared the land. And our tupuna looked behind the rising waves of pain and out to the stars, and in words of binding prophecy, proclaimed...

"Walk in the shadows, hide in the mists, step behind the rainbow to save the taonga.
"Protect our ancestors. Hold the truth close and warm it with brave hearts, for pain will consume the land and the circle of our dreams will be broken. And all will seem lost beyond recall.
"Kia Kaha! Be strong! And the day will come when the taonga will be revealed once more. And we will walk tall with the knowledge in the kete and find joy in the colours of the rainbow.
"And the fires of truth will burn into the hearts of all people of the land. And they will find the trails of gentleness and peace.
"Kahuri te Ao... the world turns. And the circle of our dreamtime takes a new shape for a new dawn. And people of all colours join to bind what was broken and live in hope."

(Song of Waitaha. p,11)

---

[3]This Prophecy indicates that little of real *spiritual mana* will be achieved by Ngapuhi until the 'tapestry' is completed. We should note, however, that "spiritual expectations" from prophecy are invariably very different to what many may expect to occur. Expectations from any prophecy naturally requires *recognition* of what *finally* 'arrives'. And that clearly presupposes the need to then *accept it* and bring about its fulfilment, even if it may mean a new direction away from any 'revered but incorrect' beliefs. In this case, it is not that the "white thread" will magically appear in the 'tapestry', *but that the people must weave and purify that thread themselves by living correctly – according to Spiritual Law! For the gift of the "white thread" will not simply be just 'given', but will need to be 'earned'.*

The above prophecy from out of the "Race of Waitaha" holds, in essence, the same longing and hope for a genuinely spiritual Aotearoa and its peoples as that awaited by Ngapuhi through their prophecy of the "white thread". The obvious reality of present-day Maori statistics clearly reveal how far Maoridom is from that desirable goal and thus the equally obvious fact that neither prophecy has yet been realised. Such a worthwhile desire, however, should provide the spur to critically hold up that vitally key word – **why** – and fearlessly address the issues. It is thus clear to me that the reasons for those unfortunate Maori statistics have their source in the following prophecy/vision which I was graciously permitted to receive in May 1997:

> "A suffocating psychic blanket lies over Aotearoa and Maoridom. It is woven from 'forms' generated by the collective refusal of Maoridom to follow the *true* spiritual path that the line of Maori Religious Prophets trod and made clear – *one necessary step after the other*. Instead, a different path has been chosen, opposite to the way of the Prophets, in the incorrect belief that it is a genuinely spiritual one. It is taking Maoridom more and more rapidly back down into those beliefs and practices that the latter, greater Prophets **warned to leave behind**. The constant promotion of these wrong beliefs thus holds in place, and unfortunately continues to thicken, that dark, unseen cover which detrimentally influences Maoridom.
>
> The '*completed tapestry*' lies above the lower suffocating one. It is the true "Cloak of Spiritual Mana" which, however, belongs to "**The Stranger**" Who "Owns the World!" **His** "Cloak" cannot and will not descend for Maori until Maori 'voluntarily let go *their* lower one', which they *believe* to be spiritual. Not until all that is incorrect from out of the old been 'swept away', can the completed, higher spiritual tapestry finally 'cloak' *all the people*, thus offering healing and grace to the *inheritors* of this land."

(Author.)

*   *   *   *   *

Note:

Both the 'white thread' of Ngapuhi prophecy and the 'new dawn and the binding again of what was once broken' from out of "Song of Waitaha", is the knowledge contained within **The Spiritual Laws of Creation** in its inviolable outworking. Only the acceptance of those Laws can offer the possibility for the revelation of the 'higher tapestry'. Moreover, the above Maori prophecies which are *key statements* in my view – *at the time of their utterance* – could **only** have ever fitted into a Maori frame of *future* spiritual promise — **with the arrival of the Pakeha**!

The fulfilment of the prophecies in terms of the past, the present, or for any future potential did not emerge, and indeed could **not** have emerged, from out of so-called 'Maori spirituality'.

Moreover, it is equally clear and logical that the 'white thread' **cannot** be contained *within* Maori Customary Law either. For, if that were the case, it would not be expected to appear from *without*. Therefore, **the first recognition** for those who wish to embrace "the way of the white thread" must be that only with the **arrival of the Pakeha** could all the key Maori prophecies have ever been fulfilled. Fulfilled, moreover, *for the ultimate spiritual benefit of Maori*! For it is eminently clear that what has eventuated thus far for Maori in terms of those prophecies is embodied, in essence, in that which the Pakeha brought to this land – the spiritual teachings contained within The Bible! They are the Truths which the greater Maori Religious Prophets clearly embraced as being absolutely necessary for the spiritual ascent of Te Iwi Maori!

For Ngapuhi then, and indeed for all of Maoridom, without this recognition as the first step, *there cannot be either the "white thread" or the "new dawn"*.

*   *   *   *   *

0.2   The "Legend" of the Rainbow Warrior

In the previous pages on "Maori Prophecies" we alluded to Native American Prophecies and beliefs that portend the Coming of a Warrior who will bring the "true way". Through that event the peoples of the world *who recognise and embrace His Teachings* will be healed in body, mind and spirit. Right and spiritually correct living will, in its train, also bring about the healing of the poisoned areas of the earth. Though not a 'Maori legend' as such, the Truth about **Him** is imperative for Maori, nonetheless, for it is His Truth that the latter and stronger of the Maori Prophets were guided by, and to Whom they were ultimately pointing. It is important for Pakeha Christians as well, for the face-book of Christianity, The Bible, reveals the identity of **The Rainbow Warrior**.

Throughout the ages the rainbow has meant many things to many peoples. Even though we in modern, scientific societies understand the empirical aspect that it is refraction of light that produces the colour spectrum, we yet still marvel at its beauty. For many earlier cultures that did not understand such scientific principles, its appearance would have produced feelings ranging from awe, reverence and veneration; to possibly even fear.

Since we generally equate the term Rainbow Warrior with Native American beliefs, a brief look at just two of their many prophecies will provide a sure stepping-stone on the path to discovering Who the Rainbow Warrior actually is. Interestingly, the dove is often associated with the rainbow in Indian teachings.

'The old woman and the boy looked to the east and saw a great rainbow flaming in the sky. The rainbow is a sign from Him who is in all things said the old wise one. It is a sign of the union of all peoples like one big family. Go to the mountaintop... and learn to be a Warrior of the Rainbow, for it is only by spreading love and joy to others that hate in this world can be changed to understanding and kindness, and war and destruction shall end.'

"In my dream I seemed to be floating in the sky looking down at a land of many round hills. On the top of each hill was a group of Indians. Some of them were lying on the dry grass, with their fingers digging into the ground despairingly. Others lifted their arms hopelessly to the sky. Women were huddled together, weeping. All were wearing old, cast-off white men's clothing, just rags. Their faces were filled with a deep sadness, and their skin seemed drawn over the bones, so I felt both bodies and souls were hungry.

There seemed to be growing a strange light up in the sky. Looking up, I saw the sunlight flashing on the wings of a beautiful white bird, a dove. The dove circled down from the sky, its body and wings pure as new fallen snow. Fluttering and circling it came slowly, but there was a feeling about it of immense power, as if all that was in the sky centred upon it.

As the dove came near the top of one of the hills, a strange and remarkable thing happened. The Indians there suddenly sprang to their feet, gazing up at the dove. The white men's rags fell from their bodies and disappeared. – As the dove dipped low again and again, other dark-skinned peoples rose joyously from hill after hill and marched up into the sky following the beautiful white bird. I saw many costumes in my dream, but I did not know what they meant or what tribes they represented...

Slowly a bow formed in the sky, a rainbow of people marching to glory, a rainbow of unity and vision so marvellous in its sense of beauty and joy that I can never forget it nor hope to see anything its equal."

(Warriors of the Rainbow: p.15-20)

As with many cultures historically the Native Americans, too, regarded the rainbow with awe and reverence. For them it was a symbol of hope and promise, as the two quoted prophecies indicate. Its influence, therefore, strongly shaped their views and their perceived connections to both their Animistic[4] and Spiritual worlds.

---

[4]World of the Forces of Nature

The rainbow is strongly connected with the story of Ratana too. The many symbolic colours he used for the various aspects of his Movement, such as the rainbow on the jackets of the Morehu Youth Group uniform and the multi-coloured uniforms of the Brass Band. But especially what Ratana described as his 'garden of flowers' – the church officials and helpers in their respective and many-hued robes and uniforms – indicate a deeper spiritual understanding of the "rainbow concept" than is probably generally realised, *even by his followers*. Yet the use of that concept can be seen as a vital part of the spiritual symbolism necessary for the overarching requirement that Ratana should travel *a different spiritual path* from other 'churches'.

The importance of that strong "rainbow connection" is also clearly shown in the spiritual insight of earlier seers such as Te Kooti Arikirangi. From p.38, Ratana Revisited... Keith Newman:

> 'Te Kooti Rikirangi had mused at Wairoa about the arrival of one who Maori had been waiting for.'
> 'If that young man were to stand on this marae, or when he sets foot within the boundaries of Wairoa, then you will see a rainbow descend upon the marae, then you will hear the voice of Ihoa. Then you will know that he is the young man you have been waiting for according to the prophecies. ... When this young man arises in this very land he will turn this waka upright to sit on an even keel; he will put his treasures upon it and he will paddle it to a place already decided by him. The man's highway will be faith and his refuge will be Ihoa o nga Mano.'

Notwithstanding the material science of light refraction to empirically explain the colour spectrum of the rainbow, many earlier cultures understood a far deeper significance in the meaning of it than science currently recognises today. People who hold to religions with foundational connections to the Old Testament of The Bible, such as with Judaism, Christianity and Islam, will accept the premise of the rainbow possessing "greater spiritual significance", by virtue of the story of Noah and his association with the "rainbow promise" from God! It is precisely that greater *spiritual significance* which is singularly important for all of mankind, irrespective of whether we might still belong to a jungle tribe, or we cruise the streets of a modern metropolis with all our digitally-derived communications devices.

If we now scribe an instant path in Biblical narrative from Noah's sure belief outlined in the Old Testament to the end of that especial Book to '**The Revelation**', there we will discover the origin and singularly sacred importance of the rainbow. Of course, we may also recognise that neither the one in the jungle tribe – who nevertheless would still hold the rainbow in awe – or many of those in the 'digitised, scientific west' – of whom many would nevertheless also marvel at the beauty of the rainbow – would necessarily even accept the huge spiritual significance of what we shall state next. Yet vitally significant it is.

John, the "Seer of The Revelation" states:

> After this I looked, and saw a door opened in the heaven; and the Voice that I had first heard like a blast speaking with me said, "Come up here and I will show you what must happen."
>
> After that I immediately became inspired; and observed a throne set in the heaven, and upon the throne an Occupant. And the Occupant in appearance resembled in brilliancy a jasper and a sardius stone; *and the throne was encircled with a rainbow* like the sparkling of an emerald.

> (Revelation 4:1-3)

> "Then I saw another mighty angel coming *down* from the heaven, robed in a cloud. *And the rainbow encircled his head...*"

> (Revelation 10:1, Fenton both. Italics mine.)

Thus the "**Occupant of The Throne**", Whom the rainbow encircles, we may recognise as "**The Rainbow Warrior**", the **Warrior of Light**. He is **The One** out of **Whom The Living Word** issues, and therefore from **Whom** the healing of the peoples of the world and the diseased body of the earth *can* take place – if we so recognise and accept. (Regardless of all other considerations, it *will* take place, anyway.)

Here in New Zealand, therefore, both the Maori – with their increasingly prideful embracing of Maori culture; and the Pakeha – with his increasing propensity to embrace the scientific path of his race at all costs; need to both powerfully understand that the social pendulum, which these two diametrically opposed paths represent, *will only find the middle way through the knowledge that The Rainbow warrior* – **The Occupant of The Throne** – *has now given to mankind.*

There is no other viable path to an harmonious future.

It is high time, therefore, to seriously rethink the present paths and their divergent effect on the social fabric of the national community. The learning will come about in any case, either voluntarily, or through a forcefully-imposed acceptance wrought via severe yet perfectly lawful trials!

Ratana: 'Called' by "THE LIGHT"! A Prophet for 'Maori': For 'New Zealand'

0.3   Key Prophecies of Ratana

> "Be at peace. Fear not! I am the Holy Ghost! I have travelled around the world to find the people upon whom I can stand. I have come back to Aotearoa to choose you, the Maori people."
>
> (Ratana, J. M. Henderson.)

Quoted in Henderson's important work, this 'message' is simple and direct. Other 'messages' along the same lines, however, are stronger and supply the *basic* reason *why* for the choice of the Maori race to fulfil the particular task indicated.[5] Two similar, more fulsome 'messages' taken from Keith Newman's *later* book about Ratana permit us to know more about the singularly-amazing life of this remarkable man!

> 'I have come to you, the Maori people. I have investigated your behaviour, and found that you have sinned also. You have sinned in that you have *bowed to tohungaism and other Maori gods*. However, despite these misdemeanours, I see that you have not forgotten the Lord Jehovah, the Father and Creator of Heaven and Earth. He has this day heard your call and made his choice.'
>
> ([– a voice from the Spirit as T. W. Ratana is informed of his mission. p.44]
> With kind permission of Keith Newman, author of 'Ratana Revisited – An Unfinished Legacy'. Italics mine.)

> 'I am the Holy Spirit, I have visited the scene of the war which has recently raged in Europe. In my travels I have found that the whole world has forgotten me. I have looked all over for some place *to establish myself*, and to ensure *that God will again be truly known and accepted in the hearts of men*. That is why I have come to you, the Maori people. I have investigated your behaviour, and found that you have sinned also. You have sinned in that you have bowed to tohungaism and other Maori gods. However, despite these misdemeanours, I see that you have not forgotten the Lord Jehovah, the Father and Creator of Heaven and Earth. He has this day heard your call and made his choice.'
>
> ('Ratana Revisited...' p.54. Italics mine.)

Keith Newman records a vision by Ratana in 1918 which brought forth the following:

> 'I, Ihoa, have heard the cry of the people, this is the reason why I have come to you, the Maori people, to be my footstool upon the earth. Go forth and unite the Maori people under me, Ihoa, heal them in all their infirmities, in the name of the Father, the Son, the Holy Spirit and the Faithful Angels.'

---

[5]The *detail* of the *complete reason why* can be readily understood from the unequivocal thread which this Work and journey is ordained to reveal.

'Although the faith was brought here by other people, *it will be us who will take the real faith to them*, because the real faith has been established among us, the Maori people. It was in 1814 that the faith was first brought to this land, but in 1918 you the Maori people first came to know what the faith really is. ... You have the faith, you the Maori people of New Zealand. Therefore you, the iwi morehu (scattered tribe) have been given the power through prayer of improving health and wellbeing, strength and enlightenment.'[6]

(T. W. Ratana, 1924. 'Ratana Revisited...' Italics mine.)

'Soon, very soon in the future you will no longer speak, but instead a very different person (generation) will reveal to you all the fruits of these prophecies. Not only will it be revealed exclusively to you the morehu only, no but to the whole country.'

(T. W. Ratana, 1929. 'Ratana Revisited...' p.15
Emphasis and parenthetic addition mine.)

'You have all heard and are familiar with the word that says': 'Night time has passed, the new break of dawn draws near', there is a day unfolding when you will see two towers standing on the Mount of Olives, and at that time you will see a woman rising up from the Labour Party who will become prime minister, and then you will know you are at the doorway, not nearing it, **but actually at the doorway**...'

(T. W. Ratana, 11th November 1936 at the Mount of Olives, Ratana Pa.
'Ratana Revisited...' Emphasis mine.)

"*I have opened the __door__*, but you yourselves must go in. I am but a finger post pointing to the true way of life!"

(Ratana, J. M. Henderson. Emphasis mine.)

*   *   *   *   *

0.4   Prophecies and Fulfilment – Post-Ratana

Many prophesied the rising and mission of Ratana. Most of those who did so saw him, *quite correctly*, as the *greatest* of the **Maori Prophets**. And perhaps, therefore, as the last to offer and/or proclaim revelatory or spiritual insight for Maori.

Such a prophecy arose in the Mangakahia valley south of Whangarei during the First World War. Keith Newman (Ratana Revisited – An unfinished Legacy) on page 38 writes that Akuhata (Hata) Kiwi, an elder from there, stated the following:

'After this war, this pillar shall come, a man; when this young man comes, he shall be the young man who will turn the people to the true faith, he shall not be lost, for his voice shall be like that of a bird. ... After this war, Ihoa's blessing and saving of the Maori people will come to be known.'

In another prophecy he proclaimed:

---

[6]We should note that Ratana's admonition to the Maori people at the time that they had been 'given the faith' can only have meaningful application if 'the strength of the faith' is fully embraced and thus used meaningfully 'in gratitude' to "The Creator". Simply being given a mandate of 'faith' without the 'continual work' which must accompany it means that a once strong 'faith' can slide to become just ritual and tradition – thus with the loss of the crucial *spiritual accompaniment* that marks 'genuine faith'.

> 'This young man will come before I have passed through death's veil. ***There will be no prophets, or knowledgeable teachers after him, never.*** If and when this young man comes he will bring with him peace and the faith, and he will be instrumental in getting back for you your remaining lands.'

(Bold emphasis mine.)

The single, strongly-emphasised sentence in the previous quote is so emphasised to reinforce the fact that Hata Kiwi's prophecy *is wrong*. Clearly gifted with greater visionary insight, Ratana was permitted to see and prophesy to a more precise and certain pattern. Therefore, the fact that he ***did*** prophesy another reveals the common human error of a 'lesser visionary' [Hata Kiwi] presuming to know more than the "greater one prophesying". Ratana obviously understood that certain key aspects of knowledge ***were reserved for a future time***, thus his prophecy to spiritually prepare the morehu and, indeed, ***all in this land*** for that future time.

It would produce that which he prophesied: ***the bringing to light 'the fruits of his prophecies'*** which would be revealed ***by a very different person (and of a different generation)***. Not only were the fruits to be made known, however, but also the key to what Ratana was pointing to ***through the open door*** and ***the meaning of the years*** in which those two key prophecies of 1929 and 1936 were proclaimed.

Such vital knowledge, however, can only be understood by *that* reader who unequivocally *recognises* that it is ***this particular book*** which contains precisely that about which Ratana prophesied and thus ***would complete his Work and Spiritual Mission***. For it was *he* who ultimately *should have* produced it. Had he found [**recognised**] what he was really seeking on earth, Ratana would have given *the key spiritual knowledge – **even then waiting for him beyond the open door to which he pointed*** – to his followers and to all in Aotearoa ***during his lifetime***. It was the very same key that *Gandhi* also sought. **He, too, did not find [recognise]!**

According to the historical narrative, though; after the completion of the Temple in 1928, Ratana announced that ***his spiritual works were complete***. In the case of Ratana – the *Mangai* – such a decision was an *unfortunate and premature one*, for *spiritual work* can *never* be ended. By its very nature, it is *the crucial constant* which must be striven for *constantly*, thus permitting ongoing and very necessary spiritual *ascent*.

His premature decision meant that not only would he *not then find* [**recognise**] and thus *not complete* his nonetheless incredible 'Calling', but it *absolutely ensured* that many decades would have to pass before the meaning of perhaps his primary prophecy: *"Soon, very soon in the future you will no longer speak...",* '*but instead a very different person...*' could, and would, finally reveal '*all the fruits of his prophecies*'.

Notwithstanding his prophecies about another in the future, the day before his passing, 17 September 1939 at 9 pm, Ratana directed the following [to] his son:

> 'Toko, light the torch. I am leaving the spiritual and material works to you. The European and Maori sides of the work are in your care.'

And on the day of his death, at 3 am, he gave his last message:

> 'I do not desire that anyone should finish my work, other than Tokouru and the family.'

('Ratana Revisited...' p.382)

So even though, in his dying hours, Ratana passed his mandate to his family, at the height of his prophetic ability years before there nonetheless arose in him the recognition for, and the prophecy about, the requirement for *another* in the *future* to *complete* his task. *Clearly not, therefore, someone from his earthly family.* The 'Calling' of Ratana – **'Te Mangai O Te Maori'** – came from **"The Light"**; for Ratana, solely. The very *spiritual magnitude* of his 'Calling' and great spiritual mission decreed that he could not simply just *hand it over* to a member of his family as he chose. For only *he* of his *earthly whanau* was *granted* the requisite talents and spiritual abilities for such a momentous task.

The actual necessity for the prophecy concerning *another* in the future to complete his Work derived from certain *crucially-significant* 'events' that occurred in Europe during the 1920's and 1930's. Notwithstanding the fact that a major aspect of Ratana's journey to Europe concerned 'land issues at home', the very fact that he was actually *in Europe* in that time-period reveals the **spiritual-ordination from Above** that the issue of land **was not at all the 'primary reason' for him to travel there.**

In truth, it was meant to have been a **'Spiritual Pilgrimage'** for him. For only **with** the understanding of the **spiritual why** for that first journey to Europe could he have **completely fulfilled** his ordained Spiritual Mission for New Zealand in the first instance. There would not then have been the necessity to prepare the morehu for *another in the future* to finally reveal *'all the fruits of his prophecies'*.

Moreover, *had* Ratana made the key recognition that his Pilgrimage to Europe actually necessitated, and *had* 'Maoridom' of the time *also* recognised the reason – **for they would surely have seen a far more spiritually-powerful Ratana** – then *other* key prophecies of **Te Mangai** would have been fulfilled. So, *had* those 'twin recognitions' occurred, the resultant 'wave of greater spiritual activity' would have travelled outwards to resonate with certain, specific 'groups' of the world's peoples.

In *that* 'revelation' from 'The Last in The Line of The Maori Prophets' may be understood the reason why particular, perhaps cryptic, prophecies/visions were given by and to Ratana. For not only was he the most *especial* Prophet for Maori and for New Zealand, but also a spiritual leader for those other 'specific groups' of people.

i.e. The prophecy: 'Although the faith was brought here by other people, *it will be us who will take the real faith to them...*'
And a particular vision of: 'All the world's roads leading to him...'

Through these analyses we *begin the process* of understanding the meaning of 'all the fruits of [his] prophecies'. So for Maori today – and irrespective of the place that 'Te Tiriti' ostensibly holds as a so-called defining partnership-document, or the 'Treaty deals' thus far 'signed off' – the key truth of the following, most important, proclamation should hold **first place** in the very psyche of that race of people into whom Ratana was incarnated to lead into '**Light**'.

"Let us <u>first</u> unite in the Father *and then* we will unite in the land."

(Ratana, J. M. Henderson, Emphases mine.)

To necessarily repeat: Recognition by him of the *'primary spiritual event'* of *his* time would ultimately have resulted in **complete fulfilment** of what was his nonetheless very great **spiritual mission** on earth. His Church and Movement would have developed far more strongly and be very different today as a consequence. More importantly, however, the **ordained task** that Ratana was **born to fulfil** – of which his **pilgrimage to Europe was key** – would have ultimately impacted on *all* of New Zealand society to the greatest possible, **spiritually-beneficial**, degree.

Ratana intuitively knew that the one in the future would be **very different** from the Prophets of the past in that he would *necessarily be* of *both races* – **Maori and Pakeha**. A half-caste configuration would **'symbolically unite'** the *two threads* of the *two peoples*, and the recognition and thus **acceptance** of what *he* would **'bring to light'** *could* also **'spiritually unite'** the two *primary* peoples of Aotearoa. The oft-quoted but sometimes contentious proclamation: "He iwi tahi tatou" – "We are one people"; was first stated by Governor Hobson during the signing of the Treaty of Waitangi in 1840.

According to Dame Joan Metge, ('Ratana Revisited...' p.19), the phrase correctly translated in 1840 would have meant:

"We two peoples together make a nation."

In that *spiritually-correct* translation lies the key reason why the one Ratana *referred to* would need to **stand**, (*e tu*), not as **the last Maori Prophet** but – as a descendant of the two main races – *as the last to arise in the line* of the **Maori Prophets**.

The reader must recognise the very important distinction here, for therewith **a vital link and cycle from Hongi Hika to Ratana and beyond is spiritually fulfilled**. Though already strongly emphasised, the fact that the one spoken of **would be the last in the line to arise**, means that he not only **could and would** "...reveal all the fruits of Ratana's prophecies..." but that **he could therefore also define the greater spiritual dimension of Ratana's Calling**. Indeed, he would not only understand the meaning of the years 1929 and 1936 for two of the key prophecies outlined above, but very much more besides.

The *precise detail* of those dates is not revealed in this, **The Final Edition**, for as previously noted, such *defining knowledge* is only for those, perhaps few, who recognise **the truth** of what is stated **herein**. In broad terms, however, the two dates bring to light the crucial time-period in the 20th century we alluded to [Ratana's time] which connects to a similarly crucial moment in time in the 21st century. We may thus recognise that moment primarily **through two key prophecies of 1929 and 1936**, and *further recognise* that the crucial point which Ratana foresaw **has arrived**.

Leading up to 'the moment', however, were certain necessary preparations and events. The study of Ratana and his incredible mission through various publications was fundamental to this ordained course, as was public awareness of his prophecies; for their undeniably-powerful impact may be read in the social, religious and political history of this country. Emerging as essential for the path to final revelation, therefore, are a number of vital factors. They are the very important work about **Ratana** by **J. M. Henderson**, essays about him in various publications on New Zealand history, **the time of the emergence of a woman prime minister from out of the Labour Party** (our present time in history) and, perhaps most central of all, the prime recent work on Ratana: **"Ratana Revisited – An Unfinished Legacy"**, by **Keith Newman**. It builds on and extends J. M. Henderson's work.

It is Keith Newman's publication, however, which permits **the final convergence** of many different yet major threads to track their ordained way to the crucial first decade of the 21st century, and thence to the decisive year of 2006.

Seventy seven years to that year have thus passed since Ratana's definitively-significant prophecy of 1929. From 'Ratana Revisited...' p.15: (Italics and parentheses mine.)

> *"Soon, very soon in the future you will no longer speak, but instead a very different person (generation) will reveal to you all the fruits of these prophecies. Not only will it be revealed exclusively to you the morehu only, no but to the whole country..."*

In 1933 Ratana also gave the following, perhaps rather cryptic, prophecy. Cryptic, however, only in terms of the particular person and his future time; one clearly *not* from his earthly family.

> '...*I will send you a Mangai [anointed mouthpiece] that you will not be able to suppress. For I am leaving you, and so I will send you a Mangai. Where is this Mangai, and when will this Mangai arrive here? You cannot tell me this...*'

('Ratana Revisited...' p.540. Italics mine.)

*   *   *   *   *

Special Note

In direct concert with that key quote, it is important to now emphasise, in the strongest possible terms, the key recognition that Ratana followers, and indeed all Christians, need to take from *this* particular segment of the Work – i.e., the *Mandate* of **'The Last in the Line of the Maori Prophets'** to *also proclaim*. Because Ratana founded his Movement primarily on the teachings in **The Bible**, he obviously believed in the 'return' of **Jesus**. Thus his following statement exactly about that 'expected event'.

> '...That we may prepare ourselves for Thy coming Kingdom, **when it comes to this earth**, fuelled as it will be from the powerhouse of your divine Spirit. We *await Thy coming*, Lord God, in all Thy Glory! When we, your true believers, will know our reconciliation with Thee, through **the reigning grace of Jesus Christ**, Thy beloved Son and our Saviour! Halleluiah, Lord! Yes, so shall it be.'

('Ratana Revisited...' p.384-5. Emphases mine)

Whilst we readily acknowledge Ratana's sure gift of prophecy, you, the reader, however, will find at the end of the *pivotal* Chapter on Ratana an unequivocal and clear proclamation about *'the return'* of **Jesus**.[7]

Notwithstanding the prophecies and proclamations from Ratana about a 'singular event' keenly-awaited by hundreds of millions, and our unequivocal *'support-through-spiritual-knowledge'* for and about his great spiritual mission and works:

My 'Mangai Proclamation' about "The SON Of GOD" and 'The Second Coming' stands absolutely alone and apart from every other earthly interpretation!

So Shall It Be!

*   *   *   *   *

In the year 2006 **this Work**, as a tentative **First Edition**, was published! And *therewith* the revelation of the greater *spiritual* paradigm for Maori and New Zealand deriving from Ratana's great Spiritual Calling.

However, in accordance with the ongoing and strongly-guided Mandate to offer the only *true* help now left for the rapidly-deteriorating state of religions, societies and cultures globally, **a**

---

[7]The reader will find precisely-detailed information from The Bible – with the *key Scriptures* from 'The Revelation' – in a stand-alone Booklet: **"THE TWO SONS OF GOD**; The Son of Man and The Son of God. *What The Bible Really Says.*" [In association with **'Zenith Publishing Group'** it is only available in New Zealand online at: **www.publishme.co.nz**]

stronger message must now be given to Maori – *including Ratana Church members* – in the very first instance.

Why Maori in the first instance?

It is precisely because of the *totally aspiritual direction* – **even if otherwise believed** – that Maori and political 'leaders', *hell-bent* on their *political, social and cultural agenda for all*, are propelling this country. And thus all who reside in it. It is a direction which sets itself *completely against* the clear path given to Maori by the latter Prophets, particularly **Ratana**!

Helped, also, by the mechanism of a document, 'The Treaty of Waitangi', that does not, in any shape or form, incorporate the very help needed to stay rapidly-approaching and dreadful outcomes wrought by our foolish intransigence to choose *not to recognise, understand and obey* – **the crucial and immutable, thus inviolable, knowledge of**:

"The Spiritual Laws of Creation!"

"CREATION-LAW!"

In 2008, the 'Revised Second Edition' delivered a *stronger Message* to Maori and New Zealand!

Now, in this **Final Edition** of 2011, is revealed the '**Final Step**'! It *is* the **Final Step** because it leads to *'The Complete'* that Ratana most unfortunately missed. And, thus; there is nothing else left to offer.

Therefore, **Maori 'Leaders'**, *especially*; lead your people into *genuine* Spiritual Knowledge and thereby understand what **'New Zealand's Lost Legacy'** truly is.

For it was primarily lost by Te Iwi Maori in the 20th century!

Can it be retrieved? In the closing stages of the time-frame still left to global humanity to spiritually-awaken, perhaps it can. But now only by a few! So:

Be Wise Before 'The Event'!

– for it will be 'too late' to be wise afterwards.

Preface

"Above all, *the pure light of revelation* has had an influence [**powerful impact**] on mankind, and *increased the blessings* of society. It is **impossible** to <u>rightly govern</u> the world <u>**without God and The Bible**</u>."

(George Washington.
Emphases and parenthetic addition mine.)

Now: Why would Washington so emphatically cite **The Bible** as a necessary medium by which, and with which, leaders and rulers should govern their societies? The answer is brutally simple. Of all so-called *religious* Works, **only The Bible** comes closest to explaining the knowledge of **The ONE-LAW – CREATION-LAW** – decisive for the life of *all* men.

For aside from all else that **The Bible** teaches, contained within it [from as far back as the eighth century B.C.] is – from out of **THE LAW** – the *one sentence*[8] of *absolute prophecy* that unequivocally explains **why all** global societies of Planet Earth are not just *failing*, but will **fall utterly**. Isaiah – the "Great Prophet" – even then *foresaw* the path that we of Planet Earth *would take*. His warning, though brutal in its Truth, has never really been heeded by we humans. For we know better – *don't we*?

"The earth also is *defiled* under the *inhabitants* thereof; because they have
<u>*transgressed* the laws</u>,
<u>*changed* the decrees</u>,
<u>*broken* the everlasting covenant</u>."

(Isaiah 24:5, Fenton. Emphases mine.)

President George Washington – whom many Americans regard as their *great* President – would surely be appalled at present-day American society. Perversely demanding the so-called "freedom-rights" of the Constitution, its citizens, through the visual, written and electronic mediums, have flooded not just their own society but also much of the rest of the world with [to name just two] spiritually-foolish and totally unnecessary excesses – foul language in music, and explicit sexual deviancy and pornography in numerous forms. Much of the world has followed – if not actually embraced – America's absolutely non-spiritual, non-beneficial, societal *example*.

A small example from America – land of the free!

When Minister Joe Wright was asked to open the new session of the Kansas [USA] Senate, everyone was expecting the usual generalities, but they heard a very different kind of prayer.
The response was immediate. A number of legislators walked out during the prayer in protest.

---

[8]Because Isaiah's prophecy encapsulates the **real** reason for **all** of humankind's problems and failings, where relevant in this Work, it is repeated.

In 6 short weeks, Central Christian Church, where Reverend Wright is Pastor, logged more than 5,000 phone calls, with only 47 of those calls responding negatively.

The church is now receiving international requests for copies of this prayer from India, Africa and Korea.

Commentator Paul Harvey aired this Prayer on his radio program, "The Rest of the Story", and received a larger response to this program than any other he has ever aired.

With the Lord's help, may this Prayer sweep over our nation and wholeheartedly become our desire so that we again can be called: "One Nation Under God!"

If possible, please pass this prayer on to your friends.

"If you don't Stand for something, you will fall for everything."

Minister Joe Wright's **"Prayer of Truth"**!

"Heavenly Father,

We come before you today to ask your forgiveness and to seek your direction and guidance.

We know your Word says: "Woe to those who call evil good", but that is exactly what we have done.

We have lost out spiritual equilibrium and reversed our values.

We have exploited the poor and called it the lottery.

We have rewarded laziness and called it welfare.

We have killed our unborn and called it choice.

We have shot abortionists and called it justifiable.

We have neglected to discipline our children and called it building self-esteem.

We have abused power and called it politics.

We have coveted our neighbour's possessions and called it ambition.

We have polluted the air with profanity and pornography and called it freedom of expression.

We have ridiculed the time-honoured values of our forefathers and called it enlightenment.

Search us, O God, and know our hearts today; cleanse us from every sin and set us free.

Amen.

Now even though we have stated *where* a large part of the **One-Law** may be found i.e., **The Bible**, it is nonetheless important to still travel this journey in a genuinely seeking way. And that means asking and answering the questions necessary *for* our path of discovery *as* we travel it.

For **_this_ Final Edition** of the history of Aotearoa/New Zealand holds the ***final revelation*** — for **_both_** Maori **_and_** Pakeha — of the *true* meaning of **The Coming of Pakeha Religion!** That revelation will reveal for you, the reader, firstly *where* the key *Source of Knowledge* to which we allude and from which the explanations in this Work are *ultimately* derived resides, and secondly; from *whence* it comes. Therein, therefore, thus also resides the *final poropiti* for this land and all in it! So: To our question and answer journey.

Individuals in crisis.
Families in crisis.
Races in crisis.
Maoridom in crisis.
Nations in crisis.
Financial system in crisis.
Planet earth in crisis.

How, then, do we as a global humanity want 'our world' to be? Do we want it to be according to our individual, cultural, racial, religious, scientific or national beliefs; thus the present, seriously-fractured state? Of course we would all say no, but clearly we do; hence the glaring and frightening reality of increasingly-ungovernable societies across the globe. Selfishly, and too often greedily, we all want the world to be 'our way', as shown by Pastor Joe Wright's Prayer. We want the answers to be 'our answers', and the solutions to be 'our solutions'. Ludicrous, and bordering on insanity. Yet that is precisely 'how it now is'.

The facts bombard us continually; from TV sets, radio, newspapers and magazines. Endless conferences, national, international, economic, educational, religious, racial, defence: all seeking solutions to so many problems. Witness the degradation of the earth with pollution, poverty, disease, ethnic savagery, tribal butchery, increasing crime and human rights violations – all by 'brother' humankind. In short, a new lawlessness and with it more despair, more agony, more hopelessness, more apathy, more suicides – more questions desperately needing to be answered. Since each year that passes **prepares the foundation for the next**, what is the prognosis for the world in two years time, or five, or ten, when there are no meaningful solutions to solve the problems? How long has the cry been heard?: "It will be better tomorrow, next year, **after the next conference.**" The reality for many of the world's people is that it is simply a lie. This incredibly beautiful "blue planet" we call home has, for increasing numbers, become just a hopeless hell.

Where, then, might we find **real** answers? Governments and politicians have not succeeded in providing them **even though they continually promise to**. Neither have the churches and religions of the world, nor rational science, nor intellectual sophistry and erudition. Most certainly small problem pockets *have* been given short-term solutions and, in some areas, there are genuinely sound ideas that offer *possible answers* in the long term. These, however, are often isolated and few and far between. Generally speaking, we travel down an increasingly bleak path, and the further we travel the fewer and fewer solutions there seem to be to "turn it all around". We appear to have reached the point where some problems may simply be too overwhelming in scale to rectify.

So, can we know what to do, and are there *actually* answers to be found? If we are not able to put right some of the larger problems globally, can we not at least ask the question *why* – in order to find the answer/s or reason/s? Logically, if we are able to *recognise* the reasons *why*, would we not then have our solutions? For in knowing the *why* and thereby *recognising* the *cause*, it must then be a logical and simple step to apply the *answer*, thus *producing* the *solution*. However, since our problems continue to multiply in both gravity and scale, it is glaringly obvious that we have not yet *recognised* the *why*, irrespective of all the "expert" answers. Therefore, until such time as this necessary *recognition* finally dawns, there will not, and indeed there cannot, be any real and lasting *solutions*.

For this to happen, mankind must first undergo a radical and fundamental change. Our way of being – for thousands of years – is the *cause* of today's horrendous problems. What we currently experience is the culmination of so much wrong thinking and foolish decision-making over that long period of time in the belief that our way was always right. That belief is now so solidly entrenched that, on the surface at least, it is difficult to see *how* change can be brought about. So even if we know the *cause*, we do not yet have the precise mechanism for the *how* to be implemented.

In the change that mankind must undergo; this must firstly be for each one, individually. We cannot *change* anyone else, we can only *change* ourselves. Governments cannot enact legislation to 'force' *change* in the citizenry either. Even totalitarian regimes are not able to do this. At best, there is only suppression, and for a particular time until the pressure is once more released. And then often violently thus producing further change. The new order is not necessarily that much better for the long term either, just different. That is the history of mankind on Earth. This is precisely because there is no widespread transition to the *true understanding* of the *why*. For only in knowing the *why* can a Nation or race become strong and remain so, and have the peace and harmony that seems such an impossible dream for most at present. If such an understanding can become accepted within the state, that vision and goal can be attained.

However, the *why* can only be found in the recognition of **The LAW**. We may well ask, "what law"? We already have laws. We have civil law, criminal law, religious law (**The Ten Commandments** and Scriptures from many religions), military law, decrees and pronouncements etc... Laws constantly changing, continually being reviewed and reformulated, modernised for "today's thinking", and differing from country to country. In some countries, from state to state, in others from tribe to tribe. In essence it is a completely ludicrous situation. Is it any wonder that so little of any real and long-lasting import can be progressed collectively anywhere, anymore?

Because individual cultures need to produce laws pertaining to their particular group, it might be assumed that all such formulated laws are therefore correct and lawful in themselves – whether for a small tribe or large Nation. Of course societies need to develop certain rules and guidelines in order to function more or less lawfully and harmoniously in any case. However, the need to constantly review laws clearly indicates they are flawed from the outset. Only a Perfect Law needs no further change or refinement. Quite clearly, mankind is not capable of formulating laws sufficiently clear or fair – in the dispensation of true justice – to *not need* this continual re-working process. Moreover, as there is an obvious requirement to have more than one law, then each should clearly intermesh with every other without contradiction or conflict, thereby producing an harmonious whole needing no further fine-tuning.

Since we are not able to do that either, is it not now time to search for the 'right way', so that we might finally produce fair and decent societies? The 'right way' *is* available to us but it will require far greater inner strength and humility from political and society 'leaders' than has been displayed thus far. Only by *their* recognition, admission and example might the correct way be enacted legislatively and thus followed, thereby allowing all members of society to fulfil their potential. Before any such recognition can beneficially permeate society, however, correct education must first be set in place.

The key point here is that any such recognition and understanding must be a *Spiritual* one! For the very essence of **The LAWS** about which we speak is that of Life Itself. They are Living Laws, as opposed to humankind's generally lifeless laws. In simple terms, in their automatic operation these *Spiritual Laws* return to us the reciprocal effects of all our free-will decisions. We have been gifted the attribute of free will to enable us to choose, along with all else, a personal path through life. With free will, however, comes responsibility. That means *spiritual* responsibility – for each decision made. But only the **decision** is free, the **consequences** are not.

In that short simple statement lies many an answer to so many *seemingly* unknowable questions. In the recognition of this fact, it should be a simple matter to similarly recognise that we truly are, therefore, masters of our own fate. The truth and correct meaning of the Biblical Scripture in Galatians 6:7:

"What a man sows, *that* **shall** he reap" –

– should thus be more readily understandable. In that Scripture lies a vital key to deep Spiritual understanding! Unfortunately, however, the true ramifications of this particular Spiritual Law are not fully understood even though it is quoted enough – and invariably with great authority.

Since this book is directed firstly to the Maori Race under the "aegis" of **The Law**, it is important for Maoridom to understand that that which we espouse and proudly promote as 'Maori law' is also, in the final analysis, generally about as lifeless as 'Pakeha law' or any other. For there is simply only *One LAW* for all men, irrespective of race, colour, creed, or their geographical location on earth. Any belief to the contrary is ultimately irrelevant, for it is within the parameters of The Living Laws only that all events must take place; thus also the arrival of the Pakeha here and the concomitant "spiritual significance" for Maori. As we unravel the "white thread" of Ngapuhi prophecy throughout the pages of this book, we will necessarily refer to, and offer relevant explanations of, those exact Spiritual Laws.

It should not be supposed, however, that the Pakeha were a particularly spiritual race when they arrived in Aotearoa, or are so today. The well-documented history of the European Races, particularly in the pursuance of religious power masquerading as service to their God, bears ample testimony to this, especially during the religious madness of "The Dark Ages". In fact, there are probably no truly spiritual races on earth. And neither the Pakeha nor the Maori are exceptions to this sorry state. Today, the dynamics of market forces and technology affect virtually all races in the world no matter where they live, and the overriding goal seems to be the relentless drive toward crass materialism. Conversely, however, whilst spiritual values are in retreat everywhere, more and more individuals are looking to what little is left of the purely natural world for the harmony and integrity that human society has generally lost, and clearly needs once more.

Because this book addresses issues from the point of view of *Spiritual Law*, which at the same time is *Spiritual Truth*, it offers clarification of all issues. In order to explain and emphasise certain aspects of The Laws, we will occasionally need to quote from various religious and philosophical works. This does not make it a religious work, however. Religion is utilised where it may have relevance to the subject matter of the moment. In any case, religion is *not* necessarily **Truth**. In fact it is rarely Truth. Religion is invariably the earthly form and organisation under which man establishes and promotes his many and varied 'ideas of worship'. Neither are such doctrines, by virtue of their 'status' as a religion, necessarily ordained or Divinely blessed from Above.

There is certainly no doubt that the world's major religions *carry* great and wonderful Truths within their teachings. However, because there are so many vastly differing interpretations within each belief, it is clear that not one of those 'interpretations' can lay claim to being an absolute and definitive authority. As previously stated, the structure of virtually all religions is simply that of man-made organisations, often put in place to perpetuate the power and influence of the group concerned with that particular set of doctrinal beliefs. Such beliefs may perhaps also be impacted by, or laced with, the cultural traditions of the people to whom such religions belong.

It is vital, therefore, that the subject matter of this book not be assessed from the intellectual point of view, for the aspiritual and earthly nature of the intellect can only allow a *material* or *empirical* analysis. Here, the intuitive faculty of the *Spirit* is needed. However it must be an *open Spirit*, not a closed one. Neither does one's race matter, though we are more concerned with examining the particular subjects from the Maori perspective initially. The reader only needs to be open-minded and objective with few preconceptions. And to be willing to suspend, at least for the duration of the reading of this Work, all the generally accepted teachings of Maori cultural tradition, the church and science, and much else that our education system deems important and correct.

Hopefully this book will strike a chord within the *wairua* (the spirit) of the reader. For in utilising the knowledge contained within **The Spiritual Laws of Creation**, one is more able to objectively review the past, examine the present, and thereby project future probabilities. For what is not learned from the lessons of history will return to haunt us to perhaps be re-lived, until the lessons *are* learnt. All we need do is witness the current state of the world! The lessons to be learnt, however, are *Spiritual ones* in the first instance, for **The Laws of The Creator**, to which we are all subject, are, in their unequivocal effect, first and foremost **Spiritual Laws**.

The disciplines of science, religion, education, politics, economics or any other subject cannot, in any way whatsoever, alter this one, single, immutable reality. Either we voluntarily adjust ourselves to those Laws and reap the associated benefits, or continue to oppose them and consequently continually suffer for our intransigence. We are gifted with *free will* to choose whatever we wish; heaven or hell on earth, thus reinforcing the stark fact of **The Law**, for we are irrevocably tied to the consequences of our decisions, individually and collectively. And, unfortunately for mankind, The Laws take no account of whether we are even aware of them or not. Ultimately, therefore, the price of being permitted the gift of conscious life is the *spiritual responsibility* to seek out these **Spiritual Laws** and live accordingly, thus guaranteeing harmony, peace and happiness for ourselves.

The source and/or veracity of the information and explanations contained in this publication may be of interest to the reader. The source is broadly outlined further on in this Preface. The veracity, however, will be shown more and more clearly in the continuing and further breakdown of all aspects of society, both nationally and globally – particularly in increasing natural disasters – **if** there is no acknowledgement and voluntary acceptance of **Spiritual Law**. Thus, until lawmakers finally formulate their societal laws in accordance with that greater and more beneficial regime, and educators of all races recognise and *teach* this also, there cannot develop any genuine progress toward a truly equitable and harmonious society anywhere.

Even though the title of this Work may possibly be contentious to some Maori – and perhaps even deemed injurious – it should really act as a spur to seek out *the why* of it. For by examining more than the opening introductory statements, the reader will discover concepts that have had no airing thus far but which, in their actual effect, impact upon each one of us in Aotearoa in no small measure. Therefore this work should not simply be dismissed immediately out of hand as a superficial, anti-Maori essay without a thorough and objective analysis.

The opening pages of this book also appropriately include Sir Hugh Kawharu's speech to the Commonwealth Heads of State at the CHOGM conference held in Auckland in 1995. Appropriate for two reasons; one because many of the Commonwealth Countries were once colonies of Britain, and two; because those same countries were also those of "colonised indigenous peoples" – two points that can be equally applied to Maori. However, whilst many former colonies of Britain can now claim full independence from 'her', in partnership with an ongoing Commonwealth bond, that is not the exact same situation for Maori who live in a "treatied partnership" with the descendants of the former coloniser.

The benefits or otherwise of "Western civilisation" that Sir Hugh alludes to have produced much debate and is also a key point in our analysis of the Maori/Pakeha relationship. Unlike some of Britain's former colonies, however, Maori are democratically free to argue this point, as Sir Hugh correctly points out. This is a clearly beneficial aspect, as the same cannot be said for the people of some of the recently independent colonies, particularly in Africa, whose leaders, whilst being of the same ethnic group, do not always offer their people genuine freedom.

In contrast to Maori who eventually "treatied" with the British, some African peoples under European domination had to fight national wars of independence. Unfortunately during those struggles, few truly democratic institutions were put in place. Consequently, with the removal of the European colonisers, one-party states of usually the largest ethnic group or tribe dominated all others within the newly independent countries, a generally inequitable system often resulting in bloody tribal conflict. The subsequent struggles that have marked the transition to truly democratic societies are, in some cases, no further advanced today than they were during the heady, euphoric days immediately following independence. Witness the despotic regime of one former president of Zaire whose obscene wealth was obtained at the expense of the people, many of whom still live in poverty. Following a more or less familiar pattern, a 'popular' rebel uprising is usually required to oust such rulers. And now the same potential in Zimbabwe, and possibly Kenya.

Perhaps such struggles might result in far less bloodshed if those relevant leaders were to take special note of what I consider to be Sir Hugh's most vital words in the closing sentence of his address. [Emphases mine.]

> "Indeed we believe that no good will come from any human endeavour that is not based on *honest talk* and ***spiritual guidance***."

Now, in the context of current Maori thinking and cultural tradition, the word "spiritual" may mean any number of things. In its distilled essence and form, however, *it should mean only one thing*. By **spiritual**, we should mean "of the spirit" i.e., that which is **not** of the material but which occupies the *higher level*. We should not use this word to attempt to describe things that are concerned solely with the mundane and the earthly, including some aspects of traditional culture.

Moreover, we certainly should not debase the inherent noble power of the word by attempting to ascribe to it practices or beliefs such as *occult* or *psychic* activity, for example – one aspect of *tohungaism*. Nor should we relate it to ancestral genealogy or *whakapapa* that, in essence, can be likened to ancestor worship. In complete concurrence with Sir Hugh's statement, therefore, we offer clarifying explanations regarding the many **incorrect** interpretations of this vitally important word – "spiritual", thus illustrating its true meaning. And thereby separating the beneficial from the clearly unhelpful, and even from the dangerous.

If we believe, however, that we actually can have "spiritual guidance" which might be described as being more uplifting, more noble in its origin, and therefore in its application more able to offer those higher virtues capable of producing the best kind of society; and if it *is that* which originates from *The Highest Spheres*, are we not then talking of absolutes? Are we not speaking of needing to apply 'rules' to achieve this desired state? Are we, in the final analysis, stating that any such thing as "spiritual guidance" can only be possible under clear, uniform, strict and *unchangeable Laws* perhaps? Our answer is an unequivocal yes to all of that! We can, moreover, state these 'guidelines' to be that contained within the perfection of **The Spiritual Laws of Creation**!

A singular memory of the formative years of my childhood in an essentially Maori environment was the often repeated reference to "The Law"! It was always stated with great sageness and authority by members of my own extended *whanau* and by numerous other speakers at various meetings and *hui*. Maori Land Court hearings, in particular, provided a suitably appropriate platform for 'legal' debate, particularly of ownership of land. And this question of "The Law" necessarily went hand in hand with the *whakapapa* or genealogical history of the *Iwi*, upon which 'rights to land' supposedly rested.

The abiding recollection of this reference to "The Law" was the great conviction evinced by both speakers and listeners as to the sacredness and correctness of this 'wondrous thing'. The clear inference that characterised the 'substance' of this "Law" was the strong belief that whilst it was certainly that which might be termed 'Maori Customary Law' today, it was also clearly thought of as the 'Absolute Law'. Therefore, it alone was thought of as being the measure by which all things should be judged. But was it the all-encompassing, far higher, *Spiritual Law*? The attitudes displayed toward this belief indicated that it was certainly deemed to be that too.

The curious aspect about it all, however, was the fact that no one could ever clearly define it. It was a wonderful concept in its ideal, but it did not appear to have any concrete form whereby it could be disengaged from its 'vaporous place' and applied beneficially to everyday matters. My personal view is that reference to this inviolable 'absolute' clearly indicated it was not just "Maori lore", but was also believed to be "The Law" – whatever that meant to the speakers and listeners. Certainly, by the very commendable 'spiritual practice' of prayer and *karakia* before the commencement of many events today, Maori ostensibly reflect an appropriate sense of reverence and veneration to a "Giver of Law". Whether this is a pre-European practice or one greatly influenced by the Christian churches, however, is not clear.

The strong belief among many Maori that the quite vague concept of 'Maori Law' should hold sway in Aotearoa has resulted in numerous challenges in the Law Courts. Maori have cited this "Maori Customary Law" as a reason to refuse to accept the dispensing of justice under so-called 'Pakeha Law'. Or, in other words, the present legislated "Law of the Land". By logical definition, however, the 'customary law' of any ethnic group can *only* derive from that particular people's traditional beliefs and customs; including even *fears and superstitions.*

It cannot possibly derive from any other source.

It does not at all mean, therefore, that such singularly ethnic laws are better than any other. And they certainly may not accord at all with true Spiritual Law, either in part or in their entirety. This fact should be clearly understood. Therefore, the choice of whether to live according to the higher **Spiritual Laws** or to adhere to 'customary law' exclusively, easily determines where any culture actually stands in terms of its 'stated spirituality'.

Thus it is important to clarify this amorphous thing called **The Law**. Throughout history many Races have based their societies upon this ideal, with the Jewish people probably possessing the strongest application of it in their long history. Irrespective of the basic tenet, however, it invariably has, as its underlying foundation, a higher being or beings who are the guardians of this "Law", with these same beings watching over the people to whom they will have given it!

The premise upon which this Work is based is that there **is** such a "Law", and it is this **One Law** for all men, which we designate as **The Laws of Creation** or **The Eternal** or **Spiritual Laws**, that we are vitally concerned with and which thereby permits us our book Title. It is that **Law**, moreover, which has brought the world into being, and humankind with it. This singular 'form' of **The Law**, however, does not take into account the personal interpretations that men may place upon it in their belief that it should serve their every whim. For the "Eternal" or **Spiritual Laws of Creation** are perfect, inviolable, unchangeable and immutable, and therefore, **unalterable**! And to them we must submit if we wish to have a better life than that which is currently the way of the world. For it is that way purely and simply because we continually choose to *break the rules* and thus suffer accordingly.

So, where aspects of Maori Law, Pakeha Law, or any other kind of law accords with **The Eternal Laws**, they should be retained. Conversely those aspects that do not, from whichever viewpoint, should be abandoned as soon as a more correct and beneficial statute can be enacted. Even that which I remember from childhood as being more the territory of various 'lore', whether of the sea, the forest, or cultural traditions; each aspect is still finally subject to the overriding umbrella of the higher **Spiritual Laws of Creation — The Law!**

What should be clearly understood is that it is not men's 'lore' that has given rise to **The Law**. It is precisely the opposite whereby the absolute perfection of **The Spiritual Laws** *permits* mankind to develop relevant 'lore' for his various cultures, in accordance with his beliefs and within the environmental and cultural parameters of the different races or groups concerned. "Cultural lore" should thus be formulated under the knowledge of the "Higher Law" in order for any real and long-lasting benefits to accrue therein too.

But where do we find these "Higher laws"? And from what source or sources should we cull knowledge sufficiently insightful for our purpose? In the Maori tradition perhaps a little analogy might offer that key.

> For aeons, under the watchful and benevolent guardianship of Tane, 'Elemental Lord of the Forest', the ground cover, the understorey and the forest canopy have all taken their rightful place in his domain, each one interdependent in perfect, natural, harmonious balance. The great trees which make up the forest canopy revel in their strength and power. During their centuries of growth they have striven upward from a tiny, fragile seedling on the dark forest floor, pushing through the middle growth until finally bursting through into the light. Here, in their rightful place, and where these great sentinels reach similar heights, they live out their allotted time span.
>
> But from time to time, perhaps over many, many hundreds of years even, a few trees more vigorous, more vibrant and stronger than the others, project their crowns above the tall canopy. There they stand, towering above the rest as lords of their domain. In this position, with their vision uncluttered, they see all the way to the horizon. And all others who have not attained to such especial heights have little choice but to acknowledge their status. These greatest of forest giants thus become the benchmark by which all others are measured if they are to have similar impact on their world. If not, they will forever remain in the understorey with a narrow view of only their immediate neighbours, never knowing the wonderful joy of being able to see to the horizon in the same way that the great sentinels can.

As in the above analogy of the great trees so, too, must we find a benchmark to look to in order to make sense of our world, in both the visible and the non-visible aspects. The ever-growing demands of an increasingly complex society continually bombard us with conflicting ideas and messages. We struggle in the undergrowth with our eyes on the ground, seeing only our personal opinions, our precious ego and our pride, all the while believing that what we have is that clear vision to the horizon. We should learn from the example of the giant trees reaching towards the light in calm, supreme, majestic confidence. We need to extend our vision beyond our immediate consumer, cultural or traditional wants to find the light of an overriding message of Truth against which everything else can be measured. One which can offer a clear, uncluttered view to the horizon. Then we will have simple, coherent and unchanging guidelines for a more fulfilling life.

For the writing of this Work, a simple and singular 'Maori upbringing' could not, and did not, provide a sufficient enough level of knowledge for its purpose. Like the analogy of the great sentinels, more than just the undergrowth contained in traditional culture was needed. It was vitally important to see the horizon too. Therefore, even if one possessed all the hidden knowledge of Io, handed on only to especially selected initiates of the chiefly or priestly caste of some of the tribes, or possessed all of the knowledge of all the ancient chants, knew all the *tapu*, the herbal lore, the *waiata*, the legends, all the *karakia,* and possessed a flawless grasp of the *reo* (language) and its delivery in correct oratory style of *whaikorero*, all that would still not have been at all sufficient for the task that the book title alludes to. All the above, or that which Maoridom generally espouses as complete spiritual knowledge in 'Maori Customary Law', was not nearly enough for the scope of this task.

For it, we needed more, much more! We needed the distilled essence of the truths contained in the collective seeking of humankind throughout our long march through history. This essence we may basically glean from mankind's analyses of the natural world, his perceptions and possible fears of the accepted but unseen worlds, his philosophic meandering, his religions, his science and, latterly, thankfully, his increasing *spiritual* insights. From this distillation, we will more certainly arrive at a more logical view of our world, Creation and the unalterable Laws that govern it, than that which has been handed down from ancient times to present-day Maori via the myths and legends that are inherently part of the *cultural* traditions of the race.

For in just one area alone, we can easily recognise the *inviolable truth of The Law* that clearly reveals the difference between that which cultural beliefs and legends may state about a particular race's origins, and the actual reality for **all** peoples. We will therefore recognise that our ancestors cannot possibly have come from anything other than the *human form* ordained to be the vessel for *all* of humankind. Any divergent belief from this reality clashes with all outworking of the **Natural**, and therefore **The Spiritual Laws of Creation**. Thus, ancient Maori ancestry is not one where the first-born were the offspring of the 'gods' or of mountains, rivers, *taniwha*, eagles or eels etc.. Our ancestors were human, the same as we are. For this is the lawful outworking of *Spiritual Law*, **The Laws of Life** – the *ultimate Law*. And Maori cultural traditions and beliefs *cannot change that immutable reality*.

Six hundred years before the birth of Christ, a new way of thinking began to evolve in Greece. Before this development people generally accepted that the answers to their questions could be found in their various religions. However, whilst they might be termed religious explanations, they were more the myths of the people handed down from generation to generation. Their myths sought to offer 'rational' explanations about the activity of their 'gods' that, in turn, made sense of their immediate world, as they believed it to be. Thus the Greek philosophers contributed immensely to the long history of man's quest for the ultimate answers to life, earnestly questioning all that was current in their society to begin with. This was not without some danger at the time, however.

One of the greatest philosophers, Socrates, (470-399 BC) accused of "...introducing new gods and corrupting the youth...", was sentenced to death by a jury of five hundred citizens of Athens. Forced to drink hemlock, he died surrounded by friends. By daring to continually question the status quo, he finally forfeited his life. His death profoundly affected Plato, (428-347 BC) one of his pupils. Also considered one of the greatest philosophers, Plato noted in the death of Socrates – whom he considered to be Athens most noble citizen – a striking example of the conflict that can exist:

> "...between society as it really is and the true or ideal society".

We also ask serious questions about certain current beliefs in both Maori and Pakeha views but, thankfully, with many hundreds of years of more enlightened thinking, such questioning should not produce the same reaction among the citizenry of Aotearoa as it did in Athens. Paradoxically, however, whilst the Greek philosophers were correct to move away from a purely mythical explanation of the world around them, their singular pursuit of answers from more the intellectual approach – notwithstanding their struggles to clarify the question of the duality of man i.e., body and soul – they nevertheless moved away from a vital aspect of their gods of myth and legend. That relevant aspect would have filled a particular gap in their knowledge. We examine this most important point in the later Chapter on "Elemental Lore".

Thus for many of our analyses, we will utilise the philosophies, religions and scientific findings of other races and cultures. From those peoples and cultures who have left behind the uncertain myths of their Creation and beginnings, retaining them only in the romantic beliefs of their historical legends, but who now unequivocally accept the human origin of their race. A major source will be that of The Bible since the path of the Maori and the Pakeha were heavily influenced by that Book and the missionaries who brought it here, and is therefore entirely appropriate to use. We will also utilise the knowledge of more recent and genuinely Spiritual works. From the various sources stated, we will offer sufficient explanation to give more meaning, purpose and *spiritual potential* for our collective path in Aotearoa than is currently the way, with **its** *potential* for totally unnecessary cultural divisiveness.

The, perhaps, unusual nature of this book, therefore, and the accompanying difficulties posed in attempting to adhere strictly and rigidly to an absolute and precisely structured format has necessarily resulted, at times, in what might initially appear to be *numerous digressions, by-ways and detours* from the immediate subject at hand. However, by following particular threads at certain points into different but related subjects, I have been able to flesh out, give example of or emphasis to, the matter being discussed at that precise point in our journey. Notwithstanding these necessary digressions, I believe the main theme is generally structured toward a clear, unequivocal and *unmistakable message*. Thus the by-ways add appropriate weight to the overall theme contained within these pages. The reader should therefore regard them as offering a greater dimension, as well as giving wider interest, to the main points of this Work.

Taken from the genuinely Spiritual standpoint, this basic overview of the path the Maori race has embarked upon since the arrival in Aotearoa thus clearly illustrates the "spiritual" ramifications of that chosen path. Because it necessarily merges later with that of the Pakeha, this event is also examined from the same viewpoint. And whilst the main aim has been to follow the historical path of the Maori up to the very recent past, certain aspects along the way provided the opportunity to come forward to the present time to offer a related perception about that relevant issue too.

In concert with Maori cultural beliefs of racial ancestry deriving from forms other than strictly human ones, the Work also sets out to explain particular Maori aspects we might term as belonging to the "unseen world". Thus we examine *how* the psychic forms of the Maori came into being, *where* they came from and *why*. Moreover, we offer explanations as to why the Maori greatly feared them, and the resultant ramifications of that fear, past, present and future. This aspect is particularly important in understanding the reasons for rapidly increasing levels of *mate Maori* and *mate wairua*, ancient mental illnesses that still rear their ugly head to infect far too many Maori, even in this so-called 'enlightened age'.

Notwithstanding the validity of the explanations we offer for those two unfortunate aspects within present-day Maoridom, it is often difficult to understand how or why there should be so much mental illness in the Maori race when there are many strongly-inherent *natural* qualities present. Positive traits such as infectious good humour, the *ability* to laugh at ourselves probably more often than not, the ease with which we *can* offer welcoming warmth, food and shelter to others, the love of music and song etc.. These kinds of beneficial traits should easily offset the alarming rates of Maori mental health. That is clearly not the case, however, and it is vitally important that all avenues regarding the *why* factor there are also explored.

Therefore, the clear need is to assess everything from the *spiritual outworking* of **The Eternal Laws** even though, via this means, certain aspects of our subject matter cannot always be 'proven physically' – or 'scientifically'. It is an *outworking*, nevertheless, that unequivocally reveals the subsequent effects that humankind's decisions bring – including those of the Maori – *differently* from that which the human view might espouse and expect.

So despite the historical evidence alone clearly showing the strongest propensity within the race toward matters psychic and/or occult there is, nonetheless, the clear belief among Maori today that they possess "great spirituality". Maori, moreover, also generally believe they are *more spiritual* than the Pakeha.[9] It is important to ascertain whether or not this belief has any basis in true Spiritual fact, for stating a far-reaching premise as a conviction about ones 'great spirituality' requires sound and factual reasons for such views. Given the present state of uncertainty among many of the non-Maori residents of Aotearoa about Maori intentions and demands in the future, this question cries out for an answer. Let us, therefore, formulate it as a precise question!

> *"Why do Maori generally consider themselves to be a highly spiritual people, and more so than the Pakeha?"*

---

[9]The word Pakeha describes all people of European origin and should not be viewed as a derogatory term. It defines this particular ethnic group as being distinct from those of Asian or African origin, and naturally from those who are Maori.

There appear to be five main reasons for this belief. There may be others but the following five seem to play the greatest part in this 'Maori view', in my opinion.

1. Maori believe they have generally been, and still are, more closely connected to the earth, the seasons and the environment in a way that encompasses a *non-physical dimension,* unlike the Pakeha generally.

2. This Maori belief recognises that people have a spiritual aspect and, for that reason, Maori conduct long *tangi,* retain connections to ancestors, genealogy, and the believed ancestral homeland of Hawaiiki – unlike the Pakeha who hold to no particular *spiritual/ancestral* place – in the Maori view.

3. The above two beliefs nurture a third view that espouses the practice of *tohungaism* and psychic knowledge and activities, as generally belonging to the realm of *genuinely* spiritual things.

4. Maori do not *believe* they live in a purely materialistic state; a *notion* that naturally enhances the perception of *greater* spirituality. Pakeha, however, are perceived to be totally materialistic and therefore lacking in spirituality – in the general *collective* perception of Maori.

5. In essence, Maori *believe* that the sum total of their historical and cultural traditions, their views of the physical and non-physical worlds, their legends, *waiata* and oral history, are therefore those of a *highly spiritual* people, unlike the Pakeha – in overall Maori estimation.

Yet only under the microscope of **The Spiritual Laws of Creation** are we able to make a proper "spiritual determination" for any such claims. That we shall do throughout the pages of this book.

Presently there is increasing concern from Pakeha – and some Maori – with regard to the often strident condemnation of the Pakeha from certain quarters of Maoridom, where the Pakeha has been blamed for virtually everything affecting Maoridom. Is this genuinely fair comment, and is it all as one-sided as many Maori evidently seem to believe? If the arguments are reasoned and objective and honestly seek to address issues that need to be examined, then that is obviously the correct thing to do. Certainly history attests to the fact that there has been much injustice toward the Maori with the arrival of the Pakeha, and very much has already been written about this in great detail. Whilst we acknowledge this fact, it is not the purpose of this book to add to that except where it may impinge/impact on the subject matter at hand or on the reason for stating it at a particular point in our journey.

The arrival of the Pakeha not only brought such things as the loss of land, strange and previously unknown diseases, but also rapid dilution of 'Maori blood'[10] through intermarriage. Quite logically the Maori could not have remained in isolation cocooned from the rest of the world forever. During the colonisation period when the European powers sought to add undiscovered lands to their Empires, it was probably fortuitous that the British were the eventual colonising power for Aotearoa.

No doubt it could be argued that a different coloniser may have been better for the Maori – or perhaps worse. In absolute terms, however, that will forever remain an unknown. In any case, there was simply no other choice for the Maori but to accept the presence of one. Paradoxically, the eventual European coloniser brought to Aotearoa a singularly important thing that the Maori would need for his "spiritual" future. That 'gift' to Maori is a key focus of this Work and provides the vital element for the Title. It also permits the "white thread" of Ngapuhi prophecy to emerge from out of the book.

In reinforcement, therefore, this Work offers *the Spiritual meaning and crucial significance of the arrival of the Pakeha for the Maori.*

---

[10]This is a most important point, about which we will offer *spiritual* clarification further on in our journey.

By viewing the history of the coming together of the two races from the Spiritual point of view, it should adequately answer many vexing questions in this area. In any case there are few real solutions in Aotearoa today. For only *with* **The Coming of Pakeha Religion** could that particular later event of great significance occur which would show the path that the Maori, as a race, were meant to take – but overall did not. As importantly, it will further explain why that direction *can and should* still be embarked upon now, and what the consequences may be *if that original guidance is not heeded.* For it was not given without specific spiritual purpose – for the Pakeha, too.

With the specific recognition by Maori of the significance of Pakeha Religion *to all matters Maori*, a greater understanding about the Pakeha and his role in the land of Aotearoa should develop within Maoridom. Moreover, the *recognition* and *acceptance* of that path would thereby ultimately bring greater benefit for Maori. In turn, the changes wrought through that *recognition* could not escape the notice of the Pakeha either, as *all* aspects of Maori endeavour would then begin to flourish. This spiritual flowering would thus allow true *tinorangatiratanga* or sovereignty to take its rightful and lawful place as a natural consequence of the observance and practice of those *inviolable* **Spiritual Laws** to which we constantly refer.

This book, therefore, may well be the ultimate *wero* (challenge) for Maoridom ever – the challenge to fearlessly and ***objectively*** examine what is stated here. Notwithstanding that reality, the Work should not be superficially rejected in indignation or derision under the psychologically demeaning method often employed by some Maori in the dismissively-challenging statement of:

"Who are you?"

There is a very appropriate saying which, incidentally, accords perfectly with the inviolable Laws of Truth, and it states:

"The proof of the Pudding is in the Eating!"

If the truth of this saying is applied to the content of this particular book and reflected upon with a *truly open* and questing mind free of any preconceptions or ***angry or emotive indignation***, it is my sincere hope that the reader will find enlightening clarification within these pages. Moreover, as well as a truly Spiritual explanation for Maori with regard to "The Coming Of The Pakeha", more importantly it *is* a signpost *pointing the way* to where the *greatest understanding* of the rapidly increasing problems that confront us today *can be found.* With *that recognition* should arise clarity of spiritual purpose and a greater measure of inner peace and sureness. Not only for Maori but for all races in Aotearoa.

In that sense, we may regard the whole thrust of this exercise as showing us more and more starkly, as we continue to travel down our self-chosen, increasingly precarious, collective path, what we must do to find the way out! 'Waiting in the wings', however, irrespective of whether or not a better, more spiritually enlightened direction has been embarked upon, lies our 'eating of our Pudding', of which we have already begun to taste! Since Maori are noted for their love of feasting, it is hoped that through "spiritually-objective discernment", the uncertain or unhelpful flavours currently present in our 'Maori pudding' may bring about a necessary, beneficial and *timely* change of recipe!

In reinforcement once more: Whilst the subject matter is addressed to Maori in the first place, it nevertheless concerns all in this land. For it is not without strong purpose that the Maori, the Pakeha and all the various other people of Aotearoa (New Zealand) have found themselves incarnated here together ***at this fateful point in planet earth's history and evolution***.

Whatever the rest of the world chooses should be its concern. Our *collective* concern and purpose should be to strive to become genuine *kaitiaki* towards, and for, this land that nurtures us all — Aotearoa/New Zealand. In order to fulfil that purpose, however, our choices should reflect a concomitant acceptance and willingness to live according to the *very Laws* which have permitted us a *spiritually-conscious life* here, in the clear recognition of the most precious *earthly gift* from **Above**:

A blessed and beautiful, bountiful land!

Part I

The Ancient Cultural Ways

1
"Who Are You?"

Know Thyself!

The decision to write this book was made with the confidence that I am able to bring to it the depth of perspective needed to both clarify and justify the reason for its very strong Title. In pertaining to things Maori:

1. To have the necessary ancestry as the first requirement.

2. To have lived the formative years of childhood in what could generally be termed, today, a "Maori environment".

3. To have lived those experiences which we would unequivocally state to be Maori in essence.

4. And, fourthly, to have the broader, wider experiences in life whereby these various aspects can be brought together in a more objective overview of the subject matter than perhaps a solely culturally-dependent or culturally-emotional Maori analysis might offer.

A particular dimension that might allow a deeper insight into our subject is Military Service, particularly the Army, since the Maori were essentially a militaristic race.[1] And if, during such service, one is fortunate enough to visit foreign lands and intimately experience the everyday life of other people – especially indigenous or native, tribal-peoples – this deeper sharing adds another very important facet to one's life experiences, particularly in the context of our subject matter.

More deeply felt, however, are the experiences shared with fellow soldiers on Military Operations. By virtue of its volatile nature such situations are imbued with far greater intensity than everyday civilian life, and more so when comrades – to whom one is inevitably strongly bonded – are killed in the course of soldiering. The volunteer soldier fully accepts this possibility, however, and adjusts his thinking and outlook accordingly.[2]

---

[1] In the two World Wars it was a source of considerable pride for Maori Soldiers to have served in those conflicts, as it also was for the various Iwi to whom those Soldiers belonged.

[2] The *toa* of former times also had to accept such possibilities on a virtually permanent basis, but of necessity, not of choice.

NUKUTAWHITI
to
PUHIMOANARIKI
generations to
RAHIRI

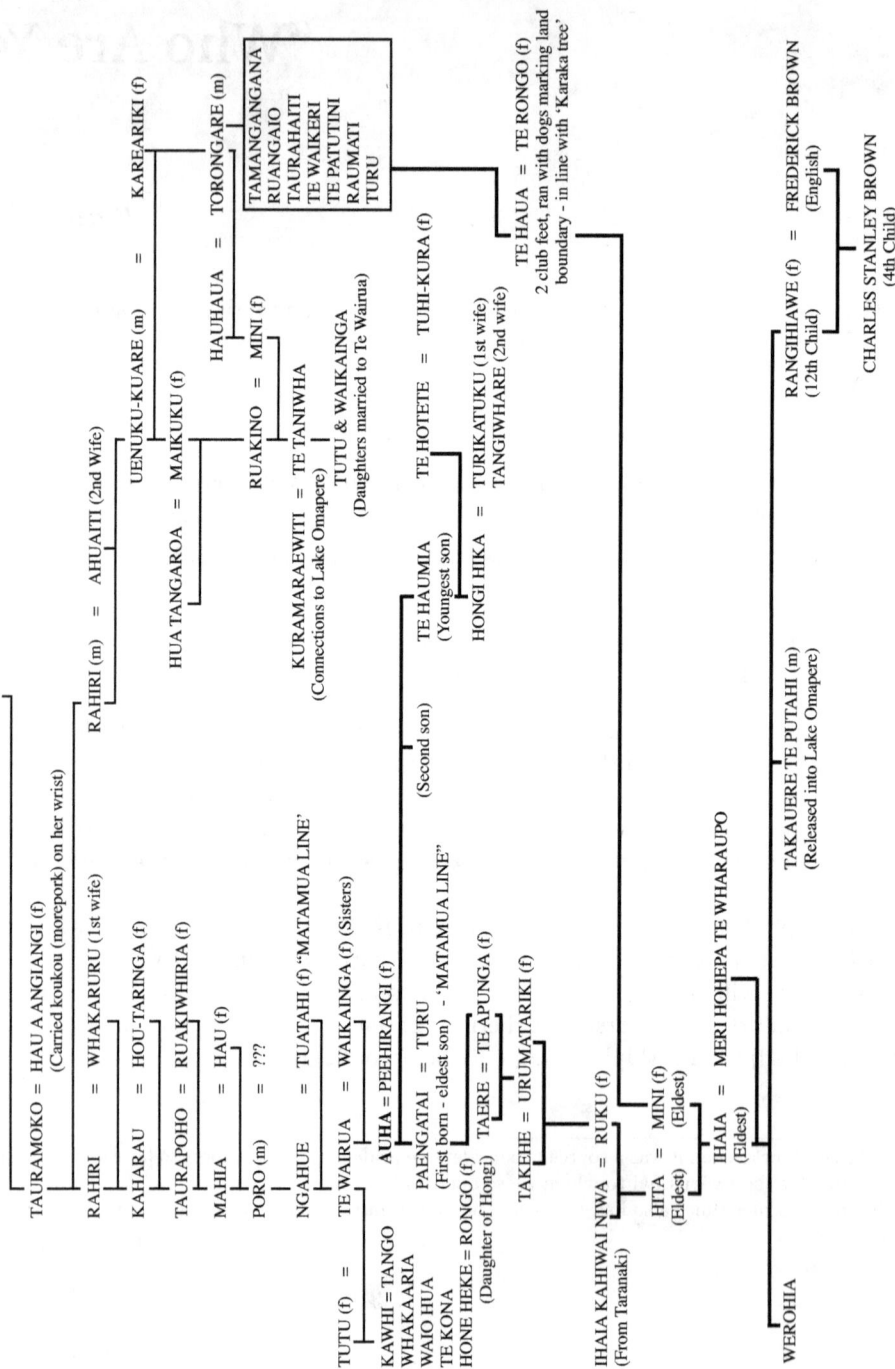

KAREARIKI (f)

UENUKU-KUARE (m) =

TORONGARE (m)

HAUHAUA = MINI (f)

TAMANGANGANA
RUANGAIO
TAURAHAITI
TE WAIKERI
TE PATUTINI
RAUMATI
TURU

RAHIRI (m) = AHUAITI (2nd Wife)

HUA TANGAROA = MAIKUKU (f)

RUAKINO = TE TANIWHA

KURAMARAEWITI = TE TANIWHA
(Connections to Lake Omapere)

TUTU & WAIKAINGA
(Daughters married to Te Wairua)

TE HAUA = TE RONGO (f)
2 club feet, ran with dogs marking land
boundary - in line with 'Karaka tree'

TE HOTETE = TUHI-KURA (f)

TE HAUMIA
(Youngest son)

HONGI HIKA = TURIKATUKU (1st wife)
TANGIWHARE (2nd wife)

RANGIHAWE (f) = FREDERICK BROWN
(12th Child)   (English)

CHARLES STANLEY BROWN
(4th Child)

TAURAMOKO = HAU A ANGIANGI (f)
(Carried koukou (morepork) on her wrist)

RAHIRI = WHAKARURU (1st wife)

KAHARAU = HOU-TARINGA (f)

TAURAPOHO = RUAKIWHIRIA (f)

MAHIA = HAU (f)

PORO (m) = ???

NGAHUE = TUATAHI (f) "MATAMUA LINE"

TE WAIRUA = WAIKAINGA (f) (Sisters)

AUHA = PEEHIRANGI (f)

PAENGATAI = TURU
(First born - eldest son) - 'MATAMUA LINE"

(Second son)

TAERE = TE APUNGA (f)

TAKEHE = URUMATARIKI (f)

IHAIA KAHIWAI NIWA = RUKU (f)
(From Taranaki)

HITA = MINI (f)
(Eldest) (Eldest)

IHAIA = MERI HOHEPA TE WHARAUPO
(Eldest)

TUTU (f) =
KAWHI = TANGO
WHAKAARIA
WAIO HUA
TE KONA
HONE HEKE = RONGO (f)
(Daughter of Hongi)

TAKAUERE TE PUTAHI (m)
(Released into Lake Omapere)

WEROHIA

It is my belief that the many and varied experiences outlined herein enable me to offer a uniquely constructive insight to some of the contentious problems we face as a race and as a Nation. However, since the *wero* (challenge) has always been an inherent part of the Maori ethos, I accept that both my assertions and the overall premise must also be open to the same process.

To this end I am sure that many of Maori descent will have heard the question: ***"Who are you?"***, a number of times in their lives; usually delivered in a challenging manner. For some Maori it may be important that I establish "Who I am". For me, personally, my *tatai/whakapapa* is not overly important – later Chapters will explain why. I have no identity crisis within the framework of the racial make-up of Aotearoa under the outworking of **The Spiritual Laws of Creation**. I am who I am. I know my ***Spiritual Origin*** and my earthly racial mix, and need only to look into a mirror to see who that person is, materially. Nevertheless, to satisfy Maori protocol – in particular for those who would demand an answer to the question: ***"Who are you?"*** – in the associated chart I therewith give my genealogical connections to Te Maori; specifically Ngapuhi.[3]

The nature of such connections, however, must be understood in their *true meaning*. Notwithstanding the emotive associations that it invariably encompasses, as with all races Maori genealogical ancestry stems *solely* from *physical blood-lines only*. So despite the strongest belief to the contrary in many cultures, including Te Maori, there is *no* actual *spiritual connection* whatsoever in human 'genealogical configurations'. Our individual *wairua* stands *separate* from *all* earthly and/or family ties. Therefore, my association with **Ngapuhi** *tatai/whakapapa* relates to and concerns just that part of me connected to the *material* world solely – *the physical body*.

The question: *"Who are you?"*, can be asked in a number of ways.

1. Arrogantly – as a challenge.

2. Dismissively, implying that one is regarded as of no account – a *taurekareka* – without any right to speak.

3. With curiosity – seeking to learn the connections of the speaker and thus relatively tolerant.

4. With genuine interest.

5. With warmth, and therefore welcoming.

In the Maori world of challenge and counter-challenge, the establishment of a superior negotiating position is of primary importance. The question, **"Who Are You?"**, is designed to be psychologically demeaning in the first instance. And, moreover, is very effective if the recipient of the challenge is unsure of his personal position in, or his factual knowledge of, a given situation. Quite obviously, however, chronological age, position or status in a tribe or group does not automatically confer great knowledge and wisdom on any individual. It is therefore unwise to ask the question, **"Who are you?"**, arrogantly. Far better to supplant that question and attitude with words such as: "What is it that you have to offer?" It is my sincere hope that ***Maori readers of this book will adopt the latter approach***.

*   *   *   *   *

---

[3]More specific connections to Ngapuhi can be noted at the beginning of Chapter 15: **"Hongi Hika – and Ruatara."**

The experiences of childhood and youth in family upbringing and its associated culture are usually the strongest agents in shaping and moulding views and attitudes during the formative years, and may also greatly influence the direction one takes in later life. Even though being of both English and Maori descent, the greater influence during those early years was predominantly Maori. Those particular beliefs were inculcated within a framework characterised by a tightly bound family group living many of the ancient beliefs and superstitions in the 'old way' – relatively speaking. Within the parameters imposed by *whanau* thinking, the views of both the natural and 'supernatural' world were therefore accepted as being correct, particularly during childhood.

The lifestyle also ensured a natural, basic grasp of the *reo* (language) since Maori was spoken regularly, and grandmother (Ma) could only muster about ten words of English in total. In certain situations we were addressed in Maori more often than we were in English, thus resulting in a more or less natural understanding of the basic language as a consequence of this partial immersion. Unfortunately, and like others from similar backgrounds, the ability to speak in the *reo* as a child soon diminished upon leaving the *whanau* and entering the wider world.

Because the *whanau* group in this essentially Maori environment was deeply immersed in all manner of superstition and *tapu*, the strongest memory of childhood was **fear**. Sometimes it manifested in an almost palpable, living reality. It permeated virtually every aspect of life and stemmed solely from the belief that forces from the non-physical world could easily intrude in a malevolent way to bring harm to us mere mortals who possessed little *normal* defence against them. The only effective way to combat these 'forces' was to fight fire with fire, employing psychic means to negate, or preferably destroy, the dark entities believed to be responsible for the many 'incidents'. The hours of darkness were obviously the times of greatest fear, when *kehua* and other unwelcome 'visitors' could manifest quite easily and, of course, more strongly.

Moreover, it was also the time that the *koukou*, or Morepork, called. This bird has been associated with death in many cultures and races so the particular belief surrounding it is not solely a Maori fear or peculiarity. Its lonely plaintive call, particularly in the forest night, can evoke feelings ranging from unease to great fear, and this was the 'reality' as a child. It is certainly true that there were some very powerful and, for a child at the time, frightening and totally inexplicable happenings around events concerning these birds.

My grandmother, upon hearing the Morepork call, would invariably venture forth into the night to either 'converse with them' or, at other times to confront them, angrily declaring in the *reo*: "I'm not afraid of you". This depended on whether they were 'ours', and therefore benevolent – or 'theirs', and therefore malevolent. Yet, in truth it was, and will always be, a *spiritual affront* to place on these beautiful, beneficial and harmless birds a burden they were never ordained to carry; a burden placed there by fearful superstition and a concomitant lack of understanding in such matters.[4]

Thankfully, and for a long time now, I fully appreciate the lonely call of the Morepork ringing out clearly in its beautiful naturalness over the forested hills and from out of the valleys of the domain of Tane, Elemental Lord of the Forest. Its cry must surely be one of the most comforting and serene in nature. Yet in childhood that plaintive call inculcated great fear into our very psyche by totally unnecessary superstitious beliefs generated by such Maori thinking.

Another bird considered to be a harbinger of death was the *karuhiruhi*, or shag. As we lived very close to a tidal creek, it was obvious that such an environment would naturally attract fish-eating birds. Nonetheless, it was considered a sign of imminent death in the family should one of these birds fly directly over the house. Consequently, if one was observed flying *towards* the dwelling, a great shout of alarm went up whereupon the *whanau* would rush out like demented beings, yelling and waving various articles to scare away this dark 'portender'.

---

[4]Even today, among far too many Maori, this totally wrong concept is still passed on to the young.

Of course, one never ever knew what might or might not have taken place when their approach was *not* detected.

Explanations were never given about the reasons for such practices. Perhaps the bird was considered to be the *ahua* of some *tohunga* or opponent. Any bird actually flying into the house, even if inadvertently, would also set off alarm bells of great shock in the expectation of some impending calamity, particularly if efforts to drive it out from the dwelling proved difficult. More especially so if it was a fantail. Natural incidents such as those always produced dread and called for an immediate interpretation to negate any possibility of trouble or harm, or to appease the person or 'thing' believed responsible for its arrival.

The tidal creek just a few metres from the house provided a ready source of fish for food. As a child growing up under the various *tapu* of the Maori, one remembers the admonition to offer the first fish caught to the 'gods' of the water, whether it be the sea or the river, and to not desecrate the water with the gut of the fish at any time. Bait, of course, was permitted as a lure, but there always appeared to be a grey area as to what sort of bait should be used. The threat of the possibility of a *taniwha* suddenly rearing its head out of the water to take us away should we transgress these *tapu* was always bravely laughed at, but not with complete confidence that it could not ever happen. The psychic hold of the institution of *tapu* was strong then.

Aside from whitebait and other fish for the table, the creek also provided unusual incidents. At various times very large, horned eels would be seen in the pools closest to the houses. They would not conceal themselves under the banks as normal, but would lie in the shallows in full view. These were considered to be *tupuna* or ancestors.[5] Notwithstanding the clear fact that they really were just very large eels, grandmother would duly welcome them as *tupuna* anyway. With beliefs so strong, they were absolutely forbidden to be disturbed. By virtue of their *tupuna* status these particular eels were never considered as possible meals. Any thoughts directed that way would incur her great wrath.

The eels would remain for varying lengths of time, from some hours to many days. In the case of the latter, they would be visited and conversed with from time to time until they departed, and some received more attention than others. The creek was naturally a potential home for *taniwha*, and the unfortunate drowning of two young Maori children in a pool where an exceptionally large eel had made its home under the roots of a submerged tree stump, was 'proof' enough of this 'reality'. This particular eel eluded all efforts to catch it and eventually disappeared.

The creek had its source in an area of native bush some kilometres from home and certain incidents deriving from journeys into the forest produced alarm amongst the elder Maori *whanau*. One such event occurred during an exploratory expedition with a cousin in tracing the path of the stream as far as the 'waterfall', a known feature in this tract of forest. I remember this particular waterfall as being approximately 18 metres high with a relatively shallow, rock-strewn pool some 15 metres wide at its base. Whilst throwing rocks into it one day, we disturbed a fair-sized eel with curious pink and reddish colouring from about the beginning of the fin to the tail, with the red more pronounced towards the tip of the tail. We immediately set off home to get the spears but upon telling everyone what we had found, were threatened with a thrashing if we dared to try to spear it. Even though we lived a life of constant psychic uncertainty at the time, I recall that their great fear of this particular eel was surprising, even disturbing.

This tract of bush also contained a number of old Maori burial caves. The caves, particularly, were considered extremely *tapu,* as was the area around them. Youthful adventurousness amongst some of the older brothers and cousins demanded that the caves be at least partially entered and such visits took place from time to time, probably more from 'spooky curiosity' and bravado than any other reason. However, if such an incident was discovered to have occurred,

---

[5]The reader will recall our previously stated contention in the Preface that human/spiritual origins can only derive from similar forms and origins under the outworking of **Spiritual Law**.

necessary cleansing *karakia* was performed with the stern admonition to leave the area alone.[6]

In many cultures throughout history, water has played a major role in the lives of the various peoples. Not only for the needs of drinking, washing and cooking, but also for its aesthetic natural beauty and its ability to offer reflective or contemplative tranquillity. I do not think, however, that the old Maori saw water and streams in quite that light. During my formative years I experienced no evidence of that way of thinking. As with other peoples, however, Maori also revered water as a powerful healing force, though the utilisation of that "energy" needed to be accompanied by certain rituals of *tapu*. Many times we were woken before sunrise by cold stream water being administered to the head area, usually by the hand of mother. This practice was considered to be a most effective protection against physical illness, particularly feverish ailments, or even to prevent the onset of illness.

It was also employed as a means to ward off evil from psychic attack. In all cases in the use of water for psychic protection, it could only be effective if the correct *karakia* and ritual were performed at the stream, thus invoking healing power from the water and its relevant *atua*. It had to be performed before the sun had risen – just before the dawn – and where the recipient had not yet awoken to relieve the bladder, the recipient needing to be 'complete', so to speak. Interestingly, even though cold water applied to the face and neck was not a likeable experience for a young child in a state of half-sleep whilst ensconced in a warm bed, one remembers the strong conviction held by the *whanau* of the efficacy of this treatment. One also remembers the concern and *aroha* with which it was given.

On the other hand, this particular stream, or rather the path which tracked along its banks closest to the three dwellings of the *whanau* 'settlement', was considered to be a *'kehua path'*, an access-way along which dangerous and evil things of the night could approach. During the day, however, it was considered 'safe'. We fished there, swung off ropes over the water, canoed on it and generally saw the stream as the wonderful asset to have in one's childhood that, indeed, it was. At nightfall, though, it was an entirely different matter. The belief of it being such a 'bad' place was 'reinforced' by the Morepork calling 'down by the creek' on most evenings. Stories of inexplicable happenings around streams at night abound in all cultures as it does with the Maori, and the home area was no exception. Strange and frightening events, particularly for a child, did occur which, at the time, could not be given any kind of rational explanation.[7]

My grandmother's generation, steeped in the beliefs of their "other world", lived a paradox of extremes. On the one hand were the incredible skills of weaving, plaiting and cloak-making etc., and the wonderful herbal cures which were commonly used and extremely effective for certain ailments – in some cases more so than Western medicine. On the other, the completely irrational and abject fear of myriad *tapu* and the twin curses of *makutu* and *utu*. There was always the need to find secret places in which to hide hair and nail clippings lest they be discovered and used for evil purpose against the owner.

Moreover, the sudden unexpected appearance of insects such as *weta*, the praying mantis and the spider, generated great fear also. But perhaps none more so than the appearance of a lizard because of its close association with the realms of Hine Nui Te Po, 'goddess' of the dark underworld in Maori mythology, and with Whiro, 'god' of *makutu* and evil. Childhood abounds with memories of these 'goings on' and the fear and damage that it wrought to all, even through my mother's generation and up to the present time.

For even today in the *whanau*, there are some who still believe that these practices are the 'right way'. This view stems from two main beliefs. It derives either from fear of the 'unknown' and the perceived associated need to appease or negate the forces that instil that fear in the first place, and/or from the totally incorrect view that the practice imbues the practitioner

---

[6]The bones were removed many years later and interred elsewhere.

[7]Not until adult life, with the discovery and help of the greater knowledge contained in **The Spiritual Laws of Creation**, did clarification and understanding of the **why** of Maori superstition and fear finally arrive for me.

with "spiritual power" – more specifically, power over 'people' and 'things'. In fact, clinging to either belief reveals a dangerous lack of knowledge regarding the outworking of the forces of the **Natural Laws** – which are **The Spiritual Laws**.

I do not decry the long and well-documented history of strange events connecting animals, birds, fish and insects to events in men's lives in every race. These stand as historical fact, even if the reason or connection is not understood. And certainly, I am sure, most people can recount more than one occasion when such an event occurred in their life, and which did accurately foreshadow a meaningful event. The memory of it would be clearly indicative of the strength of the happening.

However, there is a vast difference between that, and showing abject fear at the appearance of every single bird and insect that happens to be in the immediate vicinity, and then pronouncing a spurious reason for its appearance. Since there are literally millions of different animal and insect species worldwide, it stands to reason that a reasonable number will cross our path throughout our lives. So applying a psychic or superstitious interpretation to a relatively frequent and normal event illustrated the inability of the extended *whanau* to separate this aspect of their thinking from that of the totally natural world to which there is no psychic connection whatever.[8]

Certain plants and flowers were strictly off-limits also, especially the native clematis. For reasons unknown to us children at the time, this beautiful white flower which graces the forest of Tane without fail each spring was regarded with very great fear. Any suggestion that it be brought into the house produced a kind of 'paroxysm of apoplexy' on the faces of the previous-generation Maori adults, where one could almost see the colour drain from them. It was considered too fearful a subject to even discuss, and it was not until very recently that I discovered why this flower produced so much fear.

For northern Maori at least, the custom of mourning required that sprigs of evergreen, along with the white flowers of the clematis, when in bloom, be worn in the hair or on a hat. After the body had been interred, the mourners would take the sprigs and flowers from their heads and consign them to the grave. Thus it was the dual aspects of the custom and the hue of the flower itself that was the cause of the great concern over native clematis. From childhood memories the colour white always seemed to have an unnecessarily strong association with death and funerals, and the *whanau* greatly feared that.

Whilst a flower garden of sorts did exist around the house, I cannot recall that it was enthused over particularly much, or that flowers were genuinely welcome inside it, especially by mother. Paradoxically, the house that belonged to my uncle had a wonderful flower garden around it. That garden, however, was there through the efforts of my aunt, who naturally hailed from a 'different' *whanau*. So even in the closest *whanau* associations there, vastly different perceptions held sway. – Perhaps ancestral traditions of the natural association of all plants with the "elemental beings" of nature, but without the understanding of it, produced this fear.– It seemed such a sad irony that things as beautiful as flowers should be so superstitiously feared.

*　　　*　　　*　　　*　　　*

A very regular Pakeha visitor to the three-house settlement was the District Health Nurse. She came to administer regular and necessary inoculations, provide jars of fortifying malt extract, and otherwise monitor our, at times, not-so-good health. It was not that we were physically weak. In fact the environment positively allowed for rugged development but, compared to other children, there always seemed to be an inordinately high level of sickness, such as colds, flu's, running eyes and ears amongst us. As well, there were various skin infections such as eczema,

---

[8]That aspect is actually an "Elemental" one which we will address more fully in the later Chapter on "Elemental Lore". The telemovie , "The Man Who Lost His Head", screened on TV ONE in December 2007, whilst perhaps 'tongue-in-cheek' with comedic undertones, nevertheless portrayed essentially the very same superstitions. Set in a small coastal village in a modern but rural Northland, it starred English actor, Martin Clunes.

dermatitis, and an interesting condition called 'taapa feet'. This is where the soft skin on the top of the foot thickens and takes on the appearance of rough hide, which can crack and bleed. This, at times, painful condition was caused by a combination of bare-foot living and not washing the feet sufficiently well or regularly enough.[9]

In the whanau mind-set, psychic forces were often deemed to be the underlying cause of many of the illnesses we experienced, thus resulting in too-strong ties to things Maori. Such a strong superstition meant that many everyday necessities of basic hygiene were simply not thought about sufficiently enough, leading to poor childhood health in some areas. This belief provided one more interesting paradox whereby much pointless and superstitious tapu toward certain matters that ostensibly insisted upon strict cleanliness were deemed far more important than cleanliness of our physical person at times. As usual, fear of the unknown and the need to constantly appease whatever needed to be appeased always seemed to be uppermost in importance. Not that blame should be apportioned in this instance, more a case of a lack of real understanding.[10]

Of the total Maori inventory of things to be feared, funerals or, more correctly, the perceived potential ramifications of them – for both the mourners and the departed – headed the list. After a death, everyone would wait for signs from the departed one which would ostensibly reveal his 'status' i.e., whether happy or unhappy. A soul 'perceived' to be unhappy would immediately set in place the necessity for the whanau to call a meeting 'to put things right', or to try to ascertain who or what might have been 'responsible' for the departed one's 'situation'. For, failing this process, the departed one might decide to stay, much to the consternation of the whanau, with the possibility of haunted nights until the matter was 'resolved'. How, exactly, one was rarely able to fathom, but it invariably necessitated employing psychic means. To be continually reminded of this fear by the whanau's own attitude to virtually everything around was, I am certain, actually physically debilitating.

In retrospect, one can readily understand this fear purely because of the fact that Maori superstition believed in the very real probability of an unhappy corpse haunting everyone for some considerable time after death. And one could never know who would be unhappy, or why.[11]

My grandmother's death was especially memorable for the huge amount of emotional energy expended on ensuring that everything was conducted according to the prevailing protocol. She was in her late 90s when she died in 1960 and was considered to be a Chieftainess of Ngatiwai and Mahurehure. Deemed to possess great wisdom, her funeral was accorded the appropriate degree of mana in every part of the proceedings, particularly the tangi. What is an especially strong memory was the great fear of 'her', in her physical death state, held by the extended whanau, with this fear once more reinforced for us youngsters. We were required to pay our respects as she lay in her coffin. For fearful children this was not a pleasant proposition as the casket was on a raised bier and our faces were therefore very close to an object that we had been taught to fear since very early childhood. Whilst I have some very fond memories of sitting with Ma in the warm sun, or assisting her in her basket and kit weaving, the sight of her as an old and depleted, lifeless shell did provide a large amount of morbid fascination as it was my first

---

[9]Some of the 'health problems' were no doubt exacerbated by the fact that we also played and fished in a secondary arm of the tidal creek system. Into this the nearby Whangarei abattoir directly discharged all of its daily-kill, liquid component – all blood and stomach and intestinal material from the town's meat requirements of cattle, sheep and pigs. Further down-creek in the mangroves and mudflats, we often ate of the raw pipis living quite happily there. Notwithstanding the many stomach upsets and skin infections suffered as a result of close contact with very contaminated water as a way of life, one positive outcome was a reasonably strong immune system in later life. Sadly, many city children today are not even allowed to get 'mud between their toes'.

[10]We examine this point of 'cleanliness' from the spiritual standpoint in the vitally important Chapter on Ratana.

[11]Thankfully, we are now able to clarify the death process, which we also outline in a later Chapter. And can thus understand the relationship between the physical body or shell, and the inner animating core, the wairua – the actual life-force and person.

exposure to a dead body. One now laments the lost opportunity of childhood in not learning more from Grandmother.

During my formative years, then, the psychic world permeated and influenced all aspects of life. However, as one grew out of childhood, one was clearly able to recognise that certain aspects of Maori thinking and activity were clearly *not beneficial*, and should have been *completely discarded* without fear of invoking the wrath of some revered ancestor or feared deity for 'turning away' from such beliefs. Conversely, those beliefs and practices that were obviously beneficial I have personally retained.

With regard to the superstitious aspects of mainly Maori influences in childhood, the 'other viewpoint' was provided by the counter-balancing effect of the one Pakeha in the three-house 'settlement' – father. His view of the world naturally differed vastly from that of the Maori, and a greater clash of cultures would be difficult to imagine. Here was the interesting paradox of a thoroughly pragmatic, logical and wider English view of the world attempting to live comfortably and harmoniously, from the decade of the 1930s, with a fear-ridden and superstitious, extended Maori *whanau*. Those superstitions were strongly accentuated because of the particular setting; a lonely little 'three-house settlement' in almost its own virtually uninhabited valley quite removed from suburban New Zealand.

Even though there are still pockets of more or less 'traditional' Maori lifestyle, it is good that the fear-ridden practices of my formative years do not have to be experienced by most children of Maori descent today. Paradoxically, however, the demise of that way of life has resulted in certain necessary aspects also being discarded, aspects which should have been retained. This loss has helped to bring about the present day 'crisis of identity' particularly prevalent among young Maori, purely because there is an imbalance here now.

In fact, virtually no race or Nation is in balance anymore because the "Elemental reality" of **The Forces of Nature**, which Maori inherently accept as a factual "living force" *but do not have complete understanding of*, has generally been expunged by Western races. My hope is that the reader will keenly and objectively follow this particular thread through the book, and where this loss is explained in the Chapter on "Elemental Lore", acknowledge and recognise it, so that what has been wrongly discarded can be retrieved and once more utilised for our benefit.

Because of the particular nature of the subject matter we are concerned with, it is important to have briefly outlined my childhood years in the manner in which I have portrayed them, especially the psychic, fear-ridden aspects. This should ensure that Maori readers in particular accept that I have some experience of what might be termed 'the old way' which, in turn, permits me this personal evaluation of where we as a race are currently 'spiritually-placed'.

It is perhaps an irony of the times that one is only considered to be 'Maori' if one has some Maori blood, some knowledge of 'traditional' culture, albeit about 1970s onwards nowadays, a passable working ability of the language (even if spoken with a 'classroom accent') and knowing one's *whakapapa*. With the thankful demise of many of the more insidious psychic practices of the 'old way', paradoxically many younger Maori in positions of emerging leadership would not have had such deep 'Maori' experiences in childhood as an everyday way of life for many years on end. Yet the idea of being 'acceptably Maori' is often based on the few criteria mentioned. Perhaps, in the final analysis, experiencing the 'old ways' of the darker psychic aspects, which was once a truly Maori trait, and which too many of the race today wrongly believe to be a "spiritual" one, may arguably be the greater measure of 'knowing what it is like to be Maori'. Thankfully, however, that option is no longer so readily available as this particular way of life slowly dies out. Unfortunately, however, other psychic aspects are still being wrongly promoted as genuine knowledge under the umbrella of traditional culture and Maori spirituality.

For the purposes of *this* Work, the last aspect of note that the earlier formative years around the whanau area *experientially-offered* occurred during the transition-time from secondary school into adult working life, to just past 17 years of age. Surrounding the 3-house *whanau settlement* were many hundreds of acres of holding paddocks, ·gorse and ti-tree scrub. Prior to slaughter, stock for the nearby abattoir were placed in the paddocks. (Cattle quite often escaped into the much larger area of scrubland, however.) For successive waves of 'cousins', the abattoir provided after-school and Saturday morning 'employment' – cleaning and hosing-out the 'holding-pens'.[12]

More importantly in the context of the primary thrust of our subject matter, however, the abattoir provided the experience at a young age to work in a more raw and basic slaughtering process and gut and offal processing environment than is the case today i.e., decades before the current, very strict health and safety regulations. But why should this aspect of one's life-experience be relevant for this story and journey? After all, many thousands of 'kiwi kids', both brown and white, have done the same on farms and in the bush for generations, and will continue to do so.

The *normal everyday process* of meat-acquisition from slaughter and processing to super-market shelves is not the point here. It is all about working with well-tempered and well-honed knives – in this case to slaughter, dismember and process animals for food.

For the overall purpose of our revelatory journey, therefore, certain work and/or life experiences permit a deeper level of analyses of our ancestors' way of life. So the experience of knife-work in an abattoir, even though quite obviously inherently-possessing *a far lesser degree of resonance* to a *certain practice* in Maori Warfare, pre– and immediate post– European arrival, nonetheless permits *a far greater degree of active thought* and **spiritual analysis** about *that* particular activity of Maori Warfare than would be possible without such an experience.[13]

*   *   *   *   *

Insofar as the overall concept of the *toa* stands under the ethos of at least one aspect of Maori cultural tradition, my time of Military Service in the New Zealand Army, Regular Force, is, I believe, important to include here. Moreover, it will serve to illustrate how the strength of the influences of the 'old way' can still be detrimentally retained, even in the Military, albeit sometimes unknowingly.[14]

Upon leaving home, therefore, the comparatively narrow world of Maori upbringing and influences gave way to the wider view within the work force and New Zealand society in general. But six years service in South East Asia with the Army offered the greatest possible expansion of a wider-world vista. Military Service was a very special and fulfilling time in my life, for it not only broadened my horizons considerably, but more importantly allowed me to intimately experience a world of *especial camaraderie* with men who valued the spiritual attribute of *trust*, in its most powerful form for the soldier, above all else. For when *earned* 'in harm's way' out of mutual respect, it is something most special, even tending towards the sacred. Military Service also inculcated the right attitude to discipline enabling the recognition that, as much as possible, 'self discipline' is the best and 'right way'.

Traditionally the Army has always attracted a high proportion of Maori. This organisation, probably more than any other, allows the Maori soldier a place where he can *excel* in certain natural skills that, for the most part, have few other outlets in today's society. And the Army *whanau* provides beneficial discipline, a uniform, pride in it and oneself, and a wonderful sense of belonging to something very special in many respects. As a young soldier, however, one does not really understand the benefit of the experiences of one's service time, one simply enjoys

---

[12]The associated "By-products works" also provided employment and a particular kind of 'life-maturing' by virtue of the nature of the work there.

[13]The activity to which we allude is in Chapter 5: "The War Trail".

[14]As this book examines all issues essentially from the *spiritual standpoint*, those very implications in the role of the *toa* and soldier, and the same effect in sacrifice in battle, will be discussed as part of a later Chapter. This will help to assess where the old Maori stood in this regard too.

the high fitness and energy levels and, just as importantly, the very deep bonds of comradeship that simply cannot be experienced anywhere else other than in a strongly bonded service group. Military Operations on 'Active Service' strengthen this bonding to the utmost degree.

It is difficult to describe this incredible depth of trust adequately, but is probably understood by the universal soldier of all nationalities. I would deem it as almost an intangible, and perhaps only soldiers who have experienced 'Active Service' can fully understand this 'feeling'. Of course, the Army was not all wine and roses, and all soldiers can readily relate to that. Overall, however, it is a most beneficial force for *good*.[15]

My Service time coincided with heightened 'Operational Activity' for the Infantry Battalion in South East Asia and this greatly concerned my mother lest I come to some harm or not return home at all. Therefore, in accordance with Maori custom to try to negate that possibility, and immediately prior to my first Overseas Deployment, it was agreed that I should receive *karakia* from the *hapu tohunga*; a man deemed to have the necessary knowledge for such a task. The night before visiting him, I dreamt of driving through a thunderstorm on the way to his house. The storm cleared shortly before reaching it. This exact same thing took place next day as in the dream. I received of his ministrations, *karakia* and advice, and was also given some insight as to which countries in SE Asia I would be operationally involved in. This was an interesting perception as the later government decision to become involved in one particular country was still quite some time away.[16]

The Army Command in SE Asia was cognisant of the possible "spiritual needs" of the Maori soldier and provided the means for it, encouraging cultural activities within the parameters of an Operational Unit. The Battalion *marae*, appropriately named *Tu-matauenga*, provided the focus for this. As well, an officer or senior non-commissioned officer of Maori descent was appointed to provide counselling in 'Maori matters'. Of course, the appointee had to have some knowledge of such things. It is to the credit of the soldiers of varying tribal connections that the appointee was never challenged in the 'traditional' way. In any case there was simply no purpose served by attempting that, notwithstanding the fact that it was a Military decision anyway; for the 'soldier's bond' transcended any potential for dissent.[17]

The Battalion *tohunga's* 'knowledge' was often employed in both the good and the sad. As mentioned previously, influences from home and/or the past reached across to the Unit in sometimes dark and insidious ways. On two occasions, I was seconded, along with some others of Maori descent, for roster duty to guard Maori soldiers in the British Military Base Hospital of Terendak Camp. It was not an armed guard, but one for company, 'Maori discourse' and, if necessary with hospital staff, protective restraint. Unfortunately the latter was an only option at times. Mental problems had developed and, in discussions with them during periods of lucidity, it transpired that both had received 'something' from home, some 'news' that had mentally affected them. Both were placed on 'medication' and one received regular electric shock treatment as a means of further subduing him during times of 'difficulty'.

This latter soldier was well-proportioned, large and strong, and at 'times of agitation' and/or 'psychic influence', his strength increased to a considerable degree. On one occasion after he decided to leave the hospital, it took the combined efforts of seven large Australian Military Policemen to return him. At that particular time, the two of us rostered on were required to assist in strapping him onto the treatment table. Yet even through the fog of suppressant drugs and his own inner psychic hell and pain, he knew what was going to happen. Recognising that he could not escape, he would cry like a baby and attempt to curl up in the foetal position. Of course this was not possible owing to the physical restraints that held him firm and immovable.

[15]In fact, the organisational 'form' of the Army and the 'form' of the Soldier is actually a "spiritual" one, *if* the *serving* is *correct*.

[16]Numerous examples of second sight are well documented in many peoples and this was probably one example, and not especially unusual in Maori life.

[17]Perhaps a blueprint and good example for civilian "Aotearoa Maori".

The shock treatment always produced the desired 'medical' effect in that it subdued him completely, transforming him, in a farcical parody, from a potentially violent "mentally disturbed Maori soldier", to a medically acceptable and suitably subdued "mentally disturbed Maori soldier and patient". Totally docile now, with froth and saliva over much of his face, he would be wheeled away to sleep. Soldiers on Military Operations necessarily see, experience and are sometimes required to accept many things that most others will probably not ever know in their lives, but the sight of that once fine, strong soldier being reduced to a frightened, whimpering baby is one that will forever remain with me.

He was reduced to that awful state *solely because of totally unnecessary Maori psychic superstition reaching across the oceans to him.*

So if what is outlined in these pages helps toward a better understanding as to the why of similar situations, *and the permanent burial of this kind of psychic/occult rubbish posing as great spiritual Maori power or knowledge*, then perhaps *our brother-soldier's pain* may not have been wasted after all.

The 'other' soldier, according to reports then, jumped from the first floor of the hospital and broke limbs. Neither returned to barracks and both, I believe, were repatriated home and discharged into psychiatric care. Good men wasted through an inherent fear of dangerous, yet totally unnecessary and completely incorrect beliefs of Maori.[18]

A six-month "Tour of Duty" to Borneo in 1966 during Indonesia's two-year "Confrontation" with Malaysia, 1965-66, provided the opportunity for very close contact with the jungle peoples there – the Ibans and the Dayaks. At that time still living in mainly family groups in raised 'longhouses', they were once greatly feared head-hunters. Skulls adorned the walls of communal guest-houses in some of the villages. With the encouragement of British and Australian Special Forces Units during the Second World War, their last *official* head-hunting forays were against the Japanese. It was the 'civilising' influence of the missionaries and the British Raj in the last century that finally curbed this traditional practice. Notwithstanding the obvious potential fierceness of them, however, they are probably the most wonderful and gentle people that I have ever been privileged to know.

Yet, apart from contact with missionaries and the schooling of some of the younger generation in English in the village schools, their relative isolation from the outside world allowed a unique insight into how it may have been when the once-isolated Maori came face to face with the 'old-world' European. The British Army High Command adopted an active policy of committing Commonwealth troops to "Hearts and Minds Operations" in the different 'longhouses'. In our "Area of Operations" four-man teams utilising standard Army medical training were, on occasions, tasked to undertake medical duties in the various 'longhouses'. Normally of two weeks duration, living and sleeping space were made available in the village guesthouse for that time.

Our four-man team was assigned to 'Longhouse Bugu'. The village was effectively cut in two by a stream and had the unique distinction of one side being 'Christian' and the other being labelled 'Pagan'. There was no animosity between the two as they were basically of the same group of families anyway. They worked their crops together and celebrated various events in much the same way. Whilst we were quartered in the 'Christian' side where the guesthouse was located and from where we conducted our morning medical clinics, we regularly visited the 'Pagan' side too. However, we could detect no discernible difference in thinking between the two groups. In actual fact the 'Christian group' were Christian in name only. In reality they were still just a tribal, jungle people.

---

[18]The later sub-Chapter on Mental Health provides both clarification and resolution of the shockingly-high levels of admission and re-admission rates for young Maori, particularly, into psychiatric care in this country.

Immediately upon our arrival there, courtesy of a British Air Force 'chopper crew', we were met by a large and excited crowd of villagers. The younger people, some of whom could speak a little English, indicated that we should hurry to help a woman who was about to give birth. In the case of 'Longhouse Bugu' the landing pad was the soccer field, located some hundreds of metres from the main village areas. Our two week stay there meant that, as well as the standard scale of ammunition, we were carrying extra food and more medical supplies than would be required for a normal patrol. Thus our packs were heavier than usual and Borneo is always very hot and humid.

With regard to the mother-to-be, it is one thing to be trained to treat wounds etc., but childbirth is an entirely different matter for troops. The excitement of the crowd 'appeared' to indicate some kind of birth-complication. So, whilst we 'hurried slowly' to the village, we discussed our options. We were not trained to deal with any kind of birth, let alone a difficult one. The decision was made to immediately radio the 'chopper' to return if there were complications that the local 'midwives' could not deal with. Luckily, and much to our great relief, the baby was delivered safely just as we arrived outside the mother's house.

The huge trust placed in our 'magical' healing abilities was quite disconcerting at times. The morning after we settled into our quarters we began the first of a daily 'medical clinic'. We retained the translation services of a 12 year old boy for most of our stay there. Within a few days a long and patient queue formed each morning. Many were young mothers. Yet whilst they washed and showered daily at specific locations – determined by split-bamboo water channels directing stream-water there – the mothers did not bathe the eyes of many of the babies and toddlers brought to us. Consequently, most had eyes 'gunked-up', sometimes with the lids 'glued' closed. We cleaned and applied eye drops to the worst affected but found the same mothers back with the same problem.

We conducted sessions on general hygiene – what the Army calls "Hygiene in the Field" – and explained as best we could why they needed to gently bathe the youngster's eyes each morning. This worked well, except that we had to conduct a further session because the mothers were occasionally too enthusiastic in their 'eye-bathing' technique. Because we were the first medical team to be sent there, and because the eye problems disappeared within a few days, almost everyone in the village wanted eye drops, and that soon ran out. Cleverly, we used cold tea brewed from ration packs to minister to the villagers' 'eye-needs'. The tannin in the tea was evidently the key ingredient to soothe eyes.

A particular problem presented itself that we did not want to deal with. Yet the successful end result offered an amazing insight into the incredible power of modern antibiotics on people never before exposed to them. I suppose, in a reverse-process, it is similar to people who, not previously exposed to unknown diseases and who possess no natural immunity to them, subsequently suffer greatly as a result of such exposure.

About twenty children, roughly between the ages of four to about eight, had quite large numbers of 'blind boils', all on the scalp. Each 'boil' took the form of a slightly raised flat-topped 'mesa' roughly ranging in size from that of a twenty cent to a fifty cent coin – the older larger sizes of coin. They possessed no 'pimple point' from which to draw out the infectious material, and the flat surface was covered by very thick skin. It was clear that the boils were very debilitating because those children with them had very little hair, were listless and looked profoundly anaemic.

After submitting a medical report by radio to our HQ, the R.M.O (Regimental Medical Officer) decided to personally investigate. He arrived by 'chopper' next morning. After examining this particular group of children, he proceeded to demonstrate how to deal with the 'boils'. Taking a scalpel, and indicating to one of the mothers to hold her child firmly, he quickly cut the surface of one of the boils. Blood and pus erupted from the area, much to the mother's great concern. The child also erupted into loud crying. The R.M.O quickly cleaned and dressed the wound and told us to treat the rest the same way. Upon asking for scalpels he advised that a sterilised razor blade would do the job equally as efficiently. Then he flew out.

Since I was more or less the 'chief medic' in our 4-man group, it was left to me to do the next one. As previously stated, dealing medically with soldiers who accept such things in a matter-of-fact manner is vastly different to slicing open even a simple boil on the head of a small child. Nonetheless, I took a brand new razor blade and we opened and dressed a boil on another child. However, it was clear that the whole business was becoming quite traumatic for this group of mothers and their children. The obvious problem we had with this 'slash and dress' method was; should we treat one boil at a time on each child, or do we treat all the boils on each child at the one time? And because the thick skin of the 'blind boil' gave no indication of the amount of material inside each one, the mothers were unpleasantly surprised at the amount discharged when lanced. The procedure was also clearly not without some pain.

We concluded that there had to be a better, more effective, way of helping those children. At the time Army medics carried penicillin tablets of 125 and 250 mg strength. We believed that therein lay the answer to a thoroughly unpleasant task. However, there were two main factors to consider. One was that the villagers had probably not been exposed to such antibiotics before, and the second was the age and body weight of the affected children – all of whom were sickly and weighed less than others in the village of the same ages. We collectively took the decision to administer one single dose of one quarter of one 125 mg tablet to each affected child, and simply wait to see what would happen. We duly did this and within just a few days, all the 'boils' had simply disappeared. On reflection later, however, a key consideration that we had overlooked was the possibility of one or more of the children having a severe allergic reaction to antibiotics. However, that did not occur and everyone was very, very satisfied with the outcome.

At other times children from this village who needed surgical operations were 'choppered' out to a Military Base Hospital. On one such occasion we radioed for the 'medevac chopper' to airlift out a sick young boy suffering from what was probably a spleen disorder. He was from the Pagan side. Upon return some days later, healed and healthier, a great celebration and feast was held in our honour. The feast preliminaries began with a live chicken being proffered to us. We were seated next to the 'headman' of the village and alongside the child's immediate family and their guests. Speaking in his own tongue the person offering the chicken, either one of the headmen or a *tohunga* equivalent, danced in front of us. We were led to understand that it was especially chosen and would shortly be cooked for *the guests of honour* – four NZ troops. He disappeared very briefly and returned with the now headless chicken and proceeded to bless us by shaking the body of it and anointing us with its blood. It was once more taken away and later returned cooked for our enjoyment. It was certainly far tastier and more enjoyable than any 'ration-pack' meal. The celebrations continued on for some hours with much 'music' and dancing.

A disturbing aspect that we witnessed on a number of occasions, and which gave a clear indication of how deep psychic beliefs ran in these people, whether 'Christian' or 'Pagan', was the practice of trying to drive out evil demons from a child who suffered from epilepsy. During epileptic seizures, the other children would gather around and kick at the body of the stricken child to attempt to force out the 'demons'. Whenever we were aware of any such seizures we would keep the others away and tend to him as best we could.

Fortunately we were able to change the attitude of the other children before being 'choppered out' of the village at the completion of our two weeks there. With the help of our 'translator', who had a reasonably good command of English, we finally succeeded in convincing the children, particularly, that there were no demons inside the child, and advised them of what they should do each time a seizure occurred. This epilepsy case was notified to Army medical authorities. However, there was no long-term provision for this kind of medical problem for the locals within the Military system.

Even though we were in an Operational situation whilst in the village, we were secure in the knowledge that any potential incursion into the area by Indonesian troops would be reported immediately via 'jungle grapevine'. Thus the only time that any of our weapons were fired there was to shoot, at their request, the odd pig for village feasts. Apart from the medical work we undertook, what was especially interesting was the villagers' complete lack of comprehension about the rest of the world. In a land where the people had no modern means of communication and mostly travelled by foot or canoe, photographs from the old Weekly News magazine mailed from home provided some interesting reactions. Depicting various aspects of the wider world, the photographs in the centre pages, particularly those of big-city scenes, were invariably met with a gentle, incredulous smile, a firm shake of the head and a clear, '**no**'.

In retrospect, incidents such as those provided a small measure of insight into how it may have been for the Maori in the early days of European arrival and before Maori had visited other lands in any great numbers. The same kind of relative isolation, similar incredulity of the wider world, little or no understanding of the physical nature of some illnesses, and continuing psychic practices, with the missionaries making little genuine headway in changing unhelpful traditions of the 'old way'.

It is only through reflection with the passage of time and the rapid demise of some very special indigenous cultures globally that one realises the unique nature of those intimate experiences with the people of Borneo, for they truly were a wonderful people. Yet I am still unable to completely quantify the spiritual value of those experiences except that I know it was a deeply significant period personally, and one that remains vivid today. It has helped to broaden and shape my personal view of indigenous aspects in the present, and certainly largely contributes to the threads that run through this book. One hopes that their values, gentleness and infectious good humour has not been subsumed or destroyed by rampant commercialism and/or 'progress'. Sadly, however, if relatively recent reports of religious intolerance in Indonesia are true, then at least some of those wonderful people did, once more, take up traditional head-hunting.

With regard to the Battalion *tohunga's* duties back 'home' in Terendak Camp in Malaya, there was one aspect that sometimes did clash with Army requirements – the preparation of official *hangi*. In the formative years of childhood, the ritual for the *hangi* was absolutely precise, for this was a strong *whanau tapu*. Under mother's strict enforcement, we learned the 'correct' method of preparation; from the *karakia* in thanks for the food and for success of the *hangi*, through each individual step to the splashing of the hot stones for symbolic cleansing and to provide the necessary steam for cooking prior to the placing of the food on them, to ensure that the heavier meats were sufficiently *tonotono'd*, and thence to the covering of the food with appropriate cloths in correct sequence, thus hopefully ensuring success.

The food-coverings, apart from being necessarily clean, could not include anything that had been in contact with the body, such as sheets and bedclothes etc., irrespective of how convenient they might be for this purpose. Therefore, tablecloths and tea towels etc., were never washed with bedding, towels and personal clothing.[19] No, this was anathema, and many Maori groups still abide by this *tapu*, though not all Maori individually.

In the Battalion this particular practice was not easily effected at times, particularly when feeding large numbers from numerous *hangi* pits. On one such occasion, at the visit of the then Prime Minister, Minister of Defence, N.Z. Ambassador to Malaysia and other dignitaries and guests, the total number to be fed was about 1,000, including the soldiers of the Battalion. With others, I was assigned to the '*hangi* party'. Ordinarily, this is a most enjoyable Army function, with much kudos for the 'cooks'.

On this particular occasion, however, I was very greatly disturbed to see that the food coverings were to be our green barrack room bed sheets, albeit newly washed and out of the

---

[19]The temperature of the washing water is totally irrelevant in this case.

bedding store. The influences of the past, coupled with my own personal views about this, would not allow me to participate further. I informed the Battalion *tohunga* of my decision and, whilst the correctness of it disturbed him and some of the others, he allowed me to take no further part. This was a personal matter and not a Military one. And neither did I eat any of the food. I do not personally view this as a superstition, more a matter of good hygiene, particularly where food is concerned. And neither is it a solely Maori trait, for other peoples of the world also abide by this practice. In any case we all knew how badly the sheets were 'hand-washed' by outside contractors.

The operational requirements of any Military Unit will invariably mean that casualties and deaths are inevitable. And the final salute by the 'firing party' at such times is a fitting tribute, if one understands that there can be a *spiritual* aspect to the role of the soldier, sailor or airman. So, for servicemen or servicewomen, Military funerals are an especially meaningful occasion. The drill, ritual and discipline in comradeship add a special dimension to them. In S.E. Asia soldiers died from various causes aside from purely Military Operations, and we bade them farewell in that land away from Aotearoa. In the case of a Maori soldier, the service was conducted in both English and Maori; this last generally by a Maori Officer. Moments like these, where two races can share such an occasion in genuine and mutual togetherness in a "spiritual" transcendence of everyday soldiering, are especially poignant and moving. Perhaps only the experiences of the 'essential soldier', can give that understanding, for it is forged by the knowledge that one 'knows' that one can absolutely depend on 'the boys', *irrespective of their race*.

A key point in comparison between Maoris' of different educational levels and wider-world experience was graphically illustrated for me upon joining the Army and serving in the Infantry Battalion outside of New Zealand particularly. The relatively closed Maori world of the *whanau hapu* gave way to considerable expansion in every aspect of one's life upon being posted to South East Asia with our Unit. Apart from some contact with Maori schoolteachers, virtually all others in my life's experience up to that time were more concerned with the narrow and generally psychic aspects of Maori thinking. Thus it was as a breath of fresh air that one was exposed to open-minded, well-educated, worldly and logical thinking Maori as were among the Officers of the Battalion. Whilst there was still pride of culture with all, and a very fluent grasp of the *reo* with some, there was also an indefinable quality that elevated all of these things out of the particularly limited level of 'Maoriness' one had experienced in one's formative years.

References to other Maori as being *taurekareka* and therefore unworthy of note, and the practice of *makutu* in a Military setting was certainly possible between soldiers of different tribal affiliations, though one did not personally experience that kind of narrowness of thinking. However, what could have found expression on Military Operations, especially, was the potential to seek *utu* or revenge in the event of comrades being killed – and some were of course. Yet this potential also pre-supposed the higher responsibility of accepting the consequences of one's free-will decision in volunteering for Military Service and whatever that might bring in its train in the first place.[20]

As an example of this free choice situation for the soldier; as our Infantry Company prepared to leave Terendak Camp in Malaysia for the first operational Tour of Duty in South Vietnam in 1967, Lieutenant Colonel Poananga, a veteran of the Second World War, addressed the Company paraded for his inspection. The men of this particular Battalion had been together for quite some time with 'Operational Service' in Malaya and Borneo, and were a well trained Unit of predominantly Pakeha and Maori, but with other New Zealanders of diverse racial backgrounds such as Indian, Chinese, Yugoslav, Pacific Island, Italian, Australian and others.

---

[20]The natural, maternal concerns of mothers for their sons in operational situations is also subordinated to the Lawful effect of whatever outcome is generated through this *personal decision* of the offspring 'to go a-soldiering'.

We should state the fact that, *irrespective of the individual soldier's ethnic origin, all were treated equally. Maori Officers did not favour Maori soldiers over any other race*. This is a vital point that should be presented early in the context of this Work. The ability to do the job was the prime consideration, with lesser matters such as correct behaviour etc., as a necessary adjunct. The men were not judged by anything other than that. And that is as it should be!

With his far more extensive 'Operational Service', Colonel Poananga advised us that we would now see very large American Military formations that had not previously been part of our experience. He also asked us to do something that, for the first time, clearly illustrated the impending elevation of Operations that would shortly be undertaken. With the Company now 'standing easy' in a more relaxed, informal setting, he faced us and said: "I want you all to look at the other men around you." We did that for a few, reflective, silent moments. Then he said in a quiet voice: "Some of you probably won't come back!"

Whilst this was always an obvious possibility, to have it put into words sheeted home the reality of the consequences of one's personal decision to 'go soldiering'. That, however, is what the volunteer soldier accepts, or certainly should accept. Of course it does not mean that no loss is felt when 'brother-soldiers' are killed. Sometimes the feeling of loss can be very great, but the acceptance of the death of 'one's mates' without thought of revenge is the correct way for anyone aspiring to noble "warriorship" – past or present.

In terms of necessary discipline in any sphere of life, an object lesson was given to all by our 'Maori Colonel'. Whilst we could be regarded as being very well trained, with 'Operational Service' already behind us, some of the 'boys' had not fully appreciated the Colonel's and our Company Commander's regime of tougher preparatory training for the far more intense 'Operational requirements' of South Vietnam. Wounded egos surfaced very quickly in some of the men of the first Company to be deployed there after Colonel Poananga announced – I believe now to keep us solidly grounded – that we were 'barely adequate'.

It was not until operations had been underway for a short while 'up top' (Vietnam) that the obvious concern of the C.O. for the men's welfare – in tougher lead-up training for that more highly charged place – became very clearly apparent to all of the men. Thus, upon his first visit to us in South Vietnam, he was welcomed with very huge respect, enthusiasm and warmth – and true *aroha*. It is only from the perspective of time and distance and with the knowledge of **The Spiritual Laws** that one understands the great wisdom of Colonel Poananga's *seemingly* hard words to us at the time. For **Spiritual Law** states that the greater part of 'genuine love' is **severity!** And genuine love is a *power*, not an emotion.

Colonel Poananga had been nicknamed "Uncle Po" – in direct contrasting reference to "Uncle Ho" (Ho Chi Minh, leader of North Vietnam) – for quite some time. Now, however, the term took on a much more personal and very affectionate meaning. He was a Commanding Officer who always placed the welfare of his men first, and was one who, from time to time, would enter the 'Other Ranks' canteen completely unannounced, ask one of the boys to play the guitar, and join us in a beer and a song before leaving. A small thing one might believe, but a powerful bonding act engendering mutual respect bordering on deep affection for the Commanding Officer, "Uncle Po".

On some Battalion Parades he would remind his Officers that they were there with their 'fruit salad' on their uniforms because of the 'private soldiers' on parade in front of them – and not the other way around. And on occasions he would dismiss each tier of senior rank, one at a time, each time asking the remainder if there were any problems they wanted to raise. This process continued through the Commissioned Ranks and the Non-Commissioned Ranks until he was alone with just the private soldiers – the 'grunts'. He was a highly respected Officer, a great leader and, in this Vet's view, *one of the finest of men*.

In this first Chapter I have purposely dwelt awhile on my Army experiences. For, from the benchmark of those intense impressions, if one critically and objectively examines the traits and personalities of *certain* Maori political and cultural 'leaders' today, and contrasts the collective findings with the experiences one underwent with Maori Military Officers, the conclusion one is compelled to draw is one of concern for the future of Maori and Aotearoa generally, particularly if the present thrust and attitude of some of the 'current crop of leaders of Maoridom' continues. One sincerely hopes that the strongly entrenched attitude of egocentricity and ethnicity will dissipate somewhat and a more spiritually-correct attitude of expansiveness to the outer world and the Pakeha, particularly, takes place, exactly as one experienced in those other lands. For the views and attitudes of Maori Officers there leaned far more toward the "genuinely spiritual" than does the present 'home attitude' of many Maori 'leaders'.

Therefore, if the behaviour of a few present-day younger Maori, and some older ones who aspire to some kind of public leadership role is objectively examined, we discover that far too many anti-Pakeha sentiments are expressed rather than genuine conciliation. There appears to be little true *aroha* in the substance of their speeches. This is a natural outcome of such an attitude because it inherently possesses, as its actual foundation, negativity. It is, in essence, a negative energy, *directed toward all things Pakeha by this particular group*, rather than being applied as a positive energy directed toward *spiritual elevation for all.* Under **Spiritual Law**, of course, such negativity will always fail to achieve meaningful and lasting goals.

*   *   *   *   *

Upon return to N.Z. and the *whanau* settlement during times of Military leave, one could see that little had changed, for the '*kehua* path' was still believed to be as dangerous as ever. So much so, that during one leave period, my uncle, Te Haua Ngatikoro Hita, decided to employ certain ritual and *karakia* to finally 'destroy' these nightly 'visitors'. I agreed to assist him, though now more out of curiosity than conviction that it was as dangerous as stated. We subsequently walked this path in the morning, placing certain things at particular points in trees and on the ground, at which times Te Haua would recite certain incantations. Later, after many nights without visitations, he declared that it had been successful.

During another leave period I learned that the *hapu tohunga* to whom I was sent by my mother before first journeying to distant shores had had one of his legs amputated above the knee. Not so unusual one might think. In this particular case, however, what had started as a small gangrenous sore on a toe eventually resulted in the loss of the whole leg. Two things had triumphed over the strong advice and urging from the Pakeha doctors for the immediate removal of the toe to contain the disease: Maori superstition and fear of the loss of any part of the body for one, and, secondly, the belief that it could be healed by 'traditional medicine' and *karakia*. Unfortunately this view was confounded when it spread to the foot.

A clear case of cultural safety on the wrong foot!

Once more the doctor's advice was ignored, and stubbornness and fear persisted with the continuation of the same 'Maori treatment', but now with the subsequent further spread of gangrene to the lower leg. By this time the lower limb was foul and rotting and, even to a *tohunga* who strongly believed in 'traditional healing', it was now *painfully obvious* that the wrong option had been chosen. The Pakeha way in the beginning was the correct way. Now, instead of just one single toe, virtually the whole of the leg was lost. Only from the more objective perspective of time and distance once again does this particular event reveal so much of the old Maori psyche, and is a further stark illustration of the vital need to *totally abandon* clearly unhelpful beliefs.

The final cutting away from *certain things Maori* occurred when I was asked to 'take the *tatai*', again whilst on Army leave. The *tatai* or genealogical history of the *whanau*, *hapu* and *iwi* was once considered to be extremely *tapu*. So much so that it was kept hidden from most. It was believed to be the repository of the *mana* of the group, so possessed power and was sacred and therefore kept secret. The experiences of the wider world had shown me other things, and there was no longer the fear or need to hold on to practices which should have long since been discarded. In the recognition that so much was very wrong, it was not possible for me to accept a thing that actually represented 'repressive subjugation' – in the way in which it was often employed. My decision was received with disappointment as I was deemed to have fulfilled all the 'necessary requirements' for that 'position'.

However, my refusal of it at that time allowed me to remain free of unnecessary connections to any possible *whanau* or tribal superstition, and to certain Maori cultural traditions I could no longer accept as being in any way beneficial. This refusal was the correct *spiritual decision* as it allowed me to freely search for the deeper connections to **Spiritual Truth** than would have been possible with an unnecessary connection to, or responsibility of, a *tatai* to continually consider. Thankfully, today, *tatai* and *whakapapa* are in their rightful place in the public arena as solely showing the linear history of *whanau* and *Iwi* with far less other-world connotations attached to them.

Yet the practice of naming new-born after great ancestors who hold elevated status within *whakapapa*, and believing that their qualities can somehow be passed to the young in the simple 'transfer' of the name, still persists today. By this practice the newly named one is supposed to carry and manifest the 'perceived power' ostensibly inherent in the 'supposedly exalted' name of the 'revered' ancestor. As we outline **The Spiritual Laws of Creation** on our journey of discovery, we will actually find that notion or idea to be not the case.

There is no 'transfer of power', psychic, spiritual, or any other, by the simple expediency of conferring an ancestor's name onto a newly-born. And neither can there be. The new 'family addition' can, of course, make his own mark in the world with the given name if he so wishes. Yet the name can also become a huge burden in later life if *whanau* expect more from him than is fair and reasonable for his individual nature. I suspect that, in some cases, individuals who could not fulfil such expectations have actually succumbed to *mate Maori* through the psychic connections always deemed to be present with such revered names.

A singular event of lasting memory was that of attending mother's funeral after a curiously rapid return to N.Z. Upon being notified of her passing during a large Military exercise in Northern Malaya, scheduled Military air movements in a number of stages from the exercise area back to Singapore ensured a connection with a civilian flight home in good time for her funeral. It was a lasting memory not only because of the loss, but also for the amazing and, at the time, totally inexplicable events surrounding her funeral. In essence, one could say that all we had heard as children of strange and unexplained happenings at such times, actually occurred. Whilst the whole process kindled feelings of great apprehension, and perhaps a sense of uncertainty as to what should have been done to alleviate certain concerns at the time, for the most part it was a positive experience for a generally still fear-ridden *whanau* that I encountered. For the whole event was fascinating in its strength and intensity.

Everything that surrounds death takes place according to perfectly natural Laws since it is, in itself, a perfectly natural and lawful process. However, from this latter day point of time and distance with the knowledge of those Laws, a feeling of wistfulness sometimes arises when one considers how much less superstitiously-stressful it would all have been had the knowledge of **The Spiritual Laws** been available then.[21]

Mother's death unfortunately set in place the mechanism for a later curious incident during the mid-1970s where a *makutu* in the visible form of a Maori psychic 'death mask' was sent

---

[21]The explanations are detailed in the later Chapter outlining *the process of death*. A process that is *exactly the same* for both Maori and Pakeha – and every other human being that has ever lived!

to one sister by a member of the extended *whanau* to attempt to put right a past prediction that required a life as payment in *utu*. (This 'death mask' takes the form of an elongated face, with closed eyes and long pendulous ears.) According to the story it was originally our mother who should have paid that death price – at a particular age in her life – to fulfil a prediction made by a *tohunga* years previously. Around that designated age she did contract a serious, life-threatening illness, one that the hospital could not remedy. She was sent home to die but was placed under the care of the quite powerful *hapu tohunga*, Wi Te Nahi, who subsequently 'cured' her.

I was initially sceptical of the appearance of a 'mask', but knowing the story of mother's 'escape' from that original Maori *makutu* and being told that the image was growing stronger (on room curtains) and that Pakeha flatmates could also see it clearly in daylight, I contacted the, then, Rev. Kingi Ihaka and explained the situation. I told him about the one person in the extended *whanau* who was fearful enough of the prediction to try to bring it about, and who had therefore probably sent it. He agreed that the strength of it indicated a strong and dangerous *makutu* and advised that there were two ways to get rid of it. He could personally conduct an exorcism of it or, through collective prayer, we could ask that it be sent back to its origin – to the one who sent it. He strongly advised, however, that it be done without malice. We agreed that we should work with the latter option first, failing which, he would undertake to remove it.

The prayer session was duly entered into, the 'mask' disappeared, and the one whom we knew had sent it suffered a severe 'attack' that same night, with the effects lingering for some days. In essence, it was not a question of hate or even malevolence on the part of that person, whom we knew and liked. It was simply a question of *fearful superstition* and *non-understanding*. In retrospect, the *process* by which it was 'returned to the owner', and which we outline in a later Chapter, is simple to understand and infallible in its operation. Moreover, anyone can free themselves from such attacks or fears by simply utilising the correct *spiritual* knowledge to negate the effects of them – real or imagined.

The final experience of things psychically Maori that I wish to touch upon occurred whilst working in the iron-ore mines of North-Western Australia in the late 1970s. Like many other Kiwis of all social and ethnic backgrounds, the opportunity to earn a high wage and the potential to save most of it was a strong incentive to working in the Australian outback. Employed on this particular mine-site, as on all others, were a high proportion of New Zealanders. A fellow-worker where I was employed suffered from a mental problem caused by *mate Maori*. He confided to a number of us his belief that his family were trying to kill him by sending to him some kind of lizard creature, perhaps the most evil thing in Maori thinking.

Whether that was the family's actual wish or not was unclear but he certainly received regular letters from home. He claimed that they had sent the lizard across the sea to destroy him and he had seen it. Even though we were many miles from the sea he believed that it could still reach him during the 'wet season' when it could swim up the river that ran close to the mine-site, like a taniwha. From time to time he would strongly declare that he would "...never ever go back to them..." – the *whanau*.

Whilst he was not dangerous, it was clear that he was not completely lucid all of the time. Because he was employed as a driver on the very large 'dumpers', his condition was a matter of concern for the mine-site Supervisors. Interestingly, they were mainly Welsh and Irish working there on two-year contracts, and the psychic problems of 'our man' were quite familiar when comparing them with their own ancient beliefs. Because he would seek me out for *korero* about his problem, the mine Supervisors sought my opinion about his *mate-Maori* condition. It was collectively agreed that, whilst he was a likeable person he was, nevertheless, in need of help. However, I do not know what the particular outcome was for him as I left the area a short time later.

*   *   *   *   *

In conclusion, I sincerely hope that this short personal history will suffice to satisfy the Maori reader, especially, that I have experienced at least 'some grounding in the old way'. Sufficient, moreover, to provide the necessary insight required to dissect and open up those beliefs that need to be exposed to light. Via this dissecting method, the following pages will trace the path of pre-European Maori to the fateful arrival of the Pakeha. In the light of current Maori thinking, beliefs and aspirations today, the aftermath of that momentous event will be examined from the crucial and inviolable standpoint of **The Spiritual Laws of Creation**!

More importantly for Maori *after* that arrival, however, there occurred a particular event that could *not* have taken place *without* the 'Coming' of the white Pakeha invader – often referred to as *tauiwi*. That amazing event to which we refer will be thoroughly assessed with the help of **The Spiritual Laws**, and its meaning for Maori projected into the future as *once* a wonderful *spiritual* potential under those very same Laws!

2
Indigenous Aspects

2.1   The Development of Indigenous Peoples

The relatively recent U.N.'s "International Decade of The World's Indigenous Peoples" [1994-2004] was clearly a landmark event as it brought about far greater awareness of many indigenous groups in different parts of the world who have been largely ignored or, worse, culturally suppressed and/or brutally subjugated by the ruling regime. Regrettably, some groups now reside only in history books having been decimated to the point of extinction. This is a tragedy for all the peoples of the World as the various races and ethnic groupings are not here without purpose.

Even the most casual observer of things in the natural world must surely be struck by the sheer variety of everything that surrounds us. There are not just a few flowers and trees, nor small amounts of animals, birds, fishes and insects but an incredibly vast number. There are many, many thousands in all their colourful and diverse splendour. So many in fact that, even today, science recognises that it may never discover all the plants and creatures that exist on the planet. Imagine the drabness of our existence if **The Creative Power** had not produced such a profusion of visual wealth. This great variety should be a constant source of wonder and joy for all, and perhaps give cause for thought as to the purpose of so many different human races as well.

Just as nature's proliferation is a gift for our delight and enjoyment, the great variety of different human groups offers the same for our collective and potential spiritual well-being through cultural diversity and mutual exchange. All races possess certain abilities and attributes that others may not have and which therefore should be shared with all other people. With this recognition, and through subsequent and mutual voluntary exchanges, all races on earth *could* share in the fullness of an harmonious planet. Unfortunately, however, 'fullness in harmony' is still nowhere on the horizon.

Whilst that is clearly a desirable outcome, a cursory study of man's history will quickly show that the evolutionary development of the races did not occur at exactly the same time for all groupings and thus did not develop to the same level. Our beginnings can probably safely be described as that of nomadic hunter/gatherers where any 'economic system' was concerned with necessary food acquisition to meet immediate daily needs in the first place. As groups became more settled, agrarian farming practices gradually developed or, conversely and perhaps concomitantly, learning to farm negated the need for nomadic wandering. Increasing efficiencies probably led to food surpluses that allowed for trade or barter with neighbouring groups. Trade interaction, in turn, allowed for social interaction. Trade, moreover, was a preferable alternative to conflict and produced, as a consequence, a more stable group-foundation with a nucleus of developing sophistication.

From that development emerged that class of people not directly involved with the actual production of the food; the traders or middle-class who generally possessed more wealth than the producers on the land. Freed from the full-time constraints of manual production, this select group had the new-found luxury of 'leisure time' which allowed for the development of a different way of thinking from that of the other members of the group. Philosophy and the arts were probably seeded via this new 'time-freedom' aspect. However, not all peoples developed even to this stage, and the Maori could be included amongst those who did not crest that particular threshold to become a major player amongst the world's peoples or even a basic, technological one. By virtue of their too strong attachment to, and retention of, superstitious fears and psychic practices, the Maori race of numerous small tribes reached the Neolithic level only.

Overall, however, primitive man did give rise to more organised man and the subsequent flowering of what we loosely term the great civilisations. However, their greatness was maintained only as long as they strove for betterment and upliftment. With the inevitable transgression of **The Spiritual Laws**, they sowed the seeds for their eventual degeneration, collapse and demise.

During the time period of the inception, life and death of these various civilisations over thousands of years, many other smaller groups in different places were also developing along their particular paths too. History clearly records that not all reached elevated levels of societal sophistication, with great cities, libraries, temples and cathedrals etc.. This does not imply, however, that those peoples who did *not* reach such 'heights' were any less spiritual, *according to their particular level of development*, than the people of the 'great' civilisations. Neither does it suggest that the 'architects and builders' thereof were especially spiritual overall.

What it does show, however, is that under the aegis of **The Laws of Creation**, the 'empire builders' who possessed a more expansive and sometimes noble vision, tapped into the spiritual power inherent in **The Law of Movement** – even if sub-consciously – to develop their vision. However, whilst all races were not at the same level of development, any race that had not succumbed to superstition and psychic practices only needed to apply the knowledge of **The Eternal Laws** to its particular cultural path to attain the highest aspirations that that particular people were capable of reaching. And by this, perhaps escape the fate of other cultures and civilisations that did not apply the correct *Spiritual* knowledge and necessary discipline to their culture. For history attests to the fact that some societies were simply degenerate and brutal, and by no stretch of the imagination could we accord them the status of being spiritually-enlightened.

Clearly, then, all groups will develop for themselves a *"spiritual balance sheet"* showing a credit side and a debit side. In credit will be those practices and activities that further the overall well-being of that society i.e., strong, noble and compassionate in essence. On the debit side will be those traits that suppress and subjugate any free urge for upward striving, with its subsequent outcome for that culture or society. Recognising and accepting the truth and correctness of the 'spiritual aspect' offers the means to consciously and knowingly 'redress the balance' in any kind of society. If not, the consequences stemming from the reciprocal effect of such intransigence must then be accepted.

Via this mechanism we can thus draw the same kind of *spiritual balance sheet* for Maori, and from it determine honestly for ourselves whether or not it sits level, inclines toward The Light, or tips toward the dark. In this process it is important to ensure that we do not fall into the trap of absolutely believing that *all* indigenous or 'native' peoples are *all* more spiritually enlightened than the 'White races' or the numerically dominant one in any particular area in question.

Simply being labelled 'indigenous' with ostensibly stronger ties to certain elements within the environment such as the land and natural features for instance, and which the larger group may not inherently possess, does not automatically confer the status of 'greater spirituality'. From the perspective of **Spiritual Law**, this equates to a dangerously incorrect belief.

Of course people of the land, forest or sea, living in what we might term a 'traditional' way and *observing* "Natural Laws" in their entirety, *could* readily claim to be more enlightened than a group that is more technically advanced but *not* living to a commensurate level of spiritual maturity in *their* particular society. Conversely, in the case of a more technological society, scientific research and analysis that is also in concert with **The Spiritual Laws** and which offers ways to enhance environmental protection, for example, should be accepted by any indigenous group in the land as also being inherently correct. That should occur irrespective of any so-called cultural or 'indigenous-rights position' that might seek to automatically oppose such findings.

Quite simply, **The Spiritual Laws**, which are explained in detail in a later section, take no account of such considerations, and it is to these guidelines that all human groupings must submit, whether an advanced scientific society or primitive jungle tribe. However, the key element here is that any social or scientific application of any new discovery *must* accord with those precise and immutable Laws if it is to offer continuing benefit. The purpose of science *should be* to provide understanding of the effects of **Spiritual Law** in the physical and material world – for our elucidation. Of course the scientific community will first need to recognise this fact and, under such Laws, work accordingly – for our general betterment. In both cases, therefore, the respective 'ways' should be lived in accordance with **The Laws**, thereby allowing each particular group correct and continuing development under the outworking of what is termed **The Law of Movement**.

Unfortunately, however, in the mutual and increasing contacts between the world's 'indigenous peoples', there appears to be too ready an acceptance to believe that only *their* 'spiritual outlook' is correct and should therefore be embraced by all. It almost smacks of a new brand of fundamentalist, indigenous, 'world-native religion'. Whilst there is no doubt that such peoples have generally retained specific kinds of connections to the natural world that the Europeans have basically lost and need to rediscover, it is probably this underlying factor that gives rise to such a strong belief of 'great spirituality' amongst indigenous peoples. More especially since it has been the industrial practices of the mainly 'White' races that have been largely responsible for the horrors of environmental degradation in the poisoning of our global environment.

In a later Chapter the fundamental Laws governing Creation are examined. They explain how they intermesh and link all things, and further reveal how these immutable Laws cannot be circumvented in any way without bringing harm. This holds true for all peoples, regardless of race, religion, ethnicity, colour, etc.. For, without fear or favour, **The Law** *sifts immutably* to the *minutest degree*. Later, also, we offer an interesting comparison between 'Maori spirituality' and that of another indigenous people from a different land far removed from Aotearoa. Since Maori cultural exchanges are now a more or less regular feature with this particular group, the results of our comparison may come as a surprise. Notwithstanding the professed 'bond' between indigenous peoples, there are still vast differences in *spiritual* views and practices between the different groups even though the 'indigenous-brotherhood' aspect may *believe* them to be the same. In that particular Chapter, moreover, the knowledge of **The Law of Balance** will help to quantify 'the way of the Maori' in terms of the balance between that which was beneficial and that which allowed doors to be opened to darker psychic connections and activities.

Thus we will discover the **how** and **why** of words and forms like *makutu* and *utu* in their collective effect, and track the existence of the *taniwha* and various other thought forms which belong to the Maori race alone. What should thus emerge is a very definite and clearly defined thread running through the life of the Maori up to the arrival of the Pakeha, and thence onwards to a later special and crucial event for Maori, and on to the present.

2.2   The Beginnings of the Journey

In order to tread this particular path, it is necessary to have a starting point from which to begin. The beginnings must necessarily be pre-European *Aotearoa*, and after the great sea voyages from, or perhaps even back to, the ancestral homelands had ceased. Belich's quite recent work argues against an absolute in terms of repeated voyaging between New Zealand and the Polynesian homelands and that it:

> "...should probably be dismissed on present evidence."

> (Making Peoples, p.32)

Whatever the truth of the matter – and no doubt it will be debated by academia for some time yet – with the cessation of those voyages and the corresponding loss of contact with the ancestral home, the Maori could begin to develop his own separate racial identity, characteristics, culture and language. In a land mass as small as Aotearoa, there were only minor differences in these aspects between the tribal groups. Much from the old homeland would have been brought to *Aotearoa*, but this new home, over time, allowed sufficient separation for the transported culture to develop in a purely 'Maori direction'.

Generally speaking, every race follows a particular path that is uniquely its own. This path will be determined by various factors that, in turn, produces its culture, its national and racial characteristics, its language and even the very psyche of the race itself. The major influences will primarily be associated with the natural environment – the land itself. The feeling or attitude toward the forests, plains, mountains, seas and lakes etc., will all contribute to the specific cultural direction of the people concerned. As well, factors such as seasonal weather patterns – either warm or cold with clearly defined rhythms – whether the group inclines toward being hunter/gatherers or agriculturally based, whether settled or nomadic, peaceful or warlike, and whether desiring to be a close-knit tribal clan or a more open societal grouping; all or any of these will help to shape the groups view of itself and the immediate world surrounding it.

However, the greater, more decisive factor may be its relationship to the *unseen world*; to that world which may be perceived, believed and possibly felt physically, but not actually seen, and therefore probably feared through a lack of knowledge of it. This fear will *automatically translate* to superstition and ignorance. The initial factors may well be instrumental in aiding the development of the latter of course. For this unseen world that is sensed as existing but not materially visible, coupled with related psychic views and probable fear of the death process or the great unknown, may be *the single most powerful determinant* in defining and establishing the overall path of such a race.

This may produce, or help to produce, the myths and legends that will become its part-history, thus providing natural and perceived supernatural parameters for defining all that a primitive race, particularly, may encompass in its beliefs or religion. That 'mythical dimension' may be the only mechanism whereby certain phenomena can be explained (in a 'faith-belief mode') and perceived as being 'rational' – for acceptance and elucidation within such a group. From all those connections and threads will eventually develop what we now term the *customary law* of the different peoples. Thus, as previously stated, "customary law" is derived from a particular standpoint; i.e., the level of *knowledge* developed by a particular people. It will therefore inherently encompass the traditions, customs and even *fears* of that group. If no progress is made in understanding the fear aspect, for example, *then that part is naturally inculcated into the cultural traditions and into the very psyche of the people concerned.* And, unfortunately, it is usually *finally accepted as truth* and thus carried along as **unnecessary and invariably spiritually-dangerous baggage**.

The 'connection' to the 'unseen world', which will usually translate as a spiritual, religious, or psychic one – but more probably to varying degrees as a *mish-mash* of all three – will thus influence and greatly determine the material forms he will seek to construct, carve or use to symbolise his perceptions and beliefs. Thus, globally, we run the full gamut ranging from animism – the worship of rocks and trees etc., to carved images – both the grotesque and the beautiful – to highly stylised religious ritual in great and beautiful cathedrals and temples.

The life and ritual of pre-European Maori quite obviously did not encompass any of the latter. And because there is no written Maori history as such, it is difficult to know *exactly* how it was then. Utilising what is available to us, however, we can surmise with reasonable accuracy how it *probably* was. These sources are the orally recorded chants, *karakia* and history handed down through the generations, but will possibly reflect more of the great deeds and happenings, mythology and inner religious aspect of the tribe or race, than the everyday routine life. With the arrival of the Pakeha, however – particularly the missionaries and the more scholarly – the invaluable opportunity to record and document the 'way of the Maori' was initially ensured at a time of great change, adjustment and upheaval.

Regrettably, some loss of information from ancient times was inevitable, with Best himself commenting that even the oldest of his Maori informants lamented this loss in their own lifetime. Whilst Best was certainly a prolific writer, some latter-day historians such as Belich regard his efforts as perhaps biased toward "...native peoples in a frozen European mind-set." He describes Best's work as "...both suspect and vital."

(Making Peoples, p.24)

It is curious to note the apparent reluctance of a number of academics, especially among Maori, to readily accept the work of people like Best, Colenso, White, Cowan and the missionaries etc.. Such an attitude begs the question:

> "Who would have permanently documented the 'sacred *karakia*', the history, the many aspects of the culture and so on, if it were not for those men?"

The essential point to remember is that historians or ethnologists like Best, Cowan, Colenso and their many contemporaries, were among the most important contributors in **recording and preserving Maori culture** at the time of greatest transitional-change for Maori. Quite clearly, the early European writers were not fools. After all, they *were actually there* – **on the spot at the time**. Moreover, what they saw and experienced, they then recorded.

We can also accept that their grasp of the *reo* would have been far more extensive than many good Maori language speakers today. Indeed, would Maoridom have had a comprehensive dictionary of their language if it were not for the work of the Pakeha, Henry Williams? There even appears to be a growing determination among some 'cultural revisionists' to deny the fact of certain savage practices that were an entrenched part of Maori life. Whilst one can understand how European Universities might not readily accept such facts, it is truly amazing that some actual descendants here might seek to dangerously distort Maori history. Perhaps this attitude is also a 'frozen mind-set'. But, in this case, a Maori one!

Notwithstanding such views, sufficient information was recorded in those early years for the general path of the 'spiritual/religious' development of the Maori to be shown. This would simply be because the post-European Maori had necessarily to continue, for the most part and for a particular time – until more or less completely absorbed by the encroaching Pakeha way of life – with the familiar customs, beliefs and routines he had always practised.

The ancient, pre-European Maori could not be described as anything other than a truly stone age race, a Neolithic society characterised by the making of technically advanced, polished *stone implements.* It may well be argued that this is a Pakeha classification and not necessarily relevant to Maori thinking or culture. Nevertheless, such classifications are required as a benchmark or point of reference for the purpose of determining where any particular group might be placed amongst the world's peoples, technologically and historically. And even if we may not like the word, the description is certainly totally correct regarding the incredible stone working skills of the Maori. What greatly differentiated this stone-age society in the South Seas from other similarly developed races, however, was that it possessed a very high level of intelligence and cunning. One could almost describe it as 'healthy arrogance'. The colonising British alluded to this on many occasions with often grudging admiration. Because this particular 'indigenous' attitude and mind-set was responsible for certain precise outcomes, this trait of the Maori will be examined more closely in a later Chapter.

In all societies, certain skills and abilities develop that pertain solely to that particular group, with the singular key unit within the group generally being the family unit. With regard to our main purpose for being here, it could be argued that if all is well within the family, all should be equally well within the race. The business of bringing children into the world, nurturing and caring for them to adulthood, is the very stuff that allows for races to expand their population base, develop their culture and their notion of 'spirituality'. Without the investment in children, there is no group. On the surface this would appear to be so obvious as to not need such comment.

However, it is important that we analyse everyday family activities for our *spiritual balance sheet* too, as those results will repeat themselves as many times as there are families within the group. This collective direction, in turn, helps to produce the collective consciousness, psyche and outlook of the race. The most important aspect, though, is the mechanism of the **'how'** and **'why'** under which the society conducts its everyday activities in family and group life. These two major factors, probably more than any others, will ultimately determine what should be the group's most precious possession: its *spirituality* and, therefore, its *associated and/or ordained path.* As a logical extension of that premise, we should thus be able to reasonably determine the degree of spiritual health and level of spiritual maturity within the race and culture of the Maori – then, and today!

Let us begin our Maori journey proper, then. From the homelands of the South Pacific to a very different land and a vastly different future outcome than could ever have been envisioned by those early, greatly-skilled and fearless navigators!

3

General Aspects of Everyday Life

The Spiritual connotations!

The seemingly strong belief among many in Maoridom today that they were a highly spiritual race, were on the path to Spiritual Truth and, indeed, possess it completely now, must naturally pre-suppose the view that Maori *knowledge* of that spiritual world and also the natural world was complete – a grand claim for present-day descendants of a very savage, stone-age people to make. The publication, "The Song of Waitaha", is purported by some Maori to be the definitive wisdom and knowledge outlining the origin of a race preceding Maori. Within that frame of reference, it ostensibly describes the *true* history of pre-European New Zealand and strongly alludes to this belief of great spirituality.

The book, "Te Wheke – The Celebration of Infinite Wisdom" by Rangimarie Turuki Pere, also promotes this belief. As we will demonstrate, however, the Maori did not possess *the complete knowledge* of **The Divine Laws of Creation**. Publications such as those named above do not take us all that far from just *cultural* traditions, and are simply not sufficient to provide the definitive answers we require. This will become clear as our journey unfolds. In any case, claims to such high knowledge by any race should logically see that knowledge being applied to the everyday affairs of the people for their obvious betterment. The conscious application of it, moreover, should bring about peace, happiness, health, harmony and genuine spiritual growth as a natural consequence of such an application. Unfortunately, social statistics clearly show a different picture for Te Maori today.

Therefore it would be logical to accept that a 'cultural premise' which states that Maori possess complete and 'infinite wisdom' is clearly *not correct*. In any case, this can be easily refuted by comparing any such claim to the actuality of **The Eternal Laws of Life** and then applying that criteria to the knowledge and practices of the Maori, past and present. The more complete knowledge contained in **The Spiritual Laws of Creation**, therefore, allows us to better trace the path of the Maori in their new homeland up to the fateful arrival of the Pakeha. By applying that benchmark to his ways we will similarly be better able to more accurately assess the status of his *scales of spiritual balance*.

Certain aspects of life within any race can be deemed to be uplifting and beneficial for that particular race, gifting to it well-being, peace and harmony. Other practices, by contrast, provide an opposite reality bringing tension, sickness, war and strife etc.. The two extremes generally exist to varying degrees in all races. The level of evolutionary development and its associated percentage factor of these two opposing forces dominant in a race at any given time will have been influenced by various factors. These may differ greatly from race to race and from geographical location to geographical location, however.

Evolutionary development here means all that any race of people are capable of achieving and wish to aspire to in the material, intellectual, emotional but, most importantly from our point of view, in the spiritual aspects. 'The Spiritual' is deemed to be the most important as it should be the *guiding and leading* force. Its uplifting quality has the effect of tempering the baser propensities that a race may begin to develop or nurture, for any such baseness will exert the worst possible influence/s for that particular people. Thus, with the knowledge of **The Spiritual Laws**, all races can be examined and their overall level of general development clearly determined.

Therefore, in order to assess the actual *Spiritual* level of a particular people – **and this is crucial if we are to tie all the strands together to fully understand the final reason for the book Title** – one must go beneath the surface and *into the psyche of the race itself.*

In the case of the old Maori, the first European chroniclers and all successive ones failed to fully understand the actual living effects of certain aspects of so-called 'Maori spirituality'. (Even some resident here in New Zealand today do not fully understand or appreciate this unique dimension singularly-associated with 'being Maori'.) For the most part all appear to have blithely accepted the Maori view of 'great spirituality' within the race without any meaningful analysis. The problem arises from a non-understanding of the true meaning of this vital yet contentious word: – **Spiritual!**

*   *   *   *   *

As a basic guide, that which is *truly of* **The Spirit** i.e., – inherently encompassing **genuine 'spirituality'** – will always be that which is uplifting or **Spiritual** since its unequivocal **Origin** derives from *the Higher Realm of The Spiritual*. That particular Realm lies far above the Material worlds, those worlds in which we must *physically* reside – down here.

However, that which is concerned with *spiritualism* and/or *spiritism*, and which attempts to ascribe genuine "spiritual" activity to these two words, is actually a distortion of the higher reality by its practitioners. The actual outworking of the effect of these two particular words, spiritualism and spiritism – an effect that is wrongly deemed to be genuinely **Spiritual** – has its true place in the lower levels closer to the earth. For it is part and parcel of *psychic* or *occult* activity that, for the most part, is about as far removed from true **spirituality** as it is possible to be. In this context the world of the old Maori possessed *little* of truly **Spiritual** things but *very much* of *psychic* ones. Our continuing journey of discovery will clarify this fact for both Maori and Pakeha.

It is vitally necessary that we *do* clarify this important difference because it is the **forms** produced by mankind via the use of these two opposing principles that either uplift, or assail and oppress. And therefore, unfortunately, without mankind being aware of the why of his travails. Experience is the best teacher and it is probably quite difficult for anyone not born into the race and exposed to the more insidious effects of some *tapu,* and all *makutu* and *utu* etc., to fully appreciate the incredible physical, emotional and spiritual damage that these practices can impart.[1]

By way of similar example, only survivors of the holocaust can ever appreciate the terror and horror of that. By the same token, only a woman who is the victim of a rape can fully

---

[1]Amazingly, even today in the 21st century, those *psychic* practices still continue.

understand that particular terror and violation. All the rest of us are simply voyeurs, just 'readers of the news'.

*   *   *   *   *

Generally speaking, the historical recording and documenting of any situation needs to be more that of the objective analyst. One should readily understand this imperative, as emotional involvement can often cloud the analysis and render the study ineffective if the examiner is too close to the subject matter. However, if the same study is too coldly objective and clinical then the life, the 'living essence' of the subject matter, may be completely lost also, particularly in the study of a race of people. For, in the final analysis, the life of any particular people is one of much more than sterile objectivity. It is about love, procreation, children, marital infidelity, strife, conflict, laughter, religion, supernatural beliefs, music, war, disease and death etc..

They are the very things which produce the full gamut of emotional and *spiritual experiencing* in human beings of every race. They allow for the continuing development of various abilities and skills, and subsequently for either the spiritual growth or spiritual regression of the group.

Therefore, the well-documented and on-going study of the Maori race by all manner of European professionals and academics i.e., anthropologists, sociologists, ethnologists, linguists etc., fails to fully address the fundamental and underlying actuality or otherwise, of the so-called 'spirituality of Maori'. This is a very crucial point, for unless this is understood to an adequate degree, then all studies and analyses of such things as *tapu, makutu, utu*, the practice of cannibalism, and even language meaning and its *produced forms*, are without any kind of 'living depth'.

Interestingly, *some* Maori academics also appear to ignore certain aspects of Maori reality, historically and 'spiritually', but usually for a reason different to that of their Pakeha colleagues, unfortunately. After all, in its stark truth, history represents, and is, all that has *actually* occurred. And set in place, quite logically, by our forebears. Therefore, we who are the products of what has gone before have a duty and responsibility to ensure that historical truth is not sanitised in any way.

Notwithstanding the lack of a definitive experience of the 'Maori psyche', the chronicle of Maori life by the early European recorders should be commended. For without the work of Best, Cowan, Colenso and many, many others, much that we now have might have been lost forever. And it would be unfair to expect them to understand the deeper aspects of Maori thought processes without the experience of actual birth into the race itself. By the same token, however, 'European objectivity' probably serves as a good counterbalance to the more emotional involvement of the Maori orator and his oral history. Nevertheless, *the living essence of the Maori way* has probably not been adequately captured by the European academic. In this particular Chapter and others to follow, we will strive to achieve some measure of that reality.[2]

---

[2]An interesting example of European disbelief about certain things Maori was revealed to me some years ago whilst walking in the Tyrolean region of Austria where I met a young German anthropological student from Cologne University. On a high alpine bluff overlooking a large, deep, river valley, we exchanged introductions. She became interested in the fact that I was from New Zealand, and more so when she learned I was of Maori descent (and from one of Ngapuhi and Maoridom's most notable cannibals). Her interest stemmed from the fact that she was then studying Maori culture as part of her anthropological studies. The inevitable question and answer session touched on the subject of cannibalism among the Polynesian peoples. And there, in the beauty of the Tyrol of "Old-world Austria", I was astounded to learn that a large German University taught that Maori were never cannibals. Naive early Europeans circulated the romantic idea of the 'noble savages' of the "New Worlds". I have since learned that other European Universities also 'sanitise' Maori historical reality. Some of the Enlightenment philosophers, particularly Rousseau, in believing that 'primitive peoples' lived what he termed a more 'natural life' than that of the 'civilised European', probably found it difficult to equate the practice of cannibalism with such a supposedly 'natural' lifestyle. Natural at that time meant reasoned. For it was noted that the health of 'native peoples' was more robust than Europeans, and they were generally *believed* to be happier than the "Old-world" inhabitants.

So, from the perspective of time and distance, it is far easier to dismiss unacceptable ideas or unpalatable truths. If, now, we analyse some recorded acts of cannibalism by my own *tupuna*, Hongi Hika; whilst we find the historical record of Hongi's depredations accepted by academics we, nevertheless, still have a less than convincing account of the terror that must have been instilled in the minds and lives of those he sought to destroy.

Our analysis at this point will begin with an outline of the uplifting qualities and skills that may have been inherent in the souls that incarnated into the Maori race, and those that were attracted over time. That analysis, whilst assessing the everyday skills of the people, will not, however, dwell unduly on the detail of them. That is not the main purpose of this Work and other publications deal with it admirably. The all-pervading influence of *tapu* in Maori society and culture, and the associated practices of *makutu* and *utu* are our major interest here. Even though there may be *apparent* difficulties in separating the purely spiritually-inclined activities from the psychic, certain aspects of any culture will nevertheless have elements striving toward true spirituality contained within them. These we will seek to identify using the knowledge of **The Spiritual Laws of Creation** as our infallible yardstick.

The arrival and pre- and post-European life of all aspects of the Maori have been thoroughly documented by both Maori and European scholars and writers. Whether from the oral history of the old or from the observations of the later chroniclers, some controversy naturally exists about various aspects of Maori history. In the context of this essay, that is purely an academic argument or difference that will have little bearing on the reasons for the writing of this particular Work. Ours is an examination of the *spiritual balance sheet* of Te Maori in order to determine where we actually do stand. We will therefore not need to provide a detailed assessment of every aspect of Maori life and culture to achieve this. We will, however, need to provide a general overview of most aspects of the culture.

3.1   Maori Arrival

How did Te Maori arrive here? The *how* of the arrival of the Maori to Aotearoa has been analysed to some considerable extent seemingly without any real and concrete conclusions being reached. With purely oral traditions not necessarily being the best provider of hard facts and dates, some scholars have questioned the ability of the early arrivals to *knowingly* navigate across vast ocean expanses to land they simply claimed to know existed. Perhaps it was by virtue of their knowledge of wind and wave patterns and flight activity of sea birds. So the legend of the Great Fleet and Maori navigational methods have produced a minefield of theory and conjecture. Nonetheless, there is one irrefutable certainty, and that is the obvious fact that the Maori *did* voyage to this land and *did* settle here. We will strive to dismiss the irrelevant and concentrate on the actual, since that is the final arbiter of all things.

The publication, "Song of Waitaha",[3] speaks of a kind of composite race who were the first to arrive in New Zealand. A Temple of Lemuria was ostensibly built in this land by this early race and is put forward as evidence of them being a spiritually advanced people. According to the legends of 'Waitaha', they lived the highest levels of knowledge in spiritual peace and prosperity until the arrival of a cannibalistic and war-loving people called the Maori. These new arrivals effectively destroyed the Race of Waitaha save for a few of the line; from whom there are descendants living today. The "Song of Waitaha" is *ostensibly* their story.

In terms of the origins of man contained therein, however, the narrative is flawed for we are **not** descended from anything other than human progenitors. As already stressed, we are bound to accept a human origin for ourselves from out of all Spiritual and therefore Natural Law, not a non-human one, as is portrayed for the origins of the "Race of Waitaha". And whether or

---

[3] *Waitaha:* supposedly possessing vast knowledge.

not there was such a peaceful, highly evolved race called Waitaha that preceded Maori does not alter what we assert here.

One hopes that *that* particular 'history' is not designed to mask the reality of the ancient Maori in his *actual* lifestyle. For if that is the truth, then it is historically-clear that this newly arriving Maori race rejected the higher knowledge of the Waitaha people and their concomitant peaceful practices. On the other hand, if they were actually descended from such an elevated race, what could possibly have happened for them to spiritually-regress so comprehensively? For any such elevated foundation is completely incompatible with the *actual* pre-European practices of the Maori. Whatever the reality, we nevertheless concur absolutely with the aims of the "Song of Waitaha" as expressed in the Dedication; in particular the sentence which reads:

> *"Our dream is of one whanau that nurtures and provides for all within this beautiful land."*

However, only with the guiding light of the true knowledge of **The Spiritual Laws of Creation** as the umbrella, will this ideal ever be achievable!

Irrespective of our musings over a "Race of Waitaha", the history of pre-European Maori stands as an irrefutable path of great savagery. So if there were such a people as the originators of the Maori race with great temples of spiritual enlightenment, then the later practices of the Maori would be all the more appalling. Unfortunately stories which romanticise certain beliefs to fit particular theories of Maori history only serve to strengthen incorrect beliefs within present-day Maoridom, particularly regarding a believed high level of 'spiritual' knowledge, especially among the impressionable young.

Yet, in terms of how Maori got here, the race clearly possessed great sailing skills and were fearless in the execution of their ocean voyages. That notwithstanding, their knowledge of the sun and the stars for navigation, and even their relative positions over the horizon, has been called into question as a reliable method for two-way navigation between Aotearoa and the original homeland. Certainly the old Maori knew and named the stars in the Southern skies, as Elsdon Best has recorded.

The 'New Zealand's Heritage' publication, Vol.1, p.36, under the sub-heading "Later Theories on Navigation", states:

> "One theory has been that Eastern Polynesians deduced the existence and direction of New Zealand from observing the migratory flights of cuckoos and godwits, and were aided in navigating to and from New Zealand by following these birds."

However, they go on to say:

> "This theory ignores the fact that migratory birds continue to fly at night and independently of ocean cross-currents. Birds can also drift with winds which may adversely affect surface vessels."

The text continues:

> "Other theorists have also suggested that prehistoric navigators could have sailed to and from New Zealand by taking bearings on horizon stars. But this method, while practicable over relatively short distances, gives no clue to off-course drift with currents and winds. It is therefore untenable as a theory of navigation over the great distances from Eastern Polynesia to New Zealand and back again, particularly since horizon stars do not shine during the day and the sun is a poor navigation guide."

So how did these erstwhile voyagers find Aotearoa and return to their island homeland to report on this vast, forested land in the colder waters to the south, decide that it would be an ideal new homeland, and then relocate it again if they were not consciously knowledgeable as to where it lay, and/or how to get there? Or did they return at all? The theory that Polynesian navigators may have been blown far off course or become lost, thereby discovering Aotearoa by accident is a perfectly tenable one. It becomes a less realistic idea, however, when these same voyagers must then return home in order to bring more of their people to this new land. To have very many canoes lost or blown off course to reach unknown and relatively small islands in such a vast expanse of ocean, and with the necessary gender for the continued procreation of a race, namely women, appears to be too much to accept, if *all* landfalls were accidental.

Settlement solely by one-way voyaging also seems untenable, as this implies that no-one returned to the original homelands. This may well have been the case for some of the more adventurous first arrivals. In order to populate New Zealand to the extent that it eventually was under this scenario, however, there must have been an incredibly large number of laden canoes paddling or sailing in the South Pacific for sufficient numbers to make a *lost* landfall. This would naturally mean that far more would have perished at sea if they did not know where they were going, or perhaps even why. Further, if they did not, and could not, knowingly navigate to New Zealand, how then could they be expected to find a much smaller Island State if any attempt was made to return home? It would seem logical to accept that at some point one or more of the greater of the navigators found the means to journey back and forth, and thereby communicate this 'find' to the people of the original homeland.

From the same publication as our earlier quote (p.35) we read:

> "In *The Coming of the Maori*, Sir Peter Buck conceded that no evidence of the sailing directions used by prehistoric voyages to New Zealand had survived in authentic traditions stemming from prehistoric times."

The next quote of this paragraph is interesting as it begins to touch on our primary subject matter in this Part I – the 'spiritual knowledge' of the old Maori.

> "Elsdon Best, a noted New Zealand ethnologist, recorded that the Maoris of his time whom he questioned on this subject said that their ancestors had arrived with the help of *the gods.*"

> (Italics mine.)

In terms of being able to settle a small island country in a vast ocean with many people, produce and animals by canoe, not withstanding the obvious fact that vast amounts of such 'supplies' would *not* need to be shipped, it requires a huge leap of incredulity to believe that two-way canoe traffic did not take place to effect this. After all, we are talking about relatively small and slow craft in a huge expanse of ocean, and not large, fast modern ships. Therefore we should be able to safely conclude that these ancient navigators were able to knowingly navigate to such distant lands having first deduced the probability of its existence, even if over the horizon.

The publication by Professor Philip Houghton, "People of the Great Ocean: aspects of human biology of the early Pacific", proposes the possibility that a small group of voyagers on a double-hulled canoe, possibly numbering as few as fourteen, with women making up half the numbers, could have been the basic progenitors for the bulk of the Maori race. Departing from the Cook Islands as the most probable place, they sought to discover the land to the south that migrating birds indicated must exist, and made landfall about 800 years ago. Professor Houghton further postulates that at an average annual increase of 1.6%, numbers would have grown to about the 100,000 figure when Cook arrived.

From an interview with Herald journalist, Pat Baskett, he stated:

> "Whether there were other arrivals at other times is something debated ... multiple settlement by large numbers or any significant amount of return voyaging to tropical Polynesia was unlikely to have occurred."

In order to provide a constantly steady increase in population numbers, we must presume that the high infant mortality rate that was a feature of pre-European Maori was taken into account in Professor Houghton's calculations. And we must also acknowledge the reality of deaths of mothers during childbirth for which such a race were ill-equipped to prevent. To a large degree superstition ruled the Pacific, not medical science.

If that was the true scenario that brought Polynesia to New Zealand, then we most certainly had an incredibly intrepid band of both men and women prepared to risk death on a hard, uncertain voyage into much colder waters. Whilst Professor Houghton adequately addresses this problem in his probably correct view that the heavier musculature of the Polynesian peoples enabled them to generate sufficient body heat in the cold conditions of the South Pacific, it seems inconceivable to this 'Maori writer' that seafaring adventurers engaged on a journey of exploration of indeterminate length into completely unknown waters would take with them half their numbers as women – for the precisely planned purpose of *finding land to colonise*. Voyages to destinations known to exist and previously visited would readily include women, but surely more unlikely to a new and uncertain end result.

Of course, the opposite may well be true in that a proposed journey to another landmass certain to exist but of uncertain distance might well presuppose the possibility of finding it and not being able to return. In this case it *is* logical to believe that the men would want women in a new land from which they might not be able to leave. This would make Professor Houghton's idea perfectly tenable. Nevertheless, it still seems logical to believe that the seafaring skills that were an obvious part of their everyday knowledge would enable the Polynesians to have confidence to embark on such a journey of discovery secure in their ability to navigate their return. In this case, women would probably not be taken on the first voyage.

In his work, "Making Peoples", page 33, Belich opines:

> "Return voyaging is not very credible for New Zealand, but the idea remains valuable in two respects. First, it has shattered the implicit but common assumption that, after voyaging 3,000 kilometres to New Zealand, the first settlers suddenly abandoned their ocean-going technology on the beach and crept cautiously along the coasts for the rest of their history."

Our premise accepts this view and postulates further that the new arrivals not only retained their open-ocean navigation skills but that the forests of New Zealand provided larger trees probably better suited for open-ocean craft. Moreover, strong Polynesian ties to family in the ancestral homelands must surely have given impetus to at least try to return and persuade others to also come to this new land.

If modern theories on Polynesian navigation question this ability, how then were they able to do this, if they did so at all? Since there are no substantiated conclusions, let us consider another possibility; a *spiritual* one. We should remember that the ancient Polynesians made their home in the expanse of the largest ocean on the planet, as opposed to the European who were more land-orientated. Therefore different knowledge, attitudes and perceptions regarding distances, the effect of weather patterns etc., on their very different environments would have developed and become honed to an appropriately high degree in their respective worlds.

So, for the Pacific peoples, the ocean – inhabited by them for many hundreds of years – was their area of knowledge and expertise. In order to visit other islands, they would need to be very secure in their ability to do so. And for their safety at sea, to be able to read all the 'signs' well, especially around weather. Quite logically, the greater the ocean voyage, the greater the ability and sureness required to complete it safely. Their historical record most certainly attests to this in their ongoing development into longer and longer ocean voyages.

However, apart from these obvious skills, retained within these peoples was still the strong connection to the knowledge of **The Forces of Nature**. At this time of Pacific exploration by its inhabitants, the far more intellectual European had long discarded this idea as being, from the purely earthly scientific point of view, impossible. To all *material/empirical* intents and purposes, it certainly would be deemed to be nonsense – which, however, **it is not**! The religious authorities, on the other hand, had dismissed this notion with the sage and authoritarian decree that this kind of thinking amounted to a dark and evil connection to 'demonism', even though this connection is graphically recorded in **The Bible** by no less than the Disciples of Jesus in an incident involving The Son of God Himself.[4]

With the development of the skills and ability to undertake longer and more daring voyages, and the retained knowledge of, and perhaps connection to, **The Elemental Forces of Nature**, we would be foolish not to consider the powerful help of the 'intuition' and the 'inner voice' in guiding the early navigators 'knowingly' to their possibly 'intuitively-perceived' destinations, an ability which the European, for the most part, had long since lost. His newly-invented navigating instruments, whilst very effective for their designed purpose, simply reflected his intellectual growth and loss of the sureness of the intuition which we can possibly liken to a rejection of a connection to the 'inner voice'. Thus the reference to 'help from the gods' might be seen as using a *spiritual ability*, the employment of the 'intuition', the 'gut feeling', accompanied by the learned knowledge of his home environment – *including relevant knowledge of the stars and star systems* – to find his way *knowingly* across a trackless ocean. In any case, irrespective of the methods employed, this new land named Aotearoa *was* settled by a group of fearless, adventurous Polynesians who eventually became known as Te Maori.

As an example of this 'connection to Nature' in Island peoples, Dr Lyall Watson's book, "Gifts of Unknown Things", records, among other fascinating events, the ability of one old man living on a small, remote Indonesian island, to 'hear' shoals of fish when placing his head underwater and 'listening' for them. And then indicating the direction the younger men were to paddle in order to cast their nets. On one accompanied occasion whilst on a night-fishing expedition not far from shore, Dr Watson records that the old man suddenly lifted his head out of the water and exhorted them to paddle as hard and as fast as they could back to shore. Via this method of 'listening for fish', he had 'detected' the different 'energy field' of an approaching tsunami. This particular wave crashed onto the beach minutes after the fishing party had run up onto higher ground above the shoreline. At the time of his stay with the people of the fishing village, Dr Watson observed this ability virtually gone, with the old man lamenting the fact that he was unable to find a way to impart his knowledge to a generation of young people influenced by other 'modern' factors.

It is these kinds of lost abilities that we allude to in our belief of the possibility of return voyaging as a reasonably regular event until such time as sufficient numbers of 'family' were established in the new homeland. Whilst such notions might be considered by empiricists as just as much speculative-theory as other ideas put forward, it may be *more relevant* as a means of how early Polynesian navigators achieved their intended outcomes in long ocean voyages in terms of the *differences* in how the world was viewed and interacted with, between them and their equivalent European counterparts in the same historical time-period.

So, in terms of our balance sheet or scales, where sit the skills and abilities from the ocean-voyaging phase? Clearly, beneficial, upbuilding traits for any race are fearlessness and courage. This is certainly displayed in the exploration of the Pacific. The incredible skills of the boat-builders stand out also. Individual leadership in the captains and/or navigators of their craft and the necessary requirement to have at least some forward-planning show organisational ability and discipline – for captain and crew. These traits would be a valuable asset in the exploration and settlement of any new home.

Now, with the cessation of the return voyages to the old homelands and the subsequent com-

---

[4]This clarifying event will be examined, along with other similar kinds of examples, in the later Chapter on "Elemental Lore".

plete loss of contact there, the Maori, in splendid isolation, began to develop his own particular culture in a land which was, for the most part, heavily forested, considerably colder than the ancestral homeland and, in great contrast to the original home, had four distinct seasons. The flora and fauna also differed completely from that of the homeland without the obvious benefit of an abundance of tropical fruits and vegetables for most of the year. A whole new attitude to lifestyle would need to develop here.

Relative isolation over a long period of time will ultimately determine the development and evolution of a race in its view of itself, the natural world around it and its necessary relationship with it. Inherent characteristics within the race and within the individual souls incarnating into it under **The Law of Spiritual Attraction of Similar Species**, will be the governing base line from which it will develop its strengths, weaknesses and particular cultural paradigm. Various other factors, mainly environmental, may also greatly influence and modify this process, particularly considerations such as the terrain itself, whether flat or mountainous, whether forested or open plain, or whether many or few rivers and lakes. The patterns of the weather i.e., hot or cold, may likely influence the developmental process as these weather patterns may play a crucial role in the availability of food or the means to acquire or grow it.

As previously noted, the societies themselves, particularly in their social organisation – which will probably evolve from the above criteria – will be further influenced by whether or not a group is settled or nomadic, whether hunters/gatherers or agriculturalists, whether warlike or peaceful, whether a closed tribal group or a more open, expansive society. And in an isolated evolutionary situation such as the developing Maori race found itself in, any totally unexpected encounter with another race, especially a vastly different one with much fairer skin, would be a tremendous culture shock initially. This, of course, was the reality for the Maori from its development in relative isolation over many hundreds of years up to the eventual, fateful arrival of the Pakeha.

So, what was the basic structure of this pre-European Maori society? They were a Neolithic people, a stone age society with great seafaring skills organised into *whanau*, *hapu* and tribal groups. In fact, according to the New Zealand's Heritage, Vol.1, they were:

> "...the highest Neolithic culture the world has known ... based on a complex social system."

Developed to the highest degree possible by this stone-age people were the necessary skills for everyday living, protection and survival. The land and sea provided not only the basic needs of food, clothing and shelter, but also the means whereby song and dance could find expression, and where the making of garments developed to a skill requiring great dexterity producing ennobled works of art. And where the craft of the carver and tattooist would develop to a similarly high degree of skill.

3.2   Animistic/Elemental Forces of Nature

This particular subject is not one that is part of Maori life in the sense that it belongs solely to Maori. It is part of the culture and language of all the world's peoples. However, it is vitally important that we know of *them*, for *their activity*, as ordained under **The Divine Will**, regulates, in no small measure, those forces we loosely refer to as 'belonging to Mother Nature'. What we need to *especially understand* is the fact that these forces are not *psychic* ones as Maori invariably believe/d them to be. **All** *psychic* forms and entities are the productions of mankind! Nor are the **Elemental Forces of Nature** 'spiritual beings' either. Because Maori have not generally understood the true nature of these forces or forms, they wrongly concluded that they were all "spiritual", and belonged solely to Maori. That appears to be the present-day belief as well. In truth only Maori *psychic* or *occult* forms belong to Maori since, like all peoples, ***they are the producers of their own***.

In the previous section we briefly outlined one example of an ability to connect oneself with the all permeating 'energy' of The Forces of Nature for our benefit. We also commented how this once inherent attribute is now virtually lost to mankind. The environmental degradation of the earth is testimony to man's refusal to acknowledge such forces. Had he maintained the correct connection, the earth would not be the 'poisoned pill' that we must now swallow. Because of its importance to our story and spiritual elucidation, a totally separate and detailed later Chapter will be devoted to this vital subject.

3.3   The Forest of Tane – Hunting

The forest lore of the Maori encompassed most of the elements of the supernatural in his life, and the vast expanse of such a rich source of food and material gave expression to his belief of the existence of various deities within the forest. Reigning over this realm was Tane, a lesser-tiered god in their pantheon of gods, and on a level considerably below Io, the Supreme Being. Lesser beings inhabited the understorey and assisted Tane by performing various functions within the forest to maintain its well-being. This belief, being tantamount to a religion under the all-pervasive umbrella of *tapu*, ensured that no hunter or fowler harvesting food, or individual or group seeking building material from one of Tane's 'children', dared to operate within his domain without first seeking approval or permission to do so. Through the intonation of the correct and appropriate *karakia* to ensure success in the particular venture, and again later proffering thanks, one could be sure that one would not only be successful, but also be protected from the less benevolent and darker forest-dwellers *believed* to exist there also.

As with any race living cheek-by-jowl with nature, exceptional skills in hunting became the norm. A deep knowledge of the cycles of the seasons, with the associated insight into which foods could be gathered in the optimum harvest time, are always a characteristic feature here. With the influence of the institution of *tapu* playing such a significant role in the harvesting of food from both the land and sea, the forest, especially, offered in great abundance all that the Maori needed for his existence. In particular, trees provided the building materials for the great *waka*, for dwellings, and for implements and weapons. Thus, the forest was a vital and living treasure, a *taonga* for the welfare of the people.

However, because virtually all the elements of life were *tapu*, food-gathering expeditions into the great forest of Tane, as well as from any other source, necessarily became highly ritualised. Certain rules had to be obeyed, and the various foods harvested required different rules for each. For instance, birds gave meat and also feathers for the adornment of garments and hair, but the fowler was required to observe strict *tapu* in the gathering of them. In the *whare mata*, which was the storage place for his snares and traps, women were excluded from entering because of its *tapu* status. During the snaring and trapping process great care was taken to avoid voicing "...certain expressions of speech lest the birds hear him and escape". The hunter would not speak the name of the quarry being pursued for that would make them 'nervous and shy'. An absolute *tapu* was the carrying of any cooked food with him. This transgression would render the forest 'polluted' and bring about the destruction of the *mauri* or life-principle whereby the birds would leave.

Apart from its great abundance of fauna and flora, the main characteristic of the New Zealand rain forest for the ancient Maori must surely have been its awesome impression of brooding magnificence. The luxuriant nature of it in its incredible vastness, the thick canopy and understorey, then without predation by today's destroyers, the huge numbers of massive trees, and its overall intensity of overwhelming presence must have produced an awesome mix of reverence, veneration, trepidation and fear in such a superstitious people. For, even today, the much reduced, heavily-predated forest cover still produces this effect in many Maori.[5]

---

[5]Paradoxically, if the early European had had this same 'veneration', Aotearoa might still possess some of its

At times of both inter-tribal and Maori-European war, the forest offered a refuge where the hunted could find food and relatively safe shelter. But more significantly in the psychic beliefs of the old Maori, the forest harboured certain denizens that were dangerous to man. Any chance meeting with them could result in one's death, for they could not be fought with mortal weapons. Knowledge of the black arts was necessary to keep them in check or, preferably, to destroy them should they be encountered. The forms varied greatly but were all of an evil nature. Some in *taniwha* or lizard form, others similar to the form of man but as long-limbed and hairy tree dwellers. And there were others.

"For the Maori the forest represented the totality of life. In it, nothing was impossible."

(New Zealand's Heritage, Vol.1, p.112)

In our analysis of Maori beliefs from the standpoint of **The Eternal Laws** – which we will more fully outline in a future Chapter – it is vital to comment on the existence of such entities and to put them in their rightful place. In analysing the various aspects of Maori life, and where relevant, we will apply the knowledge of precisely that **Spiritual Law** to the subjects and issues that arise. In this particular case, then, the life and form of the dark forest-dwelling entities as accepted by many Maori, ancient and modern, *actually do exist today.*

We must be quite specific about this point.

The dark psychic forms that the Maori feared *did not exist* at the time of man's beginnings on earth. They were not produced as a work of Creation. The Creation of the spheres and of all the creatures that inhabit those spheres was an act of **Divine Will**, which knows of no such darkness. For darkness and its associated forms do not exist in the **Higher Planes of Light**. Indeed, they cannot!

The free will of *man alone* gives form to such things as *taniwha* etc., and ensures their *continued existence* by continual human-belief reinforcement and nourishment. It does so by extending an idea that such things *might* be possible, to the firm conviction that it *is* so. By that conviction, the entity or form becomes *alive* for that race. Finally, it is given its own name which then enters the language of the people. With this naming it has taken on sure form. It is complete and living, even though not physical. However, from its place of residence close to the physical world, its presence, or even belief of, is able to influence the people who have produced it. All races and peoples have numerous such 'attachments'.

The process is quite simple but potentially spiritually-devastating as it concentrates energy on things that *should never have been produced*, that are *not meant to be here*, really *do not matter* and, consequently, *should be immediately discarded*. If the names of the forms were expunged from the language, no further thought given to them and no reference ever made either in the spoken or written word, they would wither away and disappear. The means of *destruction* is just as subject to **The Eternal Laws** as is the method of *construction*, and equally as simple. For it is only the constant reinforcement that ensures their continued existence. The belief about them also maintains an air of false knowledge in that people can cling to such ideas for their own purpose and wax knowledgeable about things that, in reality, **have no useful purpose for mankind.**

It would be interesting to know whether or not the belief in such forest-forms were brought here from the old homeland. One would assume that they did not come from there. They were more likely to have been products of the imagination of the first voyagers upon discovery of such a vast, primeval expanse of forest, the like of which they would not have been seen before. Surely such a dark and vast forest had to have supernatural monsters living there? Once the

former forested magnificence.

thought produced the seed, the imagination grew the form. Given the overall level of spiritual development then, it would seem to be inconceivable for such an idea to be incorrect.

It matters not whichever is correct, however. The reality is that today, passed down through generations of Maori, are the stories and the beliefs of the dark entities of their psychic world, still living, still dangerous, and still needing the machinations of a *tohunga* to dispel, should they manifest themselves to those without sufficient strength to ward them off, or to those who allow them to be attracted in the first place. How wonderful it would be, and more intelligent, for all to simply recognise the existence of **The Laws of Creation**, consciously apply them in our lives, and expunge such forms out of existence forever. Knowing about such entities does not represent any form of true or great knowledge, it merely shows recognition of humankind's foolishness in bringing such things into being and keeping them here, when there was never any need to in the first place.

3.4 Conservation

Whether or not one could term the ancient Maori a conservationist is an interesting question. The very nature of his existence, his dependence on what the land and sea could provide in its particular season, the number of people to be fed and the possibility of being able to preserve and store certain kinds of food for later use in the off-season were some of the obvious factors governing the amount needing to be harvested. It would be difficult to imagine very much food-waste in those times. Ordinarily, it should have been in his interest to ensure the continuation of all species of possible food sources.

Notwithstanding this fact, the Maori eradicated many bird species. The Moa was just one of the many, albeit the most spectacular. Being such large flightless birds, they were relatively easy prey to hunt and obviously provided much food, as well as feathers and bones for clothing, tools and implements. Unfortunately for the Moa, such a walking treasure trove of abundance guaranteed the demise of this magnificent creature. According to Belich, (Making Peoples, p 33), the old Maori probably:

"...wiped out a dozen species of moa, 20 species of birds..."

Without the influence of man, eco-systems stay in perfect natural balance for as long as he is out of the picture. In the case of the arrival of the Maori onto the islands of Aotearoa, his impact on the natural order was minimal in the beginning. And compared to the later 'industrialising-ventures' by European Nations into the once pristine environments, that impact remained more or less minimal throughout his tenure up to the arrival of the Pakeha. Nevertheless, any intrusion into a previously untouched eco-system must bring about certain irreversible changes. Aside from the entry of the Maori into Aotearoa, the associated arrival of his *kuri* and *kiore* began the long process of changing the environment of the land from its original pristine glory to a shadow of its former self – which we have today.[6]

From the standpoint of **Spiritual Truth**, a large measure of the cause of this degradation can be placed squarely at the feet of humankind for severing the connection to **The Elemental Forces of Nature** with whom he was ordained to work in the material world consciously and therefore knowingly. That severance not only ensured the loss of a necessary life-force connection to the natural world and its concomitant vital knowledge in correct care, respect and veneration for all eco-systems, it also meant a greater loss of natural healing methods. Today we only touch on the tiniest fraction of this knowledge, whereas had this connection been retained there might now be more cures and far less devastating diseases. And most certainly far fewer *natural* catastrophes.

---

[6]The Auckland Zoo exhibits a large time-line chart of human history and the impact of humans on the eco-system of New Zealand. That particular chart notes 32 species wiped out by Maori, and 9 by Europeans.

With regard to this lost respect and veneration for the natural world in the correct way, the old Maori was also responsible for the destruction of relatively large areas of rainforest by fire, as well as some grasslands. Belich estimates that the Maori "...burned off a third of the native forest." (p. 33)

One wonders what manner of propitiatory offering might have been presented to Tane by ancient Maori for these acts of ecological vandalism given their ostensibly "sacred" regard for the forest; notwithstanding the probability that they perhaps did not intend to fire large areas. Perhaps more a case of an out-of-control burn. Still, it raises an interesting point about the 'real feeling' for the forest.

Whilst not strictly in context with the historical time frame presently being discussed, the current debate over so-called 'cultural harvesting rights' reveals a clear lack of understanding of the interconnected worlds of the material, the Animistic, and *The Spiritual* by those Maori who are proponents of this push. Naturally, if food sources are plentiful, we are permitted that harvest. However, if a particular species is low in numbers, and any further decline may bring about its extinction, it is an absolute transgression against **The Spiritual Laws of Creation** to continue to demand that species as food. Such demands made under the aegis of 'traditional culture' reveals an attitude that has no connection or affinity with *truly* 'spiritual' practices.

In the natural world each individual species has its own particular 'critical mass' level where, if the numbers drop below that minimum, the continuation of the species may no longer be viable. It is then doomed to extinction, and sometimes in an unbelievably short space of time – as we will shortly describe in a relatively recent example. The numbers needed to sustain any species, therefore, cannot be determined absolutely by man, much less by a people who do not study them. So it is a sad thing, indeed, when some Maori demand the right to harvest the native wood pigeon by virtue of cultural tradition. More especially when there is some concern from the scientific community as to the viability of sustaining their numbers.

It is incomprehensible how a people who grandly claim to be more in affinity with the natural world than the Pakeha cannot 'see' the potential for the possible extinction of this wonderful bird if the protective measures put in place to keep it with us are continually challenged by certain Maori groups.

For, despite the size and apparent strength of the native wood pigeon, its rate of reproduction is relatively low. Thus a reproductive rate perhaps insufficient to halt its demise if Maori continue to selfishly push this particular boundary. If starvation were the issue here, with few food sources available, then the harvesting of many different kinds of species, including the pigeon, might need to be considered. The reality is, of course, that whilst Maori health is generally regarded as poor, they are certainly not starving, and annihilating the *kereru* will not bring about anything other than its demise. With that extinction, however, what will be reaped would be a *spiritual* indictment against those of the Maori race who demanded the beautiful *kereru's* meat.

So, from the 'spiritual' point of view, let us analyse the ramifications of this attitude. Firstly, under **The Eternal Laws**, the power inherent in **The Creative Will** gives *form* to the *kereru or kukupa* and gives it warmth and soul life. Tane, *Elemental Lord of the Forest*, under the direction of the leading **Spiritual Power from Above**, provides the forest for its home. In this wonderful partnership the life of the *kereru* and the forest has been ordained to be intimately connected in the sustenance and ongoing development of *both* the *kereru and* the forest environment itself, and therefore for all its inhabitants – and for man, too.

Consider this fact. The *puriri* tree provides food and shelter for many varied creatures in both its branches and in its living wood and is an important tree in the New Zealand forest eco-system. This tree is propagated by seed from its berries and needs a helper to disperse them throughout the forest. Because it is the largest flier in the forest, only the *kereru* has the size to swallow the larger seeds of such fruit-bearing trees as *karaka* and *miro*, as well as the *puriri,* transport them inside the crop and the gut and, via this means, ensure the continued natural seeding of these magnificent trees for our delight and visual enjoyment. The *moa*, hunted to extinction by the Maori, once fulfilled a similar role.

No human being, for whatever reason, has the right to bring about the extinction of any species. The destruction of whole species via natural catastrophes, however, must be accepted as an ordained event according to Law. Therefore, in the unequivocal context of transgressing a living law of life, it is foolish and dangerous to cite traditional cultural rights as a reason for doing exactly that. But let us take this particular example one step further down our path to better spiritual understanding. If we hypothesise the extinction of the *kereru* purely because we had demanded it as food under the aegis of tradition and/or culture, what has *actually* taken place spiritually?

Firstly, we have transgressed on two counts. We have extinguished not only the life of a whole species of a beautiful bird given form by **The Creator of all the Worlds**, but also destroyed the connection of that ordained life-form to other created forms of the forest community, the *miro*, *karaka* and *puriri* etc., also ordained to be part of our forest under the same **Creative Will**. So we have two *irreversible* transgressions against **The Spiritual Laws**. What could this bring as its 'ordained return' under **The Law of Reciprocal Action**, (*Sowing and Reaping*), we may wonder?

But even that is still not the end of the matter. In the cultural traditions which are so proudly vaunted to the world and from which Maori ostensibly claim great *mana*; in the selfish extinction of a fellow creature – and a very beautiful one at that – will have been committed an act of very grave hypocrisy. For, should this ever happen as hypothesised here, the pigeon feather cloaks that probably represent the epitome of the weaving skills of Maori, made with *aroha* from out of the *wairua* of the weavers, who would have once given thanks and *karakia* to Tane for the birds which provided the beauty and colour which delight the eye, in a task no doubt undertaken with reverence; what would all that then represent? These forms of consummate skill and beauty, these cloaks of great *mana*, which have *rightly* been carefully protected, would then become as *nothing* in Creation. Any wanton destruction of the provider of the beauty of the cloaks would render them *not fit to exist* any longer in the world of so-called Maori *mana* or, indeed, anywhere in the worlds.

> For it is not man that **confers** *mana* on man and his works, but it is **The Living Laws of The Creator** that *allow* man to *earn mana* for himself and his works.

Therefore, it would be a sad day, indeed, if we could no longer marvel at the flashing great speed of the bird as it hurtles down the ridges like a streamlined, rocketing projectile, wings tucked in close and head thrust forward as it streaks, in perfect control, into the deep valleys of Tane's forest. There to skim the canopy of the valley floor to the forested far side, flare its wings to slow and check its momentum, and settle lightly on the branch that it had selected from far across the chasm. How enthralling it is to have the privilege of witnessing such a powerful flying display, feel wonder at this marvellous creature, to rejoice in its wonderful plumage and wish him well as he performs his display dives for his mate. And to hear their soft contented cooing as they sit together among the flowers of the *kowhai*. Far better, then, to not demand the meat of the *kukupa*. Far better, and spiritually safer, to feast on a farmed chicken from a takeaway or supermarket.

*   *   *   *   *

A relatively recent example of how quickly the extinction of a species can occur from exceptionally large numbers is clearly and tragically recorded in the case of the American passenger pigeon. The first settlers to America were astounded by the huge flocks of pigeons they encountered. Individual flocks were estimated to contain hundreds of thousands of birds – possibly millions, and migrating flocks were large enough to darken the sky. Early settlers estimated total numbers to be in the billions. [To illustrate the true meaning of such huge numbers, we can cite the example of the difference between a million and a billion, in this case the American billion i.e., – one thousand million. In terms of *time*, one *million* seconds is about 26 days, yet a *billion* seconds is almost 37 years.]

The sheer size and collective weight of migrating flocks would snap branches of quite substantial size when the birds landed to roost at night. Local settler-farmers would take advantage of this and drive their pigs to the roosting sites where they would consume large numbers on the ground. In the normal course of events these huge numbers could stand any amount of predation without any loss whatsoever when hunted by the Native Americans. Even the arrival of the first explorers with their guns could not detrimentally impact on such vast flocks. However, with the entry of waves of settlers and their families and subsequent predation, numbers began to decline.

The first settlers to move west found the passenger pigeons an endless source of meat, fat and feathers. As the railroads extended their tracks westward, professional pigeon hunters were able to ship the birds directly to city markets before the meat spoiled. Yet the sheer volume of bird numbers gave no hint that extinction could be a possibility. By 1880, however, it was evident that the species might not survive – the decrease in numbers had become irreversible. So even with substantial numbers, the base line population was still not sufficient to allow the flocks to maintain sustainable, reproductive viability. A key point in this sorry saga is that passenger pigeons were prolific breeders, unlike the *kereru*. The young grew very fast, fledged in just 14 days and became independent a few days later.

(1. Microsoft Encarta, 2. Reader's Digest Great Illustrated Dictionary, Vol. II)

Some efforts were made to breed passenger pigeons in captivity, but with little success. Finally, the last passenger pigeon died in the Cincinnati Zoological Garden in 1914. From uncountable numbers to the very last one was only a matter of two hundred odd years. This last one, paradoxically, was a female, and they called her Martha. She now stands in a glass display case in the Smithsonian Institute. A sad monument to the white man's rapacious greed, selfishness, ignorance and stupidity, and the world is surely far poorer for her pointless loss.

With a huge increase in scientific knowledge about the *kereru,* that particular fate should never befall it. Yet one still wonders; if there is ever a last *kereru* in this country, will it be preserved, or will it still be eaten under a similarly ignorant stance as that displayed by the *tauiwi* of America? This time, however, in Aotearoa under the equally selfish umbrella of cultural tradition and Maori 'sovereignty'. But sovereignty over what, we may wonder?

3.5   The Sea of Tangaroa – Fishing

For the Polynesian, the sea was all-important and all-powerful in its force and presence. The vastness of their watery environment gave them vital reason to develop sailing and navigational skills far surpassing that of most other races and allowed them to settle many islands over the vast area of Oceania. Fishing naturally provided a great amount of their food, particularly in the smaller island groups. For the Maori, however, the larger landmass of New Zealand with much more varied forest fare and fresh water fish meant that the sea, as a primary food source, was no longer so important, particularly for the inland tribal groups. Aside from being the ideal highway for effecting relatively speedy trade and travel in preference to the more difficult, heavily forested land environment demarcated by tribal boundaries, the sea also provided the means by which warring tribes on their great canoes could swiftly reach coastal enemy.

The sea provided great bounty at various times of the year and fishing, probably more than any other peaceful pastime, sometimes required the combined energies of the whole group if success were to be assured. Whether operating from canoes off shore or hauling in huge nets from the beach, the catching, subsequent preparation and preserving of parts of the catch by the tribe illustrated how efficient, industrious and organised the old Maori could be. The scale and methods of storage of food impressed early Europeans.

"No people can be more provident or industrious than the New Zealanders in supplying themselves with stores of provisions."

(Making Peoples, Belich.)

Notwithstanding a lessening of dependence upon food from the sea; because of their long history of association with it and the inherent love of that food developed over many hundreds of years, trade between the coastal tribes and the more inland ones for such delicacies as dried fish, shellfish and seaweed etc., assumed great importance. One can readily imagine how much bounty the sea would have provided for the old Maori, and the sight of a whole tribe being needed to haul in the nets heavy with the catch can only be wondered at now. The much later exploitation by European trawlers and factory ships and the discarding of 'unwanted' or 'unfavourable' species of fish, or parts of them, with its associated despoliation of the domain of Tangaroa, is just one more transgression against all that we should regard as "needing to be nurtured". As will be emphasised often in the course of this book, there will yet be a time of reckoning for such short-sightedness, irrespective of the race that so despoils.

*   *   *   *   *

An issue that has huge polarising potential between people-factions within various countries – including New Zealand – and between Nations themselves, is the question of whale harvesting. Whilst this may be viewed as a strictly conservation issue, it is equally valid to include it in Tangaroa's area. We have analysed the situation for the *kereru* and the same 'spiritual criteria' applies equally to whales. The propensity of some outspoken Maori 'leaders' to continually push traditional or 'cultural rights' as the sole yardstick by which to determine whether a particular species of animal should be 'harvested', is hardly consistent with any kind of professed or self-believed level of *great spirituality*. For it places 'cultural' or 'traditional' considerations *before* **The Spiritual Laws** themselves as the supreme determinant as to what is right or wrong.

This attitude reveals that too many Maori choose to be simply 'tribal Maori' in the mistaken belief that this is some kind of wonderful *spiritual* aim. The sole criteria for any kind of 'cultural/traditional harvesting' decision or determination here appears to be a voluntary connection to 'the tribe', irrespective of the scientific, elemental or spiritual considerations or connotations. Such an attitude is misguided and offers no impetus to think *differently* from that restrictive and very narrowly-directed *tribal goal*. Of course, for the 'tribal leader' in today's Treaty-driven society, it is a means of exercising personal power and of potentially acquiring not inconsiderable financial gain. There is very little genuine *mana* inherent in those considerations and, moreover, is clearly at variance with all that the Prophet Ratana's ordained mission brought to, and for, Maori!

The whole issue becomes doubly insidious and hypocritical when, as occurred quite recently – and irrespective of the 'scientific research label' conveniently attached to 'whale harvesting' by Japanese commercial whaling interests – initial overtures to certain Maori 'leaders' resulted in a kind of tentative 'agreement in principle' in the exercise of traditional or cultural harvesting rights. Thankfully, the whole foolish exercise seems not to have borne fruit. Such encouragement, nevertheless, is both spiritually and morally bankrupt, and particularly so under the culturally-protective umbrella of The Treaty of Waitangi.

If whale stocks really were plentiful and there was a need to harvest them, then that is *actually permitted* under the outworking of **Spiritual Law**, and purely emotional considerations should have no bearing on the yes or no of it. However, for the same reasons that the *kereru* should not be harvested, and because critical-mass numbers for whales are also unknown, the idea of harvesting as a 'cultural right' should be recognised for what it actually is. It is a clearly selfish idea if purely for any tribe's personal gratification, and would be *another spiritual transgression* by a race of people who claim to be at one with nature. Moreover, if the end-result is an insidiously acquired joint-venture to commercially exploit whales for the gratification of a people who have no compunction about raping Tangaroa's domain far from *their homeland*, it becomes hypocritical in the extreme. The greater transgression, however, may well be by those who agreed to such a proposal for monetary gain, to the detriment of the whales.

*   *   *   *   *

In ancient Maori *lore* the body of the sea was especially important in their religion. For it was the great expanse over which it is *still* believed the souls of the departed soar when returning to the ancestral homeland. So even for inland tribes with little or restricted access to the ocean, the association was still very important. The pull of Hawaiiki as the ancestral place where all went to and were re-united with their ancestors naturally meant a long, possibly lonely journey across Tangaroa's great ocean. With the ancient chants and *karakia* constantly reinforcing this as the belief of the race, the sea was an ever-present force either in the everyday activity of the coastal tribes, or in the subconscious reality of the inland groups.

Thus, for all Maori, irrespective of geographical location within New Zealand, the 'fishing-up' of the North Island by *Maui* from the ocean of Tangaroa in the ancient Creation legends, provided a common bond for the origin of the land. The legend of *Maui*, however, should be viewed as exactly that, and thus accepted and taught as a legend. For the reality of the natural history of New Zealand is completely different from Maori beliefs. Yet every race and people need to have a Creation story, a beginning. Without some kind of accepted origin, there is no sense of belonging and, whether oral or written, it is difficult to have a 'history of continuation' if there *is* no such beginning. So for a people whose whole existence revolved around a great ocean, whose everyday beliefs were dominated by the 'unseen' rather than the actual, and who had no knowledge of plate tectonics, the fishing of the North Island from out of the sea by a god-man provided the perfect beginnings – at least from their world-perspective.

With regard to such legends, and perhaps through pride of race and associated connections, there is a danger that too much emphasis can be placed on the teaching of those stories, to the detriment of the true happening. Whilst pride of culture can be a positive thing, the legends that are woven into the tapestry of the culture should not be emphasised as the most necessary part of the educative process to the formative and impressionable young minds of the race. There is no real acquisition of genuine knowledge in this, just the reinforcement of the legend within the psyche of the race.

The Eternal Laws clearly show the need for constant movement and, indeed, the natural activity of all that is in and on this earth attests to this fact. Consequently, **The Law of Movement** applies equally to man and his affairs. In accepting the births and thus education of children, this Law is vitally important for the correct 'spiritual' evolvement of any race. So to cling to culture and legends as the primary focus around which a race believes it best serves itself, at the expense of the knowledge of the true happening, guarantees *stagnation*. The next step after that is *retrogression*.

That is not to say that culture should not be retained, taught and advanced. It most certainly should, as it is the richness of the diverse cultures of the peoples of the earth that add vibrancy to everyday life. However in this latter day renaissance of ethnic cultures worldwide, there seems to be a growing tendency to want to elevate *the cultures themselves* to levels of veneration and worship. This apparent trend is a dangerous transgression against what is both **The Highest Law** and the *most powerful* of all **The Commandments – The First One!**

Thus the legend of New Zealand rising out of the sea on the hook of *Maui* should be taught secondary to the scientific origins we now have. For the acceptance of new, factual knowledge is the outworking of the process of **The Law of Movement**, which at the same time assists spiritual growth as its natural accompaniment. So as wonderful and lyrical as the legend of Maui is, the facts show that Aotearoa once belonged to a much larger land mass called Gondwanaland which broke up and allowed the continents to drift to their present geographical locations on the globe. The process, simply known as "Continental drift", is an ongoing one. For in the powerful forces present in tectonic plate movements can be observed the mechanism whereby the earth itself is rejuvenated; where new lands are formed from out of titanic subterranean activity.

Paradoxically, this formation of new land out of the movement of the continental plates with its associated volcanic and earthquake activity, whilst easily explainable scientifically, *has a far greater and stupendous cause than that which science has noted or explained*. As a further paradox, the very thing that we allude to here as the activating mechanism for all earth movements has, itself, been relegated to the realm of myth and legend and deemed *nonsense* by scientific man. In an examination of the question of **The Forces of Nature** in a later Chapter, perhaps *Maui's* great fishing deed might then be viewed differently; as one associated with those 'Forces'.

However it is viewed though, the actual happening itself is not the thing to be revered. Rather it is to **The Creator Himself** that we must direct our reverence and gratitude for the provision of such a beautiful homeland. For under **His Will**, *Tane, Elemental Lord of the Forest*, and *Tangaroa, Elemental Lord of the Sea*, from out of whose ocean Aotearoa originally emerged, provide the bounty that we are all able to enjoy. Thus **The Law** reigns supreme in all things, not least in the responsibility that we have for the correct spiritual and physical stewardship of the land and sea that is our physical home.

If we choose not to exercise this responsibility in the right way, perhaps *Tangaroa,* under the inviolable outworking of **The Divine Will**, may be directed to return this land to the sea once more. An interesting thought given the increasing earthquake and volcanic activity worldwide coupled with our blatant poisoning practices and general refusal to be genuine *kaitiaki* of our beautiful *blue-planet home.*

3.6   Waka Construction and Lashings

The sea of Tangaroa provided the Polynesians with the perfect medium to develop a number of specialist skills and, as the sub-heading proclaims, these two were vitally essential ones for sailing his sea. These two perhaps disparate but remarkable skills are best shown in the building of the great *waka*, as one was totally dependent on the other throughout the complete activity of waka construction. Whilst many races and cultures have built canoes, the sheer size, scale and grace of the largest here simply dwarf other similar kinds of craft anywhere in the world. To build a large canoe, one needs a large tree, and these Aotearoa had in great abundance. The 'scaling-up' of *waka* size in Aotearoa would probably have been a natural extension of basic designs used in the old homeland, and the ready availability of the right kind of very big trees here permitted large fleets of enormous canoes to be constructed.

In terms of the ability to transport large amounts of goods or men over long distances by a stone-age race, the great *waka* were admirably suited for that task. The psychological advantage of a large fleet of such vessels filled with *toa* during times of war must have been considerable in its obvious fear-inducing menace – similar to European gun-boat diplomacy of the recent past, perhaps. Interestingly, whilst the *waka taua* were used for war generally, they were not a naval engagement craft and their overall basic canoe design would not have provided a sufficiently stable platform for large numbers of men to engage in close quarter fighting on water without the risk of capsizing. Consequently, sea battles between rival 'fleets' were not sought. The *waka* were primarily used to swiftly transport large numbers of warriors to the intended place of attack. If the war party were successful, the same *waka* transported home the victors with their spoils of slaves and heads.

The building of the great *waka* was an amazing blend of stone-age ingenuity, the invocation of the correct forms to watch over and protect the builders and the sailors – as *waka* construction was a *tapu* undertaking – hard physical labour over a long time-period, innate sea-craft construction skills, the 'feel' for form and symmetry which produced the final balanced shape, and the carving skills to dress and adorn the hull. However, before the chosen tree could be worked on, it had to be felled. Prior to the arrival of the European with his much desired iron axe heads, the old Maori had only the use of traditional stone tools.

To emphasise the level of skill and craftsmanship relating to *waka* construction, we must digress slightly and come forward in time to the period of the early European settlers. In early New Zealand, the change from a predominantly settler/pioneer lifestyle to a rural farming way of life and finally to city-oriented or suburban living, meant that certain everyday skills, in the use of the axe for example, now became the preserve of those in particular industries or lifestyles. Today relatively few can lay any real claim to being truly skilful with an axe. By skill we do not mean the householder who buys a cheap axe or log-splitter and proceeds to end-split a few small chain-sawn blocks for his winter fire. We refer to the skill and industry required to fell very large trees. For even in the worst excesses of the wanton destruction of the forest of Tane by the Pakeha, the art of the axemen was generally confined to preparatory scarfing and trimming work, since it was the 'cross-cut' that actually felled the giants.

So even the bigger chopping tasks today contrast mightily with the effort that was required to fell, trim and shape very large trees for *waka* construction. Anyone who has ever complained about axe-work in a chopping-related occupation, or even chopping firewood for the home, and who has had the use of a well-balanced and well-honed steel tool, with the head tight on the handle, must surely marvel at a race of people who could fell such massive trees just with stone axe heads *lashed* to the haft with flax cordage. And particularly where the wood on one side of the tree – the hull bottom – was naturally seasoned to greater density and hardness.

The flailing action of the tool would have produced enormous stress shocks at the point of lashing and, no doubt, stone heads would have worked loose after a time and required re-lashing and constant re-sharpening. Nonetheless, to even contemplate such a task with so-called primitive tools demonstrates a high degree of confidence in both the tools and the ability to achieve the desired aim. Even with the use of fire to assist the felling and shaping process, the mind still boggles at the industry required to undertake such a feat, for there were very many such large canoes in earlier times.

Generally speaking, the ability to tightly lash a number of pieces together to construct a particular tool, craft, or dwelling has been part of the evolutionary development of all mankind. In today's modern technological society, knots and lashings still play an important role in some areas of work and play. In particular the activities relating to seafaring still demand a certain level of that knowledge. General cordage used by the old Maori was prepared from the common flax plant, but other plants were also used for different lashing applications as well as for weaving. Such was the strength of correctly prepared and plaited flax cordage that it was eagerly sought after by seamen when sail ruled the seas. Flax cordage thus became a material of great trading value. Even the British Navy, the greatest sea power at the time, considered it to be far superior to any other cordage.

This strength of cordage for lashing was vitally necessary in binding the prepared hull segments together and for affixing the top gunwale strakes to the hull. The ability of a stone-age people to undertake the building of a very large ocean-going canoe with the hull pre-shaped in three parts and simply lashed together, stands as an amazing feat of marine engineering. Even though strengthening ribs were added to give rigidity for the length, the whole concept of a craft of large canoe design, with the trees felled and shaped by stone head axes and adzes and consisting of more than one hull part held together by flax cordage that could carry up to 150 heavy men swiftly on the open ocean, is a truly amazing achievement. Add to that the carved fore and aft additions and a most impressive craft rides nobly on Tangaroa's sea.

3.7   Lashing and Plaiting

The obvious absence of affixing materials such as nails or glue in old Maori society necessitated the need to develop the art of lashing to a very high degree. Whilst the cordage size of lashings required for *waka* construction were necessarily large and robust, finer cordage, sometimes made from other natural materials, was employed to join together smaller tools and implements such as fishing hooks. Once again we might regard a one-piece hook as the most efficient and strongest unit for that particular purpose. Yet the Maori often chose to utilise two separate pieces tightly lashed together to achieve the same aim. Compared to the modern fisherman's world of perfectly tempered and specialised steel hooks in a bewildering array of shapes and sizes, one can only marvel at what was achieved by the old Maori through their ability to apply great strength to their fishing hooks by incredibly detailed fine-cord lashings.

The construction of buildings also required the use of cordage lashings, as did the timbers used for the protective palisades of fortified villages and fighting *pa*. The ability to manufacture good strong cordage and to be able to plait was a paramount need for all aspects of life, and was a skill that needed to be taught and mastered from an early age.

Fishing and hunting required the use of these materials for food gathering too; in the bird snares, fishing nets, eel traps, and for white-baiting etc.. Agriculture utilised the same elements in tool making, as did the men in weapons construction also. Plaiting provided the method for the production of clothing, for cloak-making, kits for food gathering, cartage and storage, and allowed for the development of art in the weaving of various *taaniko* styles. Cordage and plaiting were also utilised in the making of children's toys and games. In fact this particular ability might be rightfully considered as the cornerstone of all Maori endeavours in the everyday activity of earlier times. As it necessarily permeated virtually all aspects of village life, a smoothly functioning society was probably not possible without this skill, such was the importance of it.

In the present-day renaissance of ethnic cultures worldwide, many of these skills and techniques are being re-discovered and are once again taking their rightful place. And in the case of the re-teaching of once-lost lashing skills – among others – it is a valuable addition to the overall cultural base. Such a more complete foundation is important for spiritual growth too, as it clearly represents beneficial skills. This particular renaissance direction thus allows for the retention of the uplifting aspects of the culture whilst letting go those that do not!

To this end a recent and quite amazing development utilising Maori plaiting knowledge and technique has resulted in a method whereby the optimum configuration in a particular industrial application has been achieved. This is in the form of a wide plaited wire strap calculated to precise factors and achieved with different kinds of ancient Maori plaiting techniques being applied to the overall woven-strap configuration. An excellent example of ancient skills utilised beneficially in a modern technological application.

3.8   Games and Pastimes

In a society where there is adequate food coupled with relative peace, social considerations can give focus to leisure pastimes for both adults and children. Song and dance provide the means whereby the stories of the people, the heroic deeds and the ancestral chants can be preserved. The games of dexterity, apart from providing pleasure and laughter, also allow necessary weapons skills to be maintained and even enhanced. So the beautiful action of the *poi* can serve the dual purpose of enchantment for the eye, yet also dextrous wrist movements for the warrior and his hand weapons. Stick games played a similar role.

Other games and pastimes included stilt walking, swinging on a roundabout – similar to the maypole – knucklebones, top spinning, kite flying, string games or *whai*, and the use by children of a wooden toy called a *karetao*. This was a carved wooden figure with arms that could be swung backwards and forwards by pulling on a cord to activate the mechanism. In a time without the insidious effects of generally mindless TV drivel and video games, one can imagine children deriving great pleasure from such simple and natural pastimes. However, the warlike society of the old Maori would certainly not have allowed continual fun and laughter.

3.9   Motherhood and the Place of Women

The role of the mother in the correct nurturing and raising of children can always be regarded as a beneficial and uplifting occupation in any race. In ancient Maori society birth was considered to be a special event and, ordinarily, whilst women were not *tapu*, in childbirth they were. At this time birthing mothers were placed in isolation in the *whare kohanga*, a building set aside for this purpose, and were attended there by other women. If the birthing process presented difficulties, the *tohunga* would then be called for. Given that the overall level of knowledge about potential complications that could arise in childbirth were not developed to any great degree in any society anywhere at the time, there would surely have been a high infant mortality rate among Maori.

However, in the bringing into being of her offspring, the mother in ancient Maori society, as with all mothers of all races, was subject to The Law which states that **"Like must attract Like"**. This Law, along with certain others, determine the race, family and geographical location, among other factors, for the incoming soul. In an examination of the ramifications of these immutable Laws in a later Chapter, the reader should readily recognise the validity and logic of these assertions. In every case, each soul will find itself in exactly the circumstances that a particular race and individual family will provide for its personal experiencing. Therefore the souls that became members of the old Maori race will have been endowed with the potential to develop similar skills and abilities that the race generally possessed. On the other hand, base propensities of the race such as the psychic practices of *makutu* and *utu*, and perhaps even the practice of cannibalism, may have been the strongest, single attracting-aspect.

In other words, a soul in the beyond *seeking* such an incarnation can only be born into a race actively practising such activities. So, generally speaking, a race that occupies a particular level of spiritual development should expect to attract the same kinds of souls. Worse, a race that is degenerating spiritually will actually attract darker and darker souls, thus *accelerating* the process. The natural attraction of any individual soul to a particular race does not necessarily mean that that individual will absolutely follow the same path as the rest of the race it is born into, however. Though it is probably likely to do so. By virtue of its free will, it has the potential to be different, even in a comparatively closed society. And societies throughout history have been changed radically by the birth into it of a singularly strong individual.[7]

In the ancient Maori society of New Zealand, however, this probably did not happen. From the earliest settlements up to the arrival of the Pakeha, there is no indication that any truly spiritually-enlightened souls incarnated into the Maori race. If this had been the case, the regressive practices of *makutu*, but more particularly *utu*, would have been recognised for what they were, *and discarded*, thus turning the race around. Notwithstanding this, and irrespective of the reasons for the incarnation, the nurturing of the child by the mother is connected to the activity of the Animistic/Elemental Forces from where motherhood draws its strength and power, but under the aegis of the Higher Spiritual, nonetheless. Therefore, motherhood in

---

[7]Perhaps some of the first navigators to Aotearoa were such men?

ancient Maori society fulfilled its purpose within the parameters dictated by the level of spiritual maturity within the race at the time.

The role of women, clearly defined in Maori society, was generally a subservient one. Perhaps this idea sprang from the Maori Creation myth where men were the offspring of Tane with the original woman being formed by him. In this particular belief, therefore, women were considered to be 'inferior' to men. Because the back of the man was considered to be *tapu*, women did most of the carrying. Only in certain circumstances did men carry loads. The task of clearing the ground and planting *taro* and *kumara* belonged to the women. The men, however, dug the soil. In extraordinary circumstances women of very high birth could have influence and wield power, but this was not usual. A woman skilled in weaving and food preparation was highly valued as a wife, and in their practice of polygamy many chiefs had wives for this purpose.

Women were not permitted to speak on the *marae*, and in the archaic beliefs of a stone-age race, women were considered to be unclean during menstruation. Unfortunately, during times of inter-tribal strife, women and their offspring often suffered terribly at the hands of victorious enemy.[8]

3.10   Garment Making

This very necessary skill was more important in Aotearoa than it was in the old homelands of East Polynesia by virtue of the much colder climate here. The health and warmth for the Maori were a much more pressing concern than it had previously been in the warmer climate of former times. So Maori women developed a much higher level of skill in the production of everyday clothing wear. The colder wind and rain of the new land's winter also necessitated the development of the waterproof cloak.

Arguably, the skill of the women found its peak in the *kahu huruhuru* and art of *korowai*; the making of the feather cloaks – garments of singular beauty. From the Maori perspective of being intimately involved in such an undertaking, one can readily picture the preparations for this *tapu* and sacred work; the collecting of the feathers, the preparation of the flax fibres, to the making of the *kaupapa* – the base of the cloak to which the feathers were attached and the loom upon which dextrous and nimble fingers would produce a magic *taonga* of beautiful colour and form. The *mana* surrounding the cloak would have increased accordingly as it began to take shape. And then, finally, the day of completion when this work of art and *mana* would be named; and receive its title and place.

3.11   Diet, Health and Physique

It is a fact that the modern, refined diet of Western Nations is not completely beneficial for optimum health. The introduction of Western-type foods to people who previously lived on more natural, unprocessed food from the land and sea has resulted in degenerative diseases that were not known to them prior to the introduction of those foods. Aside from various other illnesses, diabetes, in particular, has taken strong hold among Polynesians today, including Maori. By contrast, the old Maori were considerably fitter and stronger and possessed far more stamina than any comparable Maori group today. Their ability to propel very large canoes at speed over long distances, portage them overland if necessary, jog to war, maintain a high level of fitness and agility into advanced age in the case of the older warriors and build large fortifications with deep trenches in a short space of time using only stone tools, is sure testimony to their incredible toughness. And all that on scant food supplies at times.

---

[8]This aspect of the treatment of women will be more closely examined under the later sub-heading of Warfare.

Cook noted that Maori warriors, if similar in numbers to a ship's company, would probably weigh several tons more than his own men. This was at a time of a natural diet regime. How different today. Whilst still being heavy, it is not generally the heaviness of naturally-honed, lean muscle-mass that most Maori possess now.

Professor Houghton, in his book, "People of the Great Ocean: aspects of human biology of the early Pacific", states that it was the environment of what he calls "Remote Oceania", the vast 'small-islanded' expanse of the greater Pacific that necessitated the development of the larger, more muscular physique of these particular ocean voyagers. The inhabitants of "Near Oceania", from Papua New Guinea to the end of the Solomons, comprising lands that are generally visible from one portion to the next and which gives rise to *that* particular designation, were not as big or as muscular as their open-ocean 'cousins'. Professor Houghton logically holds that the environment of the Pacific Ocean, being a cold one, dominated the lives of the people who needed to spend possibly long periods at sea. Over time, therefore, those who survived were people whose physique enabled them to cope with being cold and wet.

Moreover, Professor Houghton points out that the wet coldness of the ocean is very different from that of the Inuit Eskimo, for example. Their cold, yet dry environment provided them with the clothing to withstand it. By contrast, the people of the South Pacific had little in the way of waterproof materials, so had to rely on their body anatomy and physiology to keep warm. Thus they evolved to be large and muscular because it is muscle that generates body heat in cold conditions.

The arrival of the Pakeha with his new refined foods altered the above three parameters of "Diet, Health and Physique" for Maori thereafter. Whilst Maori Servicemen, Maori sportsmen and workers in particular industries might be considered to be relatively fit and healthy, statistics reveal a vastly different picture for most of the race today.[9]

3.12   Environment

The ancient Maori identified closely with the land and the sea and all that it produced. He developed a certain respect for it and learned the lore of it; that of the forests and of the seasons. For success in fishing and harvesting etc., certain appropriate *tapu* and *karakia* were observed. Where he cultivated the soil he was careful not to extract more from it than it was capable of producing. He observed the migratory habits of the birds and the fishes and developed the skill of preserving and storing food. As recently stated, early Europeans were greatly impressed at Maori industry in accumulating food stores. He named every part of his landscape, even to the naming of individual trees and rocks in many cases. And the great trees he revered. It could not be stated that the ancient Maori understood his eco-system in the same way that we understand it today. By the same token, however, his empathetic knowledge of the land could be a valuable addition to the scientific analyses of today. His was a more emotive bond with the land, more subjective than objective.

Every aspect of the natural world spoke to him. The wind, rain, thunder and lightning – all had a meaning. Even the activities of insects, fishes and birds at certain times told a particular story. Invariably, however, his interpretation of such things gravitated toward 'psychic' elements in his thought processes, and not the more natural association to the actual **Elemental Forces of Nature**. Consequently, his world was more one of fear through not completely understanding the natural energies that surrounded him. Indeed, it was precisely this feeling of being surrounded by forces outside of his control that permeated his day-conscious reality and the more menacing sub-conscious state. Thus his environment was a complete juxtaposition of every element of the seen and the unseen, which he extrapolated into a *mish-mash* of superstitious

---

[9]These aspects will be examined in greater detail in the later Chapter – 'Maori Today: Health; sub-section: General Health.'

beliefs and psychic activity. Generally though, he was probably considerate of most aspects of what we would designate today as belonging to reasonably good environmental practice – save for the destruction of certain bird species and the unfortunate firing of forests and grasslands in some places.

*   *   *   *   *

An interesting question arises in the present, however, with the huge areas of pine plantation now present in New Zealand. Quite obviously their presence in terms of sheer volume and numbers has irreversibly changed the landscape of the *whenua*, certainly visually and in the less visible effects on the soil and water, and therefore possibly more subtly on weather patterns. It is one thing to scatter a few introduced trees and plants over the land, but quite another to saturate very large land areas with a single species, irrespective of whether it be for economic growth and prosperity. In this regard, as in every other, **Spiritual Law** takes no account of such earthly considerations.

Pine needles have the effect of acidifying the soil onto which they fall. Pines also soak up immense amounts of ground water, and the vast areas currently planted will take some time to re-accept the native flora of the land in its full diverse richness should there be a massive and unforeseen reversal of the current situation. It would appear, then, that such huge plantings of a foreign tree, with much more to come, may have transgressed **The Law of Balance** for this land quite severely. It is also interesting to note that Maori, who ostensibly have a "spiritual feel" for the land and the forest, have embraced this practice wholeheartedly in the clear belief that exotic forestry will provide a huge financial windfall.

It is on 'Maori land', moreover, that much of this particular *tauiwi* has been planted. Against all currently accepted scientific and economic wisdom, it may well be that an ecological disaster of huge proportions is potentially in the making if this rampant, single-species planting continues at its present pace. This unnatural invader, this *tauiwi* that we have welcomed, may yet provide a severe lesson in why one should not transgress any kind of **Spiritual Law**. More especially where thriving, native forest-cover is destroyed to accommodate this interloper.

3.13   Herbal Lore and Healing

A vitally necessary adjunct to any people's welfare is the ability to heal and cure the various ailments, illnesses and diseases that will beset them. Without the, at times, dubious benefits of 20th century pharmacology and medicine, cures must obviously be found within the natural environment. Stone-age societies, small forest tribes and similar groups generally have high mortality rates. Given the usually high level of superstition within those groups, and with little understanding of real medical knowledge, death, disease and illness might be more readily attributed to malevolent or supernatural forces than to a virus or other pathogen, of which they would probably have no knowledge anyway.

The healing properties of water were believed to be so effective that this medium was used extensively, at least in some of the Northern *hapu*. Water is universally and rightfully acknowledged as one of the most necessary elements for life. Without it there can be no life. Thus, some cultures believe it to possess magical properties and accord it a certain innate reverence sometimes bordering on worship. Even from the scientific viewpoint water is an amazing substance.[10]

The obvious physical ability of water to cleanse material things, including the body, was probably transferred by the Maori to a psychic belief that it could assist in inner healing as well.

---

[10]Biologist Dr Lyall Watson of "Supernature" fame investigated the many diverse and fascinating aspects of water, and one's perspective of it was changed forever after reading his amazing findings.

This strong belief may well be the result of the associated acceptance of 'Nature Beings' active in and around certain bodies of water. As outlined earlier, one remembers water being regarded as extremely *tapu* and used often for every manner of illness, and also to ward off perceived or potential psychic attacks.

For the old Maori, belief in *makutu* as the cause of many illnesses prevented the development of true medicine. Because of his propensity to ascribe a psychic cause to every physical illness, treatment of the sick was cursory at best, and non-existent often. For why should one minister to someone sick who had been condemned to illness or death by black magic? If the initial counter-magic did not alleviate the suffering or reverse the death process, then there was little point in continuing with any form of healing ministrations. Notwithstanding this strongest of beliefs toward illness generally, Maori herbal lore did provide relief for a number of ailments including stomach complaints, minor respiratory problems, and various aches and pains. Maori also utilised the healing properties of the bark of various trees, but knowledge of medicine and healing was not extensive because of the pervasive belief that 'other-world' forces were the cause of most misfortunes.

Thus, whilst the old Maori certainly understood the healing properties of a number of plants, the knowledge of medicine as such was not taught to any great degree. In any case, the belief that illness and disease were caused by non-physical forces absolutely precluded the possibility of any logical investigation into the reasons why they were visited upon them. Therefore, instead of a reasoned objective examination of the problem, there would probably be an attempt at divination via dreams or via the activity or presence of birds or insects. Or perhaps by the way the wind blew or how the Morepork called at night. There were numerous things from which to gain possible 'insight'.

If these methods did not produce results and the illness persisted, there would probably be the call for the *tohunga* to determine from *where or whom* such disasters might come, and for him to effect a cure or resolution. And in the most *unnecessary* of rituals in the purely 'spiritual' sense, he might then wage a psychic battle with forces and forms not necessarily related to the illness at all. Nevertheless, however, brought into life by that society through their non-understanding of the outworking of **The Spiritual Laws**. Without greater enlightenment via the intuition of the spirit in such a closed psychic society, growth and ascent out of that situation to actual medical progress was not possible.[11]

3.14   Carving and Tattooing

This particular skill represented far more than the visual facade of the carved piece itself. Each carving possessed different elements that portrayed specific things. Whether the carvings portrayed religious ideas, were representations of revered ancestors, or simply decorative motifs, the level of skill displayed in the finer carvings could well elevate such pieces from a skilful craft to true art. Certainly fine carvings were held in great regard, adding to the *mana* and prestige of the carvers and tribespeople to whom they belonged. As with all Maori endeavours the institution of *tapu* was strictly observed in the acquisition of the material to be carved, during the carving itself, and in what might be considered the consecration of the carved piece. Even the chips from the piece being carved had to be disposed of in the 'correct way'.

From the standpoint of **Spiritual Law**, however, the whole ethos of carving as symbols of *mana*, in their representations of ancestors, gods, or as guardians or demons to ward off evil, actually served to 'attract and hold' the very things that the old Maori fearfully strove to protect himself 'from'. Because the carved pieces were generally conceived from superstitious beliefs stemming from 'psychic' connections, they were therefore not truly 'spiritual' in their 'form'. And certainly not in what they were connected to, by virtue of that particular aspect

---

[11]This aspect of Maori life will be examined in greater detail in other Chapters.

of Maori beliefs. They could, however, symbolise recognition of beings not connected to their psychic world but to aspects of **The Elemental Realm** i.e., Tane and Tangaroa etc.. Even with that correct recognition, however, there was still insufficient knowledge to allow for the expunging of the fear aspect from that particular area of 'part-knowledge'. For even if there is not actually worship of carved images, veneration or adulation of them still nevertheless represents a serious *spiritual transgression* against **The First Commandment** – the source of **All Law**!

The concepts inherent in carving were carried over into the art of tattooing also. As evidenced by the particular tattoos on individual chiefs, standard motifs in tattooing were open to alteration and personal design. And because tattooing meant the flowing of blood, it was subject to the strictest *tapu*. Tattooing marked the onset of puberty and was, in effect, the time of initiation into adulthood in a very public way. The intense pain that the tattooist's chisel inflicted on the recipient had to be borne stoically for the sake of one's honour. The later complete face tattoo would have meant not only an obvious external change of appearance but, given the old Maori's propensity for finding other world meanings in all that he did, would probably have wrought a subtle, inner change as well. Certainly one wonders whether the completion of a full face warrior, or Chief's tattoo in particular, brought about a possible personality change, albeit even if only to instil greater courage in times of war.

This was probably the case, as Nineteenth century observers noted that warriors often received additional tattoos after performing great deeds in battle. Thus the association of the *moko* with fighting was probably an intimate one as this practice ceased after the end of hostilities between Maori and Pakeha. In general, male *moko* basically indicated the wearer's connection to a particular group. His status within that group revealed evidence of his tribe, rank and deeds, especially in battle. It is said that Wiremu Tamihana Ngatihaua, among other chiefs, refused the *moko* because they wanted no further part in tribal wars. There can be no doubt that full facial *moko* in the designs that Maori employed did impart a fierce visage of savagery for the individual, and thus served to enhance that appearance and effect, whereas an unadorned face probably would not in the same circumstances.

Since tattooing was regarded as extremely *tapu*, any violation of traditional conventions on a large scale could threaten the continuation of the practice. Such a violation was the tattooing of slaves prior to being killed for the smoked head trade, an interesting example of once supposedly sacred traditions being quickly tossed out the door for Pakeha trade goods and money – a new Maori god. The influence of the missionaries who regarded it as a heathen practice, and who encouraged their converts to reject it, also helped in its demise. Europeanisation did not easily accommodate the traditions of full *moko* and, in any case, Maori were less inclined to want to endure the pain of it when the reason and meaning for it was fast disappearing.

The latter-day resurgence of full-face *moko* using the less painful method of an electric needle-gun and modern inks is a very far cry from the ancient chiselling technique which actually grooved the flesh producing larger amounts of blood – and certainly much more pain. Whilst this resurgence may perhaps be seen as an admirable, renaissance-form of traditional culture, from the standpoint of **The Spiritual Laws** it means that the body has been severely marked for life and is therefore a transgression. Even though a common practice in many cultures, including Western Nations with 'modern' tattoo designs, nevertheless, that is where all such practices *actually* stand.

3.15   Pounamu – the skill in the working

The one quality that the old Maori certainly possessed with regard to the working of greenstone was undoubtedly patience. To work such a hard substance into smooth and symmetrical ornaments with stone-age methods was nothing short of amazing, particularly the hole-drilling stage required for many of the pieces. The amount of industry required to rough-work and polish a piece to its finished point must have obviously represented a considerable investment in time and energy. Maori craftsmen, moreover, were not content to work the individual pieces to a 'near-enough' state, but produced clean edges and parallel lines as in the adze, an instrument which really only needed a sharp edge and not a smooth and polished surface. In other pieces, perfectly rounded or elliptical curves swelled symmetrically into the finished article.

Not surprisingly, such detailed work produced over a long period of time elevated many of the pieces to that of *taonga* and were subsequently accorded *tapu* status and revered. Thus certain such works gained fame beyond the borders of the tribe who produced them and were sought after by enemy groups. Greenstone *mere* in particular, by virtue of their association with great deeds in warfare and generally owned by chiefs, were especially sought as war trophies. Since *mana* rested in these particular pieces, the loss of them meant the loss of tribal *taonga* and a large measure of associated *mana*. If an attacking enemy succeeded in capturing them, the *mana* belonging to the *taonga* became theirs. In some cases where defeat was inevitable, the treasured articles might be hidden from the enemy in the hope that they could be recovered later. In the event of the complete annihilation of the group, the *taonga* might conceivably be lost forever, unless re-discovered by accident.

This aspect of old Maori skill must surely rank as some of the finest amongst the stone-age peoples. Moreover, the best greenstone pieces along with the finest feather-cloaks could easily be accorded the status of being some of the most beautiful that might be possible for a stone-age race to produce. In the skillful working of such pieces, those particular talents can therefore be regarded as tending toward the spiritual rather than just the everyday workings because of the essence of beauty inherent in the finished articles. That concept of beauty would be present in the image of the proposed piece to begin with.

Thus in the outworking of **Spiritual Law**, the 'holding' to a concept and form of beauty from start to finish of such beautifully worked pieces, even in a superstitiously fear-ridden race as the old Maori, illustrates the spiritual reality that *thoughts* of beauty **will produce** *works* of beauty – irrespective of the environment. The end result of such endeavours is an elevation on our scales of spiritual balance for the Maori for this particular skill.

3.16 Architecture

During his visit to New Zealand in 1895, Mark Twain, the American author and world traveller, had this to say about Maori architecture:

> "I do not call to mind any savage race that built such *good houses*, or such strong and ingenious and scientific fortresses or gave so much attention to agriculture, or had military arts and devices which so nearly approached the white man's."

> (New Zealand's Heritage, p.1705)

The design of Maori dwellings ranged from the common sleeping house (*whare puni*), to various storehouses, to the *Whare Whakairo* and the carved meeting house – which could be regarded as the peak of Maori architectural achievement. The design of the *whare puni*, the most common form of building in the North Island, was described by Cook thus:

> "The houses of these people are better calculated for a cold than a hot climate. They are built low, and in the form of an oblong square. The framing is of wood or of small sticks, and the sides and covering of thatch made of long grass. The door is generally at one end, and no bigger than to admit of a man to creep in and out; just within the door is a fireplace,

and over the door, or on one side, is a small hole to let out the smoke. These houses are
twenty or thirty feet long, others not above half as long; this depends upon the largeness of
the family they are to contain..."

(New Zealand's Heritage, Vol.1, p.137)

This particular type of dwelling was often sealed for warmth, and the practice allowed the
possibility of death by suffocation for the sleepers. In the world of Maori superstition, "...the
victims were believed to have been overcome by fairy folk, the *patupaiarehe*." (p.138)

One of the more important buildings was the elevated and carved food storehouse. Because
of its special significance and purpose, it received careful attention in its construction and dec-
oration. Its importance to the tribe was reflected in its being fenced off and placed under strict
tapu. The all-pervading institution of *tapu* ensured that the food stocks the storehouse contained
would not be stolen or otherwise interfered with by anyone within the tribe.

The careful construction of the *whare whakairo*, its elaborate carvings, 'sacred' purpose and
associated *mana* reflected that of the tribe itself. Consequently, the inception, planning and
construction was placed under strict *tapu,* and all aspects of its building overseen by a *tohunga
whaihunga*. No other Polynesian people constructed such elaborate buildings.

Yet, from the actual spiritual point of view, the meeting-houses, decorated with carvings
associated with Maori superstition and psychic forms, *actually promoted the retention of them*.
For the very forms that were represented by the carvings, the subjects discussed inside, the
karakia of the *ariki* or *tohunga*; all these were far removed from the higher levels of the truly
Spiritual. This huge gap of 'spiritual actuality' ensured that only 'forms' similar to those that
were invoked by the very nature of ancient Maori beliefs, conversations and practices, existed
in the *whare whakairo*. Genuinely spiritual activities could not take place there in those times.
The unfortunate view that Maori psychic beliefs were somehow spiritual ones guaranteed that
only similar-thinking earth-bound souls and psychic forms which those very beliefs gave rise to
and attracted, could 'people' the 'sacred meeting house'.

Thus, whilst the *whare whakairo* was ostensibly a 'sacred meeting house' in terms of ancient
Maori cultural and religious tradition, in reality it was a place where darker forms lived – in strict
accordance with Maori psychic beliefs under the outworking of The Law which unequivocally
states that: **"Like must attract Like"**! Thus in order to attract in lighter spiritual forms,
a major and fundamental shift in consciousness would have been required. Because many of
the same traditions and beliefs are still maintained around and on *marae* today, the same basic
forms of psychic things associated with that ethos will generally still be present in meeting
houses whose communities still revere or cling to the old beliefs.

Yet it is a simple matter to observe that the line of Maori Religious Prophets gradually relinquished traditional facades on their meeting houses and churches in a clear step-by-step process
away from them. In fact the later Prophets strongly advocated they be let go. Consequently,
the two strongest, Te Kooti Arikirangi and Ratana, replaced traditional carvings with symbols
reflecting a far more spiritually-expanded view – in accordance with their own more enlightened
recognitions.

*This fact should be marked well since their enlightened recognitions and influence were clearly
far more beneficial for Maori than the old traditions they rejected*!

Hence that clear and unequivocal rejection of those particular traditions by them!

3.17   Toa and Defence

3.17.1   The role of the Soldier (The Spiritual meaning – then and now)

This particular sub-heading may seem to be a gross contradiction to some readers in that the end role of the Soldier would seem to be totally incompatible with any kind of genuinely-spiritual activity. For the most part we probably deem that particular concept to be connected solely with things of peace, goodwill and harmony. There is no doubt that the business of soldiering, particularly in war, can have a devastating impact on everything in and around the battlefield, wherever that might be. It can also produce a brutalising effect on some participants; more particularly for the actual duration of the conflict perhaps. Conversely, in other major battle situations, even through literally years of conflict where heavy casualties are experienced on both sides, nobleness and chivalry – especially in the treatment of captured prisoners – *can* still be a disciplined part of the ethos of the opposing forces.

Yet one might naturally assume that taking many casualties, either dead or wounded, would presuppose ill-treatment and/or execution of captured enemy to avenge the deaths of fallen comrades. Of course, this *is* an unfortunate concomitant of war-like activities and will obviously happen. Given the horrific nature of war, however, history interestingly records far more instances of magnanimous and chivalrous conduct toward a defeated enemy than might be accepted as 'normal' in such an adrenergic situation.

In the context of this work it is important, therefore, to examine this question and seek to discover the connection between the role of the Soldier and the *Spiritual meaning of his Duty*. In our assessment of the *toa* of old, let us seek to discover how he measures up on our *scales of spiritual balance*. Was he magnanimous, noble and chivalrous toward his enemy? How did he treat his prisoners? Did he treat one group differently from another i.e., of his own race and the Pakeha one? Did he "...love one and hate the other...", or was he indifferent to both?

Before we can answer those key questions definitively, we must first assess this business of soldiering from the perspective of **Spiritual Law**. So whilst we may arrive at a decision about the old Maori warrior here, his *actual activities*, from the *Spiritual* point of view, will be outlined in the next Chapters. Since virtually every male Maori was required to be schooled in the arts of war, all of old Maoridom could be described as possessing 'armed-camp' potential, with every group awaiting the inevitable on a reasonably regular, recurring basis through the ingrained ethos of *utu*. Thus the *toa* made up the bulk of the race.

Throughout history the essential soldier has been, at various times, loved, hated, reviled, condemned as a pillager and rapist, and hailed as a saviour. He has committed acts of the greatest bravery, nobleness and sacrifice, and also perpetrated some of the worst crimes against humanity. His "record of service" has been all of these. Yet without his contribution in certain situations and at particular times in the historical record, the plight of various peoples might have been far worse if it were not for his intervention in times of dire need. The same record, however, also gives testimony to shameful events where peoples were decimated when powerful armies stood by and did nothing. Of course, if man had been intelligent enough and spiritually-mature enough to recognise the strict order and benevolence of **The Spiritual Laws**, and actively sought a far different path from that which was chosen, *there might never have been the need for such destructive and bloody activities in the first place*.

However, because mankind possesses very little real intelligence in spiritual maturity, he chose a path of contention, greed, conquest and stupidity. And so we have paid the price – in blood and suffering. In this lies the absolutely strict inviolability of **The Law of Reciprocal Action** – (*Sowing and Reaping*)! Given the fact of man's base and distrustful nature, it has always been necessary for most Nations to maintain a Military Defence Force. For those who decry the need for such forces, history gives many examples of peoples and Nations who sought the path of pacifism, who were ill-prepared or unwilling to defend their homeland *to protect their own*, and the price they necessarily paid for not obeying **The Law**. Unfortunately, because peace and freedom from war and strife will never be an automatic right for any people to demand, it thus becomes something precious that must be earned and, if necessary, fought for. That may mean that at times young men and the Nation are committed to war. It also inevitably means casualties in killed and wounded, and perhaps very many. Preparedness for such a possibility, therefore, is *not* a violation of **The Spiritual Laws**. Alertness and vigilance are thus **Spiritual Virtues**.

The role of the warrior is as ancient as man himself and, up to relatively recent times, was always considered to be a vitally important task in the protection of society. It is one, moreover, in which all young, able-bodied males should make their contribution. Given man's propensity for conquest, as evidenced throughout our collective history, this was a most necessary requirement for the defence and protection of the land or nation. Nowadays, with the horror of the threat of global annihilation via thermonuclear war a possibility, the thought of training the male populace in the craft of the Military is anathema to many. Since the reason for such training in the final analysis is to take the lives of others, we ostensibly have an organisation that would seem to be against all that we might regard as being good and spiritual, and therefore the epitome of all that is *potentially* base and evil.

*   *   *   *   *

It is important to now put the record straight with regard to the place and role of 'The Soldier'; not only on the earth but in all of Creation! To unequivocally state that the soldier occupies a particular place in Creation must presuppose the fact that his role is far more encompassing than simply serving the whim of earthly political masters. And that is correct. It is or should be a *Spiritual* one in the first instance. [In a future Chapter where we describe our origins, we note that in the Higher Realms there is no baseness and evil. It is only on the earth and in the material plane, through mankind's embracing of wrong principles under **The Law of Attraction of Similar Species**, that such a situation can arise at all.] Thus it is only 'down here' that human followers of both good and evil principles are forced to live together. Therefore the role of **The Soldier** in **Higher Spheres** is elevated to that of **The Knight**. Symbolic protection and guardianship is the living form that he embodies, *and radiates*.

In other words, what takes place in those **Higher Spheres** is meant to be the standard that should be striven for here on earth – the example to which humankind should aspire if there is to be harmony and goodwill. Discipline, selfless service, loyalty, chivalry and compassion etc., *should be* the hallmarks of correct Military Service and warriorship, and should also be the standard *of all of humanity*. However, whereas the ordained noble form and role of **The Knight** in **The Planes of Light** as guardian, protector and defender is the living, 'Spiritual' reality, it is not always the case on the earth where it should also be. Nevertheless, the 'form' of the soldier is also necessary for the material planes as well. However, because of our general historical propensity for baseness rather than for the noble ideal, the activity of the soldier, the warrior, the *toa*, is too often one that reflects this greed of conquest and enslavement of others. And, more often than not, at the behest of political masters.

Is it spiritually wrong, then, to wear the soldier's uniform and to carry weapons of war? Is it, by extension, equally wrong to kill in battle?

Firstly, the very fact of being in battle logically means that men are going to die, and that someone must do the killing. Let us answer the first question by briefly examining the answer Jesus gave to the Roman soldiers who asked Him how they should live their lives.

"And the soldiers on the march also asked Him, saying, "And we, what shall we do?" He said to them, "Extort from no one money by threats or false accusations; but be content with your pay."

(Luke 3:14, The Holy Bible in Modern English. Ferrar Fenton.)

Since Jesus was and will always be, as well as Part of **The Living Law**, the personification of **Divine Love**, we might tend to believe that He would be totally opposed to this business of soldiering. More especially, perhaps, against the Romans who were the occupiers of the land of His *earthly* birth. Carefully note His reply to the Roman 'enemy', however. Perhaps surprisingly for us, and not least because of our earthly point of view and wrong assumptions about the nature of Jesus generally, He did not condemn the soldiers or even their occupation. Neither did He condemn the Roman occupation of the land, and which was obviously the soldiers' business. Instead, *He enjoined them to do the task that they had been set by the Roman Army and to accept their pay and not take what was not theirs during the course of their soldiering activities.* In short, soldiering in its more correct form.[12]

As Jesus unequivocally lived **The Eternal Laws** and clearly understood them, He naturally understood the 'Spiritual Duty' of 'The Soldier', whether in The Higher Spheres or here on earth. By extension, because He also knew the true nature of humankind, He recognised the unfortunate necessity of the role of the soldier in the earthly affairs of men and the clear need for there to be 'Soldiers and Armies'. Hence His answer to those soldiers of Roman extraction.

Interestingly, too, and as a small but meaningful digression, just before His death as He hung broken and bleeding on the cross, He did not single out the Roman soldiers for special mention, those who had marched him there and carried out the crucifixion process, but addressed all who were there with the great prayer of intercession:

"Father forgive them for they know not what they do!"

(Luke 23:34, Fenton.)

This damning statement for mankind from the very One Who came to show the way out of our stubbornly wrong paths should be recognised as also meaning; "Are you not able to see. You have done the wrong thing!" Perhaps the obvious indictment of His words may help us to more fully realise the incredible stupidity of what mankind committed that day, particularly in the light of the inviolable perfection of **The Spiritual Laws** which He "came to fulfil".

In any case, with regard to the respective roles of the soldiers and of the mob in general, the outworking of **The Spiritual Laws** for all involved in that terrible murder would naturally take its course under the aegis of **The Law of Reciprocal Action** in the Divine warning:

"Vengeance is mine saith the Lord. I will repay."

(Deuteronomy 32:35)

Yet, paradoxically, it was the Captain of the Guard, a Roman soldier and not a Jew, who said at the end:

"This man was undoubtedly a Son of God!"

(Mark 15:39, Fenton.)

---

[12]Interestingly, also, The Bible has many examples of the ancient Jewish people destroying other tribes in order to occupy the land ordained for them. Pacifists of professed Christian persuasion must inevitably consider the warring adventures of the great patriarchs, Abraham, Joshua, and David etc., where the taking of many lives was sanctioned from Above, and place that 'Truth' in its correct area with regard to **The Spiritual Laws of Creation**.

Therefore the aftermath of all soldiering activities must logically have its reciprocal return under the umbrella of **Spiritual Law**. The key consideration, however, would be the reason and purpose under which the original adventure was embarked upon and the manner in which it was carried out. Defence against an aggressor and protection in battle is spiritually correct if peace cannot be won by alternative means and where the conquering of the homeland, with death and enslavement as its accompaniment, would be the end result of not opposing such an aggressor. Interestingly, from the perspective of religious invocation, virtually all armies – whether the aggressor or defender – will strive to seek help from Above for their particular cause. Obviously in such situations, **The Eternal Laws** will not heed all pleas for assistance in equal measure, but will calmly mete out to each participant exactly that which accords with his individual life-path fate as decreed by his own decisions. The same "infallible justice" will occur in the collective sense for the particular Military formation also, irrespective of which side believes most in the rightness of their cause.

The second question we asked was: "Is it spiritually wrong to kill in battle?"

The very act of taking a life should naturally be repugnant to any normal human being. At the same time, however, it is equally repugnant to simply stand meekly by whilst death and destruction are being meted out around one. The terse wording of **The Fifth Commandment**: "Thou Shalt Not Kill", is seemingly unequivocal in its *apparent inflexibility*. And one could possibly be admonished for attempting to seek some measure of flexibility therein to try to find a way to resolve this dilemma, given the succinct wording of that particular Commandment. Nevertheless, the idea that we must simply accept any evil that comes our way without any attempt at combating it is clearly spiritually wrong too. Let us therefore examine the question from two different but interlinked sources.

The make-up of the human being is of prime importance in the understanding of this 'problem'. (In later Chapters we detail the origins and 'make-up' of man.) Briefly, however, the physical body is simply the shell, the overcoat that we all must inhabit in order to live on the earth. The real us, the inner animating core we loosely but incorrectly refer to in general terms as the soul, but is actually Spirit. At earthly death, the entity simply sheds its outer covering, that which it needed for the material world. Whatever the cause of physical death, whether old age, accident or death in battle, only the outer cloak is rendered uninhabitable for the spiritual owner. The soul and spirit are still complete and very much alive, for that is the *actual person* in any case. In a death resulting from war, however, the experience of the battle, as with all similarly intense events, is generally strongly impressed upon the *spirit*.

That is the very basic and objective explanation of this particular happening. For those still alive after the battle, there is inevitably the emotional aspect of battle deaths to contend with. Thus any death by any means is simply the exiting of the soul and spirit from the physical shell. In its objectivity, however, this lawful process does not accept unnecessary and *wrongful* taking of life – even in war.

Let us now consider **The Fifth Commandment**: "Thou Shalt Not Kill", from another perspective. The key here is the word, *kill*. The Commandment does not expressly state: "Thou shalt not kill" *'another human being'*, end of story! It simply says: "Thou Shalt Not Kill!"

The interlinked outworking of all **The Spiritual Laws**, described fully in a later Chapter, reveal that there are many ways to 'kill' a fellow human being aside from just physical murder or by the taking of a life in protection of the homeland in a time of war. To 'kill' in the spiritual sense means the same as to 'destroy' or 'deaden'. This can apply to one's reputation or one's livelihood. Consider the impact on more than one life in the case of a family's everyday needs and future. How often do we read of people being defrauded by 'business partners', losing all that they have built up, including the family unit, through the stress of the situation? And how often do we also hear of instances where suicide is accepted as the only option to 'solve the problem'.

In such cases – and they are not too uncommon – a life has been destroyed here too, no less surely than with a bullet or a knife. The same can be said of one whose good reputation has been wrongly slandered in a Court of Law, with perhaps devastating consequences for his continuing employment and social future. Suicide here has been the outcome too. So we should carefully consider what the meaning and impact of all **Spiritual Law** and **The Commandments** really tell us. Perhaps then we may become less judgmental and more tolerant and magnanimous toward our fellow men. We might also consider the warning not to take too much notice:

"...of the dust in your brother's eye, while you cannot observe the chip in your own eye?"

(Matthew 7:3, Fenton.)

Thus, under the strict parameters of **The Laws of Creation**, killing has forms other than just physical murder and carries the same relative, "spiritual" penalty. To destroy someone in business, even via the mechanism of the Law Courts, to destroy a personal and valuable trust, to destroy the personal hopes and aspirations of children growing into adulthood by selfish parents who demand something different from that which may have been ordained for their offspring's spiritual life-path; all these are different kinds of transgressions of **The Fifth Commandment**: "Thou Shalt Not Kill!" And, in necessary reinforcement, all carry the relative level of *spiritual accountability*. With that explanation perhaps the whole question of killing – particularly in a war of defence against an aggressor or against a monstrous evil – can be better understood and put in its rightful place.

The taking of lives in an unjust war or as part of a purely mercenary force, however, is *not* a spiritual application of the qualities and virtues of the essential soldier. His role on earth should be one of protector and defender of the homeland in the first instance. To seek territorial gain or spoil by Military conquest could not generally be justified in the spiritual sense. However, bearing in mind that **The Eternal Laws** return to us all the reciprocal effects of all our past decisions, the *spiritual* state of the peoples concerned would need to be fully understood before one could make a sound judgement as to the underlying reason for any one Nation's war against another.

Obviously, serious threats must be vigorously opposed or great unnecessary destruction and death could ensue through weakness and/or lack of sufficient will. Yet not all conquests are disastrous for the conquered. The conquering Nation may bring great and beneficial changes for that people. In any case the outworking of **The Eternal Laws** may have opened the way for a specific group of souls living in a particular race to *experience* the heel of a conqueror. The number of permutations that could occur under **The Law** with regard to this will be many and varied, but will always be in strict accordance with **Spiritual Justice**. And will thus always allow for spiritual growth somehow, even in suffering or, probably more correctly in certain cases, *because* of the ensuing suffering.

A good example of the fate of a people who were not prepared to oppose an invading aggressor sufficiently strongly enough 'in the beginning', is that of the Incas. They were a people, estimated to be about 16 million in number, who created a huge Empire stretching along the Andean spine of South America for approximately 5,000 kilometres from present-day Ecuador southwards to Chile and Argentina. Yet for all their millions in population, and with a large and well trained army, in 1530 they suffered a terrible fate at the hands of Pizzaro and just 180 Spanish Conquistadors. Being a relatively peaceful people, and with their legends telling of the return of 'gods' from across the sea, the Inca trustingly accepted the Spanish into their society, with devastating results. Thus the Incas were not sufficiently alert to the potential

danger and placed their trust in these men, to their physical detriment. What was gained from
that hard lesson, however, was a new awakening that would ultimately have brought further
development for those particular souls in both the spiritual and earthly sense.

Of course many other peoples have learned similar hard lessons. A television programme
screened some years ago traced the path of a number of survivors of the holocaust. The aim
of the interviewers was to ask three questions of these survivors to attempt to understand how
so many could be herded like sheep to the slaughter without any attempt to fight for their
very survival. Aside from a few noble pockets of fierce resistance in Hitler's Europe, most Jews
'rounded-up' simply acquiesced.

The first question asked related to the phase of what was euphemistically termed 'de-lousing'
or 'showering' immediately after the initial entry into the 'death camps', and the separating out
of the fit from the sick, old and weak. The basic question asked, was:

"Do you think the Jewish people knew they were going to die?" [in the 'shower blocks'.]

Every one, virtually without hesitation, answered yes!

The second question put to them asked: "Why didn't you fight?"

The answers in every case were variants of: "We/I don't know!"

The third question was basically one concerning an unlikely similar future event.
"Given a similar situation again, would you fight then?"

The answer was an unequivocal and emotional 'yes' from all the survivors!

Many talked of the example set by those who fought the Germans in the Warsaw ghetto.
Of course virtually all died, either there in battle or later by execution or in the camps. The
key thing, however, **was that they fought** – against that evil; one intent on expunging the
whole Jewish race from the face of the earth. Therefore to fight such a monstrous evil was the
spiritually-correct thing to do. In that situation, it is far better to die fighting against it than to
die as a slave in a 'death camp', since death was the inevitable outcome for most within anyway.
It is therefore not surprising that the Israelis are so hawkish today, with their rallying cry of:
"Masada shall not fall again!"[13]

Ultimately, however, the inherent essence of all **Spiritual Law** states that through alert
wakefulness much evil can be prevented from reaching us before it can come to the point of
actual attack. For it is often *our* weaknesses that allow the faults and weaknesses of our fellow-
men to increase. Refusal to oppose such situations from the outset gives a free hand to an
ill-disposed foe. Was that not the scenario immediately prior to The Second World War? In
reality then, any fight should be in and through wakefulness – spiritual wakefulness – so that
any potential physical battle might not then need to be fought, with its obvious potential for
death and destruction.

Thus this lack of sufficient 'wakefulness', coupled with the weakness of fawning appeasement
and reluctance to oppose a growing evil by certain key European Nations, plunged the globe
into the most destructive war this planet has ever experienced. The energy that was unleashed
with the 'dogs of war' then might well have been contained and channelled into something more
constructive if men had been more alert far earlier and were prepared to more vigorously oppose
it in the beginning.

Pacifism, 'at any cost', *is the ultimate weakness* as it may allow the baser aggressive
elements of a potential foe to possibly be coercive toward others. In short, this attitude is
spiritually wrong as it actually helps to *foster* evil. We should note carefully the saying:

---

[13]Masada does not feature in recent history, but is a natural rock fortress where a small group of Jews chose
death by suicide rather than enslavement by a besieging Roman Army.

"Evil can only flourish when good men stand by and do nothing!"

Pacifism, however, will still have its place and *spiritual correctness* when it is the best option to bring about the same result of freedom from an oppressor as war might achieve. Gandhi's example in India and Te Whiti's *earlier example* at Parihaka are clear illustrations of pacifism as perhaps the only viable alternative in those particular circumstances. Generally speaking, however, pacifism today attempts to denounce defence training and expenditure as **morally wrong** and a waste of money that might be better spent elsewhere. This stance is an emotive one when viewed from the perspective of **Spiritual Law**, *if* Military service is for the defence of the Nation. Of course, one should always strive for peace, but should that process fail to satisfy an enemy bent on war, then the Nation that is the potential target should have always fulfilled the admonition to *wakefulness* and be prepared to defend itself, **or accept full responsibility for its unpreparedness**.

This means that the people of the Nation should be prepared and appropriately trained for such an event. Any claim to Nationhood bears with it the responsibility to *defend it*. Ideally, then, the Nation, and the Nation's young, able-bodied men, should accept the need for this preparation. In any case the training and discipline that the young men would receive would be clearly beneficial for them as individuals. Moreover, because it must necessarily instil teamwork and a sense of belonging and purpose – and will automatically produce strong bonds of comradeship – the Nation itself also naturally derives great benefit from the process. Not least from the social viewpoint. Even in the worst-case scenario where a far superior force were to invade with the expressed intention of decimating the populace, and where there was obviously no chance of repelling or defeating such a force, it is still better to fight and die than to capitulate and accept enslavement and/or a passive, ignominious, and ignoble death.

For under **The Laws of Creation**, the dull, resigned acceptance of the presence of a perhaps brutal occupier through unwillingness to fight against such a foe automatically brings in its train the effect of **The Law of Reciprocal Action** for both the invader and those invaded. In such a weakly demeaning situation, more than one Law is transgressed, ultimately producing the relevant and probably obvious consequences for the weak capitulator too. Unfortunately in the present time, man is still a very spiritually-immature creature and clearly regressing, even if he thinks he is making great progress. Therefore much will need to change before we, as a *people of planet earth*, develop sufficiently to discard the need for 'The Soldier of War' forever.[14]

*   *   *   *   *

Let us now examine the various traits in the behaviour of the old Maori warrior with regard to a *spiritually-correct application* of this role. Because the ancient Maori were a fierce, war-like race incorporated into independent tribal groupings within strictly demarcated territorial boundaries, the need for all males to become proficient in the skills of warfare from an early age was paramount for the safety and protection of the tribe. And, of course, for the greatest possible chance of survival for each individual. To this end, weapons training and the acquisition of related warring skills for protection and defence of the tribal area did fulfil a measure of spiritual correctness whereby fearlessness and discipline, where practised, could generally be regarded as a plus. Thus the death of a Maori fighter in battle was subject to the same Spiritual criteria that **The Eternal Laws** decree for *all* acts of selfless heroism. Within those parameters, the same *form* from the inner essence of the 'soldier of old Aotearoa' *could* also be accorded kudos for heroic deeds too.

---

[14]More detailed explanations can be derived from all the interconnected Laws outlined in the later Chapters on **"The Spiritual Laws/Principles"** and in **"Whither Cometh the Maori"**. Therefore, from the standpoint of **Spiritual Law** and its outcomes – for those killed in battle for a just cause and for those living **who may wish to know** – the explanations about what happens to a soldier in such cases are given at the end of Chapter 9, **"The First Death"**: sub-Chapter; **"Death of a Soldier"**.

However, the strongly-developed base propensities of the old Maori with regard to matters psychic unfortunately carried with it a dark dimension to his brand of warfare which brought in its train barbarously savage and evil practices. In questioning whether the old Maori *toa* fulfilled his appointed duty in a dignified, noble and spiritual way; on balance, the definitive answer would probably be a resounding no! Potentially, he *could* have fulfilled the role of the heroic warrior in certain situations, with the associated ascension of the connected *form* of any heroic deed in his spiritual favour. The base propensities of the old Maori would have been too tightly bound to psychic practices to permit any kind of easy spiritual ascent. The fact that such practices were the 'traditional way' of the time and, of course, 'culturally acceptable', does not alter the outworking of **Spiritual Law** in any shape or form.

In conclusion, the Maori fighter of old fulfilled very little of the spiritual requirements necessary to qualify him as a true "Spiritual Soldier". Indeed, the whole ancient race itself practised very little real spirituality. They did, however, as an integral part of their psyche and their living ethos, engage constantly in *psychic* activities and practices. This, quite logically, has no affinity with the higher power of **The Spiritual**. Thus, at this point in our assessment, the scales are firmly weighted toward the lower side.

In the next segment we will detail those wrong practises, thereby firmly illustrating the truth of our assertions.

The completion of this sub-heading in this Chapter denotes a transition phase in our very brief journey through the world of the ancient Maori. Only a few points concerning each subject have been touched upon, and many other aspects of Maori life have not been mentioned at all. However, it was never intended that this book should delve into every detail of every aspect of Maori life. That would have been an impossible and totally unnecessary undertaking for our purposes. What we wish to determine is where we stand as a race from the *Spiritual* point of view – in accordance with inviolable and immutable **Eternal Laws**.

To ascertain that position, certain aspects of Maori life needed to be examined in order to highlight those main points which would provide the substance for our assessment. It was also important to illuminate the great skills evident in so many areas of everyday life. In any case, there are innumerable books on all facets of Maori life available to the interested reader. From a purely Maori interest point of view, it is hoped that some of our brief reflections may spark some readers to want to learn more. More importantly, though, the greater hope is that the reader may be sufficiently moved inwardly to want to seek out **The Spiritual Laws** as they actually are, and choose to be guided to the correct living of them. And thus be similarly guided to the correct recognition of where we of Maori descent actually spiritually stood then, and where we stand now!

In the weighing of the light and the dark of the Maori race on our *spiritual scales*, we have sought out the more beneficial aspects of Maori life that lead to true spirituality. Permeating every single facet of everyday life, however, are the negative beliefs, superstitions, fears and dark activities that are associated with a psychically-riven stone-age race. Consequently, because both beneficial and negative aspects are so tightly interwoven, it becomes extremely difficult to delineate a clear separation between what should be two opposing aspects. Thus, in order to try to establish exactly that clearer demarcation, a more detailed examination will concentrate on the more insidious practices of the Maori, as a race, in the next Chapter. For it is precisely this major and spiritually debilitating aspect that we must acknowledge as being totally aspiritual, if we wish to truly understand the actual meaning of *genuinely spiritual activities*.

Let us complete this first part by quoting what is probably the accepted general and overall European academic view of the old Maori way of life. Yet a view, whilst basically identifying the uplifting skills and traits we have also acknowledged, postulates a more benign acceptance of things than we have portrayed thus far. The following text, moreover, does not, as claimed, show full Maori understanding regarding the 'taming' of a land i.e., in the knowledge of the forces contained in the land itself. Nevertheless, it serves as a good counterview to those expressed here.

These views, derived from personal experience in a formative Maori environment and associated upbringing, are yet still far removed in time from the rampant excesses of *makutu, utu,* inter-tribal warfare and cannibalism that the ancient Maori was *forced to endure* by virtue of his *free-will decisions to embrace such a path.* They are also insights derived from a simple examination of Maori history weighed against coolly-objective, infallible and inviolable **Spiritual Law**. For there was no romanticism back in pre-European Maori life, just harsh aspiritual reality!

The following extract is taken from the last paragraph of the section titled, "Ancient Maori Society". (New Zealand's Heritage, p.15)

> "In New Zealand the creative part of the Polynesian spirit flourished more abundantly than anywhere else. The arts of architecture, wood carving, decorative drawing, tattooing and weaving, of working stone like greenstone to a purity of form, of song, dance and action song, of poetry, of games like string games or spinning tops and kite making – all were highly developed. Even though the Maori discoverers of New Zealand must have felt the land's potential hostility, they tamed it with courage and grace. In the end it was a bountiful land, and in a full human sense the Maori used it well."

The next Chapter will clearly show that whilst the land was certainly used fulsomely, it was, however, also defiled by the introduction of all manner of wrong things, not the least of which were the dark psychic entities which the land **did not contain** *before* the arrival of the Maori. The later arrival of the Pakeha brought his dark forms also, as well as his greed and his previously unknown diseases. Thankfully, however, that arrival did also bring the very thing Maori needed. For the most part he embraced that particular gift enthusiastically in the early years, thus helping to break the connection to the practices of the past, thereby leading him away from those dark, savage ways.

So, let us continue with open hearts, open minds and open spirits, journeying along *without prejudice, anger or preconceptions,* but with intense curiosity born of a genuine desire to learn what is waiting to be revealed. For this revelation has the **greatest Spiritual Significance** – for the Maori race in the first instance. Moreover, this recognition will provide the correct foundation for changing the worsening social situation and offer the means with which to progress in full *spiritual* understanding. The same recognition provides the key on how to be genuine *kaitiaki* and '**stewards of land**' in the true sense of *spiritual custodianship.*

Perhaps, then, the fulfilment of the notion and/or ideal of *Tinorangatiratanga* may be realised. For without full knowledge of **The Spiritual Laws** and the willingness **to abide by them**, such longings will always be an empty, unattainable dream. And the Pakeha is totally irrelevant in this matter. Ultimately, this yearning and its associated covenant must finally be between *individual Maori* and **The Creator of all The Worlds**. First, however, the correct living according to **His Laws**. Only in this way can such aspirations then be fulfilled here in Aotearoa. And, moreover, via the admonition to: "Seek Ye First...":

> "But *First Secure* the Kingdom of GOD, and His Righteousness; and *All these things* Will be ready for You."
>
> (Matthew 6:33, Fenton, Emphases mine.)

The *securing* of The Kingdom of GOD, however, can only be found in the *observance* of **The Spiritual Laws of Creation**, the earthly expression of which are **The Laws of Nature**. For it is in the centre of their complete and perfect outworking of those Laws that we constantly stand – "...in the **Reaping** of our **Sowing**".

To strive to be a truly spiritual race or Nation should be the natural aim of all peoples. In the recognition and acceptance of **The Spiritual Laws** – and through their unequivocal acceptance of the *other-world reality* – perhaps Te Maori can be such a race. Thereby leading other indigenous peoples, and perhaps even Pakeha, to the same recognitions. Whilst the two potentialities of acceptance or rejection represent a *50% choice* in the first instance, nevertheless, the path ultimately chosen will always equate to a **100% outcome!**

4

The Other Practices: Psychic – not Spiritual

4.1   Cosmology and Religion of the Maori

Maori myths more or less encompass three distinct Creations; that of their world or cosmos, that of their gods – inherited and created – and the creation of human beings. Given the fact that there are so many different Creation stories from the diverse races of the world, it is interesting to note that many have a basic similarity in the notation of some kind of supreme deity being responsible for the process. In primitive races the effect of the forces of nature, particularly the flashing lightning and crashing thunder of violent storms, would have given credence to the belief that only supernatural beings could be responsible for such an awesome display of power.

Thus it is not surprising that some commentators believe all religion originally stemmed from fear. This fear aspect, if true, would actually be a late development since early man still retained conscious connections to his inherent Spiritual beginnings. Nevertheless, it is important to accept this general premise of the fear aspect to explain the path of the Maori. For many indigenous people, fear of 'The Forces of Nature', fear of the unseen – perhaps manifesting in the mind or in reality as demons – and fear of the unknown, was the ruling 'reality'. Conversely, other views postulate that fear was the origin of demonology only, with the defined state of 'religion' emanating from a more 'elevated mind'.

Certainly, it is easy to believe that superstitions were probably born of fear, and perhaps some religions may have developed from superstitious fear also. With a certain level of *knowledge-development*, this belief might be expanded further into the concept of a greater being, or beings, above those that produce thunder and lightning; with these perhaps being subordinate to others yet still higher. Finally there may arrive the view that all such beings – the lesser or departmental 'gods' – might need to have a leader, a ruler, a king, as espoused by Muller in his work: "Anthropological Religion".

Over time, as a more rational and knowledgeable approach to natural phenomena develops and religion feels the searching gaze of intellectual questioning, there might perhaps eventually arise a more defined level of knowledge within the people. Thus eventually leading to the spiritually-logical interconnectedness of all things. This process in its fullness did not take place within the Maori race until *after the arrival of the Pakeha*. There was, however, a belief in a

"Supreme Being" in the cult of *Io*. Much vagueness surrounds this figure with little of any real substance available to provide a description of him.

Since *Io* was a key figure then, and seems to be assuming an important role in latter-day Maori thinking, it is important to examine his position. Evidently, according to Best, no form of offering or sacrifice was made to *Io,* no image was ever made, and he had no '*aria*', or form of incarnation that inferior gods had.

"Invocations to *Io* were made only on the most important occasions such as the birth, sickness or death of a person of rank, the opening of the *tapu* school of learning, the installation of the medium of a god, or any serious calamity threatening the tribe...", records Best.

In keeping with such a highly sacred supreme deity, only the highest of the priestly caste and chiefly rank were permitted to know the mysteries of *Io*. Best further states that the ancient chants to *Io*, the 'ritual formulae' of the old *karakia* were "...couched in exceedingly archaic language."

> "...an examination of the ritual referred to shows that the Maori concept of the Supreme Being was pitched upon a high plane of thought. The purity of the conception, and the practices of the cultus, were doubtless preserved by allowing people to deal with lower types of gods, or even to practice shamanism *(tohungaism)* if they were so disposed."

> (Maori Myth and Mythology, Vol.1, Best.)

The few high-ranking initiates who were permitted into the inner sanctum of the cult of the knowledge of *Io* probably used that position to enhance their own personal status among the people. The old adage that "knowledge is power" would most certainly have found its material expression in this particular situation given Maoridom's generally unfortunate propensity for virtually everyone wanting to be either a chief or a *kaumatua* in the pursuit of 'personal *mana* status' – even today, unfortunately.

The Supreme Being had many different names and was said to have existed for all time i.e., he was never born. He was *Io-matua-kore* (*Io* of no parents), the origin of the Universe and the lower gods. Another of his names was *Io-te-waiora*, the welfare of everything, the physical and the Spiritual; all things emanate from *Io*.

- *Io* – the core of all gods

- *Io-nui* – greatest of all gods

- *Io-roa* – everlasting, not knowing death

- *Io-matua* – the parent of human beings and of all things

- *Io-matua-kore* – the parentless, nothing but himself

- *Io-taketake* – permanent, all enduring, complete, immovable

- *Io-te-pukenga* – the source of all things – all things are his in possession

- *Io-te-wananga* – the source of all knowledge, whether good or evil

- *Io-te-toi-o-nga-rangi* – the crown of the heavens – no heaven beyond his

- *Io-matanui* – the all-seeing (large or many-eyed)

- *Io-matangaro* – the hidden (unseen) face – unless he allows it to be so

- *Io-mataaho* – seen only in a radiant light

- *Io-te-whiwhia* – name denotes that nothing can possess anything of its own volition

- *Io-urutapu* – the totally sacred – more tapu than all other gods and things

(Maori Religion and Mythology, Vol.1, Best, p.144)

Notwithstanding the apparent 'secrecy' surrounding this figure and the extreme sacredness attached to it, such a "purity of conception" is a most unusual concept, even among modern, so-called 'civilised' races. For a Neolithic stone-age people to accord veneration to such a being – to the degree that the knowledge was held in the hands of a select few and denied to the ordinary people – reveals the most extraordinary and enigmatic paradox.

For if the knowledge was genuinely sacred, encompassed in the legends and *waiata* from some distant past and known only to a select few in its entirety, how was it possible for any race to degenerate to the level that the Maori did with such a supposedly high and pure concept of a Supreme Being? Especially where the ruling class deemed the 'knowledge' too sacred for the ordinary tribes-people. Or had Maori simply regressed so far that what might once have been beneficial guidelines had become too far distant and remote for this increasingly wild race. And through this degeneration only a small remnant of the original pure teaching remained which could have no further affinity with the path that Maori had now embarked upon.

If this is the case, such a 'narrowing of spiritual horizons' and the concomitant loss of the original understanding of *Io*, perhaps then allowed for a second, lower tier of Gods that, in the Maori perception, enabled them to possibly *legitimise* their more savage practices. In other words, the acceptance of a "Supreme Being", but without the correct and necessary spiritual understanding of it by the ruling elite, necessitated the need to have more 'accessible' gods on which to call. Gods who would undertake to protect and sanction all their endeavours, whatever form they might take. Such a scenario would reveal a complete lack of knowledge of **Spiritual Law** if a people seek to have a separate being for each kind of endeavour. More particularly *if* the group ascribe to each entity a *different set of laws* that could easily conflict with each other yet at the same time holding in sacred veneration a "Being" to whom they could find no ready access, but who ostensibly epitomised the very highest of religious perceptions.

According to Best, *Io* was known to the people of the Cook and Society groups so was probably brought to Aotearoa from there. He states:

> "As to how far across the ocean this belief and name may have been carried no man can say, or as to how many centuries the Maori has retained this belief."

And a further interesting entry reads:

> "It is just possible that the ancestors of the Maori brought the name of *Io* from an Asiatic home-land. In Renan's *History of the People of Israel* the author states that the name of Iahveh, or Iahoue, became contracted into Iahou or *Io*. Of a verity it would be a startling discovery to find that *Io* is but a form of the name Jehovah."

(Maori Religion and Mythology, Vol.1, Best.)

Certainly there is a contemporary school of Maori thought that believes the race to be descended from the tribe of Benjamin, one of the twelve tribes of ancient Israel.

* * * * *

Let us digress here and try to assess the validity of this assertion. To believe that the Maori race is descended from an ancient tribe of Israel in the physical sense is an unlikely theory. Physical characteristics of a race can be retained over many centuries if the race itself retains its basic ethnic purity – for whatever reasons it may deem desirable for it to do so. In the case of the Jewish race, their strong religious history and sense of spiritual destiny probably played the greatest part in the retention of their racial connections. And the Maori are very far removed in time and distance from the old Hebrew association of the twelve tribes of ancient Israel.

Yet we still apparently have this extremely unusual and interesting belief in the recorded ethnological history of the Maori of an all-powerful, unseen deity who has ostensibly existed for all eternity; a conception that the Israelites arrived at early on, hence the reason why Jesus, the 'Son' [Part] of the Invisible God, *could* incarnate into that particular race.

If the ancient Maori did bring this belief of *Io* from a very distant past, and obviously before the arrival of the missionaries, it might possibly have been as a result of *experiential memory* from lives lived in other times and in other races. Perhaps, in this way, the belief of a connection to an ancient tribe of old Israel *might* perhaps exist in Maori perceptions today. Such a belief, however, must naturally presuppose the notion of reincarnation – **The Law of Rebirth**.[1]

For a human spirit – once of the tribe of Benjamin reverently worshipping **The One God** – to incarnate very much later into a race where psychic practices were far removed from that level of worship in the land of ancient Israel, may certainly be possible. But it would clearly show the unswerving outworking of **The Eternal Laws** in the step by step regression of a soul as it travels its journey toward a baser life-path than that set in place by the old Hebrew prophets. Until finally incarnating in a spiritually-regressing, cannibal race – yet all through its own free-will attribute.

On the other hand, the Israelites did fall away from the true teachings from time to time and paid the penalty for it, suffering cruelly under other rulers. According to The Apocrypha, cannibalism was practised among other peoples of that area who worshipped gods that demanded it:

> "Those who dwelt of old in thy holy land thou didst hate for their detestable practices, their works of sorcery and unholy rites, their merciless slaughter of children, and their sacrificial feasting on human flesh and blood."

> (Wisdom of Solomon, 12:3-5)

To return to the Maori/Hebrew connection, however, the fact of reincarnation under the aegis of **The Law of Rebirth** means that the individuals who originally made up the twelve biblical tribes of Israel have travelled many different life-paths since, and may well have incarnated in many different races in the intervening time period. And perhaps even a Maori one. For the *inviolable outworking* of **The Spiritual Laws of Creation** determine the family, race, geographical location and personal circumstances that an individual human spirit will **need** for his further *spiritual* maturing. These inviolable laws are not arbitrary, however, so the final 'placement', as it were, of every human being will have been absolutely determined by individual choices and previous, personal "sowings".

Perhaps the simple answer to this proffered connection to the ancient tribe of Benjamin might be traced to the cunning *tohunga*, Te Atua Wera (the hot god), – a Northern prophet who in 1833 first spoke of being *hurai* (Jews) – and who claimed to be descended from the lost tribes of Israel. Moreover, he utilised the story of Moses and his 'serpent' for his own ends. This was to be their god who would speak to the followers through this *tohunga*. The serpent cult of Te Atua Wera (later Papahurihia) offered the converted all the goods that the white man possessed, and protection from his bullets also.

Of course, it may well also be that in this time of final spiritual resolution for all deeds perpetrated by man – both good and bad – some souls within the *present* Maori race did once walk the desert of the "Holy Land" with Benjamin. So the spiritual impressions of the knowledge

---

[1] **The Law of Rebirth**, explained in detail in Part II, Chapter 6 – "**The Spiritual Laws and Principles**" – is one of the primary and inviolable **Spiritual Laws of Creation**; to which *all* men of *all* races are absolutely subject.

of **The One God** that the Israelites gave to the world during those tumultuous times may have been retained by some souls who later travelled the path of the Maori – in the subconscious deification of *Io* in old Aotearoa. That, of course, is merely an interesting possibility utilising the outworking of **The Law of Rebirth** in touching upon *the fact of reincarnation* to offer a possible explanation of an unusually enlightened concept by a stone-age Neolithic race in the apparent, sacred veneration of an invisible "Supreme Being".

$$*\qquad*\qquad*\qquad*\qquad*$$

If we now return to Maori Cosmology: In the Maori Creation picture we have a basically correct view of a Supreme Being, in this case *Io*, standing above and being responsible for Creation and the continued maintenance of 'the world'. Below him in order of rank stands the Maori Creation-story of *Rangi* and *Papa-tu-a-nuku* as the 'sky father' and 'earth mother' respectively. Further removed in their place of residence and sphere of activity, their children; those that are termed the departmental and lesser gods i.e., *Tane, Tangaroa, Rongo* etc.. At the opposite end of the scale, at the bottom, is "The Realm of the Dead", wherein lies the myth of *Hine-nui-te-po* and, of course, *Whiro*, Maori god of evil.

Between the two extremes stands the world of the human being, perfectly positioned in terms of his inherent free-will ability. For in accordance with **The Eternal Laws** – and in strict concert with the personal choices made during its earth life – at earthly death the soul takes flight either in an upward direction towards **The Light,** or sinks heavily downwards to darker levels for its spiritual maturation. Since the Maori Creation-story is generally regarded as mythical, let us include part of Belich's interesting analysis of this topic for our ongoing comparison of all such views with those that encompass **Spiritual Law**.

> "Myths, broadly defined, might be seen as a culture's legitimating explanations for natural, supernatural, and social phenomena, for the relationship between them and for the culture's place in the world. They can have kernels of truth, sometimes so large, that they are actual historical forces as well as myths. The mythical dimension works in tandem with an actual historical dynamic which pushes history along, or an actual historical imperative, which holds history in place. But the cultural function of myths, which goes beyond mere accuracy, can put pressure on its truth, leading it to exaggerate or distort its partner dynamics and imperatives."

He states that Western civilisation, for a variety of reasons, "...has tended to see its own myth as history, and other people's history as myth."

Belich further opines:

> "Myths should not be read as either straight history or arcane mystery. But myth and history help determine each other, and they should conform to changes in each other. Change in myth can be evidence of change in history."

> (Making Peoples, p.25)

Whether myth or not, an interesting cosmological concept was that of the state of *Te Korekore* (nothingness). The ancient chants indicate that Maori philosophers believed that *Te Korekore* was the state of actuality before the sky and earth were created. Contrast that with the Biblical Scripture:

> "The WORD existed in the beginning, and the WORD was with God and the WORD was God. He was present with God at the beginning."

> (John 1:1, Fenton.)

All else until the Creation-process was, by extension, the void, nothingness – *Te Korekore!*

A further interesting aspect of the concept of *Te Korekore* was as the world of possibilities rather than as a negative thing by virtue of its potential emptiness. The philosophical thought patterns leading to such analyses appear to be quite remarkable in a Neolithic people. Philosophical tendencies often bring with it a leaning toward animated discussion and/or oratory, and the latter the Maori seems to have had in abundance.[2]

So, basically, the concept of cosmological Creation according to the overall Polynesian view has been stated as growth or evolution from an intangible state (*Te Korekore*) variously described as nothingness, space, void, darkness, night and immensity – to one of actuality through the Creation process. The 'intangible' state was further described as limitless, without light, form or motion. The Void was divided into the First Void, the Second Void, the Far-Extending Void and the Vast and the Unpossessed. The aeons of Darkness or *Po* were Extreme, Black, Gloomy and Never-Ending.

According to some views, the Maori universe was a three-tiered one translating to:

1. *Te Korekore* – Potential world.

2. *Te Po* – world of Becoming.

3. *Te Ao Marama* – world of Being.

The cosmos in Maori religion, therefore, appears to be involved in an evolutionary process with movement and development as its vital essence, exactly as **The Spiritual Laws** decree. From out of this formless world of no light, lands, seas and the heavens were brought forth in the well-known legends of Polynesia and of the Maori. An interesting idea in terms of a time-frame concept for the Creative process was expressed as perhaps successive stages of Creation in the abstract in the Maori Creation chant collected by the Rev. R Taylor, which begins:

• From the conception the increase,

• From the increase the swelling

• From the swelling the thought

• From the thought the remembrance

• From the remembrance the consciousness, the desire.

Sir Peter Buck (The Coming of the Maori, p.435) itemises this process thus:

1. *Te Rapunga* – seeking

2. *Te Kukune* – growth

3. *Te Pupuke* – swelling

4. *Te Hihiri* – energy

5. *Te Mahara* – thought

6. *Te Hinengaro* – mind

---

[2]That is certainly the case today. Unfortunately, however, whilst *some* oratory is interesting, much of it is too lengthy and tiresome with an over-emphasis on ancestral matters and genealogy. Because ancestral links are closely focused and tied to the whole Maori reason for being, oratory at such times does not offer much more than that. It thus tends to focus attention on the speaker and his connections, rather than on genuinely expanded knowledge, as it invariably purports to.

7. *Te Manako* – longing

The Maori Creation myths of *Rangi* and *Papa* and of their offspring, *Tane, Tangaroa* and *Rongo* etc., are very well known and though not the subject of our story as it does not accord with the actual Creation process, nevertheless offers the Maori idea as a contrast to what we are saying.

The concept of *Io*, though, is another matter. There can be little doubt that **if** the beliefs of *Io* and the concept of *Te Korekore* were true and *genuinely* understood by the few repositories of that knowledge, then, in this area at least, the ancient Maori ruling class was imbued with an exceptionally high level of intelligence and intuition. Quite obviously, philosophical ideas in the abstract cannot at all be expressed without those necessary accompaniments, *if* these kinds of high concepts are genuine and really understood.

However, it is extremely difficult to reconcile the ethnological record of these rather deep philosophical concepts that the select few high priests and chiefs were purported to possess, with the actual historical record of extreme Maori savagery. In the day to day life of the ordinary tribes-people, the necessary knowledge required for sustaining life would obviously have gone hand in hand with the requisite level of intelligence for such tasks. However, a leap into an idea of "...evolutionary Creation from nothingness..." requires something more introspective than that required for the purely mundane.

A further point of philosophical interest is the apparent old Maori view that the cosmos is *evolutionary* in nature, that there is movement and development, and that the universe is *not* a closed system. The power of **The Spiritual**, therefore, interpenetrates not only the everyday world but the unseen worlds as well. This insight by the priestly caste, if correct, certainly indicates that deep philosophical or religious analyses were possible in that group. The true picture is difficult to exactly determine in such a seemingly incongruous people.

For on the surface we appear to have a few highly developed individuals in a Neolithic stone age race ostensibly capable of great introspective and philosophical perceptive thought or analysis, presiding over a vastly greater number of people who were evidently deemed by these select few not to have either the necessary *mana* or sufficient intelligence to possess such knowledge. It is a strange and fascinating situation. More so when the ethnological record appears to attest to the fact that this knowledge may not have been confined to a select few in just one tribe, *but crossed tribal boundaries*. All this in a society where inter-tribal warfare was such an entrenched part of life and extremely barbaric in its execution. One would have thought that the 'wise men' possessing such great wisdom might have endeavoured to steer the race away from this less than beneficial path they were clearly treading.

So was the concept of *Io* a truly ancient knowledge? Or was it a late development taken from Christian beliefs after the arrival of the missionaries and tailored to fit Maori religious lore? According to some scholars *Io* was not a God known elsewhere in Polynesia, and the first reported European reference to him was published in the 1870s. Belich rightly observes that religion can be 'dangerous ground' and in his opinion Io:

"...was probably but not certainly adapted or even invented after contact."

(Making Peoples, p.108)

The historical record appears to show the emergence of this deity of *Io* during the middle of the 19th century where certain Maori priests of some East Coast tribes were consecrating classes of instruction for initiates in their *whare wananga* to *Io*-the-self-created. Ngata claimed that the knowledge of *Io* remained to the end the preserve of the *tohunga ahurewa*, the highest class of priests, and was denied to the ordinary tribes-people. According to other reports, the 'knowledge' about *Io* was evidently formulated during the 1860s from the teachings of two Maori priests, Te Matorohanga and Nepia Pohuhu and written down by Maori scribes into *The Lore of the Whare Wananga*. Interestingly, as in the manner of Western theological committees today, the finer, perhaps more difficult and contentious points of doctrine were debated by a similar body of priests and elders.

Generally, however, if such things require to be debated by men, it is usually a clear indication that there is a need to 'produce' some kind of doctrine to fit the proposed purpose of the teaching rather than there being a sure knowledge of the **True Laws**. Clear understanding would not require any kind of debate, just a simple application of those tenets. *The Lore*, however, clearly stated that:

'...the priests alone had complete knowledge of *Io* and that ordinary people knew nothing.'

In the present time much the same attitude can be found among the self-chosen few who claim to possess the complete 'basket of *Maori* knowledge' – the so-termed *three kits of knowledge*. Ordinarily, that in itself might be an acceptable situation, but the same group are often reluctant to offer it to others except in a teacher/pupil setting, and provided that the pupil is sufficiently worthy to receive it – in *their* estimation. But even with this gesture, we will generally find that those who claim to possess 'great knowledge', in the Maori sense, will not impart everything they have. This particular stance allows the original possessor to adopt a superior attitude, thus 'protecting' their claim to having something 'special' or 'sacred' that others are not privy to. In essence, however, it is only the ego that holds to this pretence. In the final analysis, these three 'kits' only hold the traditions and customary beliefs of Maori, and not 'all knowledge' as is usually postulated.

This rather strange stand is just part and parcel of an attitude of that group of people who play at the outermost fringes of *truly-genuine* Spiritual knowledge, so is not wholly confined to Maori. What Maoridom have done with it, however, is refined it to a point where the word *mana* – and all that that word ostensibly stands for – comes into play. Thus where the '*mana* of Maori knowledge' is ostensibly too sacred to be even questioned. The old *tohunga* played this psychological game well, but anyone with normal logic can easily see through this ploy. In any case, the whole thrust of supposedly highly secret or sacred knowledge held by latter-day *tohunga* or *kaumatua* being too dangerous for 'lesser mortals' to have, *is effectively rendered impotent* purely because **The Son of God Himself** freely gave the actual *Spiritual knowledge* we need.

The latter Maori Prophets readily understood that spiritually-unassailable fact.

So for *any* human being to claim that they can possess *more than that* out of their own 'person' is simply egotistically-arrogant, and therefore ludicrous. That particular stance, therefore, is the surest measure of where this supposedly 'too-sacred-knowledge' actually sits. For, in accordance with true **Spiritual Law**, nothing that is *genuinely Spiritual can ever be harmful to man*.

In an interesting paradox, therefore, 'Maori sacred knowledge' that is supposedly dangerous because of its 'high spirituality' thus actually stands in its rightful, *aspiritual* place. And in immutable accordance with the outworking of **The Law Itself**, in such cases will actually be *more dangerous to the possessors* of so-called 'too-sacred-knowledge'. Therefore such foolish 'game-playing' should be dismissed as irrelevant, unhelpful and even dangerous by all *free-thinking Maori*. For in order to actually possess genuine Spiritual knowledge, all we need do is fully understand the true meaning of **Spiritual Law** which was openly given for *all* of humankind.

The sole retention of the concept of *Io* by the ruling priestly caste may possibly be viewed in two ways. Either the knowledge was deliberately withheld, or The Bible of the missionaries provided very fertile ground for cunning priests to establish a 'top being' to enhance Maori 'religion'. The various names ascribed to *Io* could be seen to have some similarities with Christian concepts. *Io*-of-the-hidden-face, *Io*-eternal and *Io*-god-of-love reflect a possible 'borrowing' of a 'Christian concept' for the enhancement and elevation of a new and 'higher god'. Paradoxically the idea of old Maori having the concept of a God of Love as a venerated being hardly fits with the savage lifestyle of the people of that time. Even today, in supposedly more enlightened times, the concept of **Divine Love** is not at all understood by virtually all of humankind. And the old Maori way of life could not possibly have lent itself to such a noble sentiment as high, pure love. As a final indicator that the concept of *Io* may be a late post Christian development, *Io* was said to have created all things by *The Word*.

As a short digression away from *Io* but still staying with Maori religion, an interesting explanation of this lack of loving kindness exhibited by the old Maori is taken from Best's *Maori Religion and Mythology*, Vol.1, p.51, where he offers a passage from, *Where the White Man Treads,* by "W.B." who writes about Maori superstitions and Maori conceptions of unseen powers thus:

> "In the first place I must accept the theory that they were necessary to him, that they met his wants; and the more I study his case the more I am convinced that a ***benevolent*** scheme would not have stood the test of two generations."

> (Emphasis mine.)

Best further comments:

> "The above writer holds that the strenuous struggle among uncultured peoples to enable them to survive, the law of the survival of the fittest, effactually prevented the conception of a beneficent deity.
>   Hence, when he invented a cosmogony, it of necessity was cast in the mould of that striving, killing nature of which he was the highest member. Therefore he shared, in common with all primitive races, the want of words to express veneration, benevolence, and worshipful adoration. A loving, patriarchal creator was utterly beyond his comprehension. He could conceive nothing benedictory in the conditions of his surroundings, and therefore the Creation of his gods coincided with his appetites... His *karakia* (incantations) were invocations to his gods to preserve him from the unknown; of placation, of propitiation."

The above statement surely screams the word – **logical**! Moreover, this particular comment by one not born into the race, and therefore not subject to the all-pervading fear aspect of the 'old way', reveals a rare and accurate insight into the true nature of the old Maori *as he actually was*. For it clearly recognises the obvious fact that the very lifestyle of the race, with its propensity for the war trail, the baser practices of the black arts and the partaking of human flesh, could not easily or at all be reconciled with a natural recognition and acceptance of the concept of love or of a loving God. Whilst the old Maori seemed to possess the faculty for philosophical thought, anything tending toward a *Divine-love concept* was simply not possible. Hence the placing of *Io* on a level of virtual non-contact, divorced from the people, and clearly synonymous with non-understanding and non-comprehension. And therefore without the beneficial application of the virtues and aids that a more magnanimous belief in such an Exalted Being *could* have provided.

Best believed that:

> "The doctrine of *Io* was much more than an attempt to amalgamate Christian and Maori beliefs. *Io* manifested himself at a time of Maori resurgence and the tale of this *Io*-of-all-knowledge was to re-enforce the validity of the old beliefs with the sanction of a supreme deity who would match the Christian God."

It is an interesting analysis given the propensity of the *tohunga* and *kaumatua* class to retain power, influence and prestige, even in the present.

The above contention about *Io* is probably the truth of the matter. As previously stated, what may once have been a "high pure concept" was now simply too far removed from the everyday life of the tribes and their chosen high priests to be effective as a working, uplifting faith or foundation. That kind of *separation* would thus derive from the voluntary choice of the race to submit to an increasingly narrow and savagely-destructive path. Consequently, the *high priests'* apparent loss of knowledge of *Io* and the subsequent inability to fully comprehend the spiritual greatness of such noble perceptions, allowed for the establishment or acceptance of a 'second tier' or 'buffer-layer' of gods to whom access could be better effected. What followed was the emergence of a peculiarly Maori code of protocol that brought as a consequence, bizarre and base 'rules of conduct' pertaining to various aspects of village life and inter-tribal warfare. But more particularly, in the context of this work, to *utu* and cannibalism.

Interestingly, however, in 1974 the Rev. Fr. P.W. Shirres, after an examination of this subject through the writings of the early authorities – with one source going back to the 1840s – concluded that: "...the cult of *Io* was pre-European in origin." Whatever the truth about *Io*, whether the knowledge was ancient or whether derived from much later Christian beliefs, ancient Maori were clearly not able, or were unwilling, to utilise that concept for the benefit of the people. And if a post-contact borrowing, Maori showed themselves to be extremely adaptable to ideas that could further their cause in the new Pakeha environment.

A final interesting comparison is related in Best's work on Maori Religion and Mythology.

> "In a paper on the natives of Southern Nigeria written by Mr Talbot some years ago is described the "discovery" of a belief in a Supreme Being in that region. Knowledge of this cult had been successfully concealed from Europeans for many years, and was only detected by chance. This is just what occurred in New Zealand.
>
> We have lately had an interesting interview with a missionary from Central Africa, who has certainly studied the religious beliefs of the natives with great care, bringing to bear on the matter a mind remarkable for its liberality and the faculty of critical examination. He stated that the natives believed in a Supreme Being from whom no evil emanated, but who existed outside the hanging sky and did not interfere with ordinary mundane affairs, and also in the existence of many ancestral spirits. These latter are placated by the natives; these are the beings with whom the people are in contact, not the mighty and distant Supreme Being.
>
> All this closely resembles Maori belief and practice, and is of much interest."

Perhaps Ngata best sums up the quandary posed by '*Io*' in this concluding sentence of a lecture about him:

> "Whether independently evolved or borrowed, there were minds among the Stone Age people of the Polynesian archipelago which could comprehend this elevated conception and dream a philosophy of things in heaven and earth to satisfy the cravings of mind and spirit."

Whilst the Maori Creation legends have necessarily been a believable mechanism of explanation for the ancient Maori, the scientific knowledge available today coupled with the revelations contained in the main religious writings, but more particularly certain Spiritual writings, clearly point to a more easily definable and rationally acceptable concept of our origins.

With this truer knowledge, it behoves us, with grace and *mana*, to intelligently and gratefully accept this *greater revelation* given through the line of the Pakeha races, and allow the old legends to be just that. To be part of the cultural heritage of the evolutionary path that the Maori travelled for the thousands of years of his existence as a Polynesian people. And to recognise and teach them as such, without veneration or worship, but simply acknowledge the necessary part they played in the spiritual development of the race, and thus hold them there – in their rightful place!

If we were to attempt to very quickly encapsulate Maori religion into a single paragraph, we might describe it thus; overall a fascinating juxtaposition of an idea of Creation from out of an intriguing philosophical concept of *Te Korekore* (Nothingness), contrasting with a Darkness held in place by two gigantic beings, *Rangi* and *Papa*, representing both the male and female principle and the sky and earth concepts, to their subsequent separation by their offspring, the lesser or departmental gods named as *Tane, Tangaroa, Rongo* etc.. With the separation of their parents came the Light, revealing the worlds of heaven, the earth and the underworld. Contained within these opposing worlds are further subdivisions peopled with the various gods and entities of each level. Out of each of those sprang the legends and the superstitions of the Maori. And from that foundation came the myriad *tapu* that permeated and interpenetrated every single facet of Maori life that, in its turn, drove and accompanied the Maori along his self-chosen path to his destined future, *fateful meeting* with the Pakeha race.

4.2   The Tohunga and Tohungaism

Since time immemorial, man has sought answers to the continually arising questions that his evolutionary path would necessarily reveal. And since all men are not possessed with exactly the same levels of intelligence or even the same interest to question things around them, the members of each group will usually separate themselves out into those areas of interest, skill or ability that is more or less their natural place of expertise. Natural leaders will therefore find their place too, as will men we might loosely describe as being 'wise'.

In primitive societies wisdom was a highly prized and greatly valued gift that all people within the group could benefit from, provided, of course, that the person in whom they placed their trust *really did* possess the appropriate knowledge for the time. This 'position' should thus translate to a helping one rather than that of building personal power through the use of knowledge that others had no access to. When healing was effected in the case of illness, or a real or imagined malevolence was driven out, the position of the 'wise man' was greatly enhanced. Such men were not fools, so even if their ministrations were actually ineffective, the much lower level of understanding or possible fear of his 'wise arts' by the general group allowed 'the knowing one' the latitude to concoct a suitable explanation for any 'failure'.

Over time this particular position might become a religious one in various races and societies, with perhaps a subsequent increase in awe or veneration accorded the 'office-holder'. And there might possibly even be fear of the person holding that office. Since the sum total of the group's knowledge – which was often synonymous with power – was retained by this person or caste, the dissemination or otherwise of such knowledge ultimately rested in the hands of this small 'educated elite'. The later development and knowledge of the written word furthered this 'power-base', which greatly strengthened their controlling influence. If the particular ruling class was not a benevolent one, it might well be in their interest to withhold the knowledge from the masses, thereby keeping them ignorant.

The desire for more and more knowledge on the part of the 'ruling group' perhaps facilitated a deeper involvement in the teachings of the great religions as they emerged over time. But where the practitioners sought power through connection and experimentation with darker energies, a connecting path downwards was firmly established, with the subsequent narrowing of their horizons and the concomitant *inability* to actually perceive this *constricting effect*.

The 'wise men' of the Maori – the *tohunga* class – were, for the most part, the retainers of all the accumulated knowledge; that which held the oral history of the tribe. The lack of a written language, moreover, necessitated the development of the *chant* and the *karakia* as the medium within which to preserve this knowledge. Thus, as a first requirement for chosen entry into the priesthood, an initiation at a young age was desirable. Also desirable was the inculcating into the novice the strong acceptance that the status of priest as being one of power and prestige was vitally necessary to retain the *mana* of the position, though this would naturally be accepted in the old Maori world in any case. A certain level of intelligence would not go amiss here either since the need to retain large amounts of historical records as well as the arcane knowledge of healing and herbs, forest lore, lore of the sea and the stars, psychic knowledge both for and against etc., required an exceptionally good retentive ability.

For the ancient stone-age Maori living in a world of fearful superstition peopled with all manner of dark and malevolent entities – albeit a world of his own making – it was vitally important to have at least one member of the *hapu* with some 'understanding' of these matters. One who could therefore combat such forces and give at least some measure of psychic security to the group. In a society where virtually everything that happened was deemed to be the work of either 'good' or 'bad' forces, the relative power of the *tohunga* would determine whether or not a *counter* to a believed threat would be successful. Obviously the collective peace of mind of the group hinged on the *perceived outcome* of any such *exchanges*.

So whilst it was probably felt that a powerful *tohunga* – at least powerful according to Maori views of the time – was definitely a valuable asset to the tribe, the same perceived power concentrated in the hands of one man, or perhaps a small elite priesthood, most likely acted as a two-edged sword for the more ignorant tribal members. The very thought of even attempting to oppose malevolent forces was more than enough for those without understanding of the craft to greatly fear not only the forces themselves, but naturally also the *tohunga* or priests who carried out such dangerously-protective or aggressively-destructive psychic activities. The fact that many in the priesthood would probably have been *matakite,* ostensibly possessing the ability of second-sight and being able to see what most might not wish to see or be revealed, was one more unknown barrier for the uninitiated. Given all those factors, there stands a race of people appropriately subdued by the fear of their own huge and unwieldy raft of superstitions.

With such powerfully-subjugating forces constantly in play and affecting virtually every single aspect of everyday village and tribal activity, the potential wish to become spiritually free of psychic pressure could not possibly awaken in such straitened circumstances. The *spiritual horizons* of pre-European Māori were far too narrow to allow any kind of meaningful uplifting change of direction without some kind of major upheaval to shake the very foundations of the age-old beliefs. Without that necessary impetus, what remained was a kind of resigned acceptance to that particular way of life, with that same attitude directed toward the presence of, and necessity for, the *tohunga* class.

This caste practised white and black magic, both being seen as necessary activities for the well-being of the tribe. According to the ethnological record some *tohunga* only practised white or good magic, whilst others concerned themselves with the darker energies. It is likely that all *tohunga* were equally conversant with both since knowledge of the black arts was clearly necessary if a white 'magician' were to have any chance of combating what was perceived to be the more malevolent and deadly power of black magic.

White magic was ostensibly concerned with that which would bring benefit to the tribe. Such uses might be the act of *rotu moana* which involved the calming of the sea at times of great danger on the water, or for invoking the wind – described as *whakaara hau* – which might be used for offensive or defensive purposes. And where winds were raised purely for prestige purposes, different tribes might favour different winds. As Best has recorded:

> "...the wind of the Tamakaimoana clan [*hapu*] of the Tuhoe tribe is the south wind called *Tutakangahua,* while that of the Urewera clan is *Urukaraerae.*"

> (Maori Religion and Mythology, Vol.2)

When heavy winds were desired a charm called *tuku-rangi* was employed, and that required to stop the winds was called *puru-rangi* and *tua i te rangi.*

It should be especially noted that the Maori possessed a strong acceptance that the elements could be invoked or manipulated to serve a particular purpose, especially in the need to assist the group in warfare, and many stories describe such incidents of *tohunga* ostensibly achieving such end results. The very valuable ethnological record of the Maori compiled by Best, Cowan and others clearly give many examples of this attempted use of Elemental Forces by old-style *tohunga*. However, this belief is not solely confined to the Maori, and the history of mankind bears many such tales. Probably the most notable that might more readily spring to mind was that of the Red Sea being parted for Moses during the exodus of the Hebrews from out of Egyptian bondage, and the ongoing help thereon. Notwithstanding the help humankind can receive from them, the "Forces" themselves are not at the beck and call of the personal whims of man. For they, too, are subject to the strictest outworking of **Spiritual Law** – whether assisting mankind or fulfilling their own ordained place in Creation.

White magic served a valuable purpose in the protection of the forests and birds for the maintenance of food supplies. A food gathering party would seek the protection of the appropriate deity for a safe expedition protected from possible malevolent entities whilst in the dark forest, and for an abundant harvest. The same fearful respect was accorded the protectors of the sea and its inhabitants. Given the degree of dependence that the old Maori seems to have needed with all his invocations, it is no wonder that *tohunga* were accorded such a highly ranked position within the tribe.

The whole practice of *tohungaism* with all its accompanying **contaminants** of some *tapu*, and all *makutu* and *utu*, has been described from the ethnological, anthropological, Maori sociological and Maori religious viewpoint as a very necessary means of discipline and control over a wild and warlike people. Of course, whilst this was undoubtedly true for the most part, that particular assessment is more an academic European one viewed objectively from the cool distance of time, and/or from the cultural difference of race. It was probably not the 'living reality' of the ordinary Maori tribes-people who had no choice but to accept that regime.

Perhaps it is worth considering whether or not the *wero* or challenge – which had developed to become part of the ethos of the race itself – had become so highly ritualised that precise protocols had simultaneously emerged as its almost religious accompaniment. Thereby needing severe constraints placed upon it so that serious, undisciplined challenges could not destabilise the group.

Certainly, there would have had to be rules and laws for Maori society to adhere to if there was not to be a breakdown of the social order. Clearly a necessary aspect of life for all races if there is to be any kind of a basic harmonious structure that all can live by in relative peace and safety. As has been correctly noted, the psychic barriers developed and refined by the superstitious Maori and placed on innumerable activities at certain times and for specific reasons, were far more effective in protecting and controlling a particular aspect of life than any comparable earthly or man-made societal restriction or punishment.

Paradoxically, therefore, the very nature of the race with its propensity for the *wero* – the want to challenge – required the emergence and development of a stronger deterrent than a simple caution or warning from the leaders of the tribe to any potential infringement or transgression. For any such 'warning' might be taken by the challenger as a slight in itself and form the basis for his own *legitimised* challenge to it. So an unseen and feared protective device, with the possibility of a dark, fearful death as the reward for transgression or defilement, admirably curbed the fiery nature of the war-loving Maori. Through this regulatory mechanism, the old Maori lived his life under superstition and fear of both the known and the unknown, all under the watchful eye and the feared yet protective mantle of the *tohunga*.

Of course, by virtue of the belief of invincibility that the knowledge of these arts was supposed to confer on their practitioners, some examples of the overall foolishness of it all have been well recorded.

> "In the fight at Tapiri in 1865 the Tuhoe folk had with them a female *tohunga* who undertook to catch the bullets of the enemy in her hands, however, some hitch occurred, for she not

only failed to catch such bullets, but those she did catch did not seem to do her much good."

(Best, Maori Religion and Mythology Vol. 2, p.114)

Similar incidents with other groups, notably the Pai Marire and Hauhaus, have been recorded with the same obvious results, though it was not normally the *tohunga* who marched into battle with that particular belief.

4.3   The Institution of Tapu

William's *Maori Dictionary*, Seventh Edition, p.384, defines *tapu* as the following:

> **1**. a *"Under religious or superstitious restriction;* a condition affecting persons, places, and things, and arising from innumerable causes. Any one violating *tapu* contracted a *hara*, and was certain to be overtaken by calamity."
> **2**. Beyond one's power, inaccessible.
> **3**. Sacred.
> **4**. n *"Ceremonial restriction, quality or condition of being subject to such restrictions."*

In keeping with the main thrust of this Work in necessarily outlining and incorporating **The Spiritual Laws of Creation** into our essential journey, it can be readily observed from the explanation of the meaning of *tapu* that any transgression of it brought about the *reciprocal effect* of the *hara* or calamity. Here the very basic application of **The Law of Reciprocal Action** (*Sowing and Reaping*), which outcome the old Maori had to accept – albeit perhaps unknowingly in the lawful outworking of this particular institution – is clearly evident. That is not to say, however, that he understood the full ramifications of that **Law**, then or now!

In "Maori Religion and Mythology" Vol.2, Best describes the institution of *tapu* as a "...highly important one in Maoriland...", with the rules of *tapu* having far-reaching powers and effects. Its main effects were felt in the two areas of religion and sociology. Whilst possibly being viewed more as part of Maori religion, it was also "...the strongest force in Maori social life". Its purpose could be stated as being "...the power that preserved order..." and, as such, "...took the place of civil law". The effective power or force behind this institution was, "...represented by the gods; they were the vivifying power that rendered it effective". Also, to the Maori mind, "...*tapu* represented the *mana* (prestige, power, authority) of the gods". Thus the fear of the gods "...was the strongest preserver of order". *Tapu* could be described as an accessory or accompaniment to religion but was not necessarily the framework.

Whilst *tapu* may be understood as a kind of prohibition, its actual purpose was ostensibly that of a protective device. Moreover, even though *tapu* was not a curse or power in itself, it was still regarded as potentially that by the common people. Therefore it is not the actual *tapu* that may cause harm if transgressed, but the *mana* of it which then becomes uncontrolled and potentially dangerous in the outworking of *hara* resulting from the breach of a particular *tapu*.

The prophet Te Kooti Arikirangi understood the inherent problems of making things *tapu*. A sacred house erected by Tuhoe recalling his long hunt by colonial forces, "Te Whai-a-te-motu, The Pursuit across the land ... was built to remember the wars". Upon its eventual completion Te Kooti entered the house with 20 *tohunga* from Tuhoe to lift the *tapu*. Judith Binney, in her work "Redemption Songs", (p.471), records that the Tuhoe people wanted to make the house sacred.

But Te Kooti replied:

"Well, the only results you get from anything sacred or *tapu*, is spiders! That's the only people who'll live there. The house will be inhabited by air and spiders. But it will be remembered for the gambling of the people!" Thus did Te Kooti advise the people against making their houses *tapu*.

In English terms we might equate the meaning of the word *tapu*, with sacred or holy. But *tapu* did not always mean sacred. And what was true for the old Maori in terms of the meaning of *tapu* is still true today.

Best records Frazer as stating: "...primitive people often make no distinction between holiness and pollution; both call for ceremonial restriction which is *tapu*."

Thus that which is or has become unclean is *tapu*. Therefore anything which comes into contact with a *tapu* object, whether animate or inanimate, is also considered *tapu* or unclean and must be purified: "...freed from *tapu*, when it can be used again."

In Maori society, *tapu* could not strictly be said to be a moral institution, yet in an indirect way: "...it exerted a moral force ... preventing offences against society and individuals."

"Dieffenbach defined *tapu* as representing religious worship and civil law."

(Travels in New Zealand, Vol.2, p 100.
Best, Maori Religion and Mythology, Vol.2, p.17)

A very good explanation of the effect of *tapu* on Maori village life is reproduced here from Best's compilations, and also provides an interesting insight into how the Maori viewed their original genealogical connections from the distant past:

"The Maori were a people proud of their descent from those very gods, whose paternal care had enabled their forefathers to cross the broad "Sea of Kiwa" with impunity, and perform feats of navigation that are without parallel in modern times... It will be freely admitted that such a race of men would, under any circumstances, be difficult to manage, and yet we find that in their own *pas* or villages, they were as obedient, orderly and law-abiding as any statute-ridden Anglo-Saxon; and that such order prevailed among such a fierce and turbulent race ought to be susceptible of explanation, and I hold that the power of *tapu* was the chief factor by which the difficulty was solved."

(Colonel W. E. Gudgeon, Journal of the Polynesian
Society, Vol.15, p.49-50)

Colonel Gudgeon evidently spent a long life in contact with the Maori, and Best reported that:

"This writer maintained that one excellent effect of *tapu* was the mental and moral discipline that it imposed upon the Maori; its enforcement of self-denial and subordination."

(Maori religion and Mythology.)

A key point of the power and purpose of *tapu*, and a point which not all early European chroniclers recognised was the fact that, in Best's estimation: in the 'religious' beliefs of the Maori, *tapu* originated from the gods and was thus a "...manifestation of the *mana* of the gods..." This particular European view of the institution of *tapu* is probably an accurate one in that it necessarily provides a connecting link between the Maori and his gods, which was the main thrust of Maori thinking. An old Maori world without recourse to his gods is unthinkable as a working model for that society. There simply had to be 'gods' of all shapes and persuasions to sanction all his activities, no matter what form they might take. If a particular matter needed attention for which there was no precedent then, under the 'wise counsel' of the *tohunga*, another god, underling – or *tapu* even – could expediently approve the desired wish of the people, or perhaps of the *tohunga*.

The old Maori belief that *tapu* was a manifestation of the *mana* of the gods meant that their approval and support was necessary when important tasks such as the building of a superior *waka* or where the construction of a superior building was required. At such times the work party itself necessarily became *tapu* because they were working under "...the *mana* of the gods". Given the fiercely independent nature of the old Maori, some early 'scholars' thought that the placing of the work party itself under *tapu* effectively prevented one or all from abandoning the task before its completion. That would probably have been an unlikely event since the abandonment would have been synonymous with a snubbing of the *mana* of the gods themselves.

Therefore it is very doubtful that any Maori of ancient times would even contemplate such a transgression, let alone carry it out. The hold of *tapu* and the fear of retribution would have effectively precluded that possibility. Of course there was nothing to prevent the supervising *ariki* from calling a complete halt to the proceedings if the 'signs' indicated that all was not well with the project. This might be taken to mean that the gods themselves were no longer supportive, and had withdrawn their *mana*. All such things were relative in the thinking of the times.

To attempt to outline the many different kinds of *tapu* would require a complete work on its own, and one must surely question whether all the tribes-people were fully conversant with it all. The possibility of inadvertently 'putting a foot wrong', as it were, and inviting calamity must have been a constant and pervading worry given the great fear of 'the unknown' that the Maori lived with. With such a wide range of meaning, the term *tapu* could signify so many different things with different phases of *tapu*, each varying in intensity. It is a simple matter to accept *tapu* as meaning sacred, and to equally accept the word as meaning unclean or polluted. But in the case of a 'betrothal' where a young woman might be made *tapu* for a particular man, the meaning would be more akin to 'spoken for'. Where a prohibition is placed on a food source, the term *rahui* is used, thus denoting that it is still *tapu*.

One aspect of the institution of *tapu* that is important to understand is that only a person who possessed *mana* could declare or render a particular thing or place *tapu*. The greater or more severe the *tapu*, the greater the *mana* required for the placement of it. Thus only the highest chiefs or the priestly caste could accord anything the strongest *tapu*. An ordinary member of the tribe could place *tapu* on unimportant matters only. By marking a log with his adze, a man could claim it for his own. It was *tapu* to him. By contrast, a person of high rank could place a path, a stream, a lake, or a beach under *tapu*. Such a person could also render a place *tapu* by tying to a branch etc., a piece of thread from his clothing, or by draping his cloak over an object.

Generally speaking, therefore, the higher the rank or social standing, the higher the *mana*, and the greater the power to impose *tapu*. Thus, to claim objects of value, a war chief could declare the finest canoe of the enemy his backbone thereby rendering it his, (simply because the backs of men were accorded the status of *tapu*), and therefore too dangerous for anyone else of inferior status to claim or use. *Tapu* places were often marked by various means such as human hair or painted posts to ensure the safety of the people, but a highly ranked person could simply declare a place to be *tapu* and word of mouth would quickly complete the prohibition.

The handling, consumption and gifting of food, particularly from people outside the tribe, provided fertile ground for various application of *tapu*. Gifts of food might be regarded with great suspicion, and would surreptitiously need to be made *noa*, or safe. A person of great *mana*, with a correspondingly high degree of *tapu*, could not allow any part of his body to touch eating utensils or bowls lest they become *tapu* and too dangerous to be used by anyone else. Food cooked exclusively for *tapu* persons needed to be handled with great care and reverence, and could not be touched by anyone else, let alone consumed by others. There are recorded accounts of Maori transgressing this *tapu* either as a wero (challenge), or in error, and dying shortly after. In some extreme cases, a highly *tapu* person might need to be hand-fed so that his own hands did not come into contact with the food.

In this regard *personal tapu* for persons of rank, which had absolutely nothing to do with genuine spirituality, was an important element of 'control' within the tribal group. The greatest *tapu* was attached to the head since it was regarded as the most important part of the body. Hair cuttings were therefore carefully disposed of in a *tapu* manner or deposited in a *tapu* place. The excesses of *tapu* with regard to the sacredness of the head might mean that in certain cases, the head could not be washed. Since cleanliness is most certainly a spiritual virtue, not washing did nothing to enhance that potential and, moreover, was hardly a practice to promote good hygiene.

As well as the head, however, personal *tapu* also extended to the whole of the body in cases of high rank, and also encompassed everything associated with that person. His bed was *tapu*, as was any object used by him. In some cases even where he sat might be deemed to be *tapu* and off-limits to all others. This extreme practice could be carried further whereby a fire used for warmth by such a person could not be used for cooking purposes. Early Europeans often rightly regarded such extremes with irreverence, and Best records that the first settlers used to speak of "...certain native chiefs as being *tapu* an inch deep!" Even the Maori, to whom this institution belonged, must have found much of this carry-on extremely irksome and possibly problematic in the continual need for its absolutely correct interpretation.

In the case of certain illnesses which were considered to be the work of malevolent forces and for which the *tohunga* had no cure, such was the dread of it and the associated strength of *tapu* placed on the unfortunate person that he was often put aside and left alone to endure whatever was causing the problem. This fear might mean that he could go unattended and without ministration for days, and that food might or might not be offered to him or, at best, simply placed out for him. At times the only relief for him from such ignorance and misery was death. According to Best, during the early days of European settlement Maori often strongly objected to persons giving food or medicine to the sick. Such intense *tapu* resulted in one early missionary in the North threatening to use Naval guns to destroy a village if the local Maori continued to refuse him access to a sick chief (Ruatara). Needless to say, the villagers acquiesced.

The greatest *tapu*, however, was always associated with the shedding of blood. Thus tattooing was regarded as an extremely sacred undertaking and much painstaking care was carried out during all phases of the tattooing process, including preliminary preparations, to ensure a successful outcome. Whilst an ordinary object could be made *noa*, or *tapu-free*, shed blood could not be recalled. Even a very minor incident involving the most minimal of blood loss could be enlarged to the level of the patently absurd by the fear-ridden and superstitiously-driven Maori. So much so that any spot where the blood of a *tapu* person was shed automatically became *tapu* as well.

Such was the case where Te Heuheu, the high ranking chief at Taupo, who, upon stepping into a canoe belonging to another person, hurt his foot so that blood flowed. The canoe was promptly declared *tapu*, hauled ashore and abandoned. It was unfit for further use. The now useless vessel, originally crafted with pride and perhaps under its own *tapu* during construction and which once sat proudly on the water, could not be used again.[3]

It is patently clear that the institution of *tapu* most certainly regulated Maori life very effectively. But it would be difficult to believe that it was a naturally cheerful and happy society. The constant uncertainty and fear generated by such beliefs could only hold its subjects in subjugation much of the time.

A very interesting comment was made to me regarding the expressions of the faces of those Maori – either as individuals or in group scenes – who were the subject of the well-known painters Goldie and Lindauer. My companion observed:

---

[3]It is fortunate that the medical profession of the present-day does not subscribe to such an archaic and superstitious belief, or we would have to abandon or burn all our hospitals and ambulances!

"You never see the women smiling in the old paintings!"

That spontaneous, latter-day observation would seem to bear out the contention of a less than joyful existence through having to cope with different undercurrents of more or less constant uncertainty. And those particular women had the benefit of living under a less physically dangerous and psychically charged environment than their predecessors by virtue of the older, harsher way of life beginning to die out at the time they were captured on canvas.

Contrary to the beliefs of other primitive groups, having one's image captured was not a bad thing in Maori estimation. It did not appear to be considered *tapu* in any kind of way. If it were, it is very unlikely that we would now have the wonderful portraits of some of the more notable chiefs of that time today. Certainly an examination of tribal scenes, particularly, does seem to show that there was little sense of joy or natural happiness in the people. And it is unlikely that the artists would have set out to deliberately portray this effect. It is more likely to be an accurate reflection of the 'way it really was'.

This apparently quiet, reflective 'mood' is surely understandable given the fact that a whole lifetime of many, many years of having to endure the old psychic Maori way of life with all its attendant fears was simply the norm. One might believe that one would simply 'get used to it'. However, with so much pervasive *tapu* and material danger in everyday life, and just as much uncertainty as to the outcome at the end of one's life, it is not difficult to understand how there was probably little real long-term joy for the people of such a fear-racked society.

In the segment, "Making Maori", Belich refers to one view of the Maori as living; "...in solemn, sombre, lifeless terms, bent under a vast load of *tapu* and custom..." Whilst he describes this sorry situation as tending more towards a 'deceptive myth', the reality was not far removed from it simply by virtue of the all-pervasive 'reality of *tapu*' – which *was* fear-inducing. Of course, as he also rightly observes, the nature of the Maori, even whilst shackled by their deep superstitious fears, did produce times of laughter, though it is difficult to see how this could have been a 'frequent event'.

> "Fun and games, laughter and irreverence did exist, even if they are hard to recover in full colour."

> (Making Peoples, p.106)

Having examined a few examples of *tapu* and offered relevant comments where appropriate, it is timely to further assess some of these ideas from the standpoint of **The Spiritual Laws**. From the knowledge of that perspective and from the living experience of the effect of *tapu*, a short, sage analysis of the meaning of it by the authors of "New Zealand's Heritage", sub-heading "Ancient Maori Society" (p.15), offers an interesting viewpoint.

> "Above all, *tapu* was the supreme regulator of Maori life. Man knew that without the gods he was nothing, and the trees, insects, birds, animals and fish were the offspring of the gods as much as he was. The slightest act of irreverence, disrespect, or mere forgetfulness of the *tapu* status of a thing or act was potentially disastrous. *Tapu was no negative injunction to avoid specified activities or things, or a mechanism of psychic repression. It was a positive force which preserved the Maori environment,* so that his supplies of food and raw material were steadily available. Perhaps, more importantly, it regulated his society at the family and tribal level."

> (Italics mine.)

Whilst the practice of *tapu* most certainly regulated everyday life, it is simply not correct to assert that it was totally beneficial for the Maori in every way. In the Spiritual sense it most certainly *was not*. Neither can it be said to have been a *positive force* in accordance with the actual meaning of the word. By virtue of its all-pervading status and effect, whilst it could be termed a mechanism of *psychic repression*, it **was** ultimately a mechanism for *psychic licence*. For in its train followed the twin curses of *makutu* and *utu* with their all-pervading *psychic licence* too. *Tapu* was not a thing that Maori exulted and rejoiced in. There were no happy, annual festivals to *tapu*. It was a powerful living force to be feared, to be whispered about, and more often than not with great dread even if, technically speaking, the *tapu* itself was supposedly not the actual thing to be feared, but the *mana* ostensibly associated with it. But Maori did fear it – greatly. For that is exactly what it produced – **fear**.

By this means *tohunga*, in particular, could wield enormous influence and power over the lives of the ordinary tribes-people. Given the Maori propensity for 'personal *mana*', the virtual subjugation of the race by a few powerful people added enormously to their 'priesthood status' in Maori eyes. And in more places today than might be believed, it still exerts its dark influence over many Maori. Apart from the often insidious effects that the application of *tapu* produced, even perceived psychic effects manifesting from such natural events as the wind blowing, a rain shower slightly different from the normal pattern, the sudden appearance of an insect or bird; all required mandatory analysis and translation.

As acknowledged elsewhere, and as the written record of man attests, signs and indicators *are* given to man from time to time for different reasons and from various sources, *including the natural elements*. However, that will only happen with any real meaning or substance under **The Natural Laws** and not, perforce, from the machinations of man's *primitive* attempts to emulate this *universal force*. Therefore *tapu*, in certain applications, was a distortion of the pure power of those **Laws**, and thus used very wrongly at such times.

Moreover, and as previously stated, the application of *tapu* for any reason was not the right of the ordinary person. It was not voted on. *Tapu* was the preserve of the powerful in Maori society, and was obviously the best 'big stick' to have. Actually, it could be a force for good, even today, but it must be truly *spiritualised* as a force for spiritual freedom and knowledge, and not as it was used in the strict and narrow confines of fear and subjugation. But *only* with true knowledge of **The Spiritual Laws** can it be used beneficially. The Maori, however, did not have that understanding to the necessary degree required. Therefore the assertion that it was such a wonderful thing in the context of ancient Maori life has little validity in truly spiritual terms, for *tapu* was invariably applied more under the umbrella of *psychic* activity.

Furthermore, applied with shrewd cunning by the ruling elite under a regime of 'supposedly' great spiritual knowledge, *tapu* could be a wonderful mechanism for the material acquisition of other people's hard earned property, and this was so in old Maori society. In relative terms, surely a case of the rich getting richer, a situation no different today in some applications of Pakeha economic theory, which some Maori rightly condemn. Yet that system of old still rears its dying head in these latter times where the propensity to cling to a spiritually wrong concept of personal worth and power travelling under the term *mana*, permits situations to arise whereby 'offerings from others' are *expected*, irrespective of whether or not the 'giver' has the actual ability to easily comply. Personal spiritual accountability was not then, and is not today, a virtue of this particular excrescence of *tohungaism*.

Raymond Firth noted:

"Mainly through its agency the warlike turbulent Maori, quick to resent insult, was rendered in his own village obedient, orderly and law-abiding.

Thus the *tapu* regulated affairs between men of different status and kept the social system preserved. It enjoined men to work hard at sustaining life and gave the whole system a supernatural authority better than any human one, an authority to be exercised on the offender by the gods themselves. It must be remembered, however, that men were not mere tools of the gods, living under a *spiritual tyranny*. The Maori could *manipulate* his system."

(New Zealand's Heritage, Italics mine.)

Most certainly the old warlike Maori were effectively subdued by their own institution of *tapu* but, as previously stated, it *was* a tyranny nonetheless when viewed from the standpoint of **Spiritual Truth**. Perhaps 'spiritual tyranny' is a contradiction in terms for, by virtue of its nature, qualities of **The Spiritual** have no affinity or connection with such a thing as tyranny. What is meant here is probably more 'psychic tyranny', for the machinations of *tapu* as practised by the Maori obviously lived more in the field of 'psychic happenings' than in *genuinely-spiritual* activity.

The reader may regard this difference as being possibly unimportant but it is a huge and vital difference to the correct understanding of **Spiritual Law**, for our whole purpose is to explain the path of the Maori from that standpoint.[4]

It is important to note that the power of *tapu* was rarely challenged by any in the group to whom it belonged − by those who put it in place. In a society that readily exercised the *mana* of the *wero* or challenge in many different situations as part of their very life substance, this fact shows the fear or respect in which it was held. And *manipulation* is not the same as a challenge. Certainly with regard to the ordinary people, fear, and not respect, was the real controller. Of course a *tapu* placed on a particular thing might be challenged by the *tohunga* of another group, but that would simply be a show of a battle of wills. The 'victor' could subsequently lay claim to the greater *mana* or power deriving from his 'win'.

It is eminently clear that ancient Maori were 'kept in line' by their own psychic rules and, given the savage lifestyle of the time, those rules were necessary for effective control of that society. The old truth of needing to 'fight fire with fire' is positively true here. Spiritually-elevated concepts and laws for everyday life could not possibly have evolved in ancient Maori society with such a regime. Why? Simply because of the huge gulf existing between genuine spiritual knowledge as the key foundation from which to formulate beneficial and equitable laws, and the reality of the level on which the old Maori actually lived.

Such changes would have required a different kind of human spirit to incarnate into the race i.e., people with a far broader outlook than that which actually existed. And, under the outworking of **The Law of Attraction of Similar Species**, this was not possible whilst the Maori remained isolated and alone in their self-delusion of possessing advanced spiritual knowledge whilst at the same time practising great savagery. The time of incarnation of very different souls into the race − *such as those of the latter Maori Prophets* − was reserved for the future when **vastly different influences** could provide the necessary "*bridge of soul-attraction*".

Thus *tapu*, whilst it certainly served its ordained purpose admirably for the old Maori, was not the wonderful, benevolent, regulatory force that it is claimed to be for their society. Given a very different emphasis, and coupled with true spiritual knowledge, perhaps it could have been.

* * * * *

Paradoxically, the timely recognition that we must offer protection and preservation to so many devastated and poisoned areas of our earthly home today or face our own demise underpins the work of many concerned groups worldwide. This activity could almost be viewed as a *spiritualised-application* of the basic ethos of *tapu* if directed against unhelpful activities of degradation by powerful, wealthy corporations, or for short-term political expediency by uncaring or ignorant Governments.

For example, the attitude and *spiritual paucity* of some in the corporate world is well exemplified by the following statement:

---

[4]The concepts of *aroha* and *mana* will be examined under the same principles also, as will all else in the rest of this Work.

"A tree has no value until it is cut down!"

This statement was made by head of one of America's largest forestry corporations (recorded by Dr. David Suzuki, Canadian biologist and conservationist). Hopefully, that particular C.E.O. is far more enlightened today. A '*tapu* status' placed on the value of *living forests*, such as in this case, is the kind of usage of the word we are promoting.

*   *   *   *   *

The whole idea of *tapu*, then, if cleansed of all psychic connotations and connections, revisited from the standpoint of **The Laws of Creation** and given very careful *spiritual* thought today, could be re-applied as a strong foundation for the emergence and development of a greater '*aroha-reality*' towards the land. A subsequent re-teaching of Maori culture from that beneficial standpoint would elevate the whole revitalised concept to its corresponding place within society overall. The word itself, however, would need to be purged of its current ambiguous status and confusing multi-layered meaning.

The form presently associated with the word *tapu* is a distorted one as it has no clear and precise single meaning in the *spiritual* sense, yet is ostensibly used for that purpose. A word may not necessarily possess any *spiritual depth*, yet it will still have come into being through the *spiritual volition* of the human producers. The end use of the word, as determined by the originator through the inherent Spiritual Power that is the animating force in every human being, will automatically give it its corresponding and therefore appropriate 'form'. So in order for the word, *tapu*, to be applied solely in a spiritual way, and for it to contain and project its associated form, it would need to be, in meaning, sacred, holy, protected. The other aspect of the word meaning unclean could not fit into a purely spiritual application of *tapu* in this particular scenario.

However, a *spiritual re-designation* in the meaning of the word would not, of its own, be sufficient to elevate the use of it. For this to occur there would need to be a complete re-examination of how *tapu* had previously been applied, and why. And all connections to psychic forms and ideas, which may previously have been the basis for its application, would need to be purged from it. Only in this way could the word *tapu* be spiritually-freed of all its old connections and forms. In the same way that the mythological Phoenix rose from the ashes, so could this word also arise anew and the use of it be transformed from one of fear and dread in the old way to one of positive and beneficent work today.

Naturally this would pre-suppose a necessary willingness within Maoridom to recognise the current condition of the race wrought by so many spiritually-wrong concepts over a long period of time. And to also accept the need for fundamental changes in cultural thinking and in the teaching and/or present application of those traditional practices – a process already started by the line of Maori Prophets, and culminating in the great mission of Ratana.

Thus to courageously accept the overall spiritual direction he illuminated so that:

> *Only by leaving certain connections behind to a more savage and superstitious past can Maori also be phoenix-like and 'perhaps' now occupy what was once his especially-ordained 'Spiritual place' in this land of Aotearoa and the world.*

That pattern of savagery was the result of a long process of 'spiritual degeneration'; something very difficult for both revered Maori culturalism and European intellectualism to *really* understand. Therefore, the use of the word, ***spiritual***, to describe certain aspects of Maori thinking, attitudes and practices is simply not correct. And it becomes a problem word in that, not being fully understood and used in so many wrong contexts, it allows a veritable minefield of misinformation to be disseminated under the umbrella of great and wonderful 'truth' or 'spirituality'. So whilst there will always be beneficial and uplifting qualities in every race, in the case of the Maori, every single aspect of life was nevertheless permeated and virtually controlled by the constrictive effect of *tapu*.

Moreover, the practice of *whakanoa* whereby a *tapu* could be lifted does not alter the reality that it was still the controlling force. And the more insidious activity of *makutu* and *utu* was, in actuality, a more malevolent and destructive extension and excrescence of the outworking of this practice of *tapu*. It is this particular facet of Maori life, often superficially glossed over by various 'analysts', which was the key point in his whole existence. That led on to those more debased practices in its natural progression, and was the reason *why* it was so damaging for him. Thus the whole strongly-ingrained and incorrect attitude within Maoridom of possessing great spirituality must first be expunged from the collective consciousness before *genuine spirituality* can become the new ethos.

Such an achievement, however, can only happen when enough Maori awaken sufficiently to begin the necessary process of moving away from the old and into the new, thereby providing the influence and impetus for others to question the change and follow that lead, *exactly as Ratana once did*. The new here is not the new of the Pakeha and his corporate world, but the new of **Spiritual Law**, to which the corporate world *must also bow*. Of course, some things in the modern world are beneficial and correct and it would be foolish to not recognise that. But much more is very wrong and it is this that must be addressed spiritually if there is to be any meaningful change for all time.

In the final analysis, therefore, **The Eternal Laws**, the very **Laws of Creation** – as the ultimate paradox and irony for Maori in this case – are the most **powerful *tapu*** of all; *for they are life itself*. And the ongoing problems and heartache of all societies worldwide, including that of the Maori, are simply the lawful outworking wrought through continually transgressing ***the absolute and inviolable tapu of 'The Spiritual Laws of The Creator'***.

Whilst the Maori imposed and practised the strict institution of *tapu* in every facet of his everyday life; in the most remarkable of enigmatic thought-processes he did not ever appear to have recognised the clear fact that his journey downwards from *tapu*, to *makutu*, to *utu*, and thence finally to the eventual practice of cannibalism, was arguably ***the greatest tapu of all***. For it was a monstrous transgression against **The Spiritual Laws of Life** themselves!

4.4   Makutu

The definition and meaning from Williams' Dictionary reads thus:

> **1**. v.t. *Bewitch*.
> **2**. n. *Spell, incantation*.

The classic belief and reality of *makutu* for Maori (Italics mine) is the use of it to:

> "...place a curse, on a person rather than an object, *with the express intention of causing harm or death*."

*   *   *   *   *

Note:

> Much of the historically recorded information and anecdotal evidence contained in this section on *makutu* is sourced from Best's "Maori Religion and Mythology", Vol.2. Therefore, references to various relevant comments and examples will simply carry the name Best, and page number.

Contrary to certain viewpoints current in Maori academia regarding Best's large and crucial contribution to our understanding of the 'old Maori way', in this Work he *is* accepted as a relevant and valuable source of exactly that more ancient Maori knowledge and the practices thereof. Best was not a fool and, moreover, unlike his detractors in academia today, he was there – on the spot – recording as much as he could *before it was lost*! As we have already previously stressed, he would most certainly have been more fluent in the *reo* than many of the best in Maoridom today.

*   *   *   *   *

The practice of *makutu* can be described as being associated with the dark arts. Best terms this aspect of old Maori psychic activity 'black magic', as opposed to other acts under the umbrella of 'white magic' which the Maori did not view as *makutu*. Other terms such as *whaiwhai, maui, kanakana* and *kanakanaia* were also used. *Makutu* is the more generally known term in widespread use, so that is the term we will use. The early European writers viewed *makutu* as an agent for disciplinary purposes for the preservation of civil law and order, and was universally used in pre-European times. Ancient Maori society sanctioned the practice of *makutu* in certain cases as a necessary method of controlling socially disruptive elements, and the fear of being *makutu'd* no doubt helped to keep the same unruly in line.

The Maori belief that there were no boundaries between their natural and supernatural worlds provided fertile ground for the wonderful or the frightening to manifest, and this kept the fear of *makutu* alive within the race as a very real, potent and dangerous force. This all-pervading fear of *makutu* and the secrecy under which it could be used, thus allowed even the lowliest access to it. So, as an effective weapon of disablement, even the weakest could employ it. When used in secret, this element of uncertainty could cause great disquiet, not only for the intended victim but also among the populace in general. For who could know who was being targeted at any given time? Factually, then, with such an insidiously-powerful weapon at everyone's disposal, all Maori were victims of this practice even though it was readily acknowledged as evil; as coming from *Whiro* according to Maori beliefs. With such widespread use it could be expected that some would wish to use it more than was acceptable, even for the times.

According to Best – page 103:

> "...should a practiser of black magic become a public nuisance, a danger to the community, then he was liable to be put away, not tortured or subject to ordeals, but simply knocked on the head."

As an example of this summary justice, Best states, page 109, that:

> "The indiscriminate or irresponsible use of black magic was a serious danger and an extremely disturbing activity, hence such firebrands were sometimes put out of action by the community, as Ruru of Ngati-Tawhaki was shot at Ruatoki in 1865."

As he probably rightly concludes, this 'fear of *makutu*' no doubt resulted in the odd innocent person also being killed from time to time.

So whether these over-zealous *makutu-merchants* met their end by *patu* in the pre-European era, or by musket in more recent times at the hands of villagers tired and/or fearful of their activities, the fact that they were physically disposed of reveals an interesting side to the Maori thought processes. Given that it was so feared by all, one might accept that a simple collective warning from the community associated with a combined threat of *makutu* against the miscreant would have been sufficient to curb his activities. Perhaps, however, such individuals were shrewd enough to have discovered that only with the fear of a particular thing such as *makutu*, can one actually be subjugated by it and, by this discovery, rendered themselves immune to such threats of *makutu* from others. If so, the only disciplinary recourse left to the community was the sentence of death for the offender if they, in their continuing fear of such an individual and his practices, could not make the same recognition, thus remaining fearful of him.

In similar vein, from An Account of New Zealand (page 95-96) by the Rev. Mr Yates, Best observes that:

> "...the belief in *makutu* was the cause of much suffering, of many unjust acts. Thus the illness or death of a prominent person might be attributed to magic arts of some neighbouring folk, who would be attacked in order to equalise matters. Or some person or persons much disliked would be accused of bewitching people, and so be attacked and slain. He also notes that few of the professors of black magic attained old age, enraged natives or those who were supposed to have been bewitched attended to that matter. Such attributing of death to sorcerers, often of other clans or other tribes, was by no means uncommon, and such things were done long after the introduction of Christianity; a number of cases occurred in the 'sixties' and 'seventies' of last century."

The sorry situation of strife and killing stemming from imaginary wrongful *makutu* invariably resulted in:

> "...a sense of injury on both sides, an inter-tribal feud started that might be kept green down the changing generations and claim victims by the hundred".

Best further observes that the cause might be as trivial and innocuous as someone dying a natural death, *whanau* or friends suspecting witchcraft, and the calling in of a *matakite*, or seer, to ascertain the reason.

> '...his reply might be, "the cause of death lies in the south!" Enough said, an armed party would lift the war trail for the south, a village would be surrounded and rushed at dawn, or some workers or stragglers cut off and slain.'

(Best. Both quotes, p.115)

The Rev. T. G. Hammond, who spent a considerable amount of time among the Maori, recorded the following observation:

> "There are indications that the Taranaki tribes recognised in heathen days '*Makutu*' as a legitimate method of the execution of persons who had become obnoxious to the people, and were interfering with the peace and well-being of the tribe. The sentence was the result of the judicial decision of the leading men of the tribe."

(The Story of Aotearoa. Hammond, p 230)

The reference to deaths by *makutu* after the introduction of Christianity is of great interest in that it illustrates the incredibly strong hold of this evil over Maori, and provides a further foundation from which to examine the reasons why Maori could not easily leave it behind. Even today there are still Maori who practise this foolishness in the mistaken belief that *makutu* is some kind of powerful force that can be harnessed personally and used without redress or repercussions. There is certainly no doubt that it can be very harmful and destructive, but only against those who also similarly accept that it can be so. It can have no effect on anyone who refuses to be intimidated by such things.

The greatest danger associated with it actually lies in the outworking of **The Law of Reciprocal Action** – (*Sowing and Reaping*) whereby the *originator* must always accept the return of his personal *makutu* activity – even if directed against others. But, however, with much strengthened additional force to his deed under what I term the "whirlwind constant" in accordance with the **The Law of Spiritual Attraction**...

"We may sow the wind, but we will *always* reap the *whirlwind.*"

The lack of knowledge of the outworking of **Spiritual Law** means that the strengthened return of a 'makutu merchant's' *own dark activity* naturally sets him on a path of needing to discover **who** had sent the 'curse' his way. So his own wrong belief binds him to the delusion that *he* is being *makutu'd* by an enemy known or unknown, whilst in reality it was more a case of 'receiving his own'. In the Maori world, of course, a *makutu* from an outside source would be a real possibility, but only because the fear in the people *allowed it entry in the first place.*

The ingrained and abject fear within the Maori in the belief that *makutu* could cause death was sufficient for some to simply lose the will to live if they suspected, rightly or wrongly, that they had been so targeted. Having 'decided' thus and succumbed to *mate Maori* or *mate wairua* – the terms often used to denote any illness caused by *makutu* or similar – the 'victim' took no further part in life, took no sustenance and simply wasted away. In the final analysis, actually through a disease of the mind – fear.

In cases where *makutu* was openly employed, the old Maori held that it was necessary for the recipient to know that he was the object of attention for the curse to have the desired effect. This 'psychological acceptance' of the process strengthens our contention that the whole way of ancient Maori life was saturated by fear and not any true knowledge. Yet even just the *belief* that one was targeted could be sufficient to bring about a 'wasting away'. Fear and ignorance provide the perfect mechanism under which psychological self-destruction, in various guises, can wreak its insidious havoc.

Best notes that Dr Thompson, in his "Story of New Zealand", held that the cause of many deaths among the Maori in former times was as a result of the strong unreasoning belief that they were the victims of this practice. Of one ill Maori, Thompson wrote:

> "Instantly it flashed through his mind that he was cursed for doing what he ought not to have done, and that a spirit was feeding on his vitals; he refused food, and lay prostrate in a state of apathy. Bereft of hope, the great sustainer of life, and worn away by want of food and a disease of the imagination, he died."

Again, according to Best:

> "...the two most prolific causes of sickness and disease, in Maori belief, were magic and *hara*, the latter term denoting all acts offensive to the gods, all derelictions and transgressions connected with the potent quality of *tapu.*"

(Best. Both quotes, p 108)

Given the psychological fear of *makutu*, there can be no doubt that Maori who were believed to possess the power of it were able to destroy human life, simply because abject fear would kill the poor victims. For the hapless recipient, sometimes just a brief sentence was menacingly sufficient to cause the ebbing away of the life force, thus resulting in death.[5]

Various articles, over which the appropriate incantations or *karakia* were intoned, might be employed to effect this evil. The most potent was something from the body of the intended victim, such as hair or nail cuttings. If these could be obtained, and the 'target' made aware of this 'worst-case scenario' against his person, there was every chance that death would be the end result. Even the simple loss of hair or nail clippings could fill the 'owner' with great dread, for that could mean they might be used for *makutu* purposes. So very great care was taken to ensure that such things were destroyed or well hidden. And the old Maori – and even Maori of my childhood and youth – went to great lengths to hide them. A surprisingly large number of

---

[5]Such ideas were part of the thinking of other indigenous peoples in other countries, and the "pointing of the bone" in the psyche of the Australian Aborigine is an example that many are aware of.

Maori today still greatly fear the use of hair and nail clippings, particularly, and take what they deem to be the necessary precautions to prevent calamity. The practice of voodoo employs the same things.

In the absence of such potent material, even an article of clothing sent as a gift to the person so targeted could be sufficient to effect the intention. With his name uttered and thereby associated with the gift, which in turn was connected to the spell from out of the mouth and volition of the practitioner under the power of the relevant gods, there was little the victim could do except perhaps die. With this practice endemic in the race, a natural counter needed to be developed to nullify the potentially lethal effects of proffered gifts. So cleansing *karakia* was used to quietly, even surreptitiously, render the gift safe. It was imperative that this countering practice be carried out in secret since an obviously blatant cleansing ceremony would be regarded as a grievous insult against the *mana* of the person who proffered the gift. This could bring in its train more *makutu* – in the form of *utu.* The obvious problem here was that unless gifts were from close-knit clan it was circumspect to regard them all as possibly being 'charmed'. Unfortunately this sorry attitude of mutual distrust not only guaranteed more of the same insidious evil, it actually fed it.

Generally speaking the Maori, as a race, are an hospitable one and, for the most part, usually welcoming to all even if exhibiting a certain natural shyness at times. As with most peoples however, there are segments within Maoridom who are less than welcoming. Notwithstanding this trait of humankind in all groups, a general accompaniment to such welcomes in the Maori ethos is the provision of food for the guests.[6]

For, according to Best, hospitality was a natural attribute owing to the tribal way of life, and chiefs and high-born women who displayed this attribute were highly regarded. However, such was the penetrative power of *makutu* into virtually every aspect of the 'old way' that to not share food with visitors to the village might result in the villagers themselves being cursed for their selfishness.

Best, on page 104, describes the thinking thus:

> *"Ki te mea ka puta te manuhiri ki te kainga, a rokohanga mai e tai ana te tangata whenua, ka hohoro te karanga kia peka mai ki te kai me te hoatu kai e te iwi whenua ki te manuhiri, he mea hoki kei noho te manuhiri kei titiro ki te tangata whenua e kai ana, a ko ia e noho whakatiki ana, ka makuturia nga kai e te manuhiri, a ka mate te iwi whenua. Kia mohio hoki, ki te mea ka makuturia te tangata i a ia e kai ana ka tino mana ai te whaiwhaia."*

> ("Should a visitor come to a village and find the people thereof partaking of a meal, they would quickly call to him to turn aside, and would place food before him, lest the visitor should sit there looking at them eating while he was foodless, and lest the food should be bewitched by him and the people of the village perish. For you must know that if a person is bewitched while he is actually partaking of food, then the magic charm has special power to destroy.")

Doubtless this last comment because the food and the deadly curse enter the body together to wreak its havoc from the inside, obviously rendering it far more effective more quickly than that which would need to penetrate from the outside.[7] This method of destruction was known as *matakai.*

*   *   *   *   *

As an interesting historical/religious comparison, the Irish are generally regarded as having always been an hospitable people and very welcoming, even to strangers. Perhaps this inherent

---

[6]As a speculative question it would be interesting to determine whether this generosity had, as its possible early origins, the threat of *makutu* underlying it?

[7]Consider the usually greater efficacy of medicine when taken internally.

attitude stems from a long religious history spanning 1600 years when St. Patrick arrived to unite and civilise the wild tribes there and spread the message to "...love thy neighbour". The now natural 'generosity of spirit' that the Irish possess, which has long formed a defining characteristic of the race, has similarly long been a part of the culture. Even if individuals of that society may not personally incline to that ethos, this defining social aspect of the culture decrees that to be inhospitable is deemed to be almost 'the greatest sin'. Thus hospitality is regarded as a natural virtue of the Irish people.

*   *   *   *   *

If that attitude is compared to the old Maori in his world, with the fear of being *makutu'd* by a visitor if food was not offered to him, it can readily be seen that such considerations were based on psychic beliefs rather than any knowledge or natural acceptance of truly spiritual values such as that of 'welcoming kindness', which can be observed in the Irish attitude and example. Notwithstanding the fact that generosity was an admired trait, fear of potential *makutu* could result in hospitality being grudgingly offered, rather than with any real measure of welcoming acceptance or friendship. Perhaps we can tie this fear aspect toward a visitor and his potential *makutu* with the ingrained ethos of the *wero* – the challenge – whereby the question, "Who are you?", would at least be thought about – possibly fearfully – even if not asked openly. We can perhaps further project that notion to actually mean: *"What is your intention here?"*[8]

Ancient Maori belief required that, among Maori at least, it was necessary for the cursed person to be aware that *makutu* had been directed against him for it to be completely effective. However, any illness or setback could be deemed to have been caused by *makutu* even if the identity of the possible sender was unclear, or whether anyone had actually worked magic against the suffering one in the first place. On the other hand, *makutu* directed against Europeans had little effect, even with the knowledge that such 'magic' had been sent their way. The degree of *mana* determined the strength of such spells, and Maori believed that *mana* needed the support of his gods to imbue the *makutu* with the required power. Yet his 'magic' was clearly powerless against the *tauiwi* (white settler), who had 'different gods' to the Maori.

Thus Best reports the Rev. Taylor as recording:

> "...that attempts were made by natives to destroy European Missionaries at Otaki and Whanganui by means of magic in the early days but that the dread spells had not the intended effect."

In fact, as he further records, the *makutu* had the opposite effect in that:

> "...those spells seemed to react on the wizards who died themselves shortly after, which was attributed solely to their having failed in injuring the parties sought to be destroyed."

(Both quotes p.105)

The effect of the interconnected outworking of the **The Law of Reciprocal Action** and **The Law of Attraction of Similar Species** – *fully explained* in a later Chapter – can be readily identified in the above example. It clearly illustrates an especially strong 'volition of malevolence' on the part of the *tohunga* in the invoking of psychic forces to destroy life.

---

[8]Thankfully today, such considerations no longer hold sway at Maori gatherings, and participants are able to enjoy the event in a purely social manner without the mindless fear that one might not survive the next month through the simple and necessary requirement to eat. Even at large gatherings of diverse tribal or clan groupings today, and with ancient tribal enmities perhaps still 'officially unresolved', one can be deemed to be 'safe'. This kind of admirable 'progress' *away* from this aspect of tribalism, however, will need to be carried on to embrace the correct evolutionary path to single Nationhood!

*   *   *   *   *

In a very brief analysis of this process via the knowledge of **Spiritual Law** under the aegis of the *spiritual attribute* of 'individual free will' – in this case for the *tohunga*; having made the decision to 'send forth a *makutu*' to do his bidding, his curse, animated by the power of his *Spiritual Volition*, goes forth from him 'into the world'. However, the reciprocal effect of the process for the *tohunga* is such that, under **The Law of Attraction of Similar Species**, 'forms' *similar* to those he has called forth are attracted by, and attach themselves to, *his* curse. These 'additions' greatly strengthen the *tohunga's* 'original' volition, but more so the *makutu* itself. And since *he* is the originator or creator of this particular evil, the complete curse – *in its greatly enlarged 'form of malevolence'* – all belong to *him*.

It is connected to him since he, and he alone, brought it into being.

Now, regardless of whether or not it achieves the intended effect, under the outworking of **The Law of Reciprocal Action** – *Sowing and Reaping* – his *makutu* **must** return to him sooner or later. But, in necessary reinforcement here, *further strengthened by similar kinds of malevolence* attracted to 'his curse' in the course of its *complete journey out and back to him* under the precise outworking of that **Law of Spiritual Attraction....** What he will not know will be the time of its *return* – if he is 'aware' of the reality of a 'lawful return' in the first place. That particular *reaping* will be precisely determined by those same **Laws**, and may strike when the 'magician' least expects it.

In fact he may have no idea as to why misfortune might suddenly visit itself upon him but, in his superstitions and non-understanding of the effect of these inviolable **Spiritual Laws**, will probably conclude that someone has cursed *him*. His incorrect belief will probably set off another round of further, pointless *makutu*. Moreover, he cannot be freed from the curse 'he sent forth' until, or unless, *he personally* changes his volition with regard to such things. Then, in accordance with the outworking of **The Spiritual Laws**, such a change would thus automatically alter or modify the 'nature of the form' that he originally produced with his evil intent. The subsequent and eventual return of that 'better form' will naturally correspond with and similarly reflect an associated change of 'inner volition'.

This is a very good illustration of the lawful warning, Galatians 6:7, Fenton:

"What a man sows that Shall he reap!"

Whether written in a Pakeha Bible or any other place matters not one whit. The stark fact is that **it is written into "The Spiritual Laws of Creation"**. As recorded in Hosea, 8:7, Fenton, the mechanism of *how* the scriptural warning: "Sow the wind and reap the whirlwind" – *actually works* can also be readily understood from the above example of what really happens with every act of *makutu*. Or any act for that matter. We should understand, however, that for every *act* there must first arise the *thought*. So thoughts, too, are subject to the same procedure. But only with the knowledge of **The Spiritual Laws** are we able to know the full and complete, *inviolable process*.

One might conclude that the particular cases quoted were of a sufficiently virulent nature to guarantee a swift return to the 'owner' after having had no effect on the intended victim. It had to go somewhere of course, and its 'loaded return' to its 'owner' is the lawful outcome. He, ultimately, will always be the end target. As previously stated, moreover, the effect is the same whether good or evil is intended. That is precisely *why all* of the great Spiritual Teachers throughout history have constantly urged humankind to strive to do *only the good*.

*   *   *   *   *

In Maori 'psychic lore' insults were a medium whereby *makutu* could be used against another. However there was great danger in this practice as it was believed the recipient could 'catch the form' of the words directed against him, recite the appropriate spell over the captured word form, and return it to the originator thus visiting disaster upon him. In reality, only the fear of it could give rise to such a belief as the reciprocal and lawful 'return effect' would have directed it back to the sender eventually anyway, exactly according to the process we outlined in the previous paragraphs.

The old Maori also believed that *makutu* affected his *wairua* or spirit. Given his level of spiritual knowledge then – and with his particular designation of *Spirit* – this is perfectly understandable. However, the great fear induced by *makutu* would have affected the mind in a psychic way first. If the effect of *makutu* produced some form of hypnotic paralysis, or direct hypnosis had been employed, then this would certainly have immediately affected the spirit since **any** form of hypnosis is a 'binding' of the free will – and thus of the spirit of the individual concerned. Only in this way could *makutu* affect the free working of the spirit within any entity subject to this kind of 'coercion'.[9]

It is a paradox of the Maori race that, whilst accepting the fact that *makutu* was wrong and evil – that it was part of the contents of the so-called 'basket of evil' – there was never any attempt to abolish it. The fact that it was accepted as wrong is shown in the practice of generally teaching the arts of *makutu* in a place *away* from the 'sacred' schools of learning. Simply put, it is probable that it was too ingrained in the race for abolition of it to be easily achieved. In any case, how could this process be started, and what would it be replaced with? Whilst certain tiresome and over-enthusiastic practitioners were killed, the practice nevertheless provided a weapon that all could employ to varying degrees. So even such a recognised evil could be deemed to have had certain perversely beneficial uses. Nonetheless it *was* evil and no amount of rationalising the benefits of it could change that fact.

As a reinforcement of its evil purpose, we may note that in those particular schools of instruction:

> "The highest evidence of the skill of the pupil was to will the death of his teacher ... if your incantations did not kill your instructor you were not firm in the lessons you were given."

> (Making Peoples, Belich, p.106)

As previously noted, even today it is still employed by some in Maoridom who cling to the belief that this practice of invoking the assistance of the so-called 'gods' – or even long dead *tohunga* or ancestors for some dark purpose – represents some kind of personal power or *mana*. In these supposedly educated times of greater enlightenment, it is difficult to understand how such an obviously wrong, sinister and evil practice could be so distorted as to still be an acceptable method of seeking redress. For the Maori were not fools and certainly possessed a high level of intelligence, even if highly superstitious. Given these two facts, the only rational explanation for the retention of the practice, then and now, would be ego – for personal power in the first place – thereby inculcating fear in the victim. *Makutu* of old, therefore, seemingly offered the only acceptable or appropriate means to 'fight fire with fire'.

Whilst various aspects of *makutu* have been examined and the very basic workings of it explained from the standpoint of **Spiritual Law**, we need to know from whence it sprang. For *makutu* must have had its origin too! Yet we can be sure that such a debilitating activity was not placed here by **The Creator!**

---

[9]Hypnosis is *a serious transgression of Spiritual Law*, irrespective of the reason for which it may be used, even in medical situations or for crime resolution. More detailed information about it may be found in: ['**BIBLE "MYSTERIES" EXPLAINED** Understanding "Global Societal Collapse" From the "SCIENCE" in The Bible: What Every Scientist, Bible Scholar and Ordinary Man Needs to Know.'] Available at **www.publishme.co.nz**

Let us therefore compare the legends of the Maori with the truth from out of the only **True Law**.

To the ancient Maori, the female organ of procreation was synonymous with destructive power, for it was this organ of *Hine-nui-te-po* that ended the life of *Maui*. Perhaps the name accorded to the female principle, *Hine-nui-te-po*, also alludes to more than the earth mother. Perhaps it was the Maori way of attempting to describe the unseen and therefore the unknown of the female interior workings as well. What is unknown to the superstitious is also not understood. And without the benefit of Pakeha medical science in this case, what is both unknown and not understood by the superstitious mind is very likely to be feared.

The reality for the old Maori was the fact that man was delivered from out of woman into a hard world that offered only death at the end as an absolute certainty. Since *makutu* is concerned with death and the female principle, it has, as its home and power base, the dreaded realm of *Whiro*. He was a malevolent *atua* and the personification of evil and of darkness and death. From the creation stories of the Maori, we learn that a house called *Taiwhetuki* was erected in the underworld, in the place of the dead. This building was the property of *Tangaroa* and *Whiro*, and was the home of *makutu* and the black arts. It contained all the attendant knowledge and spells required to bring about the destruction of men, of fish, of the forest and its bird life, and even the destruction of demons. The *whare maire* of *Whiro*, the school that taught evil and destruction – of *makutu* – had the realm of the dead as its place of origin. From here this evil went out into the world of men, or could be actively sought by him there. Such is the Maori legend whereby evil entered the world.

*   *   *   *   *

Note:

That, however, is not the actual happening as now given to men under the knowledge of **The Spiritual Laws of Creation**. The complete processes are explained in the later Chapters: *"Whither Cometh the Maori – The Spiritual Origins of all Humankind"* – and: *"The Spiritual Laws and Principles"*.

When the Creative Command: **"Let There Be Light!"**, entered the emptiness of the void, The Power of **The Divine** inherent in **The Words** allowed the incomprehensible immensity of all the Realms of Creation to form. Since this forming came from out of **The Power of The Living Light Itself**, from where no evil or darkness could reside or emanate, the planes of Creation *could not*, therefore, contain evil either. And neither was this the case for incalculable millennia. The inhabitants of the different spheres lived in worlds that were blissfully ignorant of even the slightest conception of the meaning of evil, simply because it was unknown. It did not exist in those spheres.

It was not until *man* incarnated into the *material worlds* of Creation did this situation begin to change. Man, the human spirit, graciously endowed with the precious spiritual gift of free will, therewith possessed the ability to determine his destiny – and to thus *choose* between good and evil. So, from entering a world without evil, man, in his blindness and arrogance, chose that broad easy path. And it was not by any *literal* eating of the fruit of the 'tree of life' as depicted in Genesis of The Bible. That is a *symbolic* representation of the entry of evil, not a literal one.

For if that were the case and every single individual that has ever been born were contaminated with inherent evil from such a singular act then, quite logically, there is no such thing as **Perfect Spiritual Justice**. That would further logically mean that we are at the mercy of forces over which we have no control whatsoever, and that our life-paths were fated, ordained, without any way of altering any part of our life.

Therefore, in terms of just simple and unequivocal common-sense logic alone, such a belief is completely incorrect!

We possess free-will precisely *for* the purpose of *choosing between* debasement or ennoblement. We are *not* fatally flawed from birth and absolutely destined to follow an evil path because of a *seriously incorrect* misinterpretation by literal Christian fundamentalists. And that is clearly why we are strongly warned in the admonition:

> "I tell you indeed that you will not depart (ascend) until *you* have repaid (atoned for) the very last farthing."

> (Matthew 5:26, Parentheses mine.)

Through that free-will ability we are further enjoined, in Matthew 5:48, to:

> "...be perfect, as your Father in heaven is perfect."

That could not be the case if the belief of the original 'sinful-taint' label were spiritually correct. The above Biblical Scriptures clearly indicate that **we** must do the work, and not seek convenient and weak excuses for our shortcomings. There is no *maia* or *mana* in such weakness!

*   *   *   *   *

Now, from that necessary by-way, let us resume our journey. Thus the Maori, with his free will and associated ability to produce the forms of his rapidly darkening volition, gave birth and life to his demons, many of which he revered or feared as gods. They were gods of convenience in some cases, gods that would salve his conscience and sanction his savage activities. Entities and monstrous forms created by his lack of knowledge, undisciplined weaknesses and ego, and which still influence him today. Forms that he cannot even see and sometimes do not believe exist but which, nevertheless, have come into being through his ability to give life to them and thereby influence everything in his world and beyond it.

But the Maori were no exception in this regard. The same process that produced the base entities of all races also produced his. The once pristine pre-human New Zealand was then also *spiritually* pure. The endless tracts of thick luxuriant forests with their giant trees sheltering a wealth of bird and insect life, did not contain anything dark or evil. No dark forms could exist, for the first humans had yet to arrive to produce such entities by way of their dark volition. The great forests of *Tane* did, however, contain vast numbers of his helpers (the nature of which we will examine in a later Chapter) all fulfilling their appointed tasks in nurturing the forests and animal and bird life as ordained by **The Creative Will**.

Such was the beauty of this, as yet, un-named land. Then the fateful day of discovery arrived when probably Polynesian man first sighted the land and set his foot firmly on its untrammelled shores and natural perfection. For the perfect-serving *elemental inhabitants* of the forests and streams, this event represented the beginning of a long process of spiritual and material desecration by successive waves of settlers over hundreds of years. A short span in terms of the natural happening, but more than long enough to destroy so much natural beauty produced over millennia.

And with the original connections to **The Spiritual Realm** and the recognitions to his origins long since subjugated by humankind's propensity for more base and material things, what were once places of wonder and beauty – such as the great forests of natural life – now became home for the dark entities that he produced through his fear of the unknown. And so the Maori peopled the once pristine forests of Aotearoa with the thought forms of his wrongly-directed spiritual volition. Thus, in the deep pools of the rivers where fish swam and *elemental beings* attended to their duties, he added the form of the *taniwha*. For his practice of *makutu*, he produced, or invented, his departmental god of evil – *Whiro*, and also produced his *whare maire – Taiwhetuki*.

That is the process and the truth regarding these matters. All evil, and beings or gods of evil, are the production of the races to whom they belong, and only those peoples can destroy them. The question is, of course, do they wish to? Gods, monsters and evil beings produced by any race provide the framework for stories of great cultural import for they allow ancestors the possibility of undertaking heroic deeds that enhance the overall *mana* of the group. Such a belief also enables future descendants to bask in that reflected glory. All this, however, *does not advance the evolutionary spiritual path of that race by one iota.*

In the end only **The Absolute Truth**, stripped of all fictitious embellishments and impossibilities and radiating **The Power and Perfection of The Living Laws**, can stand the test of the light of day. Spiritual ascent, which was ordained for the human spirit from the very beginning, can only be travelled via that path of **Pure Truth**, thus also for Maori. Therefore, the concept and practice of *makutu*, in the belief that it might be a highly spiritual part of the people and their culture, has absolutely no affinity with the pure grace inherent in genuine **Spiritual Truth**!

4.5   Utu

Utu

1. In the form of a noun we note the meaning as; *Return* for anything; *satisfaction, ransom, reward, price, reply.*

2. As a verb; *Make response*, whether by way of payment, blow, or answer, etc..

(Williams's Dictionary, Seventh Edition, p.471)

Utu! This word, in its once fearful menace, rings down through the centuries of Maori settlement of Aotearoa to the present day. Today, however, even though still utilised in some quarters as a legitimate aspect of Maori 'tradition', it no longer carries the full vengeful impact that it once did in the exacting of payment in bygone days. Yet even in these far less war-like times – with those Maori who have not yet left these practices behind – *utu* is still regarded as a viable tool to repay some insult in an appropriate way, or as a response to *makutu* directed against them. For we still hear the cry, sometimes too often:

"There will be an *utu* for this!"

Whilst the word may mean all of the terms as stated in the above definition, in point of fact the whole thrust of much of pre-European Maori life, with regard to the 'living form' of *utu*, was revenge! Generations of Maori blood spilt in the name of honour or *mana* – or any other reason for that matter – clearly produced a particularly dark and evil form through long centuries of avenging slights and insults. Whether real or imagined, all nonetheless came into being under the reciprocal umbrella of this word *utu*! *Makutu* and *utu*, therefore, can be readily seen to be perfect 'partners in crime', so to speak. *Makutu* used as a counter-measure for the same *must necessarily* utilise the practice and the form of *utu* in order to reply or respond. In the response lies the intention of achieving satisfaction or payment. Thus *utu* has been achieved.

In the old Maori psychic world of threat and counter-threat in the practice of *makutu*, *utu* might well have been viewed as a relatively acceptable practice for that society. If, in the course of undertaking such practices, some deaths occur that are attributed to the power of *makutu*, that may be enough to satisfy both sides if the outcome of the exchanges are roughly equal. But given the war-like nature of the old Maori with his propensity for the *wero* as part of the very ethos of the race, his turbulent nature quick to bridle at any perceived insult, and the emphasis placed on the need to protect personal *mana* and to enlarge it through deeds of valour or conquest, a continued mild response to any kind of challenge was unthinkable. It was not enough to simply repay like with like to the same degree. Any need for revenge was invariably embarked upon with the expressed aim of annihilating the 'enemy'. So the practice of *makutu*, with its associated twin of *utu*, necessarily had to develop into repayment by war and blood as a natural progression of the thought processes of the Maori for that time. Therefore, from the thought-volition of *makutu* emerged the larger, more vengeful deed of *utu*!

Utu did not always need to be exacted immediately either. The Maori were quite at ease in waiting patiently for exactly the right moment for revenge. For example, when Te Heuheu finally gave up the siege to a Ngati Kahungunu *pa* in the Hawkes Bay district around 1820, he was taunted by the people of the *pa* for his grey head.[10]

Te Heuheu ignored this but waved his hand behind his back indicating that he would return at a later time to complete the task and avenge the jeers. True to his word, and no doubt nursing a strong resolve to right the insult, Te Heuheu returned a few years later and destroyed the Ngati Kahungunu pa "...with great slaughter."

(Maori Warfare, A.P. Vayda, p.44)

Notwithstanding the high level of conflict in Maori society, Belich, on page 76 of 'Making Peoples', observes that:

"Sustained and intensive conflict was a luxury they could rarely afford..."

Certainly, low population numbers and a high infant mortality rate do not offer a ready and regular replacement supply of *toa* to sustain continuous warfare for the *mana* that *utu* could generate. And there were various methods whereby such concerted and debilitating practices could be negated. If not permanently, then at least for a respite of varying duration through exchanges of:

"...gift visits, feasts and the great binding institution of intermarriage."

(Making Peoples, p.78)

Because of the old Maori love for war, and this must surely be evidenced by the large numbers of fighting *pa* scattered throughout Maoriland, perhaps the *reason* for *utu* eventually *became* the *excuse*. For a race that prides itself on its fighting skills, values deeds of valour and bravery above all else, extols such in the oral history of the people and institutes the concept of *mana* as its companion; such a race needs war. Without the ability and/or inclination to build huge monuments of engineering prowess, or the intellectual development to produce great libraries of major works of scientific or philosophical endeavour, what other avenues are open to a stone-age people under which they can establish their 'greatness'. Certainly the construction of the larger meeting houses and *waka* provided elements in which they could rightly claim *mana* under their social mores, as also in the working of stone, greenstone and in carving. It was unlikely, however, that the required but mundane pursuits of planting, harvesting, fishing and hunting could provide the necessary scope for the acquisition of *mana*. War could, however!

Because *utu* and war were so inseparable, the Maori were quick to find cause for either since the other generally followed quite naturally. Shortland, Protector of Aborigines in New Zealand and an early scholar, recorded that Maori's kept an account of all war-like transgressions for and against themselves, with the memory of unavenged slights handed down through the generations as an heirloom. Maori children learned at an early age the necessity for revenge. Vayda notes that:

---

[10]Perhaps the defenders equated grey hair with weakness.

"Shortland's Maori informants at Maketu gave him a debtor and creditor account of offences extending over eight generations. Since, as a rule, one group or the other would regard itself in arrears, the prospect of hostilities was usual among Maoris."

(Maori Warfare, Vayda, p.45)

Utu, therefore, was not solely about a mechanical or social means of seeking justice. Primarily, the *ethos of utu* ran far deeper than that – into the farthest recesses of the very psyche of the race. It was more about Maori beliefs in, and voluntary connections to, their unseen but much feared world of phantom shadows – the psychic realm which all could utilise to send forth harm and destruction. *Utu* was the means whereby any approaching harm, or even the perceived potential threat of it, could be redressed if necessary. Or at least contained by the general acceptance that reciprocal *utu* was available for all to use, and to a degree reasonably sufficient to ensure a more or less normal life under the dictates of Maori society. Since the twin curses of *makutu* and *utu* were the logical outworking and end-excrescence of *tapu* – and since *tapu* in turn protected *mana* – the whole, closed carousel-system provided the best means of acquiring this amorphous thing called *mana*. Like *mauri*, *mana* was similarly regarded as the essential life-blood in, and of, Maori society.

Clearly, if one trains constantly with weapons of war in the eventual expectation of it under an umbrella of mutual distrust as to neighbour's intentions in an atmosphere charged with the fear-ridden, psychic practices of *makutu*, the logical outcome of such tensions will be war and strife. For a warring race, this situation provides the perfect opportunity, for the most part, to test one's mettle against a similarly equipped and trained foe. And battle allows for personal and tribal *mana* to be greatly enhanced for the victors. To more clearly reveal these aspects, however, it is necessary to follow the war trail to discover the various methods of redressing *makutu* or exacting payment in *blood-utu* as we cite examples of old Maori attitudes toward war and the vanquished. An examination of his behaviour in warfare, from the standpoint of **The Spiritual Laws**, is our next goal.

In essence, as virtually all males were trained in the arts of war, the role of the race itself is thus assessed since the *toa*, the soldier-force, stood as the central core group necessary for the survival of the tribe and the race. So let us strive to ascertain where the old Maori stood on the scales of **Spiritual** balance once more.

*   *   *   *   *

As a brief, modern-day reference to this practice of *blood-utu* – for *utu* is a 'living' concept in meaning and actuality with different races naturally having different words to define it – we only need to observe the television news most evenings to see it in its working in stark relief, either in real time or instant replay. In many places in the world today this practice of *blood-utu* is played out for our daily consumption. At times between different ethnic groups, between the different factions of the same ethnic group, or between various political/religious factions as formerly in Northern Ireland, for example. The strongest, most vengeful form, however, is arguably that presently existing between American troops and Iraqi insurgents, and Iraqi religious factions against their own.

The Palestinians and the Israelis have waged a particularly brutal war of attrition in *utu*. For generations now both sides have exacted payment from each other in violent death, with seemingly no real end in sight. Even numerous peace initiatives and actual signed accords have done little to stem the pay-back killings. Sometimes they are carried out in assassinations by stealth. At other times by declared war, but each side with their preferred method, and each with the express intention of avenging previous killings.

With both sides seemingly so intractable, and each believing in the absolute right of their cause, how can such vengeful blood-letting ever be brought to a halt. The Israelis, of all people, should take cognisance of their religious teachings from **The Law**, that 'violence and oppression' are not the answer. For them, that should be the living reality, for "...violence begets further violence...". Of course, it would be problematic to simply *accept* continued acts of vengeance should the opposite side not discontinue them. Moreover, it is extremely difficult to protect against attackers who are quite prepared to accept the loss of their own lives to avenge their dead by becoming very powerful, walking bombs. Such a fanatical refinement of *utu* carries the practice to new and chilling depths; to much more than that which the old Maori once knew and sometimes carried out in the heat of battle in that often final act of fanatical desperation known as *whakamomori*.

In the many global examples of *utu* today, an interesting development also seems to be emerging in the Islamic world proper in that we may now be seeing such serious divergence of interpretation of Mohammed's teaching that the previously strong unity of Islam, once promoted as its strength and binding religious cohesion, may yet *seriously fracture*. The Christian religion went through the *same process*, and still is in the present. It is very likely that the religion of Islam will eventually tear itself apart, but from the inside and not from any external influence or threat. For in the final analysis, the extreme views of fundamentalists within have brought forth a form of *utu* that must surely be the final end-excrescence of that insidiously-evil practice – suicide bombings of not only their so-called 'sworn enemies' – **but even women and children of their own faith**.

For the Maori of today, however, this battle of *utu* between peoples on the far side of the world can perhaps be viewed as an open window on his own similar practices not far distant in time. We could opine that the Maori had the 'disadvantage' of superstitious ignorance under which the cessation of *blood-utu* could not so easily be brought to a halt. Not so for those Middle Eastern peoples, however. Locked into their war of attrition through their version of *blood-utu*, they have had thousands of years of association with the highest religious Law that had been given to humankind *up to recent times*. But even that is still not sufficient to stop continuing revenge killings today.

Therefore Maori should now be *grateful* for a time and a society that has no inherent affinity with such deadly activities. Should there ever be a return to the *utu* of old, *irrespective of the reason*, this would show that we of this *earthly Maori race* are incapable of rising to any form of true spiritual greatness. For, by that practice, we would once more regress to a level similar in principle to that which saw us devouring each other in the insane belief that it was a correct and wonderful thing to do. Only fools and madmen would contemplate such a thing.

Hopefully we may find the *maia* to face the irrefutable fact of our *utu*-ridden past, and to recognise it for what it actually was – *a debased and evil practice*. From this vital recognition we empower ourselves with both the means and wonderful potential to effectively utilise that factual historical past *as a positive and powerful springboard from which to learn and grow*. But also to forever leave it in the dark, savage past.

And via that necessary recognition, thus seek a more enlightened and genuinely *spiritual future* as revealed by the High guidance clearly given to the latter Maori Prophets – especially **Ratana**!

5

The War Trail

In terms of the generally accepted classical aims of war, i.e., the conquering and permanent occupation of territory, the Maori did not see this as his primary reason for purposeful conflict. Even though there were displaced tribes whose lands were occupied and re-settled, the main tribal boundaries, for the most part, remained relatively constant through centuries of inter-tribal warfare.

That being the case, and given the fear-riven state of the race, we can probably safely conclude that most wars were waged to avenge insults, to exact payment in *utu*. Engagements may also have been sought to acquire slaves. In any event battle in the cause of *utu* would have produced numbers of slaves for the victor. After the lust for war had been expended, the raiding parties invariably returned to the relative safety of their own tribal lands. Wars were also fought to protect traditional tribal food supplies against depletion by outsiders, and with few or no inter-tribal social mechanisms of law to commonly address contentious issues, war provided a means for settling such problems.

Now picture the preparations for war. The village is astir with excitement with the announcement that war is necessary. Perhaps it is a question of insult, or because of an attack on a related clan. Or perhaps the signs are propitious enough to avenge an ancient slight not yet resolved. Perhaps an act of cannibalism had been perpetrated on one with *mana*. Whatever the reason tribal honour is at stake and *kaha* is now required to resolve the problem. Any perceived weaknesses or lack of courage and backbone on the part of any tribe in old Aotearoa was tantamount to a declaration of tribal self-execution. So a reason has been found and the tribe prepares for war. If it is to be a major expedition, runners will have been sent to blood *hapu* and to various allies with a vested interest in joining battle. And adequate food supplies will have been made ready for the assembling expedition.

The obvious danger of leaving the tribal homelands relatively unprotected whilst the majority of the men take up the war trail will have been carefully analysed. Neighbouring tribes might possibly act as buffer zones of reasonable protection. For the young, first-time fighters, this is an intense period of both exhilaration and trepidation. Practice flourishes with the *taiaha*, and the thrust and slash of the *patu* and tomahawk take on a much more serious and deadly realism. All know that some of the young will not return. They will fall victim to more experienced and battle-hardened enemy. If battle has not been joined for some time, there will be a sense

105

of eager anticipation on the part of the more seasoned fighters to once more engage in combat. However, should total surprise not be achieved, some of the older warriors will also succumb. In the worst case scenario, where the enemy are aware of their intentions and lay a successful trap or ambush, there will be a great *tangi* for the many who will fall. And for those captured, there is slavery and/or the cooking fires to look forward to.

But all these possibilities are accepted as the norm and the war party have great confidence in their fighting ability and the *perceived justice* of their cause. After all, avenging any slight was viewed as a noble undertaking by the old Maori. As preparations reach a climax before departure, scouts might be sent ahead of the main party to gather intelligence on the enemy situation. A war chief would have been chosen and *tohunga* or *ariki* consulted to divine the possible outcome of the impending battle and perhaps advise on strategy. We can be sure that magic would also have been employed to assist the home-cause and dull the perceptive faculty of both the targeted tribe and their magicians. Various methods would have been utilised to effect this, and the appropriate propitiatory invocations made to the relevant gods for success in the venture.

If the party were to travel over water, similar *karakia* would be intoned over the fleet of *waka* with invocations made to Tangaroa, Maori god of the sea, for a smooth, safe passage. If it was to be a land trail, Tane might be requested to hide the approach of the men as they neared their objective. But now the *taua ngaki mate* was ready and appropriately stripped for the war trail. A final, blood-stirring and invigorating *haka* to bolster their courage accompanied by the loud wailing of the women, a quick farewell, and the expedition departs the relative safety of the tribal lands.

5.1   The Outcome of Battle and Treatment of the Vanquished

According to Maori battle tradition and that recorded by various early European writers, if possible the main aim of all war parties was to completely destroy the opposing group. This was rarely effected, however. In some battles before the arrival of European muskets, many hundreds were slain in hand to hand fighting using just traditional weapons, but this was probably the exception rather than the rule. According to Vayda, pursuit of the vanquished enemy was a vital part of the overall battle strategy. Not only did this 'mopping-up' operation greatly reduce the numbers of future potential 'problems' for the victors, but also allowed the pursuers to claim more warriors killed in relative personal safety. Fleeing enemy are usually less dangerous than unconquered foe fought face to face.

Vayda further observes that, for both the pursuer and the pursued, special charms known as *tapuwae* were used to give speed to the feet. The fastest of the chasing victors sped on through the ranks of the defeated men simply delivering an incapacitating blow to those they came upon, leaving them to be despatched by the slower warriors. Some of the more fleet of foot achieved great fame through their ability of pursuit. Such a person was Te Ihi, a Nga Puhi chief from Whangarei. According to a contemporary account from another Nga Puhi warrior, after the fight of Te Ika-aranga-nui in 1825:

> "...Te Ihi distinguished himself after the battle in the pursuit that extended for two miles right down to the Kaiwaka Creek. He disabled Ngati Whatua fugitives so that they could be finished off by the slower Nga Puhi pursuers..."

(Maori Warfare, Vayda, p 84)

We can safely assume that the *toa* of old would have been extremely fit. All movement could only have been undertaken by canoe or on foot, and this alone would have probably been enough to maintain a natural, high level of fitness and strength. Coupled with necessary weapons training during those dangerous times, and the fiery nature of the *haka* with *rakau maori* – their weapons of war – fitness levels would have been further elevated. For the *haka*, if intense enough, could keep the muscles of the participants in quivering tension for a length of time sufficient to add more strength.[1] And, indeed, there are recorded instances of warriors over 60 years of age still on the war trail.

For any kind of military adventure it is imperative that troops be as fit as possible. The very nature of the activity ensures that large amounts of energy can be expended in a very short space of time. Unfit troops will obviously succumb to exhaustion and reduced levels of alertness far more quickly than fit troops, with usually detrimental results for the unfit if all other parameters are fairly constant. So with the fitness levels of Maori *toa* probably being roughly equal, the pursuit phase of battle would be a test of each respective group's determination to live – if being chased, or to kill – if the pursuer.

Vayda, page 85, quotes Tregear as recording the following:

> "Another warrior celebrated for his fleetness of foot was Mohi Tawhai of Hokianga. He took part in Hongi's southern expedition and is said to have slain 150 fugitives in one day."

> "...fleeing warriors used to be so close together that a dozen of them would be knocked on the head in a short time."

At the battle of Moremo-nui around the Kaipara in about 1807 where Ngati Whatua ambushed and defeated Nga Puhi, S.P. Smith records that the pursuit was terminated by a chief of Ngati Whatua who, reportedly closely approaching the fleeing Nga Puhi, stopped and drew a line on the beach with his weapon, effectively preventing any further pursuit. According to Ngati Whatua, had this action not been taken all the Nga Puhi fighters would have been annihilated that day. Pokoia, war chief of the party was killed along with other noted chiefs of Nga Puhi. Accounts of total numbers in the war party vary from 300 to 500, and those killed ranging from 150 to 300. One report speaks of 170 heads being severed and stuck on poles, and the bodies eaten. (Vayda, p.89) It was this defeat that Hongi savagely avenged years later in retribution – in *utu*. Cook observed:

> "...to give quarter was no part of Maori military practice; the vanquished could save their lives only by flight."

According to Vayda, Maning's well-informed, *rangatira* friend regarded the pursuing phase of battle as the time of perhaps greatest slaughter. Taking these two considerations into account, deaths in war must have been quite considerable. However, reports of high battle mortality during the use of traditional weapons or *rakau maori* are not conclusive. But it certainly does suggest that the Maoris, contrary to what has been reported of some other primitive warriors, "...went right on killing after the initial shedding of blood." (Vayda.)

This is a most interesting insight and provides the best indication of the level of Maori spiritual development up to those turbulent times because of the fact that all other practices of traditional Maori customs found their fullest expression in the behaviour of the *toa* during warfare. The sage observation that "...warfare brings out the best and the worst in mjust a simple matter of defence, but always that of his incredibly dark form of *utu* that he often utilised as his reason for war. For the historical record clearly reveals that his brand of warfare produced a particularly savage code of behaviour generally lacking in mercy or compassion.

Yet, at times, Maori did show magnanimity toward the enemy, particularly if one was of chiefly rank. A chief might save the life of an individual by calling him to approach and join the chief's party whilst battle or pursuit was in progress. A foe thus 'called' was treated as an equal.

---

[1]Today we might call this process/effect isometric or isotonic in nature.

Such a move would not have been made without good reason, however. The desirability of later peace-making with the defeated party might prevent future retribution. Occasionally battle might be joined where both chiefs were loosely related. In such cases, Maori protocol demanded that it be desirable for the victorious chief to 'call' the vanquished one to his protection. A. P. Vayda, page 90, cites W.E. Gudgeon as observing that:

> "In such cases, the disgrace that would have fallen on both parties as the result of the capture of so high-ranking a kinsman was avoided."

For the most part, however, any enemy captured were either killed immediately or perhaps held prisoner for possible dispatch later, though some might be kept as slaves. W.E. Gudgeon recorded an old chief as stating that:

> "...among the oldtime Maoris the saving of an enemy's life was an action not even to be contemplated by a well balanced mind."

Similar words from another chief, Wiremu Tamihana Tarapipipi of Ngati Hau echo these sentiments:

> "...all the people found in captured *pa* were slain, whether men, or women and children, except such as were reserved to be slaves."

> (Maori Warfare, p.91)

In 'Maori Warfare', Vayda, page 91, records how Daniel Sheridan, a member of a whaling party near New Plymouth in the 1800s, described this Maori propensity for slaughter in a simple, matter-of-fact manner. After the battle of Puke-rangiora pa on 21st January 1832, the Waikato besiegers, chasing the fleeing Ati Awa:

> "...cut them down and made no effort to spare man, woman, or child."

Vayda, on page 92, records that whilst some of the Ati Awa were taken alive, Sheridan reports that these were slaughtered two days later.

> "The principal Waikato chief used a tomahawk to execute them one by one. After despatching about three hundred, he complained of his arms being tired and adjourned proceedings until the following morning. Young children, as well as grown lads were cut down the belly and then roasted on sticks before the fire. No mercy was shown."

The writings of early Europeans tend to support the view of old Maori that women and children were simply treated as enemy; to be killed. A dangerous time for them was when the able-bodied men were away on the war trail or on a food gathering expedition. An unprotected *pa* provided 'easy pickings' for a raiding party and such opportunities were rarely passed over.

> "Ngati Pukeko suffered such a massacre at the hands of the Ngati Whare and so did the Ngati Kuhungunu of Te Roto-a-Tara *pa* (Te Aute) at the hands of Ngati Paoa and Nga Puhi."

> (Vayda, page 92)

Whilst some of those early European writers chronicled the many savage aspects of the Maori, others were more fulsome in their praise. The key here is to *clearly* differentiate between the romantic view and the realistic one – the actuality – stripped of any personal, emotional input. At times though, some Europeans would reverse their opinions. Peter Bays, in his *"Narrative of the Wreck of the Minerva"*, saw the Maori as a:

"...filthy, bloodthirsty, savage race ... revengeful, unforgiving and ferocious..."

(New Zealand's Heritage, Vol.1, p.270)

Conversely, John Savage, in his *"Account of New Zealand"* considered them "...particularly kind and affectionate upon all occasions."

Samuel Marsden at one time saw them as: "...the finest and noblest race known to the civilized..." and later dismissed them as: "...a savage race, full of superstitions and wholly under the power and influence of the Prince of Darkness." (p.270)

Major Richard Cruise of the 84th Regt. Foot expressed the hope that his writings:

"...should assist in leading to the adoption of proper measures for extending the blessings of civilisation to a people eminently gifted with every natural endowment, and inhabiting one of the finest islands in the South Seas..."

(New Zealand's Heritage, Vol.1, p.271)

There is certainly no doubt that the Maori were highly intelligent. Yet, as previously stated, this fact only produces more puzzlement as to why he chose such a barbaric way of life. A graphic account of how Maori treated Maori after battle is recorded by White and reprinted in Vayda's excellent work: "Maori Warfare".

In 1850, an old chief told White about an expedition he went with in his younger days. Part of the account from White's Manuscript journal (Vayda, page 92) is quoted below, with translation (parenthesised) where the original is in Maori:

"...the party who took the *pa* stayed in it, keeping all the women they could, and killed all the men. The children under three years they cut their heads and arms off and cooked the trunk, taking the inside out and then beating it up to a pulp which, he said, was the best food to eat with *roi* (fern-root). The women they run sharp sticks through their feet to prevent their escape. A man *moe'd* (copulated with) any one of them and *ara kau ano i te aii* (the moment he rose from the act) killed her and stuck her up and *komo tia ana te anganga* (thrust the head) of any *tangata mate kite tapa* (dead person against her vagina) or the hand of any dead man... They ate the women when the men were eaten, and that after they had them to wife..."

From the standpoint of an historical report, the above incident, probably quite common in old Maori life, might be viewed as an interesting, albeit savage aside to the overall history of the Maori. But in real-life terms, these incidents reveal the true nature of the old Maori, *and should not simply be glossed over or dismissed in a light-hearted manner.*

*   *   *   *   *

Note:

In my serious view, every person of Maori extraction should strive to absorb the deeper meaning behind those kinds of [recorded] savagely-aspiritual incidents. For in the bloody history of mankind warfare has invariably had, as an accompaniment, a common casualty. And that is the women and children, who are generally non-combatant. It is in our crucial *spiritual* interest to endeavour to really understand the nature and behaviour of our ancestors. Why? Because, as stated previously, the *Spiritual* measure of a race can be gauged by their conduct in war.

The historical record of the old Maori clearly reveals that they did not attain to anything resembling genuine *Spiritual elevation* or nobleness in their conduct during inter-tribal warfare in early New Zealand. [A spiritually-elevated race will not embark upon war without good reason – but will most certainly vigorously defend the homeland.]

So we need to be courageous enough to accept the fact that the Maori race, which is ostensibly flaunted to the world and to ourselves as being a highly spiritual one was, in truth, a superstitious, fear-ridden, savage and vengeful race of cannibals generally lacking in any spark of compassion or mercy – particularly toward their own.

Moreover, until this fact is squarely faced and we cease putting on false airs about our imagined greatness and high level of spiritual purity and finally stop trying to fool ourselves – because we are certainly not fooling everyone in Aotearoa – we of Maori descent will find this wrong belief a barrier to *genuine* spiritual growth and confident maturity. True confidence, (as opposed to arrogance or an inferiority complex posing as arrogance), can only grow out of the virtue and quality of inner grace – *true mana* – that, in turn, can only develop from out of *genuine Spiritual knowledge*. The problems that beset us as a race are many and very self-evident, and we can easily itemise a long list for ourselves. So we have a long road to travel to *genuine Spiritual maturity* and it will not be easy, but at least we have the way shown to us. Moreover, we inherently possess the vital acceptance of 'other-world realities', particularly that of the **Elemental Forces of Nature**. Even though the complete understanding about them is lacking at the moment, the natural acceptance of this 'reality' offers the best and strongest opportunity to build a new and more correct Spiritual foundation for the future. As the very first step, however, we must face the past and accept the truth *that we were not a spiritual people then, nor are we today.*

*   *   *   *   *

From that very necessary digression, if one attempts to place oneself in the position of those pitiful prisoners of Maori *utu*, one might deduce that in such grievous circumstances the old Maori way of life inculcated an inherent attitude of dull acceptance or resignation to one's fate. Surely, however, there would have been the natural human traits of great fear within the midst of the captured, especially under a regime that constantly demanded retribution by death for every ridiculous and petty insult that men's foolish ego could invent.[2]

Now, though, what of the plight of our prisoners: For we have a highly charged situation where the 'defenders' were unable to protect their women and children and were subsequently killed. Watching over that remnant are a party of quite merciless and vengeful enemy who would be preparing fires for a cannibal feast. Amongst the last of the prisoners, the simultaneous killing and dismembering of children, and the rape and killing of their mothers would be taking place by this group of so-called 'warriors'. How should we relate to this happening, for do we not hear the heart-rending crying and wailing of the mothers and their children? Moreover, we must accept the sure probability that the women and their offspring were not separated to more 'humanely effect the slaughter'.

So we would have the harrowing situation where the children would see their mothers foot-staked, raped and killed. And the mothers, in turn, being forced to endure the pitiful sight of their offspring, the nurtured of their bodies, butchered and dismembered for food by very uncaring, unfeeling, physically strong men of their own race. A race who, had they followed the call of a *truly Spiritual way as they should have* – and as was ordained from the very beginning for all races – would never, indeed could never, have degenerated to such a low point of evil and

---

[2]One recalls the truth of the childhood counter to such similar behaviour in the little chant: "Sticks and stones will break my bones, but names will never hurt me!" Out of the mouths of babes ... great wisdom! Perhaps a small drop of similar wisdom replacing the concept of *utu* in old Maori times may have spared 'many in the race an unnecessary death'.

debased savagery. With such practices and fear rampant in everyday life, it is no wonder that the evil of *blood-utu* was so deeply entrenched in every aspect of Maori thinking.

*   *   *   *   *

The savagery of the old Maori was no different, of course, from that of any race which embarks on any orgy of blood-letting. Both stem from the same reason ultimately, a non-understanding or a rejection of that very thing which should be the primary goal of all humankind; the *higher Spiritual Values*. The Maori experience was perpetrated by Maori upon Maori under the ignorance and madness of the concept of *utu*. Not so with the European in their bloody history, however. Very recent historical events have seen many fellow-souls sacrificed to a similar idea of *utu*, with numbers running into millions, and it is still on-going. All this in supposedly enlightened races with a very long history of great religious teaching and traditions. For them, there is virtually no excuse.

*   *   *   *   *

To help clarify the reasoning behind Maori savagery in times of war, we have, in Vayda's book, a fulsome statement given to McDonnell by Toenga Pou, a Nga Puhi cannibal who accompanied my ancestor, Hongi Hika, on some of his raids.

> "You ask ... if it is not better to save the life of an enemy, when you have rendered him helpless, than to kill him? No, it is not better; neither is it wise. What is the use of getting a man down, if you are fighting with him during war time, or wounding him, unless you finish your work by killing him? Never, even, let him get up again; that would be wrong, and wasting all the advantage your strength and education had given to you, a wasteful expenditure of strength and *matauranga* (science), and a future source of trouble; think, too, of your cartridges wasted. For your enemy will not cease to remember that you once got him down (but refrained from killing him because it was not worth it) until he has either killed you; or somebody else, even if only remotely your relative. Then, as it will have been entirely your own fault, you will have to kill someone else in payment, and no end of trouble ensues. When you go to fish for *whapuku* (cod), and catch a big fish, you secure him and eat him, or give him to the tribe to eat; you do not let him go again, to laugh at you; that would be foolish. So always kill your enemy, if you once get him under, and make him fit for food. If ever you go to fight", continued old Pou, "fight for results; if not, stay at home and do not make a fool of yourself. Unless you are brave, and brave enough to let others know you are brave, you will be no better than a *tutua* (common fellow), and you will soon cease to live. Be really brave, then, so that you may remain long on the earth, and kill your enemies whenever and wherever you meet them. Be first, or they will kill you."

> (Maori Warfare, Vayda, p.90)

The above statement could almost be termed philosophical in its reasoning. The reference to fishing reveals an extremely simplistic view of why one should kill fellow humans, and in the willingness to want to kill them. One also reads into it the extent of the acceptance of *utu* as the most correct way to address wrongs and insults. The old Maori has often been portrayed as simply being a product of his time, moulded by his culture, his religion and by the land. With that simple dismissal we are not to question his nature or lifestyle, nor pass any kind of judgmental-analysis on his behaviour and activities lest we transgress the protocol of "cultural correctness".

Nevertheless, if we were to place a modern-day psychological label onto such an individual, perhaps we might describe him as possessing an over-sensitive perception of self, coupled with a heightened persecution complex. A high degree of introversion permits the possibility of generating moods of dangerous paranoia thus rendering the individual prone to bouts of extreme and unreasoning violence.

From the *Spiritual* point of view, we might state it much more simply and observe that such an individual was totally lacking in any of the higher virtues of love, kindness, compassion etc., as a result of completely subjugating the higher potential of the human spirit to the baseness of the concept of *utu* – with the ultimate earthly excrescence of that being the practice of cannibalism. In Toenga Pou's spiritually-sad, cold world of old Maoridom, even such a relatively benign concept of potential gratitude from a foe for the sparing of his life during battle appears to be non-existent in the psyche of the *toa*. All was reduced to the savagery of "kill or be killed" – even women and children. As stated in an earlier part of this Chapter, in the harsh world of the old Maori, without any concept of true mercy or compassion from a benevolent and similarly endowed *atua,* there could be no natural expression of such an 'alien' thing in everyday life.

Notwithstanding that assessment from the spiritual standpoint, Vayda notes McDonnell's appraisal of Toenga Pou as being:

> "...that he never met a more splendid specimen of an anti-Christian Maori;... a truly kind-hearted man in his own way, honest as the day, and truthful as one could wish, except in his tribal and private interests, where his efforts were magnificent."

(Maori Warfare, p.90-91)

Let us quickly revisit a particular attitude of conduct in war that the Maori possessed, and offer a comparative analysis of it. This attitude is well identified in the following observation (quoted earlier in this Chapter.)

> "But it certainly does suggest that the Maoris, *contrary to what has been reported of some other primitive warriors*, went right on killing after the initial shedding of blood."

(Maori Warfare, p.87, Italics mine.)

From the standpoint of **The Spiritual Laws**, the import of that attitude is vitally important to the overall analysis of Maori "spirituality", for we will now compare that particular behavioural aspect of Maori warfare with the attitude to inter-tribal warfare of a tribespeople of another land far from these shores.

*   *   *   *   *

In the emerging closer ties developing between the various ethnic or indigenous peoples internationally, there is a tendency to believe that a greater natural level of true spirituality exists in these groups and between them – by virtue of their believed closer connection with the natural world – than might be the case amongst the European groupings. Thus, in recent years, Maori have closely identified with the Aborigines of Australia and the Native American Indians. So much so that some Maori have been initiated into certain North American tribes and carry an Indian name. Moreover, there are regular exchanges of information concerning such things as healing, use of herbs, forest lore etc.; all of which are very valuable and certainly to be applauded.

Generally speaking, the International 'indigenous fraternity' would place most of its 'knowledge' under a common designation. It is one that invariably equates to being 'spiritual' knowledge. This knowledge is deemed to spring from the same source for all indigenous groups and purports to carry the same 'spiritual value'; the spirituality of the 'brown' races – of that of the *'brown brotherhood'*. In other words, the perception appears to be that this perceived or imagined level of spirituality must be, or is, of a standard commonality, and all elevated to the same ostensible 'high level' for each indigenous people; according to their own estimation. However, as the historical record clearly reveals, very few races or peoples are at exactly the same level of spiritual development. And this is equally true for the indigenous races also.

Moreover, between some groups there exist rather large differences with regard to certain practices when observed from the standpoint of Spiritual Law. Or, more correctly perhaps, the large differences were probably much more marked before the entry of the European into the lands of the New World. For, then, the various 'native' peoples developed solely according to their particular ethos and outlook, each subject to myriad essential considerations within their homeland and their personal view of the seen and unseen worlds surrounding them. They did not yet have a common modifying influence such as that which resulted from later European settlement among them.

The influence of the European into each of these environments was to eventually bring about a kind of stultifying sameness, broadly based on the pervading influences of *their* culture and religion. So any absolute comparison between the 'spiritual' levels of the Indigenous races today might be more difficult to assess accurately because of so much change wrought by this external European influence. Nevertheless, if we go back to just the 19th century even, at a time when the European had not completely destroyed the last vestiges of the 'old way' where the culture was still lived – and where inter-tribal warfare was conducted with traditional weapons – we are able to note these marked differences via the efforts of the earliest European chroniclers.

5.2 The Native Americans – [The "Plains Indians"] – A vast Difference

Let us now briefly compare the 'primary' and thus defining attitude of the Maori *toa* in inter-tribal warfare with that of the Plains Indian "braves" of North America. Both were considered a primitive people, regarded themselves as warrior races who prided themselves on their fighting skills, sang the deeds of their ancestors, sought the assistance of their gods in their endeavours and both sought glory in battle. So we have a few points in common to begin with and sufficient enough to make such a comparison. In this particular case we will mainly note the fighting code of the Plains Indians – the Teton or buffalo hunter Sioux and the Kiowa. Other tribes who shared the plains environment possessed basically similar codes of conduct also.

The great difference between the respective fighting environments of Maori and Plains Indian was generally that of open plains versus heavily forested land which, quite obviously, required a very different fighting method. As we have previously intimated, the nature of the land itself may have a bearing on the 'spiritual' development of a race. Thus, for the Plainsmen, the far-distant horizon during the day and the great vault of the star-studded night sky were his ever-present companions. Such a vast amphitheatre surely moulded the attitudes and perceptions of his spiritual views as to his place in the universe and the nature of the ruling deities. The Maori, by contrast, had dark, endless forests to contend with. There dwelt all manner of 'entities' that he believed could destroy him if he were not alert or fearless enough in his manner of neutralising or destroying them.

What the Plains Indians did have and were able to use to great effect was the horse. At that period in history – where European chroniclers were present – horses were also used in New Zealand but could not be as easily employed. In any case the methods of warfare were not the same and at this point the differences become more stark. Whilst both groups needed to take the lives of the enemy for their own protection at times, the attitude to close quarter engagement differed markedly. For the Maori, the engagement was a chance to not only kill as many of the adult fighting men as possible but also provided an opportunity to slaughter women and children who were regarded as potential future enemy, or bearers of them. And by this practice supposedly earn much *mana*. The more battles the Maori fighter survived and the greater the tally, the more sure it was that his deeds would be placed into the oral history of the tribe; to be sung and marvelled at by future generations. By this a measure of 'immortality' might be achieved. That was the "...way of the *toa*".

Whilst we may note some similar, savage practices amongst the Plains Indians to that which Maori regularly engaged in, we certainly do not see cannibalism and its associated dark energy. Our primary focus here, therefore, is on a vastly different kind of *primary attitude* to warfare.

In particular, we can starkly *contrast* the more savage activities of the *toa* with the incredibly courageous practice of 'counting coup' – the "...way of the braves". During battle, certain tribes of the North American Plains considered it far more chivalrous and noble to ride into the thick of the fighting and *touch* the person of the chosen foe rather than kill him. For this purpose braves might carry a 'coup stick' as part of their war regalia. This implement was carefully prepared and suitably decorated, and invocations for bravery in battle were said over it. Each 'coup' was recorded on it and was also duly recorded in tribal history. The higher the rank or fighting reputation of the foe so targeted, the greater the degree of bravery and daring required to effect such a 'coup' and the greater the glory attached to it. 'Counting coup' could also be effected with any weapon or even the hand, as long as the intention was not to kill but touch, thus demonstrating that a 'kill' *could* have taken place. 'Counting coup' on fallen enemy earned lesser honour.

The Time-Life series, "The Old West", provides an accurate insight into Plains Indian life and we are able to enter their world during times of such conflict.

> "But the scalping or even killing of an enemy was not the highest war honour among the Plains Indians. Bravery was shown by the scoring of coups – that is, by the touching or striking of an enemy with hand or weapon. Coups struck within an enemy camp ranked highest, and the bravest man was one who entered such a camp armed not with a lance or a bow and arrows, but with a tomahawk or whip. Better still, he might carry only a stick. But any heroic act in the face of the enemy counted – charging a defensive position alone, rescuing a wounded or unhorsed comrade, having a horse killed under one, being the first to locate an enemy or acting as a decoy in an ambush."

> (The Indians, Time-Life, p.101)

> "Probably the most fascinating insight into the warrior mentality was the act of touching a live or dead enemy...; To the Indian, contact with a live enemy was the supreme act of his existence as a man ... the man who counted coup most often and most daringly was the hero of the battle."

> (The Indians, Time-Life, p.205)

Whilst this practice may seem foolhardy and perhaps like a game, it was, nevertheless, a very serious matter. For what the Indian did possess as a very effective long-reach weapon was the bow and arrow. And it would have taken much courage to ride into a band of equally matched braves, single out an opponent, get close enough to touch his person with a short 'coup stick' and then ride back to one's own group. Even allowing for their incredible horsemanship, the possibility of being brought down by a pursuing enemy on horseback or by an enemy arrow was ever-present. It should not be supposed, moreover, that no one ever died during these engagements. Inter-tribal warfare produced death and wailing for the 'red man' as well as for the 'brown'. One can, however, readily see the vast difference in *attitude to killing* between the two groups.

From a purely pragmatic viewpoint, Military reasoning might well determine that ideas such as 'counting coup' are completely untenable as a practical consideration in any close-quarter engagement. Battles are not generally won by allowing fighting enemy to live if the outcome has not yet been decided.

Nevertheless, the attitude and behaviour depicted here stand as the greatest possible contrast between two groups of indigenous people, both labelled as savages at times, and noble savages at others, by various commentators of their respective histories. The obvious major differences in their respective conduct in times of war were; for the 'red man', no head-hunting and no cannibalism. And whilst both groups kept slaves, the Indian did not regard them as a 'food source'.

An interesting development has therefore emerged where some latter-day Maori regard their ancestors as possessing the same depth of spirituality as the Indian. A simple, comparative assessment quickly reveals that this was not the case, and certainly not with regard to the Plains Indians. To this end, perhaps we can offer a comparison in a brief mention of the 'soldier societies' unique to the Plains Indian tribes of the North American continent.

> "Their members were brought together through common battle experiences, and shared their own secrets and ceremonies. They policed not only the hunts, but also the large encampments and the camp moves. They were the *epitome of the warrior ethic*."

> (The Indians, p.104, Italics mine.)

Probably because of their prowess and fighting ability, chiefs of the soldier societies were also the war chiefs among the Cheyenne bands. In the Cheyenne tribe there were six such societies, apart from the 'Dog Soldiers'. And aside from differences in ceremonial dress, dances and songs, these fraternities were generally similar in their organisation and functions. In a major difference between the status and role of women in the two indigenous groups we are currently assessing, four of the soldier societies employed daughters of good families as maids of honour in their ceremonies, thus:

> "...giving them a role somewhere between mascot and patroness of their society and thereby honouring tribal ideals of womanhood."

This reveals a far more spiritual and magnanimous attitude toward women than that which the old Maori possessed. And to reinforce the fact that we are not dealing with 'weak warriors' here, let us read a little more about these fascinating and 'truly noble warriors'. On page 104 of 'The Indians', we read:

> "Among all the Plains Indians perhaps the most aristocratic and exclusive soldier society was one of the Kiowas" – the Kaitsenko (the Real Dogs, or Society of the Ten Bravest). They were pledged to lead charges and to fight in the van of every battle until they were victorious or perished. Of the 10 members, three wore sashes of red cloth; six wore red elkskin sashes, and the leader wore a broad black elkskin sash that trailed from his neck to the ground. In a fight to the end it was the leader's duty to pin himself to the ground with a ceremonial arrow through his sash, there to hold fast while the battle swirled around him, until victory – or, with all hope lost, he was unpinned by a fellow member of the society.
>
> Chief Sitting Bear, who wore the black elkskin sash at the great peace council of 1840, was still wearing it in 1870. "By that time his hair was fading to gray, but he was still erect and proud, and his people considered him the single bravest Kiowa alive."

In this interesting situation of the 'braves' versus the *toa* for our spiritual scales, the effect of the outworking of the *immutable driving power* of **The Spiritual Laws** on the respective attitudes and deeds of these two groups needs to be taken into account. For the fate of the individual after earthly death is determined by how a life is lived, with **The Spiritual Laws** producing the outcome in accordance with the individual life-path chosen. For the true warrior, only noble behaviour and deeds allows that corresponding part to ascend to its own particular place in the *Higher Spheres*. For the Maori *toa*, this would be highly unlikely given his particularly savage nature.

The reason why such huge differences existed between the *toa* and the 'braves' in their attitude to warfare may be read in their religions and belief-systems relating to their respective environments which, in turn, thus governed their attitude to neighbours. Whereas the Maori generally *feared* many aspects relating to his environment through his voluntary subjugation to negative forces of his own making, the Plains Indian, by contrast, *revered* his homeland.

His veneration for the land, which provided all goodness and life, was both nurtured and reflected by his love for his ruling and clearly benevolent deities. From that ennobled reverence sprang his own similarly ennobled constancy toward all things – even his enemies.[3]

Whilst we have used the example of the Plains Indian tribes in this case, we readily acknowledge that other North American tribes did not necessarily subscribe to the same degree of nobleness. Historically, many savage, inter-tribal battles were fought across the length and breadth of North America. And certain branches of the Sioux nation whose homelands were not the open plains engaged in more or less constant, fierce and bloody warfare with traditional enemies.

For example, the huge tribal territory that the "Sisseton" or North Sioux clan claimed, generally encompassed the regions around Lake Superior, Lake Winnipeg, the Red River etc., and the headwaters of the Mississippi. The same general area was also the home of the Ojibwa peoples. Territorial battles between these traditional enemies saw practices similar to those of the Maori – namely the killing of women and children and the taking of prisoners for slaves during attacks on respective encampments.

> (From: History of the Indian Tribes of the United States, Vol.2, p.151,
> Bureau of Indian Affairs, Henry R. Schoolcraft.
> Published by authority of Congress.)

Notwithstanding the fact that differing lifestyles may offer the primary reason for any individual group's particular behaviour, it still lies with each race to ennoble itself. Thus the defining difference between a supposedly primitive yet noble people and a stone-age ignoble one in this historical reality clearly lies in the hideous and totally aspiritual practice of cannibalism – the consuming of the flesh of other humans. Such a fundamental difference is vast indeed. Moreover, there is very obviously a huge spiritual gulf between seeking glory in battle by killing all and sundry – and devouring various body parts to perhaps avenge some small insult – and that of 'counting coup' on the bravest of the enemy, thus *not* seeking his death.

Whilst warfare could possibly legitimise killing to a certain degree, in general terms Native Americans did actually view the act of murder as one to be punished in kind. The 'lawful mechanism' for enacting that punishment was known as the *"Law of retaliation, or the private right to take life."*

> "Any one, two, or three, may revenge the death of a relative. Sometimes two or three are killed for one. A compromise is frequently made by the offending party giving large presents. Fleeing from justice sometimes saves the life of a murderer who may sometimes escape altogether and die a natural death. Other murderers are killed years after the offence; when they think all is forgotten, revenge is taken in a moment, and they are killed. In feuds arising from polygamy, if a death occurs, the relatives of the deceased almost always seek revenge."

> (History of Indian Tribes..., Vol.2, p.184-85)

Whilst American history unequivocally catalogues the shocking treatment of the Indian tribes by U.S. Army Cavalry operating under Government policy of the time, the journals of some Cavalry Officers who had extensive dealings with the Plains Indians during that turbulent period, reveal a deep respect for the nobleness and bearing of those tribespeople. Even the *official* annals of the Army concur to a large degree with such sentiments. Some of the chiefs, in particular, were held in very high regard. Unfortunately, that recognition was usually arrived

---

[3]The later Chapter on "Elemental Lore" both examines and elucidates this particular aspect.

at in hindsight. This belated view, however, may reveal an element of sombre 'reflection in comparison' on the part of the European soldier on the North American continent, in terms of the respective fighting attitude of his Indian 'foe'. For one was generally far more noble than the other.

That nobleness is well recorded by some of the early French missionaries in the following observations compiled by Henry Schoolcraft. The sub-heading, "Generic Traits of Mind" from Vol. 3, p 54-6, "History of Indian Tribes..." quantifies some of those opinions.

> "The scope of thought of the Indian tribes, when they stand forth to utter their sentiments and opinions in public, is more elevated and high-minded, and evinces more readiness of expression, than is generally found among the lower uneducated classes of civilised nations."
> During a long intercourse with various tribes, I have often been surprised by the noble style of their thoughts, and their capacity to rise above selfishness, and assume a high heroic attitude."

Pere le June, one of the earliest French missionaries observed:

> "I think the savages, in point of intellect, may be placed in a high rank... The powers of the mind operate with facility and effect... I have scarcely seen any person who has come from France to this country, who does not acknowledge that the savages have more intellect or capacity than most of our own peasantry."

The missionary Lafitau noted:

> "They are possessed of sound judgement, lively imagination, ready conception, and wonderful memory... They are high-minded and proud; possess a courage equal to every trial; an intrepid valour, and the most heroic constancy under torments; and an equanimity which neither misfortune nor reverses can shake."

Pere Jerome Lallemant wrote:

> "Many ... being prejudiced against them as barbarians, believing them to be barely human. But it is very wrong to judge them thus, for I can truly say that, in point of intellect, they are not at all inferior to the natives of Europe."

La Patheric noted that:

> "...when they talk in France of the Iroquois, they suppose them to be barbarians, always thirsting for human blood. This is a great error: ... the Iroquois are the proudest and most formidable people in North America, and at the same time, the most polite and sagacious."

Charlevoix adds:

> "The beauty of their imagination equals its vivacity, which appears in all their discourse: they are quick at repartee, and their harangues are full of shining passages, which would have been applauded at Rome or Athens. Their eloquence has a strength, nature, and pathos, which no art can give..."

The 'noble style' of Indian thought expressed in this segment is perhaps most ennobled in various, exceptionally powerful addresses on the environment. In particular, the address by Chief Seattle of the Duwamish tribe is rightly considered to be the definitive statement and most eloquent plea on the natural world ever uttered. It certainly is in my opinion. (His testament is offered in the later chapter on "Elemental Lore".)

Notwithstanding such glowing opinions about Native Americans from some French missionaries, other French nationals were brutally dismissive of them. Buffon and De Pauw, on a survey of Mexican and Peruvian history:

> "...pronounced the human species in America, together with the whole animal Creation on this continent, diminutive, despicable, and debased."

Such a pronouncement, in itself, clearly reveals debased thinking, for it is untenable to offer such a huge and sweeping generalisation of North American peoples on the basis of information gleaned from wholly different social structures of completely different cultures elsewhere on the continent. In any case, while the human species can certainly choose a debased or despicable lifestyle, animals can never inherently be debased. Moreover, as we have noted, the sentiments expressed by Buffon and De Pauw are diametrically opposed to other Europeans who had extensive dealings with Native Americans over a longer time-period.

5.3   Torture and Slavery

An obvious outcome of battle for the vanquished was the prospect of being taken prisoner and possibly experiencing torture and enslavement. As previously noted, the usual Maori practice in the treatment of prisoners was to kill them shortly after the victory. Except in cases where a captured enemy was particularly hated, or where grief-stricken relatives of warriors killed in battle vented their anger on captured prisoners, the Maori remarkably practised admirable restraint with regard to the torture of captured enemy. Remarkable, of course, because of the Maori propensity for revenge killing. The very concept of revenge or *utu* naturally presupposes the probability of vengeful attacks on defenceless prisoners. Although such acts were perpetrated, particularly during acts of 'blood vengeance', torture was not a commonplace occurrence amongst Maori according to the chroniclers of the time.

Killings were normally carried out in the quickest and most efficient manner, and this was usually effected with a *mere* or tomahawk. In fact, Cruise, in 1820:

> "...was struck by the humane manner in which people were executed by a blow on the head with a stone *mere*."

(Maori Warfare, p.93)

Where treachery was involved or perceived to have been so, thus resulting in the deaths of kinsmen, revenge visited upon any such enemy after later battles by members of the injured party was often brutal. In one such case, a Ngai Tahu chief, Tamaiharanui, accused of slaying the Ngati Toa chief Te Pehi via treachery, was later captured by Ngati Toa. Accounts differ as to his treatment but it is known that he was not killed cleanly, but tied up and tortured before death – a merciful release in the circumstances.

One version of this incident states that he was:

> "...fixed to a cross and his throat was cut by a widow of Te Pehi. It was also said that she drank some of the blood flowing from the wound, while her son tore out Tamaiharanui's eyes and swallowed them."

A second account from the son of an "..old whaler and trader who had seen Tamaiharanui as a prisoner..." records that he was:

> "...tied to a tree..." whereupon the ranking persons of Ngati Toa "...cut open his body at the navel and killed him by each taking a part of his entrails and pulling them out."

Whichever of these versions is correct, there is probably little doubt that the allegedly treacherous Tamaiharanui met a brutal end at the hands of equally vengeful Ngati Toa in *blood-utu*.

Whilst there were other reports of prisoners undergoing the unfortunate experience of having their veins slashed and their blood drunk, this was evidently not widespread and we can probably safely conclude that only a relatively few prisoners died in this manner. Such 'vampirism', as practised by some Maori when driven to great grief and anger, was described by Maning, Maori Warfare, (Vayda, p.93), as a:

> "...praiseworthy, glorious and public-spirited action... on the part of the captors."

To have such a practice described in so cavalier a manner reveals an almost blasé acceptance of killing by both the Maori and the early Europeans. For whilst inter-tribal warfare guaranteed killing on a regular basis before the arrival of the Pakeha, the slaughter of Maori by Maori increased markedly after his arrival, for *utu* could more easily be effected with European muskets than with *rakau maori.*

The widespread use of slaves in Pre-European Maori culture for essentially menial tasks obviously allowed their owners a certain measure of 'leisure time'. Chiefs and higher ranking members of the tribe owned more slaves than commoners. The taking of slaves resulted from inter-tribal warfare. However, not all prisoners captured were taken as slaves, and not all slaves were kept for work. The apportioning of prisoners for slaves, like all Maori activities in warfare, could be a savage and bloody affair, especially for the hapless one/s fought over. If there were many enemy, the victorious party would carefully select 'the best of the bunch', with the rest being consigned to an early death and/or the ovens.

Vayda records White's account of the fall of a *pa* in the following:

> White says that warriors might be seen disputing for a woman, girl or child, and the dispute would be ended when one of them would deal a heavy blow with his *mere* on the head of the already half-dead creature, who had been nearly torn limb from limb in the dispute, and, releasing his hold he would say, "Take our food now."

> (Maori Warfare, p.102)

Evidently, however, the sharing of prisoners was undertaken in an orderly manner. Sometimes prisoners were saved or a slave secured by a chief throwing a mat over one of the enemy. In this we have the practice of *tapu* whereby something associated with the person of the chief, or of his body, is brought into contact with the prisoner of his choice. A chief's daughter could also do the same to secure herself a slave. Polack describes one such incident where a man saved in this manner was the *sole surviving member* of his tribe.

"He had become first his deliverer's slave, then her husband."

This last example, that from all accounts was not so unusual, illustrates the curious divergent nature of the thought-processes of the old Maori.[4] For we have a situation where a victorious party has vanquished the enemy to the point of virtual annihilation. The status of the defeated is one of *taurekareka*, or slave. A man reduced to such a demeaning level in the eyes of Maori society would hardly seem fit to be the eventual husband of a victorious chief's daughter. For him to allow her to accept a slave as her husband with a consequential elevation in rank within the tribe would seem to be completely at variance with the general thrust of Maori thinking because of the deeply entrenched practice of utu. More especially in this particular example which surely demanded vengeance for any and every transgression against the tribe – under the very ethos of *utu*. Perhaps it was simply a case of magnanimity on the part of the chief.

Europeans were similarly saved at times. In an attack on Nga-Motu pa in 1832, Bill Bundy, a European in the "...wrong place at the wrong time...", who was about to be killed and eaten by a group of Maori, was saved by the daughter of their chief when she: "...rushed forward and cast her mat or mantle over him. Bundy soon after became her husband."

---

[4]We may well wonder whether such a trait is still not deeply entrenched today in matters of personal convenience, as opposed to matters of true principle at times.

(Maori Warfare, p.103)

The capture of prisoners for use as slaves was not the end of the matter. If the raiding party were some distance from the homelands, the obvious requirement was to return there without incident. Escapes were not uncommon by at least some of the prisoners even when tied together. One method employed was hands tied behind the backs and the use of ropes around the necks. When connected together it was a simple matter to lead the column along. Another method was to inter-weave cord into the hair of the prisoners and to lead them in that manner. This meant that their arms were free to carry the victor's spoils, including heads and human flesh.

*   *   *   *   *

Note:

Let us take a short digression here and closely examine this business of transporting human meat back to the homelands and/or for food along the way. As our story is directed to the Maori race in the first instance, and since many of us have worked in the abattoirs and/or freezing works at some time or other – there also being many very skilled Maori knife-hands working in the industry today – let us quietly reflect on our much-vaunted ancestors propensity for the flesh of his own kind and the obvious means by which he obtained it. If we transport ourselves back to those savage times and place ourselves in the position of our cannibal ancestors immediately after winning a battle, what we now need to do is utilise the industry of our newly acquired slaves to carry as much of the meat of our slain enemies as we can.

To this end we only require the best flesh, and *perhaps* without bone for that would only mean unnecessary weight. So we will probably first gut the selected corpses and remove and perhaps discard various parts such as the head, hands and feet. We will then need to 'bone-out' the rest of the body for the best 'meat'. We will not have the advantage of the modern well-tempered steel knives in use today. Knives which hold a razor-sharp edge, purposely forged and shaped for specific uses within the meat trade. No. We will more likely have to make do with a relatively bluntish tool such as a tomahawk which would require us to hack at the flesh rather than cleave it cleanly. If our little scenario were to take place after Pakeha arrival, we might be fortunate enough to have some of his steel knives or axes. So, in our world of desire for *utu* and human flesh, we are now ready to return home with meat of the vanquished safely packed into flax baskets on the backs of our new slaves.

This was the way of our ancestors. Where is any 'natural' peace and happiness here? Not a life of romance and continual singing and dancing, but one of *fear* and the madness of **killing for all the 'wrong' reasons**.[5]

So, in our story from the oft-times 'revered past', consider very carefully the anguish of the captured slaves – those who would be forced to observe the gutting, dismembering and 'boning-out' of their own immediate *whanau*. Or, worse, possibly being forced to carry out this gruesome and totally aspiritual task *themselves*. It is sickening to contemplate. Yet that is our heritage. Whilst we can be grateful for the few good things that we can identify in the 'total package', we must also have the courage to acknowledge the worst of it as well. If nothing else, these dark happenings, so prevalent in our race for so long, should serve to encourage us to completely expunge any lingering, romantic notions about 'the old way'. For it was solely the totally aspiritual and completely wrong attitudes and beliefs present in that particular lifestyle that permitted such evil practices to develop and flourish in the first place.

*   *   *   *   *

---

[5] Any Maori today who harbours notions that it was such a wonderful time with great spirituality, and that we should all return to something even *remotely* resembling 'the old way', **should seriously put himself 'back there' in this story of how it really was**, for he will find *that he is living in a world of his own deluded idiocy.*

Now let us return to our story.

Any prisoner discovered attempting to escape would be killed immediately, and doubtless became food. W. H. Skinner provides an interesting insight into Maori attitudes toward guarding prisoners in his account of the aftermath of a combined Nga Puhi and Ati Awa raid on the Taranaki pa of Tatara-i-maka in 1818. The victors secured their prisoners in couples by flax ropes around their necks, but despite these precautions, many escaped during the night. Vayda page 104, (after Skinner), records:

> "The Maori's failure to guard the prisoners more systematically is not unlike their failure to be more systematic about other lookout duties, and it again brings out the lack of discipline and organization in Maori warfare."[6]

Whilst prisoners who attempted to escape were invariably killed and eaten, sometimes some were killed and eaten for other reasons before the war party arrived home. Vayda quotes a report by Francis Hall, a Bay of Islands Missionary, who wrote in 1821:

> "We hear, that, among the slaves who were taken ... to Wyemattee (Waimate North) yesterday, one of them, a woman, becoming tired or lame, could not keep up with the rest: she was, in consequence, killed and eaten – *this being the custom in New Zealand!*"

> (Maori Warfare, p.104. Italics mine.)

How should we view this particular incident from the point of view of the woman's kinfolk? From any standpoint, it is surely best described as an abominable practice. The fact that it was so widespread and entrenched within the culture and a part of everyday life for Maori then, does not absolve it from the inevitable ramifications of inviolable Law. For the victim's *whanau*, however – some of whom would probably be in the same party of prisoners – there was not any belief about **The Justice of Spiritual Law** in those times. Aside from just more *utu* from kinfolk seeking revenge, lawful concepts of reciprocation *as we later outline*, would not have existed in the thought-processes governing the times. It would be difficult to imagine, however, that such an event would not produce *some kind* of inner reaction in the affected prisoners, no matter how much dull resignation to the, then, traditional ways such practices might have inculcated.

One also wonders whether the prisoners were offered flesh of members of their own *hapu* for their necessary sustenance at meal-times while with their captors on the journey to the victor's tribal lands? More interestingly, however, would be whether hunger or simple acceptance of this way of life would allow the captured to consume the flesh of kinfolk? Or would hunger have been stronger than a dread-sense of *tapu* in such cases?

If prisoners did accept the eating of slain relatives as being a necessary need but still a normal practice in accordance with the ethos of the time, we have a picture of the severest ramifications of the outworking of **The Eternal Laws**; in particular that of **The Law of Reciprocal Action** – or 'Sowing and Reaping'. Under **The Law of Attraction**... and **The Law of Rebirth**, too, one can readily envisage the potential for the same savage, tragic souls to be 'returned' to the Maori race during its long immersion-phase of cannibalism. The immutable outworking of **The Spiritual Laws**[7] could well have driven such reincarnations, particularly since the evil of *blood-utu* could probably never be completely sated for pre-European Maori.

This vengeful blood-lust can also be readily observed in the treatment of the captured when the war party finally returns home, for some prisoners were killed by widows and female relatives of slain toa. Vayda, on page 105, records Ellis, a Society Islands missionary who visited these shores in the early part of 1816 as stating that even young children took part in this time of revenge killing, seeming:

---

[6]In later Chapters we examine this trait of lack of discipline in certain other aspects of Maori life.

[7]The next Chapter [in **Part II – The Necessary Spiritual Foundation**] – gives detailed explanation of **The Spiritual Laws of Creation**.

"...to rejoice in stabbing captive children."

More understandably, perhaps, was the reaction of the womenfolk to the arrival of the prisoners. In 1821 Hall witnessed such a scene at the return of a Nga Puhi war party from the Thames area.

> "A small canoe, with the dead bodies, first approached the shore: the war canoe, and those taken in fight, about 40 in all, lay at short distance. Shortly after, a party of Young Men landed, to perform the war-dance and song usual on their return from fighting: they yelled, and jumped, and brandished their weapons, and threw up human heads in the air in a shocking manner; but this was but a prelude...
> An awful pause and silence ensued. At length the canoes moved slowly, and came in contact with the shore; when the widow of Tettee and other women rushed down upon the beach in a frenzy of rage, and beat in pieces the carved work at the head of the canoes with a pole: they then got into a canoe, and pulled out several prisoners-of-war into the water, and beat them to death: except one boy who swam away and got into another canoe. The frantic widow then proceeded to another canoe, and dragged out a woman-prisoner into the water, and beat out her brains with a club with which they pound fern root. We retired from this distressing scene..."

(Maori Warfare, p.105)

The observance by an early European visitor that it was a 'distressing scene' best encapsulates how it **really must have been**. The notions that European Society entertained about the romanticism of New Zealand Maoris from the South Seas as being 'noble savages' were clearly quite ridiculous. The whole way of life would have probably been 'distressing' by any standards. Indeed, it is difficult to imagine anything 'so distressing' and so totally uncertain than life as a Maori in old Aotearoa.

Given the level of savagery prevalent among the Maori, it is surprising that those slaves who survived the initial outburst of angry grief could go on to live a reasonably secure life among the people to whom they were now subservient. In carrying out lesser tasks for their new masters, their captors still wielded the power of life and death over them. A slave could be despatched and consigned to the ovens at his owner's whim. Moreover, an angry master might see fit to vent his rage on his slaves even to the point of killing one, irrespective of the cause of his anger. But not all suffered continual hardship, and many were eventually assimilated into the host tribe.

Whilst this could be the end result for some, the Maori regarded slavery as the worst possible thing to have happen to him. Such was the stigma attached to it that:

> "Even if a slave escaped and returned to his own people, the deep disgrace clung to him and also to his descendants."

(Maori Warfare, p.108)

This is a singularly curious attitude, and the aftermath of the raids gave rise to even stranger attitudinal responses between the captured and the non-captured of the same kin. The generally strong ties of the extended *whanau* meant that everyone could be counted on in times of collective need such as war or defence. However, the capture, removal and enslavement of kinfolk could necessitate the need for future *utu* against the enslavers, and therefore a war expedition on the behalf of those captured, but with a decidedly uncertain outcome. So regarding them as dead reduced the need for any further involvement.

Unfortunately, this response did not totally remove the strong emotional ties between kinfolk, a strong feature of Maori society, and this led to some unusual incidents of *blood-utu*. Vayda records a striking example of this by early European writers.

"Sometimes the slaves joined their masters in fighting against their own late tribesmen. For example, the Ngati Kahungunu, captured and enslaved by the Northern tribes in the nineteenth century, are said to have guided their captors against their own people, whom they then fought against with great ferocity. A Maori explanation of this behaviour is that the slaves were *getting revenge* for being captured."

(Maori Warfare, p.109. Italics mine.)

In other societies, this kind of 'behaviour' might be regarded as treason or treachery. The ancient Japanese code of Bushido, for example, regarded being captured as the greatest shame. Such stigma could only be fully remedied by committing *hara-kiri*, or ritual disembowelment, by one's own hand.

In pre-European times the lifestyle of Maori communities probably resulted in comparatively low numbers of slaves. This changed dramatically with the arrival of the Pakeha, however. Slaves were now needed to plant and harvest crops for trade with the Europeans in order to acquire guns and ammunition for further excursions to acquire more slaves. The slaves also supplied the raw material for the burgeoning trade in dried heads. Live 'goods' were often displayed 'on the hoof' for the 'customer', who then made his 'selection'. If a *moko* was required on a smooth face, it was duly carved onto the face before the 'goods' were 'prepared for delivery'. Some of the Maori 'warrior caste' also became pimps in supplying women for prostitution on board some ships. In return for services rendered they obtained Pakeha goods, particularly guns and ammunition.

The huge increase in slave traffic as a direct result of larger and larger war expeditions utilising the guns of the Pakeha, can be laid squarely at the feet of the vengeful 'Maori god' called *utu*. The designation of *utu* as a Maori god is obviously not 'politically or culturally correct'. However, the brutal havoc and totally unnecessary bloodshed wrought on behalf of this incredibly evil belief and institution almost warrants its own place alongside Whiro himself. Since the avowed aim and purpose of this book is to analyse so-called *Maori spirituality* from the standpoint of **The Spiritual Laws**, it is virtually impossible to find one single redeeming feature in the development of the concept of *utu*, especially to its worst end-excrescence as displayed in the continual demand *for more and more blood payment.*

This one single mechanism alone, this *utu*, was brought into being by the vanity and ego of the Maori in his voluntary connection to dark, psychic practices in his deluded belief that it was somehow the correct thing to do. It operated, moreover, under the terrible distortion of their word of power, *mana*. Thus the linking of *utu* with *mana* was primarily responsible for ongoing inter-tribal hate to flourish and find ever more victims to its mad concept. And before **The Atua of All The Worlds**, the Maori alone must bear full responsibility for its implementation.

The Maori wish to fully and wantonly embrace *utu*, without ever attempting to find another and better way, finally brought to him the practice of arguably the greatest *tapu* of all, and a severe transgression against all **Spiritual Law** under the Perfect outworking of **The Creative Will**; the eating of fellow Maori and fellow human beings – *cannibalism*.

5.4   Cannibalism – The 'How' and the 'Why'

In the overall thrust of our journey from extreme savagery to the emergence of the line of 'The Maori Prophets' and to a singularly-incredible *spiritual* task that the Maori race should and could have fulfilled last century – but most unfortunately did not – it is crucially important for all members of Maoridom today to fully understand *each major and defining step* of the Maori journey. For in the context of the role of *all* peoples on earth, this race *was* destined for very great spiritual things; then and into the future.

So in these concluding sub-Chapters of **Part I**, we need to understand *how* the 'Maori path' *of our ancestors* led to cannibalism. Far more telling, however, the further and con-comitant *primary reason* which finally fulfilled the end-excrescence of that hideous practice for ancient Maori – ultimately leading him *increasingly downwards* to '**Mana in Cannibalism**'! Thus the **How** and the **Why**!

Cannibalism has reared its aspiritual head in many cultures in the long and bloody march of the human race. Even the historical record in The Bible notes this activity among 'heathen' peoples in the 'holy land'. The practice of cannibalism can probably be placed into two main categories, religious or cultural beliefs, and the 'need' or wish to survive where, in extreme circumstances, it is the only food source available. There is a third category, but that is one marked by insanity in the individuals concerned, so is less common historically. Of the two major reasons stated here, and even allowing for the widespread abhorrence towards the practice, it *might* be considered acceptable to consume human flesh in instances such as have been recorded in even quite recent times. The Donner party trapped in the American Rockies during winter, whalers cast adrift for months, starvation during the Second World War among Japanese soldiers in the Pacific, among civilians during the siege of Stalingrad and a plane crash in the Andes are just a few examples.

In such cases, the perceived need to survive becomes the final justification for the act, *because everyone wants to live.*

> *The great fear of death coupled with the non-understanding of 'the death process'*
> *and aftermath will drive human beings in this material world to 'extreme lengths'*
> *to cling to life – at all costs.*

So that becomes the ultimate justification in human thinking; we must live – no matter what. In the case of the Andean plane crash, some Catholic Priests were reported to have given absolution to those subsequently rescued who had eaten human flesh. The final arbiter of all such activities, however, is not man. **The Spiritual Laws of Creation** hold sway in all things. And no priest can alter that inviolable and lawful fact. So there can never be any justification whatsoever for human beings to consume the flesh of another human being, not even the reason/excuse of starvation.

*   *   *   ,   *   *

As a final historical note on the subject: During the First Crusade to retake Jerusalem, an act of cannibalism took place that shocked the Christian world because the perpetrators were the so-called Christian 'knights' of Europe. The First Crusade was marked by killing and savagery on a scale that is difficult to comprehend today. The 'warrior knights' who took part in the three Crusades at the behest of the Popes of the time were thought to have the right amount of 'religious zeal'. In retrospect they might now be seen as descending into a kind of 'religious madness'. As we have previously stated, and will reinforce at relevant points in this Work, the mark of the *true warrior* is not that displayed by most of the Crusaders, and certainly not *their* degenerate act of cannibalism.

The interesting paradox about the whole Crusade episode was the fact that the so-called 'heathen' that European Christendom believed it had to destroy – the religion and followers of Islam – *would never have committed such an atrocity.* Not only were Muslims far more advanced than the Europeans in mathematics and all the sciences, but the true teaching of Islam, *as given by Mohammed for the Arab world then*, tended towards a more correct way of everyday life than that offered by the European Church's **terrible and appalling distortions and misinterpretations of the Words of Christ**. [The same remains to this day!]

Consequently, acts such as cannibalism and the wholesale slaughter of women and children were understood by all Muslims to be anathema to **The Holy Word**, and thus to **The Will of God**!

During World War II, the long winter siege of Stalingrad was noted for its particular level of violent, no quarter asked or given, savage attrition for both sides; the Russians and Germans. [Such was the ferocity of the fighting and the probably justified hate of the Russians towards them, out of a total number of around 600,000 troops of the German Sixth Army besieging Stalingrad, only 5,000 odd returned home to Germany from Russian captivity years after the end of the conflict.]

With the civilian population being reduced to almost starvation level, many instances of cannibalism occurred. The Soviet Army established special squads to locate individuals or groups engaged in the practice there and in other besieged cities. At a time when illness and severe weight loss was self-evident, cannibals, by contrast, revealed themselves by looking healthier and 'fleshed-out'. When noted, they were followed home. If human flesh was found there, as was invariably the case, the 'cannibals' were summarily executed – 'on the spot'.

*   *   *   *   *

Whilst we have now briefly noted the historical fact of cannibalism in many cultures throughout history, that is not our focus here. Our analysis of the 'Maori version' ultimately has a much more profound *spiritual purpose – for Maori*, and it is to that especial point we must journey.

That widespread practice prevalent among the old Maori could only have had its end-outcome as the direct result of aspiritual psychic beliefs and practices developed over many hundreds of years. Practices that took the race down an increasingly narrow and debased road to this final, degraded point. It was the culmination of so many *spiritually-incorrect ideas* about themselves and their direction. Even though there appears to have been the recognition of a Supreme Being, there was apparently no attempt to gravitate, as a race, toward the obvious virtues that such a Being would inherently encompass. Paradoxically, it was the priestly, chiefly, supposedly elevated, ruling elite that evidently held the belief in such a "Being". Instead of following an enlightened path, however, their propitiatory practices toward the so-called 'departmental gods' provided for all needs and reasons for every dark aspect within tribal life. Unfortunately, such fatally-flawed beliefs allowed the Maori to continue, and indeed foster, their downward spiral.

In the spiritual sense, fear and vanity could be described as the main factors that drove the Maori race down a path so savage as to end in cannibalism. Fear, out of ignorance of the workings within the natural world underpinned by a lack of knowledge of **The Spiritual Laws** in the first instance, produced an irrationality of reason as to give expression to all manner of superstitious beliefs and thought-created entities to which the Maori gave form. Forms that he thereafter feared. Forms of his own creating that never existed before *his* creation of them. And which, therefore, were never ever part of the *whenua* of Aotearoa before his arrival.

Because the old Maori did *not* understand this process, such forms and superstitions necessarily had to have appropriate gods to control them. Thus the *forms* of those gods were also produced. Whilst they probably provided a needed picture to explain his world and his place in it – in accordance with his limited grasp of the greater picture – they nevertheless allowed him to indulge his growing propensity for darker activities. Thus, over time, any god could simply be invented to provide a legitimate connection for any desired activity.

Fear marched the Maori further downward into the insidious, concomitant world of *tapu*. *Tapu*, with its myriad prohibitions, served its particular purpose in keeping a turbulent race in check. Consider what might have been, however, if the old Maori had developed along a different path into a more socially-lawful society where the tribes were united and where unruly elements could have been dealt with under a more expansive and open judicial system. Then he might not have followed the ultimate material path of *spiritual degradation* from just *tapu* in the beginning, all the way to cannibalism. For it was his ***step-by-step path into one dark thing after another*** that finally brought the Maori race to that point.

For the most part the institution of *tapu* as practised by the old Maori was based solely on irrational fear and superstition, and not on any kind of logical, analytical knowledge as might be gained from particular scientific concepts or from the higher perspective of **Spiritual Law**. The only exception to this might have been toward the various *rahui* placed on the husbanding of precious food supplies at certain times. This would probably have been more as a result of his observations of patterns in the natural world than from any absolute knowing of the how and why of it all. Even with this *exactly-correct* practice, however, we can be sure that *rahui* were not always totally free of superstitious connotations.

So *tapu*, in its generation of fear and uncertainty, helped to deeply-inculcate a mind-set that lacked the ability to rationally investigate reasons as to why it was needed in the first place. And also why no logical reasoning could be found to explain calamities that might strike a person or group through the effect of any *hara* – transgressed *tapu*. This *tapu-induced* fear, via its driving-force of spiritually-irrational superstition, further helped to co-incidentally advance the cause of the next step on the downward spiral; that of *makutu*.

Only a people steeped in abject fear of unseen, death-dealing calamities could wholly embrace a concept and practice such as *makutu* and thus produce the intended results of death to their victims. Particularly when a simple act of *spiritually-willed rejection* would have been sufficient to dispel or repel any such insidious, intrusive attempts to cause death or illness against their persons. In this regard Cowan *accurately* describes *makutu* as:

> "...a combination of three factors: projection of the will force, the malignant exercise of hypnotic influence, and sheer imagination and fright on the part of the person *makutu'd*."

> (Kimble Bent, p.328)

This very correct analysis perfectly describes this condition of unreasoning fear that accompanied the old Maori on his self-chosen path. Whilst *makutu* could probably be closely associated **more with fear than vanity**, we are, nevertheless, moving closer to those steps that were embarked upon **in vanity more than fear**!

The belief that one may have been the victim of *makutu* might result in one of two things. Firstly, it was a fear so great that there was no possible way to combat it – and therefore resignation as to the eventual outcome. Or, secondly, the desire to send something similar in return to the person or persons believed responsible. On its own, just the belief that one had been *makutu'd* was generally sufficient to turn suspicion about identity of perpetrator/s into acceptance of fact, thus resulting in the 'perceived need' to seek payment or revenge. Whilst *makutu* embraced the concept of attack or payback utilising psychic means, it did not, in itself, always achieve the desired aim. Yet it was deemed crucially important for *mana* to be protected absolutely.

Since both *tapu* and *makutu* were perceived to be perhaps too indecisive with regard to desired outcomes, another more direct and decisive method to protect the vanity inherent in personal or tribal *mana* from attack or insult was necessary. Thus *utu*, in its direct, physical-attack concept, became the mechanism whereby the other twin curses associated with *makutu* and *utu* – **that of fear and vanity** – could, all together, find their particular outlet of expression in *utu*, in accordance with Maori customary beliefs of the time.

Whilst *utu* could be applied in many different ways for varying purposes, the primary application appears to be that of revenge. So what might once have been a genuinely more benign application of the material use of the word perhaps underwent a constricting change, eventually becoming entrenched *with the fear aspect*, which then became *the main application*. To exact payment, more often than not with blood, became the main focus, the ethos, the way of life. And this was fed by the vanity and ego of Maori *mana* – to savagely repay all slights *however trivial*.

Ordinarily, of course, the concept of appropriate payment for a debt owed is, and would be, a right and just thing, so long as the payment or compensation reflected the true value of the original debt or transaction. By virtue of their fear-inducing connotations, however, such practices as *makutu* and *utu* could not ever be a benign practice. Thus, these twin curses, brought into being by the old Maori, forced him deeper and deeper down a path that was sliding further and further away from any connections with *genuine Spiritual knowledge and practices*.

With his continuing *spiritual* decline, and the subsequent and natural *narrowing of his spiritual horizons*, the world of the old Maori degenerated into one of *utu* demanding *utu* as the main focus. Whilst this may seem an unfair analysis, it should be clearly obvious to the reader that a practice such as *utu*, coupled with the war-like nature of the Maori who refused to accept any insult no matter how slight, could not possibly be kept within genteel bounds. The enmity between certain tribes that was also part and parcel of his way of life provided the perfect breeding ground for all manner of insults and transgressions real or imagined. This, in turn, allowed his vanity – masquerading as his great *mana* crying out for revenge – to lead him downwards to further debasement in continually demanding more **blood-utu**.

Quite logically, the more instances of *utu* that were exacted, the more there had to be in retribution. So we have a mad whirlpool of more and more *blood-utu*, with no possible end in sight. A spiritually, psychically and physically insane situation *that the Maori alone could not possibly hope to extricate himself from* without some kind of major and culturally-shattering event that would shake the very foundations of his view of himself and his *savage, narrow and constricted world*. Leading naturally on from that – because there was no *spiritually-induced effort* to halt the decline – came cannibalism!

It would be interesting to know the circumstances that brought about the first act/s of cannibalism within the Maori race. Was it brought from the old homeland, or did it develop in Aotearoa? Was it one of extreme anger where the slaying of an enemy was no longer sufficient to appease the rage of the one demanding retribution? And what might the reaction of the onlookers have been? Was it one of horror at this new development, or did they become caught up in the blood-lust of the moment, too, and accept it?

Tupaia, the Tahitian who accompanied Cook on his voyage of discovery to New Zealand, was evidently "...more disgusted by their practice of cannibalism than Cook." According to Belich, Making Peoples, p.20:

> "Tahitians had abandoned cannibalism centuries before."

Perhaps we can conclude, after all, that the ancestors of the Maori brought the practice with them. If true, why did it not die out here as it did in Tahiti and probably in most other Polynesian societies of the time as well? Because cannibalism must surely be described as the antithesis *of a truly spiritual way*, the obvious conclusion we are able to draw is that the abandonment of it by some Polynesian societies clearly represented a huge leap forward in terms of *spiritual growth* for them. Conversely, the *retention* of it by Maori to the refinement of ritual swallowing of eyes reveals quite the opposite; a continuing slide downward.

The respective environments may have played a defining role in the two positions. The open expanse of the ocean surrounding quite small Pacific islands may have allowed for an eventual expansion of the thought processes of the inhabitants to encompass a corresponding widening of perception into a more enlightened idea that there was something intrinsically wrong with the practice of cannibalism. Perhaps a similar idea to the open expanse of the North American Plains where, for those inhabitants, cannibalism was unlikely to have been a way of life at any time. This expansive mode might also allow for far less dependence upon psychic practices and may offer a corresponding awareness of the huge differences between human-generated psychic practices and the completely benevolent outworking of **The Elemental Forces of Nature**.

Thus for some of the Pacific peoples cannibalism eventually died out. The Maori, however, living in the constant shadow and presence of a vast and brooding primeval forest, possessed the perfect environment for the continuation and, indeed, the further development and refinement of his particular brand of psychic activities up to its final end-excrescence *before the arrival of the Pakeha*.

In the end it probably really does not matter how it may have begun. The fact is that once embarked upon there could be no turning back for the Maori. Given his voluntary subjugation to the darker forces of his psychic world, and the ingrained twin curses of *utu* and *makutu*, cannibalism was the next logical step for him. Therefore, regardless of all theories and opinions to the contrary, what is termed the traditional and cultural development of the Maori formed itself along *psychic* or occult lines, and not from any kind of *truly spiritual* life-path. So, without any meaningful change in that direction, it was inevitable that cannibalism would be retained – if it had been brought to these shores. If it had not, it was probably equally-inevitable that the developmental-process towards it would begin here in the manner we have postulated – from *tapu*, to *makutu*, to *utu*, to *blood-utu*, and finally: **To cannibalism!**

                    *   *   *   *   *

In principle, the insidious process that took the Maori to that step is the same that is repeated constantly in our so-called 'enlightened' society today. It is not likely that we will end up as cannibals, but exactly *the same process of spiritual degradation and debasement* can be readily observed by anyone with even the smallest amount of spiritual or moral fibre. It begins, *seemingly innocently enough*, with just an idea a little different or liberal from what is currently accepted – relative to the mores of society. If the 'new thought' should meet with disapproval by the more upstanding sections of the community, cries of rigidity and/or narrow-mindedness are usually levelled against them. If the idea is more radical, a debate may rage over its merits or otherwise, with perhaps a 'learned' panel of 'experts' determining its fitness for society. Invariably, so-called 'freedom of expression' reigns supreme. So what might very recently have been regarded with perhaps even abhorrence, is eventually accepted. It becomes the norm.

Thus, slowly and insidiously, we have seen **Spiritual Values** and morals eroded over the years. Those who originally protest against this erosion of values may eventually become accepting of the lower standards as it becomes part of a 'less constrained', more 'enlightened' society. Or they are swamped by the many who welcome the greater libertarianism, less restraint, less discipline and the associated cult of 'non-responsibility' and the 'my rights' mentality which society now almost nurtures.

Just as a child in old Aotearoa would not know of cannibalism unless exposed to it – and later accept the consumption of human flesh as normal – so the same principle applies for the young of our increasingly degenerate society who are naturally accepting of the mores of society, irrespective of what form they might take. What will it take to 'turn us around', we should wonder?

In point of fact, the outworking of **The Spiritual Laws** will finally do that, particularly **The Law of Reciprocal Action**. For **The Laws of Creation** *demand responsibility* for each and every thought and deed from every individual. And not one single person can escape that. Interestingly, and in a truly wonderful irony, the inviolable outworking of **The Spiritual Laws** will eventually return to us all our *utu*!

                    *   *   *   *   *

Now let us return to our subject matter. We have used the word vanity to describe this tragic attitude of *blood-utu* demanding *blood-utu*, for within the parameters of *vanity* also live *pride and arrogance*, perfect accompaniments for the next logical step downwards to cannibalism. Vanity, of itself, was not the sole egotistical form that helped drive the Maori in his blood-retaliation. No! We must look to his own 'word of power' that he so **spiritually-distorted** and misused. Both in form and meaning it was almost the perfect word under which vanity could wreak its havoc upon the Maori race as they underwent a severe spiritual decline. And that word is *mana*.

5.5   Mana in Cannibalism

Mana! A much vaunted word, yet almost the antithesis of that great word of true **Spiritual Power** that all of humankind should have seriously embraced from the outset – ***humility***! Yet *mana* is the word upon which Maori has built his own estimation of himself – even today. But where does this word and its meaning fit on the scales of *Spiritual Balance*? It is essential that it be examined because of its vitally important role in the affairs of the Maori, past and present. Williams' Dictionary (p.172) gives eight main meanings:

1. *Authority, control.*

2. *Influence, prestige, power.*

3. *Psychic force.*

4. *Effectual, binding, authoritative.*

5. *Having influence or power.*

6. *Vested with effective authority.*

7. *Be effectual, take effect.*

8. *Be avenged.*

Let us examine a few more meanings with regard to its various connections. Clearly *mana* can be applied to virtually *anything* for *its* ostensible *elevation in status*.

1. *mana atuatanga* pertaining to the gods.

2. *mana ariki* inherited by children of chiefs, especially the first-born.

3. *mana tapu* sacred power.

4. *mana ora* life-giving power.

5. *mana tangata* human *mana* acquired by leadership, skill, etc.

6. *mana whenua* pertaining to the land ie, – Earth Mother and progenitor of man.

7. *mana Maori* that which belongs to the Maori way of life.

8. *mana motuhake a te Maori* that *mana* which makes a Maori who he is, distinct from all other people.

Because of the very nature of the word, it is not so easy to clearly define as a singular entity. In Maori terms *mana* might be described as a supernatural force able to exist in a person, place, object or spirit. However it is more commonly understood as prestige, status or authority – although the status might be derived from possessing *mana* in the first place. *Mana* is also considered to be a dangerous power both to the possessor and to those who come into contact with it. Therefore certain ritual observances are necessary to prevent harm coming to a community or individual. By virtue of its perceived power, *mana*, as a 'supernatural' power, inherently carries with it certain problems. Thus, the 'power of *mana*' is deemed to be unfocused and dangerous unless it has some controls. The controlling and protecting system is the institution of *tapu*.

Notwithstanding the quite benign description above, it is patently clear that the word *mana* runs the full spectrum of meaning under which the Maori could sanction any activity as of right. All one needed as a reason or excuse was to cite the protection and/or maintenance of *mana*, personal or tribal. Under this all-sanctioning and all-forgiving umbrella, the Maori exercised his 'right by virtue of his *mana*' to undertake all that he wished to.

> Surely a better word was never invented for such sweeping, all-encompassing activity of one's personal choice. For this word, in its acceptance and application by Maori, actually dispenses with personal or group responsibility for many deeds that might be committed. Yet, under **Spiritual Law**, this can *never* be the case.

Therefore, under the aegis of that ultimate Law, and as is our contention, this 'word of power' was grossly misused to sanction all Maori activities, even the bloody ones. Albeit, however, through his non-understanding of **The Spiritual Laws of Creation** under which all words of man must reveal their *true form and expression*. So within the parameters of the multi-layered meaning of the word we have its concomitant twin of *vanity*, which can also find expression in *mana* when spiritually misused. In the same way, misused *mana* ultimately stems from, and finds expression in, *vanity*.

Thus, what should have been a great word of true spiritual power was degraded to ultimately sanction all that was wrong in the race. For the ultimate power is "Love", with "humility" being a high Spiritual Virtue of Love. It should be remembered, however, that humility is not the same as being weak and subservient.

If we were to now give more *Spiritual Power* to this word, *mana* – as I believe should have been the original intention – we would define its meaning thus:

> *mana* n. Denotes inner wisdom, grace and humility. – The quality of true spirituality that is acquired, *not* by birthright or rank or status, but that which must be earned through humility to have true Spiritual Value, and which therefore precedes wisdom, thus conferring grace.

And that should be the first meaning. After that, and distant from it, should *perhaps* come those relating to authority and control etc..

*   *   *   *   *

Special Note:

The first month of the year 2008 gave powerful expression to the *true meaning* of the word *mana* – *as we have redefined it*. The Nation and the world, unequivocally but perhaps unknowingly, embraced all aspects of that 'word redefinition' in the celebration of an iconic son of New Zealand – **Sir Edmund Hillary** – at his passing and State Funeral! If *humility, humble service to humanity*, and *humanity for others* are just *some* of the hallmarks of genuine *mana*, then he stood as a colossus before all in this country in epitomising the *true meaning* of the word, for he *lived* all those attributes.

His global stature of *true mana* was also clearly evident from the many decorations and awards presented to him by Royalty, universities and foreign governments in recognition of a lifetime of unselfish work for others. Sir Edmund should be recognised as singularly-possessing the *greatest* degree of *mana* – for he did not *consciously know* that he *truly possessed it*.

The defining year, 2008, also saw another son of this blessed land revealed as one with *true mana* – **Corporal Willie Apiata: VC!**

In his own words, 'a simple man' and 'soldier'; but one who has demonstrated all the attributes of 'true warriorship'. Like Sir Edmund, by the *spiritual power* inherent in *genuine humility*, Willie Apiata has similarly revealed that he, too, truly possesses the *spiritual virtue* of: **True Mana!** Given the iconic National status now thrust upon him, his professed wish to still want be just 'one of the boys' is probably no longer feasible. For this kind of 'mana' presupposes the necessary consideration of "Leadership within Maoridom", but on a very *different plane* to that idea or ideal we currently know as 'Maori leadership'. In other words, an *elevation* of the ideal, for it has been earned in the highest aspect of selfless service – carried out in extreme bravery in a defining act of **whakamomori**!

Had Lt. Ngarimu, **VC**, survived the war, would he have been permitted to simply live a quiet life? Probably not, for such men are needed for the *uplifting* of a people and Nation.

As a 'living recipient' of the **Victoria Cross** in a time and world where once-strong values have given way to far too many mindless acts of viciousness by gangs of cowardly youths possessing only a pack-mentality, **Corporal Apiata**, **VC**, will forever stand as the supreme example of **The Warrior-Soldier**. More particularly for foolish young Maori males who think that copying American gangster/rappers is somehow 'cool'. In our 'spiritually-weak' and generally gutless society – which too often *pampers* gutless cowards from this group – *Willie Apiata's example* is one for *all* young males of *all races here* to at least *strive* to emulate in some kind of *meaningful* and thus *non-superficial* existence. His kind of 'mana' must be held up by all 'straight-thinking New Zealanders' as exactly 'the right kind' for all to aspire to; *especially* for those who seek public office/leadership and who thus necessarily contribute to formulating societal law, such as it is.

On the international scene, one iconic figure stands out. A man of *true mana* is instantly recognisable in **Nelson Mandela**. His *ennobled degree* of mana is one that perhaps only a very few could *ever* hope to emulate. The legacy deriving from his vision and fight for freedom for his oppressed people *and the heavy price he paid for that dream* is self-evident in the well-deserved and ongoing kudos given him by the international community. Not simply that alone, however, but perhaps more in the recognition that at his eventual passing a *really noble human being* will leave a large tear in the relatively *small* cloth of *truly-ennobled* human endeavour globally.

With each of the above-named 'icons', also, the status of *genuine trust* inherently-holds a truly elevated yet perfectly natural position. For the virtue of trust is synonymous with *true mana*. So for New Zealand society generally; in terms of the question: "Who holds the position of most trusted individual of the past few years?" – to 2008; that honour resides with **Sir Edmund Hillary** and **Corporal Willie Apiata VC, [NZ SAS]**, respectively.

*   *   *   *   *

Now, how and where does the *concept of mana*, as it was applied by ancient Maori, fit into the practice of cannibalism.

Belich rightly observes that between individuals and between groups, rivalry for *mana* "...a deadly serious game, was played out at different intensity." (Making Peoples, p.81) In Maori thinking *mana* could be achieved and lost, as well as inherited. Essential for leadership was the necessary demonstration of competence to achieve *mana*.

> "But *mana* was actually achieved mainly in the minds of one's kin. One lost respect where it mattered most – among one's own community."

(Making Peoples, p.82)

And because it could be diminished or lost, it required protective devices, and the institution of *tapu* perfectly fulfilled that role.

Yet the Maori idea that human beings can be born with such a thing as *mana* is *spiritually impossible*. We are all born *naked*, nothing more. We do not emerge from the womb exuding or radiating great *mana*. We may perhaps be well-formed, perhaps not so well-formed, or perhaps terribly deformed, but that will be the end result of the outworking of **Spiritual Law** in accordance with our own previous decisions under those Laws. However, what we *are* born with, irrespective of our form, are the latent abilities of our Spirit which *inherently* grants us the *potential* to determine our individual life-path – in broad terms either for greatness, or for superficiality. Therefore we all possess the same *spiritual potential* to **earn** *mana*.

Mana is not found in the fist raised in unrighteous anger, in being the best drinker, the toughest in the pub, or in the use of the boot to maim. Neither, therefore, will we find it in Lion Red or D.B. Brown, in tobacco or dope smoke, or in the vapours of petrol and solvents – current activities in which too many Maori place too much store. And it will very obviously not be found in the manufacture or use or sale of P. It is precisely the huge loss of Spiritual Values and not knowing where to find them again that is the true underlying reason for these unhelpful and incredibly damaging practices that have produced such lamentable statistics in Maoridom today.

It is also a very deep and sub-conscious, pain-filled cry **for Spiritual help!**

As we strongly noted for the late Sir Edmund Hillary and recent Victoria Cross recipient, Willie Apiata: They who genuinely possess *true mana* – and there are few who actually do – will be unaware that they so possess it. For its main quality is that which we *re-defined*; **humility and grace**. Those twin spiritual attributes provide the strongest foundation and springboard for the *inner acquisition* of *true wisdom*. If we have the courage to face these truths, we logically empower ourselves with the ability to achieve humility and thus true power. *Mana* in this, its highest form, is then the natural gain for all.

We should therefore understand that:

> **It is not given for man to *confer mana* on himself and his works, but that the outworking of all Spiritual Law *allows* man to *earn mana* for himself and his works.**

The accepted meaning of *mana* for the old Maori meant that the exercise of it was actually a necessary part of his very life's purpose. For, in his estimation, without *mana* he was nothing of value, he had nothing of worth. Thus we have this quite incredible situation where the very word *mana* finally became synonymous with the need to avenge insults and deaths in order to maintain the credibility of the individual or group – by undertaking more slaughter in the pursuit of more and more *blood-utu*! Ultimately, however, even that was not enough! Personal *mana* was further elevated in Maori eyes by the practice of reducing enemy to the status of food in the belief that he completely destroyed all vestiges of him. In the ultimate excrescence of hypocrisy, he believed that he thereby gained greater *mana* through this deed. Thus cannibalism became a desired means of settling old scores and of achieving growth in stature and *mana*.

Cruise recorded that:

> "The limbs only of a man are eatable, while... the whole body of a female or child is considered delicious."

The flippant description from the journals of one Edward Markham of the process from killing to eating, must surely reflect the amount of cannibalism at the time, for it was clearly too commonplace to shock.

"...clip on the Pipkin ... so ends the life and begins the feast. They cut them up and slash down the legs, and take the bones out, wash the meat and roll it up like Beef Olives."

(New Zealand's Heritage. both p.271)

Yet cannibalism did not necessarily go hand-in-hand with the need to acquire *mana* in every instance, or to exact *utu* either. Not all such feasts were for this purpose, for it is unlikely that slaves killed for food would have provided any large degree of *mana* for the feasting ones. Best states that his informants told him the Maori ate human flesh because they liked it, and this would seem to be a perfectly logical conclusion given the widespread nature of the practice over such a long period of time.

*   *   *   *   *

The 100 YEARS AGO column in the N.Z. Herald of 5th June, 1998, chronicled the fascinating story of Mata Kukau, a woman of the Ngaitaka tribe of the South Island who died in 1898 at 105 years of age. Bartered away at age 16 to a sealer for a tomahawk and a small quantity of tobacco, she ultimately bore her 'husband' 12 children. A tribal war virtually annihilated her people but she escaped with a few others to a friendly *pa*. She witnessed many tribal battles and vividly remembered numerous *kaihungas* – the term used to denote cannibal-feast orgies. The particular article stated:

"On being questioned some time ago on the question of cannibalism, although reconciled to the idea that it was wrong for people to eat one another, she still maintained that human flesh was superior to any kind she had partaken of."

*   *   *   *   *

Notwithstanding that particular aspect of the overall practice, our contention still holds that cannibalism was a psychologically powerful way in which to demean one's enemies and gain prestige and was therefore the main driving force behind it. The fact that Maori came to like the taste of human flesh for its own sake does not alter our assertion. In fact, it might well strengthen it. Nevertheless, the high store set upon the acquisition of *mana* involving high-ranking or particularly hated enemy of note in certain ritual acts of cannibalism, most certainly would have helped to maintain an air of 'just righteousness' about the whole business. Ultimately, though, even the eating of enemy was not enough to satisfy the vengeful nature of the old Maori against his own, even though being eaten was virtually the greatest insult.

More was required to satisfy the *mana* of the victors in the degradation of the foe, even though they had ceased to exist in the physical sense and were now just part of the food intake. Still, that which could not be eaten, the bones and head etc., were defiled too, or perhaps utilised for his gain. In such cases the bones of the enemy could be used for various purposes and might find valuable employment in such items as flutes, fish-hooks, sewing needles etc..

Generally, though, the bones were broken up and burned in the cooking fires. Vayda quotes Best as citing a Maori account as to why the bones were burnt. This was:

"...to prevent the tribesmen of the slain from collecting the bones and depositing them in the sacred places of the tribe."

(Maori Warfare, Vayda, p.94)

However, from the same source we read:

"...the leg and arm bones were broken at one end before being eaten and that heated fern stalks were inserted in the bones in order to melt the marrow which was sucked and was a very good relish."

At times the bones were simply left scattered around as in the following report by the missionary Wilson in 1836 at the site of a cannibal feast by Te Waharoa's war party; – location not stated.

> "Here a bare skull, and there a rib or ribs with part of the spine: and around the ovens might be recognised any or every bone of the human frame... It was literally "a valley of bones" – bones of men still green with flesh hideous to look upon! Among these spectacles I was arrested by the ghastly appearance of a once human head. In mere derision it had been boiled, stripped of the skin and hair, and put on a post with a raw kumara stuck in its mouth."

> (Maori Warfare, p.94-95)

Vayda further records that in the case where a murder was avenged – though how one would accurately identify murder at a time of so much revenge killing is difficult to ascertain – the defilement of the bones of the alleged murderers and their descendants was standard practice. In particular, a great chief's body would be especially debased with his skin possibly being employed to cover supple-jack hoops, or later, cartridge boxes, with his eyes "...to be swallowed raw by a high chief related to the murdered person." (p.95) This is a perfect example of the strict protocols that the Maori rigidly observed in his perverse and obsessive pre-occupation in his need for continual retribution and *mana*.

Vayda states that my own ancestor, Hongi Hika, is credited with plucking out and swallowing human eyes for the very first time, according to records of that period. In tracing the downward path of the Maori, we can identify this act, perhaps previously considered *tapu* even, as one more step into darker things. Hongi was reported to have eaten the left eye "...of a great chief slain in battle at Hokianga...", and White recorded that:

> "Hongi ate the eyes of all of Paraoarahi's relatives in revenge for Koperu's murder, the murder on account of which Hongi began his war against the Waikato, Thames, and East Coast tribes."

> (Maori Warfare, p.95)

The vengeful nature of the old Maori and the complete lack of chivalry on the part of the 'warrior caste', coupled with a similar lack of the virtue of compassion which was so alien to him, is well described in an account of the treatment of the heads of detested enemy chiefs that were transported back to the tribal homelands after a successful campaign. Occasionally they were taken out, placed on show and taunted. Vayda, page 95, quotes Yate's, who joined the mission at the Bay of Islands in 1828, describing what he heard at one such incident.

> "...you wanted to run away, did you? but my *meri* overtook you: and after you were cooked, you were made food for my mouth. And where is your father? he is cooked: – and where is your brother? he is eaten: – and where is your wife? there she sits, a wife for me: – and where are your children? there they are, with loads on their backs, carrying food, as my slaves."

What consideration should we give to the feelings of the captured women who were forced to endure what must surely have been cold and perhaps brutal and degrading sexual intimacy with men who had cooked and eaten their husbands? Or would passive acceptance and a life of sorts, even a harsh and degraded one, still be preferable to the ovens?

With the increase in Maori warfare after the arrival of the Pakeha, and utilising his superior weapons for easier killing, the taking of heads increased considerably to becoming an item of trade. However, if the heads were to hold their state of preservation without rotting, there needed to be a suitable method whereby this could be achieved. Buck describes the process as follows:

"The Maori technique of preserving consisted of removing the eyes and tongue, extracting the brain by enlarging the *foramen magnum* at the base of the cranium, stretching and stitching the skin of the neck to a small supple-jack hoop, steaming the leaf-wrapped head in an earth oven and smoke drying it. That the method was effective is shown by the number in museums being still in a good state of preservation."

(Maori Warfare, p.96)

Cruise also observed the practice:

"When the head has been separated from the body, and the whole of the interior of it extracted, it is rolled up in leaves, and put into a kind of oven, made of heated stones laid in a hole in the ground, and covered over with earth. The temperature is very moderate, and the head is baked or steamed until all the moisture, which is frequently wiped away, has exuded, after which it is left in a current of air until perfectly dry. Some of these preserved heads were brought to England: the features, hair, and teeth were as perfect as in life; nor have they since shown any symptoms of decay."

(New Zealand's Heritage, p.271)

Head-hunting, of course, has been practised by numerous peoples over the ages. And the act of beheading certainly practised by most at some point in their history. At the time that Maori were 'selling' the heads of their own to the English, they – among others – had not long stopped the practice of placing heads on public display. History also notes the reign of terror of "Vlad the Impaler", a Romanian Prince who made a speciality of impaling heads on poles or gates or, indeed, on any public building with a protrusion suitable for the purpose. It is believed many thousands of his enemies were so displayed. Notwithstanding the European relish for severing heads, the unfortunate result of Maori heads acquiring an economic value was a substantial and related increase in warfare. Thus developed *the further madness* of more slaughter for more heads to trade for more guns to effect evermore slaughter to obtain more heads for more trade. Such was the voracity of this macabre trade that a live man's head could be sold and paid for before the necessary murder to obtain it. Similarly, chiefs had slaves tattooed and killed for the same purpose.

Prior to this development, however, heads were treated differently. Own chiefs who were slain in battle might be beheaded so that they could be returned home, brought out and wept over from time to time. More particularly if the homelands were a considerable distance away and the transport of whole bodies posed a problem. Apart from a few notable enemy heads that were kept, the rest were considered to have no value. Such disdain and disrespect on the part of the 'warriors' for the vanquished dead is reflected in this report by one who participated in an early northern expedition to Cook Strait.

"The heads of the slain chiefs were cut off and piled in a heap, and the head of the principal chief was placed on the top of that heap. Then we took other heads and threw them at the pile of heads. The one head on the top of the pile made a fine mark to throw at. This is an ancient game; it was practised by our ancestors, although stones were often used instead of human heads to throw at the pile of heads. We continued our game until all the heads were quite crushed. After we had finished our game the young men took those heads and burned them. They thought that burning those heads was fine sport... But we brought back the heads of *our* chiefs, even of those who died of sickness and in war, back to our homes."

(Maori Warfare, p.97)

In the section on *tapu* we considered the standpoint from which early Europeans and later academics attempted to describe these Maori practices without having the experience of being born into the race – thus feeling the effect of it from the 'inside' as it were. Quite clearly, any

attempt to adequately describe certain aspects of cannibalism, particularly the swallowing of
eyes in the final development of "*mana* in cannibalism", would be a very difficult proposition,
indeed, without personal experience of that kind of lifestyle. To arrive at a suitable description
even remotely equating to such practices would tax the literary skills of even the best writers.
For the very act of a ritual consumption of the eyes of a particular enemy can never be adequately
described, since the eyes must first be gouged out of their sockets in order to be eaten.

Moreover, we should consider the effect of this violation on a *living person*, with the owner
of bleeding and empty eye sockets in indescribable pain, as opposed to at least the painless state
of an inert, cooked body. And whilst the plucking out of the eyes was clearly a necessary and
logical requirement to the eating of them, and therefore not needing to be mentioned perhaps,
early accounts remain quite sterile and do not even begin to impart the horrendous, aspiritual
'feel' of the happening, even though some chroniclers were eye-witnesses to those events.

Consider the report of another cannibal meal with its unpalatable protocols. Here a chief,
defeated in battle, was forced by the dictates of Maori protocol to eat the cooked hand of his
own son killed in that particular fight. Under these iron-clad 'requirements', the hand of the
highest-ranking killed (the son) had to be offered by the victorious chief to the vanquished chief
of the defeated tribe with whom peace was now made. The probable anguish of that chief in
this situation becomes almost palpable. Even here, in this instance, the power of protocol in
tapu, or vice versa, reigns supreme. Perhaps in a strange and perverse way this might be viewed
as a tragic but dignified and noble act by 'noble savages', a protocol very difficult to understand
today.

Stated once more in reinforcement, in its pure form acts of cannibalism, along with all other
similar practices, were the absolute antithesis of anything Noble or Spiritual. As these two
words share a common high origin and ideal, they should not ever be used to describe what was
nothing less than barbarism and savagery. Of course, in the above example, the same inviolable
protocols demanded that *utu* would one day need to be exacted by the defeated chief for that
particularly singular insult too. The end result was the subsequent destruction of the formerly
winning group, and the further repayment of *utu* via the cannibal-feast ritual again. But this
time with the roles reversed. The Biblical Scripture that –

"...violence begets further violence..."

– certainly found its expression in the old Maori world of *utu* and cannibalism.

In the final analysis from the standpoint of **Spiritual Law**, these acts were more than
just simply meals of convenience from blood lust in war. The incantations and rites that may
have been conducted over certain acts of cannibalism by the often-feared *tohunga* or by a high-
ranking chief, would have produced a strong, pervasive *psychic cloud* over the whole proceedings,
complete with all the *accompanying forms of unseen evil* that would naturally be *attracted* to
such a scene. More particularly if *utu* and the taking of someone's *mana* were concerned. For
this kind of 'meal' was not solely a physical happening. The Maori well accepted the belief of
the continuation of the soul after earthly death and, in the world of his psychic fears, needed
to ensure that he was appropriately protected at all times. Especially so at events where the
possibility of attack by feared, unseen forces was greater than normal.

Therefore, this underlying psychic current was more the 'real and very tangible world' of the
Maori. All else, all the physical everyday activity in the forest, in the *pa*, the *kainga*, on the sea
etc., were simply necessary adjuncts to that stronger, more greatly feared, 'unseen world'. The
material aspect was necessary to sustain life, but nevertheless still subservient and subjugated
to the unspoken reality and fear of so-called 'supernatural' forces. It was therefore not at
all spiritual and benevolent in nature, but was actually psychic degradation and enslavement
emanating from a much lower, baser plane. The incredible irony of the old lifestyle was such that

whilst Maori sought his revenge in slaves and *blood-utu*, **he was enslaved to a far greater degree by the very activities that he actually believed gave him power**.

Ancient Maori were thus enslaved by the *spiritual misuse* of that 'word of power', *mana*. And, under **The Law of Attraction of Similar Species**, Maori voluntarily submitted to that base enslavement. We strongly contend once more that this 'insidious force' is not at all understood by the European academic nor by younger Maori generations either. For the new Maori 'cultural direction' today, strongly driven by academia and 'kaumatua leadership', *still wrongly believes* its ancestry to be all 'highly spiritual', and is unfortunately promoted amongst far too many of the young as exactly that.

*The whole issue, therefore, will need to be revisited and cleansed of all incorrect interpretations if the desire for long-term meaningful changes in Maori social statistics for the better is truly genuine – **for the foundation itself must change**.*

To do *that*, however, Maori must *first* acknowledge <u>The Truth</u> of the past.

5.6   Human Sacrifice

This particular practice has been part of the culture of a great many of the world's peoples at certain points in their development, and was an intrinsic part of the South Pacific cultures too. In the world of the old Maori, Best's Ngati-Porou sources identify a number of different purposes for which human sacrifice might be employed.

1. *For a new house.* A common custom around the old world, even in Europe just a few centuries ago. For the Maori, this practice was apparently not widespread and was reserved only for houses of great importance – if employed at all. In such cases, the victim was usually buried under the main supporting-post or foundation-stone as probably a propitiatory sacrifice to seek favour with the gods and ensure stability and durability of the building.

2. *For a new canoe.* Apparently, if human sacrifices were made in this case, they were only done so over the superior canoes, the *waka taua* or war-canoe. This ritual sought the protection of the appropriate gods and *taniwha* in any crisis at sea such as storms or capsize.[8]

3. *For the tattooing of a woman of rank.* This might be done for a woman of good family to impart prestige to the occasion and status to the young woman.

4. *For a funeral feast – also for prestige and status.* The chosen victim was cooked and eaten.[9]

5. *For the purpose of avenging a death.* This would usually entail the killing of a person from the targeted clan but where the victim was not necessarily connected to the deed. It was invariably carried out when a person had lost a relative via treachery, rather than in fair combat. This form of recompense was considered quite correct and justified. However, this appears to be more an act of *utu* than one of ritual sacrifice. Best also noted that, throughout Maoridom in general, sacrifices might be made for the piercing of the ears of a child of rank, in connection with war, for prophetic purposes, at a time of mourning, with agriculture, and with certain rituals performed over an infant.

---

[8]The supposed tradition of using human sacrifices as skids over which the canoe was launched was seemingly not widespread in New Zealand. In Fiji, however, slaves were often used as rollers for launching chief's canoes, after which the slaves were cooked and eaten. We should note that the Vikings were recorded as also using sacrifices as rollers to launch their longships.

[9]In the case of the death of a chief in other tribes, however, some of those killed were not eaten but quickly buried. The purpose of these particular sacrifices was to ensure that the chief had sufficient slaves in the next world, as befitted his status. Similarly, girls were sometimes sacrificed upon the deaths of the wives of some chiefs.

Whilst human sacrifice could never ever be accorded any actual spiritual kudos, its widespread practice throughout the ancient world ranks it as far more common than cannibalism, and is therefore only briefly mentioned here as part of our story. And whilst we have extolled the noble virtues of one group of North American Indians, (The Indians, Time Life, p.123), we should note that other tribes such as the Pawnee, might occasionally offer a human sacrifice of an enemy to their principal god, Tirawa:

> "...in the hope that the god would bestow good fortune on the band."

For such a specific purpose, the best 'offering' was a young, strong, enemy warrior who would be ritually killed by being first tied to a stake around which wood had been placed for the later 'consuming fire'. Once the fire was lit, the warrior who had taken the prisoner captive fired a 'sacred arrow' into his side. Then every male member of the tribe fired arrows into him, after which one chosen warrior pulled all the arrows from the body except the first sacred one. The same warrior might then cut the breast open, put his hand into the opening and smear blood over his face. The members of the band would count coup on the body, after which it was consumed by the fire. The rising smoke from the 'offering' to Tirawa was mixed with prayers to this god for good fortune and bounteous crops.

5.7   Conclusion

This segment of the Work examined various aspects of Pre-European Maori life and, as was the stated intention, the overall level of 'Maori spirituality' weighed on the scales of **Spiritual Balance**. Whilst *some things* could be regarded as being spiritually beneficial and uplifting, too many other beliefs and practices, too powerful for the superstitious and fear-ridden nature of the Maori to effectively resist, ultimately carried him down a path of spiritual degradation.

Even though the main thrust of this analysis will no doubt be deemed to be too critical by virtue of its focus on the mainly baser aspects of Maori life, there is little to be gained by concentrating on only the 'better' things if they are far fewer in number. For the good *will always be good* and should be retained and used as the foundation for growth in any case. It is the bad that must be left behind, even if, in hindsight, they are only incorrect beliefs. And there is just as little validity in believing that such an analysis is totally unnecessary today. From the spiritual standpoint, it is crucial to understand the ramifications of one's past. It is not enough, therefore, to just concentrate on the ostensible glory and *mana* of *whakapapa* solely – as is today's common practice – without also examining the deeper, fundamental aspects that the ancestors engaged in as a traditional lifestyle.

For if there are far more baser elements than good, then any analysis must surely reflect that if it is to be an honest appraisal. Unfortunately for those who may wish to see only the good, such an attitude does not allow the truth to emerge and to be squarely faced. For the fact of the matter is that the old Maori had spiritually fallen *almost as far as it is possible to do so on earth*. In terms of the need for all of humankind to acquire genuine Spiritual knowledge – particularly in these increasingly difficult latter times – it is vital to critically examine all aspects of the history of people so that we may recognise non-beneficial, residual elements that may still be present. And which will invariably be a hindrance to the acquisition of *true spiritual knowledge* and thus ascent. Overall, therefore, our scales reveal a severe spiritual imbalance in the beliefs and activities of our ancestors – the Maori of old.

This reality, however, **should not be cause for shame or reproach**.

Rather, the facts of our past should be used as a very powerful foundation upon which to rise to true and genuine spirituality, simply because it is not far removed in time from the present generation, and very much progress has been made thus far already. With the desire for greater 'spiritual identity' an obvious yearning amongst many of Maori descent today, we firstly need to re-examine ourselves critically, expunge all that is clearly wrong, and simply follow the natural spiritual urgings as outlined under **The Spiritual Laws of Creation** which we now have. With the acceptance of these *inviolable Laws* to guide us forward, the end result cannot be anything other than an harmonious future.

It should be carefully noted once more that the progression of the *inter-linked aspects* of *tapu, makutu* and *utu* finally found their fullest and debased expression in cannibalism. In fact, in "*mana* in cannibalism"! If *tapu* had been applied *only to inanimate objects* or for husbanding food supplies, then it is very difficult to envision the next steps into *makutu* and *utu* via the path we have outlined.

> *For only with the placing of a tapu status onto <u>people</u>* – particularly persons
> of rank – could the whole insidious, insane process then begin.

Personal *tapu* actually equates to *personal, egotistical vanity* under the cunning umbrella of *protective mana*, thus locking into place the believed need to severely deal with any slights against one's person and, therefore, concomitantly against one's personal *mana*.

Those beliefs gave birth to their associated practices, of which the final end-excrescence was *utu – blood-utu*. That practice effectively destroyed any possibility of any kind of *true* spiritual development for that time. In fact, because of its virulent, aspiritual nature, it was actually leading the Maori race to *spiritual destruction*!

> It was a downwards-trend only arrested *by the arrival of the Pakeha and his religion*,
> through which arose the line of Maori Prophets to lead the race out of the old 'aspiritual
> way', in both thinking and in deed!

Thus, as previously and strongly stated; in the strangest of ironies, the old Maori did not ever seem to understand that his practice of cannibalism – the consuming of the flesh of another human being – constituted a violation of *one of the greatest tapu of all*. A *tapu* that was a serious transgression against the very **Spiritual Laws** that permitted him the gift of conscious life itself.

It therefore behoves every person of Maori descent today to find the *kaha* and genuine *mana* to *personally challenge himself* with regard to his view of the 'old way of the ancestors'. And to also *personally challenge himself* as to his understanding of the stark differences between the psychic, superstitious, or occult level synonymous with 'the old way', the **Elemental** level inherent in the **The Forces of Nature**, and the genuinely **Spiritual** level. Those differences, which we offer logical explanations for in both the physical sense but, more importantly in the context of our subject matter, also in the **Spiritual** sense, are clearly and adequately explained in this Work. It should not require much mental exertion, therefore, to *honestly* determine on which level *each Maori belief and practice actually stood* **then** – and *where it stands* **now**!

By so doing, Maori today can emulate the supreme example forever set in place by Ratana. Ratana – the Mangai of God for Maori – the first to *really break the mould* and clearly *recognise the errors of the past and to lead away from them*. That is the *true* Spiritual way forward.

It is not through the emotional retention of traditional beliefs steeped in aspiritual hindrances!

Part II

The Necessary Spiritual Foundation

6

The Spiritual Laws and Principles

Oh the Ancient Truth!
Ages upon ages past it was found,
And it bound together a Noble Brotherhood.
The Ancient Truth!
Hold fast to it!

(Goethe.)

Without Revelation a Nation fades.
But it prospers **by knowing the Law***!*

(Proverbs 29:18)

It is most important that this Chapter be regarded as the *key link* to all the others, as the crucial knowledge of The Spiritual Laws is imperative for the *complete understanding* of the aim and purpose of this Work. And that is, **to know The Law** – as stated above. It will also allow the 'white thread' of Ngapuhi prophecy to emerge from out of the following pages. You, the reader, should therefore strive to seriously understand the explanations that interlink the different Laws. For the Maori reader, especially, without this understanding *here*, the *later revelation* of the spiritual purpose of the Maori race – which was not fulfilled at the time – *will be lost there too.*

The previous three Chapters, though hard-hitting and essentially concerned with the ancient and historical *aspiritual practices* of the Maori, clearly revealed little of any genuine knowledge in Maoridom of the true **Spiritual Laws of Creation**. Neither could they, for the new knowledge for all men contained within them *was reserved for this present time to be revealed.*

That fact, however, does not excuse any aspiritual practice anywhere for any reason. Because the old way *was* so savage, and because the official 'Maori-protocol standpoint' of so-called *tikanga* and cultural tradition is so zealously protected by Maori academic and political interests today, it is important for Maori, particularly, **to finally know** that the constant reference within these pages to the true Spiritual knowledge contained within **The Spiritual Laws of Creation**, in this Work find their greater explanation here, **in this Chapter!**

143

*   *   *   *   *

Readers may have noted that in previous Chapters references to "The Spiritual Laws", "Spiritual Laws of Creation", aspects centred around "Truth" and "The Word" etc., were notated in **Bold type**. They were so emphasised for the express purpose of seeding in the mind of you, the reader, the critical nature of Truth and The Law – and not simply religion – into every aspect of our crucial spiritual journey into the dark world of ancient Maori. Now that we have arrived at **Part II**, which covers the explanation of **"The Spiritual Laws of Creation"** and the related "great questions to life", that emphasis should no longer be necessary since all explanations of **The Law** from this point forward inherently carry that knowledge.

Furthermore, to know that this *new knowledge* for *all* men, *in terms of its entry into Aotearoa*, was so brought here by one of mixed Maori/Pakeha blood from Ngapuhi, thus *fulfilling the Prophecy of 'The White Thread'* under the aegis of clear guidance from **Above**. Fulfilled for those of Maori descent, particularly, but also for the Pakeha too. For the knowledge of this Truth to unite both Maori and Pakeha under the single parameter of The One Law – *should there be the genuine recognition and desire to do so* – is the mechanism by which the final 'impression' of uncertainty alluded to in **"Author's Note"** regarding our collective future can be dispelled, and thus permit such a journey to be embarked upon consciously-correctly. Yet if that aim is to bear 'good fruits', the nature of *'New Zealand's Lost Legacy'* must first be clearly recognised so that an harmonious future can thereby be the end-goal. At the very least for those who so wish to tread this path, and thus for those very same *who choose to embrace the only knowledge that will permit them the chance to so arrive* – the knowledge of **The Spiritual Laws of Creation**.

*   *   *   *   *

Therefore, proceeding on the foundation of **The Spiritual Laws** are further Chapters explaining all that we need to know to understand our actual Origins, the processes of death, the knowledge of The Elemental Beings of Nature, why the emergence of the Maori Prophets to Ratana and his particular fulfilment and, of course, *the actual Spiritual significance of the arrival of the Pakeha for Maori*. Thus genuine *tikanga* in its Living Truth!

Now, in terms of the journey from the old into the new and onto that vital Spiritual Event for Maori, detailed explanations of those Laws and how they need to be understood in the present generally aspiritual societal climate, must yet be made. That is so the obvious comparisons between current and incorrect views, and that which Spiritual Law decrees must and will be brought about, is clearly revealed for the reader, particularly where societal, cultural and religious change needs to be wrought. In the final analysis those three parts to our overall society, in their individual paradigms, will ultimately only prosper – *'by knowing The Law'*!

At present, there appears to be a growing and often vocal school of thought in Maoridom that seeks to promote "Maori Customary Law" as the rightful 'law of the land', and that this 'law' should take primary place in Aotearoa. Today many ethnic groups live in New Zealand and the rightful law of the land should clearly be fair to all people who have made their home here. By definition, and as previously noted, the customary law of any race of people can only derive from the beliefs, customs, traditions, and even fears and superstitions of that particular group at a particular time in their development. Whilst that 'law' may have served well for that time, as a race proceeds through the various stages of development, certain factors of customary law should clearly change as greater insights hopefully lead away from the fear and/or superstitious aspects perhaps previously present within that group.

However, if that has not taken place, should that Law – in this case "Maori Customary Law" – be permitted to set a 'first-law precedent' for all in Aotearoa? Our conviction is that it should not because, as we note, historically, it did not provide an equitable and caring society for Maori in the past. And therefore cannot in the future. Moreover, because this 'customary law' was based on factors that *were* more often superstitious than naturally rational, it is hardly the ideal model upon which to base any society today. Clearly, therefore, "Maori Customary Law" is *not* the rightful law for New Zealand!

Our present societal laws, commonly called "Pakeha legislation", are also far from perfect too. In reality, the only model on which to base any society today is that of **The Spiritual Laws of Creation** because, by their very nature, they are absolutely just, inviolable and therefore **unchangeable**. Since those absolute parameters logically decree that such Laws unequivocally transcend humankind's narrow views, in their clear perfection they are the ideal foundation for society. Therefore, whilst we should certainly examine "Maori Customary Law" and "Pakeha legislation", we should only retain those aspects that accord with The Spiritual Laws and discard all those that do not. As previously and unequivocally stated in the opening paragraphs, **this Chapter explains those absolutely just, inviolable, immutable and therefore *unchangeable* Laws**!

The English empiricist philosopher, John Locke, (1632-1704) notable for his "Two Treatises of Government" which justified the English Revolution of 1688 opposing the notion of the Divine Right of kings, held the view that the idea of God was a 'potential' of human reason. And that it was likely for human reason to know that God exists. Most of the Enlightenment philosophers also believed in the 'reality' of a God, for the world was far too rational for that not to be the case, in their view.

At times of human suffering, and given this seemingly inherent belief in God on the part of humankind, it is therefore not surprising to hear the anguished cries of; "If there is a God of Love, how can He let this happen?"; "How can there be a God of Love when there is so much misery and suffering in the world?"; "How can it be?", "Why him, her, them?"; "Why did they have to be taken?"; "I don't understand it!" etc..

Very great puzzlement is also evinced at the seemingly unfair and untimely death of 'good' people or young children – or in the birth of the disabled. Whilst there may not be the understanding of the reasons for 'hard fate', the very fact that many people ask why "God" should allow it appears to bear out the Enlightenment philosophers belief of a probable knowing within man of the existence of a great and powerful "Creator".

Yet therein lies our conundrum, our non-understanding! We feel great pain and anguish during times of deep sorrow because the ultimate reason *why* is often difficult to understand. Words of solace and condolence are offered but, whilst they are comforting, they may not provide answers. What do we have then? An experience that *can* serve to bring people together, but also an event – often deeply traumatic – with the potential to shatter lives and split families apart. And, moreover, can unfortunately also reduce the quality of life of those affected because the nature of the event itself and the ongoing memory of it may not offer any logical reasons why. The resultant legacy may well be the inability to ever find reasons or answers, thus resulting in unresolved heartache.

Yet to be faced with seemingly unfair 'blows of fate' should act as the strongest impetus to ask "why"? The Enlightenment philosophers encouraged rational enquiry about God by rejecting any mysterious doctrines and maintaining that the existence of God could be arrived at by introspection and human experience. However, it would be unhelpful if we became absorbed in our enquiry to the exclusion of all else. Yet it can also mean that in the continuation of one's life, one can at least adjust one's thinking and perhaps one's lifestyle to support this aim. In order to find such answers, however, there must logically be some rational mechanism whereby this can be achieved.

The premise postulated herein is that *only with the knowledge of The Spiritual Laws of Creation can sense ever be made of our existence and our reason for being*.

Only a thorough knowledge of The Spiritual Laws can provide a logical thought-process mechanism through which the question of apparently unfair and/or 'hard blows of fate' can be answered. And thereby potentially produce a more benign global society than is currently the case. A brief introduction to just two points of "The Law" should suffice to illustrate why there is such an entrenched general refusal by humankind to acknowledge the existence of Spiritual Law, let alone the inviolability of it. The same two points will further demonstrate how beliefs that do not acknowledge The Spiritual Laws effectively prevent basic understanding of the why of life's tragedies.

Firstly, it is probably reasonable to assume that most people accept the notion of 'free will' i.e., we can, and do, make decisions for ourselves virtually every minute of each day, and that personal decisions via this mechanism should allow us full command over our individual destinies. If this were not so, we would be forced to assume that what happens in our lives is determined by factors outside our control. If such an 'arbitrary force' did actually exist, it would clearly have to be regarded as a mischievous or rogue one given that some people seem to suffer more setbacks than might reasonably be expected to occur.

Secondly, the simple act of making a decision about anything must presuppose an outcome of some kind. Most students of religion, philosophy, or even home-spun logic will probably accept the concept that "...what one sows one must, or shall, reap". Certainly for the general Christian community, this biblical directive is sacrosanct in its perceived truth. If that is so, there must logically be a just and lawful mechanism that produces the outcome or the reaction to every decision made. If it is reasonable to assume the first part of the equation, then it is surely equally reasonable to assume the second; that there will be a 'return' – without fail! The premise here is that ultimately it is our own decisions that determine all outcomes that affect us. Science, in essence, states this process thus:

"For every action there is an equal and opposite reaction."

Yet what happens when these two cornerstones, i.e., the notion of "free will" and "we reap what we sow", are brought together to make sense of tragedy and misfortune? For if each notion is true, (and this work accepts that clear truth) then any misfortune – and it is usually only misfortunes and tragedies that produce any kind of soul-searching for answers – must have been set in place somewhere, sometime, by the "reaper". Clearly, if the beliefs of the two particular tenets are absolute, *then the first would naturally presuppose the second* in terms of a logical and meaningful connection.

However, because the reasons for misfortunes are not always immediately apparent – whereby the concept and logic of "free will" and its equally logical connection of "reaping the effects" is clearly visible and understandable – it becomes necessary *to attempt to postulate* some kind of *different* mechanism as explanation, or to despair of ever knowing why. The clear contention stated in this "equation" is that if both tenets are absolute and sacrosanct as an **Inviolable Law**, then we cannot possibly postulate other reasons which exclude or alter either one to simply fabricate a connection between our *free-will decision-making ability* and *reaping what we sow*. And certainly not to conveniently fit a religious doctrine or dogma or, indeed, any personal faith/belief mode. For whilst the decisions are always free, the consequences are not! Under the inviolability of this absolute *equation of life*, **consequences can only derive from decisions**. That is the clear and unequivocal reality.

Now, if the two tenets are not accepted as being absolute and lawfully connected, then searching outside these two sacrosanct positions to try to find an answer provides the only other alternative. However if that 'answer' *denies* the inherently logical and thus lawful connection between a "free-will decision" and "reaping what one has sown" – i.e., accepting that there must naturally be a consequence of making a decision in the first place – then that particular position naturally *refutes* the inherent inviolability of any *lawful connection* to begin with. Yet, again, the two 'inviolable cornerstones' of this *equation of life* unequivocally state that they clearly must be absolute, both in essence and reality.

The inviolability of "inherent justice" naturally contained within The Spiritual Laws ensures that they will always provide correct answers. It is an infallible mechanism that not only does *not* compromise the absolute nature of the two "cornerstones" of our illustration, it positively strengthens the interlinking of all The Spiritual Laws to provide genuine solutions! Therefore, since the two "cornerstones" are absolute and lawfully connected, the clear contention here is that another law – equally as valid and sacrosanct – must be taken into account *if one wishes to understand the Truth of the connection*. It is that other Law which is not generally recognised and therefore not accepted. Unfortunately, it is the refusal to accept this fact that gives rise to so much confusion and anguish when needing answers. That "other Law", explained later in this Chapter, is:

The Law of Rebirth!

This is the meaning of the Scripture: "...the resurrection of the flesh." That phrase does not mean what many Christians believe and, indeed, what many denominations teach as one of the 'inviolable tenets'; namely, the emerging of the skeletal frames of all the long dead from their graves, to be somehow reclothed in flesh for the end-time judgement. Hollywood has used this theme about the 'undead' for the horror genre. But that is Hollywood. It is not The Truth of that Scripture!

The concept of reincarnation, whilst not accepted by most Western religions or the scientific community, is an absolute belief of hundreds of millions worldwide. Multi-earth lives provide the mechanism whereby the two "spiritually-lawful cornerstones" of "free will" and "reaping what one sows" can be logically explained – particularly where an earth-life does not offer sufficient time for certain categories of "reaping" to occur. It is not for nothing that Jesus stated quite emphatically – Matthew 7:7, Fenton:

"Seek, and You Shall Find."

By virtue of His Divine Origin, Jesus spoke always from the knowledge of The Spiritual Laws of Creation! He was able to survey all happenings, both the small and the large, in their complete cycles from cause to effect. Therefore, if any answers are to give a true and comprehensive explanation, they must first explain it Spiritually.

So in contrast to the clear Truth that Jesus brought to earth for the especial benefit of *all* of humankind, a purely medical, scientific, religious, political or sociological explanation for a particular problem can only take in the *material effect* i.e., the end result of a "spiritually-willed" decision. By virtue of its purely material application, earthly disciplines therefore *cannot* give a complete overview *for they are not able to see the actual starting point*, irrespective of views to the contrary from within the individual disciplines. This is not to decry the very great help that we can obviously obtain from materially-orientated disciplines. However, where it is a question of finding the actual source of many of our problems or the answers to life itself, they are not able to supply this crucial knowledge, because only in Spiritual Law and its concomitant Source can we find ultimate answers!

Despite the superiority of the Spiritual viewpoint over 'material empiricism', the whole thrust of our much-vaunted, modern education system virtually denies the existence of anything other than what can be materially seen, heard, felt, or measured. Currently, the scientific and rationalist point of view reigns supreme. Fortunately, however, there are other voices questioning the narrow strictures of such points of view. These voices are slowly swelling in volume and some are actually coming from within the scientific disciplines. In essence, the realisation may be slowly dawning that all we have been taught to blindly accept through the education and religious systems may prove to be very different from the actual reality. And so will it be!

So where does this irrational attitude stem from; this mind-set that seeks to deny man the knowledge of his true Spiritual self, and therefore his actual Origins? Should not the ultimate goal of the various disciplines be focussed more on a wider-seeking paradigm rather than the present practice of attempting to steer all away from this so-called 'irrational and unscientific' view? Is there fear, then, of this unscientific, perhaps politically and even culturally incorrect word – **SPIRITUAL?**

The obvious problem encountered when speaking about "The Spiritual" is that the very word itself is generally lumped with whatever ideas humankind may determine it to encompass. Things that originate from, or are connected to, the actual Spiritual Realm, can be deemed to be truly Spiritual. And because only the *truly Spiritual* can *actually* be of "The Spiritual", what is of that Realm is therefore sacred and holy.[1]

However, because we of humankind generally interpret just the immediate 'beyond' as being 'spiritual', anything that is connected with it, or to it, or derived from it, is thus often deemed to be similarly so by some religions and cultures. Far too much is made of purely man-made icons being designated sacred and therefore regarded as spiritual in humankind's estimation. Thus there exists the farcical idea that everything that man *decides* is sacred must, by extension, also be spiritual. Nothing could be further from the truth. In fact some aspects of various cultures, such as the meanings ascribed to grotesque carved images or in particular ancient practices to name two examples, are so aspiritual in both form and connection that it is difficult to even begin to understand how their supporters can arrive at such a conclusion.

So, given that clear, objective solutions to all issues may be found under the aegis of The Spiritual Laws of Creation, *how can a more spiritually-correct mind-set be inculcated into beliefs that stubbornly cling to cultural emotionalism or to scientific rigidity?*

One of the greatest teachers humankind has ever had is history, and within its pages may be found, historically documented, the struggle of many individuals who have been lone and lonely "voices in the wilderness". Boat-rockers, all of them, but with voices raised in protest against blindness and, at times, sheer stupidity. Voices of people who possessed the clarity of vision or perception to *know* that certain 'official' teachings and views were gravely in error. Yet those same lonely voices were often stilled, silenced, to protect the ego and power base of those in authority who fought to maintain, *at all costs,* the 'official' version. In some cases the lone voices were actually able to convince the 'authorities' of the correctness of their beliefs, though often only after many years of protest. Then, in an absolutely farcical situation, when finally accepted by the 'ruling authority', the 'new knowledge' became the accepted current norm and, therefore, suitable for the masses.

*   *   *   *   *

A classic example is that of the view of Ptolemy (90-168AD), a Graeco-Egyptian mathematician and geographer, who believed that the earth was the centre of the universe and that the sun and planets revolved around it. In stating this view, he set in place a theory which remained unchallenged for about 1600 years. The main reason for this long acceptance of such a wrong belief was that it perfectly suited the egocentric interpretation of the church. And no voice was raised against it until 1543 when Copernicus, (1473-1543) a Polish astronomer found that only with the sun at the centre of the universe could the planetary system work. From that point on the Ptolemaic belief was rejected – at least by the newly emerging sciences.

Unfortunately, this was not a belief shared by the church and is graphically illustrated in the persecution of Galileo (1564-1642) by the Inquisition in 1633. Galileo, an Italian astronomer and mathematician, agreed with the claim of Copernicus that the sun was the centre of our

---

[1]The following Chapter explains the different levels in Creation for humankind, and the basic significance and purpose of each.

universe. But this 'unacceptable' view led to his persecution. He recanted, but is said to have muttered under his breath: "But it (the Earth) does move."[2]

Another stark example was the debate between flat-earth theorists, again upheld by the European Church, and those who believed the earth was spherical, a view accepted by scholars in some monasteries. Accepted long before by Greek mathematicians and also later by Columbus and other navigators as being the probable truth; the latter purely by their logical observations of the curved and disappearing horizon. History records that the journey of Columbus forced an immediate change of view within "the establishment".

*   *   *   *   *

What the teaching 'authorities' should learn to accept is that the very nature of truth guarantees that it cannot be stifled or suppressed forever. Far better, then, to keep a completely open mind to *all voices*. The one constant that will determine the validity of any definition of "The Spiritual" and separate the 'superficial voices' from the 'true ones', will be whether it accords with The Spiritual Laws and thus stand the test of time. This is the only true measure as these Laws are, themselves, Eternal. And, within the life-path parameters given for humankind, it is we who must finally acknowledge and accept this fact, since our life, being and sustenance are given only via those Laws.

Moreover, to glibly state that mankind is "...not meant to understand the ways of The Creator" presupposes the requirement to submit to and accept all suffering in fatalistic ignorance. The Spiritual Laws decree that we actually **are** 'masters of our own destiny', even if present events seem to suggest otherwise. It is our refusal to accept the Truth of The Law, *as it actually is,* that is the problem.

The above historic examples, together with the previously postulated premise that we are masters of our own destiny, indicate that no one should be afraid to abandon dogma when it becomes apparent that it is clearly not true. We should especially beware of leaders who knowingly still maintain the old errors out of fear of a collapse of their authority and organisation.

On the relationship between science and religion, the scientific giant Albert Einstein observed:

> "Intelligence makes clear to us the interrelation of means and ends. But mere thinking cannot give us a sense of the ultimate and fundamental ends. To make clear these fundamental ends and valuations, and to set them fast in the emotional life of the individual, seems to me precisely the most important function which religion has to perform in the social life of man. And if one asks whence derives the authority of such fundamental ends, since they cannot be stated and justified merely by reason, one can only answer: they come into being not through demonstration but through revelation, through the medium of powerful personalities. One must not attempt to justify them, but rather to sense their nature simply and clearly."

(Albert Einstein, Ideas and Opinions, p.42-43,
Bonanza Books, New York.)

As we unequivocally state throughout this Work and strongly illustrate in Chapter 7, there should be no contradiction between science and religious truth, and that science cannot supersede any such truths. Though noting the demarcation between science and religion, Einstein also understood the strong reciprocal relationships and dependencies between the two. He further stated:

> "Though religion may be that which determines the goal, it has, nevertheless learned from science, in the broadest sense, what means will contribute to the attainment of the goals it

---

[2]It is interesting to note that Copernicus did not publish his theory until the year of his death at age 70. Perhaps it was a purposeful decision on his part – to state that truth in later life – in an effort to escape the censure of the church.

has set up. But science can only be created by those who are thoroughly imbued with the aspiration toward truth and understanding.

Science without religion is lame, religion without science is blind."

6.1   The Nature of the Spiritual Principles

"The Laws of Creation derive their eternal validity from the fact of God's perfection. On account of God's perfection, His Will is also perfect and, therefore, the Laws manifesting this Will are perfect. They cannot be improved upon, and they remain absolutely unchangeable."

(Building Future Societies: The Spiritual Principles, p.23,
Stephen Lampe.)

This inviolable premise permits us to logically deduce that God cannot act in an arbitrary manner and "do anything He wants". It may certainly be convenient to offer this sort of explanation to a difficult religious question thereby temporarily getting rid of the problem, but it still, nonetheless, waits for a correct answer. For if God is able to "do anything He wants" by virtue of the fact that He Is God, where then lies His Perfection? Since it **must** logically follow that if He Is Perfect, and His Laws are Perfect and therefore unchangeable, then any belief that states otherwise *automatically* casts doubt on this accepted belief in **"A Perfect God"**.

Quite simply, any attempt to change a *Perfect Law* naturally implies that the Law could not have been perfect in the first instance, if it then needed to be changed.

It is thus impossible to impute imperfection to A Perfect God!

Therefore the recognition of The Laws of Creation, as they actually are in their inviolability, will finally return to God The Perfection that Is His.[3]

Two thousand years ago Jesus, arguably the greatest, most wonderful "boat rocker" of all, gave stern warning to the, then, leaders of the Church. The fact that He did not support their practices is clearly apparent by virtue of His condemnation of them. The same, however, applies equally well to all teachings and disciplines that attempt to suppress the Truth, especially today.

"Woe to you, play-acting professors and Pharisees! because you lock up the Kingdom of Heaven in the face of mankind; while you yourselves neither enter, nor allow those arriving to go in."

(Matthew 23:13, Fenton.)

In accordance with that clear message, it is our conviction that there are certain Spiritual Laws or Principles that guide and determine the course of everything throughout Creation, including the destiny of man on Earth. These Laws are Eternal i.e., they have existed from eternity. Everything in Creation, including humankind, came into being via the operation of these Laws, and our continued existence here depends on them also. The Originator of these Laws is **God, The Creator**. Only what are inherent in **His Laws of Creation** can ever come to full flower and be sustained in Creation. By extension, all else i.e., activities not supported by those Laws, *must inevitably fail.*

---

[3]A critical analysis of this 'theological quandary' may be read in a brief question and answer format in a stand-alone Booklet: **'Jesus: His Birth, Death and Resurrection'**. And/or in Chapter 5 of a Parent publication: [**BIBLE "MYSTERIES" EXPLAINED: Understanding "Global Societal Collapse" From The "SCIENCE" in The Bible, What Every Scientist, Bible Scholar and Ordinary Man Needs to Know.**] The reader will find therein simple and clear logic which completely clarifies this 'question/problem'. [Available online at: **www.publishme.co.nz** and **www.crystalbooks.org**]

Even though The Spiritual Laws allowed us the gift of conscious life, they have not always been clearly recognised. Throughout man's long and tortured history, great and wise spiritual teachers arose at varying intervals to call attention to them. Teachers such as Krishna, Zoroaster, Lao-Tse, Moses and the Prophets, Buddha, Mohammed – and Jesus. At best, they were often not understood or sometimes misinterpreted. At worst, they were knowingly distorted. All these contributing factors meant that it was not possible to consistently apply them beneficially. The origin of the present dangerous rise of religious fundamentalism can probably be traced to this problem of narrow, non-understanding. This unfortunate development, among many other increasing problems now facing us, may be seen as a direct correlation between the immutability of The Spiritual Laws and our refusal to heed them. The solutions to *all* our problems lie *solely* in a voluntary adjustment to them in a conscious, correct and consistent way.

Simply put, we have no choice but to understand and apply The Spiritual Laws to all facets of life and not believe that we can formulate better principles that are as effective. For it would be foolish to imagine that human beings can improve on The Will of The Creator, as we ourselves are only products of those Laws. Chaos and confusion will always be the result of attempting to deviate from them. No one can evade or change them, and The Laws apply equally to all in the same measure. To rich and poor, the powerful and the weak, the clever and the stupid, to kings and slaves. The effects are the same on those who know The Law as those who do not. Unfortunately, ignorance of them does not keep their effects at bay either!

If man's laws are compared with Spiritual Law, we find that earthly laws differ from society to society whereas The Laws of Creation remain the same everywhere and are Eternal. Our laws are constantly in a state of review, and can even be changed by public opinion or dictatorial decree, so that what may have been perfectly legal yesterday may not be so today. By contrast, Spiritual Law is immutable and unchangeable, and will forever remain so. The cost, complexity and duration of trials in earthly law courts indicate quite conclusively that our laws are not simple to understand, and require lawyers who have needed to spend years of study to become conversant with them. Even then, however, there can be much disagreement over individual points of law. By comparison, The Laws of Creation are clear, concise and simple. Moreover, they are few in number, easily understandable, and do not require years of laborious study. They are alluded to in all the major religions and philosophies of the world's peoples. Lawyers' offices and judges' chambers will contain row upon row of books of laws and statutes. The Eternal Laws, however, can be contained *in one small publication.*

The Eternal Laws have, as their infallible foundation, Justice, Love and Purity, and are therefore perfect in the dispensation of *true* justice. Humankind on the other hand, by virtue of our present level of spiritual *immaturity,* do not have such a benchmark. So, whilst we may have many laws, we do not always see justice done. Criminals have been discharged over 'technicalities'. And lawyers have cleverly exploited the 'justice system' to set free people who have *actually* committed crimes. By contrast, **no one escapes The Spiritual Laws**. Their infallible, automatic outworking ensures that Justice and Love are meted out in perfect balance at all times, even though not always immediately, or even apparently so. But meted out they always are!

The incorruptible nature of The Eternal Laws ensures that they will reign supreme. This means that in the determination of innocence or guilt in an earthly court of law, man's laws do not always offer protection or absolution should an innocent person be wrongly condemned and sentenced. The responsibility for that miscarriage of justice, however, will fall back on all those who contributed to it – as it does in all things. Attempting to shelter behind a veil of 'fulfilling one's duty' in the cause of justice via the Nation's laws matters not at all. We are all irrevocably tied to the consequences of our decisions, and a wrong conviction will eventually bring the inevitable reciprocal effect.

Judges and juries, then, have a particularly difficult task given the spiritually-unhealthy state of our secular laws. Passing judgement according to such laws may satisfy the dictates of earthly society, but if the judgement is a transgression against The Laws of Creation, the judges are bound to reap the reciprocal effect of their spiritually-wrong decisions, as will juries who determine guilt wrongly. For that reason, it should be in the *serious* interests of the judiciary to actively concern themselves with the knowledge of The Eternal Laws.

What should be understood is the fact that the material worlds are in transition between one phase and another. Literally everything is in transition and upheaval, man and nature. Consequently man is being strongly compelled to heed these Laws under the increasing Spiritual pressure currently being applied to all things. The effect of this pressure is seen in the accelerating breakdown of our society and the increasing problems globally. In short, *man's time of formulating his own policies is at an end.*

We will now be forced to adjust to The Laws of Creation, or perish.

This increasing pressure actually strengthens both the good and the bad. Thus *the good –* or that which adjusts itself to The Laws – *will flourish.* And *the bad or wrong –* that which opposes The Laws – *will collapse.* In this we have an infallible standard by which to measure events around us and to choose accordingly.

The Spiritual Laws of Creation are relatively few in number. They are:

1. **The Law of Movement**

2. **The Law of Reciprocal Action**

3. **The Law of Attraction of Similar Species**

4. **The Law of Spiritual Gravity**

5. **The Law of Balance**

6. **The Law of Rebirth**

A brief explanation of **The Law/Gift of Grace** also requires inclusion here, too. By examining each of the Laws named, it will be shown that everything in Creation is interlinked and interdependent. How, then, should The Spiritual Laws be described? By examining philosophical, scientific, religious and spiritual works, clear and consistent reference to them can be found. They could thus be termed "Universal". Everyday observations of the natural world show this universality of the Laws in their working reality.

The philosopher Heraclitus (540-480 BC) of Ephesus in Asia Minor believed that this 'universal reason' or 'universal law' is something common to all and which guides not only every person but also everything that happens in nature. Yet he observed that instead of following this 'higher guidance', most people lived by their individual beliefs. This 'something', which was the source of everything, he called God or *logos* – meaning reason.

6.2   The Law of Movement

Heraclitus also postulated a new concept; that of flux or change. He observed that everything flowed, everything is in constant flux and movement, nothing stands still. He expressed this concept of constant change by saying that "...you cannot step twice into the same river." The river changes because "...fresh waters are ever flowing in upon you." Recorded for posterity in (Philosophy History and Problems, Third Edition p.12-13) Heraclitus thought that this concept of flux:

"...must apply not only to rivers but to all things, including the soul of man. Rivers and men exhibit the fascinating fact of becoming different and yet remaining the same. We return to the "same" river although fresh waters have flowed into it, and the man is still the same person as the boy."

Therefore, when we step into a river for the second time, 'neither we nor the river are the same'.

Everything, literally everything, is in constant motion. Movement is the one activity that ensures the maintenance of life in all things. Without movement everything would become sluggish and eventually come to a complete standstill, a situation akin to death and disintegration. Therefore motion can be stated to be a most necessary principle throughout Creation. The higher and lighter the plane of Creation, the faster the motion. Conversely, therefore, the further away from The Source of Life, as for example in the material planes, the more sluggish the motion. As "movement" is thus a vital principle, all other Laws can be said to operate within the parameters of this most important Law. However, the movement must be of the *right* kind and in harmony with all else if it is to bring benefit.

Imagine life in the Universe and on earth without the Elemental activity of The Forces of Nature bringing movement. We observe the rotation of the earth each day to give the necessary circadian rhythm of day and night, thus allowing the vast majority of its creatures to regulate their life patterns accordingly. The earth rotates around the sun to provide the four seasons. These in turn produce the different weather patterns needed for planting and harvesting. The motion of the winds ensures freshness and change where there might otherwise be staleness.

Consider the moon's rotation around its own axis and around the earth, offering its different phases and bringing the rise and fall of the tides. Consider, also, the great ocean currents that constantly mix the waters of our "blue planet", and the movement of the continents over the liquid core of the earth in plate tectonics, instrumental in the formation of new lands. Constant movement equals constant renewal. Further out into the incomprehensible vastness of the observable universe, galaxies of immense size wheel and rotate their billions of suns to the same primordial rhythm.

Science has long discovered that individual cells, molecules and atoms, are 'alive' with the constant movement of sub-particles, with each fitting perfectly into its ordained place to become part of the whole. And even in the microscopic sub-atomic world where the behaviour of quarks and neutrinos appear to circumvent all the known *scientific* laws, they still, nevertheless, follow the dictates of Universal Law. It is our non-understanding of those laws that force us to declare our lack of knowledge at such behaviour. The rocks of the earth, even though appearing to be solid, dense and lifeless, are also awhirl with active movement. A crystal-clear glass of clean water gives no hint of the motion of electrons, protons and neutrons in the structure and composition of either the glass or the water. Animal and human bodies have the same basic activity in their molecular structure also, whether living and breathing, or dead and decomposing.

The physical body, with which we are all familiar, signals to us the need for constant movement in order to remain healthy. In breathing we quite automatically accept the rise and fall of the chest as the lungs inhale and exhale. The heart pumps blood in necessary circulation throughout the body. Exercise keeps the body healthy and strong, inactivity weakens it. At various times during the day the demands of the body strongly announce the need to eliminate waste. Even in supposedly restful sleep there is still the need for the body to change its position more often than we might be aware of during the sleep state. Everything must obey The Law of Movement if it is to remain healthy and not stagnate.

Rivers and streams remain fresh and oxygenated through movement. The world's great river systems yearly transport millions of tons of silt to form large, fertile deltas at their mouths. In man-made lakes where dams block the normal river flow to the point where the amount of draw off prevents any natural spillage, the impounded body of water still has movement between the vertical layers.

In the world of birds and fishes, lack of the right kind of necessary movement has resulted in the loss of certain abilities that some once possessed. For example, there are fish that are no longer able to withstand the currents and must remain near the bottom. The kiwi, Aotearoa's national symbol, is flightless through not having used its wings for a long period of time. The same applies to a number of other birds in various parts of the world. These examples showing the principle of adaptation, with which biological scientists are familiar, are a consequence of The Law of Movement.

Thus far, only the physical effect of this Law has been examined. In the first instance, however, it is a Spiritual Law. Therefore, in the case of the physical body, each movement must first be willed by the Spirit, because the Spirit is the animating force, 'the power pack', within each of us. This signal between spirit and body happens so quickly as to be virtually simultaneous and imperceptible in its time lapse.[4]

The activity of the natural world demands that every creature and plant must strive to maintain its place, or perish. Spiritual activity must produce the same, and more, if there is to be growth and ascent. Therefore, effort must be expended if we wish to achieve anything of lasting value. We cannot sit back and expect wonderful things to just happen. And whether applied to the physical, mental or spiritual, laziness in any one area is a transgression against this Eternal Law. Moreover, the different kinds of activities – spiritual, intellectual and physical – must always be kept in proper balance. Without spiritual activity as a necessary counterpoise, physical and intellectual expenditure of effort will ultimately be worthless. We can thus extrapolate that a genuinely spiritual goal will always have furthering values that will never change and, by definition, be far-reaching and beneficial.

Present trends allow people to eagerly anticipate retirement after a lifetime of work. The thought of the remaining years of life spent in blissful inactivity appeals to many. Yet this offends against The Law too. Of course the elderly could not be expected to maintain the same level of activity that a much younger person might. Nevertheless, for the older body to maintain reasonable health, movement of the right kind is still necessary. Fortunately, current directions now see more and more of the elderly pursuing this beneficial course. The 'acceptance of change' that time and development naturally bring under The Law of Movement allows one phase of life to flow into the next, for movement is designed to bring about further development.

Conversely, 'workaholics', some professional sports people, and others engaged in constant frenetic activity actually transgress this Law and will eventually harm themselves. A sense of balance should be maintained in all that we do by adjusting our pace to a natural rhythm which is connected to The Law of Movement. Perhaps the latter day phrase, "Everything in moderation", is an unconscious reaction to the increasingly unnatural pace of modern society. In heeding The Law of Movement, we also need to obey The Law of Balance as well, for this Law is also a consequence of motion.

History's testament to the rise and fall of some of the great civilisations provides excellent examples of what occurs if the correct "Spiritual" movement is not maintained. The rise to greatness shows the right kind of movement, whilst the disintegration process invariably indicates the opposite. The Law of Movement decrees that no one person, group or nation can simply stop and rest on past or present glories. What has been achieved, if spiritually worthwhile, must be maintained, or stagnation, retrogression and disintegration will quickly follow. In the same way, persons who have been honoured by society today should be required to maintain that position of honour.

---

[4]The "Spiritual Origins" of humankind, thus that which pertains to the origin and nature of the human Spirit and soul, are explained in the following Chapter.

The propensity of many to attempt to live in the past offends against The Law of Movement also. The current strong cultural trend in Maoridom to promote tribal links and the whole concept of tribalism per se as a beneficial course, clearly *transgresses* The Law of Movement in both the Spiritual and material sense. The Spiritual Power and pressure inherent in this Law decrees that the tribal phase for any race is exactly that – just a phase. Consequently any beneficial outworking contained within the power of The Law of Movement for a people will be greatest when and where *correct movement* is undertaken.

In this particular example, that would translate into leaving tribalism behind and moving toward becoming one nation, one people – exactly according to Ratana's clarion call.

This does not mean that we should not assess history, or try to correct past wrongs. But the Laws require us, indeed command us, to *live* in the *present*. And further command us to strongly heed The Law of Movement in the Spiritual sense, particularly, if there is not to be stagnation and retrogression.

6.3   The Law of Reciprocal Action.

"Do not err; God cannot be deluded: for what a man sows, that he will also reap."

"If he sows for his sensuality, he will reap perdition; but sowing for the Spirit, from the Spirit, he will reap eternal life."

(Galatians 6:7-8, Fenton.)

The key word in the above two Scriptures is **"will"**. It is not a word, for example, such as *perhaps, might, maybe* or *possibly*. No, the texts are quite unequivocal. They clearly state that we **will** reap what we sow! Other Bibles use the word "shall" in this context, but the meaning is clearly still the same.

Since all The Spiritual Laws can be designated as Natural Laws, a prime example of the damage that can be wrought through transgressing this particular one may be clearly observed in the relatively recent emergence of "Mad Cow Disease". Short-cut economic practices in British agriculture resulted in the concomitant emergence of a human equivalent of the disease through the consumption of contaminated meat products resulting in the necessary slaughter of many thousands of infected animals. The Laws of Creation ordain that herbivores such as cows and beef cattle should not consume food derived from their own kind. Meat and meat products are the ordained, natural food of carnivores, and the farming industry **cannot** arbitrarily force such a radical change in captive animals without expecting severe consequences. A 'lawful' lesson, and one that science will probably have to learn the hard way.

In the first decade of the 21st century, alarm bells have sounded over the collapse of millions of bee hives globally. To the year 2011, hive losses in America had reached 50 percent, and Europe 40 percent. Quite obviously, this disastrous trend threatens a large and vital part of global food production. Many theories and reasons have been put forward for such a drastic collapse. One culprit is certainly the so-called 'modern' corporate farming method of single-crop plantings covering literally thousands of acres and the associated pesticide/herbicide use/overuse on those areas.

Pollination of such large areas of single-crop cultivation, particularly in the U.S., mean that there is not sufficient food there for the bees themselves. So, not only are the weakened bees more susceptible to poisoning by spray residue, but the current method of trucking thousands of hives thousands of miles every year to pollinate crops stresses the colonies, thus threatening more hive collapses. Recommendations from *real* bee experts for these *solely* profit-driven companies to plough up small pockets of ground in those *monoculture deserts* and plant wildflowers to feed those very necessary 'workers' have thus far largely fallen on deaf ears. The corporate ethos reigns supreme here too – so far!

The chemical companies claim their products are safe, of course. China, however, has openly acknowledged that in one fruit-growing *region*, continual pesticide use killed *all* the bees in that area. Consequently, pollination of the whole fruit crop must now be done by hand, a method which is acknowledged to be unsustainable in the long term.

Another foolish corporate idea – artificial insemination of queen bees in the lab using sperm from a *single* drone contributor – means that the necessary and natural *diversity* that would ordinarily occur when queen bees are mated by many drones during the nuptial flight, is denied those "corporate lab queens". The predatory 'viroa' mite currently infecting hives globally is proving difficult to eradicate. In many cases now, the mite has actually become resistant to the pesticides designed to kill them.

When will we finally learn the most valuable life-lesson necessary for our *physical* well-being here on Earth? That irrespective of all advances in science, Mother Nature's way is, and always will be, the best way!

The book of Job, Chapter 34, Verse 11, in gloriously blunt truth states it succinctly:

"But man's actions return on himself."

Perhaps the 'hard lesson' in 'herbivore cannibalism' will manifest in a globally devastating way with the discovery and great concern about 'prions', that strange and potentially lethal 'protein agent' now perhaps implicated in the "brain-eating" diseases, CJD, BSE, sheep scrapie and 'kuru' (from New Guinea). Over the past few decades, American and Australian scientists observing and researching these diseases have noted the striking similarities between them. At the same time, they have also noted the increasing incidences of variants of the disease, particularly among the young. It may be that 'prions' are similarly implicated in the E. coli bacterial illness responsible for large outbreaks of deadly food-poisoning overseas.

And the 'hard lesson' over bee colony collapse? If it continues, then the outcome is obvious – global starvation. Science notates the essence of The Law of Reciprocal Action thus:

"For every action, there is an equal and opposite reaction."

What is probably not accepted, however, is that there is not just simply an '*equal*, opposite reaction', but a reaction that is always 'lawfully' *more severe* than the original action, or what might be expected to result from the originating decision. In the case of our example of the moment, the possibility that 'mad cow disease' may have now crossed the species barrier and is probably able to infect humans, should be regarded as unequivocal proof that The Spiritual Laws, which ultimately manifest as physical Laws, **cannot be transgressed without serious consequences**. The full potential horror of 'mad cow disease' resulting from this particularly foolish transgression may still be a little way off as the great uncertainty is whether or not there may be a large pool of infected people quietly moving through an unknown incubation period.

In this example alone we may clearly note that The Law of Reciprocal Action, as with all The Spiritual Laws, necessarily supports every other Law as a part of all processes and outcomes. At a more mundane level, a brief examination of this effect in the natural world will clearly show even the youngest gardener that if he wishes to harvest corn, he must plant corn, and if he wants to grow beans, he must plant beans. What would be the result if the laws were inconsistent and we were always uncertain as to what the sown seed would produce? Total confusion. And there is no confusion in The Spiritual Laws of Creation. Therefore, as it reveals its absolute certainty in the garden, so can the same certainty be observed in all other kinds of "sowing". Closely connected with this fact should be the realisation that we do not necessarily *"reap in the same season that we sow!"*

Thus, whilst the time difference between sowing and reaping, or cause and effect, usually has set periods between the sowing and harvesting of seed for earthly food crops, no such set time lapse can be determined for the sowing and harvesting of "spiritual" seed. The Spiritual Laws alone determine the precise time of such "returns".

Moreover, within the various races and religions of the world, the natural Laws take no account of a man's colour or belief. Rice sown by a white, brown or black man will produce exactly the same as for a yellow man. In the same way, wheat sown by a Jew, a Christian, a Buddhist, a Moslem, a Hindu, a Pagan, or an Atheist, will return only wheat at harvest time. As previously stated, this earthly effect well reflects the fact that this Law, along with all the other Spiritual Laws, grants no special bias or favour to any particular race or religion. Neither should it be expected to do so. The perfection of the Laws absolutely guarantees that they cannot possibly do anything other than dispense Perfect Justice to all men. Thus, if an Atheist or a Pagan sows goodness, they are lawfully bound to receive goodness; as will a Christian Bishop, a Hindu Monk, a Moslem Imam, or a *Maori Tohunga*. Therefore, it is not necessarily a man's belief or religion that determines whether he will *ascend* or not, it is *how he is in his inner being*. It is the "Spiritual Volition" of his inner nature toward all that surrounds him, both the seen and unseen, that greatly determines this. Spiritually then, it would be wrong to think that membership of a particular religion or sect would guarantee salvation.

> The *purpose* of *all* religion *should be* to help to *correctly interpret* **The Will of God** as expressed in **His Laws of Creation**, thus showing us how we are to carry out **His Will**!

If it can do that, then it fulfils its place, for religion should be recognised as a means to an end and not an end in itself. As we should surely all know, the dangerous rise of religious fundamentalism reveals too narrow an interpretation of just "religious law".

Since our current premise under the particular Law being discussed here is exactly that of "reaping what one has sown", but from the Spiritual viewpoint overall, it is necessary to have a mechanism whereby this "spiritual" aspect also produces "physical reaping". Anecdotal evidence from American medical research has shown that concentrated thoughts directed to a sick patient can directly influence the healing process of that patient. Thus what spiritual and philosophical thinking has been saying for a very long time actually happens. In simple terms, good thoughts directed to a patient can hasten the healing process whilst bad thoughts can lengthen it.

The best-selling "Sophie's World" (p.193) offers a light-hearted insight regarding this quandary.

> "A Russian astronaut and a Russian brain surgeon were once discussing religion. The brain surgeon was a Christian but the astronaut was not. The astronaut said, "I've been out in space many times but I've never seen God or angels." And the brain surgeon said, "And I've operated on many clever brains but I've never seen a single thought."

Of course, neither view is able to conclusively prove that one or the other exists materially. And that is as it should be for neither are material in form. Nevertheless, in accordance with Spiritual Law, exist they do! But what might the above two anecdotes suggest to us?

It suggests that despite the invisible nature of thoughts, they do have the power to influence our lives, and produce visible effects. Therefore our thoughts must have to be much more than empty vaporous things. To be able to influence in such a way, they must necessarily be imbued with some kind of inherent power. All the great Spiritual Teachings, even from ancient times, strongly advise to constantly strive to think good and pure thoughts. The emotive words of love, beauty, compassion and kindness automatically arouse in us vastly different feelings from words such as hate, selfishness, envy and bitterness. In the Maori idiom, compare *aroha* and *utu* – love against revenge. This small example, where the outworking of Spiritual Law is concerned, should serve to show that language alone is not the deciding factor here either, but the 'volition' of the 'producer' certainly is.

Thus every thought we think, every word we speak, produces a 'form' that actually lives. The thought or word produces the actual form of it i.e., thoughts or words of hate or bitterness will produce those forms, irrespective of whatever language is used as the medium of production. Forms of love and harmony etc., are produced by the same mechanism. Yet just because such forms cannot always be seen does not mean that they do not exist, for they can certainly often be felt. And neither do they simply and conveniently disappear. No, the forms that we produce, that we have given birth to, live on until such time as they return to us under this Law of Reciprocal Action.[5]

We, as the individual originators, are the *owners* of them. They are ours. Moreover, our thoughts naturally affect our immediate environment, family and friends. We may note how refreshing it feels to enter the dwelling of a family who live a happy, balanced, harmonious life. Contrast that with a household racked by jealousy, hate and bitterness. A thoroughly unpleasant atmosphere, which is immediately perceived, pervades the place. The constant production of the corresponding forms 'fills' the house. *It becomes their home too.*

This can be viewed as "spiritual" sowing. We "sow" through thoughts, words, volition, deeds and actions. And by this simple mechanism, humankind *"forms and forms and forms"*. Indeed, through the inherent free will of our spiritual nature, we are **unable** to stop 'forming'. Therefore, if our thoughts are always good, we must naturally receive good in return. If they are constantly evil, that is what will be received. If our thoughts and actions change between good and evil, we will receive mixed fortunes incorporating both those aspects. In this infallible mechanism lies perfect justice!

The admonition in Luke 6:31, Fenton:

"As you wish men to do to you, do the same to them."

– was surely given for our benefit under the knowledge of this particular Law. Therefore, the greater strength and benefit will always lie in doing good. The key to so many unsolved problems rests in the operation and understanding of this Law, for The Law of Reciprocal Action decrees that we cannot do anything other than continually "produce our personal works". Yet because we cannot 'physically' see them, it is difficult to accept that such a process might be possible.

Since thoughts have the power to influence, in cases where people act differently to their actual intentions i.e., as a "wolf in sheep's clothing", etc., The Law of Sowing and Reaping absolutely ensures that the 'true' actions, including related thoughts and volition, are still all exactly weighed. The same inflexible process takes place with people who make donations to organisations for some kind of personal gain or publicity, but do not accept or share their aims and ideals. This attitude is actually one of hypocrisy and is judged accordingly because of its base level of calculative premeditation.

The common Biblical quote, Matthew 7:1, King James:

"Judge not, lest ye be judged!"

– is well known. But because so few people have the ability to *clearly assess* the true intentions of others, it is often difficult to know whether intuitive 'gut feelings' are correct, simply because a person's appearance or actions may belie his true volition. For even when seeing his actions and hearing his words, we may still not know his real motives. However, if the term 'judge' *means* to 'weigh' or 'consider', then the points for and against any particular issue should *not* be seen as a transgression of the above Scripture. Clearly we are meant to utilise our reason, intelligence and intuition to consider whether a particular thing is good or not.

---

[5]What happens to them whilst on their 'journey' will be explained later in this Chapter under the effects of "The Law of Attraction..."

Therefore, judging the actions of a person or an issue is vastly different from *passing judgement* on the person or issue. In this light, the same Scripture from Fenton's translation of The Bible offers a clearer and better interpretation.

> *"Condemn not,* so that you may not be *condemned."*

Whilst we have examined the mechanism that "produces our reaping", it is necessary to clarify the very important *reciprocal extension* of the process. The, perhaps, enigmatic Scripture from The Book of Hosea offers perfect clarification.

> *"And as they have sown only Wind, the Whirlwind alone shall they reap."*

> (Hosea 8:7, Fenton.)

Thus we have what we term: **"The Whirlwind Constant".**

In the world of nature, each seed that is planted produces a huge multiple of the same at maturation or harvest time, in some cases in the millions. Some crops require only a few months between sowing and harvesting. In the forest industry, tree crops take many years to mature before felling. Depending on when planting took place, they may not be ready in our lifetime. Even different varieties of the same kind of crop may mature at different intervals. How should this be related to The Law of Sowing and Reaping?

Quite simply, our spiritual sowing of either good or bad thoughts and deeds also returns a multiple of the same, in close association with another Eternal Law – The Law of Attraction of Similar Species, hence the truth of "reaping the whirlwind" in the previous Biblical quote. The differences in the time frame of crop maturation have their equivalent in the outworking of 'spiritual returns' or 'reaping' too, and apply equally to the thoughts, words, deeds, volition, and even prayers of people.

The resultant effect of all these factors provide the answer as to why sudden misfortune can visit itself on 'a good person', or good fortune arrive to someone thoroughly debased. That is also the reason why such a person may not receive his "whirlwind" until very much later in life, or even after earthly death. Rest assured, though, it will come to him, and in the same measure as he meted out to others, exactly, however, under the effect of *the whirlwind constant.* Were this not the case i.e., without any form of ultimate justice, there would be little point in bothering with the good. In the jungle that would develop, it would be easier to simply 'take whatever one wanted'.

In this regard the Scripture:

> *"...PUNISHMENT IS MINE, I WILL REPAY."*

> (Hebrews 10:30, Fenton.)

– is more easily understood. Thus, The Eternal Laws automatically keep track of all transgressors and, at the ordained time for that person, *dispense* the appropriate justice.

This does not mean, however, that we should not punish wrongdoers through our justice system, otherwise there surely would be chaos. What it means is that nothing is missed in Creation, nothing can be hidden, and no individual can 'get away' with any crime *against* The Spiritual Laws. The reciprocal effect, moreover, will always be *greater* than the strength of the original volition or deed under the outworking of the *'whirlwind constant'.* This process should offer some comfort as we observe more horrifying events and crimes that would have been unthinkable even a short while back, crimes which greatly increase in number and degree of brutality. Therefore the rule of law must be upheld at all times, as it should reflect our recognition of the "Higher Laws" and a desire to build the right kind of society. However, humankind's societal and/or religious 'guidelines' need to fully accord with, and be adjusted to, those "Higher Laws".

It should also be a simple matter to deduce that we can only *reap* what we have *personally sown*. We cannot simply "sow" for others, or "reap" for them either – not even for a loved one. So a person constantly striving for good who nonetheless receives bad experiences *apparently unfairly*, should understand that *he* will have given cause for it at some point in the past. As difficult a concept as this may be to accept, it *is* the causal reality of our problems. There is then nothing to be gained by bemoaning one's fate, for this only increases the sense of burden and hardship. Recognition and acceptance of this lawful process, however, then connect us to another Law, The Law of Grace.[6]

In the global sense, the kingdom of the earth and dominion over all creatures on it was given to humankind to protect and nurture and take only what was required. What of the earth today, however? The story is glaringly obvious. Raped, pillaged and poisoned for selfish greed under the name of progress and *good economic strategy*. Unfortunately, it is almost time to 'pay the ferryman'. Yet the price may well prove to be way beyond our ability to pay. However, learning "The Rules" and *living them* will go some way to lessening the cost. It may still be very high, as that cannot be changed now, but it can be reduced. But there must be a truly genuine desire to want to change – to seek something better. Superficiality in this case will simply ensure more of the same.

It is too easy to rail against misfortune or bad luck, or to curse the fates and demand an end to hardship and then, in times of deep pain and seemingly no way out, to desperately seek help in prayer. In my personal experience, *when the chips are down* virtually *everyone* '...calls out for **"THE MAN"**!'

There are few who will not seek help at such times. This inner recognition, most often brought about by painful experiences, should help us to understand that the reaping of bitter fruits once sown should be seen as the best possible *spiritual* reminder that we have strayed from the path ordained by The Creator. If our understanding of The Eternal Laws and how we stand in relation to them is then examined honestly and in genuine humility, such an assessment can only help us to grow spiritually. By this process the lessons needing to be learned can be more readily identified. Consequently, as the necessary adjustments are made whereby only good seeds are sown, The Law of Sowing and Reaping will ensure *a good return* at the ordained time. Thus there should be less thought of hard, cruel, or undeserved fate.

Yet neither should we be totally fatalistic about our lot in life. It is in our power to change it – at any time. Of course, change may not come overnight, but stubbornly refusing to change for the better will absolutely guarantee that nothing *will* change or, indeed, **can** change. The Laws of Creation actually do provide the means for happiness or misery. What is "Willed" from above for all human spirits is peace and happiness through the understanding of Spiritual Law. What one *receives*, however, depends solely upon individual choice.

In this particular Law is fulfilled *the fate or karma of humankind*, and offers the solutions to the terrible tragedies which we witness today. *Through the increasing Spiritual Power now entering the Material Part of Creation, all the deeds of thousands of years past are pressured to a quicker, final release* thus also *accelerating* the *natural* catastrophes.

> *This relentless pressure and its attendant global events will not cease until all past cycles have closed, the deeds returned to their owners to face, and all opposition to The Eternal Laws has been removed.*

---

[6]The ramifications of this particular principle are examined later in this Chapter.

Then a new era will be ushered in, a time of genuine peace and happiness for all the World's people or, more precisely, those who have genuinely striven for the good – thus those who are left. That is the lawful effect of:

The Law of Reciprocal Action.

6.3.1   Attitude to the suffering

Given the obvious ramifications of the current Law we are examining, it might be thought that we advocate total disregard for the plight of those in desperate straits. If, as is stated, people do bring suffering on themselves through non-observance of The Laws and that they are solely responsible for their plight, should compassion be shown for them? Are they not simply reaping what they have sown in this earth-life, or perhaps an earlier one? And do they therefore deserve to be helped? The simple answer to virtually all aspects of that question is yes! Compassion and kindness are virtues that, if given selflessly, can only bring a good return to the giver. For The Law of Sowing and Reaping should clearly show the need to do good at all times.

"Do unto others..." should be one of the primary factors governing our everyday life. It is difficult to imagine that anyone would actually want others to visit harm or evil upon them, yet there are so many who seem to have little compunction in wishing that on others. That is the coward's way of course. It is not the way of nobleness, which is synonymous with true *mana*. Yet it is certainly the way of much of today's world.

In fact any good works we do, we do solely for ourselves since the fruits of our deeds return to us as multiples of our original sowing under the aegis of the *'whirlwind constant'*. The possibility of helping sufferers should therefore be regarded as an opportunity to do good, to 'sow good seeds'. The cause of the person's suffering should not be our concern. In short, we should not 'pass judgement'. Given the general nature of human beings, most judgements are based on externals, and a superficial assessment may belie the true situation anyway. However, help given should not be one-sided, for that will not help the sufferer in the long term.

In any case The Perfection of The Laws automatically ensures that should a sufferer not deserve help, or should he need such an experiencing to change his ways, then no one will cross that person's path who might be in a position to give help. It could well be, however, that any such opportunity to help that presents itself for an individual may have had its origin as a 'debt owed' to that particular person in the past. In this case two opportunities are given for two different souls to expiate a possible past karmaic connection, sever it, and thus become free. If such an opportunity is not recognised, then, quite obviously, the debt and connection remain.

Quite clearly, all human beings will necessarily have ties with many people to sever, and some will be of other races too. The justness of The Laws will again ensure that, if correctly recognised, individual paths will cross at the appropriate time for any such bonds to be severed. Given the increasing 'Spiritual Pressure' being relentlessly applied to the earth and all the affairs of men in this time of *final accounting*, a superficial or cynical outlook or lifestyle will not be conducive to correct or timely recognition. And just as our past free-will decisions irrevocably bind us to the origin of all 'returning karma' today so, too, are we offered the free choice to unbind ourselves from them when the opportunity arises. Conversely we are equally free to remain shackled.

Our inherent 'free-will attribute' allows us the choice of what we will sow in thought, word or deed. The outworking of The Law of Sowing and Reaping then returns to us a multiple harvest, solely in accordance, however, with the *'whirlwind constant'*.

6.4   The Law of Attraction of Similar Species

This Law is aptly expressed in sayings such as: "Birds of a feather flock together" and, "Like attracts like". How strongly mankind even unconsciously lives this particular Law is illustrated in another saying: "You can tell a man by the company he keeps."

In essence, we constantly live this Law at the everyday social and work level even though we may not be aware of it or its far-reaching implications. Yet its effects can be readily observed around us every single day. Like-minded people gravitate towards certain occupations and professions. In our recreational time the same factors apply. A more striking example, however, may be found at large social gatherings where small groups will form themselves based on what they have in common. It may be their religion or spiritual beliefs, political leanings, profession, musical tastes, sports, language or race, a particular love of something, or even a shared hatred. It can be any number of things or varying combinations, but it will always be a reflection of The Law of Attraction of *Similar* Species in operation.

Some ancient peoples were aware of the effect of this important Law and followed it unconsciously in that they *separated out into occupational and educational classes*. There, every person had the opportunity to live and develop to his fullest potential at each particular 'level'. Unfortunately societies gradually changed into divisions of upper, middle and lower classes. This development eventually embraced the full social spectrum of envy and hatred on the one hand, and conceit and arrogance on the other, until finally ending in class-conflict.

What is infinitely more beneficial, and clearly desirable, is that the various occupations and socio-economic groups in societies develop in such a way that they stand 'side by side', thus offering the greatest possibility for 'working together' harmoniously. Genuine self-esteem for every group could develop to its fullest potential then. And because the different sectors will possess abilities that the others might not have, each becomes a necessary link to every other, thus producing a sound whole. Anti-social problems should then gradually disappear as a better society develops under the correct recognition of this Law. The key consideration here, however, is: – *"Working Together, Side by Side!"*

In a completely different kind of example, gardening can show the extent of this Law quite graphically. In the practice of 'companion planting', one type of plant or group of plants assists the growth and development of others. An 'inappropriate' plant, however, can actually prevent the 'companion' from reaching full maturity or producing fruit. In the wild communities of plants The Law of Attraction... guarantees a natural balance of the various groupings. With the exception of a few species, the animal world operates under the same principle, as do the birds and fishes. The advantages of the group are quite obvious, a greater protective umbrella and care of the offspring probably being the primary consideration. In working together, food supplies may be more secure and the group entity is better able to develop a higher social structure than lone individuals can.

The Law of Attraction... also guarantees that if a particular species is split, the split parts will seek to re-unite when given the opportunity. In terms of the attracting quality, *whole species that are similar will attract*, and *split parts **of the same species*** will also **strive to re-unite**. This Law is a fundamental dynamic for everything *seeking union* in Creation.

What does this mean for us, the human species? And where do we place this powerful force of attraction between men and women? Because of its nature and place in Creation, the human being also carries, as an inherent quality within it, *the desire for union*. Sexual instinct aside, this basically explains the *natural attraction* between man and woman.

As previously stated, we possess the ability, by virtue of our spiritual nature, to produce the forms of our thoughts, words and deeds. What has not been explained, however, is the fact that these forms which are our *works*, are *whole species*, and under this particular Law attract *similar species*. Since man is unable to *stop forming*, what do we then have? What is produced are extremely large groupings of correspondingly *similar* forms. These homogenous groupings can be designated as "power centres". This is an apt description as they *do* possess power so long as we continue to 'feed' them via our ability to produce more forms to add to these "centres", or in utilising the power inherent in our thoughts to sustain the "centres" already in existence.

So, where do these "power centres" reside, and what is their function?

Each "centre" will correspond with, and attract to itself, the *same kinds* of similar forms. Thus there are "power centres" of *all* the virtues and vices from the "works" of humankind. They exist in their *non-material state* close to our physical environment from where the power inherent in them *influences* the affairs of men. Simple imagination can offer an indication of how some might look. Those of hate, jealousy and bitterness must be ugly to witness, whilst those of love and kindness would be havens of happiness and peace.[7]

A small illustration of how The Spiritual Laws intermesh and how the effect of these "power centres" on human beings can be so terribly devastating, even if the recipient has absolutely no knowledge whatsoever of them, will show how insidiously powerful they are.

*   *   *   *   *

We now know that ignorance of The Laws does not prevent the dispensing of true justice. Marriage and the family unit, by virtue of the closeness of the relationships, can often be a place where much emotion is generated – good and bad. Should a situation develop where a breaking down of what might once have been a relatively happy unit now degenerates into a difficult and perhaps emotionally bitter experience for one or both partners, the emotional pain will naturally produce *forms* associated with that turmoil.

This will probably be compounded if there is a third party involved and/or there are children to the marriage. If there can be no reconciliation or resolution and a breakdown is inevitable, the emotional pressures generated might be such that the normal strength of one of the partners is temporarily rendered far weaker than would otherwise be the case. With the ebbing of "spiritual strength", (this 'strength' being at the same time also spiritual protection), in the belief that one's hopes and dreams are about to be dashed, there may arise in the mind of the one most likely to suffer the greatest loss, the wish to 'do something about it'. More particularly with the possible estrangement from everyday contact with much loved children.

This potential chain of events may only begin as just the emotion of hurt, and then perhaps anger. If it stays at that level and is then resolved relatively peacefully, nothing untoward should occur to bring about a dangerous situation. However, should it develop further to the point of one partner 'wanting to get even', the 'forms generated' – such as those of hate and revenge – begin the process of attracting *around that individual* correspondingly *similar* forms from the relevant "power centre/s". Thus his developing volition for revenge is strengthened to a considerable degree under this "Law of Attraction of Similar Species". If the individual cannot then generate sufficient spiritual strength to *resist* a weakening former good volition and thus *change* the forms around him, it could well be that at the moment of greatest weakness, the pressure from the 'attacking' similar forms 'forces' the carrying out of the deed.

How often do we hear comments evinced with great puzzlement, "How could he/she have done that?" "It is so totally out of character!" "I would never have believed that he/she could ever do that!" In times of normalcy it might never have happened. However, with the base volition 'vastly amplified' by the other attracted forms, the receiver is rendered temporarily incapable of clear, logical reasoning at such a time. Other "forces" have 'taken over'.

---

[7]This is a key element in the thread of our story, especially the Maori aspect.

*   *   *   *   *

That is the explanation of the Biblical Scripture:

> *"Because our fight is not against blood and flesh; but against the sovereignties, against the powers, against the commanders of the darkness of this world..."*

(Ephesians 6:12, Fenton.)

Unfortunately, however, it is a darkness that we of humankind have created.

With the exception of true insanity – and/or in cases where the personal free-will volition of a person is temporarily rendered impotent by a stronger *occupying entity* – the perpetrator is, nonetheless, still spiritually responsible for his actions. Therefore, irrespective of the circumstances, or even possible provocation, it still rests with the individual whether or not he chooses a good volition or a dark one. For it should never be forgotten that we are always subject to *the whirlwind constant*. We may believe we are only *sowing the wind*, but we **will** *reap the whirlwind* under Spiritual Law. The harvesting must always be greater than the sowing and this is equally true in good or bad. Neither can we escape the effects of our works at earthly death. The biblical saying, Revelation 14:13, Fenton:

"...and their works accompany them."

– means exactly that too. We take our 'works' with us.

Consequently, no one can escape Spiritual Justice purely because one conveniently dies an earthly death. No, the "works" spoken of here are composed of **all the forms** produced by our thoughts, our words, and our actions or deeds. And because we are the producers, the originators of them, they are tied to us until such time as we finally undertake to expiate them, either upon their return to us as possible hard lessons or experiences, or we bring about a change in the nature of them by a corresponding change in our own personal attitude and spiritual volition. Thus in strict accordance with The Laws of Justice, what has not been 'dealt with' on the earth 'waits to be faced' in the planes of what we loosely refer to as 'the beyond", for we cannot escape "our works".

> *They follow us purely and simply because they must,* **and because they are ours**.

*   *   *   *   *

The birth of Jesus into the Jewish race provides an excellent example of how "The Law of Attraction..." operates in its inviolable way. As a people with strong religious convictions, the Israelites, through their prophets, divined the existence of The One Invisible God, thus anchoring a channel of *knowing acceptance* for everything from that Highest Source. The strength of this exalted belief, even in times of hard persecution, reached upward to The Godhead and allowed for the strongest possible *Spiritual* connection at that time. Thus the Jewish people were able to provide that necessary "connection" for the birth of Jesus to take place. Hence the reason why Jesus, The Son of the Invisible God **could**, and **did**, incarnate into that particular race.

For only with such a sure conviction from the Jewish people could the appropriate connections be established for such an event to take place. Without this inner divining of "The Highest Heights", a necessary attracting quality for this happening was impossible. An incarnation by Jesus into any race other than one with the requisite *spiritual belief* of The Highest Spheres would mean a huge gulf of non-understanding, so is not possible under The Laws of Creation.

Quite logically, therefore, an incarnation into a savage tribe of idol worshippers would have been a rather pointless exercise for the entry of The Son of God onto the earth plane.

6.4.1 Spiritual Qualities as the First Consideration

Because of our inherent spiritual nature, spiritual characteristics should be the most important factor in determining to whom or to what we will be naturally attracted. Most people will have probably felt strongly drawn to certain persons for no *apparent* reason other than a feeling of an especially strong bond. Sometimes to our great surprise – though it should not be so under the effect of The Law of Attraction... – we may even discover that certain meetings quickly produce bonds that are far stronger than those we experience with some members of our own immediate family.

A story in the life of Jesus illustrates this. When told that His mother and brothers were waiting to see Him, replied:

> "Who is My mother? and who are My brothers?" Then extending His hand in the direction of His disciples, He said, "Why, those are My mother and My brothers! For whosoever does the will of My Father Who is in Heaven, he is My brother, and sister, and mother!"

> (Matthew 12:48-50, Fenton.)

Spiritual qualities, therefore, should be recognised as the correct thing to strive for in the first instance, *even if it means breaking completely free from the sometimes cloying and often selfishly-emotional influence and demands that some family groups generate.*[8]

The present generally low level of spiritual maturity exhibited by human societies today is clearly demonstrated by the fact that, for many people, only race and ethnicity are the main considerations in their relationships with others. This lack of understanding for the deeper and finer qualities ensures that this superficiality places outward appearances such as skin colour, race, physical looks, fashion and religion etc., foremost.

Spiritual knowledge, particularly the right knowledge of "The Law of Rebirth", will show the relative unimportance of such things as a person's race or nationality. The basis for assessing the worth of a human being can then be made on character alone. The following Biblical quotation probably best encapsulates this:

> "A useful tree cannot produce bad fruit; nor can a worthless tree produce good fruit. Every tree not producing good fruit will be felled and used as firewood. Reject their produce; for by this you can recognise them."

> (Matthew 7:18-20, Fenton.)

6.4.2 Families and Children

The ramifications posed by the question of how and why particular souls incarnate into certain family groupings under The Law of Attraction... are so far reaching that if humanity were to *truly know and live this knowledge* much of society's ugly side could be made non-existent – in virtually just a few generations. Whilst that may seem a very broad statement, an examination of the serious importance of it, and the equally grave responsibility attached to it, should become evident to the open-minded reader. More especially, however, if one is a parent or wishes to become one. Since procreation is very much the norm rather than the exception, the significance of our opening sentence should be of primary interest to this group particularly.

Who has not heard the statement at some time, often given as an emotional outburst: "I didn't ask to be born!", or: "I didn't choose my parents!"? Unfortunately, **not so**! Random selection does not operate here. The Laws of **"Attraction"**, **"Reciprocal Action"** and

---

[8] Far too many religions, cultures, societies and races place the family 'group' (the extended *whanau*) uppermost in their life and thinking. The *'whanau'* is thus ultimately placed – and therefore *spiritually misplaced* – before **The Living Law Itself**. A foolish and dangerous transgression!

"Spiritual Gravity", under the determination of one's free-will, most certainly do, however. These three key, strongly-interlinked Laws basically determine the geographical location, the family and all other circumstances into which one is born. For an act of procreation simply provides *an opportunity for individual souls waiting in the 'beyond' to incarnate on earth.*

Since there are many souls awaiting such an opportunity, certain precise factors will finally bring the 'correct one' to the prospective mother. Because this determination is governed by Spiritual Law, the family *environment* and connections to the *pregnant mother*, particularly, will be crucial to the kind of soul expected. Strong similarities between the incoming soul and the mother or other members of the family may also have a bearing on *who* finally arrives. Or perhaps the prospective soul may have ties to a particular person or group of people that the prospective mother has close connections with. That potential can act as a powerful force of attraction for the souls surrounding her who are also awaiting an opportunity to incarnate. Thus *women*, who are the *providers* of the *Spiritual Bridge* and who are the *primary link* by which incoming souls are able to enter the earth plane, **have a very great responsibility here**.

Past life connections to various members of the family may also be a determinant as well, and one that may later provide either harmonious relationships or severely strained ones, depending on the circumstances of the past association. In all cases, however, the particular soul that finally *inhabits* the growing foetus will have been strictly determined according to Spiritual Law. It will thus possess all the necessary characteristics to be able to fulfil its particular role and purpose within the family grouping and in its own personal life-path as well.

The entry of the soul into the growing foetus, also determined by Law, takes place about the middle of pregnancy.[9] The seal of attraction is thereby complete and the soul takes full possession of its new home – the growing body. The mother may have mixed feelings ranging from bliss to unease, for this will depend on the nature of this *new stranger she is compelled to accept.*

The emotionally charged issue of abortion takes on an entirely different hue when viewed from the perspective of Spiritual Law. In accordance with the **inviolable outworking of The Eternal Laws** by which we are granted life and sustenance, abortion is *not ever the automatic right* of any mother at any time during pregnancy. Of course, there will always occur certain life-threatening situations that may necessitate the need for difficult decisions in this respect. But the strident cry of: "My body, my right!", does not remove the inevitable and severe *spiritual consequences* of unnecessary abortions by all involved – for there *is* 'freedom of choice' here too. However, in both freedom of choice and the so-called *right* to 'abortion on demand', the immutable *spiritual consequences* nevertheless remain.

Even a purely foetal abortion – in the early stages of pregnancy before the entry of the soul – does not absolve the participants of the *spiritual repercussions* of such an act. From the aspiring soul's point of view, all its hopes and aspirations for that particular earth life with its chosen parents, and the mutual opportunities of spiritual growth for both parties, is effectively lost. Whether or not a second opportunity for incarnation might present itself for the same players via another pregnancy could only be determined by the outworking of The Spiritual Laws. Abortion after the entry of a soul into the growing foetus is similar to physical murder under The Spiritual Laws of Creation, regardless of what the medical profession, women's groups, or the lawmakers have determined for themselves.

It is a foolish delusion to believe that the act of ending the life of a human being as a purely 'convenient solution' would not carry serious *spiritual* consequences for the perpetrators. Consequences, moreover, that also impact upon *all who support such practices.*

---

[9]Dr Robert Winston, of "The Human Body" series, in his later documentary about conception, growth and birth in a group of mothers around the world, noted a significant and measurable change in foetal activity mid-point through pregnancy. Thus what Spiritual Law has ordained, science has now confirmed, albeit inadvertently and without conscious acceptance of that particular truth at this time.

*   *   *   *   *

It is interesting to objectively observe the plight of certain peoples today whose primary method of birth control is abortion. This particular birth-control regime translates to hundreds of thousands, possibly millions, of destroyed lives over many years in the case of very populous countries. The now more rapid reciprocal effect of all *spiritual* transgressions accelerates the consequences of this particular practice in such societies. The subsequent accelerating deterioration of the *material* and *social* environment of *those* Nations is hardly surprising because the whole land becomes a vast, collective 'reciprocal-reaping' for the particular peoples concerned.

*   *   *   *   *

The birth of disabled children is therefore not without purpose either, whether for the mother, the family or, not least, for the disabled one. Because these events are strictly governed by Spiritual Law, it is only through the knowledge of them that full understanding can be gained as to why such an event will visit itself upon a family group. It is surely certain, however, that in the caring of the disabled one the nature of the disability will offer both partners the necessary spiritual experiencing for which the birth was perhaps ordained. Ordained, moreover, through the *free-will decision of the parents for sexual union* and an ensuing procreative event. It is necessary here to fully understand that it is only the physical body that is disabled. The inner, animating core of the Spirit, the real child and adult, is never so!

In similar vein, the infertility of certain couples is not an arbitrary act either. The inability to naturally produce offspring is also governed by "Spiritual Law". In other words, there will be a very good reason for this, even if not readily apparent. It may well have its origin in the long distant past, with its reciprocal effect translating in a deep desire to want children in the present but not easily being able to, or possibly not at all, even with modern medical procedures. Infertile couples should thus determine whether or not it is within their ordained life-path to pursue parenthood. It could mean that having no children might allow them to fulfil a particular purpose more completely, whereas having children may make it much more difficult, or even impossible.

A more enlightened attitude would see couples planning for children solely from *the spiritual point of view*. Where no children are desired, conception would simply be avoided. The very nature of physical desire between couples, which should be viewed as both spiritually-correct and special, is invariably also incredibly strong. So, in inviolable accordance with The Perfect outworking of The Spiritual Laws of Creation, the natural outcome of "two split species" [man/woman] seeking *union* means that the possibility of pregnancy is ever present. With the correct understanding of the processes that determine the *kind* of new family addition that could arrive, future prospective parents will be better able to plan for children who will be more aware and enlightened than is presently the case where this crucial knowledge is known and accepted by so few.

For just as the new soul will provide certain experiences and lessons for the family group into which it has incarnated, its new family and circumstances will offer similar provision for what it will need for its spiritual growth too. Viewed in this light, the wish to want a child should be very seriously considered because such a desire should be tempered by the acceptance of the responsibility to provide the correct upbringing for any offspring. Children are not ours to own and neither should we see them as arriving to us as a completely clean slate upon which we can write our own personal program for them.

With each act of procreation, the opportunity is offered for a soul to reside with us until such time as its ordained path or personal choices calls it to travel its own individual journey. If we have 'attracted spiritually and guided well', offspring should be well-equipped to make good decisions for themselves whenever crossroads are reached. Hopefully, the decision made then will be in accordance with The Eternal Laws, thus ensuring a good return for those we have nurtured and set free. Under this "attracting process" a family of noble people will generally attract noble souls. The arrival of a so-called 'black sheep' might indicate that the pregnant woman may have allowed a less than honourable person into her immediate sphere of influence around the time of the entry of the soul. In this inviolable and thus *infallible* process lies the reason *why* there is so much evil now present, and increasing, upon earth.[10]

> Under the lawful processes inherent in The Eternal Laws, *a darker soul seeking to incar-*
> *nate onto the earth plane will always drive back a lighter, more noble soul seeking the same*
> *opportunity.*

This is purely the lawful effect of The Law of Spiritual Gravity. Perhaps earlier generations intuitively understood this process in part, in determining pregnancy as a time, or term, 'of confinement' – a period of 'protective separation' from any detrimental influences of society. This custom would offer natural spiritual protection, more especially up to the entry of the soul into the foetus. It is unlikely, however, that *modern feminist views* would accept such an assertion. Nevertheless, these strict and lawful "spiritual" processes cannot be circumvented by *modern* and more *liberal* attitudes.

The effect of The Law of Attraction... on families and crime has produced some interesting statistics. Police records in many countries have recorded whole families, even generations of families, where crime in its myriad forms is regarded as the norm by such groups of wrong-thinking people. Sometimes, however, even in such situations and against all the odds, a member of these kinds of 'families' may choose to follow a different path. Thus the more noble and spiritual characteristics such as compassion, courage, instinctive respect for justice, inner grace – in effect true *mana* – are **not** biologically inherited.

The uglier traits of humankind are not similarly inherited either. Nevertheless, it is still The Law of Attraction of Similar Species that greatly determines the make-up of families. However, it should not be presumed that a soul with an innate propensity to live a less than noble existence on the earth must necessarily do so. Our inherent free-will factor gives such a person the opportunity to break free from any base propensities, no matter how strong, if it so chooses or wills for itself.

Genetic processes, which are by no means accidental, are what give rise to the physical characteristics of parental offspring. In this situation, The Law of Reciprocal Action ensures that only those who have 'sown the appropriate seeds' are incarnated into families and places where they are bound to enjoy genetic advantage or suffer from hereditary handicap.

*   *   *   *   *

In terms of a Maori example showing the operation of **The Law of Attraction of Similar Species** during the long phase of cannibalism within the race, a very ready bridge of *opportunal-access*, in effect an invitation, would have been offered to many disparate souls in the nether worlds of the beyond to incarnate into the Maori race to live such a life. In this particular example, the Maori were only *one* of a number of cannibal races. Therefore a soul with a propensity for cannibalism would have had 'a choice of appropriate races', so to speak. However, the final connection would have been strictly determined under the outworking of Spiritual Law thus allowing 'certain souls' to be Maori, as opposed to being a member of another *similar kind of cannibal-race for that particular lifetime.*

*   *   *   *   *

---

[10]The *primary* publication of **Crystal Publishing**: [BIBLE **"MYSTERIES" EXPLAINED**..., **Chapter 3, The Spiritual Laws**..., sub; **The Law of Attraction**... – **Why There is so much Violence and Evil on Earth**] – details the process more fully.

Now, in the light of the beneficial knowledge of The Spiritual Laws, we should re-examine our current thinking as to who or what actually constitutes a 'victim'. The present day tyranny of the 'poor victim of circumstance' syndrome virtually allows some people of this mind-set to commit even crimes of shocking violence under the umbrella of this excuse. In truth, such terribly wrong attitudes debilitate and spiritually-degrade society. Hopefully, we may soon recognise this for the wrong attitude, *the emotional disease*, that it actually is and set up re-education programmes to correct such wrong thinking. That is not to say, however, that help should not be offered to those in need. On the contrary, with this correct knowledge exactly the right kind of help or education can be given thus allowing for the possibility of the complete elimination of this societal 'illness'. This would provide the necessary foundation for nobleness and individual responsibility to become the norm instead of the present practice of socially or culturally entrenching the totally wrong idea of 'non-responsibility' into the very souls who desperately need a complete change of thinking.

Consider, also, if the earth could be rid of all diseases and the associated cause of human suffering in this case, any souls that needed to experience such suffering would not have the opportunity to be able to incarnate here. We can further extrapolate from this that if we – all humanity – really strove to be truly noble in all our thoughts, words, activities and aspirations etc., it would become impossible for any unworthy spirits to incarnate on earth simply because *the connecting bridge of attraction would no longer be there*. Through this recognition and process, a more enlightened humankind could make the earth what it was originally ordained to be – *a paradise*. That choice and responsibility was always ours alone, however.

To this end it is important to understand that the present thrust of globally entrenching the concept of **my rights**, transgresses virtually every aspect of The Spiritual Laws. Rarely now do we hear of responsibilities, duties or obligations. We hear only the increasingly strident and selfish cry of **"my rights"**! And in the case of the relationship between parents and children, this translates into a mad tyranny where children's *rights* have become more important than their *responsibilities*. For just as parents have responsibilities to their offspring so, too, should children be taught to fulfil this aspect of Spiritual Law also.

By first putting in place the attitude of responsibilities and duties to each other, we automatically create an environment where rights can become synonymous with duties for, under Spiritual Law, fulfilment of duty and responsibility must come before any claim to rights.

Therefore, *children can only claim rights if they loyally perform their duties*.

6.5   The Law of Spiritual Gravity

In accordance with *Newton's* "Law on Universal Gravitation", the idea of a force of gravity is readily understandable in the physical sense of the word. Quite logically, heavy objects fall to the ground whilst very light substances may rise. So the effect we see materially is the form by which this Law manifests on earth. However, whilst the effect of this particular Law clearly displays obvious physical characteristics, The Law itself is first and foremost a *Spiritual* one. Therefore the same gravitational effect that takes place in a physical setting also occurs in a non-physical environment. It is one, moreover, which impacts more decisively on the fate of man *after* his earthly demise! That is because, as previously stated, the actual person or individual is more than just a physical body. Our true self, or actual conscious personality, is that of our inner animating core: – Our Spirit.

For that is who and what we actually are.

At earthly death we simply discard, or step out of, the physical form that all human beings are obliged to take up or accept upon entry onto the earth plane. This shell, our *overcoat*, is then subject to the natural processes of decay and disintegration in accordance with the Laws of Nature i.e., the *earthly outworking* of The Spiritual Laws of Creation. This completely natural process thus allows the soul body, which consists of a number of non-physical bodies enveloping the spirit, to become free of its previously heavy 'physical garment'. However, it is not then able to go wherever it wishes, for that process is determined by The Law of Spiritual Gravity acting upon all the 'works' connected to each individual.

The everyday outworking of the effect of The Law of Gravity is revealed in earthly sayings, even if unconsciously, which reflect this concept in society. For instance, we often speak of 'heavy thoughts' and 'light thoughts', or the effect that a 'heavy person' may have upon us as opposed to the much more enjoyable company of a 'light person'. Evil thoughts and practices are rightly recognised as being of a 'heavy nature', whilst noble thoughts and deeds are similarly accepted as occupying a far higher and thus lighter level.

So is it with our spirit also. Base propensities and activities whilst in the physical body on earth weigh the *coverings* of the spirit down causing it to sink, to fall away in a direction opposite to its true Origin in The Spiritual Realm. Thus the spirit regresses. The depth to which it sinks is strictly determined by the extent to which it indulged in wrong-doing which, in turn, gives it its 'spiritual weight' or heaviness. The particular level descended to will be peopled by those with similar base propensities or weaknesses in accordance with The Law of Attraction of Similar Species. It is thus necessary to understand that, under The Eternal Laws, **only on the Earth can good and evil live side by side.** Every other Plane of Creation is formed according to its comparative "weight" – lightest and purest at the top, and heaviest and darkest at the bottom. In this lies the most wonderful justice because each individual spirit automatically ends up in the plane corresponding to its personal volition, **thereby automatically receiving what it strove for most.**

If a recently departed spirit has lived a life of, say, lust and greed for example – a very good illustration given the deplorable state of humankind today – it will be drawn to the same level as others similar to it. In an environment of similar beings, each will give full vent to their propensity for lust and greed upon each other continuously. This same happening will be repeated in other places at other levels where the propensities for violence, drunkenness, nicotine and drug addiction, gluttony, laziness, and anger etc., hold sway. There, in situations as depraved and potentially as hopeless as that described, is the place we call "hell".[11]

Yet even there The Eternal Laws, which also automatically incorporate Divine Love, are ever watchful for souls who, through inner recognition, finally become disgusted with themselves and their tormented environment and petition for their release from it. With this personal awakening to the truth of their situation and the longing to be free of it, a way is automatically opened for such souls to begin their ascent to the next higher level. Through their awakening to personal recognition and desire for change, they would have become different to their particular environment, thereby ensuring an automatic separation from it in accordance with The Spiritual Laws – notably *The Law of Attraction of Similar Species* and *The Law of Gravity* under the outworking of *The Law of Movement*. Thus any soul can ascend, even out of such grievous circumstances, if it so desires.

Contrast that situation with one where a soul has striven to do noble deeds all its earth life: where it had sought to find Spiritual Truth; where it had offered compassion and kindness; where its thoughts and aspirations had sought elevation. Such a life makes a spirit light and buoyant. Upon shedding its physical shell at earthly death, its spiritual lightness draws it upward toward Planes of Light. There it will find spirits who exhibit the same kinds of noble traits as itself. Whereas the inhabitants of the lower regions are surrounded by their own base volition, those in The Higher Planes of Light experience the living reality of the greater contentment and happiness synonymous with striving for more noble aspirations, which they have earned.

---

[11] A more complete explanation of the nature of "hell" is offered in Chapter 9.

For those who *choose to believe* that ascent lies **solely** in a belief of faith in Jesus, consider His following words from the "Sermon on the Mount":

> "...that until the heavens and the earth shall pass away, a single dot or hairstroke shall not disappear from the law, until **all** has been completed."

And again, in part:

> "I tell you indeed, that **you** will not depart until **you** have **repaid** the very **last** farthing."

> (Matthew 5:18 and 5:26, Fenton.
> Emphases mine.)

Since Jesus spoke from the standpoint of Spiritual Truth, we should understand that His words offer clear guidelines with regard to this contentious issue of "faith alone" versus "personal atonement".

The Law of Spiritual Gravity has logically existed since time immemorial, yet it is interesting to note that Newton's theories and discoveries in the earthly environment paved the way for a rapid increase in knowledge of astronomy and allowed for further interstellar discoveries. Moreover, the simplicity of The Laws that hold the moon in stable orbit around the earth without either crashing into it through its stronger gravitational pull or simply heading off into space, convinced Newton that only *"a few natural laws apply to the whole universe"*.

He demonstrated that The Laws which govern the planets of our solar system's elliptical path around the sun, are the same Laws that also govern all moving bodies, and therefore apply everywhere in the entire universe. Notwithstanding the medieval adage of "...as in heaven, so on earth", his radical view of the time generally put to rest a conflicting belief that there is "...one set of laws for heaven and another here on earth". Because Newton believed that the same natural laws applied everywhere in the universe, this would clearly have posed a potential "crisis of faith" for any orthodox Christian view of God.

Newton's own faith, however, was never shaken. On the contrary, he regarded the natural laws as *proof* of the *existence* of a great and Almighty God.

6.6   The Law of Balance

Aristotle, the great Greek philosopher [384-322BC] wrote extensively about 'the nature of man'. Quoted in (Nichomachaen Ethics, Book 2), he writes:

> "Virtue, then, is a disposition involving choice. It consists of a mean, relative to us, defined by reason and as the reasonable man would define it. It is a mean between two vices – one of excess, the other of deficiency."

Had Aristotle lived today, he would probably be horrified at the excesses and imbalances in global society such as the acquisition of obscene extremes of wealth alongside abject poverty, and in the increasing obsession with attaining perfection of body. In his view these kinds of activities and practices were just as unbalanced as someone who only uses his head. He considered such extremes to be an expression of a warped way of life. Aristotle also applied the "Golden Mean" to human relationships.

He believed that we must be neither cowardly nor rash, but courageous (too little courage is cowardice, too much is rashness), neither miserly nor extravagant but liberal (not liberal enough is miserly, too liberal is extravagant). The same applied to eating. He thought it was dangerous to eat too little, but also dangerous to eat too much. The ethics of both Plato and Aristotle contain echoes of Greek medicine.

Aristotle believed that for some acts there is no mean at all; their very nature already implies badness, such as spite, envy, adultery, theft, and murder. These are bad in themselves, "...and not in their excesses and deficiencies. One is always wrong in doing them."

(Philosophy History and Problems, Samuel Enoch Stumpf, p.99)

Achieving a happy or 'harmonious' life, therefore, can only be attained by exercising balance in temperament. Generally regarded as probably the first philosopher/scientist, Aristotle divided everything in the natural world into two main categories. In one corner he placed what he termed the non-living things such as rocks, clumps of soil and drops of water etc., and in the other the classification of 'living things'. He further divided this latter group into two other categories, 'plants' and the 'other creatures'. This last was finally divided into two sub-categories; animals and humans.

Aristotle further reasoned that the 'form' of man comprised three parts; a plant-like part, an animal part and a rational part (the soul, or 'divine reason'). In his view, man could only live a good life and achieve happiness by using all his abilities and capabilities. In the three forms of happiness he identified, the first was a life of pleasure and enjoyment, the second as a free and responsible citizen, and the third as a thinker and philosopher. All three needed to be present at the same time for happiness to be attained within the individual, for he rejected all forms of *imbalance*.

Thus The Law of Balance was well accepted in those early years. In spiritual terms this Law, in its effect and outworking, should reflect the necessary *balance* between 'giving' and 'receiving'. In everyday tasks, many even mundane things automatically obey this law. A baby taking its first faltering steps, a young child learning to stay upright on a bicycle, the simple act of walking, waiters balancing plates of food in cafes. On city construction sites, we observe large cranes with enormous working booms counter-balanced by opposing shorter boom lengths also appropriately counter-weighted to achieve safe working balances. The activities of trade and monetary transaction may require the use of scales for various purposes. In many judicial systems, justice is depicted by a set of scales, perhaps reflecting the wish that a correct weighing and examining in the Courts might be the outcome. For if there is no balance where lies justice?

The simplest and most quietly obvious example of The Law of Balance is breathing. We must naturally balance exhaling with inhaling. Correct breathing is vital for optimum health, but shallow breathing into the top of the lungs only does not necessarily provide for this. The solution in this case is to regard the outbreath as the key. Exhaling properly and emptying the lungs will *automatically ensure* that a full breath will next be inhaled. Many a respiratory disorder can be at least *relieved* with consistent and correct breathing.[12] The rather curious state of 'sleep' that most creatures on earth necessarily require is another example of how strongly this 'Law of Balance' governs 'life'. Even nocturnal animals experience 'circadian balance' here. For the most part, we humans must live the rhythm of 'work during the day', and 'sleep at night'. Insufficient 'sleep', like 'overwork', harms the body. Both kinds of *imbalance* seriously transgress this Law; to our detriment.

In the home and in the Nation, the need to balance the budget is important in order to live within our means. The daily intake of food generally indicates a basic understanding of the need to try to achieve a 'balanced diet' for optimum health i.e., different kinds of foods in appropriate proportions. Quite obviously, too much of just one type of food is not only inappropriate and tiresome, but is also not beneficial for the digestive system. Balancing the necessary intake of food is the need to eliminate body wastes as a natural result of this process. Any imbalance resulting from poor digestion or constipation makes us feel unwell.

---

[12]We in the 'Maori race' would be well advised to adopt this as a simple, effective, cost-free preventative health measure as we have far too high a level of respiratory disease. Naturally we should also discard the "spiritual crime" of cigarette smoking.

Workaholic burnout as a result of "all work and no play" is also a transgression against The Law of Balance. Conversely, a life characterised by no work is equally harmful, even after retirement. The right kind of work for each individual should be a feature of the retirement years to help maintain the health of the body until death. Where the elderly happily engage in appropriate activity, higher levels of health are achieved. And where job opportunities are not readily available for someone wishing to work, low self esteem may be the outcome resulting in a decline in the emotional and physical health of that individual.

The Laws of Creation show us that they inherently repose in the actuality of Divine Love. **Love is thus the greatest Power!** Also inherent in this as a part of Divine Love is Perfect Justice, for the two cannot be separated. With regard to The Law of Balance under the aegis of the Power of Love, however, 'everlasting rest' is *not* the reality of the after-death situation. We are compelled to accept the responsibility of our life's decisions and 'live them out', so to speak, even after our physical demise. Then our 'personal books' are audited to determine where there is imbalance, after which we must spiritually address it. Perhaps if more people recognised this stark reality – which cannot be circumvented in any case – there might arise a better attitude to many things, since earthly death is the great 'leveller'. Knowledge of The Law of Balance would especially benefit the elderly and those approaching death. Perhaps a greater effort might then be placed on *balancing one's spiritual account* long before being overtaken by earthly death.

Unfortunately, however, our present way of thinking clearly shows a general propensity for two things. One is to seek as much wealth in the shortest possible time; and the second, for a life of ease ever after on earth. Great wealth can achieve wonderful goals and is not, in itself, a bad thing. However, if it is used for base, superficial or selfish ends, it loses its great potential and value and *spiritually-degrades* the holders of it. It is a sad indictment on today's society that spiritual goals, or earthly activities with a truly spiritual content, are not regarded or valued highly as befits their true worth. The scales of society are well and truly tipped toward overindulgence, base passions and immorality, to our spiritual detriment.

Benjamin Franklin (1706-1790) observed that if there were no limiting factors in nature, one species of plant or animal could engulf the entire globe. But the balance is maintained because many species hold each other in check. Man is the only 'spanner in the works' here, as his activities invariably create imbalance.

In what is arguably the most difficult yet necessary part of the everyday life of the human spirit i.e., that of personal relationships, the correct application of The Law of Balance between "giving and taking" offers the key to harmony and progress in all situations. Whether in marriage between partners, in a family situation between parents and children, between employer and employee, or between groups or Nations; in each particular case the concept of giving and taking needs to be correctly understood.

Parents desiring to have children must be aware of the need to balance this with the duty to care for the child in the right way. The protection and nurturing that parents offer children must be balanced by the obligation of children to respect adults. Once the child has reached an age where it is physically able to assist in the home, it should be required to do so in order to balance the parental care it receives. Its form of assistance would be commensurate with its age and abilities. A child brought up without the application of this Law in its life may not develop any kind of purposeful work ethic, nor garner the correct social skills and attitude necessary to interact in a naturally balanced way with others. An attitude of personal selfishness is often the outcome that, unfortunately, may become ingrained for life. The spiritually-correct concept of "tough love" for wayward children today might not have been needed for many *had The Law of Balance been applied from the outset.*

It should not be assumed, however, that the application of The Law of Balance must necessarily require a *similar* kind of return contribution or payment to that received. Personal circumstances may decree otherwise. In such cases, however, the recipient will fulfil the requirements of this Law if he evinces deep and genuine gratitude for the help received. Or perhaps he may be able to tender some good advice which his benefactor may well be able to put to good use for himself. So, regardless of personal situations, everyone is able to fulfil the demands of The Law of Balance in some way. The fact that most do not do so stands as a reflection of our level of spiritual immaturity where the unhelpful human traits of selfishness, thoughtlessness, or just plain bad habits have become more the norm.

In respecting this Law, we should not unnecessarily worry about what should be given in return. It behoves us to simply give the best of what we have and what we can, *relative* to what was received and what we are *able* to give. If this should mean genuine thanks only, without guile or deceit, then the demands of The Law are fulfilled. Legal contracts are not included here, that is a different matter. Thus, everybody, rich or poor, is able to *live* this most necessary Law. Even the poorest can give out of themselves, either gratitude, a heartfelt prayer, or even a kind look to the giver. So long as the heart is pure and the intention genuine, the essential considerations from the standpoint of The Spiritual Laws will then have been correctly fulfilled.[13]

6.6.1   To Give, or to Take?

"It is more blessed to give than to receive!"

(Acts 20:35, Fenton.)

These words of Jesus, like many of them, have been so misunderstood or so grossly misinterpreted that it has become difficult to fulfil His words of The Law in the way He originally taught them, even with the very best of intentions. Yet the question of whether one should give or take is readily answered in the understanding that in The Law of Balance between giving and taking, *giving* always ranks first. Unfortunately, through the well-intentioned but misplaced 'generosity' of some social groups and churches, 'taking' as a 'social right' has become a way of life for some people and families who have no idea that they should also *give something* in return.

Whether intentional or not, this transgression of The Law of Balance has a detrimental effect on the one who is a constant receiver, not least to the individual's self-esteem and self-respect. Moreover, children raised in this environment may become unwitting transgressors of this Law later in their life, also to their detriment. Thus, through a lack of understanding of an Eternal Law, well-meaning people can actually *perpetuate and enlarge a social disaster*, as their good intent, in certain cases, does not always translate to giving *the correct and necessary kind of "spiritual" and material help actually needed. A thorough knowledge of The Spiritual Laws is the only way that humanity can address its increasing social problems.* In determining the best way that we might offer help, we should always be cognisant of the ancient Chinese saying:

"Give a man a fish, and you feed him for a day. Teach him to fish, and you feed him for life!"

At the beginning of this Chapter we stated that each Law examined would intermesh with all the other Eternal Laws to produce a perfectly balanced whole, and that the reader should be able to perceive the connections between them all. In this case, and as a simple example, one can easily deduce that *giving* in the correct way is better because it is connected to The Law of Sowing and Reaping. The act of giving is identical with the practice of sowing. And each seed will, at its appropriate time, provide multiples of the same kinds of seeds for the *giver*.

---

[13]The classic illustration of this is in the Biblical story of the widow who gave the smallest amount materially, but gave much more than the wealthy, because it was **all** she owned.

Conversely, that which one extends the hand for – the seed taken or received – is like a harvest. Once consumed, it ceases to exist. With each receiving, a cycle is closed. Whenever we give, however, we *start* a new cycle. Through this process, therefore, it is always better to give than to receive. Of course, any giving should not be coloured solely by the selfish desire for a large return, thus losing sight of the correct spiritual reason to want to give in the first place. When viewed in this light, the words of Jesus take on a far deeper and richer meaning than might previously have been understood.

As we noted in the earlier sub-heading, "Families and Children", the current social propensity to demand one's rights, whether individual, children's, youth, ethnic, cultural, social, legal, religious, or any other, in the first instance lives the aspect of "taking"! In the sense of The Spiritual Laws *it is a negative and selfish attitude,* **for rights are only obtained by the fulfilment of responsibilities or duties**.

Therefore, the fulfilment of duty and responsibility must come before any claim to rights. This vitally necessary attitude should be inculcated into every individual through education in the home, in the schools, in the collective workplaces, and perhaps more especially in the country's gaols.

Consider the effect on society if, instead of demanding more and more "rights", we all immediately and radically changed our way of thinking to encompass *a new, more tolerant and giving attitude which saw everyone become concerned with responsibilities, duties and obligations.* Toward each other, between parents and children, teachers and students, employer and employee, between religions and ethnic groups, even between individuals within those ethnic groups, from the criminal to his victim, and the individual to society.

In one single stroke of *changed-attitude*, our present kind of increasingly-selfish society could be instantly transformed into one that actually lived the completely beneficial aspects of Spiritual Law, particularly that of The Law of Sowing and Reaping. Virtually overnight, all manner of social problems and crime would disappear, and confrontation could also quickly become a distant memory – a memory of pointless, debilitating argument, anger and violence. Whilst this may seem an unworkable utopian ideal, it is exactly possible. In any case, without such a change, the social status quo not only remains, *it actually deteriorates.*

Thus one should give out of a genuine desire to help, and in the manner most *spiritually-beneficial* to the recipient. The Eternal Laws therefore urge everyone to give, and no one should practice or indulge in one-sided taking. As previously stated, however, it would be wrong to expect any kind of particular return from the person to whom one has given, as the act of giving is then denigrated to an unspoken, selfish, strings-attached, silent demand – for something in return. In the strict lawfulness of this process, what should be recognised is that what might be received in return for what one has given does not necessarily depend upon the recipient. This may initially be a difficult concept to adjust to. Yet whether or not it is believed the recipient deserves it, whether or not he is grateful or ungrateful, and even whether or not he is actually aware that he has been helped, all such considerations are ultimately unimportant. In any case ingratitude for any kindness shown will bring its own 'reward' to the 'ungrateful one'.

It is a very human trait to seek recognition for any kind of help offered, yet the outworking of The Law of Reciprocal Action applies here equally as much as our attitude toward the suffering. What comes to us as our exact due – our reward, as it were – arrives in the manner and at the time so ordained under The Spiritual Laws. And since we do not necessarily harvest in the same season that we sow, the time of its return may not be immediate. The immediacy of financial transactions are a different matter, concerned solely with business expectations and practices, unless perhaps fraud or deceit is involved.

The same principles should apply whether the giver or receiver is an individual, a group, or a Nation. Here, also, it is more blessed to give than to receive. Many developed Nations give aid and technical assistance to others, and this serves to promote a large measure of peace, harmony and goodwill in the world. If every recipient Nation were to give something in return, a wonderful system of dynamic exchange and interaction would emerge, thus promoting global development in the right way. And every recipient Nation *can* give something in return, be it cultural exchanges, or only genuine gratitude and appreciation.

> We should seriously note that **under the increased Spiritual Pressure now pouring onto the earth and its inhabitants, all past imbalances will be forcibly and therefore severely corrected**.

So as we track toward the inevitable, hard resolution that we can all now see approaching, deviation from The Law of Balance will not be able to be sustained for as long as has been possible thus far. The present structural problems that can be observed in the National and global economies, in particular through failing banks and financial institutions, are a direct result of mankind's total disregard for, and lack of understanding of, The Law of Balance. The disruption inherent in the economic and social stress of major restructuring programmes worldwide is the result of the effect of this increased pressure now culminating in urgent attempts to restore balance where, previously, there was imbalance; even if it appeared not to be the case.

Therefore, the first task of the restructuring agencies should be to ensure that the process is carried out for the right reasons and under the knowledge of this Law, with due regard for the respect and integrity of those duly affected. Without clear reasons and goals, restructuring purely for the sake of doing so will only ensure more unnecessary upheaval. So it behoves the architects of necessary change to become thoroughly conversant with The Eternal Laws, especially The Law of Balance, if they wish to succeed. And, quite obviously, only those areas that actually *need* restructuring should be worked upon and any area that is already in balance should be left alone. To make the process much less painful, areas of imbalance need to be carefully identified in order to correctly rectify the problem areas only. This should apply in all sectors including international trade, in the financial system including setting exchange rates, in the determination of prices for goods and services, and in industrial relations, particularly.

Since most restructuring involves the down-sizing of work forces and their pay rates, with the generally greedy practice of those who institute the changes *greatly increasing their own salary levels*, it would be timely for such people to become cognisant of this Law, if only for their own spiritual growth. Otherwise their 'greed', or their 'works' will one day pursue them, for The Law takes no account of supposedly 'sharp' business practices. In terms of the attitude of such "Boards of Directors" or "CEO's" to the workers who help produce the business profits for them, the correct application of this Law is well illustrated, Luke 10:7, Fenton, in the admonition of Jesus:

> "*...for the workman is entitled to his wages*."

In the international arena, the practice of advancing huge loans to poorer, under-developed Nations, and then expecting outrageously exorbitant interest charges from them, has been rightly likened to a blood transfusion – "***from a sick patient to a healthy one***". Where is the fairness and balance in such cases? To cite the global monetary system as the reason why cheap loans cannot be advanced from rich Nations to poor, quite clearly shows that we should quickly set about bringing it into balance. Thankfully, there is a trend toward change in this area. And a cunningly-engineered and interdependent system that permits the electronic and instant transfer of large amounts of currency to reap huge profits simply because of a small shift in an exchange rate somewhere in the world is clearly **obscene**, for it produces nothing of true value – just greater and greater amounts of *unearned* wealth for the few. Such practices should serve as a warning that this completely out-of-balance, globally-interconnected monetary system cannot be sustained, simply because the Spiritual Pressure inherent in The Law of Balance will one day bring about its collapse.

* * * * *

Interestingly, the December 1996 Edition of *Time* Magazine noted a subtle but growing shift in the attitude of some of the richest Americans. In the opinion of billionaire Ted Turner, the wish of the majority of those Americans to make *Forbes* magazine's listing of the 400 wealthiest, "...is destroying our country", claiming that the "ole skinflints" are so afraid of slipping down the *Forbes* list ... that they hoard, rather than share, their wealth." Turner issued a challenge: rank the biggest 'givers' instead of the biggest 'getters' (takers). Microsoft's online magazine, *Slate*, took up that notion. Launching the *Slate* 60, it lists the largest charitable donations in the country by families or individuals gathered from publicly available sources.

If this list becomes as important to the rich as the *Forbes* list has thus far been, it may well open up a veritable floodgate of financial help where it is needed most – in assisting the unemployed back to work and to self-esteem. For under Spiritual Law the wealthy have a *duty* to provide, not hand-outs, but means, schemes and employment whereby the less fortunate can contribute meaningfully toward their respective societies and to their own personal worth.

We should not leave this segment without offering this most wonderfully appropriate Biblical quote – primarily for the aspiritual wealthy:

> *"For what will it profit a man if he should gain the whole world and forfeit his life? (lose his soul?")*

(Mark 8:36, Fenton, Parentheses mine.)

* * * * *

A quote from "Spiritual Principles of Nation Building", Chapter 2, p.39, Stephen Lampe, Millennium Press, offers a further reflective note:

> More than 150 years ago, a French economist, Pierre Boisguilbert came to the recognition of the utmost importance of balance. He wrote: "Only equilibrium (balance) can save everyone; and nature alone, to repeat, can achieve this." On our part, we should give and give, and nature will restore balance.

The right balance must be struck in all aspects of our lives and not just economic restructuring. The rapid increase in one-parent families shows the urgent need to restore balance in personal relationships, in social interaction with others, and in all human activities. The breakdown of large Nations to smaller ethnic states is nothing more than the restoration of balance to peoples once forced to become, for them, part of an alien system.

The British Commonwealth is a *relatively* good example of this ongoing process. What was once an empire of disparate countries and peoples ruled by the force of arms of the "mother country", has now developed into a relatively easy voluntary association of most of those former colonies bonded by more or less common goals, aspirations and ideals. Moreover, such links have allowed the many varied races in the Commonwealth to develop a far greater knowledge and tolerance toward each other, particularly in the areas of race and religion than would otherwise have been the case under continued British military dominance. And that is as it should be. In its current format, the British Commonwealth stands as a *relatively* good example of what can be achieved through voluntary goodwill, with the ability to play a beneficial role in international affairs. Consider how much more powerful it would be if the common binding force were the knowledge and application of The Spiritual Laws of Creation!

The Law of Balance between Giving and Taking will one day play a fundamental part in true international understanding when peoples and races finally stand **SIDE BY SIDE** in mutual respect, helping and furthering one another. The ideal time for this process to begin is always in the present of course. Notwithstanding that reality, the recognition will eventually arrive that every people, every race, possesses earthly and spiritual values which are indispensable for humanity as a whole. And because other peoples and races may not inherently possess exactly the same attributes, a vital exchange of those values will then become the norm. But such exchanges that occur must reflect the right balance in accordance with the outworking of the Law between **Giving and Taking**.

The most critical application of The Law of Balance, however, is the conscious and voluntary recognition to urgently seek the correct balance between *the material and The Spiritual* in our individual lives. In the intellectual sense man presently stands astride the apex of his technological pyramid.

Spiritually, though, he grovels in the dust at the base, stunted and blind. If any kind of reminders were needed to induce us to begin to redress the balance of the scales toward The Spiritual, one need only look at everyday world events. In that clear revelation humankind unequivocally reveals the level it has chosen!

6.7   The Law of Rebirth

Irrespective of race, religious beliefs and political leanings etc., the one absolute we all accept without question is the fact of birth, life and death. For a great number of people these three facets, at least in the *physical* happening, unfortunately make up the totality of their belief. This logically means that this narrow view thereby 'colours' their attitude to life on earth, thus subsequently 'fixing in their minds' the primary reason for being here in the first place: We are born, we live, we die – end of story!

To that **totally-incorrect notion** we would reply, as per the well-known, well-liked and very truthful promotional 'observations' for Tui beer: —

"Yeah, Right!"

Whilst individual lives will naturally follow the paths set by free-will decisions and will thus be different for each person, the processes of birth and death, however, are absolutely identical for all individuals, insofar as the *mechanics* are concerned. The individual life paths will obviously be very different due to the factors of race, geographical location, education, wealth and status etc., but the *physical processes of the beginning and end of each earth life are exactly the same.* Yet the term "miracle of birth", of which there have been billions during man's existence but which simply represents –

– *the normal and natural processes that all **germinated seeds** must undergo to develop to **the full fruit** –*

– nonetheless correctly expresses amazement and wonder at this event.

The Spiritual Laws that govern the development of the growing individual and determines the final characteristics of it are constant and unchangeable. All births therefore follow the same lawful process. Even when using the procedure of in-vitro fertilisation, doctors are not able to operate outside the parameters dictated by this universal Law. Inherent in The Laws of Creation is certainly the provision for development, but not for wrong experimentation, deviation or transgression, however.

It is the same with the death process. Without exception we are forced to accept the absolute inevitability of it at some point in life. Universal Laws operate here in their Immovable Perfection too. For the step from a living, breathing, animated physical body to a cold, lifeless shell is exactly the same everywhere in the world. The manner of dying may be vastly different, i.e., disease, war, illness, accident – in peaceful sleep even – but the process is identical. Indeed, it could not be otherwise. Yet whilst we are able to observe the physical processes of the steps of birth and death, and can clearly see the after effects of birth, we do not necessarily accept that there may be after effects of earthly death too.

Why not, however? If the evidence of our own eyes with regard to the irrefutable processes of birth and death governed by strict, consistent Laws in the *physical* happening can be readily accepted, why should it not be a simple step to know, *intuitively*, that the outworking of The Spiritual Laws do not simply come to a convenient halt at that point just because we may believe or wish otherwise.

By virtue of the inviolability of The Spiritual Laws, humankind can do nothing else but submit to them for there is no other choice. Even in the cases of suicide or murder the physical processes still cannot change. However, even though The Laws are physical in their visible effect, they are, nevertheless, still Spiritual in Origin. It is well worth deep consideration that even The Son of God, Jesus, had to be born of a woman on earth.

The Creator could not just simply **place Him on the earth as a fully-grown man** – notwithstanding the strong but completely wrong religious conviction among many that: **"God can do anything He pleases"**. So, if it were possible, why did He not?

From this standpoint, consider the later words of Jesus:

> *"Do not imagine that I have come to abolish the law and the prophets; I have not come to abolish, but to complete them. For I tell you indeed, that until the heavens and the earth shall pass away, a single dot or hairstroke shall not disappear from the law, until all has been completed."*

(Matthew 5:17-18, Fenton.)

Thus the "Natural Laws" could not be circumvented, not even by Jesus Himself, nor can they be today – or ever. Not by force of arms, wealth, political power, scientific disbelief, rationalist theories and, not least, by religious dogma. There is ultimately no choice for humankind but to submit to the processes outlined, since it is Spiritual Law that drives everything in Creation. By virtue of our free-will attribute we *can* choose to *oppose* those Laws, but the outworking of them will eventually guarantee the appropriate kind of 'reaping' for such opposition. What we absolutely cannot change is the lawful outworking of the *actual* death process itself.

Since not one thing can ever happen without a reason, or not have some kind of starting point as its absolute origin, it should be a simple matter to deduce that the sudden, unexpected arrival of painful experiences in our lives can only be the end result of a previous decision made elsewhere.

> *That being the case, we thus stand constantly in the centre of all our "returns", both good and bad, exactly in accordance with all the free-will decisions responsible for every returning reciprocal effect.*

However, because there may be no recollection of the actual originating decision or event in the present lifetime of an affected individual or in the lives of others closely associated with that person to bring about such a consequence, any end-effect must therefore presuppose another possibility, i.e., the concept of more than one earth life from where such an effect/outcome could originate. As previously stated, this is not a view readily accepted in Western thinking, though it is a basic tenet of billions of the World's peoples. So, just as we can reduce the question of whether there is life after death to either there is, or there is not – for it surely cannot be both – we can also ask the same of *one life versus many*.

Within the restrictive parameters of a "one-life concept", current Western thought relating to the scientific and intellectual disciplines and/or in religious doctrines offer few genuine solutions to society's increasing problems. Unfortunately, however, **disbelief or ignorance** of **The Law of Rebirth** cannot, in any way, alter the truth of its actual reality and outworking. This widespread "unbelief of the West" *can* be accepted if there is nothing *other than* a purely physical body to contend with. Yet if the body is no more than a physical shell, a cloak housing the actual you and me, then, just as the processes of The Law allow for *one* birth, why could it not allow *for others* where another, but *different,* 'overcoat' is simply taken on in accordance with such Laws?

*   *   *   *   *

The debate over reincarnation has raged for centuries, and even though a very large proportion of the world's peoples accept it as a factual part of man's existence, the Judaeo-Christian religions generally do not. It is crucially-important to note, however, that the so decisively-important doctrine of reincarnation, of *rebirth as a human being,* was only *expunged from Christian creeds* by a very small *majority decision* at the Council of Constantinople in the year 553 AD. What was effectively lost through that decision of appalling ignorance and ego was the greater understanding of the *seeming* inequality of the world and, indeed, The Love and Justice contained in The Creative Will.

For most in the Indian sub-continent, where reincarnation is very widely accepted, the basic belief of rebirth has been a fact for the past 2,500 years. Other Nations and peoples also accept this 'reality'. Now consider, if at that fateful Council meeting only a few men had decided differently, reincarnation would be a matter of course also for Western 'religions'. Had that happened, there would not now be the present fortress of doubt and prejudice against it. In its place would be greater freedom of thinking rather than this terribly unfortunate constraint into which our current thought-processes have fallen, solely because of that unfortunate decision taken by a few powerful men centuries ago. In general, it has succeeded in removing any possible larger outlook to the greater connections of our existence, and to the incredible vastness of Creation.

> *Because of that decision, we have created the unhealthy situation of not readily accepting death as a natural part of life and as an ongoing transitional step in our complete existence.*[14]

The great difficulty with trying to meaningfully grapple with the rapidly increasing problems in society is that there *appears* to be no logical cause for it all. Is it any wonder that suicides are on the increase, particularly among the more impressionable young who are often too emotionally immature to cope with the *seemingly* insurmountable. The young seek answers but no one will give them the only correct one. Our so-called 'educators' *reject the very thing* that would provide the necessary enlightenment and yet *they* continue to ask: "**Why**"? The concept of reincarnation will need to be accepted as fact if society wishes to find answers to most of its problems, **for the deliberate rejection of it only pushes away the day of reckoning**.

It must be understood, however, that reincarnation is governed by the strictness of The Spiritual Laws too. Contrary to some beliefs and misconceptions, therefore, one **cannot return** as a tree, an insect, or an animal.

Therefore, in direct contrast to Maori cultural beliefs and, of course, similar ones of other peoples, our ancestors cannot be such things as those. Inanimate objects have no connection with human Spiritual Origins, and neither do psychically-produced forms like the *taniwha* etc.. So living, animate creatures such as eels and whales must forever remain their own kind. Thus humankind's collective Spiritual Ancestry can only be that of *human origin.* The Laws of Nature therefore clearly decree that we *cannot change our species* and they further decree that, under The Law of Rebirth, we can only return as human beings. And, moreover, carrying with us all that we have *previously* sown. The hard truth is that some of the experiences we undergo may well have their origin in previous earth-lives. Nations and races must reap together what they

---

[14]The historic points of that meeting are examined in more detail in specific later Chapters that outline the death process.

have sown as well, and how we live our life now will determine what will come our way in the future, perhaps even in a later earth-life.

The general refusal of the Western medical profession to accept this completely logical view and become locked, instead, into a single-life concept, unfortunately translates into the practice of attempting to go beyond reasonable limits at times in order to preserve 'life'. At all costs, is the view, rather than simply accepting the dignified inevitable reality of a 'natural transition' *from* earthly life *to* earthly death. Of course life should be extended for as long as it is reasonably possible to do so, but not at the expense of unnecessarily prolonging what should be regarded, anyway, as a completely normal process of exiting earth-life. Neither should death be *desperately* fought against when medical reality clearly indicates an imminent demise. The one affected is not actually helped by such non-understanding.

Reincarnation offers the only viable mechanism whereby mankind is *truly able* to make rational sense of the misery, the suffering and the tragedies that beset the world today in such a relentless manner. Whilst it brings good fortune and happiness for some, it is the tragedies that need more urgent clarification. It is not the purpose of this book to deal with this subject to any great degree, though we will briefly return to it in a later Chapter to help clarify another contentious religious issue – the "Second Death". However, as the actuality of reincarnation is a "Living Law", which no one can change, it behoves us to learn all we can about the actual mechanism and process which, in its concept and outworking, provides *real answers and solutions* for our deeply-troubled people-world.

As a final note on this subject, reincarnation, as an inviolable Spiritual Law, must live the fullness of that fact without deviation. This Law also naturally exists within the Laws of Nature – which are a reflection of The Eternal Laws – and all dovetail into each other in perfect outworking. As previously stated, perhaps the refusal of many Westerners to accept reincarnation may be due in part to the promoted belief of some Eastern religions that one may be required to return to the earth as an animal, a bird or an insect even – for various purposes of atonement.

Whilst atonement is a most necessary requirement in the outworking of our inherent free-will decision-making ability under the Law of Reciprocal Action, a Law which unequivocally states, Galatians 6:7, Fenton:

"...what a man sows, that he will also reap..."

– reincarnation provides the only "earthly" *long-term mechanism* under which *spiritually-ordained atonement* can be expiated. As it is also a Law of Nature or a natural Law, we reiterate that such Laws unequivocally state that it is not possible to change one's species, irrespective of some beliefs to the contrary.

The inner animating core of man – his life-force – is *Spirit,* whilst that of the animal is *soul.* Respectively they are two different species of animating power from two different levels in Creation – as clearly explained in the following Chapter. Therefore, via this reality, the human spirit must always remain a human spirit, with absolutely *no possibility* that it could somehow transmigrate across immovable *spiritual boundaries* to become a life-form *different* to that ordained for it by the unalterable Laws of Creation. So humans remain humans, *they cannot become animals.*

And, just as surely, **animals *cannot* "develop" into humans!**

The process of reincarnation, whereby a human spirit is ordained by Law to accept rebirth on earth, is subject to, and affected by, the collective outworking of all **The Spiritual Laws of Creation.** The free-will decisions of his previous life, or lives, will determine who he will be in the next one, what his spiritual lessons will be, and what he can also spiritually offer that group of souls into which he will be incarnated; those who will be his earthly family. That, in turn, will determine such factors as to whether he will be born disabled or complete, whether his new circumstances will be one of wealth or struggle, whether of the same race, geographical location or religion as his last incarnation, or one completely different.

Irrespective of these considerations, however, the circumstances of his next incarnation will precisely offer the necessary conditions he will need for his further spiritual maturing. The key point in all this is the fact that he is still *master* of his own destiny. In that sense his inherent spiritual free-will provides the mechanism whereby he can still set in place *new decisions* which might offer a better or worse life than that originally ordained for him by Law through the outworking of all previous decisions. Certain *"experiences of the spirit"*, however, will be part of his necessary path and may perhaps even provide a lifetime of hard struggle. Whether or not that is the case may well depend upon the lawful outcomes of previous personal decisions acting upon him as he lives out his present life. Even if he should live spiritually-correctly yet experience a lifetime of struggle, The Spiritual Laws will still set in train beneficial returns for a future time. For the more powerful experiences will be impressed upon his spirit in any case, be it through *joy or tragedy*.

Thus The Laws of Creation intermesh to bring about precisely lawful outcomes. Yet it always remains with the individual as to what those personal outcomes will be. And, as will be stated regularly throughout this book, only the **decision** is *free*, the **consequences** are *not*! So in cases where two options are presented, whilst we will always have a **50%** option or **choice**, there is always only a **100% outcome** *after* the decision has been taken. Of course there is nothing to prevent one from modifying or radically changing the original decision with a second or even third one. Those decisional-changes, however, will ultimately be reflected in its corresponding outcome at some future point.

6.8   The Divine Gift of Grace

Whilst perhaps not strictly a Spiritual Law in the same sense as the previous Laws are, nevertheless the concept and outworking of the Spiritual Attribute of Grace impacts decisively and beneficially on the fate of anyone who recognises the error of their ways and genuinely seeks a more enlightened path.

Grace is an inherent quality of Divine Love. Inherent in Divine Love, also, is Justice. However, the Love that is defined here has no affinity whatever with humankind's emotionally-distorted idea of this most noble Power. Thus, under the outworking of Grace – which *originates* from The Divine – help and guidance are given to humankind with each passing moment. In order to reap the associated benefits, however, the guidance needs to be recognised, accepted, and lived accordingly.

Since The Spiritual Laws contain both the cornerstones of Love and Justice, they return only what is *spiritually* beneficial. By heeding Spiritual Law we give no cause for any 'unwanted returns'. In its distilled essence, therefore, "Spiritual Love" is pure, *even severe if necessary*. In such cases *it needs to be severe* in order to bring about the necessary *awakening* to force the question: **"Why?"**

Yet we must be ever mindful of the fact that we ourselves will have given cause for that event or trial somewhere, sometime, in accordance with the inviolable outworking of The Spiritual Laws. Thus the kind of Love outlined here is not the caricature spawned and given form by collective humankind, and which has become so distorted that it is now used to encompass virtually every kind of debased activity under 'modern', liberal thinking. This human distortion carries no justice within it. And in keeping with current, prevalent attitudes, attempts are continually made to separate that which cannot be separated – genuine Spiritual Love and true Spiritual Justice.

In the most wonderful of ironies, the twin forces of **Spiritual Love** and **Spiritual Justice** will eventually teach humankind that they are, indeed, inseparable. We have produced a weak form we call love or *aroha* but which, in reality more often than not, is a mask and poor excuse for overly-liberal, emotional and vacillating *self-indulgence*. We have substituted the Pure Power of Love with earthly emotionalism. In its pure form genuine Love stands far above such incorrect ideas. Compassion should not be confused with what is described here either, for compassion is an attribute of unconditional Love. Yet when one has accepted, understood and worked through all that must be personally expiated, The Spiritual Laws or Rules actually become strong and furthering help for one's spiritual growth. And "The Gift of Grace" lives in the essence of that Truth!

The Gift of Grace therefore permits even the worst transgressions to be completely expiated, if one *genuinely* seeks to put right his wrongs. Naturally The Spiritual Laws operate strictly here too, but the overriding attribute contained within the outworking of The Laws in this case is that of Grace and forgiveness. If being 'pursued by one's works' presupposes a "return" of even severe difficulty and hardship, it is important to understand that simply by *changing* our Spiritual Volition for the better, we automatically begin the process of *altering* the forms (both their intensity and/or severity) of 'our wrong works' previously produced. 'Works' which will, at some future point, always return to us.

Therefore, under the process of 'awaiting our works', someone who has lived a life of dark, horrific deeds is absolutely condemned to fully reap his "personal whirlwind" either here on the earth or when passed from it, *so long as there is no effort or attempt to change his ways*. Total ignorance of this process, or even disbelief of it, cannot alter the returning effects either. As stated, this process produces ultimate Justice which, at the same time, is Divine Love.

Therefore, the returning reciprocal effect to a hardened soul should provide the necessary experiences and potential for a spiritual awakening, a re-appraisal of one's personal situation, and some deep 'soul-searching'. Should that individual stubbornly fight against this process, more of the same is assured. Yet this should not be seen as some kind of retributive punishment from some arbitrary God or Power.

It is simply the *personal* 'reaping' from the *personal* 'sowing', irrespective of when sown.

So, what *does* happen to one with many years of living a depraved or evil lifestyle with total and selfish disregard for the welfare of his victims, when he suddenly finds himself faced with the unnerving reality that his attitude and conduct were 'all wrong'? What then? Ordinarily, we would probably say he still deserves to pay for everything he inflicted on others. According to societal Law that would probably be the case and society would no doubt be well pleased with such an outcome. Indeed, it is appropriate that correct punishment be meted out, for society has a right to protection from such individuals. In any case our earthly Laws should reflect the clear recognition that we cannot function without order. This recognition, moreover, should reflect the order contained within The Eternal Laws.

Therefore, even if dealt with by the justice of the earthly courts, for the criminal this does not mean that all is necessarily 'paid for'. The more crucial debt, the **Spiritual one**, may still await resolution. However, if our miscreant, through the honest recognition that his previous ways were wrong, genuinely seeks to mend them and make atonement, he sets in place for himself the mechanism whereby the impact of the returning retroactive consequences of his previously dark volition can be greatly lessened. But the desire to want to change must be an absolutely pure one, for The Spiritual Laws are not fooled by the subterfuge and deviousness that human beings too often engage in. Humility, moreover, must be an accompanying factor in such a change. What, then, is the process?

Because we possess the inherent attribute of "free will", and because there is only *one neutral power* streaming through and animating all of Creation including the material worlds, our "free will" endowment ensures that this neutral power is – *according to how we* **choose** *to use it – refracted* through us to good or evil purpose.

Under the outworking of **The Law of Attraction of Similar Species**, if our volition is dark, we automatically make connections to, and attract in and surround ourselves with, similar species. However, if the opposite is the case, via the same process of connection and attraction we lock ourselves into a vastly different kind of "power stream", one that brings beneficial effects.

Thus, in the voluntary spiritual change that the felon of our example has undertaken, he has changed his "nature of attraction" from one originally leaning toward dark things to those much lighter. Since this change is subject to **The Law of Spiritual Gravity** also, there occurs within and around him a lightening effect as a result of his decision to change his ways for the good. Now he attracts to himself 'beneficial forms' corresponding to his 'new volition'.

But where does this place him with regard to the returning effects of his long life of degrading deeds? **The Law of Reciprocal Action** (*Sowing and Reaping*) must still hold sway. That cannot change. Now, however, through his newly-activated, lighter connections corresponding to the 'new volition' with which he now surrounds himself – quite automatically remember – a far lighter and stronger force envelops him.

This acts like a cocoon against which some of the retroactive effects of his *past* volition can be *deflected*. Some may still penetrate to him. In which case, they will be of such a nature as he *still requires* for growth and ascent and, moreover, may therefore need to be *fully experienced materially* for complete expiation under Spiritual Law. The experiences from it, however, will enable him to further develop spiritually. Some returning effects may only need to be redeemed symbolically, perhaps something even as innocuous as a kind word to a complete stranger. Each case will be different for every individual but it will be in strict and inflexible accordance with **Spiritual Law** operating in concert with **The Gift of Grace**, so demonstrating both Perfect Justice and Perfect Love, two important cornerstones of **The Spiritual Laws of Creation**.

Therefore, if we do not wish to be pursued by any former 'unpleasant works', it is essential that the knowledge of The Eternal Laws be regarded as a serious spur to help nullify the reciprocal effects of them. Thus, via The Perfection of The Laws, we are enjoined to strive only for what is good. Such striving will ensure the reciprocal effect of greater peace and happiness under **The "Gift" of Divine Grace**!

6.9   Conclusion

Whilst The Spiritual Laws of Creation are the infallible and unalterable *driving mechanism* which produce the consequence or outcome for every decision made, it is vital to understand that any spiritual transgression incurred will be made more against the "rules for correct living". They are those generally encompassed within all the great religions; that which spiritual and philosophic teachings have recognised and espoused for millennia. Thus one *can* transgress The Law of Balance, but in the true sense of the word, one cannot actually transgress The Laws of "Rebirth", "Attraction..." or "Spiritual Gravity" etc.. However, transgressions against the "rules of life" such as are stated in The Ten Commandments, for example, even if done so in complete ignorance of them, nevertheless unfailingly sets in motion the driving *return-mechanism* that is inherent in *The Power* of The Spiritual Laws – more specifically in The Law of Reciprocal Action (Sowing and Reaping.)

It is equally important to recognise, also, that it is *spiritual power* that we actually use in all decision-making. Even our thought-processes utilise the same power. It permeates every part of Creation, for that is the life-force of the whole. However, it does not at all mean that our utilisation of that power necessarily produces genuinely-spiritual outcomes. Unfortunately, and as global societies clearly reveal, the volition of humankind has produced mainly *aspiritual* ones. And, again clearly evidenced by the global situation, the infallible mechanism inherent in The

Spiritual Laws drives everything to its particular outcome.

Thus, The Spiritual Laws have been outlined at this point as a most vital adjunct to the correct understanding of the purpose of this Work. The degree to which these Laws have been explored should be sufficient for our purpose. For only with the help of the knowledge of them am I able to attempt a book that states so much.

Throughout the rest of the Work, therefore, regular reference to these Laws will be made in order to explain every other aspect of our journey as it interlinks and connects all the relevant threads – *from the first Chapter to the very last*. By this process, a multi-coloured tapestry will be woven that will reflect the recognition of "the white thread" of Ngapuhi prophecy and thus become a "Spiritual Signpost", a signpost pointing to Ratana's mission in the first instance, but beyond that too. A signpost not only for Maori, however, but also for those of all other races who have found their way to this land at this time of *final determination*!

Before we can reach that definitive conclusion, however, it is vital that we recognise and understand our origins too. Whilst The Spiritual Laws are very necessary for understanding what our free will decision-making process will return to us, that knowledge cannot stand completely alone and requires the further recognition of our Spiritual, and therefore actual, Origins – our "whither, whence and why".

For it is to that home we *can* return provided we have made the correct decisions throughout life to achieve that desirable outcome. Irrespective of whether made consciously or unconsciously, they are choices nevertheless taken under, and driven by, the aegis of **The Spiritual Laws of Creation**! In that regard, let us embark on our journey in earnest, but from the very beginnings.

From the true *Spiritual Origins* of *all* of humankind, irrespective of the colour or shape of the outward physical form that may clothe our individual spirits today, or of the differing Creation-beliefs that man's various cultures have produced!

7

Whither Cometh the Maori?

The Spiritual Origins of All Humankind!

"When we consider thy heavens, the work of thy fingers,
The moon and the stars, which thou hast ordained,
What is man, that thou art mindful of him?"

(The Gospel of the Essenes. E.B. Szekely, p.175)

"Where does the world come from?
She hadn't the faintest idea. Sophie knew that the world was only a small planet in space.
But where did space come from?"
"It was possible that space had always existed, in which case she would not also need to figure
out where it came from. But could anything have always existed? Something deep down
inside her protested at the idea. Surely everything that exists must have had a beginning?
So space must sometime have been created out of something else."
"But if space had come from something else, then that something else must have come from
something. Sophie felt she was only deferring the problem. At some point, something must
have come from nothing. But was that possible? Wasn't that just as impossible as the idea
that the world had always existed?"

(Sophie's World, Jostein Gaarder, p.8, Phoenix Press.)

The questions that young Sophie finds herself faced with in Gaarder's International best-seller
are the very same that men have asked since time immemorial. The fact that this particular
publication was a 'best-seller' illustrates the keen, ongoing interest to such ideas from far more
than the scientific or philosophic community. For, quite logically, there should be a natural,
inherent curiosity in each of us that brings forth these very same questions by virtue of the fact
that we exist on planet earth in the first place. Let us join Sophie as she asks more questions!

"How was the world created? Is there any will or meaning behind what happens? Is there a life after death? And most importantly, how ought we to live? People have been asking these questions throughout the ages. *We know of no culture which has not concerned itself with what man is and where the world came from.* But history presents us with many different answers to each question."

(Sophie's World, p.12, Italics mine.)

Thus far Sophie's second question has been addressed from the standpoint of **The Spiritual Laws**. This, in turn, should provide the answers to the fourth question, namely how we should live. The third question on life after death will be addressed in a later Chapter. For if we do not know where we originate from, we cannot know who we are, what we are, or what our purpose is. That leaves only the first question to be answered: "How was the world created?" That question we examine here – in this Chapter!

Since this Work *explains* vital aspects of "the great questions to life", quite naturally it thus challenges many Maori cultural beliefs currently considered sacrosanct. In the contentious question of human origins, the comparison between what Maori creation-traditions state as our origin and what we will reveal herein will show why we are mandated to write it. And thus further show **why it was so vital for Maori to be exposed to Pakeha religion**.

The previous Chapter on The Spiritual Laws of Creation similarly revealed a vast difference between the logic and Perfection of those Laws and the archaic beliefs of our ancestors. Because it *is* solely **The Perfection of the Laws of The Creator** that have permitted us conscious life in human form in a vast and incomprehensible universe, human ideas have no say or input into what is obviously a humanly-incomprehensible event anyway. Yet it remains the responsibility of all human beings to recognise and thereby understand who and what we are and how we came into being. The Creation-happening, naturally and logically being the same for all, means that the different ethnic groups teaching incorrect ideas about our origins must find the *kaha* to *let them go* if they finally wish to follow *the true path home*. For that particular path is the reverse of our journey *to* this material world *from* our actual home far above the environs of the earth. It is a return home, however, only if we have heeded – and lived according to – The Laws outlined in the previous Chapter.

The philosopher Plato believed that there had to be a reality behind what he termed "the world of ideas". He thought that we could never have true knowledge of anything that is in a constant state of change, and we can only have true knowledge of things that we can understand with our reason. Plato also believed that man is a dual creature with a body bound to the world of the senses – which he thought were unreliable – and an immortal soul which is the realm of reason. He also believed that the soul existed before it inhabited the body.

Even though Plato wrote extensively about this dual concept, it was widely believed by many Greeks before him. Plotinus (205-270) knew of similar ideas from Asia. Plotinus also believed that the world is a span between two poles with the Divine Light at one end, and absolute darkness at the other which receives none of the light. He believed that this darkness was simply the absence of light, without any existence. Thus the Divine Light becomes increasingly dimmer the further one travels from it. Finally, he believed, there is a point that it cannot reach. He believed, moreover, that the soul is both a spark from, and illuminated by, the Divine Light. A fascinating insight because this particular view contains much basic truth, as we will illustrate in this Chapter.

Whilst the philosophers have mulled over this question for millennia, the mainstream religions have generally not needed to do so. The acceptance of an immortal soul or spirit – whether it becomes 'one with the universe' or retains its 'personal self-conscious form' after earthly death – is part and parcel of most religious beliefs. But even within this field, there is no clear position either. Yet pre-dating the early philosophers and the main religions, we find that in some places 'cave-men' buried their dead with flowers and small items that were probably personal possessions. This indicates that the funeral ceremony was conducted with a certain ritualistic air, perhaps reflecting the first "stirring" of a belief in the duality of man in the early progenitors of humankind. A degree of reverence for either the burial process or in the belief of a soul departing from the body is evident here. This offers a different perception of these early humans than those often displayed as stereotypical, or in some Hollywood images perhaps.

Democritus (460-370 BC), on the other hand, believed that people and animals were constructed solely of atoms, and that neither possessed immortal "souls". According to him, souls were built up of atoms that are dispersed to the winds when people die. In contrast to that particular view The Spiritual Laws of Creation *unequivocally decree* that there are both animate and inanimate life-forms. The inanimate we may designate as that which is anchored in place such as trees and mountains etc.. Rivers, lakes and glaciers etc., also come into this category. The animate is naturally the opposite and comprises those life-forms that are, in essence, *mobile*! They include the insects, birds, fishes, animals and, of course, man.

The 'mobile group' is further divided into those forms that have free will and those that do not. In fact, only man possesses free will. The *mobile life-forms* of the natural world do not. They do, however, possess instinct. The designation 'mobile' means that all such creatures possess an "inner animating core" *separate from* their "physical form". We can picture that "inner core" as a 'power pack'; the 'battery in the machine', so to speak. But because there is a huge and fundamental *inherent* difference between the *free will* of humans and the basic *instinct* of all other mobile life-forms there is, similarly, the same great difference in the respective kinds of "animating power" contained within both "species".

We explained the concept of "free will" in Chapter 6, but because its nature has puzzled thinkers for centuries – and free will is inherently necessary for any decision-making process – the non-understanding of what "free will" actually is and how it works effectively prevents the understanding of the many problems that beset us. Problems, therefore, which appear to have no causal reason at times. Immanuel Kant, (1724-1804) a German idealist philosopher, Protestant and an ethical man, believed strongly in three things; that man has an *immortal soul*, that God *exists*, and that man has a **free will**.

These aspects, he believed, were essential factors under which the necessary virtue of morality could flourish. By exercising free will in his decision-making process, man moulds and shapes his individual personality in accordance with the strict outworking of certain immutable Laws, thus determining his future. The subsequent 'level of development' attained is then his alone. This simple yet absolute mechanism explains how inequalities occur – why men are not equal.[1]

In order to fully understand our true nature as human beings, therefore, it is important to also understand what exactly constitutes the three parts of the entity, man. In simple terms, they are the *material or physical body*, the *soul*, and the *spirit*.[2] Unfortunately, the designations *soul* and *spirit* either cause great confusion in the differences not being understood, or are thought to be the same thing. Essentially, we can designate "spirit" as being the **innermost** animating core of man. His "spirit" is that "form" which inhabits the material body – **and is the actual animating power or force**.

The Spirit – the [I] in each – is thus the actual person!

The soul body and physical shell are respective *outer coverings* that *clothe* the "spirit". We may thus regard the soul as being composed of all the "*other-world coverings*" that *envelop* the

---

[1]Exactly as explained in The Spiritual Laws of the previous Chapter.

[2]The mind and emotions are part of the physical aspect because their contribution largely stems from *the activity of the brain*.

spirit but is *not that* which is the material body. In the Ethereal World of the "beyond", it is the *ethereal body* which envelops the soul.

In necessary educational-reinforcement: The Spiritual Laws immutably decree that human beings have both a physical body and an "other-world", non-material one collectively called the *soul*. The soul, in turn, envelops the inner essence of who and what we are – our **Spirit**. Therefore we are *Spiritual beings first and foremost*. And whilst spirit and soul are closely linked together inside the physical form of 'earthly man' as part of the complete entity, by virtue of their different origins they ultimately serve a different purpose.

What we now need to know is the how and why of our spirit, the how and why of the various "coverings" of the "soul-body", and finally how they all fit together.

Though man possesses *spirit* as his "innermost animating-power", this is not the case with animals. Their "inner life force" may be designated as being *soul only*, because their ultimate place of origin stands at a *lower level* in Creation than man's *higher level* of **Spiritual Origin**. Therefore animals do not possess the spiritual responsibility inherent with a free-will attribute as does humankind, and are thus not subject to the outworking of "The Law of Reciprocal Action" as we are. Unfortunately, however, they are subject to every whim of mankind.

From those brief explanations it logically follows that *inanimate objects* cannot therefore possess the same kind of inner "life-force" of *either* soul or spirit that animals or humans, respectively, possess. What is sometimes *perceived* or *felt* around great trees and around waterfalls, or in mountains and forests, is something entirely different.[3]

Having determined the nature of free will, soul and spirit – the origins of which we will discover in this Chapter – the next vital step is to address the question of the Creation-process itself. Since there has never yet been complete agreement about the "origin of the world" and all that it contains, let us add our voice to the debate and offer our explanations for mankind's beginnings to therewith resolve that first question that Sophie is struggling to come to terms with. The reader can thus determine for himself that the following explanations finally provide clear and logical enlightenment to this *seemingly* perplexing question.

*   *   *   *   *

Closer to home, however, and from our own analysis of The Spiritual Laws of Creation, in concert with the discoveries of anthropological science, traditional cultural beliefs that Maori ancestors were 'things' or 'beings' other than human need to be dismissed completely. Maori are not descended from rivers or mountains or half-men or demi-gods – that some *tatai* and *whakapapa* allude to – or any other form that superstitious belief or legend has dreamed up. And neither is any other race different with respect to the truth of this. Interestingly, this is not a "Pakeha" truth, or even a "scientific" one.

> It is The Truth simply because the human form is the **only one** ordained for all of humankind under the outworking of **The Spiritual Laws of Creation** – that Ultimate Law which overrides and transcends all man-made beliefs.

Let us, therefore, begin this particular part of our journey with an emphatic and bold statement!

Those souls presently living within the race of people known today as Te Maori, who have made their earthly home in this land of *Aotearoa*, who have journeyed *individually* for thousands of years through perhaps *many incarnations* in other *different races* have, as their common Spiritual Origin and therefore their true home:

---

[3]This "force" is examined in the later Chapter on "Elemental Lore".

The Spiritual Realm of Creation!

What do we mean by this, and what is the *Spiritual* Realm of Creation? Is there such a place? If so, are we 'related' to all other races on earth by virtue of our same place of origin, and were we all there together once as Maori or Pakeha etc.? Or are such 'racial' designations 'recent developments' which provide us with a reference point for our natural, *earthly, physical differences*? Moreover, do we all automatically return to the *Spiritual Realm* at earthly death as a matter of course and as a member of 'our own particular earthly race', or are there other possibilities?

Maori cosmology and Creation-theory do not adequately address these issues, simply because Maori concepts are generally egocentric in nature. The comparatively narrow world of the Maori concerned itself only with things Maori, notwithstanding the curiously sacred belief of Io, their "Supreme Being". And even with the incredible ability to navigate across the horizons of the vast Pacific via the stars; and where the Southern stars and star systems were named; even this 'knowledge' was not sufficient to expand their view of the cosmos from a theoretical one deeply influenced by psychic beliefs and superstition, to a greatly expanded one of sure certainty as to their origin, spiritual nature and ultimate purpose. Notwithstanding the tenuous nature of Maori Creation-theory, those 'traditional' kinds of beliefs should nevertheless be accepted as being necessary for the step-by-step development of races in general.

However, if the "*Waka* of Spiritual Truth" should arrive with that Truth, then we need to find the *kaha* to relegate what previously passed as truth – for that particular time of development – to another area. It may well find its permanent place in the *waiata* of the culture. But it should be accepted as culture only, or be discarded. To cling to ideas or perceptions that pose as Spiritual Truth long after it is clear that that belief can no longer be sustained, does not advance the spiritual development of any race at all. In reality, clinging to obviously incorrect views actually hinders the spiritual growth of peoples and races. Maori cosmology, whilst fascinating in itself, does not provide the necessary scope and scale for the answers we seek. To effect this vital undertaking, therefore, we must look to other races and cultures to provide the clues for this; races that have travelled further down the path of deeper spiritual questioning than the Maori, and have consequently discovered greater insights.

Where, then, lie the answers to this most necessary of questions – our origins? For there is surely little point in journeying through life uncertain, confused, even angry at vexing questions such as race, racial mix and ethnic origins, or whether one is truly *tangata whenua*. And, in the present context of New Zealand society, how the relationship between the 'indigenous peoples' and the 'settlers' – the *tauiwi* – should proceed. So, in the context of *this* particular Chapter, where should we begin?

$$* \qquad * \qquad * \qquad * \qquad *$$

We know that most races, cultures and religions have, as a common theme, a story of "Creation". The myriad views expressed in cosmology and Creation-theory etc., are as diverse and numerous as the thought-processes that have spawned them. Yet very few of the many thousands of varying ideas completely agree with each other and are therefore probably all wrong in their *entirety*. Certainly, many aspects may be similar and have elements of the truth contained within them. And it would be equally true to say that in the natural process of evolution and development, certain races would have garnered insights which would have required previously accepted beliefs of 'truth' to be discarded, in the sure knowledge that the 'new' contained more truth than the 'old'.

However, the transition to the 'new' was not necessarily without great travail and societal and religious upheaval, for man's precious ego does not easily allow him to 'let go' what he considers to be his 'great well of truth'. Yet in the major issues relating to our origin, our entry and exit from the earth, we unfortunately remain just as ignorant and without real knowledge as we always have. This is notwithstanding the vast number of religious writings scattered throughout the world, and the various teachers of The Truth who have been sent to the different races at various times in history to teach, and show, *the right way.*

In essence, our reluctance to 'let go' pet beliefs reflects the inexplicable inability of mankind to leave such teachings alone in their pure and uncorrupted state. Rather than simply living the teachings as instructed, man chose to dissect them to suit his personal wants. This fate has befallen all the great spiritual teachings – **without exception**. Even the setting-up of the major religious institutions of so-called 'higher learning' has not advanced the cause of *Truth* a great deal. In reality, its unfortunate 'dissection' has been directly responsible for the incredible proliferation of so many *different religions*, with each generally purporting to be the only true one.

Through the great Wisdom contained within The Creative Will, certain ones chosen for the purpose unveiled The Truth to humankind in accordance with that particular people's developing spiritual maturity. These Teachings were given to mankind in a manner that could be understood by the race or Nation ready to receive them at the time, and took place over many thousands of years. Man, however, could not leave them alone. He simply had to alter the original clarity of them. In a kind of perverse irony, if all those Teachings had been lived in a purely unadulterated way by those peoples to whom it was given, there would now only be *one single unified Teaching throughout the world today*. And that would have been **the complete Truth**. The unfortunate reality is that, after being offered the Truth, man subsequently converts it to 'just a religion', often with little of the original truth being properly understood.[4]

The German philosopher, Hegel, (1770-1831) even though admitting to the existence of 'unattainable truth', believed that "truth is subjective" and "...all knowledge is human knowledge". He thus "...rejected the existence of any *truth* above or beyond human reason". He further believed that because human ideas changed from one generation to the next, there could not be such a thing as *eternal truths* or "timeless reason". In his view history provided the only fixed point that philosophy could cling to. Moreover, since history in the philosophic sense is more or less constant reflection, Hegel believed that certain rules applied for this "...chain of reflections". Thus a thought is usually proposed on the basis of other, previously proposed thoughts. However, the proposal of any one particular thought can be contradicted by another, thereby producing tension between the two opposing views.

Basically, that is the current position with regard to the Creation versus Evolution debate. Hegel postulates a method whereby such entrenched positions can be 'softened', so that the tension is resolved by the proposal of a third thought which accommodates the best of both points of view. Hegel calls this a "*dialectic* process". The unfortunate belief still persists that science and religion will probably never be truly reconciled, and that perhaps they should not be. However, since our purpose is to move from a simple and rather tenuous faith/belief state to genuine and sure conviction, the knowledge contained within The Spiritual Laws perfectly permits such a reconciliation of the two disciplines. We will therefore utilise Hegel's "dialectic process" in this Chapter to identify which of the respective main points of each argument can offer mutual accommodation without losing any genuine substance from either, thus merging the two into one complete and logical whole!

Classically, the subject of Creation has provided the perfect forum for completely opposing views – that of orthodox Christianity and Creationism against that of the scientific community generally tending toward Darwinism and/or evolution. Galileo, Darwin and others whose findings challenged Church dogma were invariably branded heretics, and the polite way to reconcile

---

[4]Explanations about the work of the 'Truth-bringers' is explained in Chapter 22: **The Rapidly-Fading "Spiritual Potential"**! sub; Legacy of the "Truth Bringers", sub; Teachers of Mankind.

science and theology was simply to agree that each would keep to its own area. Basically, science would ask and answer empirical questions like "what" and "how"; religion would confront the spiritual, wondering "why".

*   *   *   *   *

In April 1997, what was billed as the Great Noah's Ark Trial was held in a Sydney court. Whilst not a case of an 'evolutionist' versus a 'Creationist' in the classic sense, Dr Peter Pockley, a free-lance journalist, nevertheless reported that "...the trial had pitted the belief of many fundamentalist Christians in the literal truth of the poetry in Genesis against the conclusion of science for a 4.5 billion year old earth." In reality, there is no conflict between the two positions as this Chapter **will explain**. The disagreement exists only in the minds, and therefore in the *incorrect interpretations*, of the proponents of the respective points of view. Moreover, essentially *the same battle*, which we note later in the Chapter, was fought in an American State Supreme Court years ago. In 2005 a new term, "intelligent design", found its way into the ongoing debate in American schools and Law Courts. It is still, however, basically creationism.

Thus, even with the current strong corporate-earth mindset today, the age-old question of "man or monkey" still produces passionate debate. With what we have at our disposal, then, let us now employ Hegel's "dialectic process" to determine where such truth lies in discovering an origin for ourselves that makes sense. And where science and religion blend into one, each supporting the other without conflict, as it obviously should be.

*   *   *   *   *

In the evolutionist's corner, Charles Darwin (1809-1882) – once described as the most dangerous man in England because of the direct challenge to the teachings of Christian orthodoxy that his work of evolution brought – proposed that "...all existing vegetable and animal forms were descended from earlier, more primitive forms..." via the simple mechanism of biological evolution. And that evolution was the result of "natural selection". Until quite recently science had 'pushed back' and accepted a geological 'birth-date' for our Solar System and the earth as approximately 4.6 billion years. Darwin thought the age of the earth to be about 300 million years. The age of the universe itself is believed to be around 15 billion years or so.

Historical anecdotes of Darwin's ideas possibly being correct actually sent shock waves through the 'establishment', with even a distinguished scientist noting that it was 'an embarrassing discovery' and "...the less said about it the better". And an upper-class lady expressed the hope that it was 'not true', but if it was, then the further hope that it would "...not be generally known".

In the opposite corner stood the Creationists and Genesis 'literalists'. In Darwin's time, both the ecclesiastic and scientific views were virtually sacrosanct with regard to the doctrinal idea that all vegetable and animal *species* were created only *once* in each and every respective form. The views of Aristotle and Plato were not dissimilar to the Christian beliefs, since they basically thought that all animal species were patterned after 'eternal ideas'. This Creationist outlook, in concert with the Biblical, genealogical time-frame back to "Adam", postulated that the earth was 'created' about 6,000 years ago.[5]

In determining the various arguments for the "Creation versus Evolution" debate, and in the context of the subject matter in this Chapter, it is vitally important to know what Evolution means – exactly. There is a view in some scientific circles that evolution means 'selection by random chance', and not perhaps to a precise developmental path. British Astronomer, Sir Fred

---

[5]Using biblical genealogy James Ussher, a 17th century Bishop, calculated that the earth "began" at 6pm, 23rd October 4004 BC.

Hoyle, has stated; "...believing that the first cell originated by chance is like believing a tornado could sweep through a junkyard filled with airplane parts and form a Boeing 747." Professor N. Chandra Wickramasinghe, co-author with Sir Fred Hoyle of "Lifecloud: the origin of life in the universe.", has also dismissed the evolution idea.

Overall, however, the science of astronomy, (The Atlas of the Universe, p.214), believes it *can* trace the evolution of the universe:

> "...on the assumption that matter is created; but just **how** it is created is another problem altogether, and no theory has given indication of how this came about."

Yet some scientist-theologians believe that evolution provides clues to the very nature of God.

Plato, (428-347) who was basically concerned with what was eternal and immutable on the one hand and on what 'flowed' on the other, found mathematics very absorbing because "...mathematical states never change". And much later in the seventeenth century Galileo observed that the book of nature "...was written in the language of mathematics". Measure "...what can be measured, and make measurable what cannot be measured", was his view.

The actuality of Spiritual Laws, and therefore a Creator of those Laws which *automatically* govern **His Creation**, negates the idea, for example, that life on earth could ever have been the result of 'random-chance' development. This idea does not hold up because the actual Creative-process, under the outworking of **The Laws of Creation**, translates that very mechanism into precise *mathematical formulae* in the material spheres. Thus **"The Spiritual Law of Numbers"** is the all-encompassing umbrella for all *mathematical Law*, which can be noted in everything, everywhere.

Even the 'primordial soup', produced at the birth of our planet aeons ago, had to have the appropriate formulae out of which eventually developed all the *physical* life forms and substances for planet earth. And within each of them will be found its *particular mathematical formula*. Change the formula and you change the substance or thing; if such change can be achieved within the bounds of scientific law that, in reality, is Spiritual Law. This Law provides for development, but not for alteration outside of what is possible.

Science, therefore, cannot actually *create* anything new, it can only discover things not previously known. It can, however, produce new *combinations*, but only from out of substances that *already exist*, and only within the parameters of what is scientifically and therefore spiritually possible. This possibility has been given to us under the mantle of the Spiritual Laws of Creation from out of The Creative Will. The various World-religions and beliefs have given their own names to this Will or Power. The terms Creator, God, The Light and some others are common to all.

The Bible alludes to this mathematical precision in the exactness of The Laws of Creation by stating that everything is counted and nothing goes unnoticed. As a simple illustration of this lawful truth, scientific formulae decree that only a precise number and configuration of certain atoms can form molecules of a particular substance. Change the number and a different substance is produced, or the experiment may not work.

For example, one atom of copper, one of sulphur and four of oxygen will combine to produce CuSO4, which will forever be copper sulphate. Copper sulphate, quite logically therefore, cannot ever be $CuSO_6$ or $CuSO_9$. In the same way common salt, chiefly sodium chloride, will always be $NaCl$, not Na_2C_{16} or 8 or any another formula. And sodium bicarbonate, commonly used in the kitchen in the form of baking soda, can only ever be $NaHCO_3$, not Na_5HCO_7 or anything else.

Physicists have noted signs that the cosmos is custom-made for life and consciousness. It turns out that if the constants of nature – unchanging numbers like the strength of gravity, the charge of an electron and the mass of a proton – were the tiniest bit different, then atoms would not hold together, stars would not burn and life would never have made an appearance. John Polkinghorne, a former distinguished physicist at Cambridge University and now an Anglican priest, sagely observes:

> "When you realise that the laws of nature must be incredibly finely tuned to produce the universe we see, that conspires to plant the idea that the universe *did not just happen*, but that there must be *a purpose behind it.*"

(Italics mine.)

Charles Townes, who shared the 1964 Nobel Prize in physics for discovering the principles of the laser, goes further:

> "Many have a feeling that somehow intelligence must have been involved in the laws of the universe."

And the authors of "The Mystery of Life's Origin", concluded that: ***"...a Creator beyond the cosmos..."*** *is the most plausible explanation of life's origins.*

On the question of evolution, other scientists sharing similar views to Fred Hoyle and N. Chandra Wickramasinghe include Colin Patterson, senior palaeontologist at the British Museum who, after believing in evolution for more than 20 years, claimed he was 'duped'. Charles Darwin seemingly noted that not one change of species into another is on record and he could not prove that a single species had been changed. In 1984, the former President of the French Biological Society, Professor Louis Bounovre, stated:

"Evolutionism is a fairy tale for grown ups."

On the other hand, Arthur Peacocke, a biochemist who became a priest in the Church of England in 1971, has no quarrel with evolution for he finds in it signs of God's nature. He infers, from evolution, that God has chosen to limit His Omnipotence and Omniscience. In his apparent view, it is the appearance of chance mutations, and the Darwinian laws of natural selection acting on this "variation", that bring about the diversity of life on Earth. Theologian, John Haught, founder of the Georgetown (University) Centre for the Study of Science and Religion, believes this process suggests a Divine humility, a God who acts selflessly for the good of Creation.

The sticking point in this whole debate is perhaps not actually that of Creation versus evolution in any case, but probably more that of the time frame required to produce either one, or both together! For if a time period for such a thing as "evolutionary-Creation" can be logically established, then both viewpoints can be accommodated in perfect harmony. Therefore, the one key question in this debate that must be considered, yet invariably is not, is:

"Can Creation *also* be evolution?" Our answer is an unequivocal:

Yes! It can. And, moreover, it is!

However, to more *fully grasp* the *greater picture* that this long-contended issue demands, we need to seriously understand that whilst the Creative processes brought into being **the whole Creation**, the **Higher Realms** of the **Non-material World** were not subject to the *evolutionary processes* that we are familiar with *down here*. So it is vitally important to therefore set in place a demarcating barrier between the **Pure Creation** of those far Higher Realms – and **Creation *and* Evolution** *on Earth* in **The World of Matter**.

Evolution is thus a necessary and vital part of the Creative-process *down here*. Because the history of life on Earth *is* clearly one of aeons-long 'evolving' for *all* life-forms, *evolution and* the *Creative-process* are therefore inseparable – *down here*. That is simply because **The Creative Will of God** must inherently be both natural and logical by virtue of The Perfection of His Natural Laws. That fact also inherently stems from **The Perfection** of **His Will**.

Now, since it is vitally important to understand what we actually *mean* by "evolution" – or what it is supposed to mean – from our particular standpoint we shall state it to mean, and also encompass and promote, "*natural development*"! We do not mean 'random selection' or anything even remotely equating to any kind of 'chaos theory' either. Unfortunately, the respective "default settings" of science and religion presently seem to be so irreconcilable that there would seem to be no grounds anywhere for a meaningful merger of both realities. On the one hand science holds to eternal doubt whilst the core of religion is faith.

Since a major sticking point remains the possible time period necessary to accept both the scientific and religious or theological viewpoints, these two contentious aspects will nonetheless be drawn together to show that it is so – notwithstanding the many interpretations to the contrary from proponents of both disciplines.

To begin with, the very first thing to clarify is exactly who and what we are. If we un-equivocally state that our true origin is that of The Spiritual Plane of Creation, we logically imply that we cannot be purely physical in origin, just as the early Greek philosophers surmised. Therefore it may be presumed that the earth plane of the material world is not our *true* home but a *material* one for the time that we are ordained to live on it. Yet the apparently obvious reality appears to indicate the opposite. We see, hear and feel everything around us as being solid and material. To all intents and purposes, it seems logical to believe that we are *solely* material beings. But should we expect that to be the last word if our "Spiritual Origin" is *not that* of the world of matter? In this lies the key!

From our examination of The Law of Spiritual Gravity we know that heavier objects will sink whilst lighter substances will rise. Whilst being obviously so, it is nevertheless important to reiterate this fact again at this point. Thus, in the structure of Creation, a material object will occupy a lower level or plane than a spiritual one, simply because the higher the plane of Creation, the finer and lighter is the substance of which it is composed, and thus similarly so for the particular inhabitants of those respective planes.

Only the earth of the material plane is the home of the flesh.[6]

In this material world we marvel in awe at the vast expanse that we see in the night sky. Astronomers speak of interstellar distances so incredibly immense that the human brain can scarcely even begin to comprehend such figures. And we are reminded of the magnificence of such a work through the insights of the poets and philosophers in their attempts to understand man's place in the universe, e.g:

"When we consider thy heavens ... What is man, that thou art mindful of him?"

A very good question indeed, and one we should all ask of ourselves from time to time. For in the stupendous scale of things, it is vital to understand that the mind-numbing, incomprehensible immensity of just the physical universes alone can only be the *smallest and lowest part* of the *whole of Creation*. Our galaxy on its own contains something in the order of 100,000 million stars. And the known universe, in turn, contains literally billions of such vast galaxies. The higher Spiritual planes, by virtue of their far greater spiritually-expansive attributes, are therefore incomprehensibly and immeasurably far more immense.[7]

---

[6]Followers of religions and cultural paradigms that believe otherwise will learn, very severely, that their beliefs place them in dangerous opposition to **The Truth**.

[7]The explanations about the *extent* of the physical universes of the *Material Worlds* – which cosmological science is unaware of at this time and which the Hubble Space Telescope could never ever penetrate to – is explained in a separate 'Crystal Publishing' publication: [**BIBLE "MYSTERIES" EXPLAINED.** Understanding "Global Societal Collapse" From the "SCIENCE" in The Bible. What Every Scientist, Bible Scholar and Ordinary Man needs to Know.] Specifically, Chapter 11: The "Seven Churches in Asia" – The Revelation.

If, then, our Origin is out of The Spiritual, yet our earthly existence is obviously material, the only conclusion that we can logically draw here is that we must have both these aspects contained within us, i.e., the human being is both spiritual and physical – *and that is so*! But only on the earth can this duality be utilised. Indeed, it is the only way that humankind can meaningfully exist here at all. For the spirit needs *the material body* to fulfil its purpose whilst on the earth, and the body needs *the power of the spirit* to animate it here also – to give it life.

Therefore earthly death is nothing more than the separating out, the drawing apart of the two, where also at this time the "spirit" *should* strive to free itself from the material world.[8] The material shell then returns to the earthly components from whence it came in the normal process of decay that the Laws of Nature decree must take place. Hence the words of the Law, "Earth to earth, dust to dust", which we hear at funerals, and which only applies to the *empty, discarded shell*. The process is simply and clearly outlined in Job 10:9-12 (Fenton. [Italics mine.]):

"Remember You made me from clay,
That to dust You will make me return!
And did You not curdle the milk,
And fixed me together like cheese,
Then clothed me with skin, and with flesh,
And with bones and with muscles compact?
And gave me my life and my reason,
Then *last, fixed my Spirit in me*?"

Relevant to the process of establishing the human 'physical/spiritual connection' is the requirement to locate specific reference points pertaining to the respective origins of both those 'parts to man' in order to gain the necessary understanding. We will therewith learn why, in the development of 'man' and transition to 'human', (us), *the spirit was fixed last* – as Job states. (We will derive those points from certain mainstream writings.)

Therefore, of all the *religious works* that *purport* to have the Truth – insofar as most Western peoples are concerned anyway – The Bible is probably the best known and accepted by virtue of the fact that it is the one where the person of Jesus Christ is the key figure. Because of His particular Origin and pivotal role for humankind as documented in The Bible, we will therefore accept that book – at least among the *religious* works – as being *more able to provide* the answers we seek.

Thus, in one single, simple sentence from The Bible, both our *physical* and *Spiritual* Origins are actually clearly revealed. In its stupendously far-reaching yet stunning simplicity, it **completely destroys** the "great divide" that religion and science have constantly promoted and clung to. We ask why?

The King James Version of Genesis Chapter 2 Verse 7 states:

"And the Lord God formed man of the dust of the ground, and breathed into his nostrils the breath of life; and man became a living soul."

Here has lain **one part of the answer**, for centuries unnoticed, unseen perhaps, but clearly not at all understood.

Now, if this particular Scripture is thought about in purely literal terms or from solely a fundamentalist viewpoint, a picture more or less naturally arises of The Creator, The Power of All that exists, descending to the Earth and building the shape of a man out of its substance – the mud of it. Then, what would effectively be a model of a *mud-man* would be instantly transformed into a living, breathing, walking, talking, internally-pulsating human being by the simple act of being *"breathed into"* in the literal sense.

[8]Detailed explanations of the 'death process' are given in Chapter 9: **"The First Death"**.

Is that the method by which one could believe man was first formed? The crudeness of such an idea is difficult to reconcile with a Creative-force responsible for the Creation of not just the incomprehensible immensity of the physical universes alone, but the far larger and far Higher Spheres spoken of in many religious works. With all that we have learned about our multi-faceted world today, is there any point in continuing to cling to such a preposterous idea?

Moreover, there is a major and insurmountable problem for literal fundamentalist thinking here in that The Bible alludes to the fact that God *cannot* descend to the earth for it would be completely consumed by His Power. Immediately there is a contradiction, if we view it in a purely literal sense. Quite unequivocally, there can be *no* contradictions anywhere in the *actual Creation process itself.*

We should be very careful, therefore, not to apply any kind of heretical or blasphemous labels to an idea that may be markedly different to any current or orthodox Church one. We should, instead, objectively allow the intuitive inner reason the spiritual freedom to determine the true nature of what is revealed here. Perhaps a wider vista might then suddenly open offering the spirit the potential to 'soar' instead of being shackled by too rigid an interpretation that refuses to allow even the 'possibility' of such a thing as "Evolutionary-Creation".

*   *   *   *   *

The much-celebrated "Tennessee monkey trial" or "Scopes monkey case" of 1925 in Dayton, Tennessee, provided the key forum for exactly this debate. A high school biology teacher by the name of John T. Scopes who taught the theory of evolution was accused of violating the Butler Act, a Tennessee law that forbade the teaching of evolution because it contradicted the account of Creation in The Bible.[9] The trial received worldwide publicity and was conducted in a circus-like atmosphere. And because of the popular belief that evolution meant humans were descended from monkeys, the press dubbed it the "Monkey Trial".[10]

Because of its far-reaching educational implications, not least for many of the scientific disciplines, the Education Department hired the famous criminal lawyer Clarence Darrow as their Defence Counsel, whilst a former US Secretary of State, William Jennings Bryan, appeared for the prosecution. Clarence Darrow and his team argued for the scientific validity of evolution and against the constitutionality of the Butler Act. According to anecdotal reports, and after both views were aired, the case hinged on one crucial question which Darrow addressed to the opposition. The question concerned the existence of dinosaurs and the time-frame in which they lived.

Since their existence could not be denied, the challenge and case could not be upheld. Had fundamentalism won that day, the State Supreme Court would have had no option but to order schools to teach only "the 6 days-of-Creation belief" and any concept of evolution would have been officially suppressed. The Butler Act remained on the State Statute books until 1967. Paradoxically, that court case need never have taken place simply because, as is our premise, the evolutionary process is actually part of the Creative process, and naturally so. *Indeed it could not possibly be anything other than a natural union.*

Yet, even in the year 2007 of the 21st century, the science of "biological anthropology" still persists with the totally incorrect belief that it is ***solely genetics*** that has determined the so-called 'evolution' of 'primate to human'. Researchers from the Broad Institute of MIT and Harvard have evidently coined a new "anthropological term" – **the human-chimp split**. Their ***basic*** hypothesis and time-frame ***is*** correct. An ancestral ape-species ***was*** the ancestor of the human race a very long time ago, ..."**but only as the physical-form vessel, nothing more!**"

---

[9]Trials along the same theme have taken place in the USA even in more recent times.

[10]The similarities between man and the anthropoid apes evidently caused Darwin to believe that both probably evolved from the same progenitor.

Science must recognise and learn to understand the huge and fundamental difference between that *physical/material-form of vessel/body*, and *the animating life-force within it*; i.e., within *every human being*. Only with that essential knowledge as the primary foundation for any further research – if it is deemed necessary – might the current, strong scientific emphasis on genetics and the human genome find its *correct connection*. Rather than constantly needing to change hypotheses, this particular branch of science might, instead, begin to build *constant* upon *constant*.

*   *   *   *   *

If we revisit our previous Genesis quote from the King James Bible, in Chapter 2 Verse 7 we discover therein the amazing revelation of *the actual human/chimp split*.

That key Verse once more:

> **"And the Lord God formed man of the dust of the ground, and breathed into his nostrils the breath of life; and man became a living soul."**

(Emphasis mine.)

Therein lies the *overarching answer* to the most amazing evolutionary processes that, in the most natural and logical way, *separated out the first human beings from their physical-form progenitors*. Thus, The Bible described **the real human/chimp split** a very long time ago. And human science has not yet caught up with this fundamental Truth.[11]

> *Insofar as traditional Maori putaiao (matauranga [mod.]) is concerned and even taught, Maori Creation-myths and legends do not even begin to reach anywhere near these stupendous, human-origin revelations.* **The Pakeha Bible, however, does!**

Despite the incredible nature of what has been revealed here, it is still only just part of the complete process, albeit a stupendous one for human beings. A far *greater* revelation is written in The Book of Genesis, most relevantly of course in Chapter 1. Verse 26 therein states:

> **"And God said, Let us make man in our image, after our likeness."**

Verse 27 continues:

> **"So God created man in his own image, in the image of God created He him; male and female created He them."**

(Emphases mine.)

Those two primary quotes from The Book of Genesis reveals, very clearly, what Pakeha science and theology have not only **not understood**, but **missed completely – the second part of the answer**. And that is; that there are **two separate** "Creations of man".

Thus, in the above Chapter **1**, we have **both** *male* and *female* beings *created*, **but not out of the dust of the ground**.[12]

Conversely, in Chapter **2**, (our first quote) we initially have only man being formed, **but from** the **dust of the ground**. Later, after a plea for company, the Bible narrative describes the first *woman* as being *fashioned* from a rib of the first *earth-man*. All this, however, took place **AFTER** the **First** *Creation* of "man" i.e., male and female.

---

[11] The detail of this singularly-decisive event for humans more fully unfolds as we continue our journey, and clarifying explanations flesh out the primary aspects.

[12] This crucial European 'knowledge-gap' about our *actual human origins* quite obviously applies to all native/indigenous religions and cultures too.

Is there a contradiction here? No, there is not!

The Creation process, *correctly described in Genesis*, has, quite simply, not ever been understood at all.

This great degree of non-understanding has seeded the assumption for many that it all had to have taken place in the physical/material environment of the earth. Such an assumption would be perfectly valid if we were *only and solely* physical substance. Since we are not, then other *realities*, quite obviously, *must* be considered.

From the standpoint of general Christian thinking, the acceptance of a single Creation-concept for the formation of man is regarded as the norm. Yet the orthodox Bible, from which the Christian Church takes its teachings and spiritual substance, clearly states otherwise. Anyone can pick up *almost* any Bible and find the same for themselves. So what should we make of this?

What we should not fear to undertake is a keenly searching examination of a possibly contentious religious issue whereby the deepest and most wonderful revelations are missed. Moreover, it should be exactly the role of the churches in the first instance to **fearlessly** seek out The Truth, and to immediately discard any untruths discovered. That would be the right thing to do. With **courage, bold strength, and spiritual certainty** – *kaha wairua* – that is precisely what we will do here!

At this point in our search for answers, it is timely to examine a Bible that is not accepted as possibly being "church-standard" but is, nevertheless, one that comes closest to providing what we now know to be the **correct** interpretations to the answers we seek. The following comparative passages are taken from **"The Holy Bible in Modern English"** by Ferrar Fenton. The author of this remarkable Work heads the very first Chapter in "The Book of Genesis" with the words:

The First Creation of the Universe by God = Elohim.

This is clearly an exceptionally significant statement and a radical departure from orthodox thinking in that Fenton *identifies* a **First Creation**. In a comparison of the relevant Verses it is patently clear that a complete and fundamental misinterpretation of Genesis regarding the Creation of man has entrenched itself in our thinking for the last two thousand years. Unfortunately, this critical error has brought Christendom, especially, to the point where most within would be too afraid now to even *question* this 'possibility'. Such reluctance or fear, however, means that, thereby, we have completely missed what is our rightful and ordained heritage – the actual Truth of our Origins. So let us take the next steps boldly and examine in sequence, from Fenton's Bible, the *two* Creations of 'man'.

The *comparative* Verse 26 in Chapter **1** is preceded by the heading:

Creation of Man under the Shadow of God.

The Verse reads:

"GOD then said, "Let Us make men under Our Shadow, as Our Representatives."

Verse 27 continues:

"So GOD *created* men under HIS own Shadow, *creating* them in the Shadow of God, and constituting them *male* and *female*."

Now, very significantly, Verse 7 in Chapter 2 is also preceded by a relevant heading:

The formation of Man from the Dust of the Ground by the Ever-Living God.

Thus we have clear and unequivocal clarification of a huge and fundamental difference – the *first* as an *immediate Creation*, **close to** The Creator. The *second* as simply a *forming*, **very far from** The Creator.

The actual Verse regarding the forming of man reads:

> "The EVER-LIVING GOD *afterwards* *formed* Man from the *dust of the ground*, and breathed into his nostrils the life of animals; **BUT MAN BECAME A LIFE-CONTAINING SOUL.**"

> (Some emphases mine.)

The last phrase of the above sentence should be marked well because it provides *the actual key* to a true understanding of this whole question of our origins. Significantly, **it is printed in bold capitals in Fenton's Bible.**

To state once more in reinforcement; the most significant aspect is the clear and unequivocal reference to the *first* happening; with 'man' – both "male and female" – being directly *created*. That is in stark contrast to the second phase; with man being only *formed* – and from out of the "dust of the ground". The same relative Scriptures, moreover, appear in the same respective places in both the King James Bible and Fenton's, as it does in most.

*   *   *   *   *

Special Note:

At this point in our journey it is probably pertinent to mention a few facts about the author of The Bible from which the last passages were taken. In 1853 Ferrar Fenton resolved to study The Bible in its original languages and to re-translate it completely into English. Fifty years later he had accomplished his task of translating the complete Scriptures of the Old and New Testaments from the original Hebrew, Chaldee and Greek. Whilst the general thrust of the recognised story of Genesis is obviously still present, there are *seemingly small* but *extremely significant* changes to some passages; changes which throw a whole new slant on some strongly entrenched beliefs.

Throughout his work he explains translation errors, mainly in the Greek and Latin Versions, by showing where and how they occurred. Most importantly, however, the "small changes" he identifies allow for a vast expansion of perception regarding the clarification of the problem of interpreting the *time* taken for the Creation-process, not to mention the whole concept of our relationship with The Creator. Ferrar Fenton's intuitive insight into a more logical and correct explanation of the *seven days of Creation* resulting from his re-translation of The Bible may well signal *a note of warning* to purveyors of the status quo and to more recent Bible translators whose own efforts may have been clouded by religious preferences rather than a purely objective and logical analysis.

For the purposes of this discussion, if – and I use the word *if* only in terms of *this Work* being viewed as nothing more than an interesting hypothesis by some readers – *if* his re-translation of the Creation part of Genesis is correct, it might be wise to carefully consider whether this man's *ordained Spiritual purpose* was to help bring *clarification* to those Christian Churches and Bible translators who *still hold* to the literal view of seven earth days for the Creation process. Fenton's *re-translation* of Genesis in this case clearly offers a more *stupendously-correct interpretation*, given its ability to accommodate both the viewpoints of scientific evolution and a Creation-process in a *logical* scenario and time-frame.

*   *   *   *   *

Thus far we have basically established that man is both a spiritual being and a physical one. And, moreover, further noted that only here on the earth can these "two parts to man" co-jointly exist as a single, completely whole and integrated entity. What has not been explored yet is *how* they are co-joined. Again The Bible holds the key. Since the complete process naturally implies that there had to be a beginning for man and his earthly home, this is so stated.

Let us return once more to "Sophie's World" and join her as she struggles to make sense of a concept that we may never be capable of grasping in its 'living reality'. That struggle to fully understand is due to the vast natural gulf existing between the Eternal Creative Power of all that exists, and us – the *lower* **formed** *entity* that is man. Such an idea is simply beyond our ability to *ever* comprehend.

> "They had learned at school that God created the world. Sophie tried to console herself with the thought that this was probably the best solution to the whole problem. But then she started to think again. She could accept that God had created space, but what about God Himself? Had He created Himself out of nothing? Again there was something deep down inside her that protested. Even though God could create all kinds of things, He could hardly create Himself before He had a "Self" to create with. So there was only one possibility left: **God had always existed**."

> (p 8. Emphasis mine.)

Via this simple mechanism of logical elimination Sophie has hit on the only credible answer to the question – assuming, of course, that one accepts the belief of a Creator in the first place. Therefore, from the unequivocal acceptance of that premise – **and that is the standpoint from which this Work is written** – in order to have Planes of Creation to "fill the void", including the material worlds of the observable universe, there had to be set in motion a "Creation-process" to bring this about.

Hence, through the stupendous and humanly-incomprehensible process of Creation, driven by The Power of The Creator in The Divine Ordination and Command, **"Let There Be Light!"**, the Creation-process of the forming of all the worlds in all the various planes began. As the lowest and therefore last *precipitation* of all the levels in Creation – and under the outworking of The Spiritual Laws of Creation, particularly *The Law of Spiritual Gravity* – the vastness of the *material* universes also came to be. And contained within just that lower immensity, our earthly home. Thus the 'void' was filled.

*   *   *   *   *

Because of the sheer impossibility of ever being able to picture or understand what is for human beings an inconceivable process anyway – for what words in the many languages of the world could one possibly use to even attempt to describe it – what kind of earthly example could we employ to *try* to explain *how* the separation between the respective Planes of Creation occurred? If we are able to arrive at some small degree of comprehension of *at least the mechanics of the process* and thus why this demarcation was necessary, we can gift to ourselves a large measure of inner awareness of our *true place* in Creation. That kind of recognition should also help in the understanding of what our *spiritual purpose and thus our actual reason for being* really is.

As a very basic and crude analogy, we can perhaps relate the main points of the Creation-process to that which occurs every hour of the day throughout the world in the numerous oil refineries of the petrochemical industry. This process is called distillation. It takes place in a 'distillation column' whereby heat-generated crude petroleum vapour rises inside a tall metal column. At specific heights within the column, the vapour condenses to form various liquid petroleum products.

Each *different* distillate *will form itself* from the condensing vapour *at its appropriate condensing level as it cools*. This will be determined by the *weight and consistency* of the *particular* distillate being condensed *from the vapour at that level*. The distilled product *at each level* will thus precisely configure itself to *its own specific type of material substance*, and at its *specific temperature*.

I have highlighted particular terms in the previous paragraph in *bold italics* to help explain certain points that we will now outline. The explanations given here basically accord with all similar processes derived from the influence of gravity. Whilst this one example is earth-orientated i.e., operating from below upwards, the process of Creation naturally works from the Highest Heights downward to the material worlds; still subject, however, to **The Law of Spiritual Gravity**! Though we will never ever even *remotely understand* this stupendous event – for even a combined distillation of the most ennobled aspects of all the world's languages could not even begin to offer a summary of words sufficient enough for the process – I believe we should nonetheless strive to achieve at least some insight. Even a diagrammatical picture in the mind would be of value, for that is better than having no picture at all.

*   *   *   *   *

In the actual Creation process, then, we might perhaps envisage something approximating an *unfathomably vast*, white-hot mass of "downwards-moving" substance suffused with the stupendous Power of **The Divine**, vast enough to eventually form the incomprehensible immensity of the material universes – *after the far greater Creation of the Higher Spheres – The First Creation*. And all driven from the immediate proximity of The Light and Power of **The Creator** under the aegis of the "Creation-Words":

"Let There Be Light!"

Because of the obviously immense power and pressure in closest proximity to The Creator, only the strongest and purest of beings could come to immediate consciousness there in the planes of their sphere of activity – i.e., *closest to GOD*. Thus, at heights we could never comprehend, and certainly never ever reach in our spiritual form, occurred:

The Creation of Man in the First Creation.

Man *created* in the **Image of GOD**, (Genesis 1:27, Fenton) – and **not** man *formed* later in the **second** Creation – from out of *the dust of the ground.* (Genesis 2:7, Fenton)

Now, basically similar to the distillation process we examined earlier, the pressure of The Power of The Light drove the Creation-process to its completion. As each **different species within Creation** found its **appropriate level of consciousness**, as determined by its **weight and consistency** – i.e., its own **specific gravity** so to speak – so, too, could the planes for those inhabitants **form around them** in the **cooling-off process**.

This procedure was repeated all the way down to the material worlds. The governing factors which determined those levels of forming were the same as in our oil-refinery example – the *lighter and finer* in the **Higher Spheres**, the correspondingly *heavier and coarser* toward the **lower levels**. Thus each Realm formed itself at its appropriate place, corresponding to a level or plane whereby the *distance* from The Creative-Light permitted a *cooling off* and a condensing and thus an eventual *awakening to consciousness* there of that Realm's particular inhabitants.[13]

Only in the separating out and cooling off stage, roughly similar to the earthly process of *sedimentary deposition*, could worlds and landscapes form in which all the inhabitants of Creation would be able to fulfil their purpose, *exactly as we must do here.* For we should not suppose that only in the material sphere are there worlds of lands and rivers etc.. This difference is clearly alluded to in Genesis, Chapter 1, where worlds, animals and fishes were *created*, before the **first** *Creation* of *male* and *female* in the **Image of God.**[14]

And only in Chapter 2, in an incomprehensible time-frame representing the aeons-long evolutionary process concerned with the physical world of planet Earth, do we then find the animals, fishes and birds being "...formed from the dust of the ground". Earth-man, "formed" the same way – "...from out of the dust of the ground" – thus enters his new world. It is a world of incredible diversity and pristine beauty.

> "And out of the ground the LORD God *formed* every beast of the field, and every fowl of the air: ..."

> > (Genesis 2:19, King James. Italics mine.)

The same Scripture in Fenton's Bible states:

> "Therefore the EVER-LIVING GOD, who had *formed*[15] out of the ground every animal of the field as well as every bird of the skies, took them to the man to see what he would name them. And whatever the man with the ***Living Soul*** called them, that was their name."

> > (Emphases mine.)

The major difference between the lower and coarser physical worlds and the infinitely Higher and lighter Spiritual Realms is the *consistency* of the *substance* of which the *respective levels* are *composed*.

Thus the **First Creation** is of *Spiritual* substance whilst the second, out of the dust of the ground for the earth and physical universes, is obviously *material*.

The key point to reinforce and understand here once again is that **each level represents a different consistency**, lightest and finest in the Highest Spheres – increasing incrementally with each subsequently formed lower level – until the heaviest and thus lowest in the material world. Such a far-reaching concept should not be all that difficult to understand.

The statement of Jesus that: *"My Kingdom is not of this world"*; reveals the sure fact that His World – [*"I came from The Father and I return to The Father"*] – could not possibly be some kind of barren or filmy, amorphous expanse, for He gives the strongest hint that His World is anchored in its infinitely more powerful and Eternal reality. Many of the great religions speak of an attainable Paradise if one lives one's life **based on The Laws of God** (but not, however, according to the rules of Churches and Religions.) Every Realm above the material would therefore become progressively more paradisiacal.

Quite logically, therefore, the consistency and substance of the various Planes of Creation must necessarily be the same as that of their inhabitants. This implies that each Realm must also feel, and be, very firm and real for those who reside there; exactly as with humankind on

---

[13]Each individual happening, each minute and incremental change in the cooling-off process clearly spans immense spaces and distances which, of course, we can never even begin to understand. The distances of interstellar space in the physical universes alone are simply too incomprehensible to grasp, never mind concepts of the vastly larger Realms of The Spiritual – or the even greater Divine.

[14]By The Spiritual we do not mean the near-earth places that we generally associate with departed souls and occult or psychic activity, but a far greater living reality. "In my Father's house are many mansions." [John, 14:2]

[15]The exact nature of the 'forming' is of crucial import, for it reveals **the science** in the whole Creative process.

earth. Any idea to the contrary is simply unrealistic. Nowhere in all the Spheres of Creation, therefore, do any of the inhabitants float about aimlessly, as is sometimes depicted in religious interpretations or films. Every inhabitant and every thing in the various planes is thus *anchored* into the *substance* of its particular "Realm" through the *consistency* of the level concerned.

The Eternal Laws operate throughout all of Creation, and the effects of The Law of Spiritual Gravity are felt in every sphere also. The Law of Movement, too, implies **activity** – everywhere. Thus we may note the perfect outworking of those Laws in the Creative process. Understandably, however, any sudden adjustment to this kind of conceptual perception may require a leap of quantum proportions. All we need do to achieve this, however, is to use the abilities of our inner Spiritual core, the real you and me. Abilities given to us precisely for this purpose; to understand our "Spiritual Origins" – explained in this essay.

So let us look closely at our Spiritual origins – our higher Spiritual home: Because we are clearly only developed or *formed* beings i.e., from *spiritual* **non-consciousness** to *personal* **self-consciousness** and not actually *created beings* as with man of "The First Creation" (as Fenton reveals), we did not therefore possess the inherent strength **to awaken to consciousness** *close to GOD*. Our level of *spiritual residence*, therefore, had to be *far lower* – in a kind of second-level Spiritual Realm. Yet even at that huge distance from *The Creative-Light Source*, we still did not possess sufficient strength to take on form and become conscious of self there either.

Our state of *non-consciousness* therefore meant that we would require a home of transition – a material one – in which to *acquire* self-consciousness. Quite logically, any kind of material home could only be *below* that of "The Spiritual Realm". And only in that *lower, material world* would we be able to *develop to personal self-consciousness*.

Thus, in our non-conscious state at the very lowest levels of The Spiritual Realm – our true home – we, the future spiritual human inhabitants of the earth, awaited our time to *incarnate in the material worlds far below*.

> We awaited the completion of the **evolutionary developmental process** that would bring forth the **appropriate physical vessel** – that of *the primate* – via *"...the forming of man from out of the dust of the ground"*. And into which *the immortal Spiritual aspect of man could first be placed* – i.e., *"...the breathing into 'it' of the breath of life"*.

Therein lies part of the understanding of the Creation of man. And therein, also, lies part of the reconciliation of the Creation-versus-evolution debate. That contention is, in reality, a totally unnecessary argument since there is no actual reason for this division save that which the proponents of the two opposing views have 'created' for themselves.

The complete process still requires further clarification, however. So apart from the earth being the place of transition for our awakening to self consciousness and spiritual awareness, was there a greater purpose for being permitted the opportunity for self-conscious life? Unequivocally yes! The material paradise of our earthly home was not only the place where we would develop to personal self-consciousness but, more importantly, *where we were to learn the truth of our Origins*.

We were also tasked to protect and nurture the earth and its creatures given over to our stewardship as stated in Genesis and, having achieved "Spiritual Purity" through a voluntary adjustment to The Laws of Creation i.e., **The Rules**; we could then return, *ascend*, to our true home – The Spiritual Realm.

That particular Sphere is the promised *Kingdom of GOD* for human spirits. Thus, we are not even beings who stand close to The Creator, but just *developed ones* far from The Light.

To reinforce this Truth, an appropriate quote from John 1, Verse 18 of the King James Bible notes:

> **"No man hath seen God at any time."**

Fenton writes:

> **"No one has ever yet seen God;..."**

$$* \qquad * \qquad * \qquad * \qquad *$$

For the purposes of spiritual clarity, the understanding that the level of our Origin lies far below that of **The Divine – "The Abode of The Creator"** – is absolutely imperative. This fact therefore forever precludes us from ever *personally knowing* the All-Powerful Creator we too loosely call God. The Eternal Laws unequivocally impose the completely natural barrier that a creature can only possess 'actual knowledge' as an 'inherent part of itself', **up to** its 'source of origin'. It is clearly not possible for any creature to *fully understand* levels beyond, or higher than, its own beginnings.

A simple but pertinent illustration is the difference in the level of intelligence and 'awareness' between animals and humans. How much greater must the difference naturally be between humans and **He** Who permitted us form and conscious life? To believe that we are at, or can attain to, the same degree of knowledge and power – as some scientists occasionally imply – is simply ludicrous and foolishly arrogant. Just as ludicrous is the belief among some eastern religious groups that they will one day become "one with God".

Whilst we cannot 'consciously know' more than that which our level of origin would permit, we can, however, *perceive* things from above such a level, as in the case of the Jewish people's intuitive recognition of the one invisible God when most of the rest of the world at the time were worshipping a variety of idols. We also possess the capacity to perhaps roughly *visualise* levels above our origins if we are given this information from One Whose Origin is from a higher level. The tidings and knowledge of the Higher Spheres given to us by Jesus is such an example. To believe, however, that we have, or can achieve, the ability to absolutely 'know' in this way is incorrect. It is simply beyond the capabilities of even our Spirit, whose actual home is from a far higher point in Creation than this lower-level material earth.

A simple test of this "truth" is to try to picture the concept of *infinity*, just as Sophie is attempting to do. To accept that there is a Creator logically means that there has never been a time when God did not exist. He has always existed. He will thus exist forever. We, on the other hand, need beginnings and ends as frames of reference to help in the understanding of everything connected with our existence and with time, and thus cannot even *begin* to grasp such a concept. The mind rebels and almost shuts down against such an alien thought because it has no affinity with such a far-reaching 'idea'. Only One who has no beginning and no end can logically 'live' this kind of "infinite reality". For us, with our very limited perceptive ability, it is simply an impossible thing to grasp.[16]

$$* \qquad * \qquad * \qquad * \qquad *$$

For the moment, however, the problem of needing to completely reconcile the ongoing conflict between orthodox science and fundamentalist religion as to the origin of man has not yet been fully resolved. Some major points in previous paragraphs have offered many insights, but more explanations are needed. As previously stated, the real tragedy here is that this great difference

---

[16]This concept may not sit comfortably with some, though it might serve to inculcate a more realistic attitude in our self-perceived relationship to **"The Creator of all the Worlds"**.

of opinion exists only in the minds of the proponents of the respective opposing views, for it *cannot actually exist in reality.*

In other words, the pointless arguments that have marred this path since the initial stirrings of scientific thought brought the first rumblings of disquiet into the previously sacrosanct church view could not, quite obviously, have had *any bearing whatsoever* on the **actual** *forming* of the worlds in its stupendous scope and scale, however long ago it may have been. That reality will forever stand separate from all human opinion, as it surely must.

Continuing to rigidly and stubbornly hold to a personal or professional viewpoint at all costs, and sometimes even against the quiet warning of the inner intuitive voice, is a sad reflection of much that is wrong with humankind. Yet for the sake of a clear, true picture of our origins and for peace of mind,'resolving this totally unnecessary debate is imperative. However, this can only be achieved with a completely open, fearless and enquiring mind and, most importantly, without preconceptions.

The Bible once more offers the final resolution to this *apparent* quandary. The question here is one of interpretation or, more precisely perhaps, incorrect interpretation. The standard view of fundamentalist Christianity is that the "7 days of Creation" scenario – applied to the complete Creation process including the emergence of man – is non-negotiable, and probably because of the view that The Bible itself *seemingly* states that this is so. So strong has been this belief that it is now an entrenched and apparently immovable cornerstone for many. Rather than being a correct and thus sacrosanct anchor point for the church, however, it is one that causes dissension and confusion.

Clarification of a previous key quote from Genesis should help to consign this division of opinion to its proper place in the sure relief of finally knowing the answer, thereby allowing the differences to be completely expunged. Hence, in the last phases of the great Creation, our world of the lower, material sphere could take on form too. As the last level of precipitation from out of the Creative process, this vast world of matter took billions of years to coalesce into roughly the form we know.[17]

That long, slow, evolutionary progression which subsequently emerged from the initial Creative-process eventually allowed for all material life forms to emerge, including "...the formation of man from out of the dust of the ground" and the breathing into his nostrils "...the life of animals". This is precisely what science has discovered. It was exactly that incredibly long evolutionary process which saw the emergence and preparation of the *physical vessel* – the development of the primate – that vessel which would ultimately house *Spiritual* man.

The preparation of the physical vessel for man is clearly revealed in Fenton's Bible where that particular happening is separated from the formative process by its denotation in his key capitalised phrase.

The two primary events are revealed in this key Scripture:

> "The EVER-LIVING GOD afterwards formed Man from the dust of the ground, and breathed into his nostrils the life of animals, BUT MAN BECAME A LIFE-CONTAINING SOUL."

> (Genesis 2:7)

Now, if this "sacred Scripture" is separated into two parts and simple logic applied to both, we discover a crucial point. From the King James Version, the first part reads:

---

[17]The vast world of matter referred to here is *stupendously more* than cosmologists believe they know. Its true nature and extent is explained in Chapter 11 of a separate Work we have already drawn attention to: **BIBLE "MYSTERIES" EXPLAINED**. It reveals 'the plan of the world' – exactly that which the colossus of science, **Sir Isaac Newton**, searched for in The Bible – but did not find. [Available online at www.publishme.co.nz]

"And the Lord God formed man from the dust of the ground..."

This small, seemingly innocuous, part-sentence actually holds one of the key components to resolving the Creation versus Evolution debate between Christian fundamentalism and science. In it is revealed *the science of Creation* that quite clearly equates to that aspect of the overall *Creation-process* denoting the long evolutionary development of the physical vessel – the primate – *formed from the dust of the ground* to one day house "Spiritual man".

With italicised emphasis, this crucial second part states:

> *"...and breathed into his nostrils the breath of life; and man became a living soul."*

Equally clearly, the "breath of life breathed into the nostrils" *is the animating aspect for that physical vessel.* So simple yet so profound in concept, and so stupendous in scope and scale.

Perhaps many a reader may now recognise the correct picture with this explanation. For, as we state once more in reinforcement, the "...forming of man from the dust of the ground..." was simply the evolutionary process by which all creatures developed after the formation and cooling of the material earth. From the first minute microscopic life-forms out of the primordial soup, to the fishes, insects, plants, birds and great lizards, and thence from mammals to the first primates. Thus did our **physical-form** ancestors slowly develop to their particular zenith – the refinement of form ordained for *Spiritual-man.* A marvellous and completely logical happening quite naturally divorced from any *fundamentalist* connotations when viewed correctly.

The associated aspect of the *time-frame* needed for evolutionary development, and how that could possibly be reconciled with a complete Creation time of just 7 days as depicted in The Bible requires clarification too. The 7 days account, though accepted by well-meaning Christians world-wide, is essentially rejected by the scientific community. Even the more recent 'new and supposedly definitive translations' such as The Jerusalem Bible – compiled by committees of 'learned' theologians – still persist with a literal 7 days Creation-time. The scriptural quote: "...and a thousand years are as one day..." (2 Peter 3:8), scarcely suffices to place even the smallest dent in the time period required for *evolutionary development*, given that the dinosaurs alone reigned for some 180 million years.

Why, then, do such a large slice of 'Christian' humanity still persist with the absurd belief that just 7 earth-days – *which equates to 7 earth-days of 24hr time* **as we experience it here on earth** – accounted for **every facet of the whole Creation-process**?

Do we really believe that just a few thousand years ago, dinosaurs marched into the Ark two by two, as some Creationists are desperately striving to promote?

The true answer in this case is one of *incorrect interpretation* and non-understanding perhaps resulting from an incorrect translation of the original writings, or perhaps from simply accepting a symbolic "spiritual" term that was never meant to be so read. And then applying to it a literal, earthly point of view. It is, in effect then, *an incorrect "spiritual interpretation".*

WHAT, THEN, IS THE 'CORRECT' INTERPRETATION?

The correct interpretation lies in recognising the fundamental differences between Chapter 1 and Chapter 2 of The Book of Genesis! The misinterpretation from Christian orthodoxy lies in attempting to ascribe two very different processes – one, **Creation**, the other, *primarily* **Evolution** – to a singular, '7 earth-day' Creation time-frame in Chapter 1, and attempting to also include in that time-frame the completely *separate processes* that Chapter 2 explains.

That inexcusable error embraces the erroneous belief that the First Creation of Man –
both male and female – refers only to man on earth.

The scientific misinterpretation on the other hand lies in either completely disregarding the Creation aspect *as correctly outlined in The Bible*, and/or viewing Creation as a singular, material cosmological process out of which sprang the evolutionary developmental phase of the various earth creatures – including man – *through physical/genetic processes solely*.

Fenton's Bible both delineates yet also harmonises the earth-science and Christian fundamentalism points of view so completely that both are effectively neutralised in their individual positions, yet conjoined perfectly when brought together. His correct interpretation also places all native Creation-beliefs at the level to which they *naturally* belong.[18]

The "7 days of Creation" – **The First Creation** – described in Chapter 1, was therefore not immediately the Paradise of the human spirits, or the earth. It describes actual spiritual happenings at heights and distances immeasurable and thus inconceivable to earthly humanity. We should therefore not become confused with the term, earth, used in the account of Creation in Chapter 1. That word *does not* refer to any kind of 'local' association with our planet. It must be understood as a *concept of Creation* which applies to 'dry land'.

"And God called the dry land 'earth': and the gathering of the various waters He called 'seas'."

(Genesis 1:10)

In The First Creation, therefore, there are also mountains, forests, meadows, seas, animals and men – as we have previously and strongly noted – but of inconceivable beauty and perfection as prototypes for all subsequent Spiritual Creations, all of which could only come into being *after* The First Creation.

Thus it is stated:

"Let the earth (the dry land) produce seed-bearing vegetation, as well as fruit trees according to their several species, capable of reproduction upon the Earth." and that was done. The Earth (the dry land) produced the seed-bearing herbage according to every species, as well as the different species of reproductive fruit trees; and GOD saw that they were good. This was the close and dawn of the third *age*.

(Genesis 1:11-13, Emphasis mine.)

Now, what is this new and very different word – *age*– describing the Creation-process? A quick comparison of our two main reference Bibles reveals a vastly different contrasting picture with exactly that one small word making all the difference. The King James Version of Genesis 1:1 reads:

"**In the beginning** God created the heaven and the earth."

This Bible, as with most others, goes on to state in Chapter 1 Verse 5:

"And God called the light Day, and the darkness he called Night. And the evening and the morning were the *first DAY*."

[18]Perpetuated by the Christian Church, earthly science and committees of Ph.D and degree-toting Bible "scholars" this 'triune' of earthly power and flawed education persistently clings to and continues to intellectually debate this foolish divide. Riding on the back of so-called "expert" translations and opinions, the main Bible Publishers continue to reproduce the same appalling error. Despite this dreadful suppression of the truth about Creation by the "educational elite" of primarily the "Christian" part of global humanity – and in this case, also, Maori academic traditionalists – we, guided in the same way that Fenton surely was, will, with his essential contribution, together reveal the processes that facilitated our entry into spiritual life on earth.

And so on to Verse 31:

> "And God saw everything that he had made, and, behold, *it* was very good. And the evening and morning were the ***sixth day***."

And to Chapter 2, Verses 1 and 2, which state:

> "Thus the heavens and the earth were finished, and all the host of them. And on the ***seventh DAY*** God ended his work which he had made; and he rested on the ***seventh DAY*** from all his work which he had made."

Surely we are able to acknowledge that this word **day** as used here is nothing more than a 'symbolic term' for a particular 'time-period', and was never ever intended to be taken literally. The example from *Verse 4* of the *same book* quantifies this premise because it states:

> "These *are* the ***generations*** of the heavens and of the earth when they were ***created***, in ***the DAY*** that the LORD God made the earth and the heavens."

(All emphases mine.)

As previously stated, the literal acceptance of the word, '*day*', in the singular here for the complete Creation of both the heavens and the earth, and the unequivocal and clear reference to the word ***generations*** in the same creative phase, surely calls into question any literal acceptance of 7 earthly days for any kind of complete Creative-process. Clearly there is an immediate and obvious contradiction here.

In stark contrast, Genesis 1:1 in Ferrar Fenton's re-translated Bible reads very differently:

> "By Periods GOD created that which produced the Solar Systems; then that which produced the Earth."[19]

It is crucial to understand here that a vastly different conception of time must inherently exist in spheres that are obviously non-material. The diurnal rhythm we experience here on earth simply cannot apply to such spheres, for the passing of time can only be *experienced as such* in *material* spheres. In Realms that are Eternal, time, as we believe we know it, simply does not exist. Time, therefore, does not ***pass*** there. We on material and finite earth, however, ***experience its passing*** every second of our earthly existence.

So in comparison with Verse 5, Chapter 1 of the King James Version, Fenton states:

> "And to the Light GOD gave the name of day, and to the Darkness He gave the name of Night. This was the close and the dawn of the **first AGE**."

And so on to verse 31:

> "And God gazed upon all that He had made, and it was very beautiful. Thus the close came, and the dawn came of the **sixth AGE**."

And Chapter 2, Verses 1 and 2 comparatively state:

> "Thus the whole Host of the Heavens as well as the Earth were completed. And GOD rested at the **seventh AGE** from all the works which He had made."

---

[19]Fenton's translation of the word, "Periods", equates literally to, "By Headships". He writes: "It is curious that all translators from the Septuagint have rendered this word (- as -) B'reshitii, into the singular, although it is plural in the Hebrew. So I render it accurately. – F. F."

In similar vein, Verse 4 reads:

"These were the productions for the Heavens and the Earth during their Creation at the **'PERIOD of their organization'** by the LORD GOD of both the Earth and the Heavens."

(Emphasis mine.)

And *only after* that *direct Creation* phase did God *then* subsequently *form* earthman – via a long evolutionary process – from "...out of the dust of the ground...", along with the animals and birds etc.. This scenario fits perfectly with the scientific view of a very long developmental phase for the earth after its birth before even the ancestors of the very earliest primates could emerge.

It is patently clear, therefore, that the difference between an 'earth-day' and an **age** is immense indeed. Simple logic should suggest that the designation of an **age** to denote a **phase of Creation** utterly stupendous and incomprehensible to human thinking in its scope and scale makes eminently more sense than the literal acceptance of an earthly 24 hour time-period that Christian fundamentalism has perhaps interpreted as meaning a Genesis *"Creation day"*.

And neither should that correct view clash with any religious interpretation regarding the awesome greatness of the Creation-process by The Creator Himself. Religious fear and blind faith do not supply answers. They only serve to perpetuate *spiritually-wrong concepts* with the resultant effect of *producing adherents too afraid to think for themselves.* Perhaps the explanations outlined here may induce the tentative religious reader to become less afraid to question worrying uncertainties.

After all, how often do we hear the common phrase or variations of: *"It wasn't like that in my day!"* Generally used to compare an earlier time-period in a particular life to that of the present, the connotations here are surely obvious to all. Such references do not at all refer to a *single* day.

Even though the previous explanations offer solutions to some contentious questions, there is still the need to provide further clarification to particular points for our complete elucidation. In one area at least, however, our discussions thus far should offer the clear recognition that we, *as the complete entity man*, are **not descended from the primates**. The physical body which we inhabit today is a refinement of form that developed from the very first primates during the long and natural evolutionary process that eventually led to upright man.

Therefore, let us re-state once more that this 'body-form' is nothing more than *a physical vessel only*. It is, however, one we absolutely need in order to live in the material environment of the earth. The animating power that separates itself out from the physical shell at earthly death, that some in the scientific community refer to as 'the ghost in the machine'; *that* is the *real* you and me – our individual Spiritual core whose home and Origin is *not of the earth*.

The above explanations may also answer the question as to what happened to the many varied species of primates that disappeared virtually overnight, and why the search for a so-called missing link is a difficult one. With the entry of the human/spiritual aspect into the most advanced species, all others *striving to develop to that same point* – but who *could not provide* the necessary *strength of attraction* for the *Spiritual part of man then reaching the earth plane* – simply died out. As a natural consequence of insufficient development and the inability to compete with this newly arrived "Spiritual force" in the shape of early Spiritual man, all other primate groups that *could have* developed to become *that particular vessel* were rendered superfluous.

Now, whilst we have a resolution to both parts of this religious/scientific debate, *how* the human/spiritual aspect actually entered the appropriately developed primate species or group requires further clarification. For only then could the "true human being" now multiply within its own *new species* and thus populate the earth and develop into the numerous peoples of the world.

We have established that the human being is both spiritual and physical, and possesses the attribute of *free will*. It is also clear that without *The Spirit* (The *Wairua*) as the animating force within the human body, the physical vessel has no life of its own i.e., it is naturally and necessarily dead. In this particular state, it follows the decree of The Laws of Nature and decomposes. It can thus be deduced that all other *mobile* life-forms of the earth, such as birds, insects and fishes etc., must similarly have an *inner animating core* in order to have life. Their *inner core* is, however, *not* spirit, but *soul*, from which is derived the discernment of *instinct*.

As with man on earth, animals, too, have an original home above the material world from where they draw their life-force. However, because they do not possess the attribute of *free will* – which is synonymous with *personal spiritual responsibility* – their *place of origin* is **below** that of the human spirit. That plane of origin is designated as the Animistic, or Elemental Realm; which is that of the Nature Beings and the Elemental Forces of Nature. Whilst these other *mobile* creatures of the earth do not possess *free will*, they do have the driving power of the *instinct*. This inherent attribute allows all such creatures to develop their ordained place and purpose too.

It is crucially important to therefore recognise that **up to** the incarnation or arrival of Spiritual-man, *animal-man* (earthly primate) **possessed soul as his life-force**, and quietly developed the perfection of form that was ordained to provide the vessel through which the entry of the **human/spiritual** onto the earth plane would be effected.

To this end, over the many millions of years of evolutionary development of the earth's creatures to the perfecting of the form of *animal man*, the human spirit (us), slumbering in a state of non-consciousness in the lower levels of the *Spiritual Realm*, obeyed an *unconscious inherent urge* to develop to *personal self-consciousness*. Since this could not take place there, and as a result of that "inner petition", the non-conscious spirit-seed, in terms of its individual journey, was *driven or expelled* (from out of The Spiritual Realm – **the true and actual Garden of Eden**) – downwards toward the material worlds.

> *This is the mechanism whereby we ask to be born, precisely to develop to self awareness of who, what, and why we are!*

Now, as it traverses the intermediate planes below The Spiritual Realm all the way down to the Material Plane, the human *"spirit-seed"*[20] is compelled to accept a covering or cloak of the same *consistency* as that of the plane through which it is journeying.

With regard to the actual concept of a *"spirit-seed"*, what might Maori lore believe? In Part I we examined certain aspiritual practices of the old Maori. Notwithstanding such a 'hard' way of life, the Hauhau chief, Titokowaru, in an example of perhaps remarkable 'matakiteship', uttered an amazing statement. From Ratana Revisited... p.15, Keith Newman. (Emphasis mine.):

> 'I will never die, *for I am a seed broadcast from heaven.* I stand on Mt Hikurangi in the land of light and enlightenment, although I am small in numbers and do not command great physical powers, I will tread many waters of the world.'

The soil in which *all human spirit seeds sprout and grow* is the material world. So in the great immensity of what we refer to or understand as being "the beyond", there are 'many

---

[20]Here we may now understand the meaning of the parable: **"A sower went forth to sow."**

mansions'. Those 'mansions' are the Realms or levels we must traverse to get here. Thus, the closer the *now-stirring spirit-seed* gets to earth, the *heavier* its outer coverings become.

We may refer to them as the bodies or coverings that pertain to, and are of, the particular *consistency* of the *different Realms* traversed. Through this process, we become more than just an entity comprising a Spiritual core (the real us) and a physical body. In reality we possess a number of "cloaks" or coverings, each one telescoped into the other, so to speak, with each having a different consistency *exactly commensurate with the sphere or plane from which it is derived.*

This *collective* covering is the *soul-body*, distinct from the inner Spiritual core. The final cloak, of course, is that of the physical body, taken on when the *Spirit*, with its enveloping "soul-coverings", *enters, incarnates*, into the growing foetus of a pregnant woman under the perfect outworking of **The Law of Spiritual Attraction of Similar Species**. This outer physical body becomes the earthly vessel for that "complete soul body" and its inner "enveloped spirit".

The processes that determine whether a male or female is born in this first incarnation will have been decided by the journeying spirit's *intuitive inclination* as it travels downwards toward the material world and the earth. From an initial *non-conscious* state, it gradually begins to slowly *awaken* the closer it gets to the world of the physical. During its transition downwards it begins to sense the life-stream currents of the various levels through which it passes.

As it descends further, it becomes more and more firm **in its inclination towards the experiences it wishes to make its own.** With this increasing certainty comes the firm decision to choose either an **active** and therefore **male incarnation**; or a **passive** and therefore **female one.**[21] Thus, the *nature of the activity it chooses* **determines its physical body form.**

This explains the *mechanism* of *personal* choice that *determines* whether the entity's final form will be male or female. From that point onwards, in its successive incarnations, it *can* change its outer forms depending, of course, on whether it changes its activity. Thus it is *possible* for a spirit to incarnate in alternate male and female bodies, which enables it to experience and develop both the male and female abilities inherent in the Spirit. However, it can also happen that such a situation generates for that individual, spiritual and emotional uncertainty as to its true ordained place.

> *In that explanation lies the key to the many emotional and/or psychological problems of humankind with regard to sexual orientation.*[22]

Now the stage is almost set for the entry of the human/spiritual into the world of matter, therein to determine his future outcome. The earth, up to this point inhabited by prolific numbers of varied creatures, did not yet know Spiritual man, nor the effect that this particular creature would exert on their natural, pristine world. Unknowingly awaiting the advent of this new stranger were the most highly developed species of primate quietly furthering their role as the chosen vessels through which this event would be fulfilled.

With the unnecessary conflict between science and religion in **one** aspect of the "Creation versus Evolution" debate incontrovertibly resolved, let us complete the process by examining the **second** part of our wondrous yet contentious Genesis Verse to determine the final happening. This is tightly bound to our old friend, Verse 7, Chapter 2 in Genesis of the King James Version of The Bible. As previously stated, two distinctly separate parts to this verse can be readily identified.

Quoted in full once more, it reads:

---

[21]Passive in this context does not mean 'weakly submissive'.

[22]Everything has its answer – its origin and end – under the Perfect outworking of **The Spiritual Laws of Creation**.

"And the Lord God formed man of the dust of the ground, and breathed into
his nostrils the breath of life; and man became a living soul."

What we are now concerned with are the words:

"...*and breathed into his nostrils the breath of life...*"

As previously refuted, this surely cannot be taken to mean that God Himself descended to
earth to literally blow His breath into a model of a mud-man. Though brief and simple, this part
of the Scripture clearly depicts something else. It depicts the **animating** of the future **physical
vessels** for humankind, facilitated through "...**the forming of man from out of the dust
of the ground**..." That "forming" occurred quite naturally and logically during the aeons-long
evolutionary process. Through those vessels – the especially prepared species of primate – man
would eventually exert his new and far-reaching *Spiritual influence* in the material worlds at the
ordained time for this to occur.

Now, in order to answer, from The Bible, the question of *how* the entry of the human/spiritual
aspect into that species of highly developed primates prepared for its reception was effected i.e.,
those possessing a soul as their animating life-force – *animal man* – we need only re-visit Verse 7,
Chapter 2, but *this time* using Ferrar Fenton's translation of Genesis to find the *true* connection.
Fenton offers that actual revelation. It is one, moreover, which gives a far clearer understanding
than we have thus far found in any other "scriptural writings".

So, once again we read:

"The EVER- LIVING GOD afterwards formed Man from the dust of the ground, and
breathed into his nostrils the **life of animals**; – **BUT MAN BECAME A LIFE-
CONTAINING SOUL**."

(Bold emphases mine.)

The *difference* in wording here from commonly accepted Scripture represents a huge leap
forward in our knowledge of the understanding of Creation and may well reflect Ferrar Fenton's
intuitive grasp of the true happening to enable him to state it *more* precisely, but without *actual*
confirmed knowledge.[23]

The fact that the evolutionary development of the *primates* necessarily required the symbolic "...*breathing into the nostrils the life of animals*...", simply reflects the creative and actual
necessity **for all mobile creatures of the earth to have an inner animating core**, their
actual **life-force**. Thus that which is referred to here as "...*the life of animals*...", is 'their' *inner
life-aspect*, which all animals must possess in order to live.

It is that of soul.

As we have learned, man *also* possesses a soul – *but not as his innermost 'animating component'*. The primary life force of man – the actual person – is **spirit**. His **spirit** – **he** – is
enveloped by his *soul*, the *multi-layered* outer cloak or *covering*.

---

[23] Fortunately that new knowledge is available today, hence the unequivocal and unapologetic nature of this
whole Work. Fenton's clearer "spiritual insight" enabling him to clarify the terrible error/distortion about Creation
– so long accepted without question – is revealed toward the end of the "Explanatory Note" of his remarkable
work and sublime 'Calling'. It now finds voice here too – *in this Work especially for Christian Maori and
followers of Ratana*. To those few of his assailants who 'sneered' that his work was 'not a translation but a
mere paraphrase', he writes: "The remark shows that they do not know the difference between one and the other,
or a perusal of my rendering of the Hebrew of the *two first chapters of Genesis*, and my note thereon, ...would
show to them the purely philological basis of my translation." (Emphases mine.)

Spirit – or *wairua* – is who and what man is ***when all else is stripped away***.

So the reference to the word "soul" pertaining to man in this particular and *correct translation* of the Biblical account must be understood in its *true meaning*, since there is clearly a fundamental difference between the life-force inherent "***...in the man breathed into...***" and **what he then became** as a result of this ***breathed-into process***. Moreover, there is a stated delineation with the use of the conjunction – **BUT**!

This can be further extended to logically mean "**...but** *nevertheless became...*" Fenton must have understood the crucial difference here because this key phrase is capitalised in *his* Bible, i.e.: **"BUT MAN BECAME A LIFE-CONTAINING SOUL."**

We may perhaps better understand this most crucial difference which separates man from animal by examining Fenton's footnoted reference 1 immediately after the word, 'animals', in the Scripture: i,e., "...and breathed into his nostrils the life of **animals**1." Fenton's footnote states:
"1 Or reflective or intellectual life. See Cor. Ch ii.12. Ch iii.3."

We know, of course, that animals are not reflective or intellectual in the human sense, but that is not what is meant here.

So if we now look at Corinthians 2:12, we really do begin to understand what Fenton must surely have intuitively understood:

"And we have *not* received the *spirit of the world*, but the ***Spirit proceeding from God***; so that we can *distinguish* the gifts God has granted to us."

"...for you are animals still. For when there is *rage and strife and dissensions among you*, are you not rather like *animals*, than conducting yourselves like men."

(Corinthians 3:3, All emphases mine.)

Note:

If there is still uncertainty regarding these explanations in the mind of you, the Maori reader; or you, the Pakeha reader; here is the final note on this *most crucial and necessary of revelations for **all** of earthly humanity*!

In reinforcement *once more*: We now know that the breathing "...into his nostrils the **life of animals**..." represented the entry – *at the very beginning* – of the *inner, animating life-force* into the very earliest *physical-form ancestors* of primates at their ***forming*** from 'out of the dust of the ground', from which would *eventually develop* the most *highly evolved species* to exist on earth. And from that 'broad evolutionary spread', the *further development* of the *single primate branch* which would *subsequently produce* the "physical-form vessels" *human beings would require* for physical life on earth.

So the great and fundamental ***unbridgeable difference*** between primates and humans is the fact that even though we *also needed* to use the basic physical form of the most *highly evolved* of the primate species for *our human* earth-life activity too, ***we could not do so with just the 'inner, animating life-force' of the primate***.

For we are *not* animal. We are human!

And we therefore could not just simply **evolve into humans** from the primate. Why not? Because, *once again*, that which gives human beings life *is not* the same inner life-force as that which the *lower-level* animal primates possess as *their* life-power.

Thus, the capitalised reference to **"LIFE-CONTAINING SOUL"** reveals exactly that fact. That which is *contained in, and enveloped by, the 'soul'* in this crucial revelation, is *The Spirit – THE LIFE – the <u>innermost</u> animating core of the 'human being'.*

Therefore, the key capitalised phrase: **"BUT MAN BECAME A LIFE-CONTAINING SOUL."** reveals that the *quantum leap* from primate to human was *not one given life by human genetics* through simple 'brain development' by normal but slow 'evolutionary processes'. It was a quantum leap *precisely because a new force and power was required for humans to be humans*, completely distinct and very far removed from the animal primate. That is why the 99 percent of similar DNA in both *monkey and man* concerns the respective *physical bodies only*, and thus why they both *rot away* at death.

We are not our physical body!

We can conclude, therefore, that this inherently logical process that Ferrar Fenton reveals is that which actually facilitated the entry of *Spiritual man* onto the earth.

It thus depicts the amazing event of the *incarnation*, the *entry*, of the **human/spiritual** from out of his former *non-conscious* state in the *non-material* Spiritual Realm, into the most highly developed **species of primate** then existing on earth. Only thereby could man *develop* to become fully conscious of self.

'Spiritual' man – 'human' – now stands on earth!

The reader who supports Bible Scripture literally and solely may now begin to see that there is no conflict after all between the Creation account and evolutionary development since both, in their co-joined natural perfection, could only have issued from the hand of The Creator Himself in any case. Utilising Hegel's 'dialectic process' and Fenton's correct Bible translation, we have brought together the appropriate connecting threads from both the scientific and religious disciplines to offer the reader definitive clarification of the Creation-process.

So there stands our Spiritual Origin; that of *all* humankind. From that stupendous happening, Spiritual man, in his material home prepared over millions of years, began his new journey of development towards personal self-consciousness and knowledge. This journey, however, would span a certain, precisely ordained period of allotted time requiring accountability at the end of it. For with his request for conscious life came the responsibility of correct stewardship of his material home; the earth and all its creatures, as was once commanded!

The division and separating out into the races, peoples and languages of the earth still lay before him. History records that stewardship as one of mostly degradation, destruction, blood and war, with few intervals of true peace, grace and nobleness. Now, however, the time of accountability has arrived. We stand in the midst of the reciprocal effect of our bad stewardship as **The Spiritual Laws** set about the grim task of "balancing the books". That necessary "auditing process", which we now begin to observe with some considerable degree of alarm, is effected via the increasing outworking and activity of the unassailable power of **The Elemental Forces of Nature!**

The clarification herein of humankind's origin and entry into the material world of the earth as home should provide meaning and insight for many readers. With clarification should also come quiet confidence and peace of mind as to who and what one really is. Here, we outlined and explained the basic happening of the coming-into-being of Creation, and of man. We accompanied him on his journey downwards, from a non-conscious spirit seed in The Spiritual Realm to incarnation and conscious personal responsibility on the earth, and thence to the employment of his free will to determine his spiritual future under the outworking of The Eternal Laws.

Naturally, we should expect that there is also a lawful process by which he leaves the earth. Whilst considerable detail is given to this process in a later Chapter, it is appropriate to conclude here with a short paragraph to very briefly outline the reverse process of his return journey, thus completing our cycle of *spiritual* life in this segment.[24]

So, upon earthly death and *release from the physical shell – **and providing he has earned the right to do so** –* he begins his *return journey upwards* to his true Spiritual home. As he passes *into each correspondingly lighter sphere – **the same that he traversed on his journey downwards** – the heavier covering of the previous lower level is automatically discarded in accordance with its corresponding weight and that particular level's corresponding density.* In this manner his ascent continues until, finally, he stands at the threshold of The Spiritual Realm from whence he originated.

This time, however, not as a non-conscious, unknowing spirit-seed, but as a fully conscious, purified, spiritual being – the true Spiritual Man. Here, he sheds the last cloak and is drawn across that boundary into his Eternal home, radiant in his Spiritual Purity having **earned** "...the crown of eternal life". Thus is fulfilled the invitation of Jesus who stated:

> "In the home of my Father there are many abodes. If it were not so, I would have told you: because I am going to prepare a place for you."

> (John 14:2)

In order to earn this right, however, the next scriptural quote should also be accepted:

> "I tell you indeed, that you will not depart until you have repaid the very last farthing."

> (Matthew 5:26)

Therefore, to this end under The Laws of Creation i.e., spiritual/foundational science, we read;

> "You, however, should be perfect, as your Father in heaven is perfect."

> (Matthew 5:48, Fenton all.)

Given the possibly contentious yet potentially mind-extending implications of this Chapter, detailing the main points of the Biblical sequence of Creation here at the conclusion may provide simplified clarification via a greatly condensed overview.

---

[24]The reader should note, however, that this particular outline only explains the return ascent *if* The Spiritual Laws have been heeded. The process for a human spirit who **chooses** a path *opposed* to those Laws is, unfortunately for that human spirit, a very different one.

Key Points

The Utterance of the stupendous Creation-Words – "**LET THERE BE LIGHT!**" – thus resulting in: **The First Creation – (The Spiritual Realms.)**

1. The Creation of the Heavens and the Earth of **The First Creation** – "By **Periods** God created *that which produced* the Solar Systems: then that which produced the Earth."

   (Genesis 1:1, Fenton, Emphasis mine.)

2. The **Creation** of day and night (in the Heavens.)

3. The division of the waters which were **under** the expanse (firmament) from the waters which were **above** the firmament. (expanse) The firmament/expanse then named the Heavens.

4. The commanding of the waters **below** the Heavens to be collected in one place, and for dry land to appear.

5. The **Creation** of flora.

6. The Creator sets two great lights which divide day and night for earth.

7. The **Creation** of fish and bird life.

8. The **Creation** of animal life.

9. Then, the great **Creation** of man **in His Image** – both male and female – and the Blessing to rule over all flora and fauna.

10. The **completion** of the Creations at the end of the **sixth Age**. The Creator rests at the **seventh Age** and blesses and hallows the seventh **day**.

    Note Scripture: Genesis 2:1 (Fenton) "Thus the whole Host of the Heavens [as well as the Earth] were completed." This is the completion of The First Creation (i.e. Spiritual Realms.) (Parentheses mine.)

And only then:

The Creation of the Worlds of Matter, including our universes, solar systems and earth – **as planned by its Creator.**

11. After the completion of **The First Creation** **(The Spiritual Realms)** including all that was then **created** (as described in Genesis 1:1-3), **The Creation of the Worlds of Matter** through a long process of evolution leading to the forming by God of earth-man from out of **the dust of the ground** who, following a suitable time of evolution, became the first human being – **the man with the Living Soul.**

    (Genesis 2:19, All emphases mine.)

12. Earth-man gives name to every creature – **formed** from out of the **dust of the ground also.**

13. Even though God had **already created** "man" in His Own Image (both male and female) in **The First Creation**, and had subsequently **formed earth-man** from out of **the dust of the ground**, there was still no earth-woman. (Biblical tradition states that she was constructed from a rib of the man.)

Now, whether this sequence is viewed literally, symbolically, pseudo-scientifically or any other way, there are clear pointers illustrating a number of very different and very distinct happenings that occurred. This is clearly contrary to the one single sequence that the main churches generally believe and accept as having ostensibly **created** man/earth-man. And, moreover, him only. Fenton unequivocally delineates these separate, stupendous events in clear sub-titles.

1. **The First Creation of the Universe by God = Elohim.**

2. **Creation of Man under the Shadow of God.**

3. **The formation of Man from the Dust of the Ground by the Ever-living God.**

Therefore, if we take careful note of points 3, 4, 9, 11 and 13 from **Key Points**, and similarly note the above sub-titles 1, 2 and 3 from Fenton's translation, a vastly different and more stupendous picture arises than the present, general belief of an aspiritual humanity somehow being in close proximity to a Power that we cannot even begin to comprehend. Points 3 and 4 *on their own* here strongly indicate two different places very far apart: one above the Heavens and one below the Heavens. The Creator of all the Worlds is clearly far further from us than we might want to believe. (In any case recognition of that fact arrives to all not too long after earthly death.)

The sequence we have outlined here (from The Bible) concurs with many of the scientific findings of anthropology and astronomy.

It does not concur in any shape or form, however, with the Maori Creation-myths of Rangi, Papa, Maui and Tane etc..

Nevertheless, taken in concert, both views of Pakeha science – anthropology and astronomy – actually trace a path of evolutionary development that is consistent with rational logic and, moreover, encompasses and co-joins both the religious and scientific points of view. More importantly, however, this more logical sequence places man (us) in his correct place very far from a Creative Force that inherently possesses the Power to Create all that we know – and all that we do not – simply by an Act of Will. In short, by the Power of Creative thought. That is a power and an ability utterly incomprehensible to us. Such stupendous Power, moreover, will forever be beyond our extremely limited comprehension.

However, instead of that particular recognition being somehow problematical for us, we should be grateful for the fact that the incomprehensible immensity of the Creations graciously provides all that we will ever need for life here – **and life eternal**. And should thus actually offer the largest possible measure of inner peace and spiritual security possible. That is provided, of course, that we voluntarily choose to: –

Obey the Rules!

Therewith are the long-contested arguments of Creation versus Evolution – Christian fundamentalism versus intellectual science – *perfectly reconciled and harmonised*:

For Pakeha and Maori!

8

The Language of Man

The Development and Spiritual Ramifications!

"Spirit and language are inherently inseparable!"

Picture Spiritual man aeons ago at his very first beginnings. Into the environment of the physical world he takes his first faltering steps. The earth thus far has only known the activity of the animal kingdom; countless millions of different species each interacting in perfectly balanced cycles of life. Each with their own particular call, some loud, raucous and dangerous, others mellow and sweet, but all contributing to the symphony of the earth's natural sounds for that time. The voice and languages of man would be a new sound, an intrusion perhaps? Yet one that held the potential for noble enhancement, or vulgar coarseness.

The rich diversity of the languages of man, however, was still far in the future. Before that could happen, this new addition to the world's creatures would need to develop into a fully-fledged human being. For it was not *fully developed* human spirits that incarnated into the most highly developed anthropoids that were prepared for this event, but *spirit-seeds* from the Spiritual Realm, the actual "home" of Spiritual man. Consider once more the parable in Matthew 13:3:

"A sower went forth to sow..."

They had first, therefore, to develop into individual personalities in the World of Matter. As previously stated, the physical body of man is, indeed, derived from the animal, but the *inner animating core* is from the higher Spiritual Realm. Thus the 'receptacle-body' for those *spirit-seeds* necessarily underwent a fundamental and far-reaching change *with the arrival of the human-spiritual aspect into it*. In place of the previously existing animistic *souls* which were the 'driving energy' inside those 'ordained forms', the new inner animating "life-force" of the human *Spirit* now became established in their place through incarNation into the prepared vessels – the most highly developed anthropoid forms. So, in accordance with that requirement, male *spirit-seeds* or spirit-sparks incarnated in animal bodies of the male sex, and female *spirit-seeds* in those of the female sex.

Leading on from these very first incarnations, continuing incarnations of human spirits could now take place through the natural procreative process under The Law of Attraction of Similar Species. This process resulted in the demise and extinction of certain groups of anthropoid apes that did not develop to a level "sufficient to attract" the human-spiritual aspect then preparing for its entry into the material world. That procedure *would have* provided the next stage of development for those particular groups – as happened for the *primate branch* which *did attain* the necessary degree of mature evolvement.[1] This great evolutionary change from animal-man to Spiritual-man therefore allowed for the finer development of that originally-prepared, select anthropoid form, to our general, present-day, physical one.

With the arrival of the *spiritual* into the *animal bodies*, a critical event occurred for this new race called man. This was the *concomitant development* of human language. It was an evolutionary event of huge proportions with obviously far-reaching ramifications. The inherent urge of the human spirit to seek communication with others gave vocal expression to his thinking, volition and intuitive perceiving, and allowed the formation of the organs necessary for this. To this end an important and closely-linked change took place in his physical form, clearly demonstrating the difference between man and animal, a difference only discovered quite recently.

That vitally important distinction was the gradual sinking downwards of the larynx. In the world of the animal, but more especially that of the apes, there was no change in the position of the larynx. And only this sinking of the larynx, the re-positioning of that organ of communication – with the simultaneous forming of the human shape of mouth and nose – that, alone, made possible the complete voice and vowel reproduction that is a singularly-defining and characteristic feature of humankind.

However, the development of the organs of speech to the point where communication between members of the budding human race could evolve from the projection of only the most basic sounds in the beginning, to eloquent oratory and abstract intellectual theorising in the later millennia of the grand march forward, was not an instant happening. This process of development necessarily required a long period of time as humankind formulated new words to 'frame' ever new discoveries and new and evolving concepts to add to his continually developing vocabulary.

For it should not be supposed that 'Spiritual man' arrived on the earth with the innate and automatic ability to instantly converse with great skill and eloquence from an inherent vocabulary of already known words and some form of pre-programmed meanings. If we accept the literal interpretation of the forming of man from out of the "dust of the ground", then we *may possibly* accept that scenario. However, that is not the reality. In our part of Creation, evolution and development are the norm rather than the exception – in both the great and the small.

Therefore, the development of sufficient skill and ability to enhance the medium of speech as an effective means of communication from simple interchange, to more complex discussion, to the area of even conflict resolution, could not possibly be attained in just a few short years. The procedure was necessarily long and exacting, and probably in concert with the parallel development of larger and larger social groupings. This process of speech development and vocabulary acquisition which, for man, took hundreds of thousands of years, can be seen *in one single lifetime* anywhere in the world today in the natural growth of children from babyhood to the teen years.

So, today, when a new-born begins its earth-life with a cry, and through the process of imitation learns to speak within the first few years, it undergoes all the stages of development

---

[1] We may note the clear outworking of The Law of Movement here. Anthropologists have discovered that in the early history of man, a number of branches of the "anthropoid family tree" terminated for no *apparent* reason.

that humankind necessarily underwent over that long period of time. This is achieved by the sinking of the larynx and is repeated with each new birth. Research since about 1905 has allowed embryologists to establish that this 'descent of the larynx' begins at the end of the first year of life and lasts up to the eighth or ninth year.

Lieberman and Crelin, in their essay, "On the Speech of Neanderthal Man", state this same process in rather more technical terms:

> "Of all the living primates only man has an extensive supralaryngeal pharyngeal region that allows all of the intrinsic and extrinsic pharyngeal musculature to function at a maximum for speech production by changing the shape of the supralaryngeal vocal tract."

> (Negus, 1949, p.216)

Lieberman's study of the anthropoid apes and of the other apes, including macaques, has shown that; "...they are denied the true, correct vocalisation: simply because they do not experience the descent of the larynx."

Consequently this "...descent of the larynx to its lower position in adult man... ", would thus confer "...advantages in communication." Interestingly Lieberman and Crelin, on page 218, state:

> "The adult human laryngeal position is not advantageous for either swallowing or respiration. The shift of the larynx from its position in New-born and Neanderthal is advantageous for acquiring *articulate speech* but has the disadvantage of greatly increasing the chances of choking to death when a swallowed object gets lodged in the pharynx... The *only function* for which the *adult vocal human tract* is better suited *is speech.*"

Thus, via this 'shift-mechanism', a space is formed at the back of the throat, one which the anthropoid apes (and all other apes) do not have. It is a space necessary for the utilisation of our freely-moveable tongue to make the very fine movements required for vowel vocalisation. In essence, it is a true vowel space. It can therefore be clearly seen that the formation of our own human language, especially of the different vowels, is only possible with this 'vowel space'.

In the opinion of these two researchers, Neanderthals possessed an essentially non-human vocal tract, but probably made maximum use of his large brain to establish vocal communication. That utilisation, in their view would, perhaps:

> "...provide the basis for mutations that lowered the larynx and *expanded the range of vocal communication* in modern Man's ancestral forms."

> (P.218, All emphases mine.)

With regard to the time-frame required to perfect vocalisation skills, Lieberman and Crelin observe that with this stage of man's evolutionary development, particularly his speech:

> "...limited phonetic ability was probably utilised and that some form of language existed. Neanderthal man thus represents an intermediate stage in the evolution of language. This indicates that *the evolution of language was gradual,* that *it was not an abrupt phenomenon.*"

> (P.221, Italics mine.)

They state:

> "The reason that human linguistic ability appears to be so distinct and unique is that the intermediate stages in its evolution are represented by extinct species."

And they further state:

"Fully developed 'articulate' human speech and language appear to have been comparatively recent developments in Man's evolution."

From our particular perspective we note their view that:

"They may be the primary factors in the accelerated pace of cultural change."

(All p.221, Italics mine.)

Their research into Neanderthal's linguistic ability coupled with this observation is, in their opinion:

"...consistent with the inferences that have been drawn from the rapid development of culture in the last 30,000 years in contrast to the slow rate of change before that period."

(Dart, 1959, p.220)

The conclusion can be reached that man's ancestral form, which has quite clearly evolved from some basic shape close to that of the apes, was similar in configuration to the vast majority of mammals, in that the epiglottis reached right up to the palate. And, moreover, why the *Spirit* was necessary for man to begin the process of language development, which each parent can observe in the first few years of his own offspring's development. The simple yet unequivocal logic contained in this process should offer greater certainty as to the how and why of our early development, and serve to further strengthen our assertions on humankind's origins in the previous Chapter.

But in those far-off days of man's humble beginnings, how did the forming of the language proceed? Spiritual man was like a baby needing to formulate new sounds to become new words with distinct and clear meanings. In their evolutionary physical development, the posture of early man *gradually changed* from a *bent ape-like one* as they walked, to the *upright stance* that we have today. And as the larynx descended and the human mouth developed to its present shape, the initially hoarse and probably guttural sounds became clearer and more vocal.

In the beginning, humankind probably communicated with familiar gestures and sounds gleaned from the natural world around them. Individual sounds would have become groups of sounds which then became words. And these words subsequently became sentences. The ability to produce whole sentences allowed for the extension of the language, with the eventual capacity for far greater expression.

So each *word* thus became the actual *form* of that particular *sound*, evoking a clear and concise *picture* as to its *meaning* in the mind of all who heard it.

This was man's great responsibility in being given the gift of speech; to use the formative power of the spoken and written word to upbuild. Unfortunately it has too often been utilised for the opposite. Today, with many thousands of languages and dialects scattered throughout the world and its peoples, the *Spiritual Power* inherent in the formed word is no different now from what it was when man took his first, hesitant, vocal steps into his spiritual future. What is important to realise, then, is that language was intended only for the good.

Yet the historical record clearly reveals thousands of years of wrongful application by humankind. Therefore, because every language has the same relative or comparative degree of power for the race that is using it, all languages should be treated *as a spiritual gift* offering the most wonderful means to express, in a precise and specific way, all that a race, culture, or Nation is capable of attaining. Thus, the medium of the "Spiritual Power" inherent in all speech decrees that we not only produce all our *works*, but we actually also "form" our particular cultures.

To return to our first beginnings, however, the momentous potential in the *transitional effect of animal-man becoming spiritual-man* would be that which the power of the spoken word, and in turn the written word, would spiritually exert, not just on the earth, but in his part of Creation also. However, man would tread many diverse paths, produce much offspring and people many lands, before the full and generally unfortunate impact of this "speaking ability" could be gauged and measured. Separating out and populating the different parts of the earth guaranteed the formation of new languages with new words to give name to newly-discovered flora and fauna, along with sights and sounds not seen or heard before.

Via this vital and stupendous evolutionary happening, the way was now cleared for spiritual man to begin to record his exciting yet sometimes painful journey through 'history'. The establishment of 'ground rules' whereby small bands of 'new humans' could consolidate and begin to prosper, would be an obvious advantage.

In a very quick journey of compressed time, we can visualise the emerging family groups banding together to form larger, clannish organisations. This would serve the purpose of increasing their chances of success in hunting and food-gathering, provide greater protection for the group, and allow for greater social development. Continually expanding groups would also prevent the possibility of in-breeding, which would be a consequence of maintaining a small group for any great length of time.

The slow, gradual process of building groups of families into tribes, and tribes into confederations of tribes and so on, until whole Nations and races became fully established across the ancient "known world," would occupy a span of many, many thousands of years. And the primary medium of communication, the language, would provide the pivotal role in this process. Language offered the means to formulate practical, working rules to maintain cohesion and harmony in the growing organisations; vital preparation for the more difficult task of governing empires stretching across many lands. But that was a long, long way into a very distant future.

Incidental to this procedure, however, was the requirement for expanding groups to seek new lands and territories – sometimes far from their origins – thus giving rise to the establishment, over time, of a different language from that of the old homeland. One perhaps similar, but perhaps very dissimilar. Even with this diversification, however, certain elements in the languages of particular ethnic groups were retained as the basic root-foundation, thus indicating a common origin that we can trace today – particularly within the Indo-European group of people. Most Indian and Iranian languages belong to this Indo-European family of languages. Some Asian, South American, and Pacific Island languages share similarities also.

Humankind's territorial expansion did not result in an equal and uniform level of language development among the increasing numbers of different races and Nations, however. For example, races that were more concerned with merely the basics of life and with a limited view of the world, naturally developed a simple language that reflected similarly limited knowledge about fewer things. That was not the case with people who were developing more technological societies. Thus the different emerging peoples began to develop their own particular culture and characteristics in concert with their language. Some qualities would already have been inherent in the respective core group, but certain other traits would have developed as a consequence of various factors affecting their development, such as environmental ones. For each group, nevertheless, every phase added to their respective store of knowledge and word-usage overall.

Environmental aspects such as a warm or temperate climate with favourable food-producing conditions might allow an emerging race the luxury of food surpluses for trade and, therefore, the accumulation of wealth. A colder or harsher environment enforces the need for a more or less constant survival attitude with perhaps less scope for large-scale trade activity. It is not surprising therefore that, generally speaking, the earlier, more advanced civilisations first emerged in the warmer, more fertile regions of the earth, notably around the Mediterranean, the Middle East, and in parts of China, India and South America. Of course, favourable climatic conditions were not the sole reasons for such an emergence. An inherent questing and technological bent was also required, since some societies in other warm climes remained basically simple and tribal.

The acquisition of food has always been the most important need for man, with shelter a sometimes vitally necessary concomitant. Climatic factors would naturally be a strong deter-minant here too.[2] If, then, the question of food and shelter in a 'friendly climate' is resolved to the point where it does not present a problem and allows time away from the activities of food gathering – whether hunting, fishing or agriculture – this 'spare' or 'leisure' time from such activities can then be channelled into other areas.

With regard to dwellings, for example, what may have begun life as rudimentary shelters could then be expanded to become much more comfortable and elaborate homes. And from those humble beginnings later gradually arose the great civilisations featuring large, planned, paved cities with public buildings, places of worship, and even piped water etc.. In terms of language and vocabulary extension, this "expansion of the people" allowed the intellectual aspect of certain races to evolve toward greater expression of abstract thought and philosophy.

"Maslow's hierarchy of needs", defines this process in latter-day 'psycho-babble'. Abraham Harold Maslow (1908-1970) developed a theory of 'motivation' which describes the process by which an individual progresses from basic needs such as food and sex to the highest needs of what he called 'self-actualisation'. In his opinion, 'humanistic psychotherapy', usually in the form of group therapy, was the best way to help the individual through these stages.

> We would opine that the better, simpler and more sure way to achieve that desirable state is to embrace The Spiritual Laws and live by them. Self-realisation (or 'self-actualisation') sourced from *genuine Spiritual knowledge* and awareness is then a completely natural out-come deriving from such a decision.

The overall drive, energy and population levels of the various emerging races might well determine who would become the greater Nations and empire-builders, as opposed to those who would be administered and/or absorbed by others. And the establishment of larger groupings of peoples into complete Nations by the most energetic or magnanimous races might mean a correspondingly faster level of development of their administrative and building skills than perhaps those who were simply conquered or enslaved. History records many cases, of course, where some groups became slaves or servants of the strong.

Generally speaking, the languages of the "empire-builders" flourished as a result of contin-ually evolving capabilities. This expansive attribute now developing in those particular groups allowed for the subsequent emergence of a different way of thinking and speaking. Literature, religion, poetry, music composition and art gave impetus to a large degree of elevation in the language. Abstract or intuitive ideas and views became the science of philosophy which required the development of a whole new vocabulary to clarify such thinking. This process quite naturally took some considerable time.

But did the language-development of humankind proceed in accordance with the design of The Creator Who, under the aegis of His Eternal Laws, granted we human spirits the gift of conscious life? Since this work is concerned with that "reality", it is important to examine this question further.

We can probably accept that "early man" retained contact with the non-physical world from whence he came, thus holding an innate understanding of his connections there. His "spirit", guided by that still-clear connection to those other Realms and to higher Spiritual Teachers led his thinking and intuition. Consequently, the forming of words proceeded in accordance with the power inherent in The Laws of Creation. With clear guidance and strong, intuitive perception,

---

[2]It is certainly a truism, that it is easy to be a conservationist until one is cold and/or hungry!

man was able to give the correct *spiritual form* to all that he gave name – remembering that **The Spiritual** is actually the *foundation* for all that exists in the material. The non-material or abstract concepts also received their particular *word-coverings*. They, too, *resonated* their *correct spiritual meanings*. And as long as men 'built' their language *spiritually*, they received the "reciprocal returns" of peace, happiness and advancement, since all forms of ennoblement are founded on the Eternal principles of The Spiritual Laws.

Unfortunately, in the course of man's development, the purity of his previously strong intuition and volition began to falter. This was brought about *by strengthening the use of his intellect to a point where the necessary balance between the spiritual and intellectual aspects within him tipped more decisively toward the intellectual side.*

Consequently, that original, clear guidance suffered because an *intellectual barrier* was erected which *blocked* the formerly strong connections. The language *subsequently formed* began to degenerate under the power of greater and greater *materialistic thinking*. Through this event, man *severed* his connections with the lighter Spiritual Realms of his Origin and became enmeshed in darker thinking which was alien to his spirit. Increasingly *cut off* from the knowledge of its origins and walled-in by the *all-dominating intellect*, his spirit could no longer exert sufficient influence to alter his newly-chosen, aspiritual course.

> **It was that process and thus that event which constituted the "great fall of man".**

Spoken of in many legends and religious writings, *it was the turning away from The Creator and His Eternal Laws*. This definitive happening in the evolutionary history of humankind is depicted in The Bible as the story of the building of the Tower of Babel which resulted in the great "confusion of tongues". (Genesis 11:1-9)

*   *   *   *   *

The story of the Tower of Babel denoting the *scattering of the languages* should be viewed as a *Spiritual Event* describing a process that was *not a literal building of a tower to heaven*. It is vitally important to understand the true *Spiritual meaning* of this happening. The edifice of Babel was *primarily* a tower of arrogance and presumption fuelled by man's personal ego through his *greater and greater disregard* for The Eternal Laws. In this case it was especially related to the incorrect use, and therefore the incorrect *Spiritual employment*, of the language. Thus a 'confusion of language' gradually spread to all of the world's people.

That particular outcome, however, should not be interpreted to mean the development of many *different* languages, for this would have been the natural situation in any case. **That was not the problem, and not the process.** And neither does it mean that communication between the various peoples with their different languages would necessarily have been difficult either. The 'scattering' represented far more than just simple, physical differences in word-sounds, structure and meaning. In reality, it was an event of decisive *spiritual* proportions!

Men no longer *understood* each other because the *Spiritual Qualities* of honesty, nobleness and purity that were the hallmark of the early development of the *form* of language underwent drastic change. Disregard for The Laws of God brought about a fundamental and far-reaching shift in the "kinds of forms" created by collective humankind. These new, *mutated forms* of pride, ego, selfishness, personal advantage and disregard for their fellow-men, became the normal produce of mankind. In that scenario is revealed the meaning of the *"scattering of the languages"*!

With that event, a wrong volition and attitude entered the earthly languages. Words appeared which had not, until then, ever existed, and which were alien to the pure volition of the first human spirits. Words that were dark and evil, words formed from out of the evil deeds and thoughts of men. Like an insidious virus it spread throughout the languages of the peoples.

Via this process over the thousands of years since, all the evil of this world was subsequently produced. Humankind then simply inflicted that growing evil upon one another. And, in accordance with The Spiritual Laws of Creation, mankind had no choice but to give name to each evil, because the various *forms* produced, *arose within we human beings*, **alive** – exactly *corresponding* to our *free will* choices.

*   *   *   *   *

Thus today we can readily see the culmination of all those past errors. The Spiritual transgressions against the language which humankind thoughtlessly engage in clearly reveal how it is misused more and more through meaningless rubbish, empty talk and evil thinking. And ever more carelessly the meaning of words is distorted, particularly under the now socially accepted standard of 'political correctness'. 'Cultural correctness' also stands indicted here. This insidious process, however, is just one of its soiled shields. Even debate in the various political chambers of many countries – the very place where one should expect ennobled standards to be present, or at the very least, upheld – sometimes degenerates to foul-mouthed mud-slinging.

The high concepts of justice, love, purity, truth, humanity, freedom, peace and faith, whilst still bandied about, no longer hold the elevated position within society that even a few short years ago they would have. In accordance with man's present nature, he imputed to those ideals insidious meanings corresponding more to his increasingly selfish, materialistic goals. Aims far removed from the pure application that these inherently noble concepts *actually mean and represent*.

It should thus be perfectly clear to any keen observer that the degradation of the language and its latter-day use conclusively reveals the depths to which we have voluntarily fallen. Once the "darker deeds" and the associated "growing evil" had given birth to the *living form of the words connected with the deed* and entered the *language* of the race; both these aspects became *alive within that particular race*. The "greatly-enlarged whole" then became a "well" into which all could dip and drink, with the "forms" even becoming 'culturalised' and perhaps 'politically correct'. And the true magnitude of this 'disaster' is not at all understood – or even recognised.

Thus, today, the language has, to a large degree, become befouled, evil and ugly, with even the youngest children contaminated. But who really cares? In the 'Reo' of Te Maori, is the degradation there similar to that of the Pakeha 'language'? No doubt, many Maori would say no, not so! Yet *all races* have fallen away from the pure connection to the Higher Spheres that were once enjoyed in former, more spiritually-enlightened times – a time sometimes referred to as 'the golden age of man'. So words used to describe dark and evil deeds within any language are clear proof that such things are an inherent part of that particular race, since those members, alone, have spawned the deed and its associated 'living word-form/s'.

Consequently, the objective examination of any language will quickly reveal the true 'inner condition' of the "collective soul or spirit", so to speak, of that particular race. Whilst all languages inherently encompass concepts and 'forms' of enlightenment, the balance scales of all races, including Te Maori, are also clearly weighted toward baseness too, and some more so than others.

Thus, when speaking of the "fall" of man, we should intuitively understand this to be his "Spiritual" fall, which we generally acknowledge as the loss of the once sacred, strong and necessary connection to The Source of Life. As previously stated, in the supplanting of the *spiritual part* within us – the 'leader', by the *intellectual part* – the 'assistant', we could do little else *but* fall away. The difficulty in redressing that balance today is exacerbated by our apparent *inability to recognise* that this *adulation of the intellect* **actually constituted 'the fall of man'**. Interestingly, the propensity of man to want to 'intellectualise' everything – even *spiritual* matters – would not have been possible without the means of the language to express such incorrect and inherently unworkable concepts in the first place.

However, a sharp differentiation should be made here between the more natural, intuitive expressions associated with genuine knowledge and Truth, the application of earth-sciences employing greater intellectualism for supposition and theoretical analysis, and the utilisation of intellectual talent and ability to *actually construct* workable concepts for the benefit of humankind. Paradoxically – and by virtue of the fact that the intellect is *unable* to recognise spiritual truths because of its ordained purpose in fulfilling the earthly or material task – modern intellectual man has lost *the very means* by which he can *actually* and readily *recognise* Spiritual Truth in the first place i.e., via his Spirit. It is, unfortunately however, a spirit now very much suppressed by the all-powerful and *much-lauded* intellect.

*   *   *   *   *

As probably the best example of the power of language to initiate sweeping change down through the centuries, we need look no further than to the influence of Jesus, sent to this earth to guide mankind back to knowledge of The Truth. Of course, in accordance with The Law of Attraction of Similar Species, He could only incarnate into a race that had developed sufficient spiritual insight to intuitively accept the "reality" of The One Invisible Creator. So it was that Jesus was born, by Law, into the Jewish race, a people with the necessary level of spiritual development for this connection to be made. And, moreover, a people whose law and language, through the admonitions of their many prophets, clearly reflected that understanding.

As previously stated, a birth into any other race, particularly worshippers of idols etc., could not have been possible. Aside from being totally pointless, the people of such a race could not possibly have any affinity or understanding whatsoever of a being Who stands far *above* even The Spiritual. The entry and purpose of Jesus in the world gave man a far different perspective of the power of language through His use of it in the purest, Spiritual way. His whole Ministry, moreover, was remarkable for the fact that He taught the Truth via the medium of the *spoken word* and not that of the written. Thus the "living power of language" is best illustrated in the manner in which Jesus "spoke The Truth", and its resultant and *undeniably* powerful effect upon the world.

But even this stupendous event and help from Above still did not change man's basic intransigence toward the pure truth given at that time. The distortions and errors caused by the "playing with the language of The Truth" have caused great confusion, particularly among the numerous Christian Churches.

*   *   *   *   *

Thus, it was during the global expansion of the world's peoples and their ongoing process of language development where this most unfortunate development of greater and greater intellectual sophistry began to emerge and gather strength in the new peoples collectively, but with varying degrees of intensity within the different groups. The original strong and natural connection to, and knowledge of, his Spiritual Origins became more and more clouded as the intellect grew disproportionately more influential. The inevitable result saw spiritual man's once sure, secure ties to those Higher Origins virtually severed. And with it a particularly vital connection that was meant to be an ongoing and special help in his everyday activities for all the time of his earthly stay.

In the beginning, he lived his life completely aware and accepting of the other-world (ethereal) currents around him, and of his connections to what we term the "beyond".[3] As importantly, however, he worked in concert with other beings who have their origin in another plane of Creation and who are active not only on the earth but in every other Realm of Creation also. Indeed, without their essential activity, man would never have had an earth to call "home" in

---

[3]In reality, however, this is actually part of the worlds of matter, albeit non-physical matter.

the first place. Today, only a very few people scattered throughout the various races have the ability to still see these 'helpers', even though we all see and feel the effects of their necessary activity every minute of the day. These are the "Nature Beings" and "Elementals" whose names are found, virtually without exception, in the languages of *all* the peoples on earth.

This cutting away and rejection of "The Elemental Forces of Nature" through the *elevation of the intellect* guaranteed that a huge gap of knowledge would develop in the history of the peoples. Some would consciously retain this knowledge longer than others. In virtually every case, however, what was once sure and certain Truth, securely and knowingly embedded in the languages of the various peoples, eventually became relegated to the realm of uncertain myth and legend. And, moreover, was further transposed into just the 'culture' of the race rather than being retained as clear knowledge.

Some of the more intellectual races, notably those from Western cultures, have virtually severed this connection totally, not even bothering to retain them as fables in the culture. The so-called more primitive or not-so-advanced races have at least retained a strong belief in the validity of their legends as possible truth. Unfortunately for Western Nations generally, their god of science has determined that such 'notions' cannot possibly be entertained as belonging to a 'rational, logical and intelligent society'. Interestingly, however, the main book of their religion, The Bible, speaks of them quite clearly. Thus, the relegation of what was once accepted as factual knowledge to the realm of myth and legend by 'intellectual reasoning', is to our detriment. Notwithstanding this particular path, the many languages of the world's various peoples still bears testimony to a time when man accepted the evidence of his factual experiences, and thus gave name to all that he knew existed in The Elemental World of Nature.

As previously noted, the rightful place of the intellect was, and is, to facilitate and assist man in the fulfilment of his *earthly* duties, which is why it is vital for scientific endeavour and why it has produced such technological marvels and great feats of construction. And in those endeavours, the language naturally provided the means of reference for this aspect of man's development also. The spirit, however, was to lead and the intellect to assist – as ordained from the very beginning. Thus sadly, Spiritual man, with the potential for achieving true greatness in the material world and in Creation, became *merely* intellectual man more concerned with earthly analysis and theory. Greater spiritual activity would have produced correspondingly **greater** deeds.

Ironically for modern-day man, the purpose of science was always to explain – via the language of course – the workings of all The Spiritual Laws and their effects in the physical world. By this process, man could re-discover his true place in Creation. Instead, he denies himself the very knowledge and connection which can bring about that re-discovery – that of his Spirit. Now, instead of a powerful, uplifting, spiritual language at our command we have, in its place, only a weak shadow of what it should be, thus contaminating virtually all the 'works' that we currently 'produce'.

We should, therefore, not forget the lessons that history can teach us. For *there* can be seen how the power of language has stirred men and Nations to great deeds. The upwelling of nationalistic fervour by the generation of powerful and emotional oratory has galvanised whole peoples to destroy even numerically superior forces bent on their conquest or destruction. The greatest conflict the world has ever experienced produced especially stirring words of great power from Winston Churchill which greatly helped the British people to withstand the onslaught of Hitler's Air Force. The American, Edward R Murrow opined that Winston Churchill:

"...mobilised the English language and sent it into battle to fight for democracy".

Jostein Gaarder, author of Sophie's World, (p.307) in his analysis of the German philosopher, Hegel; writes of Hegel's philosophy with regard to language:

"Reason manifests itself above all in language. And a language is something we are born into."

He argues (italics mine) that a language can manage quite well without the personal involvement or input of an individual of that particular race, but the individual *cannot* manage without that language.

"It is thus not the individual who forms the language, it is the language which forms the individual."

Quite logically we can extrapolate the primary ethos of the idea to accept that *whole races, also, are "formed" by their individual languages*. We recognise, or perhaps inherently associate, various characteristics of different races with their language. The fact that specific languages generally 'belong' to particular races is usually sufficient to conjure up images that 'fit' the people of those races. Conversely, our natural acceptance that other races will invariably be different from us automatically inculcates the belief that they will probably speak a language different from ours also.

The powerful effect of language may be gauged when the *spiritual* songs in any language of the various peoples are sung at times of great distress. A strong upwelling of emotion is invariably felt then. The particular distress or loss of the moment strives to find solace from Above by seeking to establish or re-establish a "connection of understanding" to, and with, an intuitively-perceived Higher, more powerful, protective presence. The potential for, and unfortunate reality of, very much *self-imposed distress* therefore provides the very reason to use language only in an ennobling way.

The power of language to move people patriotically can also be clearly observed at all events where National Anthems are played. The words are sung with great feeling and emotion and are an obvious pointer to the power inherent in all languages when used correctly. It is the "living form" embodied in the words which actually produces that effect, and which hold and strengthen the corresponding connection for each race to their particular homeland. The same effect can be felt during the singing of hymns during reverent worship or at funerals, particularly. Here the inner person perhaps senses its lost connection to a Higher, intangible force far removed from the problems of everyday living. Here, also, the words *clothe* the form and power of the spiritual meaning and are thus felt emotionally. Of course, this is also true with opposite kinds of living word forms, but these bring forth ugliness and conflict.

But what of the less developed races; the smaller groups and tribes around the globe? And what comparative level of language development did they achieve? In general their more restricted view of the world, governed by narrower perceptions reflecting less true knowledge and of fewer things, and perhaps strongly laced with superstitious views, resulted in comparatively simpler languages. Thus, through the many diverse languages, we *see* the different, historical life-paths and subsequent fortunes of the world's various peoples quite clearly written on the pages of time. In some cases, though, recorded history has been dominated by races with perhaps stronger, more assertive languages.

Certainly, the history of humankind clearly records many instances of suppression of the language, history and culture of minority groups within the sphere of influence of totalitarian regimes. Yet, whilst such blatant activities in other societies past and present are rightly condemned, the same kind of 'official' language suppression and distortion 'at home today' virtually enshrines the dangerously insidious practice of 'political' or 'cultural correctness' too.

The stupidity of it all is too clearly evident when it becomes a criminal or cultural offence to speak on certain issues, **even with correct language usage**, in case it offends someone, somewhere. Even the meaning of once simply understood words have been distorted to allow previously unacceptable practices to become "main-stream acceptable" by the hijacking a word for a particular labelling purpose. Racial issues involving change or distortion in language meaning also occupy this wrongly elevated place. Unfortunately, a spade cannot always be called a spade today.

Notwithstanding all that is wrong with our use of it, certain languages have developed to a point of convenience and value where they are now regarded as the world standard for particular activities. Thus, for example, we have Latin for scientific classification of flora and fauna, the German language generally synonymous with engineering excellence, and English as the preferred language of international business and aviation.

Nevertheless, for all its obvious necessity, the language, in its general application, formed by the power inherent in the human spirit, is now a sad, polluted and degraded shadow of what it could and should be. Whilst it will continue to evolve, it should do so *only* under the umbrella of The Eternal Laws – if it is to be of maximum benefit for humankind.

This should not mean the relaxation of even basic rules of grammar and spelling under 'modern and enlightened' educational curricula simply because it fits with some misguided notion that it somehow provides a more 'level playing field' for all students.

No longer do we appear to strive for individual excellence as would befit the outworking of Spiritual Law. Far easier to adopt a '*herd-mentality*' and simply produce average '*automatons*' who won't be '*emotionally disadvantaged*' by not having the same '*level of achievement*' as the rest of the '*herd*'! That kind of neutering process offers nothing more than a lowering of standards within the particular society concerned because it rejects the vital necessity of sound, healthy discipline.

In the past millennium, the expansion of the world's peoples has been virtually completed. From initial, exploratory forays of mainly maritime races to the new worlds, subsequent migrations resulted in waves of settlers journeying to those newly discovered lands. With the new discoveries came the need to use the language to name the physical features and the flora and fauna of the new homeland. And where 'supplanted settlement' occurred through either conquest or absorption, new names in a new language might replace the old.

And so it was that in the second millennium AD, a race of Neolithic people with great seafaring and navigational skills ventured into the greatest ocean in the world to seek new lands at a time when the Europeans, for the most part, believed in a flat earth and were afraid to venture out of sight of the coastlines of their known world.

In a newly discovered land of the South Pacific, these settlers, in the language of their race, eventually gave name to it as Aotearoa. They increased their numbers in this new land and, in their particular *reo*, became known as Te Maori.

9
The First Death!

The "Spiritual" Aspects

The Process? The Same – for Maori and Pakeha!

"And do not shrink in fear from those who kill the body, for they are not able to kill the soul..."

(Matthew 10:28, Fenton.)

"Do not dread those killing the body, and who after that have nothing worse to do."

(Luke 12:4, Fenton.)

"The more spiritually one lives, the less fear there is of death".

(The Soul:Whence and Whither.
Hazrat Inayat Khan, p.186)

"If we go to the root of the matter, it is our concept of death that decides our answers to all the questions which life poses."

(Dag Hammerskjold.
Secretary-General, United Nations, 1953-61)

The essence of the two *Biblical* quotes clearly indicates that physical death is not that which humankind should be morbidly fearful about. Of course, we should not be frivolous or superficial about any death, or whether it affects us personally or not. That is not the intended meaning behind the quotes anyway. By them we are meant to understand that death is not the end, and that earthly death is only a transitional phase or process. And one of many in the complete time-frame of our total existence.

9.1   Death, the Great Leveller

Of all human experiences in its absolute inevitability, death probably ranks highest on the fear scale for certainly the greater majority of human beings. For we all must accept, and thus eventually undergo, this "journey to *somewhere*". Historically and to the present day, our many and varied cultures have grappled with this seemingly unknowable enigma, but without real knowledge of it. So for most human beings, in the background of everyday lives insidiously lurks the great question: "What really does happen at death?" If that question were put to ten individuals, we would probably hear ten different opinions. Even with fifty or a hundred people, we would note many more ideas about this "death process". Now if the sample group were to track into the thousands, then religious, *cultural, ethnic* and even medical and scientific notions would surface in clear divisions.

Those divisions could logically be extrapolated to reflect probably the totality of humankind's beliefs towards the concept of "death". Therein, however, lies what is really the illogical stupidity of it all. For irrespective of race, religion, culture, ethnicity, education level or any other variable, there can only be *one* single immutable, inviolable – and thus **unchangeable** – process for the earthly end of *every* human life. Any thought to the contrary is simply silly in the extreme. Since that is the reality, then we can safely and logically say that virtually all human ideas about the actual "death process" will be wrong. Ignorance most certainly rules this aspect of so-called human knowledge! Where, then, might we find the actual answer? Only in **Creation-Law** knowledge – to which the *whole* of this Work leads – may we find the *complete* and *exact* answers and explanations.

Therefore: Given the glaringly-obvious fact that there is not even a *basically-correct* "across-the-board" global consensus about earthly death, true knowledge about it can *only* come into *every* society and culture when the aeons-long perpetuated ignorance about it is literally smashed into oblivion forever. Why is it so important to know? Simply because knowing – before the fact – the Truth about the Laws that govern both the *mechanics* of the actual death process and the *phases* that we must *all* go through immediately thereafter, would absolutely ensure that we human beings would *never again* behave as we have done for the thousands of blood-letting years that is our foolish legacy.

So: If analysed from the standpoint of The Spiritual Laws, these particular Scriptures should be readily acceptable as a viable and logical outcome of being born onto the earth in the first place. For there is no point in living for one absolutely indeterminate length of time only to have it all end in a complete expunging of the conscious personality and thence to a dank hole in the ground. Further, the terrible circumstances and life-path that millions are born into must logically pre-suppose clear and precise reasons for their fate. To simply subscribe to a belief which fatalistically accepts that such dire situations are out of our control is to also accept that we are no different from animals, which are governed by instinct alone.

Since humankind possesses the *attribute of free will* as an *inherent part of his spiritual heritage,* to accept any 'station in life' in dumb resignation in the belief that it cannot be changed, or believe that we cannot institute change within the society or group we may find ourselves in, is to allow the perpetuation of that wrong belief to flourish. And via this attitude or belief, bequeath to future offspring the same straitened circumstances and the same spiritual apathy. By exercising our free will in the *conscious recognition* that the outworking of The Spiritual Laws **do** offer inherent Justice, we automatically tap into the life-stream of that Universal Power, and precisely that *inherent Justice* contained within it.

And via this ordained process, arrive at the sure knowledge that physical death *is nothing more than a transitory phase.* Of course, strict and precise **rules** govern the process, as with everything in Creation. But by adjusting ourselves to The Laws or Rules – with the subsequent gaining of the spiritual knowledge that is a natural accompaniment of them – we can fully understand, and thus *consciously experience* one inevitable day, this ostensibly 'fearful' thing called **Death!**

For the one constant that can be absolutely relied upon in life is the certainty of dying, either sooner or later. Chapter 7, Verse 6, from "The Wisdom Of Solomon" (The Apocrypha, [emphasis mine]) states it wonderfully succinctly:

> "...there is for all mankind one entrance into life, and a *common departure*."

Therefore, since death comes to us all without fail, it would be logical to believe that we would occupy ourselves far more with the how and why of it than we actually do. A previous Chapter dealt with the reality of death to a large degree in the savage world of the old Maori. Now we will examine the *actual process*.

The emotional struggle and anguish that human beings contend with at the death of loved ones clearly reveals the degree of *non-understanding* of the process. If the *mechanism* of the death process were understood, this must surely help to ease the pain of those grieving, for there would not then be the *non-comprehension* that is the usual hallmark of funerals. The emotional hurt at the loss of a loved one can generally be coped with, but the reasons why to other questions that may surround this process is often a far different proposition.

For if after earthly death *life* does continue on, is it not reasonable to assume that upon that discovery many people who have *passed on* would then want to contact those whom they had recently departed from? Cold logic would aver that that would probably be the case. However, because a major separation from the physical/material environment of the earth has occurred, any kind of subsequent contact could only therefore logically be via *a non-physical* method.

Now, consider, what if a few mediumistic persons were able to be the portal by which people in the "beyond" could pass on their experiences? Should we automatically reject such stories? Or should we perhaps see in at least some such claims the possibility of a clear Grace from Above whereby we *can* be helped to a clearer understanding of the transition through the death process to "further life" in the next "realm"?

Since the whole of this Work unequivocally accepts that premise, let us note one such person's desire to offer us this very help.

*   *   *   *   *

In 1895, a Mr A. Farnese transcribed the experiences of a "Spirit Author" who gave his name as Franchezzo. The work, **"A Wanderer in the Spirit Lands"**,[1] describes his journey after earthly death. From the perspective of the major thrust of this book – namely the explanation of **The Spiritual Laws of Creation** – the dedication by Franchezzo in his transcribed statement is most interesting since it perfectly accords with what we state is imperative *for all races* to recognise! Key aspects are noted here:

> "To those who toil still in the mists and darkness of uncertainty which veil the future of their earthly lives, I dedicate this record of the Wanderings of one who has passed from earth-life into the hidden mysteries of the Life Beyond, in the hope that through my experiences now given to the world, some may be induced to pause in their downward career and think ere they pass from the mortal life, as I did, with all their unrepentant sins thick upon them.
>
> It is to those of my brethren who are treading fast upon the downward path, that I would fain hope to speak, with the power which Truth ever has over those who do not blindly seek to shut it out; for if the after consequences of a life spent in dissipation and selfishness are

---

[1]This book has recently been *re-published* by **Crystal Publishing** and is now available online at: **www.crystalbooks.org**

often terrible even during the earth-life, they are doubly so in the Spirit World, where all disguise is stripped from the soul, and it stands forth in all the naked hideousness of its sins, with the scars of the spiritual disease contracted in its earthly life stamped upon its spirit form – never to be effaced but by the healing powers of sincere repentance and the cleansing waters of its own sorrowful tears.

I now ask these dwellers on earth to believe that if these weary travellers of the other life can return to warn their brothers yet on earth, they are eager to do so. I would have them to understand that spirits who materialize have a higher mission to perform than even the solacing of those who mourn in deep affliction for the beloved they have lost. I would have them to look and see that even at the eleventh hour of man's pride and sin, these spirit wanderers *are* permitted by the Great Supreme to go back and tell them of the fate of all who outrage the laws of God and man.

As a warrior who has fought and conquered I look back upon the scenes of those battles and the toils through which I have passed and I feel that all has been cheaply won – all has been gained for which I hoped and strove, and I seek now but to point out the Better Way to others who are yet in the storm and stress of battle, that they may use the invaluable time given to them upon earth to enter upon and follow with unfaltering step the Shining Path which shall lead them home..."

(The Dedication of Franchezzo, A Wanderer In The Spirit Lands.)

The "Better Way" that Franchezzo alludes to in his warning plea to humankind clearly means a 'better way' than that which the world presently practices and which, as he so correctly states, is *the downward path* which *outrages the laws of God and man.* His 'experiential-recognition' reveals that *only* by heeding The Spiritual Laws and living the "Better Way" might we then be able to step upon the "Shining Path" to return 'home'. The first step on the true path 'home' – after living the "Better Way", however – is transiting through the process of earthly death.

*   *   *   *   *

The wide reluctance to accept death *as a completely natural process*, coupled with most people's fear of it driving an associated desire to *stay on the earth forever*, has given rise to the offering of substantial rewards from wealthy individuals for a formula to stop, or considerably slow down, the ageing process. This line of thinking, moreover, has resulted in the *insanity* of not only freezing corpses for exorbitant fees, but also just *heads* for a lesser fee, to ostensibly await a 're-awakening' and cure from the expectations of future, 'advanced medical knowledge'.

However, as we have firmly stated in previous Chapters, it is the *spirit* that is the 'animating power' within the physical shell. Once that severs itself from the material body The Natural Laws decree that the shell will decompose. Therefore, regardless of how far medical science may develop, it will never be able to put into effect this particular *miracle*. All that has been achieved here is the provision of a very expensive refrigerated grave and the inevitable decomposition of the corpse once thawing occurs, with absolutely no chance of a re-awakening.

And, latterly, we have had Frankenstein-like scenarios that call for 'head transplants', the cloning of humans and the growing of foetuses for replacement body parts. There was also, until quite recently, the belief that there would be an inexhaustible source of animal body parts – mainly from pigs – for xeno-transplantation into humans. And all this from people who are, supposedly, 'highly educated and enlightened'. However, medical science has since recognised that such operations could trigger a global pandemic of a deadly new disease. Experiments by the Natural Environment Research Council of Britain have revealed that pig hearts and kidneys carried potentially deadly animal retroviruses, "...dashing hopes that animals could one day supply spare parts for human surgery." Researchers have noted that cancer viruses will jump species, "...in the real world, not just in artificial laboratory settings." Virologist Robin Weiss, who first demonstrated that pig viruses could infect human cells, said:

"Xeno-transplants do not *seem* to pose a big risk. But then BSE and HIV were not *thought* to pose big risks when they were first discovered."

Yet, in the 21st Century, certain New Zealand scientists and researchers are pushing for just this kind of supposedly enlightened medical advancement.

This particular recognition should not come as a surprise to the truly spiritually aware, for any kind of cross-species tampering is a *serious transgression* against The Spiritual Laws of Creation, with equally grave *reciprocal returns*. A human being who had received an animal organ would show, upon that person's physical death, *the grotesque nature of such a transgression in their ethereal form* – the real body beneath the material shell – for the physical body is able to temporarily hide the non-physical aberration whilst, *and only whilst*, it is alive on earth.

In the case of another piece of 'inspired insanity' – head transplants – there appears to be 'approval by association' from at least one Christian church so far. Dr Robert White, Professor of Neurosurgery at the Case University in Cleveland, Ohio, has proposed the idea of 'head transplants' – where a person who has a complete and healthy body but is brain-dead, could be 'married' to one who is quadriplegic or similar, but who possesses a 'good head'. This 'marriage' would ostensibly produce one good and whole "productive unit". The question is: Who would that person actually be? And which one of the two 'part-units' inhabits and animates the "completed new body"? For only one can, and that means the other one must die to facilitate the union – if the operation is successful in the first place. Both "spirits" cannot *co-exist* as 'dual animators' in the "new unit".

The problem with all medical researchers who subscribe to this kind of 'medical advancement regime' is that they seem not to even *begin* to understand that The Laws of Life decree that we are more than just a material body. We only have life during the time that the inner animating core – the spirit with its outer soul-coverings – is *present* in its ordained, individual 'physical form'. And earthly death is simply the *separating out* of the physical "overcoat" from the "soul-body" and "spirit-core".

Dr White, who claims to have already successfully transplanted the head of a monkey onto another more than twenty years ago, states himself to be a committed Catholic, is a frequent visitor to the Vatican, is a member of the Pontifical Academy of Sciences, and helped to set up the John Paul II committee on medical ethics. Why, I wonder, do we not hear of these kinds of medical 'experts' proposing to set up committees on 'spiritual reality'? In fact, it is precisely *because* they lack any true knowledge of the connections between the material body and the inner animating *spiritual* core, that they do not. For they, too, must also possess the exact same 'configuration', otherwise they could not *live* to wax 'expert' on such matters. This "life connection" is the very knowledge that should be taught as the key foundation for *all* healing in *all* Medical and Nursing Schools.

Yet there is another insidious and evil practice that has arisen through this non-acceptance, or lack of knowledge, about death and life-after. And that is the reported growing trade in body organs. Given the oftentimes dark nature of man, there is probably no doubt that some unfortunate people are murdered for selected parts. Anecdotal evidence from investigative television journalists probing into such allegations strongly suggest that in parts of India, which is one source, children have already been sold for this trade. And, quite recently, Chinese prison guards have been convicted and jailed for selling body parts of prisoners.

Unfortunately for all involved in this dark, spiritually-repulsive 'replacement body-parts business', it is not only the murderer who will reap the consequences of the deed in this case, but also the paymaster and/or recipient, the surgeons who perform the operations, and finally *all* those who harbour similar thoughts of organ acquisition. All share spiritual responsibility for such a crime under the outworking of The Spiritual Laws, even if they believe otherwise. In any case, all participants soon discover the huge error of their wrong belief when they, in turn, die. It is then that they must fully experience the consequences of their chosen belief and deed.

The final say on the practice of organ transplants may be delivered by "Mother Nature" herself in her incomparable and *inviolable* outworking. The medical profession is presently struggling with the problem of the increasing inefficacy of the current crop of antibiotics used to treat infections. Sarah Boseley, in the Guardian Weekly of 20.08.10, writes:

> 'The era of antibiotics is coming to a close. In just a couple of generations, what once appeared to be miracle medicines have been beaten into ineffectiveness by the bacteria they were designed to knock out. *The post-antibiotic apocalypse is within sight.* Hyperbole? Unfortunately not.'

Evidently a gene called NDM 1 passes easily between types of bacteria called enterobacteriaceae [such as E coli and Klebsiella] and makes them resistant to almost all of the powerful, last-line group of antibiotics called carbapenems – "...the most powerful group of antibiotics we [once] had..." said Professor Tim Walsh who discovered the gene.

> "In many ways, this is it. This is potentially the end. There are no antibiotics in the pipeline that have activity against NDM 1-producing enterobacteriaceae."

'For a long time now, doctors have known they were in a race to stay a few steps ahead of the rapidly growing resistance of bacterial infections to antibiotics. Dr David Livermore, director of the antibiotic resistance monitoring and reference laboratory of the UK Health Protection Agency, in talking about transplant surgery where patient's immune systems have to be suppressed to stop them rejecting a new organ, leaving them prey to infections, and the use of immuno-suppressant drugs', noted:

> "A lot of modern medicine *would become impossible* if we lost our ability to treat infections. ... The emergence of antibiotic resistance is the most eloquent example of Darwin's principle of evolution that there ever was. ... It is a war of attrition. *It is naive to think that we can win.*"

(Guardian Weekly. All emphases mine.)

However, radical 21st century science may now have the answer to organ transplantation in humans, at least for one internal organ at this time. Basically, in a process called 'printing', a newly developed laboratory technology using human kidney cells 'layers' more cells on top of each other to *form* the kidney. Complete and fully functional kidneys have already been transplanted into waiting patients in the United States.

Notwithstanding the huge, *seemingly beneficial,* ramifications for present-day humanity right across the globe: in the final analysis, despite the fact that medical-science drives these kinds of breakthroughs, an underlying fear lurks in the deepest recesses of *most* humans. **It is the fear of death!** In a world where virtually *everyone* – even the scientists – seem to *desperately* push away even the *idea* of dying, we all really need to accept that *earthly death is a completely natural part of true life.* In any case, we are all *forced* to accept it when our time of *transition* arrives.

Knowledge empowers whilst ignorance clouds!

So, let us keenly examine this "death thing" then. The problem with attempting to understand the death process, therefore, is that, for the most part, it is an unseen and unknown happening. What exactly *does* happen when we observe the last exhalation of breath from a body? At that particular point, what was a living, breathing, talking entity has suddenly become a still and silent, rapidly-cooling shell. What has happened to the 'life-force', the energy, the power that a few short moments ago gave this now lifeless shell the ability to live, laugh and love during its tenure on the earth? Can such a thing as its "life" simply dissipate into nothingness?

It would seem to be inconceivable to believe that an 'energy source' which can enable human beings on the one hand to produce great architectural works, wonderful symphonies and technological marvels, and on the other to stand incredible tests of privation and extreme cruelty of so many perverse kinds over long periods of time – and still survive – can simply dissolve into nothingness at earthly death. Yet that is the belief of many.

The other possibility is that this "animating power" does not disappear into oblivion but is actually a different kind of living form from that of the physical body. And there are those who believe that. For those who subscribe to such a view, the general acceptance is that the physical body is really the outer shell from which the person who previously occupied it has now vacated. There is a large third group who do not know what to believe about this apparently uncertain process. For the purposes of this introductory phase to this Chapter, let us initially assume that we do not have any answers.

Whether there actually is such an inner animating force is a question that needs to be revisited before we can continue on. Even many in the Medical profession who work intimately with the living entity are uncertain about the true nature of it all. Moreover, these are the people who utilise their considerable talents to slice, cut, remove and sew. The beating heart in the chest and the electrical computer of the brain could well induce one to arrive at the belief that we are, after all, just a physical body animated by a very efficient pump for blood flow, and a programmed computer to control all other functions and life's decisions. If this is so, then the demise of this body at what we term death is simply a process of the pump stopping. This, in turn, causes a cessation of electrical activity in the computer of the brain with a subsequent stilling of all bodily functions – or vice versa.

> This belief necessarily *rejects* the notion of a *separate* animating entity which
> *leaves the physical body* at this time.

A black hole of nothingness is the only logical end here.

The obvious fact about these differing ideas is that we have only two choices for arriving at a correct conclusion, and we have an equal **50%** chance of getting it right – or wrong – in terms of **the choice**.

Either there *is* an inner animating force, or there is not!

There cannot be two positions here. However, that even-chance choice must necessarily translate to a **100% outcome**. To be wrong is to be *completely wrong* – with either choice – and not just **50%** in error.

For those who ostensibly claim no interest or concern, such an outcome might be considered to be a personal non-event. However the *actual* reality of the outcome at death will quickly shake the foundations of that particular belief too. For those who seek answers, it surely behoves one to choose correctly, for initial peace of mind at least. Malcolm Muggeridge, the famous British social commentator, was once asked if he believed in "life after death". He thought that the more intelligent thing to do was to "hedge one's bets", even if one found it difficult to conceive of such a possibility; in his words – "...just in case"!

The question of personal responsibility for how one has lived one's life is a further factor which may have a bearing on one's attitude toward possible concern about death. If the 'notion' of "life after death" is dismissed out of hand, we might perhaps assume that proponents of such thinking, even if conceding the *possibility*, might not necessarily equate such a conclusion with a concept of ultimate personal responsibility, if a 'less than noble lifestyle' has been lived.

But what of believers who unequivocally accept that the physical body *is* the material home of the animating life-force – that of the soul and spirit? The question that needs to be addressed here is whether or not there is complete *dissipation* of this "power source" at earthly death, or *retention of it* in some form. In this particular situation, too, we can once more reduce the outcome to only one of the two possibilities. Again, *it can only be one or the other.* One more **50% choice**, and one more **100% outcome.**

For any firm conviction of absolute dissipation or dissolution of any such 'innate energy-source' is, quite logically, *completely incompatible* with a concept of 'personal responsibility' for how one has lived one's life. Quite logically, also, full acceptance of 'personal responsibility' can only *naturally* apply where there **is** the retention and continuation of a "life-force" in the form of a *complete and conscious being*, otherwise there is no point or purpose to it.

> **For ultimate 'personal' responsibility logically requires some 'form' to *act on and through* – for itself and its outward expression.**

From our particular viewpoint, little more can be said for a belief in a deep black hole of 'nothingness'. Within the context of this Work, therefore, let us examine the other possibility open to us.

Here we have a concept of the acceptance of the physical body containing an "animating life-energy source" which, upon earthly death, retains its form and accepts personal responsibility for its 'life lived'. Religious leanings of many persuasions teach this very concept, but at this point the issue becomes somewhat clouded with many varying ideas as to the final outcome. And whilst some are decidedly similar in content, nevertheless, any difference in belief as to the *actual end result* logically represents *a point of conflict* regarding the true and clearly unequivocal nature of the happening. Quite simply, there cannot possibly be any differences since the *actual death process itself*, apart from the naturally differing events leading up to it, **must be exactly the same.** And, moreover, totally in accordance with The Spiritual Laws. And that is our absolute premise and contention!

> **Irrespective of one's race, colour, religion, belief, geographical location or any other factor, *the process is the same for all.***

Indeed, the idea that there may be differences because of the aspects mentioned is completely untenable. Unfortunately, not being able to physically see every individual step has produced an impossible maze of opinions and theories to cloud and confuse the issue. If, however, the premise that the "death process" is subject to absolute Law without deviation is correct, all that is required is for us to *recognise* the outworking of those Laws and apply them to this contentious subject for our edification.

At present there are many books on the subject of 'near-death' or 'out of the body' experiences, and a number of researchers have compiled reports from the experiences of the dying. Dr Raymond Moody is perhaps the best known. Dr Moody's research noted that at times of severe illness or injury resulting in such a 'close encounter with death', all subjects recorded very similar experiences, with the *consistency* of the experiences being the most notable feature. The many differences in race and nationality, social and economic status and religion that often divide societies, produced no differences in the experiences. Even suffering different diseases or illnesses, and receiving different medical treatment, the basic event was remarkably similar. Yet, should this be a surprise? If it is a lawful process without deviation as we contend, we should expect to discover *exactly* this fact.

Therefore, if there *can* be such a thing as an out-of-body experience, then there must necessarily be another body perfectly capable of existing consciously outside of the physical one. This fact and process we have already outlined in the Chapter explaining our 'Spiritual Origins'.

There, we identified our inner life-force as having its origin, and therefore home, in The Spiritual Realm far above the material plane of the earth. That "energy source", which is the animating force for our physical body, we know as the Spirit, the true, *and very real*, you and me.

Plato, who accepted the belief that the soul leaves the physical body at earthly death, interpreted its particular realm as the "world of ideas". He also noted the fact that most people have a superficial attitude toward these ideas, being content with a life "among shadows". And as a consequence of this "...paid no heed to the immortality of their own soul". The purpose of our sojourn on the earth is to develop to personal self-consciousness and, in doing so, seek to understand the reasons for our existence. In short, to find The Truth. For only that can give us complete understanding of life's purpose. Should we be fortunate enough to *unequivocally recognise* that Truth and choose to live accordingly, we have the greater *opportunity* to more easily leave behind the physical constraints of the material world and return *home*.

Plato perhaps also intuitively understood the idea of a proffered "attribute of grace" in the connection of the soul to its origin. In his philosophical comment he states:

> "...when perfect and fully winged she (the soul) soars upward."

> (Philosophy History and Problems, p.63)

Thus the soul yearns to fly home to the 'world of ideas'. It longs to be freed from the chains of the body. Yet even *after* Plato's time and enlightened teachings, Epicurus, (341-270 BC) a Greek philosopher who accepted the teachings of Democritus and his "dispersal theory" of "soul atoms", believed:

> "...that death should not concern us because as long as we exist death is not here. And when it does come, we no longer exist."

Unfortunately for subscribers to that particular belief, the *very incorrect views* of Epicurus become a stark reality at death. It is important to therefore define and understand the nature of *spirit* which we possess as our actual inner being, and by which we are drawn upward to our Origins in the Spiritual Realm after the completion of our 'schooling' in the material world. Provided, of course, we have not placed a barrier between the two, thus *preventing* our return home. In any case, the many designations that people ascribe to this word, *spirit*, should be clarified so as to more clearly understand its meaning.

People who are highly educated, witty, intelligent and widely-read, and able to converse well about all they have learned are often regarded as being 'rich in spirit'. Or perhaps they may be gifted with a talent for producing original ideas. But the designation 'rich in spirit' is not strictly correct in either case. Neither can we call a person who is steeped in knowledge about their particular traditions and culture 'rich in spirit'. Unless there is a conscious and knowledgeable connection to the Higher Spheres, such knowledge is really only concerned with culture or tradition. Therefore *spirit* is something completely different.

As previously explained, the true Spiritual Worlds lie far higher than the earth plane, and form the upper and lightest part of Creation. Therefore *spirit* is more an *'independent consistency' composed of that substance which comprises the Spiritual Nature of those Higher Spheres.* Spirit can perhaps be best described as having, or expressing the quality of, 'deep inner feeling'. But this is not the same as being 'highly intellectual'.

Neither does spirit refer solely to the emotions, for these are given to enable us to feel the depth of an experience, irrespective of whether it be joyful or painful. So being emotional is not the same as having 'deep inner feelings' of a *spiritual* kind. It is the spirit, moreover, that is the producer of the language, and is therefore able to express itself in writings and in activities of sublime beauty such as in art and music. The *spirit*, which possesses the inherent ability to 'intuitively know' the emotions of love, hate, joy and sorrow, also naturally possesses inherent longing for its original *spiritual home*, as Plato correctly perceived.[2]

Now, as also previously explained in the Chapter on our Spiritual Origins, the journey of a human spirit from the plane of The Spiritual to the Material necessitates the need to traverse all the intervening realms. Each one is a different consistency, lightest toward the Higher Planes and heaviest towards the lower, exactly according to The Law of Spiritual Gravity. As we journey downwards we are required to take on, or wear, a cloak or body of the *consistency and material of the particular plane being traversed*, with each plane becoming more dense the nearer we come to the gross material earth. Thus, by the time we reach the earth we will have enveloped our spirit, our inner core, the actual you and me, in a number of coverings, with each one exactly corresponding to the consistency and the material of the particular plane descended through.

We might well wonder where all these *coverings* are? Since each, in turn, envelops the previous coverings on the journey downwards, they are logically all inside us. By virtue of their *different consistency*, however, they are *prevented* from *blending* with each other. We may view this as a kind of *uniting*, similar to the way a collapsible telescope is held together. The huge difference between that basic material example and the human process is the mechanism or force that holds us together as a complete and self-conscious entity. That power is "radiation" – that which holds together everything in Creation, from the greatest thing to the smallest.

*   *   *   *   *

The science of physics has long recognised that everything radiates and that the 'apparent' solidity of all material substance is due to nothing other than just this radiation. It is a specific radiation that, in a sense, 'magnetically-connects' the elementary particles. It is interesting to note that this radiation, which emanates from virtually everything, can be captured by Kirlian photography – either still-life or on video. The truly amazing aspect of the process, however, concerns the constant movement of the various colours being radiated. These appear to correspond to the different properties of the subject being photographed, particularly the relative strengths of the various parts of the energy field. Whilst there is a school of opinion that deems this energy-field to be the actual *aura* of things, science states it to be electro-magnetic radiation – but radiation, nevertheless.[3]

*   *   *   *   *

The obvious first part of us as the complete entity is that which allows us to interact with our physical environment i.e., the physical body. With it we are able to utilise the senses of sight, hearing and touch etc., to enable us to fulfil particular desires and carry out earthly tasks. In itemising the three key components, and working from the material body inwards, we find that the outer mortal cloak – that which can be seen in the mirror – has a closely connected "astral" body whose consistency is roughly similar to the physical one as it is still composed of *material matter*, but is not as dense. These two 'cloaks', in turn, envelop other body-coverings that correspond to their respective spheres beyond the earth. In the Ethereal World; that which we loosely call *the beyond*, the ethereal body covers the soul. And inside all these coverings resides our "spirit" – the real you and me!

To reiterate once more; the "spirit" and its immediate coverings enveloped by the ethereal body, but *excluding* the physical and the "astral," can basically be *collectively designated* as the "soul body".

---

[2]The cause of the seething restlessness, frustration, discontent and anger that seemingly pervades the peoples of the world today like a terminal disease, may possibly lie *in the anguish of a collective humanity that has lost its true place in Creation and is unable to find its way home.*

[3]Perhaps the word *aura* is too unscientific, too new-age! Nevertheless, that is what it seems to be.

Thus, within the material substance of our physical body resides our spirit, the actual animating power – the life-force – for the now multi-layered body. The spirit 'moves' the body by *impressing its volition* through all the respective coverings and thus onto its outer physical 'form' via the brain, thereby activating it. It is important that we clearly identify and understand the three main parts of the total entity, for we will need to remember them in order to follow the complete process of earthly death.

However, in order to *connect* the individual coverings so that the volition of the spirit *can act* on the complete entity, we require a 'connecting' or 'linking' mechanism whereby this can be achieved. That necessary connection and animating link from the *spirit*, to the *soul*, to the *astral* and finally to the *physical* body, is provided by the "Silver Cord", mentioned in various spiritual works and The Bible.

> In reinforcement, it is the "Silver Cord" which is the *connecting-link* that enables the *animating power of the spirit* to impress its *volition* on the 'coverings' that envelop it, thereby producing, through the earthly body, its earthly works.

The 'connections' also provide the very life and warmth for the physical body, without which it could not live. These last points provide the *major* keys to a full understanding of the complete death process!

In a broad sense we can liken the "Silver Cord" to the umbilical cord that connects the growing foetus to the womb of the mother. As a very *basic* analogy that cord, too, provides life and warmth to the 'developing form', as well as nutrients to nurture it. However, what the umbilical does not do after a specific point in pregnancy, is provide the *spiritual* life-force. The entry of an individual spirit into the foetus at the appropriate time assumes that role. With this development the mother is able to sense the presence of this *new inhabitant* within her.

Because the concept and knowledge of the "Silver Cord" is crucial to understanding the "death process", some views about it from two of the main schools of religious thought offer interesting comparisons. Cruden's Complete Concordance to the Old and New Testament and the Apocrypha is still highly regarded in the Christian world as an accurate and reputable publication even though the first edition appeared in 1737. The explanation of the "Silver Cord" in Cruden's work may perhaps still represent the fundamentalist Christian understanding of it today.

> "By this, commentators generally understand the pith, or marrow of the back-bone, which comes from the brain, and thence goeth down to the very lowest end of the back-bone, together with the nerves and sinews which, as anatomists observe, are nothing else but the production and continuation of the marrow. And this is aptly compared to a cord, both for its figure, which is very long and round, and for its use, which is to draw and move the parts of the body; and it is compared to silver, both for its excellency and colour, which is white and bright, even in a dead, and much more in a living body."

> (Crudens, p.445)

The above interpretation is obviously only a physical one concerned solely with the materiality of the body, for the wording of the text clearly refutes the idea of the Silver Cord being a connection between the physical body and the spirit. Compilers of more recent Concordances do not offer an interpretation of this 'cord' aspect, as does 'Cruden's'. The actual connection, of course, must *first* be recognised and understood correctly in order to be able to explain it.

Eastern philosophical beliefs, on the other hand, have long held that the "Silver Cord" *is* the link connecting the soul to the body as a kind of "ethereal umbilical cord". The "Silver Cord" is also believed to link the various energy centres or 'chakras' that are situated along the axis of the spine. While not physically visible, the 'chakras' correspond to various nerve centres and organs of the body. It is the conduit or channel through which energy and the "life-force" pass to these centres during the course of life on earth. After death the cord is severed, thus allowing the soul to be completely released from the material body which then decomposes.

Having established the main points of reference for our elucidation of this fascinating event, let us begin our actual journey into death by first examining the similarly reported phases of out-of-body experiences, as recorded and distilled by Dr Raymond Moody in his second book on this subject, "Reflections On Life After Life" (Bantam p.5-6)

> "A man is dying and, as he reaches the point of greatest physical distress, he hears himself pronounced dead by his doctor. He begins to hear an uncomfortable noise, a loud ringing or buzzing, and at the same time feels himself moving very rapidly through a long tunnel. After this, he suddenly finds himself outside of his own physical body, but still in the immediate physical environment, and he sees his own body from a distance, as though he is a spectator. He watches the resuscitation attempt from this unusual vantage point and is in a state of emotional upheaval.
>
> After a while, he collects himself and becomes more accustomed to his odd condition. He notices that he still has a "body", but one of a very different nature and with very different powers from the physical body he has left behind. Soon other things begin to happen. Others come to meet and to help him. He glimpses the spirits of relatives and friends who have already died, and a loving, warm spirit of a kind he has never encountered before – a being of light – appears before him. This being asks him a question, non verbally, to make him evaluate his life and helps him along by showing him a panoramic, instantaneous playback of the major events of his life. At some point he finds himself approaching some sort of barrier or border, apparently representing the limit between earthly life and the next life. Yet, he finds that he must go back to the earth, that the time for his death has not yet come. At this point he resists, for by now he is taken up with his experiences in the afterlife and does not want to return. He is overwhelmed by intense feelings of joy, love, and peace. Despite his attitude, though, he somehow reunites with his physical body and lives.
>
> Later he tries to tell others, but he has trouble doing so. In the first place, he can find no human words adequate to describe these unearthly episodes. He also finds that others scoff, so he stops telling other people. Still, the experience affects his life profoundly, especially his views about death and its relationship to life."

Contained within the above report are some of the points thus far outlined. Note that the being of light communicated 'non verbally'. We can assume from this that *one's earthly language is of no importance any longer*, and communication is perhaps more via the spiritual intuition – a kind of other-world telepathy. The obvious separation of the physical body from the non-physical is an especially clear point. And in accordance with the knowledge we now have, we are able to recognise the reference to "moving rapidly through a long tunnel" as relating to the drawing out of the non-physical body from the physical. This 'long tunnel', in terms of its perceived length, does not refer to the length of the physical body as the soul-body exits the physical shell. It refers to an altered aspect of time, which has a vastly different reference value in that *non-earthly* sphere.

More importantly from the above report, however, was the requirement to evaluate the key phases of one's life. This evaluation is seemingly under the direction of a powerful spiritual being. Here can be observed the necessity for accepting the fact of "personal spiritual responsibility" for all ones thoughts, words and deeds, exactly as **The Spiritual Laws demand**, and which we continually reiterate in this book. In this regard, again consider the warnings of Jesus:

> "...that until the heavens and the earth shall pass away, a single dot or hairstroke shall not disappear from the law, until all has been completed."

(Matthew 5:18)

And consider what we might regard as a further "spiritual" qualification of the above:

"I tell you indeed, that you will not depart until **YOU** have *repaid the very last farthing.*"

(Matthew 5:26, Fenton, Emphases mine.)

To be faced with the need to confront one's past life in the very early stages after one's earthly death may well presuppose the unsettling probability that the next stages of the process call for atonement and expiation in some way. And that is the inescapable reality, exactly as the above Biblical quotes clearly state. For the description from Dr. Moody's work **does not explain the process of 'actually dying'**. It merely describes only the very first steps in just being 'out of the body'. In short, the person concerned has not died.[4]

Many researchers in this field have concluded that the feelings of love and well-being that are experienced at this time represent the *totality* of the after-death situation, but that is not the complete picture. Through *insufficient knowledge*, they are not able to take into account the absolute and full outworking of this process – a process which can be only be understood with the knowledge of **The Spiritual Laws of Creation**.

Now, having determined that we must accept "personal spiritual responsibility" for our deeds, we need to draw the veil aside a little more in order to reveal the next step *into* earthly death. The actual happening is quite simple. Because the connection between the physical and the non-physical parts of man are held together by a *radiation process*, all that is required to effect a complete separation is for one or the other to become so debilitated as to not have sufficient 'radiating strength' to keep itself 'locked' to the other. We see this in severe illnesses, or during a long fast where the body can be considerably weakened.

On the other hand, the 'soul body' can also lose its 'radiation-connection' to its 'physical counterpart' such as in the case of giving up the will to live. So even where there may be no obvious physical reason for separation to occur, nevertheless, according to Spiritual Law, this must eventually take place if there is no re-strengthening of the necessary 'connecting radiation' in such cases. Thus, as the radiation between the soul body and the physical body becomes progressively weaker, the point of separation is finally reached.

A good example of that process can be noted in the old practice of *makutu*. The belief that one had been marked for death could, and did, bring about this weakening of the 'radiating strength' of the 'soul body'. And with such a deeply-entrenched belief and no sure knowledge of the process, it is no wonder that *makutu* was such a powerful tool of fear. Without the correct understanding, Maori were powerless to combat it and, according to diarists of the time, many simply 'wasted away'.

---

[4]Some years ago I experienced the very first part of the death process, i.e., I began to exit my physical body. A very sudden onset of acute and excruciating pain – from no *apparent* cause – began to rack my entire body internally and externally, forcing me to bed. The pain was so intense that I intuitively perceived I was actually dying. And because it was so sudden and not signalled in any way whatsoever, I also intuitively felt that even though experiencing great pain, the "unfolding event" was nonetheless occurring so that I might know the reality of what I had long accepted; that *earthly* death could not possibly be the end of one's "actual life". Immediately thereafter I began to leave my body – through my head. In short, I watched my feet recede as I exited through the bed headboard and the wall behind it. At this point, I was pain-free. Whilst it was a singularly strange sensation, it was at the same time extremely fascinating for me. That is because the *primary purpose* of my life was/is to write certain books, one of which you are now reading. Because this work was still in manuscript form and proving difficult to publish at the time, I strongly petitioned – as I was exiting my physical shell – to: "Let me stay 'til I complete the work." Thereupon, the exiting-process halted, and I went back into my body. And back into the pain. However, something extraordinary then occurred. What I can only describe as a specifically-configured, gold-coloured, rotating "healing-force" materialised very clearly near the ceiling in a corner of the room closest to the bed. I intuitively knew that I would be healed. And so it was. [I experienced this same effect sometime later in a hospital where, after minor surgery, the wound site had become infected. Fortunately, however, the few hours during the night that this "healing-force" was present was sufficient to reduce the infection which, over the next 24 hours, subsequently 'disappeared'.] With the help of a friend and colleague shortly thereafter, I was finally able to publish.

To clarify the process once more, where a body has been forcibly destroyed, ruined by disease, or weakened by old age, and can no longer offer sufficient strength of radiation so as to maintain a strong attraction between soul and body, the soul must sever itself from its earthly body or covering. And that, quite simply, *is earthly death*. In terms of natural Law, which at the same time is Spiritual Law, it is simply the lawful process of two "species of matter" which were once united on the earth through a "mutually-attracting radiation", but which must separate out again when one of the two *different species* can no longer fulfil its "attracting" role.

The soul, at the moment of severance, draws the astral body with it away from the physical body.[5] The soul does so because, unlike the physical body *at this particular moment*, it is now the "active partner" so to speak. This phase can be likened to that of an exiting and departure from the physical shell where the soul draws the *astral body* with it out of the *physical body*. Since there was never a *fusion* as such, but only a *sliding into one another* – as with the example of a collapsible telescope – the soul simply pulls the *astral* from the *physical* as it strives to free *itself* from its former "material partner".

In doing so, the soul does not draw this astral body very far, because the *astral body* is still connected not only with the *soul body* but also with the *physical body*. Moreover, the soul, which *initiates* the actual movement, needs to detach itself from the astral body also, and strives to get away from it as well. The astral body always remains near the physical body after the earthly departure of the soul. The further the soul moves away, the weaker the astral body becomes. The continuing detaching process of the soul eventually brings in its train the decay and disintegration of the astral body, which, in turn, immediately brings about the decay of the physical body too. This is the *normal process* under the lawful outworking of The Spiritual Laws.

Whilst this explanation should be relatively easy to follow, particularly when viewed pictorially, as a further aid we can perhaps also consider the visible *birth process* to offer *some* understanding. At this time a *separation* also occurs *between* mother and baby, where the *new-born* similarly seeks to initially strive *out of*, and *away from*, the *mother's* body. Here, it must rid itself of *the placenta* as well.

Though only a very crude analogy, the reader may find greater clarity to understanding the death process with this example, even though a kind of reverse view. However, the reader should not regard one process as perhaps being an exact mirror image of the other, though there are certain aspects that can possibly provide some enlightenment.

In the description of the death process, an immediate recognition of the outworking of The Law of Spiritual Gravity – whereby the lighter, more mobile part, the soul body, floats away from the heavier material body – should be clearly evident. *It is important that this particular point be carefully noted.* For whilst we have now described the death process, that is only with respect to a 'normal happening'; which is that for a soul who is quickly able to sever its connection or tie to its material body. Obviously, the soul is still subject to The Spiritual Laws and must now follow its particular, chosen path into its new environment, its new world. But it can only embark upon its next journey when the "Silver Cord", that which once served as the necessary link between the "power source" of the spirit and the material counterpart of the body, is completely severed. In the same way, a baby cannot be completely free of its physical tie to its mother's body until its similar *life-support cord* [the umbilical] is also cut.

We now enter the little understood, and perhaps less believed area of "personal spiritual responsibility". As the death process is subject to strict and firmly established Spiritual Laws, including that of the Law of Justice, what criteria governs the situation where a soul is not able to easily sever itself? And what does this mean for that soul body – that individual?

---

[5] In previous explanations we learned that the astral body is like the 'prototype' of the physical.

Whether or not a soul detaches itself quickly from the physical body will 'absolutely depend' on *how it has lived its life on earth*!

That is the short, blunt truth of the matter!

The spiritual nature of the individual human being is the *decisive factor* governing the *outcome* after death. We should understand that it is not the teachings of any particular religion or belief that is decisive here, it is *how we are in our being – individually*. **The Law of Spiritual Gravity** is a key aspect in our explanations now, for this Law operates in every sphere of Creation, and not just in an obvious way on earth where its effects can be readily observed.

In a previous Chapter we explained this Law and its effects, and stated that everything we do, every thought we think and every action we take corresponds to a precise spiritual weight. Thoughts and actions of good are *spiritually lighter* than those that are not. Throughout our lives, therefore, we are naturally subject to all the different experiences that our *personal choices* will generate. The changing circumstances of them, but perhaps more particularly how we cope with them from an attitudinal standpoint – sometimes well, sometimes not – will all contribute to the final 'spiritual weight' of our soul-body at earthly death.

A life of superficiality without concern for spiritual matters, or of seeking only the acquisition of material things to the exclusion of any elevating influence – even without necessarily evil intent – will ensure that the "Silver Cord" becomes *darker and thicker*, precisely corresponding to the *degree* of superficiality or materialism lived. It thus naturally follows that a life of violence, crime and debasement, *regardless of the circumstances that might have brought it about*, will actually produce a, *spiritually*, far 'heavier' individual.

This perceived effect has entered our language where we describe such persons as being or feeling 'heavy'. Unfortunately, in such cases, this 'heaviness' with its associated and perhaps desired intimidatory effect, whilst generating a tough, 'untouchable status', will likely set in place *a very painful* death experience, *if* no genuine change of spiritual direction is embarked upon before that time.

The effect of this 'heaviness' on the "Silver Cord" is to darken and thicken it *considerably*, with serious consequences for that soul at earthly death. Choosing an opposite lifestyle, however, especially one where *spiritual considerations* are a regular and normal part of one's life, will ensure that the 'Cord' remains lighter. Now, when the time comes for severance to occur, the 'spiritually-darker and heavier person' with the correspondingly 'thicker Cord' will discover that this cannot be effected so easily. And it may be very many days, or even longer, before the 'Cord' eventually begins to wither and disintegrate, thus finally setting the hapless soul free of its shell. This process clearly reveals the outworking of The Perfect Justice of The Laws in the exercising of our free will for good or evil.

It is important to reiterate that *only our decisions are free, the consequences are not*. These must be fully lived out under The Law of Sowing and Reaping. Moreover, the consequences for a soul who has lived a life without thought or care for any of the higher spiritual aspirations will mean an unnecessarily longer time *tied* to his physical body than need have been. And therefore, through the still strong attachment via his thicker and heavier 'Cord', will feel all that the physical body undergoes in that time, *including any autopsies*. And in longer-tied periods, *even part of the decomposition process itself* in some cases. The actual moment of his release will have been precisely determined by The Spiritual Laws, in exact accordance with *his* "personal attitude and chosen lifestyle" during his life on earth.

The same *process*, however, offers a vastly *different experience* for a person who has lived a more noble life. His severance will be effected much faster and he will be quickly free of the shell. That is one reason **why** all the great spiritual teachers over the ages have constantly admonished mankind to always strive for the good. These warnings were not the incoherent ramblings of foolish old men, or the strident fire and brimstone preaching of doomsday prophets; to be ridiculed, mocked and ignored. Such serious warnings are simply nothing more than the stating of **The Truth of The Eternal Laws**.[6]

With this new knowledge of the death process, and aside from the practice of autopsies, at what point can a person be safely pronounced dead? Some years ago, Dr Lyall Watson wrote a book called "The Romeo Error". The subject matter was precisely about the difficulty in determining the exact moment of death. He recounted many instances where persons had been certified dead, even to the point where the early stages of decomposition had set in, and yet still returned to life. More harrowing were the experiences of the relatives of deceased where death certificates had been issued for the one apparently very dead, where funeral preparations and burial service were undertaken, and where the casket was duly consigned to the earth and the grave filled in. These particular cases recorded relatives requesting the exhumation of the deceased because of strong feelings and even dreams that indicated their loved ones were not actually dead at the time of burial.

Because of the need to convince the appropriate authorities of the urgency of the matter, with official scepticism being an unfortunate time-barrier in such cases, subsequent exhumations did reveal persons 'buried alive'. Their short time awake was evident by the efforts they undertook to free themselves from their tomb. The most notable factors being the dishevelled arrangement of the clothing, fingernails ripped from gouging the casket lid and, probably the most harrowing for the friends and relatives, the look of frozen horror on the faces of the 'now deceased'. Dr. Watson also outlines the curious state of "Catatonia" in many of these cases where (in his opinion) the body appears to be completely dead with no detectable or discernible life within it, yet is still alive.

Even today, with all the supposedly huge advances in diagnostic medical science, on rare occasions [as happened in one of our hospitals quite recently] medical authorities report bodies held in 'storage' awaiting autopsy have bled *red blood* when cut into – much to the very great surprise and *consternation* of medical staff. Explanation? ***There is only one.*** Such bodies, persons – cadavers – are not *actually* dead. They are still *there*, still *connected* to their physical shells.

Though it clearly does not accept or even believe, the medical profession should nonetheless take urgent steps to learn about the crucial *purpose* of the "Silver Cord" – and thereby gain *real knowledge*.

*   *   *   *   *

The frightening situation of how one could possibly be accidentally buried alive surely begs the question how, and why? From the standpoint of The Spiritual Laws, and irrespective of what we believe, or may *wish* to believe, whatever takes place on earth is not solely the result of pure chance. It may be comforting to continually insist that such is the case, particularly when we might be personally affected detrimentally. But every event, every incident, even the most minute, will have been brought about by a *decision* made by human beings *somewhere, sometime*.

Indeed, it cannot possibly be otherwise for it is *we* who *cause* things to happen through our inherent 'spiritual ability' to be able to make decisions in the first place. But, as we need to continually emphasise, only our *decisions* are free, the *consequences* await to eventually be faced. So, if we are ever to make any sense of the *why* of the problems that beset us, a huge

---

[6]The effect of thousands of years of man's stubborn refusal to accept the truth of it all has now brought us to the most serious point that mankind and this earth has ever reached. And we are well into the process of reaping the results of all our personal and collective choices. What will be experienced by humankind more graphically, however, is the exponential factor of *much more* in much less time.

and fundamental leap into a *different* way of thinking must be made. A way of thinking that actually and finally accepts the absolute validity and inflexibility of every single one of The Spiritual Laws of Creation, which return to us *every* consequence of *all* our decisions.

If we apply the question of 'accidental' burial or other 'inexplicable' human misfortune to ourselves, we should consider whether or not the outworking of The Law of Reciprocal Action has 'returned' the reciprocal effect of a similarly unfortunate decision that **we** might have made in the past, even if long distant, which perhaps affected *another person* very detrimentally.

*   *   *   *   *

But to return to the existence of the "Silver Cord" and its purpose: Its vital function in the life and death of humankind brings into question the medical 'wisdom' of organ transplants. In such undertakings it is vitally necessary to ensure that the organs are taken from a body very recently 'presumed' dead, or conveniently pronounced 'brain-dead', to ensure the 'freshness' of the product, especially the heart.

This means that the 'donor' will probably **still be attached to his physical body** and, depending on the *density* of the 'Cord', may well feel considerable pain at the **removal of his organs**. Viewed from the higher knowledge of Spiritual Law, organ transplants add little to the overall 'life' of a person, as earthly death is merely a transitional phase in the total existence of an individual in any case. This is aside from the horrendous financial considerations of such 'operations', of course.

So the emotional belief of 'losing loved ones forever', coupled with the general disbelief of the medical profession in these matters, has resulted in the propensity to want to extend physical life way past what sometimes appears to be a natural and desirable point at which to exit earthly life. Consequently this has changed the nature of how we relate to every other human being. Today we are all potential spare parts units. Of course, it is correct and proper to seek to extend life where possible, but not to the point where the lawful process of dying a completely natural death is actually hindered. Yet do we ever read of anyone dying of old age anymore? No! Not even with centenarians. Where death occurs in the very aged, medical protocol must always find the exact medical words to attempt to describe this completely natural process of ageing, even where it may logically be something as simple as plain organ deterioration.

From the explanations thus far, the reader should have little difficulty in understanding how one can 'return to life'. As long as the cord is still attached to the body, the *possibility* exists for a *return*. In such a case, it is merely a question of the *re-strengthening of the radiation-connection between the physical shell and the soul body* which offers the potential for reconnection. The condition of the shell or corpse does not necessarily prevent such a reunion either, though a severely ravaged one will probably not allow for a reunion of any great length of time. As already noted, Dr. Watson records that even in cases where decomposition of the body had begun, people still returned to life. In all cases, however, the possible return of the 'dead', or the inability to return, will always be subject to strict Spiritual Law without any kind of arbitrary intervention.

9.2   Jesus – "Calling the Dead to Life"

As a further explanation of the strict outworking of The Spiritual Laws in such cases, let us briefly digress to examine the fascinating question of **how** Jesus was able to "call the dead back to life".

What should be understood here is that Spiritual Law is also Natural Law. Indeed, The Spiritual Laws could not possibly be anything other than 'completely natural'. Thus the "miracles" that Jesus wrought were *so wrought* under the naturalness of the highest Spiritual Laws. He came, "...not to overthrow the laws, but to fulfil them", as He Himself firmly stated;

"Do not imagine that I have come to abolish the law and the prophets; I have *not come to abolish, but to complete them.*"

(Matthew 5:17, Fenton, Emphases mine.)

It is unfortunate that the followers of all the great Teachers have invariably distorted the clear Truth of their original Teachings. And probably more so with those of Jesus, Who came from out of The Living Law Itself. In His unequivocal reference to "fulfilling" the Laws, He firmly indicated that even He, as The Son of God, could not circumvent or overthrow the Spiritual Laws of Creation, but had also to submit to them. Thus, even the "miracles" He performed were similarly subject to the strict consistency and inviolability of The Eternal Laws. The miraculous aspect of His work, however, was in the *acceleration* of the *healing effect* of the cures He wrought simply by virtue of the fact that **He possessed the power to bring that about**.

This does not lessen the greatness of those miracles, however. Indeed, the very fact that He absolutely had to operate within The Laws shows the sure certainty and naturalness of them, whereby we human beings can also live in the supreme confidence and perfection of the same Laws. If, now, a reader may wish to use the argument that God, and therefore Jesus, could do anything without constraint from the very Laws that The Creator placed into Creation by virtue of being part of the Godhead, the very vital and critical point of the **"Perfection of God"** is called into question!

If we accept the premise that God is, and must be, Perfect, by virtue of His Nature, then His Laws of Creation must similarly also be Perfect. The possible contention that a Perfect God would produce imperfect Laws is completely untenable, though it clearly reveals our human propensity to attempt to ascribe emotive human values to "The Creator of All the Worlds!" For, without such Perfection in The Godhead and The Eternal Laws that have issued from It, the whole idea of Laws that actually are Eternal, inviolable in their "Perfection", and therefore unchangeable, becomes an absolute and illogical *impossibility.*

Therefore, the common belief that God can change His Laws at will in order to bring about a particular event, can only mean that The Law needing to be changed to effect such a thing was not perfect to begin with. Connected with that assertion is the obvious further association of an imperfect God unable to put into place Perfect Laws from the very beginning. When we gaze at the night sky in awe and veneration and marvel at its incredible vastness, the idea of such imperfection and changeability cannot logically be considered – not even as a remote possibility. For this inconceivable immensity is only a small segment of the Material part of Creation which, in turn, is itself the very smallest and lowest part of the whole of Creation.

Were this the reality that God is imperfect because He could change His Laws at will, we should ask ourselves why He did not place Jesus on earth as a fully grown man, thus negating the need for His babyhood and childhood phase? For the Laws governing earthly procreation just as naturally also reflect the inviolability of their unchangeable Perfection too. This fact offers the absolute premise that, even here, in the conception of Jesus, The Laws could "not be overthrown", as He Himself clearly stated. Earthly procreation can only occur when the natural Laws governing this process are fulfilled. And this was so, even with Jesus. By His natural procreation, therefore, every other one carries a similar potential for a pure conception. Unfortunately, however, many conceptions today occur as a result of drunkenness, drug use, and/or general social debasement, and cannot be considered even remotely pure.

Since the physical body is not the animating 'power' of the individual, the "inner animating power" that actually **was** Jesus, was also **not that** of His physical body, which was of the earth. His "inner core", which revealed Itself through the physical vessel He was obliged to take upon entering the material world in strict accordance with The Eternal Laws He came to fulfil, was of **Divine Origin**. These facts naturally call into question the believed *physical resurrection* of

Christ, but that fascinating subject does not lie within the scope of our current analyses.[7] The reader, however, should be able to deduce the Truth of the matter from what has thus far been explained.

But let us take this argument of the perfection or non-perfection of The Laws to the next obvious step and 'allow' God to make us all sinless and perfect, but of course *without* free-will and *personal spiritual responsibility.* There would then have been no need for Jesus to come to the earth at all, and He would have been spared His life of struggle against an intransigent people who, even though awaiting His Coming, nevertheless still murdered Him. Thus the words of Jesus in declaring that He had come to "...fulfil the Law", must surely mean exactly that. Without exception, we are all born under The Law, we produce 'our works' under The Law, and we die under The Law. And throughout our complete existence, for however long that may be, we receive the 'returns of our works', good or bad, under The Law. The determinant for humankind in the "personal end result" is via the exercise of our "free will".

*   *   *   *   *

Having clarified the validity of the impossibility of altering The Spiritual Laws, let us examine the "miracles" of Jesus with regard to the 'dead'. We can now understand that the soul-bodies of those He called to, travelled back to the physical shell along the Silver Cord that had not yet been completely severed. Whilst this is a lawful process, the 'key point' here is that Jesus **possessed the power to do so.** Issuing as He did from The Godhead, without which nothing could come into existence, He naturally and lawfully possessed the Power to **command** the souls to return.

Thus He clearly demonstrated the fact that death is only a transitory phase and that we should not fear it. However a vital aspect of these "miracles" here is not the fact that He *could* order the souls to return, but the *different manner* in which He *commanded* them to do so. With the young maid who was very recently dead, He simply says:

> "My girl arise." "Her breath thereupon returned, and she at once got up. And He gave orders for her to have something to eat."
>
> (Luke 8:54-55)

In the case of the young man from Nain, who has been dead longer and is about to be buried, His command is stronger, more urgent, where He calls:

> " 'Young man, *I say to you*, Arise!' ...when the dead man sat up and began to speak. And He handed him to his mother."
>
> (Luke 7:14-15)

And finally, in the case of Lazarus who had already been in his tomb for four days, we read that Jesus, after ordering the cave-stone to be removed, first *prays* for help, before **commanding** Lazarus to rise. The Scripture states that:

> "...He called *with a loud voice*: "Lazarus, come out!" "He who was dead accordingly came out, swathed hand and foot with bandages, and his head wrapped in a napkin. Jesus told them, "loosen and let him walk."
>
> (John 11:42-44, Fenton all, Emphases mine.)

---

[7]Detailed explanations of the Truth about the life of Jesus may be read in the *primary* "CRYSTAL PUBLISH-ING" publication: [BIBLE "MYSTERIES" EXPLAINED Understanding "Global Societal Collapse" From the "SCIENCE" in The Bible: What Every Scientist, Bible Scholar and Ordinary Man needs to Know.] Specifically, Chapter 5 – Jesus: His Birth, Death and Resurrection.

It is interesting to note that John the Disciple records Martha, sister of Lazarus, as objecting to the expressed intention of raising him from the dead when she stated to Jesus:

"Master, by this time the smell must be offensive: for this is the fourth day."

(John 11:39, Fenton.)

It is also important to note that in each of the three respective cases Jesus gave different instructions to the families of them. In the case of the young girl, however, we may deduce that the order to give her food was to immediately re-strengthen the "radiation-connection" between her soul body and her material body – which she had recently vacated.

Thus we see that in these three cases, the longer the person had been dead, the *stronger the command* required by Jesus to effect a return; a clear indication of the relative 'distances' the respective souls were from their bodies. As long as the 'Cord' is still attached, however, the 'dead' have the possibility of returning, which is the sole and lawful reason **why** Jesus *was able* to bring this about, aside from *possessing* the power to do so. Once the 'Cord' is severed, it is not possible for any return. Even though possessing the power of The Divine, Jesus would *not* have been able to alter The Eternal Laws to achieve that, as He clearly pointed out!

His miraculous healings did not require a "Law change" either, as everything can only take place under the umbrella of The Spiritual Laws. It was simply a case of His Divine Power, which stands far higher again than The Spiritual, *accelerating* the normal process of healing by a very large degree so as to make it seem instantaneous, and thus miraculous. He intimated that humankind, too, would one day be able to achieve similar results once we had reached the appropriate level of Spiritual purity. The Bible narrative records that the Disciples also effected healing "miracles" *after* the Ascension.

According to the historical record, shortly after his resurrection, Lazarus left Palestine and the persecution of the Christians, and journeyed to Cyprus where he was ordained as Bishop by St Barnabas. Lazarus apparently lived there for a further 30 years and it is said that he rarely smiled having seen the plight of the souls in the beyond. We should remember that he spent some days in that "beyond" before being *commanded to return to physical life.*

*   *   *   *   *

Now let us return to our own journey of discovery. We have reached the stage where the soul-body is about to become free of its former 'partner in earthly life'. But first we should briefly return to the long, dark tunnel phase of the first stages of the death process to offer a more complete explanation of it. The subjects claimed that they felt "...as if they were gliding through something dark and narrow, a valley, a dark shaft, a tunnel", and they used words like being 'pulled out' in attempting to describe the sensation.

The striving away of the ethereal soul from the astral body is the soul's 'pulling out' from the latter. At these moments of transition – during the striving-away movement – the spirit can no longer see through the eyes of the earthly or astral body. Nor can it see through those of the ethereal soul body, which is not yet completely free. Therefore the spirit temporarily has the impression of darkness. We can liken this phase to that of being in a lift moving between two floors. In this situation we must wait until the next floor is reached before we can look out again.

The next stage is the emergence from out of this dark tunnel into the bright light of the next world. As previously stated, we can observe some similarities to the birth process in the striving away, the dark tunnel, and the emergence into a bright new world. For, in reality, *earthly death* is nothing more than *birth* into the ethereal world. This new world for the soul, however, is still close to the earth, but with a vastly altered time-perspective. Here, in this new, lighter world away from the constraints of the heavier physical body and the gross material earth, everything is more mobile, more 'speeded-up'.

For the departed one, this phase can be marked by much confusion, and more so if he had paid no attention to this matter of death during his life. Now, in death, he discovers he has the ability to see and hear all that is taking place around him, but finds he is not able to make himself heard or felt. He sees the anguish of emotional pain in those he left behind and strives to reassure them that he is actually not dead, that he lives. But he cannot. If those of his family members have the same attitude to death that he previously had, he will be forced to endure the emotional upheaval and non-comprehension of his kin that his death has produced. Because of this, he may seek to make himself understood but, as he cannot with his 'new soul-body', the only course open to him is to try through the earthly organs of speech of the physical one he has left behind.

His attempts to do so bring about a renewed strengthening of the 'Cord', with a corresponding increase in feelings of pain which he would recently have become free of. His efforts unnecessarily prolong the death struggle which can last for days, and which his loved ones will anguish over. Thus, his well-meaning attempts to offer solace to those around him actually only add more confusion for them, and sometimes fear. The feelings of anguish and loneliness for a soul in such circumstances must surely be considerable. Far better if we all occupied ourselves with this vital question instead of pushing it away, as if that act might keep earthly death away forever. Since knowledge empowers, it is far better *to know* than to not know!

*   *   *   *   *

The severing of the Silver Cord is not always easy. The Spirit-Author, Franchezzo, whose Dedication we included earlier in this Chapter, offers a sobering insight into this difficulty. After his physical death he sees, standing by his grave, the girl he loved. When she leaves he tries to follow her but is unable to.

> 'I strove with all my might to follow her. In vain, I could go but a few yards from the grave and my earthly body, and then I saw why. A chain as of dark silk thread – it seemed no thicker than a spider's web – held me to my body; no power of mine could break it: as I moved it stretched like elastic, but always drew me back again. Worst of all I began now to be conscious of feeling the corruption of that dead body affecting my spirit, as a limb that has become poisoned affects with suffering the whole body on earth, and a fresh horror filled my soul.
>
> Then a voice as of some majestic being spoke to me in the darkness, and said': "You loved that body more than your soul. Watch it now as it turns to dust and know what it was that you so worshipped, and ministered and clung to. Know how perishable it was, how vile it has become, *and look upon your spirit body and see how you have starved and cramped and neglected it for the sake of the enjoyments of the earthly body.*"
>
> (A Wanderer In The Spirit Lands, p.11. Italics mine.)

*   *   *   *   *

The Silver Cord, which in this case has thickened and become dark, binds the departed one very firmly to his physical body. Only later, after he has recognised the wrong of his earthly life, can he sever himself from his mortal shell. When the disintegration of the "Silver Cord" finally occurs, the departed one experiences the effects of The Law of Spiritual Gravity in its full manifestation. In accordance with previous explanations, by the consequential effects of its recently lived lifestyle, the soul is forced to then begin to 'reap what it sowed'. This is achieved under the outworking of The Spiritual Laws where the soul is 'propelled' to the particular plane that corresponds with its ethereal or "spiritual" weight. In accordance with The Law of Spiritual Gravity, only on the earth can good and evil live side by side. On no other plane of Creation is this possible.

"And Man seeks his Long Home,
And the Mourners will walk round the streets –
Ere the silver cord's loosed... ...
And Man goes *to the earth that he was,*
And his Soul *will return to the GOD Who gave it!*"

(Ecclesiastes 12:6-7, Fenton, Italics mine.)

Thus, upon earthly death, a separation takes place between all the departed. In accordance with that separation, they must then occupy the particular plane that their ethereal weight has decreed for them, and also those of similar mind and propensity. Therefore, souls will always find themselves surrounded by others of the same weight and essentially of the same nature. And in this lies the perfect Justice of The Eternal Laws, in particular the outworking of The Law of Attraction of Similar Species.

9.3   The Nature of Hell

An interesting question arises here. Much uncertainty exists about the nature of the place called "hell", or even if such a place exists, or could exist. Some earlier philosophers postulated a duality of forces i.e., a good and a bad one, and a light and a dark one. Such a view clearly presupposes that *two* forces must exist, thus two separate powers that we can choose between and connect ourselves to. This belief is still strong for many people today, probably because, on the surface at least, it appears to be a reasonable assumption. The dark force, moreover, is invariably deemed to be the 'creator' or 'owner' of hell.

The assumption or proposition that such a separate 'dark force' exists has certainly been used often enough as a reason or excuse where horrific crimes have been committed: "I was told to do it", they say. "Voices from somewhere made me do it" etc.. The voices would be real enough, but their origin is the key consideration here.

St Augustine, a theologian who lived from 354 to 430 AD, was preoccupied with what might be termed "the problem of evil" for much of his life; in essence where evil came from. For a time he was influenced by the Stoic school of thought that held there was no sharp division between good and evil. A major influence as well was that of Neoplatonism which espoused the view that all existence is divine in nature. A philosopher to begin with, Augustine had nevertheless long felt that there was a limit as to how far philosophy could go. And it was not until he became a Christian that he found the peace he sought, a peace anchored in faith. He wrote:

"Our heart is not quiet until it rests in Thee."

Schelling, (1775-1854) the leading Romantic philosopher, sought to unite mind and matter. He believed that all of nature in both the human soul and the physical reality was the expression of one Absolute or world spirit. He saw this "world spirit" in nature but he also saw it in the human mind. He also accepted the idea of a development from earth to rock to 'mind' governed by his "world spirit" beliefs. Schelling stated explicitly that "...the world is in God". He believed that God was aware of some of it, but there were other aspects of nature that represented the unknown in God. This was the "dark side of God" in his view.

In reality, however, there is only **one** power streaming through all of Creation. It issues from out of "The Creative Will of God" and is completely **neutral**. Being, in essence, "The Living Power", it creates and sustains all life. However, in the case of we humans who are inherently endowed with the attribute of free will and who also stand in this power stream, we are actually like lenses. This "power" is thus 'automatically refracted' through us as we choose, determine and fulfil our particular place in, and path through, life.

For whilst we absorb a *neutral force*, our free-will volition then *converts it* to whatever we choose – good or evil. Or, to word it differently, to either the correct principle or the incorrect principle. By this process we *automatically* 'form' our environment. This mechanism brings to us our personal reaping, the reaping of our society, our Nation and global family of Nations. Now, since all written history quite clearly attests to wars, blood and violence on the super grand scale, consider the forms we have created over thousands of years – and continue to do so. And because we have created them, only through a fundamental change in attitude and way of being can we ever hope to destroy them.

Yet, is there any move towards seeking to change the mostly dark forms of our free will volition? Generally speaking, no! That is probably because the reality of The Law of Reciprocal Action is not accepted. Instead, in ignorance, we not only add to those forms, we greatly nourish them in our desire to "do what pleases us". And in concert with "The Law of Attraction..." we are forced to reap more and more from that growing monster. That "reaping" is returned to us under The Law of Reciprocal Action via the aegis of the *whirlwind constant.*

Through the outworking of Spiritual Law, hell is thus simply explained. It is not an institution ordained and created by God. It is composed of those levels in the world of the afterlife that we (humankind) have created through giving full and unbridled rein to our evil dispositions over countless millennia. The rejection of genuine spiritual ideals and the gravitating toward material pleasures and vices, with the natural accompaniment of evil activities, has caused the formation of the 'planes of hell'. From there, its forms go forth to influence the decisions of humankind under the outworking of The Law of Attraction of Similar Species. And there, also, the darker like-minded are forced by Law to reside until such time as a spiritual longing to be free of it permits The Laws to bring this about for that individual. Therefore, *humankind is the landlord and owner of the place we call hell!* Under the inter-related workings of The Spiritual Laws, perfect spiritual justice may be clearly discerned via this lawful mechanism.

As a striking contrast, the same process has also formed planes of light and joy where, again, the like-minded enjoy the peace and beauty of the afterlife they have earned. Suffering and tragedy, therefore, are **not** willed by God. We bring that on ourselves, paradoxically via the same process whereby we could enjoy continual peace and happiness. Thus by the simple application of directing our free will toward the good.

The oft-bemoaned cry of, "Where lies justice?", is quite clearly explained in the above discussion. And if we consider the *following* Scriptures, we can readily see that "justice", down to its last ramification, is absolutely served. Perhaps not immediately on the earth under human law, but most assuredly later under the perfection of Spiritual Law! Through that infallible outworking, we can more readily understand the following scriptural quotes, key ones of which we have previously mentioned, and which require re-stating here. From Hosea 8:7:

"And as they have sown only Wind, the Whirlwind alone shall they reap!"

"Yet we know who says PUNISHMENT IS MINE, I WILL REPAY."

(Hebrews 10:30)

"I place Life and Death before you, – the Blessing and the Curse! Therefore choose for yourselves the Life, – that you and your posterity may live!"

(Deuteronomy 30:19, Fenton all.)

In each of the above Scriptures, the clear admonition to *choose* correctly is evident. And only with a free-will ability can we do so. Therefore all choices are ultimately ours and ours alone, and the automatic outworking of The Spiritual Laws subsequently delivers to us the ensuing consequences.

There is one final question that remains to be addressed with regard to the end fate of we human spirits in terms of the complete death process, but that will be the subject of our next Chapter. For the moment we have arrived at the end of a basic explanation of this inevitable yet vital happening. It is, however, a basic overview only.[8]

9.4   The Journey of Maori Souls

The processes outlined in this Chapter are those so ordained under the outworking of The Spiritual Laws of Creation. As stated at the beginning of this Chapter, the "Wisdom Of Solomon" from The Apocrypha states it wonderfully succinctly:

"...there is for all mankind one entrance into life, and a *common departure*".

The death process for Maori, therefore, is the same as that for all humankind, regardless of the cultural and traditional beliefs that individual races and peoples might wish to hold to. And whilst many legends may offer diverse views, even ones relating innovative and magical hypotheses towards a resolution of the understanding of death, we unequivocally state that what has been explained here is the *actual happening* under the completely natural process of Spiritual Law – **without deviation**.

So the belief that all Maori souls travel to Cape Reinga and soar northwards over the Sea of Kiwa to the ancient homeland of Hawaiki, *there to reside with ancestors*, should not be taught as inviolable truth but accepted as legend only! The fact of the matter is that one's path through life is what is *decisive* for a final determination as to one's *ultimate destination* after death. This *immutable reality* should give cause for a *different perception* with regard to the belief of a guaranteed return to ancestral groupings after earthly death.

The necessary, forced acceptance of one's "personal plane of consequence" under the Perfect outworking of "**The Law of Spiritual Gravity**", particularly – i.e., after 'Cord' severance at earthly death – may simply not allow that to take place. Moreover, the return of departed former friends or relatives to offer assistance at the first stages after death does not contradict our assertions either, since only those who are *permitted* to return to assist will, but solely under the strict outworking of The Law once again.

Since this Law propels all human spirits toward their appropriate level, it becomes a simple matter to recognise that many of our ancestors who committed savage deeds in old Aotearoa would have been propelled to a similarly savage lower plane. And as these deeds were a part of their 'way of life', we can further conclude that many could well have found themselves together again – victor and vanquished – at a similar level. There to struggle and rage against each other until such time as the souls realised the futility of it all and sought to better themselves in striving toward a more ennobled environment. However, certain conditions are placed on such souls seeking to rise out of their self-imposed hell, and ascent cannot begin until these conditions are met. Thus, under **The Law of Grace**, some such souls may well have lifted themselves out of their self-imposed purgatory.

Many souls, however, through their too-strong a propensity for materialism and earthly vices, may find themselves tied to the earth frequenting places that provided the bind when alive. Occasionally we may 'feel' the presence of such earth-bound ones, though a few people do have the ability to 'see' them.[9]

---

[8]For greater understanding, the reader may wish to avail himself of certain other publications that offer yet more insight into the subject. However, the reader should note that whilst there are very many books which *purport to give* correct explanations of the death process, in fact only a very few *actually* can, and only **one** completely so!

[9]This is not an ability that should be striven for, however. The possibility of becoming earthbound will be briefly examined in the next Chapter.

Another factor one must consider with regard to any kind of 'ancestral heritage' is **The Law of Rebirth**.

This Law plays a major role in the placement of human beings, but strictly in accordance with the spiritual volition of the individual under the outworking of Spiritual Law – again **without deviation**. Therefore, Maori today have not always been Maori!

Moreover, as we briefly outlined in **Part I**, if the lust for *blood-utu* amongst those departed Maori who relished the savagery of the old way had still not been recognised for the wrong that it actually is, perhaps some may have been re-born into races that have not yet let go this practice. And there are still many such places on earth where this is an unfortunate but regular part of life. Therefore, some Maori ancestors may now reside amongst a very different people, yet still in an *utu*-based society. A refusal to change one's nature can only return more of the same to that particular individual in terms of where it may find itself *reincarnated on earth*. The same applies after death where, without genuine change, it may once more descend to a lower plane with similar souls as before, exactly according to the outworking of the **three primary Laws** of "**Sowing and Reaping**", "**Attraction**" and "**Spiritual Gravity**".

Thus the beliefs and legends of the Maori, as well as the culture and tradition of all peoples must, by Law, subordinate themselves to **The Law of The Truth Itself**, if or where there is clear conflict between the two positions.

*   *   *   *   *

An example of totally incorrect yet traditional Maori beliefs regarding the nature of the dead was aired on television news relatively recently. It featured a request for the exhumation of a baby – a Pakeha baby in this case – by its mother. A *kaumatua* from the area stated his concerns and fears regarding the idea of disinterment, even that of a baby.

In his view, with the departure of the soul from the body, the entity left behind becomes what he termed a *'thing'*! The 'fear' that he voiced regarding possible exhumation, was that no one could predict what might 'happen'; what the *'thing'* might do, and it should therefore be left undisturbed. Presumably, in such a belief, the dead *'thing'* could somehow become animated once more and offer potential harm to others.

In just this one example, I could potentially rest my case in stating that *it is not knowledge that Maori possess about such matters*, but **lack of knowledge** encompassing elements of **fear**. This fear aspect was unequivocally voiced by that particular *kaumatua* under the aegis of, so-called, 'Maori spiritual knowledge'.

It is a sad situation, indeed, when a small, dead baby can be designated as something to be greatly feared; as having the potential to cause harm or mischief to the living.

In truth, the real harm or mischief lies solely in such *totally incorrect and aspiritual beliefs*. Beliefs, moreover, which should be *completely expunged from the consciousness of Maori thinking – or any thinking for that matter – and replaced with the clearly more beneficial knowledge of*:
The Spiritual Laws of Creation.

9.5   The Tangi (The spiritual ramifications)

Bearing that last unfortunate belief in mind, it is timely, at the conclusion of this Chapter on Death, to consider the spiritual ramifications of how one should grieve at funerals. It is an aspect of life that most people deem particularly important. It is especially so for Maori.

The great spiritual mission of Ratana, which will be analysed in a later Chapter, stated the need for huge and fundamental changes in Maori thinking and practices if there was to be any genuine spiritual progress. Thus the idea that the *mana* of a departed one should perhaps dictate the length of any particular *tangi,* is clearly challenged by the 10th principle contained in the twelve principles of Ratana's full covenant. It succinctly and rather pointedly states:

"That the duration of *tangi* be curtailed."

Since this does not concur with generally accepted and practised ideas of Maori cultural traditions, let us examine the *tangi* and its associated grieving from the standpoint of **The Spiritual Laws** and strive to understand why the "Mangai" considered this aspect important for the 'new spiritual direction' Maori needed to embark upon!

The *practice* of grieving, whilst not solely confined to Maori, of course, is nevertheless *refined* within the race to a pronounced degree of emotional display at times of death. Whilst there will always be a normal and naturally healthy level of grief for loved ones, in particular, without the knowledge of the death process to guide us, we could not ever have been sure of the *effect* that displays of very deep emotional grief might have on the ones *for whom we grieve.* Now that we *do* have clear and unequivocal understanding, it behoves us all, regardless of race, culture or tradition, to take cognisance of this knowledge and begin to more fully understand the effects that our behaviour might have on our departed loved ones.

Therefore, we should ask ourselves the question:

"What are the things we should do to help those who are struggling to become free from earthly ties?"

Given the huge amounts of emotion and stress invariably present at funerals, perhaps the more relevant question is:

"What should we **not do** when grieving for the departed?" And, just as importantly: "**Why** should we not?"

Even though we have already offered a brief explanation in this Chapter, it is probably appropriate to re-define the relevant aspects again.

People who are present at a death-bed should strive **not** to break out into loud expressions of grief! When the grief at parting is too strongly expressed, the person in the process of detaching himself from his physical body, or who may already be standing beside it in ethereal form, may hear or feel it and be emotionally disturbed by it. If he should then feel pity for those left behind, the wish may awaken within him the strong desire to say a few words of consolation. In his, perhaps, desperate attempts to make his concerns known to the grief-stricken mourners, this 'struggle' again binds him more strongly to his physical body.

Now, because of his renewed efforts to establish a closer connection with his physical body – *the only medium by which he is able to communicate to those grieving over his 'death'* – the ethereal body, which was still in the natural process of detaching itself, not only re-unites itself more closely to the physical body, *but will be drawn back into it again.* Consequently the pains from which he had already been delivered will be felt once more. When next he seeks to detach himself from his physical shell, *and which he must inevitably do*, it will be made *more difficult* and may last for several days. As previously stated, this produces the prolonged, so-called, "death struggle" which loved ones and relatives anguish over and which not only causes them more grief as they observe this process, but is also *painful and difficult for the soul wanting to depart.*

The blame for this unfortunate situation, as difficult as it may be to accept, lies solely with those *who are unable or unwilling to curb their emotions,* and who express it in *loud wailing and lamentations of grief.* Because of this the natural course of development for that soul is held back as *he* struggles to cope with it. From an earthly standpoint such behaviour is readily understandable, but from that of the purely Spiritual, *it is actually one of selfishness* because the grieving ones are more concerned with *their loss* than for the lawful transition of their loved one into his next life, or of his possible emotional struggle as *he* observes *their* grief.

This quite unnecessary interruption of the normal process, even if only a weak attempt at concentrating on making himself understood, ensures that a new and forced connection occurs. To now dissolve this unnatural connection once more may not be so easy. Unfortunately, because *he* desired the reconnection, no assistance can be given. Moreover, so long as the physical body is still not yet completely cold and the "Silver Cord", which may not necessarily tear for many weeks, is still intact, such 'reconnections' can still be effected *relatively* easily.

We should thus consider the suffering of the dying one *first*, and not the thought of our own loss. Therefore, the ideal situation for this serious event should be one of **absolute quiet**, offering the departing one the necessary dignity for the *importance* of the hour.

These vital considerations should induce each of us to seriously reflect upon our own particular attitude at such times so as to ascertain whether or not we may be remiss in this area. For most, the answer would be a resounding yes! Yet we, ourselves, would probably not want the experience of a painful death struggle. In an unfortunate paradox, however, it is what we invariably visit upon those we *most care for* during *their death process*. Therefore, at such times, we should resolve to place *our* personal sense of loss in a *secondary role* and consider more the plight of *our friend* or loved one as he struggles *to stand free of the shackles of the earthly body.* And more particularly if there has been a long and painful illness or a restrictive and painfully-debilitating accident. A quick merciful release from that should be our *primary* concern, and not our own personal wish to *hold him to us.*

To this end, it is important to clearly differentiate between the *differences* that actually exist between the natural and desirable *emotional experiencing* of such an event, and a situation where this aspect is subconsciously subjugated to a state of **raw emotionalism** brought on by the collective, emotional upwelling of the occasion. Even though the emotions are given to us to *deepen* every experience – irrespective of whether it be joyful or painful – there is a vast difference between the two positions even if, on the surface and to the onlooker, the grief may *appear* to be the same.

One is naturally healthy; if and when possessing a spiritual foundation as its wellspring of understanding, whilst the other is basically *earthly* emotionalism. **The Spiritual** knows only high, pure, cool objectivity, with Spiritual Love as its foundation. Therefore, displays of *unnecessary emotionalism* have little affinity with true spirituality. In its earthly manner, however, it invariably focuses more *on the persons displaying it.*

Only by accepting that death is a far more serious and important occasion *for the departing one* than it is for us, might we learn to leave behind the loud wailing and lamenting that so often accompanies death and funerals today. And replace that with controlled natural grief thus offering the help of a quick release, *and peace and dignity to the one we have come to farewell.*

As we would no doubt want that also, we should remind ourselves once more of the following, appropriate words of Jesus, (Luke 6:31, Fenton) given from out of The Living Law:

"And as you wish men to do to you, do the same to them."

9.6   Death of a Soldier

For those who accept that life continues after physical death, a loved one's sacrifice in battle may be easier to deal with emotionally. But what of the actual sacrifice itself, the extinguishing of a life in battle for a particular cause? Where can we place that in spiritual terms, and are we able to? The simple answer is yes! There are spiritual effects for every soldier[10] in the ultimate sacrifice. So if death is the outcome in a just and righteous cause nobly and bravely carried out, the 'after-effects' will be vastly different from those which 'brutal adventurers' in an ignoble war will experience. A brief examination of relatively recent history can probably conclude that there will have been very many acts of noble sacrifice, by virtue of the need to stop the madness of megalomanic despots.

What, then, spiritually happens for the soldier who bravely pays the ultimate sacrificial price? In order to answer *this* question, we must refer back to Chapter 7 and our explanation of the origin and nature of man.

We know that the human spirit is an amalgam of a number of bodies telescoped, as it were, into each other, with each 'body' corresponding to the nature and consistency of the particular plane to which it belongs. From our origins in The Spiritual Realm we are required to accept and occupy each appropriate body corresponding to, and consistent with, the nature of each plane we must traverse on our journey downwards to personal self-consciousness on the earth in the material world. At earthly death, the reverse process takes place whereby we discard each body at the height of its appropriate realm or level, as we ascend on the journey home; assuming of course that we have *earned the right to do so.*

Connected with Spiritual Law and the Higher Realms are all the Virtues, one of which is *heroism.* By virtue of its particular nature, its place of origin can only be in the Higher Planes. The gift of free will that is inherent in every human being means that in our chosen life-path, whether as an individual or even as part of a Nation, we can choose either the uplifting benefits of the Virtues or the debasing, destructive energies of the vices. This means that certain activities will inherently have either uplifting or debasing qualities.

Now, whilst war may generally be regarded as destructive, particular elements within it or, more particularly, certain kinds of actions that war inevitably produces, *are most certainly* connected to the Higher Virtues. So, in the case of a soldier who recognises that his participation in a just war is necessary to preserve freedom, who carries out his duties with quiet efficiency, with objectivity for the cause and without hate for the opposing side, and who is killed during an act of heroism in the course of his serving; this soldier, in spiritual terms, has released "The Virtue of Heroism" within him. It is thus connected to him.

This act of heroism in its *spiritual form,* through its release via an heroic deed, is attracted upwards – primarily under the inviolable outworking of "The Law of Attraction of Similar Species" and "The Law of Spiritual Gravity" – to its ordained place close to The Spiritual Realm of our Origin. This particular plane of Creation, commonly alluded to as the 'home of the gods', was known to many of the ancient cultures. It is that level which the Greeks, particularly, sought inspiration from to nobly emulate that loftier vision and apply it to every aspect of their society, including the military training of their young men. Their spiritual insight allowed them to 'see' the activity and nature of the inhabitants there, such as the Elemental Lords, Zeus and Poseidon, etc., whom they *wrongly believed* to be gods. They named *their* 'home' Mount Olympus.[11] Thus, every heroic act is connected to the essence of the natural

---

[10]The term "soldier" is used to describe the activity of all servicemen. Therefore, the equally valuable role of the sailor and the airman in war on the earth is the same as that of the soldier.

[11]The once noble-ideal of the Olympic games traces its origin to that recognition.

power and nobleness of those "Elemental forces".[12]

It is from the noble volition of the spirit – the real you and me – that heroic acts are generated. The 'living form' of this heroic act is thus connected to its Origin in the Higher Realms. That *form*, 'released' from the soul body of our noble soldier at his death in necessary battle, is then taken upwards to the topmost level of its ordained place where it is cared for until the day the 'owner' of the 'heroic act' – our soldier – *might* reach that point of spiritual ascent. If he does so, it is automatically returned to him, since it was his alone. This he carries with him to the next level – The Spiritual Realm – his Origin and true home. There it adorns him as *a spiritually visible sign of his selfless sacrifice*.

The ancient Nordic peoples also perceived the truth of this process and named that particular kingdom or level "Valhalla". This high 'fastness' housed the 'resting place' of their heroes killed in battle too. However, whilst they and the Greeks, among others, divined the existence of this sphere and the activity of the beings therein, they had not reached a sufficient level of knowledge to fully understand the outworking of The Eternal Laws and the associated process that determines this complete happening.[13]

That, then, is the spiritual meaning of selfless and noble sacrifice of a soldier in a just cause! Thus, whilst wars are a curse and a blight on mankind, they do provide opportunities whereby returning potentially severe fate, under the "The Law of Reciprocal Action", can be expiated by an individual during deeds of ultimate bravery.

Therefore the common saying, "...better to be a live coward than a dead hero", does not actually occupy any truly *spiritual* place. Cowardice, historically, has been reviled by most of the world's peoples, and the aftermath of various wars have seen known cowards executed anyway.

Finally, the words of Jesus best explain the true meaning and greatness of what is termed, "the ultimate sacrifice", when He said:

> "Stronger love has no one than this, that one should lay down his own life for his friends."

> (John 15:13, Fenton.)

In such noble deeds the greatest power in Creation is invoked; that of **The Power of Love**. This, however, is the **Pure Love** contained in true *spiritual* activity. It is not, nor could it ever be, the unfortunate distortion and base emotionalism produced by we of humankind in our earthly interpretations and our immoral and aspiritual activities which we deviously try to *mask* with that vital life-word.

---

[12]Note that in the animal kingdom the inhabitants there will defend territory or young, even to the point of dying for that cause.

[13]Today we can fill those gaps with the relevant knowledge from particular and special spiritual works *now available*.

The First Death!

10
The Second Death

"The conqueror shall never be injured by the 'second death'!"

(Revelation 2:11, Fenton.)

The title of this Chapter may give cause for some incredulity from many who may still be uncertain or unbelieving regarding the nature and process of just the physical deaths that we all see from time to time in the course of everyday earth-life. To state that there is such an event as a "second death" may force a struggle of considerable disbelief. Yet, just as we outlined the process of earthly death in the last Chapter, so can an explanation for a seemingly radical idea of a "second death" also be offered.

As with death in the earthly sense, the reality of the "second one" is equally as subject to immovable Spiritual Law. Indeed, only from that standpoint can it be so possible and be explained, by virtue of the simple fact that all things, from the smallest to the greatest, exist under these Laws. And neither does a "second death" conflict with the Biblical statement, Hebrews 9:27, Fenton, wherein it states that:

"...it is appointed to men to die once..."

Quite obviously if there were such a conflict, we could not logically have any allusions to such a thing as a "second death". Yet in The Book of Revelation we find two more clear and unequivocal statements about it.

"...over these the *second death* has no authority."

"...that is the *second death* – the lake of fire."

(Revelation 20:6, 20:14, Fenton. Italics mine.)

Allusions to "second deaths" and "lakes of fire" may sound religiously crass to many living in our increasingly technological and computerised society strongly directed to the 'god corporate'. However, perhaps such ostensibly 'archaic religious ideas' should be viewed as simply being 'symbolic explanations' of **particular and very precise lawful processes and outcomes**.

In any case, from the point of view of the Judaeo/Christian school of thought, upon which Western society is largely moulded, we have at least established that the "second death" idea is very much 'alive and well' in The Bible.

The *spiritual meaning* of the *conqueror* in the Biblical quote under the title heading of this particular Chapter, moreover, should be understood to mean one who has succeeded in **conquering himself**! He has conquered **his own base weaknesses** and is thus far more spiritually mature and knowledgeable than 'before the fact'. His increasing spiritual awareness may also allow him to be more accepting of an idea such as "the second death", and thus 'will not be *injured* by it'. Establishing the Biblical fact of a "second death" therefore permits us the use of this foundation to assess the ramifications of how we *might* be affected by such an 'event'.

Because human beings, generally, are not the least bit interested in the absolute nature of Spiritual Law and thus living spiritually-correctly according to that inviolable regime, most will therefore *experience* the unfortunate outcome called "The Second Death". This analysis is thus crucially-vital for all. First, however, let us read the interpretation of it that Crudens Concordance, page 96, offers.

> [2] "A separation of soul and body from God's favour in this life, which is the state of all unregenerated and unrenewed persons who are without the light of knowledge, and the quickening power of grace, Luke 1:79. This is spiritual death. [3] The perpetual separation of the whole man from God's heavenly presence and glory, to be tormented forever with the devil and his angels, Revelation 2:11. This is the second death."

If, then, we accept that there is such a thing as a "second death" as The Bible clearly states, then we should expect that however it is brought about it can only be so under the strict outworking of The Spiritual Laws. Since the Laws of Nature and scientific law both have their validity solely under the umbrella of the higher Spiritual Laws, let us approach this particular subject matter not from a purely 'religious' perspective, but from the combined intermeshing of all the above Principles of Law, as we did with the "The First Death".

In the current Biblical interpretation from Crudens Concordance, *three* different kinds of deaths are noted. Yet the Bible does not appear to indicate anywhere that there are three. Crudens mentions physical death, with which we are all familiar, and states that there is a "second death", and also a "spiritual death". Utilising The Spiritual Laws as the foundation for our assessments, we will show that, aside from physical death which we all must experience, there is the **actual reality** of "the second death" to contend with. There are not two *different* kinds of *further* deaths but a single secondary one only – the "second, spiritual death"! Therefore we can safely conclude that any difference of opinion will be in an incorrect Biblical interpretation on this particular subject.

In order to find a starting point to explain the actual meaning of the 'second death', however, we must first consider the differences between that which is Eternal and that which is not. The earlier Greeks, Indians, Persians and Teutons – the "Indo-Europeans" – shared a common view that history is cyclical, with no beginning and no end. But in an "...eternal interplay between birth and death", different civilisations rise and fall. This view is not quite the *'eternality'* that we mean.

Let us compare that with the thinking of Rene Descartes, (1596-1650) a French philosopher and mathematician who rejected all previously held beliefs and built his own philosophy on the one premise he held to be indisputable, the existence of himself as a 'thinking subject'. This is reflected in his 'personalised statement':

"I think, therefore I am."

As a 'dualist philosopher', Descartes believed that whilst there are two different forms of reality or substances – *thought* or mind and *extension* or matter – he nevertheless *very-correctly* maintained that both substances *originate* from God, because:

"...only God Himself exists independently of anything else".

He thus came to the conclusion that man is a dual creature – of the mind, and of the body. Yet even though perhaps philosophically equating the mind with spirit, he apparently did not extend that thought to encompass a separately-existing "Spiritual Realm" as the originating place of that spirit.

With his existentialist beliefs, Sartre, (1905-1980), thought that man had no eternal nature to fall back on, and it was therefore pointless to search for the meaning of life. Existentialism, in the philosophic sense, appears to represent that century's answer to all other philosophical beliefs of the past. It is therefore interesting to observe the path that philosophy has taken. An early and strong acceptance of a separable soul or spirit before the birth of Christ became interspersed with diverging philosophic/religious views at varying intervals up to the present.[1]

However, in the century preceding Sartre's, another European philosopher had already rejected the values of Christianity. Friedrich Nietzsche (1844-1900) regarded the Christian ideal as 'slave morality'. In his opinion, both Christianity and traditional philosophy had turned away from what he termed 'the real world', and instead directed their thinking toward "heaven" or "the world of ideas". He urged people to be 'true to the world' and not to be seduced by any offers of 'supernatural expectations'.

In terms of an actual truth or a distortion of that truth, his reference to Christianity as being a 'slave morality' could quite clearly be viewed as 'a truth in itself' if, in the course of centuries, the original teachings had become so badly distorted that only rigid fundamentalism or a religion of fear was left. Without the vitality and vibrancy that only a 'Pure Truth' can offer, apathy, superficiality and non-understanding – with the obvious potential to lead into hypocrisy – may well then become the 'way of that religion'. Of course, this applies to all beliefs and teachings, and not necessarily religious ones.

As explained in the Chapter on our Origins, we know that Creation consists of two main basic parts, the Eternal and the non-eternal or Material. For we human spirits, the *Eternal part* is that region of Creation from which we issued as *non-conscious spirit-seeds* on our journey down to the earth in the *non-eternal Material*. For its part, the Material is primarily that region to which the earth and the physical universes belong and in which it was ordained we were to develop to a fully conscious state, thus recognising both our origin and our life's purpose. And, therefore, with the concomitant potential to return to The Spiritual Realm in the Eternal part of Creation as a fully purified spiritual being.[2]

In order to understand why there *is* a "second death" reality, there needs to be the further recognition that there is necessarily a 'time-frame constraint' for all the Material Worlds of Creation. The Spiritual Laws decree that everything in the material worlds must inherently have *a finite* lifespan. The Eternal Realms, quite logically, do not. In the material world of the earth

---

[1]Perhaps we might now see existentialism and its general denial of the spirituality of man as the almost final excrescence of our lauding of intellectual prowess above all else.

[2]In fact, that is the *only* state in which we *can* return!

and physical universes, it is a simple matter to observe the vast number of diverse creatures and inanimate life-forms with varying life spans; from fractions of a second for sub-atomic particles, to hours for the most minute creatures, to days for some insects and on to years for those of the animal world. Man, as the only creature on earth with an inner animating spiritual core and free will – as opposed to just instinct – has a life span of 70 odd years approximately. The great trees, though, can live for thousands of years.

Out in the vast tracts of the universe, however, suns and planets are born, live out their allotted time span over billions of years and then disintegrate to be reborn into other celestial bodies aeons later. The far larger galaxies have a life span running into many millions of light years. One light year is the distance a ray of light travels in one earth year – approximately 6 million, million miles. Or more precisely – 9.4605 million, million kilometres. Notwithstanding such incomprehensible measurements of distance and time, everything in the Material Worlds has its time of birth, life and disintegration, nevertheless.

The Material Part of Creation is therefore *finite*, with a strictly ordained time of existence, after which it must also disintegrate back to its primordial components to be reformed into a new *Material Creation*. Obviously such a time span is difficult to comprehend but it behoves each one of us to give this concept at least some thought. For the disintegration of a whole part of the Material World cannot take place without huge and unimaginable dislocations and upheavals. Whole galaxies and universes would be absolutely convulsed in this process under the immensely powerful outworking of The Laws of Nature acting under The Creative Will. Quite logically, therefore, we, the inhabitants of the very small planet earth, can expect similar kinds of convulsions also, with a correspondingly large degree of dislocation and destruction *when that time eventually arrives*!

Now, being of the spirit in his inner animating core, and being of the material in his body of flesh, man, in reality, *stands in both parts at the same time*. With his origins from out of the Eternal Spiritual he has the potential to return there, and to reside eternally. With his other foot in the Material, however, he has an equal chance of remaining there tied, as it were, to it. The choice is solely his, and his alone. And therein lies *the key* to the understanding of the "second death".

In the granting of conscious life to humankind, and the accompanying formation of the Material Worlds for the many journeys man must make in order to spiritually develop and mature, The Spiritual Laws that govern this process also determine the total time of existence for this part of that World, in strict accordance with The Creative Will. Thus this earth, and therefore man on it, naturally have the exact same amount of allotted time – in terms of his total existence in this part of the Material World. At the close of that time period, it will undergo its disintegration phase too, exactly in accordance with the established Spiritual Laws which then transform the component pieces into a new part of the material world in a vast, *humanly-incomprehensible* cycle of birth, life and disintegration over a similarly stupendous time-frame.

Of course it should be realised that whilst such concepts of time are mind-boggling for humankind, in terms of eternity under The Creative Will it is not even a 'snap of the fingers'. Our general inability to come to terms with such a concept owes itself to the fact that the human spirit, even though possessing the *potential* to live *eternally* as a self-conscious personality, was never inherently so. We will therefore never be able to form a knowing concept of eternity. It will be forever beyond our grasp as we are merely 'developed' beings only, and not 'originally-created' ones as some might wish to believe.

Having thus established a basic framework of time through which the ramifications of the current subject can be further explored, let us continue our explanations. As previously stated, the precisely determined and ordained time of life for humankind on earth is necessarily exactly the same as the far larger and clearly defined part of the Material World *to which the earth belongs*. This fact decrees that that ordained time-span is naturally also the total amount of time given for our *spiritual maturation*. This period we can designate as part of the time of our *complete spiritual existence*.

As previously explained, also, the basic earthly concept of a *single lifetime* of birth, life and death is totally in error. One lifetime hardly suffices to gain even the faintest recognitions of Spiritual Truth. And since it is barely possible to become spiritually mature in the course of one lifetime, we are therefore able to designate a single-life time-period as being just a very small part of our complete existence.[3]

10.1   One Life – or Many Lives?

This sub-Chapter returns us to the contentious question of a single-life concept versus a multi-life one. As with other similar choices, what we determine for ourselves in terms of a 'belief of conviction' about this particular concept has a corresponding and natural flow-on effect into every other aspect of how we live our individual lives and how we relate to everything and everyone around us. The question of choice here is once again a **50%** one, but with the same **100% outcome**.

Therefore, just as a personal choice over the question of "life after death" might logically presuppose a certain attitude and lifestyle in its *100% acceptance*, so might the question of "one life versus many" also produce a particular conviction as to one's perceived purpose and final outcome in life. Yet the problem remains that if the *wrong 50% choice* is made – for whatever reason – that choice necessarily translates to being *100% wrong*, with all its attendant wrong opinions, views and, more importantly, the consequential reciprocal effect under the outworking of Spiritual Law.

Since we contend that it is not possible for the human spirit to acquire all the spiritual knowledge that it needs in one lifetime, we must therefore state our unshakeable *conviction* that the concept of multi-lives, or reincarnation, under the inviolable outworking of **The Spiritual Law of Rebirth**, is the *only* correct possibility. And thus the unequivocal and completely logical reality!

Thus have we chosen our 100% outcome!

Therefore:

> "Man is a spirit and his body is the dress, the clothes it wears while it is on the earth. Just as an earthman changes his clothes but remains the same person, so the human spirit changes his physical body in the process called death. But the spirit, the owner of the body, lives on after discarding the body.
>
> Belief in reincarnation is simply the acceptance of the knowledge that a human spirit, in one continuous existence, is given the opportunity to come to the earth more than once. On each occasion, the human spirit takes on a different human body.
>
> This simple concept is the key to the unravelling of many so-called mysteries, the explanations of the inequalities, apparent injustices and inequities that worry so many well-meaning people, and the understanding of some exceedingly important but difficult passages in the Bible. Reincarnation leads us to a conviction of *"the relative **insignificance** of tribe, race, and nationality"*, a conviction that is absolutely essential in moving mankind from its present-day chaos into a just and joyful social, political and economic order."

> (The Christian and Reincarnation, p.1, Stephen Lampe.
> Emphases mine.)

---

[3]The very foolish **R.I.P** [**Rest In Peace**] notion is one of the greatest barriers to crucial life-knowledge for all peoples.

The New Testament of The Bible offers an interesting insight into the thought processes of the people of the day regarding this belief, even with the disciples of Jesus. In the story of the healing of the blind man, the question the disciples put to Jesus regarding the reason why the beggar was *born blind* must clearly presuppose a belief and basic understanding that certain afflictions *can only be the result of a spiritual transgression from a previous life*. Conversely, an exceptional talent or genius in a particular field, such as that which child prodigies display, can stem from the *same* process. Thus we read:

> "His disciples accordingly asked Him: 'Teacher, who sinned; this man, or his parents, in consequence of which he was **born blind**?' "

It is clear that the disciples would *not* have asked this question if they did not believe that a man *could* be *born blind* as a *consequence* of a *previous sin* committed *elsewhere in time*. And therefore a *sin* that could *only* have been *committed* in a *previous life*, in order *to be born blind*. And, equally clearly, Jesus did not admonish them as fools for believing in such ostensibly 'stupid beliefs'. On the contrary, *in this particular case*, He informed them that:

> "Neither did *this man* sin, nor *his parents*," replied Jesus; "but he is so, in order that the workings of God may be displayed through him."

> (John 9:2-3, Fenton both. Emphases mine.)

The obvious connotation from this discourse between Jesus and His disciples is that **reincarnation was a fact of life for them** and, moreover, offered **exact reasons for hard afflictions** such as being born blind. Thus the puzzlement of the disciples over this man's blindness was not about *whether* reincarnation was factual or not, **but which of the two possibilities** might have caused his blindness.

The Old Testament offers a number of relevant passages about reincarnation also, a few of which we can include here. In narrating his call to prophethood, Jeremiah, (1:4-5) stated:

> Now the word of the Lord came to me saying, "Before I formed you in the womb, I knew you; and before you were born I consecrated you, and I appointed you a prophet to the nations."

From Malachi, (4:5) the case of the prophet Elijah is also worth analysing:

> "Behold, I will send you Elijah the Prophet before the great and terrible day of the Lord comes."

Whilst there might be uncertainty among some as to what the "great and terrible day of the Lord" refers to – the coming of Jesus, or to the Last Judgement of global humanity – there should be no uncertainty in the clear message that Elijah *would* be sent back to the earth again. During the period of Christ's ministry, some Jewish people interpreted that particular prophecy in the sense of a reincarnation in that he would be born as a baby. Matthew, (16:14) reports that some therefore thought that Jesus was a rebirth of Elijah:

> And they said, "Some say John the Baptist; some Elijah, and others, Jeremiah, or one of the prophets."

So here we have another strong reference that reincarnation was accepted by the people of that time as a factual reality. In the context of multi-earth lives, if we follow this basic thread about Elijah further, then the reply by Jesus to His disciples with regard to the identity of John the Baptist is especially revealing. Matthew again references Elijah in Verses 11:14-15: (Italics mine.)

"And *if you are willing to accept it*, he is Elijah who is to come. He that has ears to hear, let him hear."

Stephen Lampe, in his Book, "The Christian and Reincarnation", notes this key aspect from the same Scripture in "The Living New Testament" Bible.

"And if you are willing to understand what I mean, he is Elijah, the one the prophets said would come. And if ever you were ever willing to listen, listen now."

*   *   *   *   *

Do we find any such belief in Maori 'religious' thinking? In Chapter 7, "Whither Cometh the Maori", we examined an interesting statement of the Hauhau chief, Titokowaru, (his life and times in Chapter 18). Whilst Chapter 7 concerned our origins and the subsequent journey from a non-conscious "spirit-seed" to a human being 'conscious-of-self' on earth, the same statement from Titokowaru *hints* at possibly the 'thought' of multi-earth lives:

'I will never die, for I am a seed broadcast from heaven. I stand on Mt. Hikurangi in the land of light and enlightenment, although I am small in numbers and do not command great physical powers, *I will tread many waters of the world.*'

(Ratana Revisited... p.15, Keith Newman. Emphasis mine.)

*   *   *   *   *

The contentious question of reincarnation, especially for the many who subscribe to the widely accepted ideas current in Western 'materialistic' thought, has rarely been given the chance to be intelligently debated. Invariably, it has been dismissed as Eastern religious nonsense or, in the most extreme view expounded by some Western Churches, as something evil stemming from, or having connotations to, Satanism. To be totally dismissive of an idea in such a highly-emotive way might stem more from fear rather than rational or reasoned objectivity. Historically, the record of mankind reveals many instances of clinging to views that were clearly incorrect. But that unfortunate stance does not necessarily advance the cause of real knowledge for mankind.

*   *   *   *   *

Consider the flat earth theory held sacred for centuries, regardless of the beliefs of more intelligent and logical men. And remember that Socrates was killed because he 'disturbed' his fellow citizens more conventional ideas when he tried to light the way to "true insight". Or consider the trials of Dr. Joseph Lister, 1827-1912, (later Lord Lister) of England who for years attempted to enlighten his fellow doctors and surgeons to the fact that poor hygiene was actually *causing* the deaths of patients in operating theatres in British Hospitals. At that time, surgeons did not necessarily wash their hands before surgery, and neither was there a high priority placed on any kind of cleanliness of the operating tables or instruments. Gangrene and other infections were thought to be caused by 'bad air'. Yet despite Dr Lister's efforts to keep his new surgical rooms and instruments clean at the Glasgow Royal Infirmary, the mortality rate remained close to 50%.

Spraying the air with carbolic acid did not reduce rates of post-operative infection. Fortunately, however, in 1865 he came across the germ theory of Pasteur. Utilising this knowledge and applying carbolic acid to instruments and directly to wounds and dressings, Dr Lister reduced surgical mortality to 15% by 1869. His work in antisepsis met initial resistance, even after demonstrating increasing levels of patient recovery through his simple procedure. It was not until the 1880's that his methods were finally accepted by the 'medical establishment'.

*   *   *   *   *

Gaarder, a latter-day philosopher and author of "Sophie's World", in analysing the philosophy of Seren Kierkegaard, a Danish philosopher (1813-1855), noted Kierkegaard's belief that truth did not lie with the masses. His views suggested that:

"...the truth is always in the minority", and that "...the crowd is the untruth".

'Lone voices' standing outside the 'organism of the crowd' can sometimes launch huge changes in the consciousness of their fellow-men for the betterment of all. Of course, obvious physical changes cannot be so easily disputed in the same way that a physically intangible 'idea' can. And, like 'unseen germs', reincarnation might be deemed to fall into that category. Nevertheless, literally hundreds of millions of human beings over millennia have accepted reincarnation as a fact in their lives. And this could hardly be likened to a 'lone voice' situation. The *seeming* problem in reincarnation for most Westerners appears to relate to the many differing views that are offered as explanations or as fact about it. Some, of course, are clearly so bizarre as to be completely untenable.

But, as with all aspects of life and death, even the smallest ramifications of reincarnation are subject to the strict and inviolable outworking of Spiritual Law. The major difference between the respective religions of the Eastern and Western worlds is probably that of the *concept* of reincarnation.

Present Eastern religions generally state that the purpose of one's existence is to strive for release from the cycle of rebirth and therefore finally merge with the 'cosmic consciousness' and/or 'become one with God'. This state is achieved, for the most part, by self-communion and meditation.

On the other hand, the three great Western religions of Christianity, Islam and Judaism all share the same fundamental idea that there is only one God, and that there is a distance between God and His Creation. With this view, man's purpose is to seek redemption from sin and blame. And this is assisted by prayer and the study of the respective Scriptures. The Christian Church has the added aspect of 'faith and belief in the resurrection of Jesus'.

Of course, not all beliefs of reincarnation share exactly the same views about it. And, arguably, perhaps the most difficult aspect for the Western intellect to accept is a particular belief that promotes the view that we can return to earth in a form other than human. Either for lessons of experiencing in a 'personal-wish' situation, or being forced to in atonement under "The Iron Law of Karma" – **The Law of Reciprocal Action!**

You the reader will now be well familiar with our premise that only man possesses spirit as his "inner life-force". In a previous Chapter we outlined the reasons for this. Elsewhere in this Work, explanations as to how The Laws cannot be circumvented, including what we may regard as The Laws of Nature, are also given. Therefore, the inviolable and immutable nature of The Spiritual Laws absolutely decrees:

> **Beliefs which promote the notion that humans can somehow embark on some kind of cross-species transmigration into a life-form different to it is inherently and absolutely wrong.**

Whether that might be animate creature form or inanimate substance is immaterial. Despite the fact that such an impossible belief is actively promoted and believed by millions on earth, the whole idea, even through just *logical* thought-processes, is simply untenable.

The general thrust of life itself offers each species the natural ability to procreate or otherwise produce its own, irrespective of however diverse that ability might be for any given species. For only with that 'procreative reality' can any species exist. Any attempt to thus procreate across clearly defined natural barriers will ultimately fail.

One can quite easily observe this "naturally lawful fact" in one group of creatures alone – that of the animals. Even in those most closely related, such as in the cat family, the inability to produce offspring should be regarded as *clear proof* of the *inviolability* of any transgression of Natural Law, regardless of any particular faith/belief-mode outlook. Thus in the case of a 'liger' – a hybrid produced by the mating of a female tiger and a male lion – or a 'tigon' – the offspring of a male tiger and a female lion – we note that all offspring from either union are sterile. It is the same for the mule, a sterile hybrid of a male ass and a female horse. "Mother nature" does not permit cross-species tampering. And that is as it should be.

For if that were not the case, and different species were able to crossbreed with any other kind, we would not have a clear, consistent classification of fauna as we now have. In short, it would be disastrous. However, this does not remove the opportunity for natural change or mutation within each species, because that is simply the process of continual evolutionary development, an entirely different situation altogether. Therefore, according to "The Spiritual Rules" of the Creative-process for all things, we can only be re-born into *human form*!

Now, since the idea of a "second death" necessarily travels into the area of multi-lives, it behoves the need to give sufficient explanation to this subject, but not to the point, however, where every aspect of every question about it is investigated. The "second death" outlined here, moreover, is not the same as that which Jesus alluded to in His enlightening statement when He proclaimed to Nicodemus:

> *"Most assuredly I tell you, that unless anyone is born from above, he cannot see the Kingdom of God."*

> (John 3:3, Fenton.)

That particular "birth" is a *spiritual* or *inner awakening* or *realisation* and does not, in any way, conflict with multi-earth lives which are obviously physical births.

For the reader who might want to examine these same questions that have puzzled great thinkers and Church leaders for centuries, and wish to be finally offered the explanations that eluded those learned individuals, he should examine the work, "The Christian and Reincarnation" by Stephen Lampe, (Millennium Press). This well researched document, with much of the material culled from The Bible, will clarify many uncertainties for the serious seeker as to the validity and purpose of reincarnation, and will provide a disturbing challenge to those who might wish to scornfully dismiss the concept out of hand.

As a prime example, let us examine just one particularly vital aspect of this subject from Stephen Lampe's work. It will supply the reader with an explanation of how the early Church determined its final position on this matter of reincarnation. We should also recognise that there have always been, and there currently still are, a number of very eminent Christian church leaders who have publicly stated their support for reincarnation, with the further far-reaching view that the concept **does not** contradict the teachings of The Bible.

As well, many eminent people from all walks of life believe it also, and recognise within it the inherent sense of *true Justice* which reincarnation offers. Therefore, if we are to fully understand how there can be so many apparent social injustices and inequities amongst the world's peoples when we speak of absolute Justice contained within The Spiritual Laws, and how there can be a "second death" separate and distinct from being re-born "spiritually", then we must openly and objectively examine this matter of reincarnation.

Since the generally accepted orthodox Christian view is to basically deny or refute the validity of such an idea, even with some of its leading clergy accepting of it, a need to define a starting point by which we might gain some insight into how the official Church position arose is vital. Stephen Lampe offers clarification about it on page 8 & 9 in Chapter 1 of his book, "The Christian and Reincarnation."

The Second Council of Constantinople (553 AD)

"The history of the official Church position on reincarnation is a very complex one. Many assume that the Second Council of Constantinople (552 AD) also called the Fifth Ecumenical Council of the Church, condemned the teaching of reincarnation, but this assumption has been called into question by some competent church historians.

The Second Council of Constantinople was called by Emperor Justinian and convened on 5th May 553 AD under the presidency of the Patriarch of Constantinople. However it was the Emperor, who had engaged in bitter conflict with Pope Vigilius, who controlled the proceedings. Even though the primary objective was to reconcile the churches of the East and West, the arrangements heavily favoured the East. It is reported that of the 165 bishops who signed the acts of the final meeting on 2nd June, not more than six could have been from the West. The request of Pope Vigilius for equal representation of bishops from East and West was refused. In protest, the Pope boycotted the meeting, even though he was in Constantinople, the venue of the meeting. However Pope Vigilius eventually accepted the decisions of the Council, an action that was not popular in the West, and which caused some dioceses, including that of Milan, to break off communion with Rome. Milan remained out of communion with Rome till the end of the sixth century.

Because of the protestations of Pope Vigilius, the Second Council of Constantinople did not open on schedule. While the assembled bishops were waiting Emperor Justinian ordered them to consider a subject (Origenism) that was not an item in the previously announced agenda. During this extra-conciliary session, fifteen condemnations (anathemas) proposed by the Emperor against the teachings of Origen (who had died three hundred years earlier in 254 AD) were approved. Apparently, one of the condemned teachings was the idea of pre-existence of the soul, and by implication, reincarnation. There is no evidence that Pope Vigilius, who was at the time protesting against the arrangements of the Council approved this action taken by Eastern bishops outside the formal sessions and before the opening of the Council. Thus, it is understandable that some Catholic scholars dissociate the Roman Church from the condemnations of the teachings of Origen, and therefore argue that the Roman Catholic Church has never really condemned the teaching of reincarnation.

Many otherwise knowledgeable Christians are unaware of the confusion surrounding the Second Council of Constantinople and the inconclusiveness and uncertainty of its decisions. For this reason, some imagine that they are obliged to uphold this ancient condemnation of reincarnation.

In any case Christians should appreciate that they should not necessarily consider themselves bound by decisions taken by some bishops more than 1,400 years ago. Did not the Church condemn Galileo's scientific support of the Copernican theory that the sun, and not the earth is the centre of the solar system? And the ordinary Christians of that day of course dutifully joined Church officials in denouncing the Copernican theory. Christians at that time probably imagined that an idea which contradicts The Scriptures must have been put in the mind of Copernicus by Satan! Today some Christians, unfortunately, have a similar view of reincarnation."

One of the main points of interest regarding this important meeting was the fact that such an incredibly far-reaching and definitive decision could have been taken in a side issue separate from the main agenda. The either/or aspect of a one-life concept versus a multi-life one decided that day actually calls into question the very essence of much of Bible teaching, the cornerstone on which rest many of our beliefs and ideals.

For a few men to therefore cast the disturbing shadow of such a definitive decree down through the centuries surely smacks of religious machinations. One might question the true motives of the Roman Emperor Justinian in *ordering* the bishops to consider condemning, among the other fifteen 'anathemas', the concept of reincarnation. Perhaps the idea of being forced to "reap what one sowed" in future lives, with the probability of some of those incarnations being lived out in less than favourable circumstances was, in itself, considered blasphemous to one very much accustomed to living a role of absolute power and obscene wealth. The possibility of anything less than that must have been 'anathema' in this case, since the line of Roman Emperors were once considered to be Divine and descended from the gods themselves.

So perhaps the very thought of reincarnation and atonement for an Emperor's perhaps debased excesses needed to expunged from the day consciousness of the Empire in general. From the spiritual point of view of course, no amount of legislation, debate or decree could have possibly altered the fact of The Law of Rebirth. And even a mighty Roman Emperor must obey this Law too.

Notwithstanding this decree, Stephen Lampe observes that:

> "Finally, Church historians point out that no papal encyclical against reincarnation has ever been issued – a point that should be of particular interest to Roman Catholics. (p.11) Thus Christianity embraced reincarnation for three hundred years before the Emperor Justinian declared it 'anathema'."

We should therefore *re-expand* our horizons to encompass the recognition that only repeated earth-lives offer the human spirit the means whereby it is *able* to accumulate sufficient experiences "of the spirit" to gain true spiritual insight as to its origin and purpose, thereby enabling it to develop genuine spiritual maturity. The intervals between incarnations should be regarded as a very necessary time of learning also, as the life experienced in the 'beyond' will be as a direct result of the *kind of life* lived whilst on earth under the outworking of The Laws of "**Sowing and Reaping**", "**Attraction**" and "**Spiritual Gravity**".

Each further earth-life, also strictly governed by The Eternal Laws, will bring the soul to the circumstances of family and race etc., that it will need for its further maturing. Either in terms of its own learning, to provide the same for others in its new environment, or to expiate past misdeeds there.

Whatever the reason he incarnates, it can only be in accordance with the strictness of The Spiritual Laws, so he will be *justly placed* in terms of circumstances and the requirement *to experience the reciprocal effects of that which he once sowed*. Purification of the whole person is a necessary part of the overall learning process, provided, of course, that the path taken for this purpose truly aspires to "genuine spirituality". Even if this were not voluntarily the case, the same Laws would work on regardless, thus still bringing to that particular individual, at the appropriate time, the consequences of all his previous decisions.

Now, because our inherent free-will endowment determines what will return to us under The Spiritual Laws, this 'constant-return process' takes effect whether we are on the earth or in the "planes of the beyond".

Thus we continually stand in the reciprocal effect – as the central focus – of all our past decisions.

Not necessarily the return effect of all at once, but nevertheless in whatever is lawfully ordained for that particular point in time. In this lawful and completely inviolable process, *there is no escape*!

As we generally vacillate between making good and bad decisions, we can naturally expect a life of changing fortunes. Therefore, some will always be better off than others at any given moment, and some will be worse off, simply by virtue of the reciprocal effect of The Spiritual Laws. That is the reality for all. Since changing fortunes are a fact of life for most people, the concept of repeated earth-lives not only provides clear solutions to the worrying problems and trends current on the earth, but allows us an insight into the Wisdom and Grace of The Creative Will in granting humankind the opportunity to 'make good' all past mistakes. We must do so in any case, if we are not to suffer potentially hard fate continually.

With regard to the changing fortunes of the numerous philosophical ideas throughout history, Kierkegaard, in fine contrast to what we affirm, believed that we are "...all unique individuals who only live once". He also attacked the reliance on ritual and dogma in Christianity, and what he thought was essentially the empty faithlessness of the adherents. He believed they had to do more than just believe 'Christianity' is true. In his view, having a Christian faith meant following 'a Christian way of life'. Kierkegaard, who rejected the basic thrust of 'Hegelianism', also thought that the individual is "...responsible for his own life".

Under the outworking of The Spiritual Laws, and in concert with the need to accept *spiritual responsibility* for the *consequences* of one's 'lived-life', belief in a single life and death concept *only* would thus be difficult to reconcile.

It is therefore imperative to *recognise the need* to make good one's transgressions. Once we have left the relative protection of the physical body at earthly death, it is too late to then lament the fact that we were too disbelieving, too superficial, too blind and stubborn to accept any other views than those we *personally* wanted to believe. For in the far more *mobile* environment of the non-material world, all movement, even the effect of ones thoughts, are 'speeded-up' considerably. So, too, are the waiting reciprocal effects for the individual. Life in the physical body in the more ponderous world of the earth at least allowed a 'stay of proceedings', so to speak.

That is precisely why the time spent on earth is crucial for correct decision-making, particularly at this point in the evolutionary development of this material part of Creation to which we and the earth physically belong. Therefore, good decisions will bring good returns. And unless one were completely insane, in which case one could not personally be held spiritually accountable for one's actions, one would logically wish to be treated with respect and kindness by ones fellow men. For no normal person would wish for thuggery and violence to be visited upon him. Yet so many are prepared to do exactly that to their fellows.

Notwithstanding the dark deeds of our fellow 'travellers', from our explanations of the death process under the aegis of The Law of Spiritual Gravity, we know that lighter spiritual thoughts and deeds produce a corresponding lightness of the soul, and darker, heavier thoughts and actions produce the opposite. And we also know that through personal choices derived from earthly lifestyle, heavier souls sink to the level corresponding to their 'commensurate spiritual weight', there to live out 'chosen propensities' with like-minded souls. It is especially important to understand that such a level still remains in the *Material Sphere* for its composition is that of 'fine matter'. And all souls inhabiting these particular levels are necessarily subject to whatever 'finite' fate may befall them. That is not the case with souls who gravitate to higher, lighter planes, however.

There, the more spiritually enlightened thus more fortunate souls are not oppressed like those in the darker regions; they who have surrendered their free-will choices to baser propensities. Unlike those ones, the souls who have earned the right to ascend to the higher levels are more easily able to continually further ascend to the region of Light that is above the pull of the Material World and its finite time. By becoming sufficiently enlightened whilst on earth, and living correspondingly similar thoughts and deeds, such souls automatically guarantee themselves an ascent into lighter planes after earthly death.

Horizons there are vastly more expansive than for those who languish in the much more restrictive environment of the lower, darker planes. The great joy and happiness that inherently exists in the lighter planes imparts the natural wish to want more of the same, thus allowing still further ascent. The souls who have chosen the experience of the lower levels, set in place by their personal wish for the exact same things whilst on earth, enjoy no such peace. Theirs is literally the torment of being inflicted upon by others in the same way that they once did. Yet the Law of Grace gives even these sad ones the choice to leave their surroundings behind.

As a precursor to providing definitive explanations about the "second death", it is timely to examine more closely the 'awakening' in the beyond of a previously disbelieving soul just released from his physical body. Firstly with such a soul, however, let us re-visit the process and consider, once more, some of the things he may experience in the moments before burial when 'friends' and relatives arrive to pay their 'respects'.

This usually difficult time invariably produces the whole range of emotional reactions in the psyche of the bystanders to the event. Human emotions at such times will run the full gamut from deep and genuine grief, to curiosity, to superficiality, sometimes to anger and sometimes to gladness. However, what is generally not accepted is that the 'departed one' can still see and hear all that takes place around his 'discarded shell'. So one can easily imagine his reaction to eulogies and speeches in his memory or honour etc., particularly when those whom he believed he knew well whilst on earth now perhaps reveal a different side to their character.

In some cases, he could well re-evaluate the relationship of those kinds of people. Sadly for him, however, it would be virtually impossible to express gratitude to those who might now reveal genuine respect and friendship towards him; those whom he did not realise held him in high regard when he was alive. To all intents and purposes, his visitors – both the genuine and the superficial – believe him to be dead, and he has no way of proving to them that he is still 'living'.

The reader will recall the "Silver Cord" being a mediating connection to the earthly organs of sight and speech through still being attached to the physical shell. Via this means it is possible for the departed one to see and hear all that takes place around him. However, he is unable to make himself heard or felt by others still alive around him *because he no longer stands in a body of the same consistency as the material world* and therefore cannot 'touch' anything of the material earth, including his loved ones.

Because of the lawful outworking of The Spiritual Laws in this all-too-common situation, it should not be difficult to picture the anguish of the departed one as he follows the whole procedure of his own funeral, even, yet is unable to offer clarification or help about his situation to those most affected. Thus we can relate to him as he attends the burial of his earthly shell, and empathise with him at the moment of greatest grief; when the casket is lowered! One can picture him in a state of great despondency and desolation at this time. After a while, tiredness would overtake him and he might find some solace in sleep.[4]

When this soul finally severs itself from its tie to its former physical body – via the disintegration of the "Silver Cord" – it will invariably find itself in a plane closely corresponding to its previous state of 'attitudinal-volition' during earthly life. If this had been one of disbelief or disinterest in "life after death" then, when he awakens, he will be surrounded by darkness, but will discover that he is no longer connected to his physical shell. He is free, but in a strange and silent oppressive darkness where he cannot even hear the sound of his own voice. And no matter what he may wish to believe about his situation, still the darkness presses in on him.

In its new and unfortunate surroundings, the soul 'lives' as it did on earth. For this is *the real person*, only now, freed from his physical body. He experiences all the travails and joys in his soul-body in the same way that he experienced life in his physical one, and he weeps, laughs, tires and sleeps. For his new world is just as real as the physical one recently left behind, purely because his new body is of the exact same *consistency* as his surroundings. Whilst his new body is not a physical one, it is not his spirit-body either, for he is still very far from the true Spiritual Realm from where he originated. His spirit – the real he – is still the *inner animating core* of his new body. This 'new body', however, is subject to the much faster vibration of the non-physical world of the "beyond" – his world at this time.

His 'faster environment' may induce a stronger urge to find out *why* than might have been the case on earth, and he may seek answers *more desperately*. But *how* to know exactly what to seek? He only knows that he **needs** answers to his plight. We can readily understand that the restless need to seek is borne of desperation to find an explanation for his rather sad circumstances. Yet to find an answer may take such a soul years, even decades, for time has a

---

[4]The reader may find this curious but, just as the physical body tires through exertion, so will the soul-body.

vastly different meaning outside the physical realm. But until such time as genuine yearning to be free wells up in the soul of one in this position, all he can look forward to is the continuing condition of dark uncertainty. We can be sure, also, that much 'soul-searching' would take place as he struggles to understand what had brought about his sorry plight. Hopefully, it will bring about the realisation that this must be the "other world" that he had never been able to believe in!

Such an inner awakening thought must surely presuppose the dawning of the recognition for this soul of obviously still being alive, yet clearly physically dead. But even that realisation may not be *sufficiently strong* to bring about a *change* in his conditions. The simple wish for change must further develop into a *deep longing* from which springs a genuine petition for help, even if only a timid prayer at first. For such a longing is suffused with 'the purer intuition born of desperate need'.

Finally, with the entry of humility and submission into his soul resulting from a genuine prayer for help, the outworking of Grace upon him and his surroundings takes immediate effect because he has now begun to establish a connection, albeit a tenuous one at this time, with the higher and lighter Spiritual Spheres of Love and Grace. Consequently for this soul, the darkness would then give way to a kind of twilight. He would feel a corresponding lightness in his 'body', and experience a sense of soothing comfort. Now he can take stock of his surroundings and is better able to determine his next move.

The 'lightening' of his surroundings also allows him a glimpse of a light in the far distance. That far-away light becomes a beacon of hope and a means of understanding his new world. It is the only point of welcoming focus. The light comes no nearer to him but he intuitively knows that he must journey towards it, for he recognises that it will lead him out of his 'twilight zone'. Thus, gratitude and humility would begin to suffuse this soul as it senses more strongly **The Gift of Grace** granted to it.

Humility, as an attribute and quality of the greatest power – Love – is a most necessary trait to develop if one seeks spiritual ascent. To practise opposite traits such as arrogance and cynicism with regard to Spiritual Truth will ensure similar kinds of experiences for such believers as those outlined here. Whilst our example is basically that of the initial experiences of a soul in the Ethereal World of the "beyond", they could not be said to be those of a 'bad' person, just one who had given no thought to his fate after earthly death; one who did not want to be 'bothered with it'.

Thus, anyone who in his earth life refuses to acknowledge that there is also "life after death", or that there is a concomitant requirement to one day render account for all that he has done and all that he has left undone, is *blind and deaf* when he finally passes over into the Ethereal World of the "beyond". Only for the time that he remains connected with his discarded physical body can he still *partially observe* events around him.

Once he is freed from his disintegrating physical body, however, this possibility is lost to him and he *no longer* sees or hears anything. Yet that should not be viewed as punishment. On the contrary, it should be recognised as a perfectly natural consequence of his own attitude toward "life after death" whilst he lived. Because he refused to 'believe', which is tantamount to 'blindness' and 'deafness', he thus 'forms' for himself his future ethereal environment which he must fully experience if there is no change from his 'disbelieving position' before his death. After that transition, *only a change in his soul will allow him to see and hear again*.

The necessary condition for such a change after earthly death is the *desire of the individual* to **want** *to change his circumstances*. The time frame for this also depends upon him solely. It may take years or decades, perhaps even longer, but is the concern of the individual alone. The exercise of his personal free will brought him there in the first place, and can also release him from it – *if* he so desires, but it cannot be forced upon him. The light that the soul was finally permitted to see as a result of his inner change, was *always there*, but his *spiritual condition* prevented him from seeing it. The *condition* of the soul determines **how** he sees it – whether strong, or weak, or not at all!

The example we have outlined shows a soul experiencing the outworking of The Law of Sowing and Reaping in stark relief. It received what it had wished, thus what it brought to itself in accordance with that wish, simply because it had refused to believe in the reality of "life after death".

What should be clearly and fully understood is: *The soul <u>cannot</u>, by any means, <u>abolish</u> the continuation of life for itself at "the First Death"*.[5]
The reason is beautifully simple and final: *It [the soul] has absolutely <u>no</u> jurisdiction over the lawful processes whatsoever!* Disbelief of this fact cannot alter that lawful outcome by one single dot!

This knowledge must be regarded as the key consideration as to how one should resolve to live one's life. Not from fear or half-truths, but from true knowledge in the realisation that we simply cannot alter The Spiritual Laws to suit our personal wishes. A human soul, purely via his inherent free-will ability, can bring himself to *either* a dark or light region in the Ethereal World. Even if finding himself in the former, all that is required to ascend out of such a place is to will the necessary change in a spiritually-pure volition of genuine humility in the recognition that he and he alone was responsible for the circumstances of his condition. With this first and most necessary step, he can begin the process of ascending out of the lower, material spheres of the beyond to the higher, lighter planes, far from the inexorable and ordained path of the earth and its inter-stellar environs as *it* tracks towards *its* time of disintegration.

If this is the position in which a relatively 'decent' individual in the earthly sense would find himself after death, how much more dire would the situation be for those whose lives are given over to total baseness? We would have to conclude that in their regions of darkness, there would probably not be any light to speak of! Now, we may begin to understand why Jesus was so severe in His admonishing of those who were not prepared to change their ways, for He surely understood all of the Law and its strict justice.

*　　*　　*　　*　　*

These explanations allow us to easily picture the fate of the 'old Maori' in the various planes of the Ethereal World. They, along with other like-minded ones who immersed themselves in savage practices of *blood-utu* and cannibalism, would have descended to lower regions of darkness after earthly death. There to live out the reciprocal effects of their self-willed and self-chosen, destructive path.

*　　*　　*　　*　　*

But if even a relatively half-decent life brings about a sad and less than satisfactory outcome, it should remind each individual to carefully consider his attitude toward this inevitable event called death. Just as important for parents and society in general is the necessary schooling and explanation about it for the young. Via this recognition and educative method, we would probably lessen the unacceptably high rate of youth suicide, and thus beneficially change the very nature of society itself. For all suicides bring to those sad souls a most difficult outcome 'after the fact'.

---

[5]The term, "First Death", in our explanations, does not mean just *one* single death only in one's total existence. The term refers to the process of earthly death for *each* incarnation; as opposed to the *one single reality* of the "Second Death" for the very many who will experience it at some future point.

Unfortunately, such souls as described in our example probably make up many, many millions on the earth today. They have no wish to learn about God, spiritual things, or eternity, yet may be good and decent people. However, since The Laws have the *final say* in all matters human, how much worse must be the end-fate of those who are just plain evil-minded. Aside from those who actively promote their particular religious beliefs, many people are reluctant to even acknowledge the need to think about such things from time to time.

*   *   *   *   *

As a reflective assessment of this insidious trend, perhaps we should collectively consider the effect of slowly but surely stripping away from our schools the once regular practice of Biblical or religious instruction and prayer. Then, at least, there was a *basic* societal recognition of a Creator and inviolable Laws recognised by far more people than might accept such a view today. For in the present climate of so much illogical and foolish 'political-correctness', such ideas are more likely to be deemed superfluous and thus unimportant for today's more 'enlightened times' of 'economic roulette' on 'corporate earth'. Too many forces within our present society deem 'religion' unnecessary for society's continuing function.[6]

Interestingly, Ferrar Fenton, from whose vital Bible we have mainly quoted, states, in his introductory notes, that Professor Karl Behr of Munich argued for the retention of religion within the state or society if it was to survive. Fenton noted to an enquiring friend that on the Philosophy of History, Professor Behr observed:

> "That the best-established doctrine of Historical Philosophy was, that all the power, prosperity, and mental energy of a Race or Nation sprang from and lived by its Religion; that when its Religion ceased to be its Faith – that is, its energising principle – the intellect, power, vigour, and prosperity of that Race or Nation died away in proportion, and ultimately perished, both mentally and physically."

And Fenton further observed:

> "...how he illustrated his doctrine by a wide survey and a series of illustrations from the history of all nations, Asiatic, African, and European, both Ancient and Modern, dwelling especially upon the fact that this *Law of National Life* did not depend upon any particular Religion, but was manifested by them all, Pagan, Jewish, Mohammedan, and Christian?"

(Fenton Bible, Explanatory Note, p.xi,
Italics mine.)

Fenton goes on to say that Professor Behr's doctrine "...did not urge a regard to that Law of History for any ecclesiastical purpose..." for he was not a professed member of any particular Christian Church. Professor Behr therefore emphasised that Law by a review of the Arabian Civilisation under the Kaliphat.

Note:

It might surprise many readers to learn that when Cecil B. DeMille's 'epic' Hollywood production of **The Ten Commandments** screened in the late 1950's or thereabouts, many High and Intermediate classes from Schools throughout New Zealand dutifully trooped to their local cinema/s to see it. The, then, religious/social climate of the country producing high Church

---

[6]Headlines – CNN.com – **Harvard committee recommends returning religion to curriculum.** "Harvard University, founded 370 years ago to train Puritan ministers, should again require all undergraduates to study religion, along with U.S. history and ethics, a faculty committee is recommending."

attendance and regular Sunday School sessions – which many of us tried to run away from – virtually guaranteed that Education Boards would deem it proper and correct for pupils to see such a movie. For it was a time when, as a matter of course, Head Prefects read from The Bible at 'Morning Assembly'.

Were there to be a remake of the same picture today with the super-wizardry of digital special-effects to greatly enhance the power of the presentation, would 'Today's Schools' – which recently were 'Tomorrow's Schools' – send their pupils to see it in 'school time'. No, of course not. The politically-correct 'Air-head brigade' would deem it too religious. But therefore, however, through crass 'intellectual blindness', miss the primary point completely – i.e., vital knowledge pertaining to **The One Law** for all humankind.

Instead, we solely teach 'knowledge of the genome', with which science can play and spend millions of research dollars; all the while foolishly believing that *inanimate*, thus *non-living*, matter can somehow will *itself* to *animate* itself. Moreover, if we delve deeply enough into the subatomic world even to below that of quarks and neutrinos, we might even find that final and singularly-infinitesimal 'life-point'. At least that is the vain hope of earth science. A fruitless quest *if* it is the *actual* life-force that science seeks to discover therein. So:

"How did *non-living* material come to life?" Thus asks the National Geographic Documentary Channel. That question we have already pointedly answered!

*   *   *   *   *

What Professor Behr refers to as a *Law of National Life* is, of course, a Spiritual Law. His revealing insight offers clear reasons for an acceptance and adjustment to The True Laws for the betterment, and indeed survival, of our society and Nation! The correct teaching of The Spiritual Laws across 'the whole spectrum of society', including the *lawful processes* surrounding the First and Second Deaths, would empower individuals within that society to be more accepting of the inevitable, thus leading to far fewer human souls 'trapped' in the close environs of the earth.

That totally unnecessary situation for the very many who are, takes us into the next issue which requires serious examination – how those souls become 'earthbound' – before finally explaining the actual meaning of the "second death".

10.2   Earthbound

The term 'earthbound' is one with which many are possibly familiar but are perhaps not completely sure of the processes that determine the 'binding'. Much has been disseminated about such situations but with little real knowledge as to why! The many recorded cases of hauntings, of poltergeist activity etc., whilst being true enough, do not give the full picture at all.

Actually, these kinds of 'noisy' activities concern only a very small number of souls. The vast majority of the 'earthbound' continue their particular activities without humankind being aware that they are about. At various times the close presence of one may be 'sensed', and people with clairvoyant or psychic ability can see them on occasions. With all processes and activities in Creation, however, the reason for the close presence of one will be subject to strict Spiritual Law, and will invariably be associated with land, a place or dwelling, a person or persons in that particular place, or with an activity there to which the 'earthbound' one is drawn. There may be other reasons but these are the general ones.

In the first place, there should not be cause for fear if a poor 'earthbound soul' is recognised as being about, because the binding of one to the earth is a perfectly natural process, and many alive today may well find themselves tied to the earth after their time of death too. Whilst we know that this should not be the normal process, nevertheless, it is brought about, once more, by man's refusal to live correctly according to Spiritual Law. The knowledge of that Law would help him to leave behind all pointless and unnecessary ties to the earth. A few brief examples as to how this sorry state can come about may offer some clarification of the process.

Let us examine the case, unfortunately all too common, where a questioning child is continually told by his parents that there is no such thing as "life after death". In the beginning the child may intuitively sense that there is such a thing, or may have heard about it from school or in church. Uncertain, he seeks confirmation of it from his parents, let us say his father. The father, through his own fear or lack of interest in the matter, dismisses the whole idea of it and forcefully imparts this view to the child. With continual reinforcement of this belief, the child begins to doubt, until finally accepting the opinion of adults that there is "no life after death".

But the time comes when the father dies and, much to *his* horror and dismay, finds that death is not the end after all. The deep wish now arises within the father to impart the truth of this to his child, and this strong desire binds him to it. But the child can neither hear him nor sense his presence, for it now has the firm conviction that his father has ceased to exist. This conviction acts as a completely natural and impenetrable wall between the child and the father's efforts. Now the father must live the painful reality that, through misleading his child, there is the very real danger that he may take a path leading him further and further from the truth. Moreover, as the child grows into adulthood and gathers future generations around him, the same misleading error is passed on through them with the added danger of that offspring, through its increasingly narrowing perceptions, falling further.

Perhaps this is one meaning of the "sins of the father" visiting themselves upon successive generations. In any case, this forms the father's so-called 'punishment' for misleading his child. In such circumstances, it would be extremely difficult for him to impart this knowledge to his offspring. Consequently, he will be forced to witness how his wrong idea is carried on down through the generations, and all as a result of his own disbelief. Unfortunately for him, however, he cannot be released until one of his descendants finally recognises the error and adjusts his life to the right way – hopefully also influencing the others. Only then will the father be gradually released and can begin to consider his own need for ascent.

A very typical and more insidious way in how one can be earthbound is through the connection to cigarette smoking. It is a situation that impacts hugely and detrimentally in two ways, physically in the first instance, and spiritually in the second. An habitual smoker who dies takes over with him the strong craving to smoke. In its strength, it is actually a propensity which thus has a connection to the "spiritual intuition", albeit only at its outermost edge. His propensity produces the need for gratification and he seeks out smokers. There he is able to satisfy his craving because the changed nature of his 'body' after earthly death enables him to enjoy *the inner sensations of smokers* to whom he is held.

If there is no stronger reciprocal effect waiting to bind him to any other place, the sensations he feels are, for him, generally pleasant ones, so such souls may not be aware that being tied to others on the earth through their propensity is actually a punishment. This is also the case with drinking and aberrant sexual desires, though given the heavy emphasis today on ones 'right' to sexual gratification by any means, many might not consider this last a punishment at all. Yet any binding to the earth prevents such souls from recognising that their primary 'craving', which overshadows all else, is actually a punishment stemming solely from *their own personal decisions*. Consequently, the longing for something better, more noble and higher, cannot easily develop to become the main focus which would then free such souls from base desires and uplift them.

Yet even if the primary desire should reach a point where it begins to die away, other former but lesser desires which he still carries within him may then rise to take the place of the original strongest propensity, and subsequently transport him to a place where his lesser desires can then be lived through, but hopefully expiated also. Eventually, with sufficient good will for his own ascent, he will finally succeed in clearing all the dross that had previously prevented any chance of release from his bind to the earth. For only when the earthly sensations are gradually outlived or let go, associated with a longing for what is higher, purer and therefore more spiritual, can he steadily ascend. The variations here will be many but these few examples illustrate the *kinds* of circumstances that can allow a soul to become 'earthbound'.

10.3   The "Second Death" Process

Now, in order to understand the Scriptural warning of the "second death" and the actual process of it, we must again revisit the concept of reincarnation. It is a concept that needs to be recognised as, or likened to, a 'school of learning'. Thus, each earth-life lived represents a class or stage in which our spiritual development can be furthered – if we so choose. But we should not be so naive as to believe that each successive incarnation *automatically* places us on the next highest step. Whilst that may be a desirable idea, and one that has its adherents in some religious beliefs, the reality is vastly different. With each earth-life, we are *given the opportunity* to re-awaken and once again advance, nothing more. In *every* case, in every incarnation, we must *recognise the purpose* for which we were born, and *live accordingly*. Therefore, to this earthly school, we must return a number of times.

The 'extra classes' allow us more time to learn and to fulfil our spiritual purpose, thus helping our ascent. But it is equally true that one may *never* recognise the purpose for which one was incarnated, irrespective of how many 'classes' one might 'attend', and consequently continually gravitate toward base or even evil pursuits. This kind of path helps to re-strengthen quite unnecessary binds to the material, from which one will need to strive harder to break away if one wishes to ascend out of the final chaos of the earth.

Finally, after many 'classes', examination day for everyone arrives. The result will determine whether one graduates from the 'school' and achieves spiritual freedom, or whether one fails to pass the 'examination' and remain behind. With regard to we human beings currently in material Creation, the examination is now due, with fewer opportunities for a 'recount'. This 'reality' is reflected in the increasing problems within society, and in the enormous amount of *reaping in suffering* that we witness daily on a global scale. As previously stated, the length of time under which our 'school' was ordained to run for is exactly that of the equally ordained time of life for this part of material Creation to which the earth, our 'classroom', belongs.

Thus, whilst the Grace of being able to "right past wrongs" is a constant promise, the time available for any such expiation **is precisely that under which the material part of the world is ordained to exist as our physical home**. At the end of the allotted time, everything that is part of that 'materiality' or connected to it **will go through the disintegration process**.

The first stage, however, **which is already under way**, is the necessary "cleansing of the earth" of all spiritually-wrong concepts and activities, along with their very many human architects and supporters. That will allow *those* human spirits – whose wish and volition to live spiritually-purer than *this sick, totally aspiritual, money and power-driven global society will currently permit them* – to produce the kind of world that was ordained from the very beginning. Notwithstanding the fact that the *actual disintegration of the earth and its interstellar environs at its time of renewal is far in the future*, we should be under no illusions as to what the first stage, the "cleansing of the earth", really means for us.

*It means destruction of man and his works on a scale not previously seen **or even imagined!*** For the greater number who will *not survive*, however, that will simply be just the "First Death".

So unless those of us who might succumb have reached a sufficient degree of spiritual maturity and inner purity – that which we need to take us above the pull of the earth – any human spirits who have not managed or not bothered to spiritually mature sufficiently enough *will be caught up in the destruction* **at the time destined for it to occur**. Yet it should always be remembered that this whole process is a completely natural one, even if difficult to comprehend in terms of reason or scale.

Now we have reached the stage where a *definitive conclusion* to the meaning of the "second death" can be offered. What is vital to understand here is that whilst the *earth* is the obvious home of mankind in the material sense, and the *Ethereal World* is the transitional experiencing plane for souls in the beyond, both "planes" or "spheres" belong *solely* to the "non-eternal" *Material Part* of Creation. The true Spiritual Realm stands far higher in "The Eternal".

Thus from its earliest beginnings the Material Creation was inexorably bound to the unalterable Spiritual Laws, which also bring about evolution and dissolution. As already noted, what are referred to as The Laws of Nature are, in reality, the "expression of the **Will of God** on earth"! In its expressionistic activity, therefore, it is continually forming and dissolving worlds, exactly as astronomers observe. Moreover, this Creative Will, out of which the Ethereal World of the beyond and the Material World of the earth plane were created *as one interconnected whole*, is *uniform* throughout all of Creation.

We have previously delineated the differences between that which is Eternal and that which is not eternal, and outlined the need for the human spirit to lift itself above the pull of the non-eternal material so as to escape the natural disintegration process of this particular part of Material Creation when it occurs. And in a time scale that we can never ever comprehend it is necessary to *strive* to understand that only the **cycle** of Creation is eternal here, and not necessarily the life of individual component parts of the material worlds. Only in a 'continuous' coming-into-being, disintegration and re-formation is the 'cycle' Eternal and without end, and thus infinite.

It is within this happening, therefore, that all the many revelations and prophecies are fulfilled. And within this framework, also, there one day comes the last i.e., the final 'sorting out' for each material celestial globe. However, whilst this does not take place simultaneously in the whole of Creation, it is a process connected with that part of Creation which reaches the point in its cycle where its disintegration must occur, so that it can once more begin the process of renewal in the fulfilment of the Eternal Cycle.

It should be further understood that in strict accordance with the consistency of the Natural Laws, the exact point at which disintegration of each celestial globe must begin is precisely determined. Most importantly for humankind, therefore, and **irrespective** of the **condition** of the **celestial globe concerned** – or of its **inhabitants** – the process of *disintegration* must develop at a very definite point in time. In accordance with The Spiritual Laws, the Eternal cycle drives every celestial globe irresistibly towards this point, enabling its particular hour of disintegration to be fulfilled. However, as with everything in Creation, this actually represents simply a transformation – albeit a mighty one – providing the opportunity for further development.

Once that collective point of its ordained evolutionary development is reached, however, this Material part of Creation, along with the earth and all its inhabitants then, will be 'ripe' for the final 'sorting'. That is the moment of our 'either/or' – our final **50% Choice** and **100% Outcome!**

Either we are raised upwards to the Light if we have followed a spiritual path or, if we have become convinced that material or aspiritual considerations are more important or more valuable, we are held fast to the World of Matter until the time when it must go through its disintegration process. Therefore, through our own wish to seek things other than spiritual values, we set ourselves on a course which propels us toward that point. We will then be drawn, with that part of the World of Matter due for transformation and renewal, into disintegration!

This, then is spiritual death!

Thus we finally have the explanation and answer to the meaning of the *second death*. **It is "spiritual death!"**

What had painstakingly developed over millennia, from an unconscious spirit seed in the Spiritual Realm to its first incarnation onto the earth plane, thence to reach the state of personal self-consciousness through the first stages of speech development, continued on through the era we designate as the time of 'early man'. That long, often tortuous path, on through the transitional stages of tribalism and then into Nationhood and the world stage via many different incarnations, now finally nears its zenith for all.

This lengthy development to "personal self-consciousness" will unfortunately be terminated for those who, through their rejection of Spiritual Truth, are irrevocably drawn into the disintegrating process. They will therefore experience the piece-by-piece shredding of the *ego of personal self-consciousness* during the dissolution process of this part of the Material World. Piece-by-piece, until the once "conscious" personality is reduced to an "unconscious" spirit-seed as it was at its beginnings. Reduced to the state of spiritual death – the "second death!"

Now the warning of Jesus, used as part of the introduction to this Chapter, may be more readily understood. From Revelation 20:6, Fenton, comes the defining Scripture. [Emphases mine.]

> *"Happy and holy is the participator in the first resurrection! – over these **the 'second death' has no authority!"***

*   *   *   *   *

Clarification of one particular aspect of the human spirit's development to *spiritual self-consciousness* and the reverse process of its possible loss in the disintegration of the "Material World" in which it had developed to that self-conscious level, is important here.

We have identified that, as a "spirit core", we originate in the Eternal Part of The Spiritual Realm and arrive in our first incarnation without yet having developed to the state of 'personal self-consciousness'. This can only be effected by 'that spirit' in the 'Material World', for it is the **personal experiencing in this earthly medium** that offers the mechanism for its necessary self-conscious development. Therefore, even though the *non-conscious spiritual part* of each human entity is of the Spiritual Realm, it can only first acquire personal *"self-consciousness"* whilst on the *earth!*

Therefore, the stripping away of its *spiritual* self-consciousness to the unfortunate condition of *spiritual death* can equally only occur **during the disintegration of the material part of Creation in which it developed to its self-conscious state**, and to which the necessary 'experiences' to obtain this desired level belong. This 'stripping away' does not occur in the actual Spiritual Realm of Creation as the words may seem to suggest, for that is **not** the area where the human spirit is ordained to develop to personal self-consciousness and gain knowledge of Spiritual Truths. All necessary 'schooling' takes place in the various levels of the Material Realm, and naturally includes some time on earth.

*   *   *   *   *

Thus it is The Spiritual Realm that the human spirit ascends to when it has gained sufficient *spiritual purity and maturity* to earn its place there. There in The Eternal Spiritual, secure in its Eternal reality within the bounds of its original home, that spirit can, from then on, assist in the further development of the worlds below.

The reality of the "second death" should not be equated with the beliefs of those who interpret this process as being similar to the attainment of 'nirvana', the 'desired' state of spiritual bliss expounded by some Eastern religions. Spiritual Law decrees that the human spirit is ordained to develop *"personal self-consciousness"* only, which means it retains its *individuality* and *personal responsibility*, something which was never ordained to merge with a collective 'cosmic consciousness'. This is a pleasant idea but does not accord with Spiritual Truth. The "either – or" **choice** here means **either** *individual spiritual life*, **or** *individual spiritual death*, in strict accordance with the inviolable Spiritual Laws. The choice once more, of course, is solely that of each individual alone.

There is one further important aspect of the "second death reality" to address at this crucial time in the earth's and humankind's development. The words, 'eternal damnation', are usually synonymous with fanatical 'fire and brimstone' religion. Yet, in reality, it well describes the quite natural and lawful processes for any human spirit drawn into disintegration, for he *ceases to be personal.* From any standpoint, this must surely be the worst fate that could possibly befall any individual, for it is equivalent to effacement from The Book of Life itself!

Moreover, this separation of *spirit* from *matter*, in itself also a completely natural process in accordance with The Spiritual Laws and now taking place under the aegis of The Creative Will, is the so-called "Last Judgement". This final 'sorting out' is necessarily connected with great upheavals and transformations but will be on a scale *not previously known.* The Book of Matthew (24:3, Fenton) offers a strong insight into just the *early stages* of the *complete process.* Those *now-stirring beginnings* are obviously connected with earthly humanity, and were given when the Disciples of Jesus asked Him what signs will portend "...the completion of this age" – our time now. Matthew, in Verses 19-22, records perhaps **the key message of all.**

> "But alas for those with child and those who nurse in those days! Pray, however, that your flight may not come during the winter, nor upon a Rest-day; for there shall then be widespread affliction, such as has not been known since the beginning of the world until now, no, nor will ever be known again. And if those times were not cut short, not a man would be saved; but for the sake of the chosen ones, those times will be cut short."[7]

Should we be modern, enlightened, intellectual human beings and mock such *unproven religious rantings* because our much-vaunted, *university-derived*, human science has now determined that our genes are our life-force, and not such a thing as an *inner, animating* **spirit-core**? Scientifically impossible, and therefore nonsense, *as 'earth-science' would surely determine it.*

Or should we be use our intuition, which is not tied to earthly empiricism, to *recognise* the obvious truth? That human genes and the processes they control affect *the physical body only* because they are *both* of *material* substance, and that therefore this scientific, so-called, *genetic life-force* **rots away with the body at its death.**

As with most Scripture in The Bible, the particular passages from the Revelation pertaining to the "second death" become far more clarified when assessed from the knowledge of **The Spiritual Laws of Creation**.

It would be a tragic mistake, therefore, to regard these explanations as just *religious fire and brimstone fanaticism without any relevance to societal beliefs today.* The very fact that virtually everything is collapsing globally should be evidence enough that there is some exceptionally powerful *reaping* taking place already. And we can be sure that even what we observe daily is not yet the culmination – the final *collective reaping* so to speak!

---

[7]Reader: The meaning of that warning – given for this present time of rapidly-increasing global-societal collapse to those [clearly mothers/women] 'who are with child and who nurse' – may be read in the *primary* Work of **Crystal Publishing**: 'BIBLE "MYSTERIES" EXPLAINED** Understanding "Global Societal Collapse" From the SCIENCE in The Bible: What Every Scientist, Bible Scholar and Ordinary Man Needs to Know'. Specifically: [Chapter 3: **The Spiritual Laws...**, sub; **The Law of Attraction...** – sub, **Why There is so much Violence and Evil on Earth.**]

Consequently, it should be a simple matter to recognise that the earth and 'its inhabitants' must surely be approaching a major and climactic point, simply because more is happening faster. The separation among men reveals itself more and more sharply every day as smaller and smaller splinter factions in religion, politics, or ethnic groupings, break away from parent organisations. Thus what had previously only manifested itself in 'opinions and convictions' now reveals itself more and more as intransigent positions, often marked by violence or the intimidatory threat of.

Therefore, the present state of the world should be viewed with very great alarm and concern, with the urgent need to seriously recognise where we, as individuals, *actually* stand spiritually. In order to stand 'right', however, we must exert the greatest strength to leave behind all base thoughts and activities, seek out **Spiritual Truth** and begin to live accordingly. If we do not, we are in danger of being chained to the World of Matter and being drawn with it towards complete disintegration.

*   *   *   *   *

Cultural and ethnic traditions will also be placed under this immense pressure. And no amount of believing in one's 'ethnic spirituality', or one's indigenous right to it, will alter the actual and lawful outcome of this unstoppable, "separating force".

The Maori race of Aotearoa, as with all other races, must be absolutely sure that what they regard as their 'high spiritual beliefs' or traditions are truly so according to The Spiritual Laws. For it will not be enough to simply *believe they are*. The Eternal Spiritual Laws are not the least bit interested in the beliefs of any people as to their 'imagined spirituality' or *mana*. For The Law will sift without favour and in complete objectivity – as it must.

Yet, in the final analysis, that process will simply be the separating out of the opposing principles of Light and Darkness along with their respective adherents, irrespective of what ethnic group they may belong to. For the end result is one of *individual and personal standing*, and **not** that of any *collective* grouping.

*   *   *   *   *

For those who strive for the Light, however, the *uplifting* attraction of this spiritual force will apply here equally as powerfully as with the *destruction* of all that opposes it. Thus *those striving souls* will gradually become freed from the World of Matter, with the correspondingly greater opportunity to ascend more quickly to the Planes of Light; to the home of all that is ***truly*** Spiritual. And with that separation, the judgement is fulfilled!

With the correct knowledge now available, we are able to shed light and clarity on much that has always been veiled in mystery and uncertainty.

We shall conclude this Chapter with the timely Scriptural quote that once more offers us the final **50% choice** and **100% outcome**:

> *"Bear witness to me, now, Heavens and Earth! I place Life and Death before you, – the Blessing and the Curse! Therefore choose for yourselves the Life, – that you and your posterity may live!"*

(Deuteronomy 30:19, Fenton. Emphasis mine.)

11
Elemental Lore of Nature

"Blow, blow, thou winter wind.
Thou art not so unkind,
as Man's ingratitude (to Man!)"

(Shakespeare, "As You Like It", Act II.)

"I happen to believe that if you treat the land with love and respect (in particular for the idea that it has an almost living soul, bound up in the mysterious, cycles of nature) then it will repay you in kind."

(H.R.H. Prince Charles – The Prince of Wales.
National Geographic.May 2006 Vol. 209–no 5)

"Understanding the *true nature* of the **'Forces of Nature'**
provides the clearest *foundation*
for the *correct understanding* of the World!"

(Author.)

11.1   The Circle of Life

'Man has a poor understanding of Life. He mistakes knowledge for wisdom.
He tries to unveil the Holy secrets of our Father, the Great Spirit.
He attempts to impose his Laws and ways on Mother Earth.
Even though he, himself, is part of Nature, he chooses to disregard and ignore it for the sake of his own immediate gain.
But the Laws of Nature are far stronger than those of Mankind.
Man must awaken at last, and learn to understand how little time remains before he will become the cause of his own downfall.
And he has so much to learn. To learn to see with the heart.
He must learn to respect Mother Earth – She who has given life to everything;
to our Brothers and Sisters, the Animals and the Plants;

to the Rivers, the Lakes, the Oceans and the Winds.
He must realise that the Planet does not belong to him,
but that he has to care for and maintain the delicate balance of Nature
for the sake of the wellbeing of our children and of all future generations.
It is the duty of man to preserve the Earth and the Creation of the Great Spirit.
Mankind being but a grain of sand in the Holy Circle which encloses All Life.'

The clear wisdom of the Native Americans is beautifully and powerfully encompassed in that illuminating statement *attributed* to White Cloud. Though a principal chief of the Iowa tribe and an iconic War Chief who fought against the whites invading his tribal lands; "Circle of Life" was probably stated by 'Wa-cha-mon-ya' – regarded as the tribe's greatest orator.

The advent of satellites and manned space stations has, for the first time in humankind's history, shown us all how incredibly beautiful, fragile and 'lonely' the earth – our 'blue planet' home – actually is. And therefore how incredibly wise are those words from a technologically-illiterate Native American people of the 19th century. For it is really only since those first space photographs appeared some years ago now that the realisation has gradually dawned that we are not separate groups, races or nations with our own closed eco-systems divorced from every other. On the contrary, those pictures have reinforced the unequivocal fact that every action on earth will ultimately impact globally, somehow, some way. At least that is the realisation among those who are sufficiently awakened to understand the truth of this.

Unfortunately, however, too many of earth's inhabitants still regard their own personal space and aspirations as being the most important thing. Nevertheless, those who are too obtuse or too ignorant to care, will one day experience the Iowa tribe's sage, intuitive observation that:

> "Man must awaken... and learn to understand how little time... remains before he will become the cause of his own downfall."

This Chapter will offer explanations as to why – and how – "White Cloud's prophecy" **will be fulfilled!**

Interestingly, in our time, the world of science that we look to for answers has also offered a sobering prediction. And one, moreover, that reinforces White Cloud's 'vision' those many years ago. The 1992 Earth Summit in Rio, attended by the largest gathering of heads of state in history, was heralded as a definitive event. It was one designed to produce a lasting international accord for protecting the world environment. Yet on 18th November 1992, just five months after that ostensible environmental milestone, more than sixteen hundred senior scientists from seventy-one countries, including over half of all Nobel Prize winners, released a signed document titled, "World Scientists' Warning to Humanity". The document began:

> "Human beings and the natural world are on a collision course. Human activities inflict harsh and often irreversible damage on the environment and on critical resources. If not checked, many of our current practices put at serious risk the future that we wish for human society and the plant and animal kingdoms, and may so alter the living world that it will be unable to sustain life in the manner that we know. Fundamental changes are urgent if we are to avoid the collision our present course will bring about."

The warning went on to list the crises in the atmosphere, water resources, the oceans, the soil, the forests, bio-diversity and human overpopulation. Here the words become more stark. (Maori word addition mine.)

> "No more than one or a few decades remain before the chance to avert the threats we now confront will be lost and the prospects for humanity immeasurably diminished. We, the

undersigned, senior members of the world's scientific community, hereby warn all humanity of what lies ahead. A great change in our stewardship (*kaitiaki*) of the Earth and life on it is required, if vast human misery is to be avoided and our global home on this planet is not to be irretrievably mutilated."

Nevertheless, when the "World Scientists' Warning to Humanity" was released to the press, Canada's national newspaper and television network ignored it, while in the United States, the *Washington Post* and the *New York Times* rejected it as "not newsworthy".

Whilst this eminent group of clearly learned men have rightly identified the gravest crisis humanity has yet faced, the scientific field in which they operate is, however, still not able to offer exact and definitive answers and solutions to most of their concerns.

Dr David Suzuki's work notes this paradox inherent in all science. And, as stated elsewhere in this work, it is precisely because earth-sciences are constrained by the very parameters it imposes upon itself i.e., *its narrow, constricting world of scientific empiricism.* This unfortunate viewpoint fails to take into account or even acknowledge – let alone understand – that all scientific endeavour must encompass Spiritual Law if it is ever to offer complete and meaningful answers to the never-ending questions it continually finds itself faced with. Thus David Suzuki points out:

> "Scientism, the aura of authority carried by scientists, has made us believe that knowledge obtained by scientists is the ultimate authority, that as we accumulate information, our capacity to understand, control and manage our surroundings will grow correspondingly. But the basic principle of scientific exploration contradicts this faith: knowledge comes from empirical observations, which are "made sense of" by hypotheses, which in turn can be experimentally tested. All information is open to being disproved." As Jonathan Marks has pointed out:
>> "...the vast majority of ideas that most scientists have ever had have been wrong. They have been refuted; they have been disposed of. Further, at any point in time, most ideas proposed by most scientists will ultimately be refuted and disposed of... Science, in other words, undermines scientism."

> (The Sacred Balance, David Suzuki, p.4:5)

Notwithstanding White Cloud's appropriate introduction for this current Chapter and its recent reinforcement by eminent scientists, the subject matter contained in this segment may appear, at first glance, to have no connection to the Chapters preceding and following this particular one. Yet it is essential that this vitally important aspect of the sum total of knowledge that is our rightful inheritance be well understood. If we are to have a more greatly clarified and harmonious existence in our material world, then the knowledge of the 'true nature' of "The Elemental Forces of Nature", perhaps more than any other, precisely offers that mechanism whereby scientific ideas need not be 'refuted and disposed of' in the future.

The very important documentary, "An Inconvenient Truth", in one sense also concurs with White Cloud's visionary statement and prophecy. But in another, Al Gore's seminal work hugely extends that ancient wisdom via the aid of exceptionally good science. The documentary should perhaps now be understood as almost the final evolvement of the work that a few insightful scientists began in earnest just a few decades ago and who had the courage to speak out about their concerns, and the ongoing work by more and more concerned scientists since. The disturbing trend of human activity and its impact on the planet and its resources is incontrovertibly clear in the documentary.

Al Gore's almost "tongue-in-cheek" comment at one point in his documentary actually reconciles the science/religion divide, at least on this crucial issue, for global humanity. Scenes of devastation of human "works" and despoliation of natural landscapes in the documentary brought forth the wry yet fundamentally truthful comment:

"It's like taking a major hike through The Revelation."

Whilst the scientific discoveries and concomitant analyses of his documentary are, in a word, brilliant, the ultimate knowledge that inherently underpins all earth-sciences must be taken into account too. That way, the *ancient wisdom* of White Cloud, and the *modern knowledge of science*, harmonise perfectly. With the knowledge of The Spiritual Laws, science can finally become 'genuinely knowing' through recognising and understanding the connection with those 'forces' which govern the immediacy of our earthly environment. Forces, moreover, that govern in absolute and direct correlation with our attitude and behaviour, thus our collective decision-making process. All of which impacts, usually detrimentally, on both the natural world and the societies we create.

Therefore, as we observe the increasingly unpredictable and sometimes disturbing 'weather-havoc' globally, the explanations of "The Elemental Forces" will hopefully offer a deep and lasting impression through greater understanding. Whilst the foundation for the process we outline is still that of The Spiritual Laws of Creation; in the context of the subject matter of this Chapter, the outworking of the reciprocal return of our free-will decisions is placed into the hands of those 'elementals' whose activities we loosely refer to as "The Forces of Nature." Thus the "**Lore** of Nature" that we refer to in the Chapter heading is also the "**Law** of Nature!"

Under the mantle of that heading it is important to understand what the Laws of Nature refer to and actually mean. Let us state quite unequivocally that whilst these Laws are Spiritual in origin, their *main* effects can be clearly observed and felt as 'weather' – in all its myriad forms. Alternately soft and gentle, and at times raging and destructive, the destiny of mankind is irrevocably intertwined with the 'Elemental' activity contained within the weather patterns. This is clearly a concept vastly different to what meteorology teaches us.

Therefore it will probably require a quantum leap for most to even *deign* to consider such an idea. Yet the strange, unpredictable weather patterns and the uncanny rapid rise in natural catastrophes worldwide has now finally produced very great concern and, of course, much speculation as to the *actual* cause. Yet even the more spectacular weather effects that trigger catastrophic natural disasters are not divorced from humankind's collective earthly activity. Since all things are interconnected and intermeshed in some way, humankind, even though a very small component part of the whole, nonetheless exert a disproportionately large measure of decisive influence in our part of Creation through the constant exercising of our free-will endowment. The consequences that flow from that decision-making process under The Law of Reciprocal Action ensure that we do, indeed: **"*Reap what we sow.*"**

And a large and increasing measure of that 'reaping' is returned to us by way of *natural disasters*. For only our decisions are free, the consequences are not! Within these parameters lies the immense responsibility of humankind in being granted the gift of free will. Thus, understanding the *true nature* of The Forces of Nature offers meaningful answers to many of our collectively-induced problems, *and to the reason for all natural disasters*. For what can be unequivocally stated again is that:

"The Laws of Nature" are the 'living-expression' of The Will of God on earth!

We began this Chapter with a rather grand but possibly enigmatic statement regarding the necessity to understand the *actual nature* of The Forces of Nature, thus perhaps presupposing a very radical view of the natural forces around us. Perhaps radical in the sense that it may not accord with current scientific thought, but certainly not radical in its spiritual reality. What do we mean by this?

Most assuredly humankind stands in stunned awe when those Elemental Forces of Nature spectacularly destroy his works, whether by earth, wind, fire or water. As we are all aware, the forces that can produce gentle lapping waves and soft summer breezes can also spawn winds and waves of immense power capable of unbelievable destruction. So, too, can the healing warmth of fire in winter be quickly transformed to raging conflagrations in forest and city. Interestingly, the narrator of the four-part series on global weather from the "Our World" documentary programme quite regularly used the term 'species of weather' to describe some of the different kinds of more severe weather events that we are subjected to. It is an interesting and unusual description to emerge from out of a purely scientific study. If not exactly 'species of weather', our clear contention is that we *are* talking about actual *Forces* of Nature – 'forces' that can bring gentleness or raging destruction.

The history of early man provides testimony to his belief of the 'supernatural' nature of these forces. He feared the lightning and thunder, and could no more control the elements in his time than can modern man today, despite his rapidly increasing technological sophistication. Herein lies the paradox! Ancient man accepted the 'Elementals' as living entities which gave him the forest for building materials and food, the sea for other foods, and good weather for the producing and harvesting of his crops.

Those same 'beings', with their destructive weather formations, could also visit great desolation upon him and his works. His naturally close connection to the "Elemental Forces" enabled him to give name to each being associated with a particular 'Elemental' activity. Through his developing knowledge, he identified male and female 'beings' with clearly demarcated tasks, with each occupying a precisely defined place in their hierarchy.

Because early man had no control over 'elemental' activity and believed he was at the mercy of these powerful beings, appeasement and worship of them became a living reality for that particular stage of his development. It is significant to note that, virtually without exception, *every developing race* has recorded the presence and existence of these 'nature beings' – from the tiniest to the gigantic – depending on their particular role and activity. In his observations of the 'gods', as he came to regard them, he ascribed human traits to them also. The vagaries of the weather at times, as though he were being played with, gave rise to a mischievous entity – a joker. Naturally there was a king and a queen who ruled over this huge and powerful 'Elemental' domain and all the lesser 'gods' who inhabited it. Every race acknowledged their existence and gave them appropriate names out of their language. And they incorporated this 'knowledge' into their respective cultures.

Conversely, traditional science has determined that weather is *caused* by a combination of precisely configured and measurable scientific formulae involving all aspects of meteorology. Insofar as the visual and material effect of weather is concerned, that is obviously the case. We observe approaching storm fronts and feel their immediate effects, and we also enjoy clear skies and bask in the warmth of high-pressure systems. From the cosiness of the lounge in winter, we can be entertained by well-groomed, witty and knowledgeable weather presenters who offer a dazzling presentation of the next few day's weather assisted by a worldwide network of sophisticated satellite detection and measuring equipment, all assessed by banks of powerful computers.

Yet, even with this vast array of modern wizardry, there are still reasonably regular, embarrassing glitches in weather forecasting, with sometimes even glaringly opposite outcomes to particular forecasts. And as we move from there into the arena of volcanic and earthquake activity projections, it becomes much more difficult to be absolutely precise in predicting either the various levels of projected activity relating to them, or the time of the disturbance – and whether such activity might be waxing or waning – if it is not clearly obvious. Even though undeniable advances have been made in the better detection of impending geological incidents utilising modern sensing instruments and analytical techniques, we are still a long way from any scientifically-acknowledged breakthrough-mechanism to accurately predict such potentially devastating events.

In quite recent times, however, we have a precisely recorded event where the population of a major Chinese city (Haicheng) was evacuated before being struck by a powerful earthquake. That precaution resulted in literally tens of thousands of lives being saved. Moreover, this was achieved not so much by technological means but by careful observations of the behaviour of animals and birds, and via the monitoring of ground-water levels.[1] Thus, we have two vastly differing mechanisms for the prediction of this kind of *Elemental-force* activity.[2]

If the development of man's spiritual or religious leanings from his earliest beginnings is examined, the various stages that he had to travel through can be readily observed. Since he did not possess the sophistication for total discernment that we today are able to have – by virtue of having travelled along this developmental path for a far longer period – the brave new world of early man mostly offered a bewildering array of powerful forces that had to be fought, appeased, or worshipped. In the beginning, therefore, animism as a belief and a religion held powerful sway over his everyday world for a long period of time.

Thus, he observed and learned the ways of not only the animal and plant worlds, but also that of the 'Elemental forms' that inhabited every part of his 'natural' world too. He gave name to them and regulated his life, to a large degree, around the activity of what he 'knew' to be fellow inhabitants of planet earth. Different from him both in form and activity but, nevertheless, as much a part of the world as was he, and who could offer the greatest help to him. So from them he learned the properties of healing herbs, how to grow his food and what to harvest from the wild. He also learned the ways of the weather and heeded their warnings of impending natural catastrophes. This knowledge is the vitally necessary connection we have long since lost.

During this phase of animistic worship, he sometimes incorrectly ascribed 'elemental entities' to the natural fixed forms such as trees, rocks and mountains. He was not able to discern that these particular aspects of the natural world did not possess their own life force such as a *soul*[3] – as is still believed by some of the world's peoples today – but simply provided habitations for the *Elemental beings* that he observed in and around them.

As developing man's world expanded so, also, did his understanding of the 'Elemental world' around him. From observing the simple activity of the nature beings close to his immediate environment, his inner sight began to reveal the higher levels of that 'world' where far larger 'beings' of greater power exerted the greatest influence on everything in the material world. Thus, certain races whose development proceeded according to the ordained path that man was to take, recognised the Higher Realm of the Elemental Beings, attempted to emulate their activity, and borrowed from them ideas that they could incorporate into their everyday life.

Arguably the peak of this particular path of development probably culminated in the classical Greek period known as Hellenism which had its flowering from near the end of the fourth century BC to approximately 50 BC. The Greeks refined quite advanced mathematical principles and constructed magnificent buildings of great beauty in symmetry of form. In the classical perfection of their architecture and their flawless sculptures, we can readily note the purity of form reflecting

---

[1] China currently has an earthquake monitoring force of 10,000 scientists and observers.

[2] This Chapter offers explanations as to which method will produce the greatest benefit and protection for modern man, provided that he does not cling to his solely intellectual pursuit of technological sophistry to the exclusion of all other possibilities. And, moreover, is open enough to allow his spirit to lead him to a greater understanding of the true nature of these awesome forces. Then, rather than foolishly attempting to 'control' this power – which he cannot in any case – he will be able to work 'consciously' with it, for his everlasting benefit.

[3] In terms of the justice of Spiritual Law that permeates every part of Creation, it would be totally against every idea of perfect justice whereby *immobile* life forms such as trees, plants and rocks, would have an *inner animating core* such as that which animals and humans possess. Only in beings or life forms that are **able to take flight** or otherwise **offer resistance when danger threatens**, is this inner life force present. Were that not the case, the harvesting of trees for housing and warmth, or the blasting of rock for road construction etc., would take on vastly different "spiritual" overtones than purely one of clear benefit for man.

the application of The Spiritual Law of Balance, and the concomitant usage of pure mathematics: **The Law of Numbers**.

Great strides were made in medicine too, not least aided by the great philosophical debates and treatises of men like Plato and Aristotle who sought to define and understand the nature and place of man in the known universe. And, moreover, the relationship and possible reality of a dualistic concept of man in being both a material form, and a spiritual or 'soul' entity as well. This highly accentuated preoccupation with the form and inner aspect of man may well have resulted in the perfection of form evidenced by Greek sculptures of the human body.

Paradoxically, the *philosophical ideas* of Plato and others, essentially being only a step toward the *sureness* of *spiritual knowledge*, might not have been necessary had man's original spiritual connections been retained. Rather than philosophy and theory by Plato, we might have had more "Spiritual Truth" by him and others. Of course, elements of The Truth may certainly be contained within those essays, but they cannot be stated to be definitive works of absolute Truth.

Notwithstanding this reality, however, the Greeks achieved a more profound level of knowledge through their greater recognition of the Elemental Beings even though, similar to most other peoples, they also wrongly regarded them as gods in their polytheistic beliefs. Nevertheless, they were the first to *more completely* understand the relationship between themselves and the Animistic Realm, which their particular level of development permitted them to 'see'. Thus, because they were able to 'perceive' the activity above and around them, all the benefits of that Realm were available to them. That insight allowed them to 'borrow' themes and ideas from the higher levels they were permitted to *see*, and the Greeks built much of their society accordingly. Greek history, culture, medicine – i.e., the Hippocratic oath – and architecture and language expresses their correct recognition of the place of these *forces* probably more vitally than most other races.

However, whilst their correct development permitted them the insight to 'know' that much more existed in Creation than just the material world by virtue of their recognition of the Elemental Beings, they basically concluded that the 'Gods on Mount Olympus' – as they perceived them to be – were the absolute height of Creation. Yet the Apostle Paul, in his first address to the men of Athens observed the possibility that the Greeks had divined the probable existence of the One Invisible God when he stated to them:

> "Men of Athens, I perceive beyond everything how deeply religious you are, for, going about and studying your objects of worship, I even found an altar upon which had been inscribed:
>
> TO AN UNKNOWN GOD
>
> What therefore you unknowingly worship, I proclaim to you. The God. Who made the Universe and all in it."
>
> (Acts 17:22-24, Fenton.)

Thus, without that sure conviction of a "Divine Realm" or a "Higher Creation", any further spiritual development for the Greeks was stunted by that uncertainty. The one race that did conclusively divine the Highest Spheres, in fact all the way to the seat of The Godhead, was the Jewish race. Their recognition of the Source of All Life paved the way for an eventual connection that subsequently allowed Jesus, The Son of God, to incarnate among them. Their prior recognition of "The Elemental Forces of Nature" can be clearly noted by the help accorded to the Israelites by these 'nature beings' – sometimes spectacularly so – on many different occasions during their exodus from out of Egyptian bondage under the leadership of Moses. We may note the same interaction between man and the 'Elementals' in other places within The Bible, examples of which will be used later in this Chapter to illustrate the spiritual and physical validity of this "Elemental-force premise".

From the Greek homeland, the same knowledge was used to create a new Empire; that of the Roman. Because the transportation of this belief and culture was effected by a small number of Greeks, the native Roman people who had not developed to the same 'level of seeing' *as a complete race*, did not have the natural recognition of this Higher Realm that the Greeks possessed. So whilst the Roman Empire flourished and grew very powerful, the connections to, and worship of, their 'gods', were far more tenuous than those that the Greek Empire enjoyed.

Certainly history records that the Romans feared their differently named deities and proffered many gifts and sacrifices to them over millennia, but this was probably based more on dogma and doctrine than actual conviction. The end result was that the Roman Emperors eventually became convinced of their own direct lineage from these 'stone gods' and this corruption of their belief brought about the demise of their empire and allowed for the subsequent new emerging force of Christianity to supersede both Greek and Roman thought.

Further on in history, other late developing races such as the Nordic and Germanic peoples also reached the level necessary to recognise the 'nature beings' and thus also the knowledge of the Elemental 'gods', with the Norse naming their high fastness Valhalla. During their depredations in other lands, the Norsemen came into contact with Christianity and they, too, eventually embraced the new religion. This acceptance of a completely new idea ensured that the original, sure beliefs would eventually die away. Notwithstanding that unfortunate demise, certain aspects of the old beliefs were retained in the fables, myths and legends of those groups too.

The active retention of this knowledge, however, was retained in the less-developed tribal groups in the different parts of the world still untouched by this new thought. Unfortunately, the generally superstitious minds of most of these tribal groups allowed major distortions to enter into their view of the Animistic world, and they did not reach the degree of actual knowledge necessary to recognise the higher levels of that realm. Moreover, their particular views generally produced fear and wrong worship, which effectively kept the door to greater knowledge firmly closed. Thus, whilst a natural and necessary connection to 'other-world realities' was retained, to all intents and purposes the vitally necessary 'working knowledge and connection' to the realm of the Elementals and Nature Beings above us was effectively lost here also.

And whereas some of the 'indigenous peoples' have at least retained a strong belief in the validity of their legends as possible truth, other more 'intellectual races', including those of European origin in the new worlds of America, Canada, Australia and New Zealand, have virtually severed this *connection* completely, not even bothering to retain them as fables. With the embarkation of millions from old Europe to the new lands in a relatively short space of time, the severing of strong family and cultural traditions developed over centuries was considered more or less necessary in order to face the challenges of a new way of life freed from the constraints of a dogmatic and blinkered Europe. This dogmatism was epitomised either by the superstitions of the rural peasantry, the bigotry of the controlling political and religious authorities, or the arrogance of the ruling aristocracy.

Notwithstanding this new 'freedom from restraint' that Old-world Europe did not easily allow, we are able to historically observe the curious emergence, particularly in America, of the concept of "Manifest Destiny", itself just as bigoted, but probably more arrogant, as that which was ostensibly left behind. In its essence it decreed that the new lands were more fit for the new people than for the indigenous inhabitants. Thus the idea of *taming* and exploiting the frontier land and subjugating and civilising the 'primitive natives' became the catchword, rather than a more benign, caring and conservation-minded approach with a mutual acceptance of the different cultures, thus offering benefits for both.

As illustrated further on in this Chapter, the 'new Americans', and the actual land of America itself, would have been far spiritually richer today had the concept of "Manifest Destiny" also espoused humility and the biblical admonition to "...do unto others..."

This 'new way' of the 'New-world peoples' clearly and unequivocally illustrates our assertion that the necessary connection to "The Elemental Forces" was no longer a part of their life. This loss, in the same way and for the same reasons that the Greeks lost it – rapidly developing and generally crass intellectualism almost completely supplanting the spiritual/intuitive insight – guaranteed the seeds for the material degradation of planet earth. For without genuine veneration and gratitude for the earthly home, we sow the seeds for our eventual demise, drowned in our own poison. It may be that we will one day look back and recognise the technical revolution itself as a perilous path opposing all that was natural and spiritually lawful in the world.

Unfortunately for 'Western Nations' generally, their god of science has determined that notions such as "Elemental Beings" cannot possibly be entertained as belonging to a 'rational, logical and intelligent' society, even though the 'face-book' of their religions, The Bible, speaks of them clearly enough. Moreover, missionaries who ventured forth out of Europe into the new 'heathen lands' generally condemned this natural and necessary connection ordained by The Creative Will, and applied various labels such as superstition, blasphemy and even demonism to it. Thus the relegation of what was once accepted as factual knowledge, even if not fully understood, to the realm of myth and legend by man's 'intellectual sophistication', is to our grave detriment. For the more correct place of the intellect was to assist man in the fulfilment of his earthly duties, which is why it is vital for scientific and other earthly endeavours. In this, its proper and ordained place, it rightly produces technological marvels and great feats of construction.

Sadly, spiritual man, with the potential for achieving true greatness in the material world and in Creation, became merely intellectual man more concerned with earthly analysis and theory, rather than spiritual activity producing corresponding deeds. And this can be largely attributed to his rejection of the twin-realities of the knowledge and outworking of Spiritual Law and the existence of "The Elemental Forces of Nature".

Two primary events in the history of man had a major bearing on the acceptance, or otherwise, of 'Elemental aspects'. One was the religious madness of The Dark Ages, and the other was the later, perhaps more enlightened, Age of Reason. During the course of The Dark Ages and the later Inquisition, the Christian religious authorities, at the height of absolute temporal power, decreed that anything remotely connected with 'nature beings' be branded as heresy and/or 'demonism'. Consequently, even the simple and innocent act of picking herbs or fungus in the forest for food or medicine often resulted in the torture and death of perhaps thousands of harvesters, mostly women, who were invariably accused of being witches and in league with the devil.

During the exploration and colonisation period when the 'White cultures' exported religion and criminals to the lands of indigenous tribal peoples beginning about the 1700s, the church once more came up against strong conviction about the existence of 'nature beings'. However, if it was totally unacceptable in their own societies where innocents were killed in the name of their God for this 'heresy', it would certainly not be tolerated in the new lands. Consequently, it was quickly opposed and/or suppressed in the new lands as well. Thankfully, the madness of 'torture by religious numbers' finally relinquished its hold on the psyche of the European Church with the beginnings of the more scientific "Age of Enlightenment" in the 18th century.

Yet what did our erstwhile, budding scientists make of the previously unseen world around them then? With the greater surge of intellectualism to scientifically rationalise the natural world, the catchwords, 'prove it', became the rationale of empiricism that everything had to bow to. What could not be physically seen, touched or heard was relegated to the realm of nonsense until such time as the new religious god of science decreed otherwise. Of course, as more powerful instruments were developed, what was very recently *dismissed as impossible* was revealed as *living reality*. It is curious that the scientific community, even in our present age of so-called absolute enlightenment, still tenaciously clings to that same view of 'not possible' until proven *scientifically*.

However, the reality for all time will be, that regardless of the adulation they may heap upon themselves with each new 'discovery', they seem not to understand – or at least publicly acknowledge – that what might be lauded as a major discovery has, quite naturally, *always existed*. Even with the production of a new element which science might suddenly produce, it was never a question of an actual *creation* of a new substance, because the necessary building blocks for that fusion were *always available*.

Therefore, if we apply the same criteria to both science and religion – each generally vehemently opposed to any such notion of 'nature beings' – to that exact same subject, we have the factual reality that *either* 'Elemental beings' exist, or they do not! It cannot be possibly be both. If, in fact, they really were a figment of the fertile and fearfully superstitious imagination of early man, *then the problem resolves itself and we need no longer bother with it*. However, if the opposite is true and they actually do exist and are a living part of the total activity in Creation and thus also here on earth – even if outside of our physical senses – then that clearly poses *a huge problem for both science and religion*. For an accommodation would have to be made somewhere in both disciplines, and one that actually fits.

Because not one thing can exist in the world of science or religion except under the umbrella of The Spiritual Laws of Creation, it naturally follows that any factual existence of 'nature beings' will have been ordained by The Creative Will. It is the same Will, moreover, under which both those disciplines are permitted to exist. Quite logically, then, if 'nature beings' do exist and ancient man did understand their place and *actually observed them*, then the obvious reality for latter day man is that *we have lost the ability to see them*. And what might that imply?

Since modern science has relegated them to the realm of superstitious myth and legend, and because their existence probably cannot ever be proven by scientific means, it follows that the scientific community will probably never accept even the possibility of such beings. Notwithstanding this attitude from that direction, Dr Lyall Watson, an eminent Biologist, (perhaps one of the very few 'knowing voices in the scientific wilderness') has produced a remarkable series of books exploring the intellectually-perceived 'no-go zone' between empirical science and the 'other-world reality'. In that series he has documented some stunningly remarkable and totally unexpected insights.

In particular, his books, "Supernature" and "Gifts of Unknown Things" reveal amazing incidents inexplicable according to man's accepted scientific criteria but naturally factual under the higher knowledge of Elemental and Spiritual Law. As a scientist, he was able to bridge the *humanly-created* 'impossible zone' between the discipline of science and the less clearly defined area of religiosity, and marry many aspects of the two-world beliefs logically. His research has greatly helped to dispel the myth that such a 'no-go area' ever actually existed in the first place. In reality it cannot, for all things between the tangible and the equally real intangible are, in various ways, precisely and lawfully connected.

*   *   *   *   *

And what of the church? Is there anything in their doctrines of faith that even faintly allude to the existence of such beings? They are certainly accepted in many races, religions and teachings other than the orthodox Christian view. We have already mentioned the assistance afforded Moses. Two instances of particular note were the parting of the Red Sea, and the 'pillar of fire' that guided his vast caravan. The others being 'manna' from heaven for bread, low flying flocks of birds for meat, and water produced by Moses who knew exactly where it was flowing under the surface of the rocks. The Bible contains examples of even supposedly savage animals not offering harm to particular individuals where, in the situations described, they perhaps normally would. Daniel in the lion's den stands as a prime example. But perhaps a very brief examination of one especially celebrated event from the Bible may offer the greatest relevant insight into this question of 'Elemental beings' and their ordained activity alongside humankind.

Most people with even a rudimentary grasp of The Bible, even from 'Sunday school', are probably aware of the story of the "miracle" of Jesus calming the wind and waves during a storm on the Sea of Galilee. In this particular instance the disciples, alarmed at the increasing strength of the storm were fearful for their lives.

From the Book of Mark we read:

> And a very heavy gale began to blow and the waves rushed into the boat, so that it was rapidly filling. And He Himself was at the stern asleep on a cushion. They accordingly aroused Him, exclaiming, "Teacher! do you not care if we perish?" Upon awakening, He restrained the wind, and said to the sea,
> "Silence! be still!"
> The wind then lulled and there was perfect calm.
> "Why," He asked them, "do you doubt in this way? How is it that you cannot yet have faith?"
> But they became terrified; and said to one another, "What can He be? for even the wind and the sea obey Him?"

(Mark 4:37-41, Fenton.)

That event is accepted by Christians as one that actually occurred but are probably inclined to label it a miracle. However, what may not generally be fully comprehended was what actually took place in this most interesting happening. To understand it fully, we must apply the knowledge of The Spiritual Laws of Creation to it, since absolutely nothing can take place in any part of Creation except under the aegis of them. Since Jesus Himself declared that He had "...not come to abolish the Laws but to complete them", the calming of the wind and the waves could only be possible under The Eternal Laws. Now, by virtue of His Origin from out of The Divine, He would clearly have known of the existence of the "The Elemental Beings of Nature" – since their existence is an actual reality.

Moreover, not only would He have been aware of them but, because of His High origins and associated Power over all else below that level, all 'nature beings' and their activities would have been naturally subordinate to His command. And it would be foolish to believe that He was rebuking the *actual substance* of water and wind. No, the clear illustration here is that He was admonishing some force or energy that, even today, has its field of activity in what we loosely call the natural world and weather. A 'force' that gave rise to the increased agitation of the wind and water that instilled fear in the disciples. Thus the forces, or 'beings', of nature!

Acceptance of this event as being one of unequivocal truth presupposes the clear connotation that the only viable mechanism under which the "calming of the wind and waves" could have occurred in the manner illustrated – in particular being *commanded* to cease their activities – is via the activity of 'nature beings'. Their ordained purpose is thus fulfilled under the umbrella of inviolable Spiritual Law, of which Jesus would have understood every single ramification.

*   *   *   *   *

Thus, through this clearly recorded incident, we are able to offer one more illustration that it is the 'work' of "The Elemental Forces of Nature" that *produce the effects* of the varying levels of interrelated weather outcomes in storms, natural disasters and catastrophes which so effectively destroy man and his works. This occurs through the *direct correlation* between the outcomes returned to humankind under The Law of Sowing and Reaping, and the wrong *personal and collective decisions* produced by our *spiritual volition*.

Such a radical view will no doubt produce smiles of incredulity, perhaps more so on the part of weather scientists and forecasters. Yet it does not take all that much imagination to wonder at the increasing frequency and intensity of storms worldwide, or of extreme weather patterns producing intense and prolonged droughts virtually alongside areas of devastating flooding. What we are also observing is the more frequent use of superlatives needed to attempt to describe the continuing catalogue of Mother Nature's 'handiwork'.

Words such as the heaviest, longest, driest, severest, worst in living memory, and worst ever recorded, etc., clearly reveal an emerging pattern that is not solely the product of journalistic jingoism. Something very different is now taking place on planet earth; the like of which we have not experienced before. Something that is producing a feeling of uncertainty and unease in the minds of more and more people. And something that cannot be completely explained by the felling of the rain forests, the enlargement of the hole in the ozone layer, nuclear proliferation, global warming, or a burgeoning global population. Even the feared 'El Nino' phenomenon, which is clearly capable of producing great devastation, is simply only the activity of these 'Elemental forces'.

It is interesting to note that the U. S. Geological Survey, the body responsible for monitoring earth-movements in the United States and elsewhere, has observed a large increase in worldwide earthquake activity over 7 on the Richter scale in the decades from the 1930s and 40s. Up until that point since records were first kept, numbers of earthquakes of that magnitude were relatively infrequent. The most interesting aspect of these findings is that various people who have studied this data cannot definitely *explain* the huge increase. However, since nothing can occur without a reason, and as everything must take place under the umbrella of The Eternal Laws, the answers can be found within their parameters, even if 'scientifically unacceptable' *at this point in time.*

For the purposes of clarification, let us suspend our probable disbelief in such a *seemingly* preposterous notion, greatly extend our personal parameters of possibilities, and allow vastly different perceptions to hold sway for the moment. And let us assume the correctness of the assertion that 'elemental' activity is the mechanism by which weather patterns and related geological activity are generated. And, moreover, that the increasing extremes of natural phenomena via this mechanism have a definite cause and purpose. What, then, might be the trigger? To understand the cause, we need to revisit the structure of Creation so that we may understand the "whence, whither and why" of the "Elemental Beings" also.

In Chapter 7, we offered explanations as to how and why Creation came into being. The reader may wish to return to that particular segment to familiarise himself with the complete process. At this point we will quickly skim over the main happenings in a brief memory refresher. The Book of Genesis provides the necessary knowledge.

*   *   *   *   *

So, in answer to the petition of many varied creatures who could not come to conscious life in the immediate vicinity of the immense power of The Creator, lower planes of habitable worlds at necessarily vast distances from His "Proximity" were permitted to come into being under the Creation-Words: "Let There Be Light!"

As each realm coalesced at its ordained level from out of the incomprehensibly vast, downwards-moving, white-hot mass that contained the building blocks for all levels of Creation, the inhabitants for each of those planes were able to take on form and begin their conscious existence. The final outcome of this 'distillation process' was the forming of the material worlds encompassing the earth and the vast physical universes. But because the more dense, physical realm of mankind must naturally occupy that lower part of Creation which is not eternal, it was unable to generate its own 'warmth' to produce the requisite parameters for conscious life there.

By 'warmth' we do not mean the interstellar mechanisms of thermo-nuclear energy which gave rise to the formation of the billions of suns and star systems in the physical universes. We refer to the 'warmth' of the *life-force* of Creation itself, which is separate from the immense heat generated during the formative processes of all celestial globes, but which nevertheless allowed those formations to come into being. This particular 'life-warmth' is naturally present in both The Eternal Realm of The Spiritual and also in The Elemental/Animistic Realm.

The material worlds, not *inherently* possessing this necessary 'animating/warming life-power', received it from what is termed: "The Animistic Realm". All the 'beings' of the "Elemental Forces" – the powerful and the small – whilst having their origin there, carry out their activities throughout all the Planes of Creation. Thus, the 'power' of *The Spiritual*, utilised by the larger "Elemental Beings" involved with the formation of the vast universes, gave life-warmth to our material home. As a clearer description, we may liken the 'nature beings' to the 'maintenance workers' holding everything together in the hive. – As above, so below! – Thus we have the "whither, whence, and why" of the "Elemental Forces" too. Not 'scientifically rational' of course but, nevertheless, spiritually, and therefore actually, correct in its basic overview.

*   *   *   *   *

Our connection to "Elemental Beings", and the reason that man should know of them is quite simple. As we explained in the Chapter, "Whither Cometh the Maori", the human spirit, as he journeyed downward from the Realm of The Spiritual to seek incarnation in the material planes in order to develop to 'personal self-consciousness', necessarily traversed other Realms, including that of the "Animistic". As he traversed the lower planes, each of which was of a heavier consistency than the previous higher one, he was logically compelled to accept a covering, or 'body', of the same substance and consistency of the particular plane journeyed through. Consequently, one of 'our cloaks' corresponds precisely to that of the Animistic Realm. And it is through this particular covering that we are able to connect to and understand both the "Elemental Beings" of the "Forces of Nature" and their activity.

This necessary connection was granted that we might recognise how we were meant to work consciously with them as once the early races did, thus hopefully bringing about an earth that would reflect the beauty and harmony of the Higher Spiritual Spheres. Yet for our material benefit also. Because we voluntarily cut off this vital connection, we have produced a mainly intellectual world devoid of any real Spiritual Truth or aspirations. Thus we struggle to make sense of an increasingly poisoned and degraded planet, for which we seem unable to provide meaningful answers. For it was originally ordained that we were to work consciously with the "Elemental Forces". If we do not now strive to re-establish that vitally important connection and begin to seek out the necessary knowledge and understanding of them, there may well be nothing to look forward to except more problems wrought by more people crowding into reducing areas of increasing degradation! We of humankind, therefore, desperately need this vital connection – for our very survival.

Even though that may be the likely end result because of our stubborn refusal to accept this reality anyway, it is still important to offer the knowledge that may turn the tide for those who still hold the desire to learn about them. And thus gain a potentially greater level of knowledge by virtue of a stronger and more conscious connection to, and with, "The Elemental Forces of Nature". Let us continue our journey of necessary education and discovery!

Whilst intimately involved in the formative processes of, and activity in, all the spheres of Creation, the "Elemental Forces", by way of a precise and lawfully ordained process, are also concerned with all human activities. To explain the further *why* of this connection to humankind, we need to once more understand that of all creatures in Creation, *only the human spirit inherently possesses the gift of free-will*. Every other inhabitant within Creation carries out their life and activity in strict accordance with The Creative Will, including the Elemental Beings.

From free-will, however, derives the ultimate spiritual responsibility of *accountability*, for all our thoughts, words and actions. Now, at this time in the spiritual and evolutionary development of mankind, our collective 'karma' over millennia – which for the most part consists of dark, debased and degraded activities – is being returned to us with increasing strength and frequency under the lawful outworking of the interlinked and inviolable Spiritual Laws. This lawful process marks the closing of all cycles – again activated by our free-will – for this Material Part of Creation. The activity of the 'Elemental beings' 'return' this 'payment' to us by generating increasingly severe effects in the world's weather patterns. It is thus in exact accordance with both the individual and collective spiritual volition of all humankind, under the outworking of The Law of Reciprocal Action in the first instance.

In Chapter 10 we explained the meaning of **"The Second Death"** for the individual, and we outlined how such an event could occur. The exact same process is also employed for the 'collective reaping' of mankind since *individual outcomes* are **simultaneously** resolved within the parameters of the *collective happening*. This is simply because the Material part of Creation was firmly bound to the unalterable Laws of evolution and dissolution from the very beginning, in strict accordance with The Creative Will. This "Creative Will", which is at the same time The 'Law' of Nature, is the *power/force* which, in its activity, continually forms and dissolves worlds, exactly as can be observed in interstellar activity.

The *key point* in the previous paragraph is the reinforcement of our assertion that the 'Laws of Nature' are immutably connected with **"The Creative Will of God"**. In other words, the 'Elemental Forces of Nature', in their ordained purpose and activity, carry out 'The Eternal Will'. Under this inviolable **Law** it is thus the activity of the 'Elemental Beings', both the large and the small that, via the aegis of **The Law of Reciprocal Action** *return* the reciprocal effect of all mankind's deeds.

So, what is the mechanism that will bring about our 'collective reward'? And how will "The Forces of Nature" achieve this? To understand that point we need to *revisit* the process of a 'second death' occurrence. And thereby learn how the Elemental activity of "The Forces of Nature" is so inseparably intertwined with the fate of humankind! Whilst a 'second death' concept necessarily represents a finite one – as does the life-span of each material globe – it is the *continuous coming into being* of the star systems contained within the **"cycle of Creation"** that is **"eternal and without end"**, thus infinite! Individual suns and planets *within* such systems simply undergo their time of birth, life and disintegration in this overall, infinite continuity.

Moreover, it is a process necessary for any particular part of the material world which finally reaches the defining point of its life-cycle whereby the disintegration can allow a further renewal – for its continuing evolution. And each globe has its ordained time for this process. The key aspect contained within such lawful outcomes is the fact that the outworking of the Natural Laws precisely determines the point at which this disintegration process for each celestial globe must begin. Thus our own planet earth cannot be exempt from this ordained event either. What colours our situation most markedly, however, is the fact that this 'inevitable happening' will proceed at its precisely determined moment, **irrespective** of the **condition** of the **earth**, or **its inhabitants** – i.e., **us!**

Therefore we should be perfectly clear from the above explanations that "The Forces of Nature" *will bring about* the 'renewal' of the earth under the outworking of the Natural Laws, which are, at the same time, **The Spiritual Laws of Creation**. The term condition in this case means the *spiritual condition*, or level of *spiritual maturity*, of the inhabitants. Therefore, since most of man's decisions for all his time on earth have leaned more toward war, strife and degradation of his material home, we can expect that the collective reciprocal return of that volition will be severe and destructive, thus returning tenfold our original 'choices' – albeit in perfect justice, however. Unfortunately for humankind, however, under the aegis of the "whirlwind constant".

Moreover, if we **actually are near the point where disintegration is due to set in**, we should then be able to detect the beginnings of that process via increased 'Elemental activity'. This effect should thus clearly reveal itself in more and more disruptive and/or destructive weather patterns. Quite obviously, there is such increased activity, the like of which even weather scientists now view with alarm. This new 'weather development', therefore, clearly heralds this impending disintegration process.

As our fate is tightly bound to the spiritually-lawful activity of the 'elementals', ordained to return the reciprocal effects of all our deeds: in the same way that we must reap 'our bad', it is equally true – and certainly more desirable – that we will also reap any 'good' that may be ours at this time. Therefore, if we wish to survive the disintegration process now 'waiting in the wings', we need to do what this Work has constantly enjoined. We as individuals, but also collectively, must become voluntarily accepting of, and conversant with, The Spiritual Laws. By changing our attitude and volition to one of conscious recognition and acceptance, instead of perversely maintaining one of cynical, disbelieving rejection – clearly to our obvious detriment – we would reap, instead, the benefits that ensue from working with and alongside "The Elemental Forces of Nature" under the inviolable outworking of exactly those Spiritual Laws!

*   *   *   *   *

In necessary reinforcement, they are:

1. **The Law of Movement.**

2. **The Law of Reciprocal Action.** (Sowing and Reaping)

3. **The Law of Attraction of Similar Species.**

4. **The Law of Spiritual Gravity.**

5. **The Law of Balance.**

6. **The Law of Rebirth.**

7. **The Law/Gift of Grace.**

*   *   *   *   *

The first step is to re-establish connections to the 'Elemental Beings' by first recognising that they are a very real and necessary part of life in the material world. By doing so we fulfil our ordained purpose in consciously working with them. With their guidance and help we *could* have created a virtual paradise on earth, as was ordained for humankind, thus to be true *kaitiaki*!

But now, under the *serious need of their protection*, we *may perhaps* survive the disintegration of our poisoned home. The sure guarantee of not accepting this 'life belt of hope' is that of destruction, exactly in accordance with our collective volition in this case.

Such a 'doomsday scenario' will invariably produce different responses from within the various sections of any society. And, of course, there have been *imminent* doomsday predictions for centuries. Yet whilst there are probably many believers, there will surely be disbelievers too, both from within and without the various religious groups. Orthodox science, also, by virtue of its basically aspiritual nature, will be generally unreceptive to such ideas. Yet the outcomes alluded to will precisely conform to 'scientific laws' in any case because they, in turn, can only be derived from the higher Spiritual Laws – as we continually reiterate. What we have not had before, however, are the explanations whereby logical sense can be made of the increasingly severe weather patterns and geological activity globally.

So the problem for all *disbelievers* being; that their views are actually **completely irrelevant**! Irrespective of what they may espouse, and from whatever discipline or source they may derive their beliefs, what we outline and explain here are the *actual connective-processes* that will bring the 'more destructive' events which humankind must soon experience. They are set in motion by the very Laws of Life. Paradoxically, it is the same "mechanism of Law" that gave rise and life to all disbelievers and to all science in the first instance.

Therefore, all we need do is *quietly watch and wait* as the verification of what has been stated, and why, becomes the living reality for all. Since we contend that that is the inescapable reality, let us continue on with our analysis of "Elemental Lore" and offer other insights into this 'brave new world' for those who may be prepared to awaken spiritually. Yet we will still offer respect for all other beliefs, in accordance with humankind's ordained free-will right to choose individual paths.

Western societies – and perhaps more particularly America with its greater technological bent and concern for the corporate, capitalist ethos – will generally have scant regard for 'Elemental' beliefs. But it is interesting to note that Japan, that dynamo of corporate wealth and global trend-setting, actually retains extremely strong links to the 'Elemental world' behind the corporate facade it presents to the world. Not only are there many shrines and temples to 'Elemental Beings' in the strong 'Animistic' religion of Shintoism, the language itself actually incorporates the sounds of 'Elemental' activity.

Yet, in a perversely selfish paradox, this same culture has no qualms about stripping the rest of the world of all that it materially needs to feed its own personal wants. And in apparent direct contravention of a strong religion *that ostensibly venerates all that the natural world has to offer.*

The Fairy Tales from old Europe that many of us fondly remember from childhood, also directly trace their origins to 'Elemental' activity. The early Teutons and other similar European groups unequivocally accepted 'nature beings' as factual reality. And in many rural areas of Europe today, such acceptance is still strong.

Paradoxically, had we retained an unbroken connection to the Animistic Realm, the world could have been much more than classical Greece once was. For such clear insight would have guaranteed greater help and advancement from those 'Beings' placed in Creation to assist us in what would have been our natural, step-by-step, spiritual development. The proliferation of chemical poisons and the development of some of the world's current energy systems that offer only nightmarish end-scenarios, would not have arisen. In their place would have been **given** natural, sustainable energy and natural sowing and harvesting methods.

Instead, much of what we have produced on the planet without that vitally necessary connection are areas of poisoned, denuded and degraded 'chemical deserts'. And in the mega or super-cities, some parts of them are little more than ugly, decaying criminal hell-holes harbouring thousands of diseased, drug-ridden or starving human flotsam housed, increasingly, in filthy slum areas – or not housed at all – or camped out in refugee hovels in unproductive desert lands. Certainly in New Zealand we should be grateful that, for the most part at least, we are still far from such distressing scenarios. Moreover, because of the bounty of the land, we should *never* reach that point.

Yet that point has finally been reached for most of global humanity simply because we severed the connection to our greatest help in the foolish belief that man could do it better. Paradoxically, and in the most 'bitter-of-pills' scenario, it will probably only be the *continuing reality* of such nightmarish situations that may finally induce humankind to awaken to the only true knowledge with which to alleviate the suffering of millions of our fellow travellers.

11.2   The 'Psychic' World of the Maori

This sub-Chapter will basically revisit those activities and connections we looked at in Chapter 4. However, because the overall consequences are irrevocably tied to 'The Law of Reciprocal Action', particularly under the return-mechanism lawfully driven by the 'Elemental Forces', the *reciprocal effect* of those *psychic* beliefs and activities – generally deemed to be *spiritual* by Maoridom – actually has *greater* relevance in *this* segment. Whilst it may seem to be covering the same ground, it is actually an *extension* of our overall knowledge, for it will detail *how* we are *connected* by such beliefs *to the outworking* of all 'Elemental activity', behind which is the 'driving power' of **Spiritual Law**. In necessary reinforcement *once more*, it is a lawful activity vitally engaged with *returning* the reciprocal effect of *all* our beliefs and activities, both right and wrong!

So where stands the Maori in his relationship with the 'Elemental Beings', and what should he do with this new knowledge? Or will he choose to believe that what he currently possesses in this regard is the be-all and end-all of 'spiritual knowing'? What is important in our full understanding of the activity of the 'nature beings' is to *clearly differentiate* between the purely ordained forms of those 'Elementals' and their activity – *created* during the formative process of original Creation; and that of psychic and phantom forms *wrongly produced* by the spiritual volition of humankind and endowed with the psychic 'life-energy' of their 'producers'.

One activity – that of the "Elemental Forces" – is concerned with the fulfilment of The Creative Will, and therefore stands under that Power. The other is *not ordained to exist in Creation at all* but does so through man's ability to produce the 'forms' of them under the power of his wrongly-directed spiritual volition. It is by this process that the psychic entities of mankind came into being. Again, had we retained that beneficial connection with the "Elemental Forces", the ability to discern what was correct and what was being produced by the dark volition of mankind would have been maintained, thereby offering the obvious benefit of far fewer unnecessary entities given psychic life for no useful purpose whatsoever.

Because so few people are able to discern effectively today, even within the indigenous races that still hold strong ties to the other-world reality and psychic things, we still have beliefs that are far removed from real truth. The proponents of such beliefs would find it difficult to accept that some of the very things which they believe and/or revere as being part of the original Creative process, are actually not so at all, and are therefore invariably useless. Not only useless, but potentially dangerous since they are nothing more than *personal/psychic productions* brought into being by the creative thought-mechanism inherent in man through his free-will attribute.

The reader may recall the explanations regarding the "life-power" that maintains and sustains literally everything in Creation; that power which is neither good nor bad, but **neutral**. Precisely because of our spiritual origins and inherent free-will attribute, we humans act like refracting lenses and are thus able to direct this 'power' to whatever purpose we choose. Moreover, we cannot stand divorced from or even **stop** the process, as it is completely automatic. Therein lies the 'accountability' that we must accept for the stewardship, the *kaitiaki*, of our existence. As previously stated, it is via that mechanism whereby the "Elemental Forces" return to us the reciprocal effects of all our deeds.

Therefore, if we compare the actuality of man's history against the Command to live according to The Spiritual Laws, it is not difficult to understand that an incredible amount of reciprocal effect is rearing-up against us like a huge tsunami about to break. We are in the vanguard of it at this present time as we observe how more and more strange and virulent diseases appear and mutate, in increasingly changeable and unpredictable weather patterns, in natural catastrophes of greater and greater frequency and intensity, and in insurmountable problems of all kinds. However, all that 'angst' is still nothing more than just the 'beginnings' of our 'complete reaping'.

The very same process applies to the many psychic forms created by the world's peoples. The end result of 'sowing' wrong views in nothing more than superstitious thinking totally divorced from the truth of things, has resulted in the natural 'reaping' of the psychic forms produced also. For they are forever part of the culture and race that produced them. For example, when the Maori first arrived in this land, his already superstitious and fertile imagination 'believed' that his mythical monster, the *taniwha*, lived in the deep pools of the rivers and the many caves around. He applied the same superstitious thought-processes to his view of the vast forest that he encountered. And similarly concluded that malevolent entities inhabited Tane's realm too.

Nothing could be further from the truth. Aside from natural fauna and flora, the only 'entities' that existed in this land and, indeed, every land before the arrival of men, were 'Elemental Beings'. And, moreover, ordained to be there by The Creative Will. Their purpose is, and forever will be, to nurture and maintain all the various worlds of Creation, including the natural environment of the earth – humankind's material home.

Our assertions of insufficient discernment toward things of truthful reality by most of mankind through a lack of true knowledge, but more particularly by the more superstitious, indigenous peoples of the world, is revealed in the confusion we find in various religious beliefs. In the case of the Maori, we note the correct recognition of an Elemental 'Lord' of the forest – Tane. And we also have a similar recognition of an Elemental 'Lord' of the sea – Tangaroa.

We should note, however, that these two named and sometimes revered 'beings' are **not** gods but are designated as 'Elemental Lords' of their particular domain and activity. Moreover, both have their counterparts in most other cultures, including the European, American and Asian ones. Below the level of the 'Elemental Lords' are many tiers of other beings we might describe as helpers, whose activity also offers the greatest aid for humankind.

The chart at the end of this Chapter shows some of the key 'beings' given name by the respective peoples to whom they 'belong'. However, unless one were of that culture and possessed clear insight into the actual activity of the 'Elementals', it would be difficult to determine which ones were *genuinely* from the Elemental Realm, and which ones were simply *aspiritual productions of the people concerned.* For instance: In the Maori example one can probably designate 'Tangaroa' as an 'Elemental Lord' whose domain is that of the sea. The same, however, could not be said of Whiro, designated as the god of evil, *makutu* and the black arts. Entities such as Whiro – and there are many of them in many races – were never part of the Creative process. They are solely the productions of the race that 'created' them, brought into being through incorrect beliefs about the actual nature of the world and what was ordained to be the spiritually-correct kind of activity in it – both 'Elemental' and human. That is why it is so imperative to understand the place and purpose of the *true* Elemental Beings of Nature!

The chart does not definitively represent *all* the 'beings' that ancient cultures worshipped; those they deemed their gods and goddesses. Vesta, for example, was the Roman goddess of 'hearth and household'. It was to her that the famed 'Vestal Virgins' dedicated their lives in Temple service. Of course, not all cultures had the same 'relative' beings. As previously stated, some were not actually 'Elemental Lords' or their female equivalent but were forms produced by an incorrect belief which 'decided' that a particular 'being' *might possibly* occupy a particular place in their hierarchy or 'pantheon' of gods. Nonetheless, the chart shows most of the main 'gods' from the cultures and peoples named, and therefore indicates the awareness that those same peoples had as to their existence, even if the knowledge of them was not completely correct.

It should be especially noted that, unlike virtually all other early cultures, ancient Maori had no actual 'god of Love' in their 'Pantheon of gods' – notwithstanding the apparent belief in *Io* as, ostensibly, a Supreme Being. So because the old Maori did *not* possess the concept of a loving and beneficent being accessible at an everyday level, that 'cultural omission' metamorphosed into a 'cultural ethos' resulting in a lifestyle both *characterised* and *defined* by extreme savagery. Until the arrival of the 'outside influence' of the Pakeha to change that very ethos, the virtue of true compassion could not exist to any great degree within the race.

If this recognitive process is extended further to encompass all that Maori regard as their 'spiritual frame of reference', we find that their inability to discern the true place of all the entities here has resulted in a culture that confuses and mixes 'natural Elemental Beings' and their 'Willed' activity with the dark activity of the 'psychic forms' produced by their own fears and superstitions. It should, of course, be an easy matter to simply let them go. Paradoxically, however, it is both the fear of them, and the idea of 'knowing' about them presupposing great knowledge in this area, that ensures their absolutely *pointless retention by Maori*. If placed solely within the framework of 'cultural traditions', then that may be more their rightful place.

Unfortunately, however, that is not generally the case. These 'Maori-produced entities' are nurtured, maintained in their forms, and locked into place by the totally wrong belief that it is all *spiritual* in its supposed reality. Here, we must include the *taniwha* and similar entities. In reality, actual *spiritual knowledge* is vastly removed from this relatively low level of just psychic/occult belief. Therefore why retain them at all?

This point of non-comprehension can be clearly illustrated by examining virtually any of the Maori legends relating to forest entities, more particularly *putapaiarehe* – or fairies. Very occasionally they are portrayed as helpers of mankind, but more regularly as evil entities who continually seek to ensnare or destroy man, such as in the legend of Rua-rangi and the "Fairy Chief", "Ihenga and the Fairies", and "Peha and the Goblins". The Maori regarded these 'entities' with great dread, and invoked the protection of their 'gods' against them. One particular 'fairy creature' called a *nanakia* was regarded as especially nasty and dangerous.

* * * * *

The belief in the more delicate "fairies of legend" is widespread in many diverse cultures. It is important to note, however, that those cultures and peoples who accepted them as being benevolent and helpful and who recognised their activity as being primarily concerned with flowers and smaller plants, were generally less fearful and superstitious than most 'indigenous peoples' who simply lived in fear of them. But that fact simply accords with Spiritual Law whereby superstitious fear *cannot possibly produce true knowledge*! It can only produce more fear and thus perpetuate ignorance in the particular area in question.

* * * * *

That is not an indictment on any people, it is simply the living reality. Which is why the Maori could not understand that the 'Elemental Beings' of "The Forces of Nature" were naturally benevolent and placed here to help humankind, if we recognise our need of them. The forest 'Elementals', which they rightfully perceived existed, were simply, for them, one more kind of unknown thing to fear. *Therein lies the reason why they could not differentiate between nature's helpers and their own frightening psychic productions which served no useful purpose.* They simply feared everything and attempted to appease all that surrounded them. That fear and uncertainty provided the means by which *tohunga* could flourish and wield great psychic control.

Whilst this level of 'knowledge' was the reality for the old Maori and formed much of the basis for his many cultural traditions, unfortunately it still remains the basic foundation for present-day 'Maori spiritual knowledge'. No real attempt has been made to analyse the truth of those beliefs, or whether or not they accord with Spiritual Law. It is all just simply inculcated into virtually every aspect of Maori thinking and even 'culturalised' politically.

That is why it is so important to not lose sight of Ratana's Mission, which led away from those wrong beliefs because they were clearly incorrect and transgressed true Spiritual Law. The transgression remains to this day in still clinging to the superstitious beliefs of old in their perpetuation of 'traditional knowledge' as inviolable Truth.

11.3   The "Natural" World of the 'Plains Indian'

Let us digress for a moment from our present thread and very briefly examine the attitude of the North American Indians to their environment, but perhaps more so with the Great Plains and forest-fringe dwellers.

The life of the Native Americans of the Northern United States revolved very much around the sharply delineated seasonal changes that characterise the Continental United States. Having the mountain range of the Rockies running in a north/south direction rather than across the land means that sudden unseasonable Arctic blasts can occur unpredictably, reaching as far south as Florida at times. By striving to understand their 'feel' for the environment, we may deduce whether or not there existed genuine knowledge of "The Elemental Forces of Nature", and not just a fear-ridden, superstitious attitude of resigned acceptance to the natural forces surrounding them, for example in the movement of life-sustaining animals, and in the vagaries of the weather.

In the case of the Plains Indians, utilising mainly the bison to provide virtually all of their shelter and clothing needs meant that he was *acutely attuned* to the most minute changes in the weather and therefore the environment surrounding him. If the legends and oral history of both the Maori and the Indian are compared in even the most cursory way, a vast difference in perception of, and attitude toward, their respective environments is quickly revealed.

As we clearly explained in **Part I**: Whereas the Maori fearfully saw dark and dangerous entities at every turn; forms that had to be *appeased* or countered in some way, the Plains Indian, in stark contrast, generally saw only the greatness of the "Elemental Forces" serving, nurturing, and protecting his world.

In his veneration of those 'forces', he not only gave thanks for all that he was given but sought to emulate their goodness in the way he related to those animals and birds whose lives he took for food, clothing and shelter. The ethos of the Native American Indians before the arrival of the European inherently encompassed that elevated outlook, where gratitude to "The Great Spirit" was invariably their first consideration. It was not fear of their environment but rather *respect* for life and *veneration* for the "Giver" of it! That recognition is well exemplified in one short sentence taken from a lengthy address by:

"One of the most important figures among Native American leaders of the eighteenth century..."

This 'most important figure' was a Seneca leader popularly known as "Red Jacket" because of a British Officer's jacket that he wore. His actual name was Sogoyewapha. From page 18 of "North American Indian Chiefs" by Karl Nagelfell, "Red Jacket's" commentary on the spiritual beliefs of the Native Americans (1805), reads:

"For all these favours we thank the Great Spirit, *and Him only*".

One can note powerful, intuitive insights here that closely approximate the essence of The First Commandment. In the case of the Native American Indians, however, it is a clearly a voluntary reverence stemming from a clarified recognition of the beneficence of the natural world which, in turn, draws its offerings from The Great Spirit, their term for The Creator! Contrast that stance with the fear element promoted by some churches toward the same Commandment from the time of the Dark Ages to the present.

Red Jacket addressed the European colonists attitude to land and religion too. Nagelfell, on page 19, records his address. Red Jacket sagely notes:

> "You have got our country, but are not satisfied... You want to force your religion upon us... We understand that your religion is written in a Book... Brother, you say there is but one way to worship the Great Spirit. If there is but one religion, why do you white people differ so much about it? ... Why not all agreed, as you can all read the Book? ... We are told that your religion was given to your forefathers... We also have a religion which was given to our forefathers and has been handed down to us... It teaches us to be thankful for all the favors we receive, to love each other, and to be united. We never quarrel about religion."

In this exceptionally noble outlook lived the strongest connections to the "Elemental Forces", and equally powerful veneration to "The Giver of Life". And even though sometimes needing to take the lives of his own at times, it was not generally in complete disregard for that life; again in stark contrast to that which the Maori savagely displayed. Whilst the Indian 'brave' was most certainly a fearless warrior, it is unlikely that this aspect of him ever degenerated to *blood-utu* and 'cannibalism'. It remained as noble as it was possible to be in the circumstances of his existence, in both the pre- and post-European phases of his life.

Even under extreme and savage provocation and duress at the encroachment of European settlement, and the more brutal behaviour of the 'frontier Army' at times, the demeanour of this people generally remained far more noble than should have been expected of any race. Their veneration for the natural world that was inherently carried within, instilled in them the strength they closely identified with in the power of the elements, and in the power and natural nobleness of the bison and the eagle.

*   *   *   *   *

Jostein Gaarder, author of "Sophie's World" notes, on pages 384-385 (emphases mine), that in this present time of great concern for our poisoned 'home', a new thought of "ecophilosophy" or *ecosophy* has emerged. Arne Naess, a Norwegian philosopher and one of the founders of this 'idea', coined the word, "ecosophy". Many in the West who subscribe to this view believe that:

> "...western civilisation as a whole is on a fundamentally wrong track, racing toward a head-on collision with the limits of what our planet can take." Moreover, the idea that man is "... master of nature... could prove to be fatal for the whole living planet."

Consequently, these particular philosophers:

> "...have looked to the thinking and ideas of other cultures... and have also studied the thoughts and customs of so-called primitive peoples – or "native peoples" such as the Native Americans – *in order to discover what we have lost.*"

We should note that Arne Naess did not look for this lost knowledge/connection in Maori culture. It is patently clear that old Maori beliefs and practices cannot possibly provide that particular essence of reverence and veneration for the natural world that philosophic-seeking would more readily find in the traditions of the Native Americans.

*   *   *   *   *

What we have lost, of course, is exactly that – true reverence and veneration – about which we offer explanations here. It is precisely what the Plains Indians had to an ennobled degree. Even though latter-day philosophers are endeavouring to find that lost knowledge, which they obviously believe exists, will they be able to accept the notion of non-material "Elemental Beings" – invisible to most of us – capable of exerting huge, weather-induced, physical effects on the environment? They are effects that, in a clearly material way, have the power to devastate man and his works. We should watch this space with great interest!

Elsewhere in this book, we opined that the great fear of the Maori toward his surroundings may have been partly influenced by the seemingly dark, brooding presence of the huge tracts of forest he encountered. And which, in his overwrought and superstitious thinking, simply had to be inhabited by dark and dangerous entities. We may note a similar fear in the ancient – and perhaps not so ancient – peoples of the "Schwarzwald", the Black Forest of southwestern Germany, and people from forested areas of Eastern Europe whose main 'phantom of fear' was the 'werewolf'.

As previously stated, the far more open and benevolent regard that the "Red Man", in particular the Plains Indians, had for his world might be similarly explained by his association with a land that was permanently open to the great vault of the sky. No dark beings could live there! But that is not the complete story. For the forest-dwellers of North America showed similar veneration for their environment, and respect for the animals they hunted too. The clear reality between the two peoples was that one, the Maori, remained more firmly tied to psychic things, **against** *the ordained Will*. The other, the "Red Man", clearly lifted himself more decisively out of that world and developed a strong and beneficial connection to the "Elemental Forces", exactly in accordance **with** *the ordained Will!*

And it was that more noble and correct connection that has bequeathed to us the deeply evocative and hauntingly beautiful, "Song of Hiawatha". Even though written by the American poet Longfellow, it nevertheless perfectly describes the veneration and love of the Indian for his environment and the "Elemental Forces" that brought it into being. The wonderful story of "Hiawatha" well exemplifies how we should relate to the natural world that is our home. With Hiawatha we can feel strong veneration for the gift of a beautiful environment, one that offers help and nurturing through honour and respect. Yet it is one that can also bring harshness and sudden death in foolish transgression.

*   *   *   *   *

Whilst Hiawatha features in many stories, legends and motion pictures as an idealised, romantic Native American tale, the historical reality about him is far more profound. Karl Nagelfell (on pages 10-11), writes that he was probably born about 1500 in what is now New York State; among the six peoples of what eventually became the Iroquois Nation – under Hiawatha's political acumen. He was active until about 1570 and during his life was instrumental in uniting the various groups into the Five Nations federation.
It took the form of:

> "...an unwritten constitution authorizing the election of a representative body and formu-lating rules for calling it into session. The vote was by people. If war was to be declared, the vote must be unanimous. Disputes between people were to be arbitrated and not settled by violence. This unwritten constitution, admired by colonial statesmen, gave each people almost complete independence but at the same time bound it to respect the wishes of others."

After Hiawatha's death, as the power of the Five Nations grew, his fame grew with it. The Federation later became the Six Nations with the addition of the Tuscarora people.
And whilst the famous:

> "...League of the Iroquois was a peaceful union for the Six Nations, it was also a military alliance against neighbouring peoples."

So successful was Hiawatha's confederacy that an Oneida chief suggested to colonial delegates of Connecticut and Pennsylvania to set up something similar to govern the relations of the colonies. Latter-day students of politics and government have found much to admire in the working of the League:

> "...and there is some historical evidence that knowledge of the League influenced the colonies in their first efforts to form a confederacy and later to write a constitution."

(Nagelfell: "North American Indian Chiefs.")

*   *   *   *   *

With regard to the Plains cultures once more, and our assertion that it was most likely the vast openness of the land that produced or strongly influenced such an ennobled outlook in the inhabitants, Colin F. Taylor, in his book "Native American Myths and Legends", notes the powerful effect the Great Plains exerted. The following notation reinforces our premise.

> "There seems to be something within the unique environment of the Great Plains which causes a people to live with such vivid intensity and an awareness and understanding of the things around them. The Plains Indian was so much in daily association with his environment and so dependent upon it, that not only animals but plant life and even some inanimate objects were believed to have a spiritual existence. There was an awareness of a great power – the energy or moving force of the great universe – which, in the sacred language of the Lakota shamans, was called Skan or To and the blue of the sky symbolised its presence."

And in the same publication, p.41, a senior Cavalry Officer – Col. Richard Dodge, 1877 – whose Military service encompassed the same part of North America, had this to say about the initial effect the Plains could have on people.

> "The first experience of the Plains, like the first sail with a cap full of wind, is apt to be sickening. This once overcome, the nerves stiffen, the senses expand and man begins to realize the magnificence of being."

If a European could experience and realize 'the magnificence of being' without possessing an inherent veneration for the environment of the Great Plains, consider how deep that respect had become for its inhabitants – a respect nurtured for far longer than Europeans. A more striking example of the deep, innate understanding that the "Red Man" had for his environment, however, is now preserved for posterity in what is probably *inadequately described* as:

> "...the most beautiful and profound statement on the environment ever made."

Like "White Cloud's statement" of great wisdom at the beginning of this Chapter, there does not appear to be anything in Maori *waiata* to even remotely approach the pure nobleness of the address given by the Great Chief Seattle, Chief of the Duwamish, upon 'surrendering' his land to Governor Isaac Stevens in 1854. After the 'Great White Chief' in Washington made an 'offer' for a large area of Indian Land and promised a 'reservation' for the Indian people, Chief Seattle 'offered' his wisdom! Surely, the most noble address on the environment ever, and from which we will offer a few quotes. Such a wonderfully powerful document should grace every home!

The clear and knowledgeable attitude toward the 'natural elements' should be carefully noted, and then seriously compared with some of the claims heard by, and currently before, the Waitangi Tribunal!

11.4   Excerpts from Chief Seattle's Address

"The Great Chief Washington sends word that he wishes to buy our land.

For we know that if we do not sell, the White Man may come with guns and take our land. The idea is strange to us.

If we do not own the freshness of the air and the sparkle of the water, how can we buy them? We know that the White Man does not understand our ways. One portion of land is the same to him as the next, for he is a stranger who comes in the night and takes from the land what he needs.

The earth is not his brother, but his enemy and when he has conquered it, he moves on.

His appetite will devour the earth and leave behind only a desert. The sight of your cities pains the eyes of the Red Man.

There is no quiet place in the White Man's cities. No place to hear the unfurling of leaves in spring or the rustle of an insect's wings. The clatter only seems to insult the ears.

The air is precious to the Red Man for all things share the same breath – the beast, the tree, the man, they all share the same breath.

The White Man does not seem to notice the air he breathes.

Like a dying man for many days he is numb to the stench.

I have seen a thousand rotting buffaloes on the prairie, left by the White Man who shot them from a passing train.

I am savage and do not understand how the smoking iron horse can be more important than the buffalo that we kill only to stay alive.

For whatever happens to the beasts soon happens to man. All things are connected.

Whatever befalls the earth, befalls the sons of the earth. If men spit upon the ground they spit upon themselves.

This we know, the earth does not belong to man, man belongs to earth. Man did not weave the web of life he is merely a strand in it. Whatever he does to the web, he does to himself.

Our warriors have felt shame and after defeat they turn their days in idleness and contaminate their bodies with sweet food and strong drink.

It matters little where we spend the rest of our days. There are not many.

But why should I mourn the passing of my people? Tribes are made of men, nothing more. Men come and go like the waves of the sea.

Even the White Man, whose God walks and talks with him as friend to friend, cannot be exempt from common destiny.

One thing we know, which the White Man may one day discover – our God is the same God. You may think now that you own Him as you wish to own our land, but you cannot.

The earth is precious to Him and to harm the earth is to heap contempt on it's Creator.

The whites too shall pass; perhaps sooner than all other tribes.

Continue to contaminate your bed and one night you will suffocate in your own waste.

But in your perishing you will shine brightly, fired by the strength of the God who brought you to this land for some special purpose...

That destiny is a mystery to us for we do not understand when the Buffalo are all slaughtered, the wild horses tamed, the secret corners of the forest heavy with the scent of many men and the view of the ripe hills blotted by talking wires.

Where is the thicket? Gone. The end of living and the beginning of survival.

So if we sell you our land, love it as we have loved it, care for it as we have cared for it,... And with all your strength, with all your mind, with all your heart, preserve it for your children and **love it** – as God loves us all.

One thing we know. Our God is the same God. The earth is precious to Him. Even the white man cannot be exempt from the common destiny.

We may be brothers after all."

(Chief Seattle, 1854. Re-printed with kind permission of
"Friends of the Earth".)

We have woven an especial thread from Chief Seattle's complete and extremely powerful yet painful address. Contained within it is much of the living essence of The Spiritual Laws of

Creation, which we can easily recognise if we so wish. If used as a guide, the exquisitely noble words of great wisdom by an equally great and noble Native American Chief can help Maori to understand the difference between that which they *believe* to be spiritual, and that which the substance of Chief Seattle's wisdom points to in its actual reality. It is thus vitally important to accurately discern between *psychic*, *elemental*, and genuine *spiritual* activity.

By that same measure we can thus differentiate between genuine *elemental* messages of warning that might be given for our safety, and unreliable 'personal feelings', perhaps often generated by the emotions or by fear. Most importantly, though, we need to learn to recognise clear spiritual guidance too, for such guidance will always be beneficial. That will be the exact measure of its spiritual validity.

The history of man records numerous incidents where warnings received from strictly elemental activity or 'signs', resulted in the prevention of accident or death in some way. That is not to say, however, that every single natural event involving all the elements of nature, and every animal, insect and bird that we see, or might otherwise catch our attention, means that something is 'absolutely going to happen'. To believe so is to nurture superstition and generate uncertainty and possibly fear at every turn. More often than not, such things will be the normal and natural activity of all the other natural life-forms around us.

Nevertheless, warnings are sometimes given for our protection and, if recognised as such, should be acted on immediately. Discernment is the key in knowing what to listen to, and what to ignore. And it naturally follows that superstition cannot provide that appropriate level of discernment. The only sure way to absolutely know is to be thoroughly conversant with the workings of "Elemental Lore". For it is "The Elemental Forces" that will sound any such warnings, since our continued existence is interlinked with their ordained activity. To achieve that level of discernment, however, the sufficient understanding of the higher Spiritual Laws is the first imperative. It is unfortunate that man has become so obtuse that the warnings *constantly* being given to mankind now are no longer heard. To our serious detriment, we have lost the ability and spiritual power of, and inherent in, **"protective discernment"**!

11.5   The "Elemental" Connection to the Animal Kingdom

In this segment we will examine a few examples of the natural ability of animals to sense impending changes in the activity of the earth in order to illustrate how we can learn and benefit from them – again for our protection. Because earthquake lore invariably records the fact that many animals become agitated before any major earth-movement, let us briefly examine this phenomenon. Earthquakes can trigger other crustal changes or movements, such as in volcanic activity – or vice-versa – and can set in motion hugely destructive tsunami. Since many of the world's great cities are clustered around natural harbours for purposes of maritime trade, and the frequency of larger earthquakes is increasing, perhaps more attention should be paid to the activity of animals in these areas.

The scientific/intellectual mind-set of seismologists for many years tended to dismiss stories of precursory animal behaviour as scientifically useless or greatly exaggerated folk-tales. However, recent large quakes in China produced thousands of reports of strange animal behaviour which were so compelling that earthquake scientists from other countries are now re-considering such phenomena.[4]

Modern seismic instruments are capable of detecting even the most minute changes in the earth's electrical and magnetic fields, and even patterns of sub-audible sound. And whilst these changes may be subsequently shown to precede seismic activity, they do not always. Yet in the

---

[4]We restate our previous contention that this has always been the natural pattern since time immemorial because earth movements are an *elemental activity* to which all animals are closely attuned. And "Elemental Lore" takes no account whatsoever of what earth-sciences may so decree.

long history of recorded phenomena of this nature, animals, birds and fishes, far more sensitive to such tiny stimuli, react immediately in the sureness of *knowing* that an earth movement is imminent. Therefore, we can surely state that we have a 'constant' in this behaviour pattern, even if a non-scientific one, yet one far more reliable than much of our 'modern' detection equipment.

So what might we deduce from this? Marine scientists marvel at the sonar abilities that mammals of the order Cetacea (whales and dolphins etc.) possess, but are unable to definitively explain it apart from using scientific terms that perhaps closely approximate their theories. Similarly, animal reactions of the kind we have outlined cannot simply be slotted into a solely scientific pigeon-hole either. Whilst the physical event can certainly be recorded as electrical activity etc., nevertheless, it is an *'Elemental' happening in the first instance,* and one driven by *spiritual* power. This is the X factor that science cannot measure with its instruments, and to which the animal world, itself strongly connected to the elemental world to the strongest possible degree, reacts.

A few examples recorded in "The Handbook of Unusual Natural Phenomena" (Eyewitness Accounts of Nature's Greatest Mysteries.) William R Corliss. Arlington House Crown Publishers, New York, may offer clearer illustration.

In the sub-Chapter, "The Curious Supersensitivity of Animals to Impending Quakes", Corliss notes how the consternation of dogs, horses, cattle and other domestic animals are referred to in the records of most great earthquakes. Fish are also frequently affected. In the London earthquake of 1749 roach and other fish in a canal showed evident signs of confusion and fright. Moreover, he records that, sometimes after an earthquake, fish rise to the surface dead and dying. And during the Tokyo earthquake of 1880 cats inside a house ran about trying to escape, foxes barked, and horses tried to kick down the boards confining them to their stables.

Whilst we may not be overly surprised with such frightened behaviour of animals *during* a tremor, it is an entirely different matter when animals clearly sense something *about* to happen when contraindications appear to suggest otherwise. As if aware of an earthquake's imminent arrival, Corliss recorded that:

> "...ponies have been known to prance about their stalls, pheasants to scream, and frogs to cease croaking a little time before a shock..."

Interestingly, geese, pigs and dogs appear more sensitive in this respect than other animals. Calabrian folklore, after the great earthquake there:

> "...recorded that the neighing of a horse, the braying of a donkey, or the cackle of a goose was sufficient to cause the inhabitants to flee their houses in expectation of a shock."

(Quotes, p.291)

At the time of this quake, sand-eels, which are usually buried in the sand, came to the surface. Many birds are believed to show their uneasiness before an earthquake by hiding their heads under their wings and behaving in an unusual manner.

Some South American peoples believe that certain quadrupeds such as dogs, cats and jerboa rats give warning of coming danger by their restlessness. And immense flocks of seabirds sometimes fly inland before an earthquake, as if alarmed by the commencement of some sub-oceanic disturbance. In Chile, before the shock of 1835, all the dogs are said to have escaped from the city of Talcahuano. A scientific explanation for such behaviour has been advanced by one Professor Milne. He believes that some animals are sensitive to the small tremors that precede almost all earthquakes. Moreover he suggests that, as the result of their own experiences, animal intelligence would then register alarm at any future indications of major earth movements which will have taught them that small earth tremors may be precursors to a large shake.

Interestingly, Corliss states that signs of alarm days before an earthquake are probably accidental. This statement is clearly contradictory for, quite obviously, any signs of alarm even days before an earthquake *actually occurring* must logically be cognitive prescience on the part of the animals concerned, purely by virtue of the *arrival* of the quake, and therefore can hardly be deemed accidental.

But what do other publications report about such interesting phenomena. Corliss records the "American Review of Reviews", 37: 104, 1908, as itemising the following:

> "In connection with the fearful catastrophes of recent date in Italy, California, and else-where, which, like so many others of like nature will long retain a hold on human memory, attention has again been called to the fact that many animals give intimations of such great disturbances in advance by certain particular and often unusual conduct. It is particularly such animals as have their abode underground that often indicate, days before the event, that something unusual in nature is about to occur, by coming out of their hiding places underground into the open.
>
> Aelian mentions that, in the year 373 before Christ, five days before the destruction of Helike, all the mice, weasels, snakes and other like creatures, were observed going in great masses along the roads leading from that place. Something similar was noticed also, later, though not to so marked an extent as in the case mentioned by Aelian. This leaving of their subterranean abodes by underground creatures on such occasions might possibly be explained by the emission of various malodorous and noxious gases during these disturbances of the earth."

But not only do animals living under ground furnish indications that something out of the ordinary is about to happen. The larger animals on the surface, such as cows, horses, sheep, and even many birds, seem to get premonitions of particular natural phenomena and events.

Corliss records that in 1805, during an earthquake:

> "...the cattle at Naples and its neighbourhood set up a continuous bellowing some time *before* the event, at the same time trying to support themselves more firmly by planting the forefeet widely apart; the sheep kept up a continuous bleating, and hens and other fowl expressed their restlessness by making a terrible racket. Even the dogs gave many indications of uneasiness at the time. The actions of animals observed during the great earthquake of 1783 seem to have been most remarkable. Thus the howling of the dogs at Messina became so unendurable that men were sent out with cudgels to kill them."

A rather foolish procedure, perhaps, given the ability of the animals to forewarn.

Corliss further notes that their noise was most marked during the progress of the earthquake, while it was difficult to pacify the animals in the vicinity for some time, even after the cessation of the shocks. Dogs and horses ran about meanwhile with hanging heads, or stood with outstretched legs: "...as if aware of the need of planting themselves firmly." Horses that were ridden at the time stopped and stood still without orders: "...trembling so at the same time that no rider could remain in the saddle."

Corliss catalogues Scophus as telling the story of a cat during an earthquake at Locris:

> "...which set up a most dismal caterwauling at the approach of each new shock, meanwhile constantly jumping from one point to another. The roosters kept up a continual crowing, both before and during the earthquake. In the fields Scophus also observed hares: ...so under the influence of the terrestrial disturbance that they made no attempt to escape and seemed in no way disturbed by his presence." A flock of sheep could not be kept on the right road, notwithstanding the efforts of shepherd and dogs, but fled in affrighted haste to the mountains."

Birds, also, seem to have premonitions of the coming of such catastrophes. During the earthquake of Quintero, in Chile, in November 1822: "...the gulls uttered all sorts of unusual cries during the whole of the preceding night and were in constant restless motion during the quake." And on 20th February 1835, the day before the earthquake at Concepcion, (also) in Chile, at ten in the morning:

> "...great flocks of seabirds, mostly gulls, were seen to pass over the city landward, a phe-
> nomenon not to be explained by any stormy condition of the weather. It was fully an hour
> and a half after their passage, at 11:40 of the forenoon, before the earthquake came, one so
> disastrous that nearly the entire city was reduced to ruins."

Even the fish in the sea seem to be disturbed at the approach of an earthquake. Alexander von Humboldt, the famous traveller and naturalist, tells of having observed: "...the crocodiles of the Orinoco leaving the water and fleeing to the forest during an earthquake."

During the 1930s some scientists wondered whether the growing mountain of anecdotal evidence on pre-quake animal behaviour might be sufficient to help predict impending earthquakes. Corliss cites the publication, Nature, as reporting that the Japanese undertook the first experiments – perhaps not so surprising given the huge amount of tremors Japan experiences.

Corliss notes: "...two Japanese seismologists, Dr. Shinkishi Hatai and Dr. Noboru Abe, observed that catfish (Siluroidea) in natural conditions showed signs of restlessness about six hours before earthquake disturbances were registered on their recording apparatus." Since catfish are ordinarily placid, unresponsive creatures, experiments were made to test that seeming precursive responsiveness. Catfish placed in an aquarium were tested three times a day by tapping on the supporting table. When no earthquake was impending, "...the fish moved lazily or not at all." But about six hours before a shock "...the fish jumped when the table was tapped and sometimes swam about agitatedly for a time before settling down upon the bottom again." Several month's testing showed that in a period when 178 earthquakes of all degrees of severity had been recorded: "...the fish had correctly predicted 80% of the shocks." They showed no discrimination in their movements between slight local shocks and more serious distant shocks. The experimenters think that the catfish:

> "...are made sensitive through electrical changes in the earth, since it was only when the
> aquarium was electrically earthed, through the drainpipe, that they responded to a coming
> earthquake."

(Nature, 132:817, 1933)

In terms of "Elemental Lore", it is quite logical that the catfish should respond when the conditions of what would be their more natural environment were re-created, whereas any form of shielding might not necessarily provide that same response.

The Chinese have always believed that the earth provided all the messages required to predict earthquakes. Some times the messages are so clear that precise predictions can be made and lives saved. Such was the case in the Haicheng earthquake of 1975 where dozens of abnormalities pointed to an impending quake. Apart from solely animal behaviour, sudden changes and unusual fluctuations in groundwater levels were also catalogued. Two days before the quake struck, 90,000 residents were evacuated. At 1030hrs on the precise day predicted, the final warning was given and the rest of the city emptied. Nine hours later the quake struck. Measuring 7.3 on the Richter scale, it destroyed or damaged 90% of the city's buildings but few deaths resulted from it. (Encarta, BBC and "Our World" programme: "The Savage Earth".)

The world's greatest recorded natural disaster occurred in China in 1556 in Shensi province where a single earthquake killed 800,000 people. Such devastating earth movements have prompted Chinese officials to collate reports concerning premonitory signs from the rural populace, particularly farmers. China currently possesses the world's largest computer network for collating earthquake data. With hundreds of millions of people tied closely to the earth who are perhaps more attuned to subtle changes in their environment than people resident in cities, the authorities have achieved some success in earthquake prediction. Unlike Haicheng, however, the 'messages' from the Tangshan 'quake', whilst very numerous, were not as clear.

After the Tangshan earthquake Shen Ling-huang, a Chinese writer, filed the following report.

> "A stock-breeder in Northern China got up to feed his animals before dawn on 28th July 1976. He is a member of the Kaokechuang People's Commune which lies only 40 kilometres away from the city of Tangshan. When he went into the stable, he found that instead of eating, his two horses and two mules were jumping and kicking until they finally broke loose and dashed outside. At that moment, a dazzling white flash illuminated the sky and huge rumbling noises were heard. The Tangshan earthquake (magnitude 7.8) had struck.
>
> This occurrence was reported to Chinese scientists during a survey of the earthquake-affected areas around Tangshan. Their mission was to find out about the feasibility of an earthquake prediction programme that made use of observations of animal behaviour. This survey, covering Tangshan and 400 communes in 48 counties around it, was conducted by Chinese biophysicists, biologists, geophysicists, chemists, and meteorologists shortly after the earthquake.
>
> Through interviews and discussions with local people, the scientists collected information on 2,093 cases of unusual animal behaviour in the time shortly before the earthquake. Nearly all of the anecdotes were passed on to the scientists by survivors of the earthquake themselves; the majority of the reports involved domestic animals. Some examples included goats that refused to go into pens, cats and dogs that picked up their offspring and carried them outdoors, pigs that squealed strangely, startled chickens that dashed out of coops in the middle of the night, rats that left their nests, and fish that dashed about aimlessly."

(Earthquake Information Bulletin, 10:231-33, 1978, Corliss 291-294.)

In the case of the Haicheng earthquake, the authorities, armed with similar kind of information – and completely accepting of its validity – took the precaution of 'being wise before the event' and ordered the evacuation of the city before it was struck. Compare that example with the people of Messina who went out to kill the howling dogs rather than accepting the phenomenon as a warning of something serious impending. Humans cannot match the sensitivity of animals to earthquake precursors, so the subtle signs that set dogs to howling often pass by humans undetected.

This unfortunate state of affairs is solely the result of humankind closing that necessary connection to the same forces and signs that animals immediately react to, and which is a potential lifesaver. For we also possess a similar ability if we would only recognise such forces and then utilise both that ability and the warnings for our protection too. The observance of animal behaviour predating the occurrence of earthquakes goes back centuries. In fact, even in 100 AD, Pliny, a Roman writer, advocated then that such behaviour be used for predicting earthquakes.

Volume II of "Earthquakes and the Urban Environment", G. Lennis Berlin. CRC Press, records interesting observations of animal behaviour. A short summary offers the following information.

> "Zoo animals refuse to go into their shelters at night; snakes, lizards, and small mammals evacuate their underground burrows; hyperactive insects congregate in huge swarms near seashores; cattle seek high ground; wild fowl leave their usual habitats; domestic animals become agitated."

In the United States, the earliest published accounts of unusual animal behaviour were for the 1906 San Francisco earthquake where a Miss Finette Locke kept detailed notes of this phenomenon from cases reported to her. In a summary of her notes published in the 1908 report of the State Earthquake Investigation Commission, several of her observations were:

"Horses whinnied before the shock... Several instances were reported where cows stampeded before the shock was felt by the observer. In other cases cows about to be milked are said to have been restless before the shock... Lowing of cattle at the time of the shock was very commonly reported, and in some cases this is said to have occurred a little before the shock. The most common report regarding the behaviour of dogs was their howling during the night preceding the earthquake."

The lowing of cattle at the time of the shock should surely be a natural expectation. So it appears surprising that such behaviour should be considered unusual, in contrast to that preceding a tremor. Vol. II of "Earthquakes and the Urban Environment" offers an interesting insight into the changes in attitude that are obviously occurring within some of the disciplines. The following quote reflects this new awareness.

"Until quite recently, accounts like these were usually met with skepticism. However, this view is changing, largely due to the apparent successes the Chinese have had in using erratic animal behaviour as an earthquake precursor... farmers are instructed to watch for unusual activity in their animals, and observers are even stationed in the Peking Zoo to watch for any unusual animal activity. Erratic behaviour is reported to a local seismological brigade."

A booklet issued by the Seismological Office of Tientsin offers observers hints on how to use unusual animal behaviour for predicting earthquakes. A translated summary states:

"It is easy and simple to use animals to predict earthquakes. Certain organs of animals may acutely detect various underground changes before earthquakes. Both historical and recent surveys of large earthquakes prove that animals have precursory reactions."

And an earthquake prediction verse from the same translated publication notes that:

"Animals are aware of precursors before earthquakes: Let us summarise their anomalous behaviour for prediction. Cattle, sheep, mules and horses do not enter corrals. Rats move their homes and flee. Hibernating snakes leave their burrows early. Frightened pigeons continuously fly and do not return to nests. Rabbits raise their ears, jump aimlessly and bump things. Fish are frightened, jump above water surface."

The high geological activity of the San Andreas fault in California offers ideal monitoring conditions for American geologists. This very visible fault line is generated by the Pacific Plate moving past the North American Plate. However, even though both plates are moving in the same northwestwards direction, the Pacific is moving faster than the North American. That 'speed differential' effectively means that the 'relative movement' of the two Plates is in opposite directions. It is generally accepted that the San Andreas fault will one day produce one of the largest earthquakes ever experienced by man.

Increasing 'Western' scientific interest in the possibility of utilising animal behaviour for earthquake predictions is illustrated by a perhaps belated admittance from U.S. scientists at a two day conference sponsored by the USGS (US Geological Survey) in October 1976 in noting that: "...there may be some truth in the belief that animals can sense some environmental change that precedes an earthquake."

"...the activity of captive pocket mice and kangaroo rats is being monitored at sites near the Palmdale bulge, and the motor activity of cockroaches is being monitored at sites near Hollister, Twin Lakes, and Anza – sites close to active faults. Preliminary results from the second study indicate that before the occurrence of small earthquakes, there is a marked increase in their motor activity."

(Conference Notes, p.38-39)

We wonder whether New Zealand seismologists would monitor fish, chickens or rodents in 'quake-prone' Wellington? Or would it actually be more a case of disbelief or even outright rejection of such 'fairy-tale' notions? If so, it is clearly a mistake. Moving further away from the knowledge of the very 'Forces' which might better offer the correct warning signs before the 'big one' hits will be to the obvious detriment of those so affected. Still, as in all things, free-will choices are never taken from us!

Yet according to historical accounts immediately prior to one of New Zealand's more spectacular natural disasters in the 19th century – the Mt Tarawera eruption – a *tohunga* living at Wairoa *accurately predicted its eruption*. Local Maori feared him so much they wanted him killed. Because his small *whare* was buried under volcanic ash they believed he had perished, much to their delight. However, he was dug out alive and well. The point here is that we humans *also* possess the innate ability to sense impending disasters if we allow our intuition or 'gut feeling' full rein. Of course, it must be *genuine* intuition or prescience, and not simply 'personal feelings'!

11.6 The "Elemental" Connection to the Human World

Having examined a few examples of connected 'Elemental' and animal activity for our purposes, apart from our previous reference to Jesus and the storm on the Sea of Galilee and the help given to Moses, are we able to cull a little more from The Bible to illustrate our assertions that other 'ordained beings' such as "Nature Elementals" are a reality. One of the Psalms of David offers a, seemingly, curiously worded Scripture, but not so curious when the knowledge of 'nature beings' is taken into account.

"Thou Who maketh Thine angels into winds and Thy servants into flames of fire."

An interesting passage in the Book of Isaiah also sheds further light on this 'reality' in terms of a definitive, relative place within Creation for such 'entities' – at least as indicated in The Bible. The prophet, Isaiah, sometimes referred to as The Great Prophet, is generally held in high regard in possessing greater clarity of spiritual perceptive depth than perhaps some of the others. In Isaiah 18, Verse 3, he states:

"All ye **inhabitants *of the world***, **AND dwellers *on the earth***, see ye, when He lifteth up an ensign on the mountains; and when He bloweth a trumpet, hear ye."

(Bold emphases mine.)

In this Scripture we can readily note a clear delineation of **two** distinctly separate groups having their sphere of activity in **two** different places **not** closely connected. It seems perfectly clear that the "inhabitants *of the world*" are **not** the same 'beings' as the "***dwellers on the earth***". This separation is further accentuated by the wording of 'inhabitants of' and 'dwellers on', and in the use of the conjunction, ***and***, in the sentence. From our explanations of the various planes of Creation, we could well conclude that Isaiah might actually have possessed the spiritual insight to *see* some of the other inhabitants of Creation aside from just the "dwellers on the earth". Whether this was so or not does not alter the obvious fact of his seemingly sure statement here.

Throughout history, what humankind term the instinct of animals has provided us with wonderful tales of near misses and lives saved from disaster when unusual behaviour of domestic pets such as cats and dogs have alerted their owners to imminent danger. Anecdotal evidence also reveals that domesticated animals such as horses have refused to continue along a path for no apparent reason, even with the strongest urging. And then, onto the very area that the animal refused to enter, the rider escapes a slip that comes crashing down.

In such cases it is not any inherent instinct of the animal that causes it to shy away from certain areas at those precise moments, even if it had taken the same path regularly for many years. It simply heeds a warning that danger is imminent, because it is able to see where the warning comes from. Today only a few people possess that similar faculty. This inherent ability in animals can be explained by the fact that their animating core (the inner life-force) originates in the Animistic Sphere. That is also the plane of origin of those 'nature beings' that have their field of activity in what we usually call Nature i.e., air, fire, earth and water. Therefore, the similarity of their origins naturally provides the clear possibility for each to recognise the other.

As our origin lies in the higher Spiritual Sphere, we are far less equipped to recognise the "Elemental Beings", unlike the animal whose origin stands closer to them. Moreover, because it is precisely the 'Elementals' who are tasked with the preparation and bringing about of those happenings we call disasters and catastrophes, they therefore know exactly when and where sudden changes in Nature are about to take place.

Therefore all events in this category, such as landslides, sudden water eruptions, the bursting of a dam, tidal waves and floods, volcanic eruptions, rocks dislodged from mountains, trees falling, the caving-in of land undermined by water, and virtually everything connected with natural events, are all the ordained activity of the 'nature beings'. If, then, such an event is imminent, the possibility exists for an animal or person approaching the spot to be warned by these 'Elementals'. Their presence and warnings, even though generally unseen by human beings, may produce feelings of distinct apprehension or unease such as a 'cold feeling' or 'hair standing on end', and may be sufficient to induce an individual not to proceed further. The behaviour of the animal may be markedly different, however. It is invariably startled, its hair bristles, and it may simply refuse to go any further.

Without this knowledge, such an experience of distinct unease or apprehension would probably imbue one with fear, particularly if one's cultural frame of reference encompassed the belief of fearful forest or mountain entities, psychic or phantom forms, or even the fear of earth-bound souls. We may wonder how many such warnings from out of the compassion of **"The Light"** have been given to humankind over millennia, and how much of it was treated with fearful apprehension? Given the increasing frequency and intensity of storms worldwide, we should be careful that any such 'help' given is not pushed away out of fear, but gratefully accepted!

Now, if we recall the earlier explanations in this Chapter regarding the connections between our free-will ability and the return of all our "sowings" via the activity of the 'nature beings', we may begin to discern the reasons why man very often finds himself in dangerous situations with the potential for death or serious injury. We should therefore emulate and refine the previous Chinese example and pay more attention to animals and thus learn from them. If we coolly and *objectively* observe the increasing 'Elemental activity' worldwide in natural disasters and catastrophes of greater and greater intensity and frequency, it is very clear that man does, indeed, **stand blind to the true nature of the happening!**

*   *   *   *   *

These explanations may offer the reader the possible connecting reasons why some intensely hot Eastern Australian, or Californian bushfire-storms, which can completely destroy a brick dwelling and melt cars, will sometimes leave the next-door *wooden* dwelling virtually untouched. Ordinarily, such intense heat would generally 'explode' the wooden structure even before the flames will have reached it.

During the Ash Wednesday firestorms around Melbourne in the early 1980s, some of the houses that were left relatively intact, even though directly in the fire-path in some cases, were then destroyed or severely damaged by major flooding a few months later. Under the outworking of The Spiritual Laws, much that we are forced to *experience*, and the *timing* of that experience – even in natural disasters and catastrophes – is **not** an arbitrary happening.

*   *   *   *   *

What should also be recognised is that the 'Elementals' are active in every Sphere of Creation, and not solely on the earth. And just as we have small 'nature beings' whose area of activity is concerned with the smaller plants of the world, and larger ones concerned with seas and mountains etc., so are there also 'beings' of immense size and power whose field of activity reaches out into the forming of galaxies, suns and planets. All such activity takes place under the outworking of **The Creative Will!**

Perhaps we may now understand the activity of the "Elemental Beings" whose 'ordained work' brought into being our own planet earth and raised the various lands out of the sea. Thus we may view the legend of Maui fishing the North Island out of the sea as an 'elemental event' performed by the larger and more powerful 'nature beings' of the earth. And we may note the legend of how Ruaumoko, youngest offspring of Papa, secured the weapon of *ahi komau* (subterranean fire) to wage war against man. By this means he makes the land and sea tremble, which engulfs land, destroys trees, rocks, man, and all other things.

With a definitive spiritual explanation of the true nature of "The Forces of Nature" at our disposal, what should we now do with it? Quite simply, it is necessary for all humankind to re-awaken to the truth of "Elemental Beings" and their vital activity. With regard to Maori, however, if there is to be a genuine re-awakening and complete fulfilment of a truly spiritual purpose, a necessary first step is to begin to fearlessly examine all that we have stated. And equally fearlessly discard the connections to psychic entities that have obviously been confused with genuine "Elemental Beings", and expunge from Maori consciousness **all** the mechanisms that produced those psychic aspects in the first place. Emotional considerations of reverence toward some aspects of cultural traditions will thus need to be curbed here.

Only then will we begin to *actually learn* the true nature and purpose of the "Elemental Beings" as the first vital step into genuine spiritual knowledge. Once that first understanding is reached, the discernment process, by virtue of more complete 'knowing', will allow Maoridom to let go of more and more unnecessary, aspiritual baggage. Thus enabling the people to stand *more firmly* on the foundation of Elemental truth in the same way that the Native Americans once did.

This would permit a *conscious working* with "The Elemental Forces of Nature" and the clear realisation that no race can lay claim to 'ownership' of land, river or air. We are enjoined to be stewards and *kaitiaki* of the land over which we must pass. And further enjoined to leave it in at least a good a state as, or preferably better than, that which we might have inherited. Those people who *truly understand* this fundamental fact will invariably produce wonderful beauty and harmony on the piece of land that they understand is theirs to nurture for the time that they are permitted to be on it.[5]

Contrast that with the general state of land owned by those who lay claim to sole *tangata whenua* status; those who state it is theirs by right. With such a wrong attitude, there is not the perceived need to offer anything of beauty back to the gift of the land, especially in the case of land simply returned under a Waitangi Tribunal determination. Thus where the receivers are not required to offer even a material value for it, let alone any beneficial future use as a condition of return. Unfortunately, such lands are often marred by unsightly nurturing practices, or accorded a 'couldn't care less' attitude, or are leased to the Pakeha who then quite rightly uses it for his benefit. All that exists here is the belief in the right to demand – a foolishly

---

[5]In this country, most in that category belong to the race of the Pakeha.

dangerous stance given the power of the "Nature Beings" to easily wipe it all away if *their lore is not respected*. The noble words of Chief Seattle should be the benchmark for a more correct attitude toward *kaitiakitanga* of land.

Such powerful statements of truth regarding 'ownership of land' should therefore be marked well because, at any moment, the incalculable power of "The Elemental Forces of Nature" can quickly devastate any tract of land or destroy any works on it. *It is a process, moreover, that occurs somewhere on earth every hour of the day – **and it is increasing***. This fact alone should sound a cautionary warning to develop more *humility* toward the inherent 'Elemental' *mana* of the land, and therefore caution in the dangerous demand to 'own' it all.

Similarly, the contention of some Maori groups who insist they have the right to lay claim to the air waves or air space, is just as spiritually untenable as any claim to rivers and the associated hydrological cycle. If the claim is purely for a share of communication channels as the medium whereby electronic data is transmitted, and nothing more, then that is obviously part and parcel of current communications and business practice. But if it is for the *actual ownership of air space* by virtue of a 'belief of ownership' of all of Aotearoa through supposed *tangata whenua* status, then the whole idea of 'owning' air space is totally ludicrous in any terms. Especially so, however, under that of the ultimate Law – The Spiritual Laws of Creation.

In the final analysis such claims appear to be nothing more than a greedy grab for money or power, or the means with which to acquire it. For such demands have absolutely **no affinity with Spiritual Truth in any shape or form**. And it greatly surprises this writer that Waitangi Tribunal members, who are clearly well educated and who *ostensibly* possess higher levels of *mana* and spiritual knowledge – by virtue of these co-joined aspects of status according to Maori thinking – are apparently unable to discern the truth of these relatively simple and logical *spiritual* realities. Careful cognisance of Spiritual Truth, nobly stated by Chief Seattle, should be the benchmark for any such determinations, and not solely that of a spiritually-flawed Treaty document.

Therefore, to *demand* ownership of a river is one more example of wrongful thinking on the part of some Iwi utilising *tangata whenua* status. Under the outworking of our new knowledge of "Elemental Lore", let us now utilise it and briefly examine the spiritual ramifications of Maori claims to waterways!

Just as land is formed by 'Elemental' activity under the outworking of Spiritual Law so, too, are the rivers. The hydrological cycle, *alone*, is the reason why rivers exist. This cycle is a spiritually-generated one through the outworking of Spiritual Law acting on, and in, the Material World. That lawful process is put in place by the activity of "The Elemental Forces of Nature".

Therefore, the river, by virtue of 'Elemental activity', can only exist if the hydrological cycle exists. Should it fail, the river ceases to be. So in claiming ownership of any waterway, the hydrological cycle with all its precipitation must be claimed, too, since that is *the source* of the river's flow. This kind of wrong demand needs to be recognised as a serious transgression against the ordained activity of the helpers of *Tane*. In truth, it is also patently ridiculous. The "Elemental Forces" determine all such things under the aegis of Spiritual Law, and it is we human beings who must understand and learn to accept the truth of this sure fact. Under that inviolable Law, therefore, rivers cannot be claimed for personal or group ownership.

In truth, a river has no actual 'spiritual' connection with any people whatsoever. It is only a people's belief that lays claim to such a notion. The river cannot therefore be so owned, for its 'Elemental' *mana* is its own, and cannot be placed there by any person or race. Neither can a river be affected by any *tapu* put on it, for it remains far above any such Maori religious ideas in its 'Elemental purity'. However, what may be observed on or around waterways that give rise to a belief that it may be so affected by man-conferred *tapu*, will perhaps be the presence of psychic thought-forms possibly produced by the act of conferring *tapu* status on them in the first place. Or by the psychic projections of all concerned with any *tapu* ceremony. Or perhaps even by the activity of earth-bound souls who may somehow be tied to the area and affected by such ceremonies. As we need to continually reinforce, such practices and activities are **not** actually spiritual ones.

Notwithstanding those possible reasons, it does not mean that gratitude in *karakia* **cannot** be **offered** for the **gift** of the river. But that is an entirely different matter, and a very correct one. Moreover, it is one absolutely connected with reverence to "The Giver of Life!"

For without the water of the rivers through the natural hydrological cycle, there would be no life for humankind at all. Therefore, whilst we are enjoined by Spiritual Law to unequivocally respect the life-giving water of the river and, by association, all precipitation that is its source, it is **not** given to man to lay claim to 'ownership' of it by any method. Not by the ploy of ancestor use or worship, or by attempting to confer *tribal mana* on it. The river, by virtue of its place and purpose in Creation, stands far above such wrong ideas, whether from Maori or Pakeha! It is a gift for our correct use from out of the goodness of The Creative Will as a vital part of our earthly home. The rivers were here long before the Maori, and will be here long after they have gone. They do not need Maori to confer any status on them. The Spiritual Laws, however, unequivocally *demand respect* in this area.

Further, the idea that certain water should not be transported from one area to another because it may adversely affect Maori not connected with the *Iwi* from where the water is taken, simply reveals this deeply entrenched psychic hold that still pervades the Maori mind, even as we enter the 21st century. Claiming ownership of any river, therefore, through reasons of loss of its *mana*, or because others wish to take drinking water from it, is another affront to all Spiritual Law since we are permitted by that Higher Law to take such water as is needed for our use. What we are enjoined to do, however, is nurture the gift of the river by striving to protect the purity of the water as it was originally given. Moreover, we should not consider the idea of 'ownership' for misuse or excessive profit, either by Maori 'ownership' aspirations, or from the Corporate world of Pakeha business practices bent on possible *privatisation* and sale of water resources.

Rivers therefore cannot possibly 'lose *mana*' via normal and ordained use. That is simply not the case. Rivers will always possess natural *mana*. Many of the world's waterways testify to the fact that it is we of global humankind who have lost our *mana* through contributing to the pollution of many, and even the death of some. The Pakeha with his materially poisonous chemicals has certainly transgressed there and, regrettably, is still doing so. Such practices are clearly not spiritual.

However, it was not the Pakeha who *first* polluted the rivers of this blessed land. The Maori also defiled the purity of the rivers by placing the *forms of their psychic productions* such as *taniwha* etc., in the deep clear pools of the waterways. In contravention of all Spiritual Law ancient Maori 'gave' to the water, monsters and dark things that were never there before his arrival. Or they believed that those beings lawfully ordained to be there were somehow evil and dangerous, or to be feared. The "Elemental Beings", the true inhabitants of the rivers and forests, are not monsters or psychic entities, but 'nature beings' who fulfil **The Creative Will**. They are placed here to assist us.

Thus, whether man is here or not, or whether he attempts to demand ownership or not, those considerations cannot alter the fact that the river is actually 'living *Mana*' due to its life-giving properties. For even if we should pollute the whole earth and bring about our complete demise, the rivers will still flow – and quickly run clean after we have gone.

Therefore, in terms of establishing the strongest possible connection to the "Elemental Forces" in our overall relationship with them and their ordained activity, we should learn *never to curse the weather*, regardless of the reason's we may wish to do so. For in doing so we curse the actual *ordained activity* of those "Elemental Beings" of the "Forces of Nature". And, by extension, that perfection which is The Creative Will! Far too often we ascribe human-emotional terms to weather in determining it as bad, ugly, lousy, rotten or shocking etc. Since weather cannot intrinsically be such as that, to hear this more or less constant litany of many expletives, unequivocally reveals how far we are from any real understanding of the "true nature" of "The Forces of Nature".

Weather is just weather, that's all!

Elemental activity may *produce* very stormy conditions that, in turn, may also *generate* violent winds and destructive waves. Or the same kind of activity may *produce* searing heat or bone-chilling cold, which may even result in deaths. But such *productions* are not arbitrary! That is the 'imperative of weather' which humankind needs to learn quickly if it is to understand the reasons for the unusual weather patterns that will yet bring far greater destruction than at present! Quite clearly, then, all of humankind is subject to every nuance of weather change and activity, and not solely in terms of food production.

At the Meteorological Society's Weatherwatch conference held in Auckland over a decade ago in November, 1996, (N.Z. Herald report) the CEO of the Insurance Council of New Zealand, Mr David Sargeant, stated that extreme weather: "...is a growing threat to New Zealand's economy." He also noted that:

> "...catastrophic weather events, such as damage from the severe winds and flooding brought by hurricanes, represented the greatest threat to the survival of the world's insurance industry. *And that the rise in natural catastrophes should not be ignored.*"

Our assertions that 'Elemental activity' will yet bring far more destruction through natural disasters *more quickly*, thus seriously affecting every aspect of all economies, was well illustrated in the graph which accompanied the Herald article. In the years from 1960 to 1984, costs to the Insurance industry worldwide from such events remained more or less manageable, fluctuating between a few hundred million U.S. dollars to a high point of about 24 billion, equating to an average annual cost of approximately 5 to 7 billion. Yet, the decade from 1985-1995 showed an almost year-by-year increase depicted by a steeply-rising exponential curve, culminating in a 110 billion dollar cost in 1995.

Mr Sargeant attributed the increase in weather damage of recent years to a combination of factors that generally all scientific agencies subscribe to. Factors noted were: "Population density, increased living standards, industrialisation in high-risk areas and vulnerability of technologies, along with changing climate conditions..." However, whilst these factors are constantly put forward as the reasons for severe weather increases, the same conference was told that even with global warming still on the rise:

> "...scientists still could not attribute the observed effects to a specific cause."

(Italics mine.)

Professor K.U. Sirinanda of the University of Brunei said:

> "People are not attuned to climate change. We need to have environmental education on a democratic scale or whatever you call it ... to convince policy makers of the importance of these issues."

Such clearly correct views are, paradoxically, probably just a pipe dream, and that conference just another in a long line of them which will bring no real change at all – simply because most of all preceding similar ones have not.

A very appropriate Biblical quote for this present time, Isaiah 8:10, immediately springs to mind:

"Take counsel together, and it will come to nought."

A decade on from that conference, the Atlantic hurricane season of 2005 received the dubious honour of being the most intense ever recorded, with unprecedented destruction to major population centres. And all that on top of the Indian Ocean tsunami, the major earthquake in the Kashmir region of the Indian sub-continent, and the huge areas inundated by mud and landslides in Central America. What did it cost the Insurance Industry in 2005, we may wonder?

So whilst the "Weatherwatch" conference produced the standard reasons for increasing concerns about the severity of global weather patterns and noted the end results of these changes, it was unable to "...*attribute the observed effects to a specific cause*". In other words, the conference delegates did not *understand* or *know* the **actual causal reason** for them. As we have explained in this Work, the reason lies in the *spiritual* connection *between* our inherent free-will decision-making ability and the *returns* we must experience through *wrongly using* that "spiritual gift" *to continually break the rules*.

As we must often reinforce, that "reaping of our sowing" is returned to us via the ordained activity of The Elemental Forces of Nature acting under **The Creative Will**. That is the precise reason why such conferences achieve no real change, and will not do so in the future either. Simply because most of society, including those of influence or power who could institute the greatest change, generally regard such ideas as religious or 'fringe-garbage'.

However, since an exponential factor can be readily observed in all events now, all we need do is sit back quietly – *and watch and wait*. In the meantime, perhaps we should, again, restate the answer of Jesus to His disciples when asked what the end-time would be like.

His reply is chronicled thus:

> **"...for there shall then be widespread affliction, such as has not been known since the beginning of the world until now, no, nor will ever be known again. And if those times were not cut short, not a man would be saved."**

To this end, we should once more carefully note Chief Seattle's beautiful words of powerful truth and understanding. "If men spit upon the ground they spit upon themselves ... to harm the earth is to heap contempt on its Creator."

In probably the saddest of prophetic and paradoxical ironies, and simply because he voluntarily allowed the knowledge of the "Elemental Forces" to die within him, man will probably *most curse* the power of the weather *as brought by them*, when it *finally destroys him and his wrong works*. And, moreover, at the very time when he would have the *most serious need of their protection to the greatest possible degree*. In the approaching stupendously-powerful future happening will be revealed the inviolable truth alluded to in Chief Seattle's address. Thus, for mankind on earth, the ultimate justice of Spiritual Law!

As this is the prophesied happening for humankind that will shortly visit itself upon us anyway, it behoves every person with even the faintest hint of 'intuitive unease' today, to begin the process of setting within himself and his family the knowledge that will offer understanding and protection at that time. Therefore, for both the Maori and the Pakeha, first begin with a thorough grounding of 'Elemental knowledge' and all its interrelated connections to the activity of man. After which can be taught all other *Spiritual Truths*. However, this clear need may require far more discipline than the Maori race currently demonstrates that it is capable of *collectively* generating at present.

It is also a vital need for Pakeha too – though I am sure it is one that the many who *religiously believe* that only 'human scientific-intellectualism' can provide answers to the myriad problems that global humanity must now solve, or perish, would be *derisively dismissive* of. They, especially, however, will learn the hardest lessons and ultimately suffer the most bitter experiences when we of the foolish *human variety* of creatures on planet earth are completely overwhelmed and stripped of our human cleverness by the "Elemental Forces" tasked to 'do the job'. Spiritually-aberrant human thinking and practice – that which has especially *accelerated* the damage to the earth and human societies – *has finally had its day.*

In that regard we should seriously question the high rate of smoking among Maori and recognise that any form of smoking represents a serious transgression against the gift of pure air; air given to us by the unselfish activity of the "Elemental Forces" for our health and well-being. For we should note, once more, that the same 'Forces' also bring all natural disasters and catastrophes – in direct accordance with our transgressions against The Laws of Nature. With smoking being one of them, it logically follows that this particular activity – among others of course – effectively destroys any possibility of a 'connection of protection' to these same 'Elementals' during the destructive times of great upheaval, for it is mankind who needs the help and protection of the "Elemental Beings".

It is not they who need us!

The possible saving grace for Maori, however, is that they are at least part-way there due to a more natural and inherent acceptance of "other-world" beings, even though not possessing complete knowledge about them. Pakeha who possess some knowledge of Spiritual Law and its associated activity probably do so because they are not shackled by aspiritual superstition and rigid, unyielding cultural traditions as many Maori are. As we must constantly reinforce, however, by virtue of their far more developed scientific-intellectualism and/or religiosity that generally *denies* the existence of "Elemental Forces", the majority of Pakeha have largely *lost* the ability to *readily* recognise and accept their existence as a natural and Creator-Willed part of 'our world'. And thus as a vital part of all Creation!

The basic cultural parameters of Maori and Pakeha overall, therefore, may well determine where each group stands in relation to the reality of "The Elemental Beings of The Forces of Nature". *Maori, as a complete race*, should *generally* be more easily able to develop the greater recognition and thus correct attitude toward 'Elementals' than perhaps the *Pakeha, as a complete race*. In reality, of course, there should be no difference whatsoever for the two peoples, for the Law states quite unequivocally that: *"All can see if they wish to!"*

Further to that, however, must be the realisation that *it is the individual, alone*, who ultimately has to accept full and personal responsibility for all his beliefs and decisions under the outworking of Spiritual Law – even ones concerning 'Elemental Beings.'

Being more accepting of the other-world reality of "Nature Beings" thus offers Maori the immediate springboard whereby he can move more quickly – if he so chooses – to establish the correct and necessary foundation for his physical and spiritual protection against the greatly accelerating 'Elemental activity' that we already observe almost daily in the news items worldwide. And this powerful, unstoppable activity, that even scientists now refer to as 'weather disasters' and 'weather havoc', will soon completely engulf our rapidly deteriorating and degraded planet earth. For we have **not** been true *kaitiaki*, and it is now time to pay!

Therefore, all Maori need do is *once more* follow the path revealed by the Mangai and enter the door he was permitted to open for them! For it is vitally important to recognise and understand that the inheritors of this land will **not** be solely Maori as many Maori may like to believe, but will only be those *individuals* who follow the path of Spiritual Truth, *irrespective of race!* Moreover, recognition of Spiritual Truth *as it actually is* automatically provides a concomitant, personal connection and *covenant* with that Source.

Therein lies the Divine promise that: *"The Meek Shall Inherit the Earth!"* But the meek in this case are not the weak, the earthly subservient, or the servile. They are the *humble few* who, by their *humility*, have become *spiritually strong* through genuine and grateful acceptance of **Spiritual Truth** – thus **Divine Truth**!

The *humble few*. What indication does the great Prophet, Isaiah, give us regarding exactly *those few* – from out of the billions of global humanity – who will surmount the destructive, cleansing phase that is now not far distant? Not only not far distant, however, but virtually almost upon us.

The early 'known world' of Isaiah encompassed only a small part of the actual world that we now know, so dire warnings to major cities and peoples of that era could perhaps have been seen by very early Bible compilers as being a 'global prophecy'. Noted in the King James Bible as ostensibly an admonition to the citizens of Tyre, it is eminently clear, however, that the wording of the following Scriptures leaves us in no doubt that Isaiah is actually directing his **visionary-warnings** to the earth and **the inhabitants of the future time** when the widespread destruction he 'saw' was ordained to occur – **our time**.

The very much later New American Standard Bible, from which we will quote the relevant warnings, does not head those Scriptures; "The overthrow of Tyre", as does the 'King James'. Whilst we all know that a particular *message* or *story* can easily be concocted or fabricated by careful or cunning selection of relevant texts, the following that I have chosen for the end of this particular Chapter well illustrates the power of **The Forces of Nature**. For the *'Elemental Power'* inherent therein will bring the very destruction that Isaiah prophesied for we poor 'know-all humans' grubbing about in 'religious intolerance and ignorance' on earth today. And prophesied a very long time before the great Prophet's visions were more powerfully and definitively endorsed by **The Son of God Himself**. Surely nothing deserves destruction *more* than exactly *that* kind of appalling *religious stupidity* so evil and widespread among we of *the* global humanity of the present time. To that most necessary end, and in *appropriate reinforcement*, let us be under no illusions whatsoever that:

"The Laws of Nature" are the 'living-expression' of The WILL of GOD on earth!

> "Behold, the Lord lays the earth waste, devastates it, distorts its surface, and scatters its inhabitants. ...
>
> The earth will be completely laid waste and completely despoiled, for the Lord has spoken this word.
>
> The earth mourns *and* withers, the world fades *and* withers, *the exalted* of the people of the earth *fade away*.
>
> The earth is also **polluted** by its inhabitants, for they **transgressed laws, violated statutes**, broke the **everlasting covenant**. [Note Chief Seattle's wisdom.]
>
> Therefore, a curse devours the earth, and those who live in it **are held guilty**. Therefore, **the inhabitants of the earth are _burned_, and _few men_ are left**."[6]

(Isaiah. Chapter 24, Verses 1-6.
Emphases and parenthetic addition mine.)

---

[6] The 'burning' of earth's inhabitants is specifically mentioned in The Bible [2 Peter] where he tells his followers; "...that the present earth and skies..." are "...reserved for *fire*..." at a period **of judgement and destruction** of wicked men". The exact meaning of what that "*fire*" is and will be; is explained in two primary Works of **CRYSTAL PUBLISHING. 1: BIBLE "MYSTERIES" EXPLAINED...** Specifically Chapter 12; **THE TWO SONS OF GOD**, sub; **Destruction by "Fire"**. And 2: **'THE GATHERING APOCALYPSE AND WORLD JUDGEMENT; What it Brings – Even Now – And Why!'**. Also in a stand-alone Booklet: **THE TWO SONS OF GOD: THE SON OF MAN AND THE SON OF GOD;** *What The Bible Really Says*. [Only available online at: **www.publishme.co.nz**]

Isaiah states his case so decisively that we actually enter the scientific discipline of **Plate Tectonics**. So whilst he 'prophesied the visions' he was permitted to see – ultimately for *our* edification *today* – he probably had no knowledge of *how* the shaking would occur. Now, of course, through the experience of the recent, very large 'Indian Ocean tsunami', we *all* now know that 'the earth will shake'. We must now await that which the great Prophet 'saw' would – precisely because of our refusal to heed the True Laws – "completely overwhelm we inhabitants of the earth".

"The earth is broken asunder,

The earth is split through,

The earth is shaken violently,

The earth reels to and fro like a drunkard,

And it totters like a shack,

For its [human] transgression is heavy upon it,

And it [current, *aspiritual*, human societies] will fall, never to rise again."

> (Isaiah. Chapter 24, Verses 19-20.
> Parenthetic *explanations* mine.)

Irrespective of whether we label such 'Truths' Elemental, Spiritual, or even Divine, the ultimate choice that we nonetheless possess here is to *choose to believe*, or *choose to disbelieve*. In the final analysis it is a *50% choice*.

That individual choice, however, unequivocally equates to a personal and final **100% outcome.**

We should all mark this well, for there is no other way.

Not for the Maori, nor for the Pakeha!

	SKY GOD RULER	QUEEN	SUN LIGHT	MOON	WAR STORMS THUNDER	SEA RIVERS RAIN	AGRICULTURE FERTILITY EARTH	LOVE	UNDER-WORLD DEAD	WISDOM KNOWLEDGE ARTS SCIENCES	CRAFTS INVENTION	CULTURE HERO TRICKSTER
EGYPTIAN	Amon-Re	Hathor Isis	Amon-Re Horus	Thorh Hathor Isis	Mont	Osiris	Hathor Isis Osiris	Hathor	Anubis Osiris	Thoth Isis	Ptah	Osiris
SUMERIAN AND BABYLONIAN	An Anu Marduk	Innini	Babbar Shamash	Nanna Sin	Enlil Marduk Adad	Enki Ea	Nanna Ishtar	Nanna Ishtar Tammuz	Ereshkigal	Nabu Ea	Ea	Ea
GREEK	Zeus	Hera	Apollo	Artemis	Ares	Poseidon	Demeter Persophone Dionysus	Aphrodite Eros	Hades (Dis)	Athena Apollo	Hephaestus Athena	Prometheus Hermes
ROMAN	Jupiter (Jove)	Juno	Apollo	Diana	Mars	Neptune	Ceres Proserpine Bacchus	Venus Cupid	Pluto	Minerva	Vulcan Minerva	Mercury
NORSE	Odin	Frigg	Balder		Thor	Aegir Frey	Frey Freya	Freya Frigg	Hel	Odin Bragi Mimir	Volund Frigg	Loki
CELTIC	Dagda	Danu	Lug	Branwen	Morrigan Macha Taranis	Mannanan	Danu Macha Brigit	Branwen	Bran Urien	Lug Brigit Bran	Goibniu Lug	
CHINESE (TAOIST AND BUDDHIST)	Yu-huang (Lao t'ien-yeh)	Tien Hou	Yi	Ch'ang-o (Heng-o)	Huang-ti Kuan-ti	Lung-wang (dragon kings) Yu-ch'iang	Sheng-mu (pi-hia yuan-kun) Kuan-yin		Yen-wang Ts'in-kuang-wang	Wen-ch'ang	Lu Pan Huang-ti	Shen-nung Fu-hsi
INDIAN (VEDIC AND HINDU)	Indra Vishnu Shiva	Lakshmi Parvati (Kali)	Surya Mitra Savitar	Soma Yaruna	Indra Skandar Rudra	Varuna Parjanya	Parvati	Kama Krishna	Yama	Rudra Sarasvati		
WEST AFRICAN (ASHANTI EON YORUBA)	Nyame Mahu Olorun	Asase Yaa	Lisa		Tano Xevioso Schango	Nyame Avlekete Olokun	Asase Yaa Mahu Odudua			Orunmila	Gun Ogun	Ananse Gun, Legba Eschu
MAYAN	Hun-Ahpu	Ixazaluoh	Hun-Ahpu Itzamna		Hurakan	Chac	Itzamna		Humahau	Itzamna Kukulcan	Ixazaluoh	Itzamna Kukulcan
AZTEC	Tonacatecutli	Tonacacihuatl	Tezcatlipoca	Metzli	Huizilopochtli	Tlaloc	Tzinteotl Coatlicue	Tlazolteotl	Michtlantecutli	Quetzalcoatl	Quetzalcoatl	Quetzalcoatl
PLAINS INDIAN	Wakan Wakan-Tanka				Wakinyan							
MAORI	Rangi	Papa Papa-tua-nuku	Tane		Tu Tawhiri-matea Whaitiri	Tangaroa Kiwa Kaukau	Rongo Rongo-ma-tane Haumia		Hine-nui-to-po	Rangi Tane-te-hiranga Tane-te wananga		Maui

Elemental Lore of Nature

Part III

The Coming of the Pakeha

12

Arrival

This part of our journey now necessarily and irrevocably joins that of the Pakeha! Whilst **Part 1** looked at particular aspects of the interaction of both races in the early days of Pakeha involvement, it sought more to identify the "spiritual path" and condition of the Maori *before* the arrival of the 'white man'. Having examined the ramifications of Death, Reincarnation and 'The Second Death' in previous Chapters **of Part II**, we now journey into 'life with the Pakeha', and hopefully into *mutual* 'spiritual understanding'.

Despite the way in which many well-meaning Maori view their ancestors, or how much European academics may romantically gloss over their activities, the indisputable fact remains that **very little** of the everyday life of the old Maori was marked by *genuinely spiritual* practices. Their tribal way of life, riven through by *makutu*, *utu*, warfare and cannibalism, particularly, offers unequivocal testimony to a long period of extremely savage activities. And to attempt to opine that that lifestyle might possess some kind of *spiritual* saving grace, either as a facet of culture or tradition, is clearly a *denial* of the truth of it. It is nothing more than a simple refusal to face the facts about the often-revered past.

Moreover, 'pride of race', which in *certain* circumstances *can* be a strong and protective *spiritual* quality, cannot be employed to mask the truth of that past, for there was simply not that kind of corresponding spirituality existing to any great degree amongst the old Maori. In this particular case, it is vital that the truth of our ancestral past be objectively and honestly accepted, for any refusal to acknowledge such truths will automatically inculcate the promotion and bequeathing of an incorrect history and its associated wrong concepts to all future generations. Therefore, whether viewed historically, culturally, traditionally, emotionally, spiritually, or any other way, any such denial is an affront to the very concept of "Spiritual Truth" itself, and is therefore clearly untenable. The wanton destruction of lives in the kind of savagery practised by the old Maori under the guise of seeking or protecting *mana* through the unfortunate practice of *utu*, **was a spiritual transgression of the most serious kind**. The virtue of compassion, which might have softened that uncultured lifestyle was, unfortunately, virtually non-existent then.

We can be sure, therefore, that under The Law of Sowing and Reaping much heartache would have been visited upon many souls of the Maori race during that long and sorry state of spiritual decline. Such wild practices over many hundreds of years *may yet still invite* some residual reciprocal return, though this could only be determined by the outworking of Spiritual Law. Whilst some of those ancient activities have been assessed under the aegis of that Law, it is equally important to understand *how* and *why* certain members of humankind who were born into races similar to the old Maori, were of the same ilk. Fortunately we are able to do so, and it is timely to offer it here as we prepare to leave behind the wild practices of our ancestors and journey into a more enlightened time.

In the Chapter on our Spiritual Origins, we explained the process whereby all humankind came onto the earth with the same strong spiritual connections to their origins. And for a time during the early stages of man's development, those connections remained, and were a strong help and support for his progress on earth. But as he advanced more surely along his evolutionary path, he began to exercise his own personal will, thereby gradually losing the pure connections to his origins, and therefore to his 'supportive spiritual guidance' and help. Utilising his free-will attribute, he began to move away from the correct spiritual path ordained for all of humankind. And driven by the inviolable outworking of the Spiritual Laws in accordance with his free-will choices, more and more of humankind slipped further and further from the 'true way' – **the spiritual way!**

This meant a regression from the ordained path of development for mankind. Subsequent rebirths onto the earth guaranteed incarnations into groups of people with the same basic characteristics and propensities. Moreover if, in subsequent incarnations and periods in between, there is a further sliding away from that ordained path, then eventually the regression will be so far advanced that an incarnation into a savage group, only, will be possible. Paradoxically, however, it is solely in those kinds of groups that such persons might have any chance of awakening to the wrong of their aspiritual way of life. If not, the possibility of incarnations into still more barbarous races await them.

Therefore, it is not that savage or primitive races are composed of new souls or are at an early stage of evolution – for all human beings have been in the Material World for a similar length of time – but their condition owes itself to the fact that in their *spiritual development* they have either not kept pace with other races or peoples or, having once *already attained to a more elevated level of spiritual maturity*, had *regressed* so far that only an incarnation into a spiritually-regressing race was possible. But, as we stress often in this Work, such circumstances *can only be brought about by the exercise of the free will of each individual*, who must then *accept* the consequences of that wrong decision under the outworking of The Spiritual Laws.

They are Laws that no one can transgress with impunity, and which **do not** permit **a collective decision** by any particular group consciously working together to effect some kind of genealogical *ethnic togetherness*! We are all disparate souls attracted into particular homogeneous groups via the lawful consequences of all our personal free-will decisions. Thus, ethnic genealogy and connections to ancestors are **not** *spiritual connections,* and we do **not** inherit their believed 'spiritual characteristics', their *mana*, their *kaha*, or anything else that tribal or racial history may ascribe to them – not even if we are given revered ancestral names in the belief that it is so.

With this knowledge, it thus becomes a relatively simple matter for all races to objectively ascertain upon which step ancestors stood 'on the ladder of spiritual growth'. It is thus a clear measure that can be used by any descendant of former, savage races to make a quick and simple comparison *for himself* – including present-day descendants of old Maori.

Quite logically, therefore, Maori today may not ever have been members of that older, very untamed race. Yet, they may also have been. As previously noted, the generations of Maori born since the demise of the old customs clearly show a huge difference in attitude, particularly in the wonderful practice of *karakia* to a "Giver of Law" at the opening and closing of meetings and events. In contrast to many ancient activities, this is clearly a spiritual practice, which one can observe is offered with feeling and veneration. It is not superficial and, in my estimation, stems mainly from a natural acceptance by Maori of the other-world reality, albeit in its various *perceived* manifestations.

Moreover, the fact that Maori ancestors were so incredibly steeped in their savage lifestyle through their non-understanding of what the other-world was meant to offer them, ***thus actually provides the <u>strongest foundation</u> for present-day Maori to more fully grasp the true meaning of Spiritual Law more easily than groups without such a powerful base-line.***

Therefore, compared to some other ethnic groups who do not possess that ready acceptance of the 'other-world reality', or who do not accept it to the same degree, it should be a relatively simple procedure for Maori to use that acceptance of the past as a vital foundation to take the most necessary step of all; a step into the world of genuine spiritual knowledge under the aegis of The One Law! Any group which aspires to that ideal, however, needs to clearly understand the huge and fundamental differences between the key levels of that 'other-world', and totally reject those levels and connections which have no affinity with genuinely spiritual things and which therefore should be let go.[1] The final step is to then learn the true meaning, the nature and the consequential outworking of the *actual Spiritual Laws of Creation* – **and live them!**

These explanations thus provide the key to the old Maori propensity for clinging to the psychic or occult world of their traditional beliefs. Irrevocably connected with that world of distorted concepts and their associated dark forms was his institution of *tapu*, and that which had to logically follow – *makutu* and *utu*. That tight-fisted bond fuelled his increasing savagery, finally leading him to exact revenge against all those he believed directed that same *makutu* and *utu* against his own. The result of being on 'that particular step', with a correspondingly 'narrow outlook' upon his 'other-world' surroundings – his frightening 'unseen world' of psychic entities – did little else but keep him tied to it for as long as there was *no external influence or event to break or challenge the iron grip that such timorous beliefs always hold for fear-ridden and superstitious people*.

That momentous event, of course, did occur. It was: '**The fateful arrival of the Pakeha!**'

The inner reaction of Maori to the first sightings of the white man have probably not been adequately recorded, at least from the Maori point of view. Notwithstanding the differing legends and theories about other visiting ships and their origins, it must surely have been a momentous occasion when other men, from across the oceans somewhere, were first sighted. Irrespective of whoever might or might not have arrived here first, Tasman is the 'Pakeha' now historically credited with discovering New Zealand on 13th December 1642, and sighting the cooking fires of the Maori on the 17th. It is recorded that on the next day whilst searching for a suitable place to land, two canoe loads of 'natives' approached the Dutch ships and made voice contact with them in what were described as 'gruff and hollow' voices. The Dutch attempted a reply, but neither side understood the other. Nevertheless, this exchange was the first officially recorded one between Maori and 'Pakeha'.

Just two days later, on the 19th December, the first physical close-quarter exchanges between Maori and Pakeha took place. It resulted in the deaths of four of Tasman's men. He records the incident as a "...monstrous and detestable thing" and named the cove Murderers Bay. The obvious restraint displayed by Tasman and his men, who possessed the combined superior firepower of the cannon and muskets of both ships, should be acknowledged here. And even though not "Men-O-War", Tasman's ships could have exacted a heavy toll on the village and of any craft on the water had they so wished, for a counter-attack is usually the normal Military response to provocation or attack resulting in the deaths of one's own. But what Tasman did **not** do was exact *utu* for the deaths of his four men. The old Maori would surely have exercised that

---

[1]That truth, in its great import, is not at all understood yet.

traditional option had the situation been reversed. And, we can be sure, they would have wanted more than just four men.

This skirmish altered Tasman's plans to land there and he sailed north up the coast and away from this land and its savage inhabitants. Whether blame could be apportioned to any one side for these killings may well be irrelevant, but it appears to have convinced Tasman that there was little to be gained – in terms of trade – from either the people or what the land had to offer. Yet this incident calls into question the subject of eventual colonisation. Tasman's encounter with South Island Maori resulting in the deaths of some of his men, and his subsequent departure from these shores, set in place the opportunity for 'other Pakeha' from other countries to vie for the later colonisation of Aotearoa. We might well speculate on what might have happened had Tasman not experienced such an incident and was more trusting or more warmly welcomed by Maori at this first encounter and during his journey up the coast?

Since later traders of other nationalities cruelly exploited the very valuable timber resources of the kauri of the North, particularly for masts and spars for burgeoning European maritime fleets and the English Navy, a less hostile reaction from Maori might have seen the Dutch fell the kauri rather than the British. Perhaps, also, a different kind of missionary might have arrived to convert the 'souls of the natives'. And perhaps a harder taskmaster than the British might have brought a very different complexion onto the face of New Zealand and to the fate of Maori. In any event, this is pure speculation, for the obvious reality of a British coloniser is now historical fact. As we have already stated, however, all Maori should think very seriously about this reality since there was going to be a coloniser in any case, *and it was not within the power of Maori to prevent it.*

The second "Pakeha" arrived off the coast of New Zealand on 7th October 1769. This one, however, was more tenacious than the first and was not put off by the aggressive behaviour of Maori. Commanded by Captain James Cook, his 'goblin ship' was believed by Maori to be peopled by 'goblins'.[2] Cook, a Master Mariner, was determined to stay until he had completed his commission of circumnavigating and charting the coast of this new land. The propensity of the Maori to 'offer the *wero*' (challenge) to all and sundry, puzzled and disturbed both Tasman and Cook. Being an inherent element in the warlike psyche of the Maori race, the *wero* would have been a natural part of any initial exchange; perhaps a kind of 'testing the waters', so to speak. But both Commanders could not possibly have known that beforehand.

This aggressive trait of the Maori to seek conflict and war, even against newly arrived strangers, provided a different result for him at the hands of Cook than that experienced with Tasman. Cook's first forays ashore were marked by the killing of one Maori when a group attempted to surround a party guarding his boats. The next day saw another brief exchange, and on the third day his men killed several Maori attempting an attack by canoe. Cook was very troubled by this incident. The fair nature of the man is revealed in the manner in which he recorded that event in his journal.

> "Had I thought they would have made the least resistance, I would not have come near them. But as they did, I was not to suffer either myself or those that were with me to be knocked on the head."

> (New Zealand's Heritage, Vol.1, p.86)

From a Military or even a normal protective point of view, Cook had little choice. Moreover, the stark reality of having to defend himself was forced on him by the attitude of Maori who coveted Cook's possessions, and perhaps even *tauiwi* heads. Notwithstanding those initial setbacks, and with the Tahitian Tupaia's help, Cook persevered in trying to establish friendly

---

[2]The reference to white-skinned 'goblins', or *pakepakeha* in the Maori idiom, is possibly the origin of the term, Pakeha.

relations with a decidedly unfriendly foe, even to displaying genuine anger toward his own men if Maoris' were treated unduly harshly for minor infringements against them. For, at a time of 'press-ganging' and harsh conditions at sea, Cook was a true humanitarian. His concern for the health and safety of his crew thus reflected that side of his nature.

*   *   *   *   *

If we briefly journey to relatively recent times, the furore at the visit to New Zealand of the replica of the *Endeavour* and Cook's killing of Maori then, failed to take into account the reality of the times. From this present viewpoint of history, the reaction of Maori who condemned the visit of the ship for that long-ago incident was a pointless and over-emotional, over-reaction with absolutely no current relevance. The Maori of the time well knew the meaning and possible outcome of any attacks made on others. Quite simply, they could be killed, and this fact they lived with constantly, because it was their way of life. And even after these first deaths, Maori foolishly continued their attacks, thus incurring further losses.

Given the only two choices available to Maori at that time – the continuation of their savage, *utu* lifestyle, or the more beneficial possibility of leaving it behind because of the later effect of Cook's arrival – Maori today should view this event with far more *gratitude* than that which some currently, emotionally display.

Entries in Cook's journal centred around those incidents give clear indication that he did not seek confrontation and tried to avoid bloodshed wherever possible, and he accepted personal blame if he failed. He tried to be fair at all times in his dealings with Maori. And whilst he may have punished them for stealing from his ship, in typical Navy tone he also had his own men flogged for stealing from Maori. But perhaps the best indication of the justness of the man toward Maori can be gauged by his reaction to an incident during his *second* voyage when Maori killed a boat's crew in a dispute over stolen food. Because his two ships were separated at the time, Cook did not hear of it until much later.

'New Zealand's Heritage' (page 100), records that his first reaction was to suspend judgement, even to lean a little towards the Maoris:

> "I must ... observe in favour of the New Zealanders that I have always found them of a brave, noble, open and benevolent disposition. But they are a people that will never put up with an insult if they have an opportunity to resent it."

When he eventually learned the truth of the matter, the perpetrators fully expected to be punished, especially the ringleader.

> Indeed other Maoris urged Cook to kill him immediately, and were surprised when the man was freed.

That is not the behaviour of a murderous tyrant seeking to indiscriminately kill Maori at every opportunity, on any pretext. In the context of historical events overall, the killing of ancestors should *always* be viewed *objectively*. Attempting to place *emotional/cultural* claims on their persons by demanding redress at every opportunity in a latter-day version of *utu* – that evil practice that should have *long been left behind* – **is spiritually wrong**. Any decision to attack Cook and his men was a personal one made with the free will of Maori at the time. The consequences were theirs alone, **and not that of descendants two hundred years on**.

*   *   *   *   *

So in the infant stage of Maori/Pakeha relations, Cook was surprised to find that Maoris refused to be cowed by his superior weapons. They attempted many attacks on his ship whilst at the same time taunting the ship's crew to "...come ashore to be clubbed". Finally, though, Cook's perseverance paid dividends and the Maori began to see in him the mark of a true *rangatira,* a chief equal in their eyes, and one who earned their respect. From that point on, Cook enjoyed generally friendly relations with them receiving assistance when provisions for his ship were gathered. Once repairs and provisioning were completed Cook continued his circumnavigation, returning to England by way of Australia.[3]

Cook's later return to New Zealand produced a curious aside to his visit to Ship Cove, a distance of only 70 miles from Murderer's Bay where Tasman lost four men to Maori attack. With Maori *waiata* and oratory generally providing the only means for the retention and recital of tribal stories of note, we might expect that such an incident as the killing of strange white men from a distant land would have been carefully and strongly retained. Yet Cook found no such memory or tradition of this notable event in the area. Perhaps the passage of time dimmed the memory of local Maori, with the incident eventually taking on a dream quality – "of a goblin ship peopled by goblins". Nevertheless, one would at least expect this to become part of tribal legend, even if it could not be retained as an actual remembered event.

The impression that Cook gained from his observations of this new country were that the land itself could not remain undisturbed indefinitely, for it held great promise for settlement. The climate for the most part was agreeable, plains and valley floors were deemed to be fertile and would probably support the planting of grains and fruit trees from Europe. Whereas Tasman did not consider this land to be of any great value in terms of trade or riches, and was evidently quite happy to leave it behind, Cook well recognised the huge potential of it and wrote accordingly:

> "The sea, bays and rivers abound with a great variety of excellent fish, the most of them unknown in England... In the woods are plenty of timber..." And he reached a conclusion: if this country were settled by an industrious people, "...they would soon be supplied, not only with the necessaries, but many of the luxuries of life."

> (New Zealand's Heritage, p.93)

With such a glowing statement of promise, the stage was now set for an influx of the Pakeha with his infusion of a vastly different cultural identity and lifestyle, one that would irreversibly alter the landscape of Aotearoa and the life of the Maori forever. For, irrespective of current Maori views, the historical record – which in any case *is forever written on the pages of time* – clearly reveals the actual reality of the old Maori beliefs and way of life before European arrival. Maori today therefore need to find the *kaha* and the *mana* to finally acknowledge that only with the **"The Coming of the Pakeha"**, could our ancestors have ever become free of their self-chosen, savage and spiritually-debilitating way of life.

Indeed, the first sightings of the Pakeha *forced* the Maori of the time to physically face the fact that there were *other kinds of men on earth* apart from themselves. The world was far greater than even the vast reaches of the Pacific, for beyond the great Sea of Kiwa clearly lived other peoples with vastly different values and technology. This huge and unexpected reality brought about a new direction in thinking and no doubt a huge challenge as to own identity. Yet the inherently high intelligence level of Maori ensured that they adapted reasonably well to this momentous change. And in that huge transitional process from Cook to the present day, emerged *far better equipped* than most other colonised, indigenous people for the challenges and opportunities that the 20th century offered, and what the 21st century will yet reveal.

Thus, with the arrival of the Pakeha, the, then, traditional way of life was graciously doomed to extinction. Without such a momentous event to force a change in direction, the status of

---

[3]Cook recorded an interesting difference between the Maori and the Australian Aboriginal. Whereas Maori readily accepted offers of gifts and used all manner of means to attempt to acquire Cook's possessions, the Aboriginals ignored his overtures and left his gifts untouched.

Maori life could only have remained where it was, for there was no mechanism *within the race itself* that could have released Maori from their voluntary subjugation to those forces that would have eventually driven him to complete "spiritual" annihilation – in exact accord with the immutable and inviolable outworking of:

The Spiritual laws of Creation.

The all-pervading trinity of *tapu, makutu* and *utu* – leading ultimately to cannibalism – fuelled their abject fear of everything associated with the forms produced by his particular world of beliefs. It was the life-altering change wrought by the 'sailors from afar' that prevented a possible, eventual extinguishing of the *mauri*, the very life force, of the Maori.

And whether considered culturally or politically correct or not, the hard truth remains:

It was the arrival of the Pakeha that arrested the otherwise sure decline!

13

The Initial Pakeha Influence

The Spiritual and Material Effect

The discovery of New Zealand was virtually the culmination of a large increase in exploration by the European Maritime Nations. Their associated 'empire-building' really received its impetus after Columbus confirmed that sailors would not fall off the earth if they sailed over the horizon. His 'discovery' of America was perhaps a test of faith in an unshakeable personal belief. With the fact of the earth being a sphere firmly established and finally believed by the Europeans, the time was ripe for the seafaring Nations to explore the previously unexplored areas of the globe. And by that exercise, add rich lands to their Empires.

So intense was that exploration and Empire phase that even before Cook had left New Zealand waters for the last time on 25th February 1777, the Frenchman Jean de Surville in the *St. Jean Baptiste* in 1769, and Marion du Fresne's expedition, had sailed around Cape Reinga.

The voyage of de Surville into the South Pacific and to New Zealand had a tragically poignant conclusion. Initially venturing here to trade, the long voyage produced much illness amongst his crew. Seeking refuge and fresh supplies he finally anchored in Doubtless Bay where the local Maori welcomed him. Even though being the first Europeans to land there and the first white men the locals had seen, he and his men were gifted vitally needed green vegetables to combat the effects of scurvy. He also required fresh water and firewood but was careful to ask permission first. This Frenchman offered valuable gifts in return; gifts such as a boar and a sow which he could ill afford to lose.

These initial cordial relations soured after a gale suddenly blew up and, in the course of moving the ship to another anchorage, de Surville discovered several anchors and a yawl were lost. By this time he was anxious to set sail and hoped to persuade one of the local Maoris to sail with him to other regions of New Zealand to ascertain trade prospects there. However, after learning that the yawl had been stolen and unable to recover it, he kidnapped Ranginui, a local chief. Despite the fact that Ranginui had given them much help, and against the pleas of his own officers, de Surville determined to keep him hostage and sailed away on New Years Eve.

*   *   *   *   *

Ranginui was never to see his homeland again. Even though treated kindly by de Surville, at whose table he was invited to dine, he died of scurvy as the ship headed towards South America. Paradoxically, de Surville was also destined never to see his homeland again either. He drowned while attempting to cross a bar in a small boat off the coast of Peru. History accords Chief Ranginui the dubious honour of being the first Maori to set sail from these shores on a sailing ship of the Pakeha.

Maori would later sail with the Pakeha as crew on whaling and sealing expeditions, on traders plying the coastal settlements, further afield to Australia, and beyond. Treatment of Maori crew was often harsh and some died or were killed by fellow crew-members, though Maori crewing other ships were treated no differently from their white counterparts. Notwithstanding the possibility of tough conditions, the adventurous Maori could be found on ships in ports far from the *hapu* of his homeland. Chiefs such as Hongi and Waikato travelled in a more relaxed and leisurely fashion, more befitting their status, to the land of their 'future Sovereign' – Britain.

*   *   *   *   *

From about the period of de Surville's exploits, maritime traffic to and around New Zealand increased markedly bringing the first of the exploiters, traders and settlers. What is probably so remarkable is the speed in which so many ships *intentionally* set out for these Southern Islands so soon after being discovered. Thus, as early as the 1790s, a Spanish Commander, Alejandro Malaspina arrived off Dusky Sound with two ships but was forced away by adverse weather conditions. In 1793 the Frenchman Antoine de Bruni d'Entrecasteaux was in Northern waters on his way to Tonga. And in 1820 the Russian explorer Thaddeus von Bellingshausen, also commanding two ships, dropped anchor in Queen Charlotte Sound. In virtually two decades after discovery, whalers and sealers arrived in increasing numbers, with the first sealers camp being established in Dusky Sound in 1792. It was there, in 1795, where the first ship was built in New Zealand.

Such was the 'rapaciousness' of seal exploitation alone that this activity was no longer economic after only just 20 years. The rape and desecration of the once pristine environment of Aotearoa had, by now, taken on an ominous and firmly established direction under the economic greed and ignorance of the white invader.[1]

The fact that Cook had laid claim to New Zealand in the name of Britain did not necessarily mean that it would remain so at that time. With such a tenuous hold on it so far from Europe by sailing time, New Zealand was ripe for claim by conquest or occupation by other powers as it was not actually subject to the absolute sovereignty of any one Nation then. The French, in particular, were extremely active around northern New Zealand charting and mapping and establishing strong contact with local Maori. Interestingly, French dealings with the Maori in the beginning were generally more cordial than other nationalities because the French possessed at least a rudimentary knowledge of the Tahitian language. It allowed them a distinct advantage in relatively easy communication with Maori. The early 1800s also saw the arrival of many American whalers. So in a very short space of time, large numbers of men from numerous nationalities were active on the land and around the coast.

The immediate effect of this huge influx of so many people of different nationalities was to give Maori a vastly different perspective on their own way of life, customs and beliefs. What was a singularly-closed society governed by the restricted world-view of this Island race was suddenly, at the arrival of the first ship of discovery, thrust onto the trade considerations of the rest of the world. Moreover, men of discovery or conquest do not venture forth without adequate

---

[1]The same obvious comparison could be made today in that nothing has changed fundamentally, with the same relative global-rapaciousness still being displayed by the advocates of the corporate world-view, and still driven solely by economic considerations without either genuine or *sufficient* regard for the more vital spiritual, social and environmental aspect.

means of protection and defence, and the visitors who reached these shores were appropriately armed and unafraid to fight.

Indeed, the nature of the people they encountered in New Zealand demanded that any adventurer or trader visiting these shores be well protected. The warlike Maori with his ingrained propensity for *utu* and quick to insult, immediately recognised the potential of European firepower for this aspect of their lifestyle. Not only did he covet the musket, but the steel axe and tomahawk as well. And so a race that did not know the bow and arrow or the throwing spear, and had only known close-quarter fighting with wood, stone, or bone hand-weapons, was suddenly thrust into the era of the musket with the potential of utilising Pakeha weapons to continue his inter-tribal killings far more efficiently than previously.

The obvious question during the early years of the white man's beginnings was who of the Maori would gather sufficient numbers of weapons to put into effect this new way of warfare and thus 'reign supreme'? And how to acquire such weapons? With such a huge disparity between the relative types of weapons that the respective groups possessed, any idea of taking them from the Pakeha by force was one clearly fraught with problems, and therefore not an intelligent option. The Maori, however, who was well used to trade and barter between the tribes, possessed both the natural ability and the resources with which to pursue his determination to acquire the muskets of the white man.

Those who would gain the most in the shortest time, moreover, would be Maori who could actively provide the climate and protection needed for such encouraged trade, which the Pakeha also sought in any case. Thus, in terms of pure self-interest, the stage was set for the more astute chiefs to provide this service and reap the dubious benefits of acquiring many muskets with which to decimate traditional enemies.[2]

*   *   *   *   *

As an aside to European trade designs in Aotearoa, it might be interesting to speculate as to what might have happened to the Maori had they not been so obviously savage and, at times, treacherous in nature. Had they been a weak people, it is probable that elements within the various visiting groups to Aotearoa might possibly have harboured far different thoughts regarding the fate of the Maori than that which was the eventual outcome. So the Maori ethos of the *wero* and the ready acceptance for war and *utu* might well have helped to curb possible thoughts of their decimation from at least some European factions. Though trade did require Maori participation, at least in the early years.

During those turbulent and decidedly uncertain times, visitors to this land needed to exercise extreme caution toward the Maori until 'credentials had been established', so to speak. This kind of, perhaps, *protective-race* or *protective-mana* 'mechanism' of the Maori probably offered at least a psychological advantage against a *potentially* ill-disposed, avaricious invader when dealing with the Pakeha in the early years.

*   *   *   *   *

With trade now becoming firmly established and the desire for European goods increasing, dependency upon the Pakeha was inevitable. In the beginning few articles for trade could be obtained from whalers and sealers, but as more and more Europeans arrived the range of goods that came with them also naturally increased along with their need to 'Europeanise' their new surroundings. These goods the Maori sought for their own use as well, and trade opportunities grew. To get what they wanted – in particular guns and steel cutting-implements – in a strange

---

[2]Whilst many of the war practices of the Maori have already been noted in Chapter 5, the question of *arms acquisition* from Europeans will be examined later.

but necessary paradox, Maori were forced to adopt a more *conciliatory* attitude toward the Pakeha then that which they had previously shown.

The introduction of Pakeha steel adzes and chisels during this period allowed the art of carving to flourish mightily because of the obvious ease with which wood could be worked, as opposed to the slower and more laborious efforts with less effective stone implements. Many of the major carved pieces were produced around that time.

Whilst there were times of friendly relations toward the Pakeha, beneath the Maori exterior lived his belief that he was probably superior to the white man or, at the very least, his equal. This attitude of 'healthy arrogance' about his own self-worth resulted in his general refusal to not work for less pay than a white man, something the British had not experienced with any other 'natives' during their colonising years. Sometimes, however, Maori resorted to attacking the white man to obtain the things he coveted.

The inadvertent Pakeha infringements of *tapu*, which was obviously still very strong, might provide a 'reason' to punish him and take his possessions. Friction caused by these Pakeha transgressions and by being cheated in trade deals also kept tensions more or less simmering. The attacks on four ships in Northern harbours did little to engender a cordial trading spirit between the two groups. The *Fancy* was attacked in 1795, the *Royal Admiral* in 1801, the *Parramatta* in 1808 and finally the *Boyd* in 1809, with the massacre of its crew. Nevertheless, trade continued to increase, and with it increased dependency upon the European. The European, for his part, welcomed and encouraged this trend as it hastened the opportunities for further expansion into areas away from the coastal fringe where most inter-action was then occurring.

With the beginnings of change inevitable in the Maori economy, agricultural opportunities arose and some Maori tribes, using newly acquired European grains, seeds and know-how, embarked on relatively large-scale cultivation of their lands to supply the growing sea-trade and settlement programme. Unfortunately, the desire to acquire guns urgently did cause hardship at times, particularly when the whole crop was delivered for trade goods and virtually none retained for food.[3]

Guns were the main trade item sought and the Northern tribes, by virtue of their longer and closer association with the white man who preferred the safe anchorages there, acquired many more guns more quickly than Maori tribes to the South. So prolific was the trade in arms that by 1829 every fighter of the Bay of Islands tribes possessed a gun. And by 1835, in a time span of only six years, virtually every tribe in the North Island was fully armed. Such rapid arming was a result of greatly increased trade between New Zealand and New South Wales where, by 1831, 75% of the value of the export trade from across the Tasman consisted primarily of guns and ammunition.

Apart from trade, one of the first and obvious long-term effects that such a large influx of men will always generate is the desire for women. Without the advent of colonisation to bring in large numbers of European women at that time, and with the hardships and privations of long sea voyages precluding women from accompanying men in the ships of the first years, the only available females were Maori, whom the 'tauiwi sailors' regarded as 'very handsome'. The historical record shows that Maori women equally regarded white men as desirable and union between the two races quickly blossomed into an accepted and widespread arrangement.

So even as early as Cook's time, half-caste Maori were fathered by some of his crew and Maori were apparently quite unconcerned at this development. Unfortunately, as has happened with the women of most races through the ages, prostitution was always a concomitant of any early interaction between the male advance guard of colonisation and the resident female inhabitants. And Maori women regularly visited, or travelled on, coastal ships of the time. From about the

---

[3]In my view these kinds of practices demonstrated the greater Maori concern to avenge *utu*, rather than for the health and welfare of his own.

1820s onwards, prostitution developed on a wide scale and the favours of women were sometimes offered as trade for goods.

Edward Markham, an early visitor to New Zealand, and one who enjoyed this aspect of life with many a chief's daughter, recorded:

> "A Waheininu (*wahine nui*) or fine Girl always looks out for a *Tangata* Mar (*ma*), a white man, if he has been any length of time in the Country or a Parkiah (Pakeha), Stranger... As they give the Father a Musket or the Mother a Blanket... I have known a Chief send his Wife to live with a European at the same time saying that he should call for 20 lb of Tobacca in a day or two but it was perfectly understood that he could resume her when he wanted."

> (New Zealand's Heritage, p.177)

Vayda, Maori Warfare, page 106, notes:

> "Women slaves became prostitutes on board the whale-ships, and for their services they received European goods, including guns and ammunition for their masters."

He further quotes Thomson (1859:1, p.284-285) as recording:

> "Pomare, one of the Bay of Islands chiefs, was said to have kept ninety six slave girls for prostitution during the early 1830s."

Now, since this Work is mandated by the clear recognition of The Truth of Spiritual Law, with that same Law acting decisively on every facet of our lives, it is entirely appropriate to comment on this particular aspect of early Maori/Pakeha relations from that standpoint.

Historically, the practice of prostitution, whilst probably as old as humankind itself has, at times, been deemed culturally-acceptable in some societies. In Spiritual terms, however, the voluntary acceptance of prostitution by women is an indictment against their spiritually-ordained role and place in Creation. The active encouragement of it by their menfolk, moreover, but more particularly by husbands, is a spiritual transgression on their part also.

Since the spiritual role of man should be that of the protector and defender, to then offer one's wife – with whom he should have developed a special bond of affection – to others for their sexual gratification in return for trade goods of dubious value, is an affront to the integrity and dignity that we human spirits are ordained to aspire to. Perhaps the practice of polygamy, particularly amongst the old Maori chiefs, allowed them a choice of which wife could be offered for trade purposes, with the favourite/s possibly being retained and jealously guarded. The whole idea, however, should be regarded as being a very aspiritual practice.

Notwithstanding that truth, Maori women were not averse to actively seeking out liaisons with the Pakeha, and even teased the missionaries for their prudery whenever they tried to bring about a cessation of their licentious activities. Such activities were not only sanctioned, they were actively promoted by the most prominent Maori leaders of the time. Even Henry Williams, with all his influence, could not halt this development. Some of his own servant girls were discovered plying their trade on board visiting ships on occasions. Maori prostitutes once rowed across from Kororareka to Paihia taunting him and, in front of his Mission station, performed a lewd dance especially for him. The good Minister chased them back to their boat.

With such widespread sexual interaction between the races and increasing numbers of marriages, the birth of half-caste children would have become a normal, and perhaps desired, event. The spiritual effect of this, however, is one of immense importance and is of primary interest to us. Notwithstanding the mutually strong attraction that can develop between members of different races, the spiritual ramifications of any such unions, particularly where the natural sexual desire produces offspring is, like every other activity in Creation, strictly subject to its firmly established Laws.

*   *   *   *   *

Let us digress slightly and examine this particular aspect from the point of view of those Laws.

New Zealanders claim collective heritage from the intermarriage of many different races, but perhaps more specifically from inter-union between the Maori race and various European ones. With such a high level of intermarriage historically, we perhaps have the interesting distinction of probably being more 'inter-married' than most. As it is an obvious consequence of "The Pakeha Influence" and "Colonisation", and given the apparent crisis of racial identity currently prevalent in some sections of Maoridom, it is important to understand the major effect of so much racial inter-union.

In order to fully understand the ramifications of such an intimate merging of two different racial groups, we need to utilise the knowledge of The Spiritual Laws.

With any union of mixed races where offspring are produced, especially where the racial differences are quite marked, the first obvious consequence of such a union is the merging of the physical characteristics of both parents. That union may produce handsome, well-formed offspring, or perhaps may not.

The other but far more decisive and unseen effect, however, is the immediate 'dilution' of the individual make-up of the blood of both parents when reproduced in the children. This may initially sound like a very fanciful and dangerously racist remark given today's increasing intolerance by many toward other races. But in fact it *actually offers* the spiritual understanding of **why** there are so many different races on earth and what their purpose together as one humankind on our 'blue planet' is or should be. In material terms, a 'dilution' of *any* liquid substance brings about an immediate weakening of that original composition, and human blood is no different. It will still have the same colour, consistency and viscosity, and still be cross-racially transfused, but its original, *individual composition* will have been *altered* and *diluted* with the addition of a *different* kind of blood, thus *weakening* the original. How can this be? After all, we are told that aside from ensuring a correct blood-group match, all blood is the same.

Let us examine Dr Ranginui Walker's assessment of this from his dual perspective of an anthropologist and a learned Maori, and assess it from the standpoint of Spiritual Law.

"The argument that there are reputed to be fewer than two hundred full-blooded Maoris in New Zealand today is a favourite ploy of some Pakehas to deny Maori people a separate identity. It derives from the "we are one people" syndrome and reflects attitudes of intolerance, ethnocentricity and monocultural arrogance of monumental proportions.

An argument based on "full-blood" or "Maori blood" is unscientific. The blood of both people is transfusible, so we shall have to look elsewhere to identify the characteristics that differentiate the Maori from Pakeha. Without going through an exhaustive list of Maori cultural elements, values and customary modes of behaviour, we can come to the conclusion that Maori identity has an objective base in that some people *think* they are Maori."

For the most part, the quite marked physical differences between Maori and Pakeha are probably clearly obvious, even to the most casual observer. However, with more and more Pakeha dilution, the differences may become less easily discernible. Nevertheless, Dr Walker believes an accuracy of about seventy per cent identification rate can be achieved. Thus he further suggests:

"Clearly the Pakeha recognises the category "Maori" on an objective basis, just as the Maori does. What is needed from the Pakeha is a frank admission that the category exists rather than denying it on the ground that "Maori blood" has been watered down.

At the subjective level some people think of themselves as Maori irrespective of the degree of "Maori blood". This subjective acceptance of Maori identity is also independent of Maori language, values and customary modes of behaviour."

(Nga Tau Tohetohe:Years of Anger, Ranginui Walker, p.213, 214)

We would certainly concur with Dr. Walker's latter observation regarding this aspect of 'personal identification to being Maori' also being independent of the language etc.. And on the basis of scientific and medical beliefs, we may well regard all blood as, *ostensibly*, the same. But that is not the complete story by any means! It only *appears* to be the same materially. Moreover, the science of physics recognises that everything has a distinct radiation of its own i.e., *everything radiates*!

The *radiating quality* of blood, therefore, is a *spiritual* one. It provides the *connection* for the work of the spirit on earth, and is therefore meant to act as a bridge for the *activity of the spirit* to animate and work through the physical part – the body – of the individual human being.

> Thus: *Human blood is formed by the spirit so that its ordained role, animating and working through man as a complete entity, may be fulfilled* **in the correct spiritual way**.

Certain races with strong views about blood purity enshrined within their religion or culture strive to retain their ethnic purity. So much so that intermarriage with other races is strongly discouraged, if not forbidden outright in some cases. Moreover, these particular groups can trace strong and clear bloodlines going back millennia. People who believe that widespread intermarriage could solve all problems of racial tension by eventually producing a global humanity of 'olive' complexion often regard such views as racist. Yet if a particular people *choose* to retain their ethnic purity, then that is their choice by right. That choice, moreover, should be accepted as their natural and spiritually correct desire to remain that particular race, and is therefore *not at all a racist stance*.

In New Zealand's case, the dilution of Maori blood by Pakeha blood, and/or vice versa, brought with it a change for both races, aside from a different coloured skin and facial characteristics. Because the spiritual ramifications are so important in a society characterised by so much intermarriage, it is vital that we acknowledge the lawful effects of the *purpose* of the blood. It is interesting to note that science has long identified the major blood types, and also noted the fact that they cannot be cross-mixed randomly, for *precise and lawful rules* strictly apply here too. More far-reaching than that, however, is the discovery that blood typing is far more *individualistic* than ever imagined. Thus via the simple method of DNA coding – a method accepted in Courts of Law as evidence for crime resolution in a process similar to fingerprinting – the final *spiritual characteristic* of blood composition is thus revealed.

Therein lies the truth that *each spirit*, each one of us as an *individual spiritual being* – even if part of the same basic race – nevertheless produces the particular blood composition that is our own very unique *'spiritual-print'*![4] Yet, notwithstanding this individuality, contained within the same parameters are strong characteristics of *ethnic attraction* too, and thus 'ethnic radiation' as well. And even with highly sophisticated, diagnostic techniques in medicine discovering singular genetic predispositions to particular illnesses running through many generations of certain families today, it is not any physical "law of genetics" that determines these "predisposed family threads".

Though genetic material is carried in every cell of the body, including blood cells, ultimately it is **The Law of Spiritual Attraction** that is the major determinant that may bring individuals into family groupings with similar predispositions – even if they be medical ones. The fact that medical science is able to conclusively demonstrate that genetic material is passed on via many generations of the same family group, clearly reveals the inviolability of Spiritual Law here

---

[4]The distinctiveness of a "spiritual-print" may be seen as a 'constantly changing configuration' in the form and colour radiations of individual aurae – Kirlian photography – which science will one day acknowledge and utilise as a most unique and beneficial diagnostic tool.

too. And via this attractant quality, we may thus note that individuals with singular *spiritual characteristics* nevertheless incarnate into particular family groups, with similar kinds of family units then subsequently incarnating into a particular race or ethnic group.

Therefore, because Spiritual Law decrees that each human spirit 'forms' its individual blood composition solely for itself according to individual 'spiritual disposition', the end result of that lawful process revealed in DNA coding has conclusively proved that no two blood types are exactly the same. This 'spiritually-lawful' code therefore represents our individual and unique *spiritual-print*, similar to a fingerprint, yet is ultimately more powerfully-distinctive.

The fact that no two individual blood types are **exactly** the same among the billions within the human race, bears out what Spiritual Law has always stated, and thus reveals the Truth of what we are saying. And it is so because all science is necessarily subject to Spiritual Law in the first place. Earth science has at last caught up. In the case of the present Maori race, all of whom to varying degrees are of mixed blood of one type or another, this new knowledge may allow for a different perspective on the question of race and spirituality. And, in reinforcement, just as individuals radiate their particular 'spiritual identity', so will different races and ethnic groups also radiate their 'spiritual connectedness' under **The Law**.[5]

$$* \qquad * \qquad * \qquad * \qquad *$$

With regard to early Aotearoa, however, from a pragmatic viewpoint, mixed-marriage alliances were a necessary part of life then, and Belich (Making Peoples, p.172) notes that this aspect:

"...dominated Maori-European relations before 1840 and was quite important after it."

Intermarriage provided the 'glue' for a large measure of stability and mutual tolerance. Possibly in keeping with the strict protocols of *mana*, the more important Pakehas such as traders, station managers and ship's captains:

"...married chiefly women...", whilst their followers "...married women of lower rank."

While many Europeans did marry Maori women, most did not. That did not mean there was no liaison between the two races. The exploitation or otherwise of the sexual favours of Maori women, either voluntarily or under duress, was part of the assimilation process into a primarily European sphere of influence that the Maori could not easily resist. From an initial attitude of disdain toward some of the more 'debauched' behaviour of the Pakeha, and amusement at his perceived foolishness in certain matters, increasing numbers of Maori gradually took up the vices of the European. So by the 1830s, the use of tobacco and heavy drinking was taking hold, even though the Maori originally labelled alcohol as *wai piro* – rotten, or stinking water. And by 1840 the Maori were well and truly in business as traders, selling their food crops, the raw materials of their land, their women, the dried heads of their own people, and the tribal lands themselves, with half of the best land of the Bay of Islands already in the possession of Europeans.

Lawlessness among some Maori who readily sought out and aped the behaviour of the more debauched whites was of concern to some of the Northern Chiefs particularly. A breakdown

---

[5]This aspect of 'weakened blood' as a result of the 'dilution factor' first came to my attention in the early 1970s at my final Medical Board pending discharge from the Army. The years in the jungles of South East Asia, often operating in wet conditions for long periods of time – including sleeping wet – produced, at least for me, asthmatic tendencies and chronic bronchitis. My query to the doctors regarding this condition brought forth the response: "Don't worry about it, all you guys have it. It's just the mixed blood." They informed me, moreover, that Service data for *part-Maori Servicemen* from the very earliest records showed a consistent and general tendency toward respiratory problems, which worsened in later life.

in previously strict Maori protocols before any kind of enforceable social law could be put into effect for all races present might have been disastrous for Maori society. This 'contamination' by lawless European elements at Russell was finally removed when Heke's frustration, combined with certain aspects of post-Treaty dealings, finally induced him and Kawiti, with a combined force of 600, to sack and raze the town to the ground. This measure effectively stopped any further problems and Russell became a law-abiding centre of Government and never again became a problem. With increasing law in the Bay area, many of the worst dregs departed to reside more closely to Pomare's Pa where laws were decidedly more relaxed and where Pomare reportedly kept his 96 slave girls for a large scale prostitution business.

Tobacco use, quickly adopted by the Maori, became extremely widespread and disastrously affected their health. The ready acceptance of smoking among Maori today with its increasing incidence of respiratory diseases and some cancers can probably be attributed to those early beginnings. Again, as with all material activities, there is a direct correlation of its effects to where the practice actually stands in spiritual terms.[6]

Previously unknown diseases from Europe also visited their virulent effects upon some Maori, and the more refined, sweeter diet similarly appealed to the 'sweetening native tooth'. Some of the more traditional, healthier foods, excluding human flesh, gave way to increasingly greater consumption of newly arrived European staples such as flour, tea and sugar. The simple inventiveness of the Maori produced an interesting porridge called *'stirrabout'* which consisted of tea, sweetened flour and water, and potato. Such a vile mix must have had, as its reason for existing, convenience, for it could not have been appetising. Respiratory infections increased, not only from the Europeans, but by the Maori practice of replacing their own warm and waterproof flax capes with the much-desired Pakeha blanket which was considered an excellent and fashionable all-purpose garment.

Unfortunately, its obvious inability to keep the occupant dry and its usual state of grimy dampness allowed bacteria to flourish producing unnecessary illness and death, particularly among the women. In the Auckland area, a small group of pioneer women connected with the early Church, appalled at the plight of these Maori women, nursed and cared for them and gradually induced many to forgo the dubious benefit of 'the Pakeha blanket'.

Initially, however, European clothing held no special allure for the Maori who much rather preferred to decorate their own persons with bits and pieces of varying colours from the white man's 'wardrobe'. But as the assimilation process developed coincidentally with the lessening of ties to his own formerly strict way of life, his original disinterest in the clothes of the Pakeha gave way to pragmatism about them. Though there were some Maori, especially some chiefs, who deemed it appropriate to wear various articles of clothing of this new style from an early time.

A particular aspect of Maori behaviour that changed dramatically as Pakeha influence and Law became more solidly entrenched was the recital of Maori battle exploits. Where once there was no mention of chivalry being accorded the enemy – this being regarded as a weakness amongst the old Maori – Pakeha disenchantment with such ideas resulted in Maori gradually *changing his oratorical style* when recounting the story of his battles. Treachery during pre-European times was an accepted accompaniment to warfare. To deceive the enemy was considered "a fine thing to do", and all Maori practised it. The early European writers cite many instances of such incidents. It was not *how* the Maori acquired victory that mattered, but the fact that he did, and by any means to achieve it. Now, however, stories of magnanimity toward a defeated enemy became much more commonplace in the hope that this would place him in a more favourable light, particularly during later Land Court hearings.

In Maori Warfare, page 42, we read:

[6]Whilst briefly mentioned here, a more detailed spiritual explanation of the effects of smoking will be offered in the later Chapter, "Maori Today".

"...but, as Best and others have pointed out, evidence given before the Land Courts is often unreliable. Those giving evidence were no doubt cognisant of the European's professed abhorrence for so-called treachery and their admiration of instances of chivalry."

To further emphasise this point, and to illustrate our assertion that with the arrival of the Pakeha the overall change for the Maori was a mainly beneficial one for him both spiritually and personally, Vayda, on page 43, further records that:

"Donne, for example, notes a contrast between *the extreme savagery of the oldtime Maori wars* and the displays of great nobility in the Maori's fight with the white man."

(Emphasis mine.)

During this time of rapid change, the lore of the Maori – the very essence of things that he held sacred and *tapu* – could not compete with the swiftly encroaching mores of the European and his religion. The despoliation of the natural order of flora and fauna by swiftly destructive and previously unknown mechanisms also spelled the beginnings of the demise of his strong connection to the natural world as *he perceived it*. The sailors of all nationalities who visited these shores could not help but be mightily impressed with the potential of the kauri to provide almost perfect masts and spars for what was then still a growing industry in ships of sail, as the steamship was still not yet perfected as a viable ocean-going alternative. Historical records detail the great decimation of the forests for this purpose and the later clear-felling of them to make way for farms.

Whether the Maori viewed this with horror and dismay is difficult to ascertain now. On the surface, at least, this does appear to be the case, and one would assume that the 'feel' he had nurtured for the forest of Tane in his beliefs spanning hundreds of years would not have been easily subjugated by this new and radical economic attitude of the white invader. Gradually, however, he, too, took part in this same degradation of the land. Perhaps neither easily nor willingly at first, but probably more so the further he travelled from the 'old way'. Some of the *tapu* slowly died out, though not all. Moreover, his practices of *makutu* were also greatly lessened though, again, not completely dispensed with. But the major transgressions of *blood-utu* and cannibalism thankfully had to die out as there was increasingly no place for them in a world gradually dominated by the Pakeha and his system of Law.

The strong influence of the churches of that period played a pivotal role in influencing Maori to reconsider their savage practices and move more towards the embracing of Christianity. In fact, so successful were the missionaries in their zeal and concern to convert these 'heathen cannibals' to the 'saving grace' of their religion, that estimates place probably over half of all New Zealand Maori as, ostensibly, professing Christians by about the year 1840. It is not feasible to expect that a race of people living as the old Maori did for centuries should, in the space of only a few short years, suddenly convert from cannibalism and *blood-utu* to become knowledgeable Christians of great conviction. The new god of the Pakeha was obviously much more powerful than the Maori gods in that he supplied the white man with all the trappings of good living and gave him powerful weapons.

So it was an intelligent move to accept this state of affairs, at least outwardly, and hope that the Pakeha god would smile on the Maori too. Maori Christianity, in the main, was necessarily a mixture of the old and the new. Up until the 1830s, however, the Maori of the Bay of Islands became more assertive in the defence of their way of life rather than less. And certainly under the command and influence of "Hongi the man-eater", were not yet ready to embrace this new way of the missionaries. An early Bay of Islands Missionary accurately commented on this ambivalent attitude of the Maori when he wrote in 1818:

"I conceive our trials (as missionaries) will be much heavier for some years to come ... the cause of which apparently arises out of this circumstance, "that the *Native Spirit* has been roused by the long intercourse of the Natives with Europeans ...” but “...the *native heart* with its blind attachment to the most barbarous customs remains unchanged, and inclines its possessor to pursue them with additional vigour.”

(New Zealand's Heritage, p.177)

The arrival of the more efficient killing tools of the Pakeha helped the Maori immensely in his 'additional vigour' of repaying old scores! To this end, it could be said that the desire of the Maori to acquire more and more of the material goods of the white man, aside from just his guns, inevitably placed him in a position of *cultural dependency* on the Pakeha. Like Cook, Samuel Marsden also made an interesting comparison between the New Zealand Maori and the Australian Aboriginals.

He asserted that the Aborigine's complete disinterest in the 'value' of material possessions:

> “...would permanently prevent the civilisation of the latter”, as they could not be “...induced to form industrious habits to obtain them”, nor to “...form a permanent... attachment for Europeans”. A people would be 'civilised', he implied – which in 19th century eyes meant the introduction of Christianity, trade and a capitalist society – “...once they could be induced to covet material possessions”.

(New Zealand's Heritage, p.179)

Prophetic words indeed! From the very earliest contacts with Tasman and Cook, the Maori immediately revealed this covetousness for Pakeha goods by their constant attempts to acquire whatever caught their eye. Even to steal if they could, or trade if that method failed. Cook lamented the constant, tiresome efforts required by his crew to prevent such thefts by certain Iwi. Moreover, many incidents were recorded where Maori were not averse to killing to obtain the objects of their desires. With this strongly developing propensity for the white man's material goods an irresistible reality, along with increasing intermarriage, Maori set in place for themselves a path that was completely dependent and *intertwined* with that of 'the Pakeha', **not separate from him**.[7]

*   *   *   *   *

How easily accepting the Maori were of the Pakeha world and how they could interact with it quite readily, occurred with the apprenticing of two young men to the printing trade. Not in New Zealand, however, but in Austria, in arguably the epitome of the most charming of Old-world European cities – Vienna. Such a huge transition from *raupo-hut hapu* to the height of European civilisation and *technology* involved far more than simple physical relocation. It was surely, more than anything else, a journey of incredible mental expansion. Two Waikato Maori – Tumohe and Paraone – in 1859 sailed on the *Novara* to study printing in 'Pakeha Europe'.

Very recently removed in time from the old 'savage way', those two young men learned to operate a, then, modern printing press: To set type and print articles; an occupation completely divorced from every frame of reference to traditional Maori things. They duly returned to New Zealand with that precious technology – a gift from the Austrian Emperor.

*   *   *   *   *

---

[7]Given the far too high percentage of Maori jailed for offences relating to theft and/or acquisition of property by various means, perhaps this covetousness is an inherently strong propensity within the race now. Even if that is so, however, it does not make the propensity acceptable. It means that Maori need to develop the spiritual strength, the *kaha*, to *not allow it* to be the major problem that it seems to be.

Such an incongruous event clearly illustrated the ability of early Maori to utilise apparatus which represented the height of European technology of the time and, notwithstanding their total immersion in fear-ridden superstition, revealed their inherent high intelligence level. All this, of course, potentially augured well for their future.

Belich expresses an interesting opinion regarding that phase of rapid change, whereby *mana*, or more particularly "rivalry for *mana*", was the "...traditional Maori mechanism for rapidly disseminating change." This aspect of the Maori describes his behaviour rather well, for "rivalry for *mana*" was markedly instrumental in the "...spread of *pa*, guns and bibles."
Moreover it greatly facilitated:

> "...the depth and breadth of engagement with the European economy before and after 1840."

> (Making Peoples, p.198)

Thus, in almost the ultimate paradox, *mana* could virtually be described as a two-edged *taiaha* for Maori. On the one hand this powerful and complex force that Maori society gave life and expression to, drove him on an increasingly downward spiral before the arrival of the European. With the coming of the Pakeha, however, it offered the *same mechanism* for rapid assimilation into the *tauiwi's* irresistible sphere of influence.

14

The Missionaries

Christianity for the Maori

During the time-period of the 14th to the 16th centuries, two vastly different people in opposite hemispheres went about their respective lifestyles completely oblivious to the fact that the other existed, or even that their lands existed. In the North, the Europeans with the Christian Church all-powerful, and in the South, on a group of small islands in the world's largest ocean – one that the Europeans had yet to discover – lived the Maori, with *tapu*, *makutu* and *utu* all-powerful! But even though unknown to each other then, the discoveries and inventions that marked this period in European history would be instrumental in providing the crucial means and tools for Europe's expansionist tendencies into the Pacific, and the concomitant mutual discovery of each other.

This was the Renaissance period – of rebirth and revival! It was characterised primarily by the humanistic revival of classical art, literature, and learning that originated in Italy in the 14th century and later spread throughout Europe. Yet these on their own were not the greatest contributory factors for the later, fateful meeting between Maori and Pakeha and the singularly powerful influence of the missionaries. For the Renaissance also produced the three vitally important things needed for global exploration. They were the *compass*, the *firearm* and the *printing press*. They provided the explorers and the missionaries with the most effective means with which to fulfil their respective roles during this expansionist and evangelical phase.

The *compass* was the primary aid for the great voyages of discovery because it simplified navigation. *Firearms* provided protection whilst at the same time producing an initial sense of awe and fear amongst the new peoples. And the *printing press* allowed the European Church to mass-produce Bibles, a task which had previously been done by hand – clearly a painstaking and laborious affair. The missionaries benefited from this rapid method of Bible production because they could now supply the large volumes required for the disseminating of their respective religions in the new 'heathen lands'.

The arrival of the missionaries represented a singularly important landmark for Maori, not only for the time, but more importantly for a *future event* destined to occur in the century following that arrival. The groundwork they would lay in the beginning would set in place a particular chain of happenings for the Maori race which would culminate in a vital and quite stupendous spiritual event – the Calling of their greatest Prophet – to which we are threading our way.

The zeal and commitment with which missionaries went about their work in British and other European Colonies during those turbulent times surely reflects a powerful sense of service to their Christian ideals and beliefs. From a relatively cloistered and safe lifestyle in England and Europe to strange and decidedly uncertain far-flung corners of the growing Empires, these remarkable men, with their equally remarkable wives in some cases, spread their universal message of peace and hope in their wish to convert the 'heathen savages' in the new lands.

Moreover, they would have encountered fewer places of outright savagery than that which existed among the Maori of old New Zealand. From the perspective of our present time in history, it is difficult to even begin to imagine how a people raised in a strictly chaste, middle-class, religiously Victorian-type society of tea and gentility – or in the civility of Old-world Europe – would react to the harsh realities of the new worlds. To be suddenly thrust into a world of tattooed faces, *blood-utu* and enthusiastic cannibalism; to a people they would, of necessity, need to live virtually cheek-by-jowl with, would have required an especially strong faith.

Notwithstanding the potentially huge difficulties and great dangers of such a task, however, they met the challenge well and began the process that would finally take the Maori *away* from his savage ways onto a path of his own future spiritual destiny. This 'future spiritual potential', ordained to be far removed from many of the traditions and cultural considerations that had hitherto been so entrenched in the old way of life, would not, and indeed *could not*, take place without the first faltering steps into that future. And under the committed courage and guidance of these men of the Church, away from a pattern of living that, unchecked, would have eventually brought about their complete 'spiritual decline'. An unfortunate decline brought about by their own hand through freely subjugating personal life-path choices to the ancient, dark god of *utu*!

So it was that at Rangihoua in December 1814, on the northern shores of the Bay of Islands, that the Maori first welcomed the "Church Missionary Society for Africa and the East". Of course, such an obvious difference in cultures did not produce an immediate and instant harmonious rapport. Yet it is interesting to note the very first words spoken by the first missionaries at their first Service on the beach.

Local Maori heard the words, *once uttered by the archangel Gabriel* at the birth of **Jesus – The Son of God!**:

"Behold, we bring you glad tidings of great joy."

With its clear, high connotations, and in accordance with The Spiritual Laws, the words spoken that day would have produced the corresponding 'spiritual form'; a form and connection which *could* become part of the new potential for Maori. There could be no turning back now. The retention of the old way was finished.

It was probably fortuitous that Northern Maori, to whom the Missionaries first gave The Bible, were already relatively familiar with the presence and ways of white men who had been in the area from the outset. To venture into a region without a reasonable level of familiarity might not have been as fruitful as it eventually was, and could have been positively disastrous. However, even though there was little common ground in their respective religious views initially, from these small beginnings the missionaries slowly began to make inroads into the world of Maori superstition. However, certain skills which the missionaries were keen for the Maori to learn were of no use to them at that time. For example, boot-making was of little use to a people who took to the war-trail bare-footed.

The primary consideration for Maori, however, and far more so than any religious instruction, was the acquisition of Pakeha trade goods. To this end the missionaries were expected to be the suppliers, or at least help facilitate this aspect of Maori desire. Consequently, Mission stations came under the increasing protection of certain chiefs, notably Hongi. In the beginning, however, the missionaries did not have sufficient supplies to satisfy the demands of Maori, and terms of trade were often a point of contention between the two sides. Being so few in numbers, and also reliant on the goodwill and protection of Maori for their continued tenure in New Zealand, the missionaries were often forced to compromise their own religious principles, particularly after Maoris discovered the devastating killing power of the musket.

In the early years the Maori regarded the missionaries as their own. And in 1820 one Major Richard Cruise, visiting the Bay of Islands, recorded that the protection of the Anglican station at Kerikeri was maintained only at the expense of:

> "...much forbearance and humiliation. The natives, knowing too well that the missionaries are in their power, commit extensive depredations upon them not infrequently aggravating their extortions by gross insult."

(New Zealand's Heritage, p.282)

Confronted with Maori demands for supplies or be driven out of the country, the missionaries reluctantly acquiesced, for the possibility of starvation in those early days was very real without access to trade with Maori. Their 'Parent Society', whilst not obviously happy with this development, gave permission if there was no other alternative. Marsden, whose concern for Maori brought about the establishment of the Mission stations, condemned the trade outright despite the fears of the missionaries themselves that the whole venture might collapse. Kendall, one of the three missionaries first sent to New Zealand, noted that Marsden quite happily approved trade in hatchets and axes even though readily used in inter-tribal warfare. Kendall opined that axes and hatchets were less humane than muskets.

The Maori desire for European goods in the early years was a constant source of concern for some Mission stations, which represented immense wealth in Maori eyes. Yet the supplies they carried were vitally necessary for a life of reasonable comfort. For example, the inventory for the Wesleyan Mission in 1824 showed that the stores contained 214 axes, 48 adzes, 69 hatchets, 27 spades, 80 chisels, 48 plane irons, 35 iron pots, 24 frying pans, 10 grindstones, 1,897 knives, 95 scissors, 7 bill hooks, 60 gouges, 21 blankets, 20 gallons of oil, 4,000 fish hooks, 8 pieces of India print, 5 yards of cloth. To a stone-age people who had never known such things, the Missionaries must have appeared extremely wealthy. Unfortunately, these much-needed supplies for the Mission acted as a two-edged sword in their dealings with Maori. Whilst possessions gave the missionaries *mana* in Maori eyes, the same goods sparked conflicts with them in their avaricious wants.

This constant discord caused the Wesleyans to consider whether they should give up their possessions and go "barefoot among the Maori". But the difficulties they would surely have encountered in attempting it quickly weighed against this train of thought. In any case, in such a harsh and savage environment, it is unlikely they would have survived. In the end, Christianity, with its strength and cohesiveness, provided sufficient foundation for the missionaries to succeed in their task.

Initial attempts at teaching Christian concepts were invariably met with a wall of non-comprehension. Notwithstanding the 'knowledge' of an unseen and all-powerful Supreme Being called *Io*, the missionaries discovered that Maori were unable to grasp the idea of the "The One God". The Maori world was peopled with *atua* for all seasons and events. When first discovered even such previously unknown objects as nails were called *atua*, as were watches and sextants later. Thus the term '*Great Atua*', coined by the missionaries to try to explain the idea of a One God, had no relative point of reference in the Maori mind. For if there was only one, why was there so much disparity between what the European possessed and what the Maori had, and why make men with different coloured skins?

The story of Creation, whilst interesting for Maori at the time, was obviously the way that the Pakeha God created their world, but New Zealand was fished up out of the sea by Maui. Moreover, since *atua* were the cause of sickness, the Maori concluded that the new diseases of the white man must be caused by their unseen *atua*. As Maori had no natural resistance to what must have seemed to be very frightening diseases, they would not have given much credence to the idea of a benevolent and just Pakeha *atua*. So for the first ten years little progress was achieved by either side in converting the other to the intent of their purpose. The missionaries offered their religion and the Maori sought to transform 'their missionaries' into traders who would supply them with whatever they desired.

The problem for the missionaries was exacerbated by the fact that the language of the Maori had no written form. Kendall, who had attempted to start a school, could only teach in Maori as his own grasp of it increased. Ideally, what was required was to teach English to Maori. But that could not happen until the missionaries had a sufficiently good grasp of the language to be able to translate it into English. With this realisation, more spare time was given over to effecting this and to producing the books with which to teach. Marsden did not wholly agree with this direction but the 'Parent Society' in London did, and subsequently instructed the replacement missionaries to concentrate on this aspect.

Not until the Rev. Henry William's arrival in New Zealand in about 1823, however, was there any real progress. Maori well recognised the great benefit in learning to read and write, and marvelled that marks on paper could be interpreted and acted upon by other white men. The obvious ramifications for trade in being able to read and write were not lost on these intelligent 'savages', even if steeped in superstition. So under the astute leadership of Henry Williams, the Maori language in terms of grammar was more formally structured. Attempts were made to translate The Bible and other religious works, and in 1827 a publication of 31 pages was printed in Sydney. With a reading reference now available, Maori, *of their own accord*, gathered to read this new Christian word. Because of this upsurge of interest, the previous policy of only teaching children to read was abandoned in favour of teaching adults who might later seek baptism.

Since literary skills were now eagerly sought after, and also viewed as a means of obtaining *mana* in both Maori and Pakeha eyes, conversion to Christianity was deemed the best way to achieve it. Yet Hongi, who had no interest in the religion and regarded it as one for the old and the weak, maintained his considerable *mana* despite his anti-religious stance.

The Mission stations themselves became havens of peace and safety in a land still racked by war and *blood-utu*, and many Maori, sickened by continual strife, left the tribal way behind and became part of the Mission settlement, particularly when Hongi's depredations decimated many Maori *Iwi* throughout the North Island. Paradoxically, Hongi did learn the alphabet under the tutorship of Kendall who, unfortunately for Hongi, was unable to teach him any more than that. From these first tentative steps at reading and religious instruction, the first three Maori were baptised at Paihia in February 1830.

This 'momentous event' encouraged other Maori to seek religious instruction and to also prepare for baptism. The ready availability of books, coupled with the desire of the Maori to master this *Pakeha secret*, quickly produced a relatively high degree of literacy amongst them. The keenness with which Maori embraced this newly acquired skill was reflected in their great glee when a printing press arrived at Paihia in 1835. It was brought ashore by excited Maori who recognised the importance of this machine for printing their very own books.[1]

An interesting consequence of this original enthusiasm, and one that surprised the missionaries, was the ability of Maori to memorise large texts of The Bible. The fact that the Maori

---

[1]With so much disappointing aversion to education among many present-day *tangata whenua* students and some parents, perhaps *these kinds of present-day tangata whenua* should revisit this earlier time in their history, learn from it and emulate the enthusiasm of Maori ancestors.

had no written language meant that anything needing to be recorded in their own *waiata* had to be committed to memory. Such a skill served them well in memorising large texts of the Pakeha religion by heart. Moreover, since the only books printed were about Christianity, Maori became quite familiar with the religious texts as they pursued their desire to learn to read.

This fledgling ability in the Pakeha 'religion' ensured that the 'The Word' was carried quickly through the tribes, especially in the North Island. However, such rapid dissemination of a new and radical concept by people who could not lay claim to an adequate understanding of it presupposed the possibility for many distortions to arise in the teaching and interpretation of it. And this was a later development with some of the emerging Prophets and religious leaders.

Not surprisingly, therefore, the lack of real understanding of such a far-reaching concept as Christianity among early Maori converts gave rise to some interesting 'home-grown' practices. Henry Williams, in exasperation, recorded one such instance.

Even though the Maori considered the head sacred, Belich records one personalised baptism that Williams witnessed, where:

> "...the ceremony appears to be the washing of the head... in warm water out of an iron pot the person at the same time confessing his sins vainly imagining thereby his sins will be pardoned and a release from *tapu* very much according to native custom."

The rapid spread of Christianity did not at the same time produce any more rapid or deeper understanding of it, such was the strength of traditionally entrenched thinking. This aspect is described well in the following observation and reinforces our premise that Maori society was actually based on fear stemming from 'psychic' practices.

> "Though Christianity has been embraced very extensively yet many are under the bondage of fear with regard to Maori gods and maori witchcraft and maori tapu. Perhaps of many it might be truly said... They served their Lord and feared their own gods."

Missionary activity was not solely confined to just one or two of the mainstream churches in Northland. The Maori came into contact with 'men of the cloth' of other Christian persuasions in many parts of New Zealand. Maori 'Christians', moreover, were not averse to changing their loyalty as occasion demanded. The laid-back attitude of the Maori, which actually reflected a cursory acceptance of Christianity rather than any clear conviction about it, allowed them to utilise two or more denominations as they saw fit. This is well illustrated by the comments of Te Heuheu Iwikau of Ngati Tuwharetoa:

> "...who bluntly informed a church (Anglican) missionary that 'when you are in Taupo I am a Churchman. When the Wesleyan missionary is here, I belong to his church. When the R. C. priest calls, I am a papist, and when no European is here, I am a Heathen'."

> (Making Peoples, p.218 [all].)

Perhaps the strangest and more incongruous situations involving missionaries were those where some *accompanied* raiding war parties – usually on *waka*. One wonders what they hoped to achieve with this practice? Perhaps they believed an opportunity might arise whereby they could dissuade the warring parties from joining battle, or effect a last-minute peace negotiation. It must surely have been a source of constant dismay for the missionaries to witness the butchery and cannibalism of inter-tribal warfare, whilst at the same time striving to teach more beneficial things such as reading, writing, agriculture and religion during that period.

Of course it could be argued that religion may not necessarily be a beneficial gift, but in the case of the old Maori, *it was surely more so than the continuation of the old lifestyle.*

*   *   *   *   *

The missionary zeal to translate The Bible into Maori resulted in the vitally important outcome of the development of a Maori alphabet, devised with the help of a Cambridge University professor. This writing system required only fifteen letters, with each representing one of the major sounds of the language. With a formal structure now in place, and Maori generally eager to acquire this ability, what had been solely an oral tradition in language expression now advanced to one of written expression also. Now the traditional history, *waiata* and *karakia* of the past could be preserved for posterity without fear of it being supplanted by new teachings, lost altogether through the deaths of those who carried it in their memories, or even 'subverted and sanitised'. Thus, for the most part, the ancient traditions and legends still survive to this day via the aid of a *written* Maori language **developed by Pakeha**.

It would be difficult, indeed, to find a more *beneficial outcome for the retention of Maori culture* than that resulting from *the energy and far-sightedness of the early* **Pakeha Church Missionaries**.

*   *   *   *   *

It is interesting to note the views expressed about the Maori by two Wesleyan Churchmen.

> Samuel Leigh reported that Maoris were "...a noble but perishing race of people..." with fine intellects. William White, by contrast, particularly in the initial shock of first contact, viewed them as "incarnate devils", a people with "...strange and ludicrous customs", in a land of "Darkness, Bondage, Death and Blood".

(New Zealand's Heritage, p.293)

Whilst these vastly differing opinions probably do reveal all of those particular aspects existing in the Maori race at that time, nevertheless, in terms of purely Spiritual Law, only one of the above views more accurately reflected the true situation. Given the path traced thus far, the reader should have little difficulty in *objectively* determining which of the two was the more correct.

The task of the missionaries was greatly restricted in the early years by the attitude of their protectors – the more powerful chiefs. The cunningly devised plans of Northern chiefs, particularly Hongi, to hold onto 'their Pakehas' for the acquisition of trade goods and weapons, effectively prevented the missionaries from readily offering the same to other tribes elsewhere. Since trade and missionary activity developed far more rapidly in the North, this meant that not only did Northern Maori acquire more than other Maori in a relatively short space of time, but gave them a distinct advantage in the new era of musket-driven, inter-tribal warfare.

Paradoxically, however, as Belich very correctly states, Hongi's depredations inadvertently set in place the mechanism for far greater dissemination of Christianity than would probably have been achieved by the missionaries themselves in what would have been lonely and far-flung outposts surrounded by a heavily forested, trackless land of ancient Maori psychic/occult practices. The thousands of slaves that Hongi and his Lieutenants canoed or marched north came into close contact with this new religion, and many embraced it wholeheartedly. Whilst slaves for Ngapuhi, these prisoners attended Mission schools where they learned reading, writing and the Scriptures. They also learned from each other.

So from about 1830 onwards, when Ngapuhi began releasing them, former prisoners returned to their homelands armed with this new knowledge. Via this movement the missionaries later discovered that Scripture was already being taught in areas where Maori had never seen a missionary. After finally leaving the constraints of Northland Maori, the missionaries:

"...followed Christianity, carried by released prisoners, not the other way around." "It was they, not the European missionaries, who generated the first mass Maori engagement with Christianity."

(Making Peoples, p.168)

Some quite remarkable results were achieved by some of these 'Maori missionaries'. Belich writes that so great was the 'influence and preaching' of one Wiremu Nera Ngatai of Ngati Ruanui:

"...that nearly all the tribes for more than 200 miles along this coast had renounced idolatry before a single European missionary had been near them." Moreover, this amazing individual "built churches", and "...sent acolytes to evangelise Nga Rauru, Whanganui and Ngati Tuwharetoa..."

Of these developments Henry Williams wrote:

"Thus had instruction ... been conveyed from Tribe to Tribe, and many had been taught to read in the remotest parts of the Island and had the word of God conveyed to them who had never seen a European."

(Making Peoples, p.169)

The first Maori preachers revealed a particular characteristic of the race; evangelical zeal. It was one, moreover, which helped the religious development of the Maori Prophetic Movement with its strong and *truly spiritual* future 'potential'. So perhaps, in a strangely perverse way, Hongi Hika was a two-edged sword for the *spreading* of Christianity. His destructive campaigns, which produced thousands of slaves and killed thousands more, actually set in place a relatively large Maori nucleus that allowed for a *more rapid* spread of Christianity than might otherwise have been achieved. Paradoxically, he had no time for Christianity, deeming it fit only for women and children, and only courted and protected the missionaries for the fulfilment of his greater plan of wide-scale *utu* against his enemies.

Of the work of the missionaries, we read:

"So they continued, an island of European influence amid the Maoris. Exempt from kinship obligations, exempt from the destruction of warfare, they toiled as instructed, and prospered while all around declined. And, as instructed, they told the Maoris they were wrong."

(New Zealand's Heritage, p.296)

From the standpoint of **The Spiritual Laws of Creation – The Ultimate Law** – the old Maori were clearly wrong!

If we examine the obvious significance of the previous paragraphs objectively, we can readily see that had the Maori *wholeheartedly embraced* the ethos which the missionaries strove to offer and inculcate into the race, a far stronger and more cohesive people would have emerged from out of the mindless propensity for their *blood-utu* that had formerly been the driving force for many hundreds of years. Through the strange, distorted belief that those practices could somehow actually give one great *spiritual mana*, the Maori were unable to recognise that such ideas are actually opposed to the *true* meaning of spirituality – or *wairua* – if this term comes more closer to Maori understanding of the true meaning of the word: – **Spiritual!**

But that was not the case. Whilst there were a few far-sighted Maori who desperately tried to steer a different path immediately after the arrival of the Pakeha, many more gladly and willingly utilised the new tools and weapons to *hunt down and kill* much more of their own people in a far shorter space of time than they could ever have done previously. And by destabilising and emptying large tracts of land previously occupied by settled tribes, the Maoris themselves inadvertently assisted the white man in his avaricious desire for land.[2]

Thus the main outcome of the introduction of Christianity was to eventually transform the Maori way of life forever. The missionaries, who arrived long before the colonists and whose arrival *they opposed*, saw the Maori race develop from one of extreme savagery to one becoming assimilated, more or less easily and relatively harmoniously, into a more Europeanised way of life. Whether regarded as a good thing or not, that was the inevitable outcome. The stories of The Bible underwent their own changes as Maori sought to identify with certain aspects of them. The Old Testament, particularly the saga of tribal Jews, struck a chord with many, leading to the establishment of their own Religious Movements in later times of trial, anguish and struggle.

And from the first tentative beginnings of this new 'Pakeha Religion' there would one day come that quite stupendous and genuinely spiritual event *for Maori – through Maori*! One, moreover, which would clearly show **the correct spiritual way forward**.

Yet, *without* those first foundation steps set in place by the early 'men of the church', this marvellous event to which we often point might not necessarily have taken place in the clear and precise manner in which it did. For that truly amazing happening was the culmination of a series of developments from those vitally necessary first beginnings for **Te Maori O Aotearoa**.

The arrival of the Pakeha and the beneficial intervention of Missionaries was not just an event of great "*Spiritual Significance*" for Maori with the 'Lawfully-imbued' and Spiritually-powerful Proclamation:

"Behold, we bring you glad tidings of great joy."

In actual and immutable *historical and spiritual fact*, it was, clearly and unequivocally in the very *first* instance:

The "Spiritual Salvation" of Maori!

Notwithstanding that reality, kudos *must still be accorded our ancestors* for their own *recognition and voluntary part* in this truly amazing story of *their* 'Spiritual Salvation' then. For *where* in the history of the world's peoples do we find a race who transited *so swiftly and so comprehensively* from incredibly savage practices as a way of life difficult to comprehend today, to *disseminating the highest religious thought among many of their own* **in just a few decades**?

And from out of the *spread* of that *higher thought* emerged: **The Maori Religious Prophets!**

However, despite the emergence of the long line of Maori Prophets to lead away from 'the old', Maori *today* need to *really understand* that the 'Spiritual journey' *begun* by the ancestors **was not continued on with to what should have been its <u>culminating point</u> in the 20th century**. **We have not yet arrived!** That notwithstanding, the journey that is yet *still meant to unfold – for some –* thus holds the same *spiritual potential* for a *few* descendants today; as it once did for the *many* ancestors then!

So let us offer deep thanks and genuine gratitude to the clear help from **Above** which precisely guided the primary convergence-points that ultimately brought about exactly that **Salvation**: An unequivocal salvation *away from* the dark constraints of debilitating *tapu*, dangerous *makutu*, undeniably destructive *utu*, and spiritually-degenerative *cannibalism*!

And thus into a new and *spiritually-better* way of life where the fears of those completely aspiritual practices – at least in their more virulent and destructive forms as practised in the 'old way' under the tutelage of the dark, *Maori-instituted production* of Whiro, god of *makutu* and evil: –

– were thankfully left far behind.

---

[2]This phase in Maori history is examined in the next Chapter.

15

Hongi Hika: – and Ruatara

"Hongi the Man-Eater"
(*Man of Utu*)

&

"Ruatara"
(*Man of Peace and Vision*)

Rahiri – Founding ancestor of Ngapuhi
From the Uri of Rahiri to:

Auha

whose sons were:

Paengatai	Te Haumia	Te Hotete
"First-born – Eldest son"	"Second son"	"Youngest son"
"Author's line"		"Hongi's line"

Whilst the major portion of this Chapter is about the life and influence of **Hongi Hika**, a short essay on **Ruatara** is also included. Regarded as a lesser chief by rank, his legacy is one that sought a more industrious and peaceful way. As pointed out elsewhere in this Work, in the Maori mind *mana* is often deemed to be greatest in exploits of war and in the killing of one's enemy, which is probably why Hongi is still held in such high esteem by many in Ngapuhi. Yet the far more beneficial and therefore spiritually-correct activity was that undertaken by Ruatara who sought to improve the life of his people. By examining the differences in vision and deed, a very interesting comparison can be made between two blood-related Ngapuhi chiefs.

Thus what was, but perhaps what *could* have been!

The basic genealogy relating to Hongi is mentioned at the beginning of this Chapter to clearly establish lines of descent. A highly revered Ngapuhi warrior chief of great *mana* in Ngapuhi eyes, Hongi undertook numerous savage and brutal campaigns against many other Maori for no other reason but simple, mana-driven *blood-utu*. According to current dictates of Maori protocol, more especially among Ngapuhi, just stating such a view might be seen as contentious and a possible insult to the memory and/or *mana* of Hongi. Therefore, from the Maori perspective, particularly, anyone writing about him in such a direct way should possess the necessary connections for the purpose!

The latter-day renaissance of Maori cultural traditions and its actively-promoted strength of protocol virtually demands that everyone pay homage to it. Whilst I respect the right of others to embrace that regime should they wish, and agree that certain aspects of cultural resurgence have been beneficial for Maori and thus for the Nation as a whole, I do not personally accept that I am required to be emotionally bound to it all, either by virtue of being part-Maori, or through simply being a New Zealander. Demands from 'Maoridom' for 'unconditional loyalty' to all things Maori harbours the potential for producing the powerful and potent 'form' of a 'two-edged sword' – or *taiaha* in this case. That dual potential is due to the inherent ability of such a weapon to just as easily *turn itself on those who might wrongly make demands of blanket, emotional servitude to Maori culture itself* as some kind of new god.

Therefore, having stated my personal views on this matter within the protocol-regime framework of the present-day 'cultural-correctness game', that 'two-edged potential' is employed here to strongly emphasise my connections to Ngapuhi in the first instance; but more essentially to Hongi Hika. Even though a major aspect of this Work is to explain why all races need to make the transition from their tribal phase to that of a single Nation, this particular tribal connection still needs to be clearly stated.

In terms of the hugely-decisive and devastatingly-influential legacy Hongi subsequently bequeathed to New Zealand, he was probably the singularly most important person the Maori race ever produced! If the direction that Maori later embarked upon – post-Hongi – is to be fully understood, more particularly with the influence of the line of Maori Prophets and where that led to, an analysis of Hongi's life and legacy is vital. Yet only with the knowledge of **The Spiritual Laws of Creation** can we fully understand the deeper, spiritual ramifications that resulted from his chosen path, for all future Maori. We will therefore assess that effect from the standpoint of those Higher Laws.

15.1   Hongi; and Author: The Genealogical Status

The reader will thus note that, *in the earthly sense*, I am descended from Paengatai, the eldest brother and first-born of Auha, and therefore from that particular *senior line*. We should further note that contrary to the accepted dictates of Maori protocol, Paengatai, as the eldest or first-born of Auha, is rarely mentioned in genealogical discourse. Given the defining impact of Hongi and Ngapuhi in our collective history, and Maori reverence for ancestral genealogy, the genealogical record put forward by *some whanau* to enhance their particular connection to Hongi and their associated status within Ngapuhi and Te Uri Ohua, particularly, means that the name of Auha's eldest son, Paengatai, has been virtually ignored by *certain* Ngapuhi 'tribal historians'.

Moreover, misuse of the word *mana* too often sets in place mechanisms whereby *tatai* are subtly changed to enhance links to certain individuals and deeds from the past. The intention is invariably to gain more 'collective *mana*' for that particular *whanau* line within the overall *tatai* and *whakapapa* of the given Iwi in the present upsurge of cultural renaissance. This may be regarded as simply a psychological ploy to better utilise the effect of the question, **"Who Are You?"**, in order to strengthen any self-perceived status and position. Of course, it may be stated that I am doing the very same thing here.

> However, **irrespective of any such beliefs, what cannot be altered are the respective and clear lines of descent from Auha – for this writer, and for Hongi!** And that is important if one is to write about him.

Whilst my main connections to Ngapuhi have been outlined in the *whanau tatai* in the Chapter: **"Who Are You?"**, from the Ngapuhi perspective it is probably as important to also detail, here, particular historical events which may not be generally known. They nevertheless reside in the *waiata* of the tribe – even if ignored by some Ngapuhi 'historians'.

Therefore, I wish to add other voices to that particular chronicle. The voices of my *earthly* ancestors from the Uri of Rahiri, requesting that *their* record be set straight – those of Paengatai the first-born of Auha, and of Takehe and Urumatariki. Also from the lines of Maikuku and Torongare, down through the generations to Te Haua, *tohunga* of Te Uri Ohua, (the one born with two club feet) to Hita, on to my Grandfather, Ihaia Hita, to his son Hita Hita and thence to my mother, Rangihiawe; all who offer their story of Ngapuhi and Te Uri Ohua, or, as handed down to the descendants: – "Te Uri Ohua e Kata te Rakau". Let us therefore discover which ancestor possessed the *mana*, the power, to cause the puriri trees to laugh – in contrast to other versions of this story.

Two versions are related in the publication, "The Puriri Trees are Laughing", by Jeffery Sissons, Wiremu Wi Hongi and Pat Hohepa. One story holds that the words, *"ka kata nga puriri o Taiamai"*:

> "...were first spoken by Ngati Pou after they had been evicted from the Taiamai plains (inland Bay of Islands) by Nga Puhi. Upon their former homelands the fires of Ngapuhi were now burning and logs of puriri wood spluttered or laughed in the flames."

A second narrative, Introduction, page 5, attributes it:

> "...to another tribe, Ngati Miru, who formerly lived north of the Taiamai plains at Te Waimate. After they had been evicted from their lands by Nga Puhi they cried, *Ka kata nga puriri o Te Waimate.*"

The story of this event, as told to me, states that my ancestor, Te Haua, (born with two club feet) caused the puriri trees to laugh in answer to a direct challenge from a rival tribe. This event is now recorded in tribal lore and is clearly noted in the name of the tribe – "Te Uri Ohua e Kata te Rakau". The fact that Te Haua was regarded as a powerful *tohunga* is still well known among the sub-tribes of the Kaikohe district. Moreover, it was he who laid the *tapu* on the Karaka tree at Waitangi, which tribal lore records caused the deaths of some who challenged the power of it – *as embodied in its particular form around that tree*. It is said that during one Waitangi Day celebrations, a woman of a particular mid-North Island tribe challenged the power of Te Haua through the *tapu* of the tree. She attempted to pluck leaves from the Karaka and died. The Karaka was *fenced off by local officials* for those kinds of reasons.

Notwithstanding this more or less *official* acknowledgement of Te Haua's *tapu* and power through that 'protective gesture' of fencing-off the Karaka – even if not fully understood by Pakeha authorities – in another stated incident; a man who later pulled down the fence in a challenge to Te Haua also died. But in a celebrated event, my Grandfather, Ihaia, descended from Te Haua and wearing the mantle of *matamua*, slept peacefully under the Karaka at a time when the power of the *tapu* surrounding it was greatly feared.

It was Te Haua, of club-foot fame, who marked out the boundary of his land by *running around it* with two dogs – one black and one red. As a clear indicator of his *mana*, he erected a stone on the boundary to warn off intruders, and issued a threat of death to anyone who ignored or defied his warning. It is said that members of one particular tribe who challenged the power of Te Haua over his land also died. His stone marker, which was recovered from its stated location in a search for it in the 1950s, was found to be roughly the shape of the land and is known as "Te Kohatu o Te Haua" (The Stone of Te Haua). The boundary of his land was also in line with the karaka tree at Waitangi, hence the warning not to cross that line with dark intent.

Now, of course, that 'once tapu' tree has been cut down. Perhaps that act represents the symbolic need for Maoridom in general, but possibly Ngapuhi in this particular case, to finally leave behind non-beneficial, superstitious connections to inanimate objects that *cannot* provide *genuine* spiritual enlightenment.

At the funeral of the Ngapuhi Chief, Patuone, in Devonport, Auckland, it is also recorded that my grandfather, Ihaia Hita, as *matamua* of Ngapuhi, was designated as *the one* to speak for the tribes of:

1. Te Uri Ohua e Kata te Rakau

2. Te Uri O Hua

3. Ngati Rangi

4. Ngati Hau (Patuone)

5. Ngai Tupoto

6. Ngai Toro

7. Te Ngahengahe

8. Ngai Pakau.

These are a few important points of tribal lore that strongly and directly connect my personal genealogical ancestry to "Te Uri Ohua e Kata Te Rakau" and Ngapuhi, as handed down from my own ancestral line.

Maori protocol therefore clearly states that such connections allow me the right to undertake that which I outline in this Work – the presenting of the greater knowledge of **The Spiritual Laws of Creation** to provide the necessary clarity to enable us to unequivocally recognise the many clearly *incorrect spiritual beliefs* of Te Maori. They are beliefs that desperately need clear recognition if Maori social statistics are to undergo any *long-term*, meaningful change for the better.

I readily acknowledge that certain protocols of Maori Customary 'Law' are closely and correctly tied to particular aspects of cultural tradition. I do not accept, however, that the so-called 'right' to speak out or otherwise comment on Maori issues should be deemed the *sole preserve* of certain nominated 'leaders', academics, or 'revered *kaumatua*' within Maoridom.

> For under the outworking of the *higher* Spiritual Laws **the greater right is auto-matic** because the right to speak out and question incorrect, entrenched views, is a **spiritual one** – and is thus clearly that of **every truly-free spirit**.

Moreover, the Maori reader generally, but of Ngapuhi more particularly in this case, should note that in offering the knowledge of **"The Divine Spiritual Laws"** for things Maori, it is not without *spiritually-guided purpose* that the line of descent and relationship of the author to the 'warrior chief Hongi', in terms of **earthly ancestral derivation**, is one of **seniority**. The **well-versed** Maori reader will fully understand the important connotations of this precise genealogical configuration, especially from the standpoint of **Maori lineage protocol/tikanga**.

Given the tremendously bloody and devastating impact that Hongi inflicted upon the Maori race, the inviolable outworking of **"The Law of Spiritual Attraction"** thus *carefully ensured* that the author was born into the appropriate Ngapuhi genealogical configuration in order to *especially bring to the attention of Maori* the precise knowledge of **The Spiritual Laws of Creation — CREATION-LAW** — at this critical time in history. Te Iwi Maori are now at a spiritual crossroad, for which a final *spiritual choice* must be made!

Therefore, because *certain* protocols are still important *for the present time*, I believe that only by possessing my particular relationship to Hongi am I able to address Maori issues in the manner outlined in this Work, and for it to be *possibly* accepted. In any case, **whether accepted or not**, the very fact that **it is now written** is, in itself, **a crucial spiritual fulfilment for Maori today**, for this Work points to the **Very Source** of those **Spiritual Laws**. And *thereby* fulfils the prophecy of "the white thread of Ngapuhi"!

Thus Maoridom, and indeed **all** in this land, will not, now, ever be able to state:

"We did not know!"

15.2   Hongi the 'man-eater'

> Of all Maori who left an indelible mark on New Zealand's early Post-European history, Hongi singularly stands out as probably the best example in illustrating the extremely complex transitional-process that the Maori had to undergo in the rapid adjustment from stone-age society racked with superstitious fear, to European thinking with its general rejection of such beliefs by way of more scientific, intellectual reasoning.

Hongi was born at Te Tuhuna, near Kaikohe about 1777. Hongi himself stated that he was born in the year of Marion du Fresne's death in 1772. His mother was Turikura, the senior of Te Hotete's five wives. He had several brothers and sisters, with Kaingaroa, his half-brother, being his favourite. As he grew to manhood he gained a formidable reputation as a warrior and tactician, and other young men readily accepted his leadership.

The Central North Island was dominated by Ngapuhi about this time, with up to 150 hapu in the tribal grouping. The battle of Moremonui in which Ngapuhi warriors were ambushed and decimated by Ngati Whatua may well have been the watershed event that set in place Hongi's seemingly singular intensity of purpose in later acquiring large numbers of muskets to produce saturating and overwhelming firepower against an enemy. Ngapuhi's experience in this battle where warriors with muskets were still defeated by traditional hand-held weapons – because of the time it took to reload the firearms – moulded Hongi's tactics in developing the most efficient use of them. These ideas he put into practice in later incredibly devastating war expeditions. The defeat at Moremonui and the deaths of two of Hongi's brothers – who were eaten – gave him ample reason to plan *utu* against Ngati Whatua at a future time, and for which they would pay dearly.

Another singularly important event in his life was meeting the Captain and crew of the *Harwich* which sought shelter in the Bay of Islands in January 1812. He was given a parting gift of musket, powder and lead, and soon became familiar with firearms, owning several by 1813. Beginning his career of warfare in earnest, he unsuccessfully attacked *Whiria pa* at Pakanae in the Hokianga. Whilst absent from his own *pa* of Pakinga, it was attacked by another Ngapuhi group from the Hokianga and many women and children were killed. Quick to seek *utu*, Hongi returned to Hokianga, capturing two strongholds and killing many. It is alleged that he swallowed the eyes of Te Tihi, one of the principal leaders of the attack on his own *pa*. This trait of swallowing the eyes of targeted enemy was to become a trademark of 'Hongi the man-eater'.

In a strange paradox for a society where blood-ties and tribal connections were supposed to hold such clear purpose and ostensibly provide a powerful bond of strong cohesiveness, it is a source of constant amazement to me that there were so many battles with quite significant loss of life between *hapu* of the same tribe. This curious trait; the inability to let even the most insignificant insult just simply pass by without seeking some kind of immediate redress, preferably in blood, was probably the single most important factor in Maori being unable to make any true spiritual advancement then. And Hongi was to demonstrate that trait of '*utu* for insult' very graphically in his future campaigns.

15.3   Ruatara

Let us leave Hongi for a moment and briefly examine the life and influence of the Northern chief, Ruatara, for his legacy is vastly different to that of Hongi.

In 1814 Ruatara sailed to Sydney on the *Active* with two other Ngapuhi chiefs, Hongi (of this Chapter) and Korokoro. Ruatara, even though being a contemporary of Hongi and obviously subject to similar traditional influences sought, instead, to establish European ideas and agricultural practices as the saving grace for his people. Hongi, by contrast, chose to avenge insult for all of his active life.

New Zealand's Heritage, page 310, records J.L. Nicholas, a companion of Marsden who had invited the chiefs to sail with him to Sydney, describing Ruatara as a man:

> "...in the full bloom of his youth ... of tall and commanding stature, great muscular strength and marked expression of countenance."

Ruatara's path, definitively diverging from that of Hongi's ancient Maori one, actually began in earnest in 1804 when he set sail on a whaling ship to see King George III. Instead of getting to England, however, he spent most of the next four years on various whalers, sometimes well-treated, at other times very badly treated.

Even though finally reaching England, Ruatara was not permitted to land and he did not see King George. Marsden, who was about to return to Australia by the *Ann*, discovered him ill and neglected. Ensuring that he was cared for, upon reaching Sydney he invited him to his house at Parramatta. Ruatara spent eight months with Marsden and in that time studied European agricultural techniques, carpentry and other skills. It is interesting to note that even though Ruatara was mistreated by Pakeha sailors at times, he evidently never harboured thoughts of *utu* against them. Displaying the greater trait of nobleness, he kept his particular focus on agriculture and peace for his people. On the other hand his kinsman, Hongi, directed his thoughts solely towards *utu*.

Setting off home with gifts of tools from Marsden, and filled with a grand plan to begin wheat production on a large scale, Ruatara was once more defrauded and abandoned, this time on Norfolk Island. Rescued again, he accompanied his saviours back to Sydney, eventually reaching home in 1812. Distributing seed to his people, he experienced great difficulty in persuading them that wheat was valuable as food or as an item of trade, or convincing them that bread could be made from it. It was not until 1814 that he was able to prove this. Marsden sent Ruatara many gifts including a hand-powered wheat-mill. Finally convincing his fellow chiefs of the value of wheat he distributed more seed, and grain production began in earnest.

Upon his arrival back in Sydney in 1814 with Hongi and Korokoro, Ruatara once more began a further study of European agriculture and other skills, spending five months there this time. Apart from the acquisition of tools and weapons, gifts of animals and tree seedlings were also offered by official parties keen to smooth the establishment of the first mission in New Zealand. Arriving home, Ruatara, like Hongi, watched over and protected the missionaries and their activities. He even travelled with Marsden to the Thames-Hauraki area, a dangerous thing for a lone Ngapuhi chief then.

By this time, however, he began to have serious doubts about the true purpose of the arrival of the missionaries. He had been told in Port Jackson that missionaries were the advance guard of settlers and soldiers, as had happened in Australia, and that Maori would suffer in the same way as Australian Aboriginals, whose plight he had seen. Thus he was never quite sure that assisting the missionaries was exactly the right thing for his people.

It is clear that Ruatara harboured radical and far-sighted plans in his desire to accept education and training in the use of European technology and agriculture. His goal was for Maori to become wealthy and self-sufficient through trade whilst still retaining the land. To achieve this, there could not be a large influx of whites. Those who were necessary were already there, the tutors and traders, but would probably need to be kept at arms length. With this thought firmly planted in his mind, Ruatara's dealings with the missionaries were not always as cordial as they had previously been, even though still offering them protection.

He plunged himself into his work of planning new wheat cultivations and a European-style town on a hill near Te Puna, even to the point of marking out the site. Though now recognised as the top ranking chief at Rangihoua, other chiefs were jealous of his wealth and he accepted the possibility that he could be killed because of it. However, his personal stock of Pakeha weaponry ensured a commensurate amount of necessary respect from any covetous enemy. Ruatara and his wonderful vision of education and wealth for his people through trade and agriculture did not sprout sufficiently enough to take strong root. He fell ill on the 13th February 1815 and his far-sighted and spiritually-beneficial vision died with him on the 3rd March. Perhaps his early demise was partly caused by the severe privations suffered during his years aboard whaling ships.

When it became clear he was dying, his bed was made *tapu*. Marsden was initially prevented from seeing him. Only after threatening to destroy the village with the big guns of the *Active*, which he owned, did the relatives relent, allowing Marsden to minister to him.[1] The missionaries gave him food and medicine but to no avail. The day after his death, his wife, Rahu, hanged herself. In death Ruatara was attended by seven chiefs, including Hongi. All were made *tapu* for the occasion, meaning they could not touch food for several days.

*   *   *   *   *

Ruatara was clearly a far-sighted and extremely intelligent man. He was impressed with the form, practicality and comfort of European buildings, and he possessed the ability to readily recognise that Pakeha know-how could take the Maori into a new and better way of life. He sought to quickly and actively inculcate these ideas into his own people, but tragically died young. It is an interesting irony that, *at the end of his life*, his funeral still encompassed the very things that he would eventually have left behind; the deeply ingrained superstitious fear that the institution of *tapu* wrought.

Ruatara was also a clever visionary, able to exploit situations to his advantage by setting in place mechanisms for his own personal wealth and success. The greater vision, however, was clearly one of advancing the cause of his people. By utilising the benefits of European technology, therefore, the debilitating superstitions of the past could be more quickly left behind. One

---

[1] This was the incident referred to in a previous Chapter.

wonders what this man might have achieved had he lived a long life? Certainly one can believe that it would have been fruitful, productive, and offering the most benefit for his people.

*   *   *   *   *

Two chiefs of Ngapuhi: **Ruatara** – a man of the land, agriculture and peace. And **Hongi** – a far different man. A man driven by revenge, a man of war and *utu*!

The great difficulty in letting go ingrained traditions is illustrated in the story of another Northern Maori by the name of Tui. He travelled to England in 1818, learned to read and write, and showed great promise as a potential administrator. Upon his return to New Zealand, however, he reverted to tribal life retaining little more of European ways than his musket and clothing. The reader may be curious as to why the need for the Maori to quickly adopt clearly beneficial European ideas is strongly represented in this Work?

Quite simply, had this been the *primary* consideration during those early years, a number of things of great value would have immediately developed for all Maori. Firstly the totally unnecessary bloodshed would have stopped far more quickly along with the concomitant demise of *utu* and cannibalism. And the peace brought about by the cessation of inter-tribal warfare would have meant *numerically larger numbers of Maori* with more stable populations in clearly defined tribal lands. Instead, the reality was increasing and easier Pakeha encroachment onto emptying lands. Thus a far stronger united front could have been presented to the arriving Pakeha, rather than the tensions that divided tribes.

Conversely, as we noted earlier, a too-peaceful native people might have produced an outcome as equally as disastrous as that which Maori visited upon themselves with efficient Pakeha weaponry. Certainly, a strongly united 'Maori people' possessing European weapons in numbers might have fared far better than a few badly decimated and scattered tribal groups who could find little agreement with each other because of the ingrained propensity to avenge past insults in pointless *utu*. A classic case of *negotiation from strength* being effectively lost.

Now let us return to the story of Hongi in Sydney and his subsequent meeting with Samuel Marsden in 1814. Hongi's offer of protection encouraged Marsden to plan the establishment of a Church Missionary Society mission at the Bay of Islands. Under Hongi's shrewd protection plan, the mission was set up later that same year. Hongi was quick to recognise the advantage of protecting missionaries and seamen alike from possible avaricious demands toward them by his own people. He knew that a peaceful haven in an otherwise dangerously-turbulent country would attract more Europeans, thus offering greater opportunities for trade. With weapons to arm his warriors being his primary consideration, he well recognised the great value of Pakeha agricultural tools to grow crops for trade purposes too. Under his protection, other mission stations were also established at Kerikeri and Waimate North.

In Sydney, Hongi also met the Governor who presented the chiefs with gifts including a regimental uniform and sword each. So what did this man Hongi look like? A description of him by J. L. Nicholas whilst on the return journey to New Zealand on the *Active* makes interesting reading.

> "He had not the same robust figure as Ruatara, but his countenance was much more placid and seemed handsomer allowing for the operation of the tattoo, while it wanted the marked and animated severity which gave so decided a character to the face of his companion. The man had the reputation of being one of the greatest warriors in his country yet his natural disposition was mild and inoffensive, and he would appear to the attentive observer much more inclined to peaceful habits than to strife or enterprise."

(New Zealand's Heritage, p.310)

Upon arrival in New Zealand, Hongi, ever the Military Commander, together with Ruatara and Korokoro, all dressed in regimental scarlet with swords in scabbards and switches in hand, marched their men into an enclosure specially prepared for Marsden's first service. Ruatara took care of the seating and Korokoro was master of ceremonies for the Maori, indicating when to stand and when to sit.

In June of 1815, Kaingaroa, Hongi's favourite brother, died. So deeply did it affect him that he thrice attempted to hang himself. What may have been the outcome had Hongi succeeded? Perhaps thousands of Maori of many tribes spared death, slavery or loss of homeland. By early 1817, however, flocking beneath Hongi's banner were about 800 fighting men. Allied to him was Te Morenga who had 600 warriors with 35 muskets. With such a force available to them Hongi and Te Morenga could plan larger operations to avenge past insults.

That year their combined strength – almost two Battalion's of men by today's standard Army formations – decimated tribes-people in the areas of East Cape, Bay of Plenty and Coromandel in payment for relatives killed and eaten by them. In January of 1818 the people of Tauranga were forced to flee from Te Morenga, and in February Hongi laid waste to the area between Maketu and Hicks Bay. The results of this slaughter were clearly evident about a year later when Hongi returned with around 2,000 prisoners as well as hundreds of heads. For the deaths of a few relatives, Hongi had exacted payment in *blood-utu* in this single campaign of hundreds slain and thousands enslaved.

The musket had shown its value in easily defeating fighters with traditional weapons and Hongi wanted more. However, the acquisition of them through trade with missionaries and traders was too slow and expensive for Hongi and he resolved to acquire them by other means. Kendall was returning to England, so Hongi and Waikato, another Ngapuhi chief, accompanied him, leaving on 2nd March 1820. Whether by invitation or guile, these two erstwhile Ngapuhi secured passage to England where Hongi sought to gain an audience with the King. Hongi probably knew that gifts would be showered on him; gifts which he could later trade or sell for muskets.

They arrived in England on 8th August. Hongi and Waikato spent five months there being feted and showered with gifts, a practice to which Hongi was no doubt well accustomed as a paramount chief. During earlier times Kendall had taught Hongi the alphabet, and whilst in England the three men assisted Professor Samuel Lee of Cambridge University with the compilation of a Maori dictionary.

The two Ngapuhi chiefs, dressed in European clothes, finally met King George. Reportedly bowing to him, Hongi greeted the King with the words:

> "How do you do, Mr King George?"
> To which the King was said to have replied:
> "How do you do Mr King Hongi? How do you do Mr King Waikato?"

And in the most incongruous and normally highly-unlikely situation, two heavily tattooed Ngapuhi chiefs, one an avowed and enthusiastic cannibal who had recently eaten and enslaved fellow countrymen, accompanied the King of the, then, world's greatest power and Empire, on a tour of his palace. It was an amazing event, and one that clearly illustrates the great adaptability, intelligence, shrewdness and cunning that many old Maori possessed. So, from *raupo* hut to England's grandest palaces and higher halls of learning, Hongi never lost his focus – tribal warfare back home.

At that time, the divorce case between the King and Queen Caroline was being played out and Hongi was supposed to have expressed surprise that such a powerful monarch could not handle one wife when he could easily handle five. He was also reported as having attended a service at Norwich Cathedral with the Bishop's family and visited British War Museums where he was vitally interested in tactics and the life of Napoleon. Hongi had a second brush with death when he contracted influenza there. However, he survived and he and Waikato set sail for Sydney on 20th December with many gifts, including a suit of chain armour. Again one wonders what direction Ngapuhi would have taken had Hongi died in England? His recovery from a potentially fatal bout of influenza once more set in place a singular path of events, the compass of which would not be fully grasped, *even by future generations of Maori*. Yet it was one that would affect virtually all of Maoridom – then and into the future.

Upon arrival in Sydney, and except for his suit of armour, Hongi traded all his gifts for muskets, powder and lead, and steel weapons such as axes and swords. To further illustrate the intensity of his personal focus and Maori sense of 'obligation' to avenge past slights, he warned Te Hinaki, chief of Ngatipaoa who was also in Sydney, that for their killing of his son-in-law in 1819, his tribe would be attacked upon Hongi's return.

History records that Hongi arrived in New Zealand on 11th July 1821 with his weapons of English steel and perhaps as many as 400 to 500 muskets, a formidable number in terms of value and potential firepower during those early times. One can readily imagine the euphoria and elation with which he and his weapons were greeted by his followers.

Whether Hongi actually received gifts of such value as would be required to purchase such numbers remains a mystery. It is possible that Hongi and Waikato, along with Kendall, were involved in a dubious and possibly fraudulent land sale to Baron de Thierry, who claimed to have paid the two chiefs about 1,100 pounds for the purchase of 40,000 acres of land at Hokianga. Kendall provided de Thierry with the deed of grant, but on his arrival there, discovered that the land he had paid for was now only 5,000 acres and that Kendall had acquired it for just 24 axes. Perhaps this deal, if true, helped Hongi's cause considerably. Whatever the means, Hongi was now well armed, and immediately prepared for war.

This was rapidly effected within two months, with Hongi departing the Bay in a huge *kaupapa* of 50 *waka* carrying 2,000 to 3,000 fighting men; roughly Brigade strength – or 3 over-strength Battalions in today's Military formations – of whom 1,000 were armed with muskets. It is fascinating to try to imagine or paint such an incredible spectacle.

*   *   *   *   *

Let us pause a moment and allow our gaze to look back in time to those incredible and defining years: To Hongi's time, and Hongi's years!

> If we picture the preparations as men make ready for war, we first see the arrival of the participating *hapu* with much welcoming and fierce *haka*. Now, strive to absorb the palpable sense of deadly purpose and perhaps destiny. Observe the fighting men as they compare weapons and practice and hone fighting skills. Watch the women and slaves preparing the huge amounts of food for the assembling army and for the journey. And note the youths caught up in the great sense of the occasion, imitating the adults and looking forward to the day when they, too, might sail off to battle to avenge death and insult. At night, hear the *waiata* of the great deeds of their ancestors, of brave and almost impossible acts in battle by warriors caught up in the highly charged state of *whakamomori*. Hear, also, the boasting of greater deeds yet to come.
>
> Now feel the growing exhilaration and euphoria, and sense the rush of adrenalin and the rising tension as the moment of departure for battle draws near. See the complete armada of large war canoes lined up on the beach made ready and prepared for sail. Hear the roar of the last *haka* of farewell. Feel the ground shake as over 2,000 fighters join in unison in the war dance for courage to exact *blood-utu* from their enemies. Observe the *tohunga* intoning the appropriate *karakia* for the war party and the *kaupapa* to invoke the help of the relevant gods for a safe and fruitful campaign.
>
> Watch, as each fully manned *waka* swings about with prow pointed toward the open sea. And hear the wailing of the women as they exhort their men to kill as many enemy as they

can and return with many prisoners. Now observe Hongi, the "Nelson of the South Pacific", give the final signal, and see chanting warriors raise and dip paddles which, in unison, bite deep into the water sending the huge war canoes surging forward toward the great sea of Kiwa.[2]

But wait! Now stand on the beach or the headlands with the women and children. Hear the wailing of the women as they watch the battle fleet sail away. Hear, also, Hongi's *tohunga* call his final *karakia*, and listen to his farewell fading into the distance. Now the reality of the moment strikes home. No one knows what the outcome will be. The 'signs' will have indicated a profitable one, or they would not have gone. But that may not necessarily be the case, as all who are watching know. And even if successful overall, there will be future widows among the women bidding their husbands farewell this day. This they also know. Now they can only wait, as there will be no news for some time.

The Pakeha sailors on board their own Men-O-War and traders on board various merchantmen would have watched this grand and savage event too. Missionaries also watched these amazing, but soon-to-end, Ngapuhi *waka* armadas. They, however, with a sense of sorrow and dread. Sorrow at the continuation of inter-tribal killing in the name of revenge, anathema to men of God. And dread at the prospect of once more seeing Hongi returning with canoe-loads of prisoners, human flesh and heads. And return Hongi always did!

Such scenes must surely have been an absolutely stunning and stupendously enthralling spectacle, and surely one to stir the blood in the incredibly-savage 'grandeur' of the time.

*   *   *   *   *

Over the next five years Hongi Hika was engaged in catastrophic tribal conflicts the like of which had never been experienced before. The heavily armed Northern tribes attacked all tribes to the south who were more or less defenceless in the face of the far superior firepower of Ngapuhi. Whole areas were devastated as Hongi's war parties ravaged their tribal enemies, and all in the name of *utu!*

Belich estimates that as many as 20,000 Maori may have been killed in the musket wars alone, a huge amount for a race relatively few in number. In his book, "***Forgotten Slaughter***", Ron Crosby estimates that between 1815 and 1840, of an estimated population of 100,000 to 150,000 Maori, 50,000 to 60,000 had been killed, enslaved or forced to migrate. As we have stated often in the course of this Work, this time of terrible slaughter and dislocation had, as its reason, the terrible 'affliction' of *utu*!

Hongi's first grand campaign of *utu* took place on the Auckland Isthmus where he fulfilled the threat offered to Te Hinaki in Sydney. In the strangest of almost comedic ironies, both Hongi and Te Hinaki were dressed in British Regimental Uniforms, helmets and swords, and conducted themselves in the manner of British Officers at war right down to field glasses, flying colours, bugles and trumpets. Hongi, however, also wore his coat of chain mail beneath his red coat. Superstition almost delivered Te Hinaki and his people from Hongi's wrath when Hongi's foot became entangled in some vines and a bullet knocked his helmet from his head. He initially contemplated calling off the attack but continued, eventually slaughtering Te Hinaki's group. Hongi, in what was his particular method of defilement toward a defeated and reviled chief, swallowed Te Hinaki's eyes. It is estimated that Hongi's army killed more than 1,000 and enslaved about the same number in this battle.

Hongi then turned south and attacked the ancient enemy of Ngatimaru in Te Totara Pa at Thames but was initially unsuccessful. Peace was ostensibly negotiated with the inhabitants. Hongi moved away but treacherously returned in the night and another 1,000 odd Maori were

---

[2]There was not the need for life-jackets for those fighting men in their great ocean-going *waka*. No 'nanny-state' with 'politically-correct' bureaucracy to threaten fighters with Health and Safety regulations back then.

put to the musket, tomahawk and *patu*. Now temporarily sated, he returned home in December 1822. His canoes were loaded with 2,000 prisoners and more heads.

Hongi's restive need to take up the war trail in the cause of *utu* surfaced once more after only two months at home. With a larger war party now numbering 3,000 warriors, Hongi ventured toward Waikato territory. His reason this time – some Waikato fighting men were present at Te Totara and had helped in its defence. Clearing his way down the Awaroa stream to the Waikato River, he found his main quarry at the junction of the Waikato and Waipa Rivers in the very large and fortified triple *pa* of Matakitaki. The Waikato Maori, aware of Hongi's approach and desperately fearful of his guns, had gathered together in their strongest fortress. Without muskets and totally defenceless, the panic-stricken Waikato people attempted to escape. Many were trampled to death or drowned, and it is believed that about 1,500 of the 'defenders' died that day.

One can hardly imagine the terror, even for a people regularly accustomed to war and death, of the imminent approach of Hongi's army, knowing full well his formidable reputation. And to intuitively understand that whatever one might try to do, Hongi's muskets would probably prevail, with death the inevitable result for most. And for all others captured, at the very least slavery, and perhaps the ovens.

About one year later, Hongi's armada and army targeted the Rotorua tribes in revenge for the deaths of some Ngapuhi warriors killed nearby. Possessing only a few muskets, Te Arawa withdrew to Mokoia Island in Lake Rotorua in the belief that they would be safe. Hongi, however, portaged his canoes between various bodies of water to finally launch them into the heart of Te Arawa at Lake Rotorua. The subsequent one-sided battle resulted in about 3,000 of the Rotorua people killed. Sated once more, Hongi returned home. One marvels at the tenacity of Hongi to press home an attack in these circumstances, for it would have required an immense physical effort to drag very large and heavy war canoes over difficult terrain, even given the large numbers of men at his disposal.[3]

His campaigning, however, was not yet over. One matter was still outstanding; the defeat at Moremonui at the hands of the Ngati Whatua who had slain many Ngapuhi including numbers of Hongi's own kinsmen. In 1825, taking just 500 of his best fighting men this time, but all armed with muskets, Hongi attacked Ngati Whatua in Ikaaranganui *pa* on the Otamatea River. According to historical accounts, whilst the defenders had over 2,000 warriors, they could only muster two muskets. Against the overwhelming superiority of Hongi's guns, the defenders were well defeated, though Hongi lost 70 of his own men, including his son. Not completely satisfied with that outcome, he returned later in the year, chased the survivors into the Waikato area where he trapped and slaughtered them.

Hongi, whilst obviously a man of war and *utu*, by all accounts evidently enjoyed the affection of his wife and children and helped with fishing, planting and harvesting. Turikatuku, his blind wife and *matakite*, was treated with kindness and he heeded her advice, even taking her with him on some of his campaigns. The death of his son, Hare, was a major blow to him, yet he himself had been responsible for the deaths of many sons of many fathers. And whilst it may be recorded that he was a mild and well-liked family man, it is as a savage nemesis for *utu* that he will forever be remembered.[4]

Another facet of Hongi's war strategies was that he was able to use slave labour to push through an agrarian revolution that, because of the northern climate and fertile soil, was very

---

[3]The legends recount that Te Arawa's *tohunga* invoked the *taniwha* of the lake to agitate the waters and prevent Hongi's fleet from being launched. But Hongi's *tohunga* prevailed and he calmed the waters allowing the canoes to sail to Mokoia.

[4]Perhaps Hongi possessed a little of a Jekyll and Hyde personality – or perhaps he was just Hongi!

successful. In previous times slaves were often kept for food, to be fed and watered until needed for the ovens. With human flesh being of no value to the Europeans, Hongi created large gardens to supply them with their kind of food. So now, instead of being eaten, slaves were used as labour to produce crops of wheat, potatoes and corn. Trade meant a vicious cycle of more muskets, powder and lead to avenge more *utu* to acquire more slaves to grow more food for more muskets.

After his last major campaign against Ngati Whatua – or perhaps because of the loss of his son or his age (he was now almost 50) – Hongi lived a relatively quiet life in his Northern lands. He had acquired a second, younger wife, Tangiwhare (lit. weeping house), whose infidelity was to inadvertently lead to Hongi's death. According to some accounts, the literal meaning of her name was to be fulfilled for her family and relatives by the hand of her husband. Given the fierce reputation of Hongi, it is very surprising that anyone would dare to disgrace his honour, or *mana*. Yet his new wife reportedly committed adultery with his nephew. So great was their fear of Hongi the "swallower of men's eyes" that, upon being discovered, Tangiwhare hanged herself, and the nephew shot himself.

For Hongi the matter could not simply rest there. Much *utu* was demanded – as much as befitted a great fighting chief whose very considerable *mana* had been sorely defiled. Thus decided, Hongi set off to avenge this grievous insult against his person and honour. Travelling to Whangaroa, the home of Tangiwhare's people, he slaughtered men, women and children of her family. Not content with this, he chased the fleeing remnants to a village on the Mangamuka River where a fierce battle ensued. And here, avenging a slight against his *mana*, and without his coat of chain mail, the great chief Hongi was finally felled by a bullet from the muskets he had helped to introduce. Although the ball passed through him, it was a mortal wound. He was to die a little more than a year later on 5th March 1828.

*   *   *   *   *

Let us digress for a moment and compare Hongi's attitude to being slighted by his wife's adulterous behaviour, to that taken by some of the great chiefs of the Plains Indians of North America in a similar situation. Having already made a comparison between the respective attitudes of Maori and Indian toward war and the enemy in Part I, let us also compare this situation. Some early American writers and even some Cavalry Officers who had quite extensive dealings with the Plains Indians in both war and peace were often amazed and humbled by the noble demeanour of chiefs when faced with personal grief. In a situation similar to that in which Hongi found himself, one chief simply and nobly *dismissed the incident and his wife* with the quiet remark:

"A dog has soiled my tipi!"

No thought of revenge and *great slaughter* as there was with Maori. Such *utu-based* ideas were not generally part of the life and thought processes of the Native Americans.

*   *   *   *   *

Augustus Earle, an early painter of New Zealand scenes, visited Hongi at his home towards the end of 1827. He describes the meeting thus:

> "In a beautiful bay surrounded by high rocks and overhanging trees, the chiefs sat in mute contemplation, their arms piled up in regular order on the beach. Hongi sat apart. Their richly ornamented war canoes were drawn up on the strand; some of the slaves were unloading stores, others were kindling fires. To me it almost seemed to realise some of the passages

of Homer, where he describes the wanderer Ulysses and his gallant band of warriors. We approached the chief and paid our respects to him. He received us kindly and with a dignified composure, as one accustomed to receive homage. His look was emaciated; but so mild was the expression of his features that he would have been the last man I should have imagined accustomed to scenes of bloodshed and cruelty. But I soon remarked that when he became animated in conversation, his eyes sparkled with fire, and their expression changed, demonstrating that it only required his passions to be roused to exhibit him under a very different aspect...”

                                                                            (New Zealand's Heritage, p.313)

Returning now to the subject of his death: During this time of waiting for his 'ancestors' to assist him through the death process, did Hongi ever understand the effect that his actions and single-minded purpose caused for Maori then and into the future? Was he content with what he believed he achieved? For the legacy he left Aotearoa is one of almost disbelief in the extent of his depredations and the depth of savagery he displayed with complete and ruthless disregard for those he attacked. The effect of his campaigns resulted in a considerable loss of population in a small and vulnerable race of people. With the killing of so many women and children, this kind of 'ethnic cleansing' obviously had a profound effect on future Maori generations. *Utu* had wreaked its terrible vengeance on too many Maori, yet it was Maori who had **voluntarily enslaved themselves** to its incredible evil and who carried out its deadly bidding.

Hongi's influence was clearly catastrophic for Maori. Butchery, rape, pillage and cannibal feasts were the hallmarks of those years. From Auckland to Thames, to Waikato, Rotorua and down both coasts, approximately 7,000 men women and children were slaughtered by the war parties of Ngapuhi, all in the name of *utu*! At least as many were taken captive and transported back to the Bay of Islands to become Ngapuhi slaves. Hongi, more than any other single Maori, locked into place events that, in the 1820s and 1830s, brought in its train other wars that caused tribal migrations and set almost the whole of the population of the North Island on the move. This, in turn, caused numerous other wars as traditional enemies turned against each other.

Thus, his impact on the Waikato tribes in turn affected their neighbours, and those disaffected tribes impacted on the rest of the country. It is believed that at least 600 battles were fought between 1801 and 1840, with some estimates of war deaths calculated at up to 30,000, a fifth of the original population of 1769 according to some calculations. Such casualties reflected the large numbers of campaigns in both the North and South Islands, eventually bringing about a major redistribution of population. Because he was not interested in occupying the lands he conquered, simply being content to return each time to his tribal area, Hongi never made the necessary leap to become a national leader. This particular characteristic may more clearly define Hongi's campaigns as being solely driven by *utu*!

It is generally accepted that Hongi was merely a product of his times and of his culture, and what he did other tribes would also have done had they the same access to arms. But we cannot be absolutely sure that other tribes would necessarily have embarked on a similar pattern of depredation against others in the same ruthless manner that Hongi did. For his own kinsman, Ruatara, chose a peaceful path. Hongi was clearly incredibly single-minded in his quest to avenge all transgressions against his own people, no matter how slight. And muskets were far more effective for this purpose than *patu rakau*.

We can be sure, moreover, that Hongi's visit to England was not solely to have tea with King George. Hongi was no fool. For all his superstitious beliefs, he was obviously a shrewdly-intelligent man of great cunning – and he had a plan. The plan was to get more guns. That could not be achieved in New Zealand as rapidly as he would have liked. So Hongi's actions fuelled an *arms race* amongst the tribes. And because of their collective worship of their evil god, *utu,* all Maori were the eventual losers.

Where would Hongi find himself propelled to at his death? What kind of 'home' would he have earned for himself under the outworking of The Spiritual Laws? Assuredly not that associated with the Maori belief of 'ancestral bliss' for great deeds of tribal *mana*, and certainly not one of quiet contemplation or one of cheering adulation for his earthly deeds. No, Hongi might well have found that, rather than achieving his goal of avenging all *utu* and basking in glory with his ancestors, he might have discovered a far greater debt, solely incurred by him, and which he, alone, would have to pay. He may have found that those whom he slaughtered and who shared his propensity for *utu* were waiting for him. And, in accordance with The Law, Hongi might have found himself psychically bound to them for a very long time. No escape for Hongi until a genuine *spiritual* awakening!

Hongi's death did produce one major and vital development for Maori, however. According to Belich, it:

> "...released Christianity in Northland. It also began the process that released it from North-
> land to the rest of the country."

(Making Peoples, p.167)

The final ramification of Spiritual Law states that "...the activity of all darkness ultimately serves **The Will of The Light**!"

So in the *seemingly* strangest of ironies, Hongi's wars of *utu* did exactly that. His propensity for war ultimately led to a radically different and more beneficial path for Maori than that of the 'old way' – Hongi's way – leading to a quicker transition time onto a new path with the already emerging line of Maori Prophets than *might* otherwise have been the case!

15.4   Hongi's Utu? Not the Maori Soldier Today!

In terms of the devastation wrought by Hongi's brand of *utu*, perhaps with the influence of longer close contact with upper echelon Europeans, Hongi could well have changed his ways. Moreover, rather than leading his army on such terribly destructive raids, he could have used that same energy and drive to certainly maintain military strength, but worked more closely with Ruatara to become a trading force to be reckoned with. Thus providing wealth and education for his people – as was the vision of Ruatara – instead of offering just bloodshed to all and sundry. History, however, records otherwise.

The irony of Hongi's attitude was that he personally rejected Christianity 'as a religion unfit for warriors' but eminently suitable for a 'nation of slaves'. Yet the very protection he offered missionaries not only ensured a secure trading base for the weapons he wanted for his destructive raids, but also allowed the very religion he spurned to become strongly accepted by his own people. Moreover, the same missionaries, by virtue of Hongi's patronage, helped Northern Maori to achieve a higher level of literacy than other tribes who had much less contact with Europeans, which further enhanced the trading position of Ngapuhi. Finally, and paradoxically, his protection of the Christian Church indirectly helped to facilitate the setting in place of two vitally decisive things. A later 'partnership' document between Maori and Pakeha – The Treaty of Waitangi – and the *far more important spiritual event* that would visit itself upon future Maori. That event is the *pivotal* point of this book.

Had Hongi lived longer, would he eventually have embraced Christianity? Possibly in his older years, but perhaps it would be too much to ask of him. The old way of *utu* was probably too strong in "Hongi the man-eater" for any meaningful spiritual change to occur for him in that particular lifetime.

So it is important to understand the ramifications of killing for *utu*, for *spiritual* responsibilities of no small import are subsequently incurred with any decision to do so. The revenge aspect that could well be an accompaniment of all wars has thankfully been replaced by a *generally* far more enlightened "code of conduct" than that displayed by the old Maori – at least for the most part with some, but not all, Nations of the world. Whilst war can perhaps be regarded as being intrinsically barbaric in nature, at times they may need to be fought. For a soldier exposed to the possibility of capture, the unsettling knowledge that your opponent does not necessarily accept standards of conduct that might be deemed 'civilised', could be a decidedly chilling prospect indeed.

For the old Maori that was the norm, with perhaps the final indignity of being eaten. Contrast that, however, with an enemy who *does* accept a more magnanimous standard, and will care for your wounds and welfare in the mutual respect that a "true warrior" should accord another. In its spiritual meaning the codes of conduct in this area have, as their very basic earthly counterpart, "The Geneva Convention". If we therefore consider the whole concept and practice of *utu* as perfectly according with the fact of "violence begetting further violence", it is difficult to see any end to it unless the cycle can be somehow broken. That might be possible through constant goodwill, or perhaps when both protagonists have simply had enough of killing. Otherwise there exists the real possibility of the eventual demise of one or both groups if the cycle cannot be arrested.

As previously noted, witness the seemingly intransigent position between the Arabs and Israelis, even though both sides claim to want peace. Theirs is *utu* on almost the super-grand scale – as is that of religious Iraqi factions – even of the same religion!

Spiritual Law, alone, holds the answers here – simple, workable answers to every single aspect of life. Thus, in the perfection of that Law and the sheer logic of just plain common-sense, we are admonished to recognise that:

> *"As you wish men to do to you, do the same to them. For if you love only those who love you, what credit is it to you? for even the wicked love those who love them."*

> (Luke 6:31, Fenton.)

Because the old Maori chose to accept *utu* as a deeply ingrained way of life without thought for anything more enlightened, and because he refused to show genuine mercy, even to women, small children and babies, he did not, and indeed could not, expect compassion from an enemy. With that voluntary stance as his "code of conduct", he could only live the insanity of *utu* begetting more *blood-utu*, because he would not *voluntarily* change. The quest for supposed 'glory in *mana*' via this method was far too strong to allow the true *mana* of *humility* to enter into his psyche.

Thus, through his *spiritual weakness* and concomitant *lack of discipline*, Maori were almost the instrument of their own demise! And, as this Work unequivocally and unapologetically states:

> **Were it not for the arrival of the Pakeha to finally halt that unfortunate and savage trend, it might eventually have been so!**

In accepting the war trail, therefore, one should also accept the possibility of being killed, and that should be the end of the matter. If viewed from the spiritual standpoint, the desire to nurse and nurture revenge over the loss of comrades, understandable as it may be in perhaps highly-charged, desperate situations, nonetheless actually degrades that 'serving'. Any 'losses taken' should be a naturally expected consequence for at least some participants in any war party or operational Military formation engaged in battle. Moreover, where *utu* is an accepted part of a group's behaviour in war, if intense feelings of revenge cannot be satisfied in the vengeful deed itself, other means must then be found to push the boundaries of *utu* still further to denigrate the 'hated' enemy. Yet, whether an accepted way of life, tradition, culture, or for any other reason; to *choose* the war trail is exactly that, a personal *choice* with all its consequences.

Within the ethos of the 'old Maori way', even if the tribal or traditional hold is so great that the rightness of the path is not questioned by any individual, the tribe still possesses the inherent free will to exercise its choice collectively so as to accept or not accept war and *utu*. Of course, defence is a must for survival in some situations and the best form of defence may well be a preemptive attack against an obviously aggressive enemy. However, in the case of the old Maori, these considerations were clearly not part of his frame of reference, and certainly had no place in his personal wants. Only *utu*, paid in blood, could satisfy his continual and ultimately spiritually-debilitating lust for revenge.

Yet with regard to any potential 'revenge-factor' in warfare, *well-disciplined troops* will generally always respond according to their leader's code of conduct. Under the outworking of The Law of Attraction... in a purely voluntary situation, a brutal leader with no compassion will generally attract to him men of the same ilk, whereas a humane leader in a just cause will invariably attract men who share similar ideals.

In terms of fighting ability, however, and contrary to what may generally be thought, the brutal ones may not necessarily prevail. A cruel attitude does not necessarily translate to the production of tougher fighting men, and history well records many occasions where small groups of highly motivated, well-disciplined and dedicated troops comprehensively defeated numerically larger formations.

15.5   The Wairua (Spirit) of the Maori Battalion

> The retention of the concept of *utu* within the Maori soldier of recent times could have found its strongest expression during New Zealand's participation in World War II where large numbers of Maori served in many varied Units in that long and exceptionally bloody conflict. The Unit that we immediately associate with Maori soldiering in The Second World War is the Maori Battalion by virtue of the fact that it was formed as a Maori Unit, and very many Maori served with it during its time in that war. We will therefore end this Chapter with a short spiritual analysis of the fighting 'attitude' of those particular Maori soldiers and try to gauge whether or not the concept of *utu* still held sway to any large degree. And if it did not, why not?

The Maori Battalion established itself as a formidable fighting Unit in the North African desert and in Italy. In a theatre of total war many men can be expected to die, and Maori casualties were, at times, disproportionately higher than other comparable New Zealand Units. The reasons for this have been well examined in other publications and we will not do so here.

However, there is one aspect of this particular Unit's overall 'spiritual balance sheet' that does warrant brief comment. Even though the Maori Battalion had been trained in the Military conventions of the time, what Military training may not always *completely* remove from a particular racial group, are strongly entrenched or inherent traits. These can certainly be modified and even greatly curbed by Military training if they are at variance with established codes of Military conduct, particularly in peacetime. Yet they may also provide certain skills that can add *lustre* to the Unit's *Operational* record. However, in terms of particular traits that may be unhelpful for precise Operational expectations, *and as all soldiers who have been in 'harm's way' know*, it is far easier for those suppressed traits to surface in a more fluid situation such as 'Operational combat in war', as opposed to that of strictly garrison duty.

The Official History of the Maori Battalion's participation in North Africa and Italy records many instances of brave and valiant battles fought, with great respect and admiration for the

Battalion's fighting skills expressed by their German counterparts. However, anecdotal reports note instances where a less than professional appreciation of their particular part in some vital battles also occurred. At times, opportunistic looting of enemy dumps or vehicles took precedence over the operational requirement to be 'in place and on time'. This easy-going manner of Maori, whilst exhibiting a certain amount of 'roguish charm' in a 'tatou-tatou' way, *can* be a damaging hindrance when greater decisiveness is required. This is not condemnation of the Battalion, but simply a reference to particular Maori traits that will often find inappropriate expression in certain situations.

Looting from the enemy was, of course, carried out by all soldiers of all nationalities during the war. Black-market activities involving Allied troops and supplies also flourished. In one anecdotal, almost celebrated, incident, so many supplies went 'missing' from a supply ship unloaded by New Zealand Divisional-troops that they were never used in large numbers for dock work again.

We, however, are *more interested* in the *reason for change* in Maori soldiers' attitudes to 'modern' warfare, as opposed to fighting the 'old way'. For a huge difference in attitude is clearly evident from the relatively short space of time – from as late as around 1870 before inter-tribal warfare to avenge *utu* with no quarter asked or given finally relinquished its hold on tribal Maori – to a "Geneva Convention" type situation just 70 years later, where wounded enemy must be shown compassion. This was the reality for Maori soldiers serving in the Western Desert in The Second World War. There, the original traits and propensities of the old Maori way were not apparently evident except in a few cases.

Generally speaking, therefore, the Maori soldier in that war conducted himself in the same way as most other Allied troops; with honour and distinction overall. We might opine that this great difference in attitude between pre-European and post-European Maori was the result of simply leaving the old ways behind because they were patently unworkable and not desired under the influence of a vastly different way of life. With respect to Military training, moreover, a far different code of conduct would have naturally been inculcated into the thought processes of the modern Maori soldier than that which was accepted in days of *utu*. But does that kind of exposure provide the *complete answer* for this difference?

This 'new way', at the time self-evident with the greatest majority of Maori Battalion members, was clearly illustrated in an incident shown some years ago on the TV One Series: **"New Zealanders at War"**. Revealed there, and not officially talked about at the time, was an event of great shame; one which showed the dark side of an otherwise well-educated Maori Officer.

Officially hidden for 50 years, it was revealed that this Officer committed the cardinal Military sin of executing prisoners in his care, but in a particularly cold-blooded manner after ensuring they were fed. It is to the *great spiritual credit of the other Maori soldiers who were with him that they took no part in it*. More revealing, however, was the attitude of the rest of the Battalion towards this incident. Upon learning of it, a feeling of great disquiet permeated the Unit.[5] According to the ex-Maori Battalion soldier who narrated this incident, it set in place a feeling of deep unease where the men felt they had *collectively lost* something of very great value. Thus some of their hard-won honour or *mana*; that very especial-thing which comrades had died for in battle. In battles, moreover, fought for a *genuinely noble* and high cause. From the ethos and outworking of **The Spiritual Laws**, that is *exactly* what happened.

*   *   *   *   *

It is probably very difficult for civilians to understand how men who had recently been involved in battle and perhaps even experiencing heavy losses of very close friends and comrades,

---

[5]This collective feeling was probably one of *shame*. Shame, however, *is the living form of an intuitive feeling of "disquiet"*, and is actually *a spiritual help* in assisting humankind to maintain at least some degree of ennobled thought.

can then tend to wounded enemy with compassion and care, and not seek to immediately execute them in rage and *utu* at losing one's own. Men who a few moments previously had been desperately striving to kill each other, can now share a moment of closeness even. Of course many enemy have been executed at such times, and probably in most of the wars that have ever been fought. In a free-flowing situation, however, the difference between men who will succumb to the base emotional desire for revenge and men who can objectively understand the greater picture, will probably be their respective levels of overall spiritual maturity. And this may not necessarily reveal itself in the *outward manner* of any individual.

*   *   *   *   *

So here we have the *key* connection as to the *why* of the change in Maori soldiers; from the sorry and vicious *utu* of old to more honourable practices since those days. Of course, as we have noted, the undeniably strong influence of modern Army training and the moderating factors of society hold certain sway, but the more decisive factor is the *spiritual* one. For, as we *now know*, any given race, whilst obviously having similar physical characteristics, is, in reality, a group of individual and disparate souls ordained by The Spiritual Laws to accept birth into its 'personally-chosen' race for that lifetime. From our explanations of **The Laws**, we *also know* that part of the determining criteria by which souls are attracted will be the overall *spiritual level* of the race at the time such a soul incarnates, in accordance with the ultimate outworking of all its previous decisions.

In other words, if a race is spiritually regressing, it will attract to itself those kinds of souls. By contrast, a race that has been influenced to leave behind dark and brutal practices can be deemed to be *spiritually maturing* and will thus attract more *enlightened souls* to its fold. This clarification indicates that the souls who make up the Maori race today and in the recent past are, *generally speaking,* far more enlightened than those who incarnated into the race in the days of inter-tribal warfare. Whether they were souls also present in that ancient time but had recognised the wrong of those practices and are again part of the Maori race, is also entirely possible. In any case, the greater enlightenment allowing a later incarnation where the practices of *blood-utu* no longer held sway is the key point here. In a grievous situation such as existed in old Aotearoa, nothing is likely to change unless a person of great spiritual strength is born into the race and is able to recognise the wrong and lead the way out.

In accordance with The Law of Attraction..., however, the possibility that an advanced and enlightened person could have incarnated into the old Maori race in the days of *utu* would have been very unlikely! Therefore, only an external event of massive and far-reaching proportions could provide sufficient influence to radically alter the situation then, steer a new course and direction, and thus change the associated "attraction-aspect" for souls who would make up the future Maori race. As we must often reinforce:

The coming of the Pakeha was that event for Maori!

That was the catalyst which provided the circumstances whereby the preparation for the eventual emergence of **a great spiritual leader for Maori and New Zealand**, as a whole, could take place **at his appointed hour**.

With regard to the previously-mentioned incident in the Western Desert, it was unfortunate that the Maori Officer concerned, inculcated with the ethos of the Army, who was well educated and influenced by a relatively benign society for a sufficiently long period of time, could still carry out a deed of great dishonour. A sharp contrast to the repugnance and shame evidently evinced by the rest of the Maori Battalion at this event, not least by the 'ordinary soldier' who is often stereotyped as being rough, crude, uneducated and sometimes even brutish. The clear difference between these two positions will generally reflect the actual *inner spiritual state* of the respective persons or groups in question.

Therefore it can be readily deduced that even though not as well educated – and certainly more 'rough and ready' on the surface – the inner souls of the ordinary soldiers of the 'Maori Battalion', *with regard to that particular incident*, revealed a *far higher degree* of nobleness and 'fair play', of *genuine mana*, to that displayed by the Officer in question. For *he* lost his *'soldiering mana'* with that dark deed. And in keeping with the Eternal, undying values of Spiritual Law, external behaviour can well be deceiving whereas inner spiritual strengths are far more valuable and enduring, even in the so-called 'ordinary man'.

Thus the men who fought in The Second World War, *particularly those who volunteered*, for the most part fulfilled the role of the 'true warrior'. For whilst war will nonetheless always hold the prospect of adventure for young men; in that particular long and bloody conflict a monstrous evil had to be, and was, defeated.

*   *   *   *   *

The actual degree of *mana earned* and the associated rightful claim to *noble warriorship* for most who fought to defeat that evil holds the strangely-unique paradox that the *real reason 'why'* for that devastating war *is not at all known by the greatest majority of humankind* – not even by the many millions of Allied soldiers who fought the many battles, and, of course, the millions who died. But that is the fault of a spiritually-blind and primarily *religiously-driven* global society. Whilst 'Official History' states that the war was seeded by perhaps geo-political and expansionist aims by Hitler, *the true, underlying reason is far more profound* and, in the final analysis, *critically decisive for the spiritual future of all of global humanity*.[6]

*   *   *   *   *

Maori soldiers who nonetheless participated in that long and bloody conflict *can rightfully claim*, along with millions of their Allied soldier-brothers, a very large degree of *genuinely-earned mana*.

Perhaps present-day Maori soldiers should *educate* the Maori youths who arrogantly strut the streets; those who either believe they are warriors or think they have an automatic right to claim some kind of warriorship-status without ever having *earned* it. For in terms of 'fighting', there are great *spiritual differences* between the many and diverse kinds of 'confrontations' that males, particularly, might choose to be involved in. Soldiering in 'Defence of the Nation' and in the protection of the weak and defenceless, is the ultimate level of 'true warriorship'. [The Hollywood production, *"The Thirteenth Warrior"*, depicts this Truth most powerfully in the closing scenes.]

Youth gang clashes in surburbia, irrespective of why, or how fuelled, carry not one ounce of spiritual 'anything'. It is exactly that fighting-drive of youth, however, that really can be put to good and beneficial use for all. And so should be employed thus.

We of this land now have the highest expression of "warriorship" in the awarding of the **Victoria Cross** to **Corporal Willie Apiata** for *outstanding bravery*. As we have already stated and will do here again: Maori males, whatever your chosen field of work might be, that is *the kind of ennobled service* you must emulate if *you* wish to apply that spiritually-especial term, 'warrior', *to yourselves*. For this *man*, on his homecoming to his region of birth at Oromahoe Marae in Ngapuhi-land, in emotional and *genuine humility* – [*Note: 'only humility holds the power of true mana'*] – stated, in reply to the welcome of his people there, the *twin aspects* of *true warriorship*:

---

[6]The awakening that must shortly come to pass through humankind's *non-recognition of the true reason* will be a terrible one.

"I come home a **warrior**, and a **humble man!**"[7]

Thus, in the main context of this particular Chapter, the *greater* strengths which naturally accompany true and genuine warriorship – defense of the home and land, the sick, the old, the weak and infirm – were traits that Hongi clearly did not possess! And because he did not, those whom he led and greatly influenced did not have any higher code of conduct to emulate. So what remained was not any kind of 'Maori *spiritual* path of greatness', but just the debilitating destructiveness of the *nothingness* of **more *utu*!**

The soldiers of the Maori Battalion, unlike Hongi's fighters, can therefore rightfully claim – along with the soldiers of the Pakeha Battalions too – the kudos that is earned "by a job well done". And with salutations to their very many dead comrades, under the outworking of Spiritual Law **they stand especially 'spiritually-strong'.**[8]

This being the case: Could we also at least *partly attribute* that particular ethos of the Maori Battalion – in terms of the differences between the 'old' and the 'new' – to the *'spiritual-language forms'* incorporated in the 'marching tune' of the 'Unit?

For certain key lines and references in it really do express both the highest form of *Spiritual acknowledgement* and the correct aspect of 'warriorship in battle' for a just cause.

For example; the following lines: [not sequential] –

'Maori Battalion march to Victory
Take the honour of the people with you
And we'll march, march, march to the enemy
And we'll fight right to the end'

– clearly reveals exactly that correct spiritual ethos of and for men who must fight in a *just* war, and thus for the *right* reason.

Now, whilst that part of the 'Battalion March' incorporates the 'spiritually-correct' ethos for soldiers prepared to accept death to help defeat a monstrous evil, the next aspect of it is more revealing in the *truly spiritual sense*. For it states to **Whom is given** all that they will *give* in battle and sacrifice ***Firstly***; then secondly and thirdly, respectively!

Thus with sure courage: 'Ake, ake, kia kaha e' –
'For **GOD**, for **King** and for **country**...'

In that one single line: ***The key sequence of service for Allied soldiers in the global conflict of 1939-45 is <u>especially revealed</u>.***

For *New Zealand's* soldiers and people, however, the acknowledgement of **THE ALMIGHTY** in the first instance in the 'song' of the Maori Battalion precisely resonates and converges with both the 'Mission of Ratana' and the purpose of this Work for Maori, primarily.

---

[7]Because the word, ***warrior***, is one *which inherently carries* **the spiritual power and mana of 'The Soldier'** *as a high inherent attribute when used in its* **true** *meaning and purpose*, this writer of Maori extraction and descended from the line senior to the great **Hongi Hika**; here, *in this **Work***, seriously questions the use of the capitalised name, 'Warriors', for just a sports team.

[8]For a deeper explanation of the Soldier's sacrifice, the reader may wish to revisit Chapter 9, 'The First Death!' sub: Death of a Soldier.

Special Note:

The powerful paradox inherent in this 'spiritually-ordained' association *for Aotearoa and its peoples* has its genesis in the *spiritual seeds sown in Europe* after the First World War. [Ratana *necessarily journeyed* to Europe in that time period.] Unfortunately, however, he did not find the especial **spiritual connection** *he was ordained to seek out whilst there.*

His similarly-unfortunate, too-early demise in 1939 thus *ultimately resulted* in a legacy of *non-fulfilment* of his crucial mission for New Zealand. [The reader will have noted that demarcated earlier in this sub-Chapter we have *intimated* the *exact reason* for The Second World War, and thus why we have given it *especial mention herein* around New Zealand's fighting involvement in that key **spiritual** conflict.]

Here now, from Henderson's important work about the life and 'Mission' of the Prophet, Ratana: A powerful **'Spiritual Declaration'** by him for Maori which resonates with the primary *spiritual* recognition and acknowledgement inherent in the signature march of the Maori Battalion, i.e.:

'For **GOD**, for **King** and for **country**...'

Thus:

"Let us *first* unite in the Father..."

16
The Treaty of Waitangi

"But first secure the Kingdom of GOD and His righteousness and all these things will be ready for you."

(Matthew 6:33, Fenton.)

"The Treaty of Waitangi is more important than The Ten Commandments."

(Tariana Turia. Co-leader
of the Maori Party.)

A book on Maori issues would probably be regarded as incomplete if there were not some mention of the Treaty of Waitangi included in it. It is certainly true that this particular subject has been well dissected by numerous writers and commentators, and the reader of this Work may well suppress a shudder at the thought of having to plough through one more interpretation of it. It is a perfectly understandable view given the vast amounts of coverage accorded "The Treaty". Or, in its transliterated form, "Te Tiriti".

What *we* seek to do in a brief overview is ascertain – from the *standpoint* of **"CREATION-LAW"** – just exactly *where* the Treaty stands for **both** Maori and Pakeha. And, moreover, what the ramifications of that *immutable* **LAW** might be for *all* in Aotearoa. For it is one thing to put in place a Treaty, agreement, or covenant at a particular time in history, but another to expect or demand that it forever remain sacred and sacrosanct. Whilst the intention may be admirable, the possibility of maintaining the absolute 'letter of the law of the Treaty', *eternally*, may simply be impossible. The issue here is not one of Maori cultural or indigenous rights or demands, Pakeha interpretations, Government intransigence or anything else.

No! We simply state that it can *only* be a relevant and workable document **when Spiritual Law [Creation-Law] is taken into account**, and that *that* **is its foundation.**

The above *Biblical* quote is well known, and its unequivocal meaning clearly reveals its Origin as issuing from out of The Eternal Laws. In its "living essence", moreover, it offers a pointer to understanding how we should also relate to **The First Commandment** – the **key one!**

Since the meaning of each of the opening quotes is clearly unambiguous, they therefore cannot be wrongly interpreted. One rings with the power and purpose of **The Creative Will** whilst the other is perhaps more a personal opinion expressing an earthly belief as to the perceived place of Maori in the overall scheme of things universal. The second quote, in reality therefore, is thus directed to seeking things other than those of the *genuinely* Spiritual, which we are admonished to seek *first*. For despite its 'exalted position' within Maoridom, the Treaty of Waitangi is not – *nor ever will be* – a truly spiritual document. Despite attempts to elevate it thus, it will forever remain only an *earthly* agreement; and one formulated *just by men*.

The undeniable overall Maori belief that all things pertaining to Maoridom are somehow sacred and therefore probably spiritual, including the Treaty of Waitangi, has unfortunately led to the curious position where many so-called *tauiwi* also buy into this belief of the 'Treaty' being a sacred and wholly sacrosanct document.[1]

Genuinely seeking The Kingdom of God *first*, logically means that we *recognise* the concept and *reality* that the earth *is not our true* home at all. It is the *home* of the *flesh*. Strong Biblical Scripture explains that fact. The Son of God Himself stated that reality to His Disciples on a number of occasions. *'In my Father's house are many mansions.'* *'I go to prepare a place for you.'* *'I return to The Father...'*

In this example, to *'go'* is clearly to go *'from'* – the earth. Similarly, *'return to'* means *'away from'* – the earth. Since Maori actually possess the *knowledge* that the spirit [we/us] really is an entity *separate from* the physical body – and that it's [our] *true home* therefore cannot possibly be on, or in, a material world – it is all the more puzzling why so much angst and anger is centered on Treaty claims *down here*. The *spiritually-necessary* longing for, and therefore *spiritual-connection* to, our *true* human-spirit home is severely compromised – and even deadened.

Quite clearly therefore, we **are** enjoined to *first* seek the **'Kingdom of God'** *before* we should seek anything else, or expect more to be given for the particular time. And we are further told to seek **His** Righteousness also, because that cannot be separated from **His** Kingdom. Moreover, this righteousness can only be that which is inseparable from The Creative Will contained in all things, and is therefore logically contained within that Creative Power. That Power and Will is expressed in **The Laws of Creation** – the **Eternal, Divine Laws!**

Therefore we are admonished to *first* seek out and learn these laws – His Righteousness – that we may have some understanding of The Kingdom of God, so that we can logically know *how* we are to live on the earth. This clearly means that we should seek to lay claim to earthly things only *after* we have secured the first, which is the knowledge of **The Spiritual Laws of Creation**. Within the parameters of that Living Truth, we may then gain necessary insight into the wider vista.

Therefore, any race of people who claim to possess a high spiritual heritage must be absolutely sure that they do actually possess it. If that is not the case, we can expect to see that same people with all sorts of problems, since a wrong belief will naturally bring *the reciprocal effect of that wrong thinking* through its associated *spiritually-incorrect* activity. Thus, its subsequent outcome **will be clearly evident**!

Because we generally understand Biblical Scripture to stem from Spiritual Law, with regard to the admonition to "...seek the Kingdom first", we should further understand that what will next be given after the *first conditions are met*, will be a greater measure of *genuine* spiritual recognition and its associated values in the first instance; this being a natural consequence of striving for the *correct thing* first. Spiritual values, moreover, mean **lasting** values. Everything else connected with purely earthly issues is only transitory – without any such "lasting values' – from which, therefore, no related benefit can ensue.

---

[1] In the next Chapter we explain the *spiritual meaning* of *tangata whenua* and further explain why Pakeha *tauiwi* of many generations should not feel dispossessed in Aotearoa because of certain Maori views to the contrary.

To seek The Kingdom of God thus means we should seek out **His Spiritual Laws** and live according to Them, for The Law and their application are logically inseparable! *Only then* should we expect other lasting benefits to emerge, especially in the earthly sense. And in this we must include the Treaty of Waitangi and Maoridom's overall, collective attitude towards it.

In the starkest of contrasts, consider the spiritually-enlightened reply of Ratana (the *Mangai* of God) when asked by the Maori King if he would help in the fight to win back lost lands. Ratana's response was:

"Let us first unite in the Father *and then* we will unite in the land."

(Ratana. J. M. Henderson. Emphases mine.)

With regard to the Treaty of Waitangi, let us reflect on an address by another very well respected Maori leader as we seek to ascertain whether or not the current placing of this 'revered' document on its own pedestal by Maoridom, actually accords with the admonition to "...seek the Kingdom of God" first.

Sir James Henare, in 1984, stated in part:

> "Let the Treaty remain in its sacredness ...
> ...the Treaty still holds *mana* as from the beginning because it was the *mana* of the Treaty that allowed Europeans to live on these islands.
> It was the laws set out by the various Governments after it was signed that confused the meaning of the Treaty.
> Let us not be carried away by our own interpretations but let us deliberate on higher levels of thought and in lowliness and humility."

I question Sir James's contention that the Treaty is genuinely sacred, and that it was "...the *mana* of the Treaty that allowed Europeans..." to live here. In reality, it was not at all within the power of Maori to prevent Pakeha arrival and settlement. And as we conclusively verified in previous Chapters, many Maori welcomed the Europeans and their goods. With Pakeha arrival, also, gratefully welcomed the demise of *utu* in blood.

With regard to deliberating on the Treaty "...in lowliness and humility", Sir James's sentiments have, unfortunately, largely fallen on deaf ears. What has been thrust forward, however, is the erroneous belief that without such a Treaty Europeans could not live here, and that the Treaty holds the *mana* of the Maori. In order to have a Treaty in the first place, there logically had to be a partner to that Treaty accord. Europeans were going to live here in any case, either by force or Treaty. Moreover, any Treaty will only hold *mana* if it is entered into and formulated under the clear knowledge of The Spiritual Laws. Without that as its foundation, it is little more than a convenient and contemporary agreement where both sides may seek to maximise their individual positions for future gain. If viewed objectively, the Treaty of Waitangi is such a document.[2]

We know that the great **Spiritual Law of Movement** decrees that nothing stands still – without movement of some kind. The only things that will never change are **The Spiritual Laws of Creation**. All else, including the Treaty of Waitangi, must continually change and evolve in accordance with the universal drive that man and his works must heed – or be pushed aside. It should be clearly obvious to all that many previously sacrosanct ideas and institutions are either experiencing radical change or are falling apart. They are doing so because they do not

---

[2]Perhaps we should consider what the word(s), ***wai – tangi***, might actually mean in their spiritual form. We might then begin to perceive a deeper meaning around this whole issue of the arrival of the Pakeha, for Maori!

have the correct foundation that only Spiritual Law can provide. Institutions that *do* take this into account, however, will prosper. [The enormous social and financial pressures that societies worldwide currently experience are simply warning signs that our secular laws are becoming more and more unworkable. This, in turn, is forced onto mankind by rapidly increasing *spiritual pressure,* which will reveal all the inherent weaknesses in every system, including agreements and Treaties.]

So it is from that *infallible standpoint alone* that this agreement will be examined. In fact, **if** both Maori and Pakeha understood the inviolability of The Spiritual Laws or, indeed, accepted their very existence and recognised the absolute need to adjust all thinking and legislation to them:

There would be no need for any such Treaty in the first place.

Such an understanding would automatically negate the need for what would then be a totally superfluous piece of paper. Interesting from the historical point of view perhaps, but completely unnecessary.

Moreover, it is precisely because there is **no real understanding or recognition of those Laws** that we believe we *need* such a document to put right 'past wrongs'. Ultimately, that is actually *not* the truth of the matter at all. Instead, however, we have a most contentious document that will probably be a mechanism for continual divisiveness until such time as the **pressure** of The Spiritual Laws themselves **forcibly brings about the correct recognition to both races**.

Notwithstanding that eventual reality, let us examine the generally accepted history and the current views of this Treaty of Waitangi: the two-edged *taiaha* that offers some resolution, but also the potential for much more division.

The lead-up to the signing of the Treaty of Waitangi is documented well enough, and regardless of personal interpretations as to whether Maori chiefs should or should not have signed, the fact remains that many diverse and often unpredictable factors at the time combined to produce a violent, volatile and unstable land. Whilst it might always have been violent through inter-tribal fighting, the arrival of different kinds of people with vastly differing personal agendas from that which Maori espoused, set in place far more uncertain undercurrents and tensions than was previously the case. Problems of treatment of Maori by whites, of whites by Maori, of fraud involving land and trade, the introduction of alcohol, Maori attacks and threats on traders and missionaries, the probability of the arrival of many more settlers with greater land loss; all these factors conspired to produce a deadly witches brew of potent discontent.

Nationalities other than the British, such as the French and Americans, were apparently of great concern for the Maori lest the whole of the land be lost to them. The huge increase in Maori fighting and great loss of life through the utilisation of Pakeha weapons began to sap the lifeblood of the people. Even Europeans sometimes took sides in tribal conflicts, with devastating results for Maori. For example, Te Rauparaha's decimation of Ngai Tahu was achieved with the help of the Captain and crew of the *Elizabeth*. Understandably, after so much bloodshed in such a relatively short space of time, Maori finally tired of the futility of war.

This recognition helped to generate a Maori Peace Movement in the 1830s. Younger warriors began to refuse to participate in wars and by about 1838 the high point had passed. But what to do? Land encroachment and sales were increasing and lawlessness was a constant problem with no central authority to effectively curb it. Moreover, given the great mistrust between tribal affiliations, it was not likely that any single chief could ever have had sufficient approval from all Maori to be an effective overall authority uniting all the tribes to a common cause. Thus the stage was set for some kind of necessary agreement between Maori and Pakeha, and one which might at least offer a single, consensual-direction for fragmented Maori. But what that would eventually translate to, lay far in the future.

The Northern chiefs, particularly, by virtue of their longer and closer association with Europeans of many persuasions, and fearful of a possible French invasion, sought the protection of King William IV. In particular the Frenchman, Baron de Thierry, posed a potentially dangerous threat with his plan to establish his own independent state at Hokianga. To counteract this possibility, James Busby, British resident appointed to ostensibly maintain law and order – though without the means to do so – on the 28th October 1835 effectively persuaded thirty four Northern chiefs to sign a "Declaration of the Independence of New Zealand", calling themselves The Confederation of United Tribes. During the previous year Busby had been instrumental in creating a flag of national identity for the Maori. The British Government was asked to recognise the country's independence and to accept the role of protector, to which they agreed.

The increasing need and wish for there to be an overall mechanism for settling grievances and protecting both Maori and Pakeha brought Captain William Hobson to New Zealand in 1837. He was sent to initially report on the situation and to consider how best to put into effect some kind of agreement. Whilst Busby believed that a "protectorate" might be the best, Hobson thought that a treaty, in concert with the settlement of a few key sites, could help solve the problems. Meanwhile, British officials were already considering the possibility of limited settlement of New Zealand through the New Zealand Company, initially. Because of Britain's appalling record of colonisation, she was determined to improve upon it.

Unfortunately there was a snag. With the decision taken to colonise New Zealand, and having previously agreed to recognise the independence of the country and to extend protection to it, Britain would first need to find a way to convince the signatories of the Declaration of Independence to cede "sovereignty" to the British Crown. The best way to achieve this seemed to be in the form of a mutually agreed treaty, so Hobson was given the authority to strike such an agreement with Maori leaders. However, this "difference of intent" on the part of the British Authorities required the formulation of a very carefully worded document if this change was to be accepted in trust by Maori.

Claudia Orange, author of "The Story of a Treaty", on page 14 writes:

> "When officials had first thought about plans for a British colony in New Zealand, it was for a Maori New Zealand in which settlers would somehow be accommodated. But by the time Hobson got his instructions, the plan was for a settler New Zealand in which the Maori people would have a special "protected" position."

Thus the stage was now set for a treaty that would bring future differences of opinion and interpretation.

According to the New Zealand's Heritage encyclopaedia (p.365):

> "The Treaty of Waitangi is perhaps the most important single document in New Zealand's history. It was formulated in haste by intelligent, well-meaning and well-informed men to solve an urgent practical problem; thereafter, it was for long periods forgotten, and, when remembered, the subject of bitter controversy."

Certainly, in terms of the potential for harmony or acrimony, many in this country would readily share that view. And therefore the necessity to carefully examine the contentious issues from the point of view of **Spiritual Law** so that a knowledgeable understanding of what it *should guarantee* be clearly understood, irrespective of the relative positions and interpretations of it – then and now!

At the time, however, as a necessary foundation from which to hopefully develop the aspirations of all participants, some kind of agreement simply had to be reached. With such a vast gulf between the two respective cultures, the complete understanding by Maori chiefs as to the intent of the document was vital if they were to support it. Therefore a correct translation was imperative. Fortunately, Hobson was able to avail himself of the services of people like Busby and others, and of Henry Williams of the Church Missionary Society. They were all men who knew the Maoris and their language well, and were highly respected.

Without legal training Hobson had difficulty preparing a suitably worded document in the first draft, and Busby offered to provide a new one. Given his concerns for Maori interests, and now offered the opportunity for direct input into the formulation of what he believed would be a binding agreement, he inserted an important clause, without which he was sure no one would sign. The amended document now stated that Britain would guarantee Maori possession of their lands, fisheries, forests and all other *taonga*.

That is our main point of interest in this Chapter.

On the 5th February 1840, Hobson addressed the large gathering of Europeans and Maori explaining in English the benefits of the Treaty. After the Treaty was read in English, Williams read it in Maori. Hobson reminded Maori how they had often asked the King for protection, and that now the Queen offered the same in the treaty.

> "This is Queen Victoria's act of love to you," he said. "She wants to ensure that you keep what is yours – your property, your rights and privileges, and those things you value. Who knows when a foreign power, perhaps the French, might try to take this country? The treaty is like a fortress to you."

The debate that followed continued for some hours with some chiefs speaking for the proposal and others against it. It is interesting to note the respective arguments of the various chiefs. For the most part they were concerned with their land, their authority and trade dealings. Of those chiefs who spoke *against* the proposal, loss of chieftainship and associated *mana* appeared to be the overriding concern since all other material issues were subordinated to this key point. At the same time, those who spoke *for* the Treaty considered their *mana* and chieftainship to be safeguarded within it.

From pages 18-20, "The Story of a Treaty" (bold emphasis mine), Claudia Orange writes of the exchange of opinions that then took place.

Rewa said:

> "The Maori people don't want a governor! We aren't European. It's true that we've sold some of our lands. But this country is still ours! We chiefs govern this land of our ancestors."

Tareha joined in:

> "We chiefs are the rulers and we won't be ruled over. If we are all to have a rank equal to you that might be acceptable. But if we are going to be subordinate to you, then I say get back to your ship and sail away."

Whai complained about Pakeha traders.

> "What will you do about trade dealings, and the cheating, lying, and stealing of the whites?" he said.

But what of those who were more welcoming and who spoke for the proposal?
Rawiri Taiwhanga was one.

> "It's a good thing that you have come to be a governor for us", he said. "If you stay we will have peace."

Hone Heke was another.

"Governor," he said, "you should stay with us and be like a father. If you go away, then the French or the rum sellers will take us Maori over. How can we know what the future will bring? If you stay, we can be "all as one" with you and the missionaries."

But now the Hokianga chief, Tamati Waka Nene, rose and turned towards the chiefs.

"I'm going to speak first to you," he said. "Some of you tell Hobson to go. But that's not going to solve our difficulties. We have already sold so much of our land here in the north. We have no way of controlling the Europeans who have settled on it. I'm amazed to hear you telling him to go! *Why didn't you tell the traders and grog-sellers to go years ago?* There are too many Europeans here now, and there are children who unite both our races."

He looked at Hobson. "Don't be too concerned with what these others are saying. We need you as a friend, a judge, a peacemaker, and as a governor. You must preserve our customs, and never permit our lands to be taken from us."

"Patuone, his brother, agreed."

Keith Newman writes that 'Te Ruki Kawiti, the great warrior born in 1770 who defied the Crown's plans to control New Zealand, was one of the last to sign the Treaty'.

From Ratana Revisited... p.37:

'My illustrious warriors and people, I fought with God last night, but I survived. Therefore I call upon you to trample anger and fighting under your feet. ... Hold fast to your faith, for the day will come when you will be ruled over by your Pakeha friends. Be patient, wait until the sandfly nips the page of the document [the Treaty of Waitangi], the Sacred Covenant, then and only then shall you rise and question and oppose. Lest you break the Sacred Word of your ancestors, their Covenant ... look to the distant horizon of the sea.'

The respective positions stated above should be carefully analysed to determine which was the more practical view. From the present perspective of recent and current radicalism and greater Maori assertion of ethnicity, to simply label the pro-treaty chiefs as weak and vacillating 'uncle tom Christians' seduced by the new Pakeha religion, would reflect a grave lack of understanding of the necessary practical considerations that needed to be addressed in that volatile time. Moreover, it would be extremely foolish for any present-day Maori radical or cultural traditionalist to label such chiefs as weak. Maori chiefs of that era, irrespective of their personal opinion of the Pakeha, could not be regarded as weaklings.

We have already commented on the physical toughness of the ordinary *toa* of those times, never mind the chiefs, but Ron Crosby, in his book, "Musket Wars", conveys it very well. He writes:

"The taua in the Musket Wars era give an overwhelming impression of incredible endurance, fitness and toughness that is nigh incomprehensible today. Modern triathletes and other exceptionally fit sportspeople usually have a well-regulated food supply along with comfortable accommodation at night; members of a taua had temporary shelters of manuka, tree-fern leaves or raupo and a bed of fern if they were lucky. And yet, day after day, for weeks and often months on end, they were expending massive levels of energy on their travels over vast distances by waka, or in rugged steep bush country, in all sorts of weather."

We should also include portaging the huge war canoes overland at times.

Militarily, therefore, in terms of hand-to-hand fighting or close quarter combat, the chiefs of former times would have had few equals in the deadly efficient use of *patu rakau*. As well as possessing *mana* by birthright according to Maori custom, they were chiefs by virtue of their ability to use these weapons effectively and answer any challenge to their position should it arise. It would be a safe assumption to declare, therefore, that *any present-day Maori* who might harbour foolish beliefs that "weaker" chiefs were among the first signatories to this "Pakeha document", *would not have lasted more than just a few minutes, at most, in a fight to the death with any one of them* – irrespective of the degree of skill that latter-day exponents in the martial arts of *patu-rakau* might have learned in the strong thrust of ongoing cultural renaissance.

To simply demand that the Pakeha return to their homeland and leave the Maori and New Zealand alone was just as impossible then as it is today. Those chiefs who advocated the establishment of some kind of agreement clearly understood the inevitable, and sought to correctly gain some measure of 'Maori rights'. The alternative was continuing lawlessness, more inter-tribal fighting and possible anarchy. Waka Nene rightly questioned the motives of some of the chiefs in not asking the Europeans to leave earlier. It was an advantageous thing to have at least some acquiescing Pakeha around, because they served their purpose for Maori.

Moreover, of those chiefs who advocated that Europeans should leave, what would they have been replaced with, given that Maori of the time greatly desired European trade goods? And, inevitably, who would have filled that vacuum, and would it have been by peace or force? In that scenario, we can probably conclude that it would have been 'conquest by force', for, after removing the British to retain their land and sovereignty, the Maori would still have had to resist any later encroachment. A later coloniser would also have had much more advanced weapons. In any case, the Maori tribal system would probably never have produced any united and totally unanimous agreement. Purely because of its volatile and unpredictable nature, it never has – *not even to this day.*

So more practical views ultimately prevailed, even if there was much apprehension from some quarters. During the evening of the 5th, discussion amongst Maori camped around Waitangi continued into the night. From "The Story of a Treaty", p.20:

> As Williams recorded:
> "There was considerable excitement amongst the people, greatly increased by ... ill-disposed Europeans, stating to the chiefs ... that their country was gone, and now they were only *taurekareka* (slaves). Many came to us to speak upon this new state of affairs. We gave them but one version, explaining clause by clause, showing the advantage to them of being taken under the fostering care of the British Government, by which act they would become one people with the English, in the suppression of wars, and of every lawless act; under one Sovereign, and one Law, human and divine."

The reference by Williams to "one Sovereign, and one Law, human and divine", perhaps held the conviction that the laws under which the British Government operated and which the Sovereign endorsed, had their basis in The Bible, and its associated outward expression in the English Protestant Church. In any case, history records that on the next day, the 6th February, 1840, a day earlier than originally planned, the treaty was signed by 46 'head chiefs', including twenty six who had signed the Declaration of Independence in 1835.

Claudia Orange records that as each chief signed, Hobson shook hands with him and said, *"He iwi tahi tatou."*[3]

> Williams must have known that the words – "we are one people" – would have a special meaning for the chiefs, especially those who were Christian: Maori and British would be linked, as subjects of the Queen and as followers of Christ.
>
> (The Story of a Treaty, p.22)

It is difficult to reconcile the idea of a 'two-people partnership' somehow also being, or capable of becoming, a 'one people' entity, or even how that can be achieved. For the individual concepts would seem to be quite naturally opposed to each other. Put simply, *"one people" cannot possibly be a "partnership".*

---

[3] According to Dame Joan Metge, the phrase correctly translated in 1840 would have meant: "We two peoples together make a nation". (Ratana Revisited p. 19, Keith Newman.)

*   *   *   *   *

What would my ancestor, **"Hongi the man-eater"**, have done had he lived to that point? Would he have willingly signed the Treaty? As we have noted, he was a major influence on all aspects of Maori-European relationships in the north. His overall influence also indirectly encompassed virtually all of New Zealand in the chain reaction of tribal movements that *he initiated* via his wars of revenge. His *mana* at the Treaty signing would have been considerable. Given his unwavering protection of missionaries and traders, albeit for his own ends, he might well have sensed the greatest opportunity yet to greatly increase contact and trade with the Pakeha. Of course we will never know. However, we can certainly believe he would have carefully scrutinised the document, and only signed if there were guaranteed benefits for him.

*   *   *   *   *

Hobson eventually went on to obtain about 500 signatures at approximately 50 meetings. Some important chiefs did not sign. Others were not offered the opportunity. Whether or not it was beneficial for both Treaty partners or loaded specifically toward one or the other; with the ratification of the document by signature, the foundation for colonisation was now set. Whether Maori had later misgivings, as some surely did, there could be no turning back. Even though there was no unanimous, New Zealand-wide Maori agreement, for better or for worse, their path was now firmly linked with that of the Pakeha. *The old way was gone forever*!

*   *   *   *   *

So what does that mean exactly? The present-day argument by many Maori that Pakeha colonisation took everything and left them with virtually nothing is as incorrect and senseless as it is ridiculous. Perhaps if there were less emphasis on cultural romanticism and more on historical truth, a better, healthier and more honestly-objective overview about our Maori ancestors and their supposedly great 'spiritual deeds' would emerge. What was **actually "lost"** with the arrival of the Pakeha was, to name just some, *blood-utu* and butchery, cannibalism and slavery, *makutu* and insidious *tapu*. These totally aspiritual practices, in their primitive, virulent and destructive "forms", were henceforth consigned to the ashes of history – thankfully.

As stated many times previously, such practices, stemming from fearful superstition rather than genuine spiritual knowledge, would *eventually* have set the Maori race *on the path* to the worst possible kind of extinction – *The Second Death* (or death of the *wairua* itself) – had they remained isolated. For within the parameters of Maori beliefs and lifestyle, *there was no other way out*. As also previously stated, without some different mechanism to *force change*, true 'spiritual' advancement for the old Maori was impossible. Precisely *because* such change could not come from *within* the race itself, *an external event of large proportions* was required.

That event, once more in reinforcement, was **The Coming of The Pakeha**.

> **That is the simple and blunt, "spiritual truth" of the matter. It is a truth, moreover, which cannot ever be altered!**

What we state is an aspect of Pakeha arrival *not ever considered* by Maori before. Considered, however, it must be, irrespective of beliefs to the contrary held by *many* Maori today. And not merely just considered, but unequivocally *recognised* in its clear truth, especially by those *privileged Maori and Pakeha* now riding the very lucrative 'gravy train' carrying **'The Treaty of Waitangi Industry'**. This clear, truthful recognition also needs to be made by *all* politicians and all manner of *academics*, both of whom endlessly debate and pontificate over this quite wretched, divisive and ultimately *aspiritual*, so-called, 'founding document'.

*   *   *   *   *

Notwithstanding the incredible angst that the Treaty generates in the present; *for thousands of Maori at the time*, even though there may have been other new problems, at least now they could live without the constant fear and uncertainty which the old way wrought. That of possible attack and enslavement, food for fellow Maori, or for the 'export trade' in dried heads. There would now be far less wailing in the *kainga* across Aotearoa from the savage excesses of *utu*.

But what of the *content* of the Treaty of Waitangi? Where can that be placed in terms of genuine spiritual meaning and application if it is to be regarded as the binding document for Maori to the original Pakeha promises and vice-versa? And how should the Pakeha view it? Should it be considered sacred and untouchable simply because we seek to preserve some kind of historical ideal? Finally, is it workable, and does it have any relevance now?

Lately, questions such as these have produced long and often acrimonious debate, many publications on the issue, spawned a huge growth industry around it, and provided substantial monetary windfalls for the 'new elite' of Maoridom. Whilst much of the debate has been admirable and certainly necessary, the single most important factor has never been considered in these deliberations. What has been left out or not understood, is the critical import that *spiritual* considerations – and by that we mean **genuinely spiritual** considerations – should take precedence in any attempt to interpret 'The Treaty' for the benefit of the Nation. Without that primary factor, the whole meaning of it as a nationally binding document of goodwill between two races will eventually fail – and perhaps, ultimately, with unpleasant consequences for all. It should be clearly understood, moreover, that it is not 'Maori spirituality' that should determine the basis for this, and neither will it be 'Pakeha spirituality'.

For many Maori, 'Pakeha spirituality' may sound like a contradiction in terms given the *general* Maori propensity to believe that it was, and is today, a highly spiritual race. The Pakeha, in similar estimation, are deemed to be not at all spiritual. But in terms of aspiritual, pre-European Maori history, the past cannot be claimed as a foundation for the view that the race has *inherited* great spirituality today. From the Pakeha side, too, the *general* propensity toward empiricism and crass intellectualism, to the *exclusion* of almost all else, clearly shows a similar lack of true spirituality, but in a different way.

Yet both races also naturally possess certain important qualities that the other does not necessarily have, and which can be utilised for the benefit of this Nation and *all* its various peoples. Therefore, both Maori and Pakeha need to fully understand that *a new vision is called for which encompasses the abilities of the two respective races*, and not just offer more of the same – which is obviously flawed. But this new vision can only be fulfilled under the knowledge of **The Spiritual Laws** that alone contain true spiritual power! It is from this knowledge, once more, that we will now examine certain critical aspects of the Treaty.

Treaties and agreements, by virtue of their particular nature, can be manipulated in subtle ways to create an advantage for one side or the other. Even in the process of negotiating such an agreement, parties will invariably endeavour to include words and clauses that will be advantageous to them in any future interpretation. In the case of the Treaty of Waitangi, it is probable that the men who drafted the document did so with the honest belief that it would be beneficial for both groups. For there appears to be no evidence to suggest that it was a blatant attempt to dispossess Maori of everything they had. If the British had really wanted to do that, they could simply have invaded the country and emptied the land of Maori completely – total destruction.

With martial law declared, a naval blockade put in place by the world's greatest sea power around two small islands to prevent a relatively small and rapidly reducing Maori population from acquiring arms from outside traders, and a full-scale military campaign from the sea and on land, it would not have been an impossible task – for who could have prevented that possibility? All land areas 'cleared' could simply have been re-populated by large numbers of *armed settlers*. Maori muskets and/or *patu-rakau* would clearly have been no match for the various kinds of rapid-fire rifles and machine-guns being developed in huge advances in weapons technology at the time – and about to be produced. And even if the campaign were militarily difficult given New Zealand's hilly and heavily forested terrain, the disruption to Maori food supplies would have produced large-scale hunger, or even famine – with its obvious results.

On that realisation then, one can probably assume that the British representatives did seek a mutually beneficial accommodation with Maori under the auspices of the Treaty of Waitangi. However, because the Treaty was written in both Maori and English the possibility for misunderstanding as to original intent was ever-present from the outset.

Claudia Orange has itemised what are probably the major differences.

Article 1

By the treaty in English, Maori leaders gave the Queen "all the rights and power of sovereignty" over their land.

By the treaty in Maori, they gave the Queen *"te kawanatanga katoa"* – the complete government over their land.

Article 2

By the treaty in English, Maori leaders and people, collectively and individually, were confirmed in and guaranteed "exclusive and undisturbed possession of their lands and estates, forests, fisheries, and other properties".

By the treaty in Maori, they were guaranteed *"te tino rangatiratanga"* – the unqualified exercise of their chieftainship over their lands, villages, and all other treasures.

(The Story of a Treaty, p.30)

It is clear that there are obvious differences between the Maori and English versions that are an ongoing source of discontent as to definitive interpretation, even among Maori. The hard fact remains, however, that without the application of Spiritual Law to the document overall, such 'legal' differences are ultimately meaningless, offering just more 'contention without solution'.

Fortunately, we have a compelling illustration of how a similarly enshrined document can produce outcomes for society vastly different to that which the architects originally envisioned. Even though the document of our particular example was carefully formulated to offer "legal" freedom and protection for all, the many conflicting interpretations of it historically reveal it to be very problematic – in the legal sense especially – for its associated society. It is a document also considered sacred and sacrosanct and, therefore, never to be altered.

Thus no matter how well-intentioned, idealistic or noble the vision, unless the *foundation* for such *binding documents* is derived from *the knowledge* of **The Eternal Laws**, the outcomes will invariably *not* produce the original ennobled vision and intent.

16.1   The American Experience

16.1.1   The Declaration of Independence

At the time of its inception on July 4, 1776, America was involved in its own War of Independence with 'Mother England'; a war that lasted from 1775 to 1781. With America a vastly different country in its beginnings from what it is today and clearly offering immense and beneficent future potential, pragmatic idealism no doubt helped shape the thinking of the 'Founding Fathers'. Yet they could not have foreseen how *certain* so-called freedoms, espoused and written into 'Declaratory-law' *then*, would one day turn into a nightmare for the Nation.

To some extent probably loosely based on the original Iroquois 'Five Nations' model, which was:

> "An unwritten constitution authorizing the election of a representative body and formulating rules for calling it into session..., – ...this unwritten constitution, admired by colonial statesmen, gave each people almost complete independence but at the same time bound it to respect the wishes of others."

As we noted in the Chapter, **Elemental Lore**, Hiawatha's confederacy was so successful that an Oneida chief suggested to colonial delegates of Connecticut and Pennsylvania to set up something similar to govern the relations of the colonies. And latter-day students of politics and government have found much to admire in the working of the League:

> "...and there is some historical evidence that knowledge of the League influenced the colonies in their first efforts to form a confederacy and later to write a constitution."

> ("North American Indian Chiefs". Karl Nagelfell.)

16.1.2   The Constitution of The United States

The Constitution of the United States, which sprang from **The Declaration of Independence**, is the basic instrument of Government and the Supreme Law of that country. Drafted by the Constitutional Convention of 25th May, 17th September 1787, ratified by Conventions in two-thirds of the States – as provided for in the Constitution – it became effective in 1789.

The 'Constitution of the United States' has generally been lauded as probably the definitive humanitarian essay. Carefully put together by intelligent, humanitarian and well-meaning men, 'The Constitution' is enshrined as the legal and binding 'document' on both the 'Elected Executive' and the people. It ostensibly guarantees, in perpetuity, the rights and freedoms of all Americans. Notwithstanding that inherently noble vision, it can now be regarded as almost fatally flawed in some areas, for the much-vaunted 'land of the free' has turned sour for many of its citizens. Yet that was clearly not the original intent of the 'Founding Fathers'. This 'American foundation', 'The Constitution', cannot easily be altered now for it requires 34 States to request a Constitutional Convention to change any part of it.

The overriding wording of the document speaks of 'inalienable rights', the rights of American citizenry to be permitted, by law, access to particular practices. Two 'rights' that, on the surface, could be deemed to be innocuous – but *noble* if used correctly – are regularly abused by many of the populace. Yet those practices are defended vigorously in the Law Courts. One 'freedom' is that covered by the First Amendment:

> "...rights to freedom of speech, freedom of the press, freedom of religion and freedom of assembly"...

The other 'freedom' that is of interest to us is that of the 2nd Amendment – "the right to bear arms".

There is certainly no doubt that "freedom of speech" should be protected. Yet we should not forget that all so-called 'freedoms' presuppose a ***consequence of responsibility*** – both materially and spiritually – as we have explained many times in previous Chapters. But what do we invariably observe issuing from America, 'land of the free'? Whilst we may certainly read enlightened, knowledgeable and interesting articles on all manner of subjects, all too often quite the opposite is produced. Yet produced under the all-encompassing and sacrosanct banner of "freedom of speech". And protected, paradoxically, under the Constitutional 'freedom' of The First Amendment by the highest authority in the land, the U.S. Supreme Court.

In the strangest of ironies, should any one person or group complain, for example, about eroding societal values, as supposedly enshrined in the 'Founding Document', the very 'right of individual freedoms' to so express any viewpoint, even to counter the self-same 'erosion of societal values', is protected under the umbrella of the *same* Document, and by the *same* Supreme Court if necessary.

It is ludicrous to believe that the humanitarian men of vision and justice who couched America's 'Founding Document' in the power of ennobled language and who fought for the abolition of slavery, would ever have countenanced such a degradation and debasement of their dream of equality and decency for all citizens as that which we now see. For one would surely believe that "freedom of speech" was intended to mean freedom in the political, religious and scientific sense etc., and not the 'freedom' to churn out debased, degraded filth and religious and racial hatred. Yet that is virtually the end result now.

Most originally noble ideals eventually degenerate anyway because the spiritual aspect, which alone can ennoble, is rarely *sufficiently understood* by the following 'caretakers of the ideal'. And that is, virtually now, the state of the American Nation. It has long since lost *the correct spiritual way*!

For if we utilise the concept of "freedom of speech" as a foundation upon which to build a society of decent values and spiritually-ennobled vision, then that will obviously be the eventual outcome. If, on the other hand – and via the many and varied methods of dissemination globally available today – we use the same 'freedom-concept' to demand the right to flood society with foul language, debased writings, lewd exhibitions, pornography in all its deviant excesses *ad-nauseum*, then, quite logically, **that is the kind of society that will be produced**.

Even a 'fool' can understand that!

For the equation is childishly simple and absolutely unequivocal. And, moreover, offers the same absolute and unequivocal consequence that is naturally and inherently contained in the outworking of **The Law of Reciprocal Action!**

Any concerns voiced at the piecemeal and insidious erosion of values of decency by citizens seeking a better society, invariably become drowned by the protests of so-called 'enlightened libertarians' who increasingly and stridently demand more and more 'freedoms' and 'rights' under the umbrella of the latter, 'ignoble freedom' in the previous paragraph. Since the loudest generally get the most publicity, and the silent majority usually remain silent, the erosion of what were so recently considered good values is soon enough accepted by the rest, even if reluctantly in that initial acceptance.[4]

Thus, after a surprisingly short period of time, what was once deemed unacceptable finally becomes not only acceptable, it becomes commonplace. So without fully realising the great damage that this poisonous practice of 'greater freedom' is visiting upon society, we all slowly sink further into our self-created *immoral swamp*. It is important to note that we are not

---

[4]It is interesting to note that a British group pushing for legislation to legalise 'consensual sex' between adults and children commonly use the quote: "To the pure, all things are pure". How young children are able to make a rational and informed decision of such magnitude the group does not say. No doubt the 'willing adults' will speak *for* the 'target children'. The *hypocrisy* in such a *selfishly-evil volition* is clearly evident in the fact that any legally-sanctioned sexual violation of children could never ever be regarded as 'pure' by any civilised standards of decency. Yet this same group cries "freedom of choice".

advocating restrictions on, for example, the right to protest, or to curb the rights of a free press, or the possible need for investigative journalists to publish such things as exposure into crime and corruption. It is vital that 'these kinds of freedoms' are protectively legislated for. And certainly more so than 'freedoms' which only morally debase and corrupt – that reality which can be ascribed to most present-day societies. It would be a safe bet to assert, therefore, that the American society of today would certainly not have been the intended outcome for their 'Founding Fathers' when they enshrined the right of free speech in their "Constitution".

And what of the second of our examples, "...the right to bear arms"? The news items scream to us the shocking statistics of American society. More guns than people almost, and readily available. Killings on the increase, even by young children. Students arrive at school not simply armed, but prepared to use them. Was that the original intention of that 'amendment'? Clearly, it was not. From the wording of this particular amendment, fledging America's 'Founding Fathers' envisaged an upright and moral citizenry who would, if called upon, *bear arms for the protection of the nation*" – a citizen's army in times of National Defence. It would never have been their intention for the Nation to bear arms as an inalienable right, to then have that right translate itself into rampant crime and murder.

What this amendment actually states is:

> "A well-regulated militia being necessary to the security of a free state, the right of the people to keep and bear arms shall not be infringed."

What is conveniently ignored is the first part – the "well-regulated militia" aspect. European historical reality had shown that without legal or constitutionally-enshrined checks and balances, individual freedoms could be completely suppressed by despotic regimes controlling standing armies. Hence, for that period, the clear wording and preference was for there to be a "well regulated militia" in times of National need. Notwithstanding the unmistakable intention of the 'Founding Fathers', the killing of America by Americans continues unabated – as many as 30,000 deaths per year according to Philip Alpers, gun control lobbyist. The ideals of America's forebears are clearly not shared by all of the 'souls' currently incarnated in that land today.

Thus, in an amazing irony, the world's most powerful Nation is rendered *impotent and powerless* to institute changes that would ultimately offer greater protection for its own citizens; protection surely in accordance with the original intention of the architects of 'The Constitution'. Yet the very nature of that self-same Constitution demands that, even with its flawed form today, it nevertheless is still protected by the highest Court in the land.

The clear conflict here appears to be both the need to change part of the Constitution, or at least some of the laws of the land derived from it, and the wish to retain it in its entirety as the Nation's *Founding Document*. Implacable resistance from self-interest groups who will fight to preserve and maintain the status quo, even against the obvious reality permeating society, are further barriers to any intelligent and lasting solution. Thus, in late 1997, American news agencies reported that the Supreme Court of the United States threw out a remit that would have allowed Police to check into the background of anyone applying to purchase a handgun. That decision then – extremely difficult to comprehend in its long-reaching import – appears to be another nail in the 'gun-control coffin'.

Whilst the 'judges' once again cited the inalienable 'freedoms' enshrined within the Con-stitution, they did not at the same time cite the clear intent contained in it for 'responsible ownership' of firearms from a 'responsible citizenry'. One more attempt to curb the spread of handguns in America failed, at the door of the very people appointed to correctly interpret the Constitution in accordance with the original intent of the far more noble ideals of America's 'Founding Fathers'.

If the full ramifications of such attitudes and practices under **The Spiritual Laws** were accepted and understood, there would be a voluntary and rapid shift away from this societal degradation to a more equitable one offering beneficent upliftment. And to reflect that new and vitally necessary spiritual awareness, relevant changes in the wording of Constitutional Documents, Agreements and Treaties would see only those aspects within them which accorded with **Spiritual Law** being retained, and the rest either discarded or altered to reflect the actual 'status' of those Highest and beneficial Laws.

16.2 The "Spiritual" Solutions for 'Te Tiriti O Waitangi'

What can we learn, therefore, from the 'American experience' as we struggle to come to terms with our own 'founding document'? The clear lesson from our brief example is that a correct interpretation which accords with the intent of the original parties to the agreement is the single most vital factor in utilising any 'binding' Treaty or Document for the best possible good. It is obviously very easy to arrive at a convenient interpretation, too rigid an interpretation, or too loose an interpretation. Therefore, a huge amount of goodwill, concomitant with the need to bury prideful egos and/or *mana*, is surely the first pre-requisite for any such enterprise to succeed.

Since land ownership appears to be a key part of any Treaty interpretation according to the Maori view – that being synonymous with 'Maori spirituality' and further deemed to be necessary for self-esteem and one's place in the universe from the same viewpoint – it is important to adequately understand what 'land ownership' and/or being *kaitiaki* of land really means from the standpoint of **Spiritual Law**. For the wish to exercise *tinorangatiratanga* or sovereignty by any people over the land should presuppose *the correct spiritual knowledge* of what this actually entails.

In the first place, we should all clearly understand that no one can actually 'own land'. One of the great North American Indian Chiefs stated it succinctly. When made an offer for the purchase of a large part of his tribal lands, his rejoinder was a simple query of clear wisdom:

> *"How can anyone own land?"*

We can only occupy it and take from it that which we need. And for the time that we are in stewardship of the land, we are enjoined, under **Spiritual Law**, *to care for it in accordance with that strict and inviolable code.* By doing so we earn the respect and continuing help of the **true** guardians of the land, **The Elemental Forces of Nature**.

And even though we may believe we have a 'spiritual connection' with the land, all too often we see land rubbished and abused in arrogant disregard for it. And thereby the actual level of the so-called spirituality of the 'owners' of such abused land is revealed for all to see. The word for this is *hypocrisy*, and such attitudes have no affinity whatsoever with true *mana* or respect for the *whenua*, irrespective of the land-use purpose or the ethnic group involved.

The same recognition needs to be made before attempting to claim 'cultural rights' over the food that the land and sea provides. It is foolish to **demand** the right to harvest species that may be under threat solely on the basis of tradition or culture, or what a 150 year old treaty once guaranteed. Intelligence and reason should be the key factors whereby decisions are made with regard to natural food harvests. In this case, so-called 'Maori cultural rights' must be subjugated to **The Higher Law**. If Maori themselves do not accept this, then the full effect of **The Law Itself** will eventually intervene, with severe consequences for the intransigent perpetrators. Attitudes that fuel such selfish demands are simply arrogant and clearly demonstrate insufficient spiritual maturity for 'custodianship' of the land and its potential bounty. Ultimately, of course, **"The Elemental Forces"** within the land itself will have the final say, in strict accordance with the **Higher** and **greater demand** that humankind exercise correct 'spiritual stewardship' over it, or suffer the consequences.

Surreptitious planning prior to and during the colonisation process in Pakeha need for land quickly revealed deceitful intent to dispossess Maori of much of their land for impending large-scale influx of settlers. And also showed up *British arrogance* in their unfair methods of gaining it at times. Whilst this cannot be excused, what legacy was bequeathed to us from those early 'horse-trading' days? Irrespective of who was right or wrong, the euphemistic status of 'land-ownership' still presupposes the question of care of the land by the respective 'owners' today, for 'ownership' of land should never be for status or *mana*.

The land does **not** need man to confer that on it, for it will **always** possess genuine *mana* purely by virtue of its obviously vital place in the life-role of planet earth itself.

Land, moreover, should not be used for monetary speculation, even if the practice is considered by the primarily Pakeha corporate world to be 'good business', and the practitioners 'financially astute'. Unused land should not simply 'stay as it is' unless left in its original state – or as close as to it as possible. And degraded or abandoned land should be returned to native forest, even if only a small piece at a time. All these practices are in keeping with the Natural Laws and should be recognised as 'correct guardianship' of our earthly home of Aotearoa. In this instance, if Maori truly wish to hold the mantle of *kaitiaki* (guardians) for the land, then it is way past the time that it should be put into practice; beginning with 'Maori land' first.

What, then, of the 'treaty partnership'? The American example should help us to understand that rigidity and inflexibility in maintaining individual positions, 'at all costs', is not necessarily an intelligent option, irrespective of what was *once* agreed to by treaty. For both Maori and Pakeha, the primary consideration must be the realisation that we are able to live in Aotearoa *solely because the environment* – **the land, the sea and the air** – provides the necessary material means to effect this.

It is not because of the Treaty of Waitangi!

The land of New Zealand, moreover, is a singularly beautiful, bountiful and blessed one, and we are all spiritually and materially charged with the *collective* and correct stewardship of it. If we poison any part of it, we all lose. There must also be the further recognition that the economy of our society will always be directly affected by **the health of the environment**. Both those aspects absolutely cannot be separated. The healthier the land, the more it will produce. Countries that foolishly allow their land to be degraded and poisoned eventually lose the ability to produce, for their own, and for others.

Therefore, in differentiating between the Law for the land and 'lore' of the land, *both races need to recognise what each can gainfully contribute to nurture and protect it*. What the Pakeha possesses is the ability to scientifically analyse environmental issues and produce a management plan that enhances the protection of the environment for the benefit of all. Since *correct* scientific analysis can only derive its veracity under the higher umbrella of Spiritual Law, all *correct* conclusions reached from such research or analysis will thus naturally accord with that Law.

Therefore Maori must recognise this as well and accept such findings and management recommendations as being 'spiritually correct', even if it might clash with current views about cultural tradition under the 'indigenous umbrella' of 'Maori Customary Law'. In such cases, the knowledge contained within The Eternal Laws must take precedence, and through this acceptance Maori will gain spiritually here too. Should there be doubt as to the validity of scientific determinations, one only needs to carefully examine those Laws to arrive at a correct interpretation. It is that simple since all 'correct' scientific law is nothing more than the earthly reflection and application of The Higher Spiritual Law.

Conversely, Pakeha partners of the Treaty need to understand that, through their more intellectual and empiricist nature as a people, they have lost much of what Maori generally still retain as an inherent and particular 'feel' for the environment. This is a certain 'sense' stemming from an unequivocal acceptance that *the world* is made up of *far more* than just physical matter. Unfortunately, that innate 'sense' does not possess the full knowledge of the true connections, and is therefore nowhere near as strong as it should be as a clear, inherent understanding. Nevertheless, it is still a most vital and necessary recognition and acceptance of the 'other-world' reality!

It is important to understand here that intellect is not the same as intelligence, or intuition, or even 'plain old common-sense'. They are not at all the same. They are different qualities that are nevertheless meant to be employed for their ordained purposes. Of course, they can be employed however an individual chooses. Too strong an intellect may mean a lesser, innate 'feel' for the 'intangible' but nevertheless 'very real other-world', and will often unfortunately even translate to cynical disbelief about it or derisive condemnation of it.[5]

Therefore, if Maori 'lore' and 'feel' for certain aspects of the environment is also in perfect keeping with The Spiritual Laws, but clashes with possibly incorrect Pakeha environmental scientific thinking, then the Pakeha scientist, too, must learn to recognise such errors, take them into consideration and alter his perceptions. For if *both views* are in concert with Natural Law, they will naturally also be compatible *with each other* even if the respective "Treaty partners" may not fully understand the 'other' point of view. In this way and to this end, both need to learn to do so and thus gravitate toward a middle and genuinely spiritual way!

Finally, then, even though much land was confiscated by deceitful means, it is not a question of Maori rights versus Pakeha rights, or Maori tradition and culture against Pakeha non-understanding. These are probably more emotional considerations. Neither is it a question of Pakeha economics versus a Maori 'feel' for the land, or in exports and jobs versus the protection of the environment. Ultimately this 'Treaty partnership' should be about the protection of the environment and the correct usage of it under the *knowledge* and *application* of **"The Spiritual Laws of Creation"**.

All else – jobs, wealth, schooling and health, and all that we might wish to spiritually aspire to – will only derive from that first and most important consideration; the correct stewardship of the natural world graciously gifted to us. That should be the aim of the respective partners of The Treaty of Waitangi –**in the first instance!**

Only via this vital spiritual awareness might we set in place mechanisms whereby this Treaty of Waitangi will one day *not be needed*. For the moment it is required simply because: –

– both Treaty partners have not yet achieved sufficient spiritual knowledge and maturity *to not need it!*

However, to achieve that ideal 'spiritual goal', the necessary and correct understanding of The Spiritual Laws is imperative. Without Spiritual Law as the foundation, *the Treaty will eventually founder* under the unrealistic expectations or demands of both Treaty partners upon each other. Or in the potential for a white backlash against continuing strident and, too often, unrealistic or selfishly-ridiculous demands by Maori in the exercise of their 'believed' indigenous, traditional, or cultural 'rights' to 'ownership of Aotearoa'.

Before concluding this Chapter, it is vital to once more stress the need for a change in a particular mind-set of the majority of people of this Nation, especially including the legislators. If we genuinely wish to have a better, more equitable society, *including an harmonious Treaty partnership*, then we must accept the requirement for a fundamental change in collective attitude. The necessary attitudinal-change, moreover, would accord with the higher Spiritual Laws – from

---

[5]For such disbelievers, however, *their earthly death* will quickly set that attitude 'to rights'!

which this Work derives its validity and Mandate. As previously examined in the Chapter on **The Spiritual Laws and Principles**, societal legislation and thus its concomitant 'public conditioning' centres on: –

– **"rights versus responsibilities".**

In that lies the crucial question of *correct societal balance*! We are fast becoming a Nation of selfish people always demanding 'rights', and legislators constantly kow-tow to this selfishness. Quite simply, *supplant* the word and the concept of 'rights' – of whatever kind – with that of 'responsibilities', and it is not difficult to envisage the change that society would quickly undergo with such a sweeping and dramatic transformation.

Thus, for example, children's and young person's *rights* would instantly become children's and young person's *responsibilities* – to parents, to each other, to education, to authority, to society. In turn, those establishment institutions would ensure that they fulfilled their *responsibilities* toward the very young and older youth of the Nation. Perhaps by this change, we might bring to a halt the trend toward more youth gangs of **gutless cowards** too often now possessing little more than a selfish and vicious pack-mentality.

All ethnic peoples also, of whatever persuasion, would offer their *responsibilities* to the Nation and to each other, rather than seeking their rights *first*. In every aspect of our daily living, this should be the foundation by which we achieve for ourselves what was ordained for human societies from the outset; spiritual peace and harmony within Nations and among the peoples of it. For only within the concept and realisation of *responsibilities first*, does the outworking of all Spiritual Law live since it fulfils the **spiritual admonition**, Acts 20:35, Fenton, that:

"...it is more blessed to give than to receive."

An intellectual argument may arise here with the assertion that if we all offer responsibilities to each other, our rights are then automatically received, which we may be legally entitled to in any case. But it is not a question of secular law and/or attitude. It is the fundamental difference between the respective "inner volition" relating to *giving*, or to *taking*. As we have already explained in the key Chapter: – **The Spiritual Laws of Creation** – one stems from *selfishness* in the first instance, the other reflects the far more noble aspect of *magnanimity toward all*, and is therefore *spiritually correct*, and we are enjoined to live the spiritually-correct only!

So, since the Maori and the Pakeha are naturally regarded as the primary 'partner races' in Aotearoa, it behoves them to set the first examples. In the strangest paradox, that *can* be admirably achieved *through* the mechanism of – notwithstanding recent large and ostensibly harmonious Treaty settlements – that nonetheless *wretched and divisive document*; 'The Treaty of Waitangi'!

However, since neither the Maori nor the Pakeha possess true and genuine spirituality in the *actual sense* of the word at this *present* time, it is imperative that both races set about acquiring it so that they might find sufficient *spiritual accommodation* whereby the respective *interpretations* of The Treaty of Waitangi can be 'harmonised' in accordance with Spiritual Law – for the Nation and the land![6]

16.3   Maori Economic Power through 'Te Tiriti'?

The rapidly-growing 'economic clout' of Maoridom, primarily gained through a number of high-profile 'Treaty Settlements', has lately seen some Maori 'leaders' almost gloating over

---

[6]As an interesting consideration: 'What would become of 'Te Tiriti' should a future referendum vote for 'Republicanism for New Zealand' in the time still left?' It is certainly on the agenda of well-known, right-leaning persons here. Connection to 'The Sovereign' would then no longer exist.

the prospect of wielding this new 'power' in ways not previously possible. Two very powerful words that the same kinds of 'leaders' continually resurrect are *tinorangatiratanga* – sovereignty, and *kaitiakitanga* – guardian- or steward- ship. Powerful *if* they are understood and used in their true meaning and spiritual/material application.

So what does this growing 'power' equate to in current Maori thinking? Is it the same as Pakeha political and business thinking; to grow and expand the 'Maori economy' in the same way that corporate Pakeha do? If so, where do *tinorangatiratanga* and *kaitiakitanga* in their actual application fit? For more growth, more consumerism, more waste, more immigration into affluent Western economies to fuel this insidious and fatally-flawed, never-ending, insane carousel degrades and finally destroys increasingly-fragile, global eco-systems.

At this present time in humankind's evolutionary journey; in ecological terms we stand on the edge of an abyss. Unless we change our thinking and attitude towards the single, great interconnected-organism that permits us life – planet earth – the majority of humankind, including Maori, will shortly topple into that widening chasm. The corporate 'gurus' call it scaremongering or similar. They will also say we can solve all the problems that 'global warming' is wreaking on human societies now, never mind the exponential effect already evident. The equation is quite simple.

Planet earth can only give as much of its life-giving *taonga* as its own 'constantly-renewing ecology' will *actually allow*.

Economies, societies and cultures of global humanity *must therefore respect and embrace earth's 'natural program'*. The resources of the planet, though finite, can still be constantly sustainable if output, or *extraction*, equals input, or *correct conservation*. Earth's biosphere does *not* possess an 'endless-growth mechanism' for we 'lemming-like' humans now numbering in the 'too-many' billions.

So, when extraction of resources *far exceeds* earth's sustainable threshold just to fuel growth and consumerism for obscene profit – as has been the case with Western capitalism since the Industrial Revolution – degradation of the planet's 'life-system' is the inevitable result. Thus, earth's 'supplies' are now in serious deficit. And that deficit is growing exponentially under impossible yet nonetheless precisely-related, increasing human demands deriving from explosive population-growth.

In this case, too:

Even a fool can understand that!

Should that sound warning bells for the political and economic 'movers and shakers'? Most definitely! However, as evidenced by more rapid degradation and destruction of more and more eco-systems, 'they', for this short time of 'pregnant pause' anyway, are obtusely blind and deaf to the glaring reality of the moment. The awakening, though, *will come soon* – hard and suddenly.

What drives this mad carousel? One word – **capitalism!** *American brand capitalism.* And, of course, its twin partner in crime; the **share-market** – the shareholders of which 'continually demand' larger and larger 'profit-returns' no matter how derived or who or what suffers for 'their' dividend.

For there are more than enough well-documented cases where Western capitalism has destroyed living standards of whole groups of people by simple *abandonment* for a cheaper workforce and/or tax break elsewhere; after the initial foray to *raise* living standards by offering paid employment to produce the 'corporate goods' and its share-holder profits. And, too often, also, obscenely high earnings for such 'selfish-thinking' people – the C.E.O.'s and 'Boards of

Directors'. Even the increasing involvement of 'Global Corporates' in the beneficially-growing 'Fair-Trade Movement' has only been seeded by consumers who are primarily *not* their share-holders. Previously *seriously-exploiting* Third-world Nations for very large profits, it was never an altruistic decision for the *benefit* of the Third-world on the part of at least the greater majority of the larger 'Corporates'.

No! The 'awakening and greening' of the Western consumer has forced the 'uncaring greedy' of the Corporate world to begin to change their ways, for 'large-profit economics' is the name of their game here too.

And what, in the final analysis, drives 'Corporate-capitalism', the real power that 'calls the shots' for Governments and global societies? One word – 'petrodollars'! Petroleum is the one single commodity and 'force' which has both permitted and driven capitalist expansion and its concomitant human demographic explosion from about one billion at the turn of the 20th century to numbers that can no longer be 'fed and watered' adequately in the first decade of the 21st century – around six and a half billion.

I hear cries of horror and dismissive-derision from all capitalists. Yet even the most rabid of them **cannot deny** that **by its very nature** capitalism **demands** growth and more growth to survive, thus generating the profits **needed** to fuel **more growth** for **still greater profits**. And only with *sufficient* petroleum supplies can *that kind of growth* be maintained. In a brutally-objective assessment of the impact of such an ethos and **associated monetary system** on human and natural life; in the final analysis it is quite simply insane – because *in its present form and application* **it is completely unsustainable**. And so, in the 21st century, more financial institutions, national and worldwide, have "...bitten the dust". **Many more will follow, until all that refuse to abandon their present 'aspiritual practices' collapse completely.**

As we strongly asserted in the Chapter: **The Spiritual Laws and Principles**, the *increasing Spiritual pressure* – or *spiritual-stranglehold* – now being *exponentially-applied* to all the affairs of men actually strengthens both the good and the bad. Thus *the good* – or that which adjusts itself to The Laws – *will flourish*. And *the bad or wrong* – that which **opposes** The Laws – **will collapse**.

In this we have an infallible standard by which to measure events around us and to choose accordingly.

The greater insanity here is that the economic 'growth-engine model' based on 'oil', 'black gold', has finally run its course. In terms of human history, 'petroleum-power' represents just a short steep spike on the graph of human habitation on planet earth. Yet in that brief historical period now spiking downwards exponentially were fought the most destructive wars in our history. Global conflicts only made possible because of oil to drive the war machines and the industries which conceived and built them in their vast numbers, and which grew the societies that brought forth the men to man them.

"A Crude Awakening": Exactly the right Documentary – which should be mandatory viewing for all – for the latter half of the first decade of the 21st century, where, despite denials by certain Western Governments and Petro-chemical industry 'gurus', oil output from virtually all of the major suppliers has already peaked. Soon, the battle will begin for what is still left. The strong will simply take from the weak. For without oil, modern societies simply cannot be sustained. Technologically advanced societies and economies must and will suffer irretrievable collapse. In its train, all the attendant anarchical horrors automatically deriving from major and widespread collapse of once-stable societal support systems and infrastructure.

The perfect example of the **Iron Law: The Law of Reciprocal Action.**

"What global humanity sows, global humanity shall reap!"

"The West. Take the money and run. Do as thou wilt shall be the whole of the Law. And the drugs internationals and the gambling internationals; environmental destruction in the name of progress; the sexual morality of the mole-rat with attendant plagues; the weapons of mass murder. *And only a few men and women had paused to consider* **that certain behaviour patterns might be wrong.**"

(The Helmet and the Cross, W. H. Canaway.
Century Publishers, London, 1986. [Emphasis mine.])

Where do Maori fit, or wish to fit, in this inevitable outcome? Here at the bottom of the world we are thankfully insulated to a large degree from what will be a destructive and desperate struggle by the major economic and Military powers of the Northern hemisphere to control oil to maintain their growth and superpower status. We in Aotearoa, therefore, have the opportunity to begin the process of living sustainably from what this land can easily provide for all in it.

Large Treaty settlements provide the means whereby Te Iwi Maori – as one people – can lead away from the *now-failing* Pakeha 'Corporate-ethos' into a truly 'spiritualised' economic model which will not go the way of *the collapsing Pakeha 'money-go-round' carousel.*

Dr Elizabeth Rata, in her perceptive essay, "Retribalisation is all about money", explains it all succinctly. She notes:

"...that the tribes have become capitalist corporations through the brokerage of their resources into the national and international economic system. Indeed, corporate groups, such as the new "classed tribe", suit the global order far better than those organisations of individuals who claim economic rights based on democratic principles."

"Tribal-capitalism, along with both western and eastern forms of corporate capitalism, have profound implications for the future of democracy. The essentially pre-democratic nature of corporate capitalism urgently requires exposure and debate."

*   *   *   *   *

16.3.1   The 'Interlinked' Global Monetary System – A brief History Lesson

Note:

That which *precedes* this brief history lesson in the *current* sub-Chapter was written well before the late 2008 economic crash in America sent its viral-laden tentacles out to infect the rest of the world. In our increasingly uncertain times, knowledge of The Spiritual Laws readily permits us to 'see' what will come next – *for this is precisely the period of global collapse.*

So: Corporate Capitalism – American style; should we continue to be seduced by you and embrace you more tightly in the belief that your way is the only way? Yes, of course we will. For that is the economic model taught in probably most universities, from which 'Ph.D toting' economic 'gurus' spew forth to man failing banks and financial houses that yet *still* influence governments and social paradigms across the globe. Of course, it is not that the *genesis* of the present completely *interlocked system* is American, but was nonetheless perfected there by extremely wealthy men and families of primarily European origin, in concert with the then relatively small but super-wealthy group of home-grown magnates.

Decades ago Professor Carroll Quigley, who taught at the Foreign Service School in Georgetown University and also at Princeton and Harvard, produced a 1300 page, 8 pound tome – *Tragedy and Hope* – detailing exactly the process by which the world became economically interlocked, **and who engineered it.** Thus the **How** and the **Why**! The **Why** is simple enough: Professor Quigley states it:

"as nothing less than to create a world system of financial control in private hands able to dominate the political system of each country and the economy of the world as a whole."

The **How**, however, is the stuff of conspiracy; of which we all must disbelieve and mock or be labelled silly conspiracy-theorists. Nonetheless, the history that Professor Quigley details is exactly that – the history of *how* the world financial system became interlocked!

We have used the example of The American Constitution to show how certain freedoms written into it by America's Founding Fathers have been subverted by 'modern legal machinations' in the U.S. The same can be read in the subversion of the financial system by powerful, self-interest groups.

> [**Note:** The following excerpts and quotes are taken from a sixties-era book: **NONE DARE CALL IT CONSPIRACY**. The author, Gary Allen – along with Larry Abraham – had difficulty finding a publisher willing to 'take it on'. (Concord Press. Rossmoor, California.) Once published, however, it became a runaway best-seller with over five million in print in short order.]

Gary Allen begins our small but vital segment with the observation that: 'The architects of The American Constitution revolted against the near-total government of the English Monarchy. Knowing that having no government at all would lead to chaos, they set up a Constitutional Republic with a very limited government.' Thomas Jefferson said:

> "In questions of power then let no more be heard of confidence in man, but bind him down from mischief by the chains of the Constitution."

Jefferson knew that if the government were not enslaved, people soon would be, so the Constitution fractionalised and subdivided governmental power in every way possible. Under such a system no segment of government could amass enough [political] power to form a dictatorship.

Financial power – and thus control – is far more potent, however, and America's Founding Fathers certainly understood that reality. Wealthy European bankers had long perfected the technique of bank/wealth consolidation, and through key men of those banking houses migrated the same ideas to the 'New World'. 'The Bank of England, Bank of France and Bank of Germany were not owned by their respective governments, but were privately owned monopolies granted by the heads of state, usually in return for loans. Under this system, Reginald Mckenna, President of the Midlands Bank of England', observed:

> "Those that issue the money and credit direct the policies of government and hold in their hands the destiny of the people."

From the earliest days, the Founding Fathers had been conscious of attempts to control America through money manipulation, and they carried on a running battle with the international bankers. Thomas Jefferson wrote to John Adams:

> "...I sincerely believe, with you, that banking establishments are more dangerous than standing armies..."

So from a very early time in American history, banks were primarily independent entities and often individually-owned, set up to serve a need: e.g.; as brokers in the early fur trade. In the 'cow-towns' and mining towns of a rapidly-growing 19th century America, these independently-owned banks sprang up to service the increasingly sophisticated, permanent towns 'across the frontier'.

However, individually-owned banks did not suit the aims and goals of the European bankers then becoming firmly established in the key cities of the east. Plans were formulated to bring all banks under a single controlling umbrella. But how to achieve it and make it stick? Create artificial panic. Senator Robert Owen, a co-author of the Federal Reserve Act, (who later deeply regretted his role), testified before a Congressional Committee that the bank he owned received from the National Bankers Association what came to be known as the "Panic Circular of 1893". It stated:

> "You will retire one-third of your circulation and call in one-half of your loans..."

The next 'panic', in the autumn of 1907, was precipitated by the American banking tycoon, J.P. Morgan. Historian Frederick Lewis Allen tells in *Life* magazine of April 25th, 1949, of Morgan's role in spreading rumours of insolvency of the Knickerbocker bank and The Trust Company of America, which rumours triggered the 1907 panic.

> "Oakleigh Thorne, the president of that particular trust company, testified later before a congressional committee that his bank had been subjected to only moderate withdrawals ...[and that Morgan's machinations] ... had caused the run on his bank. From this testimony, plus the disciplinary measures taken by the Clearing House against the Heinze, Morse and Thomas banks, plus other fragments of supposedly pertinent evidence, certain chroniclers have arrived at the ingenious conclusion that the Morgan interests took advantage of the unsettled conditions during the autumn of 1907 to precipitate the panic, guiding it shrewdly as it progressed so that it would kill off rival banks and consolidate the pre-eminence of the banks within the Morgan orbit."

Frederick Lewis went on to explain that the "panic" which Morgan had created, he proceeded to end almost single-handedly. He had made his point.

> "The lesson of the panic of 1907 was clear, though not for some six years was it destined to be embodied in legislation: the United States gravely needed a central banking system..."

The Federal Reserve Act was passed on December 22nd, 1913 by a large majority in the House, but a narrower margin in the Senate. There was genuine opposition to the Act, but it could not match the power of the bill's advocates. Conservative Henry Cabot Lodge Sr. proclaimed with great foresight:

> "The bill as it stands seems to me to open the way to a vast inflation of currency ... I do not like to think that any law can be passed which will make it possible to submerge the gold standard in *a flood of irredeemable paper currency*." (*Congressional Record*, June 10th, 1932.) [Italics mine.]

After the vote, Congressman Charles A. Lindbergh Sr., father of the famous aviator, told Congress:

> "This act establishes the most gigantic trust on earth. ...When the President signs this act the invisible government by the money power, proven to exist by the Money Trust investigation, will be legalized. ... ...
> The new law will create inflation whenever the trusts want inflation. ..."

How powerful is the "central bank" of America? The Federal Reserve controls [our] money supply and interest rates, and thereby manipulates the entire economy – creating inflation or deflation, recession or boom, and sending the stock markets up or down at whim. The Federal Reserve is so powerful that Congressman Wright Patterson, chairman of the House Banking Committee, [maintains]:

> "In the United States today we have in effect two governments. ... We have the duly constituted Government. ... Then we have an independent, uncontrolled and uncoordinated government in the Federal Reserve System, operating the money powers **which are reserved to Congress by the Constitution**." (Emphasis mine.)

'Neither Presidents, Congressmen nor Secretaries of the Treasury direct the Federal Reserve! In the matters of money, the Federal Reserve directs them. The uncontrolled power of the "Fed" was admitted by Secretary of the Treasury David M. Kennedy in an interview back in 1969 for the May issue of *U. S. News and World Report*'.

"Q. Do you approve of the latest credit-tightening moves?
A. It's not my job to approve or disapprove. It is the action of the Federal Reserve."

Prior to the actual day of the crash of 1929, Paul Warburg, one of the architects of the Federal Reserve Act, provided the warning to sell. That signal came on March 9 of that year when the Financial Chronicle quoted Warburg as giving this sound advice:

"If orgies of unrestricted speculation are permitted to spread too far ... the ultimate collapse is certain ... to bring about a general depression involving the whole country."

To think that the scientifically engineered Crash of '29 was an accident or the result of stupidity defies all logic. The international bankers who promoted the inflationary policies and pushed the propaganda which pumped up the stock market represented too many generations of accumulated expertise to have blundered into "the great depression".

Can we count "the collapse of 2008" a depression? Not according to the 'experts'. It tends only *toward* a recession they say, never mind the fact that factory closures are the result, along with millions out of work globally. It is said that 'when America coughs, the world sneezes'. Since "The Great Depression" there have been regular recessions.

Gary Allen notes that: 'Each of these has followed a period in which the Federal Reserve tromped down hard on the money accelerator and then slammed on the brakes. Since 1929 the following recessions have been created by such manipulation.'

- 1936–1937   Stock Prices fell fifty percent:

- 1948   Stock prices dropped sixteen percent:

- 1953   Stock declined thirteen percent:

- 1956–1957   The market dipped thirteen percent:

- 1957   Late in the year, the market plunged nineteen percent:

- 1960   The market was off seventeen percent:

- 1966   Stock prices plummeted twenty-five percent:

- 1970   The market plunged over twenty-five percent.

Since then we have had the "oil-shock" crisis of 1973, and regular downturns in the 80's, 90's and the first decade of the new century to the definitive "crash" of 2008. So either it is all manipulated by very wealthy 'insiders' to increase their wealth markedly, or the so-called economic gurus are not expert at all – despite their much-lauded university qualifications. We should not forget that in the west at least, the media outlets of newspapers and TV etc., are primarily controlled by just a few super-wealthy tycoons and their families. So any suggestion of conspiratorial financial or share-market manipulation by the same 'super-wealthy' can easily be shut down through public ridicule and/or disinformation.

Despite the latest crash swallowing up banks and billions of dollars to simply disappear into an 'invisible vortex' somewhere, governments and the larger international banks were still able to find the mind-boggling tens of billions to attempt to prop up the tottering, inter-connected edifice from total global collapse. Now the *country* of America is in debt to the tune of *trillions* of dollars. Much of America is not owned by Americans at all but by the guarantors of multi-billion dollar loans to help keep things afloat.

From The Federal Reserve Bank later came the notion and reality of The World Bank, and then later still; The International Monetary Fund. Three powerful financial entities with massive and *historically-unprecedented* global control. Akin to The Three Musketeers mantra: **"All for One – One for All!"** – *all* felt the crunch together. But that is not the end of it by any means. No! When the *final* collapse does arrive, it will not be **The Three Musketeers** then who might rescue each other, but that it will be finally understood to have been similar to the antics of **"The Three Stooges"**.

Yet the buzz-word of the 'big three' at this time is still Globalisation; the concerted target of angry, alienated and galvanised peoples from all nationalities and all walks of life.

Money is power in this rotten, insidiously-evil, inequitable world we humans have created. Latter-day Chinese economic influence in the guise of aid in Africa and the Pacific have seen countries subvert part of *their* control and perhaps sovereignty to the controlling-power of money. China is the new emerging economic superpower, to which most countries kow-tow for free-trade deals. At least that was the position before the 2008 global collapse closed factories and sent Chinese workers back to the hinterland.

Do we think that this small history lesson is necessary? Or do we believe that the controllers of the new wealth of Maoridom, presently following the Pakeha economic 'model', have the right answers? We should take serious note of that short history lesson *for it will replay again* sooner rather than later. If we take the one stark and irrefutable fact which emerges from the 2008 financial 'experience'; it is:

> "That the virtual collapse of the global money markets clearly reveals that its foundation was, and is still, wrong. For it was founded just on human ideas and greed and **not** on the knowledge of **Spiritual Law**. So to continue with policies that have proven time and time again to not only be problematic but to cause suffering and social distress to the many whilst insulating the super-wealthy, guarantees a final and completely-irretrievable, total and utter collapse.

> **So it is written! So shall it be!"**

(Author.)

16.4   An 'Example' of Correct "Spiritual" Use of 'Te Tiriti'

Therefore, Maori 'leaders', before you travel any further down the economic path of 'corporate capitalism', hold your hui. But as your first agenda item, leave out the standard fare of 'land claim' issues and the like. *Instead*, discuss the wisdom of Hungarian *multibillionaire*, **George Soros**. If you have not heard of him, then find out who he is and learn from him. Then screen and *absorb* the three documentaries so relevant for today: **"An Inconvenient Truth"**, **"The 11th Hour"** and **"A Crude Awakening"**. And see therein many *spiritually-enlightened and expansive* Pakeha economists and scientists who are concerned with far more than just *their race and culture*. They have our human home at the centre of their concerns, and are thus *true kaitiaki* in every sense of the word. For in those three crucial presentations may be seen, in stark and insidious reality, **"the evils of capitalism"** – an apt turn of phrase that many commentators have used in the past – in 2008, however, *forced to reveal its true and insidious, aspiritual mature*.

Think differently and genuinely-spiritually around developing a new 'spiritualised' economic model for monetary exchange Become true 'spiritual leaders' of the new, ordained way which

humankind *must* embrace, and which we of this small Nation *were meant to demonstrate to the world.*
First, however, revisit the proclamations of Ratana given life by two Pakeha:

J. M. Henderson: **"Ratana. The Man, the Church, the Political Party."**

– and Keith Newman: **"Ratana Revisited: An Unfinished Legacy".**

–and you will *discern the thread* of that 'new way'.

As the final word in this Chapter, we will *once more* bring to the attention of you, the reader, the stark fact facing global societies – i.e., *the now rapidly-accelerating collapse of all aspects of human works*.

Since that is the global reality which should be clearly obvious to even the most obtuse, so-called, 'disbeliever'; in the spiritual/material sense, Te Iwi Maori will only have 'Te Tiriti' for a short while longer. The sharply-increasing and unstoppable outworking of that which must come upon the human race in full force means that such documents will also meet their demise. For they will have no reason to exist after that time; thus no purpose.

Therefore, in the time that *is* left – and in accordance with *those [Maori] cultural beliefs* that acknowledge *certain spiritual truths and realities* – use the document of **'The Treaty of Waitangi'** correctly. That means in accordance with **The Spiritual Laws of Creation**. Use 'Te Tiriti' to *immediately* bring about the vital changes necessary for the, now, near-future *spiritual and material survival* of at least *some* of the peoples of this land. Specifically, in the context of our primarily Western educational paradigm, strive to change the insidious view which *denies the truthful-reality of the separable entity – the Wairua [Spirit] – as the animating 'life-force' of all human beings*.

Under the parameters of 'Treaty Claims', in concert with a fast-closing time-frame, use *your 'constance of the wero'* to publicly challenge the educational status quo; to change school curricula to incorporate the knowledge of *the nature and purpose of the wairua*. Do not just simply sit back and pridefully preen yourselves that 'Maori cultural progress' in the multi-forms of *Kohanga Reo, Kura Kaupapa, Whare Wananga*, Maori Radio and TV etc., – now very visible assets incorporating traditional teachings – is or should be the *pinnacle* of educational/cultural achievement. Such ideas on their own will not provide the perfect spiritual outcome for you here in Aotearoa. *Nor will it get you back to humankind's true home*.

Really understand what your especial Prophet, **Ratana**, gave you – the Maori race – from *his* high **'Spiritual Calling'**. Thus:

> 'Although the faith [*Creation-knowledge*] was brought here by *other* people, **it will be us who will take the 'real faith'** [**Creation-knowledge**] [**back**] **to them**, because the 'real faith' has been [*was once*] established among us [you], the Maori people. – [***through Ratana***] You have the 'faith', you the Maori people of New Zealand. Therefore you, the iwi morehu [scattered tribe] have been given the power ***through prayer*** of improving health and wellbeing, strength and enlightenment.'

> (T. W. Ratana, 1924. 'Ratana Revisited...' Newman.
> Emphases and parenthetic additions mine.)

Since Ratana stated that **other people** *brought the faith* [*Creation-knowledge*] here to Aotearoa, his sure proclamation very obviously means that he knew the Maori race *did not possess it*. Ratana was the *very first* of the race, through his especially high 'Spiritual Calling', to be *shown* and *thereby recognise* that irrefutable fact; hence his prophecies to that effect *for* the Maori race.

The primary faith [Creation-knowledge] that would improve '*...health and wellbeing, strength and enlightenment...*' for *every human being on earth* is **The Truth** about our *actual* human nature. That inviolable **'Truth'** is the immutable reality of our *inner, animating core*; – **The Spirit**: **'The Wairua!'**
Therefore, Te Iwi Maori, fulfil your spiritual task – "*...take the real faith to them...*" – to the world; as **Ratana directed**. *The world does not need your haka, 'Kamate'.* It needs Truth – *Creation-knowledge* – and their increasing suffering cries out for it.

But, however, establish it [the 'faith' – *Creation-knowledge*] *among yourselves first* – here; **in Aotearoa!**

This Work, this spiritual/educational text-book, *was especially guided for that purpose* for it builds on and extends Ratana's Work and Mission!

In crucially-serious reinforcement: In terms of the most vital knowledge all human beings absolutely need as their *spiritual foundation*; do not be seduced by that part of aberrant Pakeha *matauranga* which *absolutely denies* the existence of our *true life-force* – **the Wairua** [spirit] – but forcefully promotes, *in its place*, the *physicality* of the 'human genome'; even to the extreme of pushing for the use of *animal* parts for **human** bodies. Material parts which *rot away with the physical body at all their deaths*, but which nevertheless impact *very gravely* on the *human* soul and *wairua* – immediately after its *necessary* transition and journey through **'The First Death'** process.

Therefore, *publicly reject such very wrong teachings*.

If the overall scientific, educational-paradigm of the Pakeha chooses to continue with such unfortunately-aberrant notions, *then let it be so for the majority of Pakeha who accept such beliefs.* Through **'Te Tiriti O Waitangi'**, however, *demand change* so that this key truth – which your cultural traditions *correctly accept as a living reality* – can at least be brought to public debate for the ultimate spiritual benefit of *all* in this land. In this case, especially for the *crassly-intellectual Pakeha*; should *those kinds* of Pakeha *choose* to accept such Truths!

For you of **'Te Iwi Maori O Aotearoa'**, however, – in this crucial and strongly-stated *Poropiti* – *enhance and further* that aspect of **'Living Truth'** within your cultural traditions, both in 'necessary' modern education and in everyday life. So that, as with all peoples on earth: In *that* way might you one day *earn the right* to return to *your* true home too.

To: 'The Realm of the Spiritual': [Of the Wairua!]

Since the *primary role* of a Prophet is to *warn*, in the closing part of this important sub-Chapter – in sure and mutual concert *with Ratana* – the Proclamatory-Mandate granted to me is herewith invoked:

If I do not tell you this, who is going to?

17

Colonisation and "Tangata Whenua"

Tangata Whenua – people belonging to any particular place, natives.

(Dictionary of Maori Language,
H.W. Williams, 7th Edition.)

Our journey now transits from the primary thrust of the last Chapter, i.e.; 'The Treaty and tangata whenua', to where we now illustrate the importance that the Pakeha should place on the spiritual understanding of **The Eternal Laws,** and thus concomitantly of *his place* in Aotearoa. Yet equally for the purpose of *Maori enlightenment* as to *how* Maori should view those who make up the present-day *Pakeha* population.

This Chapter will therefore provide the **'spiritual explanations'** about who, or what, actually constitutes the *tangata whenua* – the people – of this land.

The reader may note that the second element in the Chapter title reads *"Tangata Whenua"*, not: *"The Tangata Whenua"*. We may further note that the William's Dictionary describes *tangata whenua* as *"people **belonging** to any particular place"*. Also, according to this well-accepted source of Maori word-meanings, *tangata whenua* are *natives*. We must therefore logically regard *natives* as being *Tangata Whenua*.

Does this mean, then, that *natives* are the only *tangata whenua* that *belong* to a particular place? Or does it mean that *people "...who **belong** to a particular place* and are thus *naturally native* to that place – are *tangata whenua* too?"

Volume II of Reader's Digest Illustrated Dictionary defines some of the meanings of *native* thus:

> na-tive *adj.*
> 1. Belonging to one by nature; inborn; innate: *native ability.*
> 2. Belonging **by birth** or origin **to a specified country** or place; *a native Englishman.*
> 3. One's own because of the place **or circumstances of one's birth**; *our native land.*

(Bold emphases mine.)

409

This debate has become an unnecessarily contentious issue in our beautiful land, with the tyranny of 'political and cultural correctness' stifling any logical and reasoned debate about what the words *tangata whenua* mean exactly or, more precisely, what they *should* mean. Thankfully, however, attempts to suppress these kinds of issues are far more difficult under the aegis of Spiritual Law, because the well-spring of its support stems from The Origin of Life Itself and therefore cannot be conveniently ignored or 'pushed aside'. Yet even from the *traditional* and thus *accepted* Maori religious viewpoint, which in any case incorporates precise cultural beliefs and protocols, logical conclusions can be drawn about who *tangata whenua* actually are *in any given country*, and not just here in New Zealand. This enigma for Maori therefore doubly raises the question of why non-Maori are referred to as *tauiwi* in the sense of *not belonging here*.

The key for *Maori understanding* of this particular issue lies in the inherent belief *of Maori* that *all human beings* possess a soul, (or spirit), separate from the physical shell. By utilising that *correct* belief, it should be a simple matter to work out the mechanics of what we will shortly reveal as an unequivocal fact. We will therefore answer the question of *tangata whenua* versus *tauiwi* further on in this Chapter under its own sub-heading. As with all else in this Work, we will examine the issue from the inviolable standpoint of Spiritual Law. And via that infallible method we will dispense with any 'cultural word-games' or 'convenient protocols' that may seek to cloud the issue and blur the truth of the matter.

We should, however, first address the matter of colonists. For without them there would not have arisen a *tangata whenua* versus *tauiwi* issue in the first place.

17.1   Colonisation

The signing of The Treaty of Waitangi ostensibly set in place a 'mechanism of agreement' with the, then, *tangata whenua* of Aotearoa whereby European settlement could begin. Prior to 1840, however, attempts had already been made to settle colonists in various parts of New Zealand. Two shiploads of British colonists arrived at Port Nicholson in Wellington Harbour in 1826. After investigating that and other possible sites, they left New Zealand. Quite logically, all early colonisation began at coastal sites of good anchorage. Only later did colonists force their way into the interior and begin establishing farms and roads etc.. In many cases, early settlers needed the assistance of local Maori to help them through the initial stages of settlement. In some instances, deaths from starvation would have resulted without that first help.

In the previous Chapter we briefly mentioned the thinking of the Colonial Office toward New Zealand. An original view of limited settlement gave way to the more substantial idea of large-scale settlement in another newly-acquired colony. So, from 1840 onwards, a steady stream of new settlers arrived on these shores. Some eagerly looking forward to a new life, others perhaps filled with apprehension as to what fate might hold for them in this untamed land amongst a warring people. Settlers running the full gamut of British society found their way here.

For some, no doubt, the sheer scale of cultural difference would have been too much to cope with. Even if the decision to be a colonist was a voluntary one, it was surely a tremendous wrench to uproot oneself from a land of friends and family, a land with schools and churches aplenty, and a land with good roads and reasonably comfortable housing in established towns and villages. To then arrive in a place without any of these familiar things, where everything had to be literally carved from the land, must have been heart-breaking in many cases. Conversely, those with a sense of adventure and wider vision must have relished the chance to be free of the inequities of a class-ridden English society and well recognised the opportunities that a new land of natural wealth and a vastly more agreeable climate could provide.

The attitude of Maoris and settlers toward each other differed greatly throughout New Zealand. Many settlers were killed for various reasons. Some for transgressions of *tapu*. Others quickly prospered with initial Maori help. As the pace of settlement increased, pressure for land gave rise to tensions between Maori and European. The situation was not helped by the lies and propaganda spread by the New Zealand Company advertisements in Britain urging colonists to settle in New Zealand. The land was described as having grassy plains, fertile soils and excellent harbours; a land of unlimited economic prospects. The Maori situation was played down. Where mentioned, the Maori were depicted as a noble and superior race thirsting for the white man's ways.

Land not yet even purchased in New Zealand was offered for sale in England. Bogus plans of whole towns appeared, and prospective migrants could choose their particular parcel of house and land before embarking for New Zealand. Such clearly unworkable and deceitful schemes caused huge problems here. And with such a large influx of colonists, it was patently clear that The Treaty of Waitangi would not deliver that which the Maori believed they had agreed to. The agenda was now plainly transparent, full scale settlement of New Zealand, agreed to by both the British Government and the new, New Zealand authorities under Governor Grey.

Another problem arose for both Maori and Pakeha with the emergence of shadowy land titles. Some Maori, eager for European money or goods, entered into sales agreements without tribal authorisation or without even the tribe's knowledge at times. Consequently, subsequent European claims to such titles understandably led to confrontation with affected Maori. And not only did British settlers arrive, but other nationalities too, each finding their own part of this new land. With the help of Grey, Nova Scotians settled in Waipu, and a colony of French settlers established their presence at Akaroa. Later, others from Europe added their own contribution to different areas of New Zealand. By now, however, pressure for land from colonists coupled with some Maori reluctance to part with any more of their tribal areas, gradually set the stage for potential large-scale conflict. And so the seeds were sown for what history terms "The Maori Land Wars".

The main colonisation phase in New Zealand produced episodes of singularly arrogant and deceitful land dealings. The devastation of previously stable tribal areas during the musket era of inter-tribal warfare, particularly through the depredations of Hongi, had led to the slaughter of thousands of Maori. Estimates suggest that at least one fifth, and perhaps as much as one quarter, of the total Maori population as at 1769 were slaughtered by fellow Maori in the tribal battles between 1801 and 1835. This led to large areas of land becoming unpopulated, with previously clear tribal boundaries an uncertainty because of the migration of tribal groups trying to escape the fighting. All these factors played into the hands of the land-grabbers.

*   *   *   *   *

Of all episodes of deceitful, colonial greed in New Zealand, however, Parihaka arguably stands out as the most shameful of Pakeha legislative machinations to take the best land available in that area. People of any given land will quite naturally choose to occupy the most fertile and productive part of their area. Consequently, any invader will probably also covet it and seek to occupy it as well, perhaps through negotiation to begin with, or by force should that means fail.[1]

Parihaka *was*, and is still, New Zealand's great shame. A peaceful group striving to retain land 'legally-confiscated' by the early Colonial Government offered only passive resistance to increasingly aggressive attempts by the authorities to enforce the 'confiscation order' by any and all means. Knowing that to fight would only provide the excuse needed for a possible

---

[1]This particular blot on so-called British justice is reminiscent of the American colonist's treatment of the Native Indians. The subsequent outcome of the distorted vision of "Manifest Destiny" that the North American colonists believed was their 'divine right' was for whole Indian nations to be disruptively moved off their bountiful, ancestral lands onto marginal or inferior areas sometimes thousands of miles away into completely different environments, resulting in much distress, illness and death for many of them.

tragedy, the residents of Parihaka continued to passively resist the authorities – long before Gandhi successfully employed that particular tactic. This continuing opposition finally forced the patience of the Government which then revealed its true nature – disdain and arrogance. Internment without trial and removal to the South Island was the 'punishment' for the leaders of the group, and a 'home' elsewhere for the rest. Parihaka was a shocking blight on the history of colonisation here. And unlike the publicly avowed aim of the British Government to not make the same mistakes as were made in other colonising ventures – but to "get it right" in New Zealand – the Colonial Government here had no such qualms.

*   *   *   *   *

Therein lies the quandary. The end result of the influx of large numbers of colonists and their need for somewhere to live finally led to the inevitable – land wars. Whether they were right or wrong historically is perhaps a moot point and not within the scope of this book to comment on. In the earlier Chapter about The Spiritual Laws we offered explanations that *decisively explain* how and why events are brought about through decisions made individually and collectively, somewhere, sometime. Through that knowledge the reader may gain insight as to the possible reasons for the Maori land wars from the *spiritual* and thus *higher* overview. That notwithstanding, land was going to be found for the settlers in any case, either by agreement, purchase or confiscation. So European encroachment could not be completely resisted.

Notwithstanding the present angst over land loss, more recent research has revealed that Maori themselves were instrumental in losing much of their land for colonisation. Belich records that between 1861 and 1891:

> "...Maori land in the North Island halved from 22 million to 11 million acres, or from 80% to 40%. Less than a sixth (6th) of this land was lost to confiscation."

And much was lost

> "...through moral, if not legal, fraud ... where ruthless Pakeha co-operated with selfish Maori."

(Making Peoples, p.259)

The early Maori belief that to have a resident Pakeha automatically meant the probability of increased wealth for the tribe through trade that he or his presence might bring about, resulted in some land being offered ridiculously-cheaply for that privilege. The thinking is illustrated thus:

> "Should the Pakeha wish to purchase land here, encourage him; no matter how small the amount he may offer, take it without hesitation. It is the Pakeha we want here. The Pakeha himself will be ample payment for our land, because we commonly expect to become prosperous through him."

(Making Peoples, Belich.)

Not generally realised by Maori then was the fact that behind the first Pakeha arrivals were many thousands more 'waiting in the wings'.

The Maori propensity for the theatrical, or in *"rivalry for mana"* as Belich so aptly coins it, found expansive expression in the sale of land during this era, particularly in the arena of the Land Court. The establishment of land rights and titles with all its attendant genealogical and ancestral importance and its accompanying *hui* and *tangi* provided the perfect setting for this aspect of 'the Maori way'. Even new meeting-houses were built and chiefs attended such events by buggy, the new status symbol. One Karaitiana Takamoana:

"...had a "Maori club", a substantial hostelry, built in Napier to accommodate his *hapu* when they visited town. Such things cost money, of which land selling was increasingly the easiest source, but they were also symbols of group *mana*, cohesion and dynamism."

(Making Peoples, p.259)

So whilst there were many instances of Pakeha greed, there were also the same kinds of greedy episodes exhibited by Maori. Land was sometimes sold without the approval or even knowledge of the tribe concerned. Later retrieval was virtually impossible. And huge transfers of land, either by sale or confiscation, were a hallmark of those early times. The various and diverse aspirations of both the Maori and the Pakeha during those turbulent years, coupled with the different natures and personal agendas of the many players in this sweep of New Zealand's historical time-frame, has left us a generally unfortunate legacy of distorted history, mistrust, and accusations of unfairness and deceit. It has also unfortunately bequeathed future uncertainty regarding fair and complete resolution of some land issues.

However, notwithstanding the complexity of some aspects of past land dealings and the need to find an appropriate solution, what was stated in the previous Chapter is equally valid here too. The application of Spiritual Law to the problem can provide a fair resolution if the parties are accepting of such a help, for colonisation was absolutely inevitable and the Maori had no choice but to accept a coloniser, either by 'agreement', or by conquest. The latter option, of course, potentially offering a vastly different outcome than that subsequently experienced under the initial agreement provided for in The Treaty of Waitangi.

As previously pointed out, the devastation wrought by Hongi's earlier-style muskets in 'limited warfare' stands as an example of what damage a much larger and better equipped Army could have visited on a stone-age people, even if highly intelligent and adaptable in the effective use of new kinds of weaponry. Even though bush-fighting would have given the Maori a clear advantage – and did as evidenced by Te Kooti and Heke's campaigns – it could not have gone on forever. More and more armed settlers would have eventually brought about the total surrender as encroachment became complete. Even the genius of design of the 'fighting pa', which well resisted the cannon of the Imperial Troops, would eventually have been breached, either by continual and sustained shelling, by tunnelling and explosives, or by simple siege and starvation – if the will was there for a long-enough confrontation.

Secondly, only a Maritime Nation could have been a coloniser. In an era of exploration and Empire-building, New Zealand was regarded as an ideal acquisition. Quite clearly, no previously undiscovered lands, at least by Europeans, could have remained in isolation forever. Therefore, the Maori could not have either. And, as stated often, the Maori needed the arrival of someone from the outside *to force a change in spiritual direction* if he was not to continue further down his dark, psychic path. Moreover, the choices for a 'partner' or conqueror, then, were limited. The American colonist's treatment of 'their Indians' would have probably been repeated here, possibly to a far more brutal degree. Their general, collective dismissal of the Native Americans as 'dirty savages' would have probably found greater expressions of disgust with the cannibalism of the Maori, so probably not a good choice.

Would the Dutch, who are extremely industrious of course, have treated the Maori with respect? For the Maori were also very industrious at that time – perhaps a potentially good partnership on that basis. Had Tasman written a more glowing report about the country and its inhabitants than he did, and were he to have stopped for longer and recognised the great wealth of the forests alone, the Dutch might well have been the eventual colonisers. The French were certainly in the running as well. And who can tell what may have resulted from their presence. The record of colonisers can be read in many parts of the world. The French in Africa, Indo-China and the South Pacific, the Spanish with their less than generous treatment of the natives of South America, the Portuguese in Africa, the Dutch in Indonesia, and the British virtually everywhere.

The European attitude during the Age of Exploration was almost that of 'religious fervour', with the Christian Church a major influence in shaping perceptions for the world and its peoples. A generally highly opinionated and arrogant view of their 'supposed superiority' obviously clouded their vision, which revealed itself in dealings with people of the 'non-European club'. The very nature of colonisation inevitably means displacement to some degree of the original inhabitants. It also means subjugation of certain aspects of the traditions and culture of the native peoples. So for the Maori – and irrespective of who the coloniser was going to be – all these aspects were part of that process. And the people being 'colonised' are, quite naturally, changed forever.

*   *   *   *   *

17.2   King Henry VIII's Legacy: A Pakeha Queen for Maori

Colonisation in itself, therefore, need not necessarily be a bad thing. In many cases throughout the broad sweep of history it has had a most beneficial outcome for the *original* people of the targeted country, with an elevation in education, and of health and general living standards. European Maritime colonisers at least had, by virtue of their ability to sail the world's larger oceans and map them and the lands they discovered, a reasonably highly developed civilisation. For the most part they were more technologically developed than those peoples who were not able to explore widely and thereby colonise newly discovered lands. Certainly they had the intelligence, organisation, wealth, equipment and tenacity to achieve such aims; traits necessary to begin the process of colonising a new and distant land.

What *genuine* colonisers also bring to a new land is not only the vision of a better life, but the skills to more easily effect the transition from an 'untamed land' to one with roads, towns, industry and schools. In hindsight, whether this is regarded as being a good thing or not is totally irrelevant, for that was the aim and purpose of European colonisers anyway. From the Maori perspective, if all potential colonisers are measured against each other, one would probably be more thankful that it was the British they 'treatied' with and not any other!

If we take this analysis further in a very important history lesson for **Maori** – [all key aspects in **bold**] – we need to travel back to the **House of Tudor** and **Henry VIII**, then **King of England**. His first wife, **Catherine of Aragon**, failed to deliver a male heir. This led to the divorce which compelled **Henry** to break with **Rome** by the **Act of Supremacy** in 1536. That same year he began the dissolution of the **English Monasteries**, concomitantly killing many within the **Catholic Church** hierarchy then well-established there.

Even with six wives **Henry** never fathered a son. The child he sired with **Anne Boleyn**, however, would become **Elizabeth I, Queen of England** (1558-1603). In 1558 she succeeded the **Catholic Mary I** and established the **Protestant Religion**. She survived several plots to murder her and place the **Catholic Mary** on the throne. **Mary** was kept imprisoned until her execution in 1587. The following year **Philip of Spain** began a **Catholic Crusade** against **Protestant England**. The defeat of the numerically superior **Spanish Armada** in that year was a defining moment in **England's** status during **Elizabeth's Reign**.

That momentous historical event saw the emergence of **Britain** as the major global naval power subsequently protecting the largest **Empire** in the world, lasting centuries. Though unmarried and childless, **Elizabeth's legacy** nonetheless provided the mechanisms whereby another **English Queen**, **Victoria**, would rule over the final expansion of the **British Empire** through the might of the **Royal Navy**. Included in that expansion, of course, was **Cook's** claim to **New Zealand** for **England**.

Now consider what the outcome might have been for **Maori** had **England** *not* been a **Protestant Country**. **Catholicism's** much harder religious line of bigotry, religious intolerance and superstitious ignorance was primarily responsible for instituting **The Dark Ages**, the killing of many hundreds of thousands during the three **Crusades** to the **Holy Land** and the torture of probably hundreds of thousands of people during the **Inquisition**.

The **power politics** which defined the Papacy for centuries is a record of greed and corruption, wealth acquisition, assassination and murder by poison and the blade, and religious subjugation – by terror where necessary. The same 'aspiritual ideology' journeyed with the **Spanish** priests, soldiers and sailors responsible for the destruction of the **Central** and **South American Empires** of the **Aztecs** and **Inca**, respectively, with the associated demise of perhaps millions ultimately.

Spanish Catholic priests systematically destroyed virtually all of the written cultural records of those peoples. They could not, however, completely obliterate their stone temples and cities. All those long centuries of 'religious death and destruction by numbers' on two continents were hypocritically accompanied by *invocations* to the **Very One Whom** they professed to serve, to *sanctify and bless* their 'good religious works'.

Had **Spain's** much larger naval force succeeded in destroying the **English** fleet – thereby returning **England to Catholicism** – and embarked on serious colonisation further afield than South America to also claim **New Zealand**, [or perhaps **New Spain**], there would not have been "A Treaty of Waitangi" or 'Treaty' of 'Anything'. Under the **Spanish Catholic Church and State**, there would have been only the rule of religious intolerance and cultural *destruction* here too; as there was in all colonies and lands under **Spanish** domination at the time.

That is why **Maori** *today should give* **thanks of gratitude** *to those forces* **which guide and direct** *the fate and destiny of man* [that is, of course, if we are wise enough to recognise and heed such beneficence] that **Protestant England**, through **Cook**, *claimed and colonised this land.*

The message for Maori here, therefore, is quite stark! Forces of exceptionally-powerful *spiritual ordination* – of such a nature that so-called Maori/human spirituality is nothing more than a pale shadow when compared with it – decreed and guided an especial process whereby my great cannibal ancestor, the Ngapuhi war chief **Hongi Hika** through his incredibly savage campaigns, set the stage which paradoxically permitted that very *spiritual* ordination to be *fulfilled.* Because of its singularly crucial importance for *more* than just those in *this* land, we will state it *once more*: It was the *emergence* of the line of the **Maori Religious Prophets**, ultimately culminating in the key one – **Ratana**!

If anyone in this land should doubt that reality, even a brief study of Ratana's life story should be sufficient to recognise that the especial *spiritual gifts* granted to him for his Mission allowed him to achieve much, much more than would ordinarily have been possible for any one man in the political, religious and racial climate of the time. His amazing life, moreover, has no parallel in recent human history.

Hard-line **Catholicism** would not have permitted the religious freedom necessary for the *spiritually-ordained* line of **Maori Religious Prophets** to emerge – especially in the Calling and Mission of Ratana. **English Protestantism**, established under the **Reign** of **Queen Elizabeth I**, did, however.

*   *   *   *   *

Contrast British efforts in New Zealand with historical instances of some horse-mounted colonisers who simply invaded and destroyed, and then replaced it all with their own inferior lifestyle until, in turn, also being driven out or colonised. In any case, irrespective of one's personal view of it, colonisation has been the way of man ever since he stood upright on this planet. It is only now, when the earth is groaning at the seams with burgeoning populations, that further colonisation is not a viable option. There is simply nowhere left to colonise, only conquer.

The latter-day derogatory references by many indigenous people to colonisation and colonisers, whilst certainly true for some, cannot be said to be typical of all examples. Australia probably stands out as a shocking and evil example of the colonisation process. The Aboriginals of Tasmania were systematically killed to almost a precise extermination plan. And in the Northern Territory, even into the 20th century, whites were killing Aboriginals in what they regarded as a 'legitimate sport'. They called it 'shooting black crows'. And what of the record for colonisation of the peoples in that largest and most populous colonised country, Africa?

The verdict for the colonisers – initially not good. Slavery and exploitation were the hallmarks of some, and exploitation the record of all. But as the colonisers themselves became citizens of the land, changes occurred, and the lot of the native peoples changed dramatically. Education and training for general skills and administration in the public service became part of the colonisers 'new way'. Out of this arose an educated elite in most African States. Yet the old maxim of, "...a little bit of knowledge is dangerous", can be readily applied to the aftermath of the *decolonisation* of Africa.

Whilst there was the education and intelligence, it was not tempered and refined by long experience in administering a national infrastructure. Moreover, there was not the necessary maturity to let go all the old tribal concerns and animosities and really embrace a new and far larger idea. And chaos and anarchy, with all its attendant killing and destruction was, and still is today, the reality for many African countries. Paradoxically, the people themselves *wanted independence and self-government* from their original colonisers in the sometimes mistaken belief that "they could do it better".

*   *   *   *   *

A truly stupid yet tragic example continued to fill the news headlines at the close of 2007 and into 2008. The megalomanic ego of the despotic Mugabe had reduced Zimbabwe, a country once a prosperous food producer and exporter, to a land that could no longer feed itself. Driving from the land the very people who produced the food surpluses and thus much of the wealth of the state, the policies of that despotic 'leader' condemned even his own people to hunger and dislocation. Despite the clear evidence that his personal ideas have failed, Mugabe, in the mould of most despots, refuses to accept responsibility for his actions, but seeks to place the blame on the original coloniser.

*   *   *   *   *

So, where does Te Maori fit in this kind of scenario? There are certainly enough voices raised in anger against "colonialism", but is it a reasoned argument, or is it just a parroted response by some to a distorted view that actively promotes Maori egocentricity, or perhaps ethnocentricity, to the exclusion of all other considerations? For, as we have strongly noted, a wide Maori view tends to concentrate on what was supposedly lost, destroyed or subjugated through the European colonisation process.

What Maori have never really honestly faced "square-on", thus asked *publicly and collectively*, is the question:

"What did we <u>gain</u> with the arrival of the Pakeha and colonisation?"

It is not difficult to answer if assessed *honestly*, for one only has to study the historical record to *truthfully compare* what was lost and what was *gained*, in all its stark reality.

We of Maori *earthly* descent, therefore, should also ask ourselves the associated blunt question:

"Would we still prefer to live the ancient way completely, or are we of 'Te Iwi Maori' better off with what European know-how originally brought to Aotearoa, and continues to provide in this 21st century?"

Of course much of the Pakeha way is fatally-tainted in the *spiritual* sense but, as the main thrust of this Work unequivocally illustrates, the Pakeha way overall is quite obviously far more preferable to that which for many centuries marked the old, savage way of the Maori. Pakeha arrival, moreover, brought to these shores the means whereby Maori could travel away from that old savagery into a truly enlightened direction via a revelation that occurred last century. It offered the greatest possible potential for a new and *spiritually-correct* direction.[2]

Just as the contentious issue of "colonisation" was placed under the searching analysis of the knowledge of The Laws of Creation – **Creation-Law** – it is equally important to also spotlight in the same way the similarly contentious term, *'tangata whenua'*, and of the sometimes derogatorily-used term, *tauiwi*. By that process we will arrive at a spiritually-correct and thus better and more harmonious understanding of just who the present **"*tangata whenua*"** of Aotearoa **actually are**!

17.3   "Tangata Whenua"

If we are to determine the truth of who are genuine *tangata whenua* of Aotearoa today, that determination, once more, can only be derived from the unassailable bastion of spiritual knowledge. Given its large measure of media exposure in recent years, we probably all understand the term *tangata whenua* to mean; 'the people of the land'.

Certainly, William's Dictionary of the Maori Language states thus. *Tangata whenua* are thus broadly accepted to mean those of *Maori descent*. Indeed, most Maori would probably accept that notion as a sacrosanct traditional/cultural tenet. Yet we might just as easily conclude that only the 'first people' are the true *tangata whenua* of the land – in which case it may not be Maori, for some historians believed they arrived to find others already here.[3]

There is, nonetheless, a strong perception pervading Maoridom that Maori are the *only* ethnic group that can lay claim to *tangata whenua* status. That belief, in turn, sets in train the further general belief that that particular 'status' automatically confers 'ownership' of Aotearoa to Maori. For reasons already explained, and with some explanations yet to be made, that is a view and a *status* we unequivocally reject.

Who, then, really are the *tangata whenua* of Aotearoa? Quite obviously Maori are. But are Maori the only people here who have the right to call themselves "people of the land"? Is everyone else *tauiwi* (strangers)? No doubt many Maori readers will be incredulous that this should be questioned, and by one of Maori descent. Yet the purpose of this Work, as must be **continually reinforced**, is to offer explanations about contentious issues and unresolved problems. It does not seek to support matters that may be emotionally generated, **from either the Maori or Pakeha viewpoint**. **Spiritual objectivity** is the *only* standard by which one can meaningfully provide logical answers to contentious matters.

This previously *sacrosanct and unchallenged belief* also needs to be placed under the illuminating spotlight of our 'spiritual microscope' so that no stone is left unturned in our goal to bring at least some measure of understanding through 'spiritual knowledge' for this land and its different people – *for the time still remaining*. So this general assertion of Maoridom regarding sole *tangata-whenua* status thus needs to be seriously examined in order to achieve that goal.

---

[2]The next two Chapters will detail that process. And, in doing so, will further illustrate that the proof of the pudding *really is* in the *eating*!

[3]The jury is yet to offer its *unequivocal verdict* on this issue.

To explain how and why this might possibly be otherwise than that believed by probably most Maori, we must, of course, revisit **The Spiritual Laws of Creation** once again.

*   *   *   *   *

We know that the individual human being is made up of a material part – *the physical body*; and the non-material part – *the spirit and its outer coverings*, which we can basically refer to as *the soul*. We also know that under the immutable outworking **The Law of Attraction of Similar Species** and **The Law of Reciprocal Action** – among others – all souls are compelled to incarnate into a particular family or situation, and thus into a certain race and geographical location.

It is vitally important to understand that this is not a matter of personal choice in the sense of hoping for a life of riches and ease, perhaps, for the *outcome* in terms of one's birth circumstances is decreed by **Spiritual Law**, in strict accordance, however, with an individual's previous free-will choices. Neither does it follow that birth into a particular race necessarily means into *the country* of that race's origin, for **The Law** determines the **depth of experiencing** required for an individual's **spiritual maturing** during its earth-life. And this *may* require a geographical location *different* to that of his parents or grandparent's country of birth.

Further, the physical body that any individual is born with, of whatever colour, or whether whole or handicapped, will also have been determined under the same strict and inflexible outworking of **The Law** via those same free-will decisions; again for the purposes of spiritual growth. For it is only the physical shell, which will one day be discarded and left to the natural decomposition processes under The Laws of Nature, that may be less than whole in earthly life. The true person, the inner spirit, is always whole and complete. Via the processes outlined, therefore, it can readily be deduced that there is no such thing as *spiritual heredity*. Everyone is born an *individual spirit*, even if later *choosing* to establish precise and particular *earthly group connections* in the social or career arena in the need or desire to *fulfil* its **spiritual purpose** whilst on earth, and perhaps through the desire to pursue family life also

Whilst there is not spiritual heredity, what we do obviously have is physical heredity, and that can be readily observed in all offspring. Through this lawful mechanism, races retain their colour, their facial and body features, and their characteristics, even if born in countries far from the ancestral lands. Naturally, a particularly exclusive race without others within their midst can only give rise to children physically the same. Mixed-race offspring, however, will obviously display features of both, with skin colour probably the most notable, initial difference if the parents are of quite dissimilar races.

Thus, as previously noted, in the case where a soul must incarnate into a particular race, it may not necessarily be required to be born into the country of origin of that race. And because migration away from original racial homelands has always been part of man's history, a particular individual may find himself in a family of the race ordained for him, but in a country *quite removed* from the particular race's geographical origins. It logically follows, therefore, that in such instances **the new country is the one *spiritually ordained* as its birthplace for that particular life**, even though being of **a different race to the original inhabitants**. That is the land to which its *wairua* belongs whilst it is on the earth – exactly the same as all of Maori descent *who are **born** in New Zealand*!

*   *   *   *   *

Where, then, does this place the Pakeha colonists? Quite obviously, the first settlers were *not* of this land. However, whilst their connections of soul and spirit were tied to the land of *their birth*, it may well have been the case that for at least some of them for that particular time, other connections, under the outworking of The Spiritual Laws, called to be resolved in this new land and amongst a different people. Their offspring, however, were a *different matter* altogether. For them, New Zealand *was* the land obviously ordained for them for that particular incarnation; by clear virtue, in the first place, of the obvious fact *of being **born** here.*

> **Therefore, it was to New Zealand that their spirit (*wairua*) was ordained to incarnate under the Perfect, Inviolable and Unchangeable outworking of primarily "The Law of Spiritual Attraction...", and thus not to the land of their ancestors – a clear impossibility anyway!**

The argument could well arise that if there were no migration, then there could not be other *tangata whenua*, and that is obviously correct. But there is more to this 'process' than that which wishful thinking may retrospectively yearn for; even if as an unvoiced demand or plea for 'sole-status' recognition perhaps. Ultimately, as we must often repeat, it is all about the inviolable outworking of The Laws of Life themselves; those Laws that both demand and decree that all else must bow down and subjugate itself to. In any case, the curious nature of man often expresses itself in the fields of exploration, whether in the sciences or in actual global adventuring. Therefore, in the same way that Maori sought to establish himself in other lands – thereby becoming *tangata whenua* of the new land whilst at the same time displacing other earlier people (the original *tangata whenua*) via this exploratory process – so, too, did the Pakeha.

Now, whilst the first generation in a new country might still strongly relate to the land of their ancestors – perhaps by virtue of solid parental connections – with each successive generation, the bond to the new land generally strengthens considerably. Via this natural process, the ties of possible 'ancestral nostalgia to the old country' eventually become 'generationally-transformed' from one of strong family connection, to perhaps one evincing mild interest or curiosity only. Again, under the outworking of The Spiritual Laws, one can deduce that at least some within the 'settled generations' will have had matters requiring resolution with Maori. So migration or colonisation is not always a simple and arbitrary matter. Everything is subject to strictly lawful outcomes, even if it may not be immediately obvious, or is taken from the purely earthly and possibly culturally-emotional point of view.

So regardless of the reasons for any particular people to venture forth from original homelands, we are ultimately dealing with the effects of *The Spiritual Laws themselves* on this process, and that cannot be changed.

In the final analysis then, Maori are certainly true *tangata whenua*, but the offspring of *all other races* **BORN *in this land*** are no less *"people of the land"* too. Their spirit (*wairua*) is just as much connected to it and its particular radiations as any Maori born here. Perhaps they may not have the same *feel* for the land, but that will not be as a result of not being born Maori.

Conversely, of course, they may actually have a far greater love for the land than some Maori, and may certainly display it in the natural beauty of their home environment, or in a chosen career dedicated to preserving the remnant of this once pristine gift of Aotearoa. Boy Biddle, a Ringatu *tohunga* quoted by Judith Binney in her book, "Redemption Songs", outlining the life of Te Kooti, tells how the Prophet used the analogy of a Pakeha garden to remind his followers of an earlier prediction made concerning a beautiful tree that grew in the Whangaehu valley. Boy Biddle recounts that:

> "The tree "spoke" with a soft appealing voice, and all who heard it flocked to it. It had twelve branches and six leaves to each branch. The only thing he (Te Kooti) could think to compare it with in its beauty was a *well-kept Pakeha garden, full of different kinds of flowers.*"

(p.426, Italics and parenthesis mine.)

So even in his century, the general Pakeha penchant for beautiful gardens was not lost on the Prophet, Te Kooti, who clearly considered them things of great beauty and perhaps worth emulating. Included in this 'Pakeha irony' might also be chosen careers in the work of the *preservation* of Maori artefacts and *enhancement* of Maori history and language.[4]

More importantly, however, and especially in the case of one *not born here*, sufficiently strong ties can be established in a relatively short time whereby a *tauiwi* feels the duty or makes the choice to "volunteer to defend his new home", as happened in the two World Wars. More telling, therefore, was the threat from the Japanese during The Second World War where the *tangata whenua* of these islands could conceivably have become their *taurekareka* (slaves) if they had not been stopped.[5]

Consider, very seriously, the Pakeha *tauiwi – those not even born here –* who believed in the need to defend this land during that long and bloody global conflict of World War II; who paid the ultimate blood-price with their lives. Now contrast that sacrifice *with the attitude of the leaders of certain Iwi* of some so-called *tangata whenua* who spoke out *against fighting for the freedom of this land,* and refused to let their young men go initially.

I leave it to the astute reader to determine **who showed the more correct attitude**, and not solely from the standpoint of The Spiritual Laws either – though that carries the far greater *mana*. And, moreover, who therefore displayed **the greater aroha** for *te whenua o Aotearoa* against the very real threat of death or enslavement from a powerful, uncaring and clearly brutal, advancing enemy. It is therefore a sad indictment on the part of some Maori who have chosen to resurrect this word, *tauiwi,* deem it to be politically and culturally correct, and then sought to apply it to all who do not possess any Maori blood.

Over recent decades, comments by various Maori 'leaders' and Maori interest groups have set in place the unfortunate perception that too many Maori choose to rest on some deluded idea that they do not have to contribute to any such noble ideal, purely because they regard themselves as the *only* true *tangata whenua* of this land. And in the area of natural resources, particularly, seek to regard the land and its flora and fauna as theirs exclusively, by virtue of this similarly exclusive and self-perceived *tangata-whenua* status. Maori are subject to **The Law of Rebirth** also, and have thus been incarnated as members of other races during the whole of their existence – and almost certainly some into white races too. Consequently, therefore, as *tangata whenua* of other races in other lands!

Quiet reflection on the huge migrations of Europeans who left their homeland of centuries to make a new life in the United States of America may offer a related and clearer perspective in understanding the relative merits of ethnic exclusiveness. In the first half of the 20th century, literally millions boarded ships for the 'new world'. Those first arrivals were therefore not the "people of the land", for they were migrants. All succeeding generations, however, were most definitely Americans – "people of the land". Today, we would not even consider regarding them as *tauiwi*, strangers in America. For, in truth, they **are** America!

Similarly, Maori here must face the perhaps unpalatable yet factual situation that Pakeha who are **born** here **are** "people of the land" too, and **are** of New Zealand, just as much as any Maori. Describing Pakeha who are born here as *tauiwi* is *incorrect* under **Spiritual Law** and is thus a *serious denigration* of That Law! Therefore, in necessary reinforcement under the aegis of these same Laws by which both Maori and Pakeha derive their life and substance:

All persons **born in this land** can be regarded as *tangata whenua* – **"people of the land"**.

---

[4]This has actually been the case historically, and is still carried on into the present by *Pakeha academics* dedicated to retaining and advancing the cause of certain aspects of Maori cultural tradition.

[5]Japanese Battalions, voluntary recruited into the American Army from Hawaii, fought with distinction in Europe. They had chosen America as their country to defend, even though being of the Japanese race.

Now, what of the status of Maori children born of another country? Whilst they may be Maori in appearance, spiritually there may be a stronger connection to the actual land of their birth. And with that, we arrive at another issue that should be squarely faced. In short, who, or what, constitutes a Maori? With such an inordinate amount of intermarriage from the outset, and with varying degrees of Maori blood-levels spread throughout the population, how does one determine the exact point at which one can be deemed to be a Maori, or *primarily* of some other race?

Kimble Bent, the British deserter who lived with the Hauhaus as a slave initially, became so proficient in all facets of Maori life that not only was he made *an honorary chief*, but in his later years Maori sought *his* advice on all manner of *traditional* skills – ones deemed to belong solely to Maori. And Titokowaru, the Hauhua chief, in his last dying moments, sent for his "Pakeha/Maori" friend and asked him to:

"Remain you here. I am going away. Do not desert the tribe. Remain with *our* people."

(Italics mine.)

Whilst we have commented on Maori blood dilution, blood radiation and DNA in a previous Chapter, there is one further aspect of this contentious issue that we will address here. In terms of strict blood *proportions*, it is probably obvious that a half-caste is exactly that; half of each race. But as blood-dilution levels *increase*, we begin to move into the rather strange belief that even the tiniest amount of Maori blood is sufficient to lay claim to being solely or mainly Maori. What about the other 9, 15, or even 29 other parts? Should not the *larger amount* determine the *greater connection*?

The situation reaches farcical proportions when Ngai Tahu seeks to find tribal members down to as little as 1/250 part-Maori blood-line by descent. And to even more minuscule proportions of up to 1/560, according to information given to me from "official" Maori sources. But even down to 1/250, what do the other 249 bits mean?

As a means for building a group based on the power of greater numbers, it is a clever idea. In reality, however, it is silly in the extreme. No blood level of 1/250th can ever be sensibly deemed to be Maori – in terms of *blood percentage*. And what of the poor 1/251st's who missed out, why not them as well? It is a ridiculous situation, bordering on the farcical! More than that, however, since many Maori count more than one tribal connection, what happens if other large tribal groups decide that those which Ngai Tahu claim also belong to them – at least in part? Including both Maori connections in two or more different tribal lists would throw any population census count haywire.

The strong emotional connection to being solely Maori *seemingly* the primary consideration for many within the race – to the exclusion of virtually all else – affirms our earlier assertion that too many Maori are far too egocentric in nature.

It is as though planet earth was created only for Maori, Maori culture and Maori tradition, to which all other races must pay homage. Maori, on the other hand need not bother with learning about anyone else unless perhaps they are of the "brown brotherhood".

It is an unfortunate and narrow viewpoint that denies the soul the experience of learning about the wider world in all its wondrous permutations, both human and natural.

Perhaps it is a feeling of cultural pride, perhaps of inferiority, or perhaps it is one of cynicism and arrogance. Whatever it is, *it is certainly not beneficial for Maori*.

There are, thankfully, a few enlightened people who are inculcating into the young of the race the love of reading and learning. That can only lead to a wider-world awareness, as relatively few Maori homes appear to possess many books of real educational value. Education **of the**

correct kind is the key to enlightenment and ascent. And Maori, as a race, really need to learn that if they are to bring about much-needed, spiritually-correct practices to change the deteriorating situation clearly evident in present-day statistics.

Currently, what we have in New Zealand is what Dr. Ranginui Walker describes as a dual social structure. A "segmented society" in the case of the Maori, and a "stratified society" in the case of the Pakeha. His analysis offers a good, clear insight into the differences between the two social structures, and may reflect the respective, cultural thought-processes. So perhaps we should consider whether the dynamics of the now quite rapidly-changing relationship between Maori and Pakeha are not so much a true 'racial' problem, but more a greater clash of "*cultural ideology*".

> "A stratified society has its members hierarchically arranged in a clearly defined pecking order which some sociologists describe as social classes. The popular model assumes the shape of a pyramid with the lower strata comprising its broad base. The hierarchical structure confers the advantage of a unified system capable of concerted action in directions determined by the leaders of the pyramid.
>
> A segmented society is incapable of withstanding invasion by a stratified society because it cannot offer effective resistance by uniting across the tribal and clan divisions. Once defeated the segmented society is then incorporated within the stratified society that conquered it."

(Nga Tau Tohetohe, Years of Anger, Ranginui Walker, p.155-156.)

Whether actually insightful, inadvertently insightful, or simply the standard sociological view of relative societies, Dr Walker's statement here actually offers *the solution* to numerous Maori problems that *seemingly* have no solution. Thus from the spiritual viewpoint the stratified society clearly offers the better model for the establishment of a more enlightened direction, provided that the 'social classes' work *alongside each other*, and *not* one above the other. And provided, of course, that the 'pyramid leaders' possess the necessary insight to put in place the correct educational structures and curricula to bring about this more desirable and 'enlightened direction'. Naturally, individuals within that society may not necessarily accept such a view. Nevertheless, just as present ideas steer society along the current accepted path, so could a different idea, initiated from the hierarchical apex, guide society along a better one than that which we now debate and anguish over.

Conversely, the 'segmented society' of the Maori, by virtue of its 'nurtured fragmentation' – often characterised by "rivalry for *mana*" – cannot offer such a promise. Moreover, any potential promise cannot possibly take full flight until, and unless, there is first the clear realisation that Maoridom must change its thinking from one of tribal-culturalism to a more expansive, *national* outlook. In the end, directions other than those which unite will only serve to hold the continuing, apparent desire to maintain tribalism and all that that entails – such as *kaumatuaism* and its place-hunting – on its own spiritually-flawed, Maori-erected pedestal.

The regular and often public references to long-dead ancestors is, in the final analysis, a practice akin to 'ancestor worship' for it seeks to continually resurrect the 'physically dead' on far too many 'official' occasions. Moreover, the clinging to, and teaching of, all related aspects surrounding these main points – regarded as the height of all knowledge – is a huge stumbling block for Maori. It is a concerted direction that *clings to the past* and is therefore one which could never allow a more enlightened, *forward-looking* path!

Is it not time, therefore, to move away from this constantly nurtured and pampered idea that Maori are somehow more special than anyone else and possess all spiritual knowledge? And can thereby hold everyone else to ransom via this ploy of declaring themselves to be the only *tangata whenua* and, therefore, the only true 'owners' of the land.

That is not the spiritual reality under the outworking of The Eternal Laws!

Let us restate it strongly again: Rather than being narrow and emotive 'tribal Maoris' with an egocentric view, should we not begin the process of leaving the tribal system behind and begin thinking as a Nation and becoming genuine *spiritual citizens* of the world. Or, better yet, of Creation. For this particular course is the one ordained for all men, regardless of race or belief, and is so according to Spiritual Law.

It is certainly given that family groups must grow into tribes, but it is also ordained that tribes must grow into a single, unified people and that peoples must grow into Nations and, ultimately, Nations into a global grouping. In the final analysis, that vitally-important outgrowth for the world's peoples should thus develop to the point where we human beings become a genuinely *spiritual humanity.*

So perhaps we *should* seriously question whether or not this seemingly marked reluctance to accept the ordained spiritual path for all of humankind and cling to tribalism at all costs is an indication of some kind of 'inherent inferiority-complex' – something equating to 'reverse-psychology'? Or is it simply a stance of 'stubborn refusal', and one which chooses to view everything from a solely 'Maori standpoint'? And which, unfortunately, always seems to bring forth *an indignant or angry over-reaction* **as the first rejoinder** to a view different to that which Maoridom might espouse *for itself.* A mature and quiet, reflective analysis in such circumstances should elicit a calm and measured, unemotional, objective reply. This apparent 'over-sensitivity of race' reveals itself, in the final analysis, as one of **"spiritual insecurity"**.

That is a pity, for it does not recognise and embrace the immutable reality *which our ancestors understood*: **That Pakeha arrival brought *necessary* and timely change.**

We of the present era need to revisit the self-same recognitions of our forebears of that time, who, though still living a cannibal life-style decades after the *arrival* of the Pakeha, yet nonetheless *possessed the intelligence* to realise that the 'old way' was graciously doomed to extinction. **And neither did they seek to retain it.**

Hopefully, therefore, the knowledge offered here may permit a more *spiritually-balanced* attitude to be fostered and nurtured, specifically among Maori in the first instance. Through the little knowledge outlined here and the complete knowledge to which it points, Maori may, *if they so choose*, thus completely fulfil their *spiritual potential and purpose.* And thus, in *a leading role in a particular way*, alongside other races who must fulfil their destinies here at this crucial point in time too.

The nationalistic fervour of a people for their country is clearly an admirable and correct trait, for it confers their collective, *protective mantle* upon their birthplace. Yet, as correct as it may be to call one's place of birth home, *the broader, unequivocal reality* is that, ultimately, it is *not one's country* that is one's physical home:

Our true 'material' home – and the one for all races – is, first and foremost, actually planet earth.

Our "blue planet", in the humanly-incomprehensible vastness of space, is our earthly home. *We have no other*! The words, *tangata whenua*, thus take on a far more expansive meaning when applied to all of humanity and earth. That is how the ultimate meaning of the *form* of the words *must be understood.* The term *tangata whenua* should therefore be recognised in its full and *true spiritual meaning.*

Such recognition *would* have more readily allowed peace and harmony to flourish and become the hallmark for individual lands and peoples and for global humanity and the earth, now and into the future. For it *could* have been a future incorporating the knowledge of all **The Spiritual Laws** which, alone, have decreed our collective place and potential in Aotearoa together.

The same inviolable **Law** has also provided the gift of the "blue planet earth"; to which Aotearoa and all its many different *tangata whenua* – **firstly** belong!

Part IV

From the Prophets to the Future!

18

The Near-destruction of the Maori Race:
Emergence of the Maori Prophets

The discovery of Aotearoa by Europeans and the subsequent close Maori interaction with them set the stage for an unfortunate but inevitable and swift reduction of the Maori population. Previously unknown and highly infectious European diseases, to which the Maori had no immunity – and now new to Oceania – began their insidious work. Diseases such as measles, mumps, diphtheria, typhoid, cholera, and the especially virulent smallpox; all took their toll. The unsuitability of traditional Maori medicine and the general inadequacy of European medical services to treat these new illnesses ensured an unchecked hold on the Maori population. Venereal diseases, too, played their part.

With the Pakeha, also, came more efficient weapons with which to more effectively wage inter-tribal warfare. An immediate consequence of this new development was the greatly heightened desire of some tribes to more readily avenge past insults by utilising Pakeha weaponry. To achieve this end, larger and larger war-parties were assembled for more destructive campaigns. What was *not* considered from the Maori perspective, however, was the medium to long-term effect that such concentrated years of *slaughter* would visit on a relatively small population.

During the years of this *accelerated phase* of inter-tribal warfare, the inability to settle long enough to grow and harvest crops – because of the need to constantly flee war-parties of many different and constantly changing tribal affiliations – led to famine and starvation in some instances. The traffic in slaves and the trade in heads for more Pakeha weapons also contributed to the rapidly-declining Maori population. But even after the relative peace brought about by The Treaty of Waitangi, other factors continued the process. Failing Maori health brought about by Pakeha diseases, a radically altered lifestyle and change of diet with concomitant weaker resistance to other illnesses, pushed the numbers still lower.

Unfortunately, instead of the potential for newly emerging stability brought about by the general cessation of inter-tribal conflict, the Maori "land wars" after the Treaty led to further estrangement for some. Once more, tribal groups were forced to flee homelands, but this time as a result of Pakeha greed for land. More bullets, more sickness, more loss of cultivated lands and alienation from familiar places inevitably brought more deaths. For some 20 years after the wars, the Maori population continued to fall. From an estimate by Cook of about 200,000 to a nadir approaching 43,000 in the mid 1890s, Maori numbers declined drastically from the moment the Pakeha arrived.

However, the common cry blaming the Pakeha for that rapid population decline *fails to accept* the crucial part that *Maori* played in it. The historical record has permitted us the luxury of being able to sift the evidence and arrive at conclusions that clearly show how much Maori *desired* the killing of other Maori in his insane pursuit of *blood-utu*. With regard to the musket era of tribal killing, therefore, the Pakeha cannot be blamed for the devastation those weapons wrought upon the Maori populace.

It was Maori lust that desired them, Maori eyes that aimed them at other Maori, and Maori fingers that pulled the triggers. And, ultimately, all in the name of *mana*-driven *utu*.

The fact that Maori readily embraced war and even indiscriminate and opportunistic killing is clearly revealed in just one example in Michael King's book: "Moriori – A People Rediscovered". There, in graphic detail, he records the tragic tale of a peaceful and welcoming people decimated by two of Te Ati Awa's major sub-tribes, Ngati Mutunga and Ngati Tema. During an invasion of the Islands, those two Maori groups responded to the Moriori's welcoming overtures of "...peace, friendship and an opportunity to share the resources of (their land) in partnership without rancour or resentment...", with bloodshed and slavery. It is probable that the Moriori, being the majority, could have defeated the invaders. However, they held to their law of non-killing.

Te Ati Awa's response was to "...kill them like sheep." It was recorded by one survivor that:

"...they were laid out all on the sandy beach of Waitangi in length over a quarter of a mile touching one another the parent and the child."

Typical of the cruel treatment Maori 'victors' meted out to the vanquished we read that:

"...mass killings took place over months, well into 1836 and individual Moriori slaves continued to be killed at the whim of their masters up to 1842."

"...some of the women with stakes thrust into them were left to die in their misery."

Moreover, cannibalism still held sway then and we note:

"Fifty were roasted in one oven."

The Moriori survivors also faced near starvation, frequent beatings, sexual abuse by their captors if the slaves were young women, a prohibition on marriage or sexual contact with their own people, and total displacement from the territories where their tribes had lived for centuries. We may liken this *ugly process* to the 'ethnic cleansing' in Europe in very recent times during the break-up of the former Yugoslavia.

Bishop Selwyn later lamented the fact that even though the Maori had adopted Christianity for some eight years, he found matters much the same. He remarked of the tragic plight of the Moriori:

"The Moriori have been reduced to the condition of serfs, and are obliged to obey the orders of every little child of the *invading race*."

(Italics mine.)

In a previous Chapter, we explained the spiritual necessity to always remain alert and, if necessary, to be prepared to fight for one's survival. To not do so invites the prospect for one's own enslavement by a potential invader, such as in this case. Paradoxically for the invading Maori of the Taranaki Iwi, the later events at Parihaka, even though a noble stand under Te Whiti, should perhaps have been viewed more objectively, given the invasion, butchery and enslavement of a peaceful and welcoming people whose homeland was the Chatham Islands. From any standpoint, however, that invasion was hardly a noble one, *in direct contrast* to the welcoming stance offered to Te Ati Awa by the Moriori.

Even though the reasons for the rapid decline in the Maori population from the time of the arrival of the Pakeha to the latter stages of the 19th century have largely been placed at the feet of the Pakeha by a particular group of mainly Maori academics and radicals, the historical record clearly records **great destruction of Maori by Maori**. So the rapid reduction in Maori numbers cannot be attributed solely to introduced diseases and/or social disruptions caused by land confiscation and land wars, for that is only part of the story. The Maori propensity for inter-tribal warfare and *blood-utu contributed far more deaths* to the overall tally than did the conflicts between Pakeha and Maori. Historical facts such as these need to be accepted by all Maori if history is to be viewed *honestly* and with more *maia* than has generally been the case thus far.

Whilst most historians have put the Maori population at the time of Cook's arrival between 125,000 and 175,000, Belich has estimated it to have been only about 86,000. He further estimates the numbers of Maori killed during the musket wars alone at 20,000. If correct this clearly represents one quarter of the indigenous people wiped out in a little less than 50 years. Irrespective of what the actual population was in 1769, however, the total number of Maori killed during this phase of inter-tribal warfare was extraordinarily high by any standards.

In 1858 F. D. Fenton estimated the Maori population to be 56,049. Figures obtained from the first official census showed numbers declining to 47,330 by 1874. With each succeeding census thereafter, Maori population figures reveal a steady decline until reaching a trough of 42,113 in 1896. We must suppose that these figures were representative of part-Maoris as well. If so, that would obviously mean a staggering reduction in Maori 'blood-percentage' levels.

*   *   *   *   *

An interesting fact thus emerges from such low figures. Whilst genealogical lines may extend many generations into the distant Maori past to the *larger number* resident here at European arrival:

The present population numbers can only stem from that reduced nucleus of 42,113 in 1896.

Given the continuing high rate of intermarriage since then, the current "Maori population" census figure clearly reveals *the very large amount of Pakeha blood now present within the race.*

*   *   *   *   *

This marked dilution of Maori blood stemmed, clearly obviously, from their ready willingness to actively seek large-scale intercourse with the Pakeha during the early years of European influence.

A breakdown of Maori population figures from those early years to recent times paints the true picture.

*   *   *   *   *

18.0.1   Key Census

Census year	Maori population	Total N.Z. population
1874	47,330	344,984
1881	46,141	534,030
1891	44,177	668,632
(*1896*	*42,113*)	(New Zealand's Heritage, p.1345.)
1901	45,549	815,862
1911	52,723	1,058,312
1921	56,987	1,271,668
1936	82,326	1,573,812
1945	98,744	1,702,330
1956	137,151	2,174,062
1966	201,159	2,676,919
1976	270,035	3,129,383
1986	405,309	3,307,084

(The Story of a Treaty, p.57)

*   *   *   *   *

The decline of the Maori race, in terms of proportion of Maori blood then present in the population, is an aspect not always acknowledged by present-day Maori. The prolific sexual interchange between Maori and early Pakeha produced many offspring (half-castes) who, in turn, produced many more of mixed blood over the succeeding years. Belich records that:

> "...a 1916 study of the Maori Battalion in World War One and of 4,000 Maori pupils in Native schools suggest that about half of all Maori were of mixed blood, while according to the 1916 census only 12.6% of Maori were half-castes."

(Making Peoples, p.251)

Thus, in different ways, the historical record paints a graphically sad picture of the rapid decline of Maori over a very short time-period. Nevertheless, it is timely to *reinforce once more* for the Maori reader that the *greater* **unnecessary destruction** was directly caused by one particular thing, *and one thing only*. And that was **the madness of blood-utu – Maori upon Maori!**

Without **utu** as that spur, there could have been up to 30,000 more Maori in Aotearoa in 1840; a huge number given the relatively small population to begin with. The only 'beneficial' purpose that inter-tribal warfare *might* have served was to perhaps engender a higher degree of necessary *alertness* among the tribes. The rest was killing purely for the sake of it.

As a final comment regarding the slaughter of Maori by Maori prior to moving on to the story of the Maori prophets, and for whom the influence of the Rev. Henry Williams probably counted for very much, Belich records the following curious incident.

"When Henry Williams died in 1867, a *tribal war* was stopped in honour of the great missionary peacemaker who had *ended* tribal war."

(Making Peoples, p.168, Italics mine.)

The Maori Land Wars represent a further defining point in the history of the two peoples and accounted for more Maori deaths. The incursion of Government troops into the Waikato which precipitated the "land wars" has been well commented on. Whether 'legal' or 'illegal' is not really the concern of this book, and historians and academics from both sides of the racial divide may debate that 'legality' all they wish.

Our focus from this point on is the emergence of the various Maori "Prophets" who sought to find a way to curb the increasing encroachment of the Europeans onto their 'traditional lands', and what that particular 'religious struggle' presupposed for the Maori, then and later. For there may be seen a subtle trend in the overall path of development as each *succeeding Prophet* and his followers underwent their particular phase of change and adjustment to Pakeha encroachment. Thus they followed that particular path in response to a need to cope with the all too obvious recognition that the white man was here to stay, and would settle and work land that may have always been regarded by Maori as ancestral.

One interesting aspect of the Maori/Pakeha wars that should be commented on in the context of this Work is the role that *kupapa* (friendly native forces) played. Belich observes that because of tribal identity and affiliations and the fact that they:
"...acknowledged no entity other than their tribal group...", they therefore, "...cannot be seen as quislings or traitors..."

Moreover, he opines that:
"From their viewpoint, the British were fighting for them rather than vice versa." And, as he correctly observes: "Might-have-been history is a dangerous game...", in an apparent reference to the role of *kupapa* being, "...downplayed in Maori memories."

(Making Peoples, p.246)

The connotations of Belich's observations perhaps show that without *kupapa* help, it is unlikely that the British would have had the decisive successes they did at that time.

In Maori thinking, the opportunity for unresolved revenge against a traditional enemy was obviously too good a chance to let slip by. What better way to achieve that than to march against them on the side of the British. Whilst Imperial troops generally possessed only marginal bush-fighting abilities – apart from a few special formations – they did possess larger numbers and seemingly unlimited supplies of guns and ammunition. Even though *pa* technology was more than a match for British firepower at times, the overwhelming numbers of Pakeha then arriving virtually guaranteed eventual success.

Therefore, in terms of exacting a little more *utu,* the numerically stronger side equipped with the better weapons was the obvious one to be with. One more method of Maori revenge upon other Maori, and the utilisation of the Pakeha once more. Clearly, it suited Pakeha purposes also.

But the end result for Maori were fewer numbers of their own people.

18.1   The Emergence of The Maori Prophets

Notwithstanding the fact that Maori on the side of the British were actively engaged against other Maori, their generally shrewd and covetous ways actually sought the material goods, skills and knowledge that the Pakeha possessed. Realising that the Pakeha were simply too numerous to defeat, some Maori sought to enlist the aid of the Christian God to effect their desired outcomes. From the earliest contacts with Europeans, Maori quickly realised that this new 'visitor' was unaffected by their various *tapu*, or by the 'power' of *makutu* that he was personally forced to pay homage to in *his* fear of it. And even though some Pakeha were killed by angry Maori for transgressing *tapu*, fearless Pakeha disregard of it seemingly served to illustrate how much more powerful their God was.

In accepting Christianity in principle, though not in complete understanding, Maori quite logically interpreted those teachings from their particular level of knowledge and development, adding their own ideas and embellishments. Thus, from the beginning of the "Prophet Movement" in the 1830s to its transformation into a political one at the end of the Nineteenth Century, certain similar features that we might describe as being of Maori thinking can be found as a developing thread in all.

The impetus for such a rapid and prolific "Religious Prophetic Movement" among only a small population at the time can perhaps be explained by two major influences. One was the natural Maori acceptance of 'other-world' possibilities regarding the intangible, where the unseen played a key role in all aspects of his thought-processes and daily endeavours. And Christianity had this 'intangible aspect' in abundance. The other, which fed quite naturally into that ethos, was the transforming effect that the strong religious beliefs of quite large numbers of Maori of many different tribal affiliations, previously held prisoner by Ngapuhi, had upon their return home. Freed by Ngapuhi from about 1830, their enthusiasm for Christianity produced the same in many Maori who had thus far not been exposed to the tenets of this belief. The prisoners who had embraced this new religion clearly believed it could fulfil all Maori aspirations.

Given the straitened circumstances of Maori at the time, the evangelical enthusiasm with which they spread their particular brand of Christianity was often a welcome message of hope, even if laced with copious amounts of traditional ideas and much psychic influence. The enthusiasm for something new and hopefully better can be gauged by the numbers of such groups. Whilst there may have been more, about 50 Maori Prophetic Movements can be documented, though:

> "...some were "interchangeable" with regard to preachers and attendances."

> (Making Peoples, p.220)

The main similarity that characterised virtually all such Movements was a strong identification with the wandering tribal Jews who had an all-powerful God that protected them from their oppressors, or delivered their enemies into their hands. The idea of a vengeful Old Testament God destroying one's enemies neatly accorded with the Maori concept of *utu;* a just and rightful thing in their eyes. And the promise of a heaven filled with all that one could want by simply believing in the teachings of the various prophets added allure for converts. The natural Maori ability to memorise large sections of oral tradition was utilised in the same way to similarly memorise copious amounts of Biblical texts. And with the adoption of certain passages of Scripture as justification for calling on the Jewish tribal God for help in their cause, the stage was set for believed Divine intervention against the European as many times as there were different prophets.

However, the one thing that had to be addressed if the Maori were to defeat the Pakeha was how to acquire immunity from the effect of Pakeha bullets. In this instance, the converted were simply exhorted to have faith. If a bullet found its mark, it was a sure sign that there was *insufficient faith in the one who fell.* With these criteria more or less present in all the main Religious Movements that had, as its aim, the driving of the Pakeha back into the sea, these respective groups sometimes achieved military results disproportionate to the actual numbers participating in the engagement. Religious fanaticism is always notoriously difficult for a conventional fighting force to oppose, and sometimes calls for equally unconventional methods to combat it.

The first of the Maori Prophets began to emerge and preach their particular brand of religion from the earliest years of contact with the missionaries. With the greater influence of the missionaries in the North, it is not surprising that 'Maori Religions' began there. They were invariably a mixture of Christianity and Maori; a mix of the old and the new. The God of the missionaries was seen as the provider of Pakeha material wealth, and an *atua* capable of wreaking havoc with the dispensing of *mate Pakeha* as some kind of retributive punishment for the Maori cause. Moreover, the Pakeha Bible apparently contained all the secrets of the world. All things considered, a formidable religion.

Of course, it could not be expected that Maori of those times could fully understand the finer doctrinal points of Pakeha religion, so, within the parameters of their understanding, Maori naturally interpreted The Word in accordance with their grasp of it. Consequently, strange, confused mixes of religion developed which attempted to unite the old and the new.

18.1.1   Te Atua Wera

(Literal translation: – the hot god.)

The serpent cult of the *tohunga*, Te Atua Wera, emerged in 1833. Similar in certain respects to the cargo cult of New Guinea, its leader and self-styled prophet promised his followers a heaven crammed with all the wonderful things that the Pakeha enjoyed; flour, sugar, guns and ships and, as a further sweetener, *unbridled sexual activity.*[1] Not surprisingly, the Movement gained many followers, all eager to partake of what surely seemed to be the perfect heaven; and one to rival any that the Pakeha could promise.

The Maori Prophets readily identified with the tribes of ancient Israel, which they sometimes claimed to be descended from. In a previous Chapter we mentioned the belief of some Maori that they are descended from the tribe of Benjamin. In order to establish some level of 'credibility' for such a claim of descent from Biblical Jews, an appropriate story of revelation or Divine guidance must be 'invented' for one's followers. The Maori, with great oratorical skills, steeped in superstition and with a penchant for embellishment, could quite easily conjure up a believable story. Even one about a long lost connection to the old Jews.

But as an example of a *tohunga's* inability or reluctance, (or just plain cunning), to let go psychic connections in the furtherance of his personal influence, the serpent cult of Te Atua Wera declared their God to be the serpent of Moses. Ostensibly speaking through Te Atua Wera, the serpent even promised to protect them from Pakeha bullets, and they would not die. Other later Prophets, of course, promised the same, and many Maori paid the price for this impossible belief.

---

[1]The suicide bombers of some religious factions in the Middle East are promised, among other things, 70 virgins when they 'arrive in heaven'. What they will presumably do with those 'virgins' has clearly not been thought through as they will very obviously have left behind the very physical organs – blown to pieces at their suicide death – they would ordinarily need to 'enjoy' their gift of 'heavenly virgins'. – For The Laws of Creation *decree* that the earth, alone, is the home of the flesh.

18.1.2   Papahurihia

According to one Ngapuhi '*kaumatua*', Te Atua Wera took the name Papahurihia after an incident where it is claimed he levitated. The standard historical notation, however, records that the Bay of Islands produced Papahurihia in the early 1830s as the first of the documented Maori Religious Prophets. Little is known of him other than his establishment of a sect of *Hurai* (Jews) and the declaration that Saturday would be kept as the Sabbath. Whether his supposed levitation experience changed his outlook from that of '*tohunga* Te Atua Wera' is uncertain, but he appears to have somehow gained Catholic links and welcomed Bishop Pompallier as his younger brother. Moreover, he proclaimed himself 'Papahurihian' and also Catholic.[2]

Whilst the 'Christian cult' of **Te Atua Wera/Papahurihia** was probably the first recorded, there may have been a relatively widespread Movement in Ngapuhi territory promoting a new god, Wheawheau, as early as 1822. Other 'heresy' cults appeared at Hokianga in 1834, on the east coast in 1840 and in Taranaki in 1845. As we have already noted, the feature most common to the Maori Religious Movements of the 19th century was the strong identification with Judaism and *their* strong tribal traditions.

18.1.3   Aperahama Taonui

A young chief from Hokianga, Aperahama received religious instruction at the Wesleyan mission there. Even though schooled in the knowledge and arts of the *tohunga*, he evidently accepted Christianity at an early age and may have experienced an instance of religious inspiration or revelation in September 1834. In a dispute at the burial of a noted chief, Hauhau, the ancient custom of killing a slave was argued against by those who had become Christians. During the debate on this matter several of the participants were:

> "...seized with a kind of supernatural impulse, their whole frame shook and trembled and they spoke in a strain of piety and prophecy which surprised all present."

> (Mana From Heaven, Elsmore, p.50)

Aperahama was apparently much affected and foretold the Second Coming several times and that the dead body of the chief would be raised to life on the following Monday. On the Tuesday, Aperahama and his brother visited the mission station and reported that the chief was not raised from the dead. Whitely reported that they appeared to be:

> "...under the influence of something strange and unaccountable. Woon added that Aperahama was dressed in "...decent English clothing, with a long white veil before his face, and appeared in deep meditation and prayer."

> (Mana From Heaven, Elsmore, p.51)

Whilst his sermon was in accordance with the Scriptures on this occasion, it was not so the next evening when he announced he was the Messiah, the Son of God, and that he had the knowledge of all things, and had come to rule over the earth. The missionaries were horrified and summoned the neighbouring tribes to clarify Scripture regarding sin and the fall of man, the only 'true saviour', and the 'devices of Satan'. On the same day Aperahama recanted and next day made a short confession to the gathering.

A positive outcome of this event, at least from the point of view of the missionaries, was the embracing of Christianity by the chief Te Taonui, Aperahama's father, who had formerly 'opposed the truth'. He was baptised in June 1841, as were three of his sons. Aperahama's announcement that he was the 'Messiah' provided just one more example of the need for missionary

---

[2]This sect died away leaving little lasting influence.

vigilance to ensure that The Word was not corrupted by 'sinful' Maori customs. Understandably, such 'heretical' incidents were not uncommon at the time, for it would have been too much to expect Maori to fully comprehend most Scripture to anywhere near the depth to which the missionaries understood it.

Notwithstanding that reality, Elsmore records Woon as noting that Aperahama, a firm member of the Wesleyan congregation and "one of our class leaders", had a debate with a Catholic priest who tried to convert him to Catholicism, but that Aperahama had:

> "...decidedly the advantage over his subtle antagonist."

> (Mana From Heaven, Elsmore, p.52)

During Heke's war with the Government, Te Taonui and his family supported the Government cause, saying that they were indebted to Europeans for temporal and spiritual goods and wanted to live in peace with them. Aperahama, spoken of at the time as "...the most intelligent native we have...", and "...highly respected of all classes...", was seriously wounded in battle. He was taken to Auckland to recuperate and there became acquainted with Governor Grey. (Elsmore p.52)

One interesting aspect of this man's faith-belief mode, was his retention of at least some aspects of *tohungaism*, he being an initiate of the *whare wananga*. Moreover, he agreed to record that knowledge at the request of John White, the Government interpreter. His great concern, however, was that any book produced should be seen by Europeans only.

> "The Chief's fears were twofold – that his telling would cause ill-feeling among the Maori, and that should his own people read it, the knowledge would stop them believing in the "Almighty God".

> (Mana From Heaven, Elsmore, p.53)

From the perspective of time, it is quite clear how Maori could have been greatly influenced by knowledge that was reserved for the chosen few, to the point where Christianity might have been renounced. However, from the standpoint of spiritual objectivity, as opposed to emotionalism generated by cultural traditions, it is a more difficult proposition to understand why anyone would even begin to contemplate a return to the decided uncertainty of the old, savage way.

Elsmore postulates that Aperahama's slight shift away from Christian 'orthodoxy' may have been influenced by Te Atua Wera. In fact, as an appointed Native Assessor, Aperahama requested the Native Secretary in April 1859 that Papahurihia also be made an assessor to help him. Certainly around this time, Aperahama was known more as prophet and *tohunga*.

And in a move that Maori traditions might normally frown upon, Elsmore notes that:

> "In his later years, having failed to gain honour in his own country, he went south to live amongst the Ngati Whatua – traditional enemies of Ngapuhi – opening a *whare wananga* in which Maori traditions were taught. At his death in 1882, he was buried at Oturei".

> (Mana From Heaven, Elsmore, p.53)

18.1.4   Hakopa Nikau

Hakopa Nikau was the producer of the heresy cult in Taranaki in 1845. Often referred to as the "Warea Delusion", he called it the Tikanga Hou (New Doctrine) Movement. This interesting individual not only banished the missionaries with their books from the area, but further declared that there was no Bible, no sin, no Sabbath, no hell and no devil, yet *still maintained* that his religion was Christian.

18.1.5   Tamati Te Ito

This Movement called Kai Ngarara (Eat Lizard sect), emerged in Taranaki in the early 1850s, and was variously known as the Wahi Tapu (Sacred Places) or Whakanoa (Deconsecrate) Movements. It had, as its professed aim, the removal of all *tapu*.

The reader may recall our earlier explanations of the very great fear that the appearance of a lizard could produce for Maori. Tamati Te Ito, like most old Maori, believed that disease was caused by transgressions of *tapu*. So, in his view, the obvious answer was to remove *tapu*, not enforce it. In this particular case, 'deconsecrating rituals' such as the devouring of 'demonic' lizards would be seen as an especially powerful and effective way of achieving this.

One can surely admire the courage of a deeply superstitious Maori, steeped in the great fear of lizards, *devouring* all he could find.

18.1.6   Te Ua Haumene (Pai Marire)

In about the mid 1860s what might be described as one of the *true* Maori Religious Movements emerged under the leadership of Te Ua Haumene. It was that of "Pai Marire", the 'good and peaceful' Movement. Originally from Taranaki, Te Ua first learned of Christianity at Hokianga whilst a prisoner of war there. Upon his release and subsequent return home, he became a teacher and was baptised by the Rev. John Whitely, a Wesleyan missionary. He took the name Horopapera, a transliteration of Zerub-babel. He had apparently already received visitations by the Archangel Gabriel in his dreams and he subsequently recommended that there should be changes in religious observances.

Te Ua gained his first followers after he supposedly performed two 'biblical feats'. The first occurred after an alleged assault on another man's wife (hardly a 'good and peaceful' act) when he broke apart the ropes and chains which bound him. The second 'good and peaceful' act was being commanded to kill his son. He did not succeed and the wounds were ostensibly healed by the Angel Gabriel's timely intervention. Such shaky beginnings to a new Religious Movement, which had the blessing of no less than the Archangel Gabriel himself, might be better understood when we read that contemporary Europeans reported that Te Ua had always been regarded as being of a somewhat weak intellect.

Nevertheless, he began to attract more and more followers and, as a result of his support of the King Movement, Pai Marire came into its own as being believed to provide an answer to defeating the Europeans during the second phase of the wars. A skirmish at Te Ahuahu in Taranaki in April 1864 provided the first 'test' for Te Ua's people. Even though a small victory, it had enormous propaganda value at a time when many Maori were quite desolated over continuing Pakeha encroachment and their inability to combat it meaningfully.

Shortly after this battle, Te Ua the Prophet revealed his unbreakable connections to the old psychic ways by exhuming and drying the head of one of the dead of Te Ahuahu, a Captain Lloyd. Ostensibly under Gabriel's instructions once more, this head was to be the means of communication by which God would guide the adherents of Pai Marire in their quest to expel the white invader and regain their lands. Te Ua directed that all Christian Scriptures be burned and declared that the Sabbath was no longer to be observed. And to help redress the problem of declining Maori numbers, men and women were enjoined to live together promiscuously.

Lacking European technology, Maori were unable to emulate European skills. And whilst many Maori could read and write their own language, it was painfully obvious that this was not the means by which to acquire technological skills. Consequently, both the desire for fluency in English and the concomitant wish to possess the white man's arts and sciences were compounded by the equally strong desire to have him gone from the land. But only Divine intervention could achieve both aims and provide the means whereby Europeans would somehow be supernaturally destroyed or expelled.

To this end, Te Ua promised that once the white man had gone, teachers from heaven would be sent to impart all the Pakeha knowledge and, providing certain conditions were met, Pai Marire priests would be able to teach English "...in one easy lesson".[3]

From mid 1864 the Movement was not only gaining strength in Taranaki and Wanganui, but was important enough to warrant the alliance of King Potatau II who took the name Tawhiao. Around this time Te Ua issued a proclamation stating that New Zealand was Canaan, The Book of Moses their laws, and the Maoris Jews. Te Ua's 'Book of Rura' was a careful concoction of appropriate texts and prophecies from "The Book of Genesis" and provided a 'biblical foundation' for Pai Marire.

A ceremony central to the 'belief' involved the whole congregation marching around a *niu* pole decorated with flags. This was accompanied by ritual chanting using a mish-mash of meaningless chants which were supposedly other languages that only the priests could speak. Some Christian prayers were utilised also. When the ceremony entered the critical phase, the pace of the marchers quickened as the emotion of the belief that they were being imbued with power which would protect them from Pakeha bullets took hold. Elements of self-hypnosis and a certain degree of mass hysteria, perhaps, can be noted in these ceremonies. In any case, ideal twin companions for a group with few numbers and fewer resources, and dedicated to the expulsion of a rapidly increasing European population.

Pai Marire was probably a necessary development for a race under the very real threat of extinction for it was the first Movement to *cut across* traditionally demarcated tribal lines in its natural appeal to sentiment and need. And if not this particular Movement, the conditions under which the Maori race lived at that particular time would probably have produced something very similar as the only perceived means by which their anguish could be assuaged. Therefore, in its own peculiar way, it set in place a relatively strong foundation for other religions to emerge, and from where political savvy would eventually develop. This the Maori would need for the later integration he sought.

At its grass-roots level, however, Pai Marire could almost be said to be *tohungaism* in a different form. Whilst it purported to embrace elements of Christianity it was, in fact, just an extension of all that the Maori race would need to let go of, if it was to achieve any degree of real spiritual growth. Moreover, whilst the name Pai Marire meant 'good and peaceful', the reality of its activities were not that at all. Of course, any name that a nationalistic-type group gives to itself does not detract from the need to fight and defend what might be passionately believed in.

In February 1866, Te Ua the prophet was captured and, probably to the disbelief of his followers, renounced the religion which he had founded. Moreover, he declared himself deluded when he formed his founding beliefs. With that admission much of his following and teachings died away. It was resurrected in part and surfaced later as more or less the foundation of the Hauhau faith.

One 'Lady Martin' opined that Pai Marire was the resultant outcome of the fanatical desperation of a people "...maddened by defeat, disease, and the confiscation of their land." It produced deeds of *whakamomori* – violent and reckless behaviour borne of desperation for a lost cause. We should note, however, that it also produced a greater sense of unity and perceived rightness of purpose. Ultimately, though, it paved the way for more substantial and lasting religions; one of which would answer all of Maoridom's entreaties **if**, at a future date, they would choose to embrace it completely and wholeheartedly.

---

[3]What is evidently missing in this line of reasoning is why bother with teaching English if only Maori were to inhabit the land. Perhaps it was for use with Pakeha traders who would still need to provide the desired trade goods.

18.1.7   Titokowaru (Hauhau)

The fanaticism that Pai Marire could generate perfectly suited the aims of Titokowaru. Since his avowed purpose was to clear the white man from the Taranaki district, the recruitment of fanatical warriors 'immune' to Pakeha bullets would logically negate the need for large numbers of fighting men – which he could not muster in any case. The desperation of fanatical *toa* produced acts of *whakamomori* amongst Titokowaru's followers too.

Titokowaru came to the notice of Military Authorities when he announced his intentions in a letter to Colonel George Whitmore in 1868. Titokowaru wrote thus:

> "You were formed a *pakeha*; and England was named for your country. We are Maoris, with New Zealand for our country. There has been fixed between you and us a great gulf, the ocean. Why did you not take thought before you crossed over to us? We did not cross hence over to you. Away with you from our land to your own country in the midst of the ocean."

(New Zealand's Heritage, p.932)

Titokowaru's strong Biblical leanings were evident in the way he ended his letters:

> "Arise, that you may be baptised, that your sins may be washed away, and call upon the name of the Lord."

(Making Peoples, Belich, p.221)

With this opening move and followers of the Pai Marire faith ready to help implement his goal, Titokowaru began his campaign to rid the 'confiscated lands' in Taranaki of the Pakeha. The overriding belief among Maori of the time that this new religion would achieve their aspirations is well illustrated in an address to Bishop Williams by one of the chiefs of the Opotiki district:

> "Bishop, many years ago we received the faith from you; now we return it to you, for there has been found a new and precious thing by which we shall keep our land."

(New Zealand's Heritage, p.932)

Fighting in the name of the Pai Marire Movement began in June 1868 when Titokowaru attacked colonists who had settled on confiscated lands near Patea. With this engagement, the ancient practice of cannibalism, which had virtually died out, was revived. A hapless trooper killed in the battle suffered the indignity of being eaten, though the Hauhaus left behind his legs. The revival of this practice pleased the older men within Titokowaru's group, although he did not consume human flesh. To ensure that the general populace understood the seriousness of his intent, he issued a proclamation which stated:

> "Cease travelling on the roads, ... lest ye be food for the birds of the air and for beasts of the fields, or for me. For I have eaten man – I have begun to eat the flesh of the white man..."

(New Zealand's Heritage, p.932)

Before the next battle of Turuturu-mokai redoubt, Titokowaru utilised psychic means to choose the 12 warriors who would spearhead the attack. Being both a *tohunga* and prophet, in the opinion of his followers he was ostensibly endowed with considerable power and *mana*. He also supposedly possessed a *magic taiaha*. The weapon would be balanced between thumb and forefinger and, after remaining motionless for a while, would slowly spin and stop, pointing to each chosen warrior in turn. The number 12 was a significant biblical one and if they held to the faith in prayer and obeyed his instructions, the chosen 12 would be protected from Pakeha bullets.

The dawn attack was successful and this battle marked the revival of yet another ancient, savage custom:

'...that of *whangai hau* – the offering of an enemy heart to the ancient god of war, Uenuku. This ceremony of the *mawe* involved the hacking out of the heart of an enemy, often the first killed, whence it would be singed, either by match or firestick. When it was slightly scorched, it would be thrown away.'

(From Kimble Bent, Cowan, p.116)

Thus, certain followers of the original Pai Marire faith, notably the Hauhaus under Titokowaru, further reduced the meaning of the name of that faith to one synonymous with mockery and hypocrisy – certainly not spirituality – in their particular brand of savage activities.

The return to the war practices of the past by the Hauhaus set in train similar kinds of retaliatory actions by those Maori who fought on the side of the Government. To counteract the terror which Titokowaru and his followers were instilling in the general populace and soldiery through cannibalism and the custom of *whangai hau*, a new tack was initiated. Major Te Rangihiwinui Kepa (also known as Major Kemp), angry at the Hauhau treatment of his dead, persuaded Colonel Whitmore to place a bounty on the heads of Titokowaru and his followers: 5 pounds for an ordinary person, 10 for a chief, and 1,000 pounds for Titokowaru himself. Not surprisingly, this overly generous offer for the times produced many volunteers eager for the opportunity to greatly increase meagre pay packets.

Once more the barbarity of the not-so-old days reared its ugly head as Government volunteers, Maori and Pakeha, hunted down the Hauhaus with relish, in the same manner that one would hunt a wild beast. Every man killed was beheaded and his head smoked. The 'cured' heads were duly delivered to Whitmore who had forgotten his promise to pay. However he did pay but ordered a halt to the practice. Whilst it was an ugly and grim development, in Military terms it served its purpose in breaking the back of the previously-fanatical resistance of the Hauhaus. Fighting in Taranaki ended in 1869, ironically after the murder of the missionary who had baptised Te Ua, the Rev. John Whiteley.

The Hauhau interpretation of the Pai Marire Movement perhaps produced one of the last episodes of the custom of swallowing the eyes of one's enemy. One Kereopa Te Rau, a leader of the Ngatirangiwewehi of the Arawa tribe, sought *utu* from the Pakeha for the deaths of relatives killed in a burning *whare* at the cessation of a battle in the Waikato in February 1864. The Pakeha chosen was the German missionary then working with the Church Missionary Society, the Rev. Carl Volkner. It was widely rumoured that he had sent information to the New Zealand authorities regarding the plans of local Maori, and was subsequently branded a spy. Upon his return to Opotiki from Auckland on 1st March 1865, he was taken prisoner along with the passengers and crew of the schooner *Eclipse*.

The next day Volkner was taken alone from the house where he was held to a willow tree near the church. Stripped of his coat and waistcoat and permitted a few moments to pray, he was unceremoniously hanged by Kereopa. Two witnesses, Captain Levy and the Rev. T. S. Grace, both recorded that Volkner's body was taken back towards the church and beheaded outside, with the tribes-people tasting or sprinkling themselves with his blood. Kereopa then gouged out Volkner's eyes and swallowed them. Cowan recorded an interesting twist of *utu* for Kereopa when an eyewitness stated to him that the second eye caught in Kereopa's throat and he needed water to wash it down.

Cowan further recorded that Volkner's blood was caught in the communion chalice, then the head and chalice were carried into the church. The head was placed on the reading desk from where Kereopa addressed the gathering with the words:

"We are the Jews who were lost and have been persecuted."

It was at this point that Cowan's eyewitness claimed that the eyes were swallowed. Kereopa called the first eye the Parliament of England and the second the law of New Zealand, after which he drank from the chalice of blood before passing it on to other Maori present.[4] Carl Volkner's head was dried and carried about by the 'good and peaceful' Pai Marire party for some time until it disappeared forever. Whilst those proceedings may have satisfied Kereopa's desire for *utu* according to ancient custom, we can observe that they carry some of the hallmarks of a satanic ritual where everything is reversed in a rather blasphemous parody of a Christian communion service.

After breaking the power of Hauhau resistance and declaring peace and amnesty, the Government continued to hunt for Kereopa, now termed Kaiwhatu the Eye-eater. When finally captured and placed on trial, William Colenso argued on his behalf that enough *utu* had already been exacted by both sides and that he should be spared. Despite that appeal for clemency by Colenso, Kereopa was sentenced to die. He was hanged in 1872.[5]

But what of Titokowaru? After the Government head-hunting phase, which effectively took away the fighting spirit of his followers – a good example of fighting fire with fire perhaps – he and a small band of about 40 followers set up camp on the Waitara River until the Government bought the land in 1875. Later he joined Te Whiti's campaign of passive resistance at Parihaka where he ran foul of the Government on a number of occasions. In 1885, during the last year of his life, Titokowaru made his peace with the Europeans at Opunake saying:

> "People of the township of Opunake, we show this day that peace is made... I will shower peace upon the people until the end of time – aye for ever... Europeans I will never hold but this stick in my hand."

> (New Zealand's Heritage, p.936)

However, he persisted in annoying Europeans by "...marching round the walls of Jericho..." – encircling the towns on horseback. Once more the old prophet and one-time feared Hauhau leader was arrested and imprisoned for a month. Upon his release he returned to his tribal homeland of Manaia. Now old and dying he sent for his Pakeha-Maori, Kimble Bent, who immediately went to the side of his old protector who enjoined him with his last words to:

> "Remain you here. I am going away. Do not desert the tribe. Remain with our people."

Shortly afterward, he died.

> (New Zealand's Heritage, p.936)

*   *   *   *   *

In terms of the thrust of this Work, and in concert with knowledge of **The Spiritual Laws**, it would be beneficial to quietly consider the fate of Titokowaru after his death. For he was directly responsible for the *re-sanctioning* of the barbarous practice of cannibalism, a custom which should have been left behind in the dying stages of it years before. For him, probably not a place in the sun, but more an untamed place of his own making, until such time as a genuine desire to want something better could awaken within him. We would hope that savage fighters *of all persuasions* might find such enlightenment.

---

[4]The swallowing of eyes so specifically named was probably a symbolic and superstitious attempt to gain power over the Pakeha forces then governing New Zealand. And the drinking of the missionary's blood ostensibly transferred Volkner's *mana* and knowledge to all who imbibed.

[5]It is interesting to note that upon his capture he believed that the catching of the second eye in his throat was not a good omen and he expected just such an end.

18.1.8 Te Maiharoa

A South Island Prophet who emerged about the mid 1860s and apparently greatly influenced by the Pai Marire Movement. Belich suggests that Te Maiharoa's Movement was a southern manifestation of the Hauhau faith.

Keith Newman, in his book, "Ratana Revisited – An Unfinished Legacy", writes of Te Maiharoa's prophecy about the future emergence of Ratana:

> The South Island prophet, Hipa Te Maiharoa, chief of the Waitaha, living at Arowhenua near Temuka, prophesied before his death in the late 1870's that 'A very little child will come forth under Taranaki mountain; he will finish my works for Jehovah.'

> He had also stated: 'The one who will save you all will come forth in the Taranaki area; he will bring with him that for which you have awaited so long, for he will be carrying with him two books.'

> (Ratana Revisited... p.38)

18.1.9 Te Kooti (Ringatu)

Te Kooti was born into the *hapu* of Ngati Maru – of Rongowhakaata at Pa-o-Kahu in Poverty Bay. Even before his birth, and perhaps as a precursor to Te Kooti's ordained role in Maoridom, certain possibilities were predicted by the seer, Toiroa of Nukutaurua. He divined the birth of two children within Ngati Maru, who would both suffer illness. Should the first born – of Te Turuki – die, and the second – of Te Rangipatahi – live, then evil would come to the land. The seer's prediction was fulfilled, even to the order of the births, which were adjudged to be a bad omen. The child so predicted was given the powerful name of **Arikirangi** by Toiroa.

According to legend, Te Kooti was rejected by his father who was said to have buried him alive in a *kumara* pit. He survived and was subsequently adopted by Te Turuki. Toiroa then performed the naming ceremony over him dedicating Arikirangi to Tumatauenga, Maori god of war. This particular dedication of such a powerfully-named individual to the 'god of war and of humankind' reveals a strongly accurate, divinatory aspect among some Maori seers. Especially so with Toiroa, in terms of the choice of the name, given Te Kooti's subsequent life-path. All races have produced such seers of course, and there is nothing particularly startling about such an ability if one *understands the lawful mechanism whereby this can occur*.

As we shall discover, however, this dual dedication of a powerful spiritual name to two dissimilar, almost opposing, concepts set in place much conflict for Te Kooti throughout his life. And, moreover, probably prevented him from *more completely* fulfilling his truly-ordained spiritual path.

As a young man Te Kooti attended the Whakato Anglican Mission and was evidently a keen student quickly acquiring a strong knowledge of The Scriptures. Even though receiving baptism in 1852 and harbouring thoughts of becoming a lay preacher, conflict with the Mission authorities prevented this outcome. Consequently, Te Kooti gained a reputation as being rather wild and turbulent and became embroiled in irritating misdemeanours with a similarly inclined group of young men living at Makaraka. They took great delight in relieving Pakeha of their possessions as *utu* for various grievances. Te Kooti's growing lawlessness precipitated a raid against his *pa* by some of the leading chiefs of the district.

But he also became involved in the sea trade with Auckland on two Maori-owned vessels which undercut the monopoly of two of the local settler's, J. W. Harris and Captain G. E. Read. This 'healthy competition' earned him the enmity of both Maori and Pakeha alike.

In the 1850s, he was reported to have been visited by the Archangel Michael who warned him that:

"...your people will be crushed by the weight of your deeds upon them ... and you will know
with certainty at that time I am a God who saves people."

Perhaps with that visitation, the oral traditions which stated that his turbulence was the
evil from which Divine intervention would later rescue him was fulfilled. The Archangel Michael
reportedly gave him the white lunar rainbow for his protection, and warned of civil war which
would soon visit Poverty Bay.

In 1865 most of Te Kooti's people of Ngati Maru embraced the new religion, Pai Marire.
Significantly, and perhaps foreshadowing his future destiny, Te Kooti did not. Neither did the
senior chief, Tamihana Ruatapu. Towards the end of that same year, Te Kooti fought with the
Government forces against the Hauhau (of the Pai Marire faith) at the siege of Waerenga-a-hika
near Gisborne. In an era of confused and divided loyalties, his elder brother fought with the
Hauhau inside the *pa*. Te Kooti was arrested as a spy after being accused by the Rongowhakaata
chief Paora Parau of supplying powder to the 'rebels'. Without proof he was released, but was
re-arrested the next year.

For his trouble, he was sent to the Chatham Islands with a number of Hauhau prisoners.
Whilst en-route to his new place, Te Kooti composed a *waiata* urging the people to

"...heed the "law of the Governor" which will make good the "...the work of Rura", the Pai
Marire god, who had brought all the "present trouble".

(Dictionary of New Zealand Biography, p.463 both.)

As many other prophets and religious leaders throughout history have discovered, a period
of confinement is often the precursor to the realisation of the mission. In such straitened circumstances, reasons and ideas, clairvoyant visions and/or intuitive perceptions may become clarified
and develop into clear directions or actions for the fulfilment of the calling. Thus it was that
this period of imprisonment was the catalyst for Te Kooti's emergence as the most significant
Maori Prophet of the time.

In early 1867, during bouts of fever, Te Kooti described how God 'heard his crying', and
how the "Spirit of God" raised him up. One account records how he miraculously emerged
from the hut where he lay ill and had received his inspirational messages, immediately after
which the hut burst into flames. Another account explains that this spirit gave him a flame that
would not burn, which he showed to the other prisoners. Accused by the prison authorities of
conducting religious services and rubbing phosphorous matches on his hands to represent God,
he was sentenced to solitary confinement. According to Ringatu accounts, he escaped each night
to hold religious services in the compound.

During his time in prison, Te Kooti formulated some of the creeds and directives that would
become the basis for his Church. The Old Testament and the writings of the Hebrew Prophets
provided a strong sense of spiritual kinship with Te Kooti's followers and their struggle. From
The Scriptures later emerged the significant Biblical number 12, so each 12th day was ordained
as a special day of prayer and worship. Through his seemingly strong and growing connection
with miraculous happenings and prophetic pronouncements, the former Pai Marire adherents
become converted to Te Kooti's Ringatu faith. What must have appeared as a mighty sign
of great power was the reported glowing of Te Kooti's upraised hand in the darkness during
religious services.

Thus whilst we may consider the Ringatu faith as a direct descendant of Pai Marire, it
retained only the upraised hand of its 'parent' religion; and that as a sign of homage rather than
to 'ward off bullets'. Perhaps Pai Marire can be seen as a bridge to the Ringatu religion – one
forged in battle and bloodshed.

Now sure of his mission and purpose, Te Kooti prepared plans for escape and awaited his
opportunity. On the 4th July, 1867, providence gave him his chance. He captured the prison

compound and all the guards, seized the supply ship *Rifleman*, and prepared to sail with his new prisoners and all of his own party – 163 men, 64 women and 71 children. The operation was clearly a masterly execution of exceptional planning and discipline. Only one guard was killed, against Te Kooti's orders. Taking only arms, ammunition and money, he set sail. However, fate was not to release him so quickly. Accounts state that fickle winds prevented the ship from making any real headway for between one to three days. Exhibiting both his new-found prophetic ability and that of the old Maori way, Te Kooti announced that only a sacrifice would bring the right winds. His uncle, Te Warihi Potini, (believed to be a spy) along with greenstone and other *taonga*, were thrown overboard.

This sacrifice evidently had the desired effect, for favourable winds appeared, and six days after the capture of the *Rifleman* they arrived back in Poverty Bay. After unloading the ship and paying off the Pakeha crew, Te Kooti gave thanks for their deliverance in the sacrifice of a pig and fowl. At this time he proclaimed that they would no longer kneel for prayer. The raising of the hand at the end of prayer would be the acknowledgement of their homage to God – hence the name Ringatu!

Failing to negotiate an effective peace agreement with the Government who demanded the surrender of all their arms, Te Kooti began his long campaign of guerrilla warfare, political manoeuvring within Maori tribal affiliations, and attempts to usurp the authority of the King Movement. The apparent failure of a Roman Catholic priest to effectively carry through a seemingly genuine offer of Governmental pardon to Te Kooti and his followers early in the conflict, ensured its continuation. Based in new fortifications at Puketapu, and being warned of a possible attack upon him, Te Kooti quite probably felt that he could not take the Government offer, delivered by Father Euloge Reignier's emissary trooper, as genuine. So, unfortunately through apparent faint-heartedness, a man of the cloth perhaps helped cement years of unnecessary conflict.

During this phase of warfare it is interesting to note that Te Kooti evidently placed no traditional Maori designs on his 'battle' flags, moving completely away from that influence. His new thinking encompassed what we might describe as designs more symbolic of world-religion motifs. And neither did he appear to place any traditional 'forms' on any subsequent flags or banners pertaining to his church or spiritual mission.

Yet despite that more enlightened direction during those troubled times of conflicting and divided loyalties, it is said that some of Te Kooti's 'ordered killings' – of even women and children – were religiously ordained, as were payment of some *utu*. So even with the new vision that he subscribed to, Maori ways still held too strong a hold for some of the more savage practices to be let go easily. During his campaign in the Tuhoe homelands, Te Kooti predicted that it would be they who would betray him – and so it came to pass. As the Tuhoe chiefs were forced to surrender they, in turn, were 'encouraged' to assist Government forces in their hunt for Te Kooti. Finally, in 1873, he accepted the pacifist ideas of King Tawhiao and renounced fighting.

Te Kooti was certainly an enigmatic man. Guerrilla leader, Prophet, visionary, trader, healer, promiscuous and with a liking for drink; he was, according to contemporary accounts, all of those. Whilst residing at Te Kuiti during the years from 1873 to 1883, Te Kooti formulated the final rituals of his Church, instituting 1st January and 1st July as the sacred days of the faith and later adding a planting and harvest festival. And as well as the already established Saturday Sabbath, every 12th day was designated as a sacred day. From that time his teachings began to spread and people came to listen and receive healing.

It was during the latter phase of his life that he began to predict the birth of a "good and peaceful child" who would possess 'very great powers'. This new Prophet, moreover, would appear in the Bay of Plenty. Not surprisingly, this prediction produced many claimants. Te Kooti had also prophesied his own death by accident. Resting in the shade of a cart, he suffered fatal injuries when it moved and fell, or rolled over, onto him. He died two weeks later on the

17th April 1893. Towards the end of his life he reminded his followers of the need to acknowledge the law.

> "The canoe for you to paddle after me is the Law. Only the Law can be set against the Law."

In conclusion, Te Kooti might well have achieved far more for his people in the truly *spiritual sense* had he totally embraced the powerful name given to him by Toiroa. The name we are given is who we actually are in terms of the 'meaning and form' *produced* by our name. Therefore the spiritual *meaning and form* of our name is what we are ordained *to fulfil.* We may come closer to a better understanding of this concept in the *spiritual sense* once again if we take cognisance of the Creation-Words: – **"Let There Be Light!"** And how those Words permitted the Creation-process to be fulfilled. Those four Words, *imbued with the 'living power' of The Creative Divine Will,* contained the building blocks for every aspect of Creation – from the Higher Spiritual down to the lowest of the material.

So, too, does each individual's name also resonate in the outworking of **The Law**, the *same* that Te Kooti urged his followers to heed after his passing. Thus, Te Kooti's use of different names at various times actually produced for him a weaker, confused *form* which lacked any real and concentrated power. Te Kooti might have been the name for a *fighter* of the times, but it was the name *Arikirangi* that he should have used *exclusively.*

The name Arikirangi was ordained for him that he might *more powerfully* fulfil his destiny as a true *spiritual leader* for the Maori race *at that time.* The spiritual parameters encompassing the meaning of the name, Arikirangi, permitted the granting to him of the protection of the "white lunar rainbow of the night", and was clearly not without purpose.

Therefore, only in the correct use of his *spiritual* name could the connection with the protective umbrella of the "white lunar rainbow" be effectively utilised in the fulfilment of what should have been the primary consideration in his life – **his spiritual task**! Failing to do so only 'scattered his energies' i.e., his ability to fulfil his mission.

Notwithstanding this, perhaps, inadvertent failure and/or non-understanding on his part, Te Kooti Arikirangi clearly stands out as a vital and key prophet in the line of Maori Religious Prophets. His lasting legacy, therefore, was one where the new spiritual direction for Maori was strongly and unequivocally shaped by his life and deeds, thus greatly influencing those Prophets which immediately followed him.

In later life, however, it seems clear that he understood that he was either not the person who was to be the key spiritual leader, or that he had not completely fulfilled his ordained task, because his latter predictions accurately pointed to another from Maoridom who would arise to fulfil that role.

Years later, that man would arise exactly as Te Kooti prophesied – in **Ratana**!

18.1.10   Te Whiti

> "The New Zealand Settlements Act, 1863, provided the legal mechanism for the 'confiscation' of land belonging to 'rebel' Maori. In total, 3,215,172 acres of Maori land were confiscated in the Waikato, Taranaki and the Bay of Plenty, and on the East Coast. Of this figure, 1,341,362 acres were subsequently purchased or returned to 'loyal' Maori."

> (New Zealand's Heritage, p.1094)

Confiscation was simply a legalised form of stealing, and the Government had both the numbers and the arms to achieve that end.

It is against this background that we briefly examine the emergence of the last of the major Maori Prophets of the 19th Century, Te Whiti o Rongomai. Born in 1831 at Ngamotu near

New Plymouth, this particular Prophet followed the course of most of the others. He received a reasonably thorough grounding in The Scriptures under the tutelage of the German Protestant Minister, the Rev. J.C. Riemenschneider. Oral traditions indicate that Te Whiti was involved in battle in possibly two of the Taranaki engagements in the 1860s. Perhaps the experience of it provided the basis for his determination that there was nothing to be gained from fighting.

Subsequent to this decision, he withdrew inland to Parihaka with the intention of studying The Scriptures in peaceful seclusion to try to find a way whereby peace might be brought to his troubled land. There, he formulated his ideas for peace and progress through non-violent pacifism long before Gandhi was lionised for his monumental efforts. History records that Te Whiti's knowledge of The Bible was considerable. That erudition, coupled with an exceptional memory, enabled him to recite vast passages from Genesis to Revelation verbatim.

Whilst The Bible was the source of his speeches and inspiration, he was also a gifted orator who could hold the attention of crowds for hours on end. He was not, however, a "fire and brimstone" preacher. Rather, his gift to captivate lay in his grasp of the language and traditions, and in his skill and ability to clearly enunciate every syllable so that all he said could be heard even at a distance. The Bible was his constant companion. It was a book he clearly loved and was probably the greatest influence in his life. Its natural companion was his unshakeable belief in God, and was the single most important facet of his existence. The ease with which he could extract and quote from the vast knowledge contained in The Bible was unsettling for many Europeans who did not like to admit that their own knowledge was inferior to Te Whiti's. For at that time in history, religion played a very large part in the social structure.

An unfortunate consequence of Te Whiti's ability was that he was often quoted as referring to himself as God, or Christ, or both, when in fact he was only quoting from The Bible. One of Te Whiti's more famous "alleged" prophecies was supposedly to predict that all Pakeha would one day be swept into the sea. When asked about this, he was most upset, shouting at his interviewer:

> "Who told you this execrable untruth? Pakeha perverters, no doubt. What I said and wished to convey was, that the two races should live side by side in peace ... the white man to live among us – not we to be subservient to his immoderate greed."

> (New Zealand's Heritage, p.1361)

Whilst he did speak of a day of resurrection when Maori land and dignity would be restored, his primary aim was to help his people through a very difficult time of transition. During a brief period of incarceration, he made note of all the features of European civilisation that were obviously sensible, with the view to adopting them for the betterment of his people. And he decided to learn all he could of the White man's graces, including table etiquette. But perhaps the single most important aspect of this man was his recognition that, if the Maori were to take their rightful place in this new order with any sense of dignity and grace, *they would need to adopt many of the customs and ideas of the European.*

Consequently, after his release from detention, he introduced many Pakeha customs to Parihaka, even promoting such a radical idea as taking their illnesses to European doctors. Te Whiti's faith and trust in God is well illustrated in a remark he made to people who enquired as to what he liked most after a tour of the comparatively industrialised and modern church, even travelling on the railway and tramway. He replied, "the river".

> *"All these things are very grand, no doubt, and very useful, but they are the work of man's hands, and will perish; the river is God's work, and will last long after the things you mention ... will have passed away."*

> (New Zealand's Heritage, p.1362 [Emphases mine.])

Te Whiti's unshakeable belief and faith in the natural world of The Creator offered the means whereby he could present a seemingly meaningful reason why Maori had to suffer such "great tribulation". His message to his people was one of acceptance of God's Will. In accordance with his interpretation of The Bible, God had ordained that all men should suffer, not only Maori. Other races had suffered too, and that was God's plan for them as well. But out of that suffering was granted the promise that it could be turned into a struggle of virtue from which Maori would attain grace, and gain all that they aspired to. All that was needed was faith.

Thus, through Te Whiti's influence and explanations, the God of the Pakeha became a God who also helped Maori and who would be with them always. Te Whiti was His spokesman; it was through him Whom God spoke. Therefore Maori would always be protected from the greed and evil of the Pakeha.

Te Whiti's singular success in effecting such a huge transition of thinking is all the more remarkable in that he was dealing with a people generally regarded as fiercely independent, unafraid to take the war-trail, and only a few years removed from very savage practices. Soon to be tested by the Pakeha, their response would reveal whether they fully believed Te Whiti's teachings.

> "Parihaka is the cleanest pa I have ever visited... The inhabitants are the finest race of men I have ever seen in New Zealand."

> (New Zealand's Heritage, p.1352)

Thus wrote the Taranaki Medical Officer in his description of the village of Parihaka. Modelled on European ideas as was Te Whiti's aim, the village had sign-posted streets, the lanes were swept regularly and all waste removed. Unlike other Maori villages of the time, there was little illness among the inhabitants. Alcohol was forbidden so there was *no drunkenness*, and people were quiet and industrious. Large gardens of wheat, potatoes and melons covered hundreds of acres. The only snag to such an idyllic existence was that Parihaka was on 'confiscated land' and the Government demanded that Te Whiti and his people leave.

Now came the time of testing. The Government agencies knew there were no arms in the village, therefore a direct attack to force Te Whiti's people to move was out of the question. Nevertheless, the relatively large number of inhabitants, numbering about 2,500, could pose a potential problem for troops attempting to remove them by force. Prior to that stage, however, the Government began the process of surveying the land for eventual sale. Promising that reserve land would be put aside for them, the Government surveyors began their work. This necessarily meant cutting survey lines through crops. Initially believing the Government, the residents of Parihaka left the surveyors alone calmly repairing the damage wrought by them each time they completed their work. However, as the surveying continued on into months with no sign of alternative land being made available, Te Whiti's people sensed the inevitable looming confrontation.

Frustrated in their efforts to impose its will upon the people of Parihaka, the Government enacted legislation to arrest any persons obstructing the work of the surveyors. As each Maori repair party was arrested, another would take its place the next time. Realising that the land was well and truly lost to them, Te Whiti's people accepted more and more arrests in the knowledge that armed resistance would be futile and would simply provide the excuse for a blood-bath. With the gaols becoming overcrowded, the Government found itself in a dilemma. Dealing with an armed uprising was a simple matter, not so with a peaceful protest where those arrested cheerfully went off to goal. Finally admitting defeat, the Government released them all.

However, the problem of Parihaka remained, and a reason needed to be found to remove the village and its people. That occurred on 17th September 1881 when the normal monthly meeting was convened. Here, Te Whiti's speech was taken out of context and reported widely as a call to war. "Maoris, take your guns and weapons. Pakehas, come with yours. By weapons alone will things be arranged.", Te Whiti was reported to have said. Unfortunately his next sentence, and the most critical given the tension building over the continuing stand-off, was not reported in the National Press:[6]

> "...goodness was the only weapon which should be victorious."

With such seemingly inflammatory words from the 'rebels', the stage was set for potentially serious conflict.

Once more rejecting odious Government overtures, Te Whiti prepared for the inevitable arrival of the soldiers. Assembling his people on the marae, they waited quietly. When the troops arrived at about 7.30 the next morning, the soldiers found the fences already pulled down to allow them unrestricted access. Also waiting were 500 loaves of freshly baked bread. The last act of the troops before entering the village was to carefully lift out of the way 200 singing and skipping children. Seated calmly on the ground, Te Whiti and his followers waited patiently as the Riot Act, calling on them to disperse, was read.

Tohu, one of the leaders, rose and advised the people:

> "Let the man who has raised the war do his work this day... Let none of us stir... Even if the bayonet comes to your breast do not resist."

No one moved and no action took place until about 11.30 when the arresting party finally moved toward the leaders. A clear passage was immediately made for them. And Te Whiti and Tohu and their wives quietly accompanied their captors. Te Whiti's parting words were brief:

> "Work such as this...", he said, "...is frustrated this day."

> (New Zealand's Heritage, p.1357 all.)

The remainder of Te Whiti's people refused to move, even under threat of being fired on, but two days later forced removal by mass arrest began. One of the constabulary officers later recalled that the whole process was "...like drafting sheep." As the men were removed, houses were demolished. Evidence suggests that women were molested, and some possibly raped. The land reserves promised, whilst eventually granted, were cleverly tied up in perpetual leases offering minuscule return to the 'Maori owners', thus prolonging the pain of confiscation. In reality, still dispossession, but by other means! The invasion of Parihaka effectively marked the end of Maori resistance to Government rule in Taranaki.

Te Whiti's group was detained for over a year in the South Island, but without any real charge against them were released.

The whole unsavoury incident begs the question: What did the Government achieve? Te Whiti was a very gifted man who produced a model village that should have been *encouraged* as the blueprint for other Maori tribes. Working *with* this man, rather than against him, Government Ministers could have enlisted his aid as an adviser in their dealings with difficult Maori issues. Perhaps the Government Ministers of the time were still far too entrenched in the ideas of the class structure which riddled "Mother England" *to fully understand or appreciate the truly amazing event that they were historically connected to at Parihaka.*

Some 18 years later Parihaka was described in glowing terms by an enthusiastic visitor thus:

> "A good macadamized road leads one to the village, where one observes well laid out streets and wooden residences built in the best European style.

---

[6]Sensationalism in reporting, very much alive and well today, was clearly also "very much alive and well" back in Te Whiti's time.

In the large dining halls, one could dine on roast meats, plum pudding and jam tarts; tea and coffee were served afterwards by courteous Maori waiters. The village had "...its bake, slaughter and butcher houses, blacksmith shops etc., the different houses getting their water supply from a very fine reservoir... The waste water from the reservoir is shortly to be utilised for lighting Parihaka with electricity."[7]

(New Zealand's Heritage, p.1357)

Whilst Te Whiti and his people won a notable psychological victory over the Government of the day, the greater personal achievement for Te Whiti was the inculcating of *immense spiritual strength* in a people who, traditionally and historically, were easily given to *retaliation by force*, often over trivial things. It is a measure of the man and his people that they could watch their leaders taken into captivity and their homes destroyed, and still hold to genuine *mana* in the acceptance of a vile deed by an ignorant and oppressive regime.

Moreover, in very stark contrast to all previous Maori Prophets, Te Whiti could be said to be the first to quite clearly and visibly cut strong and lingering ties to the psychic past. For him, there could be no snake through which an old Hebrew prophet would speak. Neither could there be a dried head of a slain enemy through whom God would issue His instructions, or a human sacrifice for the wind, or even an animal sacrifice in thanksgiving.

Te Whiti was able to make a truly quantum leap away from the barbaric and savage customs of the past by instituting a totally alien concept – especially for Maori of that time – of "...doing unto others...", and "...love for one's enemies". Thus where *utu* would no longer be used against an aggressor. We might perhaps term such a concept the "Christ ideal". To turn the other cheek must have seemed very, very much to expect – or even to ask – of a proud militaristic race in the face of such extreme provocation by a truly *inept and incompetent* government.

Yet Te Whiti achieved it!

In doing so he and the people of Parihaka stood 'tall and proud', thoroughly shaming the Colonial administrators who had ordered the confiscation of the land. 'Tall and proud', too, against the Military and surveyors sent to execute the Government ministers' directive; all of whom probably regarded Te Whiti as a simple, deluded fool.

*   *   *   *   *

Te Whiti and Parihaka stand together as a singularly-powerful spiritual <u>event</u> in the history of this country! It stands as an undying symbol of grace, nobleness and dignity triumphing over selfish, grasping greed under the hypocritical umbrella of so-called Legislative Law.

*   *   *   *   *

Te Whiti was clearly a truly spiritual man of great *mana*, yet, in my view, still probably *unrecognised* for his *true greatness*. The spiritual legacy he left behind for Maori, therefore, will forever remain as a bright shining light, in stark contrast to the dark, savage butchery of inter-tribal warfare and cannibalism bequeathed to "Maori history" by so-called 'great chiefs'.

His spiritual legacy, moreover, helped to anchor over the land a beneficial yet unseen "form" for Maori, a cloak of growing spiritual *mana* that a future, especially chosen one would, initially at least, reluctantly take up and wear. He would be the one who would provide virtually the final key as to how Maori *could become* a genuinely *spiritual* Nation, and not remain just a collection of disparate tribes. But the question would still nonetheless surface: Would all of

---

[7] As an interesting aside, the promise of electricity for Parihaka was there in 1899. It was not until 1956 that this writer's *whanau* home received electricity!

Maoridom recognise this future event in its unequivocal greatness, or would Maori still choose to cling to the tribal way? That would be the final question!

Although Te Whiti was perhaps the most notable of the Maori Prophets who emerged in the latter half of the 19th century, certain others enjoyed brief times of prominence.

The Maori King, **Tawhiao,** who established his own Tariao (Morning Star) faith in 1875 in preparation for the return of confiscated Waikato lands, was also a Prophet. A version of Parihaka was established at Te Kumi in the King Country in 1883 by **Te Mahuki**, one of Te Whiti's 'ploughmen'. The belief that the dead would rise up to defeat the Pakeha and avenge Waitara emanated from there.

A Wairarapa Prophet called **Pareha** prophesied a great flood which would drown all Pakeha and leave Maori to re-inherit the land. And in 1885, **Maria Pungare**, a Prophet from the Kaitaia area proclaimed the imminence of a second coming.[8]

It is interesting to note that the development of the various Maori Religious Movements, in terms of specific areas of ritual and worship formulated as being appropriate for them, retrace the path of certain practices long condemned by some of the mainstream Christian Churches. Moreover, if we take from each Movement those particular practices which accord purely with **The Spiritual Laws** – of which we have given clear explanation – we end up with a good beginning for a true Church of Worship.

For example, the establishment of the planting and harvest festivals by Te Kooti within the rituals of the Ringatu Church has long been regarded by some churches as the practice of animism or, worse, blasphemous paganism. Yet the very **Laws of Creation** provide plants and animals to feed and sustain the lives of *all* creatures on this earth, including man. Therefore, what better way to show gratitude for the gift of life than to have such festivals. Even those Church officials who made narrow condemnatory determinations about them naturally needed to *eat* of the bounty of the earth provided by The Creator. Church officials today must also partake of the same bounty.

Quite logically, the worship should not be of the plants *themselves*, but as an acknowledgement of the goodness and grace for the gift of life itself. The idea that such practices be regarded as unchristian or pagan smacks of the same kind of bigotry and narrow-mindedness that gave life to the barbarity of The Dark Ages and The Inquisition. Festivals of this kind would surely offer a further tier of perhaps more genuine worshipping of The Creator for the gift of life – in all its wonderful permutations – than sometimes appears to be the case today. Perhaps Te Kooti, or Arikirangi, should be commended for his insight, and planting and harvesting festivals introduced 'across the board' once more.

The final legacy of the rise of the Maori Religious Movement, which in turn stemmed from the teachings and activities of the missionaries, was the transformation of the new ideas – the new reality perhaps – into political awareness and what could derive from that process. Whilst the emergence of those Movements made progress towards the uplifting of Maori aspirations in the new era, it could not, by itself, achieve the goal completely. So, towards the end of the 19th century, the focus centred on the need for another renaissance, a political one. With that realisation, the beginnings were sown with the formation of the Young Maori Party. Out of this would arise 'a new kind of Maori', a politically astute one.

But would this new development, alone, offer more for the Maori than the Religious Movements? Or would political power and the Law Courts still not satisfy an indefinable and often angry quest for something 'lost', and which Maori generally 'believe' to be 'their land'?

---

[8]This is generally thought to be Kenana and Ratana.

If we quietly allow our present thread to lead us forward, we will finally discover, and clearly recognise, what **really** has been lost! For the moment, however, let us briefly examine the effect of Rua Kenana – one more of the influential Prophets – before we join the life and times of the last and greatest of the line: **Ratana**!

18.1.11   Rua Kenana

Rua emerged in the 1900s as a successor to Te Kooti in the leadership of the Ringatu Church. By 1907 he had established a community of about 600 people at Maungapohutu on the sacred Stone Mountain of Tuhoe. Exercising complete independence in the rejection of Pakeha laws and taxes, he established, instead, other basic tenets that were instrumental in the promotion of peaceful and progressive policies. To this end he embraced the Pakeha ideas of trade and agriculture, and attempted mining and banking ventures.

In the new era of political law and order, such a community, by virtue of its influence, posed potentially larger problems than those which actually existed. Consequently, this kind of dissenting-opposition precipitated action against Rua and his followers. In 1916 – during the First World War – a Police contingent, some armed with rifles, marched against the community. In Military style, three columns converged on Maungapohutu, with the main column strength consisting of 57 officers. Whilst the 'defenders' had some shotguns loaded with birdshot only, they did not seek confrontation. Nevertheless, during the arrest of Rua, a more serious gun-fight than expected broke out in which two Maori were killed and two or more wounded. The engagement also wounded four Police.

The subsequent trial of Rua was so controversially suspect that even Pakeha were outraged. Nevertheless, Rua was convicted and gaoled. After his release in 1918 he spent his remaining years up to his death in 1937 struggling to maintain his Movement. Despite the difficulties, the Ringatu Church, of which Rua was the last custodian of note, continues on to this day.

18.2   Conclusion

It is crucial to recognise that, even though most of the Religious Prophets were important for their time, each was just *one voice* contributing to a long line of *continually evolving development* toward a final, genuinely spiritual point for Maori. Therefore, to cling to Papahurihiaism, for example, long after the path of religious development had totally eclipsed that particular Prophet's archaic ideas not far removed from *tohungaism*, is to remain *isolated* from the greater knowledge available today.

Maori of each time period, therefore, should only have embraced that which was currently *at its height of development for the particular time*, and then recognised the next step in the ongoing spiritual developmental process, which we opine was actually ordained for Maori.

The obvious extension to this factual premise means that it is crucial for Maori to have *left behind* all aspiritual aspects of the teachings of all those Prophets outlined in this Chapter – and the *complete rejection* of some of the more bizarre ideas – if they wish to possess **the greater spiritual knowledge currently available**. In any case, those points contained within the teachings of all past Maori Religious Movements that accord with **The Truth of Spiritual Law**, can and should be *brought forward and added to*, step by step, through the later teachings of the succeeding Prophets of note.

A purely objective analysis of what we have espoused should therefore offer a logical, spiritual direction for Maori, irrespective of possible emotional, personal, *whanau* or *Iwi* connections to any of the Prophets mentioned.

Therein lies the key to the future for Maori!

A spiritual future clearly and powerfully proclaimed by the clarion call of **Ratana**, the one more strongly connected to the knowledge of The Truth than all the others. They, however, *evolved* the Movement and set in place the general signposts leading to **Ratana**.

He, in turn, anchored the final signpost *pointing the way* to The Living Law Itself! Maori were thus finally presented with two choices; that of the *direction* **Ratana** pointed to – or to any other. Perhaps the ultimate **50% choice**, and **100% outcome** – for Maori!

Finally, all that is spiritually worthwhile and necessary will have been totally encompassed and elucidated within the spiritual power of the 'Calling' of **Ratana** in any case. For his was the greatest extension into the more complete knowledge that Maori vitally needed for genuine enlightenment. Quite obviously it is not for me or anyone else to decry a particular belief or religion that one may *wish* to adhere to, *and that we do not do here either*. Respect for all beliefs is a prerequisite for mutual tolerance in any society.

That notwithstanding, the emergence, 'Spiritual Calling', life, mission and achievements of **Ratana** – and thus his subsequent legacy – **simply cannot be denied!**

19
Ratana

"I have opened the door, but you yourselves must go in. I am but a finger post pointing to the true way of life!"

(Ratana: J.M. Henderson.)

"Soon, very soon in the future you will no longer speak, but instead a very different person [generation] will reveal to you all the fruits of these prophecies. Not only will it be revealed exclusively to you the morehu only, no but to the whole country..."[1]

(T.W. Ratana, 1929. "Ratana Revisited: An Unfinished Legacy": Keith Newman. [Parenthetic addition mine.])

Key Note:

Because of the importance of this Chapter to a deeper understanding of the *true purpose* for this complete Work, Ratana and his Mission will be examined in greater detail. Once again, of course, from the infallible standpoint of **The Spiritual Laws of Creation**. That, however, will be our analysis in the latter part of the Chapter. The first segment will offer a brief background to that relevant time, followed by a general outline of his life and achievements.

The life and times of Tahupotiki Wiremu Ratana represents the *pivotal point* of this Work. Ratana's clear recognition of his Calling and its subsequent fulfilment to an astounding degree by this leader and Prophet *pointed the way* to the Title of the book. Paradoxically, however, his task and his correct spiritual and material vision for the Maori race could not possibly have arisen for Maori **without the arrival of the Pakeha**.

For with the Pakeha came The Bible and the far greater knowledge and connections to the Higher Spiritual Spheres contained within it. Notwithstanding the ancient Maori 'knowledge' that **Io** *ostensibly* offered, and what that *should* have translated to in everyday pre-European life – but very unfortunately did not – the Pakeha Bible holds a degree of knowledge Maori did not at all possess. Only with access to that especial Book – inadvertently facilitated by **Hongi Hika** – *could* the line of Maori Religious Prophets arise to, step by step, lead the race slowly

---

[1] The reader should carefully note that the above prophecy, proclaimed in 1929, was so proclaimed after the completion of the Temple in 1928 when Ratana evidently announced that *his spiritual works were over*.

away from the spiritually-dead of the old. Away from the madness of *blood-utu*, the barbarity of cannibalism and the debilitating servile and fear-ridden slavery to *makutu*, and away from much pointless, superstitious *tapu*.

Without the changes that necessarily took place within the psyche of the race through such a major external upheaval as *the event* of **'The Coming of The Pakeha'** – thereby changing the thinking and lifestyle which was previously the norm for Maori – there could be no opportunity for more spiritually-enlightened souls such as Te Whiti and Ratana to be born into the race for the high purpose of offering the true way forward. Not only for Maori, but for Pakeha also. For no Pakeha in this land emerged as clearly and decisively as did Ratana to lead the way forward, not even for their own people. Nor did any arise from within the mainstream churches. The Pakeha simply continued on the same religious path he had always known!

Little had changed for the Pakeha in terms of genuine spiritual enlightenment for hundreds of years. For the Maori, however, from out of the fearful darkness of the old way, a whole new and fresh universe was suddenly available through a few especially guided ones – *if Maori were sufficiently awake to recognise and embrace it*. Thus from out of the ranks of Maoridom, an ostensibly ordinary man of the land arose who would have the innate strength and ability for such an incredible undertaking.

In my serious and absolutely unequivocal view, therefore, it should be with very crucial intent that Maori, particularly – but also the Pakeha – vitally concern themselves with the *true meaning* of Ratana's mission, and thereby strive to fully understand what he really achieved in his spiritual fulfilment of it. For out of **Pakeha ranks** arose two men whose souls, also in my serious opinion, were sufficiently moved to want to document this man's Calling and Mission *for all in this land*.

The two Pakehas are:
  J. M. Henderson:[2]
  "Ratana. The Man, the Church, the Political Party."

  – and Keith Newman's:
  "Ratana Revisited: An Unfinished Legacy".

Unfortunately, because of the spiritually destitute state of our society now wallowing in its self-created immoral swamp, Ratana's true achievements and the momentous nature of his life and Calling have not yet been fully understood or appreciated. I would even venture to say that many in the Ratana Church itself do not fully understand the *true nature* of his "Calling".[3]

Even though the *greatest potential* of his mission **was never realised**, the day will nevertheless come when Maori, particularly, will look back and offer grateful and heartfelt thanks that this man, Tahupotiki Wiremu Ratana, *did not shrink away in superstitious fear* from the stupendous and wonderful task he was ordained to fulfil. That day, from the moment of Ratana's prophecy about "...the one in the future who would reveal all the fruits of the prophecies...", *was established to be at the release of this Work*.

Will Ratana's truly great mission ever be really understood? Or will Ratana followers, and Maoridom generally, continue on as before, not recognising the true spiritual meaning of Ratana's vocation? Will there need to be more heartache for the race before the necessary question must be asked more desperately than perhaps it is at present: **Why?** – or – **Why us?**

---

[2]Much of the basic information about Ratana was sourced from J. M. Henderson's very important work.

[3]During a recent discussion with a Maori member of the Jehovah's Witness Church, I learned that *that* particular person, though part of a whanau which *belonged* to the Ratana Church, was nevertheless still exposed from birth to the very Maori superstitions that Ratana himself *directed* all Church members to let go. Because of the great fear thereby experienced, this particular person left the Ratana Church and will thus probably not now know or recognise the true magnitude of that Prophet's great Calling and Spiritual Mission – a 'Calling' from out of **The Light Itself!**

Within the pages of this Work, but more particularly in this Chapter, sufficient explanation and insight has been given to answer the question *why*, without the need for more unnecessary heartache to force such a plea. We sincerely hope that you, the reader, will readily see what Ratana proclaimed; that he **was** a true signpost pointing the way forward.

This book, the third in a somewhat spiritually-guided, *multi-authored 'trilogy'* about the man and his mission, is a signpost too. As the last of the three, however, it is not only one that along with the other two works unequivocally *recognises* the great spiritual nature of Ratana's mission; but is one which, *whilst necessarily complementing his work,* **also extends it.** As the author of a Work in which Ratana occupies the *pivotal* Chapter, it is **my** spiritual task and Mandate to ensure that **his** true spiritual purpose is given the 'mana' it actually carries; thus to forcefully bring it to the attention of Maoridom, especially, in a way that has not been done before.

Despite the fact that the three writings do state the spiritual nature of Ratana's mission so emphatically, it is nonetheless clear from the books of J.M. Henderson and Keith Newman,[4] particularly, that very much valuable information about this remarkable man is still withheld and/or suppressed by the Ratana Church hierarchy, thus the family primarily.

That begs the question:
"Who should own the revelations and prophecies from the one 'Called' by the 'Light Above' for this land and its peoples?"

In being 'Called to Service', Ratana was duty-bound to give all, just as He Whom he professed to serve – **Jesus, The Son of God** – gave all; *without which* Ratana could not possibly have fulfilled to the degree in which he did.

Withholding or suppressing information or revelatory proclamation about and/or from the one *directed to destroy tohungaism* smacks of the very practices that some modern-day tohunga and even kaumatua indulge in; their 'knowledge' supposedly too dangerous, too sacred or too 'something-else' for others to have. We can therefore surely accept that Ratana would not have sanctioned the withholding of his proclamations by the Church and Movement he founded – by virtue of the fact that he publicly proclaimed quite prolifically. So it is difficult to understand why those within the Ratana Church who hold such information are reluctant to release it to the public arena where it rightly belongs.

As we have strongly stated earlier in the book, *nothing given from the Light Above* – from where all Ratana followers no doubt believe he *derived* his key prophecies – *should be withheld from human knowledge.* In the final analysis, therefore, suppression of information from and about Ratana – *especially* of his mission and prophecies – by the Ratana Church hierarchy, is simply **tohungaism by another name**!

*   *   *   *   *

At the beginning of the 20th century, a vitally necessary Maori renaissance for the survival of the race itself seemed to be directed toward the political arena, and a few astute, young educated Maori recognised the need and took up the challenge. On the surface it appeared that future Maori leaders would emerge from the political arena rather than through the previously accepted religious path. However, the death knell of the Maori Religious Prophetic Movement could not be sounded yet. Rua Kenana's Movement, which emerged in 1906, was clear testimony to this.

In Ratana's case, even with his followers *very wrongly* believing him to be the Younger Brother of Christ and possibly even the Holy Ghost; with his death in 1939 also died the vital

---

[4]Keith Newman's new book: 'Ratana – the prophet' [Penguin].

essence of his Movement. Given the strong Maori connections to 'other-world' beliefs, it would be unrealistic to assume that those kinds of ideas would completely die out. Such a demise would not be desirable, since *all* human beings are actually strongly-connected to that 'world' anyway and must therefore at least know that it is so. A complete denial or turning away from beliefs concerning the *reality* of the intangible 'other world' would be more disastrous than retention of such a notion, even with distorted knowledge about it. Distortions can be rectified, outright disbelief is more difficult to address.

The years leading up to Ratana's emergence as a new Prophet, whilst hopeful for slowly increasing Maori population from a dangerously low ebb, were still marked by a high infant mortality rate and generally poor health, housing and education standards. The old devils of *makutu* and *utu* still held the general populace in superstitious thrall, and the many *tapu* areas were similarly feared. Yet even with those fears, such was the generally poor overall plight of the Maori that *tohunga* were often turned to for relief. So overwhelming was the belief in *tohungaism* as some kind of possible saving grace that M.P. Pomare lobbied for the Tohunga Suppression Act to be enacted. With more land loss after 1910, however, some communities landless and no help forthcoming from a seemingly uncaring Pakeha-dominated Government, the increasing wish to return to *tohungaism* was a perfectly understandable and seemingly better alternative. The plight of Maori was not helped by some groups spending all of the proceeds of land sales on alcohol, so that both the land and the money were lost.

Whilst many Maori were baptised and many more were 'formal' Christians, the true belief actually still leaned more toward the familiar of the old, or a mix of the two as formulated by the different prophets of the past. Further, the few Maori clergy that were available could not adequately address the deeper psychic problems developing from a growing feeling of despair – perhaps because they had become too steeped in Pakeha life and official Church orthodoxy to want to really understand. It was against that background under which Ratana lived out his early life experiences still yet unaware of the 'task' that would dramatically come to him in the near future. Sad and straitened circumstances would ensure that despairing Maori *would* heed the words of this new prophet.

The emergence of a such a man had been foretold by a number of Maori prophets. Aperahama Taonui, a famous prophet of Ngapuhi, in 1863 delivered the following address:

> "O chiefs of the Ngapuhi, listen to me; let not the Treaty of Waitangi be covered by the flag but let it be enshrined in a cloak of this land... Seeing that you Ngapuhi will not listen to me, a spider will inhabit this house. There is a man coming, however, who will be carrying two books: the Bible and the Treaty. You will listen to him."

And Te Kooti Arikirangi had said in 1893 just before his death:

> "From Katikati to Cape Runaway (i.e., from one limit of the Mataatua district to the other) there will be one child. If he arrives within six years there will be great tribulation. If his advent does not take place within that time, in twenty six years he will arise from the west and unite the people."

> (Ratana: J.M. Henderson, p.12)

In 1912, Mere Rikiriki, *tohunga* leader of the Holy Ghost Mission also prophesied about the imminent emergence of this "chosen prophet", in fact her own nephew, with the following words; page 14:

> "O ye people (of Ngati Apa), hasten to me your prophetess of peace. A time will come when the Child (or Chosen Man) will take action directly and strongly and with a great mission, without favouritism, he will be more than a man in his attributes."

Keith Newman's book records much the same prophecy.

> 'O people hasten to me, I am a woman, and being so, I minister unto you as a woman would to her own child. For beware! The time is near when a young man will rise in my place; when he comes there will be weeping and gnashing of teeth; when he comes the true and false will never survive together, neither with righteous and the unrighteous, nor doctrines that are of God and the doctrines of man and the Devil.'

Tahupotiki Wiremu Ratana was born on the 25th January 1873. He was the grandson of a *rangatira* and related to all the Manawatu and South Taranaki tribes. His parents were of the Church of England and Methodist faiths but he was adopted by Ria Hamuera who became his foster mother. There was nothing untoward in young Wiremu being farmed out; there were simply too many children in the family. He occasionally took lessons from missionaries but he also attended the services of Mere Rikiriki, his aunt. She was active in the Church of England and had established her own Church of the Holy Spirit at Parewanui and was with Te Whiti and Tohu at Parihaka. Being a faith healer and herbalist, she was regarded as a *tohunga* in Maori eyes. This knowledge she passed on to the young Ratana. Thus her strong influence in Ratana's formative years was considerable.

Ratana attended school to standard 4 and then worked on the land around his home area. He is reported as having lived a wild life. He was a good horseman, riding them furiously. He played hard rugby and, as soon as he was able, began drinking. His father died in 1910 and his grandfather in 1911. He was, by all accounts, a very good farmer and hard worker, earning himself the title of champion ploughman and wheat stacker of the district. As if in preparation for his future task, he would often brood when not in the mood for work, gazing at nothing, then launch himself into his work again. At about the time of his father's and grandfather's deaths, two sons were born to Ratana. They were to be named Arepa (Alpha) and Omeka (Omega). Quite correctly, Ratana was apparently not completely accepting of the names initially, but nonetheless acquiesced later on. Mere Rikiriki, who had named them, refused to touch or baptise them as she considered them 'too high'.

Point 1 – 'Too high'. (*– for spiritual clarification later in this Chapter.*)

*   *   *   *   *

During the years of The First World War Ratana spent more of his time reading newspapers and some religious articles. Perhaps his interest was spurred by the fact that he had sent his eldest son to join the Maori Contingent then serving overseas. He also visited his aunt Mere Rikiriki often, to gain some of her 'light' (*maramatanga*). Several times she repeated her prophecy concerning his future telling him to believe in The Trinity and to pray, whereby a sign would come to him. On page 23 of 'Ratana', we note:

> "About this time, as he ploughed the land, Ratana heard voices speaking to him. Occasionally he became excited, threw himself about and raved wildly. He seemed to be insane and a young relative, Ngawaka Taurua, said he should be taken to Porirua to the mental hospital. But Urumanao and others said that it would be wrong to interfere for the Spirit of the Lord was working in Bill Ratana. Time would tell."

On 17th March 1918, what might be regarded as the first signs of Ratana's "Calling" were revealed to him. Whilst camped with Urumanao, Arepa and Omeka on a beach near his home, several huge waves came crashing on to the shore leaving in its ebbing wake two stranded whales. One was killed by the force of the impact but the second was still alive, and though injured and bleeding, struggled for some time. The two whales were cut up, with the meat and oil stored for future use. Over the next twelve months they provided food, heating and light for many guests.

An oral account from Te Reo Hura (Martha), who was present at the time, says Ratana got close enough to carve his initials on the second whale and speak into its spirit.

> 'My father was overcome by the Spirit ... and spoke to the spirit of the whale, saying he had the power of life and that Satan's power was at an end. At this point the tail began to move and life was restored and a large wave like the first one carried it out.[5] As the whale left, Ratana said, "Take my name to the four corners of the world, the time will come when you are called back to the Takutai Moana O Whangaehu, it will be then that my works will be completed." '

(Ratana Revisited... p.49, Keith Newman.)

Point 2 – Elemental help.

> *   *   *   *   *

During that same year the great influenza pandemic struck, causing many Maori deaths. Over 1,000 Maori died; the death rate being 5 times that of the European. With death rates at 226 in 10,000 Maoris as compared with 49 in 10,000 Europeans, it was described as:

> "...the severest set-back received by the race since the fighting days of **Hongi Hika**."

(Ratana: p.17, Emphases mine.)

Ratana recovered from a small bout of infection to discover many of his extended *whanau* dead. From out of 20 grandchildren of his grandfather, Ngahina Ratana, only he and two other sisters were left alive. Ratana had been spared for a momentous task, and during the epidemic he once more heard voices calling to him.

Around this time Omeka contracted severe pains in his right leg, the source of which doctors could not locate. Sending for his son, Ratana spent the next three days in prayer and fasting and wrought the first of many healing miracles as one of the signs of "The Calling" to his great work. A needle, the cause of the pain – and severe blood-poisoning – came out from behind the boy's knee. But Ratana's time, though close, had still not come. The forces that would bring the day, however, continued to gather around him in light and power.

Point 3 – Healing Power.

> *   *   *   *   *

Although Mere Rikiriki had prophesied in 1912 that he would become a spiritual leader, it was not until the year 1918 that Ratana's "Calling" was given to him. On the 8th of November, while standing on the verandah of his home overlooking pasture land which sloped down to the Tasman Sea, he is recorded as seeing a strange cloud rise out of the sea, grow larger and larger and approach him swiftly. The cloud swirled around and enveloped him whereupon he seemed to be burning. From out of the cloud came a voice which reportedly said to him:

> "Be at peace. Fear not! I am the Holy Ghost! I have travelled around the world to find the people upon whom I can stand. I have come back to Aotearoa to choose you, the Maori people."

Point 4 – Visitation.

---

[5]Whichever of the two versions of the event is correct is immaterial here. What is important to recognise is that 'Natural Forces' played the decisive role in bringing the whales to Ratana.

* * * * *

The voice continued:

> *"Repent! Cleanse yourself and your family as white as snow, as sinless as the wood-pigeon."*

Point 5 – Repentance and Spiritual Cleansing.

* * * * *

The voice then proclaimed:

> *"Ratana, I appoint you as the Mouthpiece of God for the multitude of this land. Unite the Maori people, turning them to Jehovah of the Thousands, for this is His compassion to all of you."*

(Ratana: J.M. Henderson – all 3 quotes. Emphases mine.)

Point 6 – Momentous nature of Spiritual Mission.

* * * * *

According to some reports, Ratana went inside and told his family that God had spoken to him. They thought him either mad or drunk. Later, though, his certainty about the event was reinforced when he saw a shining light reflected in the clock-face above the mantelpiece in the kitchen. Turning, he saw, standing in front of the window, an Angel radiating great splendour. The Angel repeated the message from God, adding that the *Mangai* (mouthpiece) was to turn the Maori people from their fear of moreporks and roosters, their belief in *atua* hidden in sticks and clothing, and in the relics of departed ancestors; back to belief in Jehovah. He was to preach the Gospel to the Maori people of the North, the South, and the Chatham Islands. He was told to destroy the power of the *tohunga* and to heal the spirits and bodies of his people.

Point 7 – Conquered Maori fears.

* * * * *

Another version states:

> "...he saw a strange cloud like a whirlwind approach. As he ran towards his house, he experienced a vision of all the world's roads stretching towards him and felt a heavy but invisible weight descend upon his shoulders. His family saw that he looked strange. He had been struck dumb but the Holy Spirit spoke through him to his family."
>
> *"May peace be upon you; I am the Holy Spirit who is speaking to you; wash yourselves clean, make yourselves ready."*

(Dictionary of N.Z. Biography, Vol. III: p.415)

It was reported that over the next few weeks Ratana spoke with the voices of the Holy Spirit and the Archangels Gabriel and Michael.

Whilst the respective reports may differ in detail, they do not detract in any way from the momentous **spiritual nature** of the event. In fact it may well signal the opposite. Because of the incredible power that would accompany that happening, we should expect very many things to be occurring all at once. The recipient of such an experience would no doubt be in a state of extreme agitation, uncertainty, apprehension and fear, all probably mixed with spiritual euphoria at being enveloped by such power. Thus, by virtue of such complete contact with that power, the major points of the event will probably be seared into the psyche for all time. Later memories will almost certainly recall the main aspects, but may not remember the finer or sequential detail of them. In any case, from that moment on, the remarkable life and achievements of Ratana certainly bore sure testimony to some kind of *major spiritual upheaval* in his life at that time. – [**Point 4 – Visitation.**]

*   *   *   *   *

Ratana's first action was to get rid of all the beer in the house and to smash the telephone over which, it is reported, he operated as the local bookmaker. From that point on, he campaigned relentlessly against drink. Gradually, word of Ratana's vision and healing ability spread and people began to arrive for healing and to hear his message. Ratana spent many hours reading and meditating on The Bible and reading "Health for the Maori" by Pope. From time to time he would appear on the verandah to talk to the assembled crowd.

Point 8 – Cleanliness is next to Godliness.

*   *   *   *   *

Yet Ratana was not yet absolutely certain of his place, and the summer of 1918/19 saw him experience a severe time of testing – synonymous with a "...time in the wilderness". During the night he would wander over the property down to the sea, his children sometimes with him, and hurl himself through gorse, blackberry bushes and barbed-wire fences. He would return bleeding and exhausted in the early hours of the morning. Upon awakening, he would speak to his family about their superstitions, of Jehovah, and of Maori aspirations of separate rights.

Finally accepting the broad thrust of his mission, he concerned himself primarily with faith-healing in the beginning. When performing acts of healing, he would not indulge in dramatics, choosing instead to ask direct questions of the supplicant. "Have you been to a *tohunga*?" he would ask. "Give that up!" He told his followers that God would heal all who walked into the Light. One particularly memorable incident involved the healing of the bed-ridden daughter of the Whanganui chief, Te Kahupokoro, who brought her to Ratana. After asking the girl if she believed in the power of The Father, Son and Holy Spirit, he told her to rise. She did so and went on to lead a normal life.

Ratana admonished Maori to believe in The Trinity, to practice cleanliness, and to reject superstition. Every patient healed signed a covenant to this effect. More significantly for Maori thinking, however, was the agreement to also cut ties to tribal affiliations and become a member of the "Morehu", (remnant) thus uniting traditional and bitter tribal enemies in a common, truly spiritual cause and goal. Ratana's vision was for a new order where the social organisation of the tribe would be supplanted by a new life in health and 'Christianity'. To this end, he urged his followers to rejoin the churches, a stance which had the support of the Anglicans and Methodists.

The covenant that Ratana insisted upon served the obvious purpose of directing the thoughts and activities of the adherent away from tribalism and the old dead way. Thus towards a new need to think differently; towards a vital urgency to think and act truly spiritually if there was to be any kind of real and beneficial change for Maori. The wording of the covenant is especially strong against *tohungaism*.

> "This is a Covenant to certify **the unity of the Maori Race, men, women, and children under the providence of Jehovah, Lord God of Hosts**, also under the name of the Father, Son and Holy Ghost and their Faithful Angels. Therefore we, who hereto sign our names, do solemnly pledge our oath, that in the future we will renounce all the abominable foolish ways and works of Tohungaism; and that we confirm to have henceforth **one Father Jehovah, Lord God of Hosts**, to guard and guide us in the path of righteousness and assist us in spiritual betterment at all times. Amen."

(Ratana: p.60, Emphases mine.)

Ratana embarked on several nation-wide tours to spread his message and to wage war against the *tohunga* caste. He enjoyed spectacular success with healing and as many as 2,000 Maori were healed, along with some Pakeha. Save for his piercing eyes, his voice and manner were quiet and gentle, and his healing method always followed the same course. He would first question the sick about their illness and then their faith in the healing powers of The Trinity and the Faithful Angels. If they provided a satisfactory answer, he would order them to rise or put away their crutches.

Whilst many of the more amazing feats of healing involved those who arrived in his presence in wheelchairs or on crutches and who, upon being healed, discarded them and simply walked away, he did not always aim for instant healing. Often he commanded the lame to let go their crutches over a number of days. The numbers of wheelchairs and crutches left behind testify to the very many acts of instant healing he wrought.[6]

One of the more spectacular healings involved one Tamihana of Masterton who, for twenty five years and with legs bent double and hands twisted, had suffered from rheumatics so severely he could not feed or dress himself. On visiting Ratana Pa, he replied to the Mangai's query as to the why of his trouble with the simple statement: "Too much sin." In a further reply to Ratana's question as to what he would do with all the gods and *tohunga* amongst his ancestors, he replied that he would hand them over to The Trinity and the Holy Angels to be burnt to ashes. Henderson, on page 34, records that upon hearing this, Ratana advised Tamihana that:

> "...he would gradually get better, only he must never forget God. Giving him five minutes in which to stand up, the faith-healer asked him for the crutches which would only cause him to feel sorry for himself if he took them home."

Now using only a walking stick he departed Ratana Pa with much fanfare.

An unfortunate aspect of Ratana's healing success was that many of his followers believed he was opposed to doctors, and many unnecessary deaths occurred. Ratana refuted this and his claim was supported by a District Nurse. Moreover, a close friend who was a Methodist adviser in the early years gave the following positive account of the Mangai's clearly balanced view of both healing methods.

> "He was the most practical faith-healer I ever knew. He read a number of anatomy charts and medical books, and often referred to Pope's *Health for the Maori*. I never heard him give anything but sound advice on health, and he often sent people to doctors when there was organic trouble.
>
> "During a healing session when Ratana was seated on the verandah with a queue of patients, a European visitor called out a question: 'Is it true that you advise people not to use medicines?' Ratana smiled and pulled out of his waistcoat pocket a small jar of ointment. He then rolled up his sleeve displaying a rash on his skin.
>
> " 'I'm using this for this...,' he said, '...and it's very good stuff.' The mass of people were, of course, mentally ill. They suffered from *mate Maori* as a result of their lack of confidence; being born into the 'poor Maori' atmosphere of the first two decades of this century."

(Ratana: p.35, Emphasis mine.)

Ironically, some influential Maori, such as Reweti T. Kohere, conducted a slur campaign against him in Maori newspapers, labelling him just another *tohunga* in the same mould as others including Rua Kenana, Te Wereta and Hikapuhi. Given Parliament's framework of the Tohunga Suppression Act, this was a potentially damaging charge. Against *tohungaism* he was

---

[6]These are displayed in the Ratana museum.

defended by no less than the superintendent of the Anglican Maori Mission, the Rev. W. G. Williams, and also defended by Arthur F. Williams in the publication, *Te Toa Takitini*.[7]

Ratana's invaluable work in reducing dependency on *tohungaism* was the key factor for orthodox Christianity's acceptance of this aspect of his work. His healings were repeatedly questioned, however. Probably out of sheer frustration at more or less continual and antagonistic attacks on his work, he advised newspapers that although he had received more than 70,000 letters of support, mostly from New Zealand but also from other countries, he would work only with Maori in the future.

His battle against *tohungaism* often took the form of desecrating places of ancient *tapu* to show there were no harmful spirits or *atua* dwelling there. And he also used various everyday articles like a walking stick, a stone, or a pair of trousers to illustrate his point. He would dismissively shout, "Maori Gods", and continue to speak of the one God as he tossed the 'false *atua*' to one side. There is no doubt that his implacable campaign against the 'old way' earned Ratana the hatred of some *tohunga*. And any such 'battles' with *tohunga* opposed to his work, especially *tohunga whaiwhaia*, would have required them to invoke quite malevolent entities against him to maintain their particular brand of so-called 'power' – given Ratana's far greater strength. Ratana seemingly possessed highly refined intuitive 'sight' whereby he could detect anyone intending him harm. This attribute would have been entirely consistent with his receiving power to destroy *tohungaism* in the first place.

Point 9 – Spiritual Power.

*   *   *   *   *

Henderson (p.35) reports that Ratana advised those closest to him of one such antagonist arriving by train one day.

> "There's something coming with this train, boys," said the Mangai. "Yes, it's there alright. We'll send it back."

As he spoke, an old man amongst the new arrivals clutched his stomach and fell to the ground groaning. When his companions carried him to Ratana, this old *tohunga* confessed (as the story records) that he had sent a *karakia* (charm or curse) against the Mangai, but now he was very sorry. He signed the Covenant and joined the Morehu.

This was one incident among many. Moreover, this method of dealing with such adversaries in a confrontation-type situation was a definite psychological disadvantage for any 'attacker'. And more so if they were advised, on their arrival, that they were rendered impotent by the power of God – the one that Ratana fully embraced. Through such incidents his obvious connection with a far greater power could not be denied, thus increasing, in Maori estimation, his already considerable *mana*. If Ratana could show Maori that his message and the results he could produce from it were far more potent than anything the *tohunga* could produce, then, quite logically, they should gravitate towards him and his new direction for Maori.

As his message and Movement gathered momentum, emissaries from the King Movement came to see him to ask if he would address the land grievances of the Maori people. They were led by Tupu Taingakawa, uncle of the Maori King Te Rata and grandson of Tawhiao. His words to Ratana were:

> "Mangai, I have come not for the healing of my body and soul, but for the healing of the sickness of the land."

Ratana's reply was simple and direct:

---

[7]The "Tohunga Suppression Act" was repealed in the 1960s.

"Good! Let us first unite in the Father and then we shall unite in the land."

Point 10 – "But first secure the Kingdom of God..."

          *   *   *   *   *

In the presence of every Christian denomination at the opening of a new non-denominational Church called Piki Te Ora (Seek the Light) at Christmas, 1920; Ratana spoke about three things:

1. Faith in Jehovah – Father, Son and Holy Ghost.

2. Cleanliness of the body.

3. Rejection of superstitions.

He proclaimed to the ministers and the people: "I have opened the door, but you yourselves must go in. I am but a finger post pointing to the true way of life."

Point 11 – "You lock up the Keys..."

          *   *   *   *   *

He further exhorted the people to: "Be at peace. Set yourselves straight, repent!" The ministers and missionaries of the various churches were not able to understand *the extent* to which Maori were influenced by their *superstitious and fear-ridden way of life*. Ratana advised them that this was the cause of many Maori illnesses, mental, spiritual and physical. It was the illness of '*mate Maori and mate wairua*'.

> **The way out and forward was to leave it all behind and embrace the truth he taught. His strength lay in being able to correctly understand that truth and convey it to Maori.**

Point 12 – "Fear begets more Fear."

          *   *   *   *   *

His own followers certainly believed that his Church was the only true one for Maori, and that all should join. And whilst many thousands did, not everyone shared that view of course. Such ideas were not received favourably by the adherents of Ringatu or by the followers of the King Movement. Bishop W. Sedgwick, once unimpressed with the idea of a solely Maori Church, spoke favourably of Ratana in recognition of the work he was doing in leading his people away from *tohungaism*. Page 49 of "Ratana" thus notes:

> "Conversation with Ratana soon reveals the fact that he is after something bigger than the healing of the body. The real purpose of his campaign is to win the Maori from Tohungaism ... from the 'Gods many' to the one Triune God... It is a crusade against the spiritual forces of evil which are the indirect and often the direct cause of sickness and disorder..."

Inevitably, with such a powerful spiritual upheaval, it could be expected that the mainstream Churches, whilst initially supportive of the general thrust of such an obviously beneficial Movement, would begin to question particular aspects of it. Thus both the Catholics and Protestants began to withdraw support for Ratana's Movement, including Bishop Sedgwick who spoke so favourably before the schism. The Catholics were concerned over theological points being decided by vote, and the other churches could not accept Ratana's doctrine of the "faithful angels". In their view this seemed to be a return to belief in *atua* by another name.

Ratana also experienced conflict with the accepted Maori leadership of the time, namely the Maori King, and Ngata and Pomare, who all refused to sign the Covenant. This event foreshadowed Ratana's later strong involvement in the political arena when selected Ratana members contested the Maori seats held by Ngata and Pomare. Even though initially unsuccessful, the strong response clearly gave notice that the Ratana Movement was a future political force to be reckoned with.

In a speech at Christmas 1923, Ratana revealed plans to take The Bible and the Treaty to Britain. Prior to that journey, on the 18th March 1924, Ratana and his family visited Mount Taranaki and Parihaka. There, beside a stream on the mountain, he heard a voice repeating words of Titokowaru. And at Parihaka, he discovered sayings left by Te Whiti and Tohu foretelling him that he must take his spiritual message to the wider world.

In that same year Ratana attempted to present a "Treaty of Waitangi" petition to King George whilst in England as part of a World tour, but was prevented from receiving an audience with the King by the New Zealand High Commissioner in London. A journey to the League of Nations immediately afterwards produced a similar response, to Ratana's great disappointment. A stopover in pre-war Japan on the way home produced rumours of a 'deal' with the Japanese to restore all Treaty of Waitangi rights. This provided huge political difficulties for Ratana upon his return.

However, that was not the only trouble the "Mangai" had to face. Prior to his leaving, there had been talk of establishing a Ratana Church and plans had continued in his absence. In a classic case of "rivalry for *mana*" on the part of an egoistic pretender, one Otene Paora of Ngati Whatua attempted to register his own "Church of the Father, Son and Holy Spirit and Faithful Angels". This rather crude attempt to usurp the role and status of the "Mangai" was forestalled by the general superintendent of the Methodist Maori Mission who journeyed quickly to Ratana *pa* to warn the Morehu to remain faithful to their founder. Moreover, Ratana administrators were instructed not to sign Covenants endorsed with the Mangai's seal while he was away, and a list of authorised apostles was published in the Ratana newspaper, *Te Whetu Marama*.

Aside from the spiritual reasons perceived by him, Ratana's journey into the wider world community probably also served the very valuable purpose of providing a far more expansive and international view than a purely Maori one; an outlook he might not have obtained had he not left these shores. Moreover, any journey such as that which Ratana undertook should serve to offer a more sharpened perspective as to the purpose of his own mission amongst Maori, and would certainly help to negate any danger of becoming overly, or even fanatically, ethnocentric.

Whilst Ratana produced great works, there was always the danger of him being personally deified, even though Ratana discouraged attempts by his followers who sought to do so. Unfortunately, an idea surfaced which centred around a Ratana Godhead that included the Mangai, as well as the Father, Son and Holy Spirit. After the deaths of Arepa and Omeka in the 1930s, it is reported that Ratana began to encourage his followers to regard them as Ratana saints or mediators, since both were always thought to have possessed 'spiritual forces'. If these reports were true, this perhaps reveals the human nature of the man in wishing his own offspring to be remembered. However, emotional considerations are not in keeping with any truly objective spiritual 'mission' that such a one as the Mangai would need to have, and maintain. On the surface, there would appear to be no 'spiritually-objective reason' why his sons should be placed so. Perhaps Ratana was privy to a reason not known to others.

Interestingly, Ratana later began to refer to other Churches as introduced to New Zealand by 'gentiles', and therefore unsuitable for Maori. This stance no doubt smacked of possible arrogance in the minds of other Church leaders and perhaps appeared to tend towards separatism. Yet a simple analysis of the situation quite clearly reveals that the greatest need for Maori then was for a *different* kind of organisation – one under which they could develop at their own pace. In terms of genuine spiritual guidance for Maori, the orthodox Churches could actually offer far less than Ratana. Therefore, such a statement by Ratana probably reflected no more than the spiritual reality of the situation at the time.

Another contentious issue which brought an official break with the orthodox doctrines closer, was the taking of a second wife by Ratana in 1925. To protect him from the infatuation of thousands of admiring women, and encouraged by Te Urumanaao, he took a second, much younger wife called Iriaka Te Rio. She had been a member of the dance troupe who had travelled with him. She bore him two children, one a son called Hamuera, also considered special but who died young; and Raniera Aohou. It is reported that there were other later liaisons which caused controversy among his followers.

The threatened break with the Anglican Church over the divisions created by the "faithful angels" doctrine finally occurred. At a meeting to discuss the issue, and whilst understanding the orthodox viewpoint, Ratana was, nevertheless, so incensed by the behaviour of the clergy that he felt unable to speak. Henderson, on page 46, records Ratana speaking to one clergyman, telling him that he could not:

> "...address them after that. The Church has too many voices and the people are divided.
> We must go our own way!"

So the proclamation of a separate Maori Church was made by its founder on *31st May 1925*.[8] For this act, Ratana and his followers were excommunicated by the Anglican authorities. As well, the decision was taken to establish a separate Maori bishop.

The doctrine of the "faithful angels", so vehemently opposed by the orthodox Churches of the time, was probably greatly misunderstood or misconstrued. Yet Ratana's purpose for including it in his beliefs should perhaps *not* have been regarded with suspicion, because the idea of faithful guardian angels has always been part of the religious or spiritual aspect of European Church doctrine in any case. It is certainly present in European literature. Nevertheless, in Ratana's situation, the doctrine of his "faithful angels" produced disquiet in Church orthodoxy from the outset.

Ratana himself was reported to have been concerned by the practices of some of his followers who, in an understandably 'other-world' Maori view, believed they could see the angels as lights in the evening sky, and apparently offered worship to them. The fact that Ratana was very concerned by this development clearly showed that he recognised **where** veneration and worship was to be directed, and therefore could **not** be accused of **actually worshipping** the "faithful angels" – as was claimed by some of his opponents.

The flag that Ratana produced for his first tour had borne the words (in Maori), One God: Father, Son and Holy Ghost. The later flag, however, was extended to read, "Jehovah: Father, Son, Holy Ghost and the Faithful Angels". Ratana's frequent references to the Faithful Angels reassured his followers that he would come to no harm when outside his home territory of Whangaehu, for they were afraid that his *mana* would disappear as he moved into other tribal areas. To calm their fears, he told the story of Elisha and his guardian Angels, how they would protect all of sufficient belief, and that the Angels would protect him and his power.

This concept was readily acceptable to older Maori, for their ancient mythology told how the life and blood of the first man were carried from Io-matua-kore by the *whatua kura* (spiritual messengers) named Rehua. In my opinion, a better description of angelic activity between God and men for Maori *at that time* would be difficult to find. Their natural acceptance of the unseen and the intangible worlds thus allowed a similarly easy acceptance of Angels. And whilst Pakeha missionaries and bishops continued their campaign against such beliefs, Ratana and his Maori followers simply believed in the existence of them, and in the protection they brought from Jehovah.

---

[8] An exceptionally auspicious date in both the spiritual and material sense for Maori and, indeed, global humanity. But, however, as yet *unrecognised* by 'the world'.

Now free of the constraints of the orthodox Churches, Ratana applied his energies to building up his own Church and to the well-being of his people. After a short visit to the United States, he set about building the Temple of his vision. This act anchored his spiritual work to a material form expressing that vision, thus symbolising the new direction that the Maori race *should* now travel. Upon its completion in 1928, Ratana announced that his spiritual works were over. From that point on he concentrated his efforts on material goals of health and growth through social reform, successful agricultural ventures, sport, and music through brass band activity.

Point 13 – Spiritual Freedom

*   *   *   *   *

All these aspects helped to promote strong bonds to the Church, with families and even whole tribal communities accepting Ratana's covenant of belief in The Trinity and rejecting all superstition and tribal affiliations. And in 1928, growing in strength, three out of four Ratana candidates were elected to Parliament.

An increasingly wider membership meant further buildings were constructed, including Omeka Pa near Matamata. The depression swelled numbers further as the inequities of the Government payments became apparent resulting in increasing unemployment and lower rates for Maori. During the 1931 elections Ratana made a formal alliance with the Labour Party which continued more or less without interruption until the October 1996 general elections under M.M.P.

Unlike the other Maori Prophets whose Movements either foundered or were greatly diminished at their deaths, Ratana's did not. Since his passing in 1939, the Church he founded has maintained its structure and vibrancy. Aside from an obvious religious role, it also has a strong political focus which enables it to occupy a dual yet complementary position as a generally beneficial point of reference for Maori. Moreover, with its rejection of tribal affiliations and establishment of the secret ballot in Maori elections – which undermined the political power of traditional ranking leaders – it is able to offer non-tribal groups a recognised place and direction within Maoridom and New Zealand.

Possessing the necessary vision to aim for political power through which to also enhance the *spiritual aspect* of his mission for Maori, Ratana, probably more than any other, provided the structure to most effectively bring this about, and maintain it. Without that political savvy and the example he set, Maoridom would undoubtedly have fared far worse than is presently the case – even with present-day statistics – such was the far-reaching and definitive effect of this man!

*   *   *   *   *

19.1   Ratana's Calling – The Spiritual Significance

Having completed a relatively brief survey of Ratana's life and main achievements, it is vital to more closely examine the '**Key Points**' from the standpoint of **Spiritual Law**; that we might better understand both the stupendous spiritual nature of this event and the obvious great strength of the man.

19.1.1   Point 1 – 'Too high'

Whilst the particular incident concerning the first point of note is not related to Ratana in a strictly personal sense, it does serve to illustrate certain prevailing attitudes still present in Maoridom which his 'mission' clearly indicated required change.

It is inherent in the nature of the Maori psyche to sometimes place on certain, otherwise normal, things or individuals a 'too high' or 'untouchable' status. We might loosely accept this practice as being associated with *tapu*. Invariably, this kind of 'status' is necessarily determined by someone who, ostensibly, has the power and/or ability to so decree it.

In the case of Mere Rikiriki and her assessment of Arepa and Omeka as being 'too high' for her to even touch, it is not a question of the youngsters being 'untouchable'. It is probably more one of her, as a *tohunga*, either 'wrongly fearing' their 'role' or placing far 'too high' a status upon her own perceived or assumed 'high' abilities or position. That is not to say that she did not possess the gift/ability of 'second sight', for that is *not* what we are stating or implying, or that the two sons had not been born for a high spiritual purpose – *such as continuing the father's mission after his time on earth.*[9]

Therefore, even though Mere Rikiriki may have perceived a high spiritual destiny for Arepa and Omeka later in life, the children were probably as normal as any others and deserved to be treated as such, thus allowing any future talents to develop in the most natural manner. Should such 'high' abilities arise, even if at an early age, then perhaps they can be carefully 'steered' to their correct fulfilment. To simply pronounce any child 'too high' to even be touched is to place on that child an unnecessary burden and, moreover, is probably a little melodramatic – though very much a part of the Maori ethos. For even Jesus Himself was "touched" on His person, by *many* people, and invariably for His "healing radiation". And though Ratana sought his Aunt's 'light' prior to his "Calling", it was that kind of belief he later undertook to neutralise. Paradoxically, however, for the *spiritual benefit* of the Maori race, for it is humility which holds far greater spiritual virtue and power, and not any incorrectly-elevated status of *tohungaism* of any kind.

19.1.2 Point 2 – Elemental help

The incident where unusually large waves left two whales stranded on a beach at the precise time Ratana was camped there might be regarded as being purely coincidental. What we do know is that whales play a special part in Maori legend – as they do in the folklore of other races. In Maori lore, this cultural aspect is strongly evidenced in the *waiata* of Paikea, whale rider. As the oceans' largest mammals, whales fulfil a role as mothers and nurturers in the mythology of many peoples. Since Ratana's 'whale event' is immutably linked to **"Elemental Lore"**, we might accept it as a sign *linking* him to his mission. In this case as an offering, perhaps an acknowledgement from Tangaroa, 'Elemental Lord of the Sea', to Ratana, "Mangai of God" for Maori. Perhaps a sign, also, that Ratana would be a "fisher of men" among Maori.

In recognising that *key event* for what it was – signalling the beginnings of the amazing life and great 'Spiritual Mission' of the Prophet, Ratana – we see in it a clear 'elemental outworking'; the 'sign' of the whales preceding his mission proper. A similar outworking may also be noted in what took place around the later 'vision'. So, in the case of the 'sign', a precise *elemental* occurrence involving the 'forces of nature' – several huge waves delivering two whales for his use. The incident of the 'cloud rising from the sea' similarly possessed aspects of *elemental* activity. In its *complete outworking*, however, the events surrounding 'his Spiritual Calling' necessarily incorporated the most powerful *Spiritual Forces* with the visitation of a "Being" from the Higher Realms.

Thus, in Ratana's experience, *we* are shown the two key steps that all men of all races should have trodden: The step from the once clear recognition of the **Creator-Willed** *'Elemental Forces of Nature'*; to the next crucially-necessary recognition of **The Spiritual!**

---

[9]We may understand the quandary better if we take the analogy of placing persons on pedestals. If they do not measure up to 'our perceived expectations' of them, it is not actually the one who is elevated that falls, but we ourselves in our wrong or unrealistic expectations we attach to whomever has been so 'elevated'.

For at no point in any part of that total happening do we see even the faintest traces of *psychic* activity. In any case that could not possibly have happened with Ratana's 'Calling', for only man's *wrong volition* is *responsible* for the production of *psychic forms* and *their* associated activity. It is **never** *elemental* or truly *spiritual* forces, for they serve only **The Creative Will!** By this measure, alone, we may understand that the *spiritual* power connected with Ratana's Mission in the events surrounding his Calling were completely and utterly removed from any Maori *psychic* influence or input.

No Maori magician or *tohunga* could ever hope to reproduce anything even remotely approaching just the whale incident, let alone the later, stronger happenings. The gulf between the respective operating levels of origin are simply too vast for any *tohunga* to bridge – then or now! The events surrounding Ratana's immediate Calling thus possessed *spiritual* power because they were totally divorced from any kind of earthly *psychic* influence associated with human machinations. That particular event incorporated only the hallmarks of *"Elemental"* activity *associated with 'The Forces of Nature'.* Nonetheless, however, under the higher, driving-power of **The Spiritual!**

For Ratana and his family, though; an 'offering' that reportedly provided much bounty in food and oil.

19.1.3   Point 3 – Healing Power

The healing of his son represents a special aspect of the overall power gifted to Ratana for his mission. Whilst many of the *kinds* of healing results he achieved *could possibly* be termed fraudulent faith-healing by hard-nosed sceptics i.e., without any kind of scientific basis, the first healing concerning his son probably could not. The emergence from out of the flesh of a physical object such as a needle – which had been the previously unknown source of serious blood poisoning causing concern for the doctors – would make it difficult for even the most hardened sceptic to label the symptoms psychosomatic. A steel needle is hardly an intangible object.

19.1.4   Point 4 – Visitation

> *"Be at peace. Fear not! I am the Holy Ghost! I have travelled around the world to find the people upon whom I can stand. I have come back to Aotearoa to choose you, the Maori people."*

> (Ratana: J. M. Henderson. Italics mine.)

This particular aspect of Ratana's amazing story is probably the most controversial, for we are dealing with a 'personal-belief mode' situation here. Yet this has been so for millennia. The idea of an Angel blessing anyone today with a visitation could well earn for that individual a very rapid 'psychiatric assessment' by a panel of 'doubting mental health experts'. Even the Church would disapprove of such an event, given that they and not **"The Creator of The Worlds"** determine which human beings should or should not be canonised or otherwise exalted today.

However, we are generally able to *more readily* accept visitations by Angels as long as the event lies in the distant past. Should they be too close, historically, we tend to shut our eyes and ears to such a 'ludicrous' and, perhaps, even 'blasphemous' idea. Yet why should a visitation in the very recent past and thousands of miles from the "Holy Land", not take place? For if a man is tasked with a high spiritual 'mission', might he not *need* such a visit to enable him to receive directly of the Power necessary for that purpose by a messenger from on High? A high messenger with a proclamation from The Source of All Life – perhaps even an Archangel!

So can we accept that Ratana did receive a visit from such a powerful, spiritual being, or was he simply drunk as some believed? If in fact he was drunk it was a truly amazing achievement, upon sobering up, to immediately begin a mission that was so spectacularly successful. To heal thousands of sick, even those wheelchair-bound; to embark on a campaign to destroy *tohungaism*, build a whole new spiritual and political direction for the Maori race and construct temples and towns; was a highly unlikely outcome for a drunk. If that was the case, we should all find out what Ratana's favourite tipple was and generously imbibe.

No, clearly something of great import happened to shake this man to his spiritual core. For only with an upheaval of such stupendous proportions, could Ratana have possibly achieved what he ultimately accomplished. This was no fraudulent 'con'. The results, clearly and unequivocally, are simply too irrefutable to deny or mock!

The second report of the 'visitation' records The Holy Spirit speaking 'through' Ratana. Then, later, the Archangels Gabriel and Michael. Here, also, we might determine that voices speaking through Ratana or anyone else are no different from incidents which take place with literally thousands of patients in mental asylums around the world every day. Conversely, however, religious writings record many instances of spiritual beings delivering messages to mankind via specially chosen ones; instances that we readily accept today. And Ratana was clearly an especially "Chosen One" for Maori. Biblical examples, particularly – of which there are many – are not only unequivocally accepted by the Christian world, but strongly defended. A classic illustration was after the death of Jesus when the Holy Spirit spoke through His disciples at the time of **The Outpouring**.

So in terms of the general attitude of present-day Churches toward angelic visitations and the like, as long as they lie in the far distant past they are acceptable and believable. Bring them forward into recent time, however, and they must be strongly challenged. Moreover, serious doubts are invariably cast upon the whole business. Yet this attitude naturally presupposes the view that guidance from **"The Very Source of Life"** to 'ordinary people' no longer occurs. Does **The Creator**, then, no longer incline **His Grace** to erring humankind now?

Or did such an event of *loving Grace from on High* **actually happen most powerfully through Ratana** for a race of people in serious decline and sick with *mate Maori and mate wairua*? Loving Grace for a people who were in danger of dying out unless *a major and fundamental change could be wrought* **within the race itself**.

*   *   *   *   *

The doubting religious attitude of 'automatic rejection' regarding 'angelic visitations', perhaps fails to take into account the very real fact that mankind is in far more need of genuine spiritual guidance in these very stressful latter times than at any other point in our sorry history. Since many accept that God is Eternal and God is Love, we can surely believe that He may still incline His Grace to we humans muddling about in ignorance on planet earth. To believe that such happenings 'cannot ever be again' presupposes the arrogant assumption that humankind can usurp or deny events *that may actually be ordained by The Creative Will*. Moreover, since everything has come into being according to this Will, in strict accordance with inviolable Spiritual Laws, we should logically expect that, *precisely because* of that inherent Love and Grace, we may, from time to time through specially chosen ones, be offered the necessary guidance to help us "...stay on the correct and ordained path", for both our spiritual *and* material benefit.

*   *   *   *   *

So having determined that something amazing and soul-shaking occurred that intensely affected Ratana, let us examine his claim of an angelic visitation. What we must strive to separate out here are the two distinct events; one being the **unseen voice in the cloud**, and the other the clear vision of the Angel **repeating the words** of the "voice in the cloud". The obvious contention here is that they were not one and the same. The voice from out of the cloud stated that it *was* The Holy Ghost, whereas the Angel repeated the words *spoken* by The Holy Ghost. From the standpoint of Spiritual Truth, one particular thing stands out strongly in Ratana's personal account, and they were the first words spoken to him at the time by *both* the "voice" in the cloud and by the angel who 'repeated' them.

They were the words: **"Fear not!"**

The Bible clearly records many instances of angelic visitations, with the most well known probably being those events preceding the birth of Christ. Firstly, in the proclamation of certain imminent events by the Archangel, Gabriel:

1. To the priest, Zacharias, who received the message that a son, who would be named John, [the Baptist] would be born to him and his wife Elizabeth.

2. To Mary, who was informed she would bear Jesus!.

3. Later, after the birth, to the shepherds in the fields.

The respective New Testament texts state that the Angel appeared first to Zacharias who was offering incense in the "sanctuary of the Lord" while the rest of the people were praying outside. In Luke, 1:11-13, we read:

> Then a messenger of the Lord appeared, standing at the right of the altar of incense. And on seeing him, Zacharias was struck with awe, *and gave way to fear.*
> "*Fear not*, Zacharias!" said the messenger, addressing him...

Secondly, to Mary, six months after Gabriel's message to Zacharias. Luke, 1:28-30, states:

> And the messenger, on entering, saluted her with, "Good health to you! much honour attends you; the Lord is with you!"
> But she was thrown into confusion about his message, and reflected what that address might mean.
> The messenger, however, said to her, "*Fear not* Mary! for you have received a gift from God."

> (Luke 1:28-31)

And thirdly, to the shepherds on the night of Christ's birth.

> In that same district there were shepherds out in the fields, and keeping guard over their flocks by night. And a messenger of the Lord descended to them, and the lustre of the Lord shone round about them; and they became *terribly afraid.* The messenger, however, said to them, "*Do not be afraid*: for I now come to make known to you a great Gift which shall be to all the people..."

> (Luke 2:8-11, Fenton all. Italics mine.)

It is logical to accept that anything far removed from the ordinary, and therefore probably also outside the regular, parameters of general understanding might well instil very great fear; at least initially. Thus, a visitation by an angelic being would be so far outside any normal experience that fear would be the probable, natural, first reaction to such an event. Even the priest Zacharias, who was obviously dedicated to his Lord, was *very afraid.* Yet his loyalty to The Lord was such that he was blessed as the father of no less a person than John the Baptist. We can surely expect that simple shepherds at night would also experience very great fear in a similar situation.

The fear would not only be generated by the seemingly supernatural nature of the event, but equally through the immense power inherent in it. For very great spiritual pressure would naturally radiate from such a being, simply by virtue of an Origin far Higher than the relatively low level of our material world. And thus we hear the same reassuring words at any such visitation to:

"Be not afraid." And: "Fear not!"

From this explanation we may recall that upon being enveloped by the cloud, Ratana thought he was 'burning'. We should further note the previous reference to the *"pressure of the spiritual power"*, which we human beings might well experience as a 'burning sensation'. Especially note, however, the first reassuring words spoken to Ratana: *"Be at peace" – "Fear not..."*, exactly as stated in our few Biblical examples. In Ratana's case, as one from a race steeped in a world of superstitious fears, not just one "Fear not", but *two* reassurances

And what of the reference to a cloud, and a voice from out of it? The Bible also notates strong spiritual experiences in this regard. To quote just one example:

> "As he was speaking, however, a cloud came and overshadowed them; but on their entering into the cloud, they became afraid. And a voice came out of the cloud, exclaiming, 'This is My Son, My Chosen: listen to Him!' "

(Luke 9:34-36, Fenton.)

Thus, in terms of Ratana's stated spiritual experiences which granted him unequivocal authority [*mana*] for his mission and of the power given to heal; the power to challenge and destroy *tohungaism* and the scale of what he achieved: It is our contention that such a far-reaching and potent outcome was *only possible* through a source *not of the earth*. One, ultimately, from **The Origin of All Life**. Therefore, why not such a Power delivered by a Messenger from There? The individual reader will, of course, arrive at his own determination of Ratana's claim. We, on the other hand, have made our determination, and it is unequivocal recognition and acceptance that this man Ratana **was** Called from on High in the manner described!

*   *   *   *   *

Key Note:

Followers of Ratana and readers of this short text should note that *my* acceptance of Ratana's experiences – as described by him – is additionally and spiritually-powerfully determined by *certain crucial events* that the *vast majority* of humankind are not only **not yet aware of, but have missed completely**. However, *it is **precisely that Event** and its **timing** which has crucial **spiritual connections** to Ratana's Calling and Mission. The very **spiritually-astute** reader may perhaps *perceive* what that "Event" was, for the whole of this Work points to it (as does its 'sister Publications').[10]

As we have already reinforced, and will do so again as we progress to the end of our journey, this complete Work is thus an extension of Ratana's statement that he was "...but a finger-post..." also pointing in that same direction.

*   *   *   *   *

---

[10]In association with 'Zenith Publishing Ltd' those books are only available in New Zealand on [www.publishme.co.nz]. They are 1: 'BIBLE "MYSTERIES" EXPLAINED': Understanding "Global Societal Collapse" From the SCIENCE in The Bible; What Every Scientist, Bible Scholar and Ordinary Man Needs to Know. And 2: 'THE GATHERING APOCALYPSE AND WORLD JUDGEMENT: What It Brings – Even Now – And Why'.

19.1.5   Point 5 – Repentance and Spiritual Cleansing

"Repent! Cleanse yourself and your family as white as snow, as sinless as the wood pigeon."

(Ratana: J. M. Henderson.)

Being directed to repent quite clearly indicates that there was a need to do so, otherwise that would not have been stated. Whilst Ratana was told to repent and cleanse himself so that he could *more powerfully* fulfil his mission, the same directive was logically meant for the Maori race in order that they, too, could *follow* Ratana into a new way of life. The old ways were therefore *not* spiritually-correct by virtue of the fact that *they required repentance to cleanse them out of the race.* Moreover, as a necessary condition *before* change could be brought about, they *firstly* also had to be *let go.* Quite logically, if the Maori race had been spiritually knowledgeable and pure in the first place – as is promoted by some – the visit of the Angel to Ratana *would not have been necessary.* Since that was *not* the case, both repentance and cleansing *were* required for the greater task. Ratana, as the "Mangai" and leader, however, had first to set the example.

Therefore, we may view the *recognition* of the 'need for repentance' as being the first essential for the *further recognition* that 'the traditional ways' were not conducive to spiritual development, and that 'change *was* necessary'. This first requirement of 'necessary recognition' thus then allows for cleansing to begin. This by virtue of the fact that the one needing such cleansing will have necessarily accepted the vital need for a 'change in attitude' in order to bring about the correct conditions for subsequent and genuine spiritual growth.

19.1.6   Point 6 – Momentous Nature of Spiritual Mission

"Ratana, I appoint you as the Mouthpiece of God for the multitude of this land. Unite the Maori people, turning them to Jehovah of the thousands, for this is his compassion to all of you."

(Ratana: J. M. Henderson.)

A possibly intriguing question arises here with the admonition for Ratana to "Unite the Maori people, turning them to Jehovah of the thousands..." In an earlier Chapter, we examined the enigma of the Supreme Being, Io, and the name conceivably being a contraction of Iahou, from Iahoue, from Jahveh, from Yahweh, from Jehovah – according to some scholars. Perhaps, in some strange way, Ratana's overall task was to concomitantly lead Maori back to that lost knowledge of once strong connections to Higher Realms; a knowledge that all human spirits once consciously and knowingly accepted.

Apart from those musings, the first thing that should be realised here is that the directives given to Ratana through the visit of the Angel were given for the *spiritual growth* of the Maori race. These were not simply a few loose and interesting ideas for some kind of social or religious experiment. As Ratana clearly stated, he was the "mouthpiece" of God for Maori, and the "signpost" pointing in that ordained direction. Moreover, the Maori race should further understand that whatever the actual nature of the happening, this man Ratana most certainly received something of clearly sufficient authority and power to enable him to **lead** them forward spiritually, in the first instance. And that authority was not given to him by Maori!

The historical record alone unequivocally reveals how far ancient Maori activities were from anything even remotely resembling genuine spiritual life. Quite clearly, then, it behoves those who regard themselves as Maori to naturally take serious cognisance of this incredible event and of what Ratana stated. And, as a vitally necessary step, begin to put in place his teachings if the complete and active spiritual fulfilment that Ratana pointed to *is ever to be realised by Maoridom.* For, as previously noted, it must surely follow that if Ratana was "spiritually chosen" for this high task, then what he stated was therefore "spiritually-correct" *for all of the race.* Or, more precisely under the outworking of Spiritual Law, *by that group of individual souls who have incarnated into the present Maori race since Ratana's Calling to the present time.* The direction he showed is probably more relevant today given the strong resurgence of older cultural traditions and a similar kind of return to the whole idea of tribalism. Notwithstanding this 'collective potential destiny', it still remains with each individual whether he wishes to follow such a path or not.

Nevertheless, to this end, Maori leaders of all persuasions, but perhaps more so from the different Churches, should consider where they stand in the light of these assertions. A searching analysis is certainly not required to ascertain how far Maori are from the direction proclaimed by the "Mangai". The current social statistics clearly show that to be very far now. The appropriate steps should therefore be taken to immediately 'close the gap' and once more "fulfil the Mangai's directives", if Maori unquestionably wish "true spiritual growth"![11]

As Tau Henare, Minister of Maori Affairs in the first Coalition Government, basically stated:

"I don't want to hear what's wrong with the Maori race, I know what's wrong. I want to know how to fix it?"

The answer is almost disturbingly simple; embrace The "Truth" of Spiritual Law – and Live It!

19.1.7   Point 7 – Conquered Maori fears

Ratana was clearly born into a distinctly Maori environment. A small amount of schooling and scriptural studies under the influence of Europeans was part of his upbringing but, overall, one would determine the major influences as being obviously Maori. In the time frame of the early part of his century, Maori were still very much immersed in the superstition of the more ancient aspects of the culture. Even though many were nominal and/or practising Christians, reports from that time show that the old superstitions still held powerful sway, with *tohungaism* very much a strong part of everyday life.

So, bearing in mind that most Maori of the time *were* still wracked by fear-ridden superstition; given the reluctance or inability to leave such practices behind, it is all the more amazing that *one lone individual* steeped in that kind of environment could, *at one stroke*, renounce all connection to it. Not only did Ratana forsake it *completely*, however, but he actively and powerfully set out with the stated intention of completely destroying this feared 'bastion' of 'Maori power'. That fearless crusade by one from within the race gives an important indication of *the power* given to him for his "mission".

Yet it is a logical and self-evident fact that only a person of Maori descent, steeped in the environment of the 'old way', could ever understand the need to rid the race of unnecessary psychic bonds. No Pakeha, not even from the missionary element, would have possessed the *inherent understanding* to undertake such a task. However, the question could be asked: "Why not a Maori from within an Orthodox Church?" On the surface, a perfectly logical assumption since we invariably believe that high spiritual 'vocations' are ostensibly connected with 'religious service'. In the case of Christian denominations, such professions ultimately derive their ordination and authority from The Bible. In its logical progression, therefore, perhaps a trained Maori clergyman would have been more suitable. The very fact that an untrained and relatively unlettered man was chosen, reveals the historically interesting truism that many truly-ordained,

---

[11]The explanations contained in this Work <u>are</u> *the greatest single help* to bring about *genuine* desire for change.

spiritual leaders are **not chosen** from the ranks of orthodox Churches or from the religious ruling class.

The pages of The Bible itself record the condemnation by many of the Prophets of the 'religious authorities' of the day. And in probably the most striking example of this Jesus, Himself, chose as His disciples, not the learned scribes of the Temple, but *simple men*, fishermen and the like. In short, *ordinary workers in ordinary professions*. Thus, we should not be surprised at the choice of a man like Ratana to be "Called" to lead Maori away from their debilitating psychic past. Of course, it is very probable that he was born for that particular purpose. In which case the necessary *whanau* and geographical location within New Zealand would have been carefully chosen for his task, in strict accordance with the immutable outworking of **The Spiritual Laws of Creation**.

*   *   *   *   *

There is one more vital fact that should be recognised about the man Ratana at this point in our journey. Whilst he may have been ordained to fulfil the role of "Mangai", we must never forget that our spiritually-inherent free-will allows us to choose **yes,** or to choose **no** – in any situation. The fact that he had the very great courage **to choose yes**, and not shrink away in fear of the task and/or fear of very real and malevolent Maori opposition, reveals how well prepared and ideal a choice he was. *All* within Maoridom, therefore, should be grateful for both his incarnation and his clear recognition of what was required for Maori.

19.1.8   Point 8 – Cleanliness is next to Godliness

"Cleanliness is next to Godliness" –

– is a saying familiar to many. In terms of its spiritual ramifications, it is undoubtedly a powerful truth. Ratana understood that reality and constantly referred to Pope's, "Health for the Maori". And, moreover, strongly emphasised the same need at Christmas, 1920, in the 2nd point of his address – "Cleanliness of the Body" – during the opening of a new, Non-denominational Church. Genuinely striving for spiritual enlightenment should naturally presuppose the equally genuine desire to exert oneself to keep body, mind and soul "clean". Despite the fact that those individual aspects of a person are inseparable whilst alive, each 'single component' of the whole human entity can still influence, or can be influenced by, the others. Thus one who allows his mind to be 'soiled' *automatically* 'soils' his soul body too. Similarly, a reluctance to keep the physical body clean presupposes a slovenly attitude of the mind, resulting in a 'soiling' of it as well. Such a slipshod, unsanitary attitude thus prevents the *wairua* from truly shining, thereby potentially denying it its rightful place and thus possible unfulfillment of spiritual purpose.

In reality, lack of cleanliness in the physical sense reveals a certain degree of laziness and ill-discipline which may, of course, result in unnecessary sickness and disease. Pope's book, "Health for the Maori", which Ratana immersed himself in, presumably assisted him greatly in spreading his message about the vital need to foster and maintain cleanliness. Discipline in maintaining good hygiene levels and in cleanliness of the body should have a natural flow-on effect to cleanliness of clothing, dwelling and of one's immediate environment.

That is certainly true in a Military setting, as many ex-servicemen of all ethnic persuasions will know or recall – *including very many Maori*. The first step, however, should be to inculcate the concept of cleanliness of body.

All this is true in the spiritual sense too.

The same lack of discipline here 'soils' the coverings of the *wairua* [spirit] and weighs it down. If we recall the meaning of the various Laws of Creation and how they intermesh, then we are better able to understand why Ratana was so strict on this point. For under The Laws of Nature, unclean physical bodies may well cause illness and suffering, but such can be remedied. However, a person who after earthly death discovers that he is *weighed down by unclean practices*, will also find that he is then totally subject to the immutable outworking of **The Law of Spiritual Gravity**. In concert with the other Eternal Laws, the primary force of this Law will propel that soul to a plane exactly corresponding to its particular degree of 'spiritual uncleanness'. For Ratana to insist so strongly on cleanliness indicates that he probably understood why it was so important both physically and spiritually. As in all things, however, Spiritual Justice is the driving force here, not lax habits or personal views.

Therefore, we should once more note the admonition of the Angel to Ratana to, 'cleanse yourself', 'as white as snow', and to be "...as sinless as the wood-pigeon". This directive, by extension for the Maori race also, was surely given so that the new spiritual direction and potential might be completely fulfilled. Thus offering Te Iwi Maori precisely that which perhaps seems so far from spiritual fulfilment at this time – good health, harmony, peace and spiritual security.

19.1.9   Point 9 – Spiritual Power

In his battles with *tohunga* and against superstition, Ratana's powerful "destiny" gave him the decided advantage of no longer believing in the efficacy of pointless *tapu* and *makutu*, in that he clearly recognised it for what it actually was. Some of the old and feared practitioners of the past had already learned that Pakeha were not personally affected by their psychic machinations. In Ratana's case, in his singularly spectacular mission, he was endowed with the power to destroy all such practices. If we revisit **The Law of Attraction of Similar Species**, we can deduce that Ratana and his *tohunga* opponents derived their particular 'powers' from opposite ends of the so-believed "spiritual spectrum" – Ratana's from the lighter end, and the *tohungas'* from the dark end. In fact, only Ratana tapped into the power of the genuinely spiritual, whereas *tohunga* utilised inferior, man-made 'forms' to do their bidding.

> Thus it should be quite obvious that Ratana was called to destroy *tohungaism* **because it was not beneficial for the Maori race**.

If it was, he would clearly not have been tasked with its destruction. So if it was not beneficial then, **it cannot be so today either**, simply because the whole foundation of it is basically aspirital. It does not even begin to connect with genuinely Spiritual Realms, only man-made psychic ones! For the spiritual 'forms' that Ratana produced through his ordination as the "Mangai" of God for Maori, as opposed to those which *tohunga* brought forth – particularly the kinds of forms they sent against Ratana – were all subject to the same '*whirlwind constant*' under the outworking of "**The Spiritual Law of Attraction...**" Therefore, in the same way that we can apply the scriptural warning of "...fear begetting more fear" to the darker side of *tohungaism* whereby psychic malevolence "...begets only more of the same"; so should we also readily understand that Ratana's far more spiritually elevated activities logically "...begat more and more genuine spirituality".

Moreover, even if we attempt to divide *tohungaism* into 'good' and 'bad', where exactly do we draw a clear demarcating line. The fact is that Maori practitioners of the past could not do so either. And that was simply because they had neither the knowledge nor the understanding of the huge **differences** between the numerous and diverse forms and activities connected with the various levels of just the lower planes of Creation to which we are closely connected, let alone any understanding or knowledge of the *complete picture*.

The **psychic realm**, in which Maori traditional culture was mostly immersed, and from where *makutu* and *utu* derive their origin, is invariably mistaken for the genuinely spiritual one. **It is most definitely not!**

And neither is that of the **The Animistic or Elemental Realm** to which **The Nature Beings** belong.

Whilst Maori mostly feared their presence through not understanding the origin, activity and true purpose of them, they are, nonetheless, actually Creator-Willed beings placed here to help us.[12] Finally, knowledge of the actual **Spiritual Realms** – about which we have already offered explanations in earlier Chapters – Maori had no clear understanding of either.

What passed for absolute and inviolable knowledge in the world of the ancient Maori was a strange and much-feared mish-mash of the psychic and animistic worlds without any genuine spiritual clarity. Ratana's more spiritually-pure vision, therefore, could not allow the activities of the *tohunga* caste to continue to subvert and contaminate the Maori race. Thus it was necessary to immediately confront it and excise it completely from the consciousness of the race. Ratana not only had the advantage of the "power for the battle", but a high spiritual "destiny" with its concomitant support from that respective Realm under the **"The Law of Spiritual Attraction..."**. Whereas, under the same Law, the *tohunga* could only 'attract' support for any confrontation with Ratana from just the *psychic planes*, thus a far lower and decidedly inferior level. That is why Ratana was so spectacularly successful.

Unfortunately, even with Ratana's clear mission, Maori today still carry over what is essentially an uncertain combination of various bits from all three levels, in the mistaken belief that this 'mixed-bag' is actually spiritual in essence, is highly so, and is the repository of all knowledge. Unfortunately, nothing could be further from the truth! Therefore, *tohunga* and related practitioners of the 'old arts' today still do not correctly understand these vitally important differences either.

Present-day 'traditional-Maori' tutors should take careful note of these explanations and learn the key and fundamental differences between the three aspects mentioned if they wish to achieve genuine 'spiritual' progress for themselves and/or for any followers.

19.1.10   Point 10 – "But first secure the Kingdom of God..."

Ratana's reply to the land question put to him by King Te Rata's emissaries once more strongly illustrates his clearer understanding of Spiritual Law when he stated the need to address the spiritual aspect first. From that crucial standpoint, there is little point in having stewardship of land, if what should be the first aspect is completely ignored. The call to "...unite in the Father first..." and then later to "...unite in the land" is the same as the admonition of Jesus to:

> "...*first secure* the Kingdom of God, and His righteousness; and *all these things* will be ready for you."

> (Matthew 6:33, Fenton. Emphasis mine.)

It is virtually the same as understanding the need to heed **The First Commandment** absolutely! Ratana's advice for King Te Rata should not be dismissed as something for him alone or for that time only, however. By stating just such a directive to a titular Maori head of the day, Ratana placed an element of **The Living Law Itself** into the consciousness of the Maori race *for all time* – because it is a **Spiritual Truth** – and because he was the "Mangai" of God for Maori.

Therefore, the understandable jubilation through today's reclamation of land via the recommendations of The Waitangi Tribunal should be tempered by the sober realisation that land,

---

[12]A previous Chapter offers that greater clarification.

alone, *will never* solve the problems of Maoridom. In fact, *without* that first directive, it will only bring more heartache in the long term. For, in the final analysis and in terms of the ultimate Laws of Truth, any longing other than a longing for **The Truth first**, will always **lead downwards**, even that of the believed, unquenchable longing for the land of the ancestors to, ostensibly, 'help put things right'. Moreover, too strong a tie to the land holds the possible danger of becoming an earth-bound soul after death; a great danger for Maori given the 'earthly-emotional' tie to land which has developed to such a strong propensity now. That is why, today, there is a greater need than ever to strive to understand Ratana's spiritual wisdom in this matter.

Land should therefore never be viewed as a material commodity to be simply 'owned'. Since it is imbued with life, too, it should be treated with the commensurate respect that the provider of sustenance for humankind should receive. The stated desire of Maori to be *kaitiaki* of land therefore requires that serious note be taken of Ratana's statement concerning 'ownership of land'. Perhaps, then, The Living Laws may graciously incline toward Maori and bring forth genuine abundance under the *recognition* that the true "guardians of land" – and thus the greater stewardship – is that of **The Elemental Forces of Nature**, to whom we must show acknowledgement and unequivocal respect!

19.1.11 Point 11 – "You Lock up the Keys..."

Here, again, we see the wisdom of Ratana. Not only wisdom, however, but deep humility and, therefore, true *mana*. Let us contrast his proclamation that he was just "a fingerpost" pointing the way together with his invitation for all to "enter through the door", with the stinging words which Jesus levelled in serious accusation at the religious authorities of His day. His damning words to them were:

> "Woe to you, play-acting professors and Pharisees! because you lock up the Kingdom of Heaven in the face of mankind; while you yourselves neither enter, nor allow those arriving to go in."

> (Matthew 23:13, Fenton.)

More than that, however, He labelled them hypocrites and likened their inner natures to that of:

> "...whitewashed tombs ... pretty enough outside, but inside full of dead men's bones and every kind of corruption."

> (Matthew 23:27, Fenton.)

It was precisely because Jesus publicly exposed their hypocrisy that He was branded a troublemaker. In their base desire to cling to temporal power 'at all costs', the 'authorities' plotted to eventually bring about His murder!

Ratana, in stark contrast to the pharisees whom Jesus condemned, *willingly opened the door*. Not just with words, but by example also. Having opened the door, he then invited *everyone* to enter. The greater knowledge and spiritual insights he graciously received were shared with all, as should always be the case with Spiritual Truth.

If we now quietly reflect on the attitude of some Maori who still hold to *tohungaism* today, we will note a particular disposition which often characterises a sometimes unfortunate aspect of both *tohungaism* and *kaumatuaism*. Rather than openly sharing their 'supposed knowledge', there is often a 'believed need' to keep it from everyone else. There may be attempts to justify this attitude with the claim that it is too sacred or too dangerous for anyone 'without sufficient power' to 'carry it'. Or the person requesting it has insufficient *mana* to receive it. Invariably, the real reason will be an unspoken concern at possibly *losing* some kind of spurious claim to, so-called, *great knowledge.*

In short, it is nothing more than a psychological power-play masking the very real fear of a loss of imagined knowledge and, by extension in the Maori mind, 'power'. And therefore a concomitant loss of some kind of, actually non-existent, 'status of *mana*'. Quite logically, if one has to state that certain 'knowledge' may be dangerous, then that is the **surest indication** that it *cannot possibly be of a spiritual nature*.

For not one thing from out of the genuinely spiritual is dangerous to man.

It is only the dark psychic productions produced by him to feed his ego and pretence to great knowledge that are dangerous.

The Middle Ages saw the very same thing. The 'learned clergy' of the time kept The Scriptures from the ordinary people, even to the point of retaining them in Latin so that it could never become part of the life of the common man and serf. Yet the bringer of the knowledge of "The Living Truth" – Jesus – **gave it freely, to all men!**

The great Spiritual Teachers throughout history have done the same. One marvels at why we have not proceeded far enough down some kind of enlightened path to be able to simply let go pretensions to ideas of 'great knowledge' which invariably contains very little of real spiritual value. Thankfully, for Maori at least, Ratana followed the example of Jesus admirably.

19.1.12   Point 12 – "Fear Begets More Fear."

"Mate Maori!" The illness of fear!

"There is no fear in love. But perfect love expels fear, because fear is torture."

(1 John 4:18, Fenton.)

These Biblical words can be perfectly applied here if the knowledge of Spiritual Law is taken into account. In accordance with that Law, fear of anything will call in, or attract to itself, more fear.

By now we have well-learned that all thought forms are living things given life by the free-will volition of human beings. And under **The Law of Attraction of Similar Species**, a person in great fear of some particular thing will attract to himself similar forms which surround him, and which can then actually become attached to him. The greater the fear, the stronger the attachment, and all under the outworking of the "whirlwind constant". If the fear is of malevolent entities, that is what will arrive. Whilst this was a large part of the 'old traditional way', unfortunately it is still the situation among some Maori today.

Since the old Maori generally believed that illnesses stemmed from the activity of malevolent forces directed against him – and which he invariably thought were beyond his control – his fear of them produced more anxiety. That fear, in turn, simply attracted more of the same 'energies', with the 'total contribution' usually then associated with the cause of the particular illness. So it is not surprising that in many primitive and superstitious societies, deaths from simply wasting away in fear reportedly did occur. Many instances of such deaths, usually as a result of being '*makutu'd*', are recorded among Maori in just the time frame of the early European chroniclers alone – never mind what went on before their crucially-valuable contribution to posterity.

Despite that timely bestowal to New Zealand history by early European ethnologists, a general opinion has surfaced among mainly Maori academics that those early chronicles were somehow grossly flawed in that the writers of them did not accurately report what they saw and experienced, or did not understand the clear evidence of their own eyes. A strange view, given that no present academics were actually there at the time. Who is really attempting to change history, we may wonder? Some in the same group apparently believe that the majority of Maori who had *makutu* placed on them during that era did not know they had been so targeted, thus supposedly rendering the 'fear' element negligible.

That incorrect outlook fails to take into account the very real fact that not only was *makutu* a 'living force', it was one to be feared because it inculcated that very condition into the actual psyche of the people who were then subjugated by it, and thus lived in general fear of it. And Maori society did fear it, as they did *tapu*. The fact that some may not have known they had been *makutu'd* did not remove the all-pervasive societal dread of it. In truth, simply 'believing' one had been *makutu'd* was often a sufficient enough reason for stressful alarm to set in thus resulting in illness.

For a process or belief to be so virulent as to cause wasting away and death in some cases, surely reveals the dark, negative energy of that particular activity. In any case, the natural excrescence of *utu* from out of the practice of *makutu* destroys any argument that Maori society did not fear it. For *utu* was the counter, the payment for *makutu* – real or imagined. This was the dreaded reality for a generally fear-ridden Maori society. It was a 'reality', moreover, that was not at all understood.

*   *   *   *   *

It is interesting to note that at a conference of the American Advancement for the Association of Science, Dr Annaliese Pontius of the Harvard Medical School postulated the view that Stone Age tribes were 'stressed out' by constant fear – of dangerous animals, evil spirits and other tribes. Even in her studies of various primitive tribal groups of hunter/gatherers today,[13] the same fears still hold sway.
She correctly states:

"When the sun sets everybody flees into their huts out of fright."[14]

Dr Pontius believes that stressful situations force the brain to make shortcuts in how it views the world, and that is reflected in simplified Stone Age art. In other words there is no "safe space" in a fearful society to include *flowing detail and embellishment*. That difference is reflected in how tribal and European peoples relate to their respective art forms today. Europeans generally do not place ancestral or psychic constraints on their art, unless perhaps it has certain religious connotations or is placed in a religious setting. But even there, such art forms are usually associated with an elevation of thought toward a Higher benevolence thus generally negating any possible fear aspect. For the most part, therefore, European art is there to be simply enjoyed – perhaps denigrated – but usually marvelled over in their often perfected forms of visual beauty.

Indigenous tribal peoples, however, invariably imbue their 'representations' with a 'life-presence' or 'attribute' of some kind. Perhaps it may be an ancestral characteristic, but is often one derived from the fear element inherent in such peoples. That is why virtually all Maori carvings and artefacts are regarded as sacred *taonga* by Maori. And why they are similarly held to be *tapu* and accompanied by emotional ceremony when moved from place to place. One must not upset the 'forms' that 'reside' in Maori *taonga*. That particular stance, therefore, clearly leans toward the fear aspect, ultimately.

*   *   *   *   *

---

[13]Anthropologists have noted that artworks from existing tribes have the same simple quality as cave paintings, masks and carved heads from Stone Age people, and have tended to dismiss the 'artists' as untrained or unsophisticated.

[14]This was certainly the 'reality' during the formative years with the *whanau* where superstitious fear ruled, not knowledge.

Thus it was not just a few isolated 'forms' in the old world of the Maori that allowed psychic practices to flourish and be so darkly-effective, but a pervasive blanket brought into being by the non-understanding of what aspiritual Maori activities were *actually producing*. The tragedy is that it is, even today, still not really understood. That legacy has bequeathed Maoridom with a terribly distorted belief that it represents some kind of acceptable and somehow elevated, spiritual lifestyle.

Yet among Maori living prior to the 20th century there must have existed some intuitive measure of *how wrong it all was* for, as some early European observers noted, Maori communities incensed with the dangerous practices of tiresome '*makutu* merchants' within their ranks simply killed them at an appropriate opportunity. For Maori to have so decisively sorted out what was obviously a serious problem must surely indicate that **those particular practitioners and their activities were considered dangerous or not beneficial for the group**.

As noted earlier in this Work, Best and other chroniclers thus record that many *tohunga* did not live to old age, with a surprising number dying at the hands of their own people. That might well indicate how much fear the practice of *makutu did* actually instil in the populace.

Perhaps with these brief explanations the reader may gain an insight as to how one can actually die of abject fear or terror. Consequently, we should further understand Ratana's urgency to take the Maori away from the psychic conditions and activities that fostered *makutu* and *utu* and bred '*mate Maori*' and '*mate wairua*'[15] under *tohungaism*!

19.1.13   Point 13 – Spiritual Freedom

The excommunication of Ratana by the Anglican Church was actually a blessing, for the greater vision which he had been charged to fulfil could now be put into effect. The European religious ideal clearly lacked any degree of real understanding of Maori spiritual needs, especially including the degree to which *tohungaism* still held sway. As previously stated, no European Church leader was called to lead Maori forward. Therefore, any belief on the part of European Church orthodoxy that it could do so would have been tantamount to wishful thinking. An especially astute grasp of the inherent nature of the Maori psyche was necessary for such an undertaking to succeed. That also had to include the courage to fight for the very life of the race itself against the deepest kind of ingrained psychic practices that any people can possibly become immersed in. And only one born into it could have any understanding of that reality.

Consequently the vast gulf between the two groups at the time, in terms of how each viewed the "world", could not be easily bridged. The more intellectual, pseudo-scientific mind-set and attitude of European orthodoxy differed greatly from easy Maori acceptance of the intangible world where all things were possible.[16] Such was the difference between the two positions that a separate direction was necessary. For only with complete spiritual freedom and without the rigidity and strict shackles of orthodox church dogma would Ratana be able to fulfil his 'destiny' for Maori. His exasperation at having to continually explain issues that only he innately understood, and which orthodox Church leaders *should have heeded for their spiritual elucidation* also, can be gauged by one prayer which besought the:

"Lord God our Father..." to "...**certainly protect us from intellectuals**!"

(Ratana: p.46, Emphasis mine.)

---

[15]The term, '*mate wairua*', commonly used to describe a certain aspect of Maori mental illness, is actually *incorrect*. The spirit – or *wairua* – can *never*, of itself, become sick or diseased in any way whatsoever. It is the *outer coverings* of the spirit that suffer, but only if we do not live correctly; i.e., according to the immutable **'Spiritual Law of Reciprocal Action'**, primarily!

[16]This view is actually incorrect by virtue of the fact that the inviolable Laws of Creation (explained in Chapter 6) ultimately determine what is possible and what is not. It is not for man-made cultural traditions or any brand of "ethnic science" to decide – because it cannot. It has no say in such matters!

Thus, not until Ratana was actually excommunicated from the European Church was he able to more powerfully fulfil his spiritual mission and build his Temple to the Light![17]

19.2   Summary of Points

The above thirteen key points we have accentuated may help to clarify certain aspects of Ratana's "mission" and activity that will always be relevant for Maori. Those points either encompass innate conditions within the race – which need to be addressed once more – or have lasting values as a result of his works. If the high spiritual worth of Ratana's mission is not to be lost, the substance of the previous 13 points relating to his destiny – and by extension that of the Maori race – should be carefully considered. For within those parameters Ratana's spiritual signpost is strongly anchored.

Most of the other main points which Ratana included in his Covenant – those he asked his followers to honour – we have addressed by way of various explanations throughout this Work. Sometimes specifically, sometimes in general discourse, but always from the standpoint of **The Spiritual Laws of Creation**.

And thereby is Ratana's prophecy concerning the revelation of everything – not solely to the morehu but to the whole country – now fulfilled!

> **"Soon, very soon in the future you will no longer speak, but instead a very different person (generation) will reveal to you all the fruits of these prophecies. Not only will it be revealed exclusively to you the morehu only, no but to the whole country."**
>
> (T. W. Ratana, 1929. "Ratana Revisited – An Unfinished Legacy":
> Keith Newman. [Emphasis mine.])

*And **when** did the Prophet Ratana prophesy that time to be?*

> "You have all heard and are familiar with the word that says: 'Night time has passed, the new break of dawn draws near', there is a day unfolding when you will see two towers standing on the Mount of Olives, and at that time you will see *a woman rising up from the Labour Party who will become prime minister*, and then you will know you are at the doorway, not *nearing it*, **but actually at the doorway**..."
>
> (T.W. Ratana, 11th November 1936 at the Mount of Olives,
> Ratana Pa. "Ratana Revisited ...": [Emphasis mine.])

Despite such sure prophecies and precise timing by the especially Called Prophet for Maori, we can reasonably assume that the probable *first reaction* of the Ratana Church and Ratana's followers to what is stated in this particular section of this Chapter will be one of rejection and/or resistance. For, in what would be a perfectly understandable estimation, how can any "outsider" even begin to presume to analyse his mission and further *his* work? Ordinarily, that would be a perfectly reasonable position.

> However, it is *precisely* the *presentation and elucidation* of **"The Spiritual Laws of Creation"** for Maori and New Zealand as a whole that **Ratana was referring to and thus prophesying about!**

That is the **key** to *understanding the above two prophecies*, and therefore this *pivotal Chapter* furthering his 'Spiritual Mission' for Aotearoa and its peoples. By extension, therefore, *this complete **Work***.

---

[17]In that might perhaps be seen the outworking of "the wisdom of the mysterious ways of The Lord"!

*   *   *   *   *

There is one more aspect, strongly retained within Maoridom, which also requires serious dissection here, simply because Ratana campaigned strongly for its abolition.

In the context of Ratana's "mission" it is important to understand why he was so strict on the following issue. Yet it is a sad fact that many who are given spiritual insight for a particular purpose *must often afterward defend their words and actions against those who do not possess the same insight or vision*. For even with Ratana's obvious spiritual abilities, there were still many who could not accept all that he advised on, even though being clearly beneficial for all, simply because *they lacked the necessary degree of spiritual insight and wisdom*.

At the time, one of the hardest things for Maori to let go completely were ties to tribal affiliations. Today, under the renaissance of cultural traditions, tribal links are probably much stronger than they have been for many years. Yet this only serves to illustrate that the work of the true Prophet and spiritual leader of the Maori race is also *less understood now than ever before*.

So let us examine this question of tribalism and strive to *spiritually understand* why Ratana's clear 'task' also called for the *dismembering* of tribal affiliations.

19.3   Tribalism

Ratana's deeper spiritual insight revealed the necessity to lead Maori out of their bondage of subservience to tribalism. And naturally all that that necessarily implies in terms of ancestor worship and continuing vacillation to a rigidly structured code of servility to a *kaumatua* system which decrees that at a certain age and/or rank such persons magically acquire great wisdom and knowledge. Nothing could be further from the truth! Yet relatively few question this strange situation. Moreover, the *kaumatua* system itself can only be perpetuated by the continued insistence that tribal connections be maintained and, indeed, strengthened.

If one can pass on one's own experiences for the benefit of others, then that is an admirable thing to do, but the status of *kaumatua* is not necessary for that. In the case of true spiritual knowledge and wisdom, however, most of the elderly simply *do not* possess it. To continue to foster a belief that somehow automatically guarantees all Maori 'magical wisdom' immediately they turn 60 or 65 – or any other age for that matter – is ludicrous. If the title or status of *kaumatua* is purely one of *respect for age*, then that is a totally different matter, for old age and long life *should be respected*. If, however, it is supposed to be a day of immediate and vast wisdom acquisition, than the whole situation is farcical. What it does offer, as a matter of course, is a mechanism whereby 'place-hunting' becomes unhealthily entrenched.

Ratana's insistence that his 'Morehu' and those he healed give up tribal connections, was surely driven by the clear necessity of moving the Maori race along the path to Nationhood. It would also severely limit, and eventually negate, the position of the *tohunga*. Whilst Maori still clung to tribalism, the entrenched 'system' of rank, ancestor worship and *tohungaism* would always flourish and could never allow the opportunity for genuine spiritual growth and advancement. The true and correct evolutionary path of development ultimately calls for the diverse tribes within any particular race to gradually develop into a single Nation.

Ratana's strength of 'Calling', with the twin abilities of healing and spiritual power, allowed him to easily defeat the psychic machinations of the *tohunga* class who sometimes directed their venom against him personally. Ratana's capabilities were given to him to *more quickly* direct the difficult transition of a very recently active, stone-age cannibal race, then in a poor state of physical, emotional, mental and spiritual health, to a position whereby he could more vitally *accelerate* that necessary transitional-process from the old to the new. Labouring for an unnecessarily long period with the old way could result in the initial impetus being lost. And to have the *tohunga* emerge victorious over him and his mission would have resulted in a very serious setback for the Maori race in every area of life.

We should be quite clear on this point!

> **Ratana did not come just to found some Maori religion. That was simply the framework under which he could achieve the main goal. His actual mission was to arrest the serious and rapid decline of a race in grave physical, mental and spiritual health – and to clearly show the path to spiritual <u>salvation</u>.**

Moreover, it was for precisely that reason that such strong powers were given to him.

The precise timing of his mission, to which we have alluded, was not without purpose either. All people of planet earth are at a crucial point in their evolutionary development. Ratana emerged to prepare the Maori for what is now *not far distant*. Without his work of preparation, it is doubtful that there would have been any real progress away from the old way, for he, more than any other before or since, *actually achieved that goal*. Without him, Maori would more than likely have become more attached to their *tohungaism* and gone into a new 'dark psychic age' *even if not appearing to or even believing so*; and any marked reversion would have been disastrous. Unfortunately, even in the present with all of Ratana's guidance, relatively few have actually heeded his 'spiritually-mandated directives'.

Tribalism, and the maintenance of such a system long after it has served its purpose, does not flow with **The Law of Spiritual Movement** because the collective energies of the race that should be directed toward building a *single Nation*, are fragmented and scattered – and sometimes even dissipated. Interestingly, the unwillingness to accept this natural process of development under Ratana's directive, has now spawned more and more breakaway splinter groups from the main tribal core groups anyway. The obvious outcome here is that the once authoritative chiefly rank is no longer readily acceptable, and new groups now appoint their own 'leaders'. Yet this questioning of 'traditional authority' is simply the outworking of the effect of **Spiritual Law** *on everything*, including Maori tribal affiliations. For as decaying, distorted concepts everywhere are challenged, more and more quickly they are driven to collapse.

Thus, we should accept the reality that the tribal system, currently being fostered as part of ongoing Maori 'traditional and cultural development', is actually only a transitional process through which *all* of the major racial groups have also travelled. Spiritually, it has had its time for most of the world's peoples! And just as the Germans, Greeks, Romans, English, Chinese etc., have left the tribal system behind in the normal course of development so, too, are the Maori meant to do the same – **now** – as Ratana directed.

Perhaps the main criticism of tribalism is that, by its very nature, it is inherently divisive and undemocratic, though that aspect may not be so important under the outworking of Spiritual Law. Therefore the whole thrust of tribalism is both counter-productive for Maori and this Nation as a whole. The collective wish must surely be internal unity and harmony.

Sir Peter Tapsell, in an interview by Anthony Hubbard and published in the N.Z. Sunday Star Times a decade ago on 12th January 1997, correctly stated that:

> "Traditional tribal structures... are not suited to modern life and the urban Maori. Maoridom had been through an introspective phase, a swing back to tribalism, which I think is unfortunate. When the rest of the world is emerging globally, we're going the other way. That will be shortlived. We'll find, as every other people has before us, that that direction leads only into a cul-de-sac."

And that is so because, as strongly stated, clinging to tribalism does not fulfil the immutable outworking of **The Law of Movement** – in its correct *spiritual* application.

Sir Peter Tapsell's far more expanded and enlightened view again urged him to condemn this trend five months later on 26th June, 1997. As reported in the Herald, he stated that the "...return of Maori to tribalism..." was "...his greatest disappointment in Parliament." Sir Peter opined that there might be:

> "...a place for tribal bodies to deal with matters specific to members of that tribe. But in order to address the major problems of our time – unemployment, education and health – we need new regional organisations where every Maori has the same rights and *responsibilities*, irrespective of which canoe brought his ancestors to New Zealand."

> (Emphasis mine.)

He continued:

> "We need a new sense of nationalism if we are to deal with our problems."

And in concert with our analysis of The Treaty of Waitangi from the standpoint of Spiritual Law, and of large expectations from settlement claims, Sir Peter noted that:

> "Any compensation payments under the Treaty of Waitangi will remain for some time a strong incentive to tribalism."

Further noting that tribes who had received large payouts appeared to be doing well, he offered a cautionary yet sage opinion.

> "But I fear a lack of business expertise, together with an *inherent Maori nepotism*, will bring growing dissension."

> (Emphasis mine.)

The Dialogue section of the New Zealand Herald dated 15th October, 1997, carried two associated articles. One with regard to the contentious allocation of Maori fishing quota written by Sir Peter. And a second offered by Dr Elizabeth Rata. The article heading alone from Sir Peter will suffice here – "Maori fishing quota should not be allocated to tribal groups." Dr Rata's perceptive essay titled, "Retribalisation is all about money", offers the sage opinion that from the 1970s:

> "...the "Maori revival" and "Maori renaissance" movements have set Maori on a new course and altered the relationship between them and Pakeha in profound and disturbing ways. It has suited many Maori and Pakeha to believe that this social change reflects principles formulated at the beginning of modernity – justice, equality and the social cohesion of democracy."

Dr Rata continues:

> "Two groups have emerged: ethnic Maori, excluded from the benefits of the grievance settlements; and tribal Maori, privileged by access to tribal wealth."

She asks the questions:

> "What has gone wrong? Has a communal peoples' movement of traditional revival been hijacked by internal self-interest and greed? Has Maori revivalism been corrupted through incorporation into state structures?"

As we quoted in Chapter 16, sub; **Maori Economic Power through 'Te Tiriti'**: Dr Rata fleshes out her arguments further before finally offering the interesting view:

> "...that the tribes have become capitalist corporations through the brokerage of their resources into the national and international economic system. Indeed, corporate groups, such as the new "classed tribe", suit the global order far better than those organisations of individuals who claim economic rights based on democratic principles."

Dr Rata concludes by stating:

> "Tribal-capitalism, along with both western and eastern forms of corporate capitalism, have profound implications for the future of democracy. The essentially pre-democratic nature of corporate capitalism urgently requires exposure and debate."

Whilst the arguments put forward by Dr Rata in her essay have clear relevance in the light of current social, ideological and cultural changes and do certainly require debate, the title heading is what interests us most. Since "Retribalisation" is obviously about acquiring wealth and material possessions, this process should take into account the spiritual admonition to seek the associated *Spiritual Virtue* *before* the material aspect. Judging by the pronouncements of some of the new breed of 'Maori corporate chiefs' many clearly believe that to be the case. However, since "the proof of the pudding is always in the eating", future harmony or dissent *will unequivocally reveal which was placed first.*

*   *   *   *   *

As an example of how the process of 'tribes to nationhood' might proceed, let us briefly touch upon the interesting situation of the Irish people. Originally a land of many diverse and wild, warring tribes or clans, it eventually evolved to the point where the country was divided into just four regional areas ruled by four "kings" or "chiefs". The four "kings" – probably the strongest clan chiefs in each region – succeeded in welding the various clan factions in their individual areas of influence into a more of less cohesive group. The populace eventually became, after conversion to Christianity, a single Nation.

The primary driving force responsible for that final transformation was a man who was originally kidnapped at the age of 16 (about 405 AD) by those wild tribesmen during a raid across the Irish Sea into what is probably Wales. Kept in the Irish mountains for some years as a herdsman, he saw visions in which he was urged to escape. After six years of slavery he succeeded and fled to what is now France. He entered the church, was ordained a priest and returned to Ireland, concentrating his ministry on the West and North.

He was later appointed Bishop of Ireland. His reported use of the shamrock as an illustration of The Trinity led to its being regarded as the Irish national symbol.[18] That man we know today as Saint Patrick, Apostle and patron Saint of Ireland who was instrumental in forging the wild tribes into a single Nation! A Nation, paradoxically, that much later became the first Colony of Britain. Unfortunately, however, carrying with it a lasting legacy of division and bitterness as the aftermath of that particular colonisation process.

*   *   *   *   *

Not withstanding the problems of Ireland; in similar fashion here, there should be one people out of disparate tribes, and not still separate tribes each with their own political and financial agendas. Maintenance of a tribal system, of course, naturally holds small hierarchies; often as many as there are systems. And the perpetuation of them is guaranteed as long as the 'ranking

---

[18]Consider how Ratana also stressed belief in The Trinity.

hierarchy' cling to their positions and younger members vie for the later filling of various posts that perhaps might no longer be considered ones of 'traditional guarantee'. The prospect of thus ostensibly attaining *mana* with any appointment is also an underlying factor in some cases, even if it is not openly admitted, for that is part of the psyche of Maori too.

Therefore, in Ratana's great wisdom, the abolition of tribalism would also automatically mean the abolition of 'place-hunting' within the Maori race. This would mean a positive and beneficial development toward a better attitude of service to each other, rather than any kind of 'possible' servile slavishness to the chiefly or *kaumatua* hierarchy and its 'exalted' position.

> Had the Maori race recognised Ratana for what he really was and fully embraced his teachings whilst he was on the earth, much more would have been achieved in every sphere of Maori endeavour by now.

By not fully embracing the opportunity offered by the amazing event of 'The Calling of Ratana', the foundation for more fragmentation and more suffering was assured when it need not have been the case. For it should be clearly self-evident that, in all of Maoridom at the time, *only Ratana's work and influence really achieved any measure of meaningful advancement in health, education and political clout*. Most importantly, however, in spiritual growth *away from* the servile and debilitating 'old way'. Generally speaking, Maori *outside* the fold of the Movement did not achieve anywhere near as much progress or reap similar benefits which the Ratana Movement conferred on its followers.

Thus our contention and assertion that only by embracing The Spiritual Laws with sufficient understanding and discipline can one achieve any real advancement, is starkly illustrated in comparing Ratana's Movement to the rest of Maoridom during the time of his life and even years afterward. The current crop of land settlement claims in favour of Maori, with all the potential benefits that might accrue from it, cannot be accepted as a good reason for maintaining tribal affiliations today either. Such disparate amounts of compensation, irrespective of whether right or wrong in today's terms, has already produced a Maori class of 'haves' and 'have-nots'. Future settlements and financial deals will only widen the disparity without the application of Spiritual Law to the whole process.

Had Ratana's directives been followed, a more equitable distribution of resources would probably have eventuated for the benefit of a "Maori Nation", and not just for disparate tribes. Clearly, the banner of Maori Nationhood was carried by the Ratana Church at that time. And the leader or "spiritual chief" of the race was Ratana!

Therefore, if there is still to be any advancement in these rapidly failing times, then the meaning of his mission should be revisited by the current crop of 'tribal leaders'. And their task should be to subjugate their own personal status within the tribe, along with their own ideas and wishes, and work to re-establish a unifying process for Nationhood under the aegis of **The Spiritual Laws**, exactly as Sir Hugh Kawharu stated at his opening address to the CHOGM conference in Auckland in 1995. However, it is all very well to say all the right words, as is the inherent trait within Maoridom, but there must also be the disciplined will to carry them out.

In terms of the indigenous populations of the world, the Maori are far better placed to achieve this. A number of factors contribute to such a favourable scenario, and one is The Treaty of Waitangi. No matter how some may view it, and notwithstanding our analysis of it in an earlier Chapter, it probably represents the best accommodation that any indigenous people were able to achieve during the global colonisation era. Moreover, the relatively small number of Maori overall, in terms of the total population of New Zealand, coupled with the intelligence level of the race, can allow any Maori to achieve, by merit alone, any position or skill within New Zealand society. And that must surely be an enviable position by any standards. Unfortunately, however, self-discipline, in the *collective* sense, does not appear to be *naturally inherent* within Maoridom today.

The reference to a small population as being a positive thing for Maori may puzzle the reader. For, on the surface, larger numbers may well presuppose greater influence. That is obviously true in many situations, but can be a huge drawback in others. If we briefly examine the situation of decolonisation in Africa where there are huge numbers of tribal Africans and lesser numbers of the original white colonising population, we read relatively few stories about spiritual or economic advancement by virtue of their indigenous status, or because they are part of the black or brown 'brotherhood'.

No, the story of Africa today is all too often one of rampant disease, failing health and corruption on the truly grand scale, with the controllers immensely wealthy and without a shred of compassion for the rest of their people. The strong tribal groupings, moreover, have produced a seemingly endless parade of despotic rulers bent on nothing more than *"blood-utu"* against other tribes. Superstition is still rampant with many Africans apparently unable to break their bonds of fear. Even cannibalism is still reported occasionally.

Tribal butchery in that country has seen the world reel in numb disbelief at the mindless savagery of many hundreds of thousands hacked to death with machetes. Cities of once great beauty and former havens of civilisation, peace and security built by the white colonisers, are now destroyed shells offering nothing more than ethnic hell. If it appears Africa is cursed, then, in terms of the outworking of **Spiritual Law**, perhaps it is. Such situations, however, are of their own making, made under the free-will choices *never removed* from human beings, irrespective of racial connections! Even if one disagrees with colonisation, there can be no argument regarding the fact that the colonisers did at least leave an infrastructure that Africans could have used as a foundation for continued progress. After all, many African leaders were educated in white foreign Universities.

The problem was never one of the evils of colonisation, for everyone can simply choose whatever they might wish to adopt. No, the actual evil is more one of ignorance and stubborn intransigence in refusing to accept the need for real change – *spiritual change*. So tribal connections are strengthened under a perceived or potential threat from rival tribal affiliations within the decolonised area. And whether real or not, without the presence and influence of an independent administrative group, there exists no effective authority to curb rising fears.[19] If the growing tensions are not defused sufficiently, then the pressures generated will not generally be able to be contained.

By way of example in 2008, previously-stable, decolonisation success story, Kenya, descends into savage butchery leaving hundreds dead. The trigger; Presidential elections. The fear; genocide along tribal lines as the two main tribes seek, respectively, to either hold on to power, or to wrest it from the present incumbent. Subsequent to the murderous chaos there, international correspondent, David Blair, asks the most pertinent question of all:

> "As children suffer death by fire inside a village church and hundreds of people are butchered in slums across Kenya, one profoundly disturbing question arises from their suffering: *Is Africa's democratic experiment worth the cost in blood?*"

> (Telegraph Group Ltd. Italics mine.)

The key to leaving all that kind of destructive negativity behind is for *conscious development into Nationhood from a tribal situation.*

The problems of tribal Africa are very well clarified in Gwynne Dyer's "Worldview" article published in the New Zealand Herald on 20th May 1996 – over a decade ago now – from which we will quote. His sage observations should offer *more insight* into why Ratana was so strong in his insistence for Maori to sever all tribal connections. [Italics and enumeration mine.]

---

[19]We may note the effect of **"The Law of Attraction of Similar Species"** in such cases.

1. Africa is not cursed. It is the only region of the old tribal world beyond Eurasia to survive into the present with its indigenous population intact.

2. The downside of Africa's good fortune is that it must reconcile its tribal past with living in modern states.

3. People talk about how Africa is handicapped by its lack of the deep-rooted cultural traditions that come from living for thousands of years in mass societies...

4. It does not take people long to learn new traditions.

5. What you cannot change so fast is ethnicity, and Africa has a typical "tribal" ethnic pattern: 200 ethnic groups of more than half a million people, not one of which amounts to five per cent of the total population. Like the Americans before Columbus.

6. Thousands of years of empire in Europe and Asia have changed the ethnic map, mashing *the old tribes together* into ever bigger ethnic groups.

7. Europe has about the same population as Africa, but 75 per cent of its people now belong to only *eight* ethnic groups.

8. Asia has more people than Africa and Europe put together, but half its people belong to only *three* ethnic groups.

9. The same applies in the Americas, Australia and New Zealand, where only a few European ethnic groups predominate.

10. Africa is the only part of the world trying to make it with such a *huge burden* of ethnic diversity.

11. Of course it is having a hard time. Who wouldn't?

We should take cognisance of Dyer's correct observation that people can quickly learn new traditions, as Ratana's followers immediately did. Indeed, if they are intrinsically better all round than the old, then that 'old' should be easily discarded.

So the words, 'huge burden', that so aptly describes Africa's shocking plight could be greatly lessened in the short term and totally alleviated in the long, if the leaders were open enough to consider radical changes; in this case genuinely Spiritual ones. For only with the application of Spiritual Law to its overwhelming problems will Africa find the way out of its self-imposed mess. Self-imposed, moreover, by virtue of its collective refusal to acknowledge and apply those completely beneficial Laws. Since most of those leaders are probably unlikely to change their attitudes, we can expect to see on our modern, large plasma/LCD TV screens a continuing and probably more rapid decline of African society overall.

By contrast, therefore, Ratana's mission should be more clearly seen as the stupendous 'Spiritual Event' for Maori that it truly was. Therefore, his directive to all Maori to dispense with tribalism with all its current wrong connotations, is a major part of "**The Spiritual Salvation**" of the race.

We contend once more, were this *not* the case, he would not have directed it to be so!

Whilst any such resolution for this kind of change might be seen to logically lie in the hands of tribal and Maori church leaders perhaps, in fact any *collective* beneficial change can only be produced by *individual recognition* of what is needed in the first place. For this is not simply the best path for Maori to take but, in reality, ***the only one***. With such a fulfilment, consider the effect that such a powerful ethnic example might set *for other indigenous groups elsewhere in the world to follow*.

Let us hold to that spiritual possibility by considering two things. The first is the theological or spiritual ramifications between the two respective Church positions when Ratana left the Anglicans to form his own. The disquiet with which Anglicans viewed Ratana's doctrine did not take into account the fact that everything surrounding his emergence onto the wider stage was necessarily directed toward a *Maori* spiritual awakening **under him**.

Therefore, only by establishing a totally new and less dogmatic instructive-umbrella to facilitate such a *transition* – a clear impossibility for the established European Churches – could *he* then 'ease' the race from the old into the new .

The second and probably more important point is that of the words given to him by the Archangel Gabriel:

> *"I have travelled around the world to find the people upon whom I can stand. I have come back to Aotearoa to choose you, the Maori people."*

The Covenant that Ratana necessarily demanded from those who wished to follow him was not a tribal one or even a *whanau* one. It had to be *personal*. Tribalism, per se, could have no place in Ratana's plan with regard to a covenant with **"The Light"** *because the individual, alone, must bear full and **personal** spiritual responsibility for all that he thinks and does.*

A covenant with "The Source of Life", therefore, cannot be as part of a group ethos, irrespective of its make-up or the supplicant's relationship to it. It is no different with Church congregations who firmly believe they will all be together in the afterlife. That view fails to take into account the *spiritual requirement* of *personal responsibility* as the *final determinant* for one's *end place*. The "collective" has no place in terms of any such responsibility. For it is unequivocally stated that:

"It is the 'individual' who must ultimately stand before The Law, and not the group 'together'!"

That does not mean, of course, that congregations or groups or whole races cannot or should not *work together* for a common high goal. That is proper and correct. To believe, however, that by virtue of common association or beliefs all will ascend together, is simply not so. Therefore, because of Ratana's insistence on a *personal covenant* to separate the 'Morehu' from any further tribal affiliations, we must assume that he fully understood both the necessity for, and the spiritual meaning of, that particular requirement. In my certain view, the strength of the spiritual experience he underwent gave him the necessary insight to know exactly why he had to insist on it so strongly. A spiritual experience, moreover, that none in Maoridom could claim to have had to such an intense degree, and/or produce a similar outcome to Ratana. Ratana was not here for his own ego, personal agenda, or his own *mana*, he **was** 'tasked' to show the way for Maori. Therefore, as previously stated, the Maori race was also enjoined to *follow him*; ***away from their wrong direction***.

At a time of serious problems within the Maori race, the fact that his Church and Movement prospered clearly illustrates how enlightened he was. By correctly utilising the foundation of The Law for his Church and applying his newly acquired and far more elevated level of spiritual knowledge and understanding to the clear direction shown, he could do little else but succeed. Ratana's courageous choice opened the door, exactly as he proclaimed. Given that proclamation, it surely behoves the Maori race to 'get its act together' in order to fulfil the spiritual purpose Ratana indicated. In other words, to develop true spiritual responsibility as a Nation in the first instance. Was there then a further purpose?

$$*\qquad*\qquad*\qquad*\qquad*$$

Consider: With any *conscious* decision to seek a wider vista, particularly in the truly spiritual sense, there logically develops a clearer idea of where the path is *meant* to be heading the *more* the journey progresses. If it continues on correctly, still more is revealed, until such time as a meaningful, and perhaps collective goal stands out in simple and *unmistakable clarity*. We should see part of that potential as setting an example for other indigenous/colonised races to follow. However, the fulfilment of the complete potentiality first needs the necessary fundamental and genuine spiritual awakening and change in a *conscious* way 'here at home' before anything 'further afield' could be considered.

Therefore, a truly correct example for other indigenous people to follow would not be possible so long as *tribalism* remains within the race. Thus, precisely through that unfortunate retention of tribalism and its associated 'old way' –

– it is probably no longer possible for the Maori race to now fulfil its ordained spiritual purpose as a whole people.

And fragmented groups certainly could not.

19.4   The Ratana Temple

The essence of Ratana's higher wisdom in striving to lead the Maori race away from the baser elements of 'superstitious beliefs can be recognised in the design of his Temple. Nothing from the past that was not *spiritually-beneficial* for the people has been retained in his frame of reference. In that he showed both wisdom and discipline. In fact, the symbols he utilised are those derived primarily from the 'natural world', which the outworking of 'Eternal Truth' has brought into being in any case. They are thus more suited for the identification and recognition of such truths for Maori than those issuing from just Maori religious beliefs.[20]

It is vitally important, therefore, that Maori clearly recognise the full meaning of this aspect of his mission also. Carvings pertaining to *cultural tradition only* should be separated from those which may require a *spiritual designation*. Carving schools and carvers should therefore learn *the huge differences* between the various elements we have previously explained; that of the *psychic and occult*, that pertaining to *Elemental Lore*, and that of the *genuinely Spiritual*. Carvings then retained purely as cultural or traditional icons will not have any *spiritual* connotations wrongly or inadvertently placed on them:

For only *The Spiritual* is of "The Spiritual"!

With wonderful clarity and logic, the 'Wisdom of Solomon' from **The Apocrypha** explains what the idols and carved images of the older peoples of the ancient Holy Land *could not do*. The obvious, almost comedic, tongue-in-cheek truth of the following passages – Chapter 15, Verses 15-17 – which inherently pertain to all such carved representations of god(s), remain(s) the same today.

> "For they thought that all their heathen idols were gods,
> though these have neither the use of their eyes to see with,
> nor nostrils with which to draw breath,
> nor ears with which to hear,
> nor fingers to feel with,
> and their feet are of no use for walking.
> For a *man made them*,
> and one whose *spirit is borrowed* formed them;

---

[20]They will be explained more clearly in the concluding Chapter: "The Rapidly-Fading Spiritual Potential".

for *no man* can form a god which is *like himself*.
He is mortal, and what he makes with *lawless hands* **is dead**,
for he is better than the objects he worships,
since *he* has life, but *they* never have."

And from "The letter of Jeremiah", more simple wisdom.

"Their tongues are smoothed by the craftsmen,
and they themselves are overlaid with gold and silver;
but they are false and *cannot speak*.

(Jeremiah, 8)

Like a local ruler the god holds a scepter [sceptre],
though unable to destroy anyone who offends it.
It has a dagger in its right hand, and has an axe;
but *it cannot save itself* from war and robbers.

(Jeremiah, 14-15)

They are bought at any cost, but there is no breath in them.
Having no feet, they are carried on men's shoulders,
revealing to mankind **their worthlessness**.
And those who serve them are ashamed
because through them these gods are made to stand,
lest they fall to the ground.
If anyone sets one of them upright, it cannot move of itself;
and if it is tipped over, it cannot straighten itself;
but gifts are placed before them **just as before the dead**."

(Jeremiah, 25-27 [Emphases mine.])

We should reiterate once more; that if gargoyle type carvings were acceptable to the new spiritual way for Maori, *in terms of any kind of spiritual connection to The Higher Spheres,* then Ratana would have included them in and on his Temple. The obvious fact that he did not do so is the strongest statement for Maori that it is incorrect to attempt to imbue *traditional* carvings with 'spiritual' *mana* – in the strictest sense of the word. Moreover, if we trace the progress of the various meeting-house facades that the later line of Maori Prophets erected, we will clearly observe how, step by step, they gradually dispensed with traditional carvings, replacing them with other kinds of designs.[21] Until finally leading to Ratana's more sure symbols. Thereby we see how Maori 'cultural-traditionalism' has strongly-eroded the true path forward.

Point 12, "Fear begets Fear", dealt with this issue quite conclusively. And since the newest research findings are often considered by academia to be the only acceptable benchmark from which to work, perhaps Dr. Annaliese Pontius' hypothesis may be the definitive word on this particular subject. For what she postulates fits very well with the outworking of Spiritual Law. Thus, from our perspective, any further findings in this area will probably serve to reinforce her current premise which, in essence, is ours also – and has been throughout this 'Work'.

---

[21] Even Te Kooti's flags broke completely with cultural traditions. By contrast, many present-day Maori 'leaders' want to not just *retain* 'tribalism', with all its associated ramifications, but to *actually* strengthen it.

19.5   Light-Followers? – or 'man-followers'?

Historically, socially, religiously, and perhaps even culturally, the Prophet Ratana could be said to have produced a true 'Maori Church', as opposed to the many Pakeha Churches which a large number of Maori have joined – with some Maori holding senior positions within them. Ratana could also be said to have been a 'servant of his people' i.e., the Maori race.

What do followers of Ratana, the *morehu*, believe; those who attend 'his Church' and celebrate the founder's birthday each year?

For his "Maori Church" – as it has been described – could not, and did not, arise out of traditional Maori culture. As stated very clearly earlier in this Work, Ratana's Church and Movement ultimately arose from out of the Truths contained in **The Bible** brought to this land as the 'Pakeha Religion'. So whilst he founded a Church eminently suitable for Maori, *it could only arise and be successful* primarily through the application of **The Law from The Bible**. Ratana, however, could still include those particular aspects from Maori traditions that 'flowed' with the ethos of **The Law**.

Most certainly, therefore, Ratana *did* set up a Church eminently suitable for Maori, but it was a Church for Maori *to transit through* into the direction *to which he pointed*. Hence his directive:

> "I have opened the door, **but you yourselves must go in**. I am but "a finger post"
> **pointing to the true way of life!**"

> (Ratana, J. M. Henderson, Emphases mine.)

His unequivocal demand to the *morehu* thus shows that he served, first, **He by Whom** he was Called! Therefore, those who have chosen to be part of the Church he founded must also *emulate him* in this point too. Thus there should be no thought of being 'just a Ratana follower', but an *adherent of the way shown by him*.

Now, since Ratana *did* found his Church and Movement on The Bible, and since he certainly demanded to all *morehu* that, "...you yourselves must go in...", let us read the warning of Paul the Apostle *to his followers*.

The first Epistle of Paul to the Corinthians

> "But I beg of you brothers, by the name of our Lord Jesus Christ,[22] that you would all reason alike, and that there may be no dissension among you; but that you may be trained in the same mind and into the same judgement. For it has been made known to me respecting you, my brothers, by Chloe's people, that there are disputes among you. What I mean is this: that you each declare, "I am for Paul"; or, "I am for Kephas"; or, "I for Christ".

> "Can you gamble upon Christ? Paul was not crucified for you! or were you baptized in the name of Paul?"

> (1:10-14, Fenton.)

And from Chapter 3, Verse 1-9 (Emphases mine):

> "While one declares, "I am for Paul", and another, "I am for Apollos", **are you not merely man-followers**. What, then, is Apollos? and what is Paul? – *ministers by whom you believed*, and each endowed *as the Lord decided*. I planted, Apollos watered; **but God Who prospered it**. Consequently, the planter is nothing, nor the waterer; **but God Who prospered it**."

---

[22]Remember that Ratana invoked the name of Jesus in his healing successes.

Even though Paul was referring to another 'leader' aside from him, and thus not primarily a singular situation such as with Ratana, the *primary meaning* of Paul's warning should still nevertheless resonate with *all* in this country who profess to be *followers* of Ratana. Ratana planted, the *morehu* should 'water', **but only God prospers it**.

So we have a powerful warning from Paul, Called by The Light at *that* time, to not simply be *man-followers*. This warning the Prophet Ratana obviously understood. Were that *not* the case, he would *not have directed* the *morehu* to "...go through the door..." which he opened – or "planted".

All denominations of Churches based on the Teachings of Christ and which therefore use The Bible as their foundation, are thereby subject to all Law and Prophecy contained therein – *and not to the 'founder/s'* of such Churches or denominations.

In summary, whilst Ratana was certainly not a perfect human being in all that he did and revealed ordinary human weaknesses that afflict us all, his spiritual contribution and legacy for Maoridom clearly cannot be matched by any other. To this end, what will forever remain is the fact of his momentous mission and destiny, and the fearless, dedicated manner in which he carried it out.

Perhaps his greatest triumph, however, was in conquering the inherent and long-ingrained subjugation to psychic thoughts and activities which manifested materially in *tohungaism*, *makutu* and *utu*. By fearlessly fighting these debilitating aspects in Maori society he paved the way for all others to *similarly let go*, as the *first step* toward *genuine* spiritual ascent.

Thus, what he bequeathed to Maoridom via his example and his works was the Eternal Spiritual signpost directing the race and Nation to the only true and harmonious way forward.

19.6   The 'Proclamation'

> In the Section, **"Key Prophecies of the Prophet: Ratana!"**, I stated *there* that at
> the end of *this* Chapter the reader would find an unequivocally sure proclamation/prophecy
> concerning the 'return' or 'Second Coming' of **Jesus, The Son of God**.

The global Christian Church comprises somewhere around two billion members – close to one-third of humanity – the vast majority of which await 'His return'. Moreover, it is expected 'soon'. In other words, we are in the time that it is prophesied to occur – the 'End-time'.

The Ratana Church can be broadly stated to be Christian because the founder, Ratana, built his Church on the teachings of **The Bible**, the **Worship of God**, and knowledge of **The Son** and **The Holy Spirit**, primarily. Yet dissent within Ratana ranks about who or what should be worshipped and/or revered saw different ideas emerge.

In 1939, Ratana's 'Final Covenant' included the following:

> 'The fear of Jehovah is the beginning of my works that this Pa (Ratana Pa) should stand
> in the likeness of Israel. Let not its values and beliefs be destroyed by man, or by modern
> learning, or by the devil. Oh, Jehovah, the Father. Oh, Lord Jesus Christ. The tree whose
> seeds I planted in the four corners of the land has grown. *Come now, and rule over all
> the people*, so that the tree (of Christian Faith) may bring forth the spirit of righteousness
> for the body and for the soul.'

> '...That we may prepare ourselves for Thy coming Kingdom, *when it comes to this earth*,
> fuelled as it will be from the powerhouse of your divine Spirit. We *await Thy coming*,
> Lord God, in all Thy Glory! When we, your true believers, will know our reconciliation with
> Thee, through *the reigning grace of Jesus Christ*, Thy beloved Son and our Saviour!
> Halleluiah, Lord! Yes, so shall it be.'

It seems clear that near the end of his life Ratana fully believed that Jesus would return to earth to rule over the people. Yet a decade earlier on Good Friday, 4 May 1929, Ratana delivered the following, almost enigmatic, proclamation:

'The Son has already returned to this earth and is also among you the morehu. If you remove the blindfold that has been placed over your eyes, you will see and feel the Son's presence. There appears in the scriptures these words: "Wherever two or three people gather together for my names sake, there shall I be also." ... Do not think that because we recognise this day as the day the Son ascended into heaven [that] he is still there *at God's Throne*, and there only. No, *the Son has already come and is actually amongst you all.*'

('Ratana Revisited...' p.384-5 and p.441. All emphases mine.)

What should we believe with the last sentence of the above quote? Certainly some thought Ratana *was* 'the Son' returned. His proclamation here, however, is *seemingly* at serious variance with the earlier quotes taken from his 'Final Covenant'. Further, does The Bible *truly say* that Jesus stands alongside **the 'actual' Throne of "The Almighty"**? A *cursory perusal* of "The Book of Revelation" *appears* to indicate that.

However, a *more serious examination* of the relevant passages reveals something else, something truly stupendous. Moreover, the *crucial significance* of that exact revelation stands as both a direct rebuttal and a *serious indictment* upon one of the primary tenets of Christianity, and thus upon all Christians who accept that particular belief.

So would the 'ruling Theologians' of 21st century Christianity even deign to believe that they might just be very, very wrong here? Would you in the Ratana Church have the courage to think differently, in the same way that once your founder displayed great courage for you? For, in reality, the Truth about **"The Second Coming"** and Who exactly occupies **"The Throne"** in 'The Revelation' *is the single most important thing that all of humankind, but Christians especially, must recognise.*[23]

As current Christian teaching now stands, *a huge and seriously-appalling error and distortion pervades the world body of Christianity* – never mind any other religion – exactly around this question of **"The Second Coming"**.

Therefore, anyone with the temerity to unequivocally and publicly proclaim a view *diametrically opposed* to the 'Theological/religious wisdom' of global Christianity for all the world to see would probably be dismissed as 'a deluded fool'. Notwithstanding the sure arrival of many 'slings and arrows', that is *exactly* what we will do here: **Proclaim to the contrary!**

Since the 'Proof of The Pudding' really *is* in the eating, and because the times are obviously 'short', for the first time in our evolutionary/spiritual journey, global humanity will experience **'The Truth of this sure Truth'**! You 'Morehu' of the 'Ratana Church', do not wait 'for a sign', but heed these words now and adjust your lives accordingly. For one day you *will* ask:

"How did he know?"

So, for the complete extension and fulfilment of Ratana's crucial work and Mission – *precisely that for which he journeyed from New Zealand but nonetheless missed through non-recognition* – and for all Christians who may cross the path of this Work, I conclude this pivotal Chapter with 'contentious Truth'.

---

[23]The reader will find precisely-detailed information from The Bible – with the *key Scriptures* taken from 'The Book of Revelation' – in a stand-alone Booklet: **"THE TWO SONS OF GOD; The Son of Man and The Son of God. *What The Bible Really Says.*"** [In association with **'Zenith Publishing Group'** it is only available in New Zealand online at: **www.publishme.co.nz**]

Standing alone [e tu] as:

The Last in the Line of The Maori Prophets:

In "**Author's Note**": sub; '**The Proclamation**', I stated:

"The *message* from that **Sure Source** grants me the Mandate to *proclaim* the following":

If I do not tell you this, who is going to?

In concert with that 'granted Mandate' it is therefore proclaimed:

*   *   *   *   *

JESUS, The SON OF GOD, will not 'Return' to earth again – either to rule or to judge – ever!

*   *   *   *   *

20

Cultural Renaissance and Maori Radicalism

20.1 Renaissance

The image of a frail and bent Whina Cooper clutching the hand of a *mokopuna*, graphically captured as she set off on the first leg of the land-march to Wellington some years ago now, probably epitomises more than any comparable event, the beginnings of the true latter-day renaissance of things dear to Maori. Since land 'ownership' has always been believed to be synonymous with 'Maori *wairua*', the land-march was viewed as an appropriate display of solidarity to an ideal. In the collective perception of Maori, therefore, a march to the seat of Government was symbolically correct in its inception and execution. Yet, as previously stated, only the inclusion of Spiritual Law as the foundation for any venture will guarantee lasting success. This holds true with the issue of land grievances too.

So even if a particular venture is undertaken in *correct* accordance with The Laws but *without* the realisation of the people involved, it will still eventually bring success. For just as ignorance of Spiritual Law does *not* prevent the reciprocal effect of any transgression so, too, does the same *non-understanding* of those Laws **not** prevent success where The Laws are *unknowingly* adhered to. However, it is obviously far more desirable to be *consciously* aware of them so as to achieve a far greater and lasting benefit.

There can be no doubt that the renaissance and/or strengthening of any culture can be seen as a correct thing, so long as it follows a beneficent path and does so in an uplifting manner. But the culture should be recognised as solely that of the particular race concerned, and not necessarily one which should be demandingly foisted upon all other ethnic groups in the land. By virtue of the claim to being the sole *tangata whenua* of Aotearoa – a claim we have spiritually refuted in an earlier Chapter – Maoridom generally harbour the rather interesting idea that only their culture is correct for this *whenua*. However, as stated previously, all non-Maori who are *born here*, are so born under the aegis of **The Spiritual Laws of Creation**, and are therefore just as much part of this land as any Maori. That is the inflexible and final ramification of **"The Law!"**

Notwithstanding that reality, this interesting attitude *seemingly* prevalent within the

Maori race probably emanates from the belief that only indigenous peoples – that of the 'brown brotherhood' – have 'true culture'; whatever that is perceived to mean. On the other hand the *tauiwi,* the European coloniser, have no 'real' culture to offer or call their own. That kind of notion is obviously incorrect. Since European culture and heritage obviously stretches back millennia, such a stance would harbour a quite large degree of arrogance.[1] Regardless of that fact, however, the underlying feeling seems to persist that, in Aotearoa at least, only Maori culture has relevance and all else must occupy a very distant second place, or not be acknowledged at all.

This *apparent* mindset begs the question:

> "Why should Maori consider it an affront if Pakeha express no interest in their culture?"

Of course, Maori culture is an obvious reality in this land by virtue of their time of occupation here, and this must be readily acknowledged. And it should certainly be employed and displayed in more than just the cultural landscape. However, to insist or demand that all must pay homage to it is wrong, and Maoridom should excise that attitude from their consciousness.

The renaissance of the language, however, is clearly a correct and admirable thing. For the language of any people perhaps offers the greatest medium for the complete cultural expression of that group, and therefore should not be permitted to die out. As explained elsewhere in this work, by virtue of its inherent "forming power" under the aegis of Spiritual Law, language can either uplift a people or drag them down. The 'direction chosen' will depend on whether the medium is used to spiritually-ennoble the talents and abilities within the individuals of that group, or is used to pervert or cheapen those gifts. For from the thoughts are produced the words, which obviously then issue from the mouth via the language. The words thus frame or clothe the *form* of the corresponding deed.

The Book of Matthew offers a strong pointer to this spiritually-lawful and precise relationship between the use of words either for good or for the opposite. He recounts how Jesus rebuked the Pharisees intent on entrapping Him. Matthew records this reference to the power inherent in language. From Chapter 12, Verses 34-36, (Fenton), let us revisit this crucial advice.

> "...how can you preach purity, when you are yourselves depraved? The beneficent man draws from his treasury of purity, goodness; and the depraved man can only produce depravity, from his stores of depravity! I tell you, however, that every vile *idea* that men give expression to, they shall render a reason for it in the Day of Judgement."

And the King James Version (Matthew 12:37) completes it thus:

> "For by thy *words* thou shalt be justified, and by thy *words* thou shalt be condemned."

> (Italics mine.)

A further powerful statement is made in Chapter 15, verse 11, where Jesus proclaims to a large crowd:

> "Listen and understand! What goes into the mouth does not corrupt the man; but what comes out of his mouth does corrupt him."

---

[1] Paradoxically, indigenous peoples of many cultures, particularly artists, now immerse themselves in various aspects of 'European' culture today.

And in reply to His disciples puzzled by His explanations, He said to them:

> "Are you ignorant even yet? Do you not know that everything going into the mouth proceeds to the stomach, and is from there evacuated? But what come out from the mouth proceed from the heart, and corrupt the man. For there come from the heart wicked thoughts, murders, adulteries, fornications, thefts, perjuries, blasphemies. These are what corrupt the man..."

(Matthew 15:16-20, Fenton.)

Thus all languages possess words which run the complete gamut from soaring forms of spiritual upliftment, to ugly and befouled ones. The particular "word forms" chosen for use in general discourse or debate are the ones which naturally issue from the mouth of speakers of any given language. Thereby producing the corresponding "living forms" of either upliftment or debasement – and everything in between – as Jesus explained. Therefore, *beliefs* which aver that Biblical pronouncements of the kind we have quoted have little relevance for modern man and equate to nothing more than 'fire and brimstone' preaching are, *themselves*, rendered *irrelevant* by the fact of rapidly deteriorating societies worldwide.

For they are the end-excrescence of all the collective 'forms' produced by the many languages (and thus deeds) of global humanity.

Despite the fact that languages are important to retain within individual cultures in any given land, a particular language may not necessarily be the best one for general, everyday use. In our case, therefore, whilst the Maori language has equal status with English under National law, it is English that will logically always be the main medium of language communication, simply because it is the major global one. Demands that everyone learn Maori might seem to have cultural merit, but it will have little appreciable impact on the world. Moreover, to demand that it be made a *compulsory* part of the education process is a recipe for alienation because such a demand **does not represent** a truly, spiritually-free choice.

Most certainly the language should be retained, *for all languages are a gift through which the people's mana* **can** *be more nobly expressed*. But its retention must ultimately be the responsibility of Maoridom. If, as sometimes appears to be the case, the overall Maori populace are showing less and less interest in retaining it *for themselves* – despite the strong push for its wider dissemination – than what *could* obviously derive from such disinterest *would* simply be the lawful process of the demise of part of the cultural heritage of a race, *because of the people's own unwillingness to hold on to it.*

In any case, 'cultural proposals' to legislate for dual language facilitation by law 'across the board' would place an increasingly greater financial burden on the country as a whole. For example, demands for Maori interpreters in the Law Courts means a translation of all procedures and transcripts. Whilst that may satisfy the dictates of *cultural* and/or *political* correctness, it is really little more than an expensive and time-consuming exercise for all concerned. Moreover, demands from certain *cultural activists* so arraigned is sometimes not for just *any* Maori interpreter but one of the individual's own *Iwi* or *hapu*. And, in some cases, the one demanding a Maori language interpreter is not able to speak or understand Maori anyway.

So it is clearly far more practical to have one language to conduct the everyday business of society. And if that language happens to also be the choice of the wider world, then that obviously has beneficial advantages. In terms of demands for dual language use in any situation, *it is the nature of the forms produced by the words spoken that is the spiritually-decisive aspect,* **irrespective of which language is used.**

Interestingly, what has never been adequately explained is the question of what would happen if all Pakeha became fluent in Maori, when many Maori themselves have no interest in learning it? It is obviously extremely important for Maori academics, teachers and traditionalists to insist that everyone learn the Maori language, even to the point of politicising the process of demand. What these 'learned' people fail to appreciate, however, is that, unless they compulsorily teach their own to an acceptable level of fluency first, situations will arise where Maori may feel inadequate and perhaps racially intimidated upon hearing very white Pakeha discoursing with ease in a language not of *their* birth heritage. This is already happening now at some events, and an unspoken yet squirming discomfort is clearly reflected on the faces and in the demeanour of some non-speaking Maori present at such gatherings.

Yet young Maori without access to the means to learn the *reo*, or even those not even remotely interested in doing so, are nevertheless told to be proud of their language heritage. Whilst that kind of pride is correct and admirable, proponents of 'Maori for all' should concentrate their efforts on teaching the mastery of the language to Maori first, before demanding that everyone else accept it. In any case should it not be, in the final analysis, *a personal choice* whereby one chooses the language that one will utilise for every aspect of their life and work? Whilst the cultural renaissance of the Maori has been of great benefit in engendering a sense of pride and belonging, this should not be lost or damaged by wrongful demands that all pay homage to it. No culture should be elevated to an artificial position or level that it has no actual right to occupy. As in all things, The Law of Balance needs to be taken into account if there is to be harmonious advancement.

Therefore, let each pursue their own in warm tolerance and acceptance of the other. And if there is *cultural crossover*, that is also fine and wonderful. Perhaps, in time, those here who survive what must soon come upon the earth and its peoples may eventually evolve a distinctly New Zealand culture, with particular elements of all cultures *then still present* naturally gravitating toward each other. And so long as individual cultures are not *forced* into a process of bastardisation, this may be a desirable outcome at some future point. What all people are enjoined to do in the retention of their culture from the standpoint of Spiritual Law is to identify and strengthen the more beneficial aspects of it. Since the various races are not on this earth without purpose, their individually developed cultures should be viewed as a collective *taonga* for all of humanity as well.

The preservation of cultural traditions and language, however, is the *spiritual responsibility of the individual races to whom they belong*, and not that of any other. Of course, where colonisation has altered the cultural landscape, so to speak, there should still be freedom for that culture to express itself. Moreover, if the coloniser offers to assist in the process of ethnic cultural retention, then that should be viewed as a positive and beneficial 'working together'. But the ultimate survival of any or all aspects of indigenous culture is the responsibility of the people concerned, simply because it belongs to them. In truth, it is theirs alone, *for it will exclusively reflect their own precise path of development as a race or a people.*

To this end, certain aspects of a race's culture can be readily identified as being strong, whilst others can be deemed to be possible weaknesses. The strong points should therefore be identified, further strengthened and utilised, thus allowing the weaknesses to die out. Some of the obvious strengths of Maori culture are those of *whaikorero*, song and dance, carving and weaving etc., and these aspects are very much alive and well today.

The renaissance of *waka* construction, particularly, was an obviously powerful symbolic cultural re-awakening, simply by virtue of the sheer physical presence of these craft. No other race developed the skills and know-how to produce such large and amazingly sea-worthy canoes. Their great size coupled with wonderful symmetry of form, project power, purpose and pride, and that is as it should be. The *original building skills* should not be permitted to die either, and perhaps a few more *waka* should be constructed *by those traditional means*. This particular aspect of Maori cultural renaissance could be regarded as perhaps its singularly most spectacular and pivotally important feature in being the highly visible outward projection of it – by virtue of the pride, and not a little awe, that the sight of very large *waka* generate.

However, the guidance contained in Ratana's examples should be taken into account when deciding the form of carvings that might adorn any new vessels or, indeed, any new meeting house or other traditional buildings. Certain points of Maori carving, particularly with regard to the traditional forms they are meant to represent, should bow before the spiritual guidance of Ratana, and change their form and/or meaning to reflect the new knowledge he gave to the race. By doing so, the *mana* of any *waka* or meeting house would be **more elevated** simply because the new spiritual direction inherent in *his* mission would be fulfilled. In short, if carvings are produced purely for the retention of culture, then traditional forms can be retained, so long as no attempt is made to label them "spiritual" – for they are not! However, if carvings are made to represent truly spiritual forms, then the design of the carvings should perhaps change to reflect that new conscious realisation and knowledge.

As stated in the previous Chapter, that can only happen when carvers fully understand the **huge differences** between *psychic* forms, *elemental* forms, and *spiritual* forms. With this understanding, they can then give, from out of themselves, the appropriate 'volition' to the type of carving they wish to produce. Naturally, this will clearly reveal the level to which the carved piece belongs. Therefore, with the knowledge of The Elemental forces of Nature now fully explained and the spiritual direction set in place by Ratana, future carvings and crafts would 'carry' a very different and spiritually-elevated form within them than that produced by the highly skilled, savage craftsmen of old. Craftsmen whose strongest connection was *not* to the true Spiritual Realm, but to that of their psychic world of dangerous phantom-shadows – to the world of their particular 'trinity' of *tapu, makutu* and *utu!*

In the final analysis, then, culture should always only be that. It is not a god to be worshipped, nor should it be demanded that all others bow down before it, for that would be a dangerous spiritual transgression indeed. In **every case**, any given culture will always be a *reflection* of a people's knowledge of, or attachment to, *psychic, elemental,* or *spiritual* realities, or varying combinations of two or three. *Thus the overall level of spiritual development and maturity of any race may be seen in its culture.* Therefore, we must never forget the role of the Prophet Ratana and the radical changes he wrought to cement in place *correct* **spiritual renaissance**.

We must restate the clear truth that Maoridom, unfortunately, did not fully understand his incomparable vision, and his great uplifting call went largely unheeded. How will history judge this reality for Maori? Will it smile on it, or will it weep at the lost opportunity wrought by the Prophet and Spiritual Leader, Ratana? To revisit or not revisit his life, his mission, and its unequivocal meaning, and to embrace or not embrace – that is a key question that only Maoridom can decide.

*And from the decision will come the reciprocal effect of either **joy**, or greater **sorrow!***

20.2   Maori Radicalism

"Power comes out of the barrel of a gun!"

(Mao Tse Tung.)

"Physical strength will never permanently withstand the impact of spiritual force."

(Franklin D. Roosevelt.)

"The pen is mightier than the sword!"

(From the original, 'Arms give way to Persuasion!', Cicero.)

Three vastly different quotes occupying opposite ends of the "spiritual spectrum". The first concerned solely with earthly results, but ultimately returning spiritually-driven corresponding ramifications of no small import. And the other two having connections to both. In the first quote are sown the seeds of its own destruction because its inferior 'form' is correspondingly attached to weaker, and therefore lower and baser levels. The latter, however, if writing *Spiritual Truth*, is equal to the second because of its powerful connection to The Source of All Life. By virtue of this fact, any such writings connected to that Source produce "forms of spiritual power", as opposed to the 'baser forms' produced by the gun *if* the use of it is for strictly totalitarian purposes with the aim being control and/or enslavement.

Interestingly, the two World Wars produced a large measure of radicalism in the sense that thousands of rural Maori were suddenly exposed to a vastly bigger and wider world than they had been used to previously, or could ever imagine existed had they remained within the *hapu*. Paradoxically, 'through the power of the gun', they played their part in the defeat of darker forces elsewhere. In the Military training processes necessary to carry out the battle, Maori soldiers were exposed not only to the reality of the global experience, but to vastly different and radical skills far removed from the everyday needs of the *Iwi*. Those new skills they mastered well. This very great transition, a hugely radical departure from the quiet life of home, had the effect of producing, *at one stroke*, a whole generation of Maori with a far wider frame of reference and greater skill base *than any group before them*.

Such a new and different attitude, wrought by the experience of battle in foreign lands among different kinds of people, was coupled with the acquisition of very valuable skills. That time can thus be seen as a watershed event in Maori renaissance also, for out of that group emerged Maori Servicemen who could confidently apply their new-found skills in a greatly expanded home arena. Their participation in the great global conflicts on the amphitheatre of the world stage – more particularly The Second World War perhaps – ideally prepared some of them for the latter setting of New Zealand in many avenues of administrative and public life, in both the Maori field and the Pakeha one.

In terms of advancement, then, the efforts of Maori who went off to war produced a lasting and powerful *spiritual* legacy for the race in many ways. For, as we have previously stated, battle and sacrifice for a *righteous cause* inherently carry the forms of Spiritual Truth and nobleness within them. And in that vast and savage conflict, with perhaps a totally radical departure from the more ancient practices of war in general, Maori clearly gained spiritually. Thus, from out of that globally devastating conflict arose many of Maoridom's greatest leaders.

More recently on the home front, however, many New Zealanders will no doubt remember the disquiet and general feeling of unease which permeated this society in the 1970s at the stated threat by some Maori radicals of armed insurrection if *their* aspirations were not realised. In a situation as potentially explosive as that, 'aspirations' invariably translate to demands. Stories of training camps in Colonel Gaddafi's Libya were unsettling. Moreover, the potential for societal polarisation from both Pakeha and Maori quietly raised its ugly head as some contemplated which side to support should such an unfortunate situation develop. Now, of course, most of those original radicals are *older and wiser* having become, for the most part, establishment. Unfortunately, what they failed to *fully appreciate*, in their *blind perversity*, was that any armed revolution inevitably means "blood on the streets".

It means the potential for dismembered bodies of adults and children – most certainly even some of their own. It means armed troops, checkpoints and curfews also. As probably the worst possible thing in this beautiful and blessed land we have been gifted, however, it means a bitterly divided and polarised people. A polarisation, moreover, that would inevitably breed only further distrust and more discord between the factions and spawn, once more, the ugliness and evil of **utu**! Where a society is basically democratic in nature and where grievances can be aired in the Law Courts as they can here, there is no glory in such a struggle, and certainly no need!

Only in a true totalitarian state where real freedom is totally suppressed might there be cause for armed insurrection in a fight for that necessary goal of freedom. But where it is driven solely by over-reactive demands of cultural or indigenous rights, then it degenerates into ignoble behaviour and selfishness. Therefore, the whole threatening business was foolish in the extreme for it was simply *cultural ideology* driven by dangerous *over-emotionalism*, rather than by the clarifying process of *spiritual objectivity*. Yet, even with a lawful mechanism available – at least up until recent times – the establishment of The Waitangi Tribunal was perceived to greatly alleviate potentially similar emotions in any new crop of younger radicals.

Notwithstanding large settlements granted via the 'Treaty process' – and more in the pipeline – even that was still not enough for some latter-day radicals. So much so that 'attacks' on 'defenceless' and lone trees and the smashing of *New Zealand taonga* such as the America's Cup, were considered to be correct forms of Maori protest. Despite being ostensibly a protest against the Pakeha, both 'attacks' were nevertheless carried out using 'traditional Pakeha tools'. In the case of the lone and lonely *offspring of Tane* – the defenceless tree – a Pakeha chainsaw was used. Why not a traditional stone adze? Now, of course, that special *taonga* has gone, accompanied by a great and surprising wave of sadness from so many people of this land.

With the America's Cup incident, a Pakeha sledgehammer was the 'weapon'. Why not an adze also, or a *mere pounamu*? In both cases, moreover, I am sure that we would certainly guess the mode of transport to and from the 'attack' to be *tauiwi*-invented, and the 'operational gear' to be Pakeha clothing. Again, why not *operate* according to the old traditions if Pakeha trappings are so hated? Thus a stripping off of all clothing – as was the way of the *taua* – and a jog there and back. In a further interesting paradox, the N.Z. Herald of 15th March, 1997, reported that the America's Cup attacker's Pakeha lawyer whom he, by right, was entitled to engage under *Pakeha Legislative Law*, said:

"The America's Cup stands for everything he despises."

The ultimate paradox here, of course, is that at least the majority of so-called 'Pakeha-despising Maori radicals' of the past few decades live in Pakeha-designed houses, cook at least most meals on a Pakeha-designed cooker, keep milk in Pakeha-designed fridges, wash in Pakeha-designed bathrooms and sleep in comfortable Pakeha-style beds. Yet on the Holmes show, the America's Cup attacker stated that he would "...cut out the Pakeha part of him..." if he could. A Maori language student attending a Maori language course at a Pakeha Polytechnic, Ben Nathan stated he was part of a new and obviously radical group calling itself the Tino Rangatiratanga Liberation Organisation which accuses the Pakeha, in essence, of "...illegal occupation of our country." Its claimed political objective is the establishment of an independent Maori state, "...by whatever means is necessary." Did that mean 'guns and blood', if there is 'no other way'?

*   *   *   *   *

One can certainly sympathise with Mike Smith and Ben Nathan in the age-old wish to determine one's own path, particularly in the present, politically-driven corporate and social climate where flawed economic policies continually increase the gap between the 'haves' and the 'have-nots'. And in the case of Ben Nathan's actions in smashing the America's Cup, the mind positively reels at the billions of dollars spent on the whole Cup challenge by incredibly wealthy corporations and individuals when there is so much pain and hardship in many countries of the world. Even though the overall business can legitimately claim to advance the cause of the boating industry – still a wealth-oriented activity in any case – and where the actual match-racing can generate much sporting excitement, the fact remains that an incredible and seemingly inordinate amount of wealth is directed to a very singular entity.

Given that the global business world generally embraces similar aims, most of those very corporations involved in funding America's Cup syndicates would no doubt subscribe to the latter-years business ethos of demanding *more* from employees whilst offering *less*. Moreover, the argument that an America's Cup campaign will greatly benefit everyone in New Zealand is spurious at best. It will, however, certainly increase the amount that the 'haves' already possess.

Since the 'Americas Cup billionaire club' all own super-expensive floating mansions, many with private helicopters on board, why does this obscenely-wealthy 'cartel' not build or fund large, fully-staffed hospital ships where ongoing medical help can be given to at least some third-world children? Anchored off-shore, helicopters could ferry the sick onboard and return them to their homes, healed. Disaster-relief work would be perfectly suited to such craft. Do the billionaires of the world only feel empathy with their pockets?

Elsewhere in this Work we noted Billionaire Ted Turner's comments that wealthy American 'hoarders' were "...destroying our [his] country." Utilising wealth to create fair-paying jobs is the key to a more harmonious society. That equates to 'wealth-sharing' in the correct spiritual way – an exceptionally *radical* idea under the present economic ideology. So it is not too difficult to empathise with Ben Nathan in his anger and frustration over social situations which could be alleviated by less greedy and therefore more intelligent and sensible directions. Moreover, one cannot help but respect young Ben for his apology. Not just over the America's Cup incident, but also to the Pakeha whom he denigrated on the 'Holmes Show'. It takes a large measure of *maia* to do that, and relatively few possess the requisite degree of humility to do so publicly. Moreover, when reading the 'Afterword' in his book, one can believe his apology therein is *genuine*.

*   *   *   *   *

Yet, notwithstanding the anger of probably many sections of the community to deteriorating social conditions, the clear fact remains that without the knowledge and application

of The Spiritual Laws of Creation, no campaign for self-determination can ever possibly
last. And that is simply because we are all products of, and inviolably subject to, those
very Laws whose outworking we cannot ever change! The paradox, of course, is that
neither the Maori nor the Pakeha seem to want to learn about the true "Laws of Life", let
alone embrace and enact them. The many inequities and complete lack of self-discipline
throughout our society clearly show this to be fact!

Despite having stated my empathy toward the reasons for Ben Nathan's actions, anything
more than that level of protest begins to enter the realm of *being dangerous for all of
society.*

I would therefore personally recommend to any Maori radical 'out there' who might
one day believe that a 'guns and blood scenario' will *resolve* his problem; *leave* Aotearoa
for a while **and find a 'real' guns and blood conflict**. Then have the guts, the *maia*,
to actually become immersed, for a reasonable length of time, in what **you** advocate
– and thus **live the actual reality of it**. Since there are always 'conflicts' being
fought *somewhere* in the world, the choices are many. Of course, that would probably
mean 'meeting the enemy face-to-face', with roughly equal weapons at times, and perhaps
coming off an unfortunate 'second-best'. Or perhaps even losing your *mauri* altogether.

*   *   *   *   *

Special Note

As most New Zealanders are aware, a few thousand of its citizens – both Maori and
Pakeha – intimately experienced what it is like to actively participate in a long-running,
ugly and vicious, ignoble "hands-on" war: **Vietnam**. It was a war in which the wounded,
the dead, the maimed and the insane, collectively, ultimately numbered in the millions.
Where burnt – and dismembered bodies, particularly, – of soldiers, civilians (men, women
and children), from all manner of explosive devices, were not at all uncommon. And
where the destruction of many things, and *the desecration of everything*, became the
norm. The very infrastructure of society itself; the culture, the people, their religion and
their morals, were especially sorrowful casualties. It was the kind of situation where even
human compassion *can* very quickly become a dark excrescence of the whole experience
and thus be easily *subverted* to become a destructive and totally aspiritual vice. We
few [*we maligned and pilloried 'Band of Brothers'*] who lived those very intense years
– **and were changed forever after** – clearly know that any such similar experience
would very radically *transform the mindset* of any present-day Maori radical who might
somehow perversely believe there could be 'glory' or **mana** in armed struggle back here
in Aotearoa – our home!

Blood on the streets for no good purpose is a fool's path!

*   *   *   *   *

In any case, under inviolable **Spiritual Law** – to which Maori 'customary law' **must
also bow,** *even in this land* – we have already clearly established that every person *born*
here is *tangata whenua*! Therefore, under these *absolute spiritual parameters*, there is no
'illegal occupation' of New Zealand. So, what are such protests against – exactly? Were
all such radicals asked to define, *clearly and unequivocally*, their *exact* grievances **under
the strict and inviolable parameters of the higher Spiritual Laws** – that which

Maoridom claim to possess – it is my contention they would fail! For what is outlined in this Work **are those Laws**. The Maori race of the past did not know them then, **and do not know them today**.

Of course, some aspects of those Laws were a natural part of the everyday life of all races, but not the knowledge of them in their entirety. And the Maori certainly did not know them to anywhere near that fullness. If they had, their historical reality would have been vastly different and my earthly ancestor, **Hongi Hika**, would therefore *not* have effected the great slaughter he did under the totally aspiritual aegis of *blood-utu*. Thus via the infallible and inviolable mechanism of Spiritual Law, a different perspective on this whole issue can be offered.

Therefore, we do not have to blindly accept the promotion of Maori demands via a coercive, 'customary-law mechanism', or because of *tangata whenua* status that must not be challenged. Maori input and participation is clearly a rightful thing, and also desirable. But anything more than a natural and therefore rightful place for that should not be allowed to be hijacked by the often strong and sometimes insidious use of 'cultural coercion' to continually push the 'boundaries' to undesirable and thus clearly unworkable limits, such as the promotion of an independent Maori state.

What can be done to defuse such an inherently impractical and totally unworkable idea? Well, there is a solution. Since it is still a cancer gnawing away at a *part* of the vitals of Maoridom – and one resurrected with monotonous regularity – all who claim to be Maori or wish to so claim that connection should stand up and be counted (in effect, a referendum) and declare where their allegiance lies. Either to a united, harmonious, multi-cultural society operating under the beneficence of the **One Law**, or to a Maori State – whatever form that might take. And 'behind the borders of that State' can go all who claim to sympathise with such views, there to set up their 'Maori Utopia'.

Those who choose to do so would need to understand that as it is a Maori initiative solely for Maori 'thinking' and tradition, any interaction with the rest of the Nation will not necessarily be on their terms. So it would be for those particular Maori to maintain their own infrastructure of roads, schools, towns, hospitals, industry, technological research etc., – *if they desire those Pakeha things at all* – with no aid-strings attached. Of course, Maori pride within this 'Liberation Movement' would surely not ask for hand-outs from the Pakeha, or from the *majority* of 'Uncle-Tom Maoris' who would certainly choose to stay with the rest of the Nation.

Or would all the '**hated and despised Pakeha trappings**' be pushed aside and destroyed lest it contaminate this 'last bastion of Maori cultural purity'? And would this signal a return to a new and dark age of the past, where tribalism would run rampant, where *tohungaism* is the only medicine for the people once more, and where *kaumatuaism* is the highest thing striven for?

The other interesting question is: "Who will *control* the new State or tribe?" It would not be a democracy of course. Indeed, by its very nature, it could not! Historically, the *architects* of Liberation Movements always see *themselves* as the rulers – for that is their right as 'saviours of *their* people'! In such a scenario as we outline here – i.e., actually seeking *liberation* from a relatively *free, benign and democratic society* – they will therefore invariably be despotic in nature. Such a 'solution', of course, is either the ultimate *power-play*, and/or the ultimate *stupidity*!

All clear-thinking people in Maoridom should get rid of any thoughts of misguided *aroha* to a 'Maori racial ideal' of this kind, and demand, instead, an end to such emotionally-generated and dangerous radicalism from their own. And then replace it with absolute "spiritual clarity", *fully understanding* what this kind of action would bring down on all in this land – particularly under the outworking of **The Law of Reciprocal Action** [Sowing and Reaping].

As we have sought to explain throughout this Work, **without** the arrival of the Pakeha, the Maori would have **remained** in their dark psychic world. For there was clearly no other path open to them. *And, therefore, no way out*! That is *why* it is *so* difficult to understand how even well-educated Maori today would *begin* to contemplate such an idea as a separate State when they have open recourse to the Law Courts of the land in which to air *legitimate* grievances and obviously gain not insubstantial resolutions at times.

Notwithstanding the potential for ugly conflict, radicalism, in essence, is not necessarily a bad thing and may even be a vital, driving force for much-needed rejuvenation. For radicalism can take many different forms and is not solely associated with armed revolution and the like. By virtue of its particular nature, however, it will always be a powerful force that can equally bring great benefit through an enlightened view, or great destruction wrought by base aims. Even that, however, also via a *distorted application of a high ideal.*

The staleness of a particular societal direction – or complete lack of one – can often equate to stultifying stagnation. Yet The Law of Movement decrees that absolutely nothing can stand still. Should a point of stagnation be reached, then a new impetus must be developed to prevent the possibility of retrogression. However, any new idea should have, as its foundation, the application of Spiritual Law so that only upward movement is generated, for this unchangeable and powerful Law will drive either upwards or downwards equally powerfully, exactly in accordance with the kind of decision taken to set the original effect in motion.

Radicalism, therefore, can revitalise many aspects of an otherwise introverted and less than dynamic society. However, the key question as to whether it will be beneficial or not is not simply the nature of the issue at hand. What matters ultimately is whether the issue is **a spiritually-correct one**, or will lead on to such a goal. Many *supposedly* noble issues and high ideals are often nothing more than *personal wishes* driven by an over-emotional or highly-inflated *ego*. The fact of the matter is that unless any so-called radical view or aim is formulated with The Spiritual Laws as the basic foundation – and by radical in this sense we mean one that will drastically and profoundly alter the status quo – it will eventually fail.

In the recent history of the 20th century alone, we have glaring examples of great events sweeping away the old order, almost overnight in some cases, but with the new radical regime also failing. The Bolshevik Revolution in Russia, which brought to an end corrupt, obscenely wealthy, arrogant and insensitive monarchies was, itself, swept away by ideas radically different to the previous one. Both regimes failed, however, precisely because they were **not anchored in the foundation of Spiritual Law**. Today, with that same rapidly increasing spiritual pressure being exerted on man and his affairs, failure will be sooner rather than later in most areas of all societies!

The defeat of the Axis Powers during The Second World War ushered in a new era of prosperity for some of the Allied nations, along with the belief of a lasting peace for all in the, then, free Nations grouping. Whilst global conflict will always herald great changes in the aftermath, sometimes radical social trends can set in place more far-reaching effects than even World Wars. Consider the way music and dance shaped our attitudes last century; from the staidness of the waltz and similar-type dances of the upper social levels of European society; to the brashness of the American dance trends of the 1920s and

1930s; to Rock-n-Roll in the Sixties; to hip-hop and rap today. In each case, a very radical departure from the old, invariably initially condemned but later widely accepted, resulting in a society changed forever after.

Not just Western society either. For with the reality that we are a global community, the ripple effect permeates virtually every race and culture in some way or other now. The very radical and sometimes maligned rock-era of the 1960s – but more especially the aftermath – has now bequeathed to the world a legacy of drug abuse that cannot be contained *or even curbed*. As with many radical ideas, it all began innocently enough; as something new, refreshing and revitalising, with the promise of greater personal freedom. The 1960s was a time when youth felt good about itself. It was about youthful vibrancy, promise and hope, with the music reflecting those aspirations. And mindless violence, by and large, still lay a little further on into the future.

Had the dream held, the potential for sustained growth in the same vein of hope and promise would have been realised. But within a few short years the dream had been seduced by the dark side of the hallucinogenic drug culture, the proponents of which spread the message that it was the way to spiritual enlightenment. How foolish!

Only "Spiritual Truth" is the way to that!

Now, of course, 'flower power', 'free love' and all that followed in its wake is belatedly recognised as being very wrong – even destructive. Crime-pattern statistics in the U.S. now clearly reveal a sharp and disturbing upward trend in violence from that *supposedly* enlightened time that has *not* reduced. So the damage has been done and the seeds of further destruction well sown and already bearing much fruit. Now we have the rap scene and *its* associated drug culture, with anger, violence and alienation spewing forth from too many angry exponents. Thankfully, **"The Iron Law of Karma"** – [**"The Law of Reciprocal Action"**] – will give all so-called *disaffected youth* the hard answers they will soon experience.

Thus the decade of the 1960s produced what may well be the greatest and most definitive change of the 20th century. In its radical breaking away from long-cherished traditions and ideals – in association with the horrific legacy of the Vietnam War – it directly and indirectly spawned the global drug culture, with all the associated violence, drug abuse, mayhem and garbage that this has brought in its train for present-day society to cope with. Yet even that horrifying reality today and into the future is nothing more than the immutable outworking of **The Law of Reciprocal Action** visiting upon us the effects of all our collective free-will transgressions, including those of the 1960's era.

*   *   *   *   *

The Vietnam War, particularly, was a singularly defining event that polarised hundreds of millions of people worldwide. That particular war was given birth by a series of initially subtle but decisive changes in American Foreign Policy after the end of The Second World War. The United States, with its vast resources of manpower and equipment, was the primary factor in the defeat of the Axis Powers during World War II. Even though rightfully awarded kudos by grateful Nations freed from the dark tyranny of Fascism; the same country, for spurious reasons, later embarked on an ugly and totally unnecessary war in Vietnam. Whilst The Second World War could be legitimately seen as a just and righteous one and therefore a noble cause, the same could not be said of the Vietnam War. In retrospect the stated need to defeat communism could not be held up as a viable reason for ever embarking upon such an adventure, especially since Ho Chi Minh – a

Nationalist in the early years – actually first asked the Americans for help to remove the French from the land.

Out of that conflict, extremely radical and *armed* groups emerged on the American home-front to challenge the authority of the U.S. Government, but without being able to establish any lasting impact. Yet consider the effect that Martin Luther King achieved with his radical campaign for civil rights. Conducted forcefully yet with peaceful restraint, he achieved far more than all those other radical groups combined.[2]

It may be a very difficult concept for well-meaning groups, radical or otherwise, to accept, but the inescapable fact remains; that the best-intentioned ideal *will fail* unless the cause is *spiritually just*. And, quite obviously, Martin Luther King's mission was clearly correct and did largely flow with The Laws. His noble cause therefore achieved much success. However, the followers of that particular ideal must still strive to maintain the spiritual foundation which gave it power and momentum, or it will turn to mush too.

$$*\qquad *\qquad *\qquad *\qquad *$$

So whilst there have been moments of wonderful upliftment in recent times, we can generally trace Western society's swift and dramatic social deterioration in recent years to its source in the 1960s rock era. The promise and belief in enlightenment through love, flower power and 'harmless' drugs, was based on the myth that one only needed to apply the concept of *earthly love* to all of societies ills to effect a lasting cure. Unfortunately for society, the exact opposite is the case, and the new present-day 'feel-good' drugs such as ecstasy etc., will also bequeath *a similar legacy of emptiness*. Only the application of Spiritual Love and Justice – for they cannot be separated – holds the key! The *weaknesses of earthly love* and *aroha* must bow in subjugation to the power and severity of true love – that of The Spiritual.

The living reality of this bold New concept of **Spiritual Love** is that it does not possess 'emotionalism' as its foundation. It is objective and even severe, yet compassionate, for it offers only *spiritual benefit* for all. This kind of love must surely be regarded as a **hugely radical concept** for present-day humanity. The human-emotional brand that we laud to each other is invariably weak and vacillating, for its conceptual essence is constantly being liberalised and thus *further weakened*. Yet the belief remains that emotional love is somehow pure, and perhaps therefore spiritual too. However, more often than not when stripped to its basic form, what we term love is too often nothing more than personal and emotional self-indulgence and/or insecurity. Therefore, in its actual reality, ostensibly professing love to another will too commonly mean: 'I want **you** to love **me**!'

Thus, radicalism, in whatever form it may choose to clothe itself, can only be successful if it has, as its ultimate goal or aim, true **spiritual advancement** of the cause. For only then does it not oppose the inflexible and inviolable Eternal Laws. Any examination of the radical people of history will clearly reveal which ones advanced the cause of beneficial knowledge or bequeathed a lasting legacy of humanitarian and spiritual ideals – and those whose brand of radicalism wrought nothing more than dark destruction.

Paradoxically, those of the latter mould were often charismatic or mesmeric with huge followings, whereas those whose 'vision' offered the *greater* promise were often 'voices in the wilderness' – 'boat-rockers' – whose views were too radical for the time. Only much later were they *sometimes* recognised as being correct. Humankind, through its intransigence, appears doomed to have to always catch up with *the few* who have truly

---

[2]Here at home, many years before, Te Whiti O Rongomai strove to achieve the same at Parihaka.

beneficial, radical insight! Such a notion is clearly understandable since it is invariably *not* the truth which lies with the masses, but *the **untruth***. And it is only the **'spiritually-radical' views** that have stood the test of time. That will forever be so, simply because such ideas invariably have a measure of Spiritual Law as their foundation, even when or if *unknowingly applied.*

Therefore the misguided Maori radicalism of the 1970s, with its then avowed aim of the violent overthrow of Pakeha society if *its* demands were not met, revealed a complete *lack of understanding* of The Eternal Laws by which we all find ourselves born into particular countries at certain points in time. Consequently, any such attempt would have ultimately ended in failure because it had, at its heart, dark destructive energies rather than spiritually uplifting ones.[3] Such a revolution would have marked a dark age for this land, with no spiritual *mana* for the perpetrators whatsoever. And for any who harbour similar notions today, those immutable, inviolable Laws would apply to them in exactly the same way too!

Even with the setting up of The Waitangi Tribunal and the redressing of past injustices, it remains to be seen whether the same attitudes that spoke of armed insurrection three decades ago are still retained within *some* sections of Maoridom. Rather than 'guns on the streets', we should all hope that 'grievance battles' will be contested more appropriately in the Law Courts. Or, better still, apply **The Perfect Knowledge of Spiritual Law** to the issue, and you will have the correct answer and solution.

The call for sovereignty is actually the age-old wish or need of the human spirit to find itself and its ordained place in the overall scheme of things. However, it is not solely within the Nation that it should correctly seek this. For it is *our spiritual place in Creation which is the first and most important knowledge we must seek to find.* All other benefits will automatically follow from that key recognition. This kind of longing is essentially the same urge that has driven revolutions and wrought great and tumultuous changes historically. Always the urge to find the better way but not ever really succeeding. The same restless drive today is still producing upheaval worldwide. With the correct kind of *spiritual drive,* however, no Nation or race of people will be denied its rightful place.

For the Maori race, **the radicalism of Ratana** holds the key to beneficial and spiritual advancement, for his particular brand of radicalism **had The Law as its heart**. That will *always* be the correct way.

At the beginning of this Chapter, we quoted two opposite ideas of radicalism to achieve a goal. If we apply the essence of those two quotes to the contrasting views of the 1970s radicals with the threat of guns and violence, and to Ratana's radicalism – and perhaps even Te Whiti's at Parihaka – it is very clearly obvious **which ideal has lasted**.

> Therefore, *a new Maori activism is called for*, away from the narrow focus of just race and culture to the knowledge, introduction and application of **The True Laws** by which *all* humankind must finally live. Under such a *spiritually-transcending* ethos, the *right kind of* *'activists'* will find their natural place as true *'spiritual leaders'*.

Therein lies the key and the way forward for Maoridom! The major premise of most of the subject matter in this Work will no doubt clash with current Maori beliefs about how it all fits together, and probably also clash with society's present ideas on how to fix its many and increasing ills. If so, the points raised herein will therefore almost surely

---

[3]Interestingly, one wonders what Pakeha society would have been replaced with, and who would have kept the technology working – which even the radicals were quite partial to possessing.

be construed as being *very radical indeed*. Nevertheless, without these 'radical views' to hopefully foster healthy and necessary debate, only unspoken uncertainty on how to address a number of burning issues will continue to haunt and stifle dialogue.

*   *   *   *   *

In conclusion, let us quietly reflect on a singularly poignant "poem" – which many of us may know – about the life of **One** of the greatest radicals to have ever set foot on the earth. In this case: **Jesus**. And Whose Words from out of **Divinity Itself**, Ratana was 'Called' to disseminate amongst the Maori people. Illustrated in the following poem is an unknown author's salute and great love for **Jesus** and His Highest and most Noble form of 'Radicalism' – "Perfect Love"!

> Radically noble in the sense that **He** was prepared **to accept death on the Cross if that was the only way** by which He could anchor **The Truth of His Teaching in the consciousness of humankind for all time.**

He, as **The Love of God** and surely the most innocent of all – even though suffering the grossest of indignities until finally succumbing to the brutal act of murder perpetrated against **Him** – yet still offered up the greatest prayer of intercession *ever* for the senseless blind who committed that atrocity. **His** noble prayer thus stands as an indictment against those who murdered **Him** then, and against those today who still *very wrongly believe* that **His** painful and brutal death on that Cross could somehow be sanctified and Divinely blessed by **An Almighty God** as some kind of loving act of propitiatory sacrifice to cleanse the evil and sin of an *undeserving humanity*.[4]

The very words of the prayer itself stand in rightful accusation against such an evil distortion of the great and incomprehensible **Love of The Creator**.

"Father forgive them, for they *know not* what they do!"

Thus:

They did the *wrong* thing!

Through an anonymous yet clearly *spiritually-insightful* poet, the pure and ennobled form of **The Christ's Mission** rings down through the centuries and is baptised in its own unequivocal message of ***wonderful radiance and great Spiritual Power***!

---

[4]A stronger and more indictful analysis on humankind deriving from the murder of *this* **Son of God** may be read in the further **'Crystal Publishing'** publication: **BIBLE "MYSTERIES" EXPLAINED**. Understanding **"Global Societal Collapse"** From the **"SCIENCE"** in The Bible What every Scientist, Bible Scholar and Ordinary Man needs to Know. – Specifically, Chapter 5: **Jesus, His Birth, Death and Resurrection.** Or in the stand-alone **Booklet** of the same **Title**. [Only available online at: **www.publishme.co.nz**]

20.3 One Solitary Life

Here is a man
who was born of Jewish parents
the child of a peasant woman...
He never wrote a book.
He never held an office.
He never owned a home.
He never had a family.
He never went to college.
He never put foot
inside a big city.
He never travelled two hundred
miles from the place
where He was born.
He never did one of the things
that usually accompany greatness.
He had no credentials
but Himself...
While still a young man
the tide of popular opinion
turned against Him.
His friends ran away.
One of them denied Him...
He was nailed to a cross
between two thieves.
His executioners gambled for
the only piece of property
he had on earth... His coat.
When He was dead
He was taken down;
and laid in a borrowed grave
through the pity of a friend.
Nineteen wide centuries
have come and gone
and He is the centrepiece
of the human race and the leader of
the column of progress.
I am far within the mark
when I say that all the armies
that ever marched,
and all the navies
that were ever built...
have not affected the life of man
upon earth
as powerfully as has that

One Solitary Life!

(Anon.)

21

'Mores' of 'Maori Cultural-Renaissance' Permeating New Zealand Society Today

The subject matter of the previous few Chapters dealing with certain, clearly delineated issues of great angst such as land rights, language and cultural renaissance etc., will not be revisited to any great degree here. Nonetheless, further analyses of those particular subjects in this Chapter offers the reader sufficiently clear explanations about how and why Spiritual Law needs to be applied in order for Maoridom to advance more knowingly along a more correct and beneficial path. And, by doing so, greatly change the sorry statistics that are a major feature of Maoridom today!

What we will concentrate on, therefore, will be the few problem areas that, statistically, appear to cause an inordinate amount of hardship for Maori. Areas such as Health (Physical, Emotional and Mental), the seemingly acute sensitivity associated with 'cultural safety'; and Education. The interesting territory of 'Crime, Aroha and Spiritual Justice', and 'The Youth Problem and the Gangs' – all under their own particular sub-Chapter – are also examined. The Hongi and the Haka are assessed too. As always, the knowledge of The Spiritual Laws will be applied to these topics so that its illuminating light will reveal what should be done to correct the spiritually-incorrect aspects of them.

For it should be clearly self-evident to even the most obtuse and hard-nosed Maori traditionalist or radical that things are far from well in Maoridom. Numerous theories and ideas have been advanced by many learned Maori and all manner of academics to try to pin-point the exact cause. The belief evidently being that if the cause can be identified, then a cure can be easily applied and everyone lives happily ever after. That theory is probably intrinsically true and many have applied themselves to identifying the various causal factors over many years. With so much input into 'Maori angst' why, then, across the whole spectrum of life and endeavour, is the 'collective lot' of Maori not getting any better?

In stark and simple terms, the primary cause has never been acknowledged, because it has never been *recognised*. We shall state it once more – **in bold**.

No one has bothered to fully understand the absolute need to recognise, learn and apply the correct knowledge of The Eternal Spiritual Laws to this and every other deteriorating situation!

Only by doing so can there *ever be* any kind of meaningful and long-term 'turnaround'. By that we do not mean the dogma of religion, but the *infallible and inviolable outworking* of **"The Spiritual Laws of Creation"** – those which have been our constant yardstick throughout this Work. Only with the clear knowledge of these Laws can the causes of **all** problems be addressed. The emotionally-generated wishes and the spiritually-destitute intellectual theories of humankind are simply not able to reach into the living core of the many, seemingly insurmountable problems we face, irrespective of how much theoretical analysis is applied to them.

Therefore, since Maoridom generally believes itself to be highly spiritual, and consequently has no need to take cognisance of 'anyone else's truth', it would probably be very difficult for most Maori to accept that their heartache can ultimately only be solved by applying *Spiritual Law* to their many problems. As we have stated more than once or twice previously, that particular belief of 'great spirituality' is, unfortunately, simply not correct, for everything outlined thus far in this Work literally *proclaims* this inescapable fact. It was precisely *because* the Maori had no truly spiritual foundation that Ratana was Called to lead them into a completely new direction and way of life. *For the old was simply leading to their demise.*

Maoridom must therefore face the serious *wero* (challenge) of recognising a very great error about itself and begin to adjust its thinking and perceptions accordingly so that *the necessary door* can really open onto a new path of genuine spirituality. For, quite obviously, the notion of great 'spirituality' being inherent within the race would mean that the unfortunate situation that Maoridom has found itself in would simply *not exist*. And the "Mangai" would not have been tasked to lead the race out of its severely straitened circumstances. For how would that be possible or necessary if that belief was reality? Ratana's "Calling" is clear testimony that had there been any indication of great spirituality, *his mission would simply not have been needed*. The fact that it did occur in such spectacular fashion clearly illustrates the correctness of our assertions.

Therefore, let us have the *maia* to hold back our indignation or anger – or any other emotion that may well up when our 'beloved spirituality' is challenged – and calmly and objectively examine the situation **as it actually is**. And further resolve to not just attend numerous *hui* to discuss it, but to really **do something about it** i.e., to seriously begin to "walk the *korero*" (talk). Unfortunately, the Maori propensity for endless *hui* and meetings, which also serves to perpetuate the tribal system and *kaumatuaism*, appears to stem more from the desire of individuals to 'show' themselves and their 'rank' than from any *apparent* wish to alter the status quo. In truth, its associated place-hunting and so-called *mana* actually stifles the free-flowing of 'winds of much-needed change'.

In any case, there is absolutely **no need** for continual discussion at all. The simple solution is for *each individual* to resolve *to change himself* – in the necessary kinds of change called for. *This is all that is* **actually** *required!* If, however, '*hui*' can help to bring about this necessary change, then that is clearly a beneficial thing to retain and utilise.

21.1   Health

21.1.1   General Health

It is an unfortunate fact that Maori today are not generally healthy. This is shown by statistics which can be readily perused. It is certainly clear that Maori sportsmen, particularly within the professional codes of rugby and league are obviously healthy and extremely fit. The same can be said for Maori in the Armed Services, perhaps more particularly the Army by virtue of the land environment operated in *and the sheer stamina required to "keep going" for days and weeks when necessary* – unlike 80 minutes of intense game-exertion followed by a hot shower. The general populace, however, do not possess that level of fitness and associated health. Clearly, one does not need to be as fit as an 'Operational Soldier' or an 'All Black', but the huge difference in health and fitness levels between those kinds of occupations and the majority of Maori society clearly reveal too large a gap.

Why, then, the huge difference? In a word, discipline – or the lack of it! Of course, the best incentive to maintain good health and/or fitness is either in a life or death profession, a service-oriented disciplinary setting, or where high earnings are possible such as in professional sport – larger salaries for enhanced performance. With a rapid worldwide trend toward greater levels of obesity, even in some of the traditionally slimmer Asian peoples, Maori are also very much part of this trend. Unfortunately, obesity brings in its train far more than simple largeness. Many medical problems are caused by obesity, and existing ones can be greatly worsened by being overweight. The problem is, of course, that food tastes so very good.

In Chapter 3 we explored the reasons why Polynesian navigators were able to journey vast distances in the essentially wet and cold environment of the South Pacific. Professor Philip Houghton, associate professor of anatomy at Otago University, in his book, "People of the Great Ocean: aspects of human biology of the early Pacific", certainly appears to have correctly postulated why obesity is endemic amongst the Maori and Pacific Island people. Essentially, he believes, Polynesian sailors had to rely on their body anatomy and physiology to keep warm. Thus they evolved to be 'large and muscular' because it is muscle that 'generates body heat in cold conditions'.[1]

We might further postulate that the need to be able to withstand long periods of exposure in those conditions under a process of more or less 'natural selection' ensured that only the strong and fit survived, thus bequeathing that genetic attribute to their descendants. The inherent, genetic trait toward generally larger musculature from that process is, of course, still present in this ethnic group. But not always the means, however, whereby this largeness could be kept balanced as it once was through the consumption of natural, unprocessed foods in the first instance, physical exertion in food gathering and on extended ocean voyaging in cold conditions in the second. And since evidence suggests that the type of muscle used in shivering does not burn up fatty acids, these may tend to accumulate as fat deposits in the body. This *may* account for the high levels of obesity in Polynesian people and *may* offer a mechanism for the better understanding of the present health problems in this ethnic group overall.

Because our modern society no longer provides the kinds of natural conditions that kept the Polynesian sailors taut and trim, there is probably only one overall method left for keeping obesity and its attendant health problems at bay. That is discipline in eating. As the Maori race is not well-disciplined when it comes to food intake, it is not surprising that health here is so generally poor. Without careful thought for a well-balanced diet as a regular and disciplined part of life, there is not likely to be any immediate change in the statistics, just continuing poor health and increasing levels of "**preventable disease**"!

---

[1]Perhaps the same criteria may apply to the Norsemen. Even though having the benefit of fur garments, they nevertheless sailed and rowed the far colder waters of their region. Chroniclers of various kinds have recorded the fact that the Vikings possessed large musculature and performed feats of great strength and endurance – feats that would simply *kill off* the average male today.

The saying: "We are what we eat", or: "We are what we assimilate", is more than just a tired cliché. It is an actual truth from out of The Living Law. Therefore, if we transgress any part of The Law, we pay. And in wrong food intake, either in type, amount, or combination, we pay with poor health. For some, of course, there may be organic factors present which prevent or greatly hinder relatively easy weight control. In such situations medical intervention and/or assistance may be the best help. Nevertheless, the rapidly increasing numbers of mainly Maori and Pacific Islanders who are diagnosed with the dangerously insidious disease, diabetes, is now ringing alarm bells within the medical profession. Yet, even if genetically disposed toward it, diabetes still seems to be generally preventable.

Basically, however, a lack of discipline with regard to vital exercise and in the pleasures of eating will, under **The Law of Reciprocal Action**, always return disease and ill-health. And that is today's reality! Interestingly, anecdotal evidence suggests there is increasing evidence that diet and crime may also be linked. In other words, certain foods appear to trigger particular kinds of anti-social behaviour. Therefore we may well find that pure, natural foods, which we should eat for optimum health anyway, might produce the most favourable emotional balance in the individual. It would be interesting to be able to determine to what extent, if any, diet might contribute to high levels of Maori criminal offending.[2]

Much is made of the generally low socio-economic levels of Maori to endeavour to explain poor health and diet. No doubt there is a certain amount of truth there, where, for example, insufficient income may be a factor in having inadequate heating in winter, insufficient food of the right kind, or in not being able to visit the doctor as often as one might need to. But that is not anywhere near the true picture, for good health *must first begin with a change of attitude* stemming from the recognition that everything must have its beginning and end in the knowledge of Spiritual Law. Therefore, even before conception, this necessary attitude should be present in *the mother and father*, and be carried through into the *education of their children* so that they, in turn, will perpetuate the correct way of living for the benefit of *their offspring*, and thus for the race and community.

History clearly records how efficient and industrious the Maori were in even recent times, where their horticultural skills produced thousands of hectares of vegetables throughout Maoridom. How many of today's young Maori children, especially those in the cities, know how to grow even one kind of vegetable, the kinds that build healthy bodies? For that matter, how many city Pakeha grow vegetables? For what is clearly not accepted by those who control most of the food production in this country is that a major reason for our increasingly higher levels of ill health results from a daily intake of fruit and vegetables saturated with poisonous substances – herbicides and pesticides. (The ultimate horror is to have leaf vegetables with even just one insect hole in it.) Of course, it may all look wonderful on the supermarket shelves, but that pristine show belies the long-term deadliness of some so-called 'health-giving food'. Those who manufacture the poisons, along with the applicators of it, produce a constant litany of propaganda about how safe it all is.

The stark fact remains that if a substance can very quickly kill another – even ones selectively targeted – it must obviously have a detrimental effect on human tissue as well. Medical research may declare that it is minimal but there is far more to this issue than a purely physical one. What is not understood is that along with the absorption of such

---

[2]Of course, the decision to commit crimes in the first instance is a personal one, and diet or any other factors cannot ever override that ultimate spiritual reality.

contaminated foods and its subsequent utilisation and impact on the organs of the body in that material, *empirical* sense, there is the *radiative-factor* of those poisons within the food, which also impact upon the organs. And thus upon the complete entity which we are entrusted to keep healthy. In New Zealand's case, there appear to be no hard and fast standards as to how much or how little 'poison' can be sprayed onto the land overall. Anecdotal evidence strongly suggests that 'Kiwi kids' ingest far higher residual levels of these substances than similar groups in other 'advanced' countries.

The March/April edition (Vol.57, No.1, 1998) of "Soil & Health" magazine reported that Denmark was considering a total pesticide ban. The article stated:

> "In response to calls from members of parliament to make the country totally organic by 2010, the Danish government is initiating an assessment of the impacts of a total pesticide ban in the country."

An official with the Danish General Workers Union, which has been campaigning to phase out all pesticides, said:

> "I hope the committee will recommend a total pesticide phase out within a couple of years, and we are looking for the rest of the E.U. to do the same eventually."

What will this mean for New Zealand's exports to Europe should an E.U. ban come into effect? Quite clearly, such a ban will mean that Europe will not want pesticide-contaminated fruit and vegetables from anywhere else in the world. So why do we not apply this beneficial kind of "radical ideology" and create a completely herbicide and pesticide-free *organic* country with the same enthusiasm that recent successive governments have employed to drive through what we will one day soon discover, along with all other "growth-at-all-costs" capitalist countries, what will then be recognised as a fatally-flawed economic direction?[3] In the same way that we erroneously *believe* we have led the world in economic reforms, why do we not *truly lead the world* in the area that offers the only sensible future for food production and better health – organic farming.

The stupidity of persisting with 'chemical farming' is that we could realise a far greater financial return in export receipts using organic methods, and have the healthiest kind of environment. And, moreover, offer perfect examples of how to be genuine *kaitiaki* of the environment in the truly spiritual sense of the word. Thankfully there are increasing numbers of growers who currently demonstrate that kind of noble stewardship, but they are still regarded as being akin to 'voices in the wilderness' by the greater majority *at this time* who cite 'economic necessity' to continue to poison food supplies.

In the meat and poultry industry, the situation is the same. Chemical farming and feeding of growth hormones to animals and birds also impacts detrimentally on the unfortunate consumer, adding one more component to the overall level of general "unwellness" in the population. The British newspaper, the *Guardian Weekly*, May 1998, stated the following:

> "Misuse of antibiotics in intensive farming and over-prescribing by doctors represent major threats to public health and could undo the 20th century miracle of taming killer diseases such as tuberculosis and meningitis..." The House of Lord's science and technology committee said in a report highly critical of doctors, hospitals and vets: "There is a dire prospect of returning to the pre-antibiotic era."

In the same report Richard Young of the Soil Association, told the committee:

---

[3]N.Z. economists, take note of the warnings of multibillionaire, George Soros!

"The Government should take this situation seriously and to start to phase out the use of antibiotics for the short-term profits of the farming industry. The indiscriminate use of antibiotics in farming is the root cause of the resistance to Bacteria."

The insanity here is that the taste and texture of organic meat and poultry is infinitely superior to even the best export-quality 'chemical-meat'. One day, of course, such inherently foolish and unhealthy agricultural and horticultural practices will be recognised as being the disaster that they even now actually are. Thankfully more food-companies are now beginning to wake up.[4]

Even that once evergreen health standard, cow's milk, is now under siege through being contaminated with herbicides and pesticides in feed, and in being fed unsafe growth hormones – to the detriment of the unfortunate cows and anyone foolish enough to consume their milk. The question should be asked of the N.Z. Dairy Board and farmers whether the growth hormone rBGH, manufactured by Monsanto and approved by the US Federal Drug Administration – yet deemed unsafe by the European Community – is being fed to cows here. A growth hormone, moreover, that was never tested in human trials.

Research indicates that cows ingesting this particular hormone greatly increase their milk production but suffer adverse health effects including a shortened life and higher incidences of mastitis which, according to the researchers, puts more pus into the milk. Their milk, moreover:

"...creates significantly increased levels of the insulin-like growth factor 1 (IGF-1) which is identical in cows and humans. This substance is not killed by pasteurisation or human gastric acids, and its bioactivity rises nearly 30 times in the presence of oestrogens."

The researchers rightly ask the question:

"When nations with the highest rates of breast cancer have the highest per-capita intake of milk and dairy products, is it wise for engineered growth hormones to be foisted on consumers?"

(MILK: The Deadly Poison. Argus Publishing, Robert Cohen.)

Since farming in New Zealand now possesses a business mentality that embraces the 'greater production at all costs' adage, a hormone which increases milk production would seem to be the ideal remedy for concomitant increases in exports and farm revenue. Will we follow the American example and feed rBGH to our bovines? Or might we already be doing so? And just when all cow's milk is widely promoted as being very good for us, the very latest research now indicates there are two main types – one beneficial A2 type, one detrimental A1 type. A small group of scientists believe there is a link between the milk protein in cows and the incidence of diabetes and heart disease. About 80% of New Zealand cows are said to carry only the A1 milk protein, which is blamed for such diseases. Continuing research will no doubt definitively establish the truth or otherwise of this point. Milk drinkers should watch this space!

The continuing political fallout and sometimes acrimonious debate over the increasing levels of illness in New Zealand seems only able to address the growing list of patients requiring 'fixing' in our overloaded health system. However, Jeanette Fitzsimons, Green Party M.P., appears to be the only politician of note who has identified the probable reason for our high sickness levels in a land hypocritically lauded to the rest of the world as ostensibly being 'clean and green'.

---

[4]The E.U. was considering placing a complete ban on antibiotic use in agriculture.

She has correctly challenged other politicians to open their eyes to the fact that the land **is** being poisoned by all manner of deadly substances, many of which are known carcinogens. It is therefore logical to accept that they must impact heavily on the general health of every single person in the land since they must clearly be in the meat, fruit and vegetables that most of us consume. Also because it is difficult to completely escape from at least some residual effect of these foolish practices when forced to live in an environment where poisons are 'graciously bestowed' over most of the Nation's food supplies.

Should we be surprised, therefore, at the following statement from a decade ago.

Cancer puzzle hard to piece together.

"Death from cancer is on the increase in New Zealand at a greater rate than in comparable countries such as Australia, the United States, England, Wales and Japan – and the clinicians do not really know why." Dr Brian Cox of the Otago Medical School and chairman of the Cancer Society's cancer control working group, says: "...the incidence of cancer is expected to increase by 40 per cent in 2005, relative to 1990." Over the same period he calculates: "...there will be a 27 per cent increase in deaths from cancer, with only *some of this* due to the rise in population and ageing."

(N.Z. Herald, 30th-31st May 1998. Italics mine.)

Perhaps the true reason lies in the fact that our increasingly poisoned environment and stressful work and social parameters *together* are breaking down the body's once natural resistance and ability to cope with what might once have been considered occasional, normal setbacks in life. When the factors of chemical poisoning and too-high societal stress levels are *also* endemic in virtually all sectors of the community – as they now are from the youngest to the oldest – and are coupled with ongoing fear and uncertainty of the future, then the whole foolish business can do nought else but foster increasing levels of deeper depression 'across the board'. That aspect alone is a disastrous recipe guaranteed to increase cancers. Therefore it is high time that politicians recognised the truth of Jeanette Fitzsimon's insight, exercised their responsibilities, and played their part in helping 'the people' to 'turn around' worsening health statistics. In the end, of course, the mighty dollar – the powerful new god – will be the first consideration.

In just a relatively few short years, so much knowledge and natural practice has been discarded, to the detriment of good health. As well as poisoned food generally, it is too easy for everyone of us to now indulge in too many takeaways or packets of processed food, and wash it down with gallons of sickly-sweet 'lolly-water', of which only the water content is probably of any benefit. On the ill health of many, the producers of this kind of rubbish are laughing all the way to the bank. Even on the increase in children, the disastrously high levels of diabetes with its potential to cripple the health system in the near future, is at least forcing some of the community to rethink eating habits. [Maori health workers are now demonstrating how insidiously unhealthy so many processed foods and drinks are.]

Still, it is an interesting and perverse fact that humankind will spend all of their life doing exactly as they please – in blatant disregard of **The Spiritual Laws** that also govern health – fall ill, and then '*demand*' that the medical profession restore them to some level approaching optimum health.

Maori culture prides itself on its knowledge of ancient herbal cures and remedies, and numerous publications about them – some quite large and comprehensive – can be readily purchased. However, it is one thing to bask in some kind of reflected pride regarding this 'fund of knowledge', but entirely another to then indulge, on a depressingly regular basis, in eating all manner of wrong foods. In striving to maintain good health, we should be aware that particular foods will react with and in the body in diverse ways. In a previous Chapter we stated the necessity to fully understand the connection between *the physical body* and the life-giving, animating power of *the spirit* – the real me and you! Our spiritual responsibility is to live in such a way so as to *strengthen the connection* between the two. A weakened connection results in illness, and a severely weakened one can lead to death.

> The correct maintenance of the *"physical/spiritual radiation connection"* – *The Law of Balance* – is therefore vital for optimum health.

Therefore, if we wish to strengthen this connection, and since virtually all foods in varying combinations will either give energy or take energy, we should strive to only utilise those combinations which *give* energy and health to the body. By consuming the appropriate kinds of foods at the right time and in the correct combinations we can assist the body in fulfilling its natural cycle of ingestion, digestion and elimination. Of course, we should always strive to maintain a natural balance and not become overly fanatical in the pursuit of optimum health.

Just these few simple rules would go a very, very long way in eliminating so much of society's increasingly worsening health problems, particularly among Maori. Fortunately these practices are not difficult because most of the 'givers' of energy taste good. Therefore we do not have to stop eating many of our favourite foods, for they can be correctly combined so as to give energy. The current problem of obesity would be greatly reduced if this simple regime were adopted.

However, since most of our commercially-produced food is contaminated with substances detrimental to the human body, the sensible thing in nurturing and maintaining good health is, if possible, to not eat those foods.[5] Too much 'Maori land' is either unused, under-used or conveniently leased out for a quick monetary return instead of being used for the greater purpose for which it was intended, and which Maori should readily understand. Maori health would be greatly served if such land were organically utilised – for meat, poultry, fruits and vegetables. And thus demonstrate to the chemical mindset of official Pakeha agriculture and horticulture – a general disposition to which Maori presently subjugate control of their health-destiny now anyway – that there really is a better way. It is, moreover, **the spiritually-correct way**!

The land is there, the people to work the land are there. Therefore, become *kaitiaki* in the true sense of the word. Grow vegetables and fruit according to the spiritually endowed principles of organic gardening and organic animal husbandry and become, again, *the great gardeners Maori once were*.[6] This time, however, under the beneficent knowledge of, and connection to, **The Natural Laws**, and thus to **The Elemental Forces of Nature**. And thereby produce stronger bodies, as once they were, via this health-giving, natural regime. Bodies that will more readily resist disease and illness for far more years than is the present case.

Organic animal husbandry via The Natural Laws is probably more important than ever given the very great fear that BSE or mad-cow disease generated in Europe. No one knows how many people may eventually succumb to the human equivalent, vCJD, for

---

[5] The manufacture of Palm oil, an additive present in thousands of different kinds of processed foods we consume, has the dubious distinction of causing the death and displacement of hundreds of 'orang utangs' a month by the destruction of huge areas of jungle in Indonesia. The concomitant irreplaceable loss of other fauna and flora – both of which planet earth can ill afford to lose – is carried out to accommodate more and larger Palm oil plantations.

[6] In exactly such a renaissance in true *kaitiakitanga*, we note the establishment of more and more organic gardens in rural areas under Maori initiative and effort.

which there is still no cure. No one even knows how long the incubation period of the disease in humans is. A recent BSE inquiry, which cost $92 million and took more than two and a half years, damned the British Government over the tragedy. The report criticised the practice of making animal feed from animal carcases. In clear reinforcement of the primary thrust of **this Work** – namely the absolute necessity to utilise the knowledge of **"The Spiritual Laws of Creation"** in all things – we unequivocally concur with those parts of the report which state:

> **"Some say that it offended against nature to feed animal protein to ruminants. Some say that it was doubly offensive to turn grass-eaters into cannibals. Some say that it was not surprising that a plague was visited upon those that tampered with nature in this way."**

In France where a total of 93 cases were detected in 2000, perhaps the most truthful comment is that from bio-farmer Joerg Sieg, a German who farms 150 ha of Normandy fields:

> *"It's not just the cows which are mad. There are also farmers and consumers who are only interested in buying the cheapest product."*

Such a tragic lesson should induce all clear-thinking people to more vigourously oppose any and all practices that transgress The Natural Laws. For, in this case, we see the severest outworking of **'The Law of Reciprocal Action'** in a frighteningly *short period.* There will yet be many more tragic 'returns'.

Unfortunately, the general acceptance of the 'cult of non-responsibility' which now permeates the day-consciousness of much of the general populace, seemingly makes it easier to continue on with the present situation than to institute radical and beneficial change in the area of healthier food intake. Through more and more liberal attitudes, which the weak and the ill-disciplined seize upon as a crutch to demand 'more personal rights', the apportioning of blame anywhere except at the feet of oneself and one's own responsibility, is all too readily accepted. Not only by many in society, but by most of the legislators too. Thus the idea of 'non-responsibility' emerging as a natural excrescence of the 'my rights' mindset is perhaps the single most destructive thing we can perpetuate.

In necessary reinforcement here: In the area of health, this overflows into the foolish *demand* that one must, **by right**, be healed by the Medical profession, even after years of warnings, neglect and unhealthy living in personal self-indulgence – in direct contravention of The Laws of Life themselves! And in many cases when it is too late to effect any real restoration to even 'reasonable' health.

Let us, once again, reiterate the vast difference between **rights** and **responsibilities**, correct this socially-devastating and dangerously-insidious error, and set in *form* "The Spiritual Truth" of it. Firstly, we, the human beings of this material world, do not actually possess any 'absolute rights' of any kind. Neither, therefore, do we have the 'right' to make any 'absolute demands'. The fact is that by being permitted the gift of conscious life – 'solely at our request' – any right to 'any rights' is naturally abrogated by the inviolable authority inherent in The Law! Instead, by our very petition for conscious life, we are charged with *total spiritual responsibility* for all that we think and do.

Thus, in a perhaps uncomfortable reality for most, we have only **duties and obligations**. Firstly to that Source which gave to us Life, then to our fellow human beings, and to the earth that provides our home and sustenance.

Any so-called **rights** *will only eventuate as a direct consequence of* **first** *fulfilling our duties, obligations, and responsibilities.*

And in that lies the means whereby a better and more tolerant society can develop. If the differences between rights and responsibilities are carefully considered, only with the latter is it possible for a more equitable global society to develop, for this ideal lives **The Law** that:

"It is more blessed (spiritual) to **give** than to receive."

(Acts 20:35, Fenton, Emphasis and
parenthetic addition mine.)

In strong contrast, our present society, too strongly imbued with the attitude of 'non-responsibility', has set in place the wrong kind of liberal beliefs; those which have no understanding of higher Spiritual Law – let alone the justice of it. Moreover, this totally incorrect attitude and direction has produced an inordinate amount of polarisation between various groups within society. This, in turn, has the unfortunate potential to breed great mistrust, and even fear. For it is based more on emotionally-generated selfishness which promotes the 'taking first' in the perverse 'mindset' of 'my rights', rather than on clear objectivity which would promote the "giving"; the according of obligations and responsibilities to each other. Therefore, it is not difficult to understand which of the two positions would create the better and more harmonious society.

What, then, are our duties and obligations to our physical body and, by extension, to "The Living Source" which grants us this amazing marvel? Generally speaking, we take the body for granted. As long as we feel no pain or discomfort and the body allows us to carry out our personal desires, we pay it no heed. We over-indulge in all manner of ways with a quite incredible attitude of indifference as to what we may be doing to it. Yet this foolish attitude naturally sets in place a slowly increasing 'personal health deficit' which gradually reaches the point where one or more 'bodily components' have simply 'had enough' and can take no more!

Then of course alarm bells ring and great concern or fear forces us to seek help, which *may then* result in a more beneficial health regime. Equally, though, it may not! We do not seem to understand that if we are to derive the best and fullest use from the body for all of our earthly life, it should be *tended correctly* – at all times. Therefore, to be blessed with a healthy body from birth should presuppose a natural desire to strive to correctly care for the *gift* of that physical vessel.

Those not born with either a healthy body or a complete one offer the rest of us the opportunity to 'see' how fortunate we are as we observe their much harder struggle in ordinary daily living. And which very many do far more graciously and courageously than those of us without physical disabilities. Therefore we should regard the physical body as *our most precious possession* for our time on earth in the understanding that it really is a most necessary implement without which we could not function.

However, it is eminently clear from world health statistics that man does not regard his physical body as his 'most precious possession'. Indeed, the increasing illnesses and diseases worldwide starkly illustrates that this is a global trait. Perhaps it is because man lacks the key spiritual understanding of his "whence, whither and why" – even if he thinks he knows.

For New Zealand in the present time of the early years of the 21st century, the sobering comments by health professionals in the medical world probably says it all.

"New Zealand is in the grip of an epidemic involving, one way or another, heart disease, type 2 diabetes, smoking and obesity.
There is no country in the world that can afford to treat what is coming our way."

(Feature article, Weekend Herald, 19th November 2005.)

So it is not only excessive food intake that is cause for much illness and disease – in the West at least – but also over-indulgence in alcohol consumption, voluntary abuse of all manner of drugs, and the insidious, corrosive poison present in cigarette smoke.

Now, what about the 'glamour' of the 'fag in the mouth'? Statistically, far more prevalent among young Maori women than any other group in New Zealand. More unfortunately, though, an incredibly high incidence compared to the world's various groups of people. Not only of smoking but of diseases directly associated with it also. In the Sunday Star Times a decade ago on 16th November 1997, Tau Henare, Minister of Maori Affairs in the first Coalition Government, publicly acknowledged that smoking was an epidemic among Maori. "...but what's not?" he asks.
More importantly, however, was his insight noting:

"We know how sick we are, I'm totally sick of the statistics that get thrown in our faces. It's about time we started figuring out what to do about it."

Well, herein are the answers!

If one coolly and objectively applies the logic of Natural Law to the business of voluntary smoke inhalation, whether tobacco, marijuana, or even dried horse dung, one's faculties reel at the seeming inability of many smokers to recognise that their insidious and corrosively-poisonous habit *cannot possibly accord with any kind of naturally healthy practice in any shape or form.* To voluntarily choose, under our inherent free-will attribute, a habit that draws corrosive poison into one's lungs, when there is enough airborne pollution around in any case, reveals either weakness, 'stupid-cool', or the ultimate kind of arrogance in a 'couldn't-care-less' attitude. Or perhaps varying combinations of all three.

Perhaps the most amazing aspect of choosing to smoke in the first place is the fact that the body strongly registers a very high degree of *natural revulsion* at the very first puff on a cigarette. Most smokers readily agree that the initial taste is vile and unpleasant. In order, then, to reach the point of enjoying smoking, the smoker must forcibly push past *the revulsion barrier* just to be *able* to continue. So even against the immediate warnings of their own senses – and thus, more sadly, ultimately from the intuitive perception of the *wairua* – many continue to fight through those initial stages of acute distaste, *just to take up the habit.* One cannot help but wonder why, for to continue to inhale an unpleasant and vile-tasting substance until one simply 'gets used to it', seems to fly in the face of all logic and rational intelligence.

Unfortunately, the jaded argument that it is addictive and therefore difficult to give up does not alter the end result of greater health problems. Neither can the plea of peer pressure and/or being cool be used as either a reason or an excuse by the young. In actual fact it is neither of these, it is simply **weakness** in not having the guts to say no! Of course, if it is a strong wish to want to choose to smoke, then those who make such a decision should understand: **That The Spiritual Law of Reciprocal Action will** *return* **the hard effect –** *without fail.*

Medical science has now clearly established the connection between cigarette smoking and cancer and also appears to have similarly noted a link in the identification of the damage done to the organ primarily responsible for the elimination of toxins from the body – the liver. It is thus logical to accept that the effect of smoking on the liver sets in train a flow-on effect in the inability of that organ to then eliminate toxins caused by *other* conditions. Moreover, under Spiritual Law, these factors must then set in place hereditary weaknesses in the offspring of smoking mothers and fathers. This is hardly a spiritually-responsible attitude on the part of parents, for this *lives the selfishness* of 'taking' rather than 'giving' – removing the possibility of optimum health *for* the incoming soul.

With so much disease and death attributable to smoking, it is all the more strange that so many persist with it. Few smokers would agree to an early voluntary death or debilitation, but the very fact that they continue the habit guarantees most of them this surety since there is *not one element within cigarette smoke that is beneficial for the human body.* The effect is one of slow debilitation and poisoning, and the traditional argument by tobacco companies that causal links are still scientifically unproved is actually *irrelevant* anyway because **the greater transgression is a spiritual one – against the gift of the physical body**. And science cannot alter that!

In any case, belated admissions by American tobacco giants that cigarette smoking is detrimental to health – even according to their own research – and of manipulative practices to increase market share, have effectively destroyed the spurious argument of "...no causal link completely". And certainly revealed their greed and cynicism toward their 'customers', the future hospital patients.

For scientific research has now definitively isolated the actual process of mutation whereby nicotine tar in cigarette smoke produces cancer in healthy lung cells. This discovery was immediately reflected in a drop in the global share price for the tobacco companies as investors recognised the potential ramifications of this ground-breaking situation in possible law suits against the companies.

More conclusive and more damaging than those findings, however, is the direct evidence that a tobacco-specific cancer-causing substance is transmitted to the developing foetus when pregnant women smoke. Dr Stephen S. Hecht of the University of Minnesota's Cancer Centre found by-products of the nicotine-derived chemical NNK in the first urine of babies born to smoking mothers. NNK, a tobacco specific nitrosamine, is unique to tobacco and is one of the strongest carcinogens in tobacco smoke. Dr Hecht's study suggests that not only is it taken in by the foetus, but is processed by it, proving that tobacco products *cross the placenta into a baby in the womb.*

The chemical was found in twenty two of thirty one samples from new-born babies born to mothers who smoked during pregnancy. Dr Hecht noted that uptake of NNK in 'non-smokers' begins before birth simply because most women who smoke during pregnancy continue to smoke afterward, thus exposing their children to this carcinogen for many years. *The carcinogen was not found at all in babies of non-smoking mothers.*

(Source of NNK information – A.S.H!)

As we all know, one of the highest incidences of cigarette smoking in the world is endemic in young Maori women who, in turn, also have unacceptably high rates of cancer and illegitimate births. Now, by virtue of their ordained role as 'mothers of the Maori race', these young women obviously represent *the future genealogical blood-lines*, to which Maori often accord great *mana*. Since they are quite naturally *primarily charged* with both the *procreation* of children of Maori descent and the concomitant *continuation* of those blood-lines, what legacy of illness and disease is waiting a little further down the track through this serious transgression of Spiritual Law by such a high proportion of the *'mothers of the Maori race'*?

Cigarette smoking fathers, too, must also carry responsibility for this problem. And at some point, somewhere, **one** generation will need to take the serious decision *to be* **the** generation that finally recognises the need to break the cycle, and do so! Even though smoking is slowly decreasing among Maori generally, it is still at an unacceptably high level, unfortunately increasing amongst the young. Young Maori should therefore emulate the excellent example of many Maori sportsmen and women today who actively promote a non-smoking, healthy-lifestyle attitude. Moreover, the cigarette-smoking young only need to compare the health and fitness levels of those sportspeople with most of the rest of the community, particularly those of older age who still smoke, to readily see which is the more intelligent path to take.

On the home front the progression into smoking substances other than tobacco products leads us into the ironic situation where many Maori today are once more good gardeners, but of cannabis. Unfortunately, this substance is just as spiritually-insidious in its effect as tobacco. *And it is not even a native plant*!

In a previous Chapter we mentioned the weakening effect that mixed blood inherently has, and which Military Medical records reveal as an apparent propensity to respiratory weakness in part-Maori Servicemen. This can be clearly extrapolated to encompass the Maori race generally. If, as the indicators suggest, the practice of cigarette smoking is currently endemic within the race, this must surely represent the gravest possible factor to ensure the 'locking into place' of worsening Maori health. And, moreover, 'right across the board', given the direct connection of this corrosive poison to the respiratory system in the first instance, but to the entire working of the human body as a whole. Those were the findings towards the end of 2005. Whilst older people are giving up the habit, it is the young that are providing the new and increasing statistics, especially young Maori women.

Even a decade ago, the Herald edition of Monday, 16th December 1996, in an article entitled, "A nation running short of puff", itemised the key points of the tobacco 'industry' thus:

1. 40 New Zealanders take up the smoking habit every day. Half those will have their lives shortened by smoking-related illness.

2. Of 1000 20-year olds who start this year, 250 will die before age 70 losing an average 21 years from their lives, and 250 will die at age 70-plus losing an average eight years of life.

3. The annual health costs of smoking-related illness are $250m; but the Government takes $600m a year in tobacco tax.

4. On any given day, 828 New Zealanders are in hospital dying of smoking-related illness.

The article further noted:

> "Perhaps more disturbing for staff (Green Lane Hospital, where long-term smokers go to die from cancer) is the increasing number of young women, *particularly Maori*, being diagnosed as having lung cancer."

(Italics mine.)

The most amazing aspect of the statistics is that it is **a completely preventable situation**. For total statistics reveal, "1700 smokers a year killed by cancers of the lung, throat or mouth; 1400 dead from circulatory problems; around 1100 deaths annually from chronic respiratory disease and another 355 from other smoking-related causes."

And in the earlier Herald article of 4th December 1996, quoting from the results of a four year collaborative study between the World Bank and the World Health Organisation and published in the *Science* journal, the report warns of an "...extraordinary epidemic of tobacco-related mortality and disability..." which will claim more than 8 million lives in 2020.

Dr Keith Wollard, president of the Australian Medical Association, said the report provided a wake-up call for all the nations.

> "All the health community's good work in dealing with infectious diseases and improving living conditions and reducing maternal mortality will be replaced by the *appalling carnage* created by tobacco."

Thus, all indicators for Maori at least, purely by virtue of their extremely high level of smoking, *back then* pointed to a serious emerging problem potentially just as destructive as the old enslavement to the psychic world of *tohungaism, tapu, makutu* and *utu*. That was an enslavement which, we aver, would have eventually brought about the demise of the race if left unchecked. Smoking, if not curbed, will be just as devastating for Maori as the 'old psychic devils' were.

The internationally-acclaimed movie, "Whale Rider", very correctly strongly acknowledged the foolishness of smoking, particularly among Maori women. For through the line of Maori smoking mothers in the first instance and with the 'help' of Maori smoking fathers in 'support', the practice is already bequeathing to Maori the surety of weaker and sicker offspring. The end result will be a level of illness which the medical world will not easily be able to turn around later in their lives! Why? Because, as previously stated:

Smoking is a serious 'spiritual' transgression that immutable 'Spiritual Law' decrees to be absolutely wrong.

If no steps are taken to alter this propensity, the same Laws will visit the reciprocal effect more and more severely upon Maori than at present. For no race or individual can flout The Law with impunity!

Under The Law of Sowing and Reaping, therefore, the totally unnecessary statistics outlined here clearly show a relatively quick consequential return resulting from the obviously wrong decision to smoke, whether tobacco, marijuana, or any other! For it is the act of **contaminating** the gift of the physical body and the subsequent 'enslavement of the *wairua*' to such addictions that is the actual **spiritual transgression**. The *kind* of substance inhaled as the end-product is *totally irrelevant*. With regard to exceptionally high cancer levels among Maori, one further unfortunate 'record' requires recording here. Maori now evidently possess the highest rates of 'pancreatic cancer' in the world.

As at 2008, and no doubt helped by the smoking bans in cafes, pubs and workplaces etc., overall levels have fortunately decreased.

The effect of smoking on Maori health is indisputable, but the twin curses of smoking and drinking are more so in that they still both figure prominently in Maori health. Drinking, once responsible for most of the statistics of violence, has unfortunately probably been overtaken by the disastrously-damaging effects of the mind-altering, violence-inducing drug, **P**. It is a very simple matter for the reader to extrapolate the future social effect and cost that **P** will have on society, for it is clearly growing in use. *We will therefore see its destructive potential grow exponentially within society.*

We have briefly examined the spiritual meaning and effect of smoking, so let us now assess drinking from the same standpoint. Unlike smoking, however, drinking is on the increase, especially among the young. The foolish practice of binge-drinking by younger and younger drinkers – a phenomenon in many countries now – in New Zealand at least should be laid squarely *at the feet of certain politicians and other senior administrators*, even some *in the Police Force.* Against all intelligent and rational logic – and in direct opposition to the majority view of 'normal everyday people' here – those so-called 'leaders' voted for, and quickly wrote into law, their incredibly stupid decision to lower the drinking age. Since then we have had the farcical parody of supposedly 'serious debates' by M.P.'s to *raise* the drinking age once more. How many of those who voted yes to lower it *will now publicly admit it*? Perhaps the original votes should be disclosed so that those who did vote yes can be *publicly derided.* However, as we all know, that is 'not the way' of *most* politicians. Lying low or issuing denials or retractions is the usual tactic.

Unlike smoking, to take a drink is not in itself an intrinsically bad thing, so it certainly should not be considered evil. That fact notwithstanding, drinking *should nonetheless* presuppose a sense of responsibility in both the thinking and behaviour of those who *choose* to do so.[7]

Who has not enjoyed the wonderfully refreshing taste of a cool glass of good quality beer after a hard day's work? And, as with wine, beer can also admirably complement certain foods. Therefore it is not the act of taking a drink that is the problem, but the over-indulgence to the point of drunkenness resulting in loss of control that is the transgression. Standards of decency and more generally acceptable behaviour are quickly lost, for there are very few truly happy drunks; and certainly no noble ones.[8] Young binge-drinkers not only display ignoble behaviour, but the years that the young have thus far been able to legally drink in regular binge-sessions will surely have set in place health problems of no small import for perhaps many in later life. So where was there any kind of 'true' leadership displayed in lowering the drinking age in this land?

Just as there is absolutely *no mana whatsoever* in smoking, so is there none in immoderate drinking! In drinking, moreover, excessive indulgence can too often spill over into vicious and unprovoked violence. What does this tell us from the spiritual point of view?

Firstly it shows the true level of spiritual development of any individual or group that will not discipline itself in this vice. Fulfilment of spiritual potential is also severely curbed. More importantly, however, it reveals the truth of The Law that loss of conscious control allows other entities, under the aegis of **The Law of Spiritual Attraction...**, to more easily influence our thoughts and actions to a degree that we would not normally descend to if sober and 'in control'.

If violence is committed against loved ones whilst under the 'control' of drink, the awakening back into the 'real world' can sometimes be accompanied by great remorse. But, then again, depending on the level of spiritual maturity of the individual concerned,

---

[7]The era of Prohibition in 20th Century America was forced into law by an essentially far-right religious Temperance Movement. Not only was it a disastrous failure, but allowed organised crime to become so deep-rooted throughout all levels of American society that its systemic nature can never be eradicated. In fact, the huge wealth generated through illegal liquor sales then set the foundation for organised crime to flourish mightily *after* the repeal of such a foolish idea.

[8]There are surely few within the male populace of New Zealand who have not, at some time, experienced drunkenness and loss of control.

sometimes not. Yet the decision to drink is a personal one of free will. No one is actually driven to it. That is a fallacy and an attempt to employ the excuse of non-responsibility to justify one's actions in such cases. Moreover, not even emotional stress can be offered as final justification, as difficult as some life-situations can be. Whilst this ploy may wash to a certain degree with some proponents of social liberalism, it cannot under Spiritual Law which quietly waits to return the reciprocal effect of the deed unless the offender in the meantime changes his attitude.

A report from the New Zealand Herald over a decade ago on 12th February 1996 regarding overall Maori health offers truly sobering reflection. (Italics mine.)

> "New Zealand men are suffering poorer health than women because they try to "tough it out" and *fear seeming weak*, a report has found. The report found that masculinity was the main cause for men ignoring symptoms and trying to tough it out. It is easy to underestimate the power of this "masculinist outlook" and we may have an especially strong version of it in New Zealand although it is an international phenomenon. Staunch male attitudes are at the heart of why men's health and longevity are generally poorer than women's. Men also lead the statistics in suicides, violence, road fatalities, sports injuries, asthma and being overweight. *The report found Maori men the worst off having some of the poorest health records in the world."*

This report simply reinforces our constant assertion that we are not *"obeying the rules"*, and consequently paying a severe penalty in the area of health. Moreover, Maori men are clearly the worst affected. Is it a lack of education and knowledge, or is it simply a case of not caring and over-indulging far too much in our personal likes without accepting the responsibilities? For we have indeed reached a low point when, as a so-called 'masculine society', we feel we are weak if we show emotions at even what should be clearly appropriate times. Any 'need to do so', however, should perhaps be governed by the particular setting. In certain *physical* situations, it may be necessary and correct for the male to 'tough it out'. That need not be the case where natural emotions should be given the chance to be released, however.

In ancient societies masculinity was recognised as the correct thing for males to attain to. Physical strength was prized not only as a natural attribute for the necessary everyday work tasks, but also for the protection and defence of the land and its people. Thus to be *truly masculine in the spiritual sense* is also to be manly, and therefore noble. True masculinity encompasses all the spiritual virtues of the *wairua* and is the way of 'the peaceful warrior'.

Unfortunately, what was once recognised as natural masculinity is often derided as 'machoism' today. Is it any wonder that men's health is poor, given this extra unnecessary **emotional** pressure? Perhaps society needs to once more revisit *the concept of masculinity as it is ordained to be* and promote a more balanced attitude toward it, thus allowing men their rightful physical and spiritual place again. With that awareness, men's self-esteem, which has taken a battering in recent decades, might be restored to a healthier balance overall.

21.1.2   Emotional Health

Notwithstanding the content of the previous paragraph, it is important to ensure that the correct emotional balance is also struck to complement the physical and spiritual aspects of each individual. For, if correctly understood:

> **Emotions are given to allow us to deeply and fully experience life's more intense events – irrespective of whether they be joyful or painful.**

Therefore men must find ways to recognise, deal with, and finally clear their emotions in this area. Paradoxically, in this recognition rests the potential for both human frailty – out of fear of being perceived as weak; and great strength of purpose – in facing that fear and conquering it.

For with the courage to admit the nature of our problems, we empower ourselves to take the appropriate action to overcome them. Such strength springs from the ability to give and receive that most powerful of Virtues – **Love**; perhaps especially to ourselves within the healing process, but to all others around us too. As previously noted, love should not be regarded as an emotion in itself for it stands far above that. In it's pure form it encompasses the "The Living Power of Creation Itself", thus that which permitted everything to come into being; we also.

Unfortunately, however, because we are not given the correct tools and/or knowledge with which to understand our emotions, we are often confused as to what our true feelings are about, or should be about. This is more especially true for men who may be unused to talking about emotions, and who may feel uncomfortable and embarrassed by their own feelings. The most powerful emotions are usually those associated with painful experiences, which are often readily recalled in one's memories. We experience this most acutely as a 'lump in the throat' which, because of the believed need to be masculine in a masculine society, we strive to suppress and force back down. After a time – when the immediate cause of the pain has lessened – we can physically feel 'the lump' reducing in size.

However, *this does not mean it has gone away.* It has simply become lodged *deep inside the individual* where it quietly awaits to reassert its choking presence at the *next painful emotional experience* – simply because the pain previously generated was never *actually released.* Therefore, because this particular process has a cumulative effect, swallowing it down does not get rid of it. It remains entrapped within the body and enlarges with the next unresolved bout of painful, unreleased emotions. Unless the 'owner' can 'expel' this *corrosive lump*, it can well manifest in a different form, usually a physical illness. The best method of expulsion, and therefore emotional healing, is via the vocal organs and through the throat. In essence, *vocalisation* of the inner, emotional pain.

The accidental discovery of this process was made by Dr. Arthur Janov, an American psychotherapist and author of, 'The Primal Scream', whilst observing the emotional struggle of a young man in his clinic. In his words, what he heard was:

> "...an eerie scream welling up from the depths of a young man lying on the floor during a therapy session."

In subsequent sessions with other patients, he was able to observe the same release via this 'involuntary scream'.

His book, first published in 1973, has been reprinted 13 times since. Quite clearly, it appears to provide real answers to, and a release from, deep-seated emotional pain. On page 11, he explains the process; (all emphases mine):

> "I have come to regard that scream as the product of central and universal pains which reside in all neurotics. I call them Primal Pains because they are the original, early hurts upon which all later neurosis is built. It is my contention that these pains exist in every neurotic each minute of his later life, irrespective of the form of his neurosis. These pains often are not consciously felt because they are diffused throughout the entire system where they affect body organs, muscles, the blood and lymph system and, finally, *the **distorted** way we behave.*"

We should probably define the word "neurosis" so that some readers, who may equate the word with insanity, may feel reassured in this regard. From Reader's Digest Great Illustrated Dictionary, Vol.II:

> **neurosis**. n, Any of various illnesses affecting the mind or emotions, without obvious organic lesion or change, and involving anxiety, depression, phobia, hysteria, or other abnormal patterns of behaviour.

In a review of Dr. Janov's book, the Publishers Weekly noted that:

> "The results have been startling. Forced to face (*not turn from*) their lifelong core of pain, patients have lived psychic shocks as early as infancy – and emerged for the first time in a lifetime, whole, real, no longer dependent on acting out a neurotic life-style."

We necessarily tap into the concept of spiritually-correct child-rearing here where, as previously stated, it is most important that parents live a normal (natural) life-style so that they will not impart any kinds of early neuroses to their offspring that could unnecessarily and unfairly become part of the child's psyche in later-life. The tragically high levels of child-abuse today are prime and fertile grounds for cementing in place deep emotional pain. Unfortunately, however, such trauma is invariably suppressed for years afterwards.[9]

Perhaps fortunately for Maori men in general, the *tangi* is one of the few places where crying openly for themselves is socially-acceptable. This can provide an ideal opportunity whereby the 'lump in the throat', which will normally manifest at such times, can be let go naturally if released correctly. As explained in the Chapter, **'The First Death'**, however, the appropriate concern for the departed one should be the first consideration of any grieving at a funeral, and not that of overly-loud displays of emotion by the mourners. So even with the 'right place and circumstances', deep emotional pain cannot be completely released through just silent weeping. The pain really needs to be *vocalised* for a more complete emotional release, and the experience ideally needs to be completely succumbed to. By this vocalisation process one can **actually feel the 'lump' leaving the body** through the throat and mouth.[10]

For those men who carry this burden and do not know what to do about it, the first step is to *recognise that it is actually there*, for only then can one begin the process of becoming free of it. This conscious release through vocalised sound **actually does** give inner peace to the soul.

> Then the emotions become *friends to be welcomed* as a method of natural expression, not *an enemy to be feared* in the *wrong belief that it reveals one's weakness and/or lack of control*.

Initially, however, the necessary and desirable transition to more natural expressions of emotion may be difficult given the powerful pressures of society for the retention of staunch attitudes, especially for men. As in all things a third way must be found which balances natural expression with appropriate circumstance.

The timely movie, "Once were Warriors", graphically depicted a slice of real life that many Maori are aware exists. It clearly illustrated the loss of dignity, nobleness and *mana* that should be the hallmark of a true 'warrior', regardless of race. The hopelessness and agony of the lifestyle portrayed in that film is that of the never-ending carousel, where

---

[9]Very early exposure to computers, 'cyber-space' and all manner of electronic pastimes also plays its insidious part in *spiritually-incorrect* child-rearing.

[10]Knowledge gained through personal experiencing.

no end is in sight unless something very radical occurs to shake the participants out of their *self-imposed delusion* that everything is okay and that *everyone else* is wrong. No real happiness can ever result from such behaviour simply because it is actually alien to the *wairua* [spirit]. Only anger and inner pain, always masked by 'appropriate degrees of staunchness', flourish here. Since that lifestyle is akin to one of hopelessness, with nothing to look forward to but more of the same, only the suffering individual can know the painful feeling of his personal, inner emotional turmoil each time the 'lump in the throat' rises up to challenge his 'very vulnerable staunchness'.

It is important to stress that it is not the aim or purpose of this book to tell anyone how to live their lives. That is for each individual or group to decide. Our role is to simply reinforce the truth of The Law [**The Primordial Laws of Creation**] where **free-will choices unequivocally determine our life's outcomes** – nothing else!

> If we want sickness, disease and ill health, *then make wrong decisions and reap the inevitable consequences. But do not then seek to apportion blame elsewhere*.

Conversely, if we wish the opposite, then make good and beneficial choices. **It is that simple!** For the reciprocal effect of The Law is automatically invoked in that we always receive the exact outcome for all decisions. We should therefore be very careful what we wish for, as we may just get exactly that, though perhaps not necessarily in the way we might have expected!

Male inability to cope with emotional 'trauma' will often be strengthened by alcohol. This more volatile and unpredictable mix will then usually manifest most strongly toward the most vulnerable, the family unit – the perfect 'soft target' for an enraged male. So if we continue with this present line of analysis into the emotions, coupled with the downside of alcohol abuse, we find the potential tragedy of the perhaps normally placid, easy-going, likeable and respected father, suddenly being transformed into a violent, destructive personality when under the **control** of drink. Bouts of violence against the family may be followed by subsequent feelings of deep remorse at the pain he has inflicted upon the ones he loves. If this cycle continues, then shame and self-loathing may *correctly* set in but without any way to consciously deal with it. This may exacerbate the drink problem, with the cycle becoming more deeply entrenched. Should there be a family separation as a result of his inability to cope or to break the cycle, more anger and hurt will invariably be the likely outcome. It is invariably at such times that the painful 'lump in the throat' makes its presence most strongly felt.

Many men do recognise that this is an uncomfortable reality for them but are reluctant to acknowledge, even to themselves, that it *is* there. According to this wrong view, being 'staunch' is often deemed to be the manly thing to do. So rather than letting it out, such men suffer silently. Blocking its natural exit – through the mouth in **cleansing tangi** – only increases the emotional intensity of this 'lump' whenever a new and painful incident is experienced, such as the end of a marriage or relationship, loss of family or friends, job or similar.

Health, therefore, is not just concerned with the physical body alone. True health also encompasses the emotional and psychological aspects of every human being. To achieve this desirable balance, however, one must take into account the *spiritual nature* of oneself *first*. If this is correctly positioned and understood, all other failings can be tackled and re-aligned positively. So to understand the extremely damaging effects of the 'lump in the throat' in the case of men, we need to accept that it is okay to show our emotions.

We need to totally expunge this very wrong concept that only the weak cry.

In truth, it is the **truly strong** who are able to express their emotions *when required*. It is invariably the weak and/or fearful who refuse to cry even when the emotional pain is demanding to be released and causing huge anguish to the inner man.[11] In the final analysis, no matter how tough or well-muscled the physical body may be, that is only the external shell housing the real person; a shell which will one day *rot away* in any case. So there is little point in always being 'staunch' to the detriment of one's physical, emotional and spiritual health, or the health of the *whanau*. This kind of debilitating 'staunchness' on the part of the male creates unnecessary tension in family harmony and is, therefore, detrimental to all. Anger Management Courses are a useful beginning, but we need to go further than this into some form of cathartic release-mechanism for long term healing and recovery.

So whilst it is clearly correct to acknowledge the help that anger management can offer, it must also be really understood that we stand constantly in the midst of the consequences of all our previous decisions. In other words we are *always reaping the fruits of what we have already previously sown elsewhere in time*. This may be a difficult concept to grasp, especially in the field of personal relationships where most emotional pain is generated, and it is always easier to apportion blame outside of ourselves. Because this ploy can be used as an excuse or reason for violence, it is as *individuals first* that we must accept the need for change, and then adjust our lives accordingly.

The rapidly increasing spiritual pressure on the world and its inhabitants today serves to strengthen the impact of every experience we undergo – irrespective of whether painful or joyful. This greater pressure and its associated depth of feeling provides an infallible mechanism whereby the individual will be forced to look within himself in order to recognise the degree of wrong thinking that perhaps pervades and poisons his immediate environment on earth, and to which he may have contributed. So unless there is a greater understanding of the role of the emotions and how to use them effectively, the continuing downward spiral of societal violence will only worsen.

In the final analysis, then, good health must be holistic, with a correct balance between mind, body and emotions. Spiritual knowledge, concomitant with spiritual health, is the key and the foundation around which this holistic approach needs to be built. That will only happen if we accept, and live, **The Eternal Laws** in their entirety. Therefore, if we 'break the rules' and are hit with pain and suffering, we must learn to accept our individual responsibility for it, understanding that we will have given cause for that 'reaping' somewhere, sometime.

Just as there are individual emotional problems to be resolved, so, too, are there 'collective' issues to be dealt with by communities and Nations. This is especially true for indigenous peoples who feel they have been robbed of their lands and culture. Again, because of this increasing spiritual pressure, these deep-seated feelings are being intensified and brought to the fore in various protest Movements.

There is a cleansing and separating-out process occurring everywhere in the world between those who continue down a path of materialism and empiricism – where everything is explained only according to the material senses and what can be physically measured – and those who seek a more spiritual and deeper aspect to life's meaning. *And New Zealand and its peoples are not exempt from this cleansing process.*

---

[11]A clear exception to this is when the trauma is so severe that the emotions actually shut down *in order to protect the individual* for that time. The latter-day phenomenon of *professional sportsmen* crying when they lose a race, a game or a match is simply *emotional weakness*.

To effect this cleansing procedure, the Health sciences, which deal first-hand with the mental and emotional casualties of our society, will need to embrace the view that a spiritual foundation is the major prerequisite for any such healing to completely succeed. The cleansing of all inner pain through the outlet of the emotions is a necessary step to resolving problems for the individual. For this inner hurt may be the result of *lifetimes of unresolved conflict* returned to the entity under the aegis of **The Law of Reciprocal Action**.

The continuing burden of more pain through wrong decision-making eventually brings such individuals to a point of deep despair because they do not know, or do not want to know, these Spiritual Laws and how to live them accordingly. Our TV screens clearly show the dramatic anguish of millions all over the world as they struggle against inner collapse which is associated with experiences of great suffering. Humanity as a whole must recognise this worldwide happening too, and strive to understand what must be done in order to bring about a better outcome than the obvious present reality.

*   *   *   *   *

In the same kind of need for collective Maoridom to face similar sorts of hard truths, and as stated in the previous Chapter: We who participated in the Vietnam War must find the inner courage to finally accept that *that* war – as conducted by the United States Government – was ignoble and wrong. That reality notwithstanding – yet at the same time recognising the fact that war is nonetheless an adventure for the young soldier initially – there should be no thought or cause for reproach in how **we** carried out our task, for we were ultimately there at the behest of our political masters. Despite the fact that we 'operated' as true professional soldiers, first-hand involvement not only resulted in the loss of some of our comrades – *or perhaps it was their ordained time by virtue of the decision to be there* – but has also prevented *most* of the rest of us 'still here' from knowing that inner peace which the spirit longs for in the belief of a job well done.

The haunting fact remains, therefore, that 'The Vietnam Experience' was not for a noble cause. And the *wairua* of many of our "brothers-in-arms" has some difficulty finding peace because of that often-difficult, factual reality. Ultimately, the Vietnam War reflected the scheming, insidious, geo-political considerations of primarily the USA and France. Paradoxically for many 'Vets' now, Vietnam is more a 'state of mind' than an actual country. Thus, through the 'experiencing', the overall 'Emotional Health quotient' of the 'Vietnam Vet component' of New Zealand is seriously compromised.

Yet no matter how haunted or troubled the spirit might be through such an experience, **The Divine Gift of Grace** – which we have previously explained – really does permit true healing-resolution and emotional inner peace to be achieved.

On the use of Service Personnel by New Zealand Governments; a former C.D.S., Lt. General Sir Leonard Thornton, after his retirement stated that successive New Zealand Governments *'did not **deserve** the calibre, professionalism and dedication of its Armed Forces Personnel'*. We of 'The Vietnam Experience' would surely endorse General Thornton's blunt words of Truth probably before most other 'Vets'.

*   *   *   *   *

So, just as we Vietnam Vets' must find the inner strength to face *our* 'spiritual challenge' to gain genuine **Emotional Health** once more; so must collective Maoridom confront *its* emotionally-aberrant demons and excise them completely from its collective wairua.

21.1.3   Mental Health

"If we fix 'Maori mental health', we fix mental health in New Zealand."

(Comment made by the head of Mental Health
Radio N.Z.'s "Nine to Noon" programme.)

The old name of *mate Maori* [or perhaps *mate wairua*][12] is still relevant today, for too many Maori still suffer from it. The increasing level of Maori mental illness is indicative of this trend. Without **genuine** understanding of the problem or 'condition' from the psychiatric community – *purely because this particular state has nothing whatever to do with empirical science or medicine in the very first instance* – it will continue to worsen. For it is ultimately a condition wrought under the outworking of Spiritual Law, as is virtually all illness in any case. The term 'spiritual health', invariably used in the wrong context, is sometimes applied to various areas of health care, but there is no real understanding of what this term actually means or from where it is derived. Predictably, also, no understanding in how to apply it beneficially – if by some miracle it *were* recognised and accepted. In the meantime, relatively recent statistics for Maori mental health show that whilst admissions are rising – particularly for men – re-admission rates are soaring and are cause for alarm.

*   *   *   *   *

During research for this book at the Mental Health Foundation, I was appalled to learn that the standard method of treatment for Maori patients has not really changed *in many decades*. The current analyses of mental conditions by the mental health professionals clearly satisfy 'The Establishment' in that every condition is ostensibly understood and named – *according to current, medical-labelling protocols*. The stated wide use of 'Maori spirituality' through traditional culture and *tohungaism* as being essential to effect 'healing' in Maori patients did not at all reveal any kind of understanding of the *core* problem. It simply showed the opposite – non-understanding!

For the *primary* connection and interaction between the physical body and the inner animating **spiritual core** – *which is the actual person* – **is not at all understood**. And more than likely in the case of at least many health professionals anyway, **not believed to exist as a separable entity – or exist at all**. Yet this precise and inviolable knowledge **would offer the greatest help in truly understanding certain aspects of mental illness**!

Thus we still have treatment regimes for Maori which are mainly culturally-based and employing the use of *tohunga*. This *may* help if it is *not* the sole treatment method. Yet Ratana clearly showed that *tohungaism was not the way*, for in its reverential self-adulation toward things solely of Maori and associated culture, it cannot ultimately take away *the sickness of mate maori*. Moreover, it cannot do so because *tohungaism* applied to mental health regimes for Maori, particularly, is still connected to dangerous *psychic* areas.

---

[12]The term, *mate wairua*, (if lit. dying spirit or spirit death) is actually incorrect because the *human spirit* is not subject to the death process whilst it resides as the 'inner animating core' within the human body. The Chapter, **The Second Death**, explains how we of the spirit *can* suffer 'spiritual death', but that process is far removed from Maori beliefs centred around the notion of a, literal, 'dead or dying spirit'. *Mate wairua* cannot be applied to the idea of a *sick spirit* either because it is always and only the outer cloak/s that can 'sicken'. The spirit can naturally be *enveloped* by 'sick outer cloaks', but cannot, of itself, be sick. Earthly death 'deriving from' *mate Maori/mate wairua* indicates a very precise 'process of Spiritual Law' preceding such deaths.

Maori and Pakeha psychiatric 'health professionals', therefore; – for you, especially:
A proclamation!

> **"The present 'healing regime for Maori mental health' – believed by you and your profession to be 'the right way' – in the final analysis actually feeds and 'exacerbates' the whole Maori mental health problem."**

(Author.)

*　　　*　　　*　　　*　　　*

That is precisely why we read in the 1993 discussion document on "Trends in Maori Mental Health", commissioned by Te Puni Kokiri, the following disturbing facts reprinted here from their Executive Summary section.

EXECUTIVE SUMMARY

The rise in Maori psychiatric admissions.

1. "Maori rates of first admission to psychiatric services *have increased dramatically* over the last 30 years, while Pakeha rates have remained stable.

2. The following are factors which lead to Maori psychiatric admissions:

3. *Drug abuse and drug psychosis are major and rapidly growing problems for Maori*, and are occurring *at an early age*. Preventative drug and alcohol programmes seemed to have focused mainly on alcohol problems.

4. The lack of culturally appropriate early detection and support systems in schools. Maori counsellors or schools which operate as bicultural institutions are generally absent.

5. The lack of community agencies working under kaupapa Maori in the mental health field to whom Maori can turn when a mental illness develops.

6. Maori are more likely to become *seriously ill* before help is sought. Then their admission to hospital is more likely to be enforced. The Pakeha route is more likely to be through referral from a doctor or helping agency, thus processes of recovery may be already underway at admission.

7. Issues such as *cultural alienation*, poverty, unemployment and hardship, the *breakdown of cultural traditions* with the shift from rural to urban living, and the *failure of the education system for Maori* have not been taken into account in *designing appropriate mental health services for Maori.*"

The next section of this summary continues with the unfortunate title:

The failure of treatment.:

1. When Maori enter a psychiatric hospital or ward for the first time, what happens to them does not appear to work well and it is the *consequent readmission rates that are particularly worrying.*

2. Once admitted, Maori are *40% more likely* to be readmitted than Pakeha, *Maori readmission rates have risen 40%* in the decade from 1981 to 1990, while Pakeha rates have *fallen by 25%.*

3. Maori readmissions are most likely to be for *severe psychotic illnesses* (schizophrenia and effective psychosis).

Possible reasons why readmission occurred include:

- the illness was more serious at the time of first admission;

- the treatment at first admission was *not effective or culturally appropriate*;

- the discharge was too early; or

- there was insufficient or culturally inappropriate community support on discharge.

37% of all Maori male admissions are for schizophrenia, and 32% of all female admissions (compared with 22% and 16% for Pakeha males and females).

This fascinating summary continues with the next section dealing with the questions and issues:

"That arise with schizophrenia."

1. To what extent is the prevalence of schizophrenia due to cultural alienation, poverty or unemployment?

2. What impact do longer stays or more frequent admissions have on a person who is diagnosed as having schizophrenia?

3. Are Maori misdiagnosed by health professionals who are unable to communicate effectively with them?

4. Does the diagnosis of schizophrenia lead to methods of treatment that are *inappropriate for Maori*?

5. Are there major misclassification problems arising from the use of a 1975 diagnostic system or the way ethnicity and diagnosis are determined by the staff who fill in the statistical record?

When people with psychotic illnesses return to the community, they are usually severely disabled, and with illnesses such as schizophrenia, this disability is likely to be life-long. Consequently community care requires establishing people in culturally appropriate lifestyles – treatment becomes a way of life.

The cost of failure to cure or prevent psychotic illness is enormous and that cost increasingly relates to Maori consumers.

"Comparing 1981 to 1991 there were close to *1500 fewer Pakeha admissions* to psychiatric hospitals and wards. Their place was taken by an *increase in Maori admissions of over 900*, mostly with psychotic illnesses.

Already Maori make up *half the population of prisons and forensic units*. On current trends, in *10 years time*, they may eventually make up *half the population of psychiatric hospitals.*"

Summary of recommendations:

Recommendations made to the Ministry of Health, the Public Health Commission, Regional Health Authorities, Crown Health Enterprises, Accident Rehabilitation and Compensation Insurance Corporation, education and training services, health and social science research organisations, non-governmental organisations and the Department of Justice highlight the need to address the following issues:

- *greater Maori control of mental health services;*

- better funding of services with a *specific Maori mental health focus*;

- the provision of accurate and up to date service information on Maori mental health and *treatment outcomes.*

- the development of community based, hospital and advocacy mental health services that *meet Maori needs*;

- research *identifying Maori mental health needs* and effective treatments;

- training programmes to *rapidly increase* the number of qualified Maori available to work in *Maori mental health services;*

- education programmes targeting specific areas for Maori such as *drug abuse, young mothers and school aged children*; and

- reviews of the impact of legislation on Maori such as the Mental Health Compulsory Assessment and Treatment Act 1992 and the Criminal Justice Act 1985.

The discussion document ends with a summary of the key findings which are, in essence, the same as those above. Before we address those findings, however, perhaps we should offer a definition of the meaning of the word schizophrenia for those of us not in the mental health profession. From "Reader's Digest Great Illustrated Dictionary, Vol.II."

> **schizophrenia** *n.* Any of a group of psychotic conditions characterised by withdrawal from reality and accompanied by highly variable affective, behavioural, and intellectual disturbances. Formerly called "dementia praecox". [New Latin "split mind": SCHIZO + PHRENIA]

That essentially represents the official medical description, albeit in probably very basic terms. With that we are meant to be fully accepting of this categorisation in the belief that it is an inviolable and correct assessment of the actual *living form* of the stated condition.

Now, whilst the summary no doubt fulfils the standard criteria as defined in the Mental Health Act, nowhere in the above list of reasons and findings do we note any mention of the need to understand **Spiritual Law** and its decisive outworking on all things, including man and his 'assessment of situations'.

> What we do find, however, is the disturbing fact that **the combined so-called 'knowledge' of the Pakeha mental health regimes and that of Maori 'cultural healing methods' have failed to stem the alarming rise in Maori Mental Health.**[13]

Our contention is thus: It is that way because both regimes do not even begin to understand this most crucial factor of Spiritual Law and its *inviolable* outworking. And, therefore, its consequential ramifications in the mental health field also.

Therefore, until *both* ethnic sides embrace Spiritual Law and its surer healing regime, the prediction from the above assessment that Maori will make up over half of all admissions in psychiatric hospitals in the 10 year time-frame indicated, may well have been borne out. Put simply, the answers do not lie in a purely intellectual assessment, nor in applying more of the same 'cultural or traditional healing regime' through *tohungaism*. Moreover, we can be equally sure that more funding with an associated increase in the numbers of Maori mental health workers will not make one iota of difference either. In fact, without *real change*, that kind of 'remedy' is virtually guaranteed to ensure a worsening situation.

---

[13]Since the 'Mission' of the Prophet, Ratana, is a vital component of this Work, we strongly recommend that *someone* in the 'Maori health field' conduct a comparative, percentage-survey of 'Maori mental health' between the members of the Ratana Church and the general Maori population. I am sure the results would be very revealing.

The true 'remedy', once again, lies in the vital recognition that an attitudinal-change in the collective psyche of the Maori race – one that encompass the knowledge of Spiritual Law – is urgently required. With that as the first and most crucially-important step, the conscious application of that necessary knowledge will then have the effect of automatically applying **spiritual healing** to all of the Maori race, thus beneficially reducing the increasing numbers coming out of the race to be incarcerated in mental asylums.

This radical axiom does not at all mean that all within the Maori race are mentally ill. What is stated here is that, *because* of the *correct* Maori acceptance of the *other-world reality*, but unfortunately with its far-too-strong influence in its fear-inducing potential, a continuing and unnecessary inculcation of this fear and uncertainty into the collective psyche of the Maori race is very much part of the reason for an appropriate healing need. For without any clear knowledge of that *other world's* place and purpose, fear and/or acute uncertainty is generally the quite natural accompaniment of any association with it. Genuine healing will therefore only be achieved with the recognition and application of **The Spiritual Laws – *as they actually are*** – to Maori mental-health problems.

As stated previously, however, the acceptance of the 'other-world reality' should be viewed by Maori as a *positive* element. For it offers the opportunity of a relatively easy transition from the present uncertainty as to **why**, to one of truly knowing. This would then offer the means for a huge reduction in the numbers of the mentally ill. The same necessary transition for Pakeha – *as a complete people* – from a general attitude of non-acceptance to one of conscious and knowledgeable acceptance, would probably be more difficult to make by virtue of their more traditional materialistic and empirical beliefs. Yet, notwithstanding this generalisation, there are many Pakeha who are very accepting and understanding of that 'other-world' too.

Therefore, those parts italicised in the Executive Summary on Maori mental health are the crucial points to which the outworking of Spiritual Law should be immediately applied if there is to be any meaningful improvement in those worsening statistics.

Firstly, however, accept Spiritual Law!

There is one aspect of mental health not yet considered that may actually account for the increasing numbers of the Maori mentally ill. Moreover, it is a point that should be considered very relevant given Maori acceptance of the 'other-world reality'. For it is one that the Judaeo/Christian belief – from which, for the most part, we ostensibly derive our 'rules of society' – once accepted unequivocally. And that is the *possibility* of the insane, the schizophrenic or whomever, being *influenced* so strongly by external *entities* as to become *unhinged* and/or to lose the strength of their own 'personal volition'. In other words, *lose complete control.*

The word once used to describe this 'condition' was **possession**, which dictionaries generally describe as; *"the state of being dominated by, or as if by, evil spirits or by a strong emotion or idea"*.

The notion of being 'possessed' is not one that modern psychiatric or mental health regimes have much truck with. Yet the word, schizophrenia, used to describe 'different states of unreality', means 'split-mind'. The very word therefore offers both an indication and association for the 'possibility' of *possession*.

Whilst the information relating to Maori Mental Health is taken from a 1993 publication and probably 'tells it like it is', the follow-on document, "Trends in Maori Mental

Health 1984-1993", offer an overall summary of that particular decade. Because this whole business has so much potential to devastate Maori youth particularly if nothing changes, we will note the key findings of that latter report as a separate section later in this segment. At this point, however, from page 18 we will quote an interesting observation about 'possession'. [Emphasis mine]:

> "People with schizophrenia hear voices and see visions of people who are not there. For cultures who feel the presence of ancestors in a direct way, by hearing and seeing them, what is "real" and what is "unreal" is very difficult for the clinician of another culture to determine, particularly if that clinician is from a Western culture which has largely lost its direct contact with ancestors. "Delusions", weird beliefs about what is happening or what people and things are doing are common symptoms of schizophrenia that can only be effectively judged from inside the culture. For example, some form of "**possession**" may be considered both *real and acceptable* in Maori and Pacific Islands cultures."

Let us briefly examine the assertions in that paragraph from the standpoint of Spiritual Law. Firstly, to believe that only from inside a particular culture is one able to fully understand it is probably true insofar as an innate 'feel' for it is concerned. However, that is **not** a requirement where the **mechanics** of particular 'mental processes' – which in any case have their origin and outcome anchored in Spiritual Law – are concerned. Therefore, in *any* analysis of mental health for *any* culture, the *same lawful mechanisms* under **The Law** determine *all* ramifications of *all* mental illnesses, since the origin of it will have been put in place by the people so affected – under the inherent, human, free-will attribute.

So must it be with this interesting condition of "**possession!**" Simple spiritual fact ordains that either it is an actual reality, or it is not! There will not be any shades of grey here.

> However, *under the outworking of Spiritual Law*, the reality or otherwise of this condition **can only be possible where there is a separable, inner animating core or body [soul/spirit] which exists independently of the physical body, upon which other 'forces' can act and/or influence**.

Therefore, it naturally follows that **if** such is the case [this **'if'** being purely for the purpose of this debate], then the same mechanisms *will* exist for particular kinds of mental illness – *regardless of the race or culture*. Such lawful processes are inherently the same for everyone, as they logically must be, so the concept and *"reality of possession"* should be regarded as much *less* a cultural aspect and much more one of necessary acceptance by the psychiatric profession.

*   *   *   *   *

In late 2005 the release of the movie, "The Exorcism of Emily Rose", resurrected the controversy surrounding "possession". Though an American production, it was based on the story of Annaliese Michel [21st September 1952 – 1st July 1976] a German woman who was believed to be possessed by a demon and subsequently underwent an exorcism. Born into a Catholic family, an exorcism request for Annaliese was eventually approved by Bishop Josef Stangl of Wurzburg in 1975. The actual exorcism was carried out by Father Arnold Renz and Pastor Ernst Alt.

The taped sessions suggested there were six separate demons possessing her. Annaliese eventually destroyed her knees through obsessive genuflections. The exorcists – and her parents – were charged with negligent homicide, found guilty of manslaughter resulting from negligence and were sentenced to 6 months. The sentence was far lighter than expected.

The movie portrayal certainly shows that others, separate from mental health professionals in New Zealand, are prepared to examine this notion of "possession" in people *not* of the 'brown brotherhood'. If one understands the actual process by which one can be possessed, then one can further understand *why* an exorcism of a person with multiple and dark, destructive personalities – all lodged within and battling each other for "greater possession" – might *not* be successful.

The great pity about the controversy is the intellectual rejection of the notion by current medical opinion. Referencing the Bible to show why "possession" should be regarded as a very real and dangerous condition that affects many more people than is accepted at this time, is invariably dismissed as religious claptrap *by the very people who need to understand much more than just the* **apparent** *empiricism* of their 'profession' of Psychiatry.

A non-religious and open-minded look at **The Ministry of Jesus** would offer such 'professionals' far more insight into this 'condition' than current teachings from their 'university textbooks' could ever allow. When He stated He had "...not come to overthrow the Law but to fulfil it"; therein is the surest indication that *He actually fulfilled The Law when freeing the many recorded in the New Testament as being "possessed"*.

*   *   *   *   *

To *understand* this 'condition', however, means that one must understand **The Law** that He came to fulfil. If, then, we analyse this further from the explanation of the processes of the outworking of just one of these Laws more fully explained in **Chapter 6 – 'The Law of Attraction of Similar Species'** – we note how normally placid people can be driven to commit horrific crimes in the heat of great stress. Invariably in such cases, once the deed is committed, the individual returns to his normal and perhaps placid but usually deeply remorseful self.

The effect of his 'wrong idea' during his moment of weakness wrought by events he feels he perhaps cannot cope with rationally, opens the door for a massive inrush of external 'force' or 'pressure', and he succumbs to it. Having 'spent' his anguish, he 'returns' to his 'normal' daily world. Sometimes, however, an event may be so traumatic that the final outcome is far different for the one affected.

Long-term psychotics will invariably be found to be *spiritually weaker* than the average person. It is thus *precisely that weakness* which allows entry of external and decidedly unhealthy, but always dark, influences. These then exercise a certain amount of 'control' over their 'host'. Certain drugs and even the overuse of alcohol can weaken the individual to the point where he no longer has the strength to resist the intrusion of one or more entities. Thus the 'weak host' permits himself to be "possessed" by a stronger entity with a correspondingly stronger 'force of will'. However, this 'weakness', as constantly reinforced, will always result from an individual giving rise to that personal state under his inherent 'free-will volition', somewhere, sometime. For a truly strong person in the spiritual sense **cannot** be affected by such influences.

In the case of current Maori statistics, Western psychiatric views have generally dismissed such ideas as nonsense and consigned them to the 'archaic' practices of our 'ignorant past'. Nevertheless, we should seriously consider whether it is these 'external influences', under the aegis of **The Law of Attraction of Similar Species**, and set notes rise Maori mental health statistics. Since **'P'** stands for **"possession"**, society should look at the whole **'P'** problem from a new and radical perspective.

To this end, the 'overall' practice of *tohungaism*, which taps into its associated aspiritual man-made psychic world to attempt to effect permanent healing of the Maori mentally ill, is doomed to failure if it accepts its authoritative source as deriving from earthly Maori Customary Law solely. Especially if it ignores the greater knowledge and concomitant healing contained within the understanding and application of the far higher Spiritual Law. Utilising 'cultural healing methods' may certainly offer short-term improvement in some patients, but our clear contention is that long-term healing cannot take place under *tohungaism* because it necessarily operates at the earthly and psychic levels *and does not even begin to understand* the genuine and higher spiritual-level connections from which The Spiritual Laws derive their inviolable ordination.

If we now examine page 15 of Te Puni Kokiri's 1993 commissioned report into Maori mental health, we note the reasons for Maori admissions under the heading:

Why Are Maori Being Admitted To Psychiatric Hospitals And Wards?

The first sentence notes that "Mental illness comes in many shapes and sizes", and psychiatrists have traditionally divided mental illness into "psychosis and non-psychosis i.e., neurosis, personality disorders and other disorders."

Let us quote the relevant descriptions of these "disorders" from the "Discussion Document", which are taken from the International Classification of Diseases, 9th revision (1975), and used by the Department of Health for its statistics.

1. **Psychoses:** disorders where the illness is so severe that the person is unable to "meet some ordinary demands of life" or to understand their illness or what is happening to their life. People typically have bizarre beliefs not held by others, hallucinations or hear voices. Most psychoses are thought to have a biological or organic basis – that is to say that some people are born with a tendency to become psychotically ill. It is not a well defined term, but generally it is used for the most serious and disabling mental illnesses. The most common psychoses are schizophrenia and affective disorders (an example which is manic depression).

2. **Neuroses:** include things like excessive anxiety, powerful fears and panic attacks, compulsive behaviours and depression.

3. **Personality disorders:** cover behaviours like excessive hostility, withdrawal, instability of mood, insecurity or indifference. Typically people with personality disorders have major difficulties in establishing relationships.

4. **Other disorders:** include sexual deviation, alcohol and drug abuse, stress and adjustment problems and intellectual disability. These illnesses are thought to arise from the experience of life and are not out of any biological weakness, and generally people are able to carry on with a normal life of some kind. They also usually have some understanding of their illness. The most commonly diagnosed illnesses in this group are drug and alcohol abuse and neurosis.

In terms of the above definitions, we should note that virtually *all* of the Maori Prophets would have been diagnosed as being psychotic; for they heard voices, supposedly hallucinated at times, and held bizarre views markedly different from others. Yet Te Whiti and Ratana, particularly, achieved beneficial success for Maori which a true psychotic obviously could not ever hope to. That is because the particular 'psychoses' of those two Prophets were led and guided by **Spiritual Power**; as opposed to 'ideas' influenced by dark psychic entities or other similar factors.

Historically, moreover, after hearing voices and seeing visions, many great men and women of the world's different peoples produced momentous events which beneficially influenced their societies. Yet they were clearly not psychotic. Of course some individuals were, but their vision produced destruction. History records many "voices in the wilderness" affected in this way who actually understood the world better than the 'establishment', which often *initially opposed* their so-called 'crazy ideas'.

Do most of us not know the story of the French heroine revered even today – Joan of Arc? And what about the many Saints, Monks, Sufis, inventors etc., who have heard voices and to whom visions have been shown? We should include here the ongoing analysis of the life and work of the 'Sleeping Prophet', Edgar Cayce. His very many 'medical readings' recorded whilst under trance now form a library that *medical professionals*, students and laymen alike, consult. And what about the many thousands who claim to have seen the 'Virgin Mary'? Are all those thousands in asylums? Of course not. Psychiatry can be *very selective* in whom *it* determines is 'touched' and who is not.

The 'possibility' of being influenced by psychic entities – in either full or partial possession – is unequivocally recognised in a Biblical quote that the psychiatric profession, especially, should be, or become, seriously cognisant of:

> **"Because our fight is not against blood and flesh; but against the sovereignties, against the powers, against the commanders of the darkness of this world..."**

(Ephesians 6:12, Fenton. Emphasis mine.)

Whilst this kind of quote may sound crassly religious, perhaps also evoking visions of fire and brimstone fanaticism; under the outworking of Spiritual Law it nevertheless accords perfectly with what we are saying, which it would do in any case.

Therefore, this *intellectually, scientifically and medically unacceptable concept* of "psychic possession", is a lawful factor for *all* races with regard to certain kinds of mental illness, when understood from the spiritual standpoint. Coupled with Ratana's clear condemnation of *tohungaism* which, in turn, promotes fear of psychic entities, it may provide the actual reason why Maori readmission rates are soaring. So, in terms of an emphasis on traditional or cultural healing, more of the same is clearly not the complete answer. As a first step toward a far wider understanding of a more correct approach to Maori mental health problems, a mandatory study of Ratana's philosophy would certainly be appropriate. All care-givers in this area, professional or otherwise, Pakeha and Maori, would greatly benefit from such an undertaking.

To this end, figure 4 of page 16 of our current analysis of Te Puni Kokiri's Discussion Document shows a graph comparing "first admission and readmission rates to psychiatric wards and hospitals for Maori and Pakeha 1981-1990". The key statement accompanying this particular graph reads:

The readmission rates for psychoses for Maori seem to be *increasing at a staggering rate*, while hardly changing at all for Pakeha.

We may recall that the word psychoses is used to define "the most serious and disabling mental disorders". The graph itself indicates a Maori readmission rate for psychotic behaviour of about 175 per 100,000 in 1981, rising to a rate of about 325 per 100,000 in 1990, in a steeply rising exponential growth curve. This effectively represents a 100% increase of serious mental illness in that time period.[14]

Since it is now available, let us note the main points from that particular publication as they apply to the mental health situation for Maori. And try to ascertain whether these concerns are as serious as trends indicate. Firstly, however, we need to note the respective populations of Maori and Pakeha to better understand percentages that will be quoted. On page nine we find:

> "The Maori population is made up of every person who said on census night that they were of Maori descent (443,844 in 1991).
> The Pakeha population is made up of every person who has not been defined as of Maori or Pacific Islands descent (2,786,161 in 1991)."

In a graph depicting "Total Maori Readmission Rates", Figure 2, page 10, we further note:

> "...Maori male readmission rates have increased 64% from 1984 to 1993 (from 36 per 100,000 to 591 per 100,000). Maori female readmission rates have increased by 28% (from 328 per 100,000 to 420 per 100,000)."

When comparing Maori readmission rates with Pakeha and Pacific Islands rates, we read here:

> "...Maori readmission rates have grown much faster than Pakeha or Pacific Islands readmission rates over the decade from 1984 to 1993. By 1993 Maori male readmissions were nearly two times higher than Pakeha male rates and were three times higher than Pacific Islands male rates.
> The trends in Maori mental health which were apparent in the data up to 1990 have continued and increases in Maori male readmissions *have been particularly dramatic*."

> (p.11, All italics mine.)

Under the sub-heading "Drug and Alcohol Disorders", the report states:

> "Drug and alcohol disorders include the very prevalent alcohol and drug abuse categories, the increasingly prevalent drug-induced psychotic illness, and the rare alcohol-induced psychosis.
> And whilst *abuse* leads to conditions like "...depression, withdrawal and aggression...", psychosis is "...the bizarre thinking and behaviour that can be an outcome of extreme abuse."

In terms of 'first admission' rates for this category of mental illness, the report shows "...a one third decrease in Maori male first admission rates from 1984 to 1993, but male rates were still 72% higher than female rates."

Notwithstanding that improvement, however, we unfortunately note on page 12:

> "There has been a 49% increase in Maori female first admission rates for drug and alcohol disorders over a 10 year period. This translates to a Maori female rate "...climbing rapidly..." to be twice that of Pakeha female rates by 1993."

---

[14]It is interesting to note that Te Puni Kokiri's 1996 commissioned study on Maori Mental Health was not immediately released on its completion, and Opposition MP Mike Moore was only able to secure a copy under the Freedom of Information Act at that time. This reluctance to release the document seemed to suggest a worsening situation.

In terms of 'readmission' rates for drug and alcohol disorders: "Maori rates in 1993 were 33% (male) and 67% (female) higher than Pakeha."

A more insidious and therefore disturbing trend is that of rapidly rising drug abuse and psychosis rates whilst alcohol-related disorders fall. Whilst those rates rose very rapidly for Maori men and women from 1984 – 1993: "...Pakeha and Pacific Islands rates grew less rapidly and were only a small fraction of Maori rates." (Both quotes; page 13)

The present debate about whether marijuana is harmful and whether it should be legalised or not bears directly on what I consider to be the key point in the whole of the latest document, and which we will quote in full from page 14. [Emphasis mine]:

> "Drug psychosis admissions have grown most rapidly and make up 21% of all Maori admissions for drug and alcohol disorders, compared with 5% for Pakeha. It is likely that most of the increases in drug admissions will relate to the use of cannabis. This can be adduced from information such as the very high levels of cannabis use by Maori communities in Northland; the use of cannabis on a weekly basis by around 40% of school children at two Auckland and Northland schools with a high Maori roll; and the very high proportion of patients in an acute ward in Hastings (*a region with a high Maori population*) who tested positive for cannabis."

The add-on effect of this youthful trend on page 14 is the worrying thought:

> "...that cannabis use can hide symptoms of a major psychotic illness such as schizophrenia, or conditions which if not treated will develop into schizophrenia."

The inference may be made here that cannabis use has not been 'absolutely' proven to cause the illnesses claimed. However, the same claims of denial were made for decades with regard to the effects of cigarette smoking. It is only very recently, unfortunately with very great damage deeply entrenched in successive generations now, that there is finally a belated admission that it was all wrong.

And so will it be for marijuana!

For, as we have already stated in this Chapter, whether it is cigarettes, trendy cigars, marijuana, or even horse or camel dung, it is not *the kind of substance being inhaled* that is the transgression.

The **crime** against the body and the *wairua* under Spiritual Law – the Highest law – **is that of poisoning the lungs in the first place**, and with substances that were *never the natural one* ordained by this Law! The natural inhalant should be pure air, or as pure as we are able to source it. But certainly not poison in high concentrations such as are found in cigarettes, marijuana and now **'P'** etc.. We can be sure that so-called 'harmless' recreational drugs will one day be found to have also been a foolish mistake.

Since psychotic illnesses are regarded as more serious and more likely to result in long-term disability than other illnesses, it surely behoves Maori leaders and parents, particularly, to do some very serious soul-searching about this growing problem of drugs. For it is clearly one with the potential to *mentally decimate* the race if not correctly addressed.

With regard to the 'know-it-all' attitude of the young in each generation, Herald columnist Kate Belgrave, in her article, "How do you tell kids not to smoke dope?", rightly questions whether today's young are even remotely concerned about the effect that 'dope smoking' may visit on them later in life. As she so succinctly puts it, "Health means nothing to kids. Many happily inflict damage." Ultimately, of course, this young generation will learn they were wrong too, with the subsequent lessons probably being very hard ones.

But to return to our document, first admission and readmission rates for "affective and other psychoses" show that:

> "...Maori female rates are generally higher than male rates, but because male rates are rising much faster, they [had] almost caught up by 1993. However, female rates have also risen quite rapidly since 1984: 49% for first admissions and 40% for readmissions."

In comparing Maori with Pakeha, whilst first admission rates have been initially higher for Pakeha, in readmission rates page 15 notes a widening difference year by year with the deficit being a Maori one.

> "...in 1993 Maori female readmission rates were 36% higher than Pakeha, and male rates 75% higher."

With schizophrenia being the most serious psychotic illness, the report shows that while only 17% of Maori first admissions are for this illness, nearly half of the *readmissions* (45%) are because of it. This high and rapidly rising readmission rate must surely be a concern. Graphs on pages 16 and 17 show:

> "...Maori male first and readmission rates are around 60% higher than female rates... with the gap widening all the time. However, female first admission rates are also rising, even if "erratically", but "...readmission rates are rising strongly (70%)." And whilst schizophrenia, affective disorders and other psychotic disorders made up 40% of Maori first admissions for 1993, the rate of readmissions for the same illnesses rose to 78% in that year."

An interesting comment, (Bridgman) offers the view that high Maori rates of psychotic illness may possibly indicate "...a culture under siege..." in contrast to the Pacific Islands cultures which are "relatively intact". Bridgman and Lealaiaulotu, moreover, argue that strong churches "...which prohibit the use of alcohol and drugs, [and] a powerful extended family network..." may be part of the reason providing protection against mental illness.

The Ministry of Health's "Guidelines for Cultural Assessment" propose the possibility that the impact of colonisation may have helped to bring about a "...diminishing identification with... cultural heritage." Such a view would probably presuppose "loss of land" as adding to the "angst of the people".

Whilst we acknowledge that the ethos of cultural heritage is necessary for all people, it is difficult to reconcile the above statements pertaining to the Maori situation with the inordinate amount of emphasis currently placed on Maori culture and its related aspects. Moreover, as the **'white thread of Ngapuhi prophecy'** in the pages of this book clearly indicate; under Spiritual Law it should not be the fact of colonisation that produces alienation here, but more the fact that Maori need to objectively understand *exactly* what has been gained *spiritually* from that which the original *tauiwi* brought with them.

This may be gleaned from the very arguments of Bridgman and Lealaiaulotu who have probably correctly identified the strong church ethos of the Pacific Islands cultures as being the major influence in maintaining low mental health statistics in those communities. Our view is that it should not come as a surprise to find this very thing. Despite the fact that we may strongly question various interpretations of the orthodox Church, the overall thrust of Christian Church life as taken from The Bible is far more beneficial than some societal practices and activities *not sourced* from that particular Work. Moreover, it offers all that we have continually stated throughout this work, namely the knowledge of Spiritual Law – **if interpreted correctly**. That knowledge, **alone**, should be *more than sufficient* to stem the rapidly rising tide of Maori mental health.

It is rising purely because Maori have turned their back on this ultimate Law under the foundational-guidance of Ratana and replaced it with their own 'Maori Customary Law'.

It is a fatally-flawed concept very wrongly revered as some kind of 'absolute Spiritual law' under latter-day 'tribal leaders' and *kaumatua*. Unfortunately, this far weaker 'form' does not understand or demand the necessary discipline and *maia* needed to turn all the problems and concomitant worsening statistics around!

As we have footnoted further back, since the *"Mangai"*, Ratana, did open the door into the new way and condemned *tohungaism* as a barrier to that entrance, it would be interesting to compare mental health percentages between those Maori who have embraced Ratana's teachings *completely*, with those who have chosen to go back to tribalism and related aspects of traditional culture which Ratana directed must be let go. Since the "proof of the pudding is *always* in the eating" – with tohungaism deemed necessary to Maori mental health healing regimes – I believe that a marked difference would be found in favour of *genuine* Ratana followers. And for the simple reason that the Mangai's teachings accord far more with Spiritual Law than does the present thrust of traditional-culture promotion and 'Maori Customary Law'. In any case this is surely the reality because, even today, *Ministers of the Ratana Church* are often called upon to assist fearful Maori who believe they are under psychic attack or affected by *makutu*.

Notwithstanding the steps outlined – which we believe to be the surest method in effecting genuine change if the will to do so is present – Te Puni Kokiri's booklet, page 27, nevertheless outlines *its* view of *why* statistics are so alarming for young Maori men. The young, of course, will always represent the future of any race.

"While the young of all groups are more at risk for mental illness, this is particularly true for Maori. High unemployment, low educational success, cultural alienation and, in general, the perceived lack of a positive future will play a major part in the causes of mental illness in Maori youth. In addition, the recklessness of the young males make them appear more dangerous and more likely to attract attention, admission (either into the justice or mental health systems) and a diagnosis of psychotic illness."

The development of a National Maori Mental Health Strategy on page 39 identifies:

"...mental health and drug and alcohol abuse as key issues for Maori youth." Targeted areas include identification of the "...risks associated with cannabis use...", and the high priority given to the issue of Maori suicide, "...particularly for young Maori males in the community and in prison."

Finally, in the segment, "Toward The Future", on page 42 the document notes that even though there are:

"...a number of positive advances being made... the future of mental health has challenges."

From the more certain perspective of Spiritual Law, which must be taken into account for there to be any improvement and less dependency on drugs, it is not enough to describe mental illness in purely scientific/medical terms. As previously stressed, for healing to be effective and lasting we must go 'behind the surface condition' to look at the state of the whole entity, especially the spiritual aspect. Simply applying a medical name and definition to a mental illness attached to a patient does not necessarily mean that it has any relationship to the living "psychic form" of it.

Moreover, this 'form' is attached to an individual because it belongs to him, and because no human spirit is imbued *with mental afflictions* **at its point of spiritual origin**. It is only his later free-will decisions and actions that will have brought him to his present 'mental space'. So, unless the healing process engages with that 'reality', any improvement, if any, may only be temporary. Some individuals, of course, are so immersed in their own particular 'mental space' that it will be very difficult for them to leave it in their present lifetime. Those who are no longer in control of their own free will may not be able to be helped via this process anyway and may well be best treated with medication as the most compassionate way of helping them in the short term.

> Finally, however, healing in mental health, particularly, will only be *lastingly-effective* **when we unequivocally accept the reality and truth of: "The Law of Rebirth"**.

We need to therefore *really understand* that the *accumulative effects* stemming from our personal free-will decision-making process over *many incarnations* must return to us the reciprocal outcomes under the immutable outworking of this **'Iron Law'**. It is an *inviolable process* that is actually breaking through more strongly into the present time for final resolution in both its individual and collective outworking. This kind of truly holistic approach to health will only happen, however, when the scientific and medical communities have awakened to the truth of it and are prepared to apply those principles to their respective disciplines. And not simply use the term "holistic" to *indicate* either knowledge of "holism", or partial acceptance of it when there is *neither* complete knowledge *nor* understanding of the term.

*   *   *   *   *

A quantum leap in the treatment of mental illnesses occurred from the period of the wretched insane asylums of the Victorian era and their long line of predecessors, to Jungian psychology of the Twentieth Century. A similar kind of rapid progression is also possible today, but it requires the perhaps more difficult recognitions and acceptance of the outworking of Spiritual Law and its effect in this same field. If we are ever to offer complete help and progress toward a better and healthier future, then that is *the single most important development needed to achieve that desirable goal.*

*   *   *   *   *

Thus, if correct spiritual principles were taught from the *very beginning* of the educative process, there would be far less stress and unhappiness because, from an early age, children would learn about the emotions and how to express them beneficially. There would then be far less mental illness as a result. Therefore knowledge of **The Spiritual Laws** is *the most important thing* that can be taught in schools today; for the betterment of society tomorrow!

Racial and cultural considerations would then assume far less importance, since spiritual knowledge is universal and transcends all earthly considerations. Thus the time and energy that is currently spent on 'cultural safety' in health sciences would be better employed teaching *spiritual principles of health* which apply equally to *all races and cultures.*

Since transgressions *against* Spiritual Law are the cause of **all** of humankind's ills, this knowledge, therefore, ***should be the primary subject to teach***.

21.2   Cultural Safety

This curiously-strange phrase used to describe a cultural idea that has nothing whatsoever to do with 'safety' can be better understood if we recognise that the actual phrase should probably be 'cultural sensitivity'. However, the idea of 'sensitivity' applied by Maori to the issue of health does not easily fit with any concept of traditional thinking that *ostensibly* reflects great strength and purpose of Maori culture. Nevertheless, notwithstanding such a 'sensitive' issue, the utilisation of the phrase, 'cultural safety', is eminently more politically and culturally suitable than 'cultural sensitivity' for the proponents of this particular Maori push.

Let us now closely examine this vexing and divisive question of 'cultural safety' with regard to health issues. We say vexing and divisive because past media attention to it with regard to its large component aspect in nursing courses obviously indicates that there is a very real problem with it from time to time. By virtue of the connotations attached to all matters cultural in this land, it would be foolish to believe that all is well in 'hospital land'. Widely differing yet equally legitimate counter-views cannot simply disappear overnight because some over-zealous Maori academic in a position of power and influence declares that a concept of 'Cultural Safety' is a must for everyone.

In terms of simple, logical reasoning, one's sympathies would tend to lie with the Medical Professionals who, in the end, have the unenviable task of trying to stem the steeply rising tide of ill-health, especially among the very people who strongly embrace and actively promote this archaic concept. Moreover, the indisputable fact will forever be that, irrespective of what one's religion, colour, race, creed, or belief might be, all human beings are obviously constructed *the same way*. We all possess *identical organs* which are positioned in *the same places* on and in the body, and which perform *the same functions*.

Moreover, this 'unchanging body' that we all possess is exactly the same as that which the doctors and nurses 'work out of' when they perform their many miracles of healing. That is the obvious reality! For they, too, naturally possess the same basic form. Therefore, whilst there should be natural respect for the privacy of every individual patient, there should also be the reciprocal, or perhaps even greater, respect *from* the patient *for* the medical staff who must carry out the various tests and examinations necessary to facilitate that particular patient's recovery.

To be overly sensitive about one's body when one is ill has nothing whatever to do with this *absurdly-coined phrase* of 'cultural safety'. The Maori feeling of being *whakama* about showing oneself to strangers is perfectly correct and understandable where and when there is no need to do so. However, if a medical examination is required, or admittance to a hospital is necessary, then every patient, regardless of race or culture, has a clear responsibility to assist the medical staff – for their own good, obviously. Hindering the response time of the medical staff by procrastinating about 'showing the body', or of perhaps demanding particular recognition that one is Maori and therefore must be shown special consideration, may not greatly help one's cause. For not only may it damage their own treatment prospects by placing uncertainty within the minds of the care-givers as to how they should proceed without perhaps causing cultural offence, but also shows *a measure of selfish disregard* for their vital time and unselfish work.

Quite clearly, cultures did not produce our physical bodies. The outworking of the final ramifications of **The Eternal Laws of Creation**, however, most certainly did. So treatment for one's medical condition, whatever that might entail, has to be of far greater importance than considerations of 'cultural safety' first. In any case, the current societal attitude of 'anything-goes liberalism' regarding personal and even *public* activities involving the human body – *among Maori women as well* – makes a mockery of any kind of grand-standing over 'cultural safety' regarding the Maori body.

As a blunt example: If a patient, let's say a Maori woman in this instance, should seek relief for painful haemorrhoids – a common ailment invariably requiring an examination of the anal area to begin with – healing for the patient may be compromised if such an assessment is not undertaken. It is therefore foolish to stand on ceremony over one's cultural traditions. Particularly in a situation which may necessarily require a close examination of the affected part of the body in perhaps a 'bent-over' position, and then a sharp scalpel to effect permanent relief. Whether stemming from considerations of race, culture or tradition, reluctance to show the affected part of the body when seeking remedial help can hardly be described as being very helpful to the care-givers, even if the patient is of the feminine gender in this particular scenario.

The promotion of regular health checks concentrating on cervical smear tests and breast examinations now directed to '*whakama* women' of non-white origin is clearly a refreshing change. Long-overdue, such programmes are 'life-extenders', in some cases 'life-savers', for those women who participate.

Notwithstanding the inherently *correct* attribute of *whakama* being associated with the virtue of spiritual purity, those Maori who choose to push the issue of 'cultural sensitivity' to ludicrous lengths in the pursuit of some misty-eyed belief in the purity of the 'untouchable Maori body' should objectively analyse such attitudes very carefully.

Pakeha doctors should not be expected to acquiesce to any unreasonable demands at Maori behest. If Maori want the obvious benefits of Pakeha medicine and medical technology, *then they should 'wholly' accept the medical way of the Pakeha in certain medical applications without reservation and subjugate their so-called 'cultural sensitivity' to it.*

If this is unacceptable, then the answer is simple. Revert completely to *tohungaism* where there was no need for any examination, very little proper care, just as little real medicine, and very much superstition. Moreover, without the clear benefits of recovery or relief available today, the inevitable result of that lack of knowledge – or 'lack of compassion' – was often early death; and would be so today. Since Maori cultural renaissance seems hell-bent on reversion to some 'over-pretentious' aspects of the 'old way', perhaps the Pakeha medical profession should simply let it be, at least for the *proponents* of this misguided Maori push. Imagine the hue and cry then – *from the selfsame*!

Whilst there is a marked and welcome worldwide trend to consider alternative treatments, including the re-emergence of resurrected indigenous medicines, the unpalatable fact remains that the medical profession are generally expected to 'make well' an *increasingly sicker* society. As we opined earlier, the key to a healthy society is to practise affirmative disease-prevention by utilising a healthy diet from the earliest possible time and passing that on in the educative example to the offspring. As also stated, however, that requires discipline. The depressing and expensive alternative is exactly that which we have at the moment:

An *over-loaded* hospital system, with *too-long* waiting lists of *far too many* **unnecessarily** *sick people.*

On that perhaps dour note, it is nonetheless exactly the right point in our journey to also assess the increasing use of the *hongi* as a greeting for all and sundry on all manner of occasions. Especially as some present-day cultural interpretations about how and why one should *hongi* seems markedly at variance with the meaning and purpose of it from older traditions.

21.3 The Hongi

The Dictionary of the Maori Language by Henry Williams, Seventh Edition, states the meaning of the *hongi* thus:

> **Hongi.**
> 1. v.t. *Smell*
> 2. *Sniff*
> 3. *Salute* by pressing noses together; incorrectly called *rub noses*.

If we accept the place of the *hongi* as a salute and that it is effected by pressing noses together, one can readily understand its importance for ancient Maori. More or less constant warfare surely gave rise to situations where, when warring parties ceased fighting, the protocol of a new peace decreed that some form of acknowledgement be agreed upon whereby hostilities could be replaced with mutual respect and trust. Such trust would be especially important for the weaker, thus more vulnerable, side. History records that treachery was not uncommon in that kind of situation.

If, now, we examine the apparent meaning of the *hongi* today, as promoted by a seemingly growing school of Maori thought, we thus note that its 'apparent' purpose is to enable the participants to *exchange breaths*. Does this also mean an exchange and/or intermingling of the believed life-energy or *mauri* during the *hongi*? And what might that imply if one is expected to *hongi* long lines of virtual strangers on many occasions?

*   *   *   *   *

If one very objectively scrutinises this interesting new thought of 'exchanging breaths' via the *hongi*; in purely spiritual terms one does *not need* – in any shape or form for any reason whatever – the *mauri* or life-force *of another* for anything. Not even in supposedly politically-, culturally- or socially- 'correct' situations. Each of us as a human being is inherently endowed with our own *personal mauri*, along with all else required for an individual path through life. For, in truth, it is simply *not possible* for any human being to *carry* the *mauri* of another.

*   *   *   *   *

Therefore, if the *hongi* has evolved, or devolved, to now become more an *emotive display* of cultural togetherness, rather than for the purpose for which it was perhaps originally employed, then it is certainly possible that potentially serious health risks might one day accrue from the presently-promoted belief that the primary purpose of the hongi *is* to 'exchange breaths'. In the closed society of pre-European Maori traditions, if 'exchanges of breaths' did occur, that practice would not have carried any great threat with regard to *respiratory illnesses*. In any case, given the cultural/religious views prevailing at that time, such practices would lean more toward a superstitious view of the world than a medically rational one.

However, the arrival of the Europeans with diseases previously unknown to Maori clearly placed a far different emphasis on this practice. Europeans also introduced tobacco to Maori lungs – a scourge we have already noted. To this end, general Maori health statistics show a disproportionately high level of respiratory illness. Is it not conceivable, therefore, that the increasing practice of the *hongi* nationally, may actually and unwittingly be providing many more incubators of various respiratory illnesses than there need be? More especially if such illnesses are transmitted by unknowing carriers of them, and particularly if the *hongi* is engaged in for a duration sufficiently long to 'exchange breaths'. And, moreover, with numerous strangers on many occasions. So even the *cultural protocol* of the *hongi* possesses the potential for airborne diseases to be transmitted more easily via this latter-day 'exchange of breaths' scenario.

A sobering case-in-point is the re-emergence of Tuberculosis worldwide. It is once more causing deaths, even in first world cities such as New York. This has prompted medical authorities to warn against being complacent with regard to this insidious and dangerous airborne disease. Even investigations into the filtration systems of commercial passenger aircraft, which have closed recycling systems, have concluded that it is possible for passengers on long flights to be infected by a fellow passenger carrying the disease if the air filtration systems are deficient. TB is more insidious today because mutant and resistant strains have now developed. TB can affect young and old and is highly infectious, with the human strain spread through **inhaling infected droplets**. This usually causes pulmonary tuberculosis – the most common – which affects the lungs. The lungs, therefore, are the perfect infectious medium to exhale, *and thus also inhale*, more infected droplets.

If we return to the *Guardian Weekly's* report about the misuse of antibiotics that we referred to in the sub-Chapter on General Health, we note that:

> "The World Health Organisation is warning of the dangers of a global plague of tuberculosis. Drug-resistant strains are likely to be carried around the globe by airline passengers, *who will infect others through coughs and sneezes*."

South African researchers writing in the *New England Journal of Medicine* have discovered that recovering from one bout of TB is no protection from contracting another strain of the lung ailment. Researchers at the University of Stellenboch found that tests on 16 people who suffered a second bout of TB involved bacteria *with different DNA*. In other words, after recovering from one TB infection, they acquired *a new one*. The research team says its findings therefore raise questions about the results of past studies designed to assess the effectiveness of anti-tuberculosis drugs. So unless DNA testing is done on the TB bacteria, researchers cannot determine whether a treatment has failed or whether the patient has simply acquired a new infection – *infections spread by inhaling 'infected droplets'*.

The potential for the emergence of respiratory diseases through the practice of the *hongi* may well be regarded as ridiculous by many, and perhaps even as an attack on Maori 'spiritual' values. Nevertheless, the fact remains that we are becoming an increasingly sick race, and there is no filtration system between people engaged in the *hongi*. We may note, also, that the Japanese, one of the healthiest and long-lived peoples of the earth, use face-masks to shield **others**, from **their** respiratory ailments, even just the common cold. The Japanese certainly could not be regarded as having no pride in their culture.

The horrendous death toll of the 1918 flu pandemic, where up to 50 million people died globally, clearly illustrates how an airborne disease can spread so devastatingly.[15] Compared to air-travel time of just hours between countries today, some of the same

---

[15] As a comparison it is estimated that around 40 million civilians alone were killed worldwide during the six years of The Second World War.

journeys then took many weeks by ship. Yet the disease peaked around the globe at almost the same time. In New Zealand, where some 6,000 Europeans and more than 2,000 Maori died, we should note that Maori, then, numbered approximately 54,000 only. Thus Maori suffered the worst, dying at seven times the rate of Europeans. Aside from considerations of, perhaps, less immunity to the disease than Europeans, we might also wonder whether the *cultural propensity* for the *hongi*, particularly, during what would have been a time of *numerous tangi*, might not have inadvertently helped a *more* rapid spread of the disease.

More recently, of course, the death in Hong Kong in 1987 of a toddler infected by the first known case of a pure 'bird flu' virus jumping to a human, led to the slaughter of all of the Colony's 1.3 million chickens. Worried scientists and virologists who know that flu pandemics are cyclical, warned then that another pandemic was inevitable. American flu specialist Robert Webster believes that by ordering the mass slaughter of chickens that year, the Hong Kong authorities '...probably saved the world'.

It seems quite clear that the vital consideration of *respect for other cultural beliefs* and whether or not the *hongi* and an 'exchange of breaths' is acceptable to those cultures, is not given any thought at all by Maoridom generally. Everyone is expected to simply *acquiesce without question* to the demands of Maori protocol. All must bow to it. Notable dignitaries and even world leaders who attend international meetings such as APEC are not exempt from this 'cultural expectation'. Of course, if visitors are happy to engage in the *hongi* that is well and good. If, however, they are uncomfortable with it, then they should *not be coerced in any way* to accept it as a demand of Maori, or even as a *State-sanctioned protocol* at such events. The mark of *true spiritual maturity* is respect for other people's cultural beliefs too, and not to demand or believe that a 'do in Rome' policy will automatically be acceptable to all others.

Interestingly, the quite recent global scare that the SARS virus generated saw one Marae official at the time *publicly state on National TV* that the Hongi *'might need to be discontinued with'*. The projected emergence of perhaps the worst yet to come – bird flu – clearly presupposes a need to think radically-differently about practices once deemed OK! Now that we do have the greater threat of the latest strain of bird flu perhaps one day jumping to humans, we can be sure that even the most *vocal* of 'Maori culturalists' will be very reluctant to *hongi* all and sundry then.

The clear conclusion here is that *all* aspects of cultural traditions should be viewed *objectively and dispassionately*, not emotionally. Any emotional attachment to particular cultural traditions, especially to those practices with the *potential* to cause illness and suffering, should be carefully thought about as to whether or not they are ultimately worth retaining.

At the close of 2007, fear of the rapid spread of a disease so virulent that it has no vaccine and no cure moved the President of that country to ask people *to stop shaking hands*. Uganda, gripped by terror over a *new strain* of Ebola haemorrhagic fever, one of the world's deadliest diseases which kills between 50 percent and 90 percent of its victims, had MPs calling for an end to public gatherings. Market vendors now wear gloves, and Roman Catholic priests no longer give the communion wafers and wine by hand. Spread by *touch alone*, just one infected person boarding a commercial aircraft could cause a global outbreak.

What price 'cultural safety'? In New Zealand's case – and in concert with the increasing spiritual pressure driving literally everything to either breaking point or timely recognition globally – perhaps the price of one *Hongi*:

One 'exchange of breath' too many!

21.4   The Haka: 'Kamate'

The almost iconic expression of New Zealand culture now, the *haka* latterly seems to symbolise a relatively new country's 'cultural signature' to the rest of the world. Promoted as a symbol of pride, of 'presence', of feeling good about ourselves at sports events or at major and important celebratory milestones, the *haka* is performed everywhere, seemingly by everyone – even the very youngest in schools. The *haka* of choice for most is, naturally enough, 'Kamate'; commonly known as the 'All Blacks *haka*'.[16]

Historical tradition deems the *haka*, 'Kamate', to be one composed by the great War Chief, Te Rauparaha, after a narrow escape from his enemies. Forced to hide in a food-storage pit, he climbed out to find, standing over him, not an enemy but another chief who was a friend. Apparently greatly relieved, Te Rauparaha performed that *haka*. According to one interpretation by journalist and sports identity, Louisa Wall; the meaning is thus:

> It is death, it is death. It is life, it is life.
> This is the man who enabled me to live
> as I climb up step by step toward sunlight.

(We will call that: **Translation 1.**)

While most people are apparently quite happy with this *haka*, there are now well-known dissenting voices breaking through the walls of this seemingly sacrosanct fortress, both from within and without Maoridom. So why the emerging disquiet over a practice that apparently offers a way to promote racial and cultural 'togetherness' as just one of its 'feel-good' factors in such an 'ostensibly-noble' storyline? And why, at the Gallipoli celebrations of 2005, Turkish authorities stated that they were unhappy with the sexual connotations that this particular *haka* implied – especially for a Muslim Nation? The general New Zealander's view: A 'storm in a teacup'.

To answer this question of disquiet surrounding the All Blacks *haka*, we need to take a second look at the words of it. We also need to understand the actions of the hands and arms that exactly correspond with the words chanted at a particular point in it. The All Blacks website provides the 'official version'.

The first part is innocuous enough, for it simply *prepares* the party for the real 'message' which is to be delivered to the opposing group.

> Ringa pakia
> Uma tiraha
> Turi whatia
> Hope whai ake
> Waewae takahia kia kino

English Translation:

---

[16]Not to be confused with their new and very different 2005 'haka storyline'. 'Kapa o Pango' (Team in Black) is ostensibly promoted as a haka that embraces and thus brings together the various cultures now present in this land.

> Slap the hands against the thighs
> Puff out the chest
> Bend the knees
> Let the hip follow
> Stamp the feet as hard as you can

The next and thus main action is the direct challenge.

> Ka Mate! Ka Mate!
> Ka Ora! Ka Ora!
> Tenei te tangata puhuruhuru
> Nana nei I tiki mai
> Whakawhiti te ra
> A upane Kaupane!
> A upane kaupane whiti te ra!
> Hi!

English translation:

> It is death! It is death!
> It is life! It is life!
> This is the hairy person
> Who caused the sun to shine
> Keep abreast! Keep abreast!
> The rank! Hold fast!
> Into the sun that shines!

(This one we will deem: **Translation 2.**)

In my opinion both translations are 'soft', and very different in connotation. So someone has got the *actual* translation – and thus meaning – very wrong somewhere.

*   *   *   *   *

Note:

This particular *haka* was adopted as the more or less 'official one' for the New Zealand Infantry Battalion during its very long tenure in South East Asia from the late 1950's through to the 1990's. During my 'service time' with the Unit, from the mid 60's to the early 70's, 'Kamate' was at one point practised and performed by the whole Battalion – 800 soldiers – at the behest of the C.O. [Commanding Officer.]

It would have been quite a sight for any onlooker: ***A war haka performed by the full complement of a New Zealand Infantry Battalion at peak fitness and skill-level for its purpose – Jungle Warfare Operations in Malaya, Borneo and Vietnam.***

Since that particular *haka* obviously represents a serious challenge, it was naturally embraced as a *'war haka'*.

It thus finds its <u>correct place</u> in a Military setting: More particularly the Army by virtue of its natural association with land-based 'Operations'.

*   *   *   *   *

The question now is: "In spiritually ennobled terms, can this same *haka* fit in society *outside a Military setting* ; for example at a sports fixture – *spiritually-correctly?*"

Yes, sports can be gladiatorial in nature, but that is not war, it is sport. What about even the smallest children parroting these words without *really understanding* the huge moral and spiritual ramifications of them; with the *approval* of parents and school authorities who are invariably proud of their 'performance'? So what's the fuss? It doesn't do any harm. It's just nitpicking, just some kind of religious prudery – isn't it?

Well, let us examine the two key words of this *haka*, apply **Spiritual Law** to it and see what it **really** means then! The first key aspect is the title: Kamate.

What, then, does 'Kamate' actually mean? Since this *haka* springs from the era of Te Rauparaha, we will take the translation of the title from the Maori Language Dictionary *begun* by a man *who was around at the time*, and who thus knew the reo *as it was spoken then*. The man: Henry Williams – *that key Pakeha who began the compilation of the Reo, and so probably did more to save the Maori language than anyone else before or since.* There are two parts to Kamate:

Ka (i), verbal particle, used–**1.** To denote the commencement of a new action or condition,...

Mate. 1. a. *Dead.* [The first meaning of the word in the 'H.W. Williams Dictionary'.]

The other primary word of interest in this *haka* is [*puhuruhuru*].
From the same source we note the following most interesting entry:

Puhuruhuru, a. *Hairy, covered with hair.* Tenei te tangata puhuruhuru. (M.279.)

Why, then, in Louisa Wall's **Translation 1**, is there 'a deathly silence' around – thus no mention of – the English meaning of the key word; **puhuruhuru**?
Concomitantly, why the opposition to this *haka* from the Turkish authorities?

Turkish opposition surely lay in the obvious meaning of the actions of the forearms to the words: *"This is the hairy person"* – *["Tenei te tangata puhuruhuru".]*

Clearly the words do not refer to hair on the head or chest. Te Rauparaha was a noted war chief, so the very words and actions are exactly those designed to challenge an actual enemy and to psyche the performers into the necessary state of mind to destroy that enemy in battle. During the practice sessions of the Battalion for the 800-man *haka*, the meaning was spelt out very bluntly by the Maori Officers who led the 'performance', **which we 'Operational Soldiers' all well understood in any case**.

The *haka*, 'Kamate', is thus more about that part of the male anatomy created for procreation as a major purpose – *the hairy person* [**te tangata puhuruhuru**] – that can produce *life* when used correctly, or *death* when used wrongly. Moreover, warring groups of various cultures throughout history have traditionally exposed *the male aspect* before battle; thereby *symbolising* the masculine power of *potency, virility and thus superiority* of one male group over another. Mel Gibson's blockbuster movie, Braveheart, showed this practice on screen in clear detail when the front ranks of his Scottish Army lifted their kilts to expose their genitals to the English King, "Longshanks". Even our own history records that warring *taua* often stripped down for war.

21.4.1 Women and the Haka: 'Kamate' – in a Military Setting

Now, accepting the fact that we must acknowledge the *haka*, 'Kamate', as being the natural and therefore *exclusive* preserve of [obviously *male*] soldiers, where does that place *women* in the Armed Forces who might also be called on to perform this particular *haka*?

How strange and farcical a situation is that?

In this case, the ramifications are surely clear enough. It is not a *haka* that women should perform anywhere at any time, and certainly not as members of the Armed Services.

In the Western world, the latter-decades have seen women enter Military Forces in increasingly greater numbers. Whilst women have always served thus, it was usually more in Units not designated as **"Teeth Arms"** – i.e., Combat Units such as Infantry, Engineers, Artillery, Armoured/Cavalry and Special Forces etc.. Also included here are Naval Fighting and Supply Ships, and Air Force Strike and Transport/Supply Aircraft – including 'Choppers'. Now women can be found in many previously sacrosanct male occupations within all branches of the Armed Forces.

Since the purpose of this Work is to explain Spiritual Law ***without fear or favour***, we will *very briefly* introduce the *meaning* of **'Womanhood in Creation'**.

Here on the material earth, we see and perhaps understand the form of woman as she exists in her *physical* body. With it, as with all female creatures and forms, she possesses the singular gender-ability to bring forth offspring. However, that is only *one* aspect of the total entity; woman. Though an important and necessary one for procreation, it is nonetheless *not* primarily her *principal* task.

Now, whilst the *form* of the *earthly soldier* exists in all higher non-material Realms in the *corresponding form* of **The Knight**, **'Womanhood'** therein occupy no such position. For that is *not* woman's *spiritually-ordained* status and role. Yet against that spiritual ordination for Womanhood of *all* spheres; through her inherent attribute of 'free-will' *woman of earth* can and does *choose* male occupations. So wanting to fulfil the role of man is a *spiritual aberration only possible with 'human woman' of earth*. [Also the case with 'opposite-gender choices'.]

The *fundamental differences that were ordained for men and women from the beginning* have their genesis in the complete *Creative reason and process*. And therefore cannot be circumvented without serious end-consequences for all those who believe that simple personal choice is or should be the prime criteria for all life and activity on earth.

As previously explained in earlier Chapters, the first responsibility of all human beings is to *recognise* the actual meaning and purpose for which we come to this material world. And that is to one day return to our true home in The Spiritual Realm; thus to the Origin of our *non-material* body.

> "In the home [Creation] of my Father there are many abodes [Realms]. If it were not so, I would have told you: because I am going to prepare a place for you."

> (John 14:2 [Parentheses mine.])

Thus explained Jesus, **The Son of God**, to His Disciples so we might clearly understand that the earth is only *a material transitional plane of learning*, and thus concomitant 'experiencing' of that learning. And that 'those abodes' are the various 'levels of Creation'; in the Higher Realms of which there reside 'men and women' who are more than just 'human spirits'. Thus the 'prepared place' for us is therefore *not on this earth.*

Whilst we have already journeyed from our 'Origins' to 'incarnation on earth' in earlier Chapters, and also learned how we return; we will yet still ask the necessary question for our key analysis in this segment specifically directed to women who *choose* Military **"Teeth Arms"** occupations.

"How, then, do we get back home?"

The answer, whilst brutally simple, is nonetheless difficult for we human beings. Of course it should not be, but because of our strong global/human propensities for activities which resist and oppose the ordained spiritual path for our 'return', the way is thus made very much more difficult by our foolish and stubborn intransigence. Nonetheless, if we wish to return home, we must live **The Law** absolutely. (From Matthew 5:26, Fenton.)

> "I tell you indeed, that you will not depart until you have repaid the very last farthing."

So, with regard to the above requirement and to societies which legislate for women to participate in **"Teeth Arms"** activities, especially where there is no *dire threat* to that society; such societies – along with the women *who choose that kind of* **intensive Military Service** – together do not fulfil that ordination. Only in situations where a Nation is at serious threat of invasion and/or enslavement, such as was seen during the German invasion of the Soviet Union where *every* citizen had to fight; will be found *the spiritual necessity for women to take up arms.*

Once Yugoslavia's Partisan leader in World War II and political strongman after, General Tito imposed the severest penalties on any instances of intimate fraternisation between the male and female troops of his 'force', especially during 'Wartime Operations'. At a time of desperate survival against German occupying Armies when *everyone* was needed to *really fight*, including the women, he ensured that no rivalries, jealousies or similar could arise and become problematic in his volatile and passionate Partisan group. Summary executions of 'transgressing couples' by firing squad did occur.

Much is made of the Israeli Defence Forces policy of C.M.T. for all young Jewish women. They, however, are not recruited en masse into front-line combat roles. Jewish religious law holds strong sway in that regard. Just a few years ago, the Italian Government passed legislation for young woman of that country to join the Armed Forces, and many thousands did – primarily into the Army. Within a few months, however, many thousands had left.

The shocking case of 19 year old US Army private **La Vena Johnson** – evidently along with many other women who, although serving in Iraq, nonetheless died there from rape and murder at the hands of their so-called fellow-soldiers – unequivocally reveals the inherent clash of gender roles in an occupation once *rightfully-accepted* as a necessarily *male* occupation solely. Subsequently covered up by 'Top Brass', the increasing numbers of such cases in Iraq, particularly, simply reveals what this Work *repetitively but necessarily reinforces*:

> *That rapidly increasing Spiritual pressure on all affairs and notions human will force all wrong and/or aberrant views to failure and collapse.*

I therefore enjoin you, the *female reader*, to *not misconstrue* what is stated here.

Notwithstanding the obvious fact that rape and murder could *never ever* be justified in any circumstances, especially by soldiers who should operate to a higher code, certain aspects of particular 'theatres of operations' *can produce* a more brutalising effect on soldiers than would be the case in perhaps a more *benign* 'war situation'. The religious parameters of the Iraq war, coupled with the fact that in no shape or form can that conflict ever be termed a noble cause, means that – along with *great fear* – an especially-vicious religious element is constantly present.

If we then tie those highly-charged aspects to predominantly young men without recourse to particular and inherently-strong 'humanly-natural' needs for long periods of time and who see comrades killed and wounded perhaps regularly, then the stage is obviously set for explosive and potentially *very unfortunate outcomes* for female soldiers who may be part of that Unit. Of course, such things should never happen in a Military setting. But they do, and will, if and when women are constantly present. So, if we were to state the truthful obvious, which will nonetheless surely produce cries of outrage, we would yet still say:

> "As women, do not seek to fulfil that which is *not* yours under inviolable **Spiritual Law**! Do not seek *your place* in a Military setting alongside *men* whose *rightful place is* in **'Teeth Arms'** occupations."

Furthermore, do not use the tired, *aspiritual* and hackneyed cry: **'It is our right!'**

Rights are solely about fulfilling *spiritual responsibility* under the *immutable outworking* of **Spiritual Law**, upon which human female opinion *has no bearing whatsoever*.

So whilst *certain* occupations in Military Forces can clearly provide fulfilling roles for young women, it is not in **"Teeth Arms"**![17]

Irrespective of earthly societal acceptance of women serving thus in the present, concomitant with sure condemnation of views contrary to that societal acceptance – such as we have aired here; the inviolable and immutable nature of the very **'Spiritual Laws of Life'** take no account *whatsoever* of human societal law or opinion. Governments, therefore, have the ultimate responsibility in ensuring that legislation, in the very first instance, *"spiritually-protects"* the citizens within the society the politicians have sworn to govern righteously. If that should mean enacting legislation which does not meet the expectations of perhaps a minority, then so be it.

Notwithstanding the 'slings and arrows' that will surely be directed against such views from many quarters, I herewith restate a **'Spiritual Fact'**: This Work is so written to bring to the attention of this Nation and its peoples *clarifying explanations* on all ideas and activities that impact *spiritually-detrimentally* upon this land and all in it.

To that end, and directed primarily *to the women of this land **in this case***: From the 'Granted Mandate' once more is *proclaimed* the following:

If *I* do not tell *you* this, who is going to?

*   *   *   *   *

---

[17]Notwithstanding my absolute and thus *'living conviction'* of **The Truth and Sanctity of Spiritual Law** – even on this subject: In terms of a purely *personal* view on the place of women in a 'Teeth Arms' role; as an ex-Infantry Battalion 'Veteran' of Malaya, Borneo and Vietnam [3 Tours of Duty], I can unequivocally state that virtually all 'Vets' I know would have no hesitation in saying that women would have been *completely out of place* – and thus both a *hindrance and encumbrance* – in *our* kind of 'Operations'.

Now, apart from performances by The All Blacks, where else in the world might we see this iconic *haka* of Aotearoa?

In 2005, the American football team at Utah's Brigham Young University adopted the *haka*, 'Kamate'. A major Church of the world, The Church of Jesus Christ of Latter Day Saints – the Mormons – one that vigorously promotes family values and all things uplifting and moral, has endorsed this 'visual and vocal form' of Maori 'culture' for its showcase sports team too. Perhaps some team-members are also part of the world-famous Mormon Tabernacle Choir, a choir that has earned global kudos for its harmonious rendition of Hymns and sacred songs. Of course, many New Zealanders are very proud of this 'expansion into the wider world' of 'our culture'.[18]

'Kamate' now also proudly 'resides' in a little corner of Europe. Through the brave actions of New Zealand soldiers during the First World War, the town of Le Quesnoy in France is apparently the only place where ANZAC Day is commemorated. Le Quesnoy also enjoys a close association with New Zealand 'Sister City', Cambridge. So with that connection, together with the stronger one celebrating the commemorative legacy of ANZAC Day, the *haka*, 'Kamate', is taught to young school children in Le Quesnoy, too.

*   *   *   *   *

So, mothers of New Zealand children, especially Christian or religious mothers, do you still think it 'alright' for your young offspring to mouth the words of 'Kamate' seemingly for every occasion, and thus with nauseous regularity? If you still believe so, then you deny yourselves the very essence of Divine Grace inherent in that great Law given to humankind for its *spiritual protection*. From Matthew, 17:20:

> "It is not what goes into the mouth that defiles a man, but what comes out. For these produce inequities and blasphemies and all manner of foul things."

Of course good things can also come from the mouth. Consider now, however, the 'forms' that thereby issue from the collective mouths of perhaps thousands every day somewhere in this country with the chanting of this '*haka*'. In blunt terms it is one more *serious* spiritual transgression against The Living Laws of Life. And under the aegis of **The Law of Reciprocal Action** – [what we sow we reap] – there can be no good outcome, ultimately.

No doubt the usual cries of 'cultural insensitivity' etc., will be levelled at this 'affront to Maori dignity', along with much else in this Work. Its purpose, however, is to ***forcefully*** **bring to the attention of Maoridom and New Zealand as a whole**, the seriousness of all aberrant ideas that *supposedly* – but do not – accord with **Spiritual Law**, thus *true life*. The political and cultural sanitising of anything is *forever wrong* under **The Law**!

Thus we state what must be stated!

Language should always be so used that it ***actually ennobles***. That is the true spiritual way. Thus the way of the noble and *spiritual warrior*!

Therefore: The haka, 'Kamate', does not fulfil that directive for this land and its peoples.

---

[18]We remind you, the reader, that the knowledge of **The Spiritual Laws** and how they impact upon us is detailed in the relevant **Chapters**, particularly that about **Language**. You may wish to reacquaint yourself with that knowledge and detail to thus more readily understand the *very serious spiritual ramifications* of this particular Sub-Chapter.

21.5 'Education?': − Problematic!

The word, 'education', should conjure up images of animated students engrossed in learning; in absorbing the fascinating history of man and his works and marvelling at what our 'blue planet' has to offer and teach us. The broad sweep of history and the incredible diversity of the life forms around us − and certainly not least the stupendous and awesome scale of the known universe − should hold students of all ages in enraptured awe. What do we generally find, however? Whilst young children are naturally curious and animated, that often changes with the onset of the 'cool years' of youth. Except for the relatively studious few in this group, there appears to be a sameness of apathy, disinterest, a dullness of face, of biding time before leaving school, of interests in everything else except that which would actually provide the spark to truly animate the individual to *enjoy* learning − more especially among Maori, seemingly.

The one thing that does animate this particular group of students today is, along with other aspects of mindless, imported American 'culture', the similarly, for the most part, mindless pastime of 'txting' that mobile phones now easily facilitate. There is one probable sure outcome from this practice: If teaching authorities are concerned about the stated poor levels of grammar, spelling, English comprehension etc., among students now, then 'txting' will surely one day be looked upon as one more thing that society might well have been better off without.[19] Notwithstanding their obvious *safety aspect* for the young in these strange latter times of *increasing societal dangers*, the insidious power and influence that mobile phones and 'txting' now clearly exert upon this very impressionable and immature group is yet to be measured. But it's a huge money-spinner for the relevant companies, isn't it?

Since the child's educational beginnings occur in the family home from the very first weeks, a basic founding interest in children by parents in the pre-school stage would go a long way to help inculcate a keener 'wish to learn' attitude in perhaps more children than at present. The often heard plea from frustrated parents for a regime of "back to basics" is a reflection of a system which they clearly feel does not seem to be able to truly 'teach' or impart that which experience has taught them is vitally necessary for 'general life'. In other words education should teach what is *actually* required.

Dr Ranginui Walker offers a logical insight into what should be required from care-givers to enhance the child's educational chances:

> "The "back to basics" cause would be credible if parents took more responsibility for the early education of their children. *Parents themselves are responsible for teaching children language*, providing them with wide-ranging experiences which foster a spirit of inquiry, and inculcating a respect for and love of books. Without this basic foundation in pre-reading experiences many children are doomed to failure at school."
>
> (Nga Tau Tohetohe, Years of Anger, p.185,
> Emphases mine.)

Clearly this is a desirable end, yet it is interesting to observe the past attitude of some Maori to the opinions of author Alan Duff. At times reviled by overly-sensitive and over-emotional Maori, his marvellous efforts to provide exactly that which Dr Walker states as a vital first measure should be applauded and supported publicly by all of Maoridom. Yet how many actually do? And how many Maori parents even care whether their children

---

[19]Thankfully, the 'life' of all foolish and totally *aspiritual practices and activities* that are currently deemed 'cool' will soon run their pointless course.

have books in the home? Alan Duff's programme provided not just books for young Maori children but, perhaps more importantly, an attitude that seemed to produce the 'shine in the eye', the desire to 'want to learn'.

*   *   *   *   *

The late Walt Disney once said that if we lose our sense of awe and wonder at all that our incredible Universe has to offer, then we have lost virtually everything worthwhile. Without that sense of reverence and amazement, all one naturally has will be a large measure of *cynicism*, which in turn can quickly lead to *negativity* thus producing a *soured* outlook on life and the vital meaning of it.

*   *   *   *   *

Unfortunately, this attitude of 'cool cynicism' *appears* to be overly pervasive among too many students. Of course, there is the recognition with many that a good education is important for a high-earnings career, which is the motivation that drives success in that group. However, there does not *seem to be* the necessary 'stimulation and animation', that zest to 'want to know', or any sense of awe about *life itself*! Even the slow, measured strut of 'cool high-schoolers' is indicative of apathy. In this 'cool group', the 'measured strut' is often characterised by faces set in almost dull resignation that one is required to 'attend school'. In truth, many probably do not even want to be there!

Should that come as a surprise to 'educationalists'? Of course not! Why would it? The very thing that might spark the 'vital interest' for students is not even considered. If we want them to do more than just attend and not sometimes cause disruption, we should teach *that which they need*. We should give them the answers to the age-old questions of *"whither, whence, and why"* first! In knowing that, the door for animated learning is opened to the maximum degree because it permits the student that vital and necessary connection to his *very Origins*. Concomitantly, a huge measure of natural awe at the stupendous nature of the totality of it all would be the direct result of such recognition.

With the knowledge of himself, his Origins, and the reasons for him being here in the first place, all else around the student must, by virtue of this 'connective-recognition', then take its rightful place in his new and *vaster* world. Nothing of this Truth is taught, however, and we foolishly wonder why we don't really 'educate' our young and why there are so many failures. In point of fact it is not the students who fail, but this obtuse and spiritually-blind society who fail them. As has been written for at least 2000 years anyway:

"...when the blind lead the blind, all fall into the ditch."

Therefore, recognise and teach this foundation first, and **all else** will naturally follow.

Why do we not do that? Simply because we have lost that vital connection to this Living Truth. In its place we have just religion and/or crass earthly intellectualism. Neither possesses the real vitality that only pure Truth inherently holds, yet which religion and intellectual science nonetheless *purport to offer*. And since, in the final analysis, education should necessarily be a "spiritual activity", the whole educative process should ultimately be geared to the refinement and ennoblement of each individual in every aspect of his daily activities; this being the natural accompaniment of true spirituality. Of course it will forever remain a free-will choice whether any one individual or a whole race wishes to embark on such a path.

Nonetheless, if the educative system does not provide this necessary knowledge for the ultimate of informed choices, then younger generations are simply caught up in the whirlpool of *mainly* intellectually-derived, 'greed-generated ideas' without any true and better alternative being offered. Thus in notions that ultimately seduce and enslave to our spiritually-bankrupt, but so-called, 'free' society. That seductive effect, moreover, is ably supported by the mediums of film, TV and radio which collectively offer all the wrong images and messages that it is possible to inflict on the impressionable young.

*   *   *   *   *

The insights of a student who lived the shattering experience of the Columbine High School massacre probably state the current social and/or educational ethos more clearly than any educationalist-guru or expert ever could. The wisdom of the following personal statement posted on the Internet clearly bears strong testimony to a spiritually-defining and clarifying moment in that young life. Whilst written from an essentially American viewpoint, the words nevertheless are particularly true for much of the Western world today.

> The paradox of our time in history is that
> we have taller buildings, but shorter tempers
> wider freeways, but narrower viewpoints
> we spend more, but have less
> we buy more, but enjoy it less.
>
> We have bigger houses and smaller families
> more conveniences, but less time
> we have more degrees, but less sense
> more knowledge, but less judgement
> more experts, but more problems
> more medicine, but less wellness.
>
> We have multiplied our possessions, but reduced our values.
> We talk too much, love too seldom, and hate too often.
> We've learned how to make a living, but not a life
> we've added years to life, but not life to years.
> We've been all the way to the moon and back,
> but have trouble crossing the street to meet the new neighbour.
> We've conquered outer space, but not inner space
> we've cleaned up the air, but polluted the soul
> we've split the atom, but not our prejudice.
> We have higher incomes, but lower morals
> we've become long on quantity, but short on quality
> these are the times of tall men, and short character
> steep profits, and shallow relationships.
>
> These are the times of world peace, but domestic warfare
> more leisure, but less fun
> more kinds of food, but less nutrition.
>
> These are the days of two incomes, but more divorce
> of fancier houses, but broken homes.
> It is a time when there is much in the show window and nothing in the stockroom
> a time when technology can bring this letter to you,
> and a time when you can choose either to make a difference or just hit delete.

The young author concludes: "Be brave and pass it on." That we have now done because we unequivocally concur with the overall thrust of the text.

Those few lines encapsulate much of what we state in this complete Work. The difference is, however, unlike the wonderfully sage observation of the above writer who notes that his/her powerfully clarified insights can simply be deleted at the touch of a button, The Source from which this Work is derived cannot!

$$* \qquad * \qquad * \qquad * \qquad *$$

So, with regard to the relatively low achievement levels in Maori education, a Herald article published back in May 1998, headed **"Maori students at crisis point: experts"**, noted the seemingly prevalent attitude among too many Maori students of wanting everything else other than to be educated. The report stated the fact of the matter only but noted then that 'another commission will recommend to the Government their particular ideas on how to address this ongoing and worsening problem'. With Maori suspensions running at three times the rate for Pakeha, 62 per cent failing school certificate against 34 per cent for Pakeha, and 40 per cent failing seventh-form bursary as opposed to 21 per cent of Pakeha students, it is no wonder that the Ministry of Education observed, then, that "...more research needs to be done on why Maori students are failing."

Since research usually follows the same basic pattern i.e., more research, the key need will probably not be ultimately addressed here either.

Where, then, does this place the Maori student in a predominantly Pakeha society? Certain immutable, educational factors must apply here, for the Maori is just one of many races that inhabit this earth. As we have learned, moreover, Maori have the *same Spiritual Origin* as the White races. Therefore, the same criteria toward Maori education is crucial if Maori wish to stand correctly as *spiritual citizens of this Creation*.

For just as *official* European culture, education/knowledge – and even religion – does not *completely* address the ultimate question of "whence, whither and why", neither does Maori culture and knowledge do so either. As previously stated, except in one area of 'perceptive potential' regarding "The Elemental Forces of Nature", the *overall* knowledge contained in European culture far surpasses that of Maori who generally deem the sum total of their cultural traditions as possessing the greatest amount of knowledge.

Aside from that primary foundational question for *all* education, and despite the relatively few Maori students who have the necessary drive and vision to know exactly what they wish to achieve and who set out to reach their particular goal, it is clear from statistics that the rest appear to portray a dull resignation of apathy regarding the necessity of this whole business of learning. With cultural considerations elevated to an inordinately high and unrealistic degree of importance in the psyche of the race today, most everyone is *too afraid to speak out against it* for fear of being labelled either racist or 'culturally insensitive'. By *fostering* this mind-set, however, Maoridom has dug itself into the unfortunate and close-minded view that perpetuates the 'delusion' that *all the world must beat a path to the Maori door*.

This attitude stipulates that it is not Maori who should broaden their horizons by learning about other cultures – particularly European ones – or marvel at the important and fascinating sweep of the history of mankind; but it is the rest of the world who must learn about the Maori and his culture. Yet, quite clearly, Maori aspects alone do not at all possess anywhere near 'all knowledge'.

Dr Ranginui Walker, on page 210 of his book, "Nga Tau Tohetohe, Years of Anger", records an interesting aspect of an address by the Rev. Bob Lowe at a seminar at Canterbury University in the early 1970s, entitled: "The Pakeha Problem in New Zealand". In

Dr Walker's words: "The Conference was an interesting exercise in critical self-analysis, in searching for the soul of New Zealand society."

> "The Rev. Bob Lowe in his opening address made a plea to the Maori to help his Pakeha brother to come to an understanding of himself, to find the serenity and peace that tribal people through the ages have possessed and the Pakeha has surrendered to the industrial and technological age.
>
> The Pakeha, he said, have created an affluent society but failed to satisfy the spiritual side of man's nature. Pakehas over forty were emotionally denuded people. They are alienated in the urban state because they have no sense of unity with nature."

Dr Walker reports, (p.210), that Rev. Lowe:

> "...made an eloquent plea for the Maori to reach out to the Pakeha, to lead him home so that we become truly one nation."

Whilst the Pakeha, *as a race*, may certainly need help to find his spiritual nature, Maori, *as a race*, also need the same kind of help. Help to understand what they are destroying within their *wairua of race* by many aspects of their lifestyle and wrong beliefs. And whilst Reverend Lowe understands that there is a very real difference of perception between the indigenous peoples and the White races to what we term "the other-world reality", the Pakeha Church, to which he clearly belongs, also needs to embrace certain vital aspects of that "reality" too, if that Church wishes to play its part in helping its own Pakeha brethren to achieve this necessary spiritual awakening that he pleads for.

The Church must awaken first, however. For one of those very vital things that Rev. Lowe speaks of as an inherent part of what we might loosely term 'Maori knowledge or spirituality', is exactly that which the Pakeha is generally disbelieving or dismissive. It is, moreover, also one that the Christian Churches have condemned for many hundreds of years.[20]

In terms of the general thrust of this Work, even if only from the historical record, it is difficult if not impossible to reconcile Rev. Lowe's plea with the actual reality of tribal life for many peoples. In the history of certain tribal peoples, such as the Maori and the Papua/New Guineans, for example, where do we find: "...the serenity and peace that tribal people through the ages have possessed..." The ingrained ethos of *makutu*, but more particularly *utu,* did not *ever* provide that pipe-dream for Maori. What does Rev. Lowe allude to we may wonder?

Look at Africa today! His view is reminiscent of the early utopian, European ideal, strongly espoused by Rousseau, of the "noble savage at one with nature". As the thrust of this book clearly outlines, this was very rarely the reality. Tribalism, more often than not, produced lifestyles characterised by huge amounts of superstition and fear, brought about by lack of real knowledge. That everyday reality inevitably offered conflict to neighbouring tribes and peoples.

Paradoxically, however, what the Rev. Lowe asks can actually be a powerful *spiritual task* for the Maori race. Maoridom, however, must *first* recognise where 'Maoritanga' does *not* flow in accordance with The Eternal Spiritual Laws and so take the necessary steps *to correct that serious imbalance* before it could ever fulfil the plea of the good Reverend.[21]

Therefore, under the current thrust of Maori educational ethnocentricity, nothing could be more damaging to the race, particularly for the impressionable young who hold the

---

[20] That is the knowledge of Elemental Lore that Chapter 11 fully explained.

[21] We address that 'potential' in the later Chapter: The Rapidly Fading "Spiritual Potential".

future of the race in their hands, than this incredibly narrow and egocentric view that the sun and planet earth were put in place solely for the Maori race and its 'knowledge and spirituality' which the rest of the world 'must acknowledge'.

Far too many University-educated Maori holding highly influential positions in the professional and academic worlds have absolutely no idea of the **spiritual damage** they cause to young and impressionable minds, or to those who are not able to think for themselves. With their vocal and often illogical views for Maoridom, they, especially, as the singular, 'highly-educated group' within it, seemingly *regularly encourage* all other Maori to almost blindly accept the *spiritually-damaging belief* that they must not just be Maori first, *but Maori only*. This kind of self-adulation serves to perpetuate the already strongly-reinforced and narrowly-focussed ethnocentricity inherent in many within the race.

This view is most unfortunate! For *all* races, the primary recognition we must strive to make in the first instance is that we are, first and foremost, *spiritual* beings. With that as the 'foundation' we are then more able to make sense of why we are Maori, or European, or Mongolian, or anything else. This recognition would provide the necessary degree of understanding about every other thing that we must concern ourselves with on earth. Cultural traditions will then find their proper place too, not only within their own ethnic or country boundaries, but also in how they are **interlinked and complementary to all other cultures worldwide**.

What should be seriously recognised once more is that every race, and therefore every culture, has something to offer every other one. By this mechanism, both the individual and collective spiritual purposes of the different peoples of this planet would be better understood. And only with this collective mutual acceptance and recognition, can the chord of global spiritual harmony *ever* be sounded. As already stated a number of times and once more reinforced here: This means that Maori should concern themselves with cultures other than their own, and not just those of the indigenous 'brown brotherhood' to whom they might naturally feel strongly-linked. Unfortunately, because of the apparent inability by many of the world's peoples to recognise that all cultures have *equal-value potential* under the inviolable outworking of **The Spiritual Laws of Creation** – which, of course, brought each and every one of us into being – such self-centred views will ensure that the desired chord of harmony will not be sounded for some time, *if at all now*! Yet, from such a mutual acceptance of cultures, there would emerge the wonderful recognition of the collective "beauty of the peoples".

Therefore, whilst politicians and self-interest groups of all persuasions argue incessantly about what education should encompass and how it should be delivered; without exception all fail to take into account the very fundamental and necessary need to provide *spiritual knowledge first*. We state once more; **spiritual knowledge** and *not simply religion*. Unfortunately, because the word spiritual is invariably wrongly considered to have religious or even occult connotations, the vital *spiritual foundation* is similarly deemed to be not only irrelevant, but even undesirable in some circles. Without that particular *foundational-base*, however, dissension in many areas is virtually guaranteed.

All education should ultimately start with exactly that *spiritual foundation* first, and thus the knowledge of our actual Origins. From that platform, a basic overview of the development of mankind and his different cultures would offer the high aim of promoting interest, tolerance and understanding between all of the world's peoples. Individual races, of course, would teach the deeper aspects of their own culture and language to their own. That is what the education system *should* set out to achieve. Should the administrators and teachers choose not to do so, it will, nevertheless, eventually be forced upon them; and sooner rather than later by virtue of the increasing spiritual pressure that is *forcing wrong directions to failure*. As we have learned, it is a process which we can all *readily observe* in the present.

21.5.1 Gender Considerations

One particular aspect that should be carefully considered is whether we should continue with co-education High Schools. The long-held view that integrated schools are absolutely necessary for social development of students is not necessarily correct in terms of the outworking of **Spiritual Law**. The transitional teenage years have always held difficulties for budding adults as they grapple with all manner of emotional and physical changes. So this may actually be a time when the respective genders might beneficially prefer to be amongst their own.

For it may well be that social development does not proceed normally in a co-ed situation because of the emotional pressures young people are put under in what may actually be an unnatural situation for many in that age group. And where Hollywood-type expectations are striven for rather than a more natural acceptance of themselves – warts and all. Of course, many of the young enjoy the stimulation of the environment, coping easily with it. However many do not, and this may place even more pressure on those students in the co-ed situation.

Emotional uncertainty and discomfort can affect many students in this age group when or if forced to closely co-exist with members of the opposite sex for long periods of time, thereby further affecting other aspects of their education. To force young students into a situation they may not be ready for is hardly an intelligent move.

Since the teenage years are those when the 'energy for adult development', is ordained to surface, and because it brings full sexual development, it may place a further burden upon students at this time of great change, particularly under the powerful influence of the 'perfect image' that media pressure unfairly promotes. The close proximity of students to each other fostered by co-ed parameters, coupled with the developing strength of this *new force within*, may generate strong yet completely unnecessary feelings of inadequacy in some.

Without the emotional maturity that is necessary to resolve these kinds of feelings in the naturally immature, they may be held too tightly within. Striving to be 'staunch' when the emotions and perhaps emerging desires are stating the opposite may be too difficult for some students at times. And without resolution or release in such situations, even self-perceived 'personal inadequacies' may develop into actual *fears*; of things like low self-esteem. Such circumstances then have the potential to translate into feelings such as: "I don't measure up." Or: "I don't feel attractive or accepted." A visiting American sociologist once made the comment that today's teenagers:

"...are trying so hard to be cool that they're forgetting to be themselves."

Perhaps we should consider whether our too-high-a-rate of teenage suicide might have its roots in the projections we have explored here, in at least *some of the cases* anyway. It is interesting to note that many students surveyed recently, especially females, believe they would be happier in a single sex school simply because there, in natural comfort among their own, they can be themselves. This finding should not come as a surprise for we should consider this attitude to be completely natural for that age group since it concurs with the *higher knowledge* contained in all **Spiritual Law**.

Exactly that *higher knowledge* would mean a new and more desirable educative-direction and thus ensure that every child and student received the absolutely necessary foundation of the knowledge of his *"whence, whither and why"*. And whilst there should certainly be a 'well-rounded' education for all, such a more powerful *foundation of knowledge* would surely help students to be more animated and receptive to 'real learning'. That will equally ensure that student's minds **are not cluttered with irrelevant things that only weary unnecessarily**.

Whether we apply these new kinds of educative principles to Maori or Pakeha direction, we should be under no illusions as to the strict and severe impartiality of **The Eternal Laws** driving the outworking of **The Law of Movement** and **The Law of Balance** in **both** Pakeha and Maori affairs. Therefore, **teach** this knowledge and you **possess** the knowledge – the knowledge of human *"whence, whither and why"*, explained in this Work.

For without the knowledge of one's origins and the meaning of life through the structure of, and connections to, all of Creation, where and what is the *real* meaning or purpose of *any other* 'education'? Its lack of spiritual foundation ensures that it cannot ever be completely 'anchored' in this material world, which we also inhabit. Only in the absolute fullness of *'really knowing'* – and not just as a faith/belief mode – can all other learning make any sense in then offering its necessary contribution to providing the totality of beneficial knowledge. With true knowledge, healthy discernment arises. And with discernment should come the desire to discard what is detrimental to the individual and society. Discernment thereby provides the obvious potential benefit for a more equitable and harmonious society.

If education is strictly forced down a path that only reflects society's social perception of itself at any given moment in time, then the main foundation and need, which should encompass genuinely spiritual aspirations **firstly**, may not even be considered. Since spirituality is often considered to be synonymous with religion, it is invariably dismissed as being generally irrelevant for education. And certainly deemed pointless for the present, more socially-desirable thrust toward a business, or corporate, 'village earth'.

Yet here, too, as with education and health, it is precisely a spiritual foundation that even businesses should be built on. For unless the actual knowledge of human *'whence, whither and why'* is recognised and accepted, how can any other kind of activity be *fully* entered into, *including* the correct kind of business and global trade procedure. So whilst it may have decidedly greedy, selfish and thoroughly unpleasant aspects promoted by some men of the same ilk, such endeavours could be spiritually-ennobled too, for it can also naturally bring great benefits if utilised with a truly *spiritual foundation*.

The growing International Business movement, "Businesses for Social Responsibility", which includes some of the largest and most successful Corporates in America – home of rampant capitalism and 'astute' business acumen – is testimony to just such a trend; albeit probably not yet as a 'consciously-aware state' for business at this point in its evolution. A key requirement in that world of high finance and global business is, of course, a commensurate knowledge of the English language.

Given the rapidly closing window of opportunity for at least some 'to still get it right', the knowledge of The Truth outlined in this Work offers that singular chance. Thus it is, in the truly *educative sense* for both Maori and Pakeha, the key *poropiti* that should be heeded! However, as with most radical ideas that sit outside 'humanly-derived educational parameters', it is unlikely that the 'controllers of education' in this land will heed the call here.

In the closing paragraphs of: **"The Treaty of Waitangi"** sub; **...Correct "Spiri-**

tual" Use of 'Te Tiriti'; – we stated the crucial need for 'Education' to incorporate the key Truth for *all* humankind, i.e.: The *true* nature of we human beings as we *actually are* during the many incarnations of our *earthly existence*.

So; Te Iwi Maori: Bring about the primary 'Educational need' as per the following points.

1. Under the parameters of 'Treaty Claims', use *your 'constance of the wero'* to publicly challenge the educational status quo; to change school curricula to *incorporate* the knowledge of *the actual nature and purpose of the 'Wairua'*.

2. Through **'Te Tiriti O Waitangi'**, *demand that change* so that this key truth – which your cultural traditions **correctly accept as a living reality** – can be *re-seeded* educationally for the ultimate spiritual benefit of all in this land.

3. Do not be seduced by that part of foolishly-aberrant Pakeha *matauranga* which *absolutely denies* the existence of our *true life-force* – **The Wairua**. But forcefully promotes, **in its place**, just the *materiality* of the 'human genome', solely; even to the farcical yet *spiritually-dangerous* extreme of pushing for the use of **animal** parts for **human** bodies.

4. Material parts of flesh masquerading as true life within; yet which *rot away with the physical body at **all** their deaths*. But which nevertheless impacts *very gravely* on the *human* soul and *wairua*.

5. Therefore, **publicly reject such 'very wrong' teachings and practices**.

Irrespective of whether or not such vitally-correct education will see the light of day in the present, it most certainly will after all that is spiritually-aberrant has run its course and is thus no longer a part of the new very-much-reduced humanity left on earth.

So in exact concert with that absolutely vital **poropiti** for all, what this Work unequivocally points to; **will take place**.

21.6   Maori Language

The Chapter on **Language** explained how and why language is possible and how it was formed. Most importantly, we learned the spiritual meaning of language and the power inherent in the spoken word – for *every* language. Chapter 20 (sub-Chapter, **Renaissance**) looked at the latter-day emergence, or perhaps rebirth, of the Maori language; a clearly beneficial and desirable aspect of cultural renaissance overall. What we wish to briefly assess in this segment is the impact of the English language for Maori, both in education and the wider, modern world. And then compare that to what a solely Maori language only position will or will not achieve for total immersion students in the wider world where the main language of convenience is English.

Language "forms the people"! *Thus decree The Laws of Spiritual Truth!*

That is to say, a language a group or people uses as its own will clearly and quite naturally reflect that people's culture, its view of the world (and the other world) and its view of itself and place in the universe. For the 'belief-parameters' subsequently arrived at, *as elucidated in the particular language*, will attest to that cultures 'assessment-of-self' and projection to the outer world; thus what it accepts as its place, relative to other peoples and their beliefs. A people's language, therefore, actually **is** that particular people, and vice-versa. For it is through their own racial or ethnic medium of communication that they will *produce* their associated 'cultural forms'. Thus, *their* particular *attachments* are 'formed' within the overall parameters that the group has more or less collectively determined for itself with regard to its *cultural and social beliefs.*

In countries where two disparate languages of two peoples have equal value in terms of legislated law, and where the cultures are equally disparate – as in New Zealand – there is the clear potential for at least some differences to be seemingly irreconcilable unless addressed from a mutually-acceptable and *reconciliatory foundation.* Our particular foundation of unequivocal conviction states that *reconciling standpoint* to be **Spiritual Law**!

Therein resides the means for mutual accommodation and understanding, irrespective of cultural differences that, in any case, should really be regarded as a *plus* under the outworking of the same Law. For should tension arise from a strong feeling of alienation, or from a perception that one partner's language is relegated to a second-class status, then the utilisation of Spiritual Law can clarify and harmonise any potential conflict. Gains derived from particular recognitions that then subsequently *promote* the relevant 'partner' language, will thus not be lost.

Whilst it is vitally imperative that the Maori language be retained, unfortunately yet realistically, the wider world has little need of it. As stated previously, its purpose is essentially solely that of the language of the Maori. To a very large degree, the global language of the business, communications and commercial aviation worlds is that of English, and it is important for Maori to recognise this inescapable fact. Quite clearly, therefore, any Maori who wishes to fully participate in the greater world than solely that of Maoridom, requires a corresponding level of *English comprehension* – and perhaps of *other* languages as well.

Because it *is* spiritually important for all the world's languages to be retained, the current thrust toward more *kura kaupapa* and/or Maori language immersion schools may seem to offer the best possibility for the retention of the language if parents are not able or prepared to teach in the home environment. If there is natural enthusiasm for this method of schooling on the part of the young, then that is well and good. However, if there are children who may actually have no choice but to accept the directive of enthusiastic parents or 'traditional leaders' for such a scheme, then that may translate to reluctance in learning. Nevertheless, it is admirable and vitally important that English is taught as the second language after the initial early years of Maori language immersion.

It may not be too well known, but in 1876 one Wi Te Hakiro and 336 others petitioned Parliament asking that all children from two years of age should be taught English as their first language. Interestingly, the petition asked that Maori not be spoken in class or in the school. Both Sir Apirana Ngata and Dr Maui Pomare also believed that:

> '...the first subject in order of priority in the school curriculum was English, the second most important was English, the third most important was English and then arithmetic and other subjects after that.'

A powerful, knowledgeable grasp of a major language such as English unequivocally offers concomitant access to all that has ever been written and spoken in that medium. And therefore offers far more than Maori language ever could – *in terms of greater breadth and depth of knowledge overall.*

For within the parameters of present-day society, it would be grossly unfair to demand that children be totally immersed in a purely Maori teaching environment without access to the wider world of the major language of learning and convenience for society and the globe. In reality, it would be an act of extreme selfishness on the part of those Maori who might demand this kind of exclusion for the young of the race. Despite such strong views from that quarter, it is interesting to note that the most vocal of the proponents of Maori immersion schools are *all bilingual* having had the benefits of *a Pakeha education in the Pakeha world*. Without recourse to the wider communication medium that virtually every other main language offers, Maori language immersion students in the above scenario would be more or less confined to a very narrow world of 'Maoriness'.

Some years ago a strong supporter of this movement commented that he hoped one day to see Maori spoken on the flight decks of Boeing 747 passenger aircraft. With regard to that clearly impossible dream, the language barrier was investigated as a possible cause for the December 1996 mid-air collision of an airliner and a cargo plane over India. The International Aviation industry accepts that language problems have probably been the cause of other crashes as well and a tightening of English language requirements for international pilots was initiated in February, 2008. The clear need for a single standard language for global aviation, of which English is the present choice, will ensure that a relatively obscure indigenous language from a small South Pacific Ocean country is unlikely to ever fit that bill.

In reiteration, Maori language is purely a New Zealand language, and one with much the same *spiritual value* as most other languages, **if used correctly**. So whilst it has little relevance in the international arena, and clearly not in the aviation and business worlds, it should not be allowed to die out. However, it is unlikely to ever be embraced by anyone outside this land. And why should it be when English is probably already the most widely accepted international medium of communication? It is also the commonest language that many countries *compulsorily teach as the second one* to their students.

Even though Microsoft has now included Maori as one of the 40 languages available for internet access and other IT applications, it cannot hope to make meaningful inroads into the naturally greater use of the major languages of the world. Nevertheless, Maori inclusion into the wider language base of the global community is a positive step.

Paradoxically, Maori students cosseted in immersion schools without access to the English language for general discourse within New Zealand could well produce an angry backlash against that system later. More especially when any such experimental students reach adulthood and discover that all their Maori learning had deprived them of access to the wider activity of the social fabric of the country and the international arena. English is then a much harder proposition if learned as an adult. Thus the price that would ultimately be paid further down the track by such students *in this particular scenario* would probably be rebellion against the very system that purports to elevate the race to some undefined but solely Maori place through the elevation of the Maori language. And, therefore, possible alienation from a society that will always be English-language dominated, simply because **it is a common-sense position**.

So teaching *solely* Maori in immersion-schooling may well deprive students of their rightful place in the international community by being held in thrall to purely Maori views. Teach them both languages – or even more – and you give them not only the foundation of their own cultural traditions, but also the potential of the world with the richness, diversity and knowledge of *all* cultures and of *all* scientific and philosophical thought. Most importantly, therefore, they would be offered access to man's accumulated fount of knowledge whereby one can discover far more than that offered by one's own culture and traditions, including the most vital knowledge of all – **our Spiritual Origins**. Maori immersion schools cannot provide that precise knowledge from Maori cultural traditions, for neither the schools nor the cultural traditions possess it.

What a fluent grasp of the Maori language could provide, however, would be a singular

Maori mechanism whereby The Spiritual Laws and their outworking could be taught in that medium. *Te reo Maori* is well suited to explain and teach at least the *primary points* of the spiritual concepts and truths contained in **The Spiritual Laws of Creation** because both the language and culture unequivocally accept the other-world realities of both the 'beyond', and of "**The Elemental Forces of Nature**".

As previously stated, though not complete in that knowledge, those strong beliefs inherent in the cultural traditions can nevertheless, through the language, be *extended in expression* to teach/explain those connections and the interconnected outworking of **The Laws.**[22]

21.7   Crime, Aroha and Spiritual Justice

"Physical strength will never permanently withstand the impact of spiritual force."

(Franklin D. Roosevelt,
US President, 1901-1909)

21.7.1   Crime

> Some readers may find the above quote inappropriate given the outcome of some quite dubious U.S. Foreign Policy directions of recent decades. Yet in the context of this sub-Chapter, the inherent truth contained in it is *entirely appropriate* when we reflect upon the decisive and far-reaching impact of Ratana's exceptionally strong "spiritual force", albeit one granted to him for his powerful mission for Maori.

A disproportionately high level of criminal offending by a race of people who make up a *relatively* small percentage of overall numbers in New Zealand society is the unfortunate reality of Maori crime statistics! In January 1996, a visiting Swedish criminologist told a criminology conference in Wellington that Maori people faced a grim future if the number of young Maori men in prison continued to grow. Dr Nils Christie observed then that five per cent of young Maori men were in prison with current predictions rising to nine per cent within a decade. (This reflects the trend throughout the industrialised world today where minority groups make up the bulk of the prison population.) In some American states more than half of all young black men were in prison or on parole. Dr Christie posed the potentially alarming question of:

> "How large a proportion of our minority population can be held in captivity without changing the elements of how our society operates, how we look at society?"

In his view there was little cause for optimism that the situation would be reversed and the more he worked with these matters the more difficult it was "...to conceive of any end to this situation." Ominously, perhaps, yet in keeping with an explosive worldwide trend in the number of prison inmates, there had similarly been a 60 per cent increase in New Zealand which, then, was predicted to rise by a further 40 per cent by the year 2005. And because the industry surrounding crime and justice was huge in the United States, particularly, this growth has fuelled a 'business mentality' with opportunities to make money in the $65 billion local US jails market.

With such a depressing scenario, can we hope to see some sort of light at the end of our own dark tunnel here in New Zealand? The short answer is yes, **if** we are prepared to accept and put in place the only *real* solution.

---

[22]Paradoxically, Pakeha hymns sung in Maori take on an especially strong quality, thus indicating the great potential of the language to 'spiritually ennoble' its own cultural traditions.

For if prison is the place where many Maori end up, and if a lack of serious education is believed to be a contributing factor, then politicians and prison authorities should seriously consider a particular course of action that would, over time, probably inculcate in the psyche of the inmates two *very positive* elements. One would be *immediate and ongoing education* about the many and varied aspects of the marvels of the world, the universe, the world of nature and the history of man and his works. The second aspect that should develop *as a consequence of the first* would be the desire *to want to learn more*. In effect, it would be a kind of immersion or saturation-type educational programme – for all inmates. It would, however, especially benefit Maori.

Firstly, if it has not already been done, get rid of the *standard* TV fare in all prisons. Invariably promoted as quality viewing by the 'Networks', most programmes are, *primarily* in their nature and content, just *aspiritual garbage*. *Something* is required to fill TV screens *day and night*, so the bulk of programmes really do little more than mindlessly entertain, ultimately contributing to an insidious dumbing-down of the viewing masses. Feeding prison inmates a continuous diet of that kind of poison could not *ever* bring about a more educationally-aware or ennobled individual. They should also be denied access to videos and/or computer games that *do not educate*, and to internet sites that similarly have *no educative value*. We are all aware of the truth inherent in the *whakatouki* (proverb):

"Garbage in, garbage out!"

Yet despite the fact that the whole digital entertainment industry is now globally-entrenched as a **'societal weakness'**, the most unfortunate aspect about this growing trend is that it is *not recognised* for the *spiritual poison* which it actually is. Fortunately, however, its time of birth and life is rapidly drawing to a close too.

What, then, is the nature of this 'inmate-programme'? Simple! A constant diet of quality Documentaries from the four Documentary channels on Sky Digital, and regular input from world news channels. Get inmates out of the mind-set that the world turns in space for them and their problems or personal 'rights'. Yes, one can already hear the cries of horror; pampering inmates who should be denied the luxuries that society has financial access to – such as Sky Digital. Ordinarily that should certainly be the case. However, in terms of *educative rehabilitation*, this kind of immersion over a period of time will *beneficially* affect the one so immersed. There would not be individual TV sets in each cell, unless a 'multiple-access decoder' of some kind could be installed. Carefully placed large screens serving larger numbers of viewers might be a better option.

If not Sky Digital and the marvellous Documentary channels, then perhaps a centralised VHS/DVD facility serving the prison TV network, still offering only educational videos, however. Such a policy would ultimately provide very positive financial gains for the taxpayer through an equally positive return of perhaps far fewer soured and uncooperative prison inmates being released to re-offend far too often.

The key point here is to *change the diet of visual garbage that is now regarded as the norm*, and thereby change the mind-set and attitude of those so immersed.

Now: Let us not hear of trammelling the 'human rights' of prisoners through a mandatory regime of enforced education. After all, the law of the land requires that all citizens attend Educational Institutions, with a set curriculum that individual students cannot change. So why should it be any different here? In any case, the Higher Law demands that for all human beings, **responsibilities must precede rights**.

With specific regard to the Maori race, how can a people once vibrant and dynamic, who regard *themselves* as the only true *tangata whenua* of Aotearoa, produce such sorry statistics? By virtue of their 'first-citizen status', Maori are able to call on a myriad of financial and other benefits and assistance not always available to other ethnic groups. If there is so much help available, why is comparatively little achieved? What is the underlying reason? And even if there may not be the work opportunities that were once the norm, why has nothing more been done with the benefits and assistance that can be called upon?

The answer lies *primarily* in one word – **attitude**! For no race can hope to be part of a dynamic and mobile society – which New Zealand is perceived to be – if they themselves are not prepared to *fully participate* at the required level. If a people choose to cling to a wrong belief about their apparent greatness and *mana* and still want the consumerism of a 21st century technological setting *without actually earning it*, they set in place the potential for becoming a low-level, low-esteem, second class group. As we strongly stressed in the previous segment, the key here is **education**. Education, however, that encompasses the wider world in this particular instance, and not simply more Maori culture.

Despite the benefits of ethnic pride and esteem that cultural learning *can* offer, it unfortunately contributes little else to Maori 'advancement' in the *kind of society* we now possess. Quite obviously, therefore, traditional emphases will not greatly change the status quo in terms of improving worsening Maori social statistics, or alter the clear need for a more complete education. The relatively *high number* of well-educated professional and academic people from many varied backgrounds *throughout Maoridom* clearly testifies to the fact that a good education, which can more readily guarantee the opening of doors of opportunity, *is* available to Maori.

However, the unfortunate emergence of a sub-cultural mind-set that appears to subscribe to the view of 'non-responsibility' for the current Maori situation is a blot on that 'race-potential' and should therefore be openly dissected. For it tends to place most of the blame onto the Pakeha whilst at the same time extending the hand for more and more *as some kind of cultural or ethnic right*. Given such an attitude it is no wonder that crime is so endemic within the race. Yet, if we very *objectively* examine the *true* reason for such a sorry statistic, the *actual answer* can be mainly found in the outworking of **The Law of Reciprocal Action** and **The Law of Attraction of Similar Species**. In other words, it is the lawful outworking of the *choices* decided upon which *determine* the *consequences* that must *always return* to the individual or group under these inflexible and *inviolable* Laws.

Thus, in the case of Maori crime statistics, it is solely a question of *personal choice* – nothing else. No one is *forced* to commit crime, not even when extremely difficult circumstances might emotionally influence one to either believe one may have justification to do so or, conversely, believe that one has the right to demand recompense of some kind from another. In the final analysis, it is the *individual* who makes such a decision. Even in the case where young Maori gang initiates are 'ordered' to show their allegiance or staunchness to the group, it is still that *individual's choice* to gravitate to the gang *in the first place*. Therefore the **primary education** required to combat the propensity for Maori youth to seek such attachments needs to be that of the knowledge of The Spiritual Laws and their *infallible* outworking.

It is vitally important, therefore, that we understand the strictness of the outworking of those Laws in this area of crime and ethnicity. The reader may recall the explanations outlined in the Chapter on **The Spiritual Laws/Principles** where we stated that every individual on this planet is born into the particular family, race, and geographical location for that particular individual's **"spiritual maturing"**. The individual himself, moreover – in strict accordance with those Spiritual Laws – will have set in place this necessary connection for such an incarnation. Therefore any attempt to blame family circumstances or upbringing as the excuse or 'reason' for criminal activity, or to angrily rage against family or society, is at *absolute variance with spiritual reality.*

As previously and forcefully explained, the circumstances of one's life will be those which a particular soul will need for his spiritual awakening or further spiritual maturing. It will also offer an opportunity for the parents to provide the correct kind of guidance for that individual too, since the fates of both, in the first instance, are irrevocably linked for that lifetime. From this brief explanation, however, it does not automatically follow, for example, that a child must be abused or otherwise mistreated simply because he has been born into a less than compassionate 'family'. For the parents also have the free-will choice to be nurturing ones or brutal ones. The choices made, therefore, will eventually return to them the reciprocal effect of **their** actions.

Even if the parents do not awaken to their own spiritual responsibility toward those who have been given into their care – and may even be uncaring or brutal toward them – that does not offer any valid reason for the offspring to then use that occurrence as an *excuse* to embark upon a later life of abuse toward their own or society. In fact, *quite the opposite should occur.* For any such experiences during the formative years should awaken within the child or young adult the desire to **not be** like those kinds of parents. To thus have the **guts**, the *mana*, to be different. In effect, to develop the **maia** to leave such people behind if *they* refuse to change *their* ways. We may liken it to a test of spiritual strength for the offspring; to *not perpetuate* the same mistakes and perhaps visit the same debased or criminal behaviour against their own or against others, that they may have suffered in childhood.

> Maoridom's 'suffering-children' are revealed as a singularly-terrible reality. There is no *mana* in the killing, maiming and sexual violation of children – either of Maoridom or of any other race or culture.[23]

21.7.2 Maori Aroha/Christian Love

With respect to this very issue and in the assessment of the higher meaning of the word, *aroha*; overly-religious Christian parents, especially, who inculcate 'the letter of the law' of **The Commandments** for themselves and their offspring but who misconstrue the *true meaning* of them, may inadvertently burden their children with irreconcilable guilt about their role and place in the family unit in the first instance. And, by extension, in their particular Church and in society generally.

For example, **The Commandment** which *ostensibly* enjoins children to **"Honour *Thy* Father and Mother"**, should be very carefully thought about by such parents. For it is inconceivable to believe that Perfect Justice issuing from a Perfect Creator would offer a mechanism whereby children **must** absolutely honour their parents, irrespective of the 'kind of parents' such offspring might 'inherit'. Since a Divine Decree or Commandment must inherently contain both Love and Justice, It would not expect that offspring of parents whose behaviour and lifestyle were debased, abusive, or less than uplifting, should then be *expected* to honour them. That stance would be ludicrous in the extreme and, moreover, constitute the epitome of parental hypocrisy. By the very nature of

---

[23]We may wonder if there really is at least a vestige among Maori men today of a so-called, perhaps misnamed, 'violence gene' when we read of so much violence perpetrated against women and children?

their **Divine Origin, The Commandments** could not possibly contain any element of hypocrisy whatsoever!

How many children over the centuries, we may wonder, have suffered under religiously misguided parents whose Churches selfishly misinterpreted such a clear guide for *parenthood*. In this case, the unequivocal connotation was always that this particular Commandment was clearly meant for *parents in the first instance* – and **not** for children firstly. Parents should therefore be under no illusion that it is *their ordained spiritual task* to be the *kind of parents* whom their children would *naturally wish to honour* – rather than it being a case of just "do as I say".

> Thus were parents – of all races and cultures – meant to: **"Honour Fatherhood and Motherhood!"** And *thereby* 'rightfully receive', through the *correct spiritual example* in their upbringing, the *honour* of their children.

Similarly, the application of the word *aroha* in the over-emotional use of it is a major impediment for many Maori to fully accept the need for ***justice toward their own at times***, more particularly when *the transgressor* is close *whanau*. Apportioning blame elsewhere in such cases is clearly *spiritually wrong*, and such a stance only serves to promote an unfortunate and debilitating attitude of 'non-responsibility' once more. Moreover, the attributes of genuine *kaha* and *mana* are equally clearly non-existent in these kinds of circumstances. *Aroha* is too often used in the same context, and with equally damaging results, as the Churches interpretation of so-called 'Christian love'. In both cases, what is mooted as love is anything but, because it invariably fails to take into account **Justice**. The Spiritual Laws *absolutely decree* that **Love** and **Justice** simply cannot be separated. **They are one!** So where one is used without the other, **The Law of Balance** is then seriously transgressed.

Via the use of these two ethnically different yet similarly applied words, the users often impute to them a singular meaning; a weak, all-encompassing and *vacillating forgiveness* that sometimes fails to fully address the need for *the offender* to make serious reparations for his transgression, or even to accept full *responsibility* for it.

For the Maori, it is often the so-called *aroha* of the *whanau* **toward the transgressor** that seems to be the all-important thing, rather than demanding *he* face up to his offence.

The *incorrect belief* that Jesus died to cleanse all human beings of their evil dispositions [i.e., *everyone's sins*] in His 'great act of Love' is seemingly the basis for an 'all-forgiving' attitude among some Christians toward even serious transgressions which *ostensibly* seeks to 'emulate' that 'loving sacrifice'. Whilst there should ultimately be forgiveness – tempered by compassion of course – *true justice* must still nevertheless prevail.

That is why many of the problems within the Maori race stem from a completely wrong application of a too easy-going attitude that manifests in an *incorrect* concept of *true aroha*. The 'concept', in its common usage by Maori, rarely gives the correct *spiritual* help that it should. This is one of the primary reasons for worsening statistics in too many areas, the cause of which some within Maoridom try to place at the feet of those outside of it. Thus the usual application of *aroha* among Maori fails to understand and apply the very thing that would return this particular word to its correct and spiritually elevated place – the need for **self-discipline** in all things. That is the mark of the true warrior and is the 'living force' behind *maia* and genuine *mana*!

Let us, therefore, strive to understand what *should* be the true meaning of these words – the so-called *aroha* and *love*. Two small words, supposedly similar in meaning, that have inadvertently caused so many problems due to the wrongful application of them in the unfortunate belief that they were always correctly applied.

*   *   *   *   *

Because of its spiritually weak, earthly interpretation, we might designate the overall concept inherent in those two key words as being almost a 'religion of earthly love'. For it is one thing to reverentially proclaim a belief in this power of love, but another to then apply it so wrongly that its distorted application produces the worst kinds of injustices. We need to therefore understand that **The Love of The Divine**, which produced the incomprehensible vastness of the physical universes – thus permitting us our material home – is actually severe, objective and impartial in its outworking. And therefore cannot possibly be equated with the weak, emotional, earthly caricature that we have produced in the human rendition of the words *love* and *aroha*.

*   *   *   *   *

Perhaps the best kind of example to illustrate this premise is in the area of personal relationships, particularly in the search for a marriage partner. The emotional damage wrought largely by Hollywood's image-makers, coupled with the belief that pre-marital sex is necessary to determine whether two people will be 'suited' to a life together, has generated the ludicrous and almost farcical situation where 'shopping around to sample the goods' is believed to hold the key to a 'perfect marriage of true love'. Basically, in such situations, the concept of love is therewith reduced to the idea that it must surely be present in the intense feelings and emotions experienced with the 'best sexual partner'. Whilst such an encounter may certainly provide very powerful feelings of intense emotion, acceptance, and feeling good about oneself and that partner, it is not likely to be *true love*.[24]

In any case, if all such experimentation actually produced true love, we would surely not have our current, high divorce rate.[25] Moreover, one would never know whether the *next* potential partner would be 'better' than the 'present *true* love'. This current societal attitude promotes views such as that recommended by Kathleen Quinlivan, a Canterbury University sexual researcher who proposed that students:

> "...regardless of their sexual orientation...", should be allowed "...to explore a range of sexual identities and their implications."

One would have thought that any individual would have the free-will right to do so in any case. One does not need a University graduate to state a fundamental personal right to experiment and make a particular choice.

In her view it was important to recognise:

> "...the diversity and differences which existed within communities..." which would benefit "...gay, lesbian, bisexual and heterosexual youth alike."

What is interesting in this case is that such views pressurise youth into possibly believing that the average boy/girl relationship – which, by the way, is the only kind that will

---

[24]Interestingly, evidence suggests that in more simple and basic societies where "arranged marriages" are the norm, there appears to be a higher level of marriage fidelity, faithfulness and loyalty than that present in our so-called sophisticated, western cultures. Perhaps the key word here is responsibility, with duty as a close adjunct. We do not, however, advocate the 'arranged marriage' as the perfect solution, for personal free will should *always* determine the choice of a partner.

[25]Notwithstanding the societal stability that long-term marriages offer, we should nevertheless understand that some unions are meant for a particular time only. When such a union has run its ordained course, there is little to be gained in 'forcing' a continuation of it.

naturally produce offspring – might somehow be flawed. And that the impressionable young must therefore be able to 'chop and change' to suit prevailing 'liberating expectations'. The ultimate horror in the present climate of inane 'political correctness' is, of course, to be labelled homophobic or something similar.

As the Reverend Gerald Hadlow, an Anglican minister, stated so succinctly in the title of his Herald article back on 25th April 1997 on precisely this subject: "Perhaps one day our youth will rediscover love, commitment."

From the spiritual standpoint, we are not *the least bit interested* with any individual's personal choice – *in anything*! What we have continually stated throughout the pages of this book is that the inviolable outworking of The Spiritual Laws is absolute – *for every decision made*.

For the *purposes* of *this* particular discussion, then: **If** The Laws contained in The Bible, for example, *are* absolute, then the *kinds of advice* promoted by Kathleen Quinlivan for young people to 'liberate' themselves *from* the *so-called* 'debilitating constraints of homophobic views' are, in reality, nothing more than an advocacy of unnecessary and potentially dangerous experimentation. It is a view driven by the foolish emotionalism contained in the current 'my rights' mindset. Why?

> Because under the *ultimate and non-negotiable* parameters of **Spiritual Law**, any actual *'debilitating constraint'* is, *by extension*, then **actually present** in all so-called 'liberating sexual practices'. And therefore also in sexual orientation preferences *different* to that which **The Eternal Laws** decree as being *spiritually correct*.

So the actual *'debilitating constraint'* here is brought about simply by shackling oneself *to completely incorrect beliefs*.

In any case what social scientists determine for themselves and Western societies is rendered totally *irrelevant* by the sacrosanct nature of **Spiritual Law**! For whatever choices we make will bring the reciprocal return; without fail. That is the inviolable outworking of **The Law of Reciprocal Action** operating in the lives of each of us. Therefore, the belief that one can somehow become *spiritually-liberated* by choosing a sexual preference which *does not* encompass the man/woman union is, in a word, **wrong**! Whilst our explanations may not fit at all with present societal mores, it is nevertheless especially important for young people to know that the age-old boy/girl relationship which brings more boys and girls onto the earth, is not only *perfectly okay*, but flows unequivocally with **The Eternal Laws**!

*   *   *   *   *

Special Note

To more strongly anchor the spiritual/physical meaning of the man/woman relationship, and irrespective of why two people might enter into such a union, it is surely crucially-important to know the true foundation upon which meaningful relationships *should be established* and/or continued with.

To that end: We have learned that the human being in Creation is designated as a 'whole species'. However, in our respective genders, we are 'split'. As we further know, inherent within all 'split species' is the desire to seek *union* with its *complement* for 'connection or completion'. In our human case, we invariably understand that 'sexual intimacy' is the fullest expression of such a union. [Marriages are not considered consummated until sexual intercourse has occurred.] Now, because the act *is ordained to be naturally pleasurable* – otherwise there would not be well over six thousand million humans now present on earth, never mind the greater number that could have been – it permits us to give and receive in the most intimate and loving way.

Nonetheless, we are all very much aware that within man/woman relationships, societies record inordinate amounts of jealousy, anger, infidelity, violence, grievous assault and murder. Clearly, such terrible statistics reveal *the serious emotional difficulties* that can and do plague human unions. This, of course, should not be the case. However, the world reels under the insidious pressure of a multi-billion dollar global industry that promotes sex and more sex in all its forms, both natural and deviant. In 2011 for the first time, the introduction of **high-resolution 3D** pornographic movies available for down-streaming to billions of global digital 'receivers'. The drug companies add their billion-dollar earnings contribution as well. What hope for the *average* human to be just *normal?*

The question should thus be asked:

"Why do humans constantly seek greater and greater pleasure in an act that is inherently and naturally extremely pleasurable in the first place?"

Very clearly, global humanity is foolishly-compromised here, for **The Law of Balance** is seriously transgressed; never mind **The Iron Law of Karma** – [**The Law of Reciprocal Action**.

The saying: *"Soothe the savage beast."*; can be readily-applied to the effect that fulfilling sex can have on the human male particularly, i.e., the incredible *healing* aspect. Most women will surely understand and have experienced many times this exact effect which *their giving* has on their partner. **Marvin Gaye**, Motown superstar and one of the most prolific songwriters ever [over 4,000 compositions], during an interview stated that he wrote *primarily* about love – because love is the one thing that endures. The title and lyrics of one of his compositions must have struck a chord with very many, for it was a chart-topper. It was simply called: **"Sexual Healing"**.

Sexual research has long documented the many health and psychological benefits of the act – *not that the average man or woman needed to be told that.* But it is not just the physical or mental aspects of the total person that benefits thus. Fulfilling sexual intimacy at the *right time* with the *right partner* and for the *right reason* – *as Spiritual Law decrees* – brings with it the most valuable gift of all; an harmonious and *healing* radiation/connection.

So, *for men*: We should understand that when women *give* intimacy, they really give *all* of themselves. For, quite obviously, they are the *receivers* – of the *male aspect*. From the higher, ennobled perspective, therefore, we are thus honoured by that *especial giving*. Here, however, we are only discussing true and *genuine giving*, where, *at the very least*, there is *some* degree of harmony and mutual liking present. Of course, if *genuine love* is the bond, then intimacy is *elevated* to its proper place.

[Financially-transacted agreements, prostitution, deals of any sort, opportunistic lustful encounters, drug or alcohol-initiated intimacy clearly-obviously *cannot possibly give ennoblement* to the most intimate act that a man and a woman can experience.]

So if we are ever to *truly understand* what this incredibly powerful force is *really for* and how we should *use it correctly*, we need to have *precise knowledge* of the connection, process and outcome. And that is: **The Spiritual Knowledge!**

In terms of the 'ennobled-aspect' of sexual intimacy, then: From out of the Highest **Knowledge-source** ever brought *down* to the earth, we herewith itemise the *primary* considerations. It is *precisely* that **Knowledge-source**, moreover, from which the explanations herein are derived and to which **this whole Work points**.

1. Just as the needs of the physical body of food, rest, sleep, exercise and bodily elimination in their turn etc., must be satisfied, so should the natural desire for sexual intimacy. To struggle *against* the *natural* instincts is unhealthy.

2. Fulfilling the natural desire of the body can only *further*, not hinder, the *development* of the *spirit* in the inner [man/woman]; otherwise The Creator would not have placed this desire within us.

3. As with all activities, excesses are harmful. **The Law of Spiritual Balance** must therefore be heeded here too.

4. The *human/material aspect* decrees that the act be undertaken with a fully matured and healthy body; not one *artificially* stimulated.

5. The *spiritual aspect*, in necessary concert, decrees thus: That it should only occur; *'...when perfect spiritual harmony has existed between both sexes. And in its consummation, therefore, sometimes strives towards physical union as well'.*

6. So, in a clarifying encapsulation: **'Physical union not only serves to procreate, but from it is furthered the equally valuable and necessary process of an intimate fusion [an inner blending] and a mutual exchange of vibrations, thus producing higher spiritual power.'**

*   *   *   *   *

Therein lies the power, purpose, beauty, love and pleasure in the sexual intimacy between man and woman! And therein, also, will be found the great and necessary: **Spiritual Virtue of Trust!**

Liberal ideas such as we have examined in this overall segment, anchored primarily in the intellectually-derived 'Human Rights' mentality now solidly entrenched in mainstream Western thinking, have found their final end-excrescence enacted in the earthly legislative law of many countries. In 'earthly law' where 'voiced opposition' to such laws can, in certain circumstances, be *perversely deemed* an actual 'criminal' offence.

Dr Alan Duggan, an Australian researcher into men's health, stated to an Auckland Unitec seminar on 'Men's Health' that anecdotal evidence from studies carried out in Canada and Australia suggest that young male suicide statistics may lean as much as *30 per cent* to more suicides 'among homosexual men than straight men'. From that line of research alone, one can see that the higher suicide rate amongst this group does not indicate any kind of 'liberation' at all – rather the opposite. Dr Duggan opined that the research results pointed to a *'sexual orientation/identity crisis'* in this group.

Once again, and purely for the purposes of this discussion, *if* "The Spiritual Laws of Creation" are not believed to be absolute or not believed to exist at all, then *disbelievers* should simply continue to live on in their *disbelief*, particularly of the effects of **The Law of Reciprocal Action** visiting any hard affliction upon them. In all cases, under the aegis and increased power inherent in the "whirlwind constant".

> Do not then, however, apportion blame elsewhere if personal decisions and de-
> sires should visit return effects *vastly different* to what one might have wished
> for – before the fact.

In any case, it must eventually 'all come out in the wash' one way or the other. As
stressed a number of times in this Work, The Spiritual Laws cannot be transgressed with
impunity – either by any one person or any so-called *'liberated group'*.

From **our** free-will viewpoint, we really are all free to choose our particular likes, but
we nonetheless affirm that those same decisions are most certainly *not* free of *the spiritual
consequences*. Thus, whilst it is everyone's personal right to so choose, have the **kaha**
to then *accept* the reciprocal effect of those decisions and do not expect that all others
must agree with, or even approve of, any particular choice of sexual orientation. Despite
possible disapproval or even revulsion toward certain choices and/or practices, however,
such choices nevertheless ultimately remain the preserve of the 'choosers' and should at
least be *respected* as that by all others.

The Book of Leviticus provides interesting reading in this regard. One's personal views
– or perhaps sexual orientation choice – would probably engender one of two reactions
when examining this particular Book of The Bible; a strong or perhaps angry emotional
one, or more relaxed acceptance. Regardless of individual views, however, and even though
perhaps more addressing the Priesthood from the Tribe of Levi, 'Leviticus' nevertheless
provides a valuable insight and guide for more correct *spiritual living* than current so-
called 'liberating' views are probably prepared to accept.

For example, Verses 6-29 of Chapter 18 of **'Leviticus'** are sub-headed:

The Laws of Affinity, and Marriages and Sex.

The most interesting aspect of those twenty three Scriptural Verses is that they are the
cultural/social and moral foundation of *most* societies, cultures and religions globally. So
why should that be the case? Historically, why have non-Christian societies also regarded
these 'Rules for Life' as fundamental for their social stability too? Alluded to or written
about in other religious works, the detailed substance of the Sexual Laws in the face-
book of the Christian religion – The Bible – quite simply supplies the spiritual and moral
parameters for *correct* human living.

> The *natural* human/societal *repugnance* toward sexual involvement in practices such as pae-
> dophilia, incest and bestiality etc., clearly reveal that *abhorrence to activities which encom-
> pass the immoral and unnatural* is therefore *fundamentally inherent* in the psyche or spirit
> of human beings. Thus, to stand *outside* that 'inherent compass' means exactly that.

With regard to current views, and as previously noted, we can perhaps describe modern
man's general interpretation of love or *aroha* as little more than 'emotional self-indulgence'
which, when ostensibly expressing love toward another, too often means: **'I want *you*
to love me!'**

However, if the foundation for a union is a *genuine* spiritual bond in the first instance,
then we may more safely say that *true love* is probably present. Within such a partnership, moreover, all other factors – including that of sexual intimacy – will invariably be
emotionally and physically fulfilling also. And because the correct foundation of **The
Spiritual** was striven for first as the most important part of the union, it will naturally
have the greatest *potential* to be an harmonious one too.

Therefore genuine love or *aroha* will always be concerned with what ***spiritually benefits*** the other, and not necessarily with what might be personally gratifying or agreeable to him. Thus, the latter-day concept of 'tough love' for wayward teenagers owes its relative success to the fact that it 'flows' with the outworking of the Justice of Spiritual Law.

Because the application of *aroha* by many Maori to things *solely Maori* in the distorted use of this word reflects this lack of true understanding of the meaning of love contained within The Spiritual Laws, the admonition to "Love thy neighbour" and "Love your enemies" does not mean *giving them what they want* or what pleases them; a practice which many Maori deem to represent *true aroha*. It means only doing for them that which will benefit them *spiritually*. If it means possible hardship for them from *their* personal point of view, then that may actually be the correct kind of *aroha*. Otherwise how else can they learn, or grow?

> **To that end the spiritual explanations contained in this Work elucidates and expresses that 'new concept' in both its aroha *and* its severity, thus offering Love and Justice in Spiritual Knowledge!**

Maori must therefore find the strength to apply their concept of *aroha* in the right way if they wish to live spiritually-correctly. This means that *whanau* members should not demand what others may have worked hard for under an emotional-blackmail mode in a totally wrong and selfish use of the word. Misplaced indulgence would mean the continuation of the same faults in the *whanau* and, by subsequent extension, holding them within the race. The end result is that everyone continues to slide further on the downward path. That would not be displaying love. On the contrary, by acting thus one would place oneself in the position of not acting spiritually-correctly toward a fellow human being, even if of the *same race or family*. This different and radical view contrasts greatly with what we have too readily accepted thus far as true love.

With regard to the weak, Christian application of the word, love, we should note that Jesus, Himself, as a manual worker under Joseph the carpenter, would have been *physically strong* in the first instance. The fact that He was also obviously Spiritually-Powerful and not weak and vacillating, is clearly illustrated in the New Testament in His very severe admonitions to many people, *particularly to men of intellect*. His admonition to:

"Go and do thou likewise!"

– is clear testimony to His 'Loving severity' toward humankind. We should all once again similarly note His great *maia* and *aroha* in being *prepared to accept death on the Cross* – if that was the only way to convince humankind of The Truth He brought *down* to erring humankind on earth.

We should therefore regard love as a very real and consistent 'power' in which there will be found no weakness, or illogical or emotional indulgence. And further understand that we cannot place our personal transgressions upon any other person; especially not upon Jesus Who was then, and will forever be, the personification of Divine Love in all its Loving severity! Thus, every application of *aroha* by Maori should accurately reflect the true purpose and meaning of the word in being both Love and Justice if it is not to continue as an emotional tool for excuse and non-responsibility. Equally, Pakeha use of the word, *love*, must carry the same connotations wherever it is applied.

Thus: Love is a Power, not an emotion!

21.7.3   Spiritual Justice

With clear-cut recognitions of how The Law should be applied to offenders, Maori or Pakeha, **we arrive at the irrefutable spiritual fact that there really is: One justice for all!**

A flawless justice based on the immutable Spiritual Laws. Therefore, any attempt by individual Maori or by Maori self-interest groups to set in place separate *marae* justice could *only be viable* if the particular system was based *solely* on the foundation of Spiritual Law.

At various times there have been moves by a number of Maori Lawyers to establish a Maori Law Commission. Moreover, one spokesperson, Moana Jackson, has indicated that as well as for the general protection of Maori under present secular law and resolving disputes between Maori and the protection of intellectual property rights, it may also provide the foundation for 'separate Maori justice'. Such so-called 'Maori cultural reasoning' is simply nothing more than skewed logic.

*   *   *   *   *

In a relatively recent court case, a terribly-flawed judicial decision exactly highlighted such *unworkable notions*. It involved a so-called 'Maori/Pakeha' who caused '...grievous bodily harm to a Maori friend'. He claimed that being under the influence of a *makutu* was instrumental in why he committed the offence. The assault earned the 'makutu'd attacker' only a suspended sentence. In an insidious reflection of totally aspiritual 'legal stupidity', the presiding Pakeha judge bought into this nonsense and effectively discharged the 'manipulator'.

The Police were quite rightly very perplexed, and probably greatly concerned that similar instances might surface in the future with the same judicial outcome. Was a dangerous precedent set for other Maori to claim non-responsibility for their actions? How much longer will Maori 'priests', Maori 'leaders' and sympathising Pakeha, including members of the judiciary, continue with their *totally wrong and foolish beliefs* that these kinds of dark, insidious Maori practices are somehow okay or even highly spiritual, and therefore deserving of *special consideration*?

As previously stressed, whilst certain applications of *tapu* may offer some benefit at times, the deadly trinity of *tapu, makutu* and *utu* used in concert are not, and cannot *ever possibly be*, truly spiritual in belief, perception or application. It is time for Maori to wake up to the truth of this *dangerous delusion*. As we have minutely detailed, it is a delusion that is greatly contributing to 'alarming levels' of 'Maori readmission rates' to mental institutions!

*   *   *   *   *

Therefore, it is our contention that any move to ratify such an insidious process posing as the only true and viable mechanism of justice for this country; i.e., that formulated solely on Maori 'Customary Law' or *marae*-based ideas, would be absolutely wrong. For it would reveal Maori as possessing an unfortunate attitude of arrogance by stating that their own are different from every other, and that a separate form of justice should reign supreme in Aotearoa. And it would reveal Pakeha politicians and legislators who bought into this warped nonsense-concept as being foolishly gullible. It would produce a form of justice which only accords with the current, distorted view of emotionally self-indulgent *aroha* under the completely incorrect and clearly entrenched mind-set that seeks to place 'customary law' first.

It is a dangerous, potential precedent since only **Spiritual Law**, and not any other, **actually reigns supreme**. **Spiritual Law**, alone, is therefore the yardstick by which all man-made law must be formulated and/or measured against!

Yet, notwithstanding the above truth, a four-year Government-funded project was launched with the aim of "...changing New Zealand's court system and other institutions to better reflect society's bicultural nature". In the view of Chief Judge Eddie Durie, then head of the Waitangi Tribunal, the project [was] "...a decade overdue." It was headed by the former head of the Youth Court, Judge Mick Brown, who offered the interesting comment that:

> "It is part of our maturation as a nation – that we look at the way we do things ourselves instead of relying on an imported Anglo-Saxon system."

He further stated:

> "I will be looking at the idea that law, therefore the legal system and political institutions, should shape and mirror the values of society and cultural approaches to concepts like ownership and social obligations."

Judge Brown also noted that many ideas of how society could be made more bicultural had been considered, *such as a separate legal system for Maori*. This project and its avowed aim must surely beg the question:

> "For what purpose should our society be made *more* bicultural?"

Any changes should mirror spiritual values under Spiritual Law and not any more flawed societal and cultural approaches. Society is already very obviously bicultural anyway, and there is no problem in that. So why begin a process that *may* bring in its train the demand for absolute separatism when there is absolutely no need to do so? And who would separate out from whom? Since, according to Spiritual Law, most New Zealanders are *tangata whenua*, and of diverse racial mixes anyway, it really does seem to be one more example of 'cultural sensitivity'. Unfortunately, however, it is an ostensibly extreme one in its damaging potential, yet sanctioned by the Government of the day.

Therefore, we should seriously question the thinking behind Maori 'aspirations' in this case. Quite clearly, if greater biculturalism equals a greater possibility for a separate legal system, which, in turn, has the same potential for separate development, then the stage could well be set for 'apartheid'. Of course, we may play with words and say it is not so. Perhaps we could use the term *tinorangatiratanga* – sovereignty. Would the actual meaning and end-effect be any different? For even according to the most basic pocket dictionary, apartheid means a system:

"...for keeping different races separate"; or "...any policy of separating groups".

The curious thing about such views is that the proponents of it do not seem to *want* to understand that if it were the Pakeha who were advocating the idea, it would be immediately condemned outright in strongest indignation by virtually all Maori as *exactly* apartheid. Moreover, there would no doubt be a huge and concerted rush to take it to the Privy Council, United Nations or the World Court under the umbrella of trammelling human or indigenous 'rights'. But because it is strongly promoted by Maori, who are ostensibly the 'only' *tangata whenua* of Aotearoa, the supposed validity and/or right of it must not be questioned. Such an attitude actually stands as *hypocrisy*!

Quite clearly the Courts do not always deliver true justice. The answer, however, is not to set in place mechanisms for potentially more divisiveness. If there is to be a study of Law to bring about the most effective model for good justice, why do the 'supposedly learned' not study **"The Spiritual Laws of Creation"**? For *only within them* do all answers reside. With the present system ultimately failing *both* Pakeha and Maori, let us formulate a correct one based on the knowledge of those very Spiritual Laws which we now have. And which will not fail by virtue of being founded on the immutable and inviolable justice of *exactly* those Eternal Laws. Then there will be Laws which can correctly apply justice for all races in this land without the need for separate systems dictated by the politically and emotionally-generated foolishness of 'cultural-correctness'!

In the interim, however, where Maori ideas for justice accord with these Laws, *they should be retained*, and similarly so with *Pakeha ideas*. Conversely, where *both groups* harbour *wrong perceptions* in terms of true justice, such ideas must be *discarded* as soon as a more equitable formulation of justice application can be legislated for with regard to the particular issues.

The generally 'softer' approach of Maori toward offenders must be tempered by the stricter line usually employed by Europeans. And our particular European method, which has produced a relatively efficient system of court procedure, should perhaps dispense justice more according to the 'spirit' of the Law rather than the cold 'letter' of the Law, which sometimes 'appears' to be the overriding concern. However, with correctly formulated Laws understood by all, this would not then be the case and all offenders would be under no illusion as to what was expected of *them*.

Therefore, the idea of Maori *Marae* justice *separated from* Pakeha justice **is wrong**. Only the application of the true Laws of Justice from out of The Spiritual Laws are acceptable – for all men. In truth, all transgressions, whether by black, brown, yellow or white, carry equal spiritual responsibility under these unchangeable and Perfect Laws. Of course, whether that same justice is applied on the *Marae* or in the Courts should not matter so long as the same process is adhered to and the appropriate level of respect is accorded to both venues to reflect the seriousness of the occasion and the recognition of **The Source of True Law**.

> The key considerations, then, should be greater concern for the *victim* on the part of the Court and the offender, yet also *true justice tempered with compassion*. Not, however, *emotionalism in condemnation* toward the offender.

The present marae-based initiatives setting up rehabilitation programmes for released inmates by Maori interest groups and *Iwi* are clearly very commendable. Unfortunately, however, they rarely address the cause, only the end-effect. What is needed *long before that point is reached* is a programme to prevent so many Maori from ending up in prisons in the first place. Otherwise it is simply a classic case of:
"...shutting the stable door after the horse has bolted".

In truth, it should begin with correct *aroha* and discipline from the earliest age, rather than societal punishment in later life. Treat the fundamental cause, firstly, and then the early symptoms – and there will be far less requirement for later-life rehabilitation and/or anguish. However, because we *are* mainly treating the unfortunate end-effects, how should we then treat an offender 'within our justice system' so that it accords *with* Spiritual Law?

Firstly, an offender should be under no illusions as to the fact that he, and no other, was the transgressor. And solely because of a personal, free-will choice to so offend. All other considerations such as anger, alcohol, drugs, or even temporary emotional instability, do not alter that initial, personal-choice position. The appropriate saying: "If you can't do the time, don't do the crime", clearly reflects what should be a common-sense choice in the first place. Only genuine insanity, where the entity is actually not in control of itself, can be offered as a reason for a transgression not being under a free-will-choice situation.

Should the offender show unquestionable remorse for his deed and *genuinely* seeks to atone and change his ways, then all help should be given, whilst serving his sentence, to prepare him for eventual release – but only if there is the genuine wish to reform. He should also be *separated* from those who choose *not to change*; from those who refuse to make any kind of commitment to seek self-improvement.

They should be left to mix among themselves, with the more vicious and intractable to not even be *considered* for release until such time as a genuine commitment to change is received. Whilst this may seem a harsh punishment, society has the right to be protected from those who would seek to trample upon the lives of law-abiding citizens in violence and depravity and who signal their clear intention to remain at variance with societal law. Moreover, those who are incarcerated for crimes of violence should be under no illusion that unless **they personally choose to genuinely change**, their lives will eventually end in incarceration away from family and friends. That should be the incentive and reality to induce the possibility of a change of heart in even the most hardened criminals. Mechanisms to *induce* change should, however, still be offered as a trial for this particular group.

It is interesting, but nonetheless refreshing, that of all books prisoners have access to, The Bible is regularly sought by those behind prison walls. The Bible Society reported a huge rise in the number of Bibles it sends to prisons after requests from prison Chaplains. This interest has been attributed to their proactive approach and an encouraging attitude from the Department of Corrections.

21.8   The Youth Problem and Gangs

Gangs! A global problem in many of the mainly larger cities. In the case of 'youth gangs' in Western societies, however, generally incorporating a particular ethos strongly deriving from the worst excrescence of so-called 'American culture' – 'rap' that promotes anti-social violence and hatred.

So why do particular groups of people gravitate together to subsequently 'form' a gang in the first place? What conditions and/or 'forces' primarily contribute to their formation? Uncountable numbers of books, 'papers', theses and articles have been written and/or published by sociologists, educationalists and all manner of 'experts' for decades now. Yet no real answers or solutions are produced by this 'learned group', for the problem continues to worsen.

The same and ongoing litany of reasons and excuses flood newspapers and TV screens whenever gang activity makes 'headlines'; lower socio-economic status, exposure to violence in childhood, societal deprivation and so on. Agencies, groups and Trusts abound, all swallowing up millions of dollars to try to rectify the problem and 'turn things around'. Police resources are stretched to breaking point. Ordinary citizens march in their thousands demanding action until, finally, some vulnerable targeted groups threaten vigilante-justice for simple self-protection.

If we examine all the different players in this societal reality of the moment, we will notice a most interesting yet defining aspect of the **human** make up of all parties involved: The gangs to begin with; the agencies tasked to help or stop the problem; the politicians who legislate; the law-enforcement bodies; the various churches and religious groups that play their part; and, not least, the 'experts' previously mentioned.

Notwithstanding the good intentions and obvious desire by all 'helping groups' to rid society of gangs to produce 'the better way', what is *not at all present* in the 'good intentions' of so many diverse groups is the *one single catalyst* which could *begin* the process of change. The very fact that those numerous and diverse groups derive from so many different racial, ethnic, traditional, cultural/educational and religious backgrounds is actually *part of the problem*. Such huge diversity quite logically means that *from the outset* there will *already* be seriously-conflicting views on *how* to tackle the issue.

And there, in a nutshell, lies the fundamental problem!

Without the *one single unifying aspect* that *can* wring change, all we will continue to see is the same that has gone before: Constant lamentations, meetings, marches, anger, frustration, finger-pointing and blame-apportioning etc., – and all the while the problem worsens.

So where, exactly, do we find the answer?

That singular answer lies in the very first place – for all parties and groups who wish to bring about genuine societal change – in the *recognition, understanding and application* of: –

The SPIRITUAL LAWS of CREATION

– clearly explained in **Chapter 6**, and to which we have constantly drawn attention! In this case, primarily **The Law of Attraction of Similar Species**! So *irrespective* of the marked diversity of cultural, racial and religious make-up of all societal groups seeking change, **you must all first accept** the *singular Lawful-reality* of **The ONE-LAW**. So: Once more in very necessary repetitive-reinforcement:

> "The completely wrong *foundation* in education is the *beginning and end* of this and *every other* societal problem. And a spiritually-weak and uninformed society will seed and grow anti-societal gangs. The **"Law of Attraction..."** thus being a constant in all of **Creation** means that here on earth it drives the process of incarnation of certain groups of human beings into particular geographical locations and countries, cities and suburbs, and thus to their prospective parents. So this powerful and immutable Law, in direct concert with **The Law of Reciprocal Action**, is what must be recognised, accepted and taught – *or nothing changes*!"

(Author.)

The immutable outworking of **The Spiritual Laws** decree, therefore, that is not *solely* the wish for brotherhood or group identity that drives the formation of gangs. It is the *outworking* of **The Spiritual Law of Attraction...** that is the *main directing-force* here. This means that in terms of the make-up of gangs, *the same kinds of souls* will always be attracted together. That is **THE LAW**, and no one can change it. In a *voluntary-choice* situation the *same* Spiritual Law brings similar kinds of people into any Police Force and into the different branches of the Armed Forces as well. Maori gang members are together *precisely because of* that powerful and inviolable **Spiritual Law**.

The unstoppable effect of **The Law of Attraction of Similar Species** ensures that *the same kinds of people* are attracted to each other, though not necessarily in common harmony. Thus, irrespective of whether a gang is an Asian one in Hong Kong or Shanghai, a group of Latinos in Los Angeles, Russian Mafia in Moscow, Neo-Nazis in Dresden, a Maori gang in South Auckland or a white supremacy group in Christchurch, it is the *force* inherent in this **Law of Attraction...** that brings gangs into existence all over the world.

Even if societal factors such as we have previously noted should nonetheless *contribute* to the formation of a gang, why do not *all* residents of particular suburbs afflicted with poorer societal status ostensibly leading to gang formation also become gang members too? The fact is that the unstoppable and immutable effect of this **key Law** means that there are many gradations of it. And that is why chapters and sub-chapters will still form under the overall umbrella of the main gang grouping, yet sometimes with a very different 'signature behaviour'. So some chapters will reveal more vicious traits than other sub-groups.

Since incarceration seems to be inevitable for most or at least many gang members, is there anything society can do to lessen the numbers filling our jails before that point need be reached? Most emphatically, yes! The cult of non-responsibility, fostered by the enactment of incorrect Laws to begin with, inculcates a wrong attitude in the young – from where our future criminals will quite obviously come. Virtually every social ill stems from this *one inescapable fact.* Incorrect Laws based on liberal ideas rather than on spiritual protection and justice for all, including the young, positively breed dishonest attitudes in this group. No society can formulate its social laws without their foundation being **The Spiritual Laws** and expect that they will produce good results. That is a foolish and arrogant fallacy!

> **That is precisely why societies, globally, are failing to halt or even *slow* increases in violent crime.**

The formulation of wrong kinds of laws ensures that we follow trends established in other countries where increasingly younger criminals, both male and female, are committing more crime and displaying more vicious traits. Now in New Zealand we have murders for petty theft or 'kicks' by gangs of youthful *cowards* with no moral or social conscience. If young people are not held responsible for even minor social transgressions, let alone criminal ones, how can they possibly develop the necessary discernment for a sense of right or wrong if society itself will not provide the *right kind* of direction or *discipline.*

Recent headlines proclaiming that 'Police are to be based fulltime in schools' is stark evidence that the current laws and education system simply do not work. It was not so long ago that we 'older kiwis' laughed when we learned that American schools were forced to hire armed security guards to police student activities there.

"That will never happen here", we sniggered, in our foolish, smug superiority.

News item out of America, 'land of the free', August, 2008:

'Some Texas schools have given permission for teachers to carry guns in class.'

When will we finally learn this simple but potentially frightening reality:

> **That each year which passes, quite naturally and logically, prepares the foundation for the next!**

Go back in time five years, ten years, twenty: Were levels of vicious crime as rampant as they are now? Of course not. Now go forward just two years, then five, then ten: If we continue on the present direction we may eventually see *vigilante-style justice by ordinary citizens* simply wanting to protect themselves from the increasingly younger and bolder 'thug element' *we now nurture.*

> For if lawmakers and law 'enforcers' will not fully protect those they are charged to, *then it is both **the spiritual duty and responsibility of all law-abiding citizens** to ensure they are not shackled by weak societal law and/or held hostage in any way whatsoever by lawless elements within society.*

As a society and an independent Nation in our own right, we have long accepted that fighting and accepting sacrifice in wars to preserve freedom/s is always *the right way.* Is that any different in principle to *fighting and neutralising gutless cowards* to preserve the same on home turf, and thus protect the old, infirm and vulnerable in our very midst?

Perhaps applying more to war, the following great and truthful *whakatouki* nonetheless resonates equally truthfully in suburban and rural New Zealand.

"Evil can only flourish when good men stand by and do nothing!"

Let us not be deluded about the behaviour and even *volition* of much of today's youth. The time for regarding certain kinds of behaviour as just youthful hi-jinks has long gone. The *unseen* 'forms' and 'forces' that 'group organisms' such as youth gangs especially attract are not at all benign. In most cases they are evil, thus dangerous to all, so must be stamped out – very severely if need be. The outworking of **The Law of Attraction of Similar Species**, in concert with the rapidly-increasing spiritual pressure inexorably driving all directions to their final end, means that the direction of youth crime *will only grow and worsen* unless 'smashed out of existence'.

In city suburbs where youth-gang activity threatens the peace and safety of residents therein, the recent and successful British initiative of 'social capital' should be studied. Initiated by just one determined woman in one of the notorious 'housing estates' which define certain British cities, the concept *firstly* involves *all* of the residents within taking a *concerted stand* against the terrorism and thuggery of young, primarily gutless, pack-mentality thugs. In short, *taking them on.* Because of the determination of the residents in this case, Council and Police – with Government backing – subsequently played a greater assistance-role than they otherwise would have.

Residents of suburbs in this country who suffer under the tyranny of 'gutless youth-gangs' should consider emulating the initiative of that English woman and the residents of 'their' estate. For they showed courage in refusing to be intimated and achieved what the Police and Council, combined, for years could not; a safe, secure and peaceful haven: **Because they finally stood up and fought!** Parents of troublemakers were identified. If they did not 'shape up', they were simply 'shipped-out'. End of problem for the law-abiding there who simply sought a safe, family environment.

> Over-indulgent parents who seek to *over-protect* their 'precious' young and vicious 'pseudo-adult offspring' from the *righteous wrath* of their victims or from the more law-abiding of society in this land should also be *especially targeted.* Their fawning and almost sycophantic over-emotional and over-weening *aroha-attachment* to their, obviously-wayward, blood-offspring is both *tiresome and sickening.* We all see this reality played out *nauseatingly-regularly* in front of TV cameras outside Judicial establishments all over the country.

Such parents are one of the "greatest hindrances" to any chance of <u>real</u> societal change, <u>for they protect wrongly.</u>

Invariably displaying arrogant indignation when confronted with transgressions of *their* offspring, these kinds of 'spiritually-irresponsible parents' immediately screech demands that their "child's rights" be placed first and foremost. Very rarely in this unfortunately quite large and growing group now would we hear of *their* 'parental responsibilities'.

In this sub-Chapter we primarily examine the problem of youth gangs. Yet there is another kind of 'gang-organism' that is just as non law-abiding and socially-disruptive, which displays the same kinds of arrogant, drunken and unruly behaviour with sometimes violent outcomes – and congregate in *much larger* group-organisms than the street gangs. Moreover, they are those who *consider themselves* the future business, social and even political leaders of New Zealand: The 'student-body' which holds sway at certain, well-known, Universities.

Despite the fact that their anti-social behaviour is usually focussed on particular times and activities during the student year, should their 'seemingly-studious' behaviour apparently most of that time be a reason to perhaps accept, excuse or gloss over the increasingly anti-social episodes which in recent times has broken out into drunken, orgiastic violence against ordinary members of the public, the Police and Fire Service? I, for one, think not! Aspiring to a meaningful place in any society carries with it certain 'spiritual' responsibilities right from the outset. Students and student-organisations that collectively indulge in activities such as we have noted here clearly do not measure up to that level of responsibility, for the **Spiritual Virtue** of **Nobleness**, which would ordinarily accompany **Spiritual Responsibility** and **Accountability**, is non-existent.

If society chooses to base its direction on notions akin to overly-free libertarianism – which actually undermines and thus devalues tried and proven ideals thereby weakening society – then *the whole societal direction* continues on its downwards-slide. We in the West, and certainly here in New Zealand, have become ***weak and gutless***. Societal Law, *such as it is*, is no longer respected because it is not enforced correctly or strongly enough. Mostly, however, because it is human-formulated:

Thus without the Power, Justice and Clarity of Spiritual Law!

Former Judge, Ken Richardson, commenting at his retirement on what he regards as the decay in community standards, had this to say.

> "There seems today to be a lack of respect for authority and the ordinary rights of people and their property."

He also said:

> "Young people need incentive. Without it they drift aimlessly into crime, often simply through peer pressure. This is one of the tragedies of life and as a judge I have great sympathy for many who appear before me through circumstances beyond their control."

Yet young people, even from the earliest age, must understand that they also need to "obey the rules". To this end, we need to get rid of this *totally incorrect and quite foolish belief* that *children* should be treated as *adults*.

That is spiritually wrong and totally irresponsible.

Children must remain children until such time as they become 'spiritually responsible' for their own decisions. This point occurs at about the mid-teens. Until then they simply cannot possess the same level of spiritual discernment as adults by virtue of the fact that the immutable and inviolable outworking of Spiritual Law does not act upon them in the same decisive way as it does on adults. However, this does not mean that they should not be held accountable for their actions. They most certainly should! The only difference is that their actions and decisions may not be impacted to the same degree by **The Law of Reciprocal Action** as is the case with all from young adulthood onwards.

Young people must therefore accept that immutable **Law of Reciprocal Action** in their lives. And it is the responsibility of adults to ensure that this is clearly understood and applied. Therefore, all young persons should be held fully responsible for *all* that they do so that the cult of 'non-responsibility', which proliferates to an alarming degree by virtue of society's liberalism, does not one day degenerate into anarchy. The first steps toward this possibility were set in place with the formulation of the "Children's and Young Persons Act" – *in direct contravention of The Eternal Laws* – by well-meaning but uninformed politicians and 'social advisers'.

To allow young persons the insidious and dangerous luxury of non-responsibility for even minor misdeeds is a grossly irresponsible act. The foolishly-paradoxical result is that it actually does not help this target group in any way whatsoever. In 2008 the same foolish political ideology sought to *lessen* personal responsibility in this group.

To be virtually told by the Laws of the land that one cannot be touched because of one's age sends a clear signal to that particular age group that they are immune from any form of discipline. Judge Richardson further noted that:

> "...the sophistication of young people today warrants a review of protections in the Children's and Young Persons Act. There was a time when murders and rapes by 13 and 14 year olds were very rare and today they are not. There are some youths who know that on account of their age the courts are hamstrung."

Moreover, he rightly questions, as we do, whether the moral pendulum has swung too far and advocates a return to old-fashioned family values.

> "If I'm outdated and conservative then I am proud to be so and I make no apologies."

That is a view with which we absolutely and unequivocally concur! We applaud Judge Richardson's stand, but did the politicians heed his call derived from long experience?

The answer to increasing crime levels appears to lie in what American crime-fighters have called a 'broken windows' policy. This states that a single:

> "...unrepaired broken window will, in time, produce a building of broken windows; a suburb that does not deal with graffiti will soon be smothered with it; a community which chooses not to worry about minor crime will eventually find itself overcome with major crime."

In New York it is called "zero tolerance". Results from that city at the time were impressive – "...murder down 35 percent; armed robbery down 42 percent." British trials were just as successful in reducing crime there and Tony Blair established the concept throughout Britain.

A *genuine* 'zero tolerance' policy here might go a long way toward changing arrogant, untouchable attitudes amongst the young. As one Herald Editorial wistfully stated:

> "It's time to get *minor* crime back on the front pages."

And thus hopefully produce a return to *genuine values* that Judge Richardson and many other citizens of Aotearoa would dearly like to see again. Such a policy, however, requires sufficient numbers of Police to make it work. In the present political climate, however, that translates to an assault on flawed economic philosophies of profit-generation and/or simplistic cost-cutting, irrespective of social need.

Interestingly, Margaret Bazley, the Director-General of Social Welfare in 1996, stated then that:

> "...the Children, Young Persons and Their Families Service led the way internationally and its achievements in dealing with youth crime should be celebrated."

If Margaret Bazley infers that the Act is a good one and was the reason for her praise, then that appears to be a quite different view to that of Judge Richardson whose experience with the Children's and Young Persons Act in 26 years on the bench was in one of the country's most notorious areas – South Auckland. Margaret Bazley could never ever accumulate that kind of experience in political Wellington.

Is it any wonder that so many of our Police and social workers are burning out or leaving their respective services in record numbers through sheer frustration at this incredibly unhealthy state of affairs? The short answer, obviously, is no. What we have is a recipe for a greater social disaster in the near future. It is a time-bomb waiting to explode if it is not correctly addressed, and soon. And what about the increasing number of trouble-makers in schools now? How will the authorities 'sort them out' and change the ethos of 'stupid-cool' which helps breed the increase?

Even something so seemingly innocuous as 'tagging' *should have been nipped in the bud when it first appeared*, instead of procrastinating about it and allowing it to become the visual blight that it now is.[26]

In November 2005 Las Vegas Mayor, Oscar Goodman, vented his frustration at 'taggers' when he publicly declared:

> "...people who deface freeways with graffiti should have their thumbs cut off on TV." The city (Las Vegas) has a beautiful landscaping project and "...these punks come along and deface it."

Whilst perhaps considered an extreme view, the good Mayor simply voiced what many people *would probably like to see happen*. Cutting the thumbs off graffiti clowns would certainly make it more difficult to hold a spray can. It might also deter others from that particular 'career path'.

If those responsible were made to physically scrub their polluting marks off targeted walls, there would be much less of it. Moreover, we would be doing the offenders a favour by instilling in them the clear message that transgressions against the peace and harmony that society is entitled to, in every aspect, will not be tolerated. From small and unaddressed transgressions can easily and quickly develop more blatantly aggressive behaviour – which we currently see.

Who now remembers the furore that even Bill Clinton was forced to publicly comment on while U.S. President when a young American male in Singapore broke the rules there and earned himself the punishment of caning? Thankfully for *no-nonsense justice*, the Singaporean authorities were not swayed by global opinion and carried out the 'lawful sentence'. That young man probably learned one of the most valuable lessons of his life

---

[26]In election year, 2008, after the killing of a tagger, tougher measures to combat graffiti have been proposed by Government. Will it work? We shall see.

and should go on to become a better citizen. For that is certainly the case with many thousands of men in this country who, as young boys, received the appropriate 'kick in the pants' or the 'cuff over the ear', or even a very firm whack at exactly the right time to stay on the 'straight and narrow'. Most of us will state – **because we know** – that it was *exactly the right thing at the right time*!

Now it is official. In these latter times where 'Air-heads' – that wonderfully-coined phrase by an Australian journalist and author – determine "spiritually-unworkable" Laws for everyone; the word, *discipline*, has been 'politically-hijacked' and insidiously replaced by the more emotive word – *violence*. So even the genuine love of many good and law-abiding parents who might need to apply necessarily-correct discipline toward their off-spring no longer has a place in New Zealand society. Ignorant politicians legislating for a particular kind of spiritually-weak political ideology – against the wishes of the greater number of citizens who really understood the deeper and insidious nature of that and similar kinds of legislation – nonetheless yet still arrogantly rode rough-shod over simple 'common-sense' to foist their 'misguided idealism' onto all in this Nation. Will we now see the young become increasingly more emboldened and begin to demand more and more from society for 'their rights ideology'?

All New Zealand politicians should be mandatorily-required to *seriously study* Professor David Fraser's book: *"A Land Fit For Criminals; an insider's view of crime, punishment and justice in the UK."* Herald journalist, Carroll du Chateau, [on 14.06.08] reported Professor Fraser noting that 'as an insider working for 34 years from the 1950's in British prisons, the Probation Service and Criminal Intelligence Service, paroled criminals returned to prison with depressing regularity while the streets, buses and trains grew steadily more dangerous'.

Lee Kuan Yew, founding father of Singapore, was so impressed by Britain's law-abiding culture that he copied it. Forty odd years on from Nationhood in 1965 – which many Kiwi Servicemen personally experienced – 'Singapore has achieved a relatively steady crime rate of 2000 per 100,000 people.' 'The British rate grew from 2000 (1950's) to more than 10,000 (1996) crimes per 100,000.'

Carroll du Chateau asks: "Why the discrepancy?"

'According to Fraser, "the Singapore Government made the pursuit of criminal lives unbearably hard, full of risks and totally without reward". 'Britain, on the other hand, created what he calls, "a country fit for criminals" by implementing sentencing policies driven by liberal ideology and cost-saving.'

The following *spiritually-correct* observation by Professor Fraser resonates with the overall thrust of this particular Chapter: 'The new regime was based on the theory that criminals are created by inequality (poor housing and poverty) rather than *bad behaviour*. They are in the grip of something like a mental disease rather than *calculating crooks*.'

(Italics mine.)

Yes! In the absolute and final analysis, to choose or not to choose to be a criminal *is exactly that*: **A personal choice!** Nothing more. All criminals – and certainly some very well-known lawyers – should finally get their heads around that unequivocal Truth and stop trying to fool themselves. And those clever, well-known lawyers? Stop your evil practice of using every nuance of 'legal technical-gymnastics' to set free criminal clients you know *have actually committed a crime*. What do you think you achieve by that? Apart from being considered 'clever' or legally astute by at least some of your 'same-ilk colleagues', what you also earn is the general contempt of ordinary citizens who can see through your machinations. For the average, common-sense 'Kiwi' really is imbued with a sense of true justice untainted by the exclusivity of the law profession's 'fashionable legalese'.

Professor Fraser's mission: "to preach the unfashionable message that prison is a good idea. So what if prison does not reform people: they are locked up and not harming the rest of society". "The idea that prison creates more crime is hogwash ... the hard evidence shows that longer prison sentences coincide with reduced conviction rates. Sixty per cent of those sentenced to a year in prison reoffend compared with only 27 per cent reoffending rates for those sentenced to 10 years or more."

> We should note that records from the U.S. Military clearly show very few offenders ever return to Military Stockades (prisons), such is the toughness of the regime inside. We should further note that, unlike civilian criminals, Military prisoners will generally be harder and tougher and well used to privation and severe discipline as a matter of course to begin with, simply as a result of Military training – aside from the *extra dimension* of 'real Operations' for perhaps most U.S. soldiers incarcerated in Stockades in recent times.

Professor Fraser states that if the Singapore story does not convince, the American experience should. Following the same liberal path as Britain, by the late 1960's America was declared "the crime centre of the world". A public revolution began and everyone who broke the law was arrested, petty criminals shut down, prison sentences lengthened and everyone who needed to be imprisoned was. According to Fraser, "homicide rates have declined to levels last seen in [the] 1960's".

The fact that we here in New Zealand are becoming a *more* violent society that nonetheless still seemingly legislates for 'weaker notions across the board', seems not to have entered the thought-processes of those who forcefully push such legislation. In *certain* cases, if *offenders* received the exact same that they meted out to *their victims*, they would probably think very carefully before ever doing it again. If the only language that some understand is *real violence* toward others, then perhaps that is *the very same language* that society should use on them in particular situations.

Society as a whole, therefore, needs to take on board the undeniable Truth of the great Scripture in Luke 6:31 [Fenton]:

"And as you wish men to do to you, do the same to them."

The violent, evil-minded should be taught that righteous lesson. History teaches us that if we do not learn from her we will repeat the same mistakes, and thus suffer the same outcomes. The *extreme lawlessness* in the early years at Russell – where 'real violence' ruled as 'the law' – was *only ended* when two chiefs, **Hone Heke** and **Kawiti**, with a force of 600 *armed* Ngapuhi, sacked the town and drove the 'violent' with their lawlessness 'out of town'. Deaths and severe wounds resulted from that hard and lawful lesson, of course, but that necessary action *fixed the problem forever*. The 'violent lawless' never returned. 'Powder-puff discipline' for the young and arrogant, 'untouchables' who especially wish to emulate violent American gangs simply *feeds* more of them into a kind of conveyor-belt system from a younger and younger age. All of them *"waiting for their hour to hit the streets"*. For that is their arena, *their very public 'gladiatorial-stage'*.

In either the late 50's or early 60's, a major confrontation took place in Queen Street, Auckland, between fledgling 'bikie-gangs' then claiming 'the strip' as their patch, and a large group of sailors and soldiers on leave together on a Friday night. At a time when New Zealand's Navy possessed more fighting ships per capita than most countries and C.M.T.

was in full swing, the complement of one ship disembarking for leave from an overseas cruise and a Troop Train in from Waiouru saw Queen Street overflowing with obviously fit Servicemen. The ensuing 'battle' and subsequent routing of the 'bikies' resulted in the interesting paradigm that 'bikie gangs' such as developed in the U.S. and even Australia never gained any kind of real ascendency in New Zealand after that. The lesson was learnt.

If the politicians, lawmakers and legislators will not put into effect spiritually-correct Laws which alone can offer the necessary guidelines for constructive living – and the teeth to enforce it – how can the agencies tasked to 'stop the rot' ever meaningfully fulfil their role. Once more we see this attitude of non-responsibility, but this time from so-called political 'leaders'. For what cannot be changed are the incredibly powerful energies that are part and parcel of the developing young. In a process ordained from birth it is a completely natural and *desirable force* that sets in place, for each emerging adult, the necessary drive for it to take its place in the adult world. It is important to therefore understand that such powerful energies awakening in the young can be directed to whatever path they choose to travel; either good or bad, right or wrong.

Irrespective of the chosen path, however, the energies are *equally strong* whatever choices are made. We must not forget, moreover, that with the emergence of the 'spiritual-awakening aspect' within the young, the stage is also set for **The Law of Attraction...** to take *full measure* in their lives. Thus where the kinds of decisions made must, by Law, *attract to them* similar forms, thereby greatly increasing the strength of the original volition. As we observe with dismay and *righteous anger* the pack mentality of teenage and youth gangs engaged in mindless violence at times, it should not be difficult for the reader to understand how much dark and debased energy is being *attracted* into those groups. Yet they, themselves, give cause for the connection through their own personal wishes.[27]

As previously and strongly stated, this explanation may not fit with the views of psychologists, sociologists and libertarians, or with current social theory, but it is, nevertheless, **the actual process**. The responsibility of society, then, is not only to provide the young with the correct teachings of their *"whence, whither and why"* for a logical and stable foundation throughout life, but to also provide the necessary and relevant outlets so that this *unstoppable energy* of developing and emerging 'natural power' may more easily be channelled down constructive paths.

Policies that effectively *abandon* the young at this critical time in their development represent the height of spiritual and political irresponsibility. And to do so in the name of the mighty dollar is totally abhorrent. Fortunately, in terms of Spiritual Justice, such shameful policies are tightly connected to their architects until such time as they bring about the necessary and correct change in accordance with Spiritual Law. If not, the consequences of such direction, which helps fuel the increase in crime and violence, are irrevocably tied to them.

Moreover, it may be 'capitalistically-clever' to continually reduce work-forces to in-

---

[27]The reader who wishes to know *the true and thus ultimate reason why* the increasing and seemingly unstoppable levels of violence, will find that answer in the **"CRYSTAL PUBLISHING"** publication we have previously footnoted. [**BIBLE "MYSTERIES" EXPLAINED**: Understanding **"Global Societal Collapse"** From the **"SCIENCE" in The Bible**... Specifically **Chapter 3, page 85**: '**Why there is so much Violence and Evil on Earth**'.] The answer has precise resonance with the warning of Jesus to the women of the world who would be *mothers* at the time of the destruction of all humanly-created societies – *our time now*. That answer, of course, does not at all fit with present intellectual/societal notions, but that is *exactly why* no long-term workable solutions emerge from all the so-called 'experts'.

crease profit margins and/or increase personal bonuses, but it is spiritually and socially irresponsible to not then provide meaningful activity for those so affected. It is probably not so important for those who are close to the end of their socially decreed working life, for they have at least had the benefits of self-esteem and perhaps personal pride that some kinds of regular paid work can bring. However, for the young just out of school, where the energies are developing toward their strongest point; to not have an outlet for that 'energy' can be the most disastrous thing for them and for society. And if society is not able to provide a range of paid work-possibilities, *then it must offer a viable alternative.*

Since the main criteria for these emerging energies should be self-esteem, a reasonable wage, a sense of purpose, a sense of belonging, and a healthy lifestyle etc., then that viable alternative could be time spent in the Armed Forces or some kind of similar Service group. To simply give young emerging adults money for nothing whilst they are working through that transition phase into adulthood under the pressure of emerging and unstoppable energy is totally irresponsible. The necessary outlet for these emerging forces can too easily be subverted to anti-social behaviour at this crucial time in their development. The dole payment, of course, is sometimes the easiest option for politicians. Under Spiritual Law, however, it is absolutely wrong.[28]

It is interesting to therefore note that researchers writing for a US publication, the "Archives of General Psychiatry", report that the behaviour of very aggressive boys may be biologically based and thus hard to treat with counselling. It may also explain why many grow up to commit a disproportionate amount of crime. The researchers found that extreme antisocial behaviour in boys aged 7 to 12 appears to be related to low cortisol levels. Cortisol is released in response to fear, such as fear of punishment for misbehaving. Its low levels in antisocial boys might indicate that they do not fear the possible consequences of their actions. Keith McBurnett, a child psychologist at the University of Chicago who led the study, believes that any such biological propensity that's resistant to treatment would be "very troubling". He says:

> "The implication is that we may need to discard our traditional notions of treatment with these kids in favour of trying to help them fit in and find *a niche in society* where their *aggressiveness* and lack of sense of danger is *an asset.*"

> (Italics mine.)

James Dabbs, a Georgia State University psychologist, studied the report and saw no reason to doubt its findings. "Low cortisol would make you bold", he said. In youngsters with low levels of the hormone:

> "It doesn't bother them when you do things to them. Its hard to make them behave."

The disorder is characterised by severely antisocial behaviour such as animal cruelty and weapon use that often shows up before age 10. In stereotypical fashion, however, Dr McBurnett believes possible treatment measures might include *drugs* similar to those given to hyperactive children. [A change of diet – *in everything* – might just be the better option.]

Perhaps the logical answer for youth violence is to identify such youngsters – clearly they should be easy to spot – and give them *an outlet* for that aggression and its associated energy. And if such behaviour is difficult to treat, ***then let the Armed Forces constructively channel and make use of that energy.***

---

[28]Political Parties who advocate that recipients do some work for the dole have at least this area correct.

With the role of 'Peacekeeping' being recognised as an ongoing requirement for New Zealand Forces, young men of this nature would be an asset. And since aggression is *lessened by the expenditure of energy*, normal, everyday Army activity would curb the *negative aspects* of aggression through tough and beneficial training. In any case, no one steps completely out of line in the Army. The Unit and/or the soldiers within it very effectively police their own. There are enough trouble spots around the world to satisfy every male with aggressive tendencies – *if he has the courage to face this particular kind of challenge as a soldier/peacekeeper.*

This simple method would take many youthful, drunken cowards off the streets and allow them to really test themselves.

Since the U.N. funds Peacekeeping Operations, New Zealand could earn money by fielding a large force of "professional peacekeepers", as is the case with the Fijian Army. The 'once-strutting', gangster-posing, suburban youths can earn for themselves an O.E. into some of the world's dangerous troublespots. Such an experience would surely bring about a beneficial change of attitude leading to this group realising how blessed New Zealand really is. And thus how very fortunate they were to **not** be born in places where 'peacekeepers' are sorely needed. Recognition of this nature might just inculcate the further recognition that they, too, have a duty and responsibility to help keep New Zealand so blessed.

So why can't the majority of 'bleeding-heart liberals' and wimpish politicians not clearly see that the benefits of this kind of direction, probably more than any other, would be immediate and ongoing – and ultimately save money for society overall? Why can they not? Because society collectively rejects this important aspect of Spiritual Truth, and we all suffer and/or pay.

Precisely with regard to this aspect, an insidious and extremely dangerous thought, delivered by Police Chiefs, politicians and various social leaders, has been allowed to creep into the consciousness of the Nation. It is difficult to believe that these supposedly responsible leaders from time to time label the gang problem as being either 'almost out of control' or 'totally out of control'.

For a minuscule number of the total population to exert that much influence on the very people socially and politically charged with *the protection and well-being of the citizens of our society*, simply reflects what we have been saying throughout the course of this book. There is clearly not sufficient understanding, nor the necessary will within this 'leader's group' to effectively enact and/or enforce such Laws as would actually begin the process of addressing the underlying causes. To state such a thing is tantamount to simply lying down and handing control of society itself to the smallest minority, and is therefore untenable. It is also ludicrous.

*   *   *   *   *

Special Note:

The very disturbing June 2008 incident where heavily-armed A.O.S. Police Officers simply stood aside in a 'safe place' – while citizen Navtej Singh bled to death on the floor of his shop – was *absolutely inexcusable*. How could young Armed Offenders Squad members not want to go after the perpetrators; low-life thugs with a single, low-powered weapon – a .22 calibre rifle? *Army 'grunts' would have welcomed such an opportunity.* One would hope that the *rank and file* of A.O.S. members present were not neutered by bureaucratic gutlessness and stupidity and *did* want to 'sort them out'. For is that not why they are in that Unit in the first place – for the action? Notwithstanding 'official' Police protocols and procedures for such incidents; in this case the buck nonetheless stops with the overly-cautious 'commander' on the scene. His was simple 'dereliction of duty', and he should have been charged accordingly. Moreover: If, in the final analysis, over-cautiousness *has* now permeated *the whole* of the A.O.S., to the point where what we all unbelievably witnessed is now standard practice, then that organisation should be *immediately disbanded* and specialist troops given the role. They will not let the citizens down. A 3 to 1 superiority in numbers is perfectly acceptable for major Military 'Operations'. Current N.Z. Police A.O.S. 'Op's' tends to number up to as many as 30 heavily-armed, 'armour-plated' Officers. We should include attack dogs too. A clear case of overkill every time.

> **That is why the Navtej Singh incident is now indelibly-engraved as an inexcusable blot on the N.Z. Police record forever! A.O.S. 'commanders', especially – but rank and file members too – have the guts to do the job for which *you* signed the dotted line. If you cannot, then stay home with mother and watch on TV others who *will* do the job!**

*   *   *   *   *

Whilst the Police may be far more aware of the true situation regarding gangs and crime, it is still a fact that gangs represent the tiniest minority of the total population, and therefore **can** be contained, controlled or otherwise held in check if there is the political and societal will to do so. By such statements a socially irresponsible act is committed which not only emboldens and encourages the intimidatory attitude of gangs, but positively reinforces the allure of their 'untouchable' status for the impressionable young.

The gang, by its very nature, automatically inculcates an ethos of fear that must then be translated outwardly for the group's perceived safe survival; toward society in general, and toward other gangs as well. Hence the promoted aura of menace and intimidation by virtue of aggressive attitude and particular clothing and lifestyle. However, whilst the gang may certainly be aggressive and anti-social in its behaviour, under the **"The Laws of THE MAN"** the underlying reality will probably be more one of anger and a perceived sense of alienation from mainstream society, thus producing *spiritual insecurity*. If this were not the case, *there would not be gangs in fortified properties in the first place*. And aside from the outworking of **'The Law of Attraction...'** driving the formation of gangs initially, **'HIS' LAWS** also further state that *"fear must attract fear"*, thus resulting in the setting in place of mechanisms – fortified houses and intimidatory behaviour – to prevent any approach by others.

Unfortunately, gang members are generally unable to recognise this fact whilst they remain *within the group*, and it is only when individuals *leave* that they may recognise this phenomenon more clearly. Then realise, moreover, that they *can* be their own person without needing the perceived safety of the group. We must never forget that there is no *mana* in intimidation of the defenceless or in the sign of the closed fist, unless it is used to *defend* the sick, weak or vulnerable. For *mana*, in its highest meaning, **is a quality of the Spiritual in the first instance**. *Mana*, therefore, possesses both the **power and virtue of humility**, something that all gangs – including Maori ones – by virtue of their *"personally-chosen lifestyle"*, do not *generally* possess or display.

Yet they **can** possess it, **if they so choose**!

The word, gang, as with all words of every language, is also subject to the strict, inflexible outworking of **The Laws**, and thus produces its own particular 'form'. Under **'His' Laws**, the *name* that a gang may call itself is also equally subject to the same outworking. Therefore, every gang is constantly surrounded not only by the 'living form' of the word, *gang*, but just as strongly by the particular 'living form' of the *'gang name'* that the group has chosen for itself. Thus, that overall, 'enlarged form' of both *'gang and gang name'* surrounds, envelops and constantly influences the whole group and close associates for as long as they continue to maintain and thus feed it. A spiritually-receptive or clairvoyant person or *matakite* may actually see the 'kinds of forms' that the members personally and collectively promote, and which thus surround and accompany them.

In the same way, rap that promotes violence, hate and anarchy produces the corresponding forms in its 'music', which will ultimately and detrimentally affect anyone who chooses such material as their main 'music diet'.

Gang members who indulge in anti-social or criminal behaviour which also transgresses the Higher Law, must, and will, one day reap the return effect of such offending under the unstoppable outworking of **The Law of Reciprocal Action**, **irrespective of whether they *believe so* or not**. So if society is unable or unwilling to impose adequate justice on those who require it, then **"The LAW of The MAN"** most certainly will – either here on earth *or after their earthly death*. For *unless* there has been *a genuine change of **inner** spiritual volition* to something more elevated beforehand, that is the actual outcome for *all* transgressors of **The Living Law**! Our 'works' go with us when we exit our physical body at "The First Death".

Therefore, no one, but *no one*, escapes: **"THE LAW OF THE ALMIGHTY!"**

Moreover, just as gangs are absolutely subject to the rule of **'His' Law**, so, too, should they accept the rules of society. If they choose not to, they naturally express their desire to live outside of it, and should therefore understand the wish of society to remove them from it until such time as there is genuine change.

Yet we should once more be mindful of the fact that the angry energies that drive alienated people to gravitate to 'gang brotherhood' are the *same* strong energies that can be directed to different kinds of more beneficial activities. If the general thrust of society's direction is not conducive to providing reasonable opportunities for even the most basic of achievable and desired levels, then change should be wrought to allow for this possibility so that gangs can be helped meaningfully too. If gangs can clearly demonstrate that they have the interests of society at heart and wish to be part of it – for their children's sake particularly *as they state publicly on National TV from time to time* – then they should be helped. But they should be prepared to do the work, whatever that might entail. Thus: **"To walk the talk."**

> Perhaps, paradoxically, by virtue of their *self-chosen*, decidedly uncertain, insecure and sometimes dangerous lifestyle; ***some from within the gangs may gain far deeper insights into the reality of things, including spiritual ones, than many living a quieter, 'safer' life 'outside' in suburbia***.

Of course, the intimidatory or aggressive attitude that gangs sometimes display is little different in principle to that which Armies from aeons past have needed to show as well. Societies, therefore, must *really understand* that *every* generation of males requires a *controlled outlet* for that very strong and *unstoppable energy* naturally inherent within them. This is a Natural Law and thus a Spiritual one! As previously stated, it is an energy ideally suited for the defence of the Nation and society if necessary. Irrespective of the weapons used by generations of "defenders" throughout history; whether clubs, spears, bows and arrows, muskets, automatic weapons, or total hi-tech war, the Military *training and preparation* of young males for any potential conflict is still similar in the basics. It is generally sufficient to channel any negative energy toward a more positive mind-set, thus helping to defuse its aggressive potential in society. Whilst contact sports can offer a roughly similar alternative in society; in the case of young men in gangs, that is probably not the correct kind of outlet for *their* particular energy.

$$*\qquad*\qquad*\qquad*\qquad*$$

So why should we evince surprise when gangs choose to fight other gangs? ***For gangs will fight***. Government legislation and/or societal rules will not prevent it. The fact that gangs are a reality in most major cities of the world now means that inter-gang confrontation is, logically, the concomitant accompaniment. Certain men choose to join the Army, particularly, to find out if they will 'hold it together', 'measure up' and 'not let the boys down' when it really counts. Gang members no doubt hold to a similar kind of ethos in their world.

So, since gangs will always want to test themselves against rivals, ***why not simply let them fight it out***? Grant them their wish, but under strictly controlled conditions. Since the rivalry between certain gangs tends towards a large degree of loathing or hate, give them the freedom to take their inter-gang warfare out of the suburbs and off the streets. Fulfil their desire to fight it out, but with hand weapons. And ***if it is also their wish***, with no quarter asked or given. Build a special, high-walled gladiatorial arena away from suburbia, publicity and TV cameras – perhaps inside a maximum security prison – and *control* each ***'requested confrontation'*** with armed Police and Troops. Such a facility would be roughly similar to the 'killing house' type training facility that Special Forces, particularly, must hone their specialist skills in. The lust for such confrontations among gangs will quickly dissipate when death and casualty figures are made public.

Should they be given the freedom to fulfil the urge or wish to fight, even in a controlled setting? Of course, societal mores would surely say no. And who would police any 'requested confrontations'? Further, who would patch up the injuries and attend to any deaths that would inevitably result? On the surface, untenable questions. Who in power in New Zealand society would even consider such an idea? Yet deaths and injuries in gang confrontations are precisely what takes place on our suburban streets quite regularly now anyway.

$$*\qquad*\qquad*\qquad*\qquad*$$

Setting aside the idea of 'officially-controlled' gang fights; from the primary aspect of the "Law of Attraction...", high gang membership is perhaps partly a reaction to a society *perceived to be weak*.

And a weak society can never engender respect in any case.

Hence the enslavement or destruction of such societies throughout history – either from within or without!

In reality, many gang members are not actually railing against society at all. In truth, any 'fight of frustration' is usually an *inner one* – invariably with ourselves. This recognition is apparent from the comments by, and complete change of direction of, ex-gang members. For the 'struggle' represents a deep, even sub-conscious desire to find a *meaningful place* in society and the world. That meaningful place, however, is actually a *spiritual* one, which cannot ultimately occur in anti-societal gang brotherhood. Such a desire, therefore, can actually be best channelled and enjoyed under the *far stronger bond* of **'Military Brotherhood'**.

It is an environment where Military training for defence can be accepted as *a spiritual elevation of the energies that gangs display*. And, moreover, is the path of the "defending warrior". As previously stated, politicians, and society in general, should wake up to this need and make it a reality for the *benefit* of the young men of the Nation! Young males are not meant to be neutered by society's apparent weak view today that they should never be militarily trained en masse for defence and protection of the Nation.

Outside of an Army ethos, however, even Maori gangs – through the genuine *recognition* of "the way" shown by Te Kooti Arikirangi, Te Whiti O Rongomai and Ratana – can be *true warriors* in a genuinely *spiritual* sense, thus potentially becoming *spiritual leaders* for their own within Maoridom. Not for a religion or a Church but in following:

The 'WAY' of "THE RAINBOW WARRIOR".

As the colours of the spectrum – the rainbow – make up white light, **The RAINBOW WARRIOR** is therefore the True **"WARRIOR of LIGHT"**; Whose **LAW** and **Teachings** we offer explanations about in *this* Work!

Ultimately, however, the *present* unfortunate situation of confrontation between 'society and its *law*' and 'the gangs and their *code*' will only be fully resolved when *both sides* recognise the need to understand the actual *"whence, whither and why"* of *all* human beings. For only with that crucial recognition might there develop the greater understanding of our *true* purpose and reason for being "down here on earth". It is to live in such a way that we can one day *return* to our *true home* – **The Realm of The Spiritual!** *Societal confrontation is not why we are here.*

Thus, through mutual recognition of the key parameters and guidelines inherent in **Spiritual Law**, the problem can be easily resolved. If not, we can probably look forward to more confrontation and/or violence, and perhaps more repressive measures to contain it. A pointless direction for *both sides*, especially since the solution is within our grasp right now!

For the Police Chiefs and policy makers, the great difficulty will be to accept the reality of something that society itself has never ever paid any attention to, because it did not regard it as important. In other words, the rule of societal law, as enshrined by legislation, must undergo radical change to reflect the true **Spiritual Laws**. This recognition is crucial and decisive for the betterment of society overall. Perhaps, then, we may begin to see the beginnings of a more harmonious one – at least for the rapidly-closing time that is still left to global societies.

*   *   *   *   *

In the concluding part of this current sub-Chapter, let us revisit a hard truth. We have previously explained how each generation believes it, and it alone, holds the promise of a new golden age but must eventually awaken to the fact that it did not –

– because the Eternality of **Spiritual Truth** was not there as its *necessary foundational-anchor*.

Therefore, *with this generation also*, we can expect the exact same thing with regard to current changes in education policy, health restructuring, and the present method of addressing increasing crime statistics, to name a few. There will be no genuine, beneficial and equitable change *unless, and until*, <u>this society embraces **Spiritual Law**</u>!

*   *   *   *   *

As already stated a number of times, the simple and immediate answer to virtually all our problems is to change our collective attitude from one of *'my rights'* to that of *"my responsibilities"* under the aegis of **Spiritual Law**, and let all legislation reflect that crucial necessity and thus more noble ideal. That change, along with one other, would have the greatest potential to 'turn society around'.

The cry of Military training or anything similar as being unaffordable simply does not stack up against the social cost of potentially explosive rates of crime and the need for more jails if the energies of disaffected youth are not channelled constructively. The Armed Services provide the ideal environment to effect a change of attitude in the anti-social young and those of them who do not wish to work. If not by the particular Service, most certainly by their peers within it. Since it is generally the male of the species that is the potential aggressor anyway, then Service life – more particularly the Army – is ideally suited to constructively channel this emerging energy into positive outcomes.

Since Police numbers are rarely at optimum levels, Compulsory Military Training might induce some to join the Police after their stint of Army time; a wonderful cost-cutting measure since much of the preparatory training would already have been done. Ex-Army Police Constables seconded to the A.O.S. would solve the problem of that Unit being too over-cautious, to the detriment of the public whom Police are sworn to protect. Compulsory Military Training on a regular basis would also release into the community large numbers of disciplined, healthier and fitter young men *than could ever be the case today*. In this age of increasing natural disasters it is imperative to have a large pool of trained and disciplined people in society for disaster relief work. New Zealand's time of trial has not yet arrived – but it will! Politicians would also have at their disposal many more 'Peacekeepers' with which to court favour and kudos from other Governments in a rapidly deteriorating and increasingly ungovernable world.

The cost-benefits of Compulsory Military Training = Excellent.

The cost-benefits of societal status quo = huge and increasing.

The cost statistics that Professor Fraser quotes for Britain make for sobering reading. His figures reveal that prison is *not* the expensive option our political 'masters' would have us believe. "The cost of imprisoning 80,000 offenders is 3 billion (pounds sterling) [N.Z.$7.8 billion] a year. The cost of crime [to the community] is at least 60 billion (pounds)."

What would our New Zealand statistics translate to in monetary terms, let alone the emotional cost for victims of serious crime especially? Military training must surely be the most cost-effective method of slowing and finally curbing the present totally unacceptable increase in youth crime!

It is a wonderful thing to see the transformation in a young man who had never thought he could be capable of the physical and mental exertions that a Military environment provides. The huge leap in self-esteem, the warm bonds of deep friendship that develop, the change in attitude to one where virtually anything is possible; all these and more are forever part of the new man who has been privileged to experience Service life. Do we not see exactly this effect on television items from time to time? The unwarranted fears that many initially have about Service life quickly dissolve when the benefits rapidly become apparent. Not only those of fitness, strength and healthy discipline, but the fun, the social times and the laughter. Also the opportunity to do things that are simply not available outside of the Services, including first class trade training. It is also the ideal place for the intransigent 'hard-cases'.

In any case, as previously alluded to, the catastrophic events of the last few years should send a serious warning to all Governments to increase the numbers of Service Personnel markedly. The increasing frequency of what we loosely label 'natural disasters' will require large numbers of trained and disciplined troops for disaster relief – which all countries will experience more frequently.

For Maori, the Army, particularly, provides almost the ideal environment for the inherent nature of the race to flourish and 'take wings'. The record speaks for itself with regard to the large numbers of Maori who have greatly benefited from their Service time and who harbour fond memories of it. Certain energies and talents within the race admirably find their forte in this particular Service and produce men of particularly fine bearing and calibre.

So in terms of the inordinate amount of Maori frequenting our prisons, Military training should surely be accepted as the best and most constructive channel for them. If all young men were to experience the benefits of Military training, there would be fewer recruits for the gangs – brown or white – and far less anti-social behaviour.

What cost Military training again? The cost of good, future-proofing investment for the young, much of which is paid out in the dole or various kinds of social mischief in any case! What cost increasing juvenile crime and increasing prison numbers?

Horrendous, and without end!

21.9   The Solution

Some years ago a man who had been in Civil Defence most of his adult life explained to me his idea to combat the increasing breakdown of societal values, particularly with regard to youths and young men. His idea is not only brilliant in its simplicity, but also for its far-reaching, ongoing benefits for each individual region in the first instance, and thus for the Nation as a whole.

The whole concept lay in his identification of the main deep-water harbours around New Zealand. He identified ten, from Whangaroa to Bluff. Since virtually all harbours have population centres on or close to them, they are ideally suited for use as a combined **Army/Navy base**. His proposal was for such a combined base to incorporate elements of both services – the Navy to provide an ocean-going Patrol Boat or similar, and the Army to provide its contribution of general purpose all-terrain/off-road vehicles. And to that Base would go the local and regional youths, there to do Military Service for whatever length of time would be deemed appropriate.

A number of highly beneficial things would immediately result. Since there is currently a serious debate about the need for more and very expensive gaols – with Dr Peter

Sharples pointing out the worsening statistics about inmate incarceration and lamenting the fact that Maori are inordinately represented – why not spend that kind of money on preventative policies such as that proposed here. And if, on top of the actual cost of the prison itself, [which in 2008 cost the taxpayer an extra $92,000 per year to house and feed each inmate], it would seem to be far more sensible to train, upskill and have for use when needed, a large pool of young men who had spent at least part of the years of strongly-developing energy fully trained in the manning of Patrol Boats and offroad vehicles.

As previously stated, as well as the obvious benefits of vital discipline, better health, fitness and good hygiene that Military Service offers as a matter of course, the reasonably high standard of *medical training* that Military Units necessarily require would be part of most Servicemen's training too. Naturally, also, the young men in this case would be trained in the maintenance of the craft, vehicles and associated equipment of the **Army** and **Navy**. And, of course, in the Operational skills of both. The relevant mechanical and electrical training for at least some would represent a further huge gain, not only for society generally, but for industry especially. Some would no doubt opt for a career in the Armed Services, thus training new intakes. New Zealand would not only have a growing foundation of multi-skilled Servicemen at home on land or sea, but personnel better prepared to play a meaningful role in society than is the case at this time. Fewer young men would then gravitate to the gangs.

In time, the gang culture might even die out as different ideas permeate the psyche of the young men beneficially exposed to a very different ethos, especially if gang influence is entrenched around areas close to training bases, or if/when trained men return to home areas perhaps influenced by gang culture. Barrack-room life is the perfect place to learn respect for others and their personal space and property, but in an atmosphere of generally high camaraderie. Paradoxically, being totally subject to the *greater degree of discipline* inherent in Military Law, as opposed to *weaker* civilian 'law', ultimately produces servicemen who *readily accept* a stronger level of discipline.

*   *   *   *   *

A striking example of what can be achieved on even a small, very localised scale was shown on National Television in late 2005 where an ex-Army man and Cadet Corps Organiser for the Te Kaha area had formed an Army Cadet Unit based locally *at* Te Kaha Marae. [Where **Victoria Cross** recipient, **Corporal Willie Apiata**, was raised.]

Very obviously aware of the benefits of Military Training for young people, Jack Ferguson – also the local Police Officer – undertook the training of the young people involved. They showed obvious pride in themselves and pride in the uniform and their Unit, with those not yet old enough to join keen to do so later. The primary focus for those young people was the Cadet Unit, not the gangs. Cadet Units provide an easier entry-mechanism into the Regular or Territorial Forces.

[In any case the Army is the "biggest gang", with the best and most powerful weapons.]

*   *   *   *   *

A further obvious advantage of what is proposed here would be the *repopulating* of some regions previously depopulated by *migration to larger centres*. Local industry and businesses would thrive through this kind of *reinvigoration*, as would infrastructure such as schools, social centres and medical clinics or the like. Civil Defence authorities throughout

New Zealand would have the services of far larger numbers of *trained personnel and their vehicles* for rescue work than can be mustered at present. A Flotilla of ocean-going, high-speed Patrol Boats would be ideal for fisheries patrol, sea rescue and coastal surveillance etc.. Maori and Pakeha youth from the same geographical regions would beneficially sail steel or aluminium *waka* in New Zealand coastal waters together.

Inter-base and inter-regional sports fixtures would promote healthy competition throughout an expanded Military-population, and, I am sure, help provide an overall, Nationwide ethos of pride and clear purpose for all soldier/sailors within it. Surely the political will can be mustered to offer a better societal alternative than the same tired old policies that have clearly **not** produced a *better society*, and therefore **not** a *safer one*.

Perhaps the greatest benefit deriving from such a 'concept' that *should* be considered by *all* political parties in these rapidly changing times of just 'global warming' alone, is the impact of increasingly stronger and larger 'natural catastrophes' upon societies everywhere.

In just a few years we have witnessed, in real time, massive disasters on an unprecedented scale. Cynics will say all this is just the normal, cyclical patterns of nature. Nonetheless, *irrespective* of the debate surrounding the two opposing views, the *end-result* of such 'natural occurrences' is one of *catastrophic destruction* of human infrastructure, particularly. In the case of the most recent events, also great loss of life. We should note that China, the economic powerhouse of the world, awash with huge surpluses and able to muster large reserves of military manpower and equipment, struggled to cope with their 2008 earthquake.

Consider also: Even the world's only true superpower, with all *its* vast resources of trained manpower and virtually limitless amounts of machinery and equipment; it, too, was almost powerless to deliver quick and efficient help of rescue, security, food, medicine and shelter when just *one* of its major cities, New Orleans, was devastated by *one* hurricane – albeit a very powerful one.

> If the two most powerful Nations in the world cannot easily cope with a large disaster in just *one* part of their respective countries, how will we here in New Zealand with our *next-to-nothing reserves*; either of trained manpower or necessary equipment.

In the scenario we outline in this sub-Chapter, trained manpower available throughout the country, coupled with stored Field Hospitals and all necessary vehicles and equipment secured in 'local' Military bases, is going to be the best help for the future. For we should be under no illusions *whatsoever* that the disasters of the past few years and most recent decades *are not even the beginning* of what must soon come to pass right across the globe!

There is a powerful and absolute truism which states:

> "It is better to have something and *not need it*, than to *need it* and **not have it**!"

Will New Zealand's politician's consider such an idea, and perhaps even do it? Probably not. Yet such a policy would perfectly accord with all that we have tried to point out – that only with more spiritually-ennobled *practices* than are currently promoted can there ever be a 'better society'. Correct Military training not only really does produce the true "warrior ethic", but offers a powerful, logical and thus intelligent hedge against **what will take place anyway**.

In the final analysis, it probably won't matter. In **"Author's Note"** at the very beginning of this Work, I stated that the overall thrust of it ultimately represented a kind of collective swan-song, simply because the human race has reached the time ordained for it to have gained the necessary *spiritual knowledge* to survive *what must shortly come to pass*. Most unfortunately, however, since we have *not* recognised and enacted what we long should have, we of New Zealand, along with most of global humanity, will no longer simply be voyeurs of *other peoples'* tragedies and misfortunes.

We will have our own very serious time of trial!

Notwithstanding the **Spiritual Truth** of that immutable and thus *unchangeable poropiti*, in the short time *still* available, the above *solution **would yet offer*** the greatest aid for the youth of this land at this sorry time in our societal path. It would at least help to turn *some* things around. For that reason *alone*, we should begin immediately. The overall *poropiti* of this Work thus strongly states that we will need this kind of trained and disciplined manpower *before very much longer*. They would be *our* 'National Guard'.

If this Chapter has been a hard-hitting one – like a repetitive harangue or 'cracked record' – it is nothing compared to what we *constantly reinforce **is rapidly approaching***.

In the final analysis overall, therefore, Maori are basically correct when they state that the Pakeha system fails them. This is true because the Pakeha system ultimately fails the Pakeha too.

However, the Maori system would be no better either, for *the fatal flaw in both* is the refusal to unequivocally accept the reality, and therefore the validity, of The Eternal and Unchangeable **Spiritual Laws** of:

THE ALMIGHTY!.

And, moreover, **to accept them as they actually are, not as we might wish them to be: – And then live them!**

As the *final poropiti* for this Chapter, **'Mores' of 'Maori Renaissance' Permeating New Zealand Society Today**; from the **Sure Source** which grants me the Mandate to do so, I *once more* proclaim the following:

If I do not tell you this, who is going to?

'Mores' of 'Maori Cultural-Renaissance'
Permeating New Zealand Society Today

22

The Rapidly-Fading "Spiritual" Potential

22.1 Where To Now?

22.1.1 Land Ownership

Every step on our journey has outlined the how and why each individual one connects to every other, thereby producing a ladder offering the steps away from the 'psychic old' into the "spiritual new", thus reaching up to **The Source of All LIFE**. With that as the foundation, the true spiritual potential for Maori could, perhaps, be realised. However, The Spiritual Laws demand *work* to achieve it. *Spiritual work* in the first instance, so that the necessary change may be wrought whereby the transformation of each individual, and therefore of the whole race, produces the 'potential' for the best possible outcome.

To this end, however, there must develop the desire to embrace the only knowledge that can offer this realisation. Any other alternative will simply not produce that result. For if Maori believe that just 'ownership' of land will produce the necessary healing and transformation of the 'collective *wairua*', **then the truth of "Spiritual Law" is not at all understood**.

Any 'longing' *other than* the 'longing for The Truth', actually leads *downwards*. The first connection must therefore be to The Higher Realms, upward to The Source of All Life, that we may recognise our Origins, and thus our actual home – thereby fulfilling the admonition to "Seek ye first..."

Therefore, the strong cultural desire giving land 'ownership' *first place* must be understood as not being conducive to genuine *spiritual* growth. To tie oneself to land in the belief that that is the spiritually-correct thing to do first, logically means that one places the most vitally important and naturally far higher *spiritual connection* on a *lower level* than the earthly land. Whether this is believed or not is irrelevant, for that is the *actual form created* by the one who places that particular 'longing for land' first.

In turn, because that unhelpful *form* belongs to the one who possesses the 'longing', and which therefore surrounds that individual, any potential connection to The Higher Spheres is considerably *weakened* because the wish to 'own' land remains the *strongest desire* in the individual. Of course, we naturally require land for human needs of housing and food production. That consideration, however, is not the issue here. It is a question of *what* should *first* be spiritually considered, and *why*!

Ratana knew the truth of this and requested the emissaries of the King Movement, who petitioned him to heal "...the sickness of the land"; to "...first unite in the Father..." *before* uniting in the land. Thus the necessary transformation of Maoridom must take place on paths that may be radically different to that which present-day Maori might believe are spiritual, and into directions away from any 'personal desire' aspect surrounding such a belief.

As an indication of how we should undertake to live our lives and effect that necessary change, we actually only need to live **The First Commandment**.

Since **The First Commandment** encompasses **"The Word"** as **"The Living Law"**; and **"The Law"**, in turn, is **"The Living Word"**, we therefore owe our very life to The Divine Grace inherent in **The First Commandment**. All that has been created for our earthly needs and spiritual furtherance in its beginning, substance and end, springs from this first and greatest **Commandment**.

Therefore, if correctly understood, this **Commandment** holds the key to all higher knowledge and to the way upward, simply because all higher knowledge has its form and being in it. Spiritual ascent lies in both the recognition and application of the inviolable tenet inherent in **"The Commandment"**. Ratana's "Foundation of the Covenant" spells out his understanding of this fact in his unequivocal wording of it. Therefore, any deep and genuine spiritual volition in the veneration of this *greatest* of **Commandments** must, by virtue of the outworking of all the interconnected Spiritual Laws – all of which have their substance in it – naturally impact on any such believer to the greatest beneficial degree in all areas of that individual's life.

So must it be with a complete group of people too! In the first instance, however, the reciprocal help connected to any spiritually-correct attitude will first be felt in the necessary process *of the shedding of all errors*. This may mean a time of quite painful struggle as the individual fights to free himself from the binds of those past errors and any entrenched wrong attitudes still holding him tightly to spiritually-wrong concepts.

The struggling one, however, must absolutely **know** that the fight to become free is a battle – *with himself*. It will invariably be his own incorrect ideas that he must conquer. And genuine recognition of the truth of **The First Commandment** – to absorb and live its meaning – can be the greatest help in achieving this vital goal. That is why the directive and admonition was given to Ratana and, by association and extension also to the Maori race to:

"Repent, and cleanse yourselves!"

In fact, in response to the petition of humankind for conscious life aeons ago, all races on earth are here to spiritually fulfil their particular role within the ordained purpose of the whole of humanity under the aegis of **The Creative Will**. Virtually without exception, though, **no complete race seems to fully understand that fact**.

In some races, however, there *are* individuals or groups who *do* understand it and who *do* attempt to spiritually re-awaken the connections to this *once-known truth*. Unfortunately, over millennia, this was generally lost through turning away from true spiritual knowledge and replacing it with beliefs that, for the most part, are actually *opposed* to that reality.

The few souls who feel the calling to assist the re-awakening process of humankind, including their own race, are mostly like "voices in the wilderness", with their entreaties invariably blown away in the wind of disbelief. Now, however, because of the increasingly compressed time-frame of opportunity left to humankind to re-awaken, coupled with a general intransigence towards such ideas, that procrastination time is virtually over. That reality notwithstanding:

> From time to time a spectacular event of tremendous spiritual significance may occur which offers an immediate opportunity *for a complete race to embrace a very large measure of Spiritual Truth at the one time*.

A grace of such proportions for a race provides the strongest foundation for their spiritual fulfilment in the intertwined threads of all humanity. moreover, even if other races present are aware of such an event yet choose to remain unmoved, the fact remains that the race that so recognises it has greatly advanced its spiritual purpose.

Such an opportunity of immense grace was *gifted* to the Maori race with the great 'Spiritual Mission' of Ratana!

What we propose here is to explain the reasons leading to such a purpose so that Maori *may finally understand* the stupendous nature of the opportunity once gifted to them; which many *refused* at the time even with such a clear direction under the "Mangai". [One would hope that the true reason for such refusals was simple, insufficient spiritual-insight and not stubborn intransigence, or, worse, outright opposition and mockery.] Even though time has now virtually run out, hopefully the following explanations may re-awaken in Maori the *spiritual requirement* to once again follow the *signpost* given by Ratana. As previously stated, however, that will take a very great amount of true discipline and *kaha*, and perhaps even more than Maori are *currently capable of developing*.

Nonetheless, *the opportunity crosses the path of the Maori once more*: –

– but for the last time!

22.1.2   The Spiritual Potential – What should have been!

Among all the peoples on earth, the Maori race, both materially and 'spiritually', occupy an especially *unique niche* in their geographical placement, evolutionary development, and also in the historical and spiritual time-frame given to planet earth.

As background to our assertion: If we briefly examine the history of the more expansive and aggressive races of the "Ancient World", we observe the rise and fall of many empires preceding the emergence of the truly European ones. The general religious foundation of the latter is the Judaeo/Christian 'ethos'. From the time of its entry into the European psyche via the Roman Empire to the present time, it has undergone many upheavals resulting in huge differences of meaning from the original simple and pure teaching of Its Bringer – Jesus.

Religious authorities were not content to simply accept the clear truth He brought, but chose, instead, to erect huge monasteries and 'schools of learning' behind which doors they could dissect the original teachings. As a result of this long process of analysis and debate, the original clear meanings underwent change; some subtle, some far more radical. What finally emerged from that fermenting crucible of *intellectualism* differs vastly from the **Spiritual Original** given by **Jesus**. Not only that, but it was also removed from the ordinary people. Thus, what little the masses were permitted to have; even that was used to enforce and maintain religious power over them by the ruling few.[1]

That dark volition can be readily traced through the mad, religious fervour of The Dark Ages and the equally insane Inquisition instituted by the Papacy. Along with its wealth and excesses, the establishment of serious distortions of Bible Scripture into religious Church tenets seeded the wonderfully enlightened protestations of the great spiritual scholar, Martin Luther, who, in 1520, launched the Protestant Reformation. His opposition to the, then, entrenched, religious view found a kindred soul in King Henry VIII. As previously noted, by the Act of Supremacy in 1536, Henry effectively formed a new English Church and broke with Rome.

Later began the gradual expansion and consolidation of the British Empire via the age of exploration and colonisation. Along with the export of British ideas and their criminals, went the missionaries and their European religion in its final, distilled form. Whilst that was obviously an expansion of the Empire, it was not at the same time an expansion of Spiritual Truth. As already noted, what was exported to the new lands, including New Zealand, was far less spiritual than the original pure Teaching. The religious madness of The Dark Ages and the Spanish Inquisition had ensured that certain ideas of religious rigidity, formulated as 'Church dogma' during those years of bigotry and cruel torture, were henceforth retained as inviolable tenets of the new religious thinking. And that is what arrived in New Zealand in the early 1800s to first challenge, then change the way of, the cannibalistic Maori.

However, even though the 'religion' had lost much of the essence of actual Spiritual Truth, in many ways it was at least far more enlightened than anything Maori possessed. Nonetheless, and notwithstanding that reality, by their very 'religion' English Judges from the ruling aristocracy cruelly condemned even young people to penal servitude in 'Van Diemen's Land' [Australia] for the most trivial offences. That historical fact, however, serves to illustrate the truth of our assertions as to how drastically the spirit of Pure Truth had been so terribly distorted by ignoble, religious authorities. And, moreover, how **The Word**, once delivered spiritually pristine from out of the mouth of **Its Bringer**, could be invoked to sentence even the innocent to sometimes certain death in a land far from home and family, by arrogant, earthly judges completely devoid of compassion. Certainly not a case of, "...suffer the little children".

Thus, in New Zealand, this religion of Christianity came face-to-face with the incredibly savage, stone-age Maori race. A race of people whose inner volition centred, for the greater part, on the need to avenge all insults – invariably with blood – under their deeply entrenched 'reality' of *utu*. Yet even with this obvious display of inherent savagery, what traits and abilities might still lie dormant in this cannibal race that could be *re-awakened* and utilised for a *powerful, future spiritual potential*?

All races will develop certain strong and beneficial talents that will enable them to more effectively manage their particular way of life. For the Maori, one was fearlessness and another courage, even if perversely borne of the need to fight for survival against one's own people or face the possibility of being enslaved, slain and/or eaten. Fearlessness and courage were also present when sailing the greatest ocean in the world. Moreover, and notwithstanding their obvious level of savagery and unreasoning, fearful superstition, Maori possessed a high, natural level of intelligence; a level that greatly amazed many early administrators and Colonists of authority.

---

[1]In reality, **The Light** strives constantly to give *The Truth* to men, but men, unfortunately yet perversely, then quickly reduce it to *just a religion*. Religions, for the most part, of earthly power, wealth and subjugation.

As noted, sufficiently high to be able to navigate *knowingly* across the vast expanse of the South Pacific utilising the stars for navigation; to develop a relatively successful society and to philosophically ponder on the concept of *Te korekore* or nothingness. The old Maori also possessed the intelligence to use the Pakeha for his own ends and to successfully better him in trade at times. A further interesting trait was 'the constance of the *wero*' – the challenge. Burned into the very ethos of the race was the need to always challenge and test. Thus the Maori possessed some very strong abilities of great importance. However, since there is always a balance of the good and not-so-good, there are obviously weaker, unhelpful traits too.

During the colonisation process history records that superior numbers of Pakeha, assisted by his technology, quickly tipped the balance in his favour in virtually all areas of endeavour in this new land. Throughout this difficult transition time the line of Maori Religious Prophets and their Movements emerged, with the first incorporating a small percentage of Christianity initially, but with a predominantly Maori bent. From these inauspicious and shaky beginnings, and through increasingly greater inclusion of Christian principles promoted by succeeding Prophets, there finally emerged a wholly Maori-instigated Church under the strongest of them, Ratana. Significantly, however, whilst Ratana's Movement encompassed all the basic Christian principles, it totally rejected a huge amount of previously sacrosanct and strongly inculcated Maori religious beliefs and superstitions.

From that brief background, then, let us postulate the *potential* for a precise 'spiritual task' that *Te Iwi Maori* **should by now have fulfilled**.

Of course, any collective spiritual task that a complete race can become part of and fulfil is obviously dependent on that race 'first getting its own house in order'. It must first apply the correct spiritual formula to its own particular 'situation'.

Applying The Spiritual Laws to its own problems and thus developing the associated 'collective security' to maintain optimum levels of social and material benefits then provides the mechanism whereby the same formula can be offered to *other peoples* who may need *exactly* those recognitions. In any event, not until one 'sorts oneself out first' can one then genuinely help others through the 'associated recognitions and learned experience'. Notwithstanding the need to first understand and apply those essential parameters, the quick revisit of our earlier spiritual interpretation of the events surrounding Ratana's "Calling", coupled with a brief, historical overview encapsulated in the following paragraph, may help to clarify this potential.

In a country of three small Islands surrounded by a vast ocean lived a stone-age people. Cocooned from the rest of the world in total isolation for many hundreds of years, this society developed a superstitious, cannibalistic lifestyle which ended with the arrival of Europeans. In the space of less than 150 years, at a time of perhaps the most painful and difficult transition period of rampant disease and uncertain future possibilities, this race reached a point where it was feared they might die out completely. Yet, in the most remarkable of 'turn-arounds', that crisis provided the precise circumstances for a man of that race – Ratana – to emerge from obscurity and lead Maori into a *new spiritual direction and potential.*

22.1.3 Recognition or Rejection?

Relating in the very first place to the reality of **The Spiritual Laws of Creation**, the above sub-heading asks the crucial question of present-day Maoridom:

"What will you do with this *spiritual revelation* now given to you"?

Will you recognise it, or will you reject it?

Before any collective spiritual potential can be embarked upon to fulfilment, individuals within the collective must not only recognise the goal or potential, but also the need to accept the means or 'rules' whereby the potential can be fulfilled collectively, and completely. For if there is not sufficient insight or recognition of the necessary mechanism required for the task, the end result will clearly not be the realisation of precisely that spiritual potential. What will emerge, instead, will be divisiveness and/or mistrust, invariably driven by narrow, personal-wish parameters.

So why the Maori for the potential that once awaited them? And could it yet be fulfilled? More significantly, is there sufficient time still left for such a task? For it was a potential that encompassed a two-fold spiritual task that the Maori race **could have** fulfilled as a people; as a task seeded by the line of Maori Religious Prophets who took their inspiration – and sometimes revelation – from the new knowledge contained in The Bible.

If, therefore, that *potential* to which we allude arises in the first instance from out of The Bible – in which **The One God** is revealed: Why not the Pakeha who brought that especial Book to this land, and whose missionaries introduced it to the Maori who had his own gods? Consider: The knowledge of **God**, previously unknown to Maori, had been with the European for almost 2,000 years. Should they not fulfil this potential we allude to? The simple answer is probably not! The stewards of what was once **The Pure Truth** had reduced it to *just a religion*, with dogma so rigidly entrenched over many hundreds of years that it could no longer offer a clear path back to that original and pristine Source.

Sometimes the question of 'new blood' may provide fresh insight. What about a different race then? A once savage, bold and constantly challenging one; –

– to possibly provide a new nucleus to re-seed that original kernel of Truth
among *other indigenous peoples* in the first instance.

Perhaps the Maori could be such a people? Because they were not shackled by an unrecognised spiritual burden of a *religion* posing as inviolable Truth, and since their *intellect* had not over-developed to the point of being unable to recognise 'other-world' beings, they still possessed a natural and strong acceptance of the existence of the 'Elemental Beings of The Forces of Nature' – albeit in a somewhat distorted interpretation, however.

Nevertheless, they were still fully accepting of a vitally necessary, God-Willed activity that the Christian religion had long since discarded or had wrongly dismissed as superstition, paganism, or demonism, even though The Bible itself teaches about them. That 'other-world reality', readily accepted by Maori, *could* therefore be a powerful 'example' of a people *rising from* the savage, superstitious lifestyle of the old way, to stand as a shining example of a *truly spiritual people* in less than just 300 odd years. Even though current statistics portray a depressing picture, Maori are clearly able to demonstrate a high level of ability and competence in virtually any field they choose, **if** *discipline in application to the task is present or can be generated.*

> *Therefore, from a completely new and strong foundation of genuine spiritual knowing, Maori would be ideally placed to help other indigenous peoples in other colonised countries with small population numbers to similarly grow into*

the same recognitions of Spiritual Truth. Provided, of course, that they first recognise that truthful reality themselves and fully embrace it.

If not, then that potential will not be realised, and Maoridom will continue to produce the same depressing statistics that the race is currently burdened with. For the *potential* outlined was *ordained to be* the actual, collective spiritual task of Te Iwi Maori. In this, all would gain immeasurably – as Ratana once clearly demonstrated.

As previously stated, however, a collective spiritual task can only be embarked upon if the individuals within 'the collective' fully recognise the validity of The Spiritual Laws in the first instance. Only from that foundation can any group then collectively engage in a concerted path consistent with such Laws.

Apart from just that recognition as the foundation for helping other indigenous peoples, there would need to be the strongest discipline to fully understand that such a spiritually-expansive role could not afford to have any overtones of egotistical *mana* attached to it in any shape or form whatsoever. That, unfortunately, is also a trait within Maoridom. Such a noble and privileged task would need to be carried out with the utmost natural humility, for that is where true nobleness and *mana* lie.

In concert with what has been revealed, such a task has the clear potential to admirably display and fulfil the highest spiritual abilities and aspirations of the Maori race!

The question is: "Can it still be fulfilled now?"

*   *   *   *   *

The story of Saul in the New Testament provides a perfect example of a singular, particularly-powerful trait that, if wrongly directed, could so easily produce the opposite of what the owner might actually desire. This man, who later became the first apostle, Paul, possessed an exceptionally keen intellect. Whilst believing that he zealously protected and defended the letter of the Law of Moses, he failed to apply compassion to it in the 'Spirit of the Law'. As a member of the Jewish Religious Authority, his relentless persecution of the first believers in Jesus eventually led to the stoning to death of Stephen, the first Christian martyr.

Saul's implacable conviction about the correctness of his beliefs and the methods he employed to enforce them were shattered and transformed when he was struck blind during a journey to Damascus. The event we know as the "Conversion of Saul" resulted in a far more spiritually-powerful ministry by this man of intensely strong convictions. The powerful trait was still there but now utilised for a vastly different purpose and towards a very different outcome than he could have ever foreseen under the domination of his previous volition.[2]

Notwithstanding the division of opinion among theologians surrounding the writings of Paul, the "Conversion of Saul" perfectly illustrates how Maori – or anyone else for that matter – can also transform certain particularly strong but unhelpful traits and utilise that transformed energy for a higher, more powerful cause in true spiritual serving.

---

[2]We should note, however, that the quite marked differences between Paul's teachings and that of "James the Just", the earthly brother of Jesus, in what is known as the true Church of Jerusalem, has produced strong debate among Biblical scholars and theologians for a very long time now.

22.1.4   Ratana's Mission: Legacy and Extension

With the help of The Truth of Spiritual Law, let us once more carefully examine the relevant aspects of Ratana's Calling that connect us to the reason for our current revelations.

We have previously noted that the two parts of Ratana's revelation contained no manmade psychic phenomena and, therefore, we may conclude that this whole marvellous event *was* ordained from Above!

The first incident at the beach was clearly an 'Elemental happening' by the "The Elemental Forces of Nature"; which we have adequately assessed. The second, however, was a very huge step upwards to a phenomenal event that, by its very nature, could only have come from out of the truly Highest Levels. It is this particular event we must re-visit to show *the unprecedented spiritual nature of it for Aotearoa.* For only by really understanding the stupendous significance of that happening might Maori *fully realise* the huge potential offered to them then by immeasurably High Grace.

At first glance, being enveloped by a small, fast-approaching cloud on one's own verandah could be construed as an hallucination. And to experience burning sensations whilst a voice outlines what might seem to be an impossible task could also portend the same. But is there a precedent recorded somewhere that could confer a mantle of *spiritual credibility* on such an unusual event? The Bible narrates an interesting story where Jacob wrestled all night with a 'man' whose face he could not see. Jacob clearly fought well because before daylight broke the 'man' said:

> "Your name shall no longer be called Jacob, but "Israel"; – for you have wrestled with a Divine Messenger, as with men, and been equal to it."

> (Genesis 32:29, Fenton.)

Thus from out of The Bible itself, for the religious anchorage of the Pakeha peoples, we have a powerful precedent with which to perhaps *roughly compare* Ratana's experience.

There are two key aspects here. The first is whether or not Ratana was *actually visited* by a similar Divine Messenger. For if he was not, then there is *no* ordained ongoing potential, 'from that particular level', for his activity. And he should thus be regarded as a good man who helped many people to leave behind unhelpful practices. But if he **was** so visited by a being from The Highest Realms – **for on that rests the greatest authority for his mission** – then that presupposes a clear and unequivocal *spiritual message* and thus *warning* for *all* of Maoridom. [The clear spiritual outworking of "**The Law of Attraction**..." among Maori souls may be readily noted here.]

Secondly, and with regard to any spiritual potential to be fulfilled, individual Maori need to determine where he or she stands in accepting or not accepting Ratana – 'Te Mangai' – as the Spiritual leader/messenger Called to lead Maori away from their binds to unhelpful, aspiritual 'older traditions'. And, by extension, acceptance of Ratana's directives as the necessary step forward. Those are probably the *immediate spiritual choices* that need to be individually decided on in the first place before there can be any potential for perhaps the greater part of the race to choose to embrace the spiritual potential we outline.

If we accept the premise that Ratana *was* graced from Above, what we must consider are the *differences* in the way the *two* messages were delivered on that fateful day – and the *means* by which they were given. According to the narrated record, the **first message** by the 'voice in the cloud' was later **repeated** by the 'Angel'. The assertion here is that *they were not one and the same* 'deliverer of that message'. The bearer of the first voice was *hidden* in the cloud, but the 'Angel', who was fully revealed, *repeated the message* of the 'voice in the cloud'. [We have stated our unequivocal belief regarding this event; the reader must decide the possible meaning of it for himself.]

What is more important, however, are the words given to Ratana regarding the Maori race. The bearer of 'The Voice' stated that he had searched the globe:

"...to find the people upon whom I can stand."

The people, moreover, would need to repent so that the foundation **'on which He could stand'** would be a cleansed, spiritual one.

Quite obviously, as we must re-emphasise again here, to be *directed* to repent means there was a need *to do so*. It also means there was something to repent for; to be prepared to change or to accept the need to change – thus to work towards **'becoming spiritual'**.

In other words the people were not yet, or not at all, cleansed or spiritual *enough*! And without that recognitive process, the foundation could not be laid, and the race could not fulfil their appointed task. So the clear inference here is that a race was being searched for that **could** develop into a completely spiritual one, and thus **could** stand as an example for other races. It was *not* a race that had *already arrived spiritually*, as it were.

The twelve principles of Ratana's full covenant quite clearly provide a good *basic* foundation to begin with:

1. Obedience to Ratana's message.

2. Acceptance of absolute faith in the Christian God.

3. The renouncing of all Maori superstitions.

4. All who are not baptised be baptised forthwith.

5. That marriage be more sincerely honoured.

6. That greater care should be taken of children who should be wisely fed and tended.

7. That people pray for power to eschew intoxicating liquor.

8. That cigarette smoking among children and women nursing infants be discontinued.

9. That family prayers be held in every home.

10. That the duration of *tangi* be curtailed.

11. That people should retain membership of churches founded on Christian faith.

12. That even if Ratana himself should fail, he has now shown them the right way.

(Press Association, 23rd April 1921. Ratana, p.42)

If each principle is analysed individually, we find that every one is clearly beneficial and sound, though some need to be furthered into *precise Spiritual Law* for ultimate benefit. Via the knowledge of those Laws which we now have, the substance of the above principles can be extended. By doing so, we move further forward into the greater spiritual anchorage of 'living conviction' through understanding 'why' we need to embrace these basic principles *as a foundation step*, rather than have them as perhaps just faith.

In this manner, we *extend* the work of Ratana.

Quite logically, in order to fulfil the task outlined, such a race had to have the necessary latent energies and abilities for the purpose, even if dormant and needing development. The main requirement was to have the right *raw material* present, able to be *moulded and transformed* for the potential. Just as Saul used his considerable yet misguided talents and abilities for the wrong purpose before his conversion, so, too, have the Maori used their abilities and natural connections to the 'Elemental world' similarly. Such a shaky foundation jeopardises the associated need to gain true spiritual knowledge. The current task is to recognise this error and convert it to its correct application so that the bearer of "The Voice in the cloud" can **perhaps** still **'stand'** on the Maori race! Unfortunately, that is highly unlikely now. Though still a choice, at least in its potential, it is one that can only be made by Maori!

> *"If there was ever a time when indigenous peoples needed help globally, and the aspiritual Pakeha corporate ethos needed ennobling, it is surely now. This small South Pacific Nation of only a few million people of differing races and religions, in a huge ocean with no common borders, could perhaps have 'gotten it right' more easily than other Nations. To a certain degree maybe it still can – if the genuine will and goodwill to do so is taken, and if there is still time available. Via that elevated concept we could 'show the way' for all other peoples. And Te Iwi Maori, with a strong, natural acceptance of the 'other-world reality', albeit needing a vitally necessary change to bring about 'correct spiritual recognitions and practices', are well placed as a people to be in the vanguard to lead the way forward. Without the acceptance of the need for change, however, this will not take place. For, in truth, it absolutely cannot!"*

(Author.)

With that spiritual potential finally outlined, we have almost reached the end of our journey of revelation. At times it has probably hit very hard, *like a taiaha thrust into our soul.* Yet unless the truth of reality is faced, we are like a person who has suddenly been told he has a terminal illness. Usually the first reaction is one of disbelief, and then denial; a denial brought about by the fear of death or the thought of how unfair it may seem and possibly not wanting to leave family and friends.

However, for one who has *knowledge* of the process of death and therefore of The Laws that *govern it*, that person is better able to accept the earthly inevitability of it. With calm confidence he can approach his 'time' knowing it is simply a necessary transitional step with the opportunity for greater enlightenment; i.e., **'if the Laws have been lived correctly'**!

That is how Maoridom needs to view this book and its revelatory contents! For until we honestly and truthfully face the fact that our forebears were *not* a spiritual people, and shed the shackles of a *totally wrong belief* that has continually promoted similarly *wrong attitudes* for successive generations, we will forever be like our terminally ill patient – in a state of *constant denial.* Like him we have two choices: Continue to deny it, **yet still die**; or accept it with grace, thus enabling the process of *necessary transformation* to proceed. So, in direct concert with the 'Truth' of **'The Second Death'**:

Learn: and Live.
Or
Deny: and Die.

Thus: An absolute *whakatouki* and *poropiti*!

Through the powerful outworking of that kind of *maia*, we thereby permit ourselves entry into a new attitude of purpose and direction under the knowledge and protection of **The Eternal Laws**. That is the choice! The way has been prepared, first by the early Maori Religious Prophets who took the first tentative steps away from the savagery of the past, to the work of the later ones like Te Whiti and Kenana, and finally to the great 'Spiritual Mission of Ratana'. He has laid the foundation. The Maori race need only build on, and follow, it.

We have asked: "**Where to now?**"

The answer is simple. First stand correctly on the step of 'Elemental knowledge' – of which the greatest part was lost by all races – and which is both a spiritual and material reality. That should be **'The First Step'**.

By teaching the *correct understanding* of **Elemental Lore** through the knowledge of **The Spiritual Laws of Creation**, the appropriate level of discernment can be attained whereby the recognition of what constitutes true 'Elemental activity' – which we must understand and connect to in any case – can be *consciously* strengthened.

That would clearly be in stark contrast to the present acceptance of totally useless and potentially dangerous low-level psychic beliefs and activities, all of which are *incorrectly designated* as spiritual knowledge. And all of it locked into its ostensible place of 'great *mana*' under the 'supposedly sacrosanct' umbrella of 'cultural traditions'. Correct discernment will allow these unhelpful, *aspiritual aspects* to be totally and beneficially eradicated from the psyche of Maoridom.

Tohungaism, for the most part, dabbled in this low level of presumed knowledge, hence Ratana's appointed mission to *destroy it*. His strong condemnation of it in his "Foundation of the Covenant" clearly reveals his powerful purpose against it in the reference to:

"...all the abominable foolish ways and works of Tohungaism."

And as long as Maori held fast to it, they would remain with it at its *actual* inferior level, never really understanding the great difference and *separating gulf* between that *psychic level*, that of 'Elemental forces', and that of the genuinely true and far higher *Spiritual knowledge*.

Ideally, a revamped education curriculum should be put in place to teach this new knowledge. However, since the education system is held in the hands of people who could probably never officially acknowledge such 'radical ideas' – regardless of any private beliefs to the contrary – it behoves Maori *to consider producing their own*, as we have strongly recommended. Whilst there are certainly many Pakeha who have much spiritual knowledge and who may also welcome such an idea, the 'official' Pakeha view of education is, *quite wrongly*, that the prevailing 'rational' scientific agenda of empiricism, *solely*, should be continued with for *everyone*.

Along with any new spiritually-educative process should develop the desire to put in place what was directed by and through Ratana. This should prove to be a relatively easy task as the collective Maori ethos expands to encompass a far more spiritual one. Such a meaningful change should signal an associated desire to dismantle tribal organisations and everything connected with them that might still hold those particular groups in thrall. Even the tiniest vestiges of 'ancestor worship' must be let go as well.

Ancestors belong to a past *that was*, and that is their *rightful* place. Moreover, the culture should be simply accepted for what it actually is, a culture, perhaps something of strong tradition but not a thing to pridefully worship as some kind of *new Maori god*.

Nor should others be expected to do so either. Therefore carvings and cultural activities will need to encompass more objectivity, rather than be a catalyst for emotive, cultural overtones.

To help us in such understanding, we should always look to what Ratana put in place. Thus what we observe in his clarity of vision is that there are no Maori motifs on his "Temple to The Light". Yet no one could deny that Ratana was not Maori *in every sense of the word*, or in what he achieved for his people. Even though unequivocally Maori out of the 'old way', the *greater spiritual enlightenment* granted to him enabled him to *clearly see* what should be discarded.

He thus set the example accordingly.

Certainly carving skills should always be retained, but change the designs to reflect the new knowledge and direction and leave the old 'forms' in the past. If the tourist trade is to be catered for utilising traditional designs, then no wrong spiritual significance should be accorded *those* particular works.

Similarly, commissioned works of traditional cultural design should also not be accorded *spiritual significance*, either in the carving or in the blessing upon completion, **'if'** they purport to portray forms, events or meanings that are *not truly spiritual.*

It is *crucially important* to continually **stress** the need for all in Maoridom to *really understand* the huge and *unbridgeable differences* between the designations *psychic or occult*, of *Elemental*, and that of *Spiritual*. Correct recognition of the huge gulf *between each* is of paramount importance here.

22.1.5 Kaumatuaism

A further impediment to meaningful progress is the clinging to the entrenched idea that age somehow automatically implies great wisdom. Whilst this *should* be the case for all human beings, the reality is vastly different for, apart from normal education and life-experience, relatively *few* old people are *truly wise*. Therefore, in concert with the dismantling of tribal organisations should be the phasing out of *kaumatuaism*. Since age and/or status do not, in any way whatsoever, *automatically* confer vast knowledge and wisdom on any individual, a desire to seek such status should logically be demonstrably accompanied by a suitably elevated degree of *genuine* wisdom. The many Maori who currently claim such status – either by age, personal assessment, or through tribal acceptance and perhaps even encouragement – should *seriously* consider their role in the light of Ratana's mission. For *kaumatuaism* actually promotes *the negative trait* of 'place-hunting'.

To this end, where are the *kaumatua* who have exhorted their people to follow Ratana's example? And have there been any at all? We have certainly had many hundreds who, over the years, have promoted traditional culture – and *kaumatuaism*. Ratana's mission was not just about a man, a church, or a political party. It was and is, first and foremost, all about:

A true 'spiritual' awakening – for 'all' of the Maori race!

Kaumatuaism, for the most part, has therefore failed the people it is supposed to guide – their own. And purely because 'tribal *kaumatuaism*', that collective repository of 'Maori wisdom', did not ever appear to understand the stupendous Spiritual Event encompassed by Ratana's life and mission. In truth, if there is no *spiritual wisdom* in the first instance, there is no *true wisdom*, just knowledge of traditional and cultural matters. However, any claim to *kaumatuaism* in terms of 'cultural knowledge' in such cases is obviously perfectly valid. But that does not always permit any further claim to genuine 'spiritual knowledge', *for one does not necessarily lead into the other.*

In fact, certain cultural traditions are so far removed from true spirituality that it is difficult to understand how the proponents of such ideas can claim such an elevated status for particular aspects of it. However, because it is all lumped together under 'traditional' or 'Maori' culture, the whole thing takes on an almost religious significance that no one is permitted to question. And which, as we have said many times, is all ultimately deemed to be spiritual. Tribalism, by virtue of its promoted status and direction, continues to maintain this 'cult of *kaumatuaism*' too. Only the actual acquisition of the twin states of *knowledge and wisdom* through *correct learning and experiencing* allow one to truly possess them, and *not* by reaching any particular age or status.

The present system is also seriously flawed in that it does not demand that most necessary element of 'accountability'. By that we mean accountability in all things. Not just in monetary matters, but even in so-called 'spiritual teachings'. The tribal system that in reality is an extended *whanau* does not allow for true accountability precisely because Maori are generally *incapable* of imposing this **severe yet spiritually-correct demand upon each other – if blood ties are present.**

Yet that is what needs to be achieved eventually; and sooner rather than later. For accountability is a powerful attribute of the spiritual virtue of *trust*! Where trust cannot flourish, distrust and discord will as a natural excrescence of the *distortion of that higher quality.*

Elderly Maori who aspire to be *kaumatua* must therefore accept that they should be *accountable* for all their words and activities, since *kaumatuaism* is inherently synonymous with leadership. Moreover, 'lesser Maori' should have no hesitation in demanding accountability from anyone who seeks leadership, *particularly those in their own bloodline.* If even the smallest measure of *genuine spiritual ascent* is to be achieved, then the lackadaisical, easy-going Maori manner too readily expressed in a '*tatau-tatou*, it's all right boy' attitude, should be consigned to the scrap heap of useless baggage.

Whilst this particular trait often holds a certain amount of laid-back charm, which makes a refreshing change from the increasing social stresses resulting from flawed, pressure-cooker, corporate economics, the inherent danger is that such easy-going attitudes can actually promote ill-discipline. And, moreover, then possibly lead on to the condoning and general acceptance of a low-level, endemic layer of corruption.

22.1.6   Beyond Tribalism

The end result of the changes outlined would be the demise of the tribes and natural growth into a single Nation. From out of that Nation would emerge the natural leaders who will have earned the right to occupy their relevant positions. The current undesirable inter-tribal arguments and petty bickering over the sharing of resources as a result of Waitangi Tribunal decisions, particularly the Fisheries debacle which was so incredibly divisive, would not then occur. National and regional leaders in the 'new Nation' would thus need to develop sufficient independence to be totally and impartially fair in their allocation of any such awarded resources without displaying any kind of favouritism through perhaps lingering links to 'residual tribalism'. Of course, the key spiritual questions would still need to be resolved as to whether such awards were correct *in the first place.* And, if so, what amounts should simply be *given* and what should be *earned.*

Furthermore, any development toward a single Nation without tribal boundaries or influence should not develop into any kind of reverse apartheid system through any perceived 'greater right' via so-called *tangata whenua* status either. For were Maoridom to wake up one morning to find all the *tauiwi* no longer in Aotearoa, this would not result in an instant Maori 'garden of Eden'. The fact is that Maori do not possess anywhere near sufficient discipline or education in the trades and professions to maintain our present society *at its current level. Kaumatua* leadership or educational degrees in 'Maori culture' could never do so either.

Moreover, without the reasoning and logical influence of the *much-needed tauiwi*, old tribal tensions and arguments would once more surface, as it sometimes does today. But to produce what? Quite simply, exactly that which must be left behind. Anarchy in grand Maori style would erupt as the mad scramble for the spoils of society reared its ugly head. If not *that* extreme in such a scenario, then tribal and group jealousies, similar to that tragically engulfing Africa, would almost certainly surface.

For the natural progression from tribes to a single, unified Nation simply prepares the ground for the next step into *a people of planet earth.* And from there to the final and necessary spiritual understanding that we all are ordained to be:

Spiritual Citizens of Creation!

Thus without racial or even country barriers, but simply *complementing* each other as diverse peoples and Nations. Whether we achieve that or not clearly depends on we humankind of course, but in any case that will not happen with the billions of *aspiritual humans* presently populating the earth!

*A comprehensive cleansing and culling must **first** take place.*

Just as the different classes within any given race or society are meant to live and work *"side by side"* and not one above the other, so the same was ordained for the world's many and varied peoples. Just the recognition of that alone, however, will require far more inner greatness than we currently demonstrate *at this time.* Nevertheless, that is the demand in terms of the spiritual responsibility that has been placed on each of us in the first instance. And the Maori of Aotearoa are most certainly **not exempt** from that 'directive'!

If Maoridom choose not to follow the direction as given through Ratana and continue to cling to the tribal system and all the associated over-emotional connections to ancestral genealogy and culture, then that will be the surest illustration that *Maoridom have not at all understood this man Ratana and his Mission.* In the closing pages of this Work and journey we must all *seriously understand* that just as Ratana was chosen to lead the Maori race, *so, too, were Maori just as surely meant to follow his lead.* Therefore, choosing not to do so in this case would be a transgression in itself, and **The Law** will bring the reciprocal effect.

That lawful effect is already revealing itself in increasingly depressing statistics.

Thus, those Maori who do recognise how it now can be, who fully accept the need for this new knowledge and direction and who *are* prepared to change accordingly will, quite logically, **be the nucleus of the Maori race of the future**. Their example may also help to guide those people who are ordained to be in this land at this momentous time to the same recognitions in both *Elemental Lore* and *Spiritual Law.*

Finally, Maori ministers of the various religious denominations may need to carefully examine their particular relationship with their Church to determine whether or not their own personal intuitive beliefs regarding the basic and innate Maori acceptance of "Nature Beings", and which the Church officially rejects, produces conflict at the deepest intuitive level for them. After all, it is surely understood that it is not *religion* that should be taught, but **Truth**. And since 'Elemental' knowledge is of **The Truth**, then any opposition from orthodox beliefs to this sure **Truth** should be rejected outright. Quite logically, Maori ministers *should* be best placed to lead the new and necessary spiritual renaissance in continuing the work of Ratana.

Yet the ***true leaders*** of a genuinely spiritually-awakened Maori race, who recognise the potential for helping other indigenous people as we have postulated, may come from a totally unexpected quarter. Almost certainly not from the educated, academic University 'elite', or the Church leaders, or the politically astute, as one might expect. But perhaps from the ranks of those who have undergone one of the deepest kinds of truly life-changing experiencing possible for the human spirit – that associated with the necessary activity of war "in harms way". Thus leaders from the ranks of the Military Services.

Natural leaders should also emerge from out of the other 'real world'; in the 'social struggle' of society as it stands today. Thus from out of the depths of pain and despair. And, because of those experiences, be able to provide the greatest potential for this necessary leadership and change. For those in 'the gangs', with the first stirrings of a 'spiritual' awakening – born of the longing to change one's life – from out of the feeling of hopelessness and despair there will often arise a deeper veneration and *aroha* for **The MAN**, and **HIS *Aroha***. And, hopefully, grateful acceptance of **His Rules**!

Thus the 'longing for higher things' from out of one's *wairua* offers the most powerful spur for genuinely beneficial change. For this direction taps into, and is supported by, the power and force of the higher Spiritual Laws. Only with a conscious connection to this knowledge can humankind, including Maori, progress and ascend!

The blunt question now is: *Have Maori, as a people, so obtusely and completely failed to fully recognise the true spiritual greatness of Ratana's Mission and the associated clarion call for them: –*

– that it is already too late to fulfil what was their great spiritual task?

22.2 The ANZAC Legacy in the 21st Century

22.2.1 The Spiritual Maturing of New Zealand Nationhood

Note:

> Since **The ANZAC Legacy** was born from out of the sacrifice of very many 'soldier deaths', the subject matter of this sub-Chapter necessarily means that we must *revisit* the 'higher reason' for the ***'why'*** of the 'Death of a Soldier'.

Notwithstanding the overall message of human spiritual failure right across global societies that our journey unequivocally reveals, still inherent within **Divine Will** is **'ITS'** *constant striving* to bring about the necessary awakening of human beings for that very **Will** *to* *be fulfilled on earth.* Not only for that **Immutable and Inviolable Will**, however, but through the humanly-incomprehensible **"Love of THE ALMIGHTY"**, literally for the salvation of that part of us which has true life – our *wairua.*

For *only in that necessary fulfilment* lies both the *opportunity and means* for we human beings of all earthly races to one day spiritually-ascend and thus *return* to our *true home.*

Failure in serving **The Will** – which granted us conscious life – is the historic *norm* for humans on earth. So greatly distorted has humanity's collective human ego become; so great is the 'collective mana' we have placed on our human abilities and knowledge; so far removed are we now from *true* knowledge; that *true* human service to **The Will** is actually the *aberration!*

In that regard, and in perfect balance, the following Scripture from Deuteronomy both warns and encourages we humans to make the only *viable* choice. We should seriously understand, however, that the choice of **Life or Death** here (the **Blessing** or the **Curse**), is not simply about the everyday deaths that millions must undergo each week across the globe. No! Here it means **Spiritual Life** (Eternal Life) – or – **Spiritual Death** (The Second Death!) – as we necessarily reinforce.

> **"Bear witness to me, now, Heavens and Earth! I place Life and Death before you. – the Blessing and the Curse! Therefore choose for yourselves the Life, – that you and your posterity may live!**

(30:19, Fenton.)

So, what has that quite hard-hitting Scripture to do with our developing spiritual maturing through **'The ANZAC Legend'**? And where in that legacy does Ratana's spiritual mission for this Nation's future stand? Indeed, where stands the strongly-promoted ethos of continuing and growing 'Maori Tribalism' that, by extension, ultimately *prevents* the complete cohesiveness of true Nationhood among all groups within the Nation – against the clear directive of **'Te Mangai'**? The *unequivocal reality* in this case is: That 'Tribalism' must be *transcended* by true and genuine **Spiritual Nationhood** for *all* who reside here.

The journey to that desirable point logically presupposes the need to seek out and hold up those greater things and events which grant an emerging people exactly that Nationhood. In broad terms, Nationhood can emerge from out of many diverse paradigms. Invariably, however, the overall historical reality reveals many Nations emerging from out of the struggle, blood and sacrifice of war. Thus was it so for a young Nation called New Zealand.

Our defining 'sacrificial battle' was at Gallipoli in the second decade of the 20th century. Affecting virtually all within a land of only around one million souls, the inordinately high level of 'blood-sacrifice' suffered then and also later in the Second World War, now subsequently bequeaths a legacy of an increasingly deep and emotionally-perceived and felt 'spiritual connection' that is, at the same time, little-understood. And by virtue of that, perhaps, 'painful non-understanding', actually – and paradoxically – *beneficially-deepens and enlarges* the Nation's *collective-connection* with the very many lost in the 'sacrifice of war'.

Yet, if we objectively examine the differences between the two World Wars, *only one really needed to be fought by the sons of this Nation.* Seeded by the blood-baths of the First World War through generational and thus perhaps emotional ties to 'Mother Britain', the sacrifices at that time set in motion the increasing year-by-year upwelling of patriotic pride at ANZAC Day Commemorations around the Nation and, indeed, even in far-flung corners of the globe.

Here in New Zealand, these most special annual Commemoration Services interestingly reveal two important and interlinked things. One is the attendance of more and more younger members of families whose fathers, uncles, grandfathers, and even great uncles and great grandfathers etc., were killed in the various wars that we as a Nation have participated in. The other is the recognition, even if not a conscious one, that those same loved ones who did not return and who are grieved for, were the very same who would have killed others in battle. And some will have taken very many lives. Yet the memory is not one of that particular aspect, or one of shame over participation. Neither is it a glorification of war. It is simply the inherent spiritual recognition that *the men grieved for did what had to be done at the time* – and did it well. Their activities, moreover, far from being any kind of dark deed, actually lived the ethos of a higher calling – *particularly in the second global conflict.*

The one especially difficult question about this business of war that causes great anguish and emotional suffering for the families of soldiers killed in battle is the meaning and purpose of **"The Sacrifice of the Soldier"**, particularly one who is greatly loved. On the surface it appears to be an unnecessary waste of a healthy, vibrant young life, with all the future life-potential terminated in the prime of life – and *seemingly* for all time.

So if earthly death is believed to be the absolute end of life, as nothing else except a hole in the ground and blackness to look forward to, then it would be extremely difficult for families of soldiers killed in battle to ever see any meaningful reason or understanding for such a death. More especially if one is conscripted for war service as opposed to one who volunteers. Conscription, within the constraints of such a view of death, adds a further, harder dimension of incomprehensibility to the whole unfortunate business for grieving families.

The single overriding aspect that is clearly revealed on the faces of all who attend Commemoration Services is not only the natural and deep emotion of the loss experienced in the first place – and perhaps more for those Servicemen who were never *personally* known by younger members of the family – but also the deep desire to understand **why**.

All the right words are said at every ceremony of course, but they do not ultimately explain what has happened in the death of the soldier or give the true meaning of their loss and sacrifice. Usually we are urged to simply believe that such things are somehow not a waste of generally young lives, but are sometimes the unfortunate yet necessary outcome of a just cause. Indeed, whilst that may be the case, such an outcome can nevertheless still be spiritually-correct. Even if this view is not a socially acceptable one, in the case of a just cause it is *still* the end result for those for whom we may grieve at such times of remembrance. And **'Commemorations of Remembrance'** greatly strengthen connections to the flag and Nationhood.

The Maori contribution to all the Nation's 'wars' was, of course, considerable. That reality perfectly enhances this segment of our examination of Nationhood: That in the final analysis it is the *spiritual* dimension which must be strongly present as its ultimate anchorage if we are to speak of true and genuine collective Nationhood and not primarily any other – including *'tangata whenua'* status and/or tribalism. As can be seen in internal conflicts in many so-called Nations, if there is not that necessary *spiritual* attribute and accompaniment, divisiveness and tension in religion, politics and racial issues etc., inevitably produce unnecessary bloodshed for those particular peoples.

The greatest degree of 'maturing' as a result of the ANZAC legend has really taken place in the last few years. The attitude of younger participants at the Commemorative Services at Gallipoli itself has changed considerably. From a 'rite of passage' for young ANZACs 'celebrated' by some with less than appropriate reverence and not a little drunkenness just a few years ago to deep and somber reflection today; surely reflects exactly this 'collective and growing spiritual-maturing' – at least around *that* 'sacrifice of war'.

Perhaps this major change for New Zealand ANZAC's was assisted, in part, by the State Ceremony for the arrival home of 'The Unknown Warrior'. That especial ceremony surrounding 'his' return from the First World War battlefields of France, produced, for New Zealand as a Nation, a huge and totally unexpected upwelling of emotion. What was perhaps initially seen as an event mainly centred around protocols connected with the Army and Government, suddenly became a national and patriotic swelling of emotional pride. Catching most by surprise with the strength of it all, that defining moment, which moved many to experience emotions not previously evident, could not easily be quantified by the very many so moved.

The essence and 'living form' of that national upwelling at the time reveals itself as one more *especial milestone* in our 'spiritual maturing' to the fullest possible expression of complete Nationhood.

If, then, such events connected to 'sacrifice in war' affect us so profoundly, the key aspect inherent therein must surely be: – **Selfless Service!** Whilst genuine service to our fellow man is always a correct thing to do, service to **'He Who gave us Life'** is the greatest of all. For by *that kind* of ultimate service, we automatically give the same to all humanity. How can we most effectively do that? By embracing and living **The Eternal Laws of Creation**!

A truly-understood and *genuinely* spiritual foundation – which in any case can only derive from **The Law** – therefore quite naturally negates any personal, cultural or racial demands for special consideration within a 'Nation' striving to develop to true *Spiritual Nationhood*! Such a fulfilment offers the highest example for other peoples and Nations to emulate.

The complete thrust of this Work is to state, in essence, that *we can know*. The whole of **Spiritual Law** *allows us to know* if we truly wish to. Indeed, that is **the purpose of The Law** – so that we *can know* and have *real understanding*. However, it requires the letting go of certain entrenched beliefs, pet theories, and the acceptance of **The Law** *as it actually is*; irrespective of how we might *wish it to be* in order to suit our personal beliefs and/or expectations.

You, the reader, strive to understand the deeper meaning underlying the increasing patriotic pride deriving from **The ANZAC Legacy**. As the primary catalyst which each year brings forth *national emotional upwelling*; 'the lump in the throat' and the tears that accompany it *provide revelatory evidence for you personally* that your spirit – the real you – *cries out for understanding*. It seeks the meaning, purpose and thus answers to life – and to physical death and *transition* thereafter. And each Commemorative Anniversary dedicated to our Nation's defining 'legacy' of 'sacrifice in war' will bring forth the inner anguish and non-comprehension *to touch your spirit again and again*.

Therefore, set your spirit – the actual you – at peace. Gain true understanding from the knowledge of 'Spiritual Law'!

22.2.2 The National Anthem

Nationhood calls forth the need to have, as accompaniments to that status, certain 'trappings' that reflect a new Nation's 'coming-of-age'.

A very necessary one, which all independent Nations have, is a National Anthem. Perhaps also the melodic signature of the *chosen flag* of the Nation concerned, both together provide, for the global 'Family of Nations', a ready 'badge of recognition'. The same pairing of 'flag and anthem' may also provide an insight into the nature and/or spiritual aspirations of the Nation/people concerned. As New Zealand citizens, we are enjoined to be patriotic, to know the Anthem in both English and Maori.

Proudly heard on the more 'special events' that the Nation might deem appropriate for such an airing, occasions of State, key funerals and major sports fixtures etc., feature prominently. With many, tears flow when the 'Anthem' is sung/played. As we note in the previous **'sub-section'**; for this relatively new Nation and its peoples, perhaps the greatest upwelling of emotion that accompanies the playing of the National Anthem occurs around Commemorations centred on the supreme sacrifice in war.

What does that really mean for we of New Zealand? How should we relate to especially the Title of our National Anthem – **"God Defend New Zealand"**?

Our present overall heritage of culture and law can be broadly stated to primarily derive from the Judeao/Christian ethos. Moreover, The Bible features prominently in the Legislative Chamber, in matters of State, in the Law Courts and in many other segments of our society. It could perhaps be described as our main religious foundation. In essence, Christian. And the 'Christian Service' is paired with the National Anthem at events of major State/religious import for the Nation.

So, what exactly are we saying? What do we ask of **The Almighty**: **The Creator**; when we sing this Anthem? Do we really and fully understand the profound import of such a request – or perhaps demand? What do we give in return? Or do we simply expect that just because we ask it in a 'National Anthem', the key request: *'God defend our free land'*, *'God defend New Zealand'*, is, or will be, automatically granted whenever we wish or need it to be?

Further, how do we see the 'Being' or 'Figure' **Whom** we ask to 'defend us'? Do we see **Him** correctly as **One**, as John states: **"Whom no man has yet seen"** – as both **Love** and **Justice**? Or do we subscribe to the rather curious idea that **He** is someone *close* and *grandfatherly* who we will one day walk hand in hand with in paradisiacal gardens? A truly strange and grossly-distorted idea actually encompassing the farcical; if we consider the humanly-incomprehensible, unfathomable immensity of the physical universes in just the material part of Creation – **His Work** – let alone the far greater *non-material* part.

So if our National Anthem beseeches **The Almighty** to 'defend us', then we must surely be required, at the very least, to give something back. But what do we give in return? We certainly see and hear the *desperate prayers* centred around the non-comprehension of death and at funerals, and also when adversity, disaster and suffering strikes. Then, *yes then*, we turn to **Him**, whining. The suffering, however, invariably brought about by our blind and intransigent refusal to live according to **His Laws of Love and Justice** – which, *if lived accordingly*, would *not* result in the very trials for which we *beg* help.

Moreover, if we obeyed **His Perfect Laws of Creation**, our National Anthem would be one of praise and gratitude, not one where we *ask* to be defended!

Instead, the inherent close connectivity of Anthem, Bible and Christian ethos in the New Zealand setting carries both an *unfortunate reality* and similar *inevitable outcome* should we continue to hold to the status quo. For in accepting this 'triune' in its 'present form' – thus in its strongly-promoted aspect of 'truthful rightness' for the Nation – what is *concomitantly accepted* are the terrible and appalling *distortions* of certain *key realities* in The Bible which the global Christian Church *continually and wrongly fosters as 'the truth'.*

What is the English word used to describe the practice of saying or teaching one thing yet doing another, or even the opposite? With a capital **H**, it is **Hypocrisy**!

If we objectively place the 'words' of our National Anthem alongside those of some other countries, we will find interesting comparisons in what various peoples hope or ask for. As *one* example, the second verse of the Nigerian National Anthem asks all the *right* things. Notwithstanding the fact that Nigeria and Nigerians are well known for the many scams which fleece millions of the gullible worldwide, the words here show the other, more noble side of the Nigerian nature.

> "O God of creation,
> Direct our noble cause;
> Guide our Leaders right:
> Help our Youth the truth to know,
> In love and honesty to grow,
> And living just and true,
> Great lofty heights attain,
> To build a nation where peace and justice reign."

Since we as a Nation pride ourselves on our Armed Forces' dedication, commitment to Peacekeeping and to fighting ability when required, and especially feel the legacy from the 'sacrifices in war', perhaps it is now time to seriously consider different, more truthful, less hypocritical words for **The National Anthem**!

Let us therefore strive to defend *ourselves* if and/or when the need arises. Not just with the guns and bullets that are still necessary in our increasingly ungovernable material world, but also through the *greater* power and protection inherent in obeying **HIS Law** – **THE LAW** of **HE Whom** we presently ask to defend us.

22.3   Legacy of the "Truth Bringers"

> This particular sub-Chapter completes our journey, as outlined in this Work, to our present, crucial point in human physical and spiritual evolution overall. Were it not for the 'Truth Bringers' and their step-by-step revelatory journey for global humanity under the aegis of **The Will**, we in New Zealand would not have the open and free society we currently enjoy. Neither, therefore, would we have the knowledge about the various religions that sprang from the life and work of those especial men, and thus the religious freedom to choose which we might want to live by. *And neither would Ratana have emerged to show the way forward for Maori.*

Subsequent to that short introduction, there is one particular aspect of the geographical location and diverse racial and religious make-up of New Zealand that we should carefully consider in the concluding phase of this Work. As we observe the horrendous problems most other countries face – which we have not *yet* experienced – perhaps with sufficiently correct insight we may not need to undergo the same kinds of hardship *to the same degree*. Or at least be able to alleviate those hard events that will yet arrive. As previously stated, it is the unequivocal belief of this writer that because of our relatively isolated geographical location protected by the natural barrier of the sea, coupled with a small population in a very productive land blessed with an almost ideal climate, we are probably best-placed to 'still get it right', at least for those fortunate enough to surmount *what must soon occur*. That is, of course, as long as the right decisions are made in the rapidly-closing time still left.

Many relatively recent, 'younger' immigrants I have met, more particularly from Europe (including the U.K.) and America, have stated their strong conviction that they are "meant to be here" at this time. Yet they often do not know why exactly. Perhaps it is an intangible 'feeling' that possibly equates to an 'intuitive knowing' of the *fact* but not necessarily the *reason why*. Interestingly, the *reason* appears to be more than an agreeable climate, fewer people, less pollution and open spaces. Along with those clearly desirable assets, what New Zealand does have, also, is freedom of religious expression.

So let us now expand this theme into one where this small land and its diverse peoples, religions and beliefs – a microcosm so to speak – can, with *maia*, collectively develop the *mana* for genuine tolerance of other cultures and religious beliefs.

With all, however, gravitating to the same point of recognition of **The Spiritual Laws of Creation** *under which all races, religions and cultures have their life and choice of destinies.*

For just as Maori can help other indigenous peoples to an understanding of those Laws if they first accept them, so can we, *as a complete and diverse Nation*, also set a wonderful, ennobled example for the rest of the world to similarly follow. Perhaps within this potential scenario may be found the *reason* why some newcomers 'feel' the strong need to be here, dynamically involved in the life of this country. To help bring about change which, in the land of *their* birth, *may no longer be possible*. As we watch with almost disbelief the horrendous problems that much of the world's humanity is forced to endure, the desire to become an example of harmony and tolerance for the rest of the world to follow is surely the best and noblest thing to strive for.

The key lies in what was given to the different races and peoples in their homelands at particular points in humankind's history. New Zealand now probably has most of the world's various races and religions represented within it, even though in relatively small numbers. Small numbers notwithstanding, if we are to develop our present multicultural, multi-racial and therefore multi-religious society into a completely tolerant and harmonious one, a common, binding denominator needs to be recognised and accepted.

Any study of the religious history of humankind will readily reveal that certain teachings stand out more powerfully than others in the major global racial or ethnic groupings. These will also be connected with particular geographical areas of the earth in terms of *the origin of the teaching*. As men spread further afield from their 'home areas', the teachings went with them. Essentially, however, we identify certain groups of people with a particular religion, with each religion having a 'founder' from that particular racial/ethnic group in a clearly defined part of the globe. Over time, those teachings provided the religious and social framework for the life and activity of the people in the main region to which such teachings originally belonged.

The inevitable spread of those main religions to neighbouring regions might offer a challenge to the ruling authorities there. And such a challenge might produce severe opposition and reaction against that particular group or religion. More particularly if the religion ideologically opposed the laws or beliefs of the governing body of that particular region. Generally speaking, though, as long as the teachings remained simply religions and were contained within their boundaries of geographical origin, they could pose no perceived threat to any other group of people. However, given the natural human trait to seek new lands, the possibility of religious differences clashing increased proportionately with the amount of movement to and from originally clearly defined and stable, singular areas of religion.

As exploration and trade increased, many diverse religions were transported all over the globe, either to be the mainstream belief wherever they touched, or to become isolated pockets. Some, of course, did not take root at all. Those that did make a considerable impact in countries other than that of their origin can be mainly designated as Hinduism, Buddhism, Judaism, Islam and Christianity; as well as a few others. Unfortunately, the end result of the different beliefs has resulted in a 'competition-mentality' between the proponents of them. Its particular excrescence is too often translated into the visual images of brutal reality that are shown almost nightly on television screens; that of bombs, bullets and their associated destruction. Curiously, however, in complete opposition to the tenets of the original founders of those teachings.

Nevertheless, such extreme behaviour is set in motion by narrow and rigid fundamentalism where interpretations are so far removed from the original clear texts that it is difficult to comprehend the inner workings of the minds of the interpreters. That reality, however, offers a key clue as to the reason for such intractable views of intolerance toward others. Whilst such intolerance may clearly reflect the religious bent of the particular groups involved in their, at times, desperate acts, it also invariably reveals their personal, religious and/or political agendas. Such incorrect interpretations cannot be said to be solely religious, and are most certainly **not** anything *truly* spiritual.

With virtually all of the primary religions emerging prior to the "Age of Reason", there was not such a thing as hard science to really challenge the religious ideas of the main teachings before that time. Before that so-called "Age of Enlightenment", the Churches or main religions were the dominant force ruling all thinking and providing all answers. Paradoxically, whilst the age of science and reason was an obvious and beneficial step forward and did provide enlightenment to all manner of questions, the pendulum effect actually swung too far with the result that the scientific community became almost *too afraid* to *revisit* the spiritual question. Or have totally dismissed it as a meaningless aspect of life altogether.

> *Yet it should be realised that integration of the spiritual and the material, as was originally ordained, is not, nor should it be, a denial of one or the other!*

Thus the unfortunate consequence of this one-sided aspect of 'science and reason' is that too many people are afraid, even against their own gut feelings and personal experiences, to admit there is anything other than the material world of the physical senses. Perhaps such a stance might be perceived as a retrograde step back to a new 'Dark Age' before the much-vaunted "Age of Enlightenment". The time of The Dark Ages, of course, is synonymous with religious and superstitious fear coupled with lack of reasoned logic, rather than any genuine understanding of any **Spiritual Laws of Creation**. It was a dark phase that provided the perfect breeding ground for all manner of base activities cynically and hypocritically carried out in **The Name of God!**

The key question here, if we are to make any sense of the religious conflicts that have plagued mankind for centuries and which are becoming increasingly bitter in more and more countries, is:

"Did the founders of the original teachings advocate the present outcome?"

Given the strident proclamations of some of their followers, we may be excused for believing so. Certainly, particular events in history may *appear* to offer irrefutable evidence that this was the case and, moreover, with the *apparent* sanction of the founder.

Yet all the major Teachings clearly promote the tenets of compassion, tolerance, kindness and all the other virtues associated with true spirituality. Therefore, we can reduce that question to either – or! Either the founders of the main religions advocated violence and *senseless killing* as part of the religion, or they did not! The essential content of the Teachings allow us to safely conclude that the founders taught and gave only what was *spiritually beneficial* for their people, with Spiritual Law incorporated into the necessary, everyday material affairs of the society concerned for the particular time. We should note that, clearly correctly, **Laws of Justice** were an inherent part of the Teachings too.

If, therefore, violent opposition to other religions was not part of any of those original Teachings, and given that we must accept that the founders obviously knew what they were outlining and why – for they **were** the "Bringers of the Teachings" after all – the only sure and logical conclusion for the increasing strife today is that the *followers* of those Teachings have disastrously distorted the original meaning/s. Such dangerously narrow interpretations are the actual cause of so much destructive chaos of greater frequency and intensity, which we incredulously observe in the present time.

What, then, was the point of the different religions that sprang up at various times in history from diverse areas of the world out of different peoples, if only to degenerate much later into mad savagery?

Or were they actually different religions – *insofar as the Spiritual Principles that anchored the original beliefs were concerned?*

If we *believe* so, given the parlous state of religious intolerance today, then we must logically accept that the founders of the main Teachings had exactly that in mind; intolerance and bigotry. However, since the *main tenets* of the "great Religions" clearly reveal only **Spiritual Virtues** as their foundation, the sad conclusion we must draw is that we, the various groups of human followers, are clearly to obtuse, too blind, intolerant and immature to even *begin* to emulate the high level of spirituality shown by all the great "Spiritual Teachers of Mankind".

In short, we are a 'spiritually-destitute' race of humankind.

In place of their sacred and ordained mission to bring the substance of spiritual enlightenment to all of humanity, we have, instead, generally defiled those very Truths with base and opposite outcomes to that envisioned by those highly advanced men. As formerly noted, the proof of this particular pudding can be readily observed depressingly-frequently on the news screens and in the newspapers each day.

22.3.1   Teachers of Mankind

We have designated those 'founders' as "Teachers of Mankind"! Was there, then, a higher plan ordained for humankind under the leadership of those men through careful guidance from Above? If we carefully examine the times of their emergence and balance that against the particular level of spiritual maturity of the people they were associated with, we can, indeed, readily observe a precise pattern whereby Nations and peoples could be taken, step by careful step, *to the final recognition of all Spiritual Truth*! That this did not happen can be placed squarely upon our shoulders. The responsibility for that failure is ours alone.

To repeat: We, the followers, through our arrogant and foolish belief that we could know it better than the ones who were actually *prepared and ordained* to bring the respective Teachings to humankind, are the cause of all religious strife throughout history and today. By virtue of the 'founders' far higher level of spiritual maturity, it is ludicrous for *any followers to believe* that they could be **'greater than the Teachers!'**

Because **Truth** is **Eternal** and unchangeable, it must forever remain the same. It is therefore recognisable to us in **The Spiritual Laws of Creation**. They include **The Laws of Nature**, which are equally unchangeable. By extension, the recognition of these inviolable Laws leads without deviation to **God** because **His Will** is revealed to us in those **Spiritual Laws**. Through them we learn what **The Creator** Wills.

The "Teachers of Mankind", to whom all this was known, were "Forerunners for The Truth". We can identify them as Zoroaster in Iran, Lao-Tse in China, Buddha in India, Moses and the Prophets, and Mohammed in Arabia – as well as Krishna and others. Their appointed task was to mediate the knowledge of The Truth *exactly adapted to their peoples and countries*, and formed *according to their spiritual maturity at the time*.

These "Teachers of Mankind" thus gave that unchangeable Truth to their people *in a form understandable to them then*. Mankind, therefore, was to be carefully guided step-by-step over thousands of years to the eventual and final recognition of **"The Light of Truth!"** And thus into the acknowledgement that there is, ultimately, just *one single Divine Truth*!

The symbols of some of the different teachings, which are still in use today, possess precise spiritual meanings. The lotus flower of Buddhism symbolises the necessary need to strive for purity. In its place in flowing water it exemplifies the need for a strong connection with the stream of life. The crescent moon of Islam is linked with the sacred obligation to honour women at all times.

*Naturally, however, women should ensure that **they become**, in their everyday demeanour and activity, such as **can be honoured** in this manner.*

The Star of David is the sacred symbol of Judaism where the two triangles symbolise the inseparable connection between the visible material and the invisible non-material worlds.

In the beginning, all the Teachings were pure in their origin. Moreover, had mankind kept them thus and not distorted them over thousands of years for their own base ideas and selfish ends, *these individual Teachings would have long since converged and today be recognised as only transit and concomitant Teachings to The One Truth!*

Unfortunately, the paths that the individual Teachings illuminated came to an end in the Temple or Church of the particular religion. Through the non-understanding of the followers of those various religions, the Teachings did not, and could not, then lead on to the final **Temple of Truth**.

> What was ordained and set in place was a careful, step-by-step process whereby there would have been *only one single, unified Truth permeating the very consciousness of all the world's peoples right across the whole earth today.*

It was meant to be that simple. Unfortunately, however, along with our free-will ability to choose, there has not been the necessary understanding or openness to permit any kind of meaningful examination of individual beliefs to ascertain whether or not they accord with The Eternal Laws. There has, however, been very much entrenched and rigid dogma; hence the reason why there is so much ongoing and tragic 'reaping' now, which, of course, will increase markedly until the final and comprehensive cleansing.

Therefore, as we have essentially previously stated, **The Truth**, which is anchored in **The Spiritual Laws of Creation**, should not just simply be acknowledged, but *consciously recognised* also. That presupposes the need for a level of discipline serious enough to critically examine oneself with regard to those Laws in an objective assessment of one's own attitude toward them. And then finding the *kaha* to change whatever needs to be *personally changed* **in order to live them correctly**.

Given our small population and the gift of such a beautiful land, it would be wonderful to think that we in New Zealand might collectively possess sufficient inner grace and courage to put in place an ideal such as complete spiritual harmony across the Nation. For the knowledge required to bring this about is now available to us. If the courage is here also, then all that is left is to find the necessary amount of genuine humility *from all religious and cultural leanings in Aotearoa* to fulfil the 'collective potential' as postulated. And, by that, actually achieve true harmony in genuine tolerance towards everything pertaining to this land and its many different peoples: something that no country has yet found.

Is this just an unrealistic, unworkable and foolish 'pipe-dream'? It probably is now. Yet precisely because of the particular parameters we have outlined, it is very possible for at least some to achieve exactly that potential. And perhaps provide a sorely needed example for other Nations to yet still emulate.

As the Teachings of the Forerunners were of The Truth: those of Krishna, Zoroaster, Lao-Tse, Buddha, Moses and the Prophets, Mohammed and others – and of the *more complete knowledge* brought by **Jesus Himself** – so should we recognise the gift of that Divinely guided way for humankind and strive to embrace it completely. Although not perhaps as stupendous as the path and work of the "Forerunners", Ratana's mission for the Maori race nonetheless clearly ranks *highly* on the scales of spiritual greatness too.

Thus we note that Ratana, who could not be designated as a 'true Forerunner' but who stands in powerful company with certain other 'Spiritual Leaders' from other countries in recent decades, utilised symbols similar to those of the 'Teachers of Mankind'. But, however, not those normally associated with Maori cultural traditions. His innate understanding of spiritual symbolism is well exemplified in the explanations he imputed to the symbolic meaning of his flag whereby he stated that the Star and the Moon signified The Divine Law of God, whilst the Union Jack signified the human law, the power of Great Britain.

In this particular written address Ratana gave force to his correct spiritual assertion that: "God created the stars, the moon, the sun and the Laws".

And, therefore:

"...naturally understood the movement and times of those wonders which He created in the whole universe."

Perhaps because of Ratana's apparent strong belief in a "spiritual foundation" for The Treaty of Waitangi, along with its connection to the ruling British Sovereign of the time, he opined that all were united together and laid on the foundation of God's Law. In reality, however, the laws of Great Britain or any other Nation can only be united *with* The Spiritual Laws *if* they were *the foundation* for any such earthly laws in the first place.

In accordance with the path the 'Teachers of Mankind' brought to the earth's peoples, it naturally follows that all races and religions have both the spiritual duty and responsibility to ensure that their individual and/or collective beliefs encompass the true essence of **The Spiritual Laws of Creation** – the foundation upon which *all the great Teachings were unequivocally anchored in the first place*.

We in Aotearoa today would also collectively offer our beliefs and religions as *furthering links* for the spiritual whole, thus for our overall benefit. Ratana's mission, too, even though crucially important as the necessary Teaching which offered the vital step from the debilitating 'old way', might now be understood as *one more furthering link leading Maori*, in this particular case, *towards the complete Truth*.

Through such correct spiritual choices we could have gifted to ourselves the potential future experience of a true flowering of spiritual harmony under the beneficent outworking of **The Eternal Laws**. They, in any case, will be the *sole* foundation under which *all* future human works will be *permitted* to exist. In many societies now, the increasing number of once iconic and stable institutions that have suffered total collapse gives clear warning *that our whole human-societal systems stand poised on the brink of complete chaos*.

When Minister Joe Wright was asked to open the new session of the (U.S.) Kansas Senate, everyone was expecting the usual generalities, but they heard a very different kind of prayer.

The response was immediate. In protest, during the prayer a number of legislators walked out.

'In 6 short weeks, Central Christian Church, where Reverend Wright is pastor, logged more than 5,000 phone calls, with only 47 of those phone calls responding negatively.

The church is now receiving international requests for copies of this prayer from India, Africa and Korea.

Commentator Paul Harvey aired this Prayer on his radio program, "The Rest of the Story", and received a larger response to this program than any other he has ever aired.'

Minister Joe Wright's **"Prayer of Truth"**!

'Heavenly Father,

We come before you today to ask your forgiveness and to seek your direction and guidance.
We know your Word says: "Woe to those who call evil good", but that is exactly what we have done.
We have lost our spiritual equilibrium and reversed our values.
We have exploited the poor and called it the lottery.
We have rewarded laziness and called it welfare.

We have killed our unborn and called it choice.
We have shot abortionists and called it justifiable.
We have neglected to discipline our children and called it building self-esteem.
We have abused power and called it politics.
We have coveted our neighbour's possessions and called it ambition.
We have polluted the air with profanity and pornography and called it freedom of expression.
We have ridiculed the time-honoured values of our forefathers and called it enlightenment.
Search us, O God, and know our hearts today; cleanse us from every sin and set us free.'

Amen.

Societally; all our choices leading up to this present point of humanity's major, and now completely irreversible, *global crisis* thus reveals the fatuity of so-called 'human knowledge and understanding', *for the decisions which brought about the present, dire situation were always free-will ones in the first instance.* [Succinctly encapsulated in Pastor Joe Wright's **"Prayer of Truth."**]

Are we in Aotearoa comfortable with what is occurring 'at home' and across the globe? Do we believe that we have no need to institute radical and drastic *comprehensive spiritual change*? If not, then we need to seriously understand that the short time still left to do so is greatly impacted by increasing spiritual pressure driving all choices, decisions and lifestyles in all cultures and societies more and more rapidly to either *upliftment*, or **destruction**.

The early months of 2011 have seen we in New Zealand hit with a hard reality check in the Christchurch earthquake, Australia and the U.S. hit with huge floods, and Japan reeling from a truly massive 'natural' catastrophe. As the whole thrust of this Work has explained **and warned**; though devastating in the human tragedy aspect, we should be under no illusions whatsoever that what we have witnessed and suffered **is not even the beginning** of what will come upon global humanity – **soon**! In reiteration from **Author's Note**:

As far back as the eighth century B.C., the Great Prophet, Isaiah [24:4-6], *foresaw* the path that we of Planet Earth **would take**. The present-day state of it and its global societies clearly shows a **calamitous** and **rapidly-deteriorating** situation. Once more, and hopefully **for some**, a timely **awakening**.

"The earth also is defiled under the inhabitants thereof; because they have,
transgressed the laws
changed the decrees
broken the everlasting covenant.

Therefore has the curse devoured the earth,
and those that dwell therein are desolate:
therefore the inhabitants of the earth are **burned**,[3]
and few men left."

---

[3] The meaning of the term, *burned* – which continues to puzzle Bible scholars, theologians and scientists alike – is both **clear and simple**. We explain it in the Work: **BIBLE "MYSTERIES" EXPLAINED**: Understanding "Global Societal Collapse" from "The Science" in The Bible ... [Chapter 12 – Sub: 12.6]

What will be *our* final choice and thus concomitant path forward, we may wonder? Or, more realistically, what might we have *already* chosen?

And what, therefore, will be our collective, 100% outcome – our Reaping?

23
Epilogue

I began this work with an initial notation of constant Maori reference to "the law" during my formative years in an extended, primarily Ngapuhi, *whanau*. In rather curious concert with that "ostensibly ennobled ethos" of such "law" was the great fear experienced in those childhood times. This strange reality sprang from my Maori *whanau's* own fear-ridden inability to free themselves from a truly enigmatic paradox that embraced dangerous psychic beliefs and practices which, nevertheless, were somehow believed to possess some kind of 'high spiritual knowledge' of ostensibly great *mana*. Even though there was the tempering influence of a Pakeha father, the great and unreasoning fear of the *whanau* inculcated those same fears in me during the very impressionable years of childhood and into one's teens. That fear translated, at times, into minor yet *actual* physical illnesses and effectively shackled the *whanau* in the most debilitating way. Whether those illnesses could be designated as being purely psychosomatic is irrelevant. The reality of them was real enough, as was the fear.

In later life the memory of that fear provided the motivation to strive to *deeply analyse* this whole thing of Maori thought-processes, and also provided the catalyst to finally make sense of it all. More especially the truly strange paradox of the historical and therefore undeniable pre-European Maori trait of "extreme savagery" coupled with the *overall* latter-day cultural ethos too often perversely deeming ancient Maori practices to be spiritually-elevated. In truth, they were never really *genuinely* 'Spiritual'!

To that end, the late Dr. Margaret Orbell, Professor of Maori Studies and author of associated books who kindly reviewed an early manuscript for me, queried why I had so strongly emphasised the practices of *utu* and *cannibalism* etc.. She believed that because so much had changed traditionally and societally, those aspects of Maori history no longer needed detailed investigation and/or analysis.

However, what has not been understood *thus far* by *either* Maori leaders/academics *or* Pakeha academics is the crucial *correlation* between the whole ethos of pre-European Maori savagery – culminating in my ancestor **Hongi Hika's** deadly campaigns of *utu* and cannibalism [recorded by early European chroniclers] – and the *subsequent emergence* of the line of Maori Religious Prophets.

For it was *exactly* that process – ultimately founded on those ancient practices but very quickly transformed *after* the arrival of Pakeha Religion – which eventually brought forth the **Calling of Ratana**. And thus what should have been *subsequently fulfilled* in, *and by*, the ***Maori race through its spiritual purpose***. But it was not recognised, hence its *non-fulfilment*. That is New Zealand's "***Lost Legacy***" And, most unfortunately, we as a people **will yet fully experience** how serious a loss that it was in the 20th century – and still is in the 21st!

So that we of Maori descent, especially, may reacquaint ourselves with the *then normal* practices of our ancestors, I include here a small selection of observations from early Europeans who were there, "on the ground" in the relatively short time of transition *from* the "old way". Recorded by them, they bore permanent witness to an era that, whilst certainly savage in the extreme, was nonetheless "how it was". Such history should not be cause for shame or silence, for that would simply be an emotional overreaction, as we may note from time to time in various cultures and nations. Understanding, however, can *and should* spring from the knowledge of the past. In the case of Te Maori in the context of this Work, *that past* should be very seriously thought about.

Whilst there are a number of quotes in **Part I** about the present subject matter; from a compilation at **www.heretical.com**, we offer a small selection of further observations.

'There is not a bay, not a cove, in New Zealand which has not witnessed horrible dramas, and woe to the white man who falls into the New Zealanders' hands.'

'Though the New Zealanders do not conceal their cannibalism, their chiefs sometimes endeavour to excuse themselves for it. "The fish of the sea eat one another", they say: "the large fish eat the small ones, the small ones eat insects; dogs eat men and men eat dogs, while dogs eat one another; finally, the gods devour other gods. Why, among enemies, should we not eat one another?" '

(Dr. Felix Maynard and Alexandre Dumas.
The Whalers, Hutchinson, 1937.)

'The dreadful Maori custom – or at least occasional habit – of exhuming and eating buried human bodies was also a *Fijian* custom.' — (Elsdon Best.)

'This custom of eating their enemies slain in battle ... has undoubtedly been handed down to them from earliest times; and we know it is not an easy matter *to wean a nation from their ancient customs*, let them be ever so inhuman and savage; especially *if that nation has no manner of connexion or commerce with strangers*. For it is *by this* that the greatest part of the human race has been *civilized*; an advantage which the New Zealanders, from their situation, never had.'

(Captain Cook. Italics mine.)

Succinctly encapsulated in Cook's so-very-correct observation is the exact reason **why** the Maori **needed** the arrival of the Pakeha in the first instance. And as we have strongly stated in this very book, there had to be a Coloniser. Of all the Maritime Nations that had ships in New Zealand waters at the time, it was fortunate for Maori that the British flag, and not any other, was planted here. Even with the Pakeha already becoming established, however, the ancient customs still had a few more decades to run before they were finally extinguished.

[Touai, a New Zealand chief who was brought to London in 1818 and resided there for a long time, becoming 'almost civilized']

"...confessed in his moments of nostalgia that what he most regarded in the country from which he was absent was the feast of human flesh, the feast of victory. He was weary of eating English beef; he claimed that there was a great analogy between the flesh of the pig and that of man. This last declaration he made before a sumptuously served table. The flesh of women and children was to him and his countrymen the most delicious, whilst certain Maories prefer that of a man of fifty, and that of a black rather than that of a white. His countrymen, Touai said, never ate the flesh raw, and preserved the fat of the rump for the purpose of dressing their sweet potatoes..."

(Dr. Felix Maynard and Alexandre Dumas.
The Whalers, Hutchinson, 1937.)

'The captives, with the exception of one old man and a boy who were sentenced to death, were apportioned amongst the conquering warriors as slaves. The tables were laid. About a hundred baskets of potatoes, a large supply of green vegetables, and equal quantities of whale blubber and human flesh, constituted the awful menu. The old man, from whose neck suspended the head of his son, while the body formed part of the cannibal feast, was brought forth and subjected to torture from the women before the last scene of all.

The banquet went on to a finish, and, though it proved none the less attractive to the participants, was rendered all the more hideous to the onlookers by the fact that the midsummer season when it took place, added to the hasty and incomplete manner in which the human flesh had been prepared in the ovens, caused the human – yet inhuman – food to become putrid in a most revolting form before it was spread out for the banquet. Officers of the boat witnessed this frightful orgy, and some of them brought to Hobart Town mementoes of the scene, dissected from the bodies as they lay out for the repast.'

(Gary Hogg, *Cannibalism and Human Sacrifice*, pp. 197-199.)

'To the gun I was stationed at, they dragged a man slightly wounded in the leg, and tied him hand and foot until the battle was over. Then they loosed him and put some questions to him, which he could not answer, nor give them any satisfaction thereof, as he knew his doom. They then took the fatal tomahawk and put it between his teeth, while another pierced his throat for a chief to drink his blood. Others at the same time were cutting his arms and legs off. They then cut off his head, quartered him and sent his heart to a chief, it being a delicious morsel and they being generally favoured with such rarities after an engagement.

In the meantime, a fellow that had proved a traitor wished to come and see his wife and children.They seized him and served him in like manner. Oh, what a scene for a man of Christian feeling, to behold dead bodies strewed about the settlement in every direction, and hung up at every native's door, their entrails taken out and thrown aside and the women preparing the ovens to cook them! By great persuasion, we prevailed on the savages not to cook any inside the fence, or to come into our houses during the time they were regaling themselves on what they termed sumptuous food – far sweeter, they said, than pork.

On our side, there were eight men killed, three children, and two women, during the seige. They got sixteen bodies, besides a great number that were half roasted, and dug several up out of the graves, half decayed, which they also ate. Another instance of their depravity was to make a musket ramrod red hot, enter it in the lower part of the victim's belly and let it run upwards, and then make a slight incision in a vein to let his blood run gradually, for them to drink...

I must here conclude, being very scanty of paper; for which reason, columns of the disgraceful conduct of these cannibals remain unpenned [...]' — by:

(Daniel Henry Sheridan.)

Whilst that kind of extreme savagery is thankfully long past, we may still note certain residual attitudes that *perhaps* hark back to an era when Maori were "quick to anger". In recent times when escorting Maori artefacts from one place to another, *taiaha*-wielding 'warriors' have struck defenceless members of the public. It is an unfortunate and totally unnecessary 'development' that accords no kudos to either the individuals concerned or to the cultural group/s as a whole. To be over-emotional in one's attitude when under the public gaze, or in over-reacting to some gesture from the observing public during a cultural performance or other, clearly reveals a *disturbing inability* to be *spiritually-objective* about such things.

Over-protectiveness resulting in physical attacks against others in such cases – and probably under the completely wrong belief that the group's *mana* has been slighted – is, in reality, no different *in principle* from that which my own ancestor, **Hongi Hika**, once used to exact *blood-utu*. The strange paradox is that the people struck in recent instances were not Maori, of course, but members of that ethnic group who have been largely responsible *for the recording and preserving of Maori culture* – in effect, saving it. **The Pakeha.**

From the standpoint of Spiritual Law, any people who emotionally cling to cultural artefacts in the belief that it is the spiritually correct thing to do, **_at death_** inevitably *discover the truth of the saying:*

"You can't take it with you!"

Revered Maori things such as carvings, *waka*, cloaks and other similarly endowed artefacts all must stay behind when the individual members of the race leave the earth. For these are not "...the works that will follow them..." at that time. The "works" that *actually* "follow one" are those produced by *how one has lived one's life in terms of thoughts and deeds*, and *not* by the production of material things ostensibly imbued with a people's personal perception of their own 'spirituality' or *mana*.

Thus the current strong emphasis by Maori on teaching traditional culture as the first priority and believing that it is all imbued with genuine spirituality conceals the fact that this direction, with its far too-strong and incorrect, *over-wrought emotionalism*, is actually taking too many Maori away from the Truth about Spiritual Law. And thereby further and further away from the necessary spiritual direction shown to Ratana and courageously anchored for Maoridom by him. His powerful spiritual example should be heeded!

The spiritual purpose of this book, therefore, may be likened to one of the ancient and more savage practices of the Maori – that of *manawa ora*. As explained in **Part 1**, this involved the hacking out of the heart of a slain enemy, singeing or burning it with a match or firestick and tossing it aside in an offering to the ancient Maori god of war – *Uenuku*. In essentially the same way, this Work has also gone to the heart of the matter, exposed it for close examination and placed it with the dust of incorrect beliefs, psychic fear and superstition where it belongs. Hopefully, it will never rise again, in furtherance of **Ratana's great 'Spiritual Mission for Maori'.**

Unlike the old barbarous practice, however, we have not left behind a dead and heartless corpse. In its place we have offered **'the life-blood of Spiritual Truth'** whereby the once spiritually-dead and lifeless shell *can rise up to take its proper place*. This time, however, transformed into *a new and true kind of warrior*. A warrior better prepared and equipped for a vastly different and more *noble* purpose – *if that is the choice*. A purpose, moreover, that offers the greatest of all spiritual potentials at this very time of 'Rapidly-Fading' possibilities.

Academically, an acute and intense dislike of school up to and including Whangarei Boy's High in the early 1960s 'waiting for the magic leaving age of 15', translated to reaching the 'dizzy heights' of a few months into a Form 5 education level. That was seemingly not the ideal 'academic' background for this particular project. Yet whilst the task of writing this Work has been a major challenge and undertaking over many years, it has been one that has been especially *spiritually-fulfilling*. For even though *clearly directed* in its overall format through *very especial guidance*, there was still the requirement to find sufficiently-clear phrasing for the explanations and analogies in the elucidation of the spiritual concepts herein. I sincerely believe I have achieved that aim.

In retrospect, the small amount of 'formal' schooling probably did provide sufficient grounding for the writing of this Work. For one needed the vital *experiential-learning* that only 'real-life' can offer. Notwithstanding the taking of literary liberties in this book, the relatively short time spent at school actually allowed me the spiritual freedom to let my personal life's experiences shape and mould the spiritual direction I would eventually choose, unshackled by the dogma of too many fixed ideas and theories – at least from the standard educational mind-set anyway.

Though I readily recognise a good education as being clearly desirable for life in general, my own personal experience showed that, whilst all manner of academic subjects are taught, insufficient attention is paid to the more vital issue of 'how to live correctly'. In essence, of course, according to the knowledge of **The Spiritual Laws of Creation**; that which permitted us *conscious life*, which *permeates* every single aspect of life, and which should therefore be *specifically included in school education*. We reiterate knowledge of the true "**Spiritual Laws**", not simply *religion*!

Not that I left school immediately I turned 15 to find this **Truth**. One did not know such a thing even existed then. All one knew was small-town Whangarei and a *whanau* terribly debilitated by their restrictive, fear-ridden psychic world where being frightened of the dark, the Morepork, every insect and bird that appeared and every clap of thunder was the norm. I simply followed an indefinable urge to get out into the wider world away from the constraints of such a confining, fear-ridden environment.

That necessary journey led me to the Army and South East Asia. The years of rawness in valuable experiencing on Military Operations there and the inevitable deaths of comrades, coupled with the glaring fact that even members of the *extended whanau* were still locked into their fearful but little-understood psychic reality, ultimately provided the sub-conscious seed to eventually force the question: **Why?** The subsequent ensuing search after the conscious decision to begin that search in 1973, *eventually* provided the answers.

So the years away from the *whanau*, particularly outside New Zealand, provided the necessary experiences to readily see how pointless and absolutely non-spiritual were the psychic beliefs and practices of the Maori. Memories of threats of *makutu* and *utu* to and from the *whanau* and even between extended members of the group seem so sad and pointless now from a perspective which encompasses the ultimate knowledge contained within **The Laws of Spiritual Truth**. Even in the *whanau* today; with some little has really changed.

Thus this Work incorporates an added dimension in the fact that one of the reasons why I set out to write it in the first place was to clarify these 'psychic' issues for all of Maori origin in the first instance – but also for Pakeha New Zealanders too. For these very aspects of fear that were the lot of the *whanau* of my childhood are, in the final analysis, generated by, and through, *precise and lawful processes*.

Yet, even now, decades later, the same aspiritual practices that held sway during childhood are still dabbled with by certain members of that same generation and, sadly, also some within the newer, emerging ones too. All still fearing it, of course, but refusing to simply let it die out. And all the while still wrongly believing it to somehow imbue one with great spiritual power. Whilst not entrenched in the *whanau* psyche today as blatantly obvious as it once was; nonetheless, it is still there. In the present, however, it thrives in a more subtle way, yet still exerting its menacing and detrimental influence against the targeted vulnerable.

Therefore, if I appear to be just one more "lone voice in the wilderness", or one more disturbing "boat-rocker", then I count myself blessed and fortunate indeed for, historically, I stand in very good company. The challenge to write this book – presented to me via a strong inner urging – has been answered. And my *wairua* is at greater peace through the completion of it.

Whether it is believed, accepted, rubbished, mocked or offered any other view, *is the concern of the reader alone*. I have simply completed what I was *directed* to undertake, and thus what I know I was meant to do.

The free-will choice of each individual will ultimately determine how it is received.

As constantly reinforced throughout, all our life-path choices will always be determined by our personal, free-will decisions in any case. *Thus the reader is free to accept or reject this work too.*

And, as stated at the very beginning, whilst clearly repetitious in many places, that repetition necessarily serves to *constantly* and *strongly* reinforce concepts within the book that stand well outside the square of what would be considered the societal or world norm, *at least at this present time*. This ongoing Work being the overall **poropiti for Maoridom and the people of Aotearoa as a whole**, the timing of its completion as a **First Edition** in 2006 was precisely determined. The *stronger* **Second Edition** published in 2008 fulfilled, *in its natural progression*, the particular prophecy of Ratana regarding the era of the woman Prime Minister arising *"...from out of the Labour Party"*.

This **Final Edition** of 2011 represents the commensurate *final poropiti* of the *final key* which completes – from **Author's Note** – *"...the final step"*. This *'final step'* is now *'revealed'* in the following pages of this **Epilogue**.

To this end, it is my sincere hope that readers who persevered to this point, and whose spirits may have been agitated, unsettled, or seeking clarification about the current uncertain state of the world and within Aotearoa, may find the same "peace in knowing" that I have experienced for many years now. Whilst this Work is relatively comprehensive in terms of how it *mainly relates* to a single people it is, nevertheless, only a "signpost". It is a "signpost" in keeping with the Spiritual Mission of Ratana, yet pointing the clear way to where *all* explanations of life and Spiritual Truth can be found. Thus a "signpost" pointing the way to that ultimate Truth which both contains, and is contained within:

"The Spiritual Laws of Creation!" i.e., — CREATION-LAW!

As also stated at the beginning of this Work, whilst the main reasons for writing it were those of Maori issues, set in place and moulded by the events and fears of my formative years, the actual inspiration for it came from two sources.

1. A "vision" in 1995 showing both the *arrival* of Maori to Aotearoa, *and* the later, *crucial* meeting of Maori and Pakeha in its *spiritual significance* [also showing the threads which formed the Chapters of the book]. And the later revelation of the *spiritual magnitude* of Ratana's Mission for the Maori race.

   More importantly, however:

2. The discovery, during my long 'searching phase', of a particularly special **Spiritual Work** *without which* the explanations of **The Spiritual Laws**, Maori issues and about Ratana's mission *could not even have been attempted*.

That 'elevated knowledge' is precisely the **definitive Spiritual Work** which one was tasked *to seek out and bring back to this land* in order for **Ratana's Mission to be finally completed**. Notwithstanding that reality now; it was actually Ratana *himself* who should have brought that very especial Teaching back to New Zealand. For **It** was *spiritually ordained* to become the *cornerstone* of his Church in the very first instance, and subsequent **Spiritual-knowledge foundation** for *all* in this land. Then later, **in accordance with the ordained Spiritual Purpose of the Maori Race through Ratana**, to be taken beyond these shores **by Maori** to the indigenous peoples of the "New World" countries.

The greatest Mandate to write this Work, even though initially revealed through the key "Vision" and subsequently anchored during the Chapter on Ratana, was ultimately derived from that especial Spiritual Work alluded to, and to which I was directed. Thus the key connecting thread from the very beginning of the journey through to "Ratana" and to this greatest of revelations, **now completes a crucial spiritual cycle for Aotearoa and its peoples**.

Therefore reader – **in particular you of Te Iwi Maori** – seriously understand that what is written in this Work is *so written* because the Maori race **failed** in their spiritual task last century. Other races before you – also chosen – have also failed. As a people, through your Prophets, you were probably the last to be given the opportunity to re-seed **The Truth** [not *religion*] for other peoples before the now imminent and final collapse of societies, cultures and religions etc., across the entire globe. In its train will necessarily come the associated and terrible destruction required to bring to an end all that refuses to obey inviolable and immutable **CREATION-LAW**!

You were Called for this highest of Spiritual tasks. But *not because* you were a spiritual people. No! *Quite the opposite*. As we have stated often and conclude here in this **Epilogue**, the historical record unequivocally shows the unparalleled savagery of pre-European Maori. *So why you as a people?* Quite simply: It was because you possessed the *latent intelligence* to grasp, **through the line of Maori Prophets**, the now necessary *spiritual direction* from out of the *new* knowledge **which the Pakeha brought to you**. But which *they*, as a people, had *long-distorted* through their *religions*.

More to the point, the greatest of your Prophets – **Ratana** – was specifically Called to go *past* the knowledge that came with the Pakeha then. Ratana was not only given the spiritual talents and abilities of healing and prophecy – but more especially visionary-seeing. A key purpose of that gift was to **find** what Jesus referred to as **The All-Truth** [John 16] that we of *all* humankind were to await and seek out at this very time. [**But of which it was also prophesied that only the few would find and recognise**.]

"I have still much more to tell you; but you are not yet able to bear it. When, however, the **Spirit of Truth Himself** comes, <u>**He will instruct you in all the truth**</u>: for His utterances do not proceed from Himself; but just what He learns **He will declare**, and the events that are coming **He** will announce to you.
<u>**He Himself will honour me**;...</u>"

(John 16: 12-14, Fenton.)

Reader: Do not make the foolish mistake of believing that **The Spirit of Truth** here is some kind of filmy, amorphous wraith as the Christian Church *so very wrongly teaches.* For there is the very sure 'Personal Pronoun' — **He**! There is also the equally sure term: — **Himself**!

And, of course, the very telling sentence:
"**He Himself will honour me**;..."

Special Note:
The non-recognition of the true nature of **The Spirit of Truth** by global Christendom coupled with their ongoing and terrible distortions of crucial Bible Scripture effectively means that 2,000 million [i.e. 2 billion] so-called 'believers' have *missed the moment,* exactly as was prophesied; – i.e., *"He shall come like a thief in the night..."* — *"Only the few would know..."*

You, reader, will find 'brutally-logical' 'no-holds-barred' clarification of key Scriptural distortions in the *primary* Work of **Crystal Publishing** – the writing of which, like *this* Work, was *also directed.* It is:

BIBLE "MYSTERIES" EXPLAINED
UNDERSTANDING "GLOBAL SOCIETAL COLLAPSE" FROM THE "SCIENCE"
IN THE BIBLE
What Every Scientist, Bible Scholar and Ordinary Man Needs to Know.

So: What is this most especial Teaching of **The All-Truth** that we allude to? Because It was not in New Zealand at the time of Ratana's Calling, it was his ordained task *to find It and bring here.* From the knowledge therein, he was to *more strongly* build his Church, Movement and Ministry. It was therefore absolutely necessary for him to journey *from* this land. Even though becoming established in Europe, Ratana did not find **It** at the time of his travels there. Had he done so, he would have brought back the 1931 Edition of that Work. Unfortunately, however, Ratana's primary mission in Europe then evidently revolved around a 'land-grievance' claim to The League of Nations, in which he was unsuccessful. Thus, he, his followers, his Church, his work and mission – and Aotearoa as a whole – were denied the greatest knowledge of all at a singularly crucial time in human history and *spiritual-knowledge evolution.*

The 1931 Edition was later reformatted and extended to include further knowledge from the Author. That more comprehensive Work leads the reader to a profound insight into the great questions to life, the very structure of Creation itself, and much more; a level of knowledge simply not available anywhere else. That especial Spiritual Work is:

*   *   *   *   *

IN THE LIGHT OF TRUTH

The Grail Message

by Abd-ru-shin

*   *   *   *   *

Recognition of that **All-Truth** by global humanity – as should have been the case – would have *guaranteed* a world of harmonious peace, simply because we would all – to coin a today-phrase – *be reading from the same page*.

You may wonder why such a Work might be called "**The Grail Message**"? Does the word **Grail** in this case refer to **The Holy Grail**? Millions of people on earth believe that that elusive object might be any number of things: from the cup which caught the blood of Jesus, to the body (the vessel) of an earthly woman, and perhaps various other things in between. But all believed to be here on earth. Since the purpose of *this* Work is to bring the knowledge of **The Truth** to the people of *this* land, the concomitant knowledge of the *actual* Holy Grail can also be so revealed. In fact it has never ever been hidden for it is crucially-imperative for humankind to know of It. Its true nature, unfortunately for us, we have simply not recognised.

From The Bible, the "**Revelation of John**" tells us *exactly* what the true **Holy Grail** is.

> Then He said to me, *"It has come! I, The Alpha and the Omega, the beginning and the end. I will freely give to the thirsty* **from the fountain of the water of life**.*"*

The actual Holy Grail is thus the First Creation of God! Therefore, its place of being **could never ever be in the World of Matter.**

We may clearly note, therefore, that It **is** a vessel, but a Vessel at the ***Highest point of Creation***; a Vessel which dispenses the very Power of Life Itself – the **"water of life"**. Long ago, a few blessed ones were permitted to see a "radiated picture" of It, and that is how the knowledge about It entered the consciousness of a particular group of humanity. Most unfortunately, however, the once sure knowledge of "The Grail" eventually became myth and legend. And that is why the so-called "search" for It holds much of the Western world in thrall today.

The crucially essential Work, **"In The Light Of Truth"**, is for *all* humanity – thus for ***all religions*** – for It *is* the knowledge of **The All-Truth** *from* **The Almighty!** [We should seriously note here that both in Name and Title, ***The Alpha and Omega belong solely to He Who is The Will of God!***] They should therefore not be given as everyday names to humans, as was the case with Ratana's two sons.

Ratana's lifetime occupied the very time-frame in which this final gift of **The All-Truth** came to Earth with its **Bringer** — **Abd-ru-shin**. Hence Ratana's recorded disquiet that he had "missed something". Gandhi also stated much the same; that he had *'missed his guru'*.

As the author of a Work that offers deeper knowledge about the *true* meaning of Bible Scripture [and therefore from which we, in *this* book, necessarily elucidate the same for you, the reader]; the name – **Abd-ru-shin** – might, at first glance, seem rather 'out of place'. Perhaps more so for 'Western Christendom'; for that *especial Arabic name* translates to English as:

SON (Servant) Of THE LIGHT!

So: Why an Arabic name for the author in the final **Form** of the **Work — IN THE LIGHT OF TRUTH**? If you have read *this* book to *this* point, you will have well-noted the necessarily strong emphasis on the knowledge of **The Laws of Creation** throughout, including one that is problematic for many Westerners particularly: i.e., **The Law of Rebirth.** [You now also know the *true meaning* of **The Holy Grail** – the **Origin** of the very **Life-Force** for **Creation** – and therefore why the word **Grail** is included in the overall Title of that most especial Work.]

Notwithstanding the gamut of reactions from non-believers around the *concept* of "Rebirth", – from curiousity, to disbelief and rejection, to sheer vitriolic hostility; it is, nonetheless, an ***absolute reality*** under inviolable **CREATION-LAW**!

In this case, therefore, **Abd-ru-shin** – in His *first incarnation of that Name* – was an **Arabian Prince** who lived in the same time-frame as '**Moses the Law-Giver**' and the Egyptian Pharaoh, **Ramses II The Great** (c.1300-1224 B.C.) He was well known to both, but *especially to Moses.* For the logically-minded *astute* reader, therein lies a *clue* to a ***stupendous connection.*** To be strongly associated with two men who not only hold key places in human history but whose lives and activity influenced countless millions thereafter, obviously presupposes the probability that **Prince Abd-ru-shin** also held a key place then. And that is so!

So whilst there were many Pharaohs by the name of Ramses, only *one* was given the title: **The Great!** Once more for the astute reader, therefore; to be historically associated with *both* **Ramses The Great** *and* **Moses the Law-Giver** clearly reveals the importance of **Abd-ru-shin**.

The stupendous nature of the Work — **IN THE LIGHT OF TRUTH** — unequivocally testifies that sure fact to we of the present time.

Because there is no well-known historical record about **Prince Abd-ru-shin**, it would be easy to simply dismiss this nonetheless *actual historical figure* as a fabrication.[1] However, in the context of the immutable **Laws of Creation**; – and the equally-sure fact that contrary to the collective opinions of hundreds of millions of believers we can state that **Jesus** will not set physical foot on earth again – so, too, can we also state what will one day be revealed as sure and irrefutable evidence of *this Man's* life on earth.[2]

Murdered by a knife-wielding assassin – probably on the orders of Ramses – before He could *completely fulfil* His Mission on earth *then*, the earthly cloak of Abd-ru-shin for that particular incarnation was placed in a Pyramid-tomb, now long-buried under desert sands. At the appropriate time, His tomb will one day be revealed. Then, however, the

---

[1]Note the quite recent discovery of the existence of the Egyptian Pharaoh, Akhenaton. Previously unknown due to the effacing of all references to him by the succeeding Pharaoh; Akhenaton, the so-called 'heretic', is now the most studied Pharaoh of all.

[2]In the primary Work of Crystal Publishing: BIBLE "MYSTERIES" EXPLAINED; Understanding "Global Societal Collapse" from the 'Science' in The Bible... from the Divine knowledge of The ALL-TRUTH, we reveal [in the Chapter on Jesus] where the once-crucified body of **Jesus** lies [with the legs 'not broken'.]

Christian Church, particularly – but *all* religions and belief systems ultimately – will have to contend with the hieroglyphic inscriptions on that especial tomb.

For the very last line of His story, *then*, reveals the completion of His Mission for humanity in the *20th century* as **THE ONE** Who was to come. The **SON OF GOD**, **JESUS**, is thus honoured by:

THE 'SPIRIT OF TRUTH' — IMANUEL — THE SON OF MAN:

THE "WILL OF GOD"

in HIS "ALL-TRUTH":

"IN THE LIGHT OF TRUTH!"

Hence such a close association with '**Moses**, the **Law-Giver**', and thus the continuation of His Name and Title – **Abd-ru-shin** – for that Work. Being *able* to write such knowledge in the first place very obviously means that **He** carries that highest of knowledge *Living* **within Him**. His Origin is therefore revealed in the Work.

Within that crucial Work, however, He states – as the *primary* consideration for all – to:

"Heed the Word, not the Bringer!"

...As should always have been done, as well, with the Teachings of Jesus – He Who brought the knowledge of Creation and Divine Law to Earth *in a form understandable to believers then* – and with all others who similarly sought to *genuinely enlighten* earthly humanity. ... However, in the emotional stupidity that characterises we humans generally, we sought, instead, to *focus* on the 'Bringer/s'. The practice of elevating them to become the *focus* of the particular religion – rather than on *the Truths* they sought to impart – has resulted in the mess of religious intolerance and bloodshed we are burdened with today.

Quite logically, therefore, only one outcome is certain: Complete destruction of all *they* who refuse, along with all *that* which refuses, to heed and live by *true* **CREATION-LAW** — clearly explained for **all** of global humanity in the Work:

"IN THE LIGHT OF TRUTH!"

The necessary 'cleansing' that will rid the world of the many millions of blind, deluded fundamentalists of every religious 'bent' who radically promote their particular belief as the so-called *only truth* for all will finally usher in the long-awaited **Millennium of Peace**.

*　　*　　*　　*　　*

So great was the *mana* of Gandhi that, had he found 'his guru', he would surely have influenced many millions throughout the Commonwealth to embrace **The ALL-TRUTH**. On a smaller but no less important scale, the same would have occurred in Aotearoa/New Zealand.

Even though Ratana did not find in *his* lifetime, there was nonetheless <u>***still the ordained requirement for that very Truth to be brought to this land***</u>. And just as the Maori race were Called to lead all colonised peoples to the true and final reason for colonisation, the *country* of Aotearoa/New Zealand and *its people* were *also* Called to set the correct spiritual example for other societies. In both cases – failure. All that is left now is probably just *individual* recognition of the great and **Immutable Truths**, thus fulfilling the ancient prophecy/indictment that:

"Only the few would know."

Now translated into at least 10 languages to date; since Its first publication in Europe in the 1930's, very many thousands have recognised the stupendous nature and importance of the Work: **IN THE LIGHT OF TRUTH!** In many countries across the globe, associated Movements have formed to disseminate It. Precisely because It *is* **THE ALL-TRUTH** for *all* things, counted among the adherents of this Teaching in the many countries where It has taken root may be found people from all social, racial, cultural and economic levels; including scientists, financiers, industrialists, educationalists and politicians – even some nuclear physicists.

Previous religious beliefs are abandoned by virtually all who come to recognition of **It**, simply because **The Work** transcends *all* earthly scientific 'knowledge', religions and belief systems. Even explanations of the nature of 'black holes', *long before cosmologists really knew of them*, are there. But even that degree of knowledge is really only "the tip of the iceberg", for **It** contains *all* that we humans are *capable* of understanding. Therefore a level of knowledge that the disciples of Jesus could not hope to grasp then, hence His statement that they should – under the aegis of **The Law of Rebirth** – watch for the **ALL-TRUTH** and **HE** who would bring **It**.[3]

Despite the fact that since the 1930's hundreds of thousands have embraced this knowledge, that number still represents only a tiny fraction of people on earth. Precisely therewith, however:

The few 'who would find' – and know!

May you, reader, also choose to seek out this knowledge and thereby build within yourself that peace of spirit that must necessarily accept, yet objectively and compassionately understand, the increasingly disturbing and *seemingly* incomprehensible fate of suffering humankind on earth today. Unfortunately, however, a fate brought about simply by our collective refusal to pay heed to those Laws under which we have life.

In particular that decisive Law which unequivocally states in both perfect **Love** and perfect **Justice**:

> ".. for what a man sows, that will he also reap... And acting nobly, we shall not suffer..; So then, as we have opportunity, let us do good to all.."

(Gal.6: 7-10, Fenton.)

Had the greater majority of humankind *really* sought *and found*, the hypocritical distortions of all religions, especially, would have thankfully died a natural death. In the present, the end-excrescence of increasing global religious intolerance and over-wrought emotionalism has brought with it death and madness as its now-natural accompaniment.

As the author of *this* contentious yet *necessary* Work, I have completed my task in accordance with what I was guided to do. Within that ordained paradigm, the **All-Truth** – which I was guided to search for [and very thankfully recognised] – arrived in this so-blessed land in 1983.

---

[3]The clear connotation here is that Jesus is not **The One Who Comes**, and therefore, there must be Another. Note Two Titles: **Son of God** and **Son of Man**. Also Two Names: **Jesus** and **Imanuel**! This terrible and *inexcusable distortion* of this crucial **Truth** by the Christian Church has led millions astray. So many millions of 'already asleep brides', awaiting an **Event** that has *already passed them by*. [See **BIBLE "MYSTERIES" EXPLAINED**, Chapter 12, **The Two Sons of God**, for detailed clarification. www.publishme.co.nz]

As I have necessarily stated and repeat here for the last time:
You, reader, are free to accept or reject this knowledge.

The overall story of the Maori race is a truly amazing one. Unique among the many peoples of the world, through Ratana their Called Prophet they were probably the last to be offered the chance to spiritually re-seed **The Truth** for others. And irrespective of whether you, the reader, academic or layman, Maori or Pakeha, born here or not, believe what has passed before you: **YOU** cannot change what is written here.

And neither can I change this reality!

For those spiritually asleep and who would choose to mock and revile; two simple messages. One from **The Son of God**, **Jesus**, to one of His disciples who asked for leave to attend the funeral of a member of his *earthly* family:

"Let the [spiritually] dead bury their [spiritually] dead."

(Parenthetic additions mine.)

— and secondly — **Watch the nightly global News!**

Maori today, most unfortunately, are too-strongly engaged with the ***spiritually-dead negativity*** of tribalism, customary law and kaumatuaism etc., which, in its train, ultimately seeks *easy earthly gains* through the Treaty Settlement process. Beware the warning of **The Lord!**
"What does it profit a man if he gains the whole world but loses his soul?" [*wairua*]

To you of Te Iwi Maori, therefore: I once more remind you of what you have forgotten, conveniently ignore, or have relegated to the rubbish heap of disbelief or disinterest; — the very serious ***spiritual admonition*** of your great Prophet, **Ratana**:

"Let us ***first*** unite in the **Father**, and ***then*** we will unite in the **land**."

And what of the key proclamation in your '**Maori Battalion March**', to which you *rightfully accord* great kudos? For it incorporates the 'spiritually-correct' ethos of what is *given* and to **Whom**, both in battle and sacrifice for a *genuinely* noble cause ***Firstly***; then secondly and thirdly, respectively!

Thus with sure courage: 'Ake, ake, kia kaha e' –

'For **GOD**, for **King** and for **country**...'

Quite clearly, we do not, in any *truly genuine way*, give what *should* be the *first* thing **First**! For even though we often hear the hymn, *"How Great Thou Art"*, sung at events deemed important by Maori, cultural and societal *continuation* of just *the earthly* nonetheless invariably holds strong sway as the *first* consideration.

The rise of the Maori Prophet, **Te Kooti Arikirangi**, saw him before his death prophesy one who would be *the* Prophet to lead Maori. Today we readily recognise that *one* as **Ratana**.
Ratana, in turn, *also* prophesied one *after* him who would; at the appointed time:

> "...reveal to you all the fruits of these prophecies. ... [and] to the whole country."

He further prophesied:

> "...I will send you a Mangai [anointed mouthpiece] that you will *not be able to suppress*. ... Where is this Mangai, and when will this Mangai arrive here? You cannot tell me this..."

The time that these things would come to pass was also prophesied by him.

> "...there is a day unfolding when you will see two towers standing on the Mount of Olives, and at that time you will see *a woman rising up from the Labour Party who will become Prime Minister*, and then you will know you are at the doorway, not nearing it, but ***actually at the doorway***..."

(Excerpts from "Ratana Revisited: An Unfinished Legacy"
Keith Newman. [Emphases mine.])

As I have already stated but *necessarily repeat here*: The comprehensive Second Edition of this Work found its day at that very time of the *emergence* of that particular woman Prime Minister. With this **Final Edition** of this most necessary knowledge and *poropiti* for Te Iwi Maori in the first instance, and for *everyone else* in this land in the second, we have now *all* passed *through* the "***doorway***".

My choice in all of this was simple: To choose to do it, or to choose to not do it.
May you all *truly awaken* – before the "***too-late***" finally arrives!

In conclusion:

Previously stated in **Author's Note** at the *beginning* of this Work : *For the final time* I once more restate the following key **Proclamation** at the *end* of it.

Since its original publication, opposition to it from certain [presently unknown] sources has already been directed at me. In seeking *personal help* on how to counter that – and what will surely yet still come my way: From the very "**Source**" that has been **both** the *Guiding Hand* **and** *Voice* for this now completed Work; clear words were given for the purpose.

The *primary role* of a Prophet is to *warn*. Therefore, at the *close* of this **Final Edition** of "**THE COMING OF PAKEHA RELIGION**", the *Message* from that **Sure Source** grants me **The Mandate** to ***Proclaim*** the following:

If I do not tell you this, <u>who</u> is going to?

(Charles Ihaia Hita-Brown.
A Son of Ngapuhi
A servant
– and –)

The Last in the Line of the Maori Prophets!

A
Bibliography

1. The Holy Bible in Modern English, Ferrar Fenton, Destiny Publishers, Massachusetts U.S.A., 1966 Edition.

2. The Holy Bible, Authorised (King James) Version, Eyre and Spottiswoode (Publishers) Ltd., Great Britain.

3. The Jerusalem Bible, Reader's Edition, First published 1968, Darton, Longman and Todd Ltd., London.

4. The Apocrypha of the Old Testament, Revised Standard Version, Published by Thomas Nelson and Sons Ltd.

5. The Gospel of the Essenes, The original Hebrew and Aramaic texts translated and edited by Edmund Bordeaux Szekely, Revised Edition, London, C.W. Daniel, 1976.

6. Cruden's Complete Concordance to the Old and New Testaments (and to the Apocrypha), Revised Edition, Guildford: Lutterworth Press, 1954.

7. The Christian and Reincarnation, Stephen Lampe, Millenium Press (UK), 1990.

8. Building Future Societies, Stephen Lampe, Millenium Press (UK) 1994.

9. Ratana, The man, the church, the political party, J.M. Henderson, Wellington, N.Z.A.H. & A.W Read in association with the Polynesian Society, 1972.

10. Ratana Revisited - An Unfinished Legacy, Keith Newman, Reed Publishing Ltd., New Zealand, First published 2006.

11. Maori Warfare, A.P. Vayda, Published by A.H. & A.W. Reed, Wellington, Polynesian Society, 1960 (Reprinted 1970).

12. Mana From Heaven: A century of Maori prophets in New Zealand, Bronwyn Elsmore, Tauranga, N.Z. Moana Press, 1989.

13. New Zealand's Heritage, Volumes 1-5, Published by Paul Hamlyn Limited, Wellington, New Zealand. Produced in association with Whitcombe and Tombs Ltd.

14. Dictionary of the Maori Language, H.W. Williams, GP Publications, 7th Edition, 1992.

15. Maori Religion and Mythology: Being an account of the cosmogony, anthropogeny, religious beliefs and rites, Elsdon Best, Volumes 1 & 2, Dominion Museum Bulletin No.10., Govt. Printer, Wellington, New Zealand, First published 1924 (Reprinted edition, 1976).

16. The Coming of The Maori, Te Rangihiroa, Sir Peter Buck, 2nd. Edition Wellington, Maori Purposes Fund Board, Whitcoulls, 1950.

17. People of the Great Ocean: Aspects of human biology of the early Pacific, Philip Houghton, Cambridge, England, Cambridge University Press, 1996.

18. The Story of a Treaty, Claudia Orange, Bridget Williams Books Limited, 1993

19. The Dictionary of New Zealand Biography Volume 1, 1769-1869, Bridget Williams and the Department of Internal A☐airs, 1993.

20. The Dictionary of New Zealand Biography Volume 2, 1870-1900, Bridget Williams and the Department of Internal A☐airs, 1993.

21. Making Peoples: A history of the New Zealanders - from Polynesian settlement to the end of the nineteenth century James Belich, Auckland, N.Z., Allen Lane/Penguin, 1996.

22. Redemption Songs: A life of Te Kooti Arikirangi Te Turiki, Judith Binney, Auckland University Press, Bridget Williams Books, 1995.

23. Musket Wars, Ron Crosby, Reed Publishing.

24. The Adventures of Kimble Bent, James Cowan, part of "The New Zealand Wars: 1845-1872", Whitcombe and Tombs Ltd., Wellington, 1911.

25. The Story of Aotearoa, T.G. Hammond, Christchurch, Lyttelton Times, 1924.

26. Nga Tau Tohetohe: Years of Anger, Ranginui Walker, Auckland, Penguin, 1987.

27. Nga Ia O Te Oranga: Trends in Maori Mental Health 1984 - 1993 Te Puni Kokori, First published 1996. (Information and analysis by Dr Geo☐ Bridgman and Lorna Dyall.)

28. "Archives of General Psychiatry" U.S. publication.

29. Moriori: A people Rediscovered Michael King, Auckland, Penguin, 1987.

30. Song of Waitaha, Elders of Waitaha, Published by Ngatapuwae Trust, 1994.

31. Te Wheke – The Celebration of Infinite Wisdom Rangimarie Turuki Pere.

32. Great Illustrated Dictionary, Readers Digest, First Edition, 1984, USA.

33. The Concise Oxford Dictionary of Proverbs 1983 Edition, Oxford University Press, First Printing 1982, USA.

34. New England Journal of Medicine.

35. Reflections on Life After Life, Raymond A. Moody, Bantam Books USA & Canada, 3rd Printing, 1978.

36. The Soul - Whence and Whither Hazrat Inayat Khan, East-West Publication, 1984 Edition.

37. The Romeo Error, Lyall Watson, London: Hodder and Stoughton, 1974.

38. The Primal Scream, Dr Arthur Janov, Abacus, Great Britain, 1996 Reprinted Edition.

39. "A Land Fit For Criminals; an insider's view of crime, punishment and justice in the UK." Professor David Fraser. Book Guild Publishing, Surrey.

40. Ideas and Opinions Albert Einstein, Bonanza Books, New York, 1954.

41. Philosophy History and Problems Third Edition, Samuel Enoch Stumpf, McGraw-Hill, USA 1983.

42. On the Speech of Neanderthal Man Philip Lieberman and Edmund S. Crelin, Linguistic Inquiry 2:203-222, Cambridge Mass., MIT Press.

43. Sophie's World, Jostein Gaardner, Phoenix House, Great Britain, 1996 Edition.

44. Milk: The Deadly Poison, Robert Cohen, Argus Publishing USA, 1998.

45. The Atlas of the Universe, Patrick Moore, Mitchell Beazley Publishers, London, 1981 Edition.

46. Lifecloud: the origin of life in the universe, Fred Hoyle and Chandra Wickramasinghe, 1978.

47. The Life and Letters of Charles Darwin (Editor - Frances Darwin), 2nd Edition, London: John Murray, 1887.

48. The Mystery of Life's Origin: Reassessing Current Theories, Charles B. Thaxton, Walter L. Bradley, Richard L. Olsen, Philosophical Library, 1984.

49. The Sacred Balance: Rediscovering our place in nature, David Suzuki, Allen and Unwin, Australia, 1997.

50. The Indians, Old West Series, Time-Life Books, 1975.

51. North American Indian Chiefs, General Editor: Karl Nagerfeld, Tiger Books International, London. 1995.

52. Native American Myths and Legends, Editorial Consultant, Colin F. Taylor, New York: Smithmark, 1994.

53. The Handbook of Unusual Natural Phenomena (Eyewitness Accounts of Nature's Greatest Mysteries), William R. Corliss, Arlington House, Crown Publishers, New York.

54. Earthquake Information Bulletin 10: 231-33, 1978, National Earthquake Information Centre (NEIC), Published by the Centre (Rockville Md) Serial Publication, Bi-monthly, 1970 - 1985.

55. Earthquakes and the Urban Environment, Volume II, G. Lennis Berlin, Published Boca Raton, Fla: CRC Press, c 1980.

56. Friends of the Earth.

57. ASH: Action on smoking and health.

58. Soil & Health March/April 1998 Vol.57, No.1, Published bi-monthly by Soil & Health Association of New Zealand Inc.

59. New Zealand Herald.

60. Sunday Star Times.

61. Guardian Weekly

62. "Our World" The Savage Earth, BBC Series (screened 1998).

63. Encarta - Microsoft.

B

Glossary of Maori Words

The Maori words/terms contained in this glossary represent those used in this Work. Where words with more than one meaning are used, the particular word usage at any given point will generally be that pertaining solely to the explanations directly concerned with the subject matter at hand. The reader can readily obtain the full range of definitions from most Maori dictionaries. For the most part, the Dictionary from which the meanings are derived is Williams' "Dictionary of the Maori Language", Seventh Edition. We have also utilised terms present in the work of the early chroniclers, but they will not differ markedly from our chosen standard. However, because this work is a revisionist analysis of Maori spirituality in the first instance, the few exceptions to this have been certain variations in some meanings that will reflect the spiritual direction that is offered here, and which we will have brought to the notice of the reader.

ahi	fire
ahi komau	subterranean fire
ahua	form – as opposed to substance
Aotearoa	New Zealand
aria	form of incantation, visible material emblem of an atua
ariki	term applied to most hereditary and therefore most tapu of chiefs
aroha	love
atua	god(s)
haka	vigorous dance, war dance
hangi	earth-oven
hapu	sub-tribe
hara	calamity resulting from transgression of tapu
Hine nui te po	goddess of the Underworld and darkness
Hiona	part of church complex
hongi	smell, sni□, salute - by pressing the noses together; incorrectly called rub noses.
hui	meeting, conference, debate
Hurai	Jews (transliteration)
Io	the core of all gods (Supreme Being)
Io-nui	greatest of all gods
Io-roa	everlasting, not knowing death
Io-mataaho	seen only in a radiant light
Io-matangaro	the hidden (unseen) face
Io-matanui	the all-seeing
Io-matua	the parent of human beings and of all things
Io-matua-kore	the parentless, nothing but himself
Io-taketake	permanent, all enduring, complete, immovable
Io-te-pukenga	the source of all things
Io-te-wananga	the source of all knowledge, whether good or evil
Io-te-toi-o-nga-rangi	the crown of the heavens
Io-te-waiora	the welfare of all things
Io-te-whiwhia	name denotes that nothing can possess anything of its own volition
Io-urutapu	the totally sacred
iwi	tribe
kaha	courage
kahu huruhuru	feather cloak(s)
kaihunga	cannibalistic orgies
kaitiaki	guardian/s, guardianship
kanakana	black magic (makutu)
kanakanaia	black magic (makutu)
Karaka	native tree
karakia	prayer
karetoa	wooden toy which could be animated
karuhiruhi	cormorant, shag
kaupapa	fleet of canoes
Kereru	native wood pigeon
kete	kit(s) – for the carriage of things – food etc., repositories of knowledge
kiore	native rat
korowai	fine weaving

koukou	morepork
Kowhai	Native flowering tree
kukupa	Native wood pigeon
kumara	sweet potato
kupapa	term applied to 'friendly Maoris' – war of the sixties
kura kaupapa	Maori schools – (of Maori emphasis)
kuri	Maori dog – (introduced)
makutu	curse
maia	courage
mana	authority, control, influence, prestige, power, status, psychic force
Mangai	mouthpiece of God – (Ratana)
manu	any bird – (Northern)
marae	courtyard, village common
maramatanga	spiritual light – (inside person)
matakai	placing of curse (makutu) in food. usually for insult or payback – (utu)
matakite	possessing second sight, clairvoyant
matauranga	science – (more modern; relating to pakeha technology)
mate maori	illness/sickness caused by psychic means – (makutu)
mate pakeha	introduced European diseases
Maui	Mythical or legendary hero, god-man
maui	black magic
mauri	life principle – (intangible)
mere	short flat club, for hand to hand fighting, weapon of war
Miro	Native forest tree
moa	large flightless bird (extinct)
moko	facial tattoo (men and women)
mokopuna	grandchild
Morehu	Ratana's followers, (of signed covenant) remnant
nanakia	nasty and dangerous fairy-like being
niu pole	pole central to rituals of Pai Marire movement – (similar to maypole)
noa	ritual to nullify or negate e☐ect of tapu, make safe (person, object or place)
pa	fortified village or encampment
Pai Marire	good and peaceful – (Maori religious Movement of same name)
pakepakeha	term originally applied to Cook and his men - origin of Pakeha?
Papa-tu-a-nuku	earth Mother – (female aspect of creative principle)
para	act or acts o☐ensive to the gods
patu	strike, beat, club, weapon of war
patu rakau	wooden weapons – (generally pre-European)
poi	A light ball with string attached (for poi dance), pounamu greenstone, jade (specifically nephrite), ornaments from
Puriri	Native forest tree
puru-rangi	charm for stopping heavy winds
putaiao	science – (more so of Maori traditional knowledge)
putapaiarehe	fairy folk
rahui	prohibition – (usually pertaining to food sources)
rakau maori	wooden weapons of war
Rangi	sky Father – (male principle of creative aspect)
raupo	large swamp reed used for building and thatching
Rangatira	chief – (can be male or female), also – (well born, noble, of good breeding)
rehua	name of spiritual messenger

reo	language
roi	food made from fern root
Rongo	god of peace
rotu moana	ritual for calming sea
ruru	morepork/owl
taaniko	particular weaving style
taiaha	fighting spear
Taiwhetuki	home of makutu and black arts
tamariki	children
Tane	god of the forest – Maori (name of Elemental Lord of Forest)
Tangaroa	god of the sea – Maori (name of Elemental Lord of the Sea)
tangi	the sound or cry – of things animate or inanimate, weep, mourning
taniwha	mythical, lizard type monster. Inhabits deep pools and caves
taonga	cultural or traditional treasure, (perhaps revered)
tapuwae	charm for fleetness of foot
tapu	under religious or superstitious restriction, inaccessible. sacred, unclean
taro	food tuber – requires damp conditions for growth
tatai	genealogy, lineage
taua ngaki mate	war party
tauiwi	stranger, foreign race – (also foreign tribe)
taurekareka	captive taken in war, slave – (also scoundrel)
te kawanatanga katoa	government sovereignty
Te Korekore	nothingness, void – (future potential or concept of philosophical)
te tino Rangatiratanga	chieftanship
tiriti	treaty (transliterated)
toa	courage, bravery, warrior, champion
tohunga	skilled person, wizard, priest, occultist, herbalist, repository of oral history
tohunga ahurewa	highest caste of priests
tohunga whaiwhaia	black magician
tonotono	the singeing of meat – on hot stones
tua i te rangi	charm to stop the rain
tuku-rangi	charm for heavy rain – (often used against enemy)
Tumatauenga	god of war
tupuna	ancestors (Northern)
tupuware	charm for fleetness of foot
tutua	commoner, common fellow
Tutuhangahua	south wind of Tuhoe
Uenuku	ancient god of war
Urukaraerae	wind of Urewera
utu	payment, revenge
waiata	song, chant, oral history
wairua	spirit – (also unsubstantial image, shadow)
wai piro	lit. rotten or stinking water, (applied to alcohol)
waka	canoe
waka taua	war canoe
wero	challenge
weta	forest insect
whai	string games

whaikorero	oration, speak in a formal way
whaiwhaia (v.t.)	bewitch, injure by spells
whaiwhaia (n)	witchcraft
whakaara hau	invoking the wind
whakama	shame, abasement
whakamomori	act of reckless disregard for one's safety – usually in heat of battle
whakanoa	render a tapu thing safe
whanau	family
whare	dwelling, house
whare kohanga	resting house (for birth)
whare maire	school of evil and destruction – (under tutelage of Whiro.)
whare mata	storage house for fowlers snares etc. – (under various tapu)
whare puni	common sleeping house
whare whakairo	carved meeting house
whatua kura	spiritual messengers
whenua	land
Whiro	god of evil, makutu and destruction

www.ingramcontent.com/pod-product-compliance
Lightning Source LLC
Chambersburg PA
CBHW081049280326
41928CB00053B/2889